1995 Churchwide Assembly

Evangelical Lutheran Church in America

MAKING CHRIST KNOWN
EVANGELICAL LUTHERAN CHURCH IN AMERICA

PRE-ASSEMBLY REPORT

Volume 1

**for the fourth biennial
Churchwide Assembly**

August 16-22, 1995 • Minneapolis, Minnesota

Published by the
Office of the Secretary
Evangelical Lutheran Church in America
8765 West Higgins Road
Chicago, IL 60631

Lowell, G. Almen
Secretary

Contents

Introduction
To the Fourth Biennial Churchwide Assembly
Of the Evangelical Lutheran Church in America

We gather as members—baptized members of the Evangelical Lutheran Church in America. We gather, however, not as a random collection of baptized members. We have been assigned specific responsibility.

Among those of us who assemble in Minneapolis, from August 16-22, 1995, we will find: 1,053 who will be duly elected voting members; about seven dozen others who will be designated as advisory members, including Church Council members, executive directors of churchwide units, and board chairs; presidents of the eight ELCA seminaries and 28 colleges and universities who will be non-voting members; and several hundred others who will be visitors.

Assembly Vocabulary No Accident

No *delegates* will be present for the assembly. Voting members are not delegates!

- The terminology related to the legislative process of this church is no accident.
- The words, "Synod Assembly" and "Churchwide Assembly," rather than convention, and "voting members," rather than delegates, were deliberately chosen for our governing documents.

These words reflect the ecclesial understanding that the three primary expression of this church—congregation, synod, and churchwide organization—exist and serve within this *one* church.

1. The congregation does not meet in convention; the members gather in worship, carry out service, and assemble occasionally and properly for governance decisions and elections.
2. The people of this church in each of the 65 synods are not sent as delegates from a given caucus; they are *not* gathered to act as some politicized delegates to a regional party convention. Rather, they *assemble* as duly selected *members* of this church with *voting* responsibilities for governance and elections on behalf of the synod. The Synod Assembly is just that, an assembly of the people of this church, some of whom have been granted the responsibility of being *voting members* of the *Synod Assembly*.
3. The people of this church, when gathered as voting members of the Synod Assembly, have the responsibility of electing the *voting members* of the *Churchwide Assembly*. Persons so chosen are given the responsibility of doing the work of the Churchwide Assembly; they are *not* sent to participate as politicized delegates from some regional or agenda-specific caucus at some national party convention.

The vocabulary that we use both *shapes* and *reflects* our understanding of this church. When we recognize and understand that our "congregations find their fulfillment in the universal community of the Church, and the universal Church exists in and through congregations" (ELCA constitutional provision 3.02.), then our awareness of the significance of being voting members in a given assembly may grow. After all, as we declare of the "Nature of the Church," the Evangelical Lutheran Church in America "derives its character and powers both from the sanction and representation of its congregations and from its inherent nature as an expression of the broader fellowship of the faith" (also ELCA 3.02.).

We do need to (a) understand more clearly and (b) embrace more completely the conviction that the Evangelical Lutheran Church in America "shall seek to function as people of God through congregations, synods, and the churchwide organization, all of which shall be interdependent. Each part, while fully the church, recognizes that it is not the whole church and therefore lives in a partnership relationship with the others" (ELCA constitutional provision 8.11.).

Indeed, we together affirm and declare the primary principle of organization for our church, namely: "The Evangelical Lutheran Church in America shall be one church" (ELCA constitutional provision 5.01.).

Within this one church, we as voting members, advisory members, non-voting members, visitors, and staff will gather to carry out the work of the 1995 Churchwide Assembly.

Responsibility of the Assembly

According to the *Constitution, Bylaws, and Continuing Resolutions of the Evangelical Lutheran Church in America*, the Churchwide Assembly is "the highest legislative authority of the churchwide organization," charged with the responsibility of dealing "with all matters which are necessary in pursuit of the purposes and functions of this church" (ELCA constitutional provision 12.11.). That same constitutional provision declares:

> The powers of the Churchwide Assembly are limited only by the provisions of the Articles of Incorporation, this constitution and bylaws, and the assembly's own resolutions.

Further, the Churchwide Assembly, according to ELCA constitutional provision 12.21., must:

a. Review the work of the churchwide officers, and for this purpose require and receive reports from them and act on business proposed by them.

b. Review the work of the churchwide units, and for this purpose require and receive reports from them and act on business proposed by them.

c. Receive and consider proposals from synod assemblies.

d. Establish churchwide policy.

e. Adopt a budget for the churchwide organization.

f. Elect officers, board members, and other persons as provided in the constitution and bylaws.

g. Establish churchwide units to carry out the functions of the churchwide organization.

h. Have the sole authority to amend the constitution and bylaws.

i. Fulfill other functions as required in the constitution and bylaws.

j. Conduct such other business as necessary to further the purposes and functions of the churchwide organization.

Documents for the Churchwide Assembly

1. *Pre-Assembly Report, Volume One:* This volume, in compliance with the foregoing constitutional directive, presents the reports of the churchwide divisions, commissions, and other units as information for the voting members of the ELCA's fourth Churchwide Assembly.

2. *Pre-Assembly Report, Volume Two:* In a mailing scheduled about 30 days before the assembly under the legal regulations that govern formal notice of such a gathering of the churchwide organization, assembly members and ELCA congregations will receive the *Pre-Assembly Report, Volume Two*, which will include the rules of order for the assembly, actions of the Church Council addressed to the assembly, recommendations for assembly action, proposed revisions in the governing documents of this church, reports of the Office of the Bishop, Office of the Secretary, and Office of the Treasurer, the Board of Pensions, the Publishing House of the Evangelical Lutheran Church in America, and other items of business.

3. *Pre-Assembly Report, Volume Three:* Within the volume will be the recommendations for assembly action of the Memorials Committee, the report of the assembly's Nominating Committee, and additional material from both the Church Council and the bishop of this church.

A notebook will be provided to assembly voting members upon on-site registration in Minneapolis. These volumes may be inserted into the notebook for convenience in use throughout the assembly.

Policies Related to the Churchwide Assembly

In keeping with past practices, the Church Council adopted policies related to the mailing addresses of voting member of the Churchwide Assembly and to any distribution of materials, displays, and the operation of the assembly:

> That any organization composed entirely of members of the congregations of the Evangelical Lutheran Church in America, registering an official request to mail materials to the voting members of a forthcoming ELCA Churchwide Assembly, shall be permitted to do so if the materials are pertinent to the business of the assembly as determined by the Office of the Secretary. Such materials shall be sent to the secretary of this church for mailing to voting members of the assembly at the expense of the organization making the request and with the use of the specific organization's stationery and envelopes (CC88.7.80).

According to the policy of the Evangelical Lutheran Church in America for Churchwide Assemblies, as approved by the Church Council and as determined by the Office of the Secretary:

1. Only materials authorized by this church's secretary, with approval of the Reference and Counsel Committee, will be distributed to voting members of the assembly during the assembly.

2. Display space exists only for churchwide units.

3. Inclusion of material from related institutions, agencies, and organizations (such as church colleges related through the Division for [Higher] Education [and Schools]) will be decided by the unit, subject to approval of the secretary. The entire assembly display of churchwide units is coordinated by the . . . [Department] for Communication.

4. No display space or meeting facilities are provided to organizations that have no official relationship to this church.

5. Only the church's publishing house (Augsburg Fortress, Publishers) may offer items for sale. No commercial displays or sales booths are permitted.

6. Space for meetings or meal functions, as requested by churchwide units or synods, will be provided whenever possible.

7. Office space will be available only to assist the work of the assembly. No space will be provided to individual units for assembly offices.

8. Secretarial services are supplied only in relation to the official work of the assembly, its officers, and its committees.

9. Individuals and/or groups wishing to appear in relation to or at the assembly must secure permission from the secretary of this church. Priority for any such appearances will be given to persons or groups from within the constituency of the Evangelical Lutheran Church in America, particularly to groups or persons of the host synod. The Evangelical Lutheran Church in America assumes no responsibility for expenses—including travel, food, and lodging—nor does the Evangelical Lutheran Church in America offer honoraria of any amount [for the appearance of such groups] (CC88.7.81).

These policies were adopted for the good order of the assembly, for the effective working the voting members in conducting the official business of this church, and for the practice of fairness in response to various requests.

As we look toward the fourth biennial Churchwide Assembly of the Evangelical Lutheran Church in America, we see before us major decision that need to be made and significant issues that await the deliberation of the 1,053 voting members. We also anticipate an inspiring time as all participants in the assembly gather to hear the Word preached and to receive the sacramental meal of the faithful in Holy Communion.

We will assemble in Minneapolis as members, specific members of this church, who will explore anew the ways in which we as a church are "Making Christ Known."

THE REV. LOWELL G. ALMEN, *Secretary*

Report of the
Division for Congregational Ministries

Organization
Board
Ms. Janice Allen, Richland, Wash. (1999)
Rev. Nancy I. Amacher, Rothschild, Wis. (1999)
Rev. Gary F. Anderson, Shoreview, Minn. (1997)
Mr. Paul Ashley, Charlotte, N.C. (1997)
Rev. Richard R. Campbell, Charleston, S.C. (1997)
Rev. Julie A. Ebbesen, Prairie Village, Kans. (1995)
Mr. William S. Ellis, New York, N.Y. (1995)
Rev. Ronald B. Ferrell, Rock Island, Ill. (1999)
Rev. Lenier L. Gallardo, Miami, Fla. (1995)
Mr. Patrick M. Greene, Buffalo, N.Y. (1995)
Ms. Susan Hermodson, West Lafayette, Ind. (1997)
Rev. Donald J. Hillerich, Sarasota, Fla. (1997)
Ms. Beth Ann Lechtenberger, Bethesda, Md. (1999)
Ms. Ruth Terry Miller, Coopersburg, Pa. (1997)
Mr. Richard Moe, Sioux Falls, S.Dak. (1997)
Mr. Jim Myers, Kailua, Hawaii (1999)
Ms. Deborah A. Nystrom, Ann Arbor, Mich. (1995)
Mr. Arne ("Skip") E. Rosquist, Missoula, Mont. (1999)
Ms. Gail Adora Starr, Durham, N.C. (1995)
Rev. Dale M. Vitalis, Fargo, N.Dak. (1995)
Vacant (1999)

Advisors
Ms. Lita Brusick Johnson, executive assistant to the
    bishop, Office of the Bishop
Bishop A. Donald Main, Upper Susquehanna Synod
Mr. Charles Bruning, Minneapolis, Minn., president,
    Lutheran Men in Mission
Mr. John Moen, Eau Claire, Wis., chair, Lutheran
    Outdoor Ministries Committee
Mr. Clinton Schroeder, executive director, Lutheran
    Laity Movement for Stewardship
Mr. Vance Robbins, Oaks, Okla., president, Lutheran
    Youth Organization
Rev. Harvey A. Stegemoeller, executive director,
    ELCA Foundation
Vacant, Commission for Multicultural Ministries

Committees of the Board
Executive Committee
Mr. Jim Myers, *chair*
Ms. Susan Hermodson, *vice-chair*
Mr. Richard Moe, *secretary*
Ms. Ruth Terry Miller
Rev. Dale M. Vitalis

Worship Committee
Rev. Julie A. Ebbesen, *chair*
Rev. Nancy T. Amacher
Mr. Paul Ashley
Ms. Susan Hermodson
Ms. Beth Ann Lechtenberger
Ms. Gail Adora Starr
Rev. Dale M. Vitalis

Evangelism Committee
Rev. Gary F. Anderson, *chair*
Ms. Janice Allen
Rev. Richard R. Campbell
Rev. Lenier L. Gallardo
Ms. Ruth Terry Miller
Mr. Arne ("Skip") E. Rosquist

Stewardship Committee
Ms. Deborah A. Nystrom, *chair*
Mr. William S. Ellis
Rev. Ronald B. Ferrell
Mr. Patrick M. Greene
Rev. Donald J. Hillerich
Mr. Richard Moe
Mr. Jim Myers

Executive Staff
Executive Director: Rev. Mark R. Moller-Gunderson
Coordinator for ELCA Mission Support:
    Rev. Mark R. Moller-Gunderson
Director for Congregational Programs:
    Ms. M. Wyvetta Bullock
Director for Planning and Congregational Studies:
    Rev. Michael R. Rothaar
Director for Congregational Resource Development:
    Ms. Linda Schomaker
Director for Budget and Finance: Ms. Nancy Oakford
Associate Director for Finance and Director for
    Personnel: Ms. Emmalene Harbin
Director for Learning Ministries: Vacant
Director for Stewardship and Mission Giving:
    Ms. Betty Lee Nyhus
Director for Evangelism Resources and Programs:
    Rev. David Poling-Goldenne
Director for Churchwide Membership Initiative:
    Mr. James P. Petersen
Director for Men's Ministries and Lutheran Men in
    Mission: Mr. Douglas H. Haugen

Director for Missionary Support (shared with
  Division for Global Mission):
    Ms. Mary A. Johnson
Director for Mission Partners (shared with Division
  for Outreach): Rev. Donald D. Johnson
Director for Mission Interpreters and Resident
  Stewardship Service: Ms. Nancy L. Snell
Director for Vision for Mission Fund:
    Mr. Jerry Olstad
Director for World Hunger Appeal:
    Rev. Roger O. Livdahl
Director for Social Ministry for Congregations:
    Ms. Loretta Horton
Director for Worship: Rev. Paul R. Nelson
Acting Director for Worship: Rev. Michael R. Rothaar
Director for Lutheran Center Chapel:
    Ms. Lorraine Brugh
Director for Outdoor Ministries:
    Mr. Mark D. Burkhardt
Director for Youth Ministries and Lutheran Youth
  Organization: Rev. Walter J. ("Mark") Knutson
Director for Youth Ministries and Leadership
  Development: Vacant
Acting Director, National Youth Gathering:
    Ms. Ann Luther
Associate Director for Children's Learning Ministries:
    Ms. Mary Ingram
Associate Director for Adult Learning Ministries:
    Rev. Theodore W. Schroeder
Associate Director for Evangelism Resources and
  Programs: Rev. Marta L. Poling-Goldenne
Associate Director for Evangelism Programs and
  Resources: Rev. Dale C. Olson
Associate Director for Multilingual Resources:
    Ms. Evelyn Soto
Associate Director for Outdoor Ministries and Youth
  Ministries Resources: Mr. Rod Boriack
Associate Director for Resource Production,
  Stewardship: Mr. Steven A. Rusk
Associate Director for Stewardship and Ministry in
  Daily Life Resources: Mr. Robert A. Sitze
Associate Director for Worship: Rev. Karen M. Ward
Associate Director for World Hunger Appeal:
    Ms. Patricia J. Larsen

Resident Stewardship Service Staff
Mr. Stanley Rose, Bartlett, Ill.
Ms. Muriel Arms, McFarland, Wis.
Ms. Jeanne McCoskery, Billings, Mont.
Mr. William P. Otterson, Maumee, Ohio
Mr. Mark T. Wagner, Volga, S.Dak.

Deployed/Shared Stewardship Specialists
(with synod assignments)
Region 1
Rev. Michael L. Meier (Alaska, Northwest Washing
  ton, Southwestern Washington, Eastern
  Washington-Idaho, Oregon Synods)
Bishop Mark R. Ramseth (Montana Synod)

Region 2
Rev. Lauren ("Bud") I. Egdahl (Sierra Pacific Synod)
Rev. Alan L. Lorentzen (Southern California [West],
  Pacifica, Grand Canyon Synods)
Vacant (Rocky Mountain Synod)

Region 3
Rev. Duane C. Danielson (Western North Dakota
  Synod)
Rev. John F. Elverum (Eastern North Dakota Synod)
Mr. Mark T. Wagner (South Dakota Synod)
Rev. Richard J. Kennedy (Northwestern Minnesota
  Synod)
Rev. Rolland H. Bockbrader (Northeastern Minnesota
  Synod)
Bishop Stanley N. Olson (Southwestern Minnesota
  Synod)
Mr. David Jones (Minneapolis Area Synod)
Rev. Charles S. Anderson (Saint Paul Area Synod)
Rev. Roy E. Satre Jr. (Southeastern Minnesota
  Synod)

Region 4
Rev. Glenn H. Schoonover (Nebraska Synod)
Rev. Dennis R. Hallemeier (Central States Synod)
Vacant (Arkansas-Oklahoma Synod)
Vacant (Northern Texas-Northern Louisiana Synod)
Rev. George F. Haynes (Southwestern Texas, Texas-
  Louisiana Gulf Coast Synod)

Region 5
Ms. Beverly Moody (Metropolitan Chicago Synod)
Rev. Gary M. Wollersheim (Northern Illinois Synod)
Rev. John W. Kelly (Central/Southern Illinois Synod)
Mr. Jerold Slocum (Southeastern Iowa Synod)
Rev. Delwayne H. Hahn (Western Iowa Synod)
Rev. Richard G. Thompson (Northeastern Iowa
  Synod)
Rev. Thomas A. Skrenes (Northern Great Lakes
  Synod)
Rev. Richard J. Bruesehoff (Northwest Synod of
  Wisconsin)
Vacant (East-Central Synod of Wisconsin)
Rev. Alan T. Heggen (Greater Milwaukee Synod)
Ms. Phyllis Wiederhoeft (South-Central Synod of
  Wisconsin)
Rev. Harris A. Hostager (LaCrosse Area Synod)

Region 6

Rev. Richard C. Bosse (Southeast Michigan, North/West Lower Michigan, Indiana-Kentucky Synods)

Rev. F. Eugene Grimm (Northwestern Ohio, Northeastern Ohio, Southern Ohio Synods)

Region 7

Rev. Margaret G. Payne (New Jersey Synod)

Rev. Robert A. Hoffman (New England, Metropolitan New York Synods)

Rev. Marie C. Jerge (Upstate New York Synod)

Rev. Richard H. Stough (Northeastern Pennsylvania Synod)

Mr. Richard K. Rockstroh (Southeastern Pennsylvania Synod)

Vacant (Slovak Zion Synod)

Region 8

Rev. Robert J. Newpher (Northwestern Pennsylvania, Southwestern Pennsylvania, West Virginia-Western Maryland Synods)

Mr. Roger W. Smith (Allegheny, Lower Susquehanna, Upper Susquehanna, Delaware-Maryland, Metropolitan Washington, D.C., Synods)

Region 9

Vacant (Virginia Synod)

Vacant (North Carolina Synod)

Vacant (South Carolina Synod)

Rev. David M. Hood (Southeastern Synod)

Vacant (Florida-Bahamas Synod)

Rev. Judith A. Spindt (Caribbean Synod)

Constitutional Mandate

The Division for Congregational Ministries develops integrated programs and resources and provides services in support of congregations of this church. The division provides a financial support program for this church, as well as supporting congregations in such major areas as worship, learning ministries, evangelism, and social ministry in congregations. Through this division the church relates to ELCA Outdoor Ministries, the Lutheran Youth Organization, and Lutheran Men in Mission. The constitutional mandate of this division appears in continuing resolution 16.11.A91. of the Constitution, Bylaws, and Continuing Resolutions of the Evangelical Lutheran Church in America.

Report of Work 1993-1995

The division is organized in staff ministry teams. Each team has developed a multi-year plan approved by the board of the division. In all the areas of the division's work, there has been a deliberate effort to forge stronger ties with synods, to work in partnership with the ELCA publishing house in the development of

resources of the highest quality, and to provide leadership development opportunities for people in key positions to strengthen congregations.

During this biennium, the division has focused on raising the standards of quality in the programs and resources provided. This focus represents a deep desire to anticipate and respond to needs across this church in the various areas of ministry, and to plan creatively to meet those needs. In collaboration with the Department for Research and Evaluation, the division has actively pursued various means of assessing the degree to which we add value to those opportunities offered to congregations.

The division's concern for quality has been both quantitative and qualitative. It has involved surveys, focus groups, data analysis, and pilot testing. Given the division's emphasis on building partnerships, every ministry team has been involved in a variety of "listening sessions" with targeted groups of congregational leaders. These have ranged from a variety of settings for ministry (such as pastors of large membership congregations, and leaders of inner-city urban congregations) to a variety of particular mission foci, e.g., evangelism and social ministry. Such listening sessions have been extremely valuable in building bridges and partnerships.

The division operates on the principle that value of its work is defined by the people being served, partners in ministry in congregations, and synodical networks. The results of this focus are evident in such milestone accomplishments as the development of supplemental worship resources, and substantial modifications in approaching much of the ongoing work of the division.

The division has continued in this biennium to underscore three emphases for its work: worship, evangelism, and stewardship.

Worship

The worship staff again reached its full complement during this period, with the selection of a director for worship, and the addition (in 1995) of an associate director for worship and music.

A major task has been the work of the Sacramental Practices Study Task Force, formed in partnership with the Conference of Bishops at the direction of the 1993 Churchwide Assembly. This 16-member task force named by Bishop Herbert W. Chilstrom was charged with the responsibility of drafting a statement for this church's consideration. The original timeline development was lengthened to provide more time for congregational study and response. The draft statement with commentary, plus a study guide and response form, were mailed to all rostered leaders. Responses have been requested by June 1996. This should enable careful consideration of responses and development of a new draft in time for presentation to the 1997 Churchwide Assembly.

The division collaborates with the Office of the Bishop in support of worship. Along with planning Churchwide Assembly worship, the division manages the work of the director for the chapel in the churchwide office at the Lutheran Center. It also is responsible for managing the review process for liturgical materials offered for use in ELCA congregations and other settings.

Significant progress also has been made in planning a series of supplements to the *Lutheran Book of Worship*. *With One Voice*, a new collection of hymns and liturgical settings, was published in spring 1995 by Augsburg Fortress, Publishers. Along with partners in the ELCA publishing house, the division was deeply involved in managing the review process, as well as helping shape the content. We pray that it will be a worthy addition to our congregations' worship life. As the division worked with the Office of the Bishop in planning worship for the 1995 Churchwide Assembly, it was exciting to provide for the introduction of this new resource.

Work continues on the *Spanish Lutheran Book of Worship*, and it is expected to be available in Advent 1996. It will be the first complete resource of its kind since *Culto Cristiano*, published in 1964. The book truly will be the product of the Hispanic Lutheran community. A steering committee has involved 28 people, and has developed the content in consultation with more than 200 people from 70 different congregations. Working groups also are engaged in early stages of work on an *African American Lutheran Hymnal*. This resource is being developed in cooperation with The Lutheran Church—Missouri Synod.

During this biennium the division conducted an extensive review of the Revised Common Lectionary, an ecumenical resource that improves upon the lectionary as printed in the 1978 *Lutheran Book of Worship*. Upon recommendation from the board of this division, the Church Council authorized its use beginning in November 1995.

The division conducted a major event in September 1994, called, "Making the Connections: Evangelism and Worship." The event attracted more than 600 people to Chicago, September 23-25. Before and after the event, there were gatherings and training programs for the evangelism and worship synodical networks. The division's board directed staff to find ways in which cooperation, rather than isolation, would mark how we approach our work as a unit. This event, focusing on two of the division's stated priorities, is a highly visible example. We sought to help participants engage in thought and conversation about the intersection of these critical areas of this church's life.

Evangelism

In regard to evangelism, the board of the division approved a four-year plan including specific goals and strategies. Members of this ministry team have been in conversation with synodical evangelism committees, seeking both to serve and engage them in the plan.

The evangelism plan is being implemented with a variety of programs and resources. Synodical evangelism leaders have participated in leadership consultations and have received programmatic and resource support. Nine synods currently have contracts for our Evangelism Consultation Initiative, with nine additional visits pending. This program has been implemented by a staff member under contract. The Partners in Evangelism network has carried out events that reached more than 5,000 people during this biennium. The Member Referral System has been refined. In 1993, nearly 15,000 ELCA members who relocated were referred to other congregations for follow-up. Other programs have included the development of 13 pilot sites for teaching congregations (in partnership with the Institute for Mission and the Division for Outreach), expansion of the Partners in Evangelism network, and a small groups pilot project involving 16 congregations. The division is grateful to both Aid Association for Lutherans (AAL) and the Lutheran Brotherhood Foundation for their generous funding of evangelism programs this year.

A Church Membership Initiative (CMI) has provided an additional opportunity for evangelism work. This project was originally developed by Aid Association for Lutherans (AAL), which then invited participation by various church bodies to expand on its research and find ways to implement solutions. An AAL grant has made it possible to add a staff member under contract to carry out this work. During this biennium, in cooperation with the Department for Research and Evaluation, the division developed new research into the dynamics of growth in ELCA congregations. This material, combined with CMI findings, was presented in a series of presentations given in various parts of this church. It is now available to all congregations as an interactive video workshop. Combined with a video workshop on hospitality evangelism, it is packaged under the title "Awakenings." At each of the presentations, there was a gathering of pastors and congregational lay leaders, whose discussion and feedback have contributed to further development of the project. Additional components will include tools for congregational self-analysis, leadership training events, providing consultants to congregations, and making available further resource support.

In November 1995, the division will sponsor a national conference focused on "Making Disciples: Congregations for the 21st Century." Participants will include our synodical evangelism network and partners in evangelism, as well as congregational leaders. The focus will be on reaching and discipling unchurched people, with special emphasis on culture-specific and rural evangelism strategies.

Stewardship

In regard to stewardship, the division has been engaged in implementation of the Financial Stewardship Strategy adopted by the 1993 Churchwide Assembly. This division is charged with coordinating the efforts surrounding the annual churchwide offering and working in close cooperation with the ELCA Foundation to further the Vision for Mission Fund. The Rev. Mark R. Moller-Gunderson serves as coordinator for mission support in this church. During this biennium, Jerry Olstad was named director for the Vision for Mission Fund.

A four-year plan for stewardship programs builds on the Financial Stewardship Strategy and applies it specifically to the division's work. The heart of the plan is implementation of specific elements: building faithful lives, telling the story of the mission of this church, equipping leaders, and developing methods for financial support, coordination of partnerships, and supporting tithing as a joyful response.

During this biennium, the division developed new training opportunities in stewardship. In partnership with the Division for Ministry in its Growth for Excellence in Ministry (GEM) program, funding was provided for training events in stewardship for rostered leaders across this church. Pilot projects were developed in 1994. The division also has emphasized targeted stewardship education, mission interpreters, and other efforts being carried out in partnership with the synods through a network of deployed and shared stewardship staff, with pilot projects in 1994 and development into full offerings during the succeeding three years.

The Lutheran Laity Movement for Stewardship also is related to this division (see separate report). The organization's financial situation has stabilized, and they have been able to re-establish some of their direct fund-raising services that previously had been curtailed.

Stewardship work includes coordination of the Mission Partners and Mission Builders programs, in cooperation with the Division for Outreach, and the Missionary Sponsorship program in cooperation with the Division for Global Mission. All of these programs offer means by which the members of this church's congregations can direct contributions toward the strengthening the ELCA's missionary presence on all continents.

As part of the work in providing for this church's financial support, in 1994 the division, in partnership with other representatives of the churchwide organization, arranged for 65 consultations with synodical leaders at 11 sites. Along with 1996 commitments for mission support, it was a key time to discuss with those leaders the complex task of an overall development plan, as well as to plan for the 1995 Vision for Mission Fund appeal.

The division's work includes providing stewardship resources, both those designed for use in congregational programs, such as the resource guide distributed each spring, and those that ask congregations for mission support, such as synod assembly reports and congregational annual report covers. The annual World Hunger packet, Disastergrams as needed, Vision for Mission materials, and Peli-can materials are further examples.

Resident Stewardship Service is a direct-service program of the division through which congregational stewardship programs are strengthened by means of consultation and leadership. Approximately one hundred congregations have been served by this program during the current biennium, about one in five of them being new mission starts. New to this program is the development of self-guiding programs for use in groups of congregations. A training model is being piloted in 1995.

The ELCA World Hunger Appeal and ELCA Disaster Response are significant means through which ELCA members and congregations minister to those in need. As seen in the financial statements, disaster giving increased substantially in 1993, and in 1994 the hunger appeal surpassed its goals. The division coordinates the fund-raising aspects of this work, as well as providing educational resources, under the coordination of the Division for Church in Society.

A Stewardship Leaders Conference was held in January 1995. It was the first annual training event designed for a newly formed network of mission interpreters, as well as deployed and shared stewardship staff of the division. Some 120 stewardship leaders attended the conference, including an invited group of congregational stewardship leaders.

Other Areas of Focus

Other work of the division is carried on alongside the three areas of emphasis. The division's board approved a long-range plan for Learning Ministries that focuses on congregations and families as learning communities. An increasing focus of the strategies in this area is in the area of Christian discipleship, providing opportunities for growth in faith and life.

Significant effort during this biennium has been devoted to regionalized planning for multi-site "Jubilee" events being carried out July 6-9, 1995, under the theme, "Teach to Reach." This is a collaboration of Learning Ministries and Evangelism, in which conferences occur simultaneously on various sites, with a satellite teleconferencing link among them. Each event is being planned by its own local committee, but the featured speakers and some elements of the conference will be shared by all. This event is designed to bring together congregational members who are involved in Christian education, as well as those who focus on evangelism. The focus is on helping them work together to incorporate new members into the life of their congregation. In addition, the division has initiated seminars on small-group and prayer ministries, being offered in 14 synods in 1995.

Multicultural ministry also is a significant part of the division's work, as it responds to this church's Multicultural Mission Strategy. During this biennium, a pilot project was conducted with congregations from Milwaukee and Chicago to develop an experiential leadership model for African American males. The target group was a group of young men who would participate in a program at one of our outdoor ministry sites. This "Simba Project" model has been further developed on the basis of experience with the pilot, and now is being offered to other partners as a means of strengthening ministry. The division also is involved in the development of an anti-racism program for congregations in collaboration with the Commission for Multicultural Ministries and the Lutheran Human Relations Association.

The division's board has received ongoing reports on Ministry in Daily Life, a continuing part of the work of the division in cooperation with the Division for Ministry. The 1993 Churchwide Assembly action on the Study of Ministry included a mandate to assess the degree to which this theme is integrated into this church's life. Recommendations for further work include the strengthening of small group resources that assist people to develop their understanding of vocation.

Youth ministries are key areas of the work of the division. The Lutheran Youth Organization report is provided separately. There also are significant leadership development efforts, such as "Lift Every Voice" training, which seeks to provide this church with well-equipped speakers from the multicultural communities, and training for youth ministry interns. Youth ministries have provided leadership in promoting the inclusion of a broad spectrum of diverse people, including persons with disabilities, into the life of this church. An annual packet of resources is provided for all congregations, which includes program planning and strategy assistance, as well as guidance for "Servant Event" opportunities.

One of the most visible parts of the work of the division was the 1994 ELCA National Youth Gathering held at Atlanta, July 20-24. More than 34,000 registered participants, including 5,500 adult counselors, involved people from all 65 synods. This self-supporting event continues to be the largest five-day event for teenage young people sponsored by any church or secular youth-serving agency in the United States. Following this event, the division undertook a comprehensive evaluation of the National Youth Gathering, conducted jointly by the division and the Department for Research and Evaluation. While planning for future gatherings will be refined, the evaluation, involving perspectives from leaders throughout the synods, affirmed that these events make a significant impact on the lives of young people, and serve to strengthen and support congregational youth ministry.

The impact of the youth gathering is increased by the training and experience that it generates. For example, the national "Counselor Training Event" helped synods to assist those who worked directly with the youth from their congregation—skills that have applicability beyond the gathering itself. Hundreds of volunteers worked at putting together the many components needed to assure the success of the youth gathering, and in the process developed networks and skills that contribute to ongoing youth programs in the time between gatherings. The youth gathering also was an opportunity to develop specific leadership and participation through associated events. These included the Multicultural Youth Leadership Event (July 17-20, 1994) with 565 participants, and the Differently-Abled Youth Leadership Event (July 18-20, 1994).

Other elements of the division's work include social ministry for congregations, which during this biennium piloted a "Servant Event School" in cooperation with the Northern Illinois Synod. The model was extremely successful, and four or five additional sites have been scheduled. In December 1994, the division was a co-sponsor of a "Women's Networking Conference," held to equip women who are engaged in grass roots community organizing. Participants received a copy of a new *Social Ministry Handbook*. The division also has begun new partnerships in efforts to combat domestic violence.

The division's work with outdoor ministries has continued to strengthen. An annual curriculum is only part of a complex program that includes summer camps, day camps, retreat programs, travel and high adventure programs, and programs for older adults. The division has worked with the Division for Global Mission to expand an international counselor program to about 60 participants each year. This program, now in its fourth year, brings student counselors from Eastern Europe, Africa, South America, and Asia to serve at ELCA outdoor ministry centers. Services provided to outdoor ministry organizations include board development, personnel management, and assistance with health, safety, and regulatory responsibilities. The Association of Lutheran Outdoor Ministry Professionals has now adopted a member dues system, which will enhance the work of this organization.

In all areas of work, the division continues to develop partnership with the Publishing House of the Evangelical Lutheran Church in America, in the development of resources for congregations. During this biennium, the two units developed a revised partnership agreement, and have reconfigured the process by which related constitutional obligations are carried out through Resource Management Teams.

During this biennium, the division and its board have had to manage several key staff transitions, including the acceptance of a congregational call by one of the executive directors, the Rev. Mary Ann Moller-Gunderson. New positions were developed in the areas of worship and music, education, and evangelism. Throughout the process of reviewing staffing and organizational patterns, the division has kept foremost in mind the need to serve effectively and efficiently in support of the congregations of this church.

DIVISION FOR CONGREGATIONAL MINISTRIES
JIM MYERS, *Chair*
MARK R. MOLLER-GUNDERSON, *Executive Director*

Report of Lutheran Laity Movement for Stewardship (LLM)

Organization
Board of Directors

The Lutheran Laity Movement for Stewardship is governed by a 15-member Board of Directors with one member representing each of the nine ELCA regions and six members at large.

Mr. Dean W. Arnold, *treasurer*, Colorado Springs, Colo. (1995)

Ms. Margie Back, Fresno, Calif. (1999)

Mr. Richard P. Boynton, Bahama, N.C. (1997)

Mr. John R. Brown, Pittsburgh, Pa. (1999)

Mr. Robert O. Drange, Shawnee Mission, Kans. (1999)

Mr. Robert P. Gottlund, *vice president*, Kutztown, Pa. (1995)

Ms. Paula R. Kadel, Lower Gwynedd, Pa. (1999)

Mr. Michael Linder, *secretary*, Durham, Oreg. (1997)

Mr. Kenneth E. Milton, Wichita Falls, Tex. (1997)

Mr. Kent Richter, Eustis, Fla. (1999)

Mr. Leo F. Schwerin, Hilliard, Ohio (1995)

Mr. Donald F. Specht, Pottstown, Pa. (1995)

Ms. Hazel B. Steward, Chicago, Ill. (1997)

Mr. William E. Taylor, Chuluota, Fla. (1997)

Mr. Darrell W. Zenk, *president*, Inver Grove Heights, Minn. (1995)

Staff

Executive Director: Clinton P. Schroeder
Assistant Director: Joyce Cain
Budget and Membership Coordinator: Sylvia M. Burck

Relationships and Purpose

The Lutheran Laity Movement for Stewardship is a fellowship of 2,300 lay men and women who are concerned about the stewardship of all life and seek to impart this same spirit to others, in order that individual lives may be enriched and the stewardship response of members of this church may be enhanced.

The contributions of LLM members help to bring others to a deepened understanding of stewardship through a variety of programs, services, and publications offered by the movement:

- a one-day Seminar on Stewardship and Lifestyle available to ELCA congregations;
- *Faith in Action*, a quarterly stewardship journal distributed to LLM members in the United States and Canada and to all of the congregations of the Evangelical Lutheran Church in America and the Evangelical Lutheran Church in Canada;
- professional fund-raising and counseling service available to all ELCA congregations;
- Stewardship of Life Conferences; and
- new programs currently under development.

The Lutheran Laity Movement for Stewardship is related to the ELCA Division for Congregational Ministries and is recognized as being an organization within this church through ELCA continuing resolution 16.11.A91.f.4. The movement is committed to providing a stewardship ministry that supplements and complements that provided by the Division for Congregational Ministries.

Report of Work 1993-1995
Membership

Through its synodical representatives network, the Lutheran Laity Movement for Stewardship has had displays and special events at a number of synod assemblies and other events. Surveys have indicated that most LLM members tithe and many serve on synodical and congregational stewardship committees.

Programs

During the biennium, 62 Seminars on Stewardship and Lifestyle were presented for congregations, and it is anticipated that the demand for seminars will continue through the coming biennium. LLM members serve as volunteer discussion leaders for the seminars.

LLM Sunday was observed in ELCA congregations on September 19, 1993, and on September 18, 1994.

Fund-Raising Services

The LLM Fund-Raising and Counseling Service provided professional fund-raising guidance to 45 congregations during 1993-1994. Stewardship education is an integral part of all fund-raising campaigns directed by the LLM Fund Raising and Counseling Service.

Publications

The Lutheran Laity Movement for Stewardship publishes a quarterly stewardship journal, *Faith in Action*, which is distributed to LLM members and free of charge to all ELCA congregations through this church's Action Packet. *Faith in Action* also is available through individual and group subscriptions.

Major Program Directions

Lutheran Laity Movement for Stewardship will continue to offer the Seminars on Stewardship and Lifestyle and will begin the development of two new stewardship education programs, a series of videotaped Bible studies on stewardship and Christian giving, and a new version of Stewardship of Life Conferences, to be offered on a regional basis.

The three-part series on "The History of Stewardship" by Dr. William O. Avery, published in *Faith in Action* during 1994, will be produced as a separate publication during 1995.

The LLM Fund Raising and Counseling Service will continue to provide professional scripturally-based campaign direction to congregations of this church.

The Lutheran Laity Movement for Stewardship is in on-going dialogue with the Stewardship of Life Institute at Gettysburg Seminary to cooperate in the development and implementation of stewardship education programs.

Providing resources for multicultural congregations continues to be a high priority for the Lutheran Laity Movement for Stewardship.

The Lutheran Laity Movement for Stewardship, throughout its 88-year history, has been a strong voice for responsible stewardship in the Lutheran church in North America, and through the generous support of its members will continue to provide stewardship resources for congregations of this church.

LUTHERAN LAITY MOVEMENT
FOR STEWARDSHIP

DARRELL W. ZENK, *President*
CLINTON P. SCHROEDER, *Executive Director*

Exhibit B

Report of
Lutheran Men in Mission

Organization
Board of Directors
President: Mr. Charles Bruning, Minneapolis, Minn.
Vice-President: Mr. Steve Crane, Ilion, N.Y.
Secretary: Mr. Charles Schwartz, Refugio, Tex.
Treasurer: Mr. Richard Straub, Marion, Ohio
From Region 1: Mr. Eugene Johnson, McMinnville,

Oreg.
From Region 2: Mr. Kenneth Getzin, Rancho Palos Verdes, Calif.
From Region 3: Mr. Eldon Johnson, Hartford, S.Dak.
From Region 4: Mr. Peri Segaran, Dallas, Tex.
From Region 5: Mr. Robert Flemming, Miles, Iowa
From Region 6: Mr. Fred Wiedmann, Akron, Ohio
From Region 7: Mr. Gunter Samuelsen, East Patchogue, N.Y.
From Region 8: Mr. Arthur Johnson, Kane, Pa.
From Region 9: Mr. Clarence Pugh, Newton, N.C.
At large: Mr. Norman Briggs, Chicago, Ill.

Liaison from board of Division for Congregational Ministries: Mr. Richard Moe, Sioux Falls, S.Dak.
Liaison from the Conference of Bishops: Bishop Gerhard I. Knutson, Northwest Synod of Wisconsin
Liaison from the Board of the Lutheran Youth Organization: Mr. Philip Koch

Staff
Director: Mr. Douglas Haugen

This organization was established as provided in the ELCA constitution under the Division for Congregational Ministries (ELCA 16.31.A87.c.).

Statement of Purpose

The basic purpose of Lutheran Men in Mission (LMM) is to:
● help men of the ELCA grow in and live out their faith in the Lord Jesus Christ;
● afford men opportunities for spiritual growth and development of an evangelical attitude through prayer and study of the Word;
● invite men to faith in Christ and fuller involvement and participation in the life of the congregation; and
● enable men of this church to support the mission and ministries of the Evangelical Lutheran Church in America through leadership development and an active organization of service and fellowship.

Report of Work 1993-1995

The board has been involved in the development and implementation of a strategic plan for churchwide men's ministry. The major result of this plan is the "Master Builders: Building Men for Christ" program. Through this emphasis, Lutheran Men in Mission intends to deal with issues of men's faith, relationships, and ministry. This will be effected primarily through large-group gatherings, resources (print, video, audio, and electronic), and continuing leadership development.

In 1995, Lutheran Men in Mission will sponsor ten regional men's gatherings, publish five Bible studies, and conduct training for leaders in each of the nine regions.

The "Master Builders: Building Men for Christ" funding strategy is now under way. The goal is to raise $142,500 in fiscal 1995 with a "dream goal" of $215,000.

The third Biennial LMM Assembly was held July 15-18, 1994, at Wittenberg University, Springfield, Ohio. Delegates were present from most synods and elected the above-listed officers and regional board members to their respective positions. The "Master Builder: Building Men for Christ" program was approved at the assembly. Minneapolis will be the site of the 1996 Lutheran Men's Gathering and LMM assembly.

Synodical LMM projects are varied. The Carolinas continue to assist the establishment of new congregations; Nebraska and Illinois units make grants available to seminarians; and Central States is involved with disaster relief. Across this church, each synodical LMM unit chooses a specific ministry which assists and promotes the mission of its synod. Hundreds of hours are expended and many dollars are gathered—something that did not happen prior to the establishment of a churchwide men's organization.

In most U.S. congregations on a weekend, the worshiping congregation will be at most 40 percent male. This is a time when men are asking what it means to be a man in the home, in the work place, and in the church. Today we have a great open window for men's ministry!

LUTHERAN MEN IN MISSION

CHARLES BRUNING, *President*
DOUGLAS HAUGEN, *Director*

Exhibit C

Report of the Lutheran Youth Organization

Organization
Board 1991-1994
Mr. Vance Robbins, *chair*, Oaks, Okla.
Ms. Karris Golden, *vice president*, Waterloo, Iowa
Ms. Erin Johnson, *secretary*, Charlotte, N.C.
Ms. Traci Saalfeld, *Region 1*, Auburn, Wash.

Ms. Alyson Noel, *Region 2*, Oakland, Calif.
Mr. Yoshio Haraguchi, *Region 3*, St. Paul, Minn.
Mr. Brian Biggs, *Region 4,* Omaha, Nebr.
Mr. Philip Koch, *Region 5*, Chicago, Ill.
Mr. Keith Smith, *Region 6*, Croswell, Mich.
Mr. Gethyn Chilcoat, *Region 7*, Bridgewater, N.J.
Ms. Sunshine Keiser, *Region 8*, Greensburg, Pa.
Mr. Angel Tirado, *Region 9,* Toa Alta, P.R.
Ms. Lisa Canino, *representative for Multicultural Advisory Committee*, Oaks, Okla.
Mr. Kenzo Gardner, *representative for Multicultural Advisory Committee*, Houston, Tex.
Ms. Mandy Kent, *representative for differently-abled persons*, Manchester, Md.
Ms. Amanda Reese, *representative for differently-abled persons*, Evansville, Wis.
Mr. Chris Hanson, *chair for synod LYO presidents*, Groton, S.Dak.
Ms. Hmong Ly, *representative for synod LYO presidents*, Albermarle, N.C.
Mr. Tim Barr, *secretary for synod LYO presidents*, Rosenbert, Tex.
Mr. Ian Burch, *representative for synod LYO presidents*, Chuziak, Alaska
Ms. Cindy Peper, *representative for Church Council*, Liberty Center, Ohio
Mr. Arthur Norman, *representative for Church Council*, Houston, Tex.

Staff
Rev. Walter J. ("Mark") Knutson, *director for Youth Ministries, LYO/Hunger/Justice*, Chicago, Ill.
Rev. Marlene W. Helgemo, *LYO staff to Multicultural Advisory Committee and Multicultural Youth Leadership Event*, Plymouth, Minn.

Multicultural Advisory Committee
Ms. Lisa Canino, *chair, Hispanic Community representative*, Euramada, Bayamon, P.R.
Ms. Kenya Davis, *secretary, African American Community representative*, Durham, N.C.
Mr. DeQuan Kuntu, *African American Community representative*, Calumet City, Ill.
Mr. Carmelo Santos, *Hispanic Community representative*, Cantano, P.R.
Mr. Kenzo Gardner, *Asian Community representative*, Houston, Tex.
Ms. Khamphanh Bouakongxaya, *Asian Community representative*, Milwaukee, Wis.
Ms. Rebecca Rank, *Native American Community representative*, Portland, Oreg.
Mr. Christopher Finstrom, *Native American Community representative*, Coon Rapids, Minn.

Advisory Members

Ms. Sunshine Keiser, *LYO board liaison*, Greensburg, Pa.

Ms. Tammy Jackson, *Commission for Multicultural Ministries liaison*, Chicago, Ill.

The 1994-1997 LYO board was elected at the LYO Triennial Convention, July 20-24, 1994, Atlanta, Ga.

Constitutional Mandate

The Lutheran Youth Organization (LYO) represents close to 500,000 high-school-age young people in the Evangelical Lutheran Church in America. The Lutheran Youth Organization is mandated in the ELCA constitution in continuing resolution 16.11.A91.f.1. The Lutheran Youth Organization is housed in the youth ministries area of the Division for Congregational Ministries and relates to the division's board.

The Lutheran Youth Organization meets in convention every three years to conduct its business, elect officers, set goals, and envision the future. In the period between conventions, the organization is governed by its 21-member board. The board meets twice each year to carry on business as directed by the LYO constitution, to review the work of the organization, and through the board of the Division for Congregational Ministries make such recommendations to any council, board, committee, synod, institution, or agency of this church as it deems wise. A complete listing of the purpose and functions of the LYO and its board is provided in the LYO constitution.

"The Lutheran Youth Organization is made up of Christ-centered young people created, called, and commissioned by God to grow and participate in our baptismal relationships with our Lord, ourselves, and all creation." Those are the opening words of the LYO mission statement. With its mission statement in place, with a strong foundation from previous boards and leadership, and with the support of leaders and organizations within and without this church, the organizations's journey continues full speed ahead.

We invite everyone to celebrate with us. This year marks the 100th birth year of leadership from Lutheran youth. In 1895, the predecessor of the Lutheran Youth Organization, the Luther League, began. For a century, Lutheran youth have been given and have seized the opportunity to enhance leadership skills, join in fun and fellowship, study the Scriptures together, and serve each other, this church, our neighbors, and our God.

Through our baptism, we are called to be full participants in Christ's Church. So that everyone may fully participate in this call, the Lutheran Youth Organization works toward tearing and keeping down the walls that separate us from one another.

The leadership that comes from the Lutheran Youth Organization is strong, dynamic, and mature. This leadership, a youth perspective, and the fact that the LYO has stood up with conviction and strength to address openly many difficult issues that youth and adults alike face, benefit this church in its decision making. For these reasons, the LYO continues with great dedication its effort to see that young persons are included in every assembly, council, board, committee, and task force of this church in all its expressions. It is very satisfying to know that the Evangelical Lutheran Church in America today has more young people in leadership positions than ever before.

The Lutheran Youth Organization continues to celebrate the tremendous cultural heritages and multiple experiences that young people bring to this church, and is committed to reflect in its leadership the demographics of the youth population in the Caribbean and the U.S. more so than the demographics of the Evangelical Lutheran Church in America itself.

The Lutheran Youth Organization seeks to raise global awareness by encouraging young people to study and to learn about the gifts of other people and cultures in our global community, by encouraging synodical LYO units to strengthen their ties with companion synods, and by encouraging the use of global village themes at gatherings and workshops.

The Lutheran Youth Organization focuses on the importance of caring for our environment and being good stewards of God's creation. It also encourages that there be a reduction of waste, that there be recycling, and that recyclable materials be used at all congregational, synodical, and churchwide functions.

The Lutheran Youth Organization promotes servant leadership among youth in the Evangelical Lutheran Church in America. Servant events are also very important to the ministry of the organization. We recognize that service builds one's self-esteem and that indeed one person working with others can make a difference. Young people today are serving in many settings, from building homes for the homeless to advocating in state legislatures for many different issues. Expressions of this emphasis can be found in the rapidly expanding Churchwide Servant Event Network, at gatherings, and at leadership schools.

The Lutheran Youth Organization, through the Division for Congregational Ministries and in partnership with the Publishing House of the Evangelical Lutheran Church in America, continues to produce annually a Program Planning Guide (PPG) for use in every congregation. This is a youth-designed resource that helps the organization to address the triennial goals and resolutions that were passed during the preceding convention.

LYO in Congregations

Congregational LYO or youth ministry programs have a significant impact on their communities. Such congregational ministries not only are providing a place for fun and fellowship, but are teaching youth about the Word of God, and working on programs from world hunger to support groups for teens facing unique experiences and challenges. Congregational units are the primary reason for the existence of the Lutheran Youth Organization.

LYO in Synods

Today there are 62 synodical Lutheran Youth Organizations. These organizations strengthen congregational youth ministry programs through leadership schools, gatherings, servant experiences, and other opportunities.

LYO Churchwide Organization

Triennial Convention: The churchwide Lutheran Youth Organization is governed by its triennial convention, which takes place within the ELCA's Churchwide Youth Gathering. The third triennial convention, July 20-24, 1994, was held in Atlanta, Ga. The gathering brought together 34,000 youth to celebrate what it means "To Be Alive." The convention had 381 registered delegates and represented 60 ELCA synods.

LYO Board (BLYO): The Lutheran Youth Organization is governed between conventions by its 21-member board which is representative of the many gifts of today's generation. The board meetings are intense and very productive. The board continues to work on business that is set before them from the LYO triennial convention, and its two advisory bodies, the Council of Synodical LYO Presidents and the Multicultural Advisory Committee.

Multicultural Advisory Committee (MAC): MAC is made up of eight persons who are elected at the triennial Multicultural Youth Leadership Event (MYLE), with one female and one male each from the Hispanic, African American, Native American, and Asian communities. Liaisons also work with the committee. The purpose of the committee is to help the Lutheran Youth Organization to continue its efforts to be inclusive and to voice the concerns and needs of youth of color and/or whose primary language is other than English. The committee also is responsible for planning the Multicultural Youth Leadership Event, held three days prior to the churchwide Youth Gathering. This leadership event provides leadership training, a vision of unity, and the opportunity to celebrate diversity.

Differently Abled Youth Leadership Event (DAYLE): Two members of the board are elected at this event, which takes place two days prior to the churchwide Youth Gathering. These two board members are responsible for coordinating the Differently Abled Youth Leadership Event. The event brings together youth with disabilities for leadership training and sharing before the gathering.

Council of Synod LYO Presidents (CYCLOPS): The council meets annually as directed by the Lutheran Youth Organization constitution. It brings together presidents and representatives from every synodical LYO, as well as two adult advisors from each region. The council members come together to share what is happening in their regions, synods, and communities, and to advise the Lutheran Youth Organization and the entire youth ministries area of the Division for Congregational Ministries on many issues and concerns. One hundred-eighteen presidents, representatives, and advisors gathered for a four-day meeting held in Chicago, February 9-12, 1995. The theme for the council this year was "Stop the Violence." The primary focus of the meeting is leadership training, along with networking and sharing resources.

Looking Ahead

The Lutheran Youth Organization values its relationship with the Youth Ministry Team of the Division for Congregational Ministries and with the other ministry teams of the division.

The Lutheran Youth Organization is considered to be a premier youth organization both ecumenically and globally. This will continue to be the case in years ahead precisely because the LYO is an organization that is governed and run by youth. This fact enables the LYO to be responsive to the changing needs and diverse gifts of young people in our church and society. We celebrate the fact that the Evangelical Lutheran Church in America takes baptism seriously and recognizes that all Christ-centered persons are created, called, and commissioned by God to grow and participate in their baptismal relationships with their Lord, themselves, and all creation, and that all ages are called to be full participants in the life and mission of the Church, all to the glory of God.

ELCA LUTHERAN YOUTH ORGANIZATION

VANCE ROBBINS, *President*
WALTER J. ("MARK") KNUTSON, *Director for ELCA Youth Ministries and Lutheran Youth Organization*

Report of the Division for Ministry

Organization

Board

Mr. Herbert B. Dorr, Minneapolis, Minn. (1997)[1,5]

Ms. Andrea L. Dubler, Connellsville, Pa. (1995)[5]

Rev. James K. Echols, Philadelphia, Pa. (1997)[4]

Rev. James M. Ellison, Wheeling, W.Va. (1995)[1,3]

Ms. Nancy C. Fricke, Indiana, Pa. (1999)[6]

Mr. John R. Graff, Annandale, Va. (1997)[3]

Mr. David F. Hagen, Dearborn Heights, Mich. (1995)[2]

Rev. Susan M. Kintner, Portland, Oreg. (1995)[1,6]

Rev. Steven P. Loy, Las Cruces, N.Mex. (1999)[5]

Mr. Peter S. J. McKinney, Madison Heights, Mich. (1999)[6]

Rev. Susan E. Nagle, Montclair, N.J. (1997)[3]

Ms. Kelly R. H. Pearson, Norman, Okla. (1999)[2]

Ms. Marybeth A. Peterson, *chair*, Omaha, Nebr. (1995)[1,2]

Rev. Donna Hacker Smith, Freeport, Ill. (1999)[4]

Mr. David M. Soderlund, Geneva, N.Y. (1997)[3]

Mr. William F. Steirer Jr., *secretary*, Clemson, S.C. (1997)[1,4]

Rev. Leslie G. Svendsen, Northfield, Minn. (1995)[2]

Ms. Georgine E. Thompson, Corvallis, Oreg. (1995)[4]

Mr. Nelvin Vos, Maxatawny, Pa. (1999)[6]

Ms. Rachel Conrad Wahlberg, Austin, Tex. (1997)[5]

Rev. Donna M. Wright, Scribner, Nebr. (1999)[3]

---

[1]Executive Committee

[2]Administration Committee

[3]Theological Education Committee

[4]Candidacy Committee

[5]Leadership Support Committee

[6]Ministry in Daily Life Committee

Advisors

Bishop Roger L. Munson, Northeastern Minnesota Synod

Ms. Lita Brusick Johnson, executive assistant to the bishop, Office of the Bishop

Staff

Executive Director: Rev. Joseph M. Wagner

Assistant Executive Director:
Rev. Herbert B. Carlmark

Editor, *Lutheran Partners*: Rev. Carl E. Linder

Managing Editor, *Lutheran Partners*:
Mr. William A. Decker

Director of Strategy for Sexual Abuse Prevention:
Rev. Jan Erickson-Pearson

Director for Candidacy: Rev. A. Craig Settlage

Director for Rostered Lay Ministries:
Ms. Madelyn H. Busse

Director for Leadership Support:
Rev. William C. Behrens

Consultant, Growth in Excellence in Ministry:
Rev. Bruce D. Johnston

Consultant, Coordinator for Specialized Pastoral Care Services: Rev. Herbert B. Cleveland

Director for Ministry in Daily Life: Ms. Sally A. Simmel

Director for Theological Education:
Rev. Phyllis B. Anderson

Director for Inclusive Leadership Development:
Rev. James Y. K. Moy

Deployed Staff

(shared with the Department for Synodical Relations)

Region 1: Rev. Neal G. Buckaloo, Seattle, Wash.

Region 2: Vacant

Region 3: Rev. Hubert R. Kaste, St. Paul, Minn.

Region 4: Rev. Roger J. Gieschen, Overland Park, Kans.

Region 5: Central Staff, Chicago, Ill.

Region 6: Rev. Hermann J. Kuhlmann, Columbus, Ohio

Region 7: Vacant

Region 8: Vacant

Region 9: Rev. Gerald S. Troutman, Atlanta, Ga.

Constitutional Mandate

The Division for Ministry seeks to support the healthy and faithful ministry of all the baptized members of this church, especially pastors, associates in ministry, deaconesses, and diaconal ministers, through churchwide programs of recruitment, education, approval, support, continuing education, and theological reflection, in partnership with seminaries, continuing education centers, other churchwide units, synods, pastors, and rostered lay ministers. The constitutional mandate of this division is defined in continuing resolution 16.11.B91. of the Constitution, Bylaws, and Continuing Resolutions of the Evangelical Lutheran Church in America.

Report of Work 1993-1994
Introductory Overview

Everyone seems to have an idea of what it takes for the Evangelical Lutheran Church in America to be a vital, growing, faithful denomination. There is much written these days about the life of denominations and their promising or declining futures. But, quite aside from such research and prognostication by experts is the simple experience that you, as a member of a congregation, know as you worship and participate in the life of your own congregation, or as you visit in neighboring congregations, or churches across the country. The Christian faith is experienced firsthand in the relationships that exist between the parishioner, the pastor, and the community of faith known as the congregation. Simply put, healthy, faithful congregations served by healthy, faithful leaders are the building blocks of a healthy, faithful church body, and indeed a healthy, faithful Church of Jesus Christ.

In this equation, the Division for Ministry carries out mandated responsibilities to bring to bear the best resources this church has to produce healthy, faithful pastors, associates in ministry, deaconesses, and diaconal ministers. They serve in congregations and in the many specialized ministries of this church: hospitals, universities, seminaries, synodical and churchwide staffs, social service agencies, and myriad other places where competent, qualified, committed leaders are required to embody Christ's ministry.

Where do healthy, faithful pastors come from? How are they prepared, and how are they sustained? The Division for Ministry seeks to answer those questions and to provide the steady supply of healthy, faithful leaders the ministries of Christ's Church require. Healthy, faithful leaders are called out from our congregations. Through synodical candidacy committees, they are assisted in their struggle for vocational clarity and are guided as they learn the basic skills and knowledge required to serve as an ordained minister or as a rostered lay minister.

In the eight seminaries of this church, candidates are prepared through classroom study, field work, internships, and clinical pastoral education to be competent and faithful leaders. They are examined by their seminaries and by the candidacy committees to test their academic and ecclesial readiness to assume the responsibilities and the privileges of the leadership ministries of this church. The ministry and mission of our eight seminaries are guided by the Division for Ministry through work with seminary boards and seminary presidents and administrators. Work is now underway linking the seminaries into three clusters, which will allow those institutions to be more complementary, less competitive, and more able to serve the dramatically

changing needs for theological education in this church. A network of 15 continuing education centers, along with the seminaries, provides courses and promotes continuing education within this church.

In cooperation with the Division for Congregational Ministries, the Division for Ministry also carries responsibility for the ministry in daily life of all baptized members of this church. Through resources and various programs, this church is reminded of the crucial ministry provided by all baptized members as they go about their daily service within the world for the sake of Jesus Christ. At every point the Division for Ministry is committed to linking the ministries of rostered persons and of all the baptized, so that the work of pastors and other workers in congregations supports the ministries of lay members in their daily lives.

Through its programs and services the division seeks to discharge its constitutional responsibilities for the preparation and support of rostered ministers and all the baptized who minister in their daily lives. Thus, we assist Christ's church in preparing healthy, faithful leaders to promote the healthy, faithful life of congregations and to contribute to the health and faithful service of the Evangelical Lutheran Church in America.

Candidacy and Recruitment

Pastors, Associates in Ministry, Deaconesses, and Diaconal Ministers make up the official roster of this church. These leaders are trained to serve in congregations and other specialized settings and are carefully guided and prepared according to churchwide standards and through the network of synodical candidacy committees working in concert with our seminaries. As the circumstances of ministry change, categories of ministry have been adjusted. For example, the 1993 Churchwide Assembly established a new category of ministry—Diaconal Ministers—as a result of this church's Study of Ministry. Other actions of the 1993 Churchwide Assembly authorized non-stipendiary ministries, an extension of the guidelines for On Leave from Call status, and authorized other licensed ministries to meet emerging mission needs. The division has worked in the past biennium to develop guidelines for diaconal ministers and for new extended forms of non-stipendiary and licensed ministries.

A special focus of work during the biennium has been the revision of the candidacy process particularly in evaluating the candidate's readiness to begin theological study and potential for service as an ELCA rostered leader. The revised process, developed in consultation with synodical and seminary personnel, enables candidacy committees to begin evaluation of candidates prior to their entrance into seminary. This new approach seeks to assure that candidates can begin study in seminary with a reasonable expectation of success.

To help persons think through whether they may be receiving God's call to an occupation within this church, the division has recently produced a booklet entitled, *What Shall I Say: Discerning God's Call to Ministry*. This publication presents the theological foundations for understanding ministry and call, describes the various ministries that are available, assists individuals in their discernment of call, and identifies the gifts necessary for the ordained ministry.

Theological Education: Major developments are underway in the area of theological education and this church's relationship to its eight seminaries. The 1993 Churchwide Assembly took bold action in calling for the gathering of the seminaries into three to five clusters. Seminary boards and the Division for Ministry board have acted so that as the 1995 Churchwide Assembly convenes, there will be three groupings of seminaries: an eastern cluster comprising Gettysburg, Philadelphia, and Southern seminaries; a western cluster comprising Pacific and Luther Seminaries; and a Midwest cluster/covenant comprised of the Lutheran School of Theology at Chicago with Wartburg and Trinity seminaries. A major strategic planning process during 1995 will lead to systemwide and cluster projections of strategies, costs, and revenue streams for the emerging system of theological education. Funding proposals requested by the 1993 Churchwide Assembly will issue from this planning process.

Other recommendations of the 1993 Churchwide Assembly have led to developments in "distance learning" among seminaries, a stronger focus upon readiness for seminary studies among candidates, and a proposal requiring three years of continuing theological education during the time of a pastor's first call. This recommendation will be presented to the 1995 Churchwide Assembly for action. Other 1993 Churchwide Assembly actions undergird the priority of theological education in the funding decisions of this church and support the eleven imperatives for theological education developed by the study.

All these developments demonstrate this church's strong commitment to the solid preparation of rostered leaders through rigorous and faithful theological education. These significant changes in the system of theological education and in the ways seminaries complement one another will position this church well to adapt to the changing circumstances of ministry in the years ahead. The final report and recommendations from the Task Force on the Study of Theological Education appear elsewhere in the materials for this assembly and provide detailed background information regarding the issues summarized here.

The division sponsors two continuing opportunities for public theological dialogue. At the Hein-Fry Lecture Series of 1994, Douglas John Hall and Rosemary Radford Ruether spoke on the subject, "God and the Nations" while in 1995, Terrence Fretheim and Karlfried Froehlich lectured on the theme, "The Bible as the Word of God in a Post Modern Age." The Hein-Fry Lecture Series has become a hallmark of this church. The 1994 Convocation of Teaching Theologians met around the theme, "Renewing Biblical Authority: A Challenge for the ELCA." This event was attended by 90 invited theological faculty from ELCA colleges and universities, seminaries, and non-ELCA schools, as well as bishops and churchwide staff.

The 25th Anniversary of the Ordination of Women in the Lutheran Church in North America will be celebrated at a conference just prior to the 1995 Churchwide Assembly. This celebration is sponsored by the Division for Ministry in cooperation with the Women of the Evangelical Lutheran Church in America and the Commission for Women.

Leadership Support

Continuing growth and effectiveness in leadership requires continuing education. To meet this need, continuing education events are promoted and provided by seminaries, continuing education centers, and the synods of this church. Such programs are promoted and supported by the Division for Ministry. Participation in continuing education continues to increase among pastors and rostered lay leaders, as well as the lay members of this church. In 1993, 41 synods, 15 continuing education centers, and six seminaries reported that they had provided more than 950 separate continuing education events. A total of more than 18,000 pastors or rostered lay leaders participated in these events along with more than 21,000 lay members.

The Growth in Excellence in Ministry Program (GEM) concluded its fourth year in 1994. This massive project strengthens the leadership competence of pastors, rostered lay leaders, and key lay members of congregations by promoting written commitments to participate in continuing education, and providing financial scholarships to encourage such participation. Approximately 3,000 rostered leaders receive grants totalling more than $600,000 each year through GEM. A churchwide curriculum developed in cooperation with other churchwide units includes multicultural education events, transition workshops for pastors moving from and to new ministries, a mentoring program called the "Colleague Program," and an evangelism program focusing on evangelizing congregations teaching other congregations. The final elements of the curricula, related to stewardship development and Ministry in

Daily Life, are now under development. The GEM project will continue with strong support from Lutheran Brotherhood until it is phased out in the year 2000.

The compensation levels of pastors and other rostered leaders continues to be a source of interest and concern. Compensation (salary plus housing) for ELCA pastors in congregations grew annually at about $1,000 per year during the past six years:

Year	Average	Median
1988	$29,745	$28,825
1994	36,735	36,100

A new Special Needs Retirement Fund authorized by the 1993 Churchwide Assembly is now in place, initiated by the Division for Ministry, and managed by the Department for Synodical Relations. Voluntary contributions to this fund are being sought from congregations and individuals and will be used to supplement retirement benefits of pastors and spouses whose total income is below the recommended minimum retirement levels. Once these needs are met, additional contributions will be made to the retirement accumulations of pastors and rostered lay leaders who are serving in calls with chronic low compensation.

Continuing budget reductions have resulted in a gradual reduction of churchwide grants to continuing education centers; the phasing out will be completed in 1995. New developments in the area of leadership support include a Ministerial Health and Wellness Symposium sponsored by the Evangelical Lutheran Church in America and The Lutheran Church—Missouri Synod in fall 1994. The learnings and resolutions from this conference challenge the Lutheran church bodies in North America to focus their energies upon the promotion of health and wellness among pastors and lay workers through the development of new resources and support.

Sexual Abuse Prevention

Instances of clergy sexual abuse, while rare, are catastrophic when they occur. Management of the ELCA's strategy for the prevention of sexual abuse by clergy and other rostered leaders was assigned to the division by the Church Council. This responsibility is being carried out in cooperation with the Commission for Women, other churchwide units, and the synods of this church. Resources to assist synodical bishops, staff, and others in an effective response to alleged instances of sexual abuse are now being provided. As a part of this same strategy, synods and seminaries are providing education and training for pastors and other rostered leaders.

In December 1993, a comprehensive sexual abuse prevention training workshop for bishops and synod staff was sponsored by the Division for Ministry and the Commission for Women. Almost all synods now have developed policies regarding sexual abuse by rostered persons. A part-time staff person, the Rev. Jan Erickson-Pearson, guides this church's program for the prevention of sexual abuse. This church carries forward an increasingly effective program of education and prevention of this most serious problem.

Ministry in Daily Life

All baptized Christians perform ministry in Christ's name through their work and their relationships. Through the investment of our whole lives, we minister in Christ's name. The Division for Ministry continues to promote the understanding that work of the rostered ministers of this church is complemented by, and in turn complements, the ministries of all the baptized in the world and in the Church. There is great power in this simple idea. It is the answer to many questions now being raised as to how ministries can be extended while traditional sources of financial support and traditional structures in society and church are undergoing disruptive change.

During this biennium, Ministry in Daily Life has moved from good ideas to good actions and practices in this church. A variety of conferences were held in 1993 that deepened and broadened participants' understanding of their own ministries and ways that congregations can equip members for ministries in the world. The conference, "Booming the Church," brought together 60 baby-boomer church leaders who wrestled with their life issues of spirit, vocation, and family. The Ministry in Daily Life conference, "On Assignment From God," attracted both old-timers and new recruits to gather strength and plan for the future. The ELCA Work Group on Science and Technology was a major planner for "Science, Technology and the Christian Faith," an ecumenical international conference sponsored by CHARIS Ecumenical Center at Concordia College, Moorhead, Minn. More than 400 persons attended this event.

Following the adoption of the Study of Ministry recommendations in 1993, Ministry in Daily Life assignments are shared by the Division for Ministry and the Division for Congregational Ministries for implementation. Inter-unit staff work continues on these projects to determine how the understanding of ministry of all the baptized has been integrated into the life of this church, and to recommend more effective approaches for bringing a deeper appreciation of all the baptized into the ongoing life of this church. Reports on these efforts will be made to the 1995 Churchwide Assembly as this church increases its efforts to promote this foundational New Testament and Reformation theme into the everyday experiences of ministry within this church.

Specialized Pastoral Care and Clinical Education

While most ministries are provided from a congregational base, there are more than 850 pastors and rostered lay leaders who serve in specialized ministries. Included in this group are 181 counselors in pastoral counseling, 269 chaplains in general health-care chaplaincy, 242 chaplains in long-term care chaplaincy, 64 chaplains in mental health-care chaplaincy, 46 chaplains in correctional chaplaincy, 39 chaplains in substance-abuse chaplaincy, and 15 chaplains in mental retardation and developmental disability ministry. These ministries, fortified by the Gospel of Jesus Christ, enable this church to reach arenas of human need that are not accessible to most congregations. The Division for Ministry provides care and attention to these ministries through programmatic and staff support. Much of the work in specialized pastoral care is provided on an inter-Lutheran basis in close cooperation with The Lutheran Church—Missouri Synod.

In mid-1994, budget reductions led to a reduction to half-time for the staff position related to specialized pastoral care. Subsequent to a staff resignation, three consultants in specialized pastoral care were selected to carry out the programmatic responsibilities related to those ministries, and to maintain supportive relationships with synodical specialized pastoral care committees. As in all areas of the provision of services throughout this church, economies and the creative use of human resources are the rule for the future.

Lutheran Partners

Lutheran Partners magazine is the only publication of this church that specifically seeks to link the pastors and rostered lay leaders in practical and theological dialogue. Published six times per year and distributed free of charge to the entire roster of ordained and lay workers, *Lutheran Partners* has a unique niche in the web of connections that bind this church together. Its purpose is to encourage "rostered leaders, serving in congregations and other ministry settings, to exchange opinions and viewpoints on matters of interest and concern, especially those involving theology, leadership, mission, and service to the Gospel of Jesus Christ."

In the interest of seeking to better understand its readership, the staff of *Lutheran Partners*, in cooperation with the Department of Research and Evaluation, surveyed a random sample of its readers. The results of the survey underscored what readers read and want, the

articles they find helpful, and suggested possible improvements. The survey also demonstrated a high level of reader involvement in the publication. Fully two thirds of those who receive *Lutheran Partners* read at least some portion of the magazine every issue, and about 16 percent read the entire magazine.

Financial constraints have affected *Lutheran Partners* as well. During the biennium, the editor's position was reduced to half-time, and increasing costs of publication and distribution were met by more aggressive use of advertising as a source of revenue. *Lutheran Partners* provides a voice for the local pastor and lay worker and, hence, is an important source for building morale and connections among pastors and rostered lay leaders.

Referrals from 1993 Churchwide Assembly
Study of Ministry (CA93.6.17)

Recommendations from the 1993 Study of Ministry are too numerous to list, and have required major efforts by the division and our partners during this biennium. Assembly action to establish a diaconal ministry has resulted in the development of guidelines for this form of ministry and the designation of Gettysburg Seminary as the lead institution for training persons in this ministry. The first group of diaconal ministers will participate in a formation event this summer. Recommendations related to ministry in daily life and the relationships between diaconal ministers and associates in ministry are reported elsewhere among Division for Ministry reports to the 1995 Churchwide Assembly.

Study of Theological Education (CA93.6.18-CA93.6.25)

The recommendation regarding the clustering of seminaries was accomplished on schedule in fall 1994. Recommendations related to funding theological education, first call continuing theological education, and distance learning are reported elsewhere in materials for the 1995 Churchwide Assembly. The development of recommended standards for academic and ecclesial readiness have been accomplished in consultation with seminaries and synodical representatives during this biennium.

Twenty-Fifth Anniversary of the Ordination of Women (CA93.7.32)

The Division for Ministry, in cooperation with other churchwide units, has laid plans for a churchwide celebration of the 25th anniversary of the ordination of Lutheran women in North America. Such events are being held in synods and in congregations, with a special churchwide celebration scheduled in Minneapolis immediately prior to the 1995 Churchwide Assembly.

Study of Clergy Compensation (CA93.8.100)

Assembly actions in the area of low clergy compensation and pension benefits resulted in the establishment in 1994 of the Special Needs Retirement Fund. This new effort has begun to gather funds for supplementing the pension benefits of rostered leaders retiring with very low pension benefits. It also will provide additional pension contributions to low-compensated rostered leaders. Further studies related to clergy compensation and healthy congregations are being pursued cooperatively by the Division for Ministry, the Department for Synodical Relations, and the Department for Research and Evaluation.

Health of Rostered Persons (CA93.8.108)

The concern to promote healthy lifestyles among rostered leaders is being pursued through inter-Lutheran consultation and program development related to ministerial health and wellness. An inter-Lutheran conference, held in October 1994, focused interest on this important subject.

Interim Ministry (CA93.8.103)

The concerns addressed by this proposed amendment to the ELCA Bylaws has involved staff in work with the Conference of Bishops, the Department for Synodical Relations, and others. Interim ministry concerns are included in recommendations to the 1995 Churchwide Assembly in the report of the Church Council, where they appear as proposed bylaw amendments.

Clinical Pastoral Education (CA93.8.99)

The concerns raised by this recommendation, to remove the clinical pastoral education requirement for ordination, are being met by ongoing consideration of this issue in the Division for Ministry. No specific action is required at this time.

Social Teaching Statements on the Environment and on Race, Ethnicity and Culture

Two social teaching statements, adopted by the 1993 Churchwide Assembly, were referred to the Division for Ministry for certain aspects of their implementation. The division's responsibility involves integrating these concerns into programs produced by the Division for Ministry, and emphasizing the importance of such teaching statements as students are trained in the seminaries of this church. Through its ongoing relationships with the seminaries and continuing education centers, the Division for Ministry is promoting the concerns raised in these social statements.

Major Program Directions for Fiscal 1995-1996

The Division for Ministry exists to supply healthy, faithful leaders for the mission of the Evangelical Lutheran Church in America in the years to come. The next biennium will see the division continuing on this basic course with several special emphases.

First, the directions set by the recommendations of the Study of Ministry and the Study of Theological Education will begin to bear noticeable fruits. The new categories for ministry (diaconal ministers, non-stipendiary ministers, and licensed ministers) as well as the focus on the ministries of the laity in their daily lives, will become more apparent across this church. The reason for emphasizing these new forms of ministry is to allow this church to be flexible as it deploys witnesses to the Gospel of Jesus Christ in a rapidly changing world. These new personnel resources, used creatively, will equip this church to expand its ministries through more adaptable leadership in the coming years.

The second area of new development flows from the recommendations of the five-year Study of Theological Education, which will bring its final report to the 1995 Churchwide Assembly. The next biennium will see the clear development of a cohesive system of theological education linking seminaries, synods, and other theological education providers in an adaptable and effective network. It is anticipated that the three seminary clusters will be functioning realities, and will begin to win the support of traditional constituencies and to generate excitement throughout this church for theological education for the next century.

Finally, the task of developing leaders for this church will be achieved through shared program directions with other churchwide units, synods, seminaries, and other institutions. The working style of the Division for Ministry is characterized by close consultation with its partners and clear communication regarding plans. This style of working together results in strategies for ministry being developed out of local needs while taking into account the broader mission directions of this whole church. By being adaptable as well as firm, the division will continue to address with its partners the emerging needs for ministry that will challenge us as well as new possibilities for ministry that may surprise us.

BOARD OF THE DIVISION FOR MINISTRY
MARYBETH A. PETERSON, *Chair*
JOSEPH M. WAGNER, *Executive Director*

Exhibit A

Seminary Enrollments

Master of Divinity Enrollments
Lutheran and Non-Lutheran Students by Seminary

M.Div.Trend	1987		1988	
	Lutheran	Non-Lutheran	Lutheran	Non-Lutheran
LS[1]	457	33	467	28
LSTC[2]	172	29	183	9
LTSG[3]	154	8	145	12
LTSP[4]	94	7	93	7
LTSS[5]	79	18	82	17
PLTS[6]	101	9	101	0
TLS[7]	179	17	164	11
WTS[8]	178	9	167	7
Subtotals	1,414	130	1,402	91
Total Enrollments	1,544		1,493	

M.Div.Trend	1989		1990	
	Lutheran	Non-Lutheran	Lutheran	Non-Lutheran
LS[1]	457	36	468	31
LSTC[2]	199	9	179	7
LTSG[3]	139	9	131	7
LTSP[4]	85	18	92	12
LTSS[5]	81	16	80	15
PLTS[6]	106	1	100	1
TLS[7]	141	12	126	13
WTS[8]	177	3	177	3
Subtotals	1,385	104	1,353	89
Total Enrollments	1,489		1,442	

M.Div. Trend	1991		1992	
	Lutheran	Non-Lutheran	Lutheran	Non-Lutheran
LS[1]	470	35	480	40
LSTC[2]	171	6	178	14
LTSG[3]	153	10	143	17
LTSP[4]	96	50	104	60
LTSS[5]	100	20	125	19
PLTS[6]	92	0	88	1
TLS[7]	134	19	160	12
WTS[8]	173	6	183	9
Subtotals	1,389	146	1,461	172
Total Enrollments	1,535		1,633	

M.Div. Trend	1993		1994	
	Lutheran	Non-Lutheran	Lutheran	Non-Lutheran
LS[1]	444	66	452	46
LSTC[2]	173	8	163	5
LTSG[3]	148	11	152	9
LTSP[4]	106	63	108	60
LTSS[5]	146	25	141	17
PLTS[6]	90	0	104	0
TLS[7]	162	9	188	12
WTS[8]	168	7	157	4
Subtotals	1,437	189	1,465	153
Total Enrollments	1,626		1,618	

1. Luther Seminary, St. Paul, Minn.
2. Lutheran School of Theology at Chicago, Chicago, Ill.
3. Lutheran Theological Seminary at Gettysburg, Gettysburg, Pa.
4. Lutheran Theological Seminary at Philadelphia, Philadelphia, Pa.
5. Lutheran Theological Southern Seminary, Columbia, S.C.
6. Pacific Lutheran Theological Seminary, Berkeley, Calif.
7. Trinity Lutheran Seminary, Columbus, Ohio
8. Wartburg Theological Seminary, Dubuque, Iowa

Master of Divinity Enrollments
Lutheran Students by Gender

	1989		1990		1991	
Men	826	60%	778	58%	796	57%
Women	559	40%	575	42%	593	43%
Totals	1385		1353		1389	

	1992		1993		1994	
Men	825	56%	806	56%	814	56%
Women	636	44%	631	44%	651	44%
Totals	1461		1437		1465	

Graduate Enrollment
By Seminary

	1993		1994	
	M.A.R.	*GRAD.*	*M.A.R.*	*GRAD.*
LS[1]	89	170	99	190
LSTC[2]	24	124	28	146
LTSG[3]	26	34	21	22
LTSP[4]	31	79	33	82
LTSS[5]	18	14	15	12
PLTS[6]	27	13	25	17
TLS[7]	35	10	39	5
WTS[8]	6	13	9	13
Subtotals	256	457	269	487
Total Yearly Enrollments	713		756	

1. Luther Seminary, St. Paul, Minn.
2. Lutheran School of Theology at Chicago, Chicago, Ill.
3. Lutheran Theological Seminary at Gettysburg, Gettysburg, Pa.
4. Lutheran Theological Seminary at Philadelphia, Philadelphia, Pa.
5. Lutheran Theological Southern Seminary, Columbia, S.C.
6. Pacific Lutheran Theological Seminary, Berkeley, Calif.
7. Trinity Lutheran Seminary, Columbus, Ohio
8. Wartburg Theological Seminary, Dubuque, Iowa

Graduate Enrollment
By Degree 1993-1994

	1993	1994
M.A./M.A.R./M.R.E./M.T.S.	256	269
D.MIN.	248	258
S.T.M.	98	27
H.M./M.Th.	23	38
Th.D.	77	87
Ph.D.	11	17
Totals	713	696

Exhibit B

Educational Grants Program

Scholarship Grants Report

	1989	1990	1991	1992	1993
Advanced Degree Grants: Number of Grants (Ph.D. or Th.D)	55	48	46	46	45
Total Amount Given	$ 86,750	$ 69,500	$ 66,250	$ 72,000	$ 68,000
Average Grant	$ 1,591	$ 1,448	$ 1,440	$ 1,565	$ 1,511
Language Studies Grants: Number of Grants	10	13	8	0	6
Total Amount Given	$ 6,116	$ 7,925	$ 5,437	$ -0-	$ 5,005
Average Grant	$ 612	$ 610	$ 680	$ -0-	$ 834
M.Div. Grants:* Number of Grants	55	72	48	58	58
Total Amount Given	$136,400	$119,332	$105,750	$116,000	$103,000
Average Grant	$ 2,480	$ 1,657	$ 2,203	$ 2,000	$ 1,776

*African American, Asian, Hispanic and Native American Seminarians.

Horizon Internships
Statistical Summary

	1993	1994
Churchwide Funds	199,165	174,432
Synod Funds	109,333	104,700
Number Sites	26	26
Average Funds Per Site	5,532	6,337
Asian Ministry	0	0
African American Ministry	12	12
Hispanic Ministry	5	6
Native American Ministry	0	1
Institutional Ministry	1	1
Urban Ministry	18	19
Rural Ministry	7	12

Faithful Leaders for a Changing World: Theological Education for Mission in the ELCA

Report to the 1995 Churchwide Assembly

This report to the 1995 Churchwide Assembly of the Evangelical Lutheran Church in America has two components. Part One presents an overview of the Study of Theological Education and recommendations for action by the Churchwide Assembly. Part Two contains appendices which provide background detail.

Part I: Overview of the Study of Theological Education and Recommendations for Churchwide Assembly Action

A. Challenges That Demand Study and Action

In April 1989, upon the recommendation of the Division for Ministry, the Church Council of the Evangelical Lutheran Church in America (ELCA) approved a proposal for a study of theological education in the ELCA. The council appointed a task force to develop, in consultation with appropriate partners, a plan for a system of theological education which will:

- *prepare the leaders needed for the mission challenges facing the ELCA;*
- *be sustained financially by the ELCA through a combination of church grants and individual gifts; and*
- *be appropriately accountable to the ELCA.*

1. Leaders for Mission

The mission imperative to the Evangelical Lutheran Church in America is to proclaim the radical gospel of life and hope in Jesus Christ to all people. While overseas mission remains a high priority in this church, today the frontier of mission is at our doorstep. In the United States ethnic and religious pluralism are replacing the cultural dominance of the Christian churches and Eurocentric values. A vast and growing segment of the population has no relationship with Christ and his Church. This society is increasingly stratified, both educationally and economically. Populations in the United States are moving south and west, and from rural to metropolitan areas. U.S. racial-ethnic composition by the year 2020 will be at least one-third people of color or whose first language is other than English.

The mission of the ELCA includes members of ELCA congregations who seek deeper connections between their faith and their daily lives. It encompasses their non-Christian neighbors, co-workers, friends and family members. The mission extends beyond traditionally Lutheran congregations or culturally compatible communities to Americans of many racial and ethnic groups, economic classes, and regional sub-cultures. It includes those who have drifted from the church or left in anger. The ELCA's mission is to people without any religious background is growing in an increasingly secular society. (A description of the changing mission context from the 1993 report appears as Appendix A.)

To respond to this urgent mission the ELCA needs faithful leaders who can share the gospel with unbelievers and lead communities of faith. Many of these leaders will be parish pastors or ordained persons in specialized institutional ministries. Others will be associates in ministry, deaconesses, or diaconal ministers who bring professional competence and distinctive styles to their ministries in this church and in society. But the new mission challenge will not be borne by rostered leaders alone. Some communities will be served on a part-time or volunteer basis by designated leaders from among their ranks who earn their living in other occupations. And, most importantly, all the baptized are called to minister in the world where they live and work and form relationships.

Christian leaders are equipped for ministry first because they have personally experienced the presence of Christ in their lives and have come to faith through the working of the Spirit in Scripture and the sacraments. Whether lay or ordained, full-time or bi-vocational, rostered or volunteer, mobile or place-bound, all these leaders need appropriate forms of theological education. Their varied programs of preparation must ground them in Christian doctrine and tradition, teach them practical skills of ministry, and help them understand the lives of people and world events from a faith perspective.

Furthermore, this church and these times need lay and ordained leaders who have received a *Lutheran* theological education. Lutherans have a distinctive theological contribution to offer. As North Americans approach the close of the 20th century, they are immersed in a sea of human brokenness. They are bombarded by signs of the failure of human solutions to the human dilemma. The Lutheran confessional heritage emphasizes divine intervention into human existence by a God of compassion who literally suffers with us.

This emphasis has never been needed more. There is a hunger among North Americans today for a gracious God who can help people live together in communities of compassion and reconciliation. The conventional quest for success through material acquisition, dominance and control over others, and heedless exploitation of the creation is radically challenged by a theology of the cross, of Christ crucified and yet risen. For the Lutheran theological tradition, such a focus has been central. Lutheran Christians are called to proclaim it with a fresh and persuasive conviction as we enter the world of the new century.

At the heart of fulfilling the ELCA's mission is theological education that prepares faithful leaders. In the language of the 1993 report, the purpose of theological education is:

To foster faithful and informed discourse on God's saving activity in the world, and to equip lay and ordained leaders who, by the power of the Holy Spirit and through the gifts of grace:

1. *Know and believe the Gospel of Jesus Christ, as revealed in the Holy Scriptures and proclaimed in the ecumenical creeds and the Lutheran confessions;*

2. *Witness to the Gospel by word and deed;*

3. *Reflect theologically on the mission of God's people in a pluralistic and secularized society;*

4. *Understand and creatively appropriate the various expressions of the Gospel by diverse cultures across the centuries and around the world;*

5. *Empower all the baptized members of this church to express the Gospel in their daily lives of witness and service in the world.*

2. Partnerships for Service and Support

A thorough study of theological education was necessary early in the life of the ELCA, not only to address new leadership challenges, but also to respond to patterns of financial support and institutional relationships that are changing rapidly in this and other denominations. Even though congregational giving is strong, funds are not flowing as they once did to synods and the churchwide organization for allocation to the broader ministries and institutions of this church. In relation to their own costs and the rate of inflation, ELCA seminaries are experiencing steady decline in financial support from synodical and churchwide sources. (See figure 1.)

While resources are diminishing, the need for high quality, diversified theological education is growing. Gifts from individual donors and increased tuition are beginning to replace and augment funds that formerly came through church grants. In this changing economic environment, decisions need to be made about how the churchwide organization, synods, congrega-

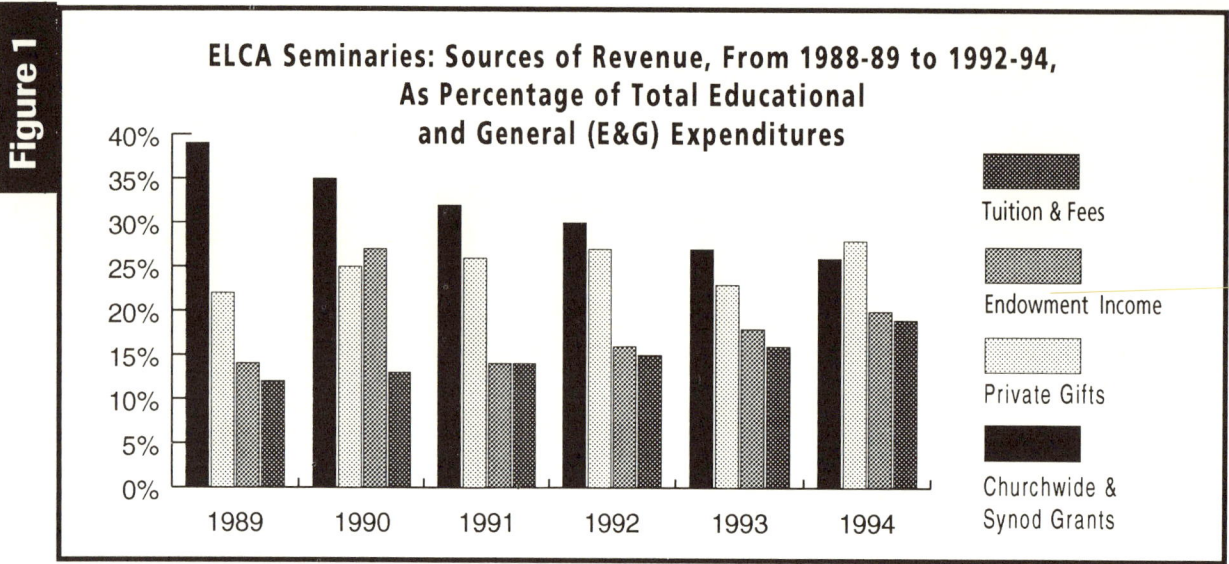

Figure 1

ELCA Seminaries: Sources of Revenue, From 1988-89 to 1992-94, As Percentage of Total Educational and General (E&G) Expenditures

Tuition & Fees

Endowment Income

Private Gifts

Churchwide & Synod Grants

The Endowment Income Contribution Ratio represents Endowment Income and Appropriated Capital Gains as a percentage of Total Educational and General Expenditures

tions, and members of this church will each support the essential and expanding services they depend upon their seminaries to provide.

The seminaries inherited by the ELCA have long understood themselves to be seminaries of the church whose primary purpose is to serve the denomination as seed beds for its future leaders and centers for theological discourse. Each seminary was originally founded to serve a specific constituency which assumed responsibility for its support. Successive mergers of Lutheran seminaries and of Lutheran church bodies have resulted in eight seminaries serving one church body. Former constituencies overlap. Seminaries with similar programs compete for students, while other potential mission leaders are asking for new services.

The study has provided the occasion for the seminaries and this church as a whole to think through and decide for new patterns of relationship among seminaries and between the seminaries and the various expressions of this church. If they succeed, these patterns will honor the distinctive character of the seminaries and maintain their common Lutheran theological identity, their formative role in preparing leaders who know and love Christ and his Church, and their responsiveness to the mission needs of this denomination. At the same time, these new patterns must yield diversity of service, greater interdependence, wise stewardship of resources, and adequate financial support for the seminaries. If positive new patterns are not forged, the ELCA will be seriously hampered in fulfilling its mission in the 21st century.

In response to these challenges, the task force proposed to the 1993 Churchwide Assembly eight recommendations, all of which were supported by at least 90 percent of the voting members. (The full text of the recommendations appears in Appendix B.) Five of the directions set by that assembly will directly strengthen and diversify the education of leaders for mission. The other three actions are structural and funding initiatives intended to undergird the seminaries in fulfilling their educational mission within an intentional theological education system.

B. Strengthening Leaders for Mission

1. Imperatives for Theological Education

The 1993 Churchwide Assembly identified 11 challenges or imperatives requiring attention at this time. (See sidebar, figure 2.) These imperatives were established as goals for an ELCA system of theological education. They were affirmed as the guiding and planning focus for preparation of leaders for this church into the 21st century. Authority to make the necessary changes in campus life, academic curriculum, and financial priorities in the seminaries to meet these imperatives resides with the boards and faculties within the seminaries.

What do we want the seminary clusters to do?

The ELCA Task Force on Theological Education has developed "11 imperatives" to develop pastors and lay leaders who have:

1. Deep faith rooted in the Scripture and a Lutheran understanding of the gospel, sustained by a disciplined devotional life.
2. The skills needed to share the faith with those who don't have it and to train others to share the faith.
3. Practical congregational skills in preaching, teaching, stewardship, evangelism and administration.
4. Knowledge of cultures of those they serve and the ability to adapt their ministry to their situation.
5. The ability to help church members connect their faith with daily life and relationships.

The ELCA seminary clusters and their partners will:

6. Identify and train African American, Asian, Hispanic and Native American leaders in ways congruent with their cultural backgrounds.
7. Identify and provide training that is flexible and readily available to indigenous lay leaders.
8. Provide continuing education opportunities to continue to develop and equip lay and ordained leaders.
9. Support theological centers where doctoral studies may be pursued.
10. Provide options for training that meet the needs of those in particular circumstances—older, unable to move, little experience of the church, etc.
11. Build cooperative relationships with seminaries and colleges of other Christian bodies.

The 11 imperatives raise up the need for pastors and lay leaders with greater spiritual and theological depth, passion for mission, practical congregational skills, and responsiveness to the context of their service. They identify the need for pastors and lay leaders from all the multicultural communities. The imperatives broaden the audience for theological education to include not only church workers of various kinds, but also laity for their ministry in daily life. The imperatives stress flexibility to make theological education more accessible for a variety of leaders in differing life circumstances. The need for continuing education over a lifetime is affirmed. Graduate theological education and scholarly discourse by seminary faculty are to be supported. The imperatives encourage ecumenical interdependence. (Complete text of the imperatives appears as Appendix C.)

Following the 1993 Assembly, the eight seminaries took immediate steps to utilize these imperatives in planning for the preparation of mission leaders. The faculties and boards of all eight have discussed the imperatives and their implications for curriculum revision. Each school has integrated the imperatives into its internal planning process. The seminaries and the Division for Ministry are developing programs and policies, are forging cooperative relationships and structures, and are committed to developing and reallocating resources in order to fulfill the imperatives.

Recommendation #1:

To direct the Division for Ministry to report to the 1997 Churchwide Assembly Continuing progress of the ELCA seminaries toward fulfilling the 11 imperatives approved by the 1993 Churchwide Assembly.

2. Quality of Candidates for Ministry

Current mission challenges demand faithful leaders who are thoroughly prepared. The degree to which candidates attain spiritual depth and ministerial competence during seminary depends in part on their readiness as incoming students to take full advantage of the learning opportunities at the seminary. Due to changes in both church and society, today's students vary widely in their readiness to begin master's level theological studies. Many bring rich educational and life experiences. Some lack familiarity with the Lutheran church, understanding of ministry, and background in academic subjects upon which the study of theology builds. Others come burdened with personal or financial problems. To develop to their full potential through the formation opportunities and graduate level academic studies offered by the seminaries, students need to have achieved certain levels of readiness before they begin.

a. Ecclesial Readiness

The 1993 Churchwide Assembly recommended that the Division for Ministry *"develop churchwide standards for early discernment of ecclesial readiness of students entering master's level programs in preparation for rostered ministries in this church."*

After consulting with many partners, the board of the Division for Ministry in March 1994 approved changes in the candidacy process which give greater weight to the entrance phase. Beginning in fall 1995, potential candidates for rostered ministry normally participate in a formal period of discernment before enrolling in seminary. During this entrance phase, a candidate completes an application for candidacy, makes contact with a synodical candidacy committee, has an initial structured interview, receives psychological and career evaluation, and is registered by the home congregation. A minimum of one year of active membership in an ELCA congregation is required. Candidacy committees may schedule retreats or interviews with potential candidates as part of this entrance stage. The Division for Ministry also has developed a resource to assist potential candidates to understand the nature and varieties of ministry in the ELCA and, with their candidacy committees, to discern their call. Reflecting on all these factors, the candidacy committee makes a formal decision regarding the readiness of the applicant to begin seminary studies in preparation for rostered ministry.

b. Academic Readiness

Another recommendation approved by the 1993 Assembly called upon the eight seminaries *"to develop common standards of academic readiness for students entering master's level programs in preparation for rostered ministries in this church."* The seminary deans responded with a statement approved by the Division for Ministry Board at its March 1995 meeting. (The full text of this statement appears as Appendix D.)

The common standard for admission to all ELCA seminaries is a baccalaureate degree from an accredited college or university, normally with at least a B average. Admissions decisions also take into account other relevant data, such as patterns of progress in the applicant's academic history, the degree of difficulty of the undergraduate program, success in other graduate programs, performance in previous occupations, and academic references.

With regard to academic readiness, the seminaries of the ELCA recommend a broad background in the liberal arts, including English, history, modern languages, philosophy, Greek, communications, and the social sciences. The applicant should possess intellectual ability for critical and reflective thinking. Beyond this, seminaries provide reading lists and study guides to candidates prior to the beginning of their seminary education. The seminaries also expect that ELCA candidates will acquire basic acquaintance with the Scriptures and the catechism as part of their ELCA congregational involvement required in the candidacy process.

The welcome diversity among today's seminary students makes it inevitable that there will be significant differences in academic readiness among entering students. Therefore the seminaries combine their stated expectations of academic readiness with introductory courses designed to bring students of varying academic backgrounds to a common level of readiness early in the program of studies.

3. Transition from Seminary to First Call

Ministry in the changing mission context requires faithful leaders with an abundant measure of the qualities outlined in the imperatives: depth in the faith, practical congregational skills, competence to communicate across cultures, capacity to reach out to unchurched people, and ability to make connections between faith and everyday life.

The foundations for these competencies are laid in the gifts people bring to ministry and the learning they receive in seminary. To a large extent, however, these ministry strengths are finally realized only in the practice of ministry in the setting of a specific congregation and its larger social, economic, and cultural context. Newly called leaders learn to do ministry and develop life-long patterns of theological reflection and spiritual discipline during their early years of service. Their transition could be greatly enhanced by collegial support and a structure for learning.

In response to these needs and opportunities, the 1993 Churchwide Assembly directed the Division for Ministry to encourage synods to develop pilot programs of continuing education for first-call pastors. As of February 1995, 59 synods have responded to the invitation to begin pilot programs of first-call theological education. Of these, 51 are working in regional or multi-synodical groups. In 11 cases, an ELCA continuing education center is designing and administering aspects of the program on behalf of a group of synods.

Based on the experience of these pilot programs and the results of numerous consultations, the task force proposes that all pastors and rostered lay leaders participate in a synodically sponsored program of theological education during their first three years of ministry under call. In order to assist the transition from seminary to parish, these programs will give special attention to three goals:

- the personal development of leadership style, spiritual discipline, and ministerial identity appropriate to the respective rosters;
- competence in and overall integration of various aspects of the practice of ministry;
- discernment of the local and regional context of ministry.

First-call pastors or rostered lay leaders in consultation with synod and congregational representatives will develop individualized learning contracts to address these goals through a combination of four educational components:

- *Core program*, that is, the common events for first-call rostered leaders in a geographical area, with flexibility provided to meet the specific needs of persons on the respective rosters;
- *Electives*, that is, offerings directed toward areas of specific need or interest which are available through a wide variety of seminars, workshops, summer school classes, synodical or churchwide events, advanced graduate courses, and distance learning programs;
- Mentoring with an experienced colleague on an individual basis or in small groups that meet regularly;

- *Structured reading* designed to support and extend the other educational components in fulfilling the overall goals of the program.

In meeting the requirements of first-call theological education the new pastor or rostered lay minister will likely utilize the two weeks already expected and commonly used for continuing education each year. About half of this time will be spent in the common events for first-call leaders; the other half will be spent in individualized learning experiences.

Normally, expenses for first-call theological education will be met within the continuing education benefits included in the compensation package. Current guidelines suggest that congregations contribute $550 for continuing education; the pastor or lay rostered leader, $250. ELCA PACE Growth awards are available to rostered leaders whose congregations are not able to provide continuing education funds at the recommended churchwide level. Synods with responsibility for a disproportionate number of first-call rostered leaders will be eligible for subsidies during the initial years of this program through external grants managed by the Division for Ministry.

The first-call theological education requirement will be included as a regular part of the letter of call. Normally, completion of this program will be presupposed prior to the bishop's recommendation of a rostered leader to a new call.

The Division for Ministry has developed churchwide standards and guidelines which appear as Appendix E. Additional resources are available from the division to assist synods in developing programs of first-call theological education.

Recommendation #2:

To require, by the fall of 1997, that all newly rostered pastors and lay leaders participate, throughout their first three years of ministry under call, in structured programs of theological education, designed and supervised by their synods, according to churchwide standards.

4. Access to Theological Education

Faithful leaders in a changing world need to be equipped for ministry in forms that meet their varied life circumstances and educational levels. Many mission leaders will receive excellent theological educations in residential seminary programs. Some, however, will need to pursue at least part of their theological studies close to where they live and work and do ministry. In the changing economic context, more leaders will need to support themselves through secular employment, not only during their studies but also as they fulfill their ministries in congregations and in the wider society. Furthermore, some local leaders will be able to minister more effectively within their cultural contexts if they do not leave their communities for theological education. Many thoughtful church members seek to enhance their discipleship in the world through theological study at a level beyond what most congregations can offer.

These varied circumstances require more flexibility in the delivery of high quality, Lutheran theological education. New developments in interactive telecommunications provide practical methods for making theological education broadly accessible where people live and work, and appropriate to their cultural patterns and values. In response to these needs and technological innovations, the 1993 Churchwide Assembly directed the Division for Ministry *"to facilitate development of models of theological education by extension and distance learning, and…to prepare a proposal for the 1995 Churchwide Assembly for a flexible system to make theological education accessible to a broader spectrum of people."*

a. Distance Learning Models

Lay and continuing education programs are available through a variety of distance learning modalities. SELECT is an ELCA continuing education program that utilizes videotaped presentations and small group interaction in the learner's locale. Education for Ministry is an intensive program of theological education prepared for Episcopalian laity by the School of Theology at the University of the South. This four-year program involves the use of print resources and small group interaction with trained mentors. After initial review of these materials, the task force has recommended that the Division for Ministry explore the possibility of adapting and authorizing Education for Ministry for use in the ELCA.

The seminaries have responded to the need for greater accessiblity by establishing extension centers, by providing courses at off-campus sites, and by adjusting calendars and schedules to accommodate commuters and part-time students. In 1994, the Division

for Ministry engaged Campbell Communications, Inc., to conduct an audit of the seminaries to evaluate their technical and human resources for venturing into distance learning through computer networks, and compressed digital, fiber optics, and satellite technology. As a result, agreement has been reached on common standards to assure technological compatibility among the schools and with the ELCA churchwide offices. All of the seminaries plan eventually to use interactive telecommunication technology to link campuses both for administrative purposes and for the delivery of educational programs.

b. Consulting Service for Distance Learning (Hub)

As these cutting-edge distance learning programs emerge, the seminary clusters each may find it useful to identify a center for distance learning for the cluster. Because this technology, and distance methodologies in general, transcend geographical boundaries, there is need for some overall technological support and coordination. A distance learning consulting service, referred to here as a hub, could provide these services for a communications network. Eventually, this network might offer ELCA members or other interested persons anywhere in the world the opportunity to pursue theological education for mission in community-based sites or at home on their own time. As programming is developed by the various educational entities, the hub would help students access degree programs, non-credit courses, and continuing education opportunities through cable television, satellite, videotape, and other communications technology.

The educational programming itself will be provided by seminary clusters, continuing education centers, colleges and universities, synods, and other educational partners. The educational providers will retain ownership and receive appropriate recognition and fees for their respective offerings.

Once established, the hub will seek to fulfill the following goals:

1. to assist theological education providers in the development of communications infrastructures for distance learning;
2. to encourage development of compatible distance education systems across this church;

3. to coordinate distance learning efforts of providers;

4. to provide consulting services to synods, seminaries, continuing education centers, and other providers that are interested in distance learning;

5. to serve as a distance learning resource and research center;

6. to coordinate workshops and conferences that will enrich teaching and learning on distance education;

7. to assist with student support services as desired by theological education providers.

The hub will require a well equipped office/studio and a small staff with expertise in distance learning technologies and educational methods. It could be located wherever technological access could be maximized.

Recommendation #3:

To request and encourage the Division for Ministry, together with the Department for Communication, the seminary clusters, and other interested partners, to develop an ELCA distance learning consulting service to be a technological, administrative, and faculty development resource for an ELCA theological education distance learning network.

C. Building an Interdependent Network of Theological Education Providers

1. The Vision

The task force identified a way of reconfiguring institutions and resources to meet the need for greater depth, variety, and accessibility in theological education. The following vision was central to the report affirmed by the 1993 Assembly:

The preparation of a wide variety of leaders, grounded in Scripture and the Lutheran confessional tradition and equipped for the church's mission in a rapidly changing environment, made possible through redeployment of resources in an interdependent network of theological education providers.

In this vision, the eight ELCA seminaries form clusters which relate to each other in a churchwide system. This system draws continuing education centers,

ELCA colleges, non-Lutheran colleges and seminaries, and other potential providers of theological education into an interdependent network that extends to every corner of this church. Each cluster with its educational partners develops a comprehensive plan for the delivery of programs needed to fulfill the 11 imperatives within its common service area. Planning and coordination of theological education involving all the clusters will be facilitated by the Division for Ministry through its Theological Education Coordinating Committee.

The vision calls for a very high level of cooperation among theological education providers and significant concentration of their resources in order to strengthen and diversify offerings. Partners will collaborate on ways to increase effectiveness and reduce duplication. (Definitions of terms related to the interdependent network are given in Appendix F.)

2. Timeline for Cluster Development

The timeline approved by the 1993 Churchwide Assembly allows for the clusters to develop in carefully planned phases between 1993 and 2003. It calls for seminaries to form cluster partnerships by formal action of the seminary and the Division for Ministry Board by the fall of 1994. The seminaries are asked to assess leadership needs on their territory, determine specializations within each cluster, explore possible structures for cluster governance, and begin developing relationships with other potential providers of theological education by the end of 1995. Between 1995 and 1999, the distribution of churchwide specializations among the clusters will be determined. The clusters will intensify cooperative planning and programming. The seminaries will determine appropriate structures for the governance and administration of each cluster for ratification by the Division for Ministry by 1999. These new structures will be implemented no later than 2003. (The full timeline appears in Appendix G.)

3. Cluster Formation, Activity, and Plans

The seminaries are responding energetically to the challenge to meet the mission imperatives as an interdependent system. All eight seminary boards have taken action to join clusters which will cooperate in comprehensive planning and program delivery and develop appropriate governance and funding structures according to the timeline. These actions were ratified by the board of the Division for Ministry in December 1994 and March 1995. (See figure 3.)

a. *The Eastern Cluster of Lutheran Seminaries:* **Lutheran Theological Seminary at Gettysburg, Lutheran Theological Seminary at Philadelphia, and Lutheran Theological Southern Seminary**

The boards of Gettysburg, Philadelphia, and Southern seminaries voted in the fall of 1994 to form an Eastern Cluster comprising the three schools. Interim structures have been put in place for coordinating and governing the Eastern Cluster, with binding decision-making powers on matters designated to it by mutual consent of a majority vote in each seminary board. A committee of the deans and faculty representatives from the cluster schools oversee academic planning for the cluster. In addition, the seminary presidents have appointed from their respective schools a person in each major area of administration, such as admissions, business, and development, to assure ongoing three-way consultation among administrative personnel to seek greater coordination and cost-effectiveness.

Student recruitment and continuing education are being done cooperatively. Compatible computerization at the three seminaries is already underway; it can use common software for development, business management, and registration. A consultation with the bishops and other synodical leaders of Regions 7, 8, and 9 is being planned for fall 1995.

In August 1994, the Division for Ministry assigned primary churchwide responsibility for developing educational programs for the newly created lay roster of diaconal ministers to Gettysburg Seminary, utilizing the resources of the entire Eastern Cluster. This is the first instance of a churchwide specialization being formally designated in the emerging ELCA system of theological education.

b. *The Covenant Cluster:* **Lutheran School of Theology at Chicago, Trinity Lutheran Seminary, and Wartburg Theological Seminary**

In February 1995, the joint planning committee of the three seminaries passed formal recommendations regarding the formation the Covenant Cluster as a means of responding to this church's need for greater

Figure 3

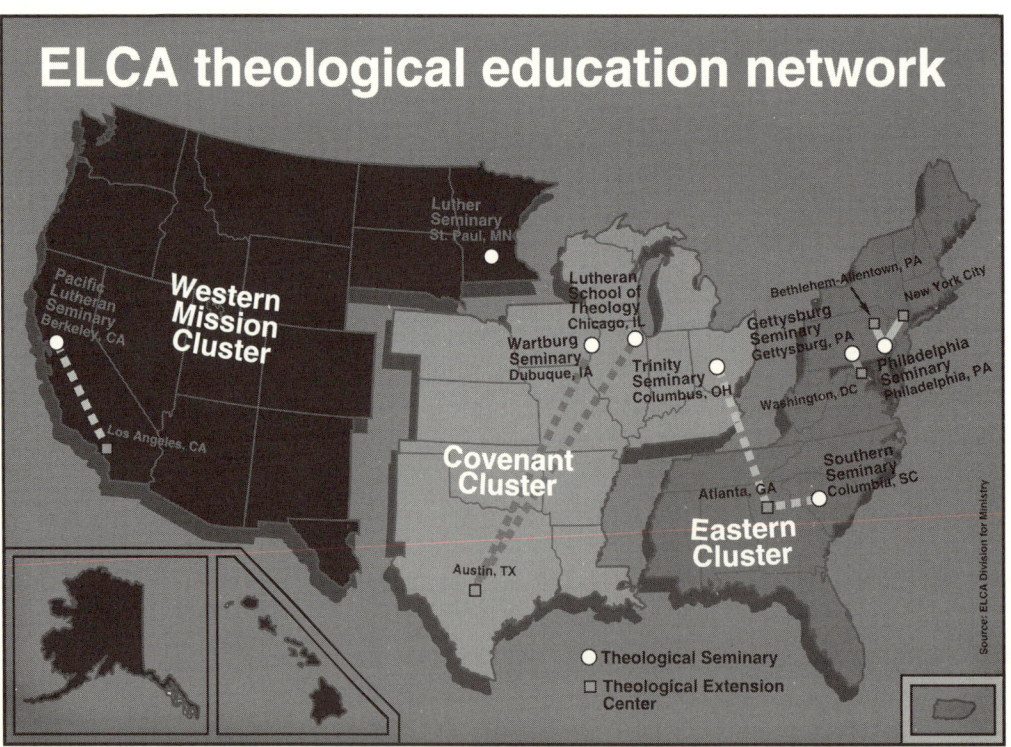

ELCA theological education network

variety and accessibility in theological education. Mission, as informed by the 11 imperatives, will guide future strategic planning for the proposed cluster. The recommendations commit the three schools to develop whatever common administration and governance structures are needed to implement and sustain their shared programmatic endeavors and further their common mission as the cluster evolves. The cluster partners will develop and deploy financial resources to undergird their shared programs. The Division for Ministry Board ratified the formation of the Covenant Cluster in March, pending action by the respective seminary boards in spring 1995.

The proposed Covenant Cluster has developed concrete plans to link the three seminaries and the Lutheran Seminary Program in the Southwest through interactive video by the fall of 1995. This technology will greatly enhance the cluster's capacity for collaboration, for sharing academic and administrative resources, and for providing programs of distance learning. The advanced graduate programs of the three schools will be structured so that they are fully compatible with each other. Action teams will be appointed to explore and propose ways to further cooperation and reduce duplication in various areas of joint work, beginning with field education and admissions.

The recommendation to form the Covenant Cluster builds upon earlier cooperative arrangements. Wartburg and LSTC, working closely together since 1988, took action in May 1994 to form the Heartland Cluster. Conversations among the leadership of Wartburg, Chicago, and Trinity during spring 1994 led to actions by all three boards to form a covenant relationship as a first step in collaborative planning and implementation in order to respond more effectively to the imperatives.

Throughout 1994, the LSTC/Wartburg cluster consulted individually with its supporting synods in Regions 4 and 5 regarding their specific leadership needs in relation to the 11 mission imperatives. Surveys of laity at all 18 synodical assemblies in spring 1994 assessed the strengths and weaknesses of the preparation of ordained ministers. Analyses of findings were shared and recommendations developed at a major consultation in October 1994 involving the two seminaries, their Lutheran Seminary Program in the Southwest, and their supporting synods. Trinity plans to pursue a similar strategy of consultation with the synods of Region 6.

c. *Western Mission Cluster:* Pacific Lutheran Theological Seminary and Luther Seminary

The boards of Pacific Lutheran and Luther seminaries approved "Principles and Strategies toward Clustering" in fall 1993, pledging their respective seminaries to work together in the formation of a cluster. This plan outlines some of the first steps these two cluster partners intend to take as they jointly develop an integrated service network across the West. One immediate challenge they face is how to extend services to the Northwest, a region which supports both seminaries but has no Lutheran theological center of its own.

Because their area of shared responsibility is so vast and comprises so many distinct cultures from the Upper Midwest to the Southwest, the Western Mission cluster will utilize satellite and other interactive communication technology to deliver resources in ways that maximize flexibility, accessibility, and cost effectiveness.

Each of these seminaries has historically taken major steps to decrease cost and duplication through creative partnerships. Pacific Lutheran Theological Seminary pools academic resources and jointly provides many academic services through the 10-member Graduate Theological Union (GTU). Because of previous mergers, Luther Seminary is considerably larger than the other ELCA seminaries and thus can realize certain economies of scale.

Recommendation #4:

To direct the Division for Ministry to report to the 1997 Churchwide Assembly continuing progress by the seminary clusters in meeting the timeline approved by the 1993 Churchwide Assembly.

4. Churchwide Coordination of Theological Education

The need for a new structure to enhance collaboration and coordination among the clusters was cited in the 1993 Report. In October 1994, the board of the Division for Ministry acted on the recommendation of the Task Force on the Study of Theological Education to establish a Theological Education Coordinating Committee, advisory to the division. This group of 14 or less will include Division for Ministry board members, seminary representatives, and others. Members were appointed by the Division for Ministry in spring 1995. The initial meeting will be held in fall 1995.

This committee will give advice and serve as a resource to the Division for Ministry in carrying out the Division's constitutional responsibility for coordination and planning for a system of theological education in the ELCA. Through this committee the Division for Ministry will provide leadership for a strategic planning process which integrates the activities of the seminary clusters as they develop and implement plans in accordance with the imperatives and the timeline outlined in the 1993 Report. (The specific functions and composition of the Theological Education Coordinating Committee are provided in Appendix H.)

D. Supporting Theological Education as a Priority for Mission

I. Churchwide Discussion of Seminary Funding

The 1993 Churchwide Assembly overwhelmingly affirmed theological education as "*a foundational priority, recognizing that the preparation of leaders for mission is essential to all the ministries of this church.*" It directed the Division for Ministry to promote study and discussion throughout the ELCA of proposals for funding theological education as a foundational priority of this church's mission, and to prepare funding proposals for recommendation in 1995.

Between January and June of 1994, synod and seminary leaders were invited to discuss and respond to a resource prepared by the Task Force on the Study of Theological Education: *A New Look at the Total Financial Support of Theological Education in the ELCA.* Synod councils or other leadership groups in 37 synods reported holding such discussions. Task force members attended 16 of these meetings personally. A total of 444 response forms was received. While the interest was encouraging, no clear consensus emerged. Commitment to strong churchly support for the seminaries was offset by concerns about the limits of synodical and churchwide resources and about the likelihood of the clusters actually achieving the efficiencies envisioned.

Based on the thoughtful reactions from seminaries and synods, the task force revised its funding proposals and presented them for response in its September 1994 Draft Report: *Theological Education for a Church in Mission.* These proposals included strategies for enhancing all revenue streams to the seminaries: grants from mission support (churchwide and synodical), support from private donors (gifts and endowment income), and income from students (tuition and fees), offset in part through a churchwide scholarship program for ministry candidates. These proposals anticipated that about half of seminary income will come from endowment income and gifts from individual donors. The ELCA Conference of Bishops took action in October 1994 to support the general directions proposed.

The 1994 draft also proposed that beginning in 1997 churchwide and synodical funds would be directed to the clusters. A further proposal called for the development of a new formula for the distribution of churchwide funds to be phased in between 1997 and 2001. The formula was to be developed in such a way as to further cluster goals.

2. Need for Comprehensive Strategic Planning: Programmatic and Financial

At the request of seminary leadership at the annual consultation on theological education in November 1994, the task force agreed to postpone final proposals for financing theological education for at least one year. It was agreed that the seminaries and the Division for Ministry needed this additional time and outside facilitation to bring their strategic planning process to the point of programmatic and financial specificity. These added steps will help them make informed estimates both of the costs involved in providing greater access and quality through an interdependent theological education network and of the savings to be realized through clustering. This information then will provide the basis for the appropriate assignment of financial responsibility for the various components of the system.

The Division for Ministry has engaged Growth Design Corporation, Milwaukee, Wisconsin, to conduct the financial planning phase. Costs for this process will be borne through a combination of external grants, contributions from the seminaries, and the remainder of Division for Ministry funds reserved for the study.

A period of intensive activity beginning in mid-December produced the following planning components for the use of the seminary presidents at their annual meeting in April 1995:

- an information system for regular reporting of comparable data regarding seminary programs, finances, and personnel;
- the compilation and analysis of such data to date;
- a financial model which enables individual seminaries, clusters, and the overall system to budget strategically on the basis of programmatic and financial projections;
- results of external market research testing assumptions and support for directions set by the 1993 assembly (clustering, the imperatives, distance learning, priority of theological education, etc.); and
- a method for quantifying the 11 imperatives to make them more effective as measurable goals in a strategic planning process.

Using these tools at a professionally facilitated session in April, the seminary presidents will make initial proposals regarding programmatic initiatives to address the 11 imperatives within the seminary system and strategies to develop and redeploy the needed human and financial resources.

During July 1995, a larger group with a wide range of perspectives and expertise will evaluate and refine the proposals from the presidents. Action teams will be assigned to further develop the most promising proposals. These groups will determine implementation steps, estimate costs, and project revenue streams related to each proposal. Such a process pursued continuously will enable seminary leadership and the Division for Ministry to determine where savings can be realized; which initiatives will have to be self-supporting; which programs have priority in receiving direct church funding; where programs can be strategically abandoned to make resources available for new projects; and how needed new initiatives should be prioritized.

The study to date has built consensus in the church and commitment in the seminaries for new directions in leadership education. The question now is how to turn those commitments into action. Action takes money. Based on the results of this comprehensive programmatic and financial planning process, the Division for Ministry and the seminaries will be prepared by 1997 to present to this church and to individual donors a case for the financial support of theological education which will prepare faithful leaders for mission in a changing world.

Recommendation #5:

To affirm the decision of the Division for Ministry and the seminaries regarding the expansion of the Study of Theological Education to include programmatic and financial planning for an ELCA system of theological education; and to request that the Division for Ministry prepare by 1997 a case and strategies for this church's increased financial support of a system of theological education.

3. Enhancing Essential Revenue Streams: Initial Funding Proposals

Revenue comes to the seminaries primarily from endowment earnings, gifts from private donors, student tuition and fees, and churchwide and synodical grants. (See figure 4.)

a. Endowment Income and Gifts from Private Donors

Current gifts from ELCA members and the return on past gifts accounted for 48.26% of the combined revenues of the seminaries in 1993–94. Revenue from these sources of income must continue to grow.

Annual gifts from tens of thousands of individual donors provide regular operating support for the institutions that prepare leaders for mission. Seminary development staffs continually add to the number of donors and encourage donors to increase their gifts and develop patterns of annual giving.

Deferred giving programs in the form of wills, insurance policies, or life income gifts have the potential for producing the greatest source of funds. Through these major gifts and bequests, donors make a profound impact upon the future of the seminary. Their gifts, deposited in the seminary endowment reservoir, provide increased flow of revenue for theological education of leaders for this church.

Growth in endowment funds is essential for a stable future for the institutions that prepare leaders for mission. In 1994, the eight seminaries held over $93 million in their endowments. The endowments of the individual seminaries ranged from a high of $22.9 million to a low of $3 million. To protect the value of the endowments for the future, financial counselors to aca-

Figure 4

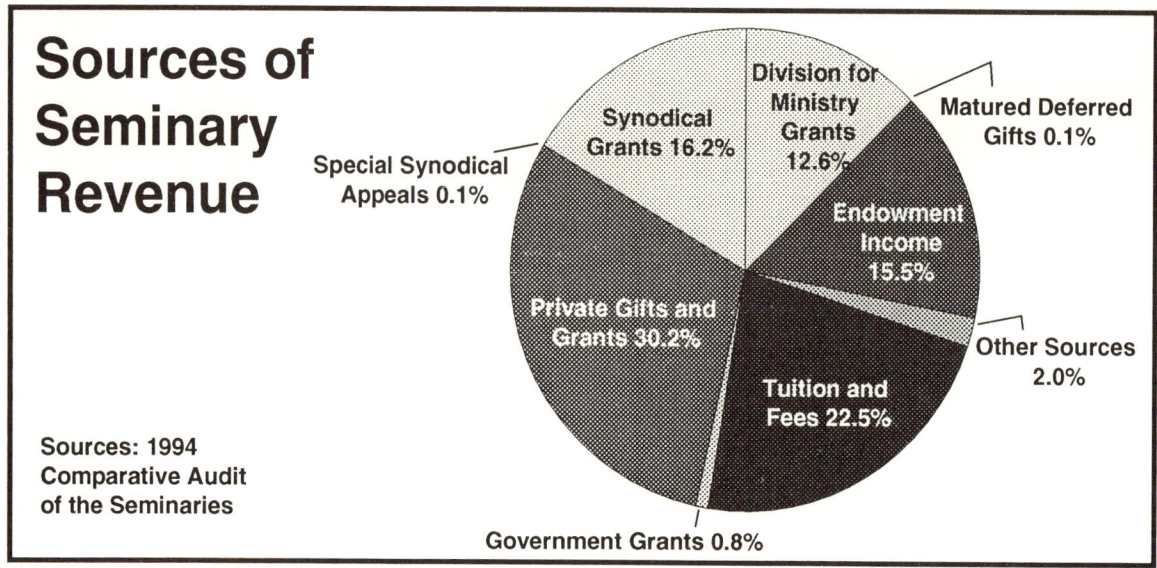

Sources of Seminary Revenue

Special Synodical Appeals 0.1%

Synodical Grants 16.2%

Division for Ministry Grants 12.6%

Matured Deferred Gifts 0.1%

Endowment Income 15.5%

Private Gifts and Grants 30.2%

Other Sources 2.0%

Tuition and Fees 22.5%

Government Grants 0.8%

Sources: 1994 Comparative Audit of the Seminaries

demic institutions recommend that annual spending from investment returns not exceed five percent. In recent years most of the seminaries have been spending at a higher rate.

This church and its seminaries need to coordinate their fund raising efforts and work in partnership to increase the flow of revenue both for theological education and for the overall mission of the ELCA. Seminary education should prepare leaders who inspire stewardship and promote connection with the larger church.

Church leaders are encouraged to foster a climate in which the fund-raising programs of the seminaries are welcomed and encouraged. Pastors and bishops play a key role in identifying potential donors and commending the cause of theological education to them. Donors need to hear that their gifts to theological education serve this church and honor the priorities it has set.

Recommendation #6:

To urge ELCA congregations, synods, and the churchwide organization to support the efforts of the seminary clusters to increase financial support by granting access to seminary representatives and commending the cause of theological education to potential donors.

Recommendation #7:

To encourage seminary clusters to invest significant time and resources for cultivating participation in deferred giving programs that will build endowments for the future.

b. Support from Students

Student tuition paid for 19.4% of the total educational and general expenditures of the ELCA seminaries in 1993-94. Costs to students are offset in part through financial aid. The major cost of theological education is provided through grants from synods and the churchwide organization, gifts from individual donors, and return on endowment investments. It is expected that tuition will rise over the next several years until tuition and fees support about 25% of the seminaries' budgets.

As costs to students increase, major initiatives must be undertaken to build endowments which can provide the financial aid needed to allow qualified ELCA ministry candidates to attend seminary without incurring crippling levels of indebtedness. Concrete proposals for such a fund are anticipated in the current financial planning process.

As part of an overall revenue strategy, many programs of continuing education, lay education, and extension education will have to be planned and priced in such a way as to be self-supporting or income-producing.

c. Grants from Mission Support: Synod and Churchwide

While support to seminaries from combined churchwide and synodical sources has remained relatively stable since the formation of the ELCA, such income represents a diminishing proportion of the overall income of the seminaries. Over this period of time, churchwide funding has decreased in terms of actual dollars and as a percentage of total theological education expenditures. (See figure 5.) Synodical support on average increased slightly between 1988 and 1993. For the sake of adequate support for theological education and appropriate accountability between church and seminaries the flow of funds from churchwide and synodical sources must be addressed rationally, realistically, and missionally.

The decision to undertake a process of system-wide financial planning, however, has postponed until 1997 any actions to change the existing formula for raising and distributing churchwide and synodical funds for theological education. Implementation of a new distribution formula will be phased in not later than 1999. The expanded process will provide the necessary framework for devising a funding system that ultimately will further mission goals and enhance giving through synodical and churchwide channels.

During the interim period from 1995 to 1999, stable income is needed from synodical and churchwide sources. In the current economic environment, the churchwide organization can demonstrate its commitment to theological education by maintaining seminary grants at not less than current dollar levels. The Division for Ministry will continue to ask synods to increase giving to the seminaries they support by 3 percent annually according to the existing Fair Share formula.

Building the relationship between seminary clusters and their supporting synods becomes a priority at this time as constituencies are shifting and financial support tends to follow those causes which are personally known and valued. Through a regular consultation process, synods and seminary clusters can begin to explore and negotiate the real needs, costs, and possibilities in leadership education on their shared territory. It is in the context of such direct conversations that seminaries can base appeals for increased fund-

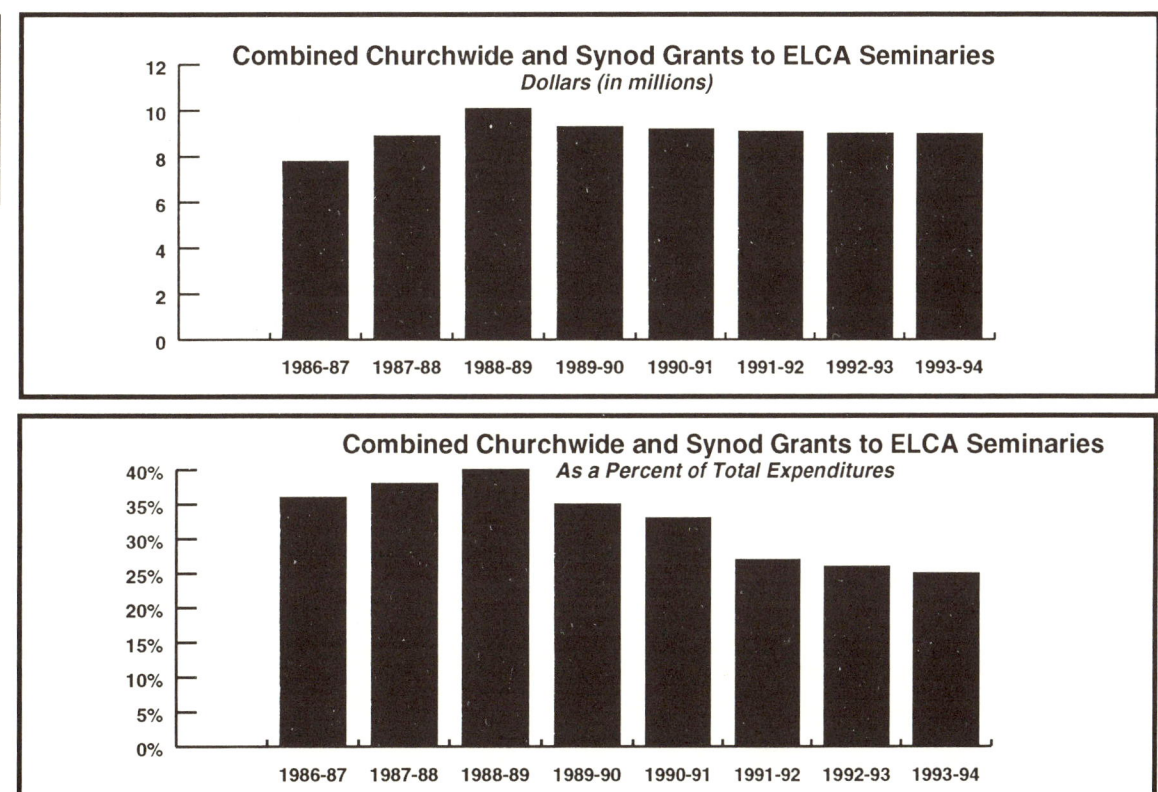

Combined Churchwide and Synod Grants to ELCA Seminaries
Dollars (in millions)

Combined Churchwide and Synod Grants to ELCA Seminaries
As a Percent of Total Expenditures

ing on factors such as the quality of their graduates, programmatic improvements, increased services valued by the synods, proposed expansion in response to mission needs, and anticipated major expenditures. Synods can give realistic projections of their capacity to support such initiatives.

Recommendation #8:

To encourage the seminary clusters, with the support of the Division for Ministry and in coordination with other churchwide units, to initiate regular consultations with their supporting synods regarding program and funding.

E. Conclusion

Since 1993, the groundwork has been laid for building an interdependent network of theological education providers that can prepare a variety of leaders, grounded in Scripture and the Lutheran confessional tradition and prepared for this church's mission in the rapidly changing environment of the 21st century. Goals for this mission-oriented system have been identified and are being quantified. The scope of theological education has been expanded to serve more kinds of ministers, both lay and ordained, full-time, bi-vocational, and volunteers. Theological education is becoming more flexible and accessible through distance learning methods. Helping people make the connections between faith and daily life is becoming a major focus of theological education.

Congregational needs for competent, missional leadership are being addressed. Standards and procedures have been established to ensure that persons considering rostered ministries in the ELCA have ample opportunity to discern their call and prepare to begin theological studies. Seminaries are committed to preparing pastors and lay leaders in ways that enhance their spiritual and theological depth, their passion for mission, their practical congregational skills, and their attentiveness to the cultures and contexts in which they serve. A three-year program of required continuing education will help pastors and rostered lay leaders move more effectively from seminary into ministerial roles and responsibilities.

The eight ELCA seminaries have formed three clusters that are planning and delivering services on their shared territories in ways that maximize resources. Structures have been put in place to facilitate the over-all strategic planning and coordination of theological education in the ELCA. Recommendations are proposed for enhancing the various revenue streams to the seminaries for the preparation of mission leaders.

The Division for Ministry and the seminaries are committed to an intensive financial planning process in 1995-96, which will enable them to anticipate costs, set priorities, effect savings, and assign responsibilities. Based on this deliberative process, the Division for Ministry will bring to the church in 1997 a clear case for an ELCA system of theological education that is adequate to prepare mission leaders for the 21st century. With that case will come a comprehensive plan to enlist the members, the congregations, the synods, and the churchwide organization of the ELCA in providing the necessary financial support to undergird the preparation of faithful leaders for a changing world.

F. Acknowledgments

The Task Force on the Study of Theological Education recognizes with gratitude grants from the Lilly Endowment, Lutheran Brotherhood, and Aid Association for Lutherans which have enabled this study and some early phases of its implementation. The approach of the study has depended upon the active participation of many partners in the seminaries, the synods, and the churchwide organization in identifying issues and developing and testing proposals. Regular support and advice from the board of the Division for Ministry, the Church Council, and the Conference of Bishops have been appreciated and liberally utilized. Special thanks go to Rev. Phyllis Anderson, staff director for the study, and to Rev. Joseph Wagner, Executive Director of the Division for Ministry. The task force also commends Chris Alexander and Pat Wilder for extraordinary administrative support. The seminary presidents have served as our chief critics and closest allies in responding to the mandates of this study and finding a way toward the future to which we believe God is calling this church.

The Task Force for the Study of Theological Education

Ms. Dorothy Marple, Philadelphia, Pa., chair
The Rev. Beverly Burkum Allert, Tigard, Ore.
Ms. Mary Chrichlow, Elmont, N.Y.
Mr. Charles Lutz, Minneapolis, Minn.
The Rev. Charles Mays, Port Angeles, Wash.
The Rev. Paul Rorem, Princeton, N.J.
Bishop Harold Skillrud, Atlanta, Ga.
Ms. Martha Stortz, Berkeley, Calif.
Ms. Marybeth Peterson, Omaha, Nebr., Division for Ministry board liaison

G. Recommendations

1. To direct the Division for Ministry to report to the 1997 Churchwide Assembly continuing progress of the ELCA seminaries toward fulfilling the 11 imperatives approved by the 1993 Churchwide Assembly.

2. To require, by the fall of 1997, that all newly rostered pastors and lay leaders participate, throughout their first three years of ministry under call, in structured programs of theological education, designed and supervised by their synods, according to churchwide standards.

3. To request and encourage the Division for Ministry, together with the Department for Communication, the seminary clusters, and other interested partners, to develop an ELCA distance learning service center to be a technological, administrative, and faculty development resource for an ELCA theological education distance learning network.

4. To direct the Division for Ministry to report to the 1997 Churchwide Assembly continuing progress by the seminary clusters in meeting the timeline approved by the 1993 Churchwide Assembly.

5. To affirm the decision of the Division for Ministry and the seminaries regarding the expansion of the Study of Theological Education to include programmatic and financial planning for an ELCA system of theological education; and to request that the Division for Ministry prepare by 1997 a case and strategies for this church's increased financial support of a system of theological education.

6. To urge ELCA congregations, synods, and the churchwide organization to support the efforts of the seminary clusters to increase financial support by granting access to seminary representatives and commending the cause of theological education to potential donors.

7. To encourage seminary clusters to invest significant time and resources for cultivating participation in deferred giving programs that will build endowments for the future.

8. To encourage the seminary clusters, with the support of the Division for Ministry and in coordination with other churchwide units, to initiate regular consultations with their supporting synods regarding program and funding.

Part II: Appendices

Appendix A: Context for Mission

This contextual analysis as described int he 1993 Report of the Task Force on the Study of Theological Education reflects several recent studies that describe the contemporary context and project future trends. In developing proposals for a system of theological education that will prepare leaders for mission, the task force was mindful of the following aspects of the contemporary religious and social context.

A. Demographic Trends

By the middle of this decade, the population of the United States will be growing at a rate of less than one percent per year. Population will decrease steadily around the middle of the 21st century. Along with this slow growth, the population is aging.

Where population is growing rapidly, the increase results more from family unit relocation and immigration from abroad than from birth rate. Families have been moving from rural to metropolitan areas. In 1950, 30 percent of the population resided in metropolitan areas of 1,000,000 or more. Today that proportion has grown to 50.2 percent. In major metropolitan areas population is shifting from the central cities to suburban fringes.

Only 25 percent of the population in the United States lives in rural areas, but 45 percent of ELCA congregations are located there. Consequently, a number of pastors are being asked to serve in rural areas which are unfamiliar to them by virtue of their own background. Only 55 percent of ELCA congregations are located where 77.5 percent of our population now lives. There is a significant under-supply of calls available in more populated areas where most pastors are interested in serving.

Residential moves are concentrated in the sunbelt regions of the West and South. The population increase over the past decade in these two areas has been 22.3 percent and 13.4 percent respectively. In contrast, population in the Northeast has increased by only 3.4 percent and in the Midwest by 1.4 percent. Within the latter areas significant declines in population have occurred. Currently, 76 percent of ELCA members are concentrated in the Northeast and North Central regions of the country. The ELCA's resources for theological education are located primarily in areas which have a high concentration of Lutheran members, rather than in the areas where population growth is most rapid.

The racial and ethnic composition of the United States is changing. The change results both from immigration from Asia, Latin America and the Caribbean, and from the relatively high birth rates among women from these areas and women of African American and Native American descent. It is projected that African Americans, Asians, Pacific Islanders, Native Americans, Eskimos, Aleuts and Hispanics will grow from one-fifth of the population in 1980 to one-third by 2020. Currently 98 percent of the ELCA membership is white. To be in fact the Evangelical Lutheran Church in America, this church must find ways to proclaim the gospel to all Americans.

The face of the American work force is changing. By the year 2000, over 80 percent of all new labor force entrants will be people immigrating to the United States from Asia, Latin America, the Caribbean region and Africa, or native born African Americans, Asians, Hispanics, Pacific Islanders, Native Americans, Eskimos and Aleuts, and women. This is the pool from which the church will increasingly draw its leadership.

Over the last decade there has been a 6.1 percent decline in mainline Protestant church membership. During the same period Southern Baptist membership grew 16 percent and the Church of Jesus Christ of the Latter Day Saints increased 30 percent. Reflecting the general decline in membership among mainline Protestants is the fact that

Lutheran membership in the United States decreased by 500,000 persons between 1970 and 1990. The single fastest growing group in America is the unchurched population.

All Christian groups combined continue to claim a majority of the population. Apart from the Christian groups, the American Jewish community is the most prominent religious community in the country. Major influx of population from Asian and Middle Eastern countries since the mid-sixties, however, has led to greater religious pluralism in this country. As a result of immigration and significant support among African Americans, the Islamic community has grown rapidly and now virtually equals the Jewish community in size. Eastern religions have extended their presence in America through both first generation immigrant organizations and the conversion of thousands of young adult Americans to both Buddhism and guru-led Hindu religions. The Buddhist and Hindu communities each claim from three to five million adherents. The rate of growth of these two communities continues to be among the highest in the country.

Demographic trends will radically affect the future of the Evangelical Lutheran Church in America, its mission, ministry and institutions of theological education. To minister effectively as a national church on the North American continent, it will have to relate to the entire geographical area, become inclusive of the growing populations of the United States, and communicate the Gospel to people unrelated to any church. At the same time, it will need to be concerned about retaining membership and providing leaders for ministry in areas of diminishing population and economic resources.

B. Global Interdependence

The global scope of contemporary economic, political, environmental, and social issues underscores the complexity and interdependence of the human family. The implications of global realities in the area of religion alone are staggering.

Over two-thirds of the world's five billion people live outside the Christian faith. Many of these people live in the highly secularized Western World where there are large numbers of nominal church members and large numbers of persons with no religious commitment. That two-thirds majority also includes 800 million Muslims; 750 million Hindus; 350 million Buddhists; and 1 billion Chinese who are Confucianist, Buddhist, Taoist or Marxist.

The Christian population is shifting from North to South. As recently as 1900, 87 percent of all Christians lived in Europe and North America. By the year 2000 as much as 60 percent of the Christian world will live in Latin America, Asia, and Africa.

A global perspective leads North American Christians to greater awareness of the need for evangelization and re-evangelization at home and abroad. It also opens the way for greater interaction with southern hemisphere Christians. It reveals the need for interfaith understanding and cooperation. Theological education for the church's mission in this global context needs to prepare leaders who are able to work with

and learn from people of many faiths and with Christians whose faith is shaped by very different cultural realities.

C. Economic Factors

While Americans continue to be among the most economically privileged people in the world, rapid economic growth is not assured in an increasingly competitive global market or in the midst of an increasingly needy world and endangered environment. Both business and non-profit sectors in this society are under pressure to improve productivity and cost effectiveness in their operations. Church bodies are not immune to this economic stress.

There is strong evidence that since the 1960's people in the lowest economic brackets have steadily lost purchasing power while the wealthiest segments of society have gained it. For each year between 1967 and 1987, the percent of all income received by families whose income is in the bottom 20 percent has slipped by at least two-tenths of one percent. At the same time, families in the top 20 percent bracket have gained as much as one percent. Women who are single parents, their children, and elderly people living alone will form the new class of the poor in the United States. Leaders are needed who can address the problems and minister within an increasingly economically stratified society.

Economic realities affecting the larger economy also affect ELCA congregations, synods, and the churchwide organization. While congregational giving increased 3.5 percent in 1991, a larger proportion is staying at home to fund local ministries and meet local expenses, including the rapidly escalating cost of health insurance. Operating budgets of congregations increased 5.5 percent in 1991. Congregational support of synodical and churchwide ministries increased by only 0.5 percent. These factors make it progressively more difficult for synods and the churchwide organization to maintain support for seminaries and other institutions of this church. As a consequence, total synodical and churchwide grants to seminaries dropped from $9,559,042 in 1988 to $8,812,528 in 1991.

Growing numbers of congregations will find it increasingly difficult or impossible to support even their own pastor. Out of the eleven thousand congregations in the ELCA, more than one third have fewer than 175 confirmed members. The average size of these four thousand small congregations is 100 confirmed. The ELCA's Division for Outreach estimates that 2,500 rural congregations have fewer than 70 persons at worship each Sunday. An additional 900 urban congregations are in similar situations. If present demographic and economic trends continue, within five to ten years these congregations will be seeking alternative forms of leadership or cooperative arrangements with other congregations to secure the ministry they need.

The general economic realities become personal for individuals preparing for leadership in the church. According to a recent study of US seminaries, the average debt of the graduating seminarian is approximately $10,000. This debt may be much higher for a student with responsibility for family living expenses. Older graduates and graduates with significant indebtedness will find it difficult to accept calls to smaller congregations which cannot pay adequate salaries.

As the flow of funds from congregational offerings diminishes, this church and its institutions are turning more and more to individual church members for support in the form of major gifts or bequests. The majority of those who make major gifts to charitable institutions are now more than fifty-five years old. Twenty-two trillion dollars will be left in bequests in the next 30 years by persons currently in that age group. According to present projections, however, subsequent generations will not enjoy the same level of disposable income and assets; nor will they share the same loyalty to the church and its institutions that marks the current older adult generation.

These sobering economic realities must be taken into consideration in responsible planning for theological education. Such planning must be responsive to the financial burdens of students, the economic stratification of the society that seminary graduates will serve, and the changing forms of ministry that are being shaped in part by economic conditions. Furthermore, such planning will have to be fiscally realistic about any proposed expansion of theological education services.

D. Communications Technology

We live in the "information age," where the now commonplace miracles of telephones, public access television, audio and video tape players are being superseded by interactive systems. These developments have changed how people think, learn and communicate. They present three challenges to theological education.

First, advances in communication technology present challenges to a church and educational system that has been highly dependent on reading and writing and deeply committed to personal interaction and community. These advances change the whole context of theological education because this pervasive communications technology impacts and changes people. In a church which historically has sought to be aware of its context in the world, the changed context today calls us to approach the people of our culture differently. In preparing people to communicate in a post-literate environment we need both new teaching methods and an awareness of the communication culture.

Second, new communication technologies afford new possibilities as tools in the educational process. They offer unprecedented opportunities for communicating the gospel and for making educational resources, including theological education, widely accessible.

Finally, the new communication culture is a mixed blessing. It demands critical evaluation by the church. Mass media and the information industries are structures of power. These structures often unjustly affect the basic human right to communicate and reduce people to the status of media consumers. This church needs to prepare leaders who can advocate in the public arena for fairness and right to access in the realm of mass media.

E. Cultural Pluralism

The demographic, economic, global, and technological developments described in this section all contribute to a pervasive sense of cultural pluralism, which is among the most distinctive characteristics of the current context for mission. Cultural pluralism shapes the context in two ways.

First, cultural pluralism presents itself as sheer diversity. It is manifested in the diversity of races, genders, ethnic groups, religions, life styles, and values in this society. Demographic factors indicate that we are experiencing the influence of an increasingly broad spectrum of people from other cultures and ethnic groups with all their attendant values and life styles. Economic conditions mean that the context of American life crosses various class boundaries, from the very rich to the very poor, and includes a wide range within a large middle class. Communications technologies make this demographic and economic diversity a part of our everyday lives.

Secondly, cultural pluralism represents an approach to this diversity. It argues for the peaceful coexistence of those various groups, insisting that every part contribute equally to the functioning of a vital and newly configured whole. In this regard, cultural pluralism supports the access of each group to the public forum and champions individual rights and responsibilities and equal opportunity for all.

Cultural pluralism has a critical impact on theological education. The fact of diversity is both indispensable and irreversible. More difficult is the question of how to regard such diversity — as opportunity or threat? On one hand, cultural pluralism has meant radical shifts in the composition of seminary student bodies, with all the attendant impetus for change in the curriculum, pedagogy, and character of the institution. Over 30 percent of all students in theological schools in this country are women. In the 1992–93 academic year, 43 percent of Master of Divinity students at ELCA seminaries were women. Feminist principles and pedagogies are increasingly reflected in the curricula and character of many American seminaries and divinity schools. To meet the increasing demographic diversity, theological schools have worked to attract a broader ethnic and racial range of students. The language of instruction has changed. These factors have diversified and enriched theological schools and now present an opportunity and challenge to theological education itself.

On the other hand, cultural pluralism may be seen as a threat. Diversity brings with it a variety of truth claims. Within such diversity it is difficult to make absolute statements or to engage in prophetic critique. The threat of pluralism is demonstrated by the difficulty of forming theological consensus among so many competing claims to truth without privileging one or another claim. In this sense, the problems created by cultural pluralism have often been pitched in terms of a dichotomy between diversity and unity or relativism and absolutism. Debates between these two poles wrack seminary campuses and divide student bodies and faculties.

While acknowledging the challenges cultural pluralism presents, it is possible that these perceived poles are false dichotomies. The ability to hold the poles in tension may be a distinctive contribution of the Lutheran theological tradition which began as a protest against long-held traditions of theological discourse and practice and sees itself as continually being reformed. Lutheran theological education is one arena in which the dynamic exchange between the Word of God and the world should be nurtured and encouraged.

F. The Ecology of Education

One last aspect of the context of theological education is the network of educational institutions and the values which surround and support the work of the seminaries themselves. Dorothy Bass, a researcher for the study of theological education in the Presbyterian Church (U.S.A.), employs Lawrence Cremin's concept of an "educational ecology" to describe this larger educational context. She indicates how radically that ecology has changed since most American seminaries were founded in the mid-nineteenth century.

…the secularization of the common school, the privatization and fragmentation of family life, the reported weakness of Christian education in the congregation, and the near-demise of the religious publication, the student Christian movement, and the recognizably denominational college have made it far more difficult for theological schools to do their job. Vast networks of spiritual formation, leadership recruitment, and pre-seminary academic preparation have dissipated. Those responsible for the theological education of clergy are now charged with accomplishing many tasks and dimensions of preparation that were once shared within a vital configuration. (Dorothy C. Bass, "Historical Context of Presbyterian Theological Institutions", 1990)

As a result of these changes in the educational ecology, we no longer have a general population that has absorbed Christian literature and history as a part of its cultural heritage. Children are not exposed to Bible stories and prayer in public school. Young people are not groomed for leadership in the church through Christian student organizations and congregational youth groups to the extent that they once were. The influence of Sunday school and confirmation has diminished in many places. Few parents see themselves as teachers of the faith for their family.

While the influence of many institutions that once undergirded the seminary in its specific task has been weakened, the influence of the secular college or university has increased. More people in this society go to college. In 1988, 75 percent of persons aged twenty-five and older were high school graduates and 20 percent were college graduates compared to less than 25 percent high school graduates and 4 percent college graduates in 1940.

The highly educated population is balanced by a large population that cannot read. Twenty to 30 million U.S.-born citizens are functionally illiterate, that is, read at a fifth grade level or below. An additional 35 million function at a second grade reading level.

These issues in the broader educational environment impinge upon the task of seminaries in several ways. First, the mission context is changed. Seminaries now need to prepare candidates to minister both to the increasing number of highly educated men and women in the population and to a large sector of functionally illiterate people.

Second, the changed educational environment affects the readiness of candidates to engage in theological studies. They come to seminary with widely divergent academic and ecclesiastical experiences. There is no assurance that even a student who has grown up in a Christian congregation and has a college degree will have a basic understanding of biblical content and the teachings of his or her church.

Third, seminaries are now playing a larger role in providing educational opportunities for the laity. Today some adults look to seminaries for nurture in the faith which earlier generations found more frequently in youth and campus ministries, denominational colleges, and congregational adult education.

This study proposes new approaches to a wide range of theological education tasks. Although once shared by many partners, in recent times these tasks increasingly have fallen to seminaries, sometimes diffusing the focus and over-extending the faculties of the seminaries.

Appendix B: Recommendations Approved by the 1993 ELCA Churchwide Assembly

The Task Force on the Study of Theological Education proposed eight recommendations to the 1993 Churchwide Assembly. All were approved by margins of 90% or more.

1. **Foundational Priority.** To affirm theological education as a foundational priority, recognizing that the preparation of leaders for mission is essential to all the ministries of this church.

2. **Eleven Imperatives.** To adopt the eleven imperatives for theological education, as presented in the Report of the Study of Theological Education for Ministry to the 1993 Churchwide Assembly, as the planning and guiding focus for preparation of leaders for this church into the 21st century. (The full text of these imperatives is given in Appendix C.)

3. **Seminary Clusters.** To call upon the eight seminaries of the ELCA to form by the fall of 1994 three to five clusters for leadership education, each cluster (a) providing a full range of theological education for mission on its territory and (b) developing a consolidated governance structure for decision-making that can plan and implement a comprehensive program of theological education, in consultation with the Division for Ministry and in accordance with the timeline contained in the Study of Theological Education for Ministry, which provides for cluster governance and administrative structure recommendations to be developed out of a planning process for approval by the boards of the seminaries involved.

4. **Academic Readiness Standards.** To call upon the eight seminaries of the ELCA, during the 1993–1995 biennium, to develop common standards of academic readiness for students entering master's level programs in preparation for rostered ministries in this church for recommendation to the Division for Ministry.

5. **Ecclesial Readiness Standards.** To commend to the Division for Ministry, as it reviews the ELCA candidacy process in consultation with seminaries and synods, the development of churchwide standards for early discernment of ecclesial readiness of students entering master's level programs in preparation for rostered ministries in this church.

6. **First-Call Theological Education.** To direct the Division for Ministry, during the 1993-1995 biennium, to encourage synods and other providers to develop pilot programs of structured theological education in the first three years of ordained ministry; to monitor such programs in order to develop churchwide standards and guidelines; and with the Task Force on the Study of Theological Education for Ministry, to prepare a proposal for churchwide implementation of a first-call education requirement for the 1995 Churchwide Assembly.

7. **Theological Education by Extension (TEE).** To direct the Division for Ministry to facilitate development of models of theological education by extension and distance learning, and with the task force to prepare a proposal for the 1995 Churchwide Assembly for a flexible system to make theological education accessible to a broader spectrum of people.

8. **Funding.** To direct the Division for Ministry, through its Task Force on the Study of Theological Education, to promote study and discussion, throughout the ELCA during the 1993–1995 biennium, of proposals for funding theological education as a foundational priority of this church's mission, and prepare funding proposals for recommendation to the ELCA Church Council for consideration by the 1995 Churchwide Assembly.

Appendix C: Imperatives for Theological Education

These 11 imperatives for theological education were approved by the 1993 ELCA Churchwide Assembly as the planning and guiding focus for preparation of leaders for this church into the 21st century.

(Note: These imperatives, prepared between 1991 and 1993, do not reflect the present reality of three lay rosters—associates in ministry, diaconal ministers and deaconesses—officially recognized by action of the 1993 Assembly on the Study of Ministry. In most instances, where *associates in ministry* is used, all lay rosters **can be assumed.)**

1. Depth in the Faith

This church needs pastors and lay leaders whose various ministries are rooted in the Bible, history and theology, and shaped by the Lutheran confessional heritage. We seek men and women whose personal faith in Jesus Christ is nourished and renewed through a disciplined devotional life. No longer can we depend on a Christian culture to transmit basic Christian knowledge and values. Leaders must be competent to teach and preach the truth of the faith with accuracy and clarity. Secular ideologies, spiritual movements and world religions offer competing faith claims to which Christians must be prepared to respond out of the depths of their tradition. People look to their lay and ordained ministers for theological and spiritual leadership that is based on an intimate knowledge of scripture, a distinctively Lutheran theological understanding, and contemporary methods of theological reflection.

2. Mission Outreach

God's mission requires leaders in all the ministries of the church who are prepared and committed to proclaim the good news of salvation in Jesus Christ. Evangelical outreach by faithful and articulate leaders is obedient to Christ's Great Commission and essential to the identity, vitality, and continuity of this church. Approaches in theological education are needed which help pastors and other leaders recognize and respond to the spiritual hunger of people in their congregations and in the communities beyond their congregations.

Pastors must themselves be equipped so that they can equip others to join with them in sharing their faith with those who have never heard, those who have not believed, and those who are out of touch with the means of grace within the community of faith. They must learn to lead congregations which serve as mission outposts for the faith.

3. Practical Congregational Needs

Congregations are asking for leaders with a high level of competence in the practice of ministry. Practical competence includes not only specific skills of ministry, but also the integration of practice with spiritual and theological depth, sensitivity to interpersonal relationships, and beyond that an overall capacity for leadership. If congregations are going to become mission outposts for the renewal of the faith in our secular context, they need pastors who inspire through their teaching, preaching and leadership at worship, who empower members for their ministry, and who provide vision and direction for the ministry team. They need associates in ministry and other lay leaders who provide expert leadership in specific areas such as education, evangelism, music, and youth ministry. In order to meet the demands of congregational ministry today, leaders need both the gifts that come from the Spirit and practical competencies that must be learned. Seminary education provides an introduction to basic ministry skills and the art of theological and practical integration. These must be refined and expanded through continuing education, practice, supervision, and reflection. Most seminary graduates need to develop competence in a variety of practical areas, including evangelism, stewardship, and administration.

4. Cultures and Contexts

With the growing diversity and interdependence of cultures that increasingly mark contemporary American society, we need lay and ordained ministers who are sensitive to and knowledgeable about the cultures of those they serve and who are able to adapt their ministry to different contexts. Global economic, political, and cultural realities shape the overall setting of contemporary ministry. At the same time, ministry is always carried out in a particular culture and a local context. The practical demands of ministry are more complex and difficult to meet when one is ministering in cultures and contexts other than one's own. This church needs leaders who can minister effectively with people from a diverse range of life situations including ethnic origins, vocational and educational experience, family situations, regional variations, types of community, and political value systems. Awareness of cultures and contexts should also lead Christian leaders to speak out against trends in society that are contrary to the faith they hold.

5. **African American, Asian, Hispanic and Native American Candidates**

This church needs to invite Christian leaders from the African American, Asian, Hispanic and Native American communities to consider service in the church as pastors or associates in ministry. It also must provide these candidates with theological education that is congruent with their varied cultural perspectives and that prepares them for rostered ministry throughout the ELCA. Mission in North America requires that the ELCA learn how to relate the Gospel to the growing number of African American, Asian, Hispanic and Native American persons who live here. These communities are often better served by pastors and associates in ministry from these communities. Furthermore, people from all communities will be nurtured in the faith more effectively within the ELCA if this church body recognizes the particularity of each community and becomes more inclusive of a variety of cultural values and styles. This second task belongs to this whole church, but it will not happen without the leadership of a growing number of pastors and associates in ministry who are themselves Asian, African-American, Native American, and Hispanic.

6. **Indigenous Lay Leaders**

This church needs to find appropriate ways to provide indigenous lay leaders identified by their communities with the basic theological education they need for ministry in their settings. Many of those

with potential for being effective ministers in their communities are not able to leave their communities for extended periods of time for training. Furthermore, there may be ways in which their effectiveness for certain ministries is enhanced by their continuity in their community. Some indigenous leaders are already being licensed for local service by their bishops. Various training programs are being developed locally and synodically to serve them. If the ELCA authorizes a wider range of ministries, such as lay catechists and evangelists, the demand will increase for approaches to theological education that are highly accessible, adaptable, and portable.

7. **Life-Long Learning**

Because of the changing, diverse context of our mission, it is necessary that leaders continually grow in faith, expand their skills and increase their knowledge through continuing education. Even at their very best, seminary degree programs cannot teach all one needs to know for the practice of ministry. While continuing education is expected of all pastors and associates in ministry, it is certainly needed during the early, formative years of ministry in a specific context. Continuing education is critically important at other points of personal and professional transition which call for fresh theological reflection, refinement of skills, response to changing societal issues, or orientation to new ministry contexts. This church must encourage and provide resources for its lay and ordained leaders to continually develop and renew their gifts for ministry through disciplined patterns of life-long learning.

8. **Ministry in Daily Life**

The education of ordained pastors and other leaders in the church should prepare them to assist the people of the church to integrate their life and faith. In addition, an increasing number of Christians who are not pursuing a church occupation seek intellectual exploration of their faith and theological reflection on their ministries in the world. Many have the time and interest to study theology with the same academic thoroughness that they apply to secular and professional fields of study. These lay members live on the cutting edge of mission. They engage structures of society and are in regular contact with people of other faiths and with people scarcely related to organized religion. Their faith and ministry could be enhanced if, in addition to congregationally based adult education, they had access to programs of theological education at an advanced level. Such programs would have to relate to their ministries in the world and be adaptable to the demands of their primary commitments to family or work.

9. **Scholarly Discourse and Reflection**

How the church engages its mission is constantly challenged, focused, and refined by lively and critical theological reflection. Since their origin in a sixteenth century university context, Lutherans have been committed to preparing pastors, teachers and other leaders to engage in theological reflection in congregations, colleges, and seminaries. The seminaries of the Lutheran church have had a special responsibility for transmitting the Lutheran theological tradition to successive generations of leaders. For the sake of the integrity and vitality of the Lutheran theological tradition and the contribution it makes to the ecumenical church, it is essential that all Lutheran theological faculties not only prepare leaders, but also serve as communities of theological discourse, which are a resource to this church in the development and review of theological positions. Furthermore, to ensure the continuation of a strong Lutheran theological tradition, this church needs to encourage and support some centers where theological education at the doctoral level can be pursued: major divinity schools where a strong Lutheran presence is consciously developed and maintained, ecumenical consortia in which a Lutheran institution collaborates with institutions of other denominations, seminary-based academic doctoral studies which may draw in scholars and expertise from neighboring academic institutions.

10. **Life Circumstances of Candidates**

Just as the context of the ELCA's mission is diverse, so also are those who come to be prepared to serve that mission: candidates young and old; candidates just out of college and candidates with a variety of work and life experience; single candidates and candidates with families; candidates who carry high debt loads and work to support themselves and their families while they prepare for ministry; candidates with advanced degrees and candidates who lack academic preparation for theological study; candidates steeped in the Christian tradition and Lutheran ethos and new Christians with little experience of the church; candidates who are mobile and candidates who are bound to particular places and communities; candidates who bring a variety of perspectives as women and men, as members of the dominant culture, and as members of various racial and ethnic communities. Some within this diversity have experienced systemic discrimination. This church needs to provide options in theological education that are responsive to the varied circumstances in the lives of ministry candidates.

11. **Ecumenical Interdependence**

Since a diversity of religions and Christian communions is part of our context for mission, people preparing for leadership in the ELCA need to learn how to work and study together with people of other traditions. It is vital that theological education in the ELCA build ecumenical understanding and model patterns of dialogue and cooperation among Christians and adherents of other faiths. Wherever possible, cooperative relationships and scholarly exchange programs should be fostered between Lutheran seminaries and those of other traditions and among Lutheran seminaries around the world. Major ecumenical seminaries which prepare some leaders for service in the Lutheran church play a role in fostering ecumenical interdependence.

Appendix D: Statement on Academic Readiness

In response to the call of the 1993 ELCA Churchwide Assembly for the seminaries to develop common standards of academic readiness for students entering master's level programs in preparation for rostered ministries of this church, the deans of the eight ELCA seminaries prepared the following statement for recommendation to the Division for Ministry board the following statement.

With regard to common admissions standards, as these pertain to academic prerequisites, the seminaries of the ELCA, in accordance with ATS standards, require a baccalaureate degree from an accredited college or university, or its equivalent, for admission to the M.Div., M.A., M.T.S., M.R.E., M.A.R., AND M.S.M. programs.

The standard of academic performance at the undergraduate level that normally obtains an admissions decision is a "B" average (2.5 or above on a 4.0 scale). However, admissions decisions also take into account patterns of progress in an applicant's academic history, the degree of difficulty of the undergraduate program, the standards of the school attended, performance in course-work most relevant to theological studies, academic letters of reference, success in other graduate programs, performance in career life, and other measures such as Graduate Record Exams, where these become a factor.

With regard to academic readiness, the seminaries of the ELCA recommend a broad background in the liberal arts, including such courses as English, history, modern languages, philosophy, Greek, communications, the natural sciences, and the social sciences. The applicant should possess intellectual ability for critical and reflective thinking.

The seminaries also expect that ELCA candidates will acquire basic acquaintance with the Scriptures and the catechism as a part of the experience of ELCA congregational involvement that is anticipated in connection with ecclesial readiness, as defined in the ELCA candidacy process.

Furthermore, the seminaries desire to build upon the candidates' knowledge of the Bible and catechism by incorporating biblical introduction and theology of the catechism into their various programs of the introduction to theological study. In this way, the biblical and catechetical components of ecclesial readiness are joined to academic readiness in the initial stages of theological study.

Beyond this, seminaries provide reading lists and study guides to candidates prior to the beginning of their seminary education, and usually incorporate these pre-seminary academic preparations into their introductory level course work.

The welcome diversity of today's seminary student bodies makes it inevitable that there will be significant differences in academic readiness among entering students. Therefore, the seminaries pursue a pattern for insuring academic readiness that blends stated expectations, assessment in key areas of competence, and a strategy for introductory studies which brings students with different academic backgrounds to a common level of participation in theological discourse early in the program of studies.

It is also important to note that introductory courses offered for credit are, in all cases, genuinely masters level courses. Even when they incorporate remediation, they do so in the context of developing the base of seminary theological studies. Furthermore, all seminaries of the ELCA provide opportunities for well-prepared students to test out of introductory requirements, gain advanced standing, or enter into an honors program.

Both the seminaries and the Division for Ministry stand ready to provide advice on specific resources to candidates, congregations, and candidacy committees.

Appendix E: First-Call Theological Education Churchwide Standards and Guidelines

Preface

First-call theological education was introduced in the Report on the Study of Theological Education to the 1993 Churchwide Assembly. That assembly directed the Division for Ministry to encourage synods to develop pilot programs of structured theological education in the first three years of ordained ministry. The 1995 Churchwide Assembly took action to require all pastors and rostered lay leaders, during their first three years under call, to participate in structured programs of theological education. These programs are to be designed and supervised by the synods, following churchwide standards. On the basis of broad consultation and the experience of pilot programs sponsored by more than forty synods, the Division for Ministry has prepared these churchwide standards and guidelines.

The *churchwide standards* define what is required of all programs of first-call theological education. They describe common outcomes to be achieved, the essential elements in the program design, and the administrative flexibility and responsibility necessary for the program to be effective. The standards do not prescribe specific courses or procedures. The *guidelines* which follow offer concrete examples and practical advice for those responsible for developing programs of first-call theological education.

First-call theological education needs both churchwide standards and synodical flexibility. Agreement on overall purpose and intended outcomes is essential for churchwide coherence and for the general compatibility of the various synodical or regional programs with one another and with basic seminary education. Synodical flexibility is essential for local initiative and for genuine contextualization, which is one of the principal values of the program. Every phase of implementation should thus attempt a creative balance of churchwide coherence and local variations.

Part I. Churchwide Standards

All newly rostered pastors, associates in ministry, diaconal ministers, and deaconesses in the Evangelical Lutheran Church in America will participate in structured programs of theological education during their first three years of service under call. Qualified programs of first-call theological education will meet the churchwide standards promoted here.

A. Goals

The common purpose of first-call theological education is to enhance the transition from seminary to parish. The desired outcome is that during their first three years under call, pastors and rostered lay leaders in the Evangelical Lutheran Church in America will have made the initial transition into their respective leadership roles and will have grown in knowledge of God's Word and the Lutheran confessional witness, in love for Jesus Christ and his Church, and in commitment to its mission.

In order to address this common purpose, ELCA programs of first-call theological education will give special attention to three goals:

1. The personal development of leadership style and collegiality, spiritual discipline, and ministerial identity appropriate to the respective rosters;
2. Competence in and overall integration of various aspects of the practice of ministry;
3. Discernment of the local and regional context of ministry.

B. Design

1. Components

Every ELCA program of first-call theological education will include the following four learning components:

a. *Core program,* that is, the common events designed for and by all rostered leaders in a geographical area: synod, multi-synodical, regional. These events are to total approximately one week per year (i.e., 25 contact hours). Core programs should provide the flexibility to meet the specific needs, patterns, and geographic distribution of persons on the respective rosters: ordained ministers of Word and Sacrament, associates in ministry, diaconal ministers, and deaconesses. First-call rostered leaders should participate in planning the core programs.

b. *Electives*, that is, offerings directed toward areas of specific need or interest which are available through a wide variety of seminars, workshops, summer school classes, synodical or churchwide events, advanced graduate courses, distance learning programs. These programs are to total approximately one week per year (i.e., 25 contact hours.)

c. *Mentoring* with an experienced colleague on an individual basis or in small groups that meet regularly. In consultation with the synod, new pastors will establish a relationship with a mentor or a colleague group.

d. *Structured reading* designed to support and extend the other educational components in fulfilling the overall goals of the program.

2. *Integration*

First-call theological education programs will include a balance of contextual awareness, theological analysis, and action/reflection methodology. Theological study is to be integrated with reflection on the practice of ministry.

3. *Individualized Learning Contracts*

First-call pastors or rostered laypersons in consultation with synod and congregational representatives will develop individualized learning contracts to achieve the stated purpose and goals through the four educational components. Programs will vary according to the creativity of the planners and the possibilities of the context.

C. Administration

Every synod is responsible for providing a program of first-call theological education, either alone or with other synods, in which all first-call pastors and rostered lay leaders participate for three years. The synod or synods working together are free to create and adapt specific programs as they see fit, within the stated standards regarding the goals and the design. Synods are encouraged to call on seminaries, continuing education centers, and/or churchwide units as partners in providing the first-call theological education programs.

As synods develop programs of first-call theological education, they should consult regularly with ELCA seminaries in order to assure that this phase of ministerial formation is in continuity with and complements the degree programs offered by the seminaries in preparation for rostered ministries. These conversations will provide data and insight for the ongoing curricular adjustment at the seminaries.

Part II. Guidelines for Implementation

These guidelines provide a commentary on the standards and offer fuller explanations and examples of the goals, design, and administration of first-call theological education programs. The guidelines are intended to stimulate thought and provide practical advice, not to impose restrictions upon local flexibility.

A. Goals

First-call theological education programs focus on three dimensions of developing leadership of pastors and rostered lay leaders. To assist synods in their planning, each dimension has been developed in greater detail by a working group, including representatives from synods, seminaries, continuing education centers, churchwide units, and first call-pastors.

1. *Ministerial Identity*

• Believing in God and living from the promise that God's Word will accomplish God's purpose in the lives of people and congregations.

• Moving from being a ministerial candidate to being a pastor or rostered lay leader involved in lifelong learning.

• Articulating a vision of evangelical pastoral or diaconal ministry.

• Balancing ministerial and personal identity through the development of appropriate boundaries and an understanding of appropriate and inappropriate conduct.

• Collegiality in ministry, accountability, and mutuality of the various rosters.

• Developing spiritual discipline that deepens one's relationship with God.

• Learning to wrestle with the complexity of demands, expectations, challenges, and disappointments of ministerial leadership.

• Finding fulfillment and joy in ministry.

• Addressing one's own personal, emotional, physical, and interpersonal health.

- Learning to live in the conversation between God's Word in scripture and human life in the concrete context of one's ministry.

In addition, an in-depth study specifically related to Pastoral Identity, is available through the Division for Ministry.

2. *Discernment of Context*

Listening, respecting, and attending to the following contextual realities:
- the history and present character of the congregation and its members
- the neighborhood and wider community
- the state and region
- the nation and the world
- synodical, churchwide, and ecumenical expressions of the church

Bringing the following factors to bear in the consideration of these contextual realities:
- interpersonal relationships
- cultural/ethnic presence
- socio-economic conditions
- historical and contemporary dynamics
- geo-political issues
- religious pluralism

Giving special attention to the outcast, the unbeliever, and the spiritually impoverished.

3. *Ministerial Skills and Practice*

Integrating ministerial skills and practice with the gospel.

Assessing and developing capabilities in the following specific areas of congregational ministry:
- preaching
- worship leadership
- teaching
- evangelism and intentional outreach
- stewardship
- community building in the congregation
- encouragement and support of the laity in ministry
- administration
- work with conflict
- youth and family ministry
- social ministry
- ecumenical dialogue and cooperation

Learning to understand and implement these various capabilities as dimensions of apostolic ministry within the ministry of the whole people of God, by bearing witness to the gospel of Jesus Christ to all the world and by showing concern for the poor.

B. Core Program Participation

Some core program events could integrate persons from several roster groups in order to explore shared areas of concern such as faith issues and spiritual development as well as the complementarity and interdependence of ministries. In order to honor the particularity of the rosters and to meet practical needs, core programs may be offered for each specific roster group:

a. **Ministers of Word and Sacrament**

Core programs will normally include all the first-call pastors within an individual synod or a group of synods working in cooperation with each other, sometimes on a region-wide basis.

b. **Rostered Lay Ministers**

Diaconal Ministers. As an alternative for diaconal ministers, synods might utilize a core program provided to one common site for one week during the summer, in conjunction with the ELCA formation program for diaconal ministers. A summer program for all new ELCA diaconal ministers would enhance their group identity within the ELCA. Even where attendance may involve considerable travel costs, it is expected that at least one such week will be part of every diaconal minister's three-year plan.

Associates in Ministry. For first-call associates in ministry, some core program events could be part of the annual synodical or regional events provided for all associates in ministry in the area.

Deaconesses. The core program for deaconesses could be tied to their biennial assembly.

Because of the geographic distribution of rostered lay ministers, it may be difficult in some cases for synods to provide them with core programs that are appropriate and accessible. In such cases the entire first-call requirement (two weeks or 50 contact hours) could be met through electives, designed by consultation among the first-call rostered leader and representatives of the synod and the congregation.

Participation in an area's core program of first-call theological education for several days each year will provide a context for developing mutual collegiality. The core program is intended to enhance the relationship of new pastors and rostered lay ministers with one another, with their mentors, with synodical staff and with the leaders provided by a continuing education center and/or seminary. The fresh perspectives, insights, and discoveries of the recently rostered ministers can be shared with their more experienced colleagues in the core events to enrich the ministry of all.

C. Accountability and Supervision

This entire process of first-call theological education involves a consensus among the individual, the congregation or agency, and the synodical representative. The mechanism or leverage to require participation in this program must be found within the ongoing life of the synod, since a seminary has already granted its degree and a candidacy committee has given its final approval for rostered ministry. Following direct discussions with the calling body and the candidate, the bishop will make sure that support for such a program is written into the letter of call. Once an individual plan is agreed upon within the terms of the call, a person designated by the synod has the responsibility of overseeing its progress. Upon completion of the program there could be a certificate or other formal recognition by the synod.

Normally, participation and completion of this program by the first-call pastor or rostered lay minister will be presupposed prior to the bishop's recommendation for a new call to a congregation or specialized ministry. A few bishops have expressed an interest in linking this three-year program with a three-year term call. Whatever the specific mechanism, this program involves mandatory participation, just as the M.Div. is a normal requirement for ordination to the ministry of Word and Sacrament. In extreme cases, willful disregard of the letter of call could occasion the process of discipline according to the governing documents of this church.

1. The First-Call Pastor or Rostered Lay Leader

In accepting and signing the letter of call, the first-call pastor or rostered lay leader expresses her/his commitment to involvement in first-call theological education.

The pastor will make use of the time provided by the congregation for participation in all components of the program.

The pastor will contribute PACE funds as fully as possible, and will apply for ELCA Growth in Excellence in Ministry PACE Growth Awards should that assistance be needed.

The pastor will work with the congregation's Staff Support Committee (or other designated group) and the synodical representative to develop the learning contract or continuing education covenant, and to provide periodic reports of progress toward the goals of the contract or covenant.

2. The Congregation/Institution/Agency

The congregation (or other calling body) will express its commitment to providing both time and financial support for first-call theological education in its call documents.

Time will be provided for the first-call pastor to participate in all components of the program.

Financial support will be provided to the best of the congregation's ability. It is hoped that in most cases PACE standards can be met. Where this is not possible, the congregation will support the pastor's application for an ELCA Growth in Excellence in Ministry PACE Growth Award.

The congregation's Staff Support Committee, or other designated group, will work with the pastor and synodical representative to develop the learning contract or covenant, and to provide periodic review of progress toward the goals of the contract or covenant.

3. Synod

The initiative and responsibility for this program will reside with the synods. A synodical program should focus on the particular needs and strengths of that synod. The new pastors assigned to a given synod will have been educated at many different seminaries and approved by the candidacy committees of many different synods. The rostered lay ministers will also vary in educational background, number, and distribution from synod to synod.

The synods may delegate responsibilities for the core program to another entity. Pilot projects have shown the complexities in developing core programs, especially in the second or third year when multiple groups are involved. Potential administrators or providers for a given area's core program include an ELCA seminary, a specialized unit of an ELCA seminary cluster, and the continuing education center(s) related to that area. Actual staffing of the sessions could come from many sources, such as local pastors or laity with special expertise, churchwide or synodical staff, and the staff of social service organizations.

Flexibility in planning and the maintenance of churchwide standards for theological education are two basic values to be considered by the synod in designing and administering first-call theological education.

Synods are encouraged to work together to develop inter-synodical or regional programs, especially for the "core program."

The Leadership Support Committee or its equivalent may be assigned the responsibility for all components of the program. Consultation with first-call pastors, providers, synod staff, churchwide units (Division for Ministry and Division for Congregational Ministries), experienced pastors, and others (e.g., community resources) should be an integral part of the planning. Decisions regarding the development of the program shall be lodged with the synod.

Below is a suggested list of steps a synod may follow in the start-up of the program and its implementation in congregations.

a. Develop the synodical or multi-synodical planning group.

b. Invite and train mentors or colleague leaders.

c. Integrate newly rostered ministers into the program.

d. Initiate, within 3 months of installation, a consultation among the pastor or rostered lay leader and the congregational representatives, to approve an overall covenant or contract.

e. Receive the annual continuing education report.

f. Assess the results of their program, in consultation with their providers, other synods, and the Division for Ministry, in relation to these standards and guidelines.

4. Churchwide Organization

The Division for Ministry, in consultation with the Division for Congregational Ministries and other churchwide units, assists in the overall implementation, research and evaluation of the program. This includes:

a. Appointing and staffing an advisory committee.

b. Preparing these standards and guidelines and distributing them to synods, congregations, and rostered leaders.

c. Distributing information about the program to seminaries and seminarians.

d. Serving as a consultant and communications link with those administering the program throughout the ELCA.

e. Assessing the results of synodical programs in relation to these standards and guidelines.

f. Reviewing these churchwide standards and guidelines.

D. Timeline

The requirement for all rostered ministers to participate in first-call theological education programs will become effective in fall 1997. Synods are encouraged to begin planning in the fall of 1995 and, where possible, to have programs in place for first-call rostered leaders in the fall of 1996. Most of the synods that are participating in pilot programs will begin holding events for first-call pastors in the fall of 1995. The pilot programs demonstrate that it takes considerable time, energy, and long-range planning for a synod or group of synods to launch such a program.

E. Costs

The costs for first-call theological education should be distributed among several parties:

1. The first-call pastor or rostered lay leader ($250 annually is expected, but not always possible given their indebtedness and low starting salaries);

2. The congregation's compensation package ($550 annually is expected, but not always possible since many first calls are carved out of small budgets);

3. Grants from ELCA PACE Growth funds administered by the Division for Ministry are available to rostered leaders whose congregations are not able to provide continuing education funds at the recommended churchwide level;

4. Subsidies from the synod for administrative costs, need-based scholarships, and travel equalization, as determined by the synod;

5. Churchwide subsidies for administrative, travel, and program costs for those synods with a larger than average number of first-call pastors and rostered lay leaders.

Subsidies are necessary and appropriate since this program is assisting leaders not only within the first call, but for future calls throughout this church. It would be unfair for the graduates and the first-call congregations to shoulder a churchwide responsibility on their own. Therefore, churchwide and synodical support will be provided as needed and possible.

F. Further Development and Resources

As with any new program, this initiative will need considerable creativity. It will require periodic review and adjustment. There should be substantial latitude for regional variations and attention to specific contexts. Even the nomenclature used in this proposal (e.g., "first-call theological education" or "core program") is intentionally generic rather than specific, in order to leave room for regional creativity also in the names chosen. The Division for Ministry should monitor all programs carefully, facilitate an exchange of insights, and conduct a general review by 1999.

As resources for those who will be planning and administering these programs, the Division for Ministry is preparing a number of documents:

1. Churchwide standards for first-call theological education;

2. Guidelines, which contain ideas and examples for planning and administering the program;

3. Questions and options for synods starting a first-call theological education program;

4. A substantial study regarding the meaning of pastoral identity and the experiences which may enhance its development;

5. Information regarding resources available from other churchwide units;

6. Appropriate programs that can be accessed electronically; and

7. Reports of learnings from pilot projects.

These resources will be available upon request from the Division for Ministry following the 1995 Assembly.

Appendix F: Cluster Terminology

The various structural relationships and components of the interdependent theological education network envisioned in the Study of Theological Education and affirmed by the 1993 Churchwide Assembly are defined as follows:

A **"seminary cluster"** is an interdependent educational entity comprising formerly independent seminaries which function corporately to provide the needed range of theological education for mission in their common geographical area. By deploying resources and specializations among cluster members and through cooperative relationships with other providers of theological education on the territory, a cluster is expected to meet a wide variety of needs for professional degree programs, continuing education, and degree and non-degree training for indigenous lay leaders, pastoral assistants, and for the baptized for their ministry in daily life. In addition, a seminary cluster may provide an educational program or service as a specialization on behalf of all the clusters for the sake of the whole church.

"Cooperative relationships" as used in this report means the partnerships being developed between a seminary cluster and other providers of theological education on their common territory in order to provide aspects of needed leadership education from their respective resources.

"Interdependent theological education network" is the comprehensive term that includes the seminary clusters and the various educational partners with which they have formed cooperative relationships in order to meet overall needs for leadership development.

Appendix G: Timeline for Cluster Development

The 1993 ELCA Churchwide Assembly called upon the ELCA seminaries to develop into fully functioning clusters with common governance and administrative structures in place no later than the year 2003. The timeline referred to in the 1993 Assembly action outlines the major tasks and dates by which they are to be completed.

a. 1993–1995

1. Cluster Formation

   By the fall of 1994 cluster alignments are to be approved by the respective seminary boards and ratified by the board of the Division for Ministry according to Criteria for the Formation of Clusters. These criteria were formulated in consultation with seminary faculties and boards and affirmed in spring 1994 by the division board.

2. Leadership Needs Assessment

   Seminaries working with potential cluster partners are to assess needs for new or improved theological education offerings to meet emerging leadership needs on their common territory. Consultation with synodical and churchwide leadership is expected.

3. Specializations

   By the spring of 1995 cluster partners are to determine specific programs and specializations to be offered by their cluster and a plan for deploying these responsibilities among the cluster partners. The Division for Ministry will initiate a process for identifying churchwide specializations to be offered on behalf of the entire theological education system by one seminary or cluster and not duplicated elsewhere.

4. Exploration of Appropriate Structures for Governance

   Potential cluster partners are to begin exploring possible forms of joint decision making and governance which would provide the necessary legal framework to allow for and support the accomplishment of cluster goals. Decisions about such structures must be made no later than fall 1999.

5. Cooperative Relationships with Other Theological Education Providers

   Conversations should begin among cluster partners and other potential providers of theological education on the territory to see how responsibilities can be shared and what resources can be contributed toward fulfilling the imperatives.

b. 1995–1999

1. Churchwide Specialization

   By 1997, specializations offered by one cluster for the sake of the whole church will be negotiated through the Theological Education Coordinating Committee and assigned by the Division for Ministry.

2. Cooperative Relationships with Other Theological Education Providers

   Efforts will be intensified to identify and prioritize theological education needs and work with partners to design and implement plans to provide needed services and programs on the territory.

3. Formation of Cluster Governance and Administrative Structures

   Decisions regarding cluster governance and administrative structures are to be made by seminary boards by spring 1999 and by the Division for Ministry by fall 1999.

c. 1999–2003

1. Implementation of Cluster Governance and Administrative Structures Seminary boards and the board for the Division for Ministry will take all necessary actions regarding academic programs and structures of cluster governance and administration no later than the spring of 2003.

Appendix H: Functions and Composition of Theological Education Coordinating Committee

The Theological Education Coordinating Committee serves in an advisory capacity to the Division for Ministry in the coordination and planning for a system of theological education.

a. Functions of the Theological Education Coordinating Committee:

1. Keeping before the ELCA and the seminaries a vision for a system of theological education which is open to meeting new needs and opportunities in the preparation of ordained and lay leaders for mission;

2. Advancing strategic planning by identifying and analyzing needs, conducting inventories of the entire system of theological education on a regular basis, evaluating resources, assessing new opportunities, and proposing strategies for action;

3. Monitoring the responsibilities and timelines assigned to various partners in the 1993 Report of the Task Force on the Study of Theological Education, including the progressive stages of cluster development, and reporting on progress made;

4. Advising the Division for Ministry regarding the funding of the ELCA system of theological education, giving special attention to the allocation of funds to the seminary clusters;

5. Identifying the needs for churchwide specializations and negotiating their placement among the seminary clusters for recommendation to the Division for Ministry board;

6. Initiating and coordinating conversations between and among seminary clusters and other theological education providers with a view to promoting cooperation;

7. Identifying issues related to educational standards and other policy issues affecting theological education within the ELCA and advising the Division for Ministry in addressing these issues;

8. Advocating for theological education as a foundational priority for the ELCA and articulating the seminary clusters' contributions, aspirations and needs in preparing ordained and lay leaders and as centers for theological discourse and research;

9. Assuming other functions as assigned by the Division for Ministry.

b. Committee Membership

Members of the Theological Education Coordinating Committee will bring experience in theological education and competence in dealing with issues and trends in theological education, in the ELCA and in society as they affect the preparation of ordained and lay leaders. For the 1995–1997 biennium, 12–14 persons will be named to the committee by the Division for Ministry board. During this initial two year period, as the clusters begin to function, each seminary will be represented on the committee. Other committee members will be persons working in continuing education, in ELCA related colleges and universities, and in non-ELCA theological institutions. Two members will be from the Division for Ministry board currently serving on its theological education committee, with one serving as chairperson of the coordinating committee. A staff member from the Division for Ministry will serve in an advisory capacity.

At the close of the 1995–1997 biennium, one representative will be named from each seminary cluster rather than from each individual seminary. The overall size of the committee will decrease accordingly.

c. Evaluation

In recognition of the ongoing evolution of theological education in the ELCA, the continuing need for this committee, its specific functions and composition shall be reviewed each biennium by the board of the Division for Ministry.

Report of the Division for Outreach

Organization
Board
Rev. Jonathan K. Bomgren, Farmington Hills, Mich. (1997)[3, 6, 7]

Rev. Julius Carroll IV, Oakland, Calif. (1999)[4, 6]

Ms. Marlene M. Case, Rochester, Minn. (1997)

Mr. Alan W. Chen, Bayside, N.Y. (1999)[1, 4, 5]

Mr. George S. Edwards, Philadephia, Pa. (1999)[4, 6]

Mr. Ira Frank, Auburn, Wash. (1995)[4, 5, 7]

Mr. Luis F. Goyzueta, Macungie, Pa. (1995)[3, 5]

Ms. Patricia J. Hardwick, *secretary*, Doylestown, Pa. (1997)[1, 3, 6]

Rev. Jane E. Jenkins, Springfield, Ill. (1995)[3, 5]

Ms. Dora Johnson, Washington, D.C. (1999)[3, 5]

Rev. Ronald K. Johnson, Minneapolis, Minn. (1995)[2, 6]

Ms. Anna-Marie Klein, Kirkland, Wash. (1995)[4, 5]

Ms. Patricia Knodel, Wilmington, Del. (1995)[2, 6, 7]

Mr. Michael Kohn, *vice chair*, West Columbia, S.C. (1997)[1, 2, 6, 7]

Rev. Gary A. Marshall, Escondido, Calif. (1999)[4, 5]

Rev. John F. Nelson, *chair*, Allendale, N.J. (1995)[1, 3, 6, 7]

Rev. Richard W. Owens, Bismarck, N.Dak. (1997)

Ms. Era M. Smith, Cleveland, Ohio (1999)[1, 2, 5]

Ms. Barbara L. Strobel, Houston, Texas (1999)[2, 6]

Rev. Hector Vasquez, Eagle Pass, Texas (1997)[2, 5]

Mr. Donald W. Vogt, Aberdeen, S.D. (1997)[4, 5, 7]

Advisors

Rev. Lee S. Thoni, executive assistant to the bishop, Office of the Bishop

Bishop Reginald H. Holle, North/West Lower Michigan Synod

---

[1] Executive Committee

[2] Program Committee—New Ministries

[3] Program Committee—Newly Organized

[4] Program Committee—Urban, Rural, and Community

[5] Program Committee—Mission Partners and Education for Mission

[6] Program Committee—Church Building, Real Estate and Finance

[7] Budget and Planning Committee

Executive Staff
Chicago-Based Staff:

Executive Director: Rev. M. L. Minnick Jr.

Associate Executive Director and Director for Administration: Rev. E. Taylor Harmon

Director for Program, New Congregations: Rev. Robert S. Hoyt

Newly Organized Congregations: Ms. Susan A. Thompson

Congregational Outreach Services: Rev. Warren A. Sorteberg

Leadership for Outreach Ministries: Ms. Catherine I. H. Braasch

Mission Education and Mission Partners: Rev. Donald D. Johnson

Mission Builders: Rev. William J. Hanson

Director for Building, Real Estate and Finance: Mr. David Opgrand

Loan Administrator: Ms. Elaine B. Graton

Church Architect: Mr. Peter Norgren

Real Estate Coordinator: Ms. Karen Sumner

Mission Directors—Deployed and Shared Staff:

Rev. Donald D. Parsons (Synod 1A)

Rev. Ludwig H. Siqueland (Synods 1B, C, D, E, F)

Mr. James L. Sims Jr. (Synod 2A)

Vacancy (Synod 2B)

Rev. Yutaka Kishino (Synod 2C)

Rev. Paul J. Halvorson (Synod 2D)

Rev. Richard A. Magnus (Synod 2E)

Rev. Dale A. Skatrud (Synods 3A, B, C, D, E)

Rev. Marshall P. Pechauer (Synods 3F, G, H, I)

Rev. Jearald J. Shaft (Synods 4A, B, C)

Rev. Raymond Legania (Synods 4D, F)

Mr. Rafael Ruiz (Synod 4E)

Rev. Ruben Duran (Synod 5A)

Rev. Gary Wollersheim (Synod 5B)

Rev. John W. Kelley (Synod 5C)

Rev. John N. Carlson (Synod 5D)

Rev. Delwayne Hahn (Synod 5E)

Rev. Lowell R. Hennigs (Synod 5F)

Rev. Dale R. Skogman (Synod 5G)

Rev. Gerhard I. Knutson (Synod 5H)

Rev. Carl W. Peters (Synod 5I)

Rev. Alan T. Heggen (Synod 5J)

Rev. Ronald E. Mach (Synod 5K)

Rev. Harris A. Hostager (Synod 5L)

Rev. James C. Kocher (Synods 6A, D, E)

Vacancy (Synods 6B and C)

Sr. Elizabeth Ann Steele (Synod 6F)

Mr. Wolfgang D. Herz-Lane (Synod 7A)

Rev. Frederick G. Wedemeyer (Synod 7B)

Rev. Grace C. Olson (Synod 7C)
Rev. David W. Preisinger (Synod 7D)
Rev. Glenn L. Simmons (Synod 7E)
Rev. Claire S. Burkat (Synod 7F)
Ms. Helen R. Harms (Synods 8A, B, C, D, E, H)
Rev. Jerrett L. Hansen (Synods 8F, G)
Rev. Boyce D. Whitener (Synods 9A, B)
Rev. J. Richard Gantt (Synods 9C, D)
Rev. Joseph W. Walker Jr. (Synods 9C, D)
Rev. Ronald J. Ryckman (Synod 9E)
Rev. Edelmiro Cortes (Synod 9F)

Building Consultants
Mr. Philip Roe (Regions 1 and 3)
Mr. Andrew K. Waters (Region 2)
Mr. Richard P. Linde (Regions 3, 5, and 6)
Ms. Patricia E. Dever (Region 4)
Mr. John D. Reisch (Regions 7 and 8)
Mr. Willis E. Shanks (Synods 9A, B, C, D, E)
Rev. Edelmiro Cortes (Synod 9F)

Maritime Ministry Consultant
Rev. Andrew E. V. Krey

Mission Founders Resource Developer
Rev. Frederick A. Marks

Constitutional Mandate

The Division for Outreach provides leadership to this church as it reaches out with the Gospel of Jesus Christ in the United States and the Caribbean and invites all people to a faith relationship with God. The mandate of this division is defined in continuing resolution 16.11.C91. of the Constitution, Bylaws, and Continuing Resolutions of the Evangelical Lutheran Church in America.

Statement of Intent

"Making Christ Known," this year's theme, is particularly appropriate for the work of this division. The following statement of intent was prepared by the division's board:

> The overriding intent of the Division for Outreach for the 1990s is to embrace with all partners engaged in outreach a shared vision to proclaim the Gospel of Jesus Christ throughout the United States and the Caribbean by:
> - Expanding the network of Lutherans committed to outreach with the Gospel. This would include individuals, congregations, synods, and agencies and institutions of this church.
> - Becoming more effective in responding to changing ministry context. This would include new outreach ministry developments that

would be appropriate to not only the cultural, but also the ethnic diversity of the United States and the Caribbean.
- Communicating and interpreting outreach issues and opportunities to all ELCA members. This would include "telling the story of God's wonderful deeds through his Church" and also moving in the direction of developing effective missionary efforts to reach the unchurched.

As this division works in partnership with synods, congregations, ministries, and ministry leaders, the focus continues to be on "Making Christ Known" to all people, for it is only through Christ that we can truly come to know our God: "If you know me, you will know my Father also. . . . Whoever has seen me has seen the Father" (John 14:7,9).

Outreach as a Priority

The division understands the priority for outreach with the Gospel to include the development of new ministries of this church in ways that are culturally and contextually appropriate, and that reach those who are not in a faith relationship with God through Jesus Christ.

The division understands the priority for outreach with the Gospel also to include support to older congregations to expand their ministry in the place they are located. Not only must there be vision, but there must be ways and means to help leaders and congregational members take ownership of opportunities and implement ministry with the resources available to them.

The synods and the churchwide units will work together to help every congregation of this church see itself as a center for mission. Being a center for mission means there is a vision, an understanding of God's mission, in which this church participates; there is clarity in regard to the context of where the congregation is located and the opportunities before it. There is intentionality on the part of the leadership of the ministry to empower all the people of the congregation to proclaim, to witness, to serve, and to be advocates for justice.

The Church, as the Body of Christ in the world, is to be the faithful servant of God. It sows the seeds, and trusts in the work of the Holy Spirit to bring growth and fruit.

Report of Work 1993-1994

The "Evangelism Strategy" and Mission Founders: To assist in the establishment and nurturing of new congregations, and in order to fulfill the resolution of the 1991 Churchwide Assembly (related to the "Evangelism Strategy") that the division "work toward establishing a minimum of 50 new congregations per year, and seek designated gifts so that by 1997 there will be 100 new congregations established each year," an active giving program, Mission Founders, has been started with the employment of the Rev. Frederick A. Marks. Through this program, contributions from major donors and congregations that have met their mission-support expectation will be sought to provide full financial support for new congregational development. This effort will be a part of this church's "Vision for Mission" efforts.

"Multicultural Mission Strategy" *and the* ***Development of Ethnic-Specific Strategies:*** Working with the Commission for Multicultural Ministries, synods and representatives of the various ethnic communities, the division seeks to define a rationale, goals, and methods for achieving the inclusiveness goals of this church. The division has received grants from Lutheran Brotherhood that provide financial resources for bringing together members of the ethnic communities who serve as co-developers with the division for these ethnic-specific strategies. By February 1, 1996, the division will begin implementing some of these strategies. The intent is to continue to use the resources of the ethnic-specific communities as implementation moves forward.

During the biennium, the African American strategy group has planned the start-up of a regional church development in 1995. Connected with this congregation will be a leadership center that can assist all congregations of this church to carry out more effective outreach to African Americans.

Planning for new ministries among Arab populations in this country continued in 1994. In cooperation with synods, progress was made toward new ministries in five of six areas originally identified in consultation with the Association of Lutherans of Arab and other Middle Eastern Heritage (ALAMEH).

With assistance from Lutheran Brotherhood, the division sponsored a Chinese consultation that brought together pastors and lay people from throughout the country to develop this church's strategy for Chinese ministry in the United States. The Korean, Arab, and Chinese strategies help the division start new ministries among the members of these communities.

The division is working with Hispanic, Native American, and other ethnic communities to develop strategies in the coming biennium that will continue to strengthen the work of this division and enhance the partnership with synods and others who reach out to all God's people with the good news of Christ our Savior.

Area Strategy Planning: During this biennium there have been increased requests from synods and congregations for technical assistance and consultation in the strategic planning for outreach in a specific area. The division has provided planning materials and consultation through Chicago-based and deployed staff members. A task force has been formed to help the division develop more effective methods of delivering area strategy resources.

Area Strategies—Multicultural: During this biennium the division continued to support multicultural strategies in the Pacifica, Sierra Pacific, Grand Canyon, and Rocky Mountain synods. In addition, the division continued its partnership with the Northern Texas-Northern Louisiana Synod in the development of an African American strategy with congregations in the Dallas-Fort Worth area. Work continues on a comprehensive strategy with congregations in Puerto Rico.

Area Ministries—Rural and Urban: Area ministries—interdependent ministries formed by synods, congregations, agencies, and churchwide units—strengthen congregational membership, community outreach to unchurched persons, and advocacy for justice in the area covered by the ministry strategy. Some 11 rural area ministries were supported in 1994; three of the funded activities are multi-synodical: US-Mexico Border Ministry, Appalachian Coalition (ELCMA) and the Appalachian Regional Assembly, and the Great Plains Coalition for Rural Ministry. More than half of the remaining area ministry activities are ethnic-specific or multicultural in emphasis. Over 30 urban area ministries, coalitions, and cooperatives (21 in 1993; 15 in 1994) have received start-up grants as they seek to provide interdependent ministry in urban communities.

Regional Consultations with Synods: The division conducts consultations with synods in regional settings to foster the interdependent partnership relationship mandated by this church. In 1995, the division held consultations in all nine regions of this church, during which outreach committee chairs, synod staff, and deployed staff discussed the "new program categories" of the division, as well as the realties of the partnership between synods and the division and the allocation of financial resources to help congregations fulfill their potential. Continued emphasis is placed on synodical planning, including this church's commitment to inclusivity.

Mission Research: During this biennium the division continued to provide financial support to the Institute for Mission in the U.S.A. and as the designated lead unit, continues to coordinate the efforts of involvement of other churchwide units in using the services offered by that Institute.

The division also worked with the firm of Percept (formerly, Church Information and Development Services) in the development of maps and related demographic data utilized by the division to identify areas in which this church needs to plant new congregations.

New Ministry and Congregational Development: The division's primary responsibility is to initiate new congregations, nurture them to organization, and care for them until they become financially self-sustaining. The process of initiating and nurturing congregations toward organization may take anywhere from 18 months to five years, depending on the context in which the ministry is placed and the community's response to a new Lutheran congregation.

During 1994, there were 137 ministries under development, 47 of which began during this biennium (24 in 1993; 23 in 1994). Twelve of the 47 ministries received significant funding from synods or Mission Partners. Of the 47 ministries begun during this biennium:

Ethnic Communities

Anglo or White	31
African American	1
Asian	4
Hispanic	10
Ministry for the Deaf	1

Socioeconomic Communities

Extreme Poverty	1
Working Class	10
Middle Class	29
Upper Middle Class	7

Every region in the country initiated at least one new ministry, with Regions 2 and 4 each initiating 11 new ministries. Five ministries under development were recessed or closed and five merged with existing congregations or another ministry under development. As congregations under development gain momentum, they are asked to participate in a salary-reimbursement process that generates additional income for the division to use in initiating ministries. Each of the ministries under development, therefore, is engaged in mission development.

Synodically Authorized Worshiping Communities: The 1993 Churchwide Assembly authorized this new category for ministry development. During the biennium the division worked closely with the Office of the Secretary and the Conference of Bishops in developing the criteria for such ministries. Sixty-six ministries—begun as small groups meeting in homes or a community building, often with appointed ministry leaders—were recognized as being in this category. Many of these new ministries are growing and may move toward recognition as a congregation. This has become a significant tool for mission planning.

Newly Organized Congregations: The program for newly organized congregations helps new congregations grow toward maturity in ministry and full partnership with this church. Assistance includes partnership support, where needed, and programmatic resources from the division and other churchwide units, including leadership training, stewardship education, counsel, supervision, and assistance in the construction of first-unit church buildings. Normally, there is a goal of fiscal self-reliance five years after organization.

During 1993, 259 congregations were served through this program and at the end of 1994, 255 congregations were related to the division:

	1993	*1994*
Ethnic-Specific or Multicultural Congregations	49	55
Poverty-Level Communities	38	42
Received Partnership Support	226	221
Staff Addition Short-Term Grants*	3	9
Became Self-Supporting	29	28
Organized Self-Supporting	7	2
TOTAL	259	255

* To Fast-Growing Congregations

Note: There is overlap in the various categories reflected in this table.

In 1994, a study was undertaken of five fast-growing congregations. It identified factors that will enhance the division's work with developing congregations in the future. Learnings from the study included factors that contributed to the growth of these five congregations and the challenges they face as result of their fast growth. The pastors, lay leaders, and congregations visited in this study were a source of learning and encouragement. The work of the Spirit is strong among them, and the division's work is well informed by them.

Urban Ministries: Our world continues to change as the process of urbanization accelerates in this nation and around the globe. The complex dynamics of urbanization challenge ELCA congregations, synods, and the churchwide expression as this church seeks to be more effective in its outreach to the urban masses.

This program served 208 congregations in 1993 and 202 in 1994, with some congregations remaining in the program for the total period of the biennium while other congregations became self-supporting, so that during this biennium, the division provided assistance to over 300 urban congregations in their outreach with the Gospel to their communities. Most of these congregations are in inner-city neighborhoods, many in desperately poor neighborhoods where resources are scarce. Most of these congregations are older and are facing or are engaged in racial, ethnic, or socio-economic transition. Assistance consists of consultations by staff for planning and evaluation, technical and financial assistance (partnership support), and training of leaders to achieve their mission goals.

The goal of each ministry receiving support is to develop outreach to new people and to reach self-reliance. Some of the ministries served are intentionally seeking to become multicultural or ethnic-specific in scope, while others are in a process of redevelopment, attempting to turn around a congregation in decline. "Ministry adjustment congregations" are attempting to make short-term, mid-course changes to strengthen their outreach to their community.

The division also provides support to approximately 20 Lay Workers in Ministry (LWIM) who serve in congregations to strengthen outreach to neighborhoods and communities.

In January 1995, the division established an urban ministry outreach team consisting of three deployed staff located in the Eastern, Midwestern, and Western regions of the nation. This urban ministry team will relate to synods, clusters of congregations, and congregations in planning and resourcing outreach ministry in urban areas. The team will develop and utilize a network of 50 or more urban specialists to consult with synods and congregations to strengthen outreach ministry from Lutheran congregations in urban communities.

Urban Initiative: The division has developed a process for developing an urban initiative. The statement chronicles the history of Lutheran presence in the cities of the nation as well as the need to re-examine the current realities and challenges of today.

The cities of the United States offer a rich field of opportunity for mission outreach among both the poor and the rich, the privileged and the underclasses. The goal is for urban congregations to be strong, effective, and faithful in ministry in their settings.

The division will bring a report of the findings of this process to the 1997 Churchwide Assembly.

Rural Ministries: During 1994, 54 congregations received financial support, seven of which became self-reliant by the end of 1994. Considerable focus was placed on ministry reviews and moving congregations to self-support, both through increased local commitment and more sustainable models of ministry programming and leadership, such as yoked ministries or shared ministry agreements.

Three rural ecumenical organizations received financial support in 1994. The purpose of these grants was to enhance cooperation between churches and rural organizations in matters of sustainability of land and communities. In addition, an emphasis was placed upon building synodical ownership in those territories where the organizations operated. While churchwide support (both dollars and leadership on boards) is important in launching the cooperation, synodical support is important if the work is to be a true partnership between this church and other organizations.

Rural Ministry Resolution Update: Implementation of the 1993 Churchwide Assembly's Resolution on Rural Ministry has involved building networks and engaging partners in dialogue regarding planning and practice of rural ministry in the late 1990s and beyond. In addition, we have sought to expand our rural constituents' knowledge of how many people in the churchwide organization address rural ministry in their work. In February 1995, a Consultation on Sustainable Outreach through Small Town and Rural Congregations was held. This was a major event in the history of this church and a key component in implementing the rural resolution. This consultation, funded through a grant from Lutheran Brotherhood, brought together a sampling of 25 of this church's key ministry leaders and practitioners from a variety of rural and small town settings, representing the faithful creativity that is the best of what the rural church offers. Dialogue addressed the needs for outreach planning congregational life materials and leadership approaches appropriate to the full range of rural and small town contexts.

Church in Community: Through this program the division encourages congregations and like-minded organizations to put faith into action among the people, neighborhoods, and areas around them. In 1995, ministry activities related to this program will be a part of the new congregational outreach services program of the division.

Japan American Evangelism Program: The Rev. Ikuo Takatsuka, missionary from the Japan Evangelical Lutheran Church, began his second five-year term at Lutheran Church of the Resurrection, Huntington Beach, Calif., in April 1992 and continues to serve as a consultant to the division regarding a strategy for ministry among persons of Japanese origin living in the United States. The fifth anniversary of the Japanese ministry was celebrated on November 7, 1993, with more than 130 people at the worship service. In March 1994, plans were shared by Pastor Takatsuka to enter into dialogue about the possibility of establishing a sister church relationship with one of the Japan Evangelical Lutheran congregations, as well as to continue dialogue related to a Japanese Center and church growth seminar in California.

Maritime Ministry: During this biennium there has been a transition in the maritime ministry program, with Lutheran World Federation area secretaries now carrying full responsibility for international work. In

December 1993, the Rev. Roald Kverndal officially retired as the maritime ministry consultant. The final transition of the international work of the consultant was completed in May 1994. The Rev. Andrew V. Krey is now related to the division as a domestic maritime ministry consultant. Pastor Krey works with staff of the division and synodical outreach committees in targeted synods to explore the possibility of establishing ministry to seafarers, assists the division in general interpretation related to maritime and seafarers ministry, and represents the division in maritime ministry associations such as Lutheran Association for Maritime Ministry and North American Maritime Ministry Conference.

Summary: At the end of 1994, 763 new and existing ministries related to the work of the Division for Outreach received financial assistance and consultative services from staff members. Of that number, 405 are in ethnic-specific and multicultural communities (81 African American, 41 Asian, 113 Hispanic, 133 multicultural, one Muslim, 33 Native American, and three ministries with persons who are deaf). In addition, approximately 1500 congregations are assisted by the church architect and church building consultants.

Church Building, Financing, and Real Estate: This division, together with the Mission Investment Fund (MIF) of the Evangelical Lutheran Church in America, provides services for church building, loans, and real estate to new ministries and established ELCA congregations. The church building and financing consultants' services cover the total spectrum of the building process, from planning for new space to assisting in placing long-term loans on completed construction. The church building and financing consultants provide building and financial consultant services to approximately 1,500 congregations each year. Consultant services are provided without charge to the congregation.

In 1993 and 1994, the division approved 210 MIF loans, totalling $84,902,000. Eighty-one loans were for mission congregation building programs and 129 were for additional building programs for established congregations. The demand for church building loans continues to grow. During the next two years the Mission Investment Fund is expected to provide loans totalling $95,000,000 to 240 congregations.

The division has continued to defer the purchase of church building sites until the time a mission congregation is ready to organize. This practice, along with the sale of excess sites, has significantly reduced the inventory of real estate assets. During 1993-1994, the MIF purchased 46 sites and parsonages totalling $6,104,476, and sold properties totalling $13,631,095. At the end of 1994, the MIF real estate assets were $51,000,000.

Seventy-seven properties, totalling $14,000,000, are currently on the market for sale.

The division works closely with the church loan departments of Lutheran Brotherhood and Aid Association for Lutherans in placing long-term loans for building programs. During 1993 and 1994, the division provided letters of recommendation to the fraternals for 148 loans, totalling $101,600,000. We are fortunate to have two strong Lutheran fraternals that actively seek to provide loans to ELCA congregations.

Future with the Mission Investment Fund: On January 1, 1996, the personnel assigned to the department for church building, real estate, and financing will join the staff of the Mission Investment Fund (MIF) and become part of its new operations department. The division's responsibilities in this area have included architectural and building consultant services, loan management, and real estate procurement and management. Movement of this group to the fund will make it possible to add the additional field staff necessary to manage the real assets in a more professional manner and attend to the growing investments that the fund has in congregations. Twelve positions will be involved in this move, seven of which are currently funded by service fees received for loan services from Lutheran Brotherhood, Aid Association for Lutherans, and by MIF loan origination fees. Two positions are already funded by the fund and three positions are funded from the division's operating budget. Under the agreement with the fund, the division will continue to fund those three positions until it is mutually determined that the fund has the resources to absorb the additional personnel costs. New staff positions added after January 1, 1996, will be funded by the Mission Investment Fund.

Mission Partners, Mission Builders, and Education for Mission

Mission Partners: The major purpose of Mission Partners is to establish direct and personal relationships with congregations and individuals to ministries related to the division. In partnership with synods, financial, material, and personal assistance is provided to outreach ministries, thereby developing concrete expressions of partnership with them. Since 1992, more than $5 million has been given annually by mission partners to ministries related to the division.

Mission Builders: From the inception of this program, mission builders projects have been undertaken coast to coast, border to border, across the United States and the Caribbean, with its priority being new ministry first-unit buildings. Mission builders give of their time, energy, skill, and talent in partnership with members of congregations, assisting in the building of first church facilities. Eight church building projects were completed in 1994. There are currently 94 rostered builders and spouses related to this program. The Mission Builders Endowment Fund was established in 1994 and plans are now under way to publicize this opportunity for individuals to contribute toward the work of this program through contributions and estate planning.

Mission Education: The Division for Outreach joins the Division for Global Mission in planning the annual Global Mission Events. Two events were held in 1994 at Concordia College, Moorhead, Minn., and Howard University, Washington, D.C., with a total of 2,667 persons participating. The events in 1995 are scheduled for July at Luther College, Decorah, Iowa; Kent State University, Kent, Ohio; and Colorado State University, Fort Collins, Colo. These two divisions also coordinate the publication of "Prayer Ventures," a day-by-day prayer calendar for domestic and international missions and missionaries. The mission education team, comprising staff members of the divisions for Global Mission, Congregational Ministries, Outreach, and staff from the publishing house of the ELCA (Augsburg Fortress), continue to work together in developing resource materials that can be used by a variety of age groups to achieve a better understanding of God's mission and this church's participation in that mission.

Leadership Development Program

A new staff position, "leadership for outreach ministries," has been created. This position carries responsibility for the recruitment, selection, training, utilization, support, and affirmation of ministry personnel related to the division. The ministry personnel will include mission developers, lay workers in ministry, and rostered indigenous leaders recruited and trained for ministry in a contextual situation.

Indigenous Leadership: During this biennium, the division provided support for the Black Leadership Project carried out by the Lutheran Theological Center in Atlanta (Ga.), a project directed toward recruitment and training of African American persons for leadership in the Church. The division also supported the Hispanic Leadership Project carried out in Los Angeles by Pacific Lutheran Theological Seminary, a highly successful program of recruiting and training indigenous Hispanic leaders for ministry in this church.

Interns and Residents: The division, together with the Division for Ministry, continues to support the Horizon Internship Program. More than 50 seminary interns have been placed in rural and urban congregations to train them for future ministry in these settings.

Intentional Ministry Conferences: The program for newly-organized congregations coordinates and provides resources for synod-sponsored, three-day events for pastors serving congregations with new or unmet mission opportunities. The division provides written resource materials for each event, and secures and funds a resource leader. Two hundred and fourteen persons participated during this biennium in these conferences—15 conferences during fiscal year 1993, and 11 in fiscal year 1994. The conferences are designed to meet participants' needs for a specialized focus on urban, rural and small town, or city and suburban ministry.

Training Conferences: Leadership development and training also occurs through the various programmatic units of the division:

Conference Types 1993-1994

Training and Orientation for Pastor Developers	3
Leadership Conference for New Congregations	4
Post-Building Conferences	2
Mission Partner Coordinators Training Event	2
Mission Builders Foremen Event	2
Redevelopment Conferences	4

Thirty-five persons, representing 18 congregations in Regions 3, 4, 5, and 6, were served through the post-building conferences. The conferences, attended by pastors and lay leaders, cover transition issues, new visions, and skill development for new ministry circumstances.

Over 200 urban and rural pastors and lay leaders, representing 150 congregations, were served through conferences on redevelopment ministry during this biennium. Redevelopment conferences focus on urban ministries but also accommodate rural and suburban congregations that are attempting to develop effective ministry. Study is under way regarding the needs for redevelopment training, development of curriculum, and a process design for future training events to meet the emerging needs of this church. The division expects that redevelopment of existing congregations will be a major issue and concern for the next decade.

The division co-sponsored and co-led, with the Division for Congregational Ministries, an Aid Association for Lutherans-funded training program in 1994 related to growth through small group ministries. Congregations from two synods participated in this pilot project.

Lutheran Brotherhood Foundation and Aid Association for Lutherans

The Division for Outreach gratefully acknowledges the partnership of Lutheran Brotherhood Foundation and Aid Association for Lutherans. These fraternal organizations have continued to assist the division's work by providing special grants, some of which have been noted earlier in this report and some which are being shared at this point, and on-going financial resources for the work of this division. The division's relationship with Aid Association for Lutherans and Lutheran Brotherhood enables the division to carry out many of its experimental and research possibilities.

Over the past 20 years, the division and its predecessors have received a significant grant from Lutheran Brotherhood, enabling the division to start many more new ministries. The grant has averaged $900,000 each year since the formation of this church. Funding from Lutheran Brotherhood assists in the budget-initiated ministries during the first and second year of development. On behalf of this church, the division expresses gratitude to the Lutheran Brotherhood Foundation for its nearly $25,000,000 subsidy to new congregations under development and added staff programming, and for its support in undergirding the division's ethnic strategy development.

Lutheran Brotherhood provides a church extension interest-subsidy program to young congregations that are refinancing their initial unit Mission Investment Fund loans. During 1993 and 1994 Lutheran Brotherhood provided $415,283 in interest subsidies to 22 congregations that refinanced their Mission Investment Fund loans with Lutheran Brotherhood. These subsidies are paid out over a five-year period and enable the congregations to refinance their Mission Investment Fund loans earlier than normal.

Lutheran Brotherhood also has enabled the division to participate in an experimental ministry (regional start) in Yorba Linda, Calif., during this biennium. This regional start, with multiple staff, did not produce the desired results. The ministry has been merged into Messiah Lutheran Church as a regional church. Additional grant money from Lutheran Brotherhood, of approximately $200,000 each of the last two years, helped fast-growth congregations add staff. This appears to be a more effective strategy in regional church development. In one or two years, these congregations have gained enough new members to continue funding these staff additions.

One additional project—a video introduction for potential new members of congregations under development—also has been initiated with the assistance of Lutheran Brotherhood. This introductory video will be used by mission developers with persons seeking a new relationship with Jesus Christ and with potential members in a congregation. It will answer such questions as: "What does Jesus have to offer me today?" and "Who are Lutherans and why should I join a congregation?" When completed and tested, this video may be available to all ELCA congregations.

The division also recognizes the significant contribution that Aid Association for Lutherans has provided in the preparation and development of the new "Selection, Screening and Recruiting" process for mission developers. This process, developed during this biennium, has enabled the division to become more effective in recruiting and selecting pastors with the skills needed to develop new congregations. An additional grant has been received to help standardize this process so that interviews carried out anywhere in the country will assist other locations in the screening and selection process.

Major Directions for Fiscal 1995-1996

The Evolution of the "Concept": At the beginning of the biennium, the staff and board of the Division for Outreach were working toward a re-formation of the work of the division and its staffing pattern. This re-formation document was entitled, the "Concept."

The development of such a plan was prompted by the mission opportunities that are present in the United States and Caribbean society. There are literally millions of people who have not been reached with the Gospel. There is urgency not only to establish new congregations, but to work with synods as they foster a vision for existing congregations to become centers for mission. A second factor in the development of the "Concept" was the establishment of the network of persons, both lay and clergy across the United States and in the Caribbean, who have effective skills and methods of reaching people with the Gospel and empowering them for God's mission. The third factor, which has been present since the inception of the Evangelical Lutheran Church in America, is the diminishing financial resources available to the Division for Outreach.

The "Concept" was developed with all of these concerns before the planners. The "Concept" stated that the primary responsibility for establishing new congregations should rest with the Division for Outreach as it works with synods. To accomplish this planting of the church, it was proposed that a staff of 10 persons would be employed and trained to serve as specialists across this church to develop new congregations and bring them to maturity. The "Concept" went on to state that the primary responsibility for working with existing congregations should rest with the synod, with financial assistance and specialist services available from the division. It was proposed that a staff of eight to ten persons would assist in the development of networks of "ministry practitioners," which could be available to congregations and synods for work with existing congregations.

The "Concept" was reviewed by the Conference of Bishops' Committee on Synodical-Churchwide Relations, which called for a churchwide consultation on services and staffing for congregations based on issues raised by the "Concept." The consultation was held at Chicago in October 1993. All churchwide units participated in the consultation with representatives from each of the 65 synods. Funding for this event was provided through grants from fraternal organizations.

The "Concept" was not reviewed at the consultation. Follow-up conversations were held with the bishops of each of the ELCA's nine regions. It was hoped that the conversations might clarify the "Concept" for synodical bishops. Once again, this was done with inter-unit teams from the churchwide organization entering into conversations with bishops regarding staffing and services for congregations and for ministry leaders.

At the conclusion of these "Conversations with the Bishops," a report was prepared and shared with the Conference of Bishops. Immediately prior to the distribution of this report, the Church Council had decided to appoint an "Inquiry" panel to articulate future directions for this church. As the "Inquiry" process began, the Division for Outreach was asked to put on hold the work it was doing in connection with the "Concept" and its planned implementation by January 1, 1996. The division honored the request and the division's board subsequently authorized the executive director to proceed with plans for reorganizing the Chicago-based staff of the division and to put in place interim plans for program directions and staffing patterns through fiscal year 1997. The plan has been approved by the board and is now in the process of implementation.

Future Directions: The board and staff of the Division for Outreach analyzed the use of financial resources available to the division for existing congregations. As the board reviewed this analysis it requested the staff to prepare new program categories for the division. The categories were prepared with input from the deployed staff of the division and from information gathered through other sources such as the Department for Research and Evaluation. The staff developed four program categories that will become effective February 1, 1996. They include: 1) Division Services; 2) Synodical Outreach Services; 3) New Congregations; and 4) Congregational Outreach Services.

Underlying the new program categories is an understanding that the churchwide organization must be a service organization to synods, ministries, and to ministry leaders.

Major changes were made in the program for congregational outreach services. There are four ministry activities in this program. Each activity is descriptive of the desired outcome of the division's relationship with the congregation and its use of churchwide funds. Each activity can apply in rural,

small town, suburban, or urban contexts. The four ministry activities are: 1) Ministry Adjustment, which anticipates assisting a congregation to make mid-course adjustments within a three-year period that can assist it to be more effective in its outreach ministry; 2) Redevelopment, which anticipates the willingness of a congregation to make major changes over a five year period that will re-direct its ministry into one that is appropriate and effective for the place it is located; 3) Transition to Racial and Ethnic Inclusivity, which assists a congregation to become multicultural in its membership, worship, and program; and 4) Strategic Mission Partnerships, which reflects assistance of partners such as the churchwide organization, synods, Mission Partners, and the ministry in providing the financial resources necessary for congregations located in low income communities or in areas where special ministries are needed and appropriate.

Inherent in this new approach is the understanding that an existing congregation has acknowledged what it needs to do, has a plan of action, and a definite timeline for doing it. The partnership with the churchwide organization in assisting the congregation to accomplish its goals for change is granted for a stated period of time.

Extensive orientation to the new program categories already has been accomplished with the deployed staff of the division, with synodical outreach committee chairs, synodical staff, and synodical bishops.

In addition to the programmatic changes, beginning February 1, 1996, the division will begin to use functional teams within its Chicago operation and work teams in the field as it provides services to congregations, synods, and ministry leaders.

The first teams appointed will be an urban ministry team and a small town and rural (STaR) ministry team. Three deployed staff of the division will make up each of the teams. Their purpose will be program development as appropriate to the needs of the ministries in these settings. The teams also will develop networks of urban and rural specialists who will serve as ministry advisers to congregations and synods needing counsel and assistance.

There also will be other work teams, such as a development team, that will have responsibility for working with synods in the development of new congregations and bringing them to maturity.

As the division moves to new programs and to a new mode of operation, it will also have a new staff relationship to the Mission Investment Fund. Beginning January 1, 1996, the staff members related to church building, real estate, and finance will be transferred into the staff of the Mission Investment Fund (MIF). This will consolidate the functions of a real estate holding company, a lending agency, and services to congregations regarding church building and the purchase of real estate. This will broaden the MIF services to congregations and synods while affording these services to the Division for Outreach for new congregations and congregations with special circumstances.

As we participate in God's mission, it is our privilege and responsibility to make Christ known to all people, that they may come into a living relationship with the God revealed in Jesus Christ.

BOARD OF THE DIVISION FOR OUTREACH

JOHN F. NELSON, *Chair*

M. L. MINNICK JR., *Executive Director*

Report of the Division for Higher Education and Schools

Organization

Board

Rev. Paul H. Andrews, Columbus, Ohio (term expires 1995)[4]

Rev. Stephen P. Bouman, *chair*, New York, N.Y. (1995)[1,5]

Mr. Kirk Downey, Richmond, Va. (1997)[5]

Mr. Kenneth A. Erickson, Eugene, Oreg. (1999)[5]

Mr. Richard S. Froiland, Hendricks, Minn. (1995)[1,6]

Rev. S. Philip Froiland, Waverly, Iowa (1999)[3,6]

Mr. Carl T. Fynboe, Fox Island, Wash. (1997)[3]

Ms. Gladystine B. Hodge, Teaneck, N.J. (1997)[1,5]

Rev. Wi Jo Kang, Dubuque, Iowa (1997)[3]

Mr. Ryan A. LaHurd, Hickory, N.C. (1999)[4]

Rev. John K. Luoma, Stow, Ohio (1995)[2,3]

Rev. Nancy Anderson Milleville, Snyder, N.Y. (1999)[3]

Ms. Mary Hull Mohr, Decorah, Iowa (1999)[4]

Ms. Maxine H. O'Kelley, Burlington, N.C. (1995)[4]

Ms. Chickie J. Olsen, Pompano Beach, Fla. (1999)[5]

Rev. Karen S. Parker, Englewood, Colo. (1995)[1,5]

Rev. H. Frederick Reisz Jr., Columbia, S.C. (1997)[1,4,6]

Ms. Mary Ellen H. Schmider, Moorhead, Minn. (1995)[4,6]

Ms. Mary Ann Shealy, Newberry, S.C. (1997)[1,2,4,6]

Mr. Adolph C. Streng Jr., Mesquite, Tex. (1997)[5]

Ms. Kathryn Swanson, Thousand Oaks, Calif. (1999)[3]

---

[1] Executive Committee
[2] Finance Committee
[3] Campus Ministry Committee
[4] Colleges and Universities Committee
[5] Schools Committee
[6] NLCM, Inc.

Advisors

Rev. Lee S. Thoni, executive assistant to the bishop, Office of the Bishop

Bishop Dale R. Skogman, Northern Great Lakes Synod

Mr. Carl L. Hansen, ELCA Council of College Presidents

Ms. Julia Sieger, Evangelical Lutheran Education Association

Mr. Minh Nguyen, Lutheran Student Movement

Staff

Executive Director: Rev. W. Robert Sorensen

Director for Administration and Finance: Ms. Sue Rothmeyer

Assistant Director for Budget Management: Ms. Valerie Maggitt

Director for Campus Ministry: Rev. James R. Carr

Director for Colleges and Universities: Mr. James M. Unglaube

Director for Schools: Vacant

Assistant Director for Campus Ministry: Vacant

Assistant Director for Colleges and Universities: Ms. Naomi E. Linnell

Deployed Director for Campus Ministry, Regions 1 and 2: Rev. Adrianne Heskin

Deployed Director for Campus Ministry, Regions 3 and 4: Rev. Marcus D. Pera

Deployed Director for Campus Ministry, Region 5: Rev. Thomas F. Loftus

Deployed Director for Campus Ministry, Region 6:
Rev. James R. Carr (interim for Indiana-Kentucky);
Rev. Thomas F. Loftus (interim for Michigan);
Rev. Marcus D. Pera (interim for Ohio)

Deployed Director for Campus Ministry, Regions 7 and 8: Rev. John B. Hougen

Deployed Director for Campus Ministry, Region 9: Rev. William H. King

Constitutional Mandate

The mission of the Division for Higher Education and Schools (DHES) is to advocate for the work of this church in education and for the work of education in this church. The mandate of this division is defined in continuing resolution 16.11.D91. of the Constitution, Bylaws, and Continuing Resolutions of the Evangelical Lutheran Church in America.

Report of Work 1993-1994

The Evangelical Lutheran Church in America received gifts when it was born. Among the most important were the educational ministries built by those who had gone before us. Our mothers and fathers in the faith saw to it that this church came to life with campus ministries, colleges and universities, early childhood education centers, and elementary and secondary schools, all of which carry forward and undergird the mission of this church in fundamental and irreplaceable ways. They comprise an extraordinary gift for ministry in the increasingly important setting of education.

They strengthen this church's global mission.
International students seek out institutions of higher learning in this country. Thus, colleges and universities are places where conversations and understandings among the young people of the world can occur. When people come together on Sunday morning to worship in our campus ministries across the nation, some 14 percent of those who gather around Word and Sacrament are international students. Our ELCA colleges and universities, through efforts carried forward in this division and with the assistance of the Division for Global Mission, are about to complete one of the most significant achievements of this church's early efforts. It is called the "Higher Education and Namibia Program," designed to prepare 100 leaders for Namibia, a largely Lutheran country that has in recent years freed itself from apartheid and become an independent nation. These young graduates of our ELCA colleges have returned to their homeland to become nation builders for their church and society. The colleges and universities and campus ministries have always produced leaders for this church. Increasingly, they produce leaders for the global Church, particularly among those from the developing world.

Our campus ministries, colleges and universities, and schools strengthen this church's multicultural mission. The Evangelical Lutheran Church in America undertakes its multicultural efforts not only for reasons of justice, but primarily because it bears witness to the promise and power of the Gospel to create a new being in Christ—neither Jew nor Greek, neither male nor female, neither slave nor free—but a new creation in Christ. Some 10 percent of those who attend Sunday worship in campus ministries are persons of color. Since 1987, the number of students of color attending ELCA colleges and universities has increased by 52.7 percent. Most impressive of all are the figures from our congregation's elementary and secondary schools. In 1991, some 28 percent of the students enrolled were students of color. In 1993, their number increased to 31 percent while, over the same period, the number of faculty members of color increased from 12 percent to 18 percent. These schools are the most multiculturally rich setting in this church. We still have far to go to achieve the ends we desire, but clearly without these educational ministries the multicultural work of this church would be considerably weakened.

These educational ministries develop leaders for this church. Virtually all of the bishops and half the missionaries of this church have graduated from ELCA colleges and universities or have been participants in campus ministries. Campus ministries and colleges and universities are major sources from which come students who enter our seminaries. The elementary and high schools are places where faith formation occurs in those who will be future leaders of this church. And, perhaps most significantly, all these areas produce large numbers of lay leaders for our congregations. Among the important tasks carried out in these ministries is that of helping to develop the next generation of leadership for this church and nation.

These ministries enable this church to serve society in specific ways. Education, through which the neighbor is served, always has been fundamental to the mission of the Lutheran church. Through these ministries, this church serves others by helping to form people who will benefit society through such vocations as teachers, doctors, nurses, artists, industrialists, scientists, social workers—to name but a few of the fields students enter. Because our theological heritage looks upon education as one of the God-given structures of society through which good can come to people, it is understandable that Lutherans create campus ministries, colleges and universities, early childhood education centers, and elementary and secondary schools not only for their own needs, but for the needs of the larger society as well.

Campus Ministry

The purpose of campus ministry is to assist persons in academic settings to discover and fulfill their vocation in Jesus Christ. This effort is led by the 144 ordained and lay staff members who serve under letters of election from our ELCA campus ministry agencies. In partnership with these professional staff are the students, faculty, administrators, and staff who are living their faith in the context of higher education as well as the dedicated persons who represent the synods and the churchwide organization on boards and councils. These persons, along with the 65 synods, the nearly 800 contact congregations located in communities that have colleges, and the churchwide organization, are in a partnership providing and supporting an ELCA ministry presence on the campuses of state and other publicly supported colleges and universities across this land.

Campus ministry is an investment in the future because the center of its activity is developing leaders. Christian students enter the university as stewards of the gift of the mind God has given them. Most campus ministry activities are tied into leadership development. Students are challenged to *think theologically* and grapple with God's call to be faithful in all aspects of life, including the choice of a major and of life work. At the university they are encouraged to *think critically,* and our ministries help them apply this to the faith. The rise in volunteerism among students is a response to the challenge they have been given to *act compassionately*. Our ministries organize and support students in helping others as we encourage them to do so in the name of Jesus Christ. Virtually every ELCA-supported campus ministry has a number of volunteer projects that serve others.

Our partnership and support of the Lutheran students' own organization, Lutheran Student Movement-USA (LSM), also is centered in leadership development. The 15 students who serve as officers and regional representatives on the national LSM council have a unique opportunity to hone their leadership gifts. This also is true for the hundreds of students who join with other Lutherans in local campus ministries and contact congregations across America. As these students lead worship, plan ministry activities and programs, learn about the truths of Scripture and Lutheran doctrine in study groups, speak in congregations about their ministry, sweat alongside others in building housing for Habitat for Humanity, and serve the elderly or learning impaired with tutoring visits they are sharpening their leadership skills for use in church and world.

Since 1993, our worship and evangelism emphasis, "More Boldly," has involved the professional staff who serve at 60 campuses. This movement invites staff and students to reconceptualize their ministries around the areas of worship, evangelism, and hospitality. Student evangelists are supported by local "More Boldly" committees who think, pray, study, and plan about sharing the faith. They form groups of students who discuss how their stories are connected to the Jesus story. The Church may benefit from this student witness as they "more boldly" share their faith with their peers—a generation the rest of the Church has great difficulty in reaching.

Global education is basic to any education in today's world. Marshall McLuhan, the Canadian futurist, looked at modern travel, communication, computer modeling, and economic interdependence and wrote that we are a global village. Students today know about the global dimensions of world community through the media. Campus ministry seeks to enhance that education with personal experiences in global community. It is difficult not to meet and interact with students from other countries and cultures when more than one million of the more than 14 million students attending American universities today are international students. The LSM-USA National Council has one of its three elected offices filled by an international student. This secretary of international multicultural concerns has the responsibility to keep global education before this national council as they carry out their planning. Local campus ministries seek to involve international students, and this often takes the form of allowing international student groups the free use of our campus centers.

The 1993 National Gathering for Lutheran University and College Students was held at year's end in Toronto, Ontario. The theme dealt with living our Lutheran faith in different countries and cultures, and more than 10 percent of the 350 students attending that event were international students. Scholarship assistance enabled them to attend, and they shared their faith and theology in small groups with American students. Students heard the Lutheran doctrines familiar to them and learned how this faith was practiced in different cultural settings.

The 1994 gathering was an ecumenical event held at St. Louis at year's end. More than 1,800 students gathered, among them a delegation with several students from each of the six regions of the World Student Christian Federation (WSCF). The international flavor and dialogue also were enhanced by special international guests sponsored by the several denominations. The Rev. Dr. Lobi Sifobela, dean of students at Zimbabwe's National University of Science and Technology, was our guest. He has been carrying on conversations about how we might assist them in beginning a campus ministry at this three-year-old university of 2,000 students. The Division for Higher Education and Schools, the Division for Global Mission, and the Lutheran Student Movement-USA are in conversation in this planning, along with the Lutheran Church in Zimbabwe and the Zimbabwe Council for Churches. He spoke with the LSM Council and Caucus and visited Purdue University, Iowa State University, Wartburg and Dana Colleges, and Wartburg Seminary.

For the past 100 years, the World Student Christian Federation (WSCF) has brought together Christian students from more than 90 nations to share with one another in their Christian and global education. The WSCF is celebrating its centennial in 1995 with a variety of activities. A liturgy of thanksgiving will be held in July at the Vadstena Castle in Sweden, where the WSCF was constituted. The Quadrennial General Assembly Celebration will be held the first two weeks in September at Yamoussoukro, Ivory Coast. LSM-USA is an associate member movement and will have a representative in attendance.

Campus ministries plan events to further this global education, and the ministries at Berkeley, Palo Alto, and Albuquerque are among many that have organized overseas experiences for students. Professor Larry Rasmussen, Niebuhr Professor of Ethics at Union Theological Seminary in New York, suggests that what is needed today is *earth education*, which is a matter of survival as we face the threats to our common global home. This is in harmony with the World Council of Churches' emphasis on the integrity of the creation.

This aspect of global education is integral to any meaningful education about God's creation.

We live in a society and world where youth are at risk. The horrors of life for children in Brazil and the drive-by shootings in America's cities confirm in physical ways what have become levels of abuse not radically different from the earlier sweatshop era. Violence has also touched America's campuses, where rape and assaults are all too common. Campus ministries have been among the active campus leaders in education about rape, assault, sexual discrimination, and harassment. Several ministries have provided students with escorts to evening classes and events.

Physical abuse and harm are not the only risks for youth. Many are denied the opportunity to attend college if they choose, and the escalating costs of a college education may return this nation to the situation of many other nations, where only the children of the wealthy, or the exceptionally gifted, may attend colleges or universities. This subtle risk impedes the good stewardship of the mind.

By carrying out our ministry of gathering to celebrate the Eucharist, preaching the Gospel, teaching the Word, caring and counseling those in need, challenging the community to serve others and organizing such activities, and meeting people in fellowship, we encourage students and others involved in campus ministries to discover and fulfill their vocation in Jesus Christ. These acts of ministry that go on each day at ELCA campus ministries convey the good news to youth at risk that things can change. Youth, too, can change and break the patterns and forces that bind them. In such ministry we contribute positively to the future of all God's creation.

ELCA Colleges and Universities

The *Mission Statement for Colleges and Universities* of the Division for Higher Education and Schools speaks of the church being in partnership with these institutions in order "to equip people for the vocation of leadership and service in church and society." The colleges and universities are called to be *faithful*: to be faithful to the Lutheran tradition, to be faithful in service and freedom, to be faithful to community.

The 29 colleges and universities of this church live out this call to faithfulness in a variety of ways. They offer the finest academic programs possible. They provide spiritual life programs under the leadership of an ELCA chaplain, offering ministries of Word and Sacrament along with many opportunities for learning and service. They create settings in which students learn to live and work and support one another in community. Indeed, in such settings a sense of vocation

and a call to responsible global citizenship is nurtured among the members of campus communities.

Service has grown in importance on the campuses as students, faculty, and staff reach out from the classroom to express global citizenship. In growing numbers, they serve in a variety of settings in the communities where the colleges and universities are located, from assisting in social service agencies and institutions to working with Habitat for Humanity. They engage in service learning where classroom and community meet in hands-on experiences. Such service and learning opportunities more and more frequently extend beyond the local community to the corners of the globe.

The colleges and universities of this church, like most institutions of American higher education, are in transition between two periods, one dating from the mid-1970s to the present and the other reaching into the foreseeable future. The past two decades have been ones of dramatic shrinkage in the number of high school graduates in the population. While predictions suggested that enrollments would tumble during the period, such was not the case. For the ELCA colleges and universities as a group, this was a period of remarkable stability. Enrollments fluctuated very little, and the full-time enrollment in fall 1994 was just below a record high reached in 1993. Success in this regard is attributable to several factors; these factors can be summarized by saying that ELCA institutions reached out to communities of students who were under-represented on the campuses, be they students of color, international students, or older students. These institutions also did a better job of retaining students once they were enrolled. The fact is that the faces of the campuses changed.

**ELCA Colleges and Universities
Enrollment Patterns: 1988-1994**

Academic Year	Full-Time Enrollment	Full-Time Students of Color	Full-Time International Students
1988/1989	42,549	2,656	1,301
1989/1990	43,675	2,770	1,286
1990/1991	43,371	2,866	1,399
1991/1992	43,589	3,257	1,600
1992/1993	43,708	3,694	1,571
1993/1994	44,140	4,058	1,448
1994/1995	44,064	3,996	1,351

The future presents a new challenge. Tuition and fees charged the students have risen as the economy has grown. Concern is being expressed throughout society about the high price of a college education. The institutions seek to make education more affordable through financial aid in the form of grants, loans, and work. Much of this assistance has traditionally come from state and federal governments. Those sources of aid are not growing as educational costs increase. Greater burden in providing student aid has fallen to the institutions themselves; the limits to which such aid can grow are close to being reached. There is growing resistance on the part of students and their families to assume indebtedness in pursuit of college educations. Finding a solution to this growing problem will be a major challenge for higher education in the years ahead.

The campus communities have been on a steady path toward greater diversity. Over the period from 1979 to 1994 the representation of students of color in the student bodies has risen from 5.0 percent to 9.1 percent. African Americans represent about half of this total increase with most of the balance split evenly between Hispanic and Asian students. The number of Native American students, while modest, has more than doubled during the period. The number of persons of color serving on college faculties has grown steadily but more slowly, moving to 6.1 percent of the total in 1994. Representation on the administrative staffs and the boards of trustees is at about the same level as the faculties.

The work of the division is focused in several areas. A "Student Search" program identifies high school youth in the congregations, and is used by the colleges and universities in recruitment. The file includes some 190,000 names. This program helps the division fulfill one of its goals in assuring that all ELCA families with members contemplating college attendance are aware of the opportunities offered through this church's colleges and universities. Lutheran student enrollment at the 29 institutions stands at 32.4 percent of the total. While this figure has declined in recent years, the decline is less than the drop in high school age youth in ELCA congregations.

Staff members of the division are active in assisting ELCA colleges and universities in their searches for new presidential leadership. The position of college president is key for the continuing nurture of church-college relationships. Since the formation of this church, new presidents have been selected at 17 of the 29 institutions. Staff are represented on the college and university boards, and their presence serves as a bridge between educational institutions and this church. An electronic mail project on the Internet helps persons seeking campus teaching or administrative positions to connect with vacancies. An institutional research activity assists the institutions in their planning processes by offering comparisons between their own operations and those of other institutions.

Upsala College in East Orange, New Jersey, experienced in recent years unfortunate difficulties that its closing. Within the ELCA community of colleges and universities, Upsala had represented the most significant effort in serving students of color, who constituted 60 percent of its student body.

By summer 1995, the "Higher Education and Namibia Program" will have reached its completion. The two-fold dream of educating 100 Namibian students at ELCA colleges and universities, and of achieving Namibian independence, has come true. Over a period of nine years, beginning in 1986, these students have come to the campuses, graduated, and returned home to assume leadership roles in their newly independent country. Many are enrolled for graduate degrees in education, mathematics, business, engineering, law, medicine, and dentistry. In Namibia, they are serving as teachers, principals, hospital administrators, bankers, and scientists. Many are serving in a variety of governmental positions, while others are working in business and industry (One works for the U.S. Agency for International Development in Namibia.). A more recent development in this area is an agreement encouraging scholars from ELCA colleges and universities to spend a period of time at the new University of Namibia. The first three faculty members went to Namibia in spring 1995.

Early Childhood Education Centers and Schools

Lutheran schools strive to offer educational excellence imbedded within a Christian context for children and young people. Lutheran schools are understood increasingly to be a means through which this church is able to re-root itself in communities that no longer are traditionally Lutheran. Approximately one-third of the students at Lutheran schools are unchurched, and similarly, one-third are persons of color or persons whose primary language is other than English.

These schools are financially supported by tuition, congregations, individual donors, and small outside sources of public or private funding. Every effort is made to keep the tuition affordable for people in the community. Interest has been growing on the part of individuals and agencies to provide some financial assistance to children and youth at serious socio-economic risk, enabling them to attend a Lutheran school.

Philadelphia Lutheran School, housed in historic St. John Lutheran Church, was founded in the early 1800s by Henry Melchior Muehlenberg. It is an ELCA school serving primarily African American students in a disadvantaged neighborhood. Few of these students have a church home. The school becomes their church. The ELCA pastor who is the chaplain of the school leads students in worship, teaches religious instruction, and is their guide and confidant. The school and the police department are cooperating to sponsor an after school and evening leisure activities program in the church basement under the supervision of police officers. Police and youth relate to one another with respect and enjoy the arrangement.

Lutheran schools are one means through which this church touches the lives of young people spiritually and develops leaders for the church and society. Epiphany Lutheran School in Brooklyn, N. Y., serves the African American youth of that community. Its principal attended the school from kindergarten through high school when it was under the direction of a white pastor and principal. She felt so committed to the Lutheran church and its school that she chose to stay in the community and become the principal, effectively touching lives of a new generation of young people as she had been touched. From First Lutheran School in Blue Island, Ill., the torch of leadership was passed on. Graduates went on to become principals of other Lutheran schools in such places as Miami, Florida, and Detroit, Michigan, and pastors of Lutheran congregations in Baltimore, Maryland, Columbus, Ohio, and St. Thomas, Virgin Islands.

A number of synodical bishops, many pastors, and the current secretary of this church attended Lutheran schools and early childhood education centers. Countless other graduates of these schools were touched by Christ in these settings and chose to make their light shine in settings other than Lutheran ministry—business, medicine, teaching, industry, science, technology, entertainment, music, homemaking, and parenting.

Lutheran schools seek ways to connect with others, to build community, and to promote global education. Oak Grove Lutheran High School in Fargo, North Dakota, the only ELCA boarding school, has been a school renowned by students from other continents for nearly a century. Such students become familiar with the language, customs, and educational system of the United States as they prepare for study in colleges and universities in this country. Their presence on campus enriches the lives and increases the global awareness of students from the United States mainstream culture.

Students at Grace Lutheran School in Appleton, Wisconsin, connected through correspondence and with scholarship money for a student from Liberia, making it possible for him to attend a Lutheran school in that country. Students from St. Paul Lutheran School in Waverly, Iowa, correspond with students from Japan. A group of Japanese teachers came to visit the school and brought gifts that are on display at the school. In recent years, students from Lutheran schools have raised money to help students from other Lutheran, Roman Catholic, and public schools across the country that were damaged by natural disasters. Students from rural Iowa provided scholarship money enabling students from low-income housing projects in Chicago to attend a Lutheran school. Lutheran school educators from Namibia, Norway, Germany, Australia, Canada, and Japan have visited ELCA schools and invited our schools to engage in exchange visits or correspondence. Plans are underway to host an international conference for Lutheran high schools in 1997.

With more than one out of ten ELCA congregations sponsoring of Lutheran schools, this church makes Christ known to thousands of children and young people everyday. And, Lutheran schools have been making Christ known for generations. The oldest elementary school, St. Peter, near Niagara Falls, was founded in 1843. Frederick Lutheran Churh at St. Thomas, Virgin Islands, one of the oldest congregations of this church, hosts a Lutheran school.

The desire to make Christ known through Lutheran schools is alive and growing. More than 18 elementary schools and an unknown number of early childhood centers have been started in the past two years, and interest has been expressed in starting one high school.

All Lutheran schools, sponsored by more than one ELCA congregation or jointly sharing the ministries of congregations of the Evangelical Lutheran Church in America and The Lutheran Church—Missouri Synod congregations, follow a formal process of affiliation. Having gone through the process, they are acknowledged and affirmed by the ELCA churchwide office as an ELCA ministry. This affiliation process is described in a document available from the Division for Higher Education and Schools. All Lutheran schools and early childhood centers that are sponsored by a single ELCA congregation are viewed as a ministry of the Evangelical Lutheran Church in America through the congregation. Guidelines to strengthen the relationship between the congregation and its center of weekday Christian education for children are available from the Division for Higher Education and Schools.

The professional ELCA-related membership organization for schools and early childhood centers is the Evangelical Lutheran Education Association (ELEA). ELEA works in partnership with this division to promote the ministry of Lutheran early childhood education centers and schools and to provide services that enhance this ministry, e.g. conferences, workshops, and resources.

Major Directions 1995-1996

It is apparent that the great gift of educational ministries, handed to the Evangelical Lutheran Church in America when it was born, is increasingly important to the mission of this church. These ministries play a central role, in partnership with this whole church, in developing the next generation of leaders for church and society. They are vital to this church's efforts in multi-cultural ministry. They are significant settings for global understanding and for carrying forward elements of global mission. They touch, in significant ways, the lives of children and youth at risk.

Education today has been identified as one of the most secularized segments of American society. Such writers as Stephen Carter (*The Culture of Disbelief*) and George Marsden (*The Soul of the American University*) are among those who thoughtfully have made this case. The well-known sociologist, Robert Bella, speaks of the fact that Christian theology and theological ethics are largely banished from the curriculum in most of higher education. ELCA campus ministries, colleges and universities, congregational early childhood education centers, and schools are among those places so vitally important to the Church and to the nation where Christian theology and ministry are integrated into the academic setting. This division will continue its task of strengthening this effort in the years ahead. It will also strengthen its work with children and families in urban areas. Its continued focus on helping college and university students tell the story of Christ more boldly will be advanced. And, it will work in new ways to develop leadership in academic settings. The work is as exciting as it is important. Although these educational ministries have all been under severe stress because of financial pressures, they remain fundamental to this church as it works to make Christ known throughout the world.

BOARD OF THE DIVISION FOR HIGHER EDUCATION AND SCHOOLS

STEPHEN P. BOUMAN, *Chair*
W. ROBERT SORENSEN, *Executive Director*

Report of the Division for Church in Society

Organization

Board

Ms. Ruby Anderson, Sacramento, Calif. (term expires 1995)[1, 4]

Mr. Per Anderson, Moorhead, Minn. (1999)[4]

Ms. Marjorie F. Bailey, Aurora, Colo. (1997)[2]

Mr. Bill D. Brittain, Raleigh, N.C. (1997)[3]

Rev. Joy K. Bussert, Minneapolis, Minn. (1995)[4]

Ms. Ingrid Christiansen, *chair*, Chicago, Ill. (1999)[1, 2]

Rev. Robert E. Duea, Milwaukee, Wis. (1995)[1, 3]

Mr. C. David Hartmann, Annandale, Va. (1997)[3]

Rev. L. Edward Knudson, Portland, Oreg. (1997)[4]

Ms. Janet R. Line, Minneapolis, Minn. (1997)[3]

Mr. Richard D. Mandsager, Anchorage, Alaska (1995)[2]

Rev. Margarita Martinez, Levittown, P.R. (1999)[2]

Rev. Lawrence A. Miller, Atlanta, Ga. (1995)[2]

Mr. Willard Moseng, Haslett, Mich. (1999)[4]

Ms. Betty Olson, Lincoln, Nebr. (1999)[2]

Rev. Harvey S. Peters, Madison, Wis. (1999)[4]

Mr. Damon Roye, Philadelphia, Pa. (1995)[3]

Ms. Patricia W. Savage, Cresco, Pa. (1995)[3]

Rev. Arnold L. Tiemeyer, Philadelphia, Pa. (1997)[4]

Rev. Daniel D. Wee, Woodbury, Minn. (1997)[4]

Rev. Lee H. Wesley, New York, N.Y. (1997)[1, 3]

Advisors

Bishop Steven L. Ullestad, Northeastern Iowa Synod

Ms. Lita Brusick Johnson, executive assistant to the bishop, Office of the Bishop

---

1. Executive Committee
2. Program Review Committee 1
3. Program Review Committee 2
4. Studies Committee

Staff

Currently there are 20.5 full-time-equivalent executive staff positions. During 1994-1995, the staff operated within seven areas of responsibility: Administration, Advocacy, Education and Program Resources, Leadership Development, Studies, Support to Social Ministry Organizations, and World Hunger Ministries.

There are 13 full-time-equivalent support-staff positions provide administrative and secretarial support services to the division.

Executive Staff

Executive Director: Rev. Charles S. Miller Jr.

Associate Executive Director: Ms. Fran Burnford

Director for Finance: Ms. Karen J. Bruce

Director for Leadership Development: Ms. Ruth H. Reko

Director for Advocacy: Ms. Kay Dowhower

Director for Corporate Social Responsibility: Ms. Marian Nickelson

Director for Lutheran Office for Governmental Affairs: Ms. Kay Dowhower

Assistant Directors: Ms. Kay Bengston, Rev. Mark B. Brown

Director for Lutheran Office for World Community: Mr. Dennis Frado

Director for State Public Policy Advocacy: Ms. Fran Burnford

Director for Education and Program Resources: Ms. Josselyn Bennett

Director for Community Development Services: Mr. Gaylord Thomas

Director for Disability Ministries: Mr. Dennis Busse

Director for Domestic Disaster Response: Rev. Leon A. Phillips Jr.

Director for Environmental Stewardship and Hunger Education: Mr. Job Ebenezer

Director for Health Ministries: Ms. Sally Camp

Director for Refugee Ministries: Rev. Leon A. Phillips Jr.

Project Director for Women and Children Living in Poverty: Ms. Romenita Henderson

Director for Leadership Development: Ms. Ruth H. Reko

Director for Board Development Services: Rev. Harold B. Everson

Director for Center for Ethics and Social Ministry: Rev. Adele Stiles Resmer

Director for Studies: Rev. Karen L. Bloomquist

Associate Director for Studies: Rev. John R. Stumme

Director for Support to Social Ministry Organizations: Rev. Gary D. Stubenvoll

Regional Staff for Support to Social Ministry Organizations: Rev. Adele Stiles Resmer, Rev. Harold B. Everson, Ms. Ruth H. Reko, Mr. Dennis Busse, Ms. Sally Camp

Director for World Hunger Ministries and Coordinator for World Hunger Ministries: Rev. John L. Halvorson

Director for Environmental Stewardship and Hunger
Education: Mr. Job Ebenezer

Constitutional Mandate

The Division for Church in Society of the Evangelical Lutheran Church in America witnesses to Jesus Christ who frees us to do justice and give our lives in service in God's world. Through our ministry we work for the common good, confront obstacles to local and global community, and promote care for creation and for all people according to their needs. The mandate of this division is defined in continuing resolution 16.11.E91. of the Constitution, Bylaws, and Continuing Resolutions of the Evangelical Lutheran Church in America.

Report of Work 1994-1995

The board of the Division for Church in Society (DCS) held regular meetings in October 1993, March 1994, October 1994, and March 1995. The board conducts the majority of its work through four board committees: executive, program review(s) 1 and 2, and studies. During the 1994-1995 biennium, the board has spent intensive time on the continuing development of the Division for Church in Society Strategic Five-Year Plan. The board also provided direction and oversight for all of the work described below.

Advocacy

Corporate Social Responsibility: Transnational corporations affect every area of life around the world. Some have assets greater than the gross domestic product of other whole nations. Through the unit's Corporate Social Responsibility program, this church challenges corporations through letter writing, dialogue, and the filing of shareholder resolutions. Seven resolutions were filed with 22 companies during the 1993-94 season on issues related to the environment, South Africa, equality in the workplace, and community reinvestment and development.

State Public Policy Advocacy: In cooperation with synods and social ministry organizations, this division oversees state public policy advocacy offices in 18 states and contributes to ecumenical public policy advocacy efforts in three additional states.

The public policy issues that made up the major part of the agenda of the state offices during this period include: food, nutrition, homelessness, shelter and related housing concerns, environmental stewardship, job employment training for low-income persons, and access to health care.

In October 1995, the oversight of the state public policy offices will be moved to the Lutheran Office for Governmental Affairs. This move will further strengthen the continuum of Lutheran public policy advocacy

covering state, national, and international concerns. Efforts also continue to focus on developing cooperative interdependent relationships among social ministry organizations, synods, and state offices in carrying out this vital ministry.

Lutheran Office for Governmental Affairs (LOGA): The Lutheran Office for Governmental Affairs (LOGA) fulfills this church's witness for social justice on domestic and foreign policy issues facing the nation, and through it, the world. Semi-annual "Issue Reports" document this church's policy base for these advocacy efforts and the status of current issues. Based on adopted Working Principles, LOGA participates in advocacy for health care reform and welfare reform. Other issues include human and civil rights, religious liberty, Central America, the Middle East, and Southern Africa.

Collegial staffing partnerships continue with Lutheran Immigration and Refugee Service (LIRS) and the Lutheran Volunteer Corps. Interns and volunteers also supplement an issue staff of three.

The office publishes a periodic "Legislative Update" that is mailed to 5,000 recipients and is available on computer networks. Supplemental information is shared via "Action Alerts" and a toll-free legislative hotline. Advocacy information and training is also shared through speaking and workshops.

Lutheran Office for World Community (LOWC): A first-of-its-kind Young Adult Global Hunger Justice and Peace Seminar at the United Nations (UN) in April 1994 was co-hosted by the Lutheran Office for World Community (LOWC) and the Youth Ministries desk in the Division for Congregational Ministries.

Follow-up activities at the UN related to the World Conference on Human Rights (June 1993, Vienna, Austria) included interpretation with church and secular media following the decision of the UN's General Assembly to establish a UN High Commissioner for Human Rights. The office is monitoring UN and non-governmental organizations' preparations for the World Summit for Social Development (Copenhagen, March 1995) and World Conference on Women (Beijing, September 1995) in support of and in cooperation with the relevant desks in the Lutheran World Federation (LWF) offices in Geneva, as well as LWF member churches. LOWC planning and participation continues in UN and ecumenical events leading up to the 50th anniversary of the United Nations in 1995.

Education and Program Resources

Age-Span Ministries: In the area of Age-Span Ministries, multiple issues received attention during 1993-1994. The training of Black Family Ministry Consultants and a final draft of a manual has been completed. The manual, entitled, *Church and Family Together: A Congregational Manual for Black Family Ministry*, will be available to congregations in the spring of 1995.

Participation with The Lutheran Church—Missouri Synod in the Older Adult Consultant Training funded by Aid Association for Lutherans has provided this church with more than 70 people trained in 14 synods. In cooperation with other denominations participating with the National Interfaith Coalition on Aging, resources for use by congregations are being produced. A collection of 21 articles focused on positive aspects of aging entitled, *Can We Uplift the Spirit As The Body Slows Down?* is now available.

The work of the Committee on Justice for Children and Their Families of the National Council of the Churches of Christ in the U.S.A. has brought together the talents of denominational representatives to produce new resources for families. The group is producing annotated bibliographies on Child Abuse, Children's Health, and Violence. In addition, the committee has produced a video entitled, "Welcoming the Child."

Community Development: During 1993-1994, Community Development has included three focus areas in addition to the normal functions of this program which include consultation services, technical assistance, resourcing, and networking.

The director has placed more intentional focus on job creation activities as a function of community economic development efforts. A pilot project that established the New Day Maintenance & Supply Company yielded some helpful data for future endeavors in job creations.

Several events and encounters over the past two years have led to the development of a total new ministry with males who traditionally have been unchurched. This new ministry has evolved from the result of some intentional hands-on work in the arena of street violence among youth. The director assisted in the development and implementation of a two-week summer camp pilot project for young African American males who are living in crisis. In three regions of this church, further assistance will be provided in the development and training helping congregations and coalitions of congregations to implement a prototype of this pilot (the Simba Circle) at the local level.

There has been continued analysis and review of congregationally-based community organizing and its effectiveness on the Church and within the community. The director is involved with a number of religious and secular funders in the creation of a new initiative to increase the number of persons of color organizing in their communities.

Disabilities Ministry: The major theme for all activity in Disability Ministries (presently a half-time position) continues to be the development of leaders and networks within the disability communities of this church. Experience has demonstrated that persons living with disabilities and their family members usually are the most effective spokespersons and experts on the issues of accessibility and participation.

Many synods now have Disability Committees that work to assist congregations in becoming accessible to members with disabilities. The Lutheran Network on Mental Illness supports congregations in their efforts to provide support and care for families experiencing mental illness, and the Evangelical Lutheran Deaf Association focuses upon leadership training. Other networks are being developed, including one to address the needs of ELCA members with disabilities who are seminarians, clergy, and seminary graduates awaiting call.

Disaster Relief: During the past biennium, this church responded to 20 disasters through Inter-Lutheran Disaster Response. In addition, response to hurricane Iniki in Hawaii continued throughout 1993, and response to hurricane Andrew was continuing at the close of 1994. Both hurricanes occurred in 1992. Major disasters during the biennium included the Midwestern floods of 1993, the southern California earthquake of January 1994, the Georgia floods of July 1994, and the Texas floods of November 1994. The floods in the Midwest devastated the largest territory ever affected by a disaster in the history of the United States. Lutherans provided emergency assistance to families, help to communities, emergency supplies, and volunteers and material for rebuilding.

Long-term grants also were provided for rural and farm assistance and for permanent housing needs. Major response efforts were mounted by Lutherans in Illinois, Iowa, Kansas, and Missouri, and large relief projects also were carried out in North Dakota, South Dakota, Wisconsin, and Minnesota. Lutheran social ministry organizations in Iowa, Illinois, Missouri, Kansas, North Dakota, South Dakota, and Minnesota were involved in the flood response. Together with the Inter-Lutheran Disaster Response, Lutheran Social Services of Southern California managed relief operations following the 1994 Los Angeles earthquake, providing food, urgently needed supplies, and counseling. Efforts there continued throughout 1994 while new relief efforts were begun in Georgia and Texas following major flooding.

Environmental Stewardship and Hunger Education: Over the past three years, the Millennium Institute's "21st Century Studies" program has grown into a strong and important program at 27 colleges and universities throughout the United States and Canada. The director is working with a task force on curriculum development at a consortium of seminaries affiliated with the National Council of the Churches of Christ in the U.S.A. (NCCC) and made a presentation at the "Down to Earth Theology" conference at Wartburg Seminary (Dubuque, Iowa). Funding from Aid Association for Lutherans was provided to the Lutheran School of Theology at Chicago for upgrading their lighting system and for the "Energy Conservation at Church-Related Institutions" conference.

Interest-free loans to churches for initiating lighting efficiency projects were established at the Metropolitan Chicago, Florida-Bahamas, and Upper Susquehanna synods. The director worked with the Delaware-Maryland Synod to hold an urban gardening conference and supported work with urban gardening in Baltimore.

Printed materials produced in partnership with other organizations include: *George Washington Carver and Global Sustainability*; *Make Your Church a Creation Awareness Center*; *From Eco-Lighting to Eco-Justice*; *What Is Congregation Supported Community Gardening?*; *Environmental Tithing*; *Conserving God's Gifts through Simple Actions*; *God's Earth Our Home: A Manual on Environmental Stewardship for Congregations*; *To Till and Keep*.

Audio: "The Bible as an Ecological Handbook."

Video: "Making Your Church a Creation Awareness Center"; "Straw Bale Construction and Global Sustainability"; "Growing Season."

Health Ministries: The division carries on its work in health ministries through the Strategy Team on Health, a group made up of health-care professionals, churchwide staff, and staff from affiliated social ministry organizations. The Strategy Team supports advocacy efforts directed at achieving universal access to health care. Support is provided to the National Interreligious Health Care Access Campaign through financial contributions to the campaign and by providing leadership on the campaign's steering committee. Materials also are being provided to congregations to help them study the issue of access to health care. In 1992, the Strategy Team developed a paper on access to health care and worked with the division's board to prepare a resolution on reform of the health-care system. The resolution and paper were printed in booklet format for distribution to congregations.

The Strategy Team also developed a resource to be used by congregations to develop a wide range of congregationally-based health ministries. The team received a grant from Lutheran Brotherhood Foundation to provide a pilot training program in ten congregations in three synods. The team also supports congregational

health ministry by using ELCA publications to promote health- and healing-related materials.

Lutheran Immigration and Refugee Service (LIRS): Lutheran Immigration and Refugee Service (LIRS) is an Inter-Lutheran agency, enabling this church to participate in immigration and refugee ministries. This agency also provides a first asylum concerns program that assists persons seeking asylum in this country to obtain fair access to equal protection under the law. The agency supports projects providing social service, legal representation, and community education directly to, or on behalf of, those seeking safe haven.

During the past biennium, LIRS resettled 8,646 refugees through 26 regional affiliates and their 32 suboffices under a cooperative agreement with the United States Department of State. For the fourth year in a row, LIRS was ranked number one among national agencies in an informal evaluation by the State Department for their performance in resettling refugees.

Leadership Development

Leadership development staff provide four basic services.

1) *Public presentations* during 1994-95 included: Board training events for 10 social ministry organization (SMO) boards per year, churchwide unit boards and officers, and other church-based governance groups; ethics seminars for 12 social ministry organization (SMO) staff and board groups; five synod gatherings; eight workshops at Global Mission Events; two dialogues with leaders of Women of the ELCA; and lecture series at two ELCA seminaries. In addition there were presentations on AIDS at regional and national Lutheran and Episcopal events; presentations on servant leadership for two state-wide SMO Days of Sharing events; and presentations on volunteerism for two retiree groups.

2) *Resource development* involving the research, writing, and production of print materials includes: A monograph entitled *The Corporate Mind*; papers on aspects of ethics for symposia and a guidebook entitled *How to Start an Ethics Committee*; regular columns on ethics written for several newsletters that reach social ministry organization executives and chaplains and one article per year for *Lutheran Woman Today*; a recruitment brochure designed to interest young people in church-related human service care occupations distributed at the Youth Gathering and by social ministry organizations; Personnel and Referral Bulletin mailed each month to 1500 individuals and organizations; a history of Lutheran social ministry in the United States in the last century now in process.

3) *Planning and consultation* activities included: Frequent telephone and in-person problem analysis and recommendations provided to social ministry organiza-

tion executives and board leaders in the areas of governance, ethics, and executive search; participation with Stanford University to plan a conference on "Multicultural Influences on Ethical Issues in Death and Dying"; assistance with aspects of strategic planning and committee formation for social ministry organizations and synod committees.

4) *Support to networks* has involved conference planning to facilitate formation and growth of a variety of groups such as Days of Sharing for nursing home staff and three affinity groups of staff members of social ministry organizations.

The work of these staff members aims to provide assistance to leaders of this church body, both professionals and volunteers. Staff members interact regularly with staff and boards of social ministry organizations; staff, rostered persons, and committees in synods; students and faculties of seminaries and colleges; and other churchwide units.

Support to Social Ministry Organizations

Goals:

- Undergird and relate to the ELCA's affiliated 250 parent social ministry organizations;
- Provide for affiliation studies, financial reviews, consultation, and crisis intervention services; and
- Assist synods and congregations to begin new social ministry organizations

A Blue Ribbon Committee was appointed by the board of the Division for Church in Society "to develop a new shared vision for the corporate social ministry of the Evangelical Lutheran Church in America, and the goals and strategies to achieve this vision, so that the life of this church is strengthened by the witness and service advanced through a strong social ministry presence in the world."

The committee has developed a preliminary theological statement, surveyed bishops and social ministry executives, and identified preliminary issues and strategies. Focus groups are providing feedback for the committee to present a final report in September 1995.

The 1994 Annual Report indicates a remarkable network of services to needs in our society on behalf of this church, inspired by the Gospel. Highlights from the 1994 report are provided in the accompanying chart.

Studies

Staff members produce and distribute adopted social statements that undergird and are central expressions of this church's witness in society. They make available the considerable legacy of social statements developed over the years by The American Lutheran Church and the Lutheran Church in America, and

produce and distribute the five social statements that have been adopted thus far at ELCA churchwide assemblies.

1994 Annual Report Highlights

"The Gospel must be lived as well as told, or people disregard it . . ." —(William A. Passavant). From very humble beginnings, Lutheran social-ministry organizations have become one of the nation's largest human service networks. Lutheran Social Ministry reflects partnerships with congregations, synods, communities, government, and individuals.

This report summarizes the work of 250 ELCA-affiliated Lutheran social-ministry parent corporations in the United States and the Virgin Islands. Lutheran Social Ministry services are provided in every state except Vermont and Rhode Island.

Services

Total persons served	1,809,969
Persons served in non residential services	1,703,946
Persons served in residential services	106,023
Total number of volunteers	7,744
Total number of volunteer service hours	4,889,262
Total number of employees	80,073
Total Income	$2,296,376,000
Total Expenses	2,195,041,000

At the 1993 assembly, such statements included "Caring for Creation: Vision, Hope, and Justice" (order code: 69-1380) and "Freed in Christ: Race, Ethnicity, and Culture" (69-3952). Implementation of "Caring for Creation . . ." is occurring especially through the division's program of environmental stewardship. A congregational study guide for "Freed in Christ . . ." has been jointly produced with the Division for Congregational Ministries and the Commission for Multicultural Ministries. The latter also coordinates implementation of other aspects of the statement.

ELCA social statements grow out of this church's confession, and are intended to help carry out God's mission in our world today.

Social statements (1) are theological documents, which bring this church's understanding of its faith to bear on social issues; (2) are teaching documents, which inform, guide, and challenge this church and its members; (3) involve this church in the ongoing task of theological ethics; (4) result from an extensive, inclusive, and accepted process of deliberation; (5) guide the institutional life of this church; and (6) are intended to be used widely in the life and mission of this church.

In 1993, after an extensive four-year process of participatory input and deliberation, the first draft of a possible social statement on human sexuality was developed and authorized for publication by the division's board, together with a related video. In 1994, a working draft of a possible social statement was developed and distributed.

In 1993, a study document entitled, "Peace: God's Gift, Our Task" was authorized and published for feedback prior to the development in 1994 of the first draft of the statement, "Peace, God's Gift, Our Task." In light of responses received in writing and at hearings throughout this church during fall 1994, this statement was revised in early 1995; the proposed statement will come before the 1995 Churchwide Assembly for its consideration.

In 1994, the division's board authorized the initiation of work on a social statement on economic life (anticipated since 1988). A task force was appointed and has had its first meetings. During fall 1994, an extensive series of listening posts on economic life were held in a number of areas across this church, in which hundreds of ELCA members shared their perspectives of what is occurring economically and the role of their faith and the church in relation to such developments. This was pivotal to the task force as it began to focus and plan their work. A study and discussion document is being developed in 1995, and a first draft of a statement is expected in 1996.

During 1995, a review committee on social statements is convening to review the bases, purposes, procedures, and authority of social statements, and is expected to bring a report to the division's board and the Church Council at their fall 1996 meetings.

During spring 1994, a "Message on Community Violence" (order code 69-6598) was developed, approved by the division's board, adopted by the Church Council, and distributed that summer to all congregations for study, discussion, and action. It suggests a number of ways in which this church is and can be further involved in countering the reality and fear of violence in communities.

In 1995, a two-part study on educational choice is expected to be completed, one for congregational discussion and the other for more in-depth exploration of the issues at stake.

Studies staff consult with and advise those who represent this church in public policy advocacy and corporate social responsibility work, for the purpose of clarifying and interpreting the policy bases established by the social statements of the predecessor bodies of this church as well as those of the Evangelical Lutheran Church in America. In 1994, staff members worked with the Lutheran Office for Governmental Affairs (LOGA) in development of the "Working Principles for Welfare Reform" document, which clarifies the bases for ELCA advocacy on this issue.

Through statements, messages, studies, and other resources, a central intent is to develop documents in such a way that they result from and engender continuing moral deliberation throughout this church. What is important is not necessarily the final product or position but the ongoing process through which the Holy Spirit is at work in the many settings where critical social issues of the day are deliberated in light of the faith we confess.

World Hunger Ministries

Hunger staff members coordinate the churchwide World Hunger Program on behalf of the Division for Global Mission, Division for Church in Society, and Division for Congregational Ministries, and the Department for Communication. Staff monitor hunger program budget expenditures and coordinate the production of a yearly hunger resource packet and periodic hunger newsletters for distribution to all congregations of this church.

Staff members also direct the domestic hunger relief and development grants, as well as hunger education and advocacy grants.

Hunger Program Coordination: The Hunger Program coordinator chaired monthly meetings of the Interunit Hunger Staff Team. Eight churchwide units have representatives on this staff team.

Two world hunger resource packets for congregations were produced (one each year). Ten hunger newsletters were produced (five per year). Other resources produced included: 1992 Hunger Program annual report; 1993 Hunger Program annual report; "Standing With People Living in Poverty," highlighting three state public policy advocacy offices' hunger work; "Loving Neighbors Far and Near, U.S. Lutherans Respond to a Hungry World," by Charles P. Lutz.

The biennial gathering of the synod world hunger leadership network took place August 25-28, 1994 at Augsburg College, Minneapolis. One hundred and forty persons attended, 110 being synod hunger leaders.

The domestic grants team continues to critique and analyze the current funding procedures and processes. At present, it is reviewing the possible changes in the funding year to facilitate distribution of funds collected versus our current situation of distributing funds projected. These discussions evolved since the World Hunger Appeal Program experienced the first income shortfall in its seven year history.

A long-range partnership that ultimately will affect funding from both secular and religious entities presently going to communities of color is the National Fund for Community Leadership, of which the director has been a part for the past three years.

Domestic Hunger Relief, Development and Organizing Grants		
1993	**187 Projects Funded**	
Direct Relief	88	$240,200
Community Development	46	$191,000
Community Organizing	53	$198,000
1994	**186 Projects Funded**	
Direct Relief	187	$230,550
Community Development	58	$245,750
Community Organizing	41	$168,300

Hunger Education Grants: In 1993, World Hunger Education grants in the amount of $132,760 were given to 36 agencies. In 1994 (for the period ending October 1994), 30 organizations received a total of $71,680 in grants. The recipients of the grants included regions, synods, congregations, colleges and universities, seminaries, ecumenical organizations, and secular organizations with Lutheran ties. Regions and synods received grants for training leaders in hunger and global sustainability education. Congregations received hunger grants to initiate gardening projects in urban areas, initiate energy conservation programs, and train former drug addicts in greenhouse management. Colleges and universities affiliated with this church received grants to pursue global sustainability studies. Studies of Haiti, Ecuador, and the Dominican Republic have been completed. Nearly 24 such studies are being conducted for countries such as Nepal, Vietnam, Jamaica, Mozambique, and Namibia.

Two ELCA colleges also received grants to demonstrate resource conservation. Several seminaries received grants to publish a resource book on the *Care of Creation*, to study the feasibility of congregationally-supported agriculture in urban congregations, and to develop curriculum involving earth stewardship. A grant was given to publish two books on sustainable agriculture, *Common Harvest* and *To Till and Keep*. One grant was awarded to a group in San Francisco called The Garden Project, to train women prisoners on parole in urban agriculture. Grants were made to the National Council of Churches' Eco-Justice Project to produce a resource packet entitled "God's Earth Our Home." A book on George Washington Carver entitled, *George Washington Carver and Global Sustainability* was commissioned as part of a newly formed Christian environmental organization called The Christian Society of the Green Cross.

Hunger Advocacy Grants: In 1993, grants totaling $119,525 were given to 25 organizations for their hunger-related advocacy work. In 1994, $88,250 were committed to 22 organizations for their hunger-related

advocacy work (as of November 30, 1994). Long time recipients of these advocacy grants include Bread for the World, Interfaith Impact, Interfaith Center for Corporate Responsibility, NCCC World Community, Food Research Action Center, Coalition on Human Needs, and the Center for Budget and Policy.

Referrals from 1993 Churchwide Assembly
Community Violence Part 1—Gun Control

a. Assembly action on gun control was forwarded to all ELCA public policy offices.

b. Along with a summary of other actions related to the Division for Church and Society, a summary of the gun control action was included in the interpretive piece sent to all the congregations of this church through the Action Packet, regarding social statements acted on at the 1993 Churchwide Assembly.

c. Bishop Herbert W. Chilstrom sent a letter to President William Clinton and the United States Congress addressing the issue of Community Violence and Gun Control.

d. The board of the Division for Church and Society approved and the ELCA Church Council approved in April 1994, a Message on Community Violence developed by the studies staff and disseminated to this church through the Action Packet.

North American Free Trade Agreement (NAFTA)

Principles for Consideration of the North American Free Trade Agreement were developed by an Interunit Team and affirmed by the Executive Committee of the board of the Division for Church in Society on July 7, 1993, as the basis for deliberation and advocacy by the Evangelical Lutheran Church in America.

U.S. and Cuba Relations

The board of the Division for Church in Society, at its March 1994 meeting, voted to recommend to the ELCA Church Council that it request the relevant entities of this church to implement the resolves in the Minneapolis Area Synod memorial to the 1993 Churchwide Assembly as follows:

1. To support Lutheran congregations in Cuba through prayer, information sharing, and material support, in cooperation with the Division for Global Mission and the Lutheran Coalition on Latin America;

2. To participate in sending humanitarian aid to Cuba through Lutheran World Relief, Church World Service, and Pastors for Peace;

3. To petition the United States government to end its embargo against Cuba, and

4. To seek further reconciliation and normalization of relations between the United States and Cuba.

Conflict in Bosnia

In February 1994, The Lutheran Office for World Community and the Lutheran Office for Governmental Affairs provided background material and a list of church leaders that were utilized for a letter which was sent by Bishop Herbert W. Chilstrom later that year.

State and National Health-Care Policies

The Division for Church in Society continues to participate in the Interreligious Health Care Access Campaign, a national association of more than forty faith groups that advocates for universal access to health care. During 1993-1994, the division provided significant leadership to this organization. The division distributes materials to congregations to help them address health care system reform on the local level, and also distributes copies of the 1992 resolution of the board concerning health-care system reform. Professional chaplaincy services were affirmed as essential to total health care.

U.S. Immigration Policies

As requested in the memorial, the Lutheran Office for Governmental Affairs continues to work with Lutheran Immigration and Refugee Service to advocate for justice in immigration laws and policies. Concerns about justice for immigrants are contained in the first draft of the social statement on peace. The series of Listening Posts on Economic Life, related to preparations for a possible social statement on the economy, include foci on migrant farm workers, Hispanic farm labor, the economic effects of immigration, border issues, and trade between the United States and Mexico, including the *maquiladoras*.

ELCA Hunger Appeal

The division has worked with the Hunger Appeal Office in the Division for Congregational Ministries to promote increased giving through:

greater visibility for the appeal in the World Hunger Newsletter (produced five times a year);

additional fund appeal items in the yearly hunger resource packet;

hiring Ms. Patricia Larsen to work in the foundation for the Hunger Appeal, especially in major donor giving and special gifts;

the biennial gathering of synod hunger leader persons in Minneapolis, August 26-28, 1994. One hundred and ten leaders from 59 synods participated. Much emphasis was placed on ideas and strategies for increasing Hunger Appeal giving in the synods.

Transmissions from 1993 Churchwide Assembly
Namibia and Angola

The Lutheran Office for World Community prepared for Bishop Herbert W. Chilstrom a letter, sent November 4, 1993, to Assistant Secretary of State for African Affairs George Moose, Ambassador Madeleine Albright, Representative Harry Johnson, and Senator Paul Simon, urging that adequate resources be provided to the United Nations for peace-keeping in Angola. The Division for Church in Society has been active with the Division for Global Mission in the ELCA Southern Africa network that advocates for peace and justice in the entire region. The Lutheran Office for Governmental Affairs has pressed for reforms in foreign assistance which would allocate a greater proportion of United States aid to the neediest regions of the world, of which southern Africa is one.

ELCA Deaf Community

A 1993 Churchwide Assembly resolution calling for affirmation of the deaf community "by giving them the visibility and voice of being one of the five emphasis groups in the Commission for Multicultural Ministries" was referred to, and thoroughly discussed by, staff of the Division for Church in Society, the Commission for Multicultural Ministries, and deaf members of this church. The division's board recommended to the Church Council, and it concurred, to address the needs of the deaf by affirming its 1991 Church Council statement, recognizing the uniqueness of the deaf culture and directing the churchwide offices to address the needs of this culture through a multi-unit approach, with the division taking lead responsibility.

Christians in the Holy Land

Whenever the Resource Guide on the Middle East is requested or distributed by Lutheran Office for Governmental Affairs (LOGA) staff to members of Congress or of this church, LOGA includes the 1993 Churchwide Assembly resolution on Christians in the Holy Land. Bishop Herbert W. Chilstrom sent the letter requested in the resolution.

Major Program Directions 1994-1999

1. We will lead and support this church's commitment
   to identify and analyze causes of injustice;
   to challenge individuals and systems that perpetuate oppression;
   to work toward removing obstacles that prevent people from living justly in community.
2. We will assist this church's development of servant leaders for ministry in society.

3. We will help equip church leaders and members to connect and apply the language and values of Christian faith to public realities.
4. We will bring together, support and strengthen people and organizations to contribute to the common good.

Areas of Urgency (1994-1995)

As a part of the division's strategic planning, staff and board identified six areas of urgency, which will receive priority attention during 1994-1995. Those areas are: activities which directly address poverty, especially among women and children, domestically and world-wide; development of a church culture and leaders committed to the social dimensions of the mission of this church; development of a vision and strategy for this church's corporate social ministry; health and safety concerns; migration and refugee concerns; and a possible Social Statement on Human Sexuality.

BOARD OF THE DIVISION FOR
CHURCH IN SOCIETY

INGRID CHRISTIANSEN, *Chair*
CHARLES S. MILLER JR., *Executive Director*

Report of the Division for Global Mission

Organization
Board
Mr. Timothy A. Bennett, Springfield, Ohio (term
   expires 1997)
Rev. June Nilssen Eastvold, Seattle, Wash. (1999)
Ms. Ann Foltz, Mt. Jackson, Va. (1995)
Rev. Ruth Fortis, Humble, Tex. (1997)
Ms. Fern Lee Hagedorn, Philadelphia, Pa. (1997)[1]
Rev. David L. Johnson, Jerusalem, via Israel (1995)
Ms. Patricia R. Johnson, Detroit, Mich. (1999)
Ms. Sue S. Lane, New Market, Va. (1995)
Ms. Harolyn C. Light, Jefferson City, Mo. (1997)
Rev. Nancy Maeker, *chair*, St. Paul, Minn. (1997)
Ms. Ida M. Martinson, St. Paul, Minn. (1999)
Dr. Richard J. Meier, Hialeah, Fla. (1999)
Mr. Mark Monono, Omaha, Nebr. (1999)
Mr. Robert Munson, *vice chair*, Brooklyn Center, Minn.
   (1995)
Rev. Roberto Navarro, Tampa, Fla. (1997)
Mr. David L. Perry, *secretary*, Seattle, Wash. (1995)
Rev. Winston D. Persaud, Dubuque, Iowa (1999)
Mr. Denis A. Radefeld, Lorain, Ohio (1995)
Ms. Jane Rossing, Ithaca, N.Y. (1999)
Rev. Merlyn Seitz, Dayton, Ohio (1995)
Mr. Ronald J. Solimon, Albuquerque, N.Mex. (1997)
Ms. Diana M. Valdez, Spokane, Wash. (1997)

Advisors
Bishop Rev. Howard E. Wennes, Grand Canyon Synod
Mr. Richard L. McAuliffe, treasurer, Evangelical
   Lutheran Church in America

---

[1]Resigned January 11, 1994.

Executive Committee
   The executive committee is composed of the three
officers and two additional members elected by the
board at its first meeting following the biennial Churchwide Assembly. The executive committee may act on
behalf of the board between meetings, within established
policies and stated directives.

Staff
Executive Director: Rev. Mark W. Thomsen
Director for Personnel and Office Management:
   Ms. Deborah Moffa

Director for Global Community and Overseas
   Operations: Rev. Will L. Herzfeld
Director for Planning and Evaluation and Program
   Director for Papua New Guinea and the South
   Pacific: Rev. Bonnie L. Jensen
Program Director for East Africa, Mexico, and the
   Caribbean: Ms. Lynda Tidemann
Program Director for French-speaking Africa and
   Madagascar: Rev. Olin K. Sletto
Program Director for English-speaking West Africa and
   Southern Africa: Rev. Daniel W. Olson
Program Director for East Asia:
   Rev. Delbert E. Anderson
Program Director for South Asia:
   Rev. Warner W. Luoma
Program Director for Latin America:
   Rev. Rafael Malpica Padilla
Program Director for Europe and the Middle East:
   Rev. David H. Nelson
Director for Finance: Mr. Philip A. Jacobson
Assistant Director for Finance:
   Ms. Christina L. Jackson Skelton
Director for Development: Ms. Belletech Deressa
Director for International Scholarships:
   Rev. H. Karl Reko
Director for International Personnel:
   Mr. Harold T. Hanson
Director for Lutheran World Mission Volunteers and
   Associate Director for International Personnel:
      Rev. Jack F. Reents
Associate Director for International Personnel:
   Ms. Joyce Bowers
Directors for Global Mission Education:
   Rev. David G. Dennison and
   Rev. Julianne Dennison
Associate Directors for Global Mission Education:
   Ms. Stacy D. Kitahata, Ms. Martha C. Pedersen,[1]
   and Ms. Sandra Holloway[2]
Director for Missionary Sponsorship and Global
   Mission Designated Giving: Ms. Mary Johnson

---

[1] Contract completed March 10, 1995.
[2] Began employment March 1, 1995.

Constitutional Mandate
   The Division for Global Mission (DGM), in partnership with Lutheran and other Christian churches and

agencies, develops and implements programs that witness to Jesus Christ through proclamation, teaching, leadership development, service, and advocacy around the globe. The constitutional mandate of this division is defined in continuing resolution 16.11.F91. of the Constitution, Bylaws, and Continuing Resolutions of the Evangelical Lutheran Church in America.

Report of Work 1993-1995
Evaluation of Program Budget for 1993-1995

During the 1993-1995 biennium, the Division for Global Mission conducted a major evaluation of its work. This evaluation focused upon the priorities established by the division's board in 1990 for the 1990-1995 time period, namely: evangelism, leadership development, south-south, relief and development, and mission to the Evangelical Lutheran Church in America (ELCA). The board of the division has voted to extend the use of these priorities into 1996 when they will be re-evaluated in conversation with the new executive director of the division, who is to be elected in October 1995. This church's organizational principles also were used as criteria for the evaluation, namely: inclusivity, interdependence, flexibility, resource stewardship, and servant leadership.

The Church Council, through its Program and Structure Committee, also decided to evaluate the work of the division in order to ascertain its effectiveness in carrying out the division's constitutional mandates. The Church Council evaluative process was coordinated with that of the division.

The division board had major discussions about the division's work during this evaluation process. Leadership development was the focus of the spring 1994 board meeting. The fall 1994 meeting centered on an evaluation of a multiplicity of evangelism programs, and included the presentation of a report on a major staff evaluation of the unit's program budget. During a ten-day period, August 24-September 2, 1994, a divisional staff-committee reviewed every program, activity, and project funded by the division. Affirmations, concerns, recommendations, and decisions concerning future programming were made. This evaluation process revealed significant major trends which have developed between 1988 and 1994. At its spring 1995 meeting, the board heard reports on the effectiveness and efficiency of the unit's administrative process and the Global Mission Education Program.

During spring 1995, the Department for Research and Evaluation also reported on the results of their findings received through questionnaires sent to 400 congregations and 250 partner churches and agencies. The findings from these surveys were not available when this report was written. Surveys of 300 missionaries and other overseas personnel, synodical leadership, and congregations that sponsor missionaries also are being conducted in 1995. Responsibility for this part of the process was borne by the Program and Structure Committee of the Church Council.

At this point in the process, the division shares with this church the most valuable information identified to date: the major program trends and the summaries of the findings dealing with evangelism and leadership development (Exhibits A and B to this report).

Major Program Trends 1988-1994
Evangelism

Major Trend One: There has been an increase of personnel and resources designated for dialogical witness among people of other faiths. Dialogical witness is defined as witness to the crucified and risen Jesus Christ within conversations concerning life and faith and accompanied by activity devoted to fullness of life for the whole human family.

Much of the Division for Global Mission's work in the past has been carried out among peoples belonging to traditional and popular folk religions. This work may be distinguished from witness among people of other major religious traditions such as Muslims, Buddhists, and Hindus. Effective witness among these major religious traditions has not received adequate attention and the division is, therefore, prioritizing work in these areas. The division began this effort with a program to develop a more effective witness among Muslims and is expanding this focus to include Buddhism, Hinduism, and developing secularism in Asia. Furthermore, this focus has led the unit to take more seriously the study of traditional and folk religions, the context in which many of our partner churches work.

Witness Among Muslim Peoples

The Division for Global Mission has prioritized work among Muslim peoples because: (a) it is the second largest faith community in the world—with one billion adherents; (b) historical tensions and political conflicts between Christians and Muslims call for a mission of reconciliation in Jesus' name; (c) theological differences and misunderstandings demand a corrective evangelism; and (d) the ELCA has partner churches and missionary personnel located in many areas of the world where Muslims and Christians meet each other. The budget for the witness among Muslims totals approximately $2 million, or 14 percent of the division's program budget.

Equipping for Dialogical Witness. This division has attempted to improve the Evangelical Lutheran Church in America's effectiveness in engaging with Muslim peoples in two ways. First, the division's personnel have been involved in graduate programs in Islamic studies. The purpose of these Christian-Muslim study programs is to train persons who can in turn teach the local church or missionary personnel in engaging with Muslim people. Second, the division has supported or initiated training programs for missionaries or local leaders that equip persons for Christian-Muslim dialogical witness.

Thirteen of the division's staff have graduate degrees in Islamic studies and are engaged in teaching programs that equip persons for Christian witness among Muslims. These teachers are listed regionally and represent approximately $500,000 annually in financial resources: *International*—Rev. Harold Vogelaar, Ph.D. (Lutheran School of Theology at Chicago, Chicago, Ill.); Rev. Roland Miller, Ph.D. (Luther Seminary, St. Paul, Minn.); Rev. Sigvard von Sicard, Ph.D. (Selly Oaks Colleges, Birmingham, England, UK); *West Africa*—Rev. Ronald Nelson, Th.M. (Cameroon); Rev. Mark Nygaard, Th.M. (Senegal); *East Africa and Madagascar*—Rev. James Gonia, completing Th.M. in 1995 (Madagascar); Rev. Samuel Wolff, completing Th.M. in 1995 (Tanzania); *South Asia*—Ms. Nelly van Doorn, Th.D. (Duta Wacana, Indonesia); Rev. Steve Haggmark, Th.D. and completing a Th.M. in Islamics (Indonesia); Mr. Fred Nelson, Th.D. Candidate (Bangladesh); Rev. Steven Benson, M.A., Ph.D. program to begin (India); *Middle East*—Rev. Michael Shelley, Ph.D. (Cairo, Egypt); Rev. Mark Swanson, Th.D. (Cairo, Egypt).

Fifty missionaries and one partner church person attended the division's summer Islam seminars held in 1992, 1993, and 1994. Seventeen of these persons teach and train local persons for dialogical witness. Cost for these educational programs was approximately $75,000.

Ten persons from partner churches were trained through graduate studies to teach courses in dialogical witness among Muslim people. This initiative has just begun, and to date the division has made a scholarship investment of approximately $220,000.

Support of Local Initiatives Among Partner Churches. This division has supported a number of local initiatives through: (1) a financial grant for the training of Ethiopian Evangelical Church Mekane Yesus (EECMY) evangelists through a four year program ($50,000); (2) the financial support of a 1993 Christian-Muslim consultation in Nigeria ($8,000), which is to be followed by a second consultation in 1995; (3) the salary of Robert Wandersee, who directs the Joint Christian Ministry in West Africa, an ecumenical ministry among Fulani people implemented by approximately 20 churches and agencies throughout West Africa; (4) the placement of Mr. Lon and Ms. Mynna Kightlinger (primary health care personnel) in northern Madagascar to accompany local pastors and evangelists in outreach

to Muslim people; (5) the relocation of DGM leadership development personnel within the Evangelical Lutheran Church of Cameroon to equip persons for witness among Muslim people, and a center established at Ngaoubela for the education of Muslims seeking baptism; and (6) the reassignment of a missionary family in the Central African Republic to work among the Fulani.

New Initiatives in Bangladesh and Senegal. The Division for Global Mission is now working in two geographical areas where there is no primary partner church. In Southern Bangladesh entirely new work in an area that is 100 percent Muslim is beginning with a community development program in Dumki directed by Edwin and Karen Scott. The annual budget will approximate $120,000 (one-half being raised by a consortium of ELCA congregations in the Minneapolis-St. Paul, Minn., area). The work also is supported by the presence of Fred and Bonnie Nelson in Dhaka, where Fred teaches at the ecumenical Evangelical Seminary.

This division's work in Senegal has been strengthened because of the priority on Islam. The number of people in ministry here has increased from five in 1988 to nine in 1994. Six of these positions are in direct evangelism. The baptisms of three Fulani men were conducted in the spring of 1993—the first baptisms since the beginning of the program about fifteen years ago. The Senegal budget is now $480,781.

Witness Among Asian Peoples of Other Faiths (Buddhism, Hinduism, Secularism in Asia)

The Division for Global Mission has also prioritized evangelical outreach in Asia in the form of dialogical witness among peoples of other faiths. As in the case of Islam, the unit historically has partner churches and personnel in these areas. The division has focused upon better preparation for personnel serving in dialogical witness.

Six divisional personnel have undertaken graduate studies in Asian religions and cultural studies or the relationship of Christianity to Asian history and cultures: Rev. Michael Fonner, completing the Th.D. in 1995 (Buddhism); Rev. Craig Moran, Ph.D. (Chinese culture); Rev. Mark Luttio, completing the Th.D. in 1995 (Japanese folk religion); Rev. Kenneth Dale, Ph.D. (Japanese folk religion); Rev. James Sack, Th.D. (Japanese cultural values); Rev. John LeMond, editor of *Areopagas* and completing the Ph.D. in 1995 (Chinese history). All of these persons are or will be involved in the training of local theological leaders.

The Division for Global Mission has also initiated regional studies of the cultural contexts in which the division carries out its witness to the Gospel. Studies are being done in Japan, the China area, and South Asia.

These studies will become the basis of an evaluation of present activity and future directions for work in Asia.

Major Trend Two: Since the disintegration of the USSR and the opening up of Eastern and Central Europe, the Division for Global Mission has begun to increase resources and personnel in Eastern and Central Europe while decreasing resources in Western Europe (1989—$189,045; 1994—$101,280; a decrease of 41 percent).

The Division for Global Mission recognizes that after 50 years of communist oppression, suppression of religious freedom, and ideological propaganda, there are vast numbers of people in Eastern and Central Europe who have not encountered the Gospel. However, because of the strong involvement of the Lutheran World Federation (LWF) and of the European Lutheran churches in supporting churches in Eastern and Central Europe, the division has not made this region a major priority and therefore has only slightly increased financial resources for this area. In spite of this fact, the program director for Europe has made creative use of volunteers, persons under contract, and small financial grants in order to support mission outreach by Lutheran churches in Eastern and Central Europe.

At the present time four contract persons (a clergy couple, a third ordained minister, and one English as a second language professional), along with 19 volunteers, serve with the Lutheran church in Slovakia. A volunteer theologian from this church is a theological consultant to the Lutheran church in Estonia. Lutheran World Mission Volunteers have served an English-speaking congregation in Tallin, Estonia. A woman pastor, the Rev. Austra Reinis, serves in a Latvian-speaking parish in Ventspils, Latvia. Two volunteers will serve in Hungary. Another theologian from the Evangelical Lutheran Church in America serves as a theological consultant with the Lutheran church in Russia. The Rev. William Anderson serves as pastor of the English-speaking Warsaw International Church in Poland. A Global Mission Associate teaches at the Warsaw Christian Academy, an institution serving Polish Lutheran theological students.

Approximately $140,000 a year is channeled via the Lutheran World Federation's Department for Mission and Development to Lutheran churches in Eastern and Central Europe. The Rev. Gerhard Krodel, professor emeritus of the Lutheran Theological Seminary at Gettysburg, raised over $500,000 within the Evangelical Lutheran Church in America for building a seminary in Russia. The division at present is working with a private United States citizen, the Estonia Evangelical Lutheran Church, and the Kogudus organization (a church renewal group within this church that has Estonian roots) in order to initiate a Christian renewal

center in Estonia. This project includes a 25-year free lease to the Estonian Evangelical Lutheran Church of an Estonian manor house on the Baltic Sea, where the center will be located.

Major Trend Three: There has been a decrease of missionary personnel dedicated to traditional DGM evangelism positions (from 116 to 55 personnel; financial resources from $5.7 million to $3.9 million or 30.79 percent). Equipping local evangelists and pastors has become the priority.

Within the category of "traditional evangelism," the number of missionary personnel has declined from 116 to 55 salaried units between 1988 and 1994 (a decrease of 61 missionary salaried units, or 52 percent). The primary reason for this radical change is the rapid emergence of local leadership within partner churches. Local evangelists and pastors have assumed responsibilities for these ministries and perform them effectively and efficiently. The Division for Global Mission, working with partner churches, has refocused its priority to training local personnel for this work. These training statistics will be noted subsequently in this report, under Leadership Development.

Staff discussions noted that, even if given a million-dollar increase within the budget, these traditional "evangelist" missionary positions among present partner churches, with a few exceptions, would not be refilled. However, if funds were available, the division would add "evangelist" positions in, for example, the Central African Republic (one or two), Papua New Guinea (one or two), and Madagascar (one or two). The primary purpose for these additions would be to give missionaries necessary cultural and church experience which would, in turn, prepare them for future leadership training within the church.

It should be noted that there is a great need for "evangelist missionaries" in other parts of the world where the Gospel is first being preached or where the church is just beginning to develop its own leadership.

Leadership Development

Major Trend Four: Funding for leadership development within partner churches has increased between 1988 and 1994 from $2,352,524 to $2,834,635 (20.5 percent). There has been a small decrease in missionary personnel in this category, from 55 to 48 salaried units or 12.7 percent. Scholarship funds have increased from $650,459 to $842,426 or 29.5 percent. Most of these funds are matched by this church's theological seminaries, giving the Division for Global Mission an annual scholarship program of approximately $1.5 million.

The Division for Global Mission has made leadership development within our partner churches a priority, as this trend indicates. An evaluation during the division's spring 1994 board meeting of leadership development activities revealed the quality and numbers of the division's missionaries serving in teaching roles in seminaries and Bible schools. The summary report of the director for planning and evaluation of the leadership development evaluation, Exhibit B, indicates that approximately 70 education programs (including seminaries, Bible schools, theological education by extension [TEE], and continuing education programs), along with many more scholarship programs, accounted for approximately $3.8 million, 25 percent of the division's program budget. The report noted that missionary personnel are assigned to 55 theological schools, six TEE programs, and six other training programs. Fifty-five assigned staff and 45 spouses have 25 earned doctorates and 42 master's degrees. The evaluation noted the quality and contributions of the division's efforts.

Within the priority of leadership, this division places a special emphasis upon leadership development among women. This initiative begins with the office at the churchwide center where 40 percent of the executive staff are women. The number of ordained women within the missionary community increased from five to nine, 1988-1994. Women in dual assigned and team positions increased from three to seventeen. Scholarships for international women increased to 21 percent of the recipients. Three women from partner churches have earned doctorates and now teach in theological seminaries in India, Brazil, and Madagascar. Significant changes have occurred within the partner churches. Each year there has been an increase in the number of churches ordaining women (approximately 10 Lutheran partner churches have begun to ordain women since 1989; the latest is the Lutheran Church of Malaysia—Singapore). The Ethiopian Evangelical Church Mekane Yesus recently established a policy that all elected assemblies should have 25 percent to 50 percent women in attendance. Consciousness-raising efforts within the division's programs and advocated by the Ecumenical Decade Staff Committee have increased, with the best efforts being made within the division's global mission education program.

Scholarship funds have increased by 29.5 percent and make possible studies for many future leaders within partner churches. The Report of the Director for International Scholarships to the fall 1994 meeting presented statistics indicating the results of the more than 180 scholarships administered by division staff since 1988. The following facts are noteworthy: scholarship students came from 42 countries and earned 38 Master of Theology degrees, 10 Master of Divinity degrees, 13 Doctor of Theology degrees, two Doctor of Ministry degrees, 20 Master of Arts degrees, four Doctor

of Philosophy degrees, four Bachelor of Arts degrees, and three Bachelor of Science degrees. These students serve as professors (37), deans of educational institutions (eight), department heads (eight), pastors (35), bishops (six), administrative assistants (12), program directors (13), social workers (10), chaplains (four), government service (12), and continuing graduate study (11). The growth of this program has required one additional part-time support staff person.

South-South

Major Trend Five: There has been an increase of South-South missionaries (from none in 1988 to nine in 1994) and South-South scholarship programs (from zero percent of the International Scholarship budget to 20 percent). South-South programs enable partner churches to participate in the international life and mission of the body of Christ.

The purpose of the South-South program is to: (1) enhance relationships between churches in the South; (2) tap the gifts of the South and facilitate the exchange of personnel resources and international mission outreach from the South; (3) increase self-reliance in the South; and, (4) reduce costs for mission outreach.

South-South missionary programs have included: two Nigerian missionaries in Sierra Leone, two Malagasy doctors in Cameroon, one Malagasy pastor in Zaire, one Malagasy doctor in Papua New Guinea, one Brazilian pastor in Mozambique, and an Indian professor in Tanzania. The financial investment is approximately $150,000.

Scholarship programs include Sierra Leone students in Singapore, Nigeria, and Tanzania; Central African Republic students in Cameroon; Cameroon students in Nigeria; a Batak student in Java; Papua New Guinean students in Fiji; two Japanese students in Lima, Peru; a Zimbabwean and a Namibian student in South Africa; and Guyanese students in Jamaica.

Mission to the
Evangelical Lutheran Church in America

Major Trend Six: There has been a tremendous increase in personal contacts between members, congregations, and synods of the Evangelical Lutheran Church in America and partner churches around the world. The Companion Synod Program (65 synods are now participating at some level) and the Global Mission Events to a great extent have made this possible.

One of the constitutional mandates given to the Division for Global Mission is to be a catalyst and facilitator in enabling the global Church to share its witness to the Gospel with this church. The purpose of this division's education program is to make possible this witness of the global churches to the Evangelical Lutheran Church in America.

The Companion Synod Program, which was initiated in 1988, grew rapidly because of the *Mission90* Program and soon included 15 relationships; all 65 synods of this church are now participating. This program has facilitated synod-to-synod, leader-to-leader, and person-to-person exchanges; scholarship programs; resource exchanges (devotional books written by companion synod members, for example); grants and gift exchanges; and, in one case, the development of a new seminary.

As this report is being written, a survey of Companion Synod activity (39 synods reporting) reveals that to this date: (1) there have been 50 companion visits to partner churches, involving 255 people; (2) there have been 60 partner church visits to the U.S.A., involving 94 people.

Three annual Global Mission Events gather nearly 4,000 persons for an immersion in global awareness. More than 50 young people from seven partner churches served three-month periods as camp counselors in camps and retreat centers of this church during the summer of 1994. This on-going program is co-sponsored by the Division for Global Mission and the outdoor ministries program of the Division for Congregational Ministries.

Development

Major Trend Seven: Relief and development programs have been maintained through use of the ELCA Hunger Program. These ELCA Hunger Program funds enable the Evangelical Lutheran Church in America to be involved in relief and development programs among the poorest and most marginalized persons around the world.

The Division for Global Mission has made development and relief work among the poor and marginalized a priority. Approximately 36 percent of the division's total budget is committed to this task. These funds are made available from the ELCA Hunger Appeal. With the sharp reduction of general program funds in 1989-1990, the division found it necessary to eliminate general benevolence funds from its grants designated for administrative costs for the Lutheran World Federation's Department for World Service (LWF/WS) and Lutheran World Relief (LWR). For this reason, $1,000,000 given annually from general proportionate share dollars prior to 1988 to LWR for administrative costs and $400,000 from the same source given to LWF/WS for similar costs, were replaced by ELCA Hunger Appeal dollars. Except for this change, financial resources committed to relief and development have remained rather constant between 1988 and 1994 (1988—$7,128,450; 1993—$7,318,003).

In 1994, approximately $3.7 million of these funds were channeled through Lutheran World Relief and $3.7 million were sent through the Lutheran World Federation's Department for World Service and Department for Mission and Development. Other funds are channeled through organizations such as the World Council of Churches, Church World Service, and Witness/National Council of the Churches of Christ in the U.S.A., Technoserve, etc., as well as the division's own programs integrating evangelism with service.

A slight decrease in funds occurred in 1993 and 1994. Surveys of congregations within this church indicate that the decrease can be attributed to alternative giving in support of relief work related to the natural disasters experienced in the U.S. during those years.

Belletech Deressa, the division's director for development, has done an excellent job in focusing this church's dollars on countries of the world where people are most in need. Grants from the Evangelical Lutheran Church in America, along with the Lutheran World Federation's Department for World Service (LWF/WS) include: Bangladesh ($235,000), Haiti ($405,000), Israel—West Bank ($185,000), El Salvador ($210,000), Mozambique ($210,000), Ethiopia ($140,000), and Liberia ($100,000). Members of this church also contribute to international disaster relief with many of these funds being channeled through LWF/WS. In 1994, more than $875,000 was sent by the division for the relief effort in Rwanda. Examples of the division's holistic ministry are: a primary health care worker and a veterinarian in Senegal, a community development person in Chile, a rural development person in Peru, and agricultural consultants in Cameroon and Madagascar.

The Evangelical Lutheran Church in America is a large, extremely wealthy Lutheran church centered in the most wealthy and powerful country in the world. When compared to much of the world, most this church's members live in a country club surrounded by incredible poverty and suffering. When Christ says "I was hungry and you did or did not feed me," Jesus is looking directly at us. We have financial resources. We have some of the best relief and development work in the world. We are called to assume our responsibilities!

Overall Program

Major Trend Eight: There has been a large reduction in missionary personnel, from 299 to 203 salaried units (–32 percent). This reduction of missionaries is primarily due to the 20 percent reduction in the Division for Global Mission budget from 1989-1994. This reduction has made it impossible for the Division for Global Mission to respond to many new challenges and requests for missionary personnel. Greater reduc-

tions have been made in financial resources devoted to missionary personnel than to grants to partner churches and agencies. There is approximately a 60/40 division between reduction in funds for missionary costs (60 percent) and reduction in funds for grants to partner churches and agencies (40 percent).

This trend reveals another priority with which this division functions, namely, a commitment to the empowerment of local churches, equipping local leaders, and self-reliance regarding local control of programming and funds. This was a major priority for this church's predecessor church bodies and has been continued by the ELCA Division for Global Mission.

While allowing the reduction of personnel in order to maintain church grants and scholarship programs, the Division for Global Mission has also emphasized increasing the expertise of the missionary personnel who still serve in long-term positions. Many missionaries have received some form of continuing education grants for seminars and courses varying in length from three weeks to one year; 14 of those have been at the graduate school level.

The reduction of the division's total budget has made it impossible to respond to challenges and requests for new missionaries or new financial resources. For example, if funds were available the division would increase personnel in: (1) Central African Republic, Cameroon, and Madagascar (one or two pastors in each country who would become theological teachers); (2) Nigeria (a theologian for Bronnum Theological Seminary and an Islamicist for the reconciliation project); (3) Namibia, Ethiopia, India, Peru and Eastern/Central Europe (theological and Bible teachers/professors); (4) Cameroon, Central African Republic, Liberia, and Tanzania (medical, health, and development personnel); (5) Peru, Nicaragua, and Haiti (pastors in leadership development). These are just a few examples from countries where we are already at work. The Division for Global Mission continues to receive requests to enter into new areas of work. Late in 1994, Bishop Mano Rumalshah from the Diocese of Peshawar of the Church of Pakistan, a small church surrounded by a Muslim majority of 97 percent, asked for funding of a small medical hospital which he could no longer support. Former mission partners were no longer active. I dreamed of the possibility that I could say, "This is a priority of the Evangelical Lutheran Church in America and we will support you; we will commit $100,00 annually." I pray that in the future we can.

There also is a tremendous need for capital funds. Present requests include: $400,000—seminary in Namibia; $300,000—seminary construction, Lutheran Church of Christ in Nigeria; $250,000—reconciliation center in Nigeria; $300,000—theological seminary in Slovakia; $300,000—reconstruction of damaged medical and theological facilities in Liberia. In addition, relief and development needs are virtually endless.

Major Trend Nine*: There has been a significant increase in the number of volunteers and contract persons called by the Division for Global Mission. Volunteers for global ministries have increased from approximately 15 in 1988 to 125 in 1994 (an increase of 800 percent).*

In order to compensate for the loss of salaried missionary personnel, the Division for Global Mission greatly increased the use of volunteers. In order to administer this program, the Lutheran World Mission Volunteer staff increased from one-half of an executive staff position and one full-time support staff to one full-time executive staff and two full-time support staff. Division volunteers raise approximately $500,000 annually for their own support.

The report on Lutheran World Mission Volunteers will be included in the Report of the Director for International Personnel to the spring 1995 meeting of the board and will give further details of the growth and value of the volunteer program.

This division also has increased the number of contract persons employed for overseas positions. Contract persons fulfill defined tasks for specific terms (two to five years) and normally receive a lower level of financial support than long-term missionaries serving under the "Division for Global Mission/Evangelical Lutheran Church in America Personnel Polices and Handbook."

Major Trend Ten: *There has been a rapid increase in new forms of DGM financial resources from a variety of non-budgetary sources.*

The Division for Global Mission has been able to compensate partially for regular budgetary losses through the initiation and use of other income sources. These sources include: (1) The Shadan (a joint Evangelical Lutheran Church in America-Japan Evangelical Lutheran Church financial fund in Japan), $1.5 million annually; (2) Lutheran Health-Care Bangladesh (a consortium of congregations in the Minneapolis/St. Paul, Minn. area), $50,000 annually; (3) World Hunger Appeal funds (small increase); (4) other restricted funds, $100,000 annually.

Continuing development of new funding sources will be essential in the division's future. It should also be noted that there has been a gradual reduction of regular missionary sponsorship funds from approximately $3,963,571 (1989) to $3,843,575 in 1994. Division studies indicate that congregations of this church give another $1.25 million to missionaries of other church bodies, most of whom are members of their congregations.

Major Trend Eleven: *The Division for Global Mission program from 1988 through 1994 is marked by many new, creative initiatives.*

New initiatives for the Division for Global Mission include:

- starting of new congregations in Sierra Leone, Senegal, and Peru; participation in development of the new churches in Nicaragua, Guatemala, and Honduras;
- new relationships with churches and agencies such as the Evangelical Lutheran Church of Zimbabwe, the Bolivian Evangelical Lutheran Church, the All Africa Conference of Churches, and the Evangelical Church of the Augsburg Confession in Slovakia;
- new programs in countries such as Tibet and Bangladesh;
- new forms of financing already noted in Major Trend Nine;
- new forms of cooperation, such as the companion synods and the consortium of congregations in the Minneapolis/St. Paul, Minnesota area;
- new ways of placing personnel through special contracts and volunteer service; and
- the development of the South-South Program.

Major Trend Twelve: *Progress has been made in increasing cultural diversity and inclusivity within the Division for Global Mission staff and missionary personnel.*

Since 1988, three persons of color have been called to the following positions: Director for Global Community and Overseas Operations; Area Program Director for Latin America; and one Associate Director for Global Mission Education. Since 1988 a person of color has served as Director for Development and another as Associate Director for Global Mission Education. At present, eight persons of color serve in support staff positions. It was significant that at a recent meeting with partner churches in South America, this division was represented by a delegation of six, four of whom were persons of color.

The Division for Global Mission has worked closely with this church's Commission for Multicultural Ministry in order to increase contacts with the various communities of color within the United States. The goal is to recruit a larger percentage of this church's missionaries from these communities. In spite of the drop in total missionaries between 1988 and 1994, the number of persons of color has remained constant: 1988 (11) and 1994 (12).

The Global Mission Education team has made positive steps to increase diversity within all synod and Global Mission Events committees. Serious efforts are continually made to make the Global Mission Events and global mission education resources more inclusive, reflecting the global Church's diversity.

Major Trend Thirteen: *There has been constant change of work assignments within the DGM churchwide office staff.*

Two former mission education personnel now serve as Area Program Directors. A former Area Program Director now directs the Lutheran World Mission Volunteer (LWMV) program. A previous Director for International Scholarships now serves in Mission Education. Many changes have occurred within the support staff. Almost all of these reassignments were caused by retirements and resignations.

Efforts to maintain the quality of the program with a decreased number of staff also have led to changes. The number of area program directors has decreased from ten to seven and one-half, though responsibilities have expanded through the increased number of volunteers and the many companion synod relationships. On the other hand, the increased number of recipients of U.S. international scholarships and Lutheran World Mission Volunteers has required additional staff in those areas (LWMV—an increase of a one-half executive position to full time and from one full-time support staff to two full-time support positions; International Scholarships—an increase of one-half an executive position to full time, and one-half a support staff position to a full-time position.)

Overall executive staff positions have decreased from 24 to 21 positions, or 12.5 percent. The division's staff is thanked for their committed and hard work which has made the Division for Global Mission's program possible.

The Division for Global Mission wishes to express its gratitude to the Evangelical Lutheran church in America—its members, congregations, synods, churchwide units, seminaries, colleges, Bible camps, hospitals, and social service organizations for their cooperation, as this church participates in the global life and mission of the body of Christ. It is our privilege to be among the followers of the risen Jesus Christ, who addresses us: "And you shall be my witnesses in Jerusalem, Judea, Samaria, and to the ends of the earth" (Acts 1:8).

BOARD OF THE DIVISION FOR GLOBAL MISSION

NANCY L. MAEKER, *Chair*

MARK W. THOMSEN, *Executive Director*

Summary of Evaluation: Evangelism Programs

Board of the Division for Global Mission
October 22-24, 1994

This report is a condensed summary of the full report of the evaluation of the Evangelism program of the Division for Global Mission.

The Priority

The Division for Global Mission's (DGM) emphasis on evangelism gives priority to reaching out among peoples who have not heard or fully heard the Gospel of Jesus Christ. This emphasis supports evangelistic efforts (especially into new arenas) by the churches with whom this division cooperates, witness among Muslims, among people of the major religions of Asia, and within the context of secularism in Asia. In some cases this means a gradual diversion of funds from maintaining ongoing church programs toward new outreach efforts.

Evangelism Activities
The Global Invitation

Each geographic region and each local context presents its own particular invitation to the Evangelical Lutheran Church in America through the Division for Global Mission to be faithful in proclaiming Jesus Christ globally. Of the world's population of more than five billion people, over three billion have not embraced the Christian faith. The Christian Church still faces a major challenge to witness to the Gospel of Jesus Christ in today's world.

Local Responsibility

The Evangelical Lutheran Church in America and the Division for Global Mission recognize that the mission of God in each place is primarily the responsibility of the church living in that context. This church and the division are committed to listening to the local church and setting the division's goals and priorities within the relationships with those churches and their callings to mission. In two countries, Senegal and Bangladesh, this church's Division for Global Mission works in first-stage evangelism in anticipation of forming Christian congregations and eventually a church.

Activities and Programs
Ongoing Programs

In partnership with other churches, the Evangelical Lutheran Church in America, through its Division for Global Mission, supports evangelism activities that bring people to faith in Jesus Christ. Most evangelism programs in which the division is involved are primarily congregation-based, that is, established congregations support new outreach efforts whose goal is the establishment of new congregations in which believers are called and nurtured in the Christian faith. Most Lutheran churches continue to reach out, developing new preaching points and a variety of ministries among peoples where the Lutheran church is not established.

A wide range of proclamation ministries support the witness of the congregations: radio broadcasts, cassette tape ministries, student ministries and university centers, and Christian publications. Education, teaching of English, social ministries, health ministries, relief and development work, agricultural work, and community development remain stalwart ministries where the Good News of God's abundant life is witnessed to and made a reality in Jesus' name.

The Division for Global Mission offers gifts and resources from this church for these ministries in primarily two ways: (1) people (missionaries, volunteers, seminary interns) and (2) funds (financial grants directly to churches and indirectly through ecumenical agencies such as the Lutheran World Federation). The total allocation for these ministries in 1995 is $4,206,443. The division also offers the gifts of partnership in prayer, fellowship, exchanges and visits, training, scholarships, and consultation. In all these ways, members of this church are answering God's call to proclaim the good news of Jesus Christ.

New Directions

Islam. Building on the relationships this church has established within and near Muslim communities, the Division for Global Mission is developing strategies to assist churches toward more effective witness among Muslims. Muslims number about one billion people, representing the largest single community of faith outside Christianity.

Not only do Christians live in close contact with Muslims in northern and eastern Africa, the Middle East, southeastern Europe, and southern Asia, but we are aware of their growing presence in the United States and throughout the western hemisphere. Historically and currently there is much misunderstanding and, in some areas, violence between Christians and Muslims. For the most part Christians have not been successful or creative in building positive relationships with Muslims and in sharing their Christian witness among them.

Given the large numbers of Muslims, this history of failures, and our close proximity to Muslim peoples, this church's Division for Global Mission is concentrating effort on this concern within its priority on evangelism.

Much of the planning for this new effort grew out of a report and recommendations submitted by the Rev. Roland Miller after visits to the Division for Global Mission ministries located in Islamic contexts. Through a deepened understanding of Islam both by study and through encounters with Muslims, two main areas give focus to the division's activities with its partners: (1) training and equipping for effective Christian witness among Muslims, and (2) reconciliation and peacemaking between Christian and Muslim communities.

Special Islam study programs and placement of professors at Luther Theological Seminary, St. Paul, Minn., and at the Lutheran School of Theology at Chicago provide special study opportunities for this church's missionaries, partner church leaders, and international scholarship recipients (Ethiopia, Indonesia, Nigeria, Papua New Guinea, and Tanzania). The Division for Global Mission has conducted two-week study programs for missionaries in Bangladesh, Cameroon, the Central African Republic, Finland, Ghana, India, Indonesia, Jerusalem, Kenya, Madagascar, Nigeria, Senegal, Singapore, and Tanzania) and church leaders (Ethiopia) for three consecutive summers. A fourth is planned.

Overseas, this division has provided seminar funding for local evangelists, pastors, and church leaders (Ethiopia). Several missionary professors teach Islamic studies in institutions overseas and conduct seminars for local Christians (Great Britain, Egypt, and Indonesia). Others are strategically placed in outreach programs of partner churches (Cameroon, the Central African Republic, and Madagascar).

The Division for Global Mission is supporting efforts at peace-making and reconciliation especially where tensions are high. The establishment of a Christian-Muslim center in Nigeria, for example, is underway. Additional study centers and seminars have been requested (Cameroon and the Middle East). The division participates in an ecumenical organization, Program for Christian-Muslim Relations in Africa (PROCMURA), that educates and supports churches' ministries among Muslims of West Africa. Occasionally advocacy efforts are made in Washington, D.C., or elsewhere.

Major Religions and Secularism in Asia. Given the overwhelming numbers of people in Asia who have not heard or fully heard the Gospel, missionaries of this church and partner church leaders are making new efforts in studying and analyzing the religious context in Asia. They hope to deepen our understanding of the role of Hinduism, Buddhism, and Chinese folk religion in people's lives. Missionaries with special expertise in these religious traditions are already placed in a variety of learning-teaching settings in Asia (Thailand, Indonesia, India, Hong Kong, and Singapore). A staff team is receiving reports from these resource persons and will take a critical look at a variety of approaches and methods for witness in Asia. The team will present a proposal for priorities and concrete strategies for the division's involvement in Asia.

Poor, Marginalized, and Suffering People. Christian churches, and particularly the "rich" churches of the North are challenged to examine God's calling to mission in many places where poverty and oppression are a daily experience. Churches caught in economic downturns become more sensitive to witness with love and compassion among and on behalf of the poor (Suriname and Tanzania). A number of predominately middle-class churches in Latin America are reflecting on God's calling to mission among poor and disadvantaged persons. Churches are examining their structures and policies to ascertain what influence middle class values might have on their faithfulness to poor people (Brazil, Argentina, and Chile). Brothers and sisters in Christ in the so-called third world are inviting this church through its Division for Global Mission to reflect on our responsibility to accompany and support Christ's mission in these contexts. Churches in Latin America, the Caribbean, and North America, whose members are primarily immigrant in background, face new challenges to reach out creatively and effectively among the indigenous peoples in their country.

Urbanization. In general, the Lutheran churches around the world have their roots and often the majority of their membership in rural areas. Much of the mission movement of the 19th and 20th centuries has been rural in its orientation and tended to neglect outreach opportunities in urban areas. With the rapid urbanization of today's world populations, Christian churches are being challenged to examine the scope of their commitments and to make new resolves to give sufficient energies to Christ's mission in the cities.

The Witnesses

In areas where the Church has experienced significant growth (Africa, Madagascar, and Papua New Guinea), the *lay evangelists* are almost without exception the critical factor in sharing the Gospel. They often serve(d) without salary or with very low compensation. *Women* normally play a key role in the growth of the Church, often being quite creative and innovative in their approaches, witnessing to God's love in Christ through song, drama, soup kitchens, and a variety of social ministries witnessing to God's love in Christ

(India, Peru, and Nicaragua). The lay ministries of health, education, agriculture, and other development areas communicate the love of the Gospel and open the way for baptisms into the Christian faith.

In 1995, 54 missionaries of this church's Division for Global Mission serve in evangelism assignments in 25 countries. Some develop new areas of outreach, usually partnering with a local pastor or evangelist. Others serve in congregations with unique ministries such as English language congregations. Missionaries often teach and equip evangelists and other church workers and members for their ministries. They support the ongoing church life, women's and youth programs, translation and communications ministries. A growing number of missionaries are teaching in the areas of witness among peoples of other faiths. As the churches continue to meet the mission challenge and to nurture subsequent generations of Christians, leadership development goes hand in hand with an effective evangelism program. As the churches develop their own workers and leaders, the task of the missionaries becomes more specialized and more focused on the development of local leaders.

Financial Support for Mission

Even though a dynamic witness or a faithful response to the Gospel cannot be "purchased" by funds given to support the mission of Christ, the churches' programs and workers need financial support to carry out their goals. Lack of funding means the Church cannot send pastors and evangelists into new areas. When churches grow as people respond to the Gospel, support for pastors and leaders to nurture new Christians is critical. Declining support can require that theological education and training programs for evangelists and pastors be trimmed back.

The area program directors provided examples of needs that could be met by this division if the funding was available. The following list from the Latin America, Caribbean, and Mexico programs is a small sample of the opportunities we are given. This concrete invitation to the members of this church calls us to a more faithful response of sharing the Gospel of Jesus Christ in today's global village.

Latin America, Caribbean, Mexico

Argentina: missionary personnel and funding for ministry among working class people

Brazil: support for South-South missionaries from Brazil

Chile: outreach ministry strategy needs to be created

Colombia: (1) funding of evangelist program
(2) missionary personnel in Saliva

Cuba: train Cuban ordained pastors and others at Martin Luther Institute and Ecumenical Seminary in Matanzas, including a missionary for these two institutions.

El Salvador: (1) coordinated outreach strategy by regions, including training and mission coordinator position
(2) expansion of Centro do Pastoral faculty at Salvadorean Lutheran University

Guyana: encouragement of evangelism efforts

Haiti: identify and train Haitian pastoral leadership

Mexico: (1) encourage joint training efforts and networking among Lutheran church bodies in Mexico
(2) support evangelism efforts of the new Mexican National Lutheran Church in northern Mexico

Nicaragua: missionary personnel to assist pastoral teams and this church's outreach strategy

Peru: missionary for leadership development and to assist with outreach ministry

Suriname: (1) seminars on Islam for leaders and members
(2) expansion of Mattenshoop outreach program
(3) evangelism workshops for members

Exhibit B

Summary of Evaluation: Leadership Development

**Board of the Division for Global Mission
March 17-19, 1994**

This report is a condensed summary of the full report of the evaluation of the Leadership Development program of the Division for Global Mission.

The Priority

The Division for Global Mission's priority of Leadership Development allocates the division's resources to the discovery, formation, and undergirding of persons who are or can be leaders within the churches with whom the division relates. Three areas of emphasis give direction to the priority: (1) the development of the potential and leadership of women; (2) programs of theological education and programs that support lay and clergy ministries; and (3) sending missionaries who equip and empower others for leadership.

Activities and Resources

The board of the Division for Global Mission reviewed the churches' leadership development programs and institutions, in addition to international scholarships and education for witness among Muslims. This worldwide program represents slightly over 15 percent of the 1994 global mission budget. This amount includes grants to institutions and church leadership programs, scholarships (in-country and international), and the cost of this church's missionaries serving in leadership development. The funding for personnel and programs underway in 1994 at the time of the reporting was:

Missionary support	$2,519,805
Grants to institutions/programs	530,134
In-country scholarships	134,502
International scholarships (1993)	645,652
TOTAL	$3,830,093

The churches with which the Division for Global Mission cooperates have taken responsibility for the development of their leaders. These programs (almost 70) include seminaries, Bible schools, theological education by extension programs, and continuing education programs. Although most leadership development programs focus on theological education for pastors, training and continuing education for evangelists, catechists, women, and other church workers are provided. Globally, the faculties of schools are predominantly staffed by local teachers. Their education programs range from short courses to certificate and diploma programs, to bachelor's, master's, and doctor's degrees.

The challenges facing the churches vary greatly depending on many factors including age of the church, education levels in the society, church growth, historical commitment to lay and clergy development, and access to graduate programs for the development of local faculties. An emerging emphasis on leadership development opportunities for women has caused churches and their mission partners to review the grassroots and undergraduate opportunities that are, or in many cases are not, available to women. These preliminary opportunities are crucial for women for entry into seminary and other upper level programs.

Historically, American churches have provided crucial assistance for local faculty development through their international scholarship programs. Most often these programs brought students to the United States for study. One of the needs in many areas is development of local and regional graduate programs. The Division for Global Mission is reviewing graduate programs offered in the various regions and intends to increase support for placement of students in contexts outside the United States (South-South). This allows students to study closer to their local context and increases the number of students able to engage in graduate programs.

In reviewing this division's *missionaries* involved in theological and church leadership development programs, the global picture reveals a highly trained, strategically-placed theological training staff serving with sister churches in more than 25 countries. The missionary staff of this church is assigned to 52 theological schools, six TEE (theological education by extension) programs, and six other training programs. Among these deployed staff are approximately 55 full-time missionary teachers (plus two part-time). Six long-term volunteers and many short-term volunteers (including seminary professors on sabbaticals) add to the teaching staff the division offered in 1994. This missionary faculty is equivalent in size to that of Luther Seminary, this church's largest seminary.

Though the majority serve in programs where English is the medium of instruction, at least 14 other languages are used: Arabic, Chinese, French, Fulani, Fulfulde, Gbaya, Japanese, Malagasy, Melanesian Pidgin, Portuguese, Sáliba, Sango, Spanish, and Swahili.

A review of the academic background of 55 assigned persons and their spouses (more than 100 persons) reveals 25 with doctorates plus three candidates soon to complete their programs. Four women are among the 25 holding doctorates. Forty-two hold master's degrees including Master in Theology, Master of Divinity, and numerous other fields.

A small portion of the teaching positions are filled by women. Among the total number of women are 20 holding master's degrees and 24 holding bachelor's or registered nurse (2) degrees. Most women serve "informally" as spouses in related teaching responsibilities such as English, education, and social sciences. The Division for Global Mission, in reviewing its priority on the full participation of women in the life of this church, will be seeking to more clearly identify and formally recognize the contributions of these women whose service often goes unrecognized and unaffirmed. A review of their expertise and contributions is a first step in this process.

The eight theological *seminaries of the Evangelical Lutheran Church in America*, through grants and scholarships to international graduate students sponsored by the Division for Global Mission, literally double the division's resources in training global leaders through ELCA institutions. A recent survey reveals that the seminaries match the division's resources, dollar for dollar, in the investment made to support international students from sister churches. The division's 1994 budgetary commitment in assisting students to study outside their home country is $648,047. Currently, 41 jointly-supported students study at the eight institutions. In addition to the monetary support is the investment of mentoring, hospitality, family support, and caretaking.

Lutheran School of Theology at Chicago (Ill.)	10
Lutheran Theological Seminary at Gettysburg (Pa.)	2
Luther Seminary (St. Paul, Minn.)	11
Pacific Lutheran Theological Seminary (Berkeley, Calif.)	2
Lutheran Theological Seminary at Philadelphia (Pa.)	2
Lutheran Theological Southern Seminary (Columbia, S.C.)	1
Trinity Lutheran Seminary (Columbus, Ohio)	5
Wartburg Theological Seminary (Dubuque, Iowa)	9

Report of the
Commission for Multicultural Ministries

Organization
Steering Committee

In its composition, the steering committee of the Commission for Multicultural Ministries is unique among ELCA governing entities. The steering committee is composed of 20 persons, including four each from the African American, Asian, Hispanic, Native American, and White membership of this church. The steering committee is formed on the basis of parity within each community of peoples, with each having equal representation and participation in the processes of decision making.

Two African American, Asian, Hispanic, and Native American members are nominated from the membership of their respective associations. The boards of the six churchwide divisions each nominate one additional member from the collective membership of those four communities. The ELCA Church Council nominates the remaining six members. The Church Council then elects the nominees to the steering committee.

The current members are:

Rev. Duane L. Addison, Fridley, Minn. (term expires 1997)
Ms. Inez Torres Davis, Chicago, Ill. (1995)
Rev. Jose Gustavo Guerrero, Dallas, Tex. (1995)
Ms. Daphne Gustafson, *secretary*, Fairbanks, Alaska (1995)
Mr. George E. Harris, Carson, Calif. (1995)
Rev. Callon W. Holloway Jr., *vice chair*, Columbus, Ohio (1999)
Ms. Juliet Yuen Hsia, Honolulu, Hawaii (1995)
Rev. Margrethe S. C. Kleiber, San Diego, Calif. (1999)
Ms. L. DeAne Lagerquist, Northfield, Minn. (1999)
Rev. Ivis J. LaRiviere-Mestre, Allentown, Pa. (1997)
Ms. Jennie Lightfoot, New Brighton, Minn. (1997)
Mr. Ezekiel Martin, Santa Ana, Calif. (1997)
Mr. Joel D. Mugge, Minneapolis, Minn. (1997)
Mr. Erik Phelps, Eau Claire, Wis. (1995)
Ms. Audrey Russell, Philadelphia, Pa. (1999)
Mr. Jack Russell, Fincastle, Va. (1997)
Mr. Alfred Sagar, Kalamazoo, Mich. (1999)
Rev. Kenneth W. Wheeler, Milwaukee, Wis. (1995)
Rev. Edmond Yee, *chair*, Berkeley, Calif. (1995)
Mr. LeRoy D. Zimmerman, St. Louis, Mo. (1999)

Advisors
Rev. Lowell G. Almen, secretary, Evangelical Lutheran Church in America
Bishop George P. Mocko, Delaware-Maryland Synod
Ms. Joanne Chadwick, executive director, Commission for Women

Ethnic Associations

The mandate of the Commission for Multicultural Ministries is to organize itself into African American, Asian, Hispanic, and Native American communities. The commission has developed a process for the recognition of ethnic associations. The commission's steering committee recognizes the following ELCA-affiliated associations (ELCA 16.22.A91.c.):

- African American Lutheran Association in the Evangelical Lutheran Church in America; the Rev. Cheryl Stewart-Pero, *president*;
- Asociación Luterana de Ministerios Hispanos de la Iglesia Evangélica Luterana en América; the Rev. Arthur B. Wyse, *president*;
- Association of Asians—Evangelical Lutheran Church in America; the Rev. Dwight Ong, *president*; and
- Native American Lutheran Association—Evangelical Lutheran Church in America; Ms. Lynda Jarsocrak, *president*.

While the ethnic associations are a part of this church through affiliation with this commission, they also are independent. They are responsible for their own operating budgets and programs. They determine their own criteria for membership and elect their own officers. The commission provides some financial support for the associations. Its steering committee may withdraw affiliation from any association that acts in violation of the ELCA constitution or related procedures.

Staff

Executive Director: Rev. Frederick E. N. Rajan
Assistant Director for Administration: Ms. Doris Christine May
Coordinating Director for Ethnic Ministries: Ms. Carmen Rabell-Freire
Director for Multicultural Mission Strategy: Rev. William E. Wong
Director for Synodical Ministries: Ms. Tammy Jackson

The Commission for Multicultural Ministries has a total of five executive and three support staff members. Two executive and one support staff members have primary responsibility for administration, and three executive staff members have primary responsibility for commission programs, such as the Multicultural Mission Strategy, ethnic ministries, and synodical ministries.

In addition to their programmatic responsibilities, executive staff persons work with regional and synodical multicultural ministries committees. This work is coordinated through the synodical ministries program.

Constitutional Mandate

As Lutheran Christians, we are heirs to a tradition that confesses Jesus Christ as Lord. Christ, through faith by the power of the Holy Spirit, calls us, a diverse people, to reconciliation in his name and sends us among other peoples with a unique mission to baptize and teach God's creative, redeeming, and sanctifying activity (Matthew 28: 18-20). Jesus promises to be with us always even to the end of the age.

God created us with unique characteristics; our diversity is first and foremost a gift from God. As human beings, we have developed a wide variety of cultures that express our diversity. We celebrate this diversity—that we are at once distinct from one another and yet joined to one another through our Creator.

In recognizing our cultural differences, we affirm that Christ was crucified, died, and was raised for the people of every culture and race. As members of one Church, we meet each other in our diversity as the body of Christ. In this church, as in the rest of society, our cultural differences are a reality. As culture-bearing people carrying out God's mission of proclaiming the Gospel "to the ends of the earth," we encounter each other and each other's cultures.

God places people in a variety of ethnic families and cultures. Those differences, however, are more than genes and color. The incarnation—God taking on human form—is an event that by its very nature suggests that the Gospel will take on cultural forms. While the Evangelical Lutheran Church in America is an ethnically diverse church including persons whose heritage is Danish, Estonian, Finnish, German, Latvian, Norwegian, Slovak, Swedish, etc., its predominantly Western European membership does not reflect the pluralistic character of U.S. and Caribbean society.

Persons in all cultures who have come face-to-face with God in Christ Jesus have an internal imperative to share the good news. The love of God, revealed in Jesus Christ, compels us to reach out with the Gospel. Christian mission can be authentic only when it struggles against injustices that are dramatically opposed to the

kingdom of God and when it looks for a response in an act of faith that issues in commitment.

The effort is not easy. The Church's mission is an act of hope rather than a manipulation of the future. We are mindful that even though many may toil in tears without seeing much result, sooner or later God will honor their witness and many will respond in faith to the Gospel's invitation, for as the psalmist reminds us "those who go out weeping, bearing the seed for sowing, shall come home with shouts of joy, carrying their sheaves" (Psalm 126:6).

The goal of God's mission is expressed clearly by Christ who said, "As the Father sent me, so send I you" (John 20:21). Christ expressed that ministry of mission when he said, "Preach good news to the poor, proclaim release to the captives and recovering of sight to the blind, set at liberty those who are oppressed" (Luke 4:18-19). The essential mission work of this church, therefore, consists of evangelism, advocacy for justice, social ministry, and the nurturing of people and congregations to serve as God's instruments of mission. The result of this ministry in mission depends upon the power of God.

The purpose of the commission is to assist this church in working toward the goal of full partnership and participation of African Americans, Asians, Hispanics, and Native Americans in the life of this church and society. The constitutional mandate of this commission is defined in continuing resolution 16.22.A91. of the Constitutions, Bylaws, and Continuing Resolutions of the Evangelical Lutheran Church in America.

Response to
1993 Churchwide Assembly Referrals
Deaf Ministry (CA93.8.107)

As directed by the Churchwide Assembly, the Commission for Multicultural Ministries worked with the Division for Church in Society and the Church Council in addressing the question of making the deaf community one of the five emphasis groups in the commission. A response on this matter will be transmitted to the 1995 Churchwide Assembly by the Church Council.

Representational Principles (CA93.7.47)

In response to the actions taken by the 1993 Churchwide Assembly and the subsequent meetings of the Church Council and the Executive Committee of the Church Council, the Commission for Multicultural Ministries prepared reflections on this church's representational principles. Fifteen reflections on the representational principles were presented to the Church Council at its fall 1994 meeting. These 15 two-page reflections were prepared by African American, Asian,

Hispanic, Native American, and White members of this church who are clergy and lay, male and female, and from many age groups and from different geographical areas. The Commission for Multicultural Ministries forwarded the 15 reflections to the Church Council as information and called on the Evangelical Lutheran Church in America to maintain the representational principles as presently stated in the ELCA constitution.

Report of Work 1993-1995

Anti-Racism Training Institute: The Commission for Multicultural Ministries developed this institute in response to the reality of the sin of racism, the commission's constitutional responsibilities, and God's mission of reconciliation. Invitations were sent to all synods. In 1993 and 1994, the institute provided anti-racism training for nine synodical teams. Each team is multicultural and composed of four to five members selected by the synod. The institute provided information and skills training so that the teams can better understand and identify racism, conduct anti-racism education workshops, and work and organize against racism. The synod teams work within the context of their synod and its congregations. In 1995, four synod teams will participate in this training.

Arab/Middle Eastern Ministries: Following up on the Multicultural Mission Strategy adopted by the 1991 Churchwide Assembly and the 1992 ELCA Arab/Middle Eastern Consultation, this church committed itself to developing ministry with Arab and other Middle Eastern persons in the United States. To assist in this effort, the Commission for Multicultural Ministries provided the services of a consultant. The consultant's responsibilities included assisting the Association of Lutherans of Arab and Middle Eastern Heritage; producing a quarterly ELCA Arab/Middle Eastern newsletter; and providing assistance related to Arab/Middle Eastern ministries. These efforts have resulted in the formation of the Association of Lutherans of Arab and Middle Eastern Heritage in 1993; the recruiting of several future Arab pastors; and the ongoing development of ELCA Arab/Middle Eastern ministries.

Multicultural Mission Institute: The 1993 Multicultural Mission Institute was held at Chandler, Ariz., under the theme, "Together in Mission: A Multicultural Church in a Changing World." The 1994 institute, under the theme, "Generations Together in a Multicultural Church," was held at Minneapolis. The institutes focused on and shared information about ministry in African American, Asian, Hispanic, Native American, and multicultural settings. A total of 500 people from all parts of this church participated in these events. The institute is part of the Commission for Multicultural Ministries' Multicultural Mission Strategy effort.

Multicultural Mission Strategy: The 1991 Churchwide Assembly adopted the "Multicultural Mission Strategy: A Strategy for Proclamation of the Gospel." The director for Multicultural Mission Strategy serves in the Commission for Multicultural Ministries. The director convenes the Multicultural Mission Strategy staff team, composed of staff from other churchwide units. Together, they monitored churchwide unit strategy implementation efforts, held discussions with churchwide unit boards and steering committees, encouraged churchwide unit implementation plans, and made recommendations to the cabinet of executives. Work with the Department for Research and Evaluation continues in developing instruments and processes to evaluate the strategy's progress. A more detailed report of churchwide unit activities in implementing the Multicultural Mission Strategy will be presented during the 1995 Churchwide Assembly.

African American, Asian, Hispanic, and Native American Advisory Meetings: Focused on issues of advocacy, leadership from the African American, Asian, Hispanic and Native American communities met to consider key advocacy issues vital to the life of each community within this church.

African American, Asian, Hispanic, and Native American News Bulletins: Quarterly news bulletins or occasional letters were developed and mailed to rostered people and leaders of the ethnic communities. These bulletins provided support and affirmation to the leadership and communicated ELCA churchwide programs and activities that were relevant to African American, Asian, Hispanic, and Native American communities.

African American, Asian, Hispanic, and Native American Ministry Reports: The commission developed and distributed ministry reports for each ethnic community to provide as much data and information as possible about ELCA efforts in ministering among African Americans, Asians, Hispanics, and Native Americans.

Ethnic Associations Support: Operating grants, technical assistance, and training, as well as advice and counsel, are provided to the African American, Asian, Hispanic and Native American ethnic associations to support their efforts in serving their communities.

Ministries Visits: Visits to ethnic and culture-specific ministries were made by African American, Asian, Hispanic, and Native American ethnic directors to affirm and support mission in these places and to assess needs, opportunities, and challenges for future development of programs and activities in this church.

Rooted in the Gospel: In partnership with the Division for Congregational Ministries, African American leaders were brought together for a national event to evaluate an African American spiritual formation congregational resource. They also participated in a training event designed to help African Americans in the ELCA connect or reconnect their faith journey with their African American heritage. People trained in this national event were chosen in teams to assist in five regional events held in 1994 and 1995.

Black Family Ministries Project: An ecumenical project involving ten other church bodies provided training for consultants to assist congregations in planning and implementing ministries with African American families. A Black Family Ministries manual was produced.

ELCA Black Family Ministries Consultants Training: In partnership with the Division for Church in Society, further training was provided for all ELCA Black family consultants trained at the Black Family Project.

Chinese Ministry Consultation: In partnership with the Division for Outreach, a consultation with Chinese pastors in southern California was held to develop a Chinese ministry and outreach strategy for the Division for Outreach.

Hispanic Area Meetings: Seven meetings were held in areas of high concentration of Hispanics. They provided a forum for dialogue among the participants, as well as information for the development of future programs and activities for Hispanics in this church.

Hispanic Lay Educators Conference: In partnership with the Division for Ministry, a conference for coordinators and directors of Hispanic lay training programs was held to share information and to assess needs and opportunities to enhance the programs and explore new ways of theological education for Hispanics in this church.

1993 Planning Guide for Native American Awareness Sunday: A planning guide was produced for groups and congregations that expressed an interest in observing a Native American Awareness Sunday in 1993. The packet included worship materials, a Bible study, worship inserts, adult forum materials, and additional information on other resources.

Multicultural Seminarians Conference: Approximately 45 African American, Asian, Hispanic, and Native American master of divinity candidates were brought together in Chicago for a three-day conference. This conference was planned in partnership with the Division for Ministry. The purpose of the conference was to increase the seminarians' knowledge of this church, to improve their leadership skills, and to strengthen their cultural identity in order that they might become more effective as leaders in this church.

Synodical Ministries: Multicultural ministries committees have been established in 58 synods of this church. These committees comprise 575 volunteer members. The Commission for Multicultural Ministries

provides a full-time director to work in partnership with synods to support the work of the multicultural ministries committees. Activities of this program include leadership education and training, on-site consultations, an annual grant program, and resource development. During 1994-1995, the commission held several town meetings in synods with the synodical multicultural ministries committees to listen and dialogue about opportunities and concerns of this ministry from the perspective of local leadership.

ELCA Multicultural Writers Workshop: This project grew out of an increasing need for diverse writers in the Evangelical Lutheran Church in America. It seeks to identify experienced African American, Asian, Hispanic, and Native American writers who are interested in writing for ELCA publications and resources. During the 1993-95 biennium, a total of 23 writers were identified and introduced to the range of writing opportunities within this church. The project already has borne fruit. The work of many of the writers has been published in ELCA publications and resources. The commission leads this interunit project with the Department for Communication, the Division for Congregational Ministries, *The Lutheran*, Women of the Evangelical Lutheran Church in America, and the Publishing House of the Evangelical Lutheran Church in America.

Ethnic Ministries: In 1993, an extensive and thorough report on the state of African American, Asian, Hispanic, and Native American ministries in the Evangelical Lutheran Church in America was proposed in partnership with all churchwide units. This resource was distributed widely to African American, Asian, Hispanic, and Native American congregations, ELCA seminaries, college and university libraries, and synodical offices.

In 1994, ethnic ministries in the commission underwent a significant change. Ethnic ministry director positions were replaced by ethnic ministry consultants. This action resulted in more funding for ethnic ministries programs of the commission. In the African American, Asian, Hispanic, Native American and White communities, many have voiced concern over this change.

In February 1995, the CMM steering committee again addressed the question of ethnic ministries staffing. After considering different options, the steering committee opted for a staffing arrangement of program directors with shared responsibilities. The new ethnic ministry staffing arrangement includes:

- Director for African American Ministries and Synodical Ministries
- Director for Asian Ministries and Multicultural Mission Strategy

- Director for Hispanic Ministries and Leadership Development
- Director for Native American Ministries and Racial Justice Ministries

The implications of this new staffing arrangement are that:

- there will be an ethnic ministry director for each African American, Asian, Hispanic, and Native American community;
- ethnic ministries directors will spend approximately 50 percent of their staff time on other responsibilities of the commission, such as support for the synodical multicultural ministries, coordinating the Multicultural Mission Strategy efforts of this church, support of leadership development needs of the various communities, and addressing the racial justice ministry of this church;
- the services of ethnic ministry consultants will be terminated, effective April 15, 1995; and
- funding of some of the current plans and activities of the commission gradually will be reallocated to pay for the additional ethnic ministry staffing.

An extensive network has been established with the African American, Asian, Hispanic, and Native American membership by meeting regularly with community leaders, congregations, and the leadership of each ethnic association. In 1994, each ethnic association received training in membership and fund development. Ethnic association presidents' summits were held to address issues and concerns of the associations. Meetings were held with churchwide units to address the strategies of supporting the ethnic-specific ministries of this church.

"You Can't Do It Alone: Fighting Racism": This study guide and videotape was produced by the Commission for Multicultural Ministries to assist young adults, ages 15-25, to respond to issues of racism in church and society. The resource presents an overview of the issue of racism for youth in congregations or local gatherings. Each of the six sessions has a brief (three to six minute) video introduction, followed by suggested group activities outlined in the 30 page study guide.

No Hate Allowed: The commission produced a resource for congregations for action against racial hate crimes. Racial hate-crime violence is real—and it hurts. When violence and injustice are allowed to flourish and when people are attacked because of their race, it is not only the victims, but also their families, congregations, and communities that stand to lose. Christians, now more than ever, need to be the ambassadors of reconciliation and to be messengers of peace and good news. How can we become stronger ministries to victims, agents of love, builders of community, and advocates for peace? And what resources are available to help us?

This resource offers theological reflections; a litany and Bible study; stories about the ways people are affected by racial violence; an action section, including ways to prevent racial hate crimes and to move from debate to dialogue; and a resource listing of organizations, publications, and people to contact for further education and networking. This resource is available in both English and Spanish.

God's People Building Bridges: This guide for conducting basic cultural awareness workshops is available from the ELCA Distribution Service. The commission is working with synods to train individuals to conduct training events utilizing this resource.

Major Program Directions 1995-1997

The ELCA constitution states that commissions are assigned the responsibility of assisting this church to address specific tasks of particular urgency by providing advice, counsel, and services in the areas of the commission's specific function to the divisions, other churchwide units, Church Council, congregations, and synods of this church (ELCA constitutional provision 16.22.). This commission provides advice and counsel to all expressions of this church through its staff, consultants, and by consultations. Services to all the expressions of this church include providing training, resources, and funding. The functions of this commission include:

1. review and monitoring of program directions and plans;
2. development and recommendation of strategies, plans, policies, and procedures;
3. assistance in developing and implementing strategies;
4. assistance in leadership development and support;
5. assistance to this church in dealing with racism and in ministering within a multicultural context;
6. assistance in assessment and response to ethnic-specific needs and opportunities;
7. facilitation of dialogue among and between all five ethnic communities;
8. assistance in development and implementation of cooperative efforts with the ethnic communities in society, in other Christian communities, and in other religious traditions.

Within this context, the following major program directions were developed for the commission:

Association Leadership Development: In consultation with the associations, the commission offers leadership development training for association leaders.

African American, Asian, Hispanic, and Native American Ministries Report: The commission prepares and distributes a biennial "state of the church" report about the African American, Asian, Hispanic, and Native American communities in 1995 and 1997.

Church Workers Directory: The commission maintains accurate mailing addresses of African American, Asian, Hispanic, and Native American ordained and lay leaders, and publishes an annual African American, Asian, Hispanic, and Native American church-workers directory.

Consultations: The commission annually brings together leaders from the African American, Asian, Hispanic, Native American, and White communities to address community concerns and explore ways to address these concerns. Through the consultants and ethnic-specific consultations, it addresses community concerns with all the expressions of this church.

Multicultural Leadership Skills Event: The majority of multicultural ministry committees at the synodical and regional level have been given the task of assisting their synod and region to function more multiculturally. Beginning in 1995, regional Multicultural Leadership Skills Events will be organized. These events will offer participants basic knowledge and skills needed to effect change individually and institutionally.

Consultative Services: This program will provide consultative services to regional and synodical multicultural ministry committees that will assist them in committee organization and development, strategic planning, multicultural and culture-specific programming, and resource planning and development.

Synodical Multicultural Mission Strategy: Beginning in 1995, efforts will be made to develop the multicultural mission strategy at the synodical level. This activity will include assisting synods with strategic planning and training.

Support for Arab and Middle Eastern Ministry Development: Arab and Middle Eastern population is on the increase in this nation. The purpose of this program is to create a ministry of witness and service with and among these persons both within this church and within their communities that affirms the dignity and worth of the Arab and other Middle Eastern people and their culture.

Multicultural Mission Institute: Beginning in 1995, the annual Multicultural Mission Institute will become an inter-generational event with activities and programs for persons of all ages.

Anti-Racism Training Institute: Synods are an important partner in this church's effort to address racism. Synods must be equipped to conduct anti-racism training events in their own setting. This commission will continue to train anti-racism teams in synods. Beginning in 1995, four synodical teams will be trained each year.

Anti-Racism Videotape Resource: Providing anti-racism educational resources to this church is one of the responsibilities of this commission. In 1995, an educational videotape resource with a study guide will be released by this commission. A decision on any new videotape production will be made in 1996.

Multicultural Writers Workshop: The workshop serves as a vehicle to identify and train skilled writers from the African American, Asian, Hispanic, and Native American community as writers for this church. In 1995, another Multicultural Writers Workshop will be held.

Multicultural Seminarians Conference: This event supports ELCA African American, Asian, Hispanic, and Native American master of divinity candidates by increasing their knowledge of this church, improving their ministry skills, and strengthening their cultural identity, so that they will become more effective leaders in this church. A Multicultural Seminarians Event is planned for 1996.

Multicultural Leadership Data Bank: As this church moves along the continuum toward building a more multicultural church, leadership opportunities for African Americans, Asians, Hispanics, and Native Americans will continue to increase. This data bank of leadership information will undergo a significant updating in 1995.

Newsletter: A quarterly Commission for Multicultural Ministries newsletter, "CMM Messenger," will be published and distributed to all African American, Asian, Hispanic, and Native American congregations, ELCA seminaries, synods, churchwide units, and synodical multicultural ministry committee members.

COMMISSION FOR MULTICULTURAL MINISTRIES
EDMOND YEE, *Chair*
FREDERICK E. N. RAJAN, *Executive Director*

Report of the
Commission for Women

Organization
Steering Committee
Rev. Petunia Chung-Segré, Oakland Park, Fla. (1997)
Rev. Loren E. Halvorson, Stanchfield, Minn. (1995)
Ms. Heidi Helgemo, Plymouth, Minn. (1997)
Mr. Ronald K. Jacobson, Marysville, Wash. (1999)
Rev. Nancy K. Jewell, Wheaton, Minn. (1995)
Ms. Patricia Lemmerman, Allentown, Pa. (1999)
Mr. Eddie Martin, Erie, Pa. (1995)
Ms. Audrey R. Mortensen, Springfield, Mo. (1995)
Rev. Ann M. Tiemeyer, Van Nuys, Calif. (1999)
Mr. Reinaldo Valenzuela, El Paso, Tex. (1997)
Ms. Bea N. Vue-Benson, St. Paul, Minn. (1997)
Ms. Venice R. Williams-White, Milwaukee, Wis.
    (1999)

Advisors
Ms. Lita Brusick Johnson, executive assistant to the
    bishop, Office of the Bishop
Ms. Charlotte E. Fiechter, executive director, Women
    of the Evangelical Lutheran Church in America
Rev. Frederick E. N. Rajan, executive director,
    Commission for Multicultural Ministries
Bishop E. LeRoy Riley, New Jersey Synod

Staff
Executive Director: Ms. Joanne Chadwick
Director for Cross-Cultural Advocacy, Leadership
    and Budget Control: Ms. Charlotte D. Williams
Director for Studies and Leadership:
    Ms. Jean Martensen
Contract Staff for Special Projects:
    Rev. Jan Erickson-Pearson

Constitutional Mandate
It is the purpose of the Commission for Women to assist this church to acknowledge and utilize fully the gifts of women. The constitutional mandate of the Commission for Women is provided in continuing resolution 16.22.B91. of the Constitutions, Bylaws, and Continuing Resolutions of the Evangelical Lutheran Church in America

Report of Work 1993-1995
At the spring 1993 steering committee meeting, committee members ratified the following focus areas for the 1993-1994 biennium:

- Support the leadership of African American, Asian, Hispanic, and Native American women.
- Foster mutual understanding and support between women and men.
- Encourage women's networking.
- Promote safety.

The Commission for Women's vision of partnership was realized during the past biennium. With the reality of shrinking financial and human resources, the Commission for Women continued to nurture alliances with other churchwide units as it sought to carry out its mandate. Projects, training events, resources, and other accomplishments were achieved through a greater use of expertise and partnerships with congregational, synodical, and churchwide leaders. Much of the energy of the commission's staff is directed towards providing technical assistance, advice, and counsel to the ongoing work of other churchwide partners.

Support the Leadership of African American, Asian, Hispanic, and Native American Women
The commission worked to develop a network of women of color who are leaders in their congregations, synods, and other agencies of this church. A "Face-to-Face" video was completed and a "Spiritual Fast" resource was developed and distributed.

The Commission for Women sought to involve the members of its steering committee in more practical and relevant ways when it began to use the Women of Color Consulting Panel. The women of color who sit on the commission's steering committee are given a structured time frame in which to share information, hear what is going on in the communities in which they live and do ministry, and engage in learning from the expertise of other women of color. This process grew out of a project jointly sponsored by the Commission for Women and the Commission for Multicultural Ministries, the Consultation for African American, Asian, Hispanic, and Native American Women, and the Visioning Project (1992) in which women at the churchwide offices held a day of dialogue. The opportunity for mentoring and sharing knowledge has been a most fruitful and innovative method of utilizing the gifts of women of all cultures while continuing a process of leadership development.

At the 1993 Multicultural Women's Gathering sponsored by the Women of the Evangelical Lutheran Church in America, an announcement of a "Spiritual

Fast" initiative was made. A one-page resource giving biblical imperatives for fasting and providing suggestions for carrying out a fast was developed early in the process. Several congregations signed on to this initiative which was developed to model the "fasting" that people in ancient times did to face the challenges and adversity in their society. This comprehensive resource, which includes litanies, songs, and suggested readings, is available through the ELCA Distribution Service.

Foster Mutual Understanding and Support Between Women and Men

The commission was invited to attend the 1994 Lutheran Men in Mission Assembly held at Springfield, Ohio. An opportunity for listening and dialogue, the assembly provided the beginnings of a framework for the continuing work of the commission as it continues to create new paradigms in which women and men truly can be in partnership with one another.

The Commission for Women is pleased to be working on a major project with Lutheran Men in Mission and the various churchwide units to end domestic abuse. A "Stop the Violence" project envisions training events and resources for men's and women's groups on this topic.

Encourage Women's Networking

The commission receives numerous calls for recommendations of women to fill congregational, synodical, regional, and churchwide positions of leadership. The commission is able to respond through the *Name Exchange* project, solid relations with synod staffs, and participation in churchwide events.

Name Exchange: In an effort to identify the names of women who are in leadership, or exhibit leadership potential, the *Name Exchange* project was initiated. With a small grant from Lutheran Brotherhood for the start-up and development of the *Name Exchange* project, the commission moves into the age of technology. The project consists of the maintenance of a database of women who would be available for service in various leadership roles in every expression of this church. The comprehensive software allows ranking, processing, cross-referencing, and inventory of the women and their skills in order to facilitate more efficient and effective participation of women in the life of this church. To date, more than 500 names are listed in the *Name Exchange* system.

Synodical Relations: Another networking opportunity was created by the Commission for Women when the first meeting of the Women Assistants to the Bishops was held in February 1993. This event was an opportunity for women assistants to synodical bishops to meet one another, share information, and identify

concerns. Subsequent dialogues prompted the planning of another such gathering. The second gathering is planned for December 1995.

Various churchwide events have provided opportunities for initiating and supporting partnerships, and sustaining women's networks. For example, as a result of the 1994 consultation on clergy and sexual abuse, we now have a list of persons trained to provide related services within each of the 65 synods. Collegial work on the planning of the 25th anniversary celebration of Lutheran women's ordination, to be held in August 1995, has identified women who are supportive of women in ordained ministry. A newly formed network of women who organize around issues that affect women and children who live in poverty was formed in December 1994.

Promote a Safe Environment In Church and Society

The Commission for Women continues to receive calls and to respond to requests for information regarding sexual abuse by directing those who need assistance to the appropriate source. Listening continues to be an ongoing service of the commission as it assists this church to be a safe place for all.

As the Commission for Women continued its work to "Make this Church a Safe Place," three new resources were produced. "Support Groups for Victims of Sexual Abuse in the Church" and a fact sheet, "How Lutherans Responded to Rape in the Former Yugoslavia," were timely pieces developed to respond to inquiries, calls, and needs. The video, "New Faces of Courage," urges young men and women to train for peace building and to serve on unarmed intervention teams where there are conflicts at home and abroad. The resource, "If You Have Been Sexually Abused or Harassed," has been reprinted and continues to provide clear and concise information to ELCA members who are victims of sexual abuse and harassment.

The Commission for Women was instrumental in preparing and conducting a *Synodical Leadership Training Event* on the sexual abuse and misconduct of ordained ministers. Synodical leaders were equipped with resources, practical skills, and intervention processes that would assist persons within this church who have been so affected. Leadership for the ongoing work of implementing and coordinating this strategy is now lodged in the Division for Ministry. Monitoring this church's progress will remain the responsibility of the Commission for Women.

Resolution on Ending Violence against Women: The Commission for Women has continued to speak out on the issue of violence against women. In 1994, the Commission for Women met with the Women of the Evangelical Lutheran Church in America and the Division for Global Mission to frame a resolution on the ending of violence against women. This multi-unit effort was adopted by the boards of several churchwide units, as well as the Lutheran Youth Organization board. This resolution condemned violence against women at both the local and global levels, and called for the ELCA Church Council to "denounce and seek to eliminate the beating, sexual abuse, raping, and killing that threaten the lives and safety of women everywhere; urge members of the ELCA to make their homes and places of employment safe places where all may be free from physical abuse and those elements of the mass media which extol violence and the exploitation of women . . .." and, "to reiterate its support for the ratification of the Convention on the Elimination of Discrimination Against Women (CEDAW) in the near future."

Ongoing Work of the Commission

The commission continues to maintain statistics that examine closely the level of participation of women in this church. These statistics assist in the direction, development, and prioritizing of the work of the commission as it assists this church in achieving the full participation of women. The results and implications of this monitoring and gathering of data enable the commission to identify issues, suggest solutions, and to act in an "urgent and special" manner.

The steering committee of the Commission for Women initiated a dialogue on this church's representational principles. A dialogue by the steering committees of the Commission for Women and the Commission for Multicultural Ministries was held jointly at their spring 1993 meetings. The commissions were directed by the ELCA Church Council to collect stories from church members on the subject of representational principles as the ELCA sought to evaluate their effectiveness. Concept papers, personal stories, and testimonies enabled good discussion and a greater appreciation and understanding of the need for continuing such a mandate. Both the Commission for Women and the Commission for Multicultural Ministries recommended to the ELCA Church Council that use of the representational principles be retained.

The Commission for Women has provided leadership for the training of churchwide staff on sexual harassment in the form of workshops and resources. The commission also has been instrumental in the development of models that examine issues of equity, e.g., compensation, benefits, and pensions. The Commission for Women works cooperatively with other units in the planning and conducting of commemorative activities during Women's History Month. With the conclusion of the part-time staff agreement between the Commission for Women and the Lutheran Office for Governmental Affairs (LOGA), the commission celebrated the accomplishments made in regard to advocacy. Advocacy efforts on legislation that affected women were supported through a grant that the commission provided to the Lutheran Office for Governmental Affairs.

Leadership for Churchwide Emphases

The commission provides leadership in assisting this church in the implementation and development of two churchwide emphases:

Women and Children Living in Poverty

The Commission for Women staff played a major role in the writing and development of a comprehensive resource on the ELCA strategy on "Women and Children Living in Poverty: A Plan to Listen and Act." The resource includes stories of hope from women who have experienced poverty and the faith that brought them through very difficult times. In addition, the resource clearly spells out directives for congregations, synods, churchwide units, and ELCA-related agencies. It names the responsibilities each has to eradicate poverty and its consequences for women and children in our society.

In response to directives listed in the strategy, the Commission for Women and the Division for Congregational Ministries' social ministries program, jointly sponsored a Women's Organizing and Networking Event held at Louisville, Kentucky, December 9-11, 1994. Eighty men and women came from across the United States and Caribbean to exchange knowledge and information and to develop a network of women who organize around poverty and justice issues within their communities. Speakers, work groups, and dialogues better equipped the participants to network, serve and organize around issues that affect women. A resource will be produced to assist this church to understand better the gifts of persistence and perseverance that women so effectively utilize when they network and organize to empower women who are oppressed or abused.

Ecumenical Decade of Churches in Solidarity with Women (1988-1998)

The Ecumenical Decade of Churches in Solidarity with Women is a global movement now in its eighth year of a ten-year program. The "Decade" has three goals:

(1) full participation for women in the life of this church and in society;
(2) hearing and encouraging of women in theology and teaching; and
(3) the promotion of justice for women in this church and in society.

These goals make this commission's participation vital as it seeks to accomplish those goals as a church-wide unit of the Evangelical Lutheran Church in America.

Living Letter

In cooperation with the Women of the Evangelical Lutheran Church in America, the Division for Congregational Ministries, and the Division for Global Mission, the Commission for Women hosted one of the four-member "Living Letter" teams of the World Council of Churches that visited member churches worldwide. The members of the team visited the ELCA churchwide offices and various local ministries in the Chicago area, e.g., Bethel New Life, Isaiah Housing, and a nursing home, to gain a sense of the variety of roles women are now playing in church and community-based groups.

Major Directions 1995-1997

After a two-day process in which staff gave prayerful, thoughtful, and realistic reflection on the commission's mandate, its call to serve, and its financial restraints, the Commission for Women put forth the following two focus areas for the coming biennium:

(1) Promoting justice and full participation for women of all cultures in the life of this church and in society; and

(2) Assisting this church to create a safe environment for all women in this church and in society.

The constitutional mandate of the commission calls for the promotion of justice for women of all cultures. As in previous years, cross-cultural efforts will promote the leadership of African American, Asian, Hispanic, and Native American women. During the next biennium, the commission will work to foster a greater understanding of the relationship between women of color and white women. The connections, similarities, and differences between racism and sexism will be researched. The staff of the commission will explore more deeply the richly diverse ways that women engage in theology, work for justice, and live their lives in the hope that Jesus Christ gives. The commission will seek to formulate opportunities for women of all cultures to identify and exchange their gifts of ministry, leadership, and spirituality.

Assist this Church to Create A Safe Environment

As its constitutional mandate states, the commission will continue to assist this church in creating a safe environment for all women. During the next biennium, the Commission for Women will be engaged in a process of monitoring the efficiency and effectiveness of the "ELCA Strategy for Responding to Sexual Abuse in the Church." The commission will continue to address barriers and challenges that would hinder the elimination of sexual abuse in this church and in society. Broadening the definitions and developing a language that is conducive to both the victim's and the perpetrator's healing and recovery is a critical element in the development of a safe environment for the women of this church. Continued education and awareness of the implications and harmful nature of sexual abuse also will be lifted up.

Networking

During the past biennium, the commission was engaged in consultations, training, and research in order to uncover the most effective and productive methods by which to address the challenges of achieving full participation for women in this church. The Commission for Women began to use networking as a tool for communication, learning, and progressive action as the commission seeks to facilitate better the completion of its mandate.

With diminished financial resources, the commission seeks new and innovative ways in which to accomplish its mandate. In October 1994, a process was begun that would engage other units in the work of the commission in a more effective and efficient manner. A group was formed of resource persons from churchwide units in order that the many concerns and issues that affect women could reach a larger and more comprehensive audience.

The commission has received funding from Lutheran Brotherhood for a churchwide gathering of synodical leaders. These liaisons will act as contacts for the Commission for Women as it seeks to have the concerns of women addressed by every expression of this church. This two-day event will equip synodical leaders to "get the work of the commission done" at the synodical level.

The Commission for Women will provide leadership for continued fostering of partnerships and support between women and men, as well as for addressing the issue of sexism and the intricacies of women and men working together. The commission will focus on creating models and opportunities for dialogue and alliances between women and men through mutual understanding, commitment, and action as they witness to God's grace in the shared body of Christ.

Other Work

In August 1995, the Commission for Women, the Division for Ministry, the Women of the Evangelical Lutheran Church in America, and other supportive entities will celebrate the 25th anniversary of the ordination of Lutheran women in the U.S. Commemorative activities include a two-day event preceding the 1995 Churchwide Assembly in Minneapolis, Minn. The Commission for Women has provided scholarships to the eight seminaries of this church in order that a seminarian from each institution might attend this event. The commission will invite all ordained women to participate in a survey that will seek to identify issues and concerns of women in the ordained ministry, while helping also to set directions in some areas of the commission's work. The commission will update the statistical study on ordained women that was produced in 1990 in order to provide some comparative analysis.

The commission will continue to provide technical assistance and expertise when called upon. It also will continue to monitor, engage in research, and create opportunities and models to ensure the full participation of women of all cultures in the life of this church and in society.

STEERING COMMITTEE OF THE COMMISSION FOR WOMEN

AUDREY R. MORTENSEN, *Chair*
JOANNE CHADWICK, *Executive Director*

Report of the Department for Communication

Organization

Advisory Committee

Mr. Cliff Albert, El Cajon, Calif. (term to 1999)
Rev. Barbara Berry-Bailey, West Lawn, Pa. (1999)
Ms. Eva Reque David, Worcester, Mass. (1999)
Ms. Christine L. Davis, Hartford, Conn. (1997)
Ms. Gloria L. Jensen, Moorhead, Minn. (1995)
Rev. Randall R. Lee, Evanston, Ill. (1997)
Rev. Mark R. Ramseth, Great Falls, Mont. (1995)
Mr. Charles R. ("Dick") Reeves, Williamsburg, Va. (1997)
Mr. Barry G. Wittchen, Bethlehem, Pa. (1995)

Staff

Director: Rev. Eric C. Shafer
Director for Planning and Budget:
    Mr. Jerrold H. Bents
Director for Internal Communication:
    Ms. Sanda Horeis
Associate Directors for Internal Communication:
    Mr. Robert Elliott; Rev. Kurt A. Reichardt
Associate Director for Internal Communication
    (Hunger): Ms. Laurel M. Hensel
Assistant Director for Internal Communication
    (*Mosaic* producer): Mr. Tim Frakes
Assistant Director for Internal Communication
    (Spanish language translator):
    Ms. Magdalena Meza
Director for News and Information:
    Ms. Ann E. Hafften
Associate Director for News and Information:
    Mr. Frank F. Imhoff
Assistant Director for News and Information:
    Ms. Lia Christiansen
Director for Public Media: Mr. John L. Peterson
Senior Producer for Public Media (Lutheran Vespers
    Producer): Ms. Susan V. Greeley
Production Manager for Public Media:
    Ms. Rhonda Campbell
Director for Program Services and Administration,
    Lutheran Vespers: Ms. Irene Stangland
Speaker for Lutheran Vespers:
    Rev. Walter M. Wangerin Jr.
Director for Resource Information and Networks:
    Mr. Paul D. Edison-Swift
Editor for "Seeds for the Parish" and the "Action
    Packet": Ms. Marcia Erickson Bates

Specialist for Resource Information and Networks:
    Ms. Miriam L. Woolbert

Constitutional Mandate

The Department for Communication's mission statement is "to assist, inspire, and challenge the units, synods, and congregations of the Evangelical Lutheran Church in America to communicate God's grace with diverse publics and among themselves." The constitutional mandate of this department is defined in continuing resolution 15.31.B91. of the Constitutions, Bylaws, and Continuing Resolutions of the Evangelical Lutheran Church in America.

Report of Work 1993-1995

In order to fulfill its mission, the Department for Communication is divided into four work groups: News and Information, Internal Communication, Resource Information and Networks, and Public Media Ministry. The director now attends Office of the Bishop staff meetings as well as meetings of the Conference of Bishops. In cooperation with Ms. Lita Brusick Johnson of the Office of the Bishop, the director chairs the churchwide office crisis management team.

News and Information

The News and Information service of the Evangelical Lutheran Church in America gathers and disseminates news related to this church and its members and responds to inquiries from the media about this church, its decisions, programs, and policies. News reporting provides the public media with information about the church's mission and ministry.

News releases: Each year more than 200 stories are sent, in about 70 mailings, to 700 media outlets, news services, religion writers, and columnists. News is increasingly distributed via computer networks. News releases also reach the Church Council, synodical editors, bishops, seminary presidents, and churchwide staff. Breaking news is faxed to major media outlets and other media in strongly Lutheran markets. Newsbriefs (shorter news reports) are distributed by mail and computer networks.

Radio news: The radio hotline is the Evangelical Lutheran Church in America's ongoing broadcast news resource. Radio news directors can place a free phone call and gain access to a 40-second news story with taped actualities, updated weekly. Between 30 and 60 direct calls were received each month in 1994. Each taped radio news story was mailed to major radio networks, reaching at least 500 markets. A monthly promotional mailing was sent to 1,000 broadcast news outlets.

Media placement: The department provides the media with qualified ELCA representatives to discuss current issues. During 1993 and 1994, consultants working with ELCA news staff arranged for more than 540 radio, television, and newspaper interviews in cities nationwide. There were additional placements on national television networks, Armed Forces Radio, shortwave, and more.

Video News Releases (VNRs)*:* The department distributes video news releases either by satellite or direct mail with varying degrees of success. Television news directors have mixed responses to this new form. In 1993, two VNRs highlighted the 1993 Churchwide Assembly. During 1994, three VNRs were produced: the Peace Prize Forum at St. Olaf College, Northfield, Minn.; the Global Mission Event at Concordia College, Moorhead, Minn.; and the ELCA Youth Gathering at Atlanta, Ga.

Major events: The department provides comprehensive services for the media. Complete news room services were provided at the 1993 Churchwide Assembly and the Triennial Convention of the Women of the Evangelical Lutheran Church in America, 1993 and 1994 Global Mission Events, and the 1994 Youth Gathering. Special reporting via fax and computer was done at these and other events.

Internal Communication

Through telling the good news of this church's ministries, Internal Communication (interpretation) helps to inform, inspire, and challenge the people of the Evangelical Lutheran Church in America. The six-member staff:

- coordinates churchwide interpretation;
- creates video and print materials; and
- consults with churchwide units, synods, and congregations.

Coordination

The ELCA Calendar of Emphases provides structure for planning, production, and distribution of both interpretive and programmatic items. The internal communication staff coordinates the annual calendar, calendar planning guide, and calendar devotional booklet for congregation councils. In 1994, staff provided clip art related to the calendar to voting members at synod assemblies.

Churchwide themes and related subthemes help to convey a unified message to the members of this church as well as to the general populace. Internal Communication provides leadership in planning and coordinating themes.

Displays interpret churchwide ministries at important gatherings. Recently, internal communication staff members have:

- coordinated churchwide participation in the interactive area of the 1994 Youth Gathering at Atlanta, Ga.;
- coordinated and executed the display area of the 1993 and 1995 churchwide assemblies;
- begun to plan for churchwide participation in the display area of the 1996 convention of Women of the Evangelical Lutheran Church in America;
- provided traveling displays to congregations upon request; and
- coordinated unit displays in the lobby of the churchwide office.

Video and Print Materials

Spring, summer, fall, and winter issues of *Mosaic,* the video magazine of the Evangelical Lutheran Church in America, tell stories of ministries throughout this church. In spring 1994, budget constraints dictated that four, rather than five, issues of *Mosaic* be produced annually. To increase *Mosaic*'s usefulness to congregations, internal communication staff member are working with the Department for Research and Evaluation to obtain information from both present and former subscribers.

More than 20 percent of ELCA congregations currently subscribe to *Mosaic.* Congregations that do not subscribe can borrow *Mosaic* from area resource centers. To promote the use of *Mosaic,* its stories are highlighted regularly in *Seeds for the Parish,* and in 1995, a guide giving specific advice on how to use *Mosaic* in various settings will be added to users' guides that accompany each issue of *Mosaic.* Free subscriptions are available to deployed and shared stewardship staff of the Division for Congregational Ministries, as well as to churchwide unit and seminary libraries. In 1994, newly ordained pastors and newly certified associates in ministry were offered one-year complimentary subscriptions.

Synodical bishops continue to localize *Mosaic* by adding tags of interest for their synod's viewers. Special rates for taping and editing are available, as are reduced rates for synod-wide distribution.

Post-production work on *Mosaic,* formerly contracted out of house, is now done in the Department for Communication studio on new computerized editing equipment. Use of this technology reduces the production cost of each issue by approximately $6,000.

Other recent videos, in addition to *Mosaic*, include the 1994 and 1995 synodical assembly videos and a video for the Department for Ecumenical Affairs produced in late 1993.

Major churchwide print projects often are designed to be reproduced by congregations for use in Sunday bulletins or newsletters. Interpretation pieces, which may be freely reproduced, include Hunger Appeal pieces and *ELCA World Hunger News; Pericope Partners*, a reproducible resource that connects churchwide ministries to lectionary texts; *Voices of Congregational Life*, an interpretation piece for the Division for Congregational Ministries; *Prayer Ventures*, a cooperative effort of Internal Communication, the Division for Outreach, and the Division for Global Mission; a series of print ads for congregations released in spring 1994, with another scheduled for release in 1995.

Consultative and Direct Services

Each churchwide unit may rely upon a member of the Internal Communication staff to interpret its ministries and to help and inform in matters related to communication. Staff members also respond to questions from synods and congregations.

Resource Information and Networks

The Evangelical Lutheran Church in America is rich with resources--human, print, and media resources--resources found and produced from across this church and around the world. To equip ELCA members and staff for mission, resource information and networks staff members "mine" these resources--locate and develop them, interpret, and promote them. Staff members serve as connectors, bringing the people, the congregations, and the resources of this church together for the sake of the Gospel. Connecting is achieved in many ways, including:

Resource Information
- *Seeds for the Parish* is a resource paper reaching 195,000 congregational leaders six times a year (down from seven issues in 1994). To keep this popular paper afloat, staff work to improve production methods, change paper stock, purchase paper in advance, and seek limited advertising, as well as coping with changing postal standards.
- The *Action Packet* continues to deliver resources and resource samples to the congregations and rostered personnel of this church in other ministry settings (18,800 in all), now on a bimonthly schedule.
- The Resource Information Service (RIS) 800 telephone lines average nearly 15,000 calls per month

(see chart for monthly comparison with 1990). RIS staff members answer questions, transfer callers to other churchwide staff, and mail out more than 3,000 items a year in response to requests from this church's members.

Networks
- In 1994, more than 80 synodical staff and volunteers attended the ELCA Communicators' Consultation, exchanging ideas and resources for communicating the Gospel throughout this church.
- In an effort to build communication partnerships, departmental staff initiated regular phone contacts with ELCA synodical communicators, using a contact database to log information about the communicators and their activities.
- LutherLink computer network membership doubled in 1994 to 650 members from all expressions of this church. Synod sub-networks are providing new ways for sharing information and support within and among synods. Faculty from ELCA seminaries are coming on-line, with the first on-line course appearing in February 1995. Churchwide units are using the network for communicating with constituents and deployed staff. In fall 1994, the wide-area network concept received important support from the ELCA Church Council and the Cabinet of Executives.

Public Media

The Rev. Walter M. Wangerin Jr. was named the "Lutheran Vespers" speaker in 1994. Within the first two months of Pastor Wangerin's presence, 22 new stations were added to the lineup. The enthusiasm of listeners and radio station executives grows daily.

The "StoryBarn Christmas" television special aired on 99 NBC affiliates in 1993. The NBC relationship is through the National Council of Churches. More than three million people saw the first airing of the program. The special was repeated in 1994 with more than 100 National Broadcasting Company (NBC) affiliates airing the program; it also was placed on the VISN network on the Faith and Values Channel for two air plays.

We have added non-linear editing equipment which helps lower editing costs for video production. Non-linear editing is to video what word processing and desktop publishing are to print.

Two television spots and three radio spots were produced and released in 1995. Synods and congregations will be able to customize these ads for local use.

The staff of the department hosted the World Council of Churches communicators' network in Chicago in fall 1994. That group of 40 communicators represents development and relief agencies from around the world. A prime topic of discussion was a jointly operated umbrella organization to coordinate communication in times of emergency. It was implemented successfully during the Rwanda crisis.

ELCA staff provided key leadership to the development of the policy statement of the National Council of the Churches of Christ in the U.S.A. (NCCC) on "Violence in Electronic Media and Film." The policy was passed unanimously during the fall 1993 session of the NCCC General Board.

Ecumenical relationships remain key components of our work. The World Association for Christian Communication, the WCC communicators' network, the NCCC, and the Vision Interfaith Satellite Network (VISN) on the Faith and Values Channel are important relationships, which help us do our work in the best and most cost-effective manner.

"Networking" has been a buzzword for the 1990s and it will continue to be a priority for this unit in the next biennium. As our computer networking capabilities increase, more and more interpretive and news materials will be delivered via computer networks. As our ability to network with people increases (through computers, telephone contact, satellite technology, conferences, and visits), new colleagues in our work will be found and opportunities for outreach will increase. Tight funding and good sense will make more cooperative work with synodical communicators and churchwide units a priority. New computer-based video editing equipment will allow for more video editing at the churchwide office building, saving many dollars and much time. Close cooperation with staff of the Office of the Bishop and members of the Conference of Bishops will continue.

Departmental staff members hope to continue to expand news room services for major churchwide events, including the installation of the bishop-elect later this year. Other news priorities will include more video news releases (VNRs), increased delivery of news via computer, and continued strengthening of media placement services and activities.

Computer networking also will allow us to interpret the work of this church better and more directly to congregations. The internal communication staff, with the help of a Lutheran Brotherhood grant, also will develop a comprehensive video library. Disciplined, intentional listening will continue as a priority for them. In addition to providing more materials via computer network, more interpretation materials will be provided in "camera-ready" format for quick and easy reproduction.

Key interpretation resources such as *Seeds for the Parish*, the *Action Packet*, and *Mosaic* will continue as unit priorities. We will continue to look for opportunities to expand services via the Resource Information Service.

Public Media staff expect continued growth and expansion of "Lutheran Vespers." The "StoryBarn" format will continue with a special "StoryBarn: World Friends" production later in 1995 (in cooperation with Lutheran World Relief, Canadian Lutheran World Relief, the ELCA World Hunger Appeal, the National Council of the Churches of Christ in the U.S.A., and NBC). Marketing efforts will include the newly developed radio and television spots and new interests in "Davey & Goliath" (CD-ROM versions, and related products). Additional radio and television outreach opportunities will be sought.

We will continue to do all of this in the name of and for the purpose of the Gospel of Christ Jesus, our Lord and Savior!

DEPARTMENT FOR COMMUNICATION
ERIC C. SHAFER, *Director*

ELCA 800 number calls
January-November, 1990 & 1994

Months: January, February, March, April, May, June, July, August, September, October, November

800 # Calls: 0, 2000, 4000, 6000, 8000, 10000, 12000, 14000, 16000

■ 1990   ■ 1994

STORYBARN CHRISTMAS

MOSAIC
A video magazine of the ELCA

Report of the
Department for Ecumenical Affairs

Organization
Advisory Committee

Bishop Herbert W. Chilstrom

Ms. Terry L. Bowes, Longmont, Colo. (1995)*

Rev. James G. Cobb, Norfolk, Va. (1995)*

Rev. Franklin D. Fry, Summit, N.J. (1995)*

Rev. David F. Lindblom, Minnetonka, Minn. (1999)

Rev. Donald G. Luck, Columbus, Ohio (1995)

Mr. Charles F. Ruthroff, Oakland, Calif. (1997)

Rev. Ernest L. Simmons Jr., Moorhead, Minn. (1997)

Rev. Jane E. Strohl, St. Paul, Minn. (1997)

Rev. Stephen D. Swenson, *chair*, Carmel, Ind. (1999)

Advisors

Bishop James S. Aull, South Carolina Synod
(1993-1994)

Bishop Stanley N. Olson, Southwestern Minnesota
Synod (1995)

* Church Council Member

Staff

Director: Rev. William G. Rusch

Associate Director: Rev. Daniel F. Martensen

Associate Director: Ms. Darlis J. Swan

U.S.A. National Committee of the Lutheran World Federation

The advisory committee of the Department for Ecumenical Affairs—with the addition of the Rev. Mark W. Thomsen, executive director of the Division for Global Mission, and the Rev. Charles S. Miller, executive director of the Division for Church in Society—serves as the U.S.A. National Committee of the Lutheran World Federation. Mr. Dennis Frado, director for the Lutheran Office for World Community, New York, N.Y., serves as an advisor to the national committee.

Bishop Stanley N. Olson serves as an advisor to the advisory committee of the Department for Ecumenical Affairs and to the U.S.A. National Committee of the Lutheran World Federation, as representative of the ELCA Conference of Bishops. Bishop James S. Aull served with distinction as an advisor to the committee from 1993 to 1994.

Constitutional Mandate

This department assists the bishop and this church to coordinate inter-Lutheran, ecumenical, and interfaith activities. The mandate of this department is defined in continuing resolution 15.31.C91. of the Constitution, Bylaws, and Continuing Resolutions of the Evangelical Lutheran Church in America.

Report of Work 1993-1995

The work of the Department for Ecumenical Affairs (DEA) has centered around certain program areas including: (1) assisting the bishop of this church as its chief ecumenical officer; (2) guiding the process of reception of theological and ecumenical agreements that include proposals for full communion with the Episcopal Church in the USA and with three Reformed churches, and "lifting" certain condemnations against the Roman Catholic Church; (3) coordinating theological studies and research; (4) conducting ecumenical dialogue with African Methodist Episcopal and Moravian Churches, and interfaith conversations; (5) administering membership in the Lutheran World Federation (LWF); (6) administering membership in the World Council of Churches (WCC); (7) administering membership in the National Council of the Churches of Christ in the U.S.A. (NCCC); and (8) assisting the regions, synods, congregations, and churchwide units of this church to carry out their ecumenical, inter-Lutheran, and interfaith responsibilities.

Lutheran World Federation

ELCA membership in the Lutheran World Federation was determined at the constituting convention of this church. At its June 1987 meeting, the Church Council voted that the Office of the Bishop, in the name of the Evangelical Lutheran Church in America, secure membership for this church in the Lutheran World Federation. Since that time this church has been active in the work of the federation, which involves hundreds of projects worldwide, inter-church liaison and consultancy, theology and study programs, and communication and advocacy.

ELCA involvement in and support of the work of the Lutheran World Federation is coordinated by its U.S.A. National Committee through the Department for Ecumenical Affairs. Under the leadership of the department, a staff working group on international conciliar relations oversees the financial and program involvements of this church in the work of the federation.

WCC Ecumenical Decade:
Churches in Solidarity with Women 1988-1998

In January 1987, the Central Committee of the World Council of Churches accepted sponsorship of an "Ecumenical Decade for Churches in Solidarity with Women: 1988-1998" (the decade). At its April 1988 meeting, the Church Council resolved that the Evangelical Lutheran Church in America would join with other WCC member churches to support the stated goals of the decade. The work of the decade has been focused in three areas: (1) full participation of women; (2) women's visions and perspective—justice, peace, and the integrity of creation; and (3) theology and spirituality—integrative sharing, acting, and celebrating.

The Department for Ecumenical Affairs has supported the goals of the decade through funding and through representation on the ELCA inter-unit committee and the U.S.A. National Committee of the Decade. The most recent activity of the Ecumenical Decade is a series of visits of WCC staff and others to member churches. An official visit was made to the Evangelical Lutheran Church in America in October 1994.

ELCA Statement on Ecumenism

In 1991 the second Churchwide Assembly of the Evangelical Lutheran Church in America adopted by a large margin "A Declaration of Ecumenical Commitment: A Policy Statement of the Evangelical Lutheran Church in America" as the policy of this church. This document—Part II of "Ecumenism: The Vision of the Evangelical Lutheran Church in America"—provides, under the constitution and bylaws of this church, an ecumenical commitment and direction for this church especially as it faces major ecumenical decisions in 1997. A major part of the responsibility of the department is to challenge this church to continue to live out that commitment. The text of "Ecumenism: The Vision of the Evangelical Lutheran Church in America" is now available in French, German, and Spanish translations.

Lutheran-Episcopal Relations

The Evangelical Lutheran Church in America, at its constituting convention, accepted the 1982 Lutheran-Episcopal Agreement with the Episcopal Church in the U.S.A. Interim eucharistic fellowship, projects of joint study and mission, and the dialogue have continued. In 1988, the first part of the mandate of Lutheran-Episcopal Dialogue III was completed with the publication of *Implications of the Gospel*, a text that has been studied in both churches.

The mandate established in 1982 by the sponsoring churches included agreement on the implication of the Gospel, and attention to the "historic episcopate, and the ordering of ministry (bishops, priests, and deacons) in the total context of apostolicity." As a result of the work of the dialogue commission, the 1991 Churchwide Assembly had before it the proposed "Concordat of Agreement" and "Toward Full Communion between the Episcopal Church and the Evangelical Lutheran Church in America." That assembly deferred formal study until 1993 and official action until at least 1995. There now is a mutual commitment that both churches will take official action in 1997. Since the 1991 Churchwide Assembly, the ELCA Department for Ecumenical Affairs has worked with the Ecumenical Office of the Episcopal Church to provide assistance for the Lutheran-Episcopal Coordinating Committee, which includes representatives from both churches.

In response to the 1982 agreement and in a cooperative fashion, the coordinating committee has guided the process for interpretation of the results of Lutheran-Episcopal Dialogue III. This has been done through a series of projects focusing on the common Christian witness shared by the Evangelical Lutheran Church in America and the Episcopal Church: a consultation, a commentary, a book of essays, a congregational resource packet, an audio tape, and a video tape. The projects were used in a formal study of the "Concordat" and "Full Communion" in the Evangelical Lutheran Church in America. A churchwide study process, including selected congregations, took place in spring 1995.

Lutheran-Reformed Relations

The Lutheran-Reformed Committee for Theological Conversations began its work in 1988 and completed its final report in 1992. Titled, "A Common Calling," this report was distributed to voting members of the 1993 Churchwide Assembly with recommendations for action. The 1993 Churchwide Assembly voted to affirm that the recommendations, made in the report from the committee for conversations for full communion between the Evangelical Lutheran Church in America and three Reformed churches, i.e., the Presbyterian Church (USA), the Reformed Church in America, and the United Church of Christ, be voted in the same year, not earlier than 1995 and not later than 1997. Subsequently, a mutual decision was made, and affirmed by the Church Council, that the vote be taken in 1997.

A Lutheran-Reformed Coordinating Committee of representatives from all the churches participating in the proposal was formed to guide the reception process. That committee has: encouraged the use of "A Common Discovery," congregational study materials; visited congregations to discuss the proposal for full communion; drafted a "formula of agreement" for further clarification of the proposal; and planned a church-wide study. Additional projects may include a newsletter and a scholarly commentary. A vote on full communion is anticipated in all four churches in 1997.

ELCA-African Methodist Episcopal Dialogue

In September 1992, bilateral dialogue began between the African Methodist Episcopal Church and the Evangelical Lutheran Church in America. This is the first dialogue between a Lutheran and an historic African American church in the U.S.A. It is anticipated that this present round of dialogue will come to a close in late 1995 with the conclusion of work on a study document to be used in the respective churches. A coordinating committee may be established to facilitate ongoing relations between the two churches and to plan for a second round of theological dialogue to begin in 1996.

ELCA-Moravian Dialogue

A dialogue carried out at the regional level between the Evangelical Lutheran Church in America and the Northern and Southern Provinces of the Moravian Church began in 1992. As of 1994 the dialogue has included national representatives from both churches. The dialogue commission is presently drafting a common statement and report which will document a significant consensus on basic theological and ecclesiastical questions and propose the establishment of full communion between our churches. Action on such a proposal would take place at the 2000 Churchwide Assembly of the ELCA.

ELCA-Roman Catholic Relations

After 27 years of Lutheran-Roman Catholic dialogue in the United States, a consultation was held in February 1993 to determine the next steps to be taken in the relationship between the two churches. The results of the most recent round of dialogue, the ninth, is being published under the title, *Word of God: Scripture and Tradition*.

A Lutheran-Roman Catholic Coordinating Committee was established and met for the first time in 1994. Its tasks include planning for and coordinating in 1997 the effort to declare the inapplicability of the mutual condemnations on the doctrine of justification dating from the 16th century, and planning for the next round of official dialogue in the U.S.A.

ELCA-Orthodox Dialogue

A third round of dialogue between the Evangelical Lutheran Church in America and the Orthodox churches in the USA began in 1994. The dialogue is building upon Lutheran-Orthodox dialogue results of earlier years and is closely related to the international Lutheran World Federation-pan-Orthodox dialogue dating from 1981.

Lutheran-Jewish Dialogue

The Department for Ecumenical Affairs works cooperatively with the newly founded Institute for Jewish-Christian Understanding in Allentown, Pennsylvania. With the help of a consultative panel on Lutheran-Jewish dialogue, three pilot dialogue projects are being carried out. In this area as well as in interfaith dialogue with Muslims and Buddhists, the ELCA Department for Ecumenical Affairs works with the national and world councils of churches. A departmental staff member recently was appointed by the World Council of Churches to serve as one of three U.S. representatives on the "Consultation on the Church and the Jewish People" (CCJP) until the next WCC Assembly in 1998. The staff member also serves as a consultant to the "Lutheran European Commission on the Church and the Jewish People" (LEKKJ).

Work proceeds on the development of an ELCA Statement on Christian-Jewish relations. The ELCA Church Council made public a "Declaration to the Jewish Community" on April 18, 1994. The declaration repudiates the anti-Jewish writings of Martin Luther which date from 1543-1546. Action of the 1993 ELCA Churchwide Assembly instructed the Department for Ecumenical Affairs to develop the one-page document. Positive response from the Jewish community across the U.S.A. has been noted. The statement reads:

THE DECLARATION OF THE EVANGELICAL LUTHERAN CHURCH IN AMERICA TO THE JEWISH COMMUNITY

In the long history of Christianity there exists no more tragic development than the treatment accorded the Jewish people on the part of Christian believers. Very few Christian communities of faith were able to escape the contagion of anti-Judaism and its modern successor, anti-Semitism. Lutherans belonging to the Lutheran World Federation and the Evangelical Lutheran Church in America feel a special burden in this regard because of certain elements in the legacy of the reformer Martin Luther and the catastrophes, including the Holocaust of the twentieth century, suffered by Jews in places where the Lutheran churches were strongly represented.

The Lutheran communion of faith is linked by name and heritage to the memory of Martin Luther, teacher and reformer. Honoring his

name in our own, we recall his bold stand for truth, his earthy and sublime words of wisdom, and above all his witness to God's saving Word. Luther proclaimed a gospel for people as we really are, bidding us to trust a grace sufficient to reach our deepest shames and address the most tragic truths.

In the spirit of that truth-telling, we who bear his name and heritage must with pain acknowledge also Luther's anti-Judaic diatribes and violent recommendations of his later writings against the Jews. As did many of Luther's own companions in the sixteenth century, we reject this violent invective, and yet more do we express our deep and abiding sorrow over its tragic effects on subsequent generations. In concert with the Lutheran World Federation, we particularly deplore the appropriation of Luther's words by modern anti-Semites for the teaching of hatred toward Judaism or toward the Jewish people in our day.

Grieving the complicity of our own tradition within this history of hatred, moreover, we express our urgent desire to live out our faith in Jesus Christ with love and respect for the Jewish people. We recognize in anti-Semitism a contradiction and an affront to the Gospel, a violation of our hope and calling, and we pledge this church to oppose the deadly working of such bigotry, both within our own circles and in the society around us. Finally, we pray for the continued blessing of the Blessed One upon the increasing cooperation and understanding between Lutheran Christians and the Jewish community.

Synodical Ecumenism

The Department for Ecumenical Affairs is responsible for coordinating a network of ELCA synodical ecumenical representatives (LERN). The network was created as the result of a request from the first National Consultation on Synodical Ecumenism sponsored by the Office for Ecumenical Affairs in November 1988. Synodical bishops have selected representatives to help them with their ecumenical responsibilities and to serve on the network. In addition, the bishops have named other interested people from their synods to receive materials and share information. The department has helped the representatives with their work by publishing a DEA Ecumenical Update, distributing a list of local ecumenical contacts, sponsoring ecumenical continuing education events, disseminating information on local, national, and global ecumenical developments, and working cooperatively on an individual basis to create

covenants, guidelines for ecumenical committees, and models for local studies and ecumenical celebrations.

Since the creation of the network, the representatives, in addition to contributing to a bank of information about the ecumenical activities at the synodical level, have been working with similar networks sponsored by ELCA dialogue partners to promote grass-roots ecumenical endeavors. The Department for Ecumenical Affairs cooperates with the network in publishing a newsletter.

The Reception Process

The means whereby ecumenical agreements become part of the faith and life of the churches is called reception. This translation into reality, as some have called the development, takes place in all expressions of this church and calls for reciprocity and interdependency as mandated by the ELCA constitution.

The Department for Ecumenical Affairs is responsible for motivating and stimulating the reception process, in order to help the members of this church decide whether ecumenical documents and other developments are appropriate to their self-identity and serve to proclaim the Gospel. Part of the task of reception is interpretation and communication.

The 1997 ELCA Churchwide Assembly will have two proposals for full communion (as delineated in the Lutheran-Episcopal "Concordat" and in the Lutheran-Reformed "A Common Calling"), and a declaration on mutual condemnations between Lutherans and Roman Catholics, on its agenda. The Department for Ecumenical Affairs bears responsibility for ensuring that a careful study process occurs.

The Department for Ecumenical Affairs has participated in the reception process in a variety of ways including speaking at synodical and regional training events. In 1994, the staff, plus an international consultant, presented a lecture series on "Ecumenism and the ELCA" at three of the ELCA seminaries. Plans are being made to present the lectures at the other five seminaries in 1995 and 1996.

Additional projects include an audio, a video, and a brochure, "Why Unity?," produced in cooperation with the Department for Communication. Two churchwide studies, Lutheran-Episcopal and Lutheran-Reformed, will take place in 1995 to help determine the mind of this church on the two proposals for full communion. A Lutheran-Roman Catholic study also may take place.

National Council of the Churches of Christ in the U.S.A.

The Evangelical Lutheran Church in America participates in a variety of ways in the ongoing work and leadership of the National Council of the Churches of

Christ in the U.S.A. (NCCC). At a time when budgetary constraints have reduced this church's financial support of the council to historically low levels, it is important to recognize that through membership on the General Board, the Executive Coordinating Committee, various working groups, and special task forces, representatives of this church are involved actively in the continuing work of the council and in shaping its future.

The Department for Ecumenical Affairs has initiated and provides leadership to a NCCC working group on conciliar relations, an inter-unit committee composed of representatives of the staff of various churchwide units. The working group coordinates funding from this church and representation from churchwide units to the council, and provides interpretation of NCCC resolutions, actions, and programs.

World Council of Churches

Since its seventh assembly in Canberra, Australia, in 1991, the World Council of Churches has undergone a process of restructuring. In August 1992, the Central Committee elected the Rev. Konrad Raiser as general secretary to succeed the Rev. Emilio Castro. Although levels of financial support by the Evangelical Lutheran Church in America are low, this church contributes to the work of the World Council of Churches by participation in the Central Committee, several unit committees, and the Commission on Faith and Order. In 1993, the Fifth World Conference of Faith and Order was held at Santiago de Compostela, Spain. The Evangelical Lutheran Church in America provided leadership and financial support for this important ecumenical event. A staff working group under the leadership of the Department for Ecumenical Affairs coordinates ELCA involvement in and support of the work of the council.

Referrals from
1993 Churchwide Assembly

Three memorials from this assembly were addressed to this department or to this department and other churchwide units.

The assembly requested the department to prepare a declaration to the Jewish community on some of the writings of Luther and anti-Semitism. As reported above, this declaration was approved by the Church Council and shared with Jewish leaders and other interested persons.

The Department for Ecumenical Affairs and the Division for Church in Society were asked to explore the feasibility of communication with religious leaders in the former Yugoslavia and to invite religious leaders in the United States to prompt care of refugees and wounded. These matters were taken up in correspondence that

Bishop Herbert W. Chilstrom addressed to a number of appropriate persons.

The assembly addressed a number of churchwide units, especially the Division for Outreach, to speak to the issue of rural ministry. This department indicated to the Division for Outreach its willingness to be of assistance and to participate in a consultation on congregations in small towns and rural settings in February 1995.

Program Directions 1995-1997

During this biennium, the department intends to place its highest priority on the reception process leading to three major ecumenical decisions by the Evangelical Lutheran Church in America in 1997. This priority will involve all the staff of the department and the maximum amount of funding available to engage all aspects of this church in a process of study and reflection on the three ecumenical proposals.

Fundamental to this process is the policy statement, "A Declaration of Ecumenical Commitment," which was adopted by the 1991 Churchwide Assembly. The policies, aims, and goals of this department are provided as basis and framework by this document. The "Declaration" states that the ecumenical goal of this church is a relationship of "full communion" with all those churches that confess the Triune God. Now after three decades of intense ecumenical dialogue with three partners, there is the possibility of entering into full communion with the Episcopal Church in the USA, three Reformed churches (Presbyterian Church [USA], Reformed Church in America, and United Church of Christ), and of taking a decisive step with the Roman Catholic Church regarding the sixteenth century mutual condemnations on justification. To bring these possibilities to reality will require extensive activity by this department.

The department has developed a detailed process for study and interpretation that includes the production of various materials, as well as lectures and presentations throughout the Evangelical Lutheran Church in America. These programs are carried on and overseen by three coordinating committees, one for each of the three proposals. These committees intend to have prepared the specific texts for churchwide action by early 1996, so that synod assemblies in that year will be able to evaluate the proposals.

Although much ecumenical work has roots in the past, new ecumenical opportunities clearly are present in this church. This department seeks to use these occasions to challenge this church to the possibility of further ecumenical progress.

While the three proposals for 1997 will have the highest priority, other ecumenical activities continue.

Lutheran-Orthodox, Lutheran-Moravian, and Lutheran-African Methodist Episcopal dialogues will continue.

Channels of communication will need to be kept open and relations of trust cultivated with a number of churches and ecumenical organizations. The encouragement and participation of the new bishop of this church as its chief ecumenical officer will be indispensable.

Theological study and research will be ongoing. Here the department seeks out and enlists the theological talents in this church; the quality of an ecumenical dialogue is related directly to scholarly research. Such research on the nature of the Church and ministry will be key topics in ecumenical discussion.

Studies on the nature of unity, and the closely related topic of *koinonia*, will produce clearer understandings of such issues as confessional integrity, communion identity, and local cooperation. This church will play a major role in such studies.

The department is responsible for the administration of this church's relationship to inter-church and conciliar agencies. During this biennium, attention will be given to the next assembly of the Lutheran World Federation in 1997 and the assembly of the World Council of Churches in 1998. Continuing responsibilities include the nomination of representatives to serve in the name of this church, and the formation of delegations. A major concern is to identify and nominate capable delegates and committee members. This is a time when major conciliar agencies are examining their structure and assessing budgets and programs. The Evangelical Lutheran Church in America with its ecumenical commitments will wish to have a continuing voice in these discussions.

The department is committed to an intensive effort of interpretation and education about the ecumenical movement as well as the decisions in 1997. Ecumenism thrives when it is a reciprocal process: all expressions of this church contribute to the endeavor and provide valuable insights and information. For Lutherans ecumenism is a priority and responsibility of the entire church. Thus, this department provides resources for pastors and other congregational leaders so they can communicate the Gospel with an ecumenical awareness. In order to do so, this department will continue to assist synods in their task of fostering ecumenical relations.

As the Department for Ecumenical Affairs is attentive to relations with other churches, it also is aware of other religious communities in the U.S.A. The pluralistic character of American society and the global interests of this church call for serious interfaith dialogue and the study of the major religions of the world. Within the limits of its priorities and resources, the department intends to pursue its working Lutheran-Jewish relations.

Cooperation among the churchwide units, seminaries, congregations, and others is important in all of these programs. Churchwide collaboration, certainly in regard to the decisions in 1997, with its mutual support and critique, assures that the statements, policies, and goals of this church related to ecumenism participate in the rich biblical, theological, and pastoral wisdom that this church enjoys in all areas of its life.

DEPARTMENT FOR ECUMENICAL AFFAIRS
WILLIAM G. RUSCH, *Director*

Report of the
Department for Human Resources

Organization
Coordination and Services Committee

The Department for Human Resources and Management Services report to the Office of the Bishop through the Executive for Administration. The Coordination and Services Committee of the Church Council provides oversight of the work of this department. The members of the Coordination and Services Committee are:

Mr. William E. Diehl, *chair*, Emmaus, Pa.
Ms. Karen Dietz, Danbury, Wis.
Rev. David K. Johnson, Fargo, N.Dak.
Mr. Loren W. Mathre, St. Petersburg, Fla.
Mr. Carlos Peña, Galveston, Tex.
Ms. W. Jeanne Rapp, Pontiac, Ill.
Ms. Susan Huber Stapell, Cheektowaga, N.Y.
Rev. Nelson T. Strobert, Gettysburg, Pa.

Advisor:
Bishop Peter Rogness, Greater Milwaukee Synod

Advisory Committee for Human Resources

The Department for Human Resources receives advice and counsel in areas of human resource management and development from this committee. The committee is composed of experts in various fields related to human resources. The group meets annually. Its members are:

Ms. Barbara M. Despenza, Chicago, Ill. (1995)
Mr. Terry M. Ihlenfeld, Louisville, Colo. (1995)
Ms. Doris Pagelkopf, Minneapolis, Minn. (1997)
Mr. Roy J. Prigge, Sioux Falls, S.Dak. (1997)
Mr. Larry M. Smith, *chair*, Golden Valley, Minn. (1999)

Constitutional Mandate

"Through service and advocacy, the Department for Human Resources of the Evangelical Lutheran Church in America shall seek to provide the staff resources and the personnel policies and practices for all who carry the responsibility for advancing the purpose of this churchwide organization, and to bring to all staff justice and wholeness in the fulfillment of their tasks. The department shall strive constantly to achieve economy and quality in its service, as an expression of good stewardship for the people of this church. In all its endeavors, the Department for Human Resources shall embrace the mission of this church, to give joyfully in witness and service."

The mandate of this department is defined in continuing resolution 15.31.D91. of the Constitution, Bylaws, and Continuing Resolutions of the Evangelical Lutheran Church in America.

Internal Committees

Two internal committees comprising churchwide staff assist this department.

The Personnel Representative Committee is composed of one staff member, executive or support, from each unit. The purpose of this committee is: (1) to provide personnel policy information and application from the Department for Human Resources to each of the units through personnel representatives, (2) to advocate policies and practices that promote effective working relations within the churchwide organization, (3) to promote productivity in the work place, and (4) to provide a communications link between the Department for Human Resources and the units.

The Position Evaluation Team evaluates new positions and establishes executive and support position categories. The team's mandate is to maintain equity among churchwide units and external comparisons in the evaluation process. The Position Evaluation Team also provides a consistent and systematic approach to determining the relative position values throughout churchwide units.

In addition, the Department for Human Resources is the lead unit of the Inter-Unit Staff Team on Diversity, and serves as staff to that team.

Staff
Director: Rev. A. C. Stein
Assistant Director: Ms. Agaliece W. Miller
Manager, Building Services: Ms. Marilyn V. Schmidt
Manager, Purchasing Services: Ms. Elaine D. Hall

Report of Work 1993-1994
Inclusive Staffing

In faithfulness to the Gospel and this church's commitment to be inclusive in the midst of division within society, the churchwide units are staffed to reflect the inclusive unity that is God's will for this church.

Analysis of Churchwide Staff

Total Staff

Year	Total	Executive	Support	Male	Female	Clergy	Lay	White	POC
1992	505	298	207	216	289	140	365	393	112
	100%	59%	41%	43%	57%	28%	72%	78%	22%
1993	482	291	191	209	273	137	345	373	109
	100%	60%	40%	43%	57%	28%	72%	78%	22%
1994	478	283	195	198	280	113	347	361	117
	100%	59%	41%	41%	59%	24%	72%	76%	24%
1995*	465	277	188	186	279	102	345	347	118
	100%	60%	40%	40%	60%	22%	74%	75%	25%

Associates in Ministry

1994	18
	4%
1995*	18
	4%

*as of March 22, 1995

Compensation

The churchwide organization uses the HAY Compensation System. As the accompanying table demonstrates, nineteen grade levels have been set for positions within the churchwide organization. The 1994 pay ranges for the executive for administration, executive director of the ELCA Foundation, and the general

Analysis of Churchwide Salary Grades And Pay Practices for 1993

	Salary	Actual Pay	
Clerical Support	Grade	Minimum	Maximum
Data Entry Operator	4	$15,208	$16,640
Remittance Processing Clerk	5	16,267	22,009
Mail Clerk	5	16,267	22,009
Secretary	6	17,525	23,751
Accounting Clerk II	6	17,525	22,067
Senior Secretary	8	20,504	28,365
Purchasing Clerk	8	20,504	26,730
Executive Secretary	9	22,291	30,159
Telecommunicator	9	22,291	30,113
Technical Support			
Administrative Assistant	10	$24,410	$33,025
Editorial Specialist	10	24,410	33,025
Computer Operator	10	24,410	33,025
Telecommunication Specialist	11	26,859	32,336
P. C. Support Specialist	11	26,859	32,336
Sr. Computer Operator	12	27,025	32,272
Programmer Analyst	12	27,025	32,272
Executive Staff			
Supervisors	13 & 14	$28,610	$39,519
Entry Level Executives	14	30,519	39,519
Associate Directors	15	32,264	47,164
Program Directors	16 & 17	36,789	59,408
Asst. Exec. Directors	18	48,788	61,624
Unit Directors	19	53,141	65,064
Unit Executive Directors	20 & 21	58,534	73,082
Assistants to the Bishop	20 & 21	58,534	67,898

counsel were $80,333 to $89,000.

Salaries for support staff are within the middle pay range for comparable nonprofit organizations in the Chicago area. Executive staff salaries are in the lower range for comparable organizations.

The 1994 salary and housing allowance for the bishop of this church was $116,181. The 1994 salary and housing allowance for the secretary of this church was $87,916, and the 1994 salary of the treasurer of this church was $86,176.

Salaries of the full-time officers are set by the Church Council's Executive Committee within ranges established by the Church Council.

The three officers receive the normal pension, medical, and dental coverage provided to employees of the churchwide organization. The bishop and all staff who are ordained are required to pay out of their salaries the full 15.3 percent self-employment Social Security tax up to the required maximum. Ordained staff receive no allowance to cover the 7.65 percent of the Social Security tax paid by the employer for lay staff members.

For perspective, it is noted that, while the bishop's salary is the highest one at the Lutheran Center, it is not the highest within other organizations related to this church. Some Lutheran college presidents and deans, as well as executive directors of social service agencies and institutions, receive higher salaries and a wider range of benefits. In the context of the Chicago metropolitan area, for comparison purposes, the bishop's salary is in the low to middle range of that of suburban high-school principals and superintendents.

Performance Appraisal System

The churchwide organization performance appraisal process has been revised. The new system is more flexible and participative, while, at the same time, providing an increased focus on the results expected of the staff member. Copies of performance appraisal materials are available upon request.

Personnel Policies

Additional changes have been made to the *Personnel Policies of the Churchwide Organization*. The policies have been written so that they may be used as a congregational resource and are available upon request.

Staff Development

Through the three-year staff-development plan, a series of "core" courses are provided for every staff member. In addition, a wide variety of "elective" or specialized courses is available to assist staff members with individual development needs. Copies of the 1995 Course Catalog are available upon request.

Lutheran Children's Center

The churchwide organization has an on-site child-care center, licensed by the City of Chicago and managed by Lutheran Social Services of Illinois. The center's capacity (42 children ranging in age from two to five years) currently is fully enrolled.

Management Services

Management Services is responsible for the facility administration of the churchwide office building at Chicago, Ill., the churchwide Archives at Rosemont, Ill., the Lutheran Office for Governmental Affairs in Washington, D.C., and the Lutheran Office for World Community in New York City.

The Lutheran Center is an 11-story building occupying 220,000 square feet of floor space. Approximately 380 churchwide staff are housed on 5.5 floors. The remaining 4.5 floors are leased to other nonprofit organizations. Current tenants are: Lutheran General HealthSystem, Big Brothers/Big Sisters of America, the Retirement Research Foundation, Child Serv, Lutheran General Foundation, and the Northern Illinois Conference of the United Methodist Church.

Facilities within the Lutheran Center include a day-care center, resource library, visitor's center, chapel, and a conference center. More than 3,000 visitors are welcomed each year. The conference center is used every day, including weekends. In addition to administering these special facilities, Management Services provides receptionists, mail service, copy-center operations, purchasing services, and telephone-system service, and manages tenant-leased spaces.

ELCAdvantage Program

This stewardship program began in May 1993 and is designed for use by congregations, affiliated agencies, institutions, and organizations of the various expressions of this church. The goal is to offer reduced prices on high-quality products and services through collective volume purchases of commonly-used goods and services. These products and services, as well as excellent customer service, are provided by the companies specifically selected as our business partners. Participation in the program by entities connected to this church is voluntary, and the savings realized can be used to further mission and ministry endeavors of congregations and communities throughout this church.

Through the ELCAdvantage Program, the churchwide organization develops partnership agreements with "preferred providers" of high-quality products and services. When an agreement is negotiated, all entities affiliated with this church are included. The agreements include pricing and performance standards, and periodic evaluations are conducted before agreements are renewed or renegotiated.

Ten vendors are currently working in partnership with the churchwide organization to provide products and services through the ELCAdvantage Program. By utilizing each of these business partners, the churchwide organization is able constantly to monitor and evaluate their levels of service and commitment. Our administrative costs for managing the program are offset by vendor contributions.

DEPARTMENT FOR HUMAN RESOURCES
AND MANAGEMENT SERVICES

A. C. ("CHRIS") STEIN, *Director*

Report of the Department for Research and Evaluation

Organization
Advisory Committee
Mr. F. Paul Carlson, Tacoma, Wash. (1993)
Mr. Charles Y. Glock, Sandpoint, Idaho (1997)
Ms. Pamala M. Jolicoeur, Thousand Oaks, Calif. (1977)
Rev. Martin Rafanan, St. Louis, Mo. (1995)
Ms. Jayne Rose, Rock Island, Ill. (1995)

Staff
Director: Mr. Kenneth W. Inskeep
Associate Director for Demographic Analysis:
    Ms. Stella U. Ogunwole
Demographic Associate: Ms. Patricia J. Simonik
Research and Demographic Associate:
    Ms. Jacqueline A. Mroczek
Research Associate: Ms. Gretchen R. Olson
Research Associate: Mr. Martin H. Smith

Constitutional Mandate
The department is responsible for assisting the bishop, other leaders, and staff of the churchwide organization by providing reliable, relevant information and appropriate evaluation related to the purposes of this church. The mandate of this department is defined in continuing resolution 15.31.E91. of the Constitution, Bylaws, and Continuing Resolutions of the Evangelical Lutheran Church in America.

Report of Work 1993-1995
The department divides its work into general research, evaluation, and demographic research.

General Research
The department designs the majority of its projects to support the work of the Office of the Bishop and to meet the research-based information needs of the churchwide units.

Office of the Bishop
The department worked extensively in cooperation with the Office of the Bishop to support and promote discussion about this church's future in a process called the "Inquiry." The department helped develop an extensive literature review on the future of mainline denominations. It also provided a workbook summarizing a variety of societal and religious trends in the United States in order to provoke additional thinking and discussion. The workbook was used by the planning team of the churchwide organization, the executive as well as the program and structure committees of the Church Council, the synodical vice presidents, and in the mission support consultations.

The department, along with the Office of the Treasurer and the Division for Congregational Ministries, also prepared the materials used for mission-support consultations with synods. Those materials presented stewardship trends to help inform the discussions.

Departmental Support
Division for Congregational Ministries

In 1993, the department shifted its focus from constituents to congregations. Approximately 400 congregations of this church were systematically selected and asked to participate in a program of surveys designed to produce a better understanding of congregational life within the Evangelical Lutheran Church in America. Of the 400 selected congregations, 350 agreed to participate and completed a first round of the program. The department mailed questionnaires to the pastor, the council president, an additional council member, and a new member from each congregation. Return rates averaged 62 percent. Several significant findings from the program are presented at the end of this report. Based upon that initial study, the department published "A Profile: Facts about the Congregations of the Evangelical Lutheran Church in America" in August 1994. Since its publication, the department has distributed approximately 3,000 copies. The department sent "The Profile" to the participating congregations, synodical bishops and staff, churchwide program and communication staff, deployed outreach and stewardship staff, members of the evangelism network, board members of the Publishing House of the Evangelical Lutheran Church in America (Augsburg Fortress, Publishers) and its marketing staff, college and seminary presidents, members of the Church Council, and the churchwide Cabinet of Executives.

Along with the Division for Congregational Ministries, the department participated in producing the second phase of the Church Membership Initiative sponsored by Aid Association for Lutherans (AAL). The department compiled and summarized data from the congregations to supplement and expand the findings of the Church Membership Initiative. The presentations in six sites across this church used these facts and figures to explain the need for renewed interest in evangelical outreach. In addition to the presentations, the department conducted "focus groups" with lay and clergy members of this church in each site. The focus groups explored the congregational challenge of evangelism along with clergy and lay perspectives on membership growth. The findings assisted the evangelism staff of the Division for Congregational Ministries in setting program directions.

The department also worked with the Division for Congregational Ministries to field and analyze a survey of worship practices among congregations of the Evangelical Lutheran Church in America. Results informed plans for resource development.

Division for Higher Education and Schools

The department conducted constituency surveys for the Division for Higher Education and Schools with the design and distribution of four questionnaires. The questionnaires reviewed the work of the division and explored the future needs of the groups served by the division. Bishops, campus ministry staff, college and university officials, and administrators of elementary and secondary schools and early childhood education centers completed questionnaires. Reports were presented to the board of the Division for Higher Education and Schools.

Division for Church in Society

In cooperation with the Division for Church in Society, the department conducted an extensive survey of ELCA social ministry organizations. The survey focused on identifying social, governmental, and economic changes affecting the work of social ministry organizations and explored possible strategies for strengthening the partnership between social ministry organizations, synods, and the Division for Church in Society. Findings were presented to the "Blue Ribbon Committee" of the division.

Division for Outreach and
Division for Congregational Ministries

The department developed a computerized congregational trend report that provides church leaders with membership and stewardship data for any of the 11,000 congregations of this church. The information covers 1980 to 1993 for membership and 1988 to 1993 for stewardship. The department distributed the program to synods and deployed outreach and stewardship staff. It is possible to load and use the program on nearly all MS-DOS computers. For the first time, church leaders have convenient access to trend information on individ-

ual congregations. Demand for the program is high. A second computerized report also is available that provides demographic trend data for each of the more than 3,000 ZIP code areas in the United States. In 1994, the department processed more than 600 such requests from congregations, synodical staff, and deployed outreach staff.

Division for Ministry

The department completed a report on the supply and demand for clergy in this church and presented the report to seminary presidents, deans, and board presidents. It concludes that the supply of clergy is appropriate and will continue to be so for the foreseeable future. At the same time, congregations in some settings will continue to have difficulty in calling a pastor.

Women of the Evangelical
Lutheran Church in America

The department conducted focus groups at the triennial convention of the Women of the Evangelical Lutheran Church in America. The focus groups studied programs and resources available to WELCA units in congregations, as well as the challenges those groups face.

Evaluation

The Division for Ministry requested a survey to determine how well *Lutheran Partners* meets the needs of the rostered leaders of the Evangelical Lutheran Church in America. The department also conducted an extensive review of the continuing education program, Growth and Excellence in Ministry, commonly known as GEM.

The department participated with the Division for Global Mission in congregational survey work reviewing the activities of the division, through several different questionnaires. A sample of 400 congregations was selected to learn the role global mission plays within the lives of the congregations of this church. The questionnaire also explored the use of global mission resources.

The department also fielded questionnaires to the division's partner churches and from the division's newsletter, *Global Contact*.

A review of giving to the World Hunger Appeal indicated that, in 1993, monetary gifts declined by $1 million. The department fielded questionnaires to a sample of congregations whose decrease in gifts to hunger ministries ranged from $1,000 to $45,000. The department shared the results at the meeting of the 65 synodical World Hunger leaders and the World Hunger staff team.

Working with the Department for Human Resources, the department conducted a survey of employee attitudes toward their work in the various units of the churchwide organization. The results were presented to the Coordination and Services Committee of the Church Council, the Office of the Bishop, and the Department for Human Resources.

The department participated with the Division for Congregational Ministries both in a review of the 1994 Youth Gathering and in an extensive evaluation of "The Visionary Planning Project," sponsored by Lutheran Brotherhood. The project funded consultation services to congregations, helping them to plan and implement outreach strategies. Finally, the department conducted focus groups for camp directors evaluating outdoor ministries curriculum.

Demography

The department continues to provide timely and accurate demographic information to decision makers, particularly in the area of outreach. The department produces presentation-quality demographic maps and tables detailing relevant changes in the characteristics of the population. That information is particularly useful to church leaders as they adjust their ministries to meet the most pressing needs of their community. The department devotes much of its energy to area studies. Over the past two years the department's largest projects included Youngstown, Ohio; New City Parish, Los Angeles, Calif.; Kannapolis, N.C.; and suburban Detroit, Mich.

The department also trains individuals to use demographic information in decision making. Ms. Stella U. Ogunwole recently published, "Demographics in Area Ministry Development: The Planning of Congregations," in *Studies of Applied Demography, The Proceedings of the International Conference of Applied Demography*, Bowling Green, Ohio, edited by K. Vaninadha Rao and Jerry W. Wicks.

Cross-Denominational Research

The department participated in two major research projects involving several denominations. Patricia Chang of Hartford Seminary headed a Lilly funded study of women in ministry that focused on the particular issues women face in ministry and is a follow-up of a similar study conducted more than a decade ago. The department also participated in a cross-denominational study of giving headed by Dean Hoge of the Catholic University of America in Washington, D.C., and funded by the Lilly Foundation. In preparation for the study, Mr. Hoge commissioned papers, some of which were published in the December 1994 volume of *The Review of Religious Research*. The volume includes an article by Mr. Kenneth W. Inskeep entitled, "Giving in the Evangelical Lutheran Church: A Test of Several Hypotheses." Preliminary results of the study are available through the department.

DEPARTMENT FOR RESEARCH AND EVALUATION
KENNETH W. INSKEEP, *Director*

Exhibit A

Research and Evaluation: Some Examples

Examples of studies conducted by the Department for Research and Evaluation follow on pages 134-136.

CONFLICT

How Many Congregations Have Experienced A Serious Conflict in the Past Five Years?

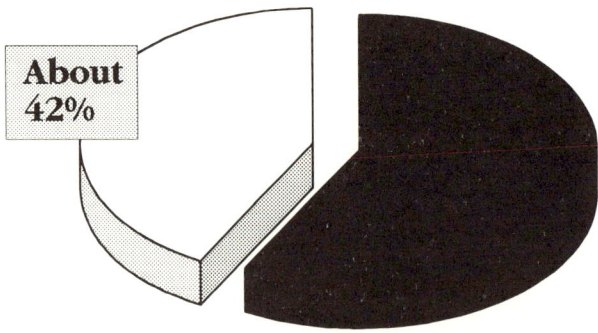

About 42%

☑ According to the pastors' reports, 37.5% of ELCA congregations have, in the past 5 years, experienced conflict that has resulted or has nearly resulted in either the pastor or a significant number of members of the congregation leaving the congregation. The frequency went as high as 48.9% based on all reports of conflict from council members. But in some of those congregations the two council members who responded disagreed as to whether this kind of serious conflict had occurred. **Based on the reports of both pastors and council members, the best estimate of the number of congregations experiencing serious conflicts is about 42%.**

☑ About 55% of those conflicts involved "an issue of pastoral leadership."

> About 5% of pastors and council members say their congregation is definitely in a perpetual state of conflict and disagreement.
>
> About 33% say strongly that disagreements and conflicts in their congregation are dealt with openly and are understood as a natural part of their congregational life and growth.

PLANNING

How Many Congregations Have Developed
A Plan for the Future?

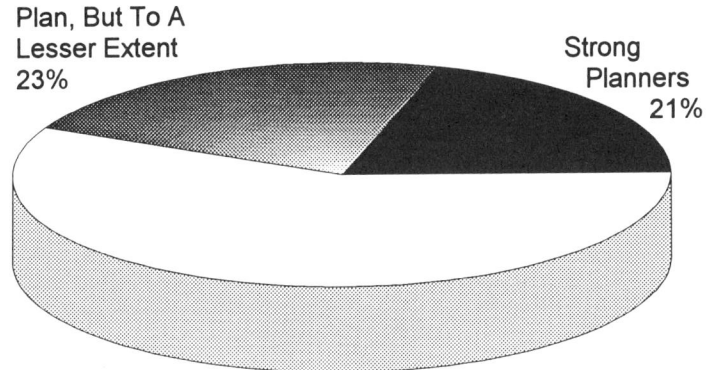

Plan, But To A
Lesser Extent
23%

Strong
Planners
21%

Do Little to No Planning
Over 50%

☑ About 21% of pastors and council members indicated that their congregation has definitely developed a plan for the future; another 23% have also been engaged in congregational planning, but to a lesser extent. The remaining congregations have not made planning a priority. Pastors and council members responded almost identically in rating the extent to which their congregation has developed a plan.

☑ About 27% of congregations are extremely conscientious in regularly studying the needs of members as a basis for mission planning; another 20% regularly study members' needs, but to a lesser extent. About 15% of congregations are very deliberate in regularly studying the needs of the local community as a basis for mission planning; another 14% engage in community study, but to a lesser extent. The remainder do little to no study of the local community.

What Percent of Congregations in Each Size Category Are Planners?			
Baptized Members	Strong	Somewhat	Little/No Planning
1 - 175	12.3%	20.3%	67.4%
176 - 350	18.8%	13.9%	67.3%
351 - 500	8.8%	36.0%	55.2%
501 - 700	18.2%	32.6%	49.2%
701 - 950	42.3%	11.2%	46.6%
951 - 1500	39.0%	34.1%	26.9%

WORSHIP

What Proportion Offer Differing Styles Of Worship Services Within Their Weekly Schedule?

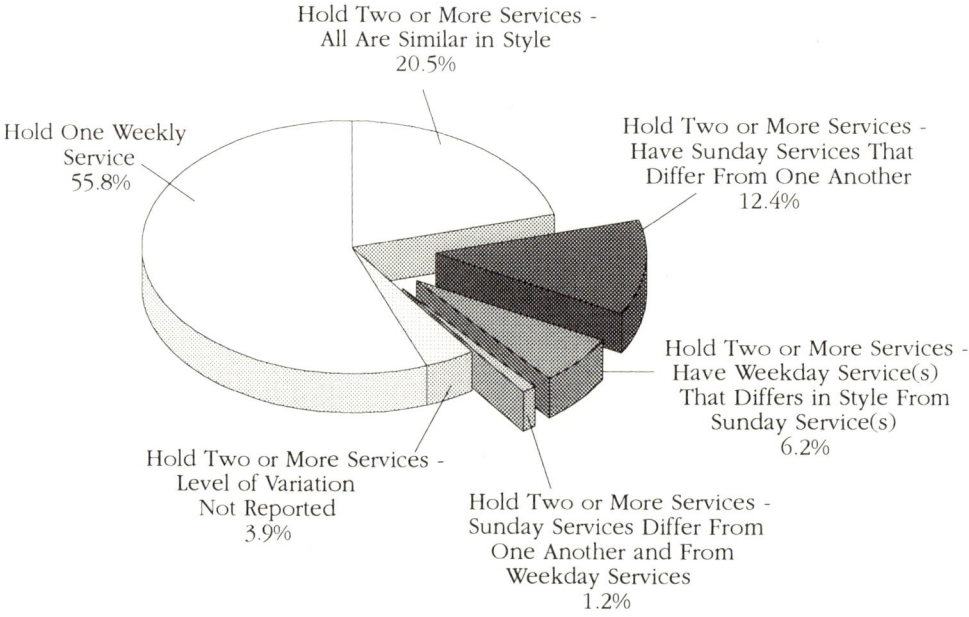

Hold Two or More Services -
All Are Similar in Style
20.5%

Hold One Weekly
Service
55.8%

Hold Two or More Services -
Have Sunday Services That
Differ From One Another
12.4%

Hold Two or More Services -
Have Weekday Service(s)
That Differs in Style From
Sunday Service(s)
6.2%

Hold Two or More Services -
Level of Variation
Not Reported
3.9%

Hold Two or More Services -
Sunday Services Differ From
One Another and From
Weekday Services
1.2%

How Often Do Congregations Celebrate Holy Communion As Part of Their Their Principal Sunday Worship Service?		
	In 1989	In 1993
Weekly	16.5%	20.4% *
Twice A Month	14.9	20.4
Twice/Month Plus Festivals	20.4	18.2
Monthly	15.6	15.0
Monthly Plus Festivals	29.0	21.4
Other	3.0	3.4

*Another 10% of congregations do not provide the sacrament weekly through their principal service but do have another worship service available that offers Holy Communion every week.

Report of the Department for Synodical Relations and Conference of Bishops

Organization
Staff
Director: Rev. Michael L. Cooper-White
Coordinator for Synodical Services: Glenndy L. Sculley
Assistant for Federal Chaplaincies:
 Rev. Lloyd W. Lyngdal
Shared-Deployed Staff, Region 1: Rev. Neal G. Buckaloo
Shared-Deployed Staff and Coordinator, Region 2:
 Vacant
Shared-Deployed Staff, Region 3: Rev. Hubert R. Kaste
Consultant, Region 4: Rev. Roger J. Gieschen
Shared-Deployed Staff and Coordinator, Region 5:
 Vacant
Shared-Deployed Staff and Coordinator, Region 6:
 Rev. Hermann J. Kuhlmann Jr.
Shared-Deployed Staff and Coordinator, Region 7:
 Vacant
Consultant, Region 8: Vacant
Shared-Deployed Staff, Region 9:
 Rev. Gerald S. Troutman

Constitutional Mandate
"This department shall coordinate the relationships between the churchwide organization and synods, including regions, develop and implement synodical-churchwide consultations and services, render support for synodical bishops and synodical staff, and provide staff services for the Conference of Bishops" (ELCA 15.31.F91.a.).

Report of Work 1993-1995
Ongoing Departmental Functions
The department supports synods through the following:

1. *First-Call Assignment Process:* Annually, approximately 350 candidates for ordained ministry and for service as associates in ministry are assigned to regions and the 65 synods of this church. The department collects and disseminates information on all candidates and conducts the three annual assignment consultations.

2. *Mobility:* Departmental staff assist synodical bishops and staff in their work with rostered persons who seek new calls. Regional mobility conferences are held to facilitate personal interviews between candidates for call and synodical bishops and staff. The standard mobility form has been converted to computer disk format and exploration continues regarding development of an electronic mobility system.

3. *Consultation:* Along with other churchwide units, the regions and synods, the department is involved in planning and conducting the synodical-churchwide consultations. In addition, departmental staff regularly consult with synodical leaders, providing resources and leading retreats and leadership development efforts.

4. *Good Samaritan Fund:* The department administers the Good Samaritan fund. The fund provides emergency assistance to rostered persons, their families, and survivors.

5. *Shared-Risk Fund:* This fund, in which two-thirds of the synods currently participate, is a form of "self-insurance" for costly disciplinary proceedings.

6. *GEM Continuing Education Grants:* In partnership with the Division for Ministry, the department administers "Growth in Excellence in Ministry" (GEM) continuing education grants to synodical bishops and staff, as well as to churchwide staff.

7. *Federal Chaplaincies:* The Rev. Lloyd W. Lyngdal, assistant to the bishop for federal chaplaincies, provides support for military chaplains, as well as chaplains in federal prisons and other institutions. Budget for the work of this office in Washington, D.C., is provided by this department.

8. *Regional Coordination:* Together with the Office of the Bishop, this department provides support for coordination in the nine regions of this church. Synods and the churchwide organization carry out significant work together through the regions.

Special Projects and Inter-Unit Collaboration
During the past biennium, the department has collaborated with other churchwide units in work on the following special projects: Special Needs Retirement Fund; Interim Ministry Development; Compensation Study; Process for Reflection on Bishops' Elections; and Symposium on Ministerial Wellness.

A Synodical Services and Resources staff team is chaired by the department director and meets regularly to coordinate work with synods and strengthen the churchwide organization's services to synods.

New Initiatives and Future Directions

With the addition of a staff position in which Ms. Glenndy L. Sculley serves as coordinator for synodical services, the department now has enhanced ability to respond to requests from synods for assistance and support in strategic planning, staff training and development, and management audits.

The following are new departmental initiatives under way or proposed for priority focus during the coming biennium:

1. *Transition Services:* A stronger level of support in the bishop's office will be offered to synods undergoing change. A synodical transition checklist has been developed, along with a synodical bishop's and staff handbook to assist those newly assuming office. Orientation and training for new synod staff persons will be offered regularly in addition to the annual new bishops' orientation.

2. *Synodical Initiatives Grants:* Together with the fraternal grants coordinator in the Office of the Bishop, the department will oversee allocation of grants totalling approximately $200,000 annually for leadership development and creative ministry initiatives in synods. Funding priorities will be established annually by the Conference of Bishops.

3. *Synodical Leaders' Support:* Through budget re-prioritization and special funding, the department intends to work collaboratively in organizing gatherings of key synodical leadership groups for networking, training, and mutual support.

And A Vision . . .

In our work in the coming biennium, staff of the Department for Synodical Relations will be guided by commitment to a vision of service and support--to the Conference of Bishops and to the synods of this church. In all we do, our efforts will seek to foster empowered, effective leaders in healthy, mission-driven synods.

DEPARTMENT FOR SYNODICAL RELATIONS

MICHAEL L. COOPER-WHITE, *Director and Assistant to the Bishop*

Conference of Bishops

The Conference of Bishops consists of the 65 synodical bishops, the bishop of this church, and the secretary of this church. The members of the Conference of Bishops on February 1, 1995, were the following:

Rev. Roy G. Almquist, Southeastern Pennsylvania Synod

Rev. James S. Aull, South Carolina Synod

Rev. L. Paul Bartling, Northwest Washington Synod (interim)

Rev. Richard F. Bansemer, Virginia Synod

Rev. John C. Beem, East-Central Synod of Wisconsin

Rev. James E. Bennett, Southwestern Texas Synod

Rev. Allan C. Bjornberg, Rocky Mountain Synod

Rev. L. Alexander Black, West Virginia-Western Maryland Synod

Rev. Paul J. Blom, Texas-Louisiana Gulf Coast Synod

Rev. Juan Cobrda, Slovak-Zion Synod

Rev. Guy S. Edmiston Jr., Lower Susquehanna Synod

Rev. Paul W. Egertson, Southern California (West) Synod

Rev. Norman D. Eitrheim, South Dakota Synod

Rev. Jon S. Enslin, South-Central Synod of Wisconsin

Rev. Lowell O. Erdahl, Saint Paul Area Synod

Rev. Richard J. Foss, Eastern North Dakota Synod

Rev. Lavern G. Franzen, Florida-Bahamas Synod

Rev. Ronald K. Hasley, Northern Illinois Synod

Rev. Mark B. Herbener, Northern Texas-Northern Louisiana Synod

Rev. Sherman G. Hicks, Metropolitan Chicago Synod

Rev. Reginald H. Holle, North/West Lower Michigan Synod

Rev. Robert L. Isaksen, New England Synod

Rev. E. Harold Jansen, Metropolitan Washington, D.C., Synod

Rev. Richard N. Jessen, Nebraska Synod

Rev. Robert M. Keller, Eastern Washington-Idaho Synod

Rev. Robert W. Kelley, Northeastern Ohio Synod

Rev. Ralph A. Kempski, Indiana-Kentucky Synod

Rev. Gerhard I. Knutson, Northwest Synod of Wisconsin

Rev. April C. Ulring Larson, LaCrosse Area Synod

Rev. Robert D. Lynne, Western North Dakota Synod

Rev. Charles H. Maahs, Central States Synod

Rev. A. Donald Main, Upper Susquehanna Synod

Rev. Robert W. Mattheis, Sierra Pacific Synod

Rev. Donald J. McCoid, Southwestern Pennsylvania Synod

Rev. Mark W. Menees, North Carolina Synod

Rev. Curtis H. Miller, Western Iowa Synod

Rev. Lee M. Miller, Upstate New York Synod

Rev. Robert L. Miller, Pacifica Synod

Rev. George P. Mocko, Delaware-Maryland Synod

Rev. Roger L. Munson, Northeastern Minnesota Synod

Rev. Glenn W. Nycklemoe, Southeastern Minnesota Synod

Rev. David W. Olson, Minneapolis Area Synod

Rev. Stanley N. Olson, Southwestern Minnesota Synod

Rev. Donald D. Parsons, Alaska Synod

Rev. Gregory R. Pile, Allegheny Synod

Rev. Mark R. Ramseth, Montana Synod

Rev. James A. Rave, Northwestern Ohio Synod

Rev. E. LeRoy Riley Jr., New Jersey Synod

Rev. Arthur V. Rimmereid, Northwestern Minnesota Synod

Rev. Peter Rogness, Greater Milwaukee Synod

Rev. Kenneth H. Sauer, Southern Ohio Synod

Rev. Floyd M. Schoenhals, Arkansas-Oklahoma Synod

Rev. Harold C. Skillrud, Southeastern Synod

Rev. Dale R. Skogman, Northern Great Lakes Synod

Rev. Paull E. Spring, Northwestern Pennsylvania Synod

Rev. James E. Sudbrock, Metropolitan New York Synod

Rev. Paul R. Swanson, Oregon Synod

Rev. Steven L. Ullestad, Northeastern Iowa Synod

Rev. Gregory J. Villalón, Caribbean Synod

Rev. J. Philip Wahl, Southeast Michigan Synod

Rev. Harold S. Weiss, Northeastern Pennsylvania Synod

Rev. Howard E. Wennes, Grand Canyon Synod

Rev. Paul M. Werger, Southeastern Iowa Synod

Rev. David C. Wold, Southwestern Washington Synod

Rev. Alton Zenker, Central/Southern Illinois Synod

Rev. Herbert W. Chilstrom, bishop of this church

Rev. Lowell G. Almen, secretary of this church

The following bishops retired or accepted other calls in 1993 and 1994: Rev. Charles D. Anderson, Rev. J. Roger Anderson, Rev. Robert H. Herder, Rev. Lowell E. Knutson, Rev. Rafael Malpica-Padilla, Rev. Michael G. Merkel, Rev. Gerald E. Miller, Rev. Lyle G. Miller, Rev. Henry Schulte Jr., Rev. Robert H. Studtmann, and Rev. Wayne E. Weissenbuehler.

Rev. John P. Kaitschuk, Central/Southern Illinois, died on April 1, 1994. He served as bishop from 1987 until his resignation on March 21, 1994. He had struggled with cancer since 1990.

Committees

The Conference of Bishops organizes itself according to its identified needs and mandated tasks. The officers of the Conference of Bishops are:

Rev. Kenneth H. Sauer, *chair* (1991-1995)

Rev. Charles H. Maahs, *vice chair* (1991-1995)

Rev. Lowell G. Almen, *secretary* (1991-1995)

Executive Committee

The officers serve as the executive committee, evaluating the director, budget, and activities of the staff, and appointing conference members to committees, boards, and task forces. The Rev. Kenneth H. Sauer served as chair from 1991 to 1995.

Agenda Committee

This committee prepares the agenda and program for the semiannual meetings of the Conference of Bishops (ELCA 15.41.A91.a. and b.). The Rev. Harold S. Weiss served as chair from 1991 to 1995.

Orientation and Bishops' Academy Committee

The orientation of newly elected synodical bishops and an annual continuing education event for all bishops (the Academy for Bishops) are the responsibility of this committee (ELCA 15.41.A91.g. and h.). The Rev. Gerhard I. Knutson served as chair from 1991 to 1995.

Roster Committee

The conference responds to applications for call to "ministry in unusual circumstances," exceptions to the three-year parish ministry requirement, and other exceptions to normal roster management (ELCA 7.41.11., 12., 13., 14., and 15.). The Rev. Guy S. Edmiston Jr. served as chair from 1991 to 1995.

Synodical-Churchwide Relations Committee

The Synodical-Churchwide Relations Committee is established to assist churchwide units and related organizations in securing review, advice, consultation, and recommendations by the Conference of Bishops on policies and programs. It is available to churchwide units and other ELCA entities that do not have a continuing liaison committee established by the conference. The Rev. Reginald H. Holle served as chair from 1991 to 1995.

Theological and Ethical Concerns Committee

Assisted by this committee, the conference serves as a forum for reflections upon the theological and ethical implications of issues that affect this church (ELCA 15.41.A91.h.). The Rev. E. Harold Jansen served as chair from 1991 to 1995.

Committee for Liaison with Division for Ministry

The conference works closely with the Division for Ministry in matters of roster definition, management, and supervision through this committee (ELCA 15.41.A91.c., e. and f.). The Rev. Richard N. Jessen served as chair from 1991 to 1995.

Committee for Liaison with Department for Ecumenical Affairs

The conference works closely with the Department for Ecumenical Affairs on ecumenical documents and the promotion of the unity of the Church through this committee (ELCA 15.41.A91.i.). The Rev. Ralph A. Kempski served as chair from 1991 to 1995.

Committee for Liaison to the Church Council

One synodical bishop from each region serves as an advisor to the Church Council and provides counsel to the conference on concerns related to the Church Council. The Rev. Robert L. Isaksen has served as chair since 1992.

Report of Work 1993-1995
Meetings of the Conference of Bishops

At each of the meetings of the Conference of Bishops, time is devoted to worship, synodical bishops' concerns, consultation regarding churchwide programs and emphases, and reports from the committees of the conference.

Meetings:

March 5-8, 1993--Savannah, Ga.

October 5-8, 1993--Chicago, Ill.

March 3-7, 1994--San Antonio, Tex.

October 1-6, 1994--Door County, Wis.

March 2-7, 1995--Newport Beach, Calif.

Other Meetings:

January 7-12, 1994--Academy for Bishops, Mundelein, Ill.

January 7-12, 1995--Academy for Bishops, Mundelein, Ill.

January 6-7, 1994--Orientation of Newly Elected Bishops, Chicago, Ill.

January 5-6, 1995--Orientation of Newly Elected Bishops, Chicago, Ill.

Referrals to the Conference of Bishops

The 1993 Churchwide Assembly referred the following to the Conference of Bishops:

Inadequate compensation and pension, referral on (CA93.8.98): The Conference of Bishops is cooperating with the Division for Ministry and the ELCA Board of Pensions to establish and manage the ELCA Special Needs Retirement Fund.

Interim ministry, referral on (CA93.8.101): Staff of the Department for Synodical Relations are consulting with other churchwide units and the Conference of Bishops in the development of guidelines for synodical calls to interim ministry and expanded support for interim pastors.

25th anniversary of the ordination of women, referral on (CA93.7.30): The Conference of Bishops received a report on how the ordination of women as pastors has enhanced the ministry of this church.

Rules governing disciplinary procedures, response to synodical memorial and referral to (CA93.8.107): The Conference of Bishops concurred with the Church Council recommendation to call for analysis of the issues involved in the burden of proof standard in discipline cases. The Conference of Bishops reviews and advises ELCA legal counsel on proposed changes to disciplinary procedures.

Major Areas of Study and Consultation

In addition to working on matters of concern to synodical bishops, the Conference of Bishops responds with advice and counsel as requested by the Church Council and boards and staff of churchwide units. Major issues and agenda for consultation since the 1993 churchwide assembly have included: Study of Ministry implementation; Study on Theological Education; development of social statement drafts on "peace" and "human sexuality"; process of reflection on this church's representational principles; discussion of this church's global mission outreach, including outreach in the United States and Caribbean; the "Inquiry" process, which looks toward the future of this church, synods, and congregations; continued development of this church's understanding of sacramental practices; ecumenical initiatives and preparation for major decisions in 1997 regarding ecumenical partnerships. The Conference of Bishops is engaged in an ongoing study of how the call process is carried out in synods and has recently reviewed results of synodical-churchwide consultations regarding staffing patterns.

Appreciation

Appreciation is expressed to all bishops who in 1995 conclude four-year terms as officers and committee chairs. Likewise, appreciation is expressed to all bishops who serve on committees and task forces, and as liaisons to boards of churchwide units and related entities. Finally, the Conference of Bishops expresses deep appreciation to its members who have left office for retirement or other calls.

CONFERENCE OF BISHOPS

KENNETH H. SAUER, *Chair*

MICHAEL L. COOPER-WHITE, *Director and Assistant to the Bishop*

Report of *The Lutheran*

Organization

Advisory Committee

The ten members of the committee elected by the ELCA Church Council are:

Rev. Robert E. Allen, Macon, Ga. (1997)

Ms. Mary Ann Bengtson, *chair*, Avoca, Iowa (1995)

Mr. Scott Bosley, Gary, Ind. (1999)

Mr. Daniel F. Kaercher, Urbandale, Iowa (1997)

Rev. Nadine F. Lehr, Gettysburg, Pa. (1995)

Ms. Jean M. LemMon, Des Moines, Iowa (1999)

Rev. Walter H. Mees Jr., *secretary,* Culver City, Calif. (1997)

Ms. Hazel H. Reinhardt, Edina, Minn. (1999)

Mr. Mark A. Staples, Landsdale, Pa. (1995)

Rev. Richard N. Stewart, Philadelphia, Pa. (1995)

Advisors

Rev. Lowell G. Almen, secretary, Evangelical
    Lutheran Church in America

Bishop Robert M. Keller, Eastern Washington-
    Idaho Synod

The committee met on March 15, 1993, November 5, 1993, March 11, 1994, and October 27-28, 1994.

Staff

Editorial Staff:

Editor: Rev. Edgar R. Trexler

Managing Editor: Rev. Roger R. Kahle

Senior Features Editor: Rev. David L. Miller

Features Editor: Ms. Kathleen H. Kastilahn

Senior News Editor: Ms. Sonia C. Groenewold

News Editors: Ms. Rosemary Dyson,
    Ms. Andrea S. Pohlmann

Production Editor: Mr. Rod Gerlach

Art Director: Mr. Harvey (Jack) Lund

Desktop Manager: Ms. Constance M. Gallagher

Editor of *Voces Luteranas*: Ms. Carmen Rodriguez,
    Meriden, Conn.

Publishing House Staff:

Director of Periodicals: Mr. Sigurd A. Hadland

Managing Editor, Periodicals: Mr. James Huber

Manager, Periodical Sales: Mr. Jim Pinkowski

Production Planner: Mr. John Rydeen

Subscription Order Supervisor: Ms. Jane Olson

Constitutional Mandate

The Lutheran is the monthly magazine of the Evangelical Lutheran Church in America, nurturing understanding of the mission and ministry of this church and providing informed editorial content about relevant concerns in the church's common life. The constitutional mandate for the church periodical is defined in provisions 17.20.ff of the Constitution, Bylaws, and Continuing Resolutions of the Evangelical Lutheran Church in America.

Report of Work 1993-1995

The Lutheran has a "new look." After 18 months of staff planning, the January 1995 issue ushered in a reorganized and redesigned magazine, the first major change in the church's periodical since the beginning of the Evangelical Lutheran Church in America in 1988.

Reader response was quick and positive. "Every publication I receive has undergone some major design changes in the last few years," wrote Kathy Bradley of Valparaiso, Ind. "Some of them overuse the capabilities afforded them, and the design does nothing to enhance the readability. But yours is by far and away the best I have seen. You have kept your readers foremost in mind."

The fresher, more contemporary design produced pages the staff calls "clean, neat, uncluttered, airy, bold, and striking." Additional "white space" was introduced, and full-color photo reproduction make every page colorful. Graphs, charts, maps, and other devices enable readers to absorb large amounts of information quickly. The cover logo was enlarged, and bold illustrations enhance the cover.

The staff worked hard at making the magazine more reader-friendly, primarily through shorter stories, and through writing that is personal, often using "you" and "we" language once considered too informal for good journalism. Using the concept of "entry points" for each page, the staff focuses on brighter, more inviting headlines, high-quality photography, and photo captions with increased content and information. Information in a story have been "quantified" so that readers can grasp it easily ("Ten ideas for healing your grief," "Seven ways to make Advent count"). "For more information" and "How you can help" boxes were added to provide "news you can use."

The Lutheran's reorganization of content moved the magazine away from its pattern and those of its predecessors that put longer feature articles in the front of the magazine and shorter news stories in the back. Longer and shorter stories about congregations, for example, formerly could be found in two different places in the magazine--for reasons understood by editors but not by readers. The magazine reorganized topically in four sections--Living the Faith, Values and Society, In Our Congregations, and Our Church at Work. Similar material--both long and short, features and news--were gathered together in each section to make it easier for readers to find specific material. The various columns of the magazine--Arts and Books, From the Bishop, Reader's Viewpoint, etc.--were retained, each placed in the section most appropriate for it. The popularity of a "theme" for each issue increased the frequency of such content from four times a year to monthly.

Each month *The Lutheran* prints synodical news supplements, which are stapled into issues going into the territory of a synod. Sixty-two synods have supplements at least four times a year. The magazine is received on audio tape by 627 persons, most of them visually impaired. A four-page wraparound section in Spanish, *Voces Luteranas*, is produced for each issue and distributed along with the magazine to congregations with worship services in Spanish and to some Spanish-speaking Lutherans. *Voces'* circulation is 2,450.

The Lutheran was honored in 1993 with the "People's Choice" award at the annual Associated Church Press Convention. Some 180 representatives of the church and religious press selected *The Lutheran*'s 1993 Christmas issue for the honor. Each magazine represented at the convention entered a single issue in the contest. During the convention, *The Lutheran* also received an award of merit for its "Letters" page and an honorable mention for its "reader response" article on subscribers' views of heaven and hell. In 1992, *The Lutheran* won three ACP awards for biblical exposition, professional resource, and for titles, kickers, and captions.

The September 1993 issue of *The Lutheran* included a special 20-page commemorative section, "The ELCA at 5." The special section was distributed at the 1993 ELCA Churchwide Assembly.

Editorial Content

The magazine's editorial guidelines state: "This magazine shall address the total constituency of the church in its diversity by:

1. proclaiming the Christian faith and relating it to the life of the people;
2. nurturing understanding of the mission and ministry of this church, its various units, its affiliates, and its related agencies;
3. reporting information of significance to the church and its people;
4. offering a forum for the responsible discussion of issues important to the life of this church and its people;
5. providing informed editorial content about relevant problems, needs, and concerns in this church's common life;
6. introducing the members of this church to personalities and institutions; and
7. publishing official notices as required by the constitution, bylaws, and continuing resolutions of the Evangelical Lutheran Church in America."

In the topically organized magazine, a substantial first article opens each section, followed by a number of other articles of varying lengths. Sections vary in size, usually from eight to twelve pages, depending upon the amount of news during a given month. Heavy emphasis is placed on using charts and graphs to help the reader comprehend the subject more quickly, as well as for adding liveliness and excitement to the page layouts.

Research during the biennium showed that readers were less interested in institutional church news and more interested in articles that help them live their faith amid the hassles of life. This information led to the formation of the "Living the Faith" section and to a decision to position it early in the magazine. Although articles of personal Christian experience had always been published in *The Lutheran*, the new section highlights this reader interest, focusing on heartwarming articles of personal experience, stories of interesting personalities, Bible study, and similar material. Such stories included "Ordinary Saints," "God's Gardener," "You Can Keep Your Spiritual Focus," " Heart of Joy," and "Have We Forgotten How to Forgive?"

Other sections flow logically from "Living the Faith." The "Values and Society" section contains ethical reflections on issues in society and allows for the probing of some new arenas, such as Christian perspectives on science and technology, personal finance, health and wellness, entertainment, and travel. Stories within recent months included "Investing with a Conscience," " 'My Genes Made Me Do It'," "Is TV Tuning Out God?", "Jesus Is Not a Republican (Or a Democrat)," and "Gambling: Who Wins, Who Loses?"

The third section, "In Our Congregations," tells about innovative and inspirational activities of congregations from Anchorage to San Juan. Stories included "Take Back the Streets," "Dining-Room Evangelism," "Six Marks of Growing Churches," "New Ministry for a 'New City'," and "User-Friendly Worship."

The final section, "Our Church at Work," highlights the wider work of the Evangelical Lutheran Church in

America, its synods, agencies, institutions, ecumenical, and international relations. Articles included such variety as "35,000 Youth in Atlanta," "Social Ministries Serve Two Million," "China Renews Religious Oppression," "Lutheran Lifeline to 250,000 Rwandans," "After the Quake" (Los Angeles), and "ELCA Schools Give You More."

Since *The Lutheran* is used for group study as well as for personal information, the staff increased the frequency of the "theme" section during the biennium from four times a year to every issue, adding a study guide in late 1994. The themes in 1994 were: aging; overcoming shame; finding Easter; why are we so angry?, whatever happened to loyalty?; Jesus: more than you think; social ministries; church shopping; culture of disbelief; how churches keep growing; and Christmas in the home. Themes scheduled for 1995 are: what's happening in worship?, healing your grief, how Lutherans interpret Scripture, fifty postwar years that shaped the church, prayer and personality, congregations and the environment, substance abuse, nourishing marriage, Lutheran identity, comparative religions, God's will for my life, and incarnation and healing. The "theme" section usually runs from eight to ten pages.

The reorganization did not change *The Lutheran*'s continuing commitment to being the news magazine of the Evangelical Lutheran Church in America and of the world of religion. It did mean, however, that the news stories were mixed with features in each section.

Continuing upheavals pushed editors to the limits in keeping up with the disintegration of church and society in the former Yugoslavia, famine in Somalia, genocide in Rwanda, church resurgence in the former Soviet Union, and the "breaking out of peace" in the Middle East. During 1993-1995, *The Lutheran* published first-hand reports from Tanzania, Poland, India, Germany, Singapore, Somalia, Hong Kong, Senegal, Sudan, Israel and the West Bank, Guyana, Bosnia, Angola, Switzerland, El Salvador, China, Slovakia, and Rwanda. In addition, *The Lutheran* daily monitors Lutheran news electronically from the Associated Press, United Press International, and Reuters, and the news bureaus of the Lutheran World Federation, the World Council of Churches, the National Council of the Churches of Christ in the U.S.A., and from church news organizations in Africa, Asia, Finland, Norway, Sweden, and Germany.

At home, the crush of news was almost as heavy. Church involvement after a major earthquake in Los Angeles, floods in the midwest, reaction to the release of the first draft of a proposed ELCA social statement on sexuality, articles on increased ELCA giving while membership decreased, the ordination of the first Eskimo and the first Hmong woman, Augsburg Fortress

closing its printing operation, the planting of 36 new ELCA missions in 1994, and a continuing series of retirements and elections of bishops, college and seminary presidents, and church executives crowded the news columns. Correspondents in each of the 65 synods contributed valuable information from across this church. Pages called, "At a Glance" and "Faces," helped to make a variety of material manageable for the reader.

A crossword puzzle is a new addition to the departments that appear in each issue. Creator of the puzzle, which is based on the theme of the issue, is Bishop Richard F. Bansemer of the Virginia Synod. Other departments continue. "Reflection," a short meditation, opens each issue. A column by the Rev. Walter M. Wangerin provides spiritual insights with a literary touch. A biblical or doctrinal study provides specific educational content ("Nurturing Faith at Home," by David W. Anderson, "Reclaiming Revelation," by Walter F. Taylor Jr., "Job," by William Matthews)." Arts and Books" focuses on the relationships between these areas and religion. "Since You Asked," co-authored by the Rev. Burton L. Everist and the Rev. Norma J. Everist, gives practical answers to frequently asked questions about church practice and doctrine. "Reader's Viewpoint" and "Letters" allow feedback from readers, along with a new effort, "Reader to Reader," in which readers are asked to share their ideas and questions about major articles. Responses are published two months later. "Lite Side" reflects on the humorous side of church life. The young readers' page, "Youngchurch," attracted 2,696 responses to its 1993 theme, "What would you tell people about God?" and 1,770 entries to the 1994 theme, "Thank you, God." ELCA Bishop Herbert W. Chilstrom authors a monthly page, and the editor concludes each issue with an editorial.

Color and Design

Each issue of the magazine is enhanced by extensive use of four-color photography. Contemporary design and high-quality, full-color illustrations, charts, maps, and graphs are high priorities for the staff. A major staff need for the future is the employment of a graphic artist to increase the use of charts and graphs.

In January 1994, *The Lutheran* moved to desktop publishing. Much of the staff is involved in on-screen editing of pages, utilizing QuarkXPress. Pages are now sent to the printer on SyQuest disk, a development that may soon be superseded by sending pages via modem. We are also contemplating going "direct to plate," which means all production from *The Lutheran* office to the printing press would be digital.

Publishing

The ELCA constitution states that *The Lutheran* "shall be published by this church through the ELCA publishing house." In consultation with the editor, the publishing house produces and distributes the magazine, supplies editorial services for the synodical supplements, and provides staff for circulation, promotion, subscription fulfillment, advertising solicitation, billing, collection of accounts, and other services. Quad Graphics, Hartford, Wis., prints the magazine under a new three-year contract. The contract also brought a reduction in the number of pages per issue from 68 to 60.

Advertising

Advertising is accepted in each issue, following advertising acceptability guidelines approved by the Advisory Committee for *The Lutheran* and the ELCA Church Council. During 1993, advertising revenue totaled $876,592; in 1994, the total was $771,921.

Promotion and Circulation

Some 95 percent of *The Lutheran*'s circulation comes through group subscriptions. In January 1994, the magazine's synod-wide and congregation-wide plans were combined into a single Every Home Plan. The region-wide plan was dropped. Congregations that belong to the plan are billed directly.

As of January 1, 1995, 5,611 congregations participated in the Every Home Plan with 700,676 subscriptions. Individual subscriptions total 36,830. Subscription rates changed in 1995 from $5.35 on the Every Home Plan to $5.95 per subscription, and from $10.50 for individual subscriptions to $11.90. Subscription income for 1993 totaled $4,627,791. In 1994 the total was $4,338,326.

In spite of vigorous marketing efforts, economic pressures on congregations and synods and other factors brought a slippage of total circulation from 912,417 in January 1993 to 783,578 in January 1995. The publishing house sends tailored promotion mailings to Every Home Plan and non-Every Home Plan congregations and makes presentations to synodical assemblies and to some individual congregations. *The Lutheran*'s circulation remains the largest among denominational publications in North America and is the largest Lutheran publication in the world. It goes into about one-half of the homes of ELCA members.

Budget

The editor and the president of the Publishing House of the Evangelical Lutheran Church in America prepare the magazine's budget. In addition to advertising and subscription revenue, the magazine receives an annual subsidy from the churchwide budget. In 1993, the subsidy was $276,530; in 1994, $250,000; in 1995, $245,000. Operating budget for *The Lutheran* was $5.6 million in 1993, $5.5 million in 1994, and $5.4 million for 1995.

Major Directions 1995-1997

The staff's continuing emphasis is to hone the quality of the magazine. In times of fast-paced life, reduced reading time, and decreased interest in institutions, the challenge is to produce a publication that invites and holds readers. In its twice-a-year planning retreats, the staff produces content analyses of its work, and reviews the magazine's written and visual content to see whether balance has been maintained in such categories as geography, gender, age, persons of color, etc.

Members of the Advisory Committee for *The Lutheran*, along with outside consultants, provide critiques at the committee's two meetings each year. The magazine is fortunate to have three editors of major publications on the advisory committee. Jean LemMon is editor of *Better Homes and Gardens*, Daniel Kaercher is editor of *Midwest Living*, and Scott Bosley, now publisher of the Gary (Ind.) *Post Tribune*, recently was editor of the *Journal of Commerce*, New York. The staff has relied upon the committee for insight and guidance in the redesigned and reorganized magazine.

Another emphasis in the years ahead will be maintaining an editorial balance between what members of this church want for their personal reading and providing the information about the life and work of the church that this church expects the magazine to deliver. Research has been clear in suggesting that undergirding personal living is a prime expectation of the magazine by readers, even to the point of being dubbed "Lutheran Living." But, *The Lutheran* is also the chief information tool of the Evangelical Lutheran Church in America, and willingly carries the responsibility of communicating our common life together to as many members as possible. Understanding this balance and working to achieve it will be a major factor in guiding *The Lutheran*'s future.

As these words were being written, the vice-president of the Oregon Synod, Kenneth Erickson, wrote about the "new" *The Lutheran*: "I commend you particularly for your primary emphasis on 'living the faith' right where I am . . . amid the struggles of daily life. I'm also enthusiastic about your section, 'In Our Congregations.' While it may be challenging to search out these unique practices, you perform a genuine service when you discern, share, and give credit to local leaders who have discovered a better approach to problems most of us face. 'Our Church at Work,' plus 'Values and Society' have important background contributions to make. We might wish these were the primary interests of our members, but from my observation that's not the case. I believe you have made an insightful shift that will increase the value and readership of the publication."

ADVISORY COMMITTEE FOR *THE LUTHERAN*

MARY ANN BENGTSON, *Chair*
EDGAR R. TREXLER, *Executive Director and Editor*

Report of the ELCA Foundation

Organization

Board

In 1993, the ELCA Church Council and the Churchwide Assembly approved the separate incorporation of the Evangelical Lutheran Church in America Endowment Fund under ELCA bylaw 17.31.01. The Church Council subsequently approved the Articles of Incorporation.

The Endowment Fund, Inc., will function under the continuing resolutions of the ELCA Foundation as one of the "other churchwide units." The adopted articles establish a founding board of five to bring about the actions necessary for the new corporation to function. There are issues dealing with legal, regulatory, and securities matters. Attorneys are working on the various applications and filings that are necessary.

The founding board includes these persons:

Rev. Robert N. Bacher, Executive for Administration, Office of the Bishop

Rev. Lowell G. Almen, Secretary of the Evangelical Lutheran Church in America

Mr. Richard L. McAuliffe, Treasurer of the Evangelical Lutheran Church in America

Mr. David J. Hardy, ELCA General Counsel

Rev. Harvey A. Stegemoeller, Executive Director, ELCA Foundation

When the Endowment Fund, Inc., is in place with necessary approvals from the Internal Revenue Service, Securities and Exchange Commission, et al., the Church Council will elect a board of directors of nine members to serve with one member from each of the nine regions of this church. It is anticipated that this election will take place in fall 1995.

Staff

The ELCA Foundation has 19 executive staff serving as representatives of the foundation to the members and congregations of this church. Most of them serve as shared staff with synods and consortia of Lutheran agencies and institutions.

The ELCA Foundation has seven executive staff and five support staff in the Chicago office.

Executive Director: Rev. Harvey A. Stegemoeller
Associate Director: Rev. Melvin L. Johnson
Associate Director: Rev. Kenneth R. Olsen

Area Representatives

Rev. Jeannette Bauermeister: Arkansas-Oklahoma; Missouri-Kansas

Ms. Patricia A. Bilow: Women of the Evangelical Lutheran Church in America

Ms. Gwen M. Boeke: Iowa

Rev. Franklyn A. Caron: Grand Canyon

Rev. Duane Danielson: Western North Dakota

Ms. Kathryn L. Glotfelty: N.W. Pennsylvania; S.W. Pennsylvania; West Virginia-W. Maryland

Rev. Mark W. Halaas: Minneapolis; St. Paul

Mr. Carl L. Johnson: S.E. Michigan; N.W. Lower Michigan

Mr. Gary D. Kovar: Florida

Rev. William F. Krenz: Lower Susquehanna

Ms. Patricia J. Larsen: World Hunger Appeal

Ms. Lois I. Leffler: S.E. Pennsylvania

Rev. Keith T. Nelson: Nebraska

Ms. Charles H. Oestreich: Texas

Rev. M. Franklin Pudas: South Dakota

Mr. Paul M. Quello: Wisconsin

Rev. Arlyn D. Saathoff: Metropolitan Washington, D.C.

Rev. Jerold B. Salveson: Northwestern Minnesota

Rev. Arthur W. Sorensen: Sierra Pacific

Constitutional Mandate

The constitutional mandate of the ELCA Foundation is defined in provision 17.30., ff., of the Constitution, Bylaws, and Continuing Resolutions of the Evangelical Lutheran Church in America.

Report of Work 1993-1995

The ELCA Foundation has as its purpose to increase the financial resources for all the ministries of the Evangelical Lutheran Church in America--the churchwide organization, synods and congregations, as well as agencies and institutions related to this church.

The primary objective of the ELCA Foundation is to motivate members of the Evangelical Lutheran Church in America to extend their commitment of Christian stewardship to their accumulated assets. Almost all ELCA members accumulate some assets of value—personal property, savings accounts, money market funds, certificates of deposit, stocks, bonds, mutual funds, annuities, retirement plans, pension funds, life insurance, and real estate. How are such accumulated assets managed, disposed of, or eventually left behind at death in the context of our commitment to

Christian stewardship on behalf of the ministries of Christ? Since its founding in 1988, the ELCA Foundation staff has conducted about 2,000 estate planning seminars in congregations and has provided personal, one-on-one, estate planning guidance and assistance to about 20,000 individuals and households that have expressed a desire to use this free service.

Specific ways to exercise Christian stewardship--trusteeship, our discipleship--are dependent on individual circumstances. Every member of this church, however, should ask some basic questions: When the Lord calls me from this life, what will I leave behind? How should I express my thanksgiving and accountability for the material blessings that I have accumulated? How much of what I leave behind should be dedicated to the mission of Christ, to help to do what Christ wants done? In which ministries in particular do I want to participate to fulfill Christ's Great Commission to preach the Gospel and to do deeds of love and mercy?

Exhibit A reports the work of the ELCA Foundation for the past biennium, 1993 and 1994, and for the seven years, 1988-1994. The life-income plans are investment gifts that provide income to the donors for their lifetimes and then provide funds for ministry after the donors are deceased. Though attention is focused on deferred and planned gifts, there are significant current, direct gifts.

The beneficiaries of the funds are quite diverse, including almost every type of ministry being done in the Evangelical Lutheran Church in America. The ELCA Foundation staff assists donors to determine which ministries of Christ they care most about as their own ministries for Christ. General undesignated gifts are always needed, but the donors are the ones who make the decisions. The exhibit will show you where the income through the ELCA Foundation has been distributed. The second pie-chart indicates where the life income deferred gift funds will be distributed.

If each ELCA family would dedicate a portion of its accumulated assets and a portion of its life insurance to support and strengthen the ministries of Christ in the Evangelical Lutheran Church in America, greater and more wonderful things could happen in and through this church. Members of the 1995 Churchwide Assembly are encouraged to make such dedication and to encourage others to go and do likewise.

ELCA FOUNDATION

HARVEY A. STEGEMOELLER, *Executive Director*

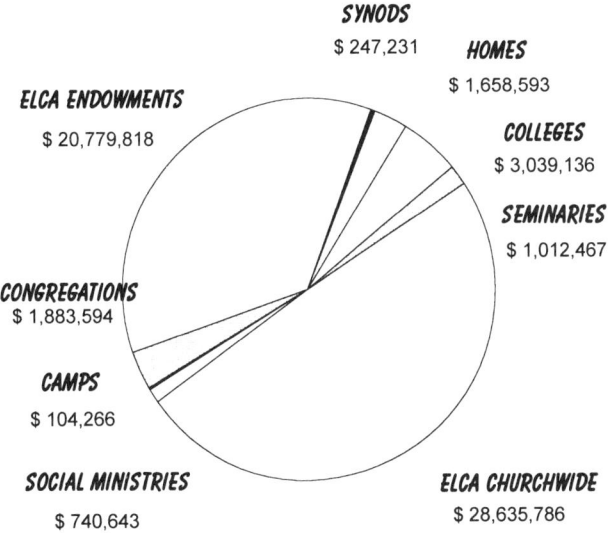

ELCA Foundation
Gift & Bequest Dollars to ELCA Ministries

SYNODS $ 247,231
HOMES $ 1,658,593
COLLEGES $ 3,039,136
SEMINARIES $ 1,012,467
ELCA CHURCHWIDE $ 28,635,786
SOCIAL MINISTRIES $ 740,643
CAMPS $ 104,266
CONGREGATIONS $ 1,883,594
ELCA ENDOWMENTS $ 20,779,818

$59 Million Distributed, Jan. 1, 1988 - Dec. 31, 1994
Outright Gifts, Bequests & Matured Income Agreements

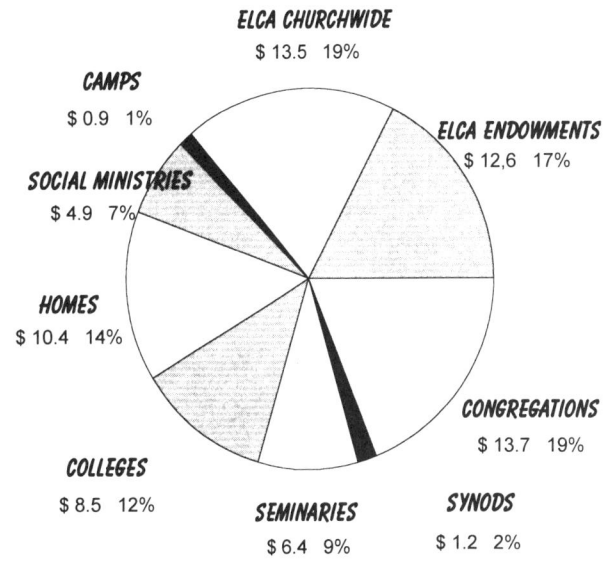

ELCA Foundation
Deferred Gift Dollars to ELCA Ministries

ELCA CHURCHWIDE $ 13.5 19%
CAMPS $ 0.9 1%
ELCA ENDOWMENTS $ 12.6 17%
SOCIAL MINISTRIES $ 4.9 7%
HOMES $ 10.4 14%
CONGREGATIONS $ 13.7 19%
COLLEGES $ 8.5 12%
SEMINARIES $ 6.4 9%
SYNODS $ 1.2 2%

$74 Million Total as of January 1, 1995
Gift Annuities, Pooled Income Funds, Charitable Trusts

Exhibit A

Beneficiaries of ELCA Foundation Gifts
February 1, 1994 through January 31, 1995

Beneficiary	Outright Gifts	Bequests & Trusts	Matured Contracts	Life Income Gifts
ELCA Undesignated	$ 3,672.75	$ 203,349.08	$ 34,349.80	$ 226,483.32
Department for Ecumenical Affairs	0.00	91,087.60	0.00	0.00
Division for Congregational Ministries	0.00	2,007.23	0.00	0.00
Division for Church in Society	0.00	5,745.56	0.00	0.00
Division for Global Mission	506,733.63	1,346,903.56	63,351.16	26,334.00
Division for Higher Education	25.00	0.00	0.00	28,800.00
Division for Ministry	35.33	0.00	7,577.60	5,000.00
Division for Outreach	843.96	415,318.38	11,104.38	3,333.00
ELCA Foundation	50,000.00	305,565.86	0.00	50,000.00
ELCA Vision for Mission Fund	12,419.17	128,228.00	557.67	2,000.0
ELCA CHURCHWIDE UNDESIGNATED	573,729.84	2,498,205.27	116,940.61	341,950.32
Division for Global Mission	0.00	40,000.00	0.00	0.00
ELCA Life Insurance Premiums	115,135.67	0.00	0.00	0.00
ELCA Mission Investment Fund	0.00	196,062.84	31,692.80	18,333.00
ELCA CHURCHWIDE DESIGNATED	115,135.67	236,062.84	31,692.80	18,333.00
ELCA Endowments	7,188,172.61	4,291,651.47	119,607.11	3,981,753.07
Lutheran Laity Movement	0.00	0.00	0.00	5,000.00
Lutheran Men in Mission	1,110.94	7,459.15	0.00	0.00
Lutheran Vespers	200.00	127,452.57	4,381.11	3,000.00
Lutheran World Relief	19,102.56	6,652.07	2,360.59	12,500.00
Women of the Evangelical Lutheran Church in America	0.00	7,459.15	0.00	186,543.68
World Hunger Appeal	29,347.22	189,804.53	101,471.35	147,403.47
ELCA CHURCHWIDE OTHERS	7,237,933.33	4,630,478.94	227,820.16	4,336,200.22
ELCA Seminaries	3,500.00	10,245.90	115,508.00	667,222.73
ELCA Colleges and Universities	41,400.00	0.00	446,930.27	970,775.49
ELCA Social Ministry Organizations	12,699.69	10,702.69	497,153.53	2,150,225.27
ELCA Congregations	308,261.64	0.00	274,764.24	1,402,801.36
ELCA Synods	1,000.00	76,142.47	64,735.35	392,056.91
Non-ELCA Charities	0.00	20,054.08	13,122.11	207,023.69
SUB TOTALS	8,293,660.17	7,481,892.19	1,788,667.07	10,486,588.99

GRAND TOTAL . . . . $ 26,262,141.35
(excludes matured contracts subtotal)

ELCA Foundation Report on Giving
February 1, 1994 through January 31, 1995

Type of Gifts Coming to the ELCA Foundation	1994 Fiscal Year to Date	1993 Fiscal Year to Date	Total Since Jan. 1, 1988
Current Major & Special Gifts			
Outright Gift - Endowment Funds	7,187,972.61	1,476,763.61	9,939,052.18
Outright Gift - CWO Division	570,021.76	107,896.98	1,124,813.28
Outright Gift - CWO Designated	0.00	7,200.00	184,159.58
Outright Gift - CWO Other	49,760.72	49,331.65	277,447,82
Outright Gift - Outside	367,061.33	102,749.96	1,226,079.05
Outright Gift - Undesignated	3,672.75	195,068.00	430,052.73
Life Insurance Premium Payments	115,135.67	163,812.50	672,572.39
Miscellaneous Gifts	35.33	30.55	26,849.94
SUBTOTAL	8,293,660.17	2,102,853.25	13,881,026.97

Current Income from Matured Bequests, Trusts & Life Insurance			
Trust Income - Undesignated	48,139.38	42,115.89	306,182.77
Trust Income - CWO Division	228,484.28	180,298.11	1,581,036.64
Trust Income - CWO Other	62,198.95	15,256.04	181,556.13
Trust Income - Outside	53,292.43	10,241.98	312,366.80
Bequests - Undesignated	145,834.97	677,820.49	7,215,514.37
Bequests - CWO Division	2,103,494.33	936,411.35	9,534,285.22
Bequests - CWO Designated	196,062.84	113,255.63	1,911,475.59
Bequests - CWO Other	276,628.52	359,266.24	2,538,297.14
Bequests - Outside	97,196.55	89,043.38	593,642.61
Bequests - for Endowment	4,219,591.02	972,895.40	9,980,103.56
Life Insurance Death Benefits	50,968.92	147,115.31	278,016.61
SUBTOTAL	7,481,892.19	3,543,719.82	34,432,477.44

Life Income Agreements for Future Benefit of ELCA Ministries	1994	1993	1988-1994			
Gift Annuity 1-Life	200	508	1727	4,128,131.11	6,954,719.17	24,930,017.77
Gift Annuity 2-Life	91	200	626	1,351,484.73	4,201,302.08	12,427,670.09
Deferred Annuity 1-Life	9	2	50	91,340.01	280,800.00	666,600.56
Deferred Annuity 2-Life	15	15	61	213,398.10	204,656.07	684,624.21
Pooled Inc. Fund #1	2	8	16	7,500.00	65,185.50	103,996.00
Pooled Inc. Fund #2	2	3	25	141,067.05	68,844.31	663,207.54
Annuity Trust	2	0	5	557,500.00	0.00	886,400.00
Unitrust	25	24	138	3,524,167.93	3,377,552.83	19,109,385.17
Life Estate	1	1	6	472,000.00	74,500.00	792,717.77
SUBTOTAL				10,486,588.93	15,227,559.96	60,264,718.11
CURRENT YEAR TOTAL				26,262,141.29	20,874,133.03	108,578,222.56

	1994 Fiscal	1993 Fiscal	Total Since
ECA Mission Investment Fund	2,477,913.35	1,153,113.83	10,213,933.66

Matured Life Income Agreements

	Number	Amount Paid Out
ELCA Churchwide Ministries	35	256,288.79
ELCA Endowments	20	119,607.11
ELCA Local Ministries	149	1,412,771.17
Total Agreements Matured Fiscal 1994	157	1,788,667.07
Distribution Pending	19	203,655.28

Living and Deceased Expectancies

Wills: Churchwide	62,766,264.00
Wills: Local Ministries	18,386,118.00
Life Insurance	18,625,504.31
Deceased Estates/Trusts	12,234,133.44
Deferred Gift Principal	73,589,427.39
TOTAL EXPECTED	**$185,601,447.14**

Beneficiaries of ELCA Foundation Gifts
January 1, 1988 through January 31, 1995

Beneficiary	Outright Gifts	Bequests and Trusts	Matured Contracts	Life Income Gifts
ELCA Undesignated	$ 468,293.13	$ 7,547,741.42	$ 1,303,258.81	$ 3,549,412.12
Dept. for Ecumenical Affairs	0.00	448,204.23	0.00	1,500.00
Div. for Congregational Ministries	0.00	4,077.02	0.00	5,000.00
Division for Church in Society	27,825.19	531,299.15	80,622.92	56,500.00
Division for Global Mission	693,692.60	6,605,789.23	355,469.75	1,086,187.41
Division for Higher Education	47,600.00	25,247.33	520.88	96,850.00
Division for Ministry	35.33	46,638.30	25,780.14	415,549.80
Division for Outreach	128,491.23	2,453,715.90	320,404.94	884,103.42
ELCA Foundation	140,207.24	593,245.36	,423.11	181,347.52
ELCA Vision for Mission Fund	29,171.17	252,297.63	557.67	102,000.00
Ingathering-1992-ELCA	17,300.10	0.00	0.00	0.00
Ingathering-1992-Global Mission	8,784.96	0.00	0.00	0.00
Ingathering-1992-Outreach	3,580.00	0.00	0.00	0.00
Ingathering-1992-Seminaries	2,160.00	0.00	0.00	0.00
National Lutheran Campus Ministry	5,000.00	0.00	0.00	18,960.00
ELCA CHURCHWIDE UNDESIGNATED	**1,572,140.95**	**18,508,255.57**	**2,089,038.22**	**6,397,410.27**
ALC Commitment to Mission	81,025.38	0.00	49,821.27	2,000.00
Board of Pensions	0.00	2,794.38	2,978.65	10,000.00
Dept. for Ecumenical Affairs	0.00	25,000.00	0.00	0.00
Division for Church in Society	300.00	500.00	0.00	0.00
Division for Global Mission	9,275.00	83,774.69	0.00	0.00
Division for Ministry	0.00	92,431.43	0.00	0.00
Division for Outreach	0.00	26,474.90	0.00	0.00
ELCA Life Insurance Premiums	672,572.39	0.00	0.00	0.00
ELCA Mission Investment Fund	74,111.05	1,819,503.03	52,394.37	267,801.92
LCA One in Mission Appeal	29,023.15	89,178.18	112,630.97	0.00
ELCA CHURCHWIDE DESIGNATED	**866,306.97**	**2,139,656.61**	**217,825.26**	**279,801.92**
ELCA Endowments	9,939,252.18	10,231,362.18	609,204.26	10,650,496.26
Lutheran Laity Movement	3,919.30	7,922.00	0.00	31,286.70
Lutheran Men in Mission	1,160.94	56,937.31	0.00	2,504.62
Lutheran Vespers	35,588.52	1,030,468.81	75,465.83	57,668.70
Lutheran World Relief	41,293.56	229,042.45	25,748.83	522,750.43
Women of the ELCA	0.00	64,238.99	2,465.61	328,335.44
World Hunger Appeal	195,485.50	1,345,408.22	127,415.31	638,675.97
ELCA CHURCHWIDE OTHERS	**10,216,700.00**	**12,965,379.96**	**840,299.84**	**12,231,718.12**
ELCA Seminaries	135,716.68	222,440.93	654,309.03	5,494,743.92
ELCA Colleges	328,276.33	0.00	2,710,859.89	5,243,181.62
ELCA Social Ministr Organizations	137,904.69	303,845.61	2,362,858.35	16,094,596.99
ELCA Congregations	593,741.37	27,215.66	1,262,637.11	11,871,978.46
ELCA Synods	14,700.00	81,142.47	151,388.19	1,147,715.96
Non-ELCA Charities	15,539.98	184,540.63	129,300.49	1,503,570.89
SUB TOTALS	**$ 13,881,026.97**	**$ 34,432,477.44**	**$ 10,418,516.38**	**$ 60,264,718.15**

GRAND TOTAL . . . . **$.108,578,222.56**
(excludes matured contracts subtotal)

Report of
Women of the Evangelical Lutheran Church in America

Organization
Officers and Executive Board

Churchwide officers and board members of Women of the Evangelical Lutheran Church in America for the 1993-1996 triennium were elected at the Second Triennial Convention, August 7-10, 1993.

Officers
President: Ms. Jan Peterson, Thief River Falls, Minn.*
Vice President: Ms. Jannene Sass, Omaha, Neb.*
Secretary: Ms. Peggy Bowker, Las Vegas, Nev.*
Treasurer: Ms. Iva Kjosnes, Zillah, Wash.*

Board Members
Ms. Faith Ashton, Chapel Hill, N.C.
Ms. Carol Bell, Cambridge, Minn.
Ms. Sharroll Bernahl, Ft. Morgan, Colo.
Ms. Mary Blake, Port Charlotte, Fla.
Ms. Joyce Breen, River Falls, Wisc.
Ms. Merle E. O. Freije, Mayville, N.Dak.
Ms. Angeline Haines, Lutherville, Md.
Ms. Victoria Hamilton, Slidell, La.*
Ms. Hattie Hammer, Priddy, Tex.
Ms. Carol Hines, Miller, S.Dak.
Ms. Mona Laughlin, Lancaster, Ohio
Ms. Borgne McClelland, Grafton, Wisc.
Ms. Nan Richard, Rome, N.Y.
Ms. Georganne Robertson, Olympia, Wash.*
Ms. Mary Sagar, Kalamazoo, Mich.*
Ms. Marilyn Sorenson-Bush, Cape Canaveral, Fla.
Ms. Judy Wagner St. Pierre, Newport News, Va.

Advisors
Rev. Lowell G. Almen, secretary, Evangelical Lutheran Church in America
Ms. Joanne Chadwick, executive director, Commission for Women
Bishop Gregory R. Pile, Allegheny Synod

---

* Executive Committee

The standing committees of the executive board for the 1993-1996 triennium are:

Executive Committee (see board listing)

Affirmative Action
Ms. Nan Richard, *chair*; Ms. Sharroll Bernahl,
    Ms. Carol Hines, and Ms. Marilyn Sorenson-Bush

Constitution
Ms. Angeline Haines, *chair*,
    Ms. Faith Ashton, Ms. Joyce Breen, Ms. Hattie
    Hammer, and Ms. Borgne McClelland

Printed Resources
Ms. Mona Laughlin, *chair*; Ms. Carol Bell,
    Ms. Mary Blake, Ms. Merle Freije, and Ms. Judy
    Wagner St. Pierre

Executive Staff
Executive Director: Ms. Charlotte E. Fiechter
Associate Executive Director: Ms. Patricia A. Robertson
Director for Finance and Administration:
    Mr. Jonathan C. Kalkwarf
Director for Planned Giving: Ms. Patricia Bilow
Director for Service and Development:
    Ms. Doris E. Strieter
Director for Literacy: Ms. Faith L. Fretheim
Director for Peace with Justice: Ms. Joan B. Pope
Director for Community Organization and
    Development: Ms. Dolores Yancey
Director for Communications and Stewardship
    Interpretation: Ms. Bonnie B. Belasic
Director for Leadership Development:
    Ms. Beckie M. Steele
Director for Growth and Witness: Ms. Valora K. Starr
Director for Educational Resources: vacant
Editor, *Lutheran Woman Today*: Ms. Nancy J. Stelling
Managing Editor, *Lutheran Woman Today*:
    Ms. Sue Edison-Swift
Assistant Editor, *Lutheran Women Today*:
    Ms. Cynthia Mickelson

Women of the Evangelical Lutheran Church in America serves participants in almost every ELCA congregation and in 64 synodical women's organizations. It is a network of women who are supported, challenged, and committed to grow in faith and ministry. The organization provides a place and a purpose for women throughout this church to discover and use their gifts and to serve others locally and globally.

Women of the Evangelical Lutheran Church in America is an incorporated and self-supporting organization governed by an executive board of 21 members. The triennial convention is the highest legislative authority of the organization.

The congregational unit, which consists of participants in congregational or inter-congregational groups, is the basic component of the women's organization. Congregational units relate to 64 synodical women's organizations which, in turn, relate to the churchwide executive board and the churchwide staff. One of the major responsibilities of the churchwide unit is providing organizational support to congregational units and synodical organizations in matters such as constitutional development, financial management, and programmatic resources.

Constitutional Mandate

The purpose of Women of the Evangelical Lutheran Church in America is to enable the women of this church to grow in faith and mission and to assist them in committing themselves to full discipleship, in affirming their gifts, and in promoting healing and wholeness in the church, the society and the world. The constitutional mandate of Women of the Evangelical Lutheran Church in America is provided in provisions 17.40., ff., of the Constitution, Bylaws, and Continuing Resolutions of the Evangelical Lutheran Church in America. The program and structure of the organization are defined in the constitutions and bylaws of both Women of the Evangelical Lutheran Church in America and the Evangelical Lutheran Church in America (ELCA 17.40.).

The consitution of Women of the Evangelical Lutheran Church in America defines the organization's purposes, principles of organization, governance processes, and responsibilities. The women's organization of this church is challenged to provide programs and resources that enable women to grow in faith, to articulate their faith and act on it in all areas of life, to work for the wholeness of church and society, and to build and celebrate relationships that are global, diverse, and interdependent.

The organization is mandated to facilitate local initiative in creating programs, to work for peace and justice, to advocate for the oppressed and voiceless, to promote change in systems and structures that exclude and alienate, and to relate to other women's organizations ecumenically and globally.

Women of the Evangelical Lutheran Church in America is committed to interdependence with the Evangelical Lutheran Church in America. The organization cooperates with all ELCA churchwide units, works closely with the Commission for Women, relates to interchurch entities and operates within the financial and personnel policies of this church. The ELCA constitution emphasizes such interdependent relationships. Women of the Evangelical Lutheran Church in America is an integral part of the life and ministry of

this church and it endeavors to live out this relationship in all of its work.

Report of Work 1993-1995

The organization's purpose statement serves as the basis for all unit activities:

> As a community of women created in the image of God,
>> called to discipleship in Jesus Christ, and
>> empowered by the Holy Spirit,
> We commit ourselves to grow in faith, affirm our gifts,
>> support one another in our callings,
>> engage in ministry and action, and
>> promote healing and wholeness in the church, the society, and the world.

Throughout the biennium the organization has worked in this church and ecumenically to fulfill this statement of purpose and to affirm women and seek full partnership for them in this church. During the period 1993-1995, the executive board has taken, in addition to its ongoing work of governing the organization, the following actions:

- continued work on the development of goals and policies for the organization;
- revised the organization's governance document;
- established goals and planning timetables for the 1996 Triennial Convention;
- designated sites for future Triennial Conventions (San Antonio in 1999; Philadelphia in 2002);
- adopted new working arrangements with the Publishing House of the Evangelical Lutheran Church in America.

Triennial Emphasis:
"Women and Children in Poverty"

"Women and Children in Poverty" is the organization's triennial emphasis from 1993 to 1996 and will continue as the emphasis in the next triennium. As part of the organization's commitment to improving the condition of women and children in poverty, Women of the Evangelical Lutheran Church in America has engaged in a broad array of activities and has supported the development of a number of resources, including:

1. A churchwide "Women and Children Living in Poverty" event to train volunteers from all 64 synodical women's organizations for implementation of the triennial emphasis.
2. Development and presentation of consultations on "Women and Children in Poverty" in six ELCA regions in cooperation with Lutheran Men in Mission and the Division for Congregational Ministries. The purpose of the consultations was to educate partici-

pants about issues related to poverty and ways to effect change.

3. Use of income from the New Ministries Fund, the Fund for the Development of Human Resources, the Designated Fund for Women and Children in Poverty, and the triennial convention offerings to support programs and projects designed to alleviate the condition of poverty for women and children. Among the projects funded were:

   - job training, employment, and leadership training programs for low income women in Kentucky, Pennsylvania, and Massachusetts;
   - a program providing care and training for homeless and abused children in Oklahoma;
   - an adoption project for children of persons affected by AIDS in Illinois;
   - community advocacy programs for immigrants and refugees in California and Wisconsin;
   - health-care assistance for Native American children in Montana;
   - housing rehabilitation projects in the District of Columbia and other areas;
   - safe houses for women and children who are victims of abuse and shelters for the homeless; and
   - primary health-care and development projects in Kenya, Guatemala, India, and Cameroon.

4. Development of resources to inform participants about the situation of people in poverty and to educate them about ways to effect change (see section on resources).

5. Development of "An Opportunity for Public Witness," a pilot empowerment project designed to focus on public policy advocacy at the state and local levels. The purpose of the program is to train women in advocacy and to move them from dealing with the effects of poverty to designing and implementing systemic change. The pilot project and related resources focused on Illinois, but the program has been designed to be replicated in other states.

6. Co-sponsorship of a conference on "Women and Children Living in Poverty" with Region 7, the Division for Outreach, and the Interunit Staff Team on Women and Children Living in Poverty.

7. Work in cooperation with other units and ecumenically to address this issue.

Literacy

In 1993, Women of the Evangelical Lutheran Church in America celebrated the 25th anniversary of the establishment of the Volunteer Reading Aides, the foundation of the organization's literacy program.

Women of the Evangelical Lutheran Church in America remains the only denominational women's organization with a literacy desk, and serves as the coordinating agency for the literacy work of the major denominational women's organizations through the Working Group on Literacy and Basic Education of the National Council of the Churches of Christ in the U.S.A..

Leadership Development

During this biennium, the organization initiated a new leadership program, "Embracing Self and Others," designed to enable all women to discover and develop their leadership gifts. It is anticipated that by the end of 1995 more than 10,000 women will have participated in this program. The organization also initiated training programs for new synodical presidents and treasurers, and an orientation program for new churchwide board members. The Conference of Presidents convened annually and addressed issues such as organizational development, community building, and conflict management.

The Witness of Women

The organization's evangelism strategy was introduced in 1994 with "Rediscovering my Story," a six-part learning module designed to help women rediscover their personal stories and how these relate to evangelism. As of this writing, the strategy is being used in more than 2,000 congregational units. "Revitalizing our Story," introduced in 1995, explored the way Christian witness affects the lives of others our understanding of evangelism. Part three, "Reaching Out With God's Story," will be introduced in 1996 and will focus on intentional evangelism. The strategy will be available in English and Spanish.

Cross-Cultural and Ecumenical Programs

Major budget cuts in 1993 led, among other program reductions, to the suspension of the organization's two major cross-cultural programs, "One in Christ" and "Woman to Woman." The organization made a commitment to the continuation of cross-cultural programming, and a staff committee was assigned to make recommendations. Those recommendations led to the appointment of a consultant to work with the organization and to propose the development of programs and resources for the organization's cross-cultural and anti-racism efforts.

Planned-Giving Program

With the appointment of Patricia Bilow as director for planned giving, Women of the Evangelical Lutheran Church in America initiated a three-year pilot program in planned giving. The purpose of this program is to assist women with their financial and estate planning and to begin the development of financial resources to support the organization in the future. Through a program of presentations to synodical conventions and congregations, printed resources about planned giving, and individual consultations, the director for planned giving has made a promising beginning to this important work.

Theological Conferences

Women of the Evangelical Lutheran Church in America sponsored and organized several regional theological conferences in 1994 and 1995. These conferences, developed on the theme of "Grace," offered participants an opportunity to explore a theological concept and to understand how they themselves could think about theological issues.

Scholarships

As part of its effort to empower women to become full partners in church and in society, Women of the Evangelical Lutheran Church in America provides scholarships to mature participants who wish to return to school to continue their educations. Funds to support this program come from endowments established by women of faith and vision and from current gifts.

The *Academic Leadership Scholarship* enables women faculty and staff members of ELCA colleges and seminaries to participate in leadership and management development programs. The goal of this scholarship program is to develop and promote women's leadership in ELCA colleges and seminaries and to prepare women to move into senior leadership positions at their institutions.

Research Initiative

During this biennium, the organization initiated a comprehensive research project to learn more about its constituent base. With the assistance of the ELCA Department for Research and Evaluation, the organization conducted focus groups with the presidents of synodical organizations and developed a series of questionnaires seeking demographic data, evaluative information about programs and resources, and general information about constituent perceptions and needs. These questionnaires were directed toward approximately 3,000 women in 600 congregations. Plans call for this research project to continue through the entire triennium.

25th Anniversary of the Ordination of Women

In cooperation with the Division for Ministry and the Commission for Women, the women's organization has been active in planning the celebration of the 25th anniversary of the ordination of women in the Evangelical Lutheran Church in America. The planning commit-tee has organized a three-day commemorative conference, "Breaking the Jar: Twenty-Five Years of Remembrance," to be held in Minneapolis prior to the 1995 Churchwide Assembly, and helped to plan a celebration of the ordination of women, which will be held during that assembly. The organization's gift to the celebration is a book of essays by Lutherans who participated in the decision to ordain women and those who were among the first women to attend seminary and to be ordained.

Development of Resources

Developing resources is a major activity of the organization. Such resources include Bible studies, resources on organizational development and management, programmatic and interpretive resources, and resources for individual spiritual growth.

Lutheran Woman Today, the magazine of the women's organization, is one of the organization's outstanding resources and evangelism tools. With the largest circulation of any denominational women's magazine, *Lutheran Woman Today* provides information and inspiration to some 225,000 subscribers 11 times a year in regular, large-print, and audio-cassette editions.

Lutheran Woman Today continues to receive recognition from religious press associations. In 1993, the magazine received awards for "general excellence" from the Associated Church Press in the special interest magazine category and for two special feature articles. *Lutheran Woman Today* also received four awards from the Religious Public Relations Council in its DeRose/Hinkhouse competition: an award of merit and three honorable mentions, in the national magazine category, for black and white photography and for graphic design. In 1993, the magazine won two certificates of merit in the DeRose/Hinkhouse Awards contest. Special issues included two triennial convention issues, an issue on "Heaven and Hell," which was featured in an Associated Press release, and "Seize the Hope," the July-August 1994 issue on Women and Children in Poverty.

During the past biennium the organization's newsletter was reshaped and redesigned and is now *Women of the Evangelical Lutheran Church in America Interchange*. This publication, published three times a year, is mailed to all congregational units and also is available by subscription.

Bible study and related educational programming always have been central to the purpose and work of the women's organization. Each year participants in thousands of congregational units use one or more of the Bible studies prepared by Women of the Evangelical Lutheran Church in America to learn more about the Bible and its meaning for their lives.

Bible studies published in this biennium included:

- "Faith, Hope and Love: A Study of First Corinthians" (*Lutheran Women Today* 1993);
- "The Unshakable Kingdom: A Study of Hebrews" (*Lutheran Women Today* 1994);
- "The Hidden Promise: A Study of the Ten Commandments" (*Lutheran Women Today* 1995).

A reader guide, resource book, and companion pieces (theme programs, bulletin covers, posters, calendars, daily Bible readings, etc.) were published for each Bible study.

Other printed resources included:
- "The Witness of Women, Year One" (evangelism strategy) and
- "The Witness of Women, Year Two," in English and Spanish;
- "Weaving Your Faith and Life: The 1994 Program Idea Book";
- "Programs, Retreats and Devotions: The 1995 Program Idea Book";
- "Building Blocks of Hope for Women and Children Living in Poverty";
- "We're All in This Together: Building Blocks of Hope Resource" Packet 2;
- "Breaking the Barriers: Women and Development";
- "The Volunteer Reading Aides: 25 Years";
- "Women and Children in Poverty: The Literacy/Education Connection";
- "*Ser Pobre*? (To Be Poor?): Poetic Reflections from Peru";
- "Activity Planning Calendar for Women and Children in Poverty";
- "The Action Flash," which is sent to all peace with justice, literacy, and service and development coordinators;
- "Charitable Connections," the planned giving newsletter; and
- The WELCA Resource Packet, distributed to all congregational units twice a year.

The organization also produced several videos, including a promotional video for the 1996 triennial convention; an interpretive video for use by synodical organizations, conferences, and clusters, and congregational units; and a video to interpret the designated-gifts program of the organization.

Gift to the Evangelical Lutheran Church in America

As an expression of the partnership of Women of the Evangelical Lutheran Church in America in the ministries of this church, the organization gives an annual gift to support the total outreach of the Evangelical Lutheran Church in America. This gift is made possible by the contributions of women throughout the organization through their support of Designated Gifts and Thankofferings.

In 1993, Women of the Evangelical Lutheran Church in America gave $1,067,400 to the churchwide work of the Evangelical Lutheran Church in America. For 1994 and for 1995, the "Gift to the Church" was budgeted at $1,100,000.

These annual gifts, representing more than 30 percent of the annual organizational budget, were in addition to the gifts to this church and its institutions and related operations (e.g., scholarships to ELCA colleges and seminaries, support for social ministry organizations, contributions to food pantries and homeless shelters supported by congregations, support for physical improvements in congregations, etc.) given by congregational units and synodical organizations of Women of the Evangelical Lutheran Church in America throughout this church.

Major Program Directions 1995-1997

Major program directions for the next biennium include:
- continuing the development of programs and resources to support the triennial emphasis of Women and Children in Poverty;
- expanding the number of congregational units and providing more support for existing units;
- the development of phase two of the new leadership program;
- working to make the organization more inclusive and to bring more younger women into the organization;
- continuing to affirm the changing roles of women in our society and in our church; and
- supporting and enabling women in their efforts to grow in faith and ministry.

In keeping with its purpose statement, Women of the Evangelical Lutheran Church in America will continue to affirm women in this society and in the Evangelical Lutheran Church in America, empowering women in their efforts to grow in faith and ministry, working to identify and respond to the needs of women, and helping them meet their spiritual and personal needs. A biennial report such as this can cite only major events and programmatic highlights. It tends to focus on specific events and programs, rather than on continuing efforts to create change. The ongoing life of the organization occurs day by day, with dedicated staff members working to achieve organizational goals and purposes in a multitude of ways.

The past two years have been rich in dreams and rich in accomplishments. For the future, Women of the Evangelical Lutheran Church in America will remain committed to its purpose statement, to making a difference in the world for its participants and for women and men everywhere in the service of God.

WOMEN OF THE EVANGELICAL LUTHERAN CHURCH IN AMERICA

JAN PETERSON, *President*
CHARLOTTE E. FIECHTER, *Executive Director*

Report of the Board of Pensions

Organization

Board of Trustees

Mr. Floyd O. Arntz, Newton, Mass. (term expires 1995)
Ms. Barbara L. Bauer, *secretary*, Boise, Idaho (1997)
Mr. Ulysses Bell, Greensboro, N.C. (1995)
Ms. Mary Alice Bjork, Salem, Oreg. (1999)
Ms. Linda J. Brown, Moorhead, Minn. (1995)
Mr. Irving R. Burling, Birchwood, Wis. (1999)
Mr. Ralph J. Eckert, *chair*, Dillon, Colo. (1997)
Mr. Noel I. Fedje, Fargo, N.Dak. (1995)
Rev. Kenneth C. Feinour Jr., Jenkintown, Pa. (1997)
Ms. Sandra G. Gustavson, Athens, Ga. (1995)
Mr. William R. Halling, Bloomfield Hills, Mich. (1999)
Ms. Carla P. Haugen, Darien, Conn. (1999)
Ms. Carolyn S. Nestingen, Minneapolis, Minn. (1997)
Ms. Emma Graeber Porter, New York, N.Y. (1999)
Rev. J. Christian Quello, Appleton, Wis. (1999)
Ms. Ruth E. Randall, Lincoln, Nebr. (1999)
Ms. Rochelle D. Reed, Golden Valley, Minn. (1997)
Mr. Theodore S. Rosky, *treasurer,* Louisville, Ky. (1995)
Mr. David A. Russell, Allentown, Pa. (1997)
Rev. Viviane Thomas-Breitfeld, *vice chair,* Waukesha, Wis. (1995)
Rev. Wilson Wu, Monterey Park, Calif. (1997)

Advisors

Rev. Lowell G. Almen, Secretary, Evangelical Lutheran Church in America
Bishop Glenn W. Nycklemoe, Southeastern Minnesota Synod

Executive Committee

Mr. Ralph J. Eckert, *chair*
Ms. Barbara L. Bauer
Ms. Linda J. Brown
Rev. Kenneth C. Feinour Jr.
Ms. Sandra G. Gustavson
Ms. Carolyn S. Nestingen
Mr. Theodore S. Rosky
Rev. Viviane Thomas-Breitfeld

Audit Committee

Ms. Linda J. Brown, *Chair*
Mr. Floyd O. Arntz
Ms. Barbara L. Bauer
Mr. Ralph J. Eckert *(ex officio)*
Mr. William R. Halling
Ms. Carolyn S. Nestingen
Ms. Ruth E. Randall

Benefits Committee

Ms. Sandra G. Gustavson, *chair*
Ms. Barbara L. Bauer
Ms. Mary Alice Bjork
Mr. Irving R. Burling
Mr. Ralph J. Eckert *(ex officio)*
Mr. William R. Halling
Ms. Carolyn S. Nestingen
Ms. Emma Graeber Porter
Ms. Rochelle D. Reed
Rev. Viviane Thomas-Breitfeld
Rev. Wilson Wu

Investment Committee

Mr. Theodore S. Rosky, *chair*
Mr. Floyd O. Arntz
Mr. Ulysses Bell
Ms. Linda J. Brown
Mr. Ralph J. Eckert *(ex officio)*
Mr. Noel I. Fedje
Rev. Kenneth C. Feinour Jr.
Ms. Carla P. Haugen
Rev. J. Christian Quello
Ms. Ruth E. Randall
Mr. David A. Russell

Nominating Committee

Ms. Rochelle D. Reed, *Chair*
Ms. Mary Alice Bjork
Mr. Ralph J. Eckert *(ex officio)*
Mr. Noel I. Fedje
Rev. Kenneth C. Feinour Jr.
Ms. Sandra G. Gustavson
Ms. Emma Graeber Porter
Rev. Wilson Wu

Personnel and Compensation Committee

Rev. Viviane Thomas-Breitfeld, *chair*
Mr. Ulysses Bell
Mr. Irving R. Burling
Mr. Ralph J. Eckert *(ex officio)*
Ms. Carla P. Haugen
Rev. J. Christian Quello
Mr. Theodore S. Rosky
Mr. David A. Russell

Investment Committee Advisors

Mr. James A. Greenleaf, Bethlehem, Pa.
Mr. Deryl F. Hamann, Omaha, Nebr.
Mr. Norman M. Jones, Minneapolis, Minn.
Mr. Richard L. McAuliffe, Chicago, Ill.
Mr. Howard I. Rundquist, Chatham, N.J.

Executive Staff

President: Mr. John G. Kapanke
Vice President, Finance: Mr. David G. Adams

Vice President, Pension Administration:
    Mr. Lyle N. Anderson
Vice President, Administrative Services:
    Mr. Vernon S. Bolte
Vice President, Medical and Dental Administration:
    Ms. Kathryn A. Helmke

Constitutional Mandate

The mission of the Board of Pensions is to provide pension, health, and other benefits, and related services that will enhance the lives of pastors, associates in ministry, lay employees, and their families, and support the well-being of congregations and institutions of the Evangelical Lutheran Church in America.

The constitutional mandate of this churchwide unit is provided in provisions 17.60., ff., of the Constitution, Bylaws, and Continuing Resolutions of the Evangelical Lutheran Church in America (see *1995 Pre-Assembly Report, Volume 1,* pages ###-###)

Report of Work 1993-1994

Two years ago the Board of Pensions embarked on a Strategic Planning Project to develop a long-term strategy for managing the liabilities and risks of the Pension and Other Benefits Program. The Strategic Planning Project dealt with challenges facing the board in three major areas: governance, medical-dental, and pension/investments. Significant changes have been carried out in the first two areas. The Pension/Investment Strategy Project continues to identify improvements in the pension plan design. The staff project team is working to accommodate both the plan members' desire for flexibility in investment choices and the church's need to convert pension contributions effectively into retirement benefits.

Governance

Governance generally doesn't rank high on the interest scale. But, according to Ralph Eckert, Chair of the Board of Trustees of the Board of Pensions: "Governance is of the highest importance because it ensures a continuance of a fiscally sound operation in which our members can put their trust. The decisions we make today about the Medical and Dental Benefits Plan or about investments are exceedingly important. But as time changes, so will those specific decisions. What we need above all is superior leadership that will ensure sound decision-making for the future. Good governance provides us that."

Governance changes affect the selection of trustees for the Board of Pensions and the way trustees function. With respect to recent changes in the governance of the board, Eckert states: "We evaluated how trustees are elected and how we as a board are organized. We added a personnel and compensation committee and are moving toward a corporate model of governance. Committees now meet just prior to the quarterly board meetings. This format has been very successful."

These changes in governance will allow the trustees to focus on strategic management while the staff of the Board of Pensions assumes responsibility for operations management.

Medical and Dental

During 1993–1994, more than 800,000 medical and dental claims were received and processed under the internally-administered plans. Total benefits paid under the plans in 1993 and 1994 exceeded $135 million. During this period, board staff also responded to more than 80,000 telephone inquiries and answered thousands of letters concerning plan benefits.

During the past several years, the board has undertaken initiatives to evaluate and implement "managed care" programs under the ELCA health plans. Effective January 1, 1993, a mail service drug program through Express Pharmacy Services (EPS) became effective for members covered under the three medical plans. Member satisfaction with the program has been high and savings to members and the plans during 1993 totaled approximately $2.9 million.

Effective January 1, 1994, a managed mental health program through Value Behavioral Health (VBH) was implemented for members covered under the ELCA Medical and Dental Benefits Plan. The program is unique in that only treatment for inpatient mental health and any chemical dependency treatment must be pre-certified and managed by VBH. Plan members may access outpatient mental health care at any time they wish.

The first phase of an ELCA national managed care program for members of the ELCA Medical and Dental Benefits Plan was implemented on January 1, 1995. Over 11,400 individuals, approximately 33 percent of plan members, in 18 different locations became covered under a point-of-service managed care program administered by Aetna. The second phase of the program will be implemented on January 1, 1996, when an additional 12 percent of plan members in 20 areas will become covered under the point-of-service program.

Projected savings from the managed care programs, along with a lower rate of escalation in health care costs, enabled the Board of Pensions to substantially reduce medical plan contribution rates for 1995. For active members, 1995 contribution rates decreased by an average of 16 percent, producing total savings of $9 million for congregations and other sponsoring employers. Favorable rate action was also taken for retirees, with contribution rates for retirees covered by Medicare decreasing by 22 percent and contribution rates for retirees not yet eligible for Medicare remaining unchanged. The recent favorable experience also has enabled the board to build adequate reserves for future adverse fluctuations in experience.

In April 1995, a pilot program for the implementation of a toll-free telephone service began. Plan members in four states are able to contact the Board of

Pensions by dialing a toll-free number. The service will be implemented nationwide by the end of 1995.

Pension and Investment

In 1993 and 1994, the Board of Pensions continued its program to improve investment fund management as international and private market investments were expanded. The funds and the market value for each fund's assets (in millions) as of December 31, 1994 are listed below:

Frozen Funds
ALC Balanced Fund ($723)
LCA Fixed Income Pension ($616)
LCA Variable Income Pension (VIP) ($430)
AELC Retirement Plan ($11)

Current Funds
ELCA Equity Fund ($70)
ELCA Balanced Fund ($130)
ELCA Bond Fund ($106)
ELCA Social Purpose Equity Fund ($81)
ELCA Social Purpose Balanced Fund ($87)
ELCA Social Purpose Bond Fund ($72)
ELCA South Africa Free Equity Fund ($36)
ELCA South Africa Free Balanced Fund ($53)
ELCA South Africa Free Bond Fund ($44)

Funds Related to Survivor, Disability, Medical, and Dental Benefits:
Survivor Benefits Fund ($46)
Disability Benefits Fund ($22)
Medical/Dental Benefits Fund ($41)
ALC Medical and Dental Fund ($80)
LCA Ministerial Health Benefits ($9)

The events leading up to the scheduling of multiracial elections in South Africa in April 1994 led the board to review its policy on South Africa and adopt policy changes in late 1993. The changes included (1) elimination of the South Africa free screen in the Social Purpose Funds, (2) elimination of the South Africa policy statement, and (3) approval of pension plan amendments to allow pensioners to transfer their interests out of South Africa Free Funds.

Plans to eliminate the South Africa Free Funds were approved in 1994. As of December 31, 1994, over $130 million remained in these funds. Effective April 1, 1995, the assets in the South Africa Free Funds were transferred to the other existing funds.

The expansion of the board's international investment program has continued over the past two years. In 1993, the Investment Committee made an allocation to emerging markets equities, which led to the hiring of Schroder Capital Management as portfolio manager. In late 1994, the target allocation to non-U.S. equities was increased from 20 percent to 30 percent of the total equity portfolio. Gradual fundings to the four non-U.S. equity portfolio managers will bring the board's international equity allocation to 30 percent of the total equity portfolio by the end of 1997.

One of the most significant changes in the past two years has been the expansion of the board's private markets investment program. The target allocation to private equity investments remains 10 percent of the total equity portfolio. During 1993 and 1994, a total of over $46 million was committed to a broad range of private equity investments, such as venture capital and corporate finance funds. To assist in this process, the board retained the services of Brinson Partners to help implement the investment in venture capital opportunities. The board will continue to gradually build the private equity investment program, and will bring the actual allocation to the 10 percent target allocation over a minimum period of three years.

For the balanced funds, the target allocation to real asset investments is 10 percent, with a primary role to be served by private real estate investments. During 1993 and 1994, a total of $26 million was committed to private real estate investments. This program also will be built gradually, with the board achieving the 10 percent target allocation over at least three years.

In further developing investment strategies to domestic fixed income markets, in 1993 the board retained the services of BlackRock Financial Management as portfolio manager in order to invest in mortgage, corporate, and United States government fixed income securities. In 1994, the Investment Committee approved a strategic allocation to the investment grade commercial mortgage-backed securities market, which led to the hiring of Pacific Investment Management Company (PIMCO) in late 1994.

The domestic component of the Social Purpose Equity portfolio has relied on a passive investment management approach due to its smaller size. As the Social Purpose Equity portfolio has grown in size over the past several years, utilizing active portfolio management strategies became a viable complement to passive management for the domestic equity investments. In late 1994, the board began implementing an approach to active domestic equity management which involved the existing five managers for the unconstrained equity portfolios (Internal Equity, J.P. Morgan, Rosenberg Institutional, RCM Capital, and Alliance Capital). Gradual funding of the actively managed portfolios will occur over approximately two years, until a target allocation of 50 percent active and 50 percent passive investment management is reached.

The Investment Committee approved overall investment strategy statements for asset allocation, real assets, and high yield assets, and updated those for the equity and fixed income asset classes. These statements provide the board with a clear set of strategic guidelines for implementing and monitoring investment programs in a consistent manner.

During 1993 and 1994, the Internal Fixed Income team expanded its community development investment program for the Social Purpose Bond and Social Purpose Balanced Funds, both in terms of increasing investment commitment levels and increasing the number of intermediaries. By the end of 1994, a total of 13 investments had been made through seven intermediaries. The board's existing and pending commitments put it well on its way to achieving the board's goal of targeting 25 percent of the Internal Social Purpose fixed-income assets portfolio to prudent market return oriented vehicles in low and moderate income communities around the country.

Declining fixed income market returns led to slightly lower crediting rates in the board's bond portfolios in 1993 and 1994 compared to recent years. Nevertheless, crediting rates were above the general level of interest rates in the economy as well as above those available from competing high quality fixed income investment vehicles. Balanced funds, which benefited from the generally stronger performance of equity and high yield markets, provided consistently higher crediting rates to plan members. The crediting rates for 1993 and 1994 were:

Allocation of Investment Fund Income	1993	1994
South Africa Free Bond	8.0%	7.7%
Social Purpose Bond	8.3%	7.7%
Bond	8.1%	7.5%
LCA FIP (Bond)	8.5%	7.5%
South Africa Free Balanced	9.5%	10.0%
Social Purpose Balanced	10.0%	10.0%
Balanced	9.5%	10.0%
ALC Balanced	10.0%	10.4%

Based on unit value changes, the net annualized returns of equity funds for participants were:

Net Equity Fund Returns—Based on Unit Value[1] (Annualized for Periods Ending 12/31/94)			
	1 year	3 years	5 years
LCA Variable Income Pension (VIP Fund)	2.1%	8.9%	9.7%
ELCA Equity Fund	2.0%	8.3%	9.1%
ELCA Social Purpose Equity Fund	1.8%	7.2%	9.8%
ELCA South Africa Free Equity Fund	0.8%	7.2%	NA

[1] Source: 1994 Annual Report

Several factors have contributed to the differences in returns for the equity funds. Owing to their smaller size, the Social Purpose and South Africa Free Equity Funds have relied more on passive investment approaches. Active management strategies are expected to add value over longer time periods, although passive strategies may perform better in some periods. Also, owing to their smaller size, the international investment programs for the Social Purpose and South Africa Free

Equity Funds began approximately three years subsequent to that of the Equity and LCA VIP Funds.

Following a review of the financial impact on ELCA congregations and other organizations, and approval by the ELCA Church Council, the minimum Regular Pension Plan contribution rate was increased from 9 percent of defined compensation to 9.5 percent in 1993 and 10 percent in 1994. The higher contribution rate is believed to be necessary in order to meet the plan's goal of providing long-term church workers with a replacement income, including Social Security, at a level that enables them to maintain their pre-retirement standard of living.

The ELCA Institutional Pension Plan has been changed to be more flexible for participating organizations. Sponsoring employers now can choose between quarterly crediting of contributions throughout the year or an annual allocation of pension contributions, with restrictions on eligibility to hold down costs. All members now are able to allocate pension contributions to any of the seven investment funds.

In response to rising costs, revisions to the ELCA Disability Benefits Plan were implemented effective January 1, 1994. During the first two years of disability, one-half of employment earnings between 20 percent and 80 percent of pre-disability income are offset against the ELCA disability benefit. After the first two years, the ELCA benefit is offset by all earnings. In addition, after two years of disability, the definition of disability changes from an inability to perform one's own occupation to an inability to perform in any occupation for which the member is or may become reasonably suited by education, training, and experience and be expected to earn at least 70 percent of pre-disability earnings.

Major Directions 1995-1996

In 1994, the Board of Pensions identified 10 critical success factors to guide the board. They are:
- Provide high-quality benefits and services to plan members at below-market costs.
- Maintain a fiscally sound operation by establishing appropriate reserve and plan surplus positions.
- Instill confidence in the work of the Board of Pensions to plan members and other expressions of the Evangelical Lutheran Church in America.
- Maximize long-term investment returns while controlling investment risk.
- Attract and retain competent people with high ethical standards and integrity, providing a challenging work environment that recognizes the value of each individual.
- Communicate effectively with plan members and other outside entities.
- Anticipate and respond to changing member needs, regulations and benefit delivery systems.
- Coordinate policy planning for benefits, investment, financial reporting, and information technology.

- Maintain interaction with other parts of this church, recognizing the interdependence among churchwide units.
- Identify and offer services, where appropriate, to other expressions of the Evangelical Lutheran Church in America.

By focusing on these critical success factors, the board can fulfill its mission of providing outstanding service to plan members and to the Evangelical Lutheran Church in America.

RALPH J. ECKERT, *Chair*, Board of Trustees of the Board of Pensions
JOHN G. KAPANKE, *President*, Board of Pensions

Exhibit A

Financial Statements

Statements of Net Assets Available for Plan Benefits and Benefit Obligations
As of December 31,

(Dollars in thousands)	1994			1993
	Pension funds	Other benefit funds	Total funds	
ASSETS				
Investments, at fair value				
Bonds, U.S.	$ 1,088,670	$ 64,283	$ 1,152,953	$ 1,250,616
Bonds, foreign	87,060	4,550	91,610	88,747
Common and preferred stocks, U.S.	953,820	58,205	1,012,025	1,030,505
Common and preferred stocks, foreign	231,312	14,128	245,440	196,054
Short-term investments	113,272	44,097	157,369	164,358
Mutual funds	33,251	3,368	36,619	23,308
Other	58,721	2,933	61,654	54,028
Total investments	2,566,106	191,564	2,757,670	2,807,616
Foreign currency contracts	111,468	6,147	117,615	105,182
Accrued interest and dividends receivable	22,376	1,625	24,001	22,984
Cash	15,961	15,208	31,169	17,355
Other receivables	350	2,333	2,683	2,618
Due from brokers for security sales	23,699	1,424	25,123	17,355
Furniture, equipment and computer software, net	—	1,097	1,097	1,891
Total assets	2,739,960	219,398	2,959,358	2,975,001
LIABILITIES				
Foreign currency contracts	111,659	6,162	117,821	103,484
Cash overdraft	23,279	6,531	29,810	17,219
Payables for securities purchased	72,809	4,036	76,845	76,240
Deferred revenue	939	1,351	2,290	2,581
Accounts payable	2,773	2,174	4,947	5,277
Collateralized lease obligation	—	65	65	686
Total liabilities	211,459	20,319	231,778	205,487
NET ASSETS AVAILABLE FOR PLAN BENEFITS	2,528,501	199,079	2,727,580	2,769,514
BENEFIT OBLIGATIONS (See Note 2)				
Accrued health claims payable	—	12,920	12,920	13,220
ELCA postretirement medical obligation	—	121,665	121,665	178,272
Pension obligation for active plan members	1,702,024	—	1,702,024	1,636,796
Pension obligation for retired plan members	792,791	—	792,791	723,088
Optional pension plan obligation	24,492	—	24,492	20,561
Institutional pension plan obligation	27,043	—	27,043	23,583
Institutional savings plan obligation	9,262	—	9,262	6,013
Disabled life obligation	—	30,466	30,466	28,268
Survivor benefit obligation	—	21,457	21,457	20,909
ALC minimum pension obligation	4,388	—	4,388	4,787
LCA supplemental pension obligation	6,221	—	6,221	6,183
LCA non contributory pension obligation	2,891	—	2,891	3,138
AELC retirement plan obligation	11,178	—	11,178	11,222
Other obligations	—	91	91	55
Total benefit obligations	2,580,290	186,599	2,766,889	2,676,095
Excess/(shortage) of net assets over benefit obligations	$ (51,789)	$ 12,480	$ (39,309)	$ 93,419

See accompanying notes to financial statements.

Statements of Changes in Net Assets Available for Plan Benefits and Benefit Obligations
For the Year Ended December 31,

(Dollars in thousands)	Pension funds	1994 Other benefit funds	Total funds	1993
ADDITIONS TO NET ASSETS ATTRIBUTED TO:				
Net investment income				
Interest income	$ 96,875	$ 7,141	$ 104,016	$ 102,717
Dividend income	32,086	1,904	33,990	29,706
Market appreciation/(depreciation)	(159,598)	(9,673)	(169,271)	184,217
Other investment income/(loss)	(297)	(19)	(316)	1,782
Investment expenses	(6,138)	(290)	(6,428)	(8,077)
Total investment income/(loss)	(37,072)	(937)	(38,009)	310,345
Contributions				
Pension contributions	67,596	—	67,596	63,169
Disability contributions	—	9,467	9,467	4,149
Health benefit contributions	—	78,584	78,584	81,287
Survivor benefit contributions	—	44	44	1,930
Other contributions	1,181	1,875	3,056	2,996
Total contributions	68,777	89,970	158,747	153,531
Church allotments	1,157	5,078	6,235	6,169
Gifts, bequests and other	64	1	65	85
Total additions	32,926	94,112	127,038	470,130
DEDUCTIONS FROM NET ASSETS ATTRIBUTED TO:				
Benefits				
Health benefit payments		66,116	66,116	72,290
Pension payments	84,048		84,048	76,308
Disability payments	—	5,232	5,232	4,811
Lump-sum death benefit payments	—	1,689	1,689	1,733
Other benefit payments		591	591	428
Withdrawals, transfers and adjustments	(495)	51	(444)	1,733
Total benefits	83,553	73,679	157,232	157,303
General and administrative expenses	3,731	8,009	11,740	12,231
Total deductions	87,284	81,688	168,972	169,534
Net increase/(decrease) in net assets available for plan benefits	(54,358)	12,424	(41,934)	300,596
Increase/(decrease) in benefit obligations	144,919	(54,125)	90,794	254,835
Net change in excess/(shortage) of net assets over benefit obligations	(199,277)	66,549	(132,728)	45,761
Excess/(shortage) of net assets over benefit obligations at beginning of year	147,488	(54,069)	93,419	47,658
Excess/(shortage) of net assets over benefit obligations at end of year	$ (51,789)	$ 12,480	$ (39,309)	$ 93,419

See accompanying notes to financial statements.

Notes to Financial Statements

NOTE 1: Description of plans administered by the Board of Pensions

The following plan descriptions provide only general information. Participants should refer to Summary Plan Descriptions and other documents for a more complete description of each plan's provisions.

The ELCA Regular Pension Plan is a non-contributory "money-purchase" plan. The plan is authorized under the provisions of Section 403(b)(9) of the Internal Revenue Code and has been approved by the IRS. It provides retirement and survivor benefits based on the accumulated pension contributions and investment earnings of a member's individual account at the time of retirement or death. There are nine investment funds: South Africa Free Equity, South Africa Free Balanced, South Africa Free Bond, Social Purpose Equity, Social Purpose Balanced, Social Purpose Bond, Equity (formerly Alternative Equity), Balanced (formerly Alternative Balanced), and Bond (formerly Alternative Bond), in which members may choose to invest contributions. The LCA VIP (Equity), ALC Balanced and LCA FIP (Bond) Funds were merged into the ELCA Regular Pension Plan effective January 1, 1991. The ALC Balanced Fund, LCA FIP and LCA VIP include employee contribution accounts that provide payments to members based upon their own contributions. Due to the multiracial elections in South Africa in 1994, the Board of Pensions will eliminate the South Africa Free Funds effective April 1, 1995. In addition, on December 1, 1994 the word "alternative" was dropped from the Alternative Equity, Alternative Balanced and Alternative Bond Funds.

All non-retired participants have individual account balances, by fund, which represent the accumulation of all contributions made on their behalf, plus credited investment earnings. At retirement, members' accumulations are converted to monthly annuities, and the accumulated balances are pooled with all other retirees participating in that fund. Initial pensions are calculated on the basis of an assumed interest rate of 4.5 percent using a gender-neutral mortality table. After retirement, investment earnings in excess of 4.5 percent are used to increase pensions.

Congregations and other employing organizations contributed 10 percent of salary in 1994 on behalf of members who were not active participants in a predecessor church plan at December 31, 1987. Persons who were participants in a predecessor plan were credited with employer contributions ranging from 10 percent to 12 percent of salary, based upon their age at December 31, 1987. Within limits, organizations are also allowed to make additional contributions to the plan on behalf of employees. All contributions are fully and immediately vested.

The ELCA Optional Pension Plan is also a 403(b) plan approved by the IRS which allows for employer contri-

butions and for contributions by members on a salary reduction basis. Participants may choose among five mutual funds. The plan charges members $6.00 or .125 percent of assets per quarter, whichever is less, for administrative work performed by the Board of Pensions.

The ELCA Continuation of The ALC and LCA Minimum and Non Contributory Pension Plans provide defined benefit pensions to certain ALC and LCA ministers and lay workers, surviving spouses, and children whose rights were established primarily by the antecedent churches of The ALC and LCA.

The ELCA Institutional Pension and Savings Plans are 403(b) money-purchase plans for ELCA institutions. The employer chooses its contribution rate to the pension plan as a percent of employee salary with a minimum contribution rate of 3 percent. The Savings Plan may also be chosen by the employer. This plan allows for employee salary reduction contributions, "matching" employer contributions, and other contributions under certain circumstances.

The AELC Retirement Plan is a qualified plan authorized under the provisions of Section 401(a) of the Internal Revenue Code. It is a defined contribution plan that has provisions for purchasing individual annuities at retirement or death. All contributions and earnings are vested.

The ELCA Medical and Dental Benefits Plan provides reimbursement of hospital, surgical, and other medical expenses incurred by plan members and eligible dependents. Like other medical reimbursement plans, the ELCA medical and dental plan contains deductibles and copayments which are paid by the member. Within certain salary minimums and maximums, contributions for the 1994 medical and dental benefits ranged from 9.7 percent to 17.3 percent of defined compensation. The plan also provides optional supplemental coverage which reduces the deductibles and copayments by one half. Costs for the supplement ranged from $492 to $1,416 annually in 1994 based on the dependent coverages in force. Effective January 1, 1995, the supplement will be eliminated.

The ELCA Continuation of The ALC Medical-Dental Plan for Retired Participants provides retiree health benefit coverage to eligible retired participants and their dependents. Eligible participants may also purchase supplemental coverage to reduce deductible and copayment amounts. The cost for certain members and their spouses is subsidized from a trust fund established by The ALC.

The ELCA Continuation of the LCA Ministerial Health Benefits Plan for Retired Members provides retiree health benefit coverage for eligible retired ministers, certain lay employees and their dependents. The ELCA subsidizes the cost for certain members on a current basis.

The ELCA Disability Benefits Plan provides for three types of benefits, after a specified waiting period, for plan members who suffer injury, or physical or mental disorders which prevent them from engaging in substantial gainful activity for which they are suited by education, training or experience. The benefits include (1) a monthly disability income benefit equal to two-thirds of monthly defined compensation (increased by 3 percent per year), less Social Security and other governmental disability benefits, (2) a pension supplement in retirement based on required pension contributions that would have been made if the individual had not been disabled and had received salary increases of 4 percent per year, and (3) medical, dental and survivor benefits coverage at no cost to the member or to her or his employer. Disability contributions were 2.0 percent of defined compensation for 1994.

The ELCA Survivor Benefits Plan provides four different benefit coverages. Subject to a minimum of $4,000 and a maximum of $50,000, the plan pays a lump-sum benefit based on the age at death and the defined compensation of the member during the 12 months prior to death or retirement. The second benefit is the augmentation of pensions, with annual increases for inflation for surviving spouses of non-retired members whose pension would otherwise be below a specified percentage of defined compensation. Third, for a retired member or spouse who dies after commencing her or his pension, the survivor is paid the greater of the annuity specified by the form elected or a single life annuity computed on the basis of the original accumulation, less payments received prior to the first death. The fourth benefit includes a monthly benefit for children under age 18 and an education benefit for post-secondary schooling by children under age 26. In 1994, there were no employer contributions made to the survivor plan because of the large surplus in this plan.

The Government Chaplaincy Program. The ELCA Pension Plan for Government Chaplains provides pensions to those eligible members who retire without receiving a minimum government-paid retirement pension. No claims were made on this plan in 1994 or 1993. The ELCA Welfare Benefits Plan for Government Chaplains provides benefit coverages to government chaplains at cost to the chaplain.

Administrative and other. Effective January 1, 1991, congregations and other employing organizations were charged .6 percent of defined compensation to defray the costs associated with administering the ELCA Pension and Other Benefits Program. Allocated costs in excess of the administrative charge are deducted from a plan's investment income or funded through the plans' contribution rates. The administrative charge covered 21.6 percent of the board's operating expenses both in 1994 and in 1993.

Figure 1

(Dollars in thousands)	Postretirement benefit obligation	
	1994	1993
Current retirees	$ 80,356	$102,800
Other participants fully eligible for benefits	30,381	49,434
Participants not yet fully eligible for benefits	10,928	26,038
	$121,665	$178,272

Figure 2

(Dollars in thousands)	Total fixed assets at cost	Accumulated depreciation	Net fixed assets
Office equipment and fixtures	$ 3,512	$ 2,719	$ 793
Capitalized lease—computer	1,487	1,420	67
Capitalized software	846	716	130
Leasehold improvements	447	340	107
	$ 6,292	$ 5,195	$ 1,097

Figure 3

(Dollars in thousands)	Realized and unrealized gains and losses	
	1994	1993
Bonds	$ (161,167)	$ 50,794
Common and preferred stock	(6,978)	131,851
Other	(1,126)	1,572
	$ (169,271)	$ 184,217

NOTE 2: Significant accounting policies

Postretirement medical obligation

The ELCA postretirement medical obligation represents the actuarial present value of the estimated future contribution subsidies from the church that are attributed to employee service rendered at December 31 for certain categories of participants (including their beneficiaries and dependents) as shown in figure 1.

The actuarial present value of the expected ELCA postretirement medical obligation is determined by an actuary and is the amount that results from applying actuarial assumptions to historical claims-cost data to estimate future annual incurred claims costs per participant and to adjust such estimates for the time value of money (through discounts for interest) and the probability of payment.

For measurement purposes, an 8.75 percent annual rate of increase in the per capita cost of covered health care benefits after age 65 was assumed for 1995. The rate was assumed to decrease gradually to 6.5 percent for 2001 and to remain at that level thereafter. Costs for coverage prior to age 65 are assumed to increase 11 percent for 1995, decreasing to 6.5 percent for 2001 and to remain at that level thereafter. If the assumed rate increased by one percentage point in each year, that would increase the obligation as of December 31, 1994 and 1993 by $16,627,000 and $29,262,000, respectively.

The following were other significant assumptions used in the valuations as of December 31, 1994 and 1993 based on the assumption the plan will continue.

Weighted-average discount rate: 1994 – 8 percent
1993 – 7 percent

Average retirement age: 64.7 years

Mortality: 1983 Group Annuity Table for male lives with ages set back 2 years for males and 8 years for females

The shortage of $32,348,000 of net assets over the ELCA postretirement medical obligation will be funded by the church. See Note 3.

Benefit obligations—other

Other plan benefit obligations at December 31 for health claims incurred by active participants but not reported at that date, for survivor benefit liability, and for future disability payments to members considered permanently disabled at December 31 are actuarially determined. Such estimated amounts are reported at present value based on an 8 percent discount rate for 1994 and a 7 percent discount rate for 1993.

Pension plans

All non-retired participants have individual account balances, by plan and investment fund, which represent the accumulation of all earnings and contributions made on their behalf. The present value of members' accounts is their account balances; therefore, no actuarial valuation is required. After retirement, pension benefits are valued on the basis of the 1983 Group Annuity Mortality Table (male lives) with an eight-year setback for females and a two-year setback for males. The pension obligations for retired members are determined by the plan's actuary. Annuities eligible for excess interest adjustments are valued on the basis of the assumed interest rate of 4.5 percent. All other annuities are valued using an assumed interest rate of 8 percent.

Investments

Investments are stated at fair value, as measured by quoted market prices in active markets. Security transactions are accounted for on a trade date (the date securities are purchased or sold) basis. Dividend and interest income is recorded as it is earned. In accordance with the policy of stating investments at fair value, unrealized appreciation or depreciation is reflected in the statement of changes in net assets available for plan benefits.

Accrual accounting

The financial statements are prepared on an accrual basis. Contributions due but unpaid for benefits, including pensions, are shown as a receivable. Contributions for benefits, including pensions, that are paid prior to the due date are shown in the liability section as deferred revenue.

Fixed assets

Fixed assets are stated at cost, less accumulated depreciation. Depreciation is computed on a straight-line method over the estimated useful lives of assets at the time of installation. See figure 2.

Reclassifications

Certain prior year amounts have been reclassified to conform with the current year presentation.

NOTE 3: Related party transactions

The board received $6,235,000 and $6,214,000 in 1994 and 1993, respectively, from the church for current supplemental minimum pensions and retiree health benefits.

The board also charged investment management fees of .3 percent of assets, or $319,000 and $286,000 in 1994 and 1993 respectively, for managing the Endowment and Deferred Giving investments for the ELCA Foundation.

NOTE 4: Derivative financial instruments

The board has an established investment policy prescribing the uses of derivative instruments by internal and external investment managers. This investment policy expressly identifies the permissible uses of derivative instruments and contains accounting and management controls designed to ensure the conformance with these policies. These derivative instruments carry off-balance sheet risk that results mainly from fluctuations in interest rates, equity markets, and exchange rates. The board's investment policy uses derivative instruments to hedge foreign currency exposure and to implement the tactical asset allocation program.

The board hedges against short-term currency fluctuations in foreign securities by purchasing foreign currency contracts. These contracts are marked-to-market. The gains and losses on these contracts are netted against the gains and losses in the underlying foreign securities. As of December 31, 1994, the foreign currency contracts receivable was $117,615,000, and the foreign currency contracts payable was $117,821,000. These contracts mature between January 6, 1995, and June 19, 1995.

The board's tactical asset allocation program uses financial futures and options to adjust the fixed income and equity portfolio allocation in the balanced funds. Financial futures and options provide a more effective and efficient financial instrument compared to cash market alternatives. These financial futures and options are exchange traded and marked-to-market daily. As of December 31, 1994, the board has U.S. Treasury futures maturing in March and June of 1995 with a notional value of $72,219,000, and S&P 500 Index futures maturing in March of 1995 with a notional value of $47,288,000. The realized and unrealized gains and losses for fiscal 1994, the average fair value for fiscal 1994 and the fair value as of December 31, 1994, of these futures contracts are not material. The board also has written futures options outstanding on December 31, 1994, that mature in March of 1995. These written futures options are not significant and are shown as a liability based on the current market value.

NOTE 5: Investments

The plan's realized and unrealized gains and losses on investments by major category at December 31 are shown in *figure 3*.

NOTE 6: Commitments

At December 31, 1994, the Board of Pensions was obligated under non-cancelable leases for equipment ranging from two months to three years.

Rental expense (including taxes, insurance and maintenance when included in rent) amounted to $753,000 in 1994 and $727,000 in 1993, respectively.

Future minimum rental payments under capital leases and non-cancelable operating leases with terms of one year or more, at December 31, 1994, were:

	Capital leases	Operating leases
1995	$ 65,000	$ 802,000
1996	—	853,000
1997	—	866,000
Total minimum rental payments	$ 65,000	$ 2,521,000

NOTE 7: Plan activity by fund for the years ended December 31, 1994 and 1993

(Dollars in thousands)	Net assets beginning of year	Contributions and other receipts	Investment income/(loss)
1994 ELCA Regular			
Equity Funds			
South Africa Free Equity	$ 56,634	$ 1,532	$ 783
Social Purpose Equity	57,320	7,845	1,118
Equity (formerly Alternative Equity)	55,412	9,022	1,168
LCA Variable Income Pension (VIP)	439,947		8,141
Total Equity Funds	609,313	18,399	11,210
Balanced Funds			
South Africa Free Balanced	89,238	2,096	(505)
Social Purpose Balanced	54,982	6,676	(381)
Balanced (formerly Alternative Balanced)	106,905	12,886	(254)
ALC	758,193	54	(4,963)
Total Balanced Funds	1,009,318	21,712	(6,103)
Bond Funds			
South Africa Free Bond	70,628	2,188	(3,567)
Social Purpose Bond	53,082	3,254	(2,899)
Bond (formerly Alternative Bond)	97,140	9,707	(5,177)
LCA Fixed Income Pension (FIP)	673,739		(31,434)
Total Bond Funds	894,589	15,149	(43,077)
Total ELCA Regular	2,513,220	55,260	(37,970)
ELCA Optional	20,561	4,429	189
ELCA Minimum and Non Contributory	8,257	1,214	78
ELCA Institutional	29,599	9,095	(29)
AELC Retirement	11,222		660
Total Pension Plans	2,582,859	69,998	(37,072)
Other Benefit Plans			
ELCA Medical-Dental	27,008	77,012	899
ELCA Continuation Plans	92,719	8,313	(1,081)
ELCA Disability	17,614	9,678	(270)
ELCA Survivor	49,038	45	(744)
Other	276	1	259
Total Plans	$ 2,769,514	$ 165,047	$ (38,009)
1993 ELCA Regular			
Equity Funds			
South Africa Free Equity	$ 51,780	$ 1,572	$ 6,209
Social Purpose Equity	44,070	6,324	5,991
Equity (formerly Alternative Equity)	42,253	7,722	6,754
LCA Variable Income Pension (VIP)	399,140		59,022
Total Equity Funds	537,243	15,618	77,976
Balanced Funds			
South Africa Free Balanced	80,571	2,736	9,827
Social Purpose Balanced	39,141	5,881	5,132
Balanced (formerly Alternative Balanced)	83,351	12,974	11,937
ALC	695,634	69	91,390
Total Balanced Funds	898,697	21,660	118,286
Bond Funds			
South Africa Free Bond	63,741	2,460	7,468
Social Purpose Bond	41,547	3,381	4,874
Bond (formerly Alternative Bond)	78,706	10,759	9,259
LCA Fixed Income Pension (FIP)	630,016		68,044
Total Bond Funds	814,010	16,600	89,645
Total ELCA Regular	2,249,950	53,878	285,907
ELCA Optional	15,868	4,003	1,358
ELCA Minimum and Non Contributory	7,167	1,215	950
ELCA Institutional	22,351	6,679	2,714
AELC Retirement	10,808		752
Total Pension Plans	2,306,144	65,773	291,681
Other Benefit Plans			
ELCA Medical-Dental	16,066	77,920	508
ELCA Continuation Plans	84,630	8,539	10,402
ELCA Disability	15,442	4,149	1,940
ELCA Survivor	46,068	1,930	5,633
Other	568	1,474	181
Total Plans	$ 2,468,918	$ 159,785	$ 310,345

Investment Portfolio

The Board of Pensions will send a detailed listing of all securities held at December 31, 1994 to any interested member, congregation or employing organization. If you would like a copy of the portfolio, please contact the board's Communications/Publications Department.

Funds managed (checkmark matrix)

Columns: Equity (formerly Alternative Equity) · Social Purpose Equity · South Africa Free Equity · LCA VIP · Balanced (formerly Alternative Balanced) · Social Purpose Balanced · South Africa Free Balanced · ALC Balanced · Bond (formerly Alternative Bond) · Social Purpose Bond · South Africa Free Bond · LCA FIP · Optional

Asset managers

Asset managers	Assets managed (dollars in thousands)	Assets managed (percent of total)
DOMESTIC EQUITIES		%
Internal Equity	$ 127,262	4.62
JP Morgan	120,067	4.35
Rosenberg	98,015	3.55
Alliance	117,399	4.26
Rosenberg Capital Management	97,375	3.53
Wells Fargo S&P 500	165,756	6.01
Wells Fargo Extended	119,506	4.33
Internal Social Purpose Equity	4,010	.15
JP Morgan Social Purpose	3,004	.11
Rosenberg Social Purpose	4,121	.15
Alliance Social Purpose	2,638	.10
Rosenberg Capital Management, Social Purpose	2,701	.10
Wells Fargo Social Purpose Equity	90,421	3.28
Wells Fargo South Africa Free Equity	58,849	2.13
Other	901	.03
Total Domestic Equity	1,012,025	36.70
INTERNATIONAL EQUITIES		
Acadian	87,306	3.16
Acadian II	25,565	.93
Acadian III	14,259	.52
UBS Philips & Drew	49,439	1.79
Schroder Pacific Basin	48,398	1.76
Schroder Emerging Markets	17,303	.63
Other	3,170	.11
Total International Equity	245,440	8.90
Private Equity	19,460	.71
DOMESTIC FIXED INCOME		
Internal FIP	483,819	17.54
Internal Investment Grade Bond	344,445	12.49
Internal Social Purpose Bond	82,973	3.01
Internal South Africa Free Bond	50,556	1.83
PIMCO	17,364	.63
BlackRock	112,810	4.09
Total Domestic Fixed Income	1,091,967	39.59
International Fixed Income, JP Morgan	90,876	3.30
International Fixed Income, Other	735	.03
High Yield Securities, Pacholder	60,985	2.21
REAL ASSETS		
Cohen & Steers	14,016	.51
Private Real Assets	9,818	.36
Other	1,540	.05
Total Real Assets	25,374	.92
TACTICAL ASSET ALLOCATION		
JP Morgan	0	0.00
QuantiLogic	0	0.00
Total Tactical Asset	0	0.00
OPTIONAL AND INSTITUTIONAL SAVINGS		
Vanguard	28,146	1.02
Calvert	3,209	.12
Total Optional and Institutional Savings	31,355	1.14
SHORT-TERM INVESTMENTS		
Boston Company Asset Management	109,031	3.95
CDS, CASH, GICS, AND OTHER	70,422	2.55
TOTAL INVESTED ASSET PORTFOLIO	$ 2,757,670	100.00 %

Statement of changes by fund

Benefits paid	Withdrawals, transfers and adjustments	General and administrative expenses	Net assets end of year
$ (63)	$ (23,092)	$ (43)	$ 35,751
(314)	14,952	(266)	80,655
(277)	5,377	(324)	70,378
(9,845)	(7,562)	(342)	430,339
(10,499)	(10,325)	(975)	617,123
(275)	(37,085)	(66)	53,403
(514)	26,769	(239)	87,293
(1,113)	12,455	(502)	130,377
(30,061)	(23)	(527)	722,673
(31,963)	2,116	(1,334)	993,746
(376)	(25,323)	(71)	43,479
(722)	19,675	(145)	72,245
(1,217)	6,279	(441)	106,291
(32,619)	7,499	(704)	616,481
(34,934)	8,130	(1,361)	838,496
(77,396)	(79)	(3,670)	2,449,365
(1,098)	411		24,492
(2,344)	31	(79)	7,157
(2,530)	156	18	36,309
(680)	(24)	—	11,178
(84,048)	495	(3,731)	2,528,501
(56,191)	(4)	(7,755)	40,969
(9,913)	(16)	(705)	89,317
(5,232)	4	(285)	21,509
(2,272)	(15)	(22)	46,030
(20)	(20)	758	1,254
$ (157,676)	$ 444	$ (11,740)	$ 2,727,580
$ (50)	$ (2,830)	$ (47)	$ 56,634
(191)	1,319	(193)	57,320
(140)	(931)	(246)	55,412
(8,396)	(11,800)	(461)	439,947
(8,777)		(947)	609,313
(304)	(3,507)	(85)	89,238
(216)	5,226	(182)	54,982
(557)	(360)	(440)	106,905
(27,370)	(819)	(711)	758,193
(28,447)	540	(1,418)	1,009,318
(305)	(2,659)	(77)	70,628
(486)	3,888	(122)	53,082
(814)	(366)	(404)	97,140
(32,126)	8,766	(961)	673,739
(33,731)	9,629	(1,564)	894,589
(70,955)	(1,631)	(3,929)	2,513,220
(2,405)	169		20,561
(1,808)	1,425	(95)	8,257
(315)	(337)		29,599
	(20)	(1)	11,222
(76,320)	(394)	(4,025)	2,582,859
(62,251)	1,588	(6,823)	27,008
(10,119)	64	(797)	92,719
(4,811)	1,041	(147)	17,614
(2,089)	(2,475)	(29)	49,038
20	(1,557)	(410)	276
$ (155,570)	$ (1,733)	$ (12,231)	$ 2,769,514

Independent Auditors' Report

Board of Trustees
Board of Pensions of the
Evangelical Lutheran Church in America

We have audited the statements of net assets available for plan benefits and benefit obligations of the Board of Pensions of the Evangelical Lutheran Church in America as of December 31, 1994 and 1993, and the related statements of changes in net assets available for plan benefits and benefit obligations for the years then ended. These financial statements are the responsibility of management of the Board of Pensions. Our responsibility is to express an opinion on these financial statements based on our audits.

We conducted our audits in accordance with generally accepted auditing standards. Those standards require that we plan and perform the audit to obtain reasonable assurance about whether the financial statements are free of material misstatement. An audit includes examining, on a test basis, evidence supporting the amounts and disclosures in the financial statements. An audit also includes assessing the accounting principles used and significant estimates made by management, as well as evaluating the overall financial statement presentation. We believe that our audits provide a reasonable basis for our opinion.

In our opinion, such financial statements present fairly, in all material respects, the net assets available for plan benefits and benefit obligations of the Board of Pensions of the Evangelical Lutheran Church in America at December 31, 1994 and 1993 and the changes in net assets available for plan benefits and benefit obligations for the years then ended in conformity with generally accepted accounting principles.

Deloitte & Touche LLP

Deloitte & Touche LLP
Minneapolis, Minnesota
March 10, 1995

Management's Report

The management of the Board of Pensions of the Evangelical Lutheran Church in America has prepared and is responsible for the content of the financial statements and all information in the annual report. Information is consistent between what is presented in the financial statements and that shown elsewhere in the annual report. The financial statements have been prepared in conformity with generally accepted accounting principles. The statements necessarily include amounts based on management's best estimates and judgments.

The board's system of internal control plays an important role in meeting its responsibilities for reliable financial statements. It is designed to provide reasonable assurance that assets are safeguarded and that transactions are properly recorded and executed in accordance with management's authorization. The control environment is enhanced by the selection and training of competent management, maintaining and reinforcing the highest standards of conduct by employees in carrying out the board's affairs, organizational arrangements that provide for segregation of duties and delegation of authority, and the communication of accounting and operating policies and procedures to the board's employees.

To properly oversee the effectiveness of the board's internal controls, the board maintains an internal audit department. In the event of unforeseen irregularities or errors, management believes that the board's internal accounting control system provides reasonable assurance that errors or irregularities that could be material to the financial statements are prevented or would be detected on a timely basis and corrected in the normal course of business.

The Board of Trustees oversees these financial statements through the Audit Committee comprised of six Trustees. All Trustees are independent of the board's internal management. The committee meets periodically with management and the internal auditors, who are each, of its responsibilities. The independent auditors, who are engaged to express an opinion on the financial statements, meet periodically with and have free access to the Audit Committee or the Trustees, without management present, to discuss internal accounting controls, auditing and financial reporting matters.

John G. Kapanke

John G. Kapanke
President
March 10, 1995

David G. Adams

David G. Adams, F.S.A.
Vice President, Finance

Target asset allocations

Equity Funds

Equity *(formerly Alternative Equity)*

Social Purpose Equity — 20%

South Africa Free Equity — 20%

LCA VIP — 1%

All Equity Funds
60% Domestic equities
30% Non-U.S. equities
10% Private equities

■ Domestic equities
▨ Non-U.S. equities
▨ Private equities

Balanced Funds

Balanced *(formerly Alternative Balanced)*

Social Purpose Balanced

South Africa Free Balanced

ALC Balanced — 40%

Balanced *(formerly Alternative Balanced)* and South Africa Free Funds
60% Equities
25% Fixed income
5% High yield
10% Real assets

Social Purpose Funds
60% Equities
30% Fixed income
10% Real assets

ALC Balanced Funds
55% Equities
30% Fixed income
5% High yield
10% Real assets

■ Equities
▨ Fixed income
▨ High yield
▨ Real assets

Bond Funds

Bond *(formerly Alternative Bond)* — 90%

Social Purpose Bond — 11% / 87%

South Africa Free Bond — 11% / 89%

LCA FIP — 9% / 91%

All Bond Funds
90% Domestic bonds
10% Non-U.S. bonds

■ Domestic bonds
▨ Non-U.S. bonds

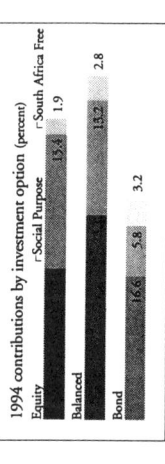

Pension plan accumulations (dollars in millions)

Equity — Social Purpose 81 / South Africa Free 36

Balanced — 67 / 53

Bond — 106 / 72 / 43

1994 contributions by investment option (percent)

Equity — Social Purpose 13.6 / South Africa Free 1.9

Balanced — 13.2 / 2.8

Bond — 16.6 / 5.8 / 3.2

Report of the Church Council

Summary of Meetings December 1993

The nineteenth meeting of the Church Council of th Evangelical Lutheran Church in America was held in the Church Council room of the Lutheran Center at Chicago, Ill., December 3-5, 1993. Vice President Kathy J. Magnus, chair of the Church Council, called the meeting to order at 2:06 P.M.

Adoption of the Agenda

Chair Magnus reviewed the agenda for this meeting of the Church Council and welcomed newly elected council members.

William H. Engelbrecht requested that a discussion on the policy for the issuance of social statements be included in the agenda for the executive session. Chair Magnus reviewed recent discussion by the council's Executive Committee regarding the agenda for the executive session; the committee had concluded that personnel issues regarding the draft document be conducted in executive session, but that other discussion be held in open session.

William H. Engelbrecht then moved the following:

MOVED;
SECONDED;   *YES–11; No–21*
DEFEATED: To include in the executive session during the evening of December 3, 1993, discussion of procedures followed in the release of study documents.

The Rev. H. George Anderson inquired how executive sessions are called. Secretary Lowell G. Almen reviewed the rules of procedure related to executive sessions. Pastor Anderson commented that matters of procedure related to social statements seem best handled in open session.

The Rev. Franklin D. Fry questioned whether the present situation could be disentangled through procedural means. Chair Magnus reviewed the agenda for the executive session and the open session, in order to clarify the matter. The Rev. Donald M. Hallberg suggested that the chair could direct the conversation to divide personnel from procedural matters.

VOTED: *CC93.12.68*
To adopt the agenda and to permit the chair to call for consideration of agenda items in the order she deems most appropriate.

Report of the Bishop

Chair Magnus called upon the Rev. Herbert W. Chilstrom, bishop of the Evangelical Lutheran Church in America, who presented his report. Basing his remarks on the Old Testament lesson for the First Sunday in Advent, Bishop Chilstrom noted the awesome charge given to the Church Council, but also noted its dependence on God.

He characterized the 1993 Churchwide Assembly as a business-oriented session and underscored the significance of concluding the Study of Ministry, the last "transition task" to be completed in the formation of this church. He pointed in addition to the importance of the ongoing Study of Theological Education and the work to be completed before the 1995 Churchwide Assembly. Bishop Chilstrom also reviewed other actions of the 1993 assembly in setting the agenda for Church Council meetings in the future and for the 1995 assembly.

Recalling his decision not to seek re-election in 1995, Bishop Chilstrom outlined the areas of emphasis he intends to highlight in the coming biennium. The issue of human sexuality was one on which he had commented during the 1993 Churchwide Assembly, he said. He noted that responses to the content of the initial draft of a social statement on the church and human sexuality confirmed his belief that these issues must be discussed in this church.

Regarding finances, Bishop Chilstrom reported that the churchwide organization has received less mission support than was budgeted in 1993 and, in fact, less than was received in 1992. He observed that the "dip" in income occurred before the release of the statement on human sexuality. Synods have detected no reason for the reduced income.

Bishop Chilstrom commented on *Mission90* events being held throughout this church from January 1993 through October 1995. Certain basic elements are common to those events, including worship with Holy Communion, an opportunity for Bishop Chilstrom to reflect on the six major emphases outlined in his Kansas City report, workshops aimed at enhancing congregational ministries, and dialogue between himself and participants.

A synodical-churchwide consultation on mission support was held in October 1993, designed primarily to discuss financial commitments for 1995. Bishop Chilstrom reported that a positive spirit characterized the consultation in which congregations were viewed as "mission outposts," and in which a clear sense of unity in the Body of Christ was experienced. He announced that in the report of the Executive for Administration the council would be given a proposal for planning the future of the churchwide organization, reflecting on the most effective ways to serve this church. Finally, he quoted the great "O Antiphons" of the Advent season, which pray, "O King of the nations, the Ruler they long for, the Cornerstone uniting all people; Come and save us all, whom you formed out of the clay."

Report of the Vice President

Vice President Kathy J. Magnus, chair of the Church Council, commented on the appropriateness of having the chairs of churchwide boards present at this meeting of the Church Council. It reflects the interconnectedness between boards and the agenda of the council, she said. In October 1993, Chair Magnus reported, she had the opportunity to represent the bishop of this church at the 100th anniversary celebration of the Evangelical Lutheran Church in Tanzania. She characterized it as a learning and growth experience as she witnessed the passion for the Gospel evident there. But, important as the major celebrations were, the most fascinating and moving experiences came in small villages where she met with many people and talked about the Gospel. Chair Magnus observed that one third of the council members were newly elected, and that in the face of the heavy conversations before the council, she hoped a community would form quickly.

Report of the Secretary

Chair Magnus called upon the Rev. Lowell G. Almen, secretary of this church, to present his report. Secretary Almen referred to his printed report, but continued to reflect on his preparation for this meeting. He termed the appearance of the initial draft of a social statement on human sexuality as an early frost coming upon this church. He noted that much had been accomplished from the close of the Churchwide Assembly through late October. This work began with publication of revisions of the Model Constitution for Congregations, the Constitution for Synods, and the churchwide constitution, including the extensive changes resulting from the Study of Ministry.

He commented that in all his years of observing close at hand the workings of churchwide offices, never had he witnessed so many missteps as occurred in the release of the draft statement. The greatest problem of this incident is its damage to the work of six years of building a sense of trust throughout this church. He found himself greatly discouraged until Thanksgiving when the Almen family traveled to North Dakota, which was a poignant time. He was sharing his private experience, because it reminded him that focusing on the problems generated by the release of the initial draft obscured the wider picture of one's own life and of the life of the church. What previous generations have given to us can be passed on to others as the heritage of faith, he said. He called attention to chapter two of the constitution of this church, which reminds us of God's mission that we carry out on behalf of Christ. That bigger picture should inform the discussion of all the matters before the Church Council, "that bigger picture of the whole march of faith through the ages, that in all that we do here may

we together pray that we in our time and in our tasks of leadership may finally be found faithful in the end."

Report of the Treasurer

Chair Magnus called upon Treasurer Richard L. McAuliffe to present his report. He drew attention to his printed report. Treasurer McAuliffe reviewed the current operating funds, comparing revenue versus expenses. He noted that mission support (formerly, "proportionate-share commitments") was down $1.4 million from the previous year. On the expense side of the ledger, he noted that total spending by churchwide units was at 72.7 percent of budget at the ninth-month point of this fiscal year. He also reported on the revenue and expense of World Hunger funds. Finally, he called attention to $1.523 million received by the Lutheran Disaster Response fund for assistance to victims of the Midwest floods.

During discussion, the Rev. Franklin D. Fry asked for clarification regarding receipts from synods for the churchwide offering and the disaster response program, especially given the "competition" from other programs, for example, the Lutheran Brotherhood request for relief funds. The Rev. Robert N. Bacher, executive for administration, indicated that Lutheran Brotherhood had initiated a national campaign for donations; that action violated a written agreement between this church and the fraternal benefits societies, which the societies had subsequently promised not to repeat. Lita Brusick Johnson, executive assistant to the bishop, reported that Lutheran Brotherhood had received approximately $1.8 million, half of which came from ELCA congregations. D. Mark Klever asked how funds designated for relief are distributed. Pastor Bacher indicated that such gifts are dispensed through ELCA channels, especially social service agencies.

Report of the Conference of Bishops

Chair Magnus called upon Bishop Kenneth H. Sauer, chair of the Conference of Bishops, to report on behalf of the conference. Bishop Sauer drew attention to his written report, and to the items on the council's agenda that had been transmitted from the conference for the council's consideration. He reviewed the work of the conference, including the Academy for Bishops, an annual continuing-education event. Bishop Sauer expressed appreciation to the Rev. Harold R. Lohr, who has served as interim director of the Department for Synodical Relations. Bishop Sauer noted that synodical bishops in this church operate in the fulcrum of various areas of this church's life, for example, such matters as finances and confessional integrity (expressed at the most recent meeting of the conference in a statement rejecting the blessing of same-sex relationships). He noted that synods are actively planning for ministry in the 21st century and that congregations are utilizing new forms of outreach. Good things are happening in this church and we dare not let those things be lost in light of other problems, he urged. Finally, Bishop Sauer said that he believes the conference has arrived at "where it wants to be," in relationship to the churchwide organization.

During discussion, the Rev. James G. Cobb inquired whether the conference has ever considered the question of the number of synods in this church. Bishop Sauer responded that the issue has been addressed both formally and informally, especially in light of fiscal concerns.

Referrals from the 1993 ChurchwideAssembly Directed to the Church Council

1. Election Process: Bishop of the Evangelical Lutheran Church in America

Background: Acting upon the recommendation of its Reference and Counsel Committee, the 1993 Churchwide Assembly took the following action related to two resolutions submitted by a voting member of the assembly:

To refer the following resolutions to the Church Council for such consideration as it deems advisable:

Resolution:

WHEREAS, Bishop Herbert W. Chilstrom has declared his resolve to conclude his service as bishop of the church in 1995; and

WHEREAS, the choice of a new bishop for the Evangelical Lutheran Church in America will be one of the most important decisions of the Churchwide Assembly in 1995; and

WHEREAS, some voting members in synod assemblies who have participated in electing a synod bishop have expressed the desire to be better prepared to make this decision and have asked for some planned means for giving careful consideration to it in advance of voting; and

WHEREAS, some synods have experience with processes which help to surface names of persons who might be considered and give opportunity for church members to talk together in various settings about the needs of the church for leadership at this time and to pray together in preparation for making a decision; therefore, be it

RESOLVED, that this assembly direct the Church Council to develop a process in the period prior to the next Churchwide Assembly that will facilitate an open and prayerful consideration of persons who might serve as the next bishop of this church, with the understanding that the provisions of the constitution and bylaws governing election of the bishop (specifically 19.31.01.a.) will not be changed in any way.

Motion:

WHEREAS, Bishop Herbert W. Chilstrom has served this church faithfully and with distinction since its founding; and

WHEREAS, Bishop Herbert W. Chilstrom has declared that he will not seek reelection in 1995; and

WHEREAS, the times continue to call for an open and informed discussion throughout this church of our mission, our vision, and the role of leadership; therefore, be it

RESOLVED, that the Church Council appoint a select committee to receive names of persons who might faithfully and competently serve as a successor to Bishop Herbert W. Chilstrom, selecting from among them four to eight persons to engage in a thoughtful, public dialogue on the mission of the Evangelical Lutheran Church in America, a vision for our future, and the leadership role of the bishop of this church; and be it further

RESOLVED, that the work of the select committee will begin no sooner than November 1, 1994, and will conclude no later than June 1, 1995.

During discussion, William E. Diehl asked whether the recommendation would empower the Executive Committee to determine the action, or to appoint a select committee as mandated by the Churchwide Assembly. Secretary Almen noted that the Executive Committee would explore possible responses and prepare recommendations for possible action at the April 1994 meeting of the Church Council. Mr. Diehl said that he assumed the intent of the assembly's directive was to involve people from throughout this church, rather than the Executive Committee. Pastor Almen indicated that the Executive Committee might make such a recommendation, but the full Church Council would make the final decision. He noted that, if the Executive Committee were to recommend bylaw changes for revision of the election process, it would do so in consultation with the Legal and Constitutional Review Committee. Edith M. Lohr observed that as one possibility the Executive Committee might simply reaffirm the present process.

VOTED: *CC93.12.69*

To refer the resolution relating to the election of the bishop of this church to the Executive Committee of the Church Council; and

To request that the Executive Committee develop a response and/or recommendations for action, to be reported to the April 1994 meeting of the Church Council (in consultation with the Legal and Constitutional Review Committee, if appropriate).

2. Length of Terms of Synodical Officers

Background: Acting upon the recommendation of its Reference and Counsel Committee, the 1993 Churchwide Assembly took the following action related to a resolution submitted by a voting member of the assembly:

To refer the following motion to the Church Council for consideration with other constitutional provisions:

To amend ELCA bylaw 10.31.05. and section S8.51. in the Constitution for Synods by substituting the word, "six," for the word, "four".

Council Action: In response to an inquiry from Edith M. Lohr, Secretary Almen clarified that the resolution referred to the duration of terms of *synodical*, rather than churchwide, officers.

VOTED: *CC93.12.70*

To refer the resolution of the 1993 Churchwide Assembly on the length of terms of synodical officers to the Legal and Constitutional Review Committee of the Church Council; and

To request that the committee recommend a response to the Church Council at its April 1994 meeting.

3. Long-Range Planning

Background: Acting upon the recommendation of its Reference and Counsel Committee, the 1993 Churchwide Assembly took the following action related to a resolution submitted by a voting member of the assembly:

To refer the following motion to the Church Council:

WHEREAS, ever-accelerating societal changes will continue to have profound implications for the role of the Evangelical Lutheran Church in America within our society; and

WHEREAS, analysis of the existing structure of the Evangelical Lutheran Church in America reveals that there is no division, department, office or other churchwide unit charged with primary responsibility for developing long-range plans and future strategies for the Evangelical Lutheran Church in America; and

WHEREAS, declining financial resources require difficult decisions and prioritizing of the services and support available through the various churchwide units, synods, and related organizations of the church; and

WHEREAS, the continuing decline of church membership and worship attendance suggests ever more creative approaches to ministry and greater sensitivity to the changing needs of society as we seek to reach the unchurched with the Gospel; and

WHEREAS, in light of the above challenges, it is important that this church be proactive in establishing its ministry priorities and direction for the next decade and beyond; therefore, be it

RESOLVED, that the 1993 Churchwide Assembly of the Evangelical Lutheran Church in America call upon the Church Council to establish a task force or council committee which would include representation from the Conference of Bishops and which will be responsible for long-range planning and out of which the task force or committee will establish key priorities, which will be expressed in measurable objectives; and be it further

RESOLVED, that the task force or committee recommend the structural adjustments and the reallocation of resources necessary to accomplish these key priorities; and be it further

RESOLVED, that the process begin as quickly as possible following the close of the 1993 Churchwide Assembly, and that those recommendations made by the task force or committee that can be implemented without Churchwide Assembly action be initiated immediately upon approval by the Church Council, which shall receive a report from the task force or committee at its April 1994 meeting; and be it further

RESOLVED, that a process be established for the ongoing review of progress on any goals adopted and appropriate updating of the planning process; and be it further

RESOLVED, that a complete report of the work of the task force or committee including actions taken by the Church Council and actions required by the Churchwide Assembly be reported to the 1995 Churchwide Assembly.

A proposal, which deals with the subject addressed in the foregoing referral was distributed to council members under the Report of the Executive for Administration. Further action related to this matter is reported elsewhere in these minutes.

4. Commission for Multicultural Ministries: Deaf Community

Background: Acting upon the recommendation of its Reference and Counsel Committee, the 1993 Churchwide Assembly took the following action related to a resolution submitted by a voting member of the assembly:

To refer the following resolution to the Church Council for appropriate action after conferring with the person who submitted the resolution, the Division for Church and Society, and the Commission for Multicultural Ministries; and

To request that a response regarding ministry with the deaf community be transmitted to the 1995 Churchwide Assembly.

WHEREAS, the language and culture of the deaf population is unlike any in this nation; and

WHEREAS, the language of the deaf, American Signed Language (ASL), is truly a language other than English, being strongly based in a French signing system, and is the primary language of members of the deaf culture; and

WHEREAS, 94 percent of the deaf population in the United States is unchurched; and

WHEREAS, specialized ministry, skills, and sensitivity are necessary to reach this population; and

WHEREAS, four years ago the deaf community asked the Churchwide Assembly to view them not as "persons with handicapping conditions" but rather as a unique and diverse community and as such to be "inclusive" in the work of the church through the efforts of the Commission for Multicultural Ministries; and

WHEREAS, this was subsequently addressed by the Church Council, at its April 1991 meeting, affirming the uniqueness of the deaf community and then resolved to take a "multi-unit" approach leaving the Division for Social Ministry Organizations or its successor carrying the responsibility; and

WHEREAS, this approach has continued to confuse the issue of the deaf as either a community or as individuals with handicapping conditions; and

WHEREAS, further attempts were made by the deaf community at the 1991 Churchwide Assembly, to ensure that a desk position be created for deaf ministry to serve the deaf community by advocating the "Multicultural" approach to this ministry; and

WHEREAS, the Division for Social Ministry Organizations or its successor unit has chosen not to create a desk position because of financial constraints; and

WHEREAS, Women of the Evangelical Lutheran Church in America at its recent assembly enthusiastically recognized deaf culture as a culture of its own and American Signed Language (ASL) as the primary language of this culture; and

WHEREAS, the Metropolitan Chicago Synod has successfully included the deaf community in its Commission for Multicultural Ministries for several years; therefore, be it

RESOLVED, that the 1993 Churchwide Assembly, after hearing several years of prayerful requests from the deaf community, open its arms to this unique community, to affirm this ministry by giving them the visibility and "voice" of being one of the five emphasis groups in the Commission for Multicultural Ministries.

Council Action: Following an inquiry for clarification from Ramona S. Rank, the council adopted the following:

VOTED: *CC93.12.71*

To refer the matter of the inclusion of the deaf community as an additional community served by the Commission for Multicultural Ministries jointly to the commission and the Division for Church in Society;

To request that a report and recommendation on this matter be developed following consultation with the ELCA deaf community and with the Division for Outreach and the Office of the Bishop; and

To request that this report and recommendation be brought through the Program and Structure Committee of the Church Council to the November 1994 meeting of the Church Council.

5. Calls to Interim Ministry

Background: Acting upon the recommendation of its Reference and Council Committee, the 1993 Churchwide Assembly took the following action:

To refer the following motion to the Church Council for consideration, in consultation with the Conference of Bishops, Board of Pensions, and Division for Ministry, and to report back to 1995 Churchwide Assembly:

To adopt a new bylaw, ELCA 7.41.13., and renumber existing bylaws accordingly, to provide for uniform standards of call status for pastors serving in interim positions at the request of their synods, as follows:

7.41.13.   **Calls to Interim Ministry.** Pastors as ordained ministers serving as interim pastors, at the request of the synod, shall serve under letter of call, if the pastor so requests. This shall be a term call extended by the Synod Council. The period of call shall be defined by the Synod Council upon recommendation of the office of the synodical bishop. An ordained minister serving under call as interim pastor will be reviewed annually by the synodical bishop.

Council Action: During discussion, Loren W. Mathre observed that the recommendation formulated might necessarily address the issues of uniform and specific training, as well as expectations for those who serve in interim ministries. Thus, he suggested that there may be a need for consultation with seminary faculties in addition to the entities listed in the recommendation.

VOTED: *CC93.12.72*
To refer the proposed amendment of ELCA 7.41.13. to the Conference of Bishops (Department for Synodical Relations) and Division for Ministry;

To request that a report and/or recommendation be developed by the Conference of Bishops, the Division for Ministry and the Board of Pensions, for Church Council consideration (following review by the Church Council's Legal and Constitutional Review Committee); and

To request that this recommendation be brought to the Church Council for consideration at its November 1994 meeting.

6. Financial Support of Church Workers on Leave from Call

Background: The Minneapolis Area Synod, at its 1993 assembly, adopted the following memorial:

WHEREAS, pastors of the Evangelical Lutheran Church in America are not eligible for unemployment compensation; and

WHEREAS, a pastor's profession is unique, in that opportunities to seek calls may be limited; and

WHEREAS, circumstances sometimes arise in which a call is terminated, leaving a pastor with no sustainable income; therefore, be it

RESOLVED, that the Minneapolis Area Synod memorialize the 1993 Churchwide Assembly to request the Board of Pensions to develop a plan to provide basic financial support to pastors and other self-employed church professionals who are on unrequested or involuntary leave from call or appointment and are without other sources of sustainable income.

The following background information was provided by the Memorials Committee to the 1993 Churchwide Assembly:

The Board of Pensions of the Evangelical Lutheran Church in America could develop and administer an Unemployment Compensation Plan. A plan administered by the Board of Pensions would ordinarily be a "contractual" arrangement under which each covered member of the plan would be entitled to benefits, regardless of need. Before such a plan can be devised, however, many issues would need to be resolved and clarified. Some of the more important issues include:

1.   It should be determined whether there is consensus among the synod bishops for the establishment of an unemployment compensation plan. The concept should be introduced to the Conference of Bishops for consideration prior to the development of a proposed plan.

2.   It needs to be determined whether a proposed unemployment compensation plan should be optional or mandatory for ELCA pastors, associates in ministry, and lay employees and/or for congregations, synods, seminaries, ELCA churchwide units, and other ELCA affiliated organizations. The matter of coverage for ELCA ordained ministers serving non-ELCA organizations also would need to be considered.

3.   It needs to be determined how the proposed plan would be financed. While the Board of Pensions would be able to administer a plan, the board could only administer a plan that was adequately financed. A determination would need to be made as to whether the cost for the plan would be paid from ELCA benevolence, from synod budgets, or from assessments of congregations. Considerations for the financing mechanism are very closely related to the considerations for the makeup of the group of eligible persons and the participation requirements for the congregations and other employing organizations.

If it is believed that congregations should pay the premiums for the coverage, it needs to be determined whether those premiums would be assessed on a per member basis, a flat fee per covered individual, etc. It also would need to be determined whether coverage would be lost or what other consequence would occur if a congregation did not remit the required payments on a timely basis.

It should be determined whether the unemployment compensation benefits would be based on a percentage of salary, a flat dollar amount, or some other formula.

The ELCA Pension and Other Benefits Program is mandatory only for synods, seminaries, and churchwide units (other than the publishing house). This fact would add to the challenge of establishing a viable plan applicable to all persons in need.

4.   Would the ELCA be the sponsor of the plan? The plan sponsor is the entity that would be committed to covering any financial shortfall.

5.   The resolution refers to support for persons who are without other sources of sustainable income. The ELCA Department for Synodical Relations administers a Good Samaritan Program to assist ELCA pastors, associates in ministry, and lay employees with emergency financial needs. If the Unemployment Compensation Plan would have a needs test, consideration should be given to financing the plan through

the existing Good Samaritan Program. In cooperation with the synod bishops, the program already provides assistance to persons based on their need.

Before such a plan could be designed, determination would be needed on whether there would be support for such a plan throughout the Evangelical Lutheran Church in America and on whether it be deemed to be economically feasible.

Upon recommendation of the Memorials Committee, the 1993 Churchwide Assembly took the following action:

To refer the memorial of the Minneapolis Area Synod on financial support of pastors and other professional staff to the Church Council and the Board of Pensions to determine the financial feasibility and wisdom for such a plan and to provide a report to the 1995 Churchwide Assembly.

Council Action: During discussion, William T. Billings observed that, from the tenor of the proposed action, the recommendation favored the provision of financial support. He expressed concern that the council not be predisposed to a particular position on the matter. Chair Magnus suggested that the word, "possible," be added editorially so that the resolution would read, ". . . a report and *possible* recommendation . . . ."

The Rev. John O. Knudson concluded that addition of the word, "possible," was inappropriate, since the council could decide to take no action. Secretary Lowell G. Almen observed that the work of the study might result in a report to be received only as information. Pastor Knudson withdrew his objection. The Rev. David A. Andert noted that in referring the matter to the Church Council, the 1993 Churchwide Assembly presumed no implication of endorsement.

VOTED: *CC93.12.73*

To request that the Board of Pensions, following consultation with the Conference of Bishops and the Office of the Bishop, bring to the November 1994 meeting of the Church Council a report and possible recommendation for action on this resolution related to financial support of church workers on leave from call.

7.   Disciplinary Procedures

Acting upon the recommendation of its Reference and Counsel Committee, the 1993 Churchwide Assembly took the following action related to a resolution submitted by a voting member of the assembly:

To refer the following resolution to the Church Council for consideration, in consultation with the Conference of Bishops and legal counsel:

WHEREAS, the teachings contained in the Confessions of the Evangelical Lutheran Church in America, and named in the Confession of Faith of this church, have played a role in setting norms for the life as well as the faith of the church; and

WHEREAS, in the Large Catechism (on the Eighth Commandment) Luther writes: ". . . God will not have one neighbor deprived of his reputation, honor, and character any more than of his money and possessions; [God] would have every [person] maintain his self-respect before his [spouse], children, servants, and neighbors" (Tappert, p. 399); and "[N]o [one] should be deprived of his honor and good name unless these have first been taken away from him publicly .

. . . Every report that cannot be <u>adequately proved</u> is false witness . . . . For honor and good name are easily taken away, but not easily restored" (Tappert, p. 401, emphasis added); and

WHEREAS, serious accusations against the integrity of a congregation can imperil its mission and damage the faith of its members; and

WHEREAS, serious accusations against the integrity of an ordained minister endangers his/her reputation, honor, name, as well as his/her livelihood, and may damage the reputation and mission of the church; and

WHEREAS, the standard of preponderance as defined in the guidelines requires the disciplinary committee to find only a "greater probability of truth" in the accusations, than in the defense; and

WHEREAS, this church should be convinced of wrongdoing by the pastors or congregations when speaking judgment and applying discipline against them; therefore, be it

RESOLVED, that the "Rules Governing Disciplinary Procedures Against an Ordained Minister or a Congregation of the Evangelical Lutheran Church in America" be amended to require the following standards:

1.   That this church require the accuser(s) or an ordained minister of a congregation to have the burden of proving by means of "clear and convincing evidence" the allegations brought in the charges; and

2.   That if the charges are serious enough to merit removal of a pastor from the roster of ordained ministers or the expulsion of a congregation from this church, the accuser(s) of an ordained minister or a congregation be required to have the burden of proving their accusations "beyond reasonable doubt"; and

3.   That these standards shall <u>not</u> limit the ability of the discipline hearing committee to use of the findings of a secular court to establish a presumption for or against the accused (regardless of the burden of proof used in that court proceeding).

A recommendation for action on this matter provided by the Legal and Constitutional Review Committee is reported elsewhere in these minutes.

8.   Discipline Process in Congregations

Background: The following memorial was adopted by the Lower Susquehanna Synod at its 1992 Synod Assembly:

WHEREAS, we are of the opinion that the Congregation Council must be formally involved in efforts to resolve disputes within the congregation before the dispute is brought to the synodical bishop, and we do not believe that informing the congregation president that the bishop is being contacted in the event of disagreements would serve the containment and resolution of difficulties as well as the procedure outlined below; and

WHEREAS, Chapter 15 of the Model Constitution for Congregations has been changed from "Discipline of Members" to "Discipline of Members and Adjudication," it would appear consistent that, in addition to the subtitle, "Adjudication," that now appears at C15.10., there be a subtitle, "Discipline of Members," perhaps C15.00.; and

WHEREAS, paragraphs pertaining to discipline of members have been well defined over time, it would be good if the sections devoted to adjudication could be just as carefully worked out; therefore be it

RESOLVED, that to clarify procedural matters, the following paragraphs be proposed to replace C15.11.:

C15.11.   When there is disagreement among factions within this congregation on a substantive issue that cannot be resolved by the parties, members of this congregation shall refer the disagreement to the Congregation Council.

C15.12. Should the disagreement not be resolved by the Congregation Council in a manner that is satisfactory to the parties involved and the Congregation Council, members of this congregation shall have access to the synodical bishop for consultation.

C15.13. Should the disagreement not be resolved with the help of the bishop in a manner that is satisfactory to the parties involved and the Congregation Council, the disagreement shall be referred to the synodical Consultation Committee.

C15.14. Should the disagreement not be resolved by the Consultation Committee in a manner that is satisfactory to the parties involved and the Congregation Council, the disagreement shall be referred to the Synod Council. The decision of the Synod Council shall be final and binding upon the parties involved and the Congregation Council.

The following background information was supplied to the 1993 Churchwide Assembly by its Memorials Committee:

Provision C15.11. in the *Model Constitution for Congregations* regarding "Adjudication" is identical to required provision S17.11. in the *Constitution for Synods*. Both relate to stipulations in constitutional provision 20.84. in the churchwide constitution.

Although the *Model Constitution for Congregations* may be amended by the Churchwide Assembly in the manner provided for the bylaws of this church (ELCA 9.53.02.), mandatory provisions in the *Constitution for Synods* that incorporate constitutional provisions of this church may be amended only in the manner prescribed for amendments to the constitution of this church (ELCA 10.13.).

In view of the fact that final action on such proposed amendments could not be completed by the 1993 Churchwide Assembly and in recognition of the need for study of the implications of such amendments, the 1993 Churchwide Assembly acted upon the Memorials Committee recommendation and adopted the following resolution:

To refer the memorial of the Lower Susquehanna Synod on adjudication related to members of congregations to the Legal and Constitutional Review Committee of the Church Council for study in connection with preparation of any possible amendments to be proposed by the Church Council to the 1995 Churchwide Assembly.

Council Action: The Church Council adopted the following recommendation without discussion:

VOTED: CC93.12.74

To refer this resolution to the Office of the Secretary; and

To request that a report and/or recommendation be prepared for review by the Church Council, through its Legal and Constitutional Review Committee of the Church Council, at the November 1994 Church Council meeting.

9. Process of Consultation and Discipline

Background: The following memorial was adopted by the Slovak Zion Synod (7G) at its 1993 Synod Assembly:

WHEREAS, we the voting members of the Slovak Zion Synod, meeting in assembly at Muhlenberg College the 16th day of June 1993, after prayerful consideration of Matthew 18:15-17 ("If another member of the church sins against you, go and point out the fault when the two of you are alone. If the member listens to you, you have regained that one. But if you are not listened to, take one or two others along with you, so that every word may be confirmed by the evidence of two or three witnesses. If the member refuses to listen to them, tell it to the church; and if the offender refuses to listen even to the church, let such a one be to you as a Gentile and a tax collector."), wish to convey to the Evangelical Lutheran Church in America and its presiding bishop, Herbert Chilstrom, our dismay at the handling of issues regarding our bishop, Kenneth Zindle; and

WHEREAS, we believe that it is incumbent upon the leadership of the church to deal with questions of discipline of bishops and pastors in a manner consistent with Christian fairness, equity, love, and due process. The presumption of guilt or innocence should in no way be arrived at without the most careful review of the facts and exhaustive investigation. It is our feeling that the person accused of impropriety should be informed immediately of the charges and should be made aware of those who have made the accusations. Accusations in themselves should not be construed to presume guilt. Indeed, the burden of proof, according to the standards of American common law presumes innocence until proven guilty. This standard must pertain in all cases; and

WHEREAS, consistent with these standards of fairness and due process we object to the following:

1. that the allegations against Bishop Zindle were not shown to him when they were given to Bishop Chilstrom and an inordinate period of time lapsed (seven months) before he was informed of them;

2. that the biblical guidelines as stated in Matthew 18 were not followed;

3. that unwarranted assumptions seem to have been made;

4. that the accusers were not subjected to the same scrutiny as the accused;

5. that privileged information was disclosed and not repudiated by the bishop of the church as a breach of pastoral confidence;

6. that the threat of a protracted investigative process, which would lead to the extension of personal pain to all concerned, resulted in the resignation of Bishop Zindle;

7. that there appears to be a double standard for bishops and pastors, i.e., "you are not fit to be a bishop but you could serve as a pastor," seems contradictory to the documents on the Study of Ministry, which recognizes that there is no difference between bishops and pastors; therefore, be it

RESOLVED, that in the light of these concerns, not only for the life and ministry of Bishop Kenneth Zindle, but also for the integrity of the pastoral ministry (bishop of the Evangelical Lutheran Church in America, synodical bishops, and pastors) and the significant impact these kinds of accusations and discipline affects a professional career, we [memorialize the 1993 Churchwide Assembly to]* recommend the following:

1. that a committee be appointed by the Conference of Bishops to investigate the process used in dealing with these allegations against Bishop Zindle and establish guidelines to be adopted for the future handling of similar situations where discipline against pastors or bishops is considered;

2. that Christian love, fairness, equity, and due process be the ever-present standards under which these investigations are conducted;

3. and that pastoral care be extended to all so accused, so that there will be given emotional, spiritual support and rehabilitation;

4. that copies of this memorial be sent to the Slovak Zion Synod office; the Rev. Bishop Herbert Chilstrom, ELCA bishop; the Conference of Bishops; the Rev. Lowell Almen, ELCA secretary; and the pastors of congregations of the Slovak Zion Synod.

---

*Text in brackets added to reflect the apparent intention of the Synod Assembly as reported by the synodical secretary.

The following background information was provided by the Memorials Committee to the 1993 Churchwide Assembly:

1. **Removal from Office of Synod Officers:** The process for consultation and potential ecclesiastical discipline in this church is prescribed in Chapter 20 of the *Constitution, Bylaws, and Continuing Resolutions of the Evangelical Lutheran Church in America.*

As specified under ELCA continuing resolution 20.53.A92.a., the recall or dismissal of a synodical bishop and the vacating of that office "may be effected: (1) for willful disregard or violation of the constitution and bylaws of this church or the constitution and bylaws of the synod; (2) for such physical or mental disability as renders the officer incapable of performing the duties of office; or (3) for such conduct as would subject the officer to disciplinary action as an ordained minister . . . ."

Under continuing resolution 20.53.A92.b., the sources of a written petition for removal from office of a synodical bishop are defined, including the Synod Council, Synod Assembly, at least ten synodical bishops, or the bishop of this church.

Prior to the filing of formal charges in a written petition, continuing resolution 20.53.A92.g. specifies that "the petitioner shall first meet with the Executive Committee of the synod in which the officer serves. The Executive Committee shall function as a consultation panel to give advice to the petitioner." If no petition is filed, the proceedings end. If a petition is filed, the Committee on Appeals serves as the discipline hearing committee.

All proceedings that may lead to removal from office are ended upon the resignation of the office holder.

2. **Adoption and Revision for Disciplinary and Removal Procedures**: In April 1991, the Church Council initiated a process that gathered together synod bishops, churchwide staff, and experts to develop a strategy by which the Evangelical Lutheran Church in America would respond to matters of discipline in this church. The work of this committee was reviewed by the Conference of Bishops. In 1992 the council adopted recommended key elements of policy and procedure for use by synods in developing their own processes. This was part of a broader strategy affirmed by the Church Council, which also included the goals of education, training, and prevention as central elements of this strategy.

The bylaws of this church assign responsibility to the Committee on Appeals for the development of processes and rules of procedures related to discipline of pastors and congregations (ELCA 20.21.16.) and for removal of synod and churchwide officers (ELCA 20.53.11.). In the development of the current documents, the advice of the Conference of Bishops was sought. Responsibility for ratification of such rules is assigned to the Church Council.

At its November 1991 meeting, the Church Council also authorized a continuing mechanism for review and revision of these documents. A subcommittee of the Committee on Appeals is developing recommendations for changes in the current process and rules of procedure that take into account actual experience in a growing number of discipline cases and the proposed bylaw changes that are before the 1993 Churchwide Assembly. At its October 1993 meeting the Conference of Bishops will be asked to provide advice relating to proposed amendments to those documents, prior to Church Council action anticipated in December 1993.

3. **Slovak Zion Memorial:** To address fully the memorial of the Slovak Zion Synod would require presentation of extensive information that would have the result of making details of a preliminary investigation part of the permanent record of a Churchwide Assembly. *The Memorials Committee deems this to be an unwise precedent.* Furthermore, the Churchwide Assembly lacks the authority under the governing documents of the Evangelical Lutheran Church in America to review specific cases of discipline.

The 1993 Churchwide Assembly voted:

To acknowledge receipt of the memorial of the Slovak Zion Synod regarding the process of consultation and potential discipline related to synodical officers; and

To refer the memorial of the Slovak Zion Synod to the ELCA Church Council for consideration in its ongoing review and revision of the documents governing ELCA processes for discipline and removal from office of synod officers in the Evangelical Lutheran Church in America, such ongoing review and revision to be done in consultation with the Conference of Bishops.

Council Action: The Church Council received the foregoing as information.

Ecumenical Affairs: Lutheran-Roman Catholic Coordinating Committee

Background: In February 1993, a consultation on the future of Lutheran-Roman Catholic relations in the United States was held. Two conclusions of the consultation were:

1. That priority should be given to a declaration that certain condemnations of the sixteenth century between Lutherans and Roman Catholics no longer apply to the present ecumenical partner; and
2. That a new series of Lutheran-Roman Catholic dialogues should be planned to address the topic of ecclesiology.

Work on the first priority would be done in close collaboration with the Lutheran World Federation.

In order to address these two topics, "lifting" of condemnations and a new dialogue, ELCA Bishop Herbert W. Chilstrom presented the slate of names that follows for ELCA members of a Joint Lutheran-Roman Catholic Coordinating Committee. Two additional names were to be supplied at the time of the December 1993 Church Council meeting (see below).

The U.S. Conference of Catholic Bishops presently is appointing Roman Catholic members to the committee. It is envisioned that the Joint Coordinating Committee would function between 1994 and 1997.

Council Action: Chair Magnus called upon the Rev. William G. Rusch, director of the Department of Ecumenical Affairs, to introduce a resolution related to the creation of a joint coordinating committee for Lutheran-Roman Catholic relations. He noted that there would be only one additional candidate for appointment to the committee, namely, the Rev. Joan A. Mau.

William H. Engelbrecht requested that brief biographies of the candidates to be appointed be provided. Pastor Rusch reviewed the vitae of the nominees.

VOTED: *CC93.12.75*

To approve the following persons as ELCA members of the Joint Lutheran-Roman Catholic Coordinating Committee:

- **Rev. H. George Anderson (Decorah, Iowa);**
- **Rev. Sherman G. Hicks (Bishop, Metropolitan Chicago Synod);**
- **Rev David W. Lotz (New York City, N.Y.);**
- **Rev. Joan A. Mau (Sioux City, Iowa);**
- **Rev. John H. P. Reumann (Philadelphia, Pa.);**
- **Rev. Harold C. Skillrud, chair (Southeastern Synod); and**
- **Rev. Trudy A. Thorleifson (Edmonds, Wash.)**

The Rev. Franklin D. Fry inquired whether this church's other ecumenical partners (i.e., the Reformed and Episcopal churches) had been informed that this church was entering into another study process with the Roman Catholic Church. Pastor Rusch indicated that is was clearly understood by those other partners that the outcome of the study process had not been predetermined.

Slate of Appointments for Church Council Committees

Background: Listed below is a slate proposed by the chair of the Church Council for council committees and related advisory committees to which council members must be appointed. A proposed chair for each council committee was suggested. In proposing this slate, the chair attempted to provide for the necessary balance of male/female, clergy/lay in the membership of all committees; attention also was given to providing both desired expertise for the committee's work and balance between experienced and new members of the council. The chair tried to honor, insofar as possible, the preferences submitted to the chair.

Council Action: During discussion, Karen M. Dietz inquired about the duration of appointments to Church Council committees. The duration is the current biennium.

VOTED: *CC93.12.76*
To approve the slate of appointments to Church Council committees and related advisory committees as follows:

Budget and Finance Committee
Charles A. Adamson
H. George Anderson
Richard G. Deines
J. David Ellwanger
John O. Knudson
Edith M. Lohr, chair
Philip L. Natwick
Ramona S. Rank

Coordination and Services Committee
David K. Johnson
William E. Diehl, chair
Karen Dietz
Loren W. Mathre
Carlos Peña
W. Jeanne Rapp
Susan Huber Stapell
Nelson T. Strobert

Legal and Constitutional Review Committee
David A. Andert
William T. Billings
William H. Engelbrecht
Dale V. Sandstrom, chair
Deborah S. Yandala

Program and Structure Committee
Lorraine G. Bergquist
David G. Gabel
Patsy Gottschalk
Donald M. Hallberg

Cynthia P. Johnson
Mark Klever
Robert S. Schroeder
Stephen M. Youngdahl, chair

Advisory Committee: *The Lutheran*
Nadine F. Lehr

Advisory Committee: Ecumenical Affairs
James G. Cobb
Terry L. Bowes
Franklin D. Fry

Following several announcements, the Church Council recessed at 4:48 P.M. for dinners hosted by the staffs of churchwide units. The council reconvened at 6:30 P.M. in executive session.

Executive Session

The Church Council convened into executive session at 6:37 P.M. on December 3, 1993, in the Church Council room of the Lutheran Center at Chicago, Ill., for the purpose of discussing personnel matters related to the development of a social teaching statement on the church and human sexuality.

The Church Council reconvened in plenary session at 7:55 P.M. Chair Magnus indicated that the council would meet at this time as a committee of the whole in order to consider the initial draft of a social teaching statement on the church and human sexuality. No legislative action would be taken during this session, she stated.

Social Teaching Statement on the Church and Human Sexuality

Background:
1. History
Where did the process start for development of a possible social statement on human sexuality? Although the various social statements of predecessor church bodies were recognized as historical documents, discussion in the Commission for a New Lutheran Church and in the early operational life of the Evangelical Lutheran Church in America pointed to the need for development of social statements by the church.

a. *Synod Memorials and Resolutions.*

In various synods, calls for churchwide response and studies began to come as early as the spring of 1988 and in subsequent years.

Resolutions from the Sierra Pacific Synod (1988), Alaska Synod (1988), Nebraska Synod (1988), and Southwestern Texas Synod (1988) on the ordination of homosexual persons were referred by the Church Council's Executive Committee (October 16-17, 1988) to the Division for Ministry as it developed a statement on "Expectations Concerning Sexual Conduct of Candidates" and to the Commission for Church in Society "for use as the commission develops a process for a possible study of human sexuality" (EC88.10.40).

A review of 1989 Churchwide Assembly minutes reveals that memorials from the following synods asked, in one form or another, that the ELCA churchwide organization address questions related to sexuality, homosexuality, and family life: South Dakota (1988), Saint Paul Area (1988), Lower Susquehanna (1988), Southwestern Pennsylvania (1988), Delaware-Maryland (1988), Eastern Washington-Idaho (1989), Eastern North Dakota (1989), Central States (1989), Sierra Pacific (1990 and 1991), and Greater Milwaukee (1991). The text of the resolutions and additional background material were distributed to council members.

b. *Initiation of Study by the Commission for Church in Society and Appointment of Task Force.*

In the churchwide organization, the board of the former Commission for Church in Society (later merged with the Division for Social Ministry Organizations to form the Division for Church in Society) took action at its September 30-October 2, 1988, meeting (CS88.10.11):

> WHEREAS, concern about issues of human sexuality and Christian faith has been strongly raised by many in the Evangelical Lutheran Church in America; therefore, be it
>
> RESOLVED, that the Executive Director [the Rev. Jerry Folk] of CCS [Commission for Church in Society], in consultation with the studies department, appoint a task force to facilitate a churchwide study of human sexuality, a study process which would develop varieties of participatory models to listen to the church's many voices, and help form the church's understandings of human sexuality. This study will be a focus of the CCS [Commission for Church in Society] studies department in cooperation with the other units of the ELCA [churchwide organization], synods, and congregations.

The Church Council, at its November 1988 meeting, received a report from the Commission for Church in Society on its plan to develop social statements in the coming biennium, including plans for this statement on human sexuality.

At its March 9-11, 1989, meeting, the board of the Commission for Church in Society voted:

> To ratify the proposed appointments for the task force for the human sexuality study (CS89.3.27).

(Edith Lohr was appointed to serve on this task force as liaison to the Church Council.) This action was reported to the Church Council at the council's April 15-17, 1989, meeting.

Following the Church Council meeting, the task force began the process of developing a study booklet on human sexuality ("Human Sexuality and the Christian Faith").

c. *1989 and 1991 Churchwide Assemblies.*

In response to memorials (cited above), the *1989 Churchwide Assembly* noted (CA89.2.12) that a task force had been appointed to guide the development of a churchwide study of human sexuality (1989 Minutes, page 655). "This will be a participatory study involving other units of the Evangelical Lutheran Church in America, synods, and congregations. As part of its work, this representative

task force will address the broad issue of human sexuality, including concerns related to homosexuality and homophobia" (Ibid.).

The 1989 Churchwide Assembly, in a resolution on sexual harassment, also voted (CA89.4.18) to "call upon the Commission for Church in Society to include sexual harassment and abuse in its forthcoming society statement on sexuality."

The *1991 Churchwide Assembly* received in its pre-assembly material a report that the Commission for Church in Society was proceeding on a possible social statement on human sexuality (*1991 Reports and Records, Volume 1, Part 1*, pages 166-167). The 1991 assembly also received a report that the Church Council approved at its October 20-22, 1990, meeting the commission's proposal for a series of social statements (CC90.10.76), including the development of a social statement on human sexuality, which at that time was scheduled for the 1993 assembly.

In response to memorials from the Sierra Pacific Synod (1990 and 1991) and the Greater Milwaukee Synod (1991), the 1991 Churchwide Assembly noted that development of a social statement on human sexuality was under way. The assembly also voted (CA91.7.51): "To encourage individuals and congregations throughout the Evangelical Lutheran Church in America to engage actively in the process of deliberation and discernment that will shape the social teaching statement on human sexuality, prior to action by the Churchwide Assembly."

d. *Study Document: "Human Sexuality and the Christian Faith."*

At its October 31-November 2, 1991, meeting, the board of the Division for Church in Society reviewed and authorized for distribution a study document developed by the task force, which was shared with the Church Council at its November 8-11 meeting. Extensive discussion on the study document occurred at the Church Council's November 1991 meeting; the council also discussed the possibility of extending the time line for preparation of this possible social statement, but did not vote to extend the timeline at that time (Minutes, pages 96-99).

Following that meeting, the study document was distributed widely throughout the church, responses were received until the end of 1992, and regional hearings were conducted throughout the church.

In the meantime, anticipating that more time was needed for the development of a statement on human sexuality, the board of the Division for Church in Society voted at its March 12-14, 1992, meeting: "To affirm the recommendation of the executive committee [of the board] that the process for development of a social statement on human sexuality be extended to 1995" (DS92.3.43). At its

April 4-5, 1992, meeting, the Church Council received this as information.

e. *First Draft of the "Social Statement on the Church and Human Sexuality: A Lutheran Perspective."*

In August 1992, the task force held a consultation with a number of theologians, biblical scholars, and church leaders. Throughout the remainder of 1992 and the first part of 1993, staff and the task force continued to review the responses and develop a draft statement. In late May 1993, a "pre-draft" was sent to approximately 60 persons for comment and counsel, including those at the August 1992 consultation, three to five faculty members from each ELCA seminary (nominated by their deans), studies and executive committee members of the board of the Division for Church in Society, the theology and ethics committee of the Conference of Bishops, the executive committee of the Church Council, and the Office of the Bishop. Comments from this group were considered by the review committee of the task force in late June. In July 1993, the task force reviewed the entire draft, made additional recommendations as to its revision, and reached consensus regarding strategic aspects of the draft. Revisions in the draft continued to be made until mid-September, when the draft was shared with the board of the Division for Church in Society.

At its September 30-October 3, 1993, meeting, the board of the Division for Church in Society reviewed the text of the draft, made several changes in the draft, and authorized distribution of this draft statement.

The Conference of Bishops, at its October 5-8, 1993, meeting, reviewed the draft statement and took the following action:

We, as the Conference of Bishops of the Evangelical Lutheran Church in America receive the first draft of a proposed "Social Statement on the Church and Human Sexuality—a Lutheran Perspective" with appreciate but also with reservations.

As this church takes the opportunity to discuss and shape the statement, we as the Conference of Bishops, express concern about the unity of this church and call upon all to participate in a climate of mutual respect.

Within the Conference of Bishops, numerous theological and biblical concerns were raised. These initial reservations about the statement include such concerns as the way Scripture is interpreted and objections to the judgments rendered in Section III.E. (cf., especially the commentary regarding "Response 1" of Section III.D., page 16, lines 34-42).

We encourage congregations to review the comparable social statements of the predecessor church bodies ("Human Sexuality and Sexual Behavior," The American Lutheran Church, 1989, and "Sex, Marriage, and the Family," Lutheran Church in America, 1970).

We recognize that a final draft is expected to be considered at the 1995 Churchwide Assembly of the Evangelical Lutheran Church in America. We trust that God will give to this church sufficient will and wisdom to accept, reject, alter, delay, or withdraw this statement in a manner pleasing to the Holy Spirit. As members of the Conference of Bishops, we will continue to participate in that process (CB93.10.24).

The draft, "Social Statement on The Church and Human Sexuality: A Lutheran Perspective," was mailed to pastors and other church leaders on October 21, 1993.

Church Council members were asked to bring with them subsequent mailings that outline events of the past month. Additional copies are available upon request.

2. **Process for the Development of Social Teaching Statements**

The procedure for the development of social teaching statements, and the role of various governance bodies within the Evangelical Lutheran Church in America, have been stipulated by action of the 1989 Churchwide Assembly:

(1) The board of the [Division] for Church in Society shall oversee the development of social teaching statements.

   (a) The board shall consider the proposals made by its department for studies, the synods, and other churchwide units, and approve the issues to be dealt with in social teaching statements; the ELCA Church Council or the Churchwide Assembly may direct the [Division] for Church in Society to address an issue.

   (b) The board shall oversee the study process leading to a social statement, assuring that an appropriate group be named to study the issue and the way be found to encourage broad participation by the congregations and members of our church.

   (c) The board shall review, if need be, revise, and approve proposed social teaching statements, and recommend through the Church Council (ELCA 14.21.03.) that they be adopted by the Churchwide Assembly; it shall recommend to the Church Council that they be on the agenda of the next Churchwide Assembly.

   (d) The board shall cooperate with the Division for Congregational [Ministries] and other churchwide units and synods to encourage the use of social teaching statements in this church; it "shall monitor the faithfulness of this church to its social statements" (ELCA 16.41.A87.f., 1989).

(2) The Church Council shall review and act upon the recommendations of the board of the [Division] for Church in Society [ELCA 14.21.01., 14.21.02., 14.21.03.]; the council may offer a report expressing its observations and recommendations on social teaching statements for the consideration of the Churchwide Assembly.

(3) Only the Churchwide Assembly shall adopt ELCA social teaching statement (ELCA 12.21.d.).

(a)   A two-thirds vote of the voting members of the assembly shall be required to adopt a social teaching statement . . . (CA89.3.14).

3.   Synod Council Resolutions

In response to the release of the draft statement on human sexuality, several synod councils took action relating to this statement. The full text of resolutions from the following synods was printed the council's agenda: Southwestern Pennsylvania, Indiana-Kentucky, Northwestern Pennsylvania, Upper Susquehanna, Metropolitan New York, Delaware-Maryland, and Minneapolis Area synods.

4.   Staff Team on Social Statement Development

A staff team was put in place at the request of Bishop Herbert W. Chilstrom in mid-November 1993. This staff team is to responsible for planning and coordination related to the development and release of study documents, preliminary drafts, and assembly-approved texts of social statements. The establishment of this staff team and this explicit statement of the responsibilities and expectations of staff represent an attempt to learn from and to prevent the recurrence of the difficulties that characterized the October 1993 release of the draft statement on human sexuality.

5.   Proposed Revision in the Process for the Development of a Statement on Human Sexuality

In the weeks following the release of the draft statement on human sexuality, there was substantial communication between churchwide staff and leaders throughout this church, in particular synodical bishops. Reflecting on the churchwide reaction to this statement and the advice received, the Division for Church in Society, after consultation with Bishop Herbert W. Chilstrom, brought forward to the Church Council a proposal.

Council Action: Chair Magnus urged that council members continue to listen to one another with care and respect, in order that this might be "a safe for discussion and differences of opinion." She stated that she was certain that council members had opinions as diverse as those that had been expressed across this church. She also observed, "Whatever action the council takes is not going to please everyone in the Evangelical Lutheran Church in America, but I would ask you to remember that you are not in this position to please everyone, but you are here to be leaders."

Chair Magnus called upon Bishop Herbert W. Chilstrom to comment on his perceptions on this church's reception of the initial draft of the proposed social teaching statement. A transcript of his remarks and those of council members follows:

Vice President Kathy J. Magnus: ". . . We are now functioning as a committee of the whole. There will be no legislative action taken this evening and I call on Bishop Chilstrom for his perception of what has happened."

Bishop Herbert W. Chilstrom: "My perceptions of what has happened: I often say in places around this church that I have both the best and the worst place from which to observe it. You can understand why I would say that. I first learned of the difficulty of the release of the document when I was in the Ozarks of Missouri enjoying myself–leading a pastors' retreat; looking forward that day to Bible studies with the pastors, which is one of my favorite things to do. And about half-way through my lecture, I noticed a stir in the room. Newspapers began coming in. And I soon found out what was happening. That was October 20. And I would have to say that the six weeks since that time have certainly been one of the more stressful times of my 35 years in ministry. As soon as I returned to Chicago, as you heard in executive session, we met with the three units that were involved and I think we can say now in this open session that, while there was initially, as Secretary Almen has mentioned in his report, some defensiveness on the part of each of those units, that quickly changed. And I have to say that I have been pleased with the cooperation of all three of those units in looking very carefully at what happened, in admitting mistakes that were made by them, and in putting together a process where, so far as is humanly possibly, that will not happen again. I want to underscore something that needs to be said over and over again, because it comes in letters; and that is that there was nothing deliberate or cavalier about this mistake. A serious mistake–a very serious mistake–but nothing that I can determine that was either deliberate or cavalier, and there was no deliberate leak of the story in order to embarrass this church or that particular unit. What we faced was what I call a genuine crisis. I mentioned in my message to you this morning that I have received over 700 letters–500 from lay people and 200 from pastors–over the last six weeks. Early on, the letters were almost exclusively reacting to the story of the Associated Press and for that reason were almost 100 percent negative. Now, in the last week, it is becoming much more balanced in terms of the numbers of letters that are very much opposed to the statement, and to the press reports and letters that are urging us to move ahead and that are commending the church and are reacting very favorably to those reports and to the document itself.

"I have to say that we are all over the map in every corner of this church. Today, came two letters from bishops. One said, 'I would suggest immediate withdrawal of the document and dismissal of the task force, which produced it.' The other says, 'I think the statement is well done and the discussion on sexuality long overdue in this church.'

"From parishes, if I can give you just some samples of the diversity, this would be an example–I think, a good example–of many similar letters where a congregation writes and says, `We were dismayed, frustrated, angered, and disappointed as we were confronted in the local newspapers, television, and radio with the latest Associated Press release about the first draft. Since then, we have received the task force's document itself. Our people are deeply disturbed and disillusioned. We find it hard to believe that the scholars who authored this document, supposedly as a teaching moment, would not see how it has become, rather, a vehicle of persuasion instead of information. We cannot help but feel that we are being systematically massaged into accepting beliefs and behavior that would have been considered nothing short of heresy by the apostles and the reformers. Indeed, the lay people of our church seem to be better informed in the traditional interpretation of Scripture on this issue.'

"In the same mail, just to give you an example of what crosses my desk, is a letter from another congregation saying, `We as one congregation cannot provide answers for the whole church, but, frankly, we wish we could. For the issues dealt with in the church and human sexuality are ones we certainly live and deal with every day. Within our congregation, we have come to just about every type of existing familiar relationship: ordinary heterosexual two-parent families; single-parent families; multi-generational families, where children are being raised by grandparents; one-person families; families with both parents who are gay or lesbian; and both heterosexual and gay and lesbian couples in committed relationships. And we all worship together, we pray together, and learn together. Every Sunday, we recall our common Baptism in the name of the Triune God, and we share God's gift of bread and wine. Together we yearn for justice–for God's healing presence.' And they go on to say that `we believe that the traditional biblical interpretation is in error, which condemns all homosexual acts as morally debase, deviant choices of inherently heterosexual people,' and urges us to remember that the church has changed its mind on issues in the past. An example of two congregations at both ends of the spectrum.

"Theologians also differ considerably. Again, from today's mail alone: one who says, `I cannot believe that my church would ask me to negate my understanding of Scripture to accommodate a concern for gay and lesbian families. Love them in Christ, yes. Pray for them and for all of us who sin in whatever way, yes. But rationalize sin, no.' Another theologian who says, `I am not alone when I offer you my support and thanks. Please do not let this draft be withdrawn. As a mother raising a child in a society that gives mixed and damaging messages about sexuality, as a sister in Christ who cherished gay and lesbian friends, I read the document with hope and finished it consoled that now, at last, we can talk about these matters.'

"These are examples of the kind of mail that I am reading in the 700 that arrived each day. I will also say that, in most cases, the vast majority of cases that are negative on the proposal, go directly to the section on homosexuality. There are some letters concerned about the position on marriage and are hoping that they can be made sharper and clearer in a subsequent document. There are some letters that also are concerned about the section regarding teenagers, and the issue there is that folks are saying, we know that teenagers are active sexually. We do not think we ought to say anything to them about birth control. We believe we should simply say to them, do not do it, period. Many letters are to that effect, but I have to say that most of them go directly to the subject of homosexuality. There is no question that that is the flash point in a very difficult subject matter.

"I would say this from a general perspective, that I find that, if I were to sit in my office reading my mail only, it would be quite overwhelming–particularly in those [initial] few weeks. I find, however, that as I move out into the churches, both at synodical meetings and at congregational settings–which I have done, both of which I have done–that I do not feel hostility and the violent reaction in that setting that I do in the letters that cross my desk. In the past week, I have been in two congregational settings. In one case, a large congregation–I think there were 75 to 80 people who came out for a discussion about the statement–we spent a good evening together. There were no volatile comments made that evening. It was a good, balanced discussion, and the pastor of the congregation says that there were probably three or four persons who were upset in the congregation and each of them was dealt with pastorally.

"I find great variety among the synods as well. As the bishops have been reporting, you will find that even in contiguous synods, the pictures tend to be very different–one bishop reporting the phone jumping off the hook and the bishop in the next synod indicating very little response.

"Now, we do have a crisis. What do you do in a crisis? A crisis can destroy–whether it is personal or family, in your work, or in the church–or a crisis can be a doorway to new ways of looking at things and, above all, a teaching moment. And I would hope that we in the ELCA [Evangelical Lutheran Church in America] would see this as a teaching moment. As I said in my report to you earlier today, the main thing we have to do is put this into perspective. And, for that reason, in my opportunities to speak about this, I usually take a blackboard–oh, we do have it here[1]. I like to remind folks that in Chapter 2 of the "Statement of Faith," you have that

which we will not negotiate. And that includes the confession of the Trinitarian Formula: that God is revealed as Father, Son, and Holy Spirit; secondly, that Jesus Christ is the Living Word of God in the center of the Gospel; thirdly, that we rely on the Bible as the written Word of God for the purpose of understanding, most of all, the Gospel; fourthly, that we embrace the ancient creeds; and, fifthly, that the Augsburg Confession is for us not only a good ecumenical document, but also the way in which we in particular as Lutherans understand the Christian faith, and the point to be made here is that we as a church of Word and Sacrament are centered here. This is essential.

"Then, to point out that in terms of social statements, this church has said, along with our predecessor churches, that they are important, but not essential. And so we may have a statement on the death penalty. We have a statement on abortion. We have one now on the environment, and one on racism in the clash of cultures. And I have tried to help people understand that my conception of social statements is that they do not belong within this [central] circle. Even though they are developed on the basis of our understanding of this circle, they belong outside the circle in terms of not being binding on the conscience of an individual. And, if there is value to what I have pointed out here, then it means that the social statement in its present form is sitting about over here someplace [far outside the inner circle of confessional documents]. And yet, most of the letters I receive are trying to move it into this area. And so, our teaching opportunity is to help folks understand that the way we go about developing social statements in the Evangelical Lutheran Church in America is quite different from, say, the tradition of the Roman Catholic Church. It is not to say that their tradition may be the wrong one, or that we have found the magic way of doing this, but that this is, in fact, the way we agreed at our first Churchwide Assembly that we would do things like this. So the process is a long one, until finally it takes its place here, maybe someday, along with the other social statements that we have already developed.

"The other thing that is occurring in the letters I receive and in the discussions I am having in congregations is that back of this crisis and underneath this issue is probably the issue that this church needs to face up to, and that is, 'How do we use the Bible in the church?' I get many letters which in effect say, 'Dear Bishop, If you would only read this or that Bible verse'–they usually point me to Leviticus, Chapter 20, verse 13–'then you would understand exactly what it is this church needs to say about this particular issue. Do not bother to spend all that money bringing people together, because it is really very simple.' And, in the minds of these folks, the Bible is interpreted on a straight line, with every verse being of equal value. But, one man called me and said, 'If you just read Leviticus 20:13, you would know the answer.' I said, `Hold the phone,' and I grabbed my Bible and we read Leviticus 20:13 to the end, which says that, if a man lies with a man, you put them to death by stoning. I said, 'Shall we take that literally?' He said, 'Well, not all of it.' And I said, 'Let us back up three verses where it says that, if a man commits adultery with his neighbor's wife, he, too, and she should be put to death. What about that one?' Well, he was not aware of that one. And this certainly indicates the problem, I think, we have with the way so many of our folks are looking at Scripture.

"I was taught–and I assume most of you in this room were taught–that our Lutheran understanding of the Bible is more like this: We accept it as the Word of God, but recognize that at the heart and center of the Bible is the good news about Jesus Christ, the living Word of God. And that the whole of Scripture, above all else, is intended to lead us to faith and trust in Jesus Christ. It does not mean that the other things are not important. But, we would have to push, I think, out to the edges some things in the Bible that we would say are no longer relevant for us today, such as the dietary laws of the Old Testament, the keeping of the Sabbath, maybe the Song of Songs, which is a very erotic love story that will match most things you could find on the best-seller list today. Maybe the Bible could get along without that and maybe it sits out here closer to the

---

[1] Bishop Chilstrom drew several concentric circles on the blackboard.

edge, and yet it is a very beautiful story of love and passion. Now, as you deal with things like the death penalty, abortion, and human sexuality, it gets a little bit more complicated, because these certainly are not out at the edge, and certainly our faith does not depend on our opinion about certain aspect of sexuality; and yet we try to draw on the resources of the Scriptures that are there and try to interpret it in terms of what is at the center.

"What bothers me about many of the letters I receive now, is that there seems to be developing what I call a *sexuality hermeneutic*. What do I mean by that? That so many of the folks who write to me are wanting to establish biblical principles of interpretation, which they will apply to, let us say, homosexuality, but they are not willing to apply to other difficult issues in the Bible, such as divorce, for example, or the ordination of women, or what have you. If Paul is the last word on a given subject, then he must be given the last word on all subjects, for example.

"And then the question comes up, too, how do we treat tradition and how does that play into this issue? Many folks say—and I think that there is value in this—that it has been the tradition of this church, our understanding of the Bible, that, for example, homosexual relationships—intimate relationships—are wrong. Well, what then do you do about tradition? Do you never look at something which has not fit the tradition for 500 or 1,000 years? If that were the case, of course, we would not be ordaining women today. The bottom line of this, as I said before, is that I think we have a very serious issue in the church about `How do we interpret the Scriptures.'

"In The American Lutheran Church—those of you who were part of that church—when you went through the inerrancy debate in that church, which really was very intense, as you may recall, one of the things that came out of that was a wonderful volume called *The Bible Book of Faith*. We had something like it in the LCA [Lutheran Church in America] in Bob Marshall's book, *The Mighty Acts of God*. Both books were written in such a way as to help people understand how we use the Bible when we deal with difficult issues of this kind. I would say we are very ripe for that kind of thing in the ELCA [Evangelical Lutheran Church in America] right at this point in time.

"Let me make just a couple of more comments. The first is about the financial impact of this crisis. It is very, very difficult to measure that. We know that you have heard the report today that even before this story broke and the crisis came, we were facing some very difficult problems financially, and we cannot measure at this point what the impact of this statement and the news releases is going to have. Surely it will have some impact, but the only thing we know now is by anecdotal evidence. I think we will simply have to wait and see.

"Now, where do we go from here with the draft and with the process? Because of the confusion at the Conference of Bishops meeting regarding the release of the document, they did not make any recommendation. The motion on the floor was withdrawn, and so, given the confusion over that, I surveyed the bishops to find out what their attitude was. Forty-one of them have said, `let us continue the process at least one more step.' Eleven said, `no, let us stop it at this point.' Three indicated that they were really undecided about whether to go ahead or not. But, you have them voting by approximately four to one that we should go ahead with the process.

"That raises the question of what options do we have at this time—and I am guessing that in addition to the six that I am going to mention right now, there are people in the group who have thought of other possibilities. But, as I see it, here are the options that you may have to look at as a Church Council. The first would be to take action to stop the process right now and in the section P.1.a., you have a resolution from the Southwestern Pennsylvania Synod asking you to do that. You have also had similar requests from congregations and from a number of individuals who have said, in effect, `This is too divisive. Stop it right now.' Another possibility would be to recommend to the Division for Church in Society to dismiss the present task force, to forge a new one, and to start all

over again. This, of course, would mean that you would be redefining the process in the case of the human sexuality statement. A third possibility would be to continue at least to a revised draft, that is, the second draft, and then decide what we ought to do. Whether we should continue or stop the process at that point. A fourth option might be to refine the draft and issue it as a study resource, rather than try to develop a statement at all. These suggestions come from one of the task force members. Take what is there, work on it to the point where we can simply use it as a kind of study resource in the congregations of the Evangelical Lutheran Church in America. It would not have the force of a statement. A fifth possibility would be to postpone action until at least 1997. A number of folks have expressed concern about bringing this to the 1995 assembly when we will be electing a bishop for the Evangelical Lutheran Church in America, believing that all candidates will somehow be subjected to this as a litmus test.

"The final [sixth] possibility that I have thought of and the one that I favor is to continue the full process, but with the understanding that the recommendations from Chuck Miller [Rev. Charles S. Miller Jr.], as head of that division, which you will hear, will guide the process. And we have at least two synods which have said in that same section, [council agenda Exhibit] P.1.a., let us do this: continue the process, because the church needs to do so in this day and age. Again, I favor this last possibility. I know it is not easy. I know it is a very explosive situation. I thought abortion was a lively, divisive issue, but this certainly is much, much more divisive than that. Some folks have said that the issue of homosexuality alone is probably the most divisive this culture has faced since we dealt with slavery. I would like to believe that we have the maturity to move ahead and to deal with this in the way that will be explained to you by Chuck Miller.

"I should let you know that we have invited a number of folks in addition to—say, to the whole church—react to this. We have invited each of our seminaries and our colleges, by letter from me, to look at this document carefully in their own best way and give us their measured reaction and their recommendations. And a letter like the one from Paul Dovre [president, Concordia College, Moorhead, Minn.], today, I think indicates the kind of resource, we have in the institutions of the church. Paul says, Thanks for your recent letter about the draft statement on human sexuality. We have already initiated plans for a campus forum, perhaps in late January. We hope to have a member of the task force, as well as someone who participated in preparation of the Luther Northwestern [Theological Seminary] statement. We will probably invite area pastors to join us for discussion around the report. I agree that this draft report has created a teaching moment for the church. Indeed, it seems to me, it has created a teaching mandate for the church. You can count on our partnership.' And that is typical, I know, of the kind of cooperation we will get from all of our colleges and seminaries—or most of them, at least.

"Now, I guess the last thing I want to say is this—two things: First of all, suppose we go all the way to 1995. Suppose by that time the Division for Church in Society is able to bring to us a revised document that they believe ought to go to the church. Suppose that, at the Church Council in April of that year, you agree to recommend to the Churchwide Assembly that it be adopted. Suppose that the assembly, after dealing with it, probably revising it, votes and it fails to get the two-thirds vote needed for adoption. What happens then? I would like to hope, and I do believe, that the church goes on. And, why? Because the following Sunday, in 11,000 congregations of the Evangelical Lutheran Church in America, we will gather for Word and Sacrament and be back to the center of the circle we believe. And that to me is what is most important for us to keep in mind as we, as a church, move through discussion of a very difficult issue.

"The last word is to encourage you to pray, asking that God will give us the Spirit in this very important discussion, recognizing that we need a word for the church and, hopefully, that this church can be a vehicle for giving a very necessary word to the world around us. Thank you very much."

Chair Magnus: "Thank you, Bishop Herb. Now I would like to call on Chuck Miller [Rev. Charles S. Miller Jr., executive director of the Division for Church in Society] to report to us on the response of the board for Church in Society. And you will want to turn in your council agenda Exhibits to P.1.d."

J. David Ellwanger: "Can I just have a moment of personal privilege?"

Chair Magnus: "Yes, you may have a moment of personal privilege."

J. David Ellwanger: "Bishop Chilstrom, I wish we had had a video camera on tonight. You were just terrific and you are at your best as a teacher. And I just was sitting here as I had new thoughts brought to me in a way that I never had them brought before. I just wish that five million other Lutherans could have heard you tonight."

Bishop Chilstrom: "Well, we do plan to do something like this. It will be more extensive than this, but like this, in a video opportunity for me and it will simply be offered to congregations to those that want to use it."

J. David Ellwanger: "Terrific."

Rev. Charles S. [Chuck] Miller Jr.: "I hope you have had an opportunity to read [council agenda Exhibit] P, Part 1, d., pages 1 through 4. I am not going to paraphrase the material in that report and only simply repeat what is there for you to read, but add some information for you. Since the release of the first draft, the Division for Church in Society alone has received 1,100 phone calls. As you might guess, they have naturally moved from the first week or two of phone calls that were largely critical of the process of release of the document publicly before to rostered persons, but have moved since then almost entirely to calls related to the content of the document. And our experience would be similar, very similar to Bishop Chilstrom's, in terms of the topics raised up in those phone calls. In addition, we have received a total of 600 letters. It is our practice now to respond within 24 hours to each letter, except to the most complicated of the letters we receive, in which case it takes much longer to develop a response. We have responded to about 95 percent of those 600 letters then as received and within 24 hours. Like the phone calls, they, too, have moved from letters mostly critical about the process to now letters that solely focus on the content of the document and, again, similar to the experience of the bishop's office, a vast majority focus on the subject of homosexuality, but in addition to that, many others are referring to such issues as marriage and adolescent sexuality and matters related to divorce. Very little comment is received in relation to the latter part of the document on such matters as promiscuity, pornography, and sexual abuse. We have printed—I use the word, a record number, and that is true, at least for a social statement—140,000 copies of the document, and have ordered a reprint of an additional 100,000. That, in comparison to the 7,000 copies of the first draft of the document on the environment, gives you some idea of the great contrast in terms of interest in this document—some of it, no doubt caused by the media headlines with which we all had to contend.

"That is, then, background for me to call your attention to what I believe is the key—on the first page of this document —namely, under the second assumption—a deeply-held belief by me and I think by many persons in the church—that the trustworthiness of the process for the development of this statement is in great peril. And later in that paragraph, if members of this church do not believe the process is trustworthy, then progress in developing a social statement on human sexuality will be greatly impaired, if not permanently poisoned by the cynicism, disillusionment, suspicion, and sense of betrayal now felt by a significant number of persons.

"What follows in this paper, then, is our division's response to that climate of distrust and our proposal of a way to move from a climate of distrust to a climate of trustworthiness. Our proposal offers you details as to how we would handle the oversight of the process for the next 20 months, staffing, the process of widening the circle of those engaged in review of the responses, both to the study document and to the first draft, and in crafting the subsequent

drafts—also a data base that would provide a much more sophisticated presentation of the responses received by the division to the first draft.

"What I would say to you about this proposal is that we believe that it is characterized by a high expectation of ourselves of regular reporting to a large number of partners throughout the church, many in leadership positions, who need to know about all of the important steps along the way in the development of the next, and subsequent drafts, of the social statement. Secondly, that this proposed plan is characterized by collaboration between the key persons in the leadership positions of the church, mainly the Church Council, the Conference of Bishops, the seminaries of the church, along with the Division for Church in Society. And, thirdly, that this proposal brings to you a series of bench marks to address the question of whether along the way we will wish to make a decision to either delay, postpone, or suspend the process. You will see in the time line, for example, that we will assess along the way the deadline and our success at crafting a document that can be more widely embraced by the church. We believe that this proposal does achieve those goals, and we offer it to you as what we believe will create a trustworthy climate and will offer us an opportunity to bring a successful conclusion to the development of a statement of excellence and integrity for the church speaking to the subject of human sexuality."

Chair Magnus: "Thank you, Chuck. At this point, we are going to widen the responses and, if there are those of you around the tables that have other options that you would like to have considered, now would be a good time to throw those out onto the floor, or the table, and then we will begin the discussion of this. Chuck?"

Charles A. Adamson: "Just picking up on what Dave [Ellwanger] said, and earlier tonight when I went to the dinner meeting, Mark [D. Mark Klever] was telling us about Bishop Chilstrom being at one of the churches that he mentioned. That it was one of those magic teaching moments, like Dave felt this was, and I did, too. And, like Edie [Edith M. Lohr] said earlier, the letters, I thought, Bishop Chilstrom, were terrific. It would seem to me that there should be some way to capitalize on that on a rather grand scale. I mean, to get this out in a dramatic way to not only the 5 million people that we represent, but the general public, as well. I am just thinking of some kind of a general forum where you would be the teacher, Bishop [Chilstrom], but there would be questions asked from the people there present—that type of thing. I am not saying this very well, but to try to: I think you called the teaching moment I refer to as, I think, the best opportunity that I can think of—since I can recall—in the church where we can really do some terrific good because we have got everybody's attention. And I would encourage you to work out some plan that can be a very grand thing."

Bishop Chilstrom: "This is [possible] and I had alerted the bishops to the fact that we would try and do this—but it touches on a very important question. I get lots of pressure from people telling us, `What do you think?' and I have resisted answering the question, because I do not want the debate to center on what I think. I think it needs to center on the statement itself. However, I see my calling as bishop of the church to frame the questions and to help folks understand how this issue fits into the larger picture. So, my goal in developing a video will be exactly that."

Chair Magnus: "Bishop Spring."

Bishop Paull E. Spring: ". . . do you want to have a proposal, Kathy [Chair Magnus]? I mean, I do not have anything in writing, as an option, but another approach. I am not prepared to present anything, but just orally I can give out parameters."

Chair Magnus: "Yes."

Bishop Spring: "This is before we had Pastor [Charles S. Jr.] Miller's presentation in front of us, but some of us were talking and I think that others will have to speak for themselves—but, I know we have, some of us have, talked about the possible value of a review team where somebody in addition to look and review the material as it comes forward from the review, from the processes.

But, we have some serious reservations about tying it in with the Church in Society Division, and the task force. I cannot go into the details of why there is that, but I think that that is another option–the development of another review team, a panel or whatever you want to call it, whose task would be to review the responses that come in and then make recommendations directly to the Church Council. Now, I have since seen this and that it is not doable. I realize that. I do not think you can do that. You can not bypass the Division for Church in Society. But that is another option. I am not prepared to present anything in writing now, but that has been discussed by several."

Chair Magnus: "Thank you. We have lots of hands. Keep your hands up right now. And, Rick?"

Rev. Richard G. Deines: "Ready?"

Chair Magnus: "Yes, you may go."

Pastor Deines: "Okay. Well, first of all, just to clarify kind of where I am coming from, I want to really affirm the work of the bishop [Herbert W. Chilstrom] and the staff [of the Division for Church in Society] and the different groups that have been working on this and the opportunity for us to discuss it in this kind of forum, because I was not sure, coming into this meeting whether we were really going to have a chance to share. So, I really want to say a word of appreciation about that.

"If we have only the six options, I would go for number six without hesitation. I think that is the one that sends the kind of message that I want to send. But, I think, I have been thinking about a three-step or along-side-of [——]. As we have talked about the teaching moment and the fact that this response has gotten our attention, I have said, `Who needs to be taught and what do we need to be taught?' I am not assuming that what we need to be taught is that statement. I am assuming who needs to be taught is me and us. And just as we talk, when we talked about the stewardship stuff, we say we are the first ones that need to tithe and show where we are coming from, it seems to me that what we need to be taught is that we can begin to break our own silence about sexuality. And I think this: the teaching moment is this council, the council of bishops, the churchwide staff, saying we are willing to do something like the `Can we talk about this?' resource that came out of Central States Synod a few years ago. I believe, unless we start talking about our own sexual journeys, our own lack of assistance over the years–my own; I can not speak for you–by the church, everything I have learned from the church relative to sexuality has been unhelpful to my journey. And it seems to me that this is an opportunity to say the Word of Jesus Christ does have something to do with that dimension of life. I happen to believe that some of the same things–and I want to be careful here–some of the same things that guided us in the debate over racism and that led the civil rights movement of the 1960s, I think some of those same things apply. Bishop Chilstrom has already referred to the ordination of women–and I think as this unfolds, particularly the homosexual dimension of this, we have a great opportunity to provide some leadership. But I am not so much interested at this point about teaching people what I believe. I am more interested in our struggling together with what our own sexuality, our own sexual journey, and beginning to unblock us from the kind of fear that has begun to lead to the violence, which, I think, is finally underneath all of this. The kind of violence response that has gone on in parts of the church and has definitely gone on in any other number of sexual–Don [Donald M. Hallberg] mentioned AIDS–crisis, we can mention domestic violence and so forth–and that begins, for me at least, to go the direction Frank Fry [Rev. Franklin D. Fry] was saying, `What is deeply underneath all this?' I think that is a piece of it."

Chair Magnus: "Thank you, Rick. Lorrie?"

Lorraine G. Bergquist: "I had prepared a possible approach, another option, for discussion and to answer some of the concerns that I have heard and some of my own concerns. It would be an option on procedure on how to proceed, and, I think, before I would share that with you, I would like to say I think we need to ask some really hard questions–Is there a distrust of the task force? And, secondly, built on that, is there a distrust of the division? Is

there a distrust of the Lutheran Center staff? Those are hard questions, but, I think, we have to ask them, in order to get to where we need to be. Would you like me to read this whole thing that I have?"

Chair Magnus: "I think so."

Ms. Bergquist: "Okay.

That the Church Council declare the work of the task force responsible for the development of the social statement, "The Church and Human Sexuality: A Lutheran Perspective," to be ended;

That the social statement, "The Church and Human Sexuality: A Lutheran Perspective," not come before the 1995 Churchwide Assembly;

That a study committee be established to receive responses from members and congregations of the Evangelical Lutheran Church in America, faculties of the ELCA theological seminaries, as well as other theologians within this church, and additional interested parties. This study committee shall consist of two seminary professors named by the joint seminary presidents, two bishops named by the Conference of Bishops, two persons named by the Division for Church in Society, and three persons named by the Church Council. Staffing for this study committee shall be provided by the Division for Church in Society in consultation with the Office of the Bishop;

That the study committee be charged to articulate faithfully and clearly the mind of the church as faithful people of God, consider the social statements of the predecessor church bodies, the LCA "Sex, Marriage and Family" (1970), and The ALC "Human Sexuality and Sexual Behavior" (1980), as well as the paragraph on page 13 of "Visions and Expectations: Ordained ministers in the Evangelical Lutheran Church in America," regarding sexual conduct, and the work of the task force on the draft of the social statement, "The Church and Human Sexuality: A Lutheran Perspective"; and,

That the study committee produce a report that will be provided to congregations and rostered persons, synods, and the churchwide organization of the Evangelical Lutheran Church in America. The report from the study committee will be received by the Church Council at its March 31-April 2, 1995, meeting, and will be reported to the 1995 Churchwide Assembly as information."

Chair Magnus: "Do you want to speak to that, Lorrie?"

Ms. Bergquist: "No, not right now."

Chair Magnus: "Okay. John Knudson."

Rev. John O. Knudson: "One of the concerns I have had as I read the document is to somehow reflect on my role as a council person in seeking to assure the church that careful consideration will be given to all voices in the church. And I would perhaps offer a motion when we are in the [plenary session] that would indicate that as we receive, or to continue to review, the process, if it becomes clear to the council that it does not reflect the wide spectrum of the church's understanding, we would, as a council, stop the process. I am not saying when that would be. Perhaps, it would be 1995. But, I think, I feel a need to signal to the church at large that as a council we are hearing their concerns and that we will try to reflect on them as a part of the process of deliberation."

Chair Magnus: "Thank you. Stephen?"

Rev. Stephen M. Youngdahl: "A couple of comments, I guess, more on the council agenda Exhibit that Chuck [Rev. Charles S. Miller Jr.] brought to us, if that is in order."

Chair Magnus: "Yes."

Pastor Youngdahl: "I do not have another to add to the list. I would echo what Lorrie [Bergquist] said in terms of the trust, and that is a lot of what I have heard and we have dealt with that the last two years–while I have been on the council anyway–of trying to build up relationships and trust. I like the council agenda Exhibit. Basically, I think, the one thing that bothers me is [that] in Roman Number III the advice and consent group [is] very heavily chosen by the Division for Church in Society–or they are involved in all of those choices. One of the things that I have heard up for question is how task forces are chosen. I think we have to be really careful, if we choose another advice and consent group, that we do–maybe as John [O. Knudson] just said–that we reflect the nature of the reality of the church and not always look for specific–this is going to sound funny–but specific expertise. You can get so [much] expertise, that you get people in a very narrow line of thought and, if this is going to be an advice and consent [group], I think it would be more helpful to have that group chosen by somebody other than the Division for Church in Society, which is really coming under fire now. You may even appreciate that or not appreciate that, Chuck [Miller]–I do not know–but to take some heat off of this in-house-appearing kind of thing. So, if we go with that, I would want us to be really careful on how we choose these people to be on that group."

Chair Magnus: "Thank you. Bishop Lyle?"

Bishop Lyle G. Miller: "Mine relates to the proposal also, and it has to do with the relationship between the panel and the existing task force. As I understand it, the task force presently constituted would continue to exist and would–I am not sure what their role would be–would they be the primary persons nonetheless responsible for a creation of whatever new draft or revisions; and what would be the relationship of this new panel to that, and so forth, and then in that relationship of that to the board? I am just not clear as to [that], because we really do have a problem with the existing task force as regards the issue of confidence and trust, and whether or not it has within itself the kind of flexibility of viewpoint that would allow it to come up with any revisions."

Chair Magnus: "Are you asking for a response from the executive director or are you just lifting this up for us?"

Bishop Miller: "Well, . . . can you respond at all in terms of the relationship between say, the panel–I like your ideas, I mean, the team approach, the panel approach–but I am not clear as to their relationship to the task force as it is presently constituted?"

Rev. Charles S. Miller Jr.: "The way the proposal is conceived is that the new staff team, the present task force, and the consorting panel, would be working in tandem on a mutually-shared objective, and that is to develop a subsequent draft and a final draft that the division board can receive and with confidence pass on to the Church Council. They would, then, share that objective, but have different roles. There would have to be symmetry between those three, but the responsibility–what we would be suggesting is that the task force would still have the final responsibility to bring a final draft to the division board, but it would not do so in isolation. It would do so in tandem, with the advice and counsel of the consulting panel, and the new staff team. Because the work of all three would be exposed, both to the division board, as well as to the Conference of Bishops and Church Council, with none of their interchange hidden, the task force then would be publicly account-able to the advice and counsel of that consulting panel which is conceived to be as broadly representative as possible of some key leadership sectors in the church."

Bishop Miller: "May I just ask a follow-up question?"

Chair Magnus: "Yes, you may."

Bishop Miller: "Is it then your sense that the task force is open to this,to this idea and, in your mind, do they have the capability within themselves of accepting other viewpoints?"

Rev. Charles S. Miller Jr.: "I have had three conference calls related to the task force. One with the whole task force and two with the steering committee of the task force. I am more convinced that the steering committee could immediately embrace the idea. There will be some members of the task force who will resist it. I do believe, however, that in the end, if this were the proposal that were supported by the Church Council, that the majority, if not the entire task force, would rally behind the proposal and would work with the consulting panel. So, I am operating on, it is another assumption Lyle [Bishop Miller], and another belief. It comes from the interchange that I have had so far with those people; admittedly, not a great deal."

Chair Magnus: "Thank you, Chuck [Miller]. I have Jim, Terry, Bill D., Nadine, Bill B., Paull Spring, and Frank. Jim?"

Rev. James G. Cobb: "Mine has been asked. Thanks."

Chair Magnus: "Thank you. And Ken. Terry?"

Terry Bowes: " To be a leader in the church means to think not about what is difficult for me to talk about, but what kind of a church am I indeed handing on to those children and, hopefully, someday, grandchildren–if those children ever move out! On the flight here from Denver, I was a faithful council member and I reviewed a lot of material, including my folder of mail that has come in with good cogent arguments on both sides–47 form letters from Florida–and then decided to do my devotions by reading United Airlines *Hemispheres*. There is an article in here you should all steal from the airplane: "An Interview with Maya Angelou." The question that this interviewer asks this incredible woman is, `What do you hope your students will take away with them from this course?' She says, `I hope they will see themselves on the stage of life and see which side they really want to commit themselves to. I would like my students to learn how to learn. To be involved in the process of teaching themselves. And to make commitments not to be in love with a position, but to be in love with the search, so that, if they find themselves not able to hold a position, if it turns out to be untenable, then they should be able to have enough courage to say, `You know what I said last week? I no longer believe that.' I would ask everybody to have patience with them-selves and with others, but do not give up the struggle to make it a better world.'

"I think that this church is indeed at a teaching moment and I think that this is the place where, if we choose to continue the process–to take option number six–then we have the opportunity to be a sign of hope and wisdom and compassion in this world."

Chair Magnus: "Thank you. Edie?"

Edith M. Lohr: "I have to admit to have not written down all the options by number, so I can not remember which one is which. The letters that I have received and read that are letters of people who are genuinely angry with the document, I read them as saying that the Church Council should act to remove the document, because `We do not want to talk about this' and that, to me, is a very frightening situation to be in as a church. It is my understand-ing of the process that we go through, as Lutherans, when we deliberate on moral and ethical issues, that we are free to say, `no,' as well as `yes.' And that, if we do not talk about this subject and get to a place where the church can vote against this or against something, or respond to something, and we take away the subject, the problems that underlie what is going on in our lives will not go away, but a lot of people will go away; because the church is saying nothing to them as it relates to how they are trying to live in this world. I think I may have said this once before, but we have a lot of children. I think I am listed, as a matter of fact, on the document that the bishop sent out describing the different people on the task force, as one with many children. . . . My children have difficulty finding relevance for the church speaking to them about things that are really important in their lives. I have, among the children we have, one who is a highly-educated pediatrician, who is devoted to working in the community and whose wife is a pediatrician and is devoted to working in the community and works in inner-city Chicago. The church does not have a point of connection with the work that they are doing, nor with their lives. Is it because we are afraid to talk about tough issues? I am not sure that after all this time on the task force that I know what the right answer is, but I guess I began to believe that I understood what the questions were we needed to address. And that is what I think this document is talking about. And we need to talk about this, folks. And I would advocate for, I think, its position six, but I can not remember."

Chair Magnus: "Thank you, Edie. Bill Diehl?"

William E. Diehl: "Well, I also agree that option six is desirable. I think Chuck Miller's explanation of the process will ensure that we have the best possible document we can get out. But, if I put myself in the mind of those who are very upset about it, I do not think what is proposed here will create the trust that

Chuck [Miller] is trying to recreate. I think it will just continue in the mind of those people who say, `Well, they have just moved the chairs around a little bit and they are still going to go ahead with the same thing." So, I am wondering, would it be wise to take the steps that Chuck [Miller] is proposing, but instead make the deadline 1997, instead of 1995? What is so important about 1995? I think, if the people who are very upset about this see the deadline has been moved out, they may feel, `Well, you know, they are listening to us and something is going to happen and, perhaps, I can, perhaps, I can trust a little bit more.' Also, give them a lot more entry points into the whole process to find out what is going on. So my question is, what is so important about 1995?"

Chair Magnus: "Do you want an answer to that question?"
Mr. Diehl: "No."
Chair Magnus: "Nadine?"
Rev. Nadine F. Lehr: "I guess most immediately I would like to respond to that and, if there, I guess, if the concern is that the chairs are simply being moved around, I am not sure what extending the deadline would do to address that. So, I have some questions about that. But I wanted to respond to this issue of trust, I guess, and just make a comment about that. I do think we have a problem, obviously. But I want to make a very personal comment and you may do with that what you wish.

"I am a little disturbed that [the position of] this task force is perceived to be the churchwide kind of position. It seems to me that we all took part in approving a constitution, and this task force was appointed accordingly. And no one raised a problem with that process until after the fact. And, I think, we need to take responsibility for that lack of foresight. And I am not sure it is a just kind of perception to make this a churchwide versus–kind of an us/them sort of thing. This is our task force. It is our statement. These people were duly appointed and they did their job. So, it is our problem. I think the other issue has already been addressed and I feel very strongly that this is our issue, but I also do see that there is a perception of mistrust that needs to be addressed and I would look for an alternative way to deal with that and the appointment of the new consulting panel and staff panel and the use of the task force."

Chair Magnus: "Thank you. Bill Billings?"
William T. Billings: "I would like to read Matthew, the 7th chapter, the 13th verse: `Enter through the narrow gate, for the gate is wide and the road is easy that leads to destruction and there are many who take it.' [Verse] 14: `For the gate is narrow and the road is hard that leads to life. There are few who take it.'

"I read this [the draft document], actually as most of us, maybe twice, at least. I studied it very carefully when we were given the pre-pre-document that we were not allowed to even discuss with our family. They sent you this big thing across the top, `Do not discuss this with anybody, because it has not been released'–and, then again, when after all the furor hit and I got this one, because I knew that we would have to come here. And I did not know what was making me feel bad about it, because I looked at it and they were quoting scriptures and all of that. But then it occurred to me that the impression that I get from the task force's whole outlook is not [that] they are trying to bring a change in society that is needed and is against all odds, but the opposite–that we are trying as a church to rationalize a behavior that we have traditionally been against. And it is not just homosexuality. It seems like on everything there, it is whatever is happening in society. Look, wake up, recognize it–it is here. We have to deal with it. We have to live with it. So, therefore, we have to accept it. I was not, I did not come into the Lutheran Church for that. I was brought up–I used to tell people when I was called upon to speak at congregations that I was born a Lutheran and raised a Baptist, because I was raised in the Baptist Church and with the Scriptures and all the rest of it, but there was always a little bit of an uneasiness with the freedom of the Baptist church with the uncontrol of it that I found in the Lutheran church. I found a biblically-based church, but with controls like this–and like our seminaries, and so forth. Not to say anything against the Baptist church, but the Lutheran church

spoke to me, because I felt that it was rooted in the same kind of thing. I read the story of Martin Luther. He did not look to see what the council thought, or what the [Roman] Catholic Church thought, or even what his friends thought, or even what he thought. He got on his knees and he prayed and he fasted. He walked up steps until his knees bled, trying to come to grips with his faith–and it did not matter to him, if only one person believed in those 95 theses. He felt deep down that that was the Word of God speaking to him.

"And that is what I do not see here. What I would hope in from this body is not that you agree with me. I have very strong beliefs that most people know around here, but I could be wrong. I could be dead wrong. But that you let the Holy Spirit speak to you and do as Bishop Chilstrom said, pray about it. Do not worry about the letters. But, do not worry about what people will say about you either, because there is another scripture that says we should be happy, if men–how was that again?–`revile you and say all manner of evil against you for Jesus' sake; rejoice and be exceedingly glad. I do not mean to preach to preachers, but I do mean to say, I do mean to say, that we are a church. We are not a synod, we are a church, and we should not be ashamed of it. We should not be ashamed, ask the . . . right where it is, folks. Thus, says the Lord. That is the way it is. Crucify me, or whatever you want to do with me, but that is the way it is. If that is what this statement said, even if I disagreed with it, I could not oppose it, but it does not say that to me. And I hope that the new statement does say just that. Point to me and say, `you are wrong, because the Holy Spirit speaks to me and says you are wrong,' or `because Scripture says that you are wrong.' Not because this is the way things are, because things may be entirely wrong and we may be the only ones going down that narrow road."

Chair Magnus: "Thank you, Bill. I have Paull, Frank, Ken, Loren, Patsy, Dave, Mark, Jim, Nelson, Peter, and Deb. We are going to go until 10:00 and we want to keep hearing, but keep in mind, be concise. Paull?"
Bishop Spring: ". . . You just started with a question, `Are there other options,' you know, and, from there, went. I think we should be aware that as we speak, probably, or next week, or sometime already, options are being developed relatively independently. Individual people–theologians, pastors, lay persons, groups, clusters–are developing options already, and I think we should be aware that we are not the only group of people who are thinking about this document, or even thinking about alternatives, but the church out there, which is part of us, is also in some circles, I am aware, developing alternative proposals that we need to be on and that is another problem as to how to handle that. I just put that forward as an issue."
Chair Magnus: "Thank you, Paull. Frank?"
Rev. Franklin D. Fry: "Two preliminary comments before speaking directly at the issue. The first is that it is striking to me again that on the consulting panel described in the second paragraph of Roman [numeral] III, again, we have no specific reference to what I would call resident theologians. No parish pastors are identified at all."

"Secondly, I would like to identify with our bishop's [Herbert W. Chilstrom] comment about Bible study and say that, again, if we want to ask ourselves, `How do we get ourselves into such a pickle and such a situation?,' I think it is substantially because we have not helped our people understand how to understand the Bible and read it." And we as a church killed "Word and Witness," which is the best adult Bible study I ever knew of."

"To the point now: although we were promised at least there would be materials left on the shelves, they are not even being printed anymore for those who want to use them. Secondly, when I called, and I believe that was the division's decision, I called the publishing house asking, `I have someone who is an adult, thinking adult, [who] said I never read the Bible; what do you have to offer me that I can put in this person's hand?.' And the best thing that was suggested by the resource people was the *Mission90* document created by the Trinity Seminary faculty, which is a very good introduction, but Jesus appears on page 73."

"It has nothing to do with what we are saying. So, we have to, I think, if nothing else, learn we have got to help our people understand how to understand the Bible. And we simply are not doing it on materials, be that research projects, through this search, people, whatever. They said that our goal is to help people have more faith, which is totally un-Lutheran. It goes violently against the father in Mark who says, `I believe. Help my unbelief.' I think we need to help people come to more mature faith. Am I the only one in this room who believes in God less securely now than when I was five years old? I do not have more faith than I did as a five year old. But I sure hope I have a more mature faith. That is no small measure—understanding how to understand the Bible.

"Now specifically to the point, I think that it is imperative for us to proceed in some fashion with materials that our people can study and chew on and be confronted by and challenged by. Luther said the church is the community of mutual conversation and consolation of the faithful. I would like to drop a "c" into the middle of that—conversation, *correction*, and consolation—because I need a lot of it, and the rest of us do. We ought to have that. It is imperative. Again, you people just do not stand still, so I do not know how to be a pastor to you. It was not that long ago that probably at least a third of the brides at a wedding were pregnant, but none of them lived together. Now, nobody is pregnant and about 90 percent are living together. And that is in one man's time of ministry. I just read that one-fourth of all the children in this country—*all* children, right now, are being born to a single parent. . . .

"I have some fear about number six, so I would go that way, incline that way, as long as we said we do not intend to be a slave to the time line, if *en route* we see it does not come to majority, appropriately. Then maybe 1997 or whatever. Or, maybe it is, [presented as] a study document instead of a statement. I think we ought to go full bore into the issue, but I would not like to have you ask me now to guarantee what form it is going to have? Let us see how we can make it a teaching moment through the church. And that means we have got to teach biblical theology, not just Bible—and a critical distinction between those two.

"And that runs directly into the ideological strains in our church. I think that is one of the reasons we had the fire storm. The first document I think was appalling—the study material a year and a half ago. Just appalling! It was almost entirely ideological, without biblical theology. So, we should have expected a bit of that. And then, when we were told—some of us in private sessions in Kansas City—that there is nothing ambiguous about racism, I wonder, how can we think there is anything that is not ambiguous? I think that one of the things that keeps me Lutheran is that it says everything is ambiguous. Everything! And that means our acceptance and use of our sexuality.

"We talk as if some people are still in Genesis 1 and 2 with their sexuality and have it all set up, and only some of us have it post-Genesis 3 and are living east of Eden. And yet, we had some eloquent comments about how all of us are struggling with the reality of our own grasping and understanding and being faithful in our sexuality. I do not see this really said that well in this present draft. I think that is one thing the Lutheran tradition clearly has to say and I still believe the Lutheran confessions make sense.

"And when you speak of the 95 Theses, I went to the library this afternoon to get the 95 Theses to remind us that the first thesis is—you remember—`When our Lord and Master, Jesus Christ, said repent, he willed the entire life of believers to be one of repentance.' In other words, we have got nothing that cleans, yet everything is mixed. And people may want a simple answer on this side or that side to help follow up in what you said in your sermon, too. People want simple answers to complex questions. And that great Lutheran, Mark Twain, said, `And they're always wrong.' The simple answer is always wrong. Now we have known that. The thesis starts in that—from that—premise. So, why can not we relativize everybody's self-righteousness about their sexuality and say, `Well, I am the mess?' And now, we have got to figure some

way in which to organize our life appropriately so that we are not just dogs in heat running all over the place, but to organize ourselves some way in society and in the teaching of the Church. But recognize that, unfortunately, this noon I did not get a chance to confess that I am in bondage to sin and get absolution. But that is really where we are. All of us. And I think we can make a contribution to this debate within the Christian community and within our society, because I do not know any other tradition that comes at it quite the same way. Why can not we just say, `We are in bondage?' Now we have got to figure out the best way we could live with this and that, and organize this and that, and then live by grace. And this way, we are not tied to specifics. I do not think we are equipped to do and I do not . . . provides this."

Chair Magnus: "Thank you, Frank. Ken Sauer?"

Bishop Kenneth H. Sauer: "I want to affirm that the division's proposal ought to offer us a good place to begin to debate. I want to follow up by saying that much that has been said about trust proves to me to be a primary expectation that our constituency has of the Church Council, and that in some way you will acknowledge what has been shared and written and phoned in to you by the constituency. And I would like to report back to you what I heard you saying about the constituency.

"You have said that the constituency really does not want to talk about sex, that they probably do not understand the Bible right, that they probably are not faithful supporters of their church, and that they could indeed have been racist, pro-life, anti-environment, and anti-ordination of women before, that the church has totally failed in its teaching of sex, marriage, and family in years gone by.

"I think that we are in great danger of blaming some victims here who are trying to respond to us and, if we are concerned about the return of credibility and trust, one thing I would hope you would find to do is to acknowledge that those who have written to you, even if they are not adequately informed, were well-enough taught that somehow you could acknowledge to them that they are sexual beings and know something about that—that they have been to catechism and surely know something about the Gospel and the Law, and that they surely are faithful members of the church or they would not have taken the trouble to write to us. If we want to begin to restore credibility, I hope that we can begin with . . . how can we proceed to acknowledge to our constituency—pastors, congregations, all the rest—that we acknowledge that they were writing to us with the best construction. There is a meaning to commend, but this says we assume the best construction on what people are saying—and to try to restore then a way of affirming where those hopes are, so that the dialogue can continue. My primary concern with the proposal of the panel is that the reports of the panel will go to the Conference [of Bishops] and the Church Council and that there is no provision somehow so that the dialogue can be shared with a constituency so that they know that dialogue is going on."

Chair Magnus: "Thank you, Ken. Loren?"

Loren W. Mathre: "Going back to what Bishop Chilstrom said, it bothers me a little bit that I think our basic problem here is interpretation—biblical interpretation. And I see a problem of setting up a social statement and I see a problem in this looking as if we are going to get a social statement. We collect a committee and, unfortunately, I believe that the committee or in the selection, I think there was some pre-determined indication of what they wanted, to bring us along. And I am not a theologian, but I do read some books, and I depend upon a theologian. And I am looking at what we are doing in the church—if we have determined that we want to have somebody other than a theologian, or other than the seminaries, be our leaders in the biblical interpretation of our social [statements]. And I am bothered with—here, we have got a very effective data base, but what do we do with our theology if it is determined by the number of responses we get from one point or the other? And that bothers me: putting ourselves up to a position where we get an overwhelming response or we get some pastor, like we have got one in Florida, who did a campaign of letters. If we get campaigns of letters on that to try to determine the number of people saying one thing or the other, we are dividing ourselves. I would like to see something re-looked at. And maybe what you said–talking about having a teaching statement by our seminaries or our theologians, or some other group–but I am concerned with the way we are going to go on just with this as a basis."

Chair Magnus: "Okay. Thank you, Loren. Patsy?"

Patsy Gottschalk: "Well, I really think this violent reaction is more a symptom of other things. And I think the constituency out there is waiting to hear from us. I do not think we can let this thing be status quo without doing something or I think we, too, will lose our credibility. And I honestly feel that since the task force has been given two opportunities, I do not think there is any trust level with that group. And I do not think we can really at this point stop the process as far as the study. . . . I think it is a wake-up call. I think a lot of people in the pews have been very complacent. They have not paid any attention to anything we have been doing. And I think they will now. I think it is time. They are ready to look. And they are ready to learn. And we are going to miss an opportunity, if we would, you know, stop the study. But, I honestly believe the task force, as it is now, does not have credibility. And, if we do not make a real strong statement, as Bishop Sauer said, to the people that wrote us, and the people in the pew, we are going to lose our credibility, too. And it will be worse than it ever has been."

Chair Magnus: "Thank you, Patsy. Dave?"

Rev. David K. Johnson: "I am glad that Bishop Sauer raised some of the things he just did, because, as a new member of this Church Council, I have been just a little surprised at what I have heard, . . . [with assertions] that the problem is with our people. They are fearful. They are faithless. They do not read the Bible enough. They do not get in touch with their sexuality. The problem is not us, it is them. And we have presented this. I am not–we will make some modifications and we will study this. But the thing that I have seen, the thing that concerns me, is that we will talk 10 minutes about sexuality. We are going to talk a long time about interpretation of the Word. The people that have come to me have not come to me to talk about homosexuality. They have come to talk to me about that very thing–about interpretation of the Word and what this church believes in. And these are great people. These are fantastic people. And, if these people walk from this church–wow!

"And I want to say one other thing. I think that we are talking about sexuality for a while. We will get by sexuality. I think the issue that has been raised, that needs to be heard, is `How are we going to do church?' You talk about suspicion there. How is this church going to do church? Is it going to do it from the top down? Are we going to wait for something else to come down the pike? Where I live, what I hear is, `Chicago is going to do it to us again.' I think that we have tremendous staff. A tremendous presiding bishop [Herbert W. Chilstrom]. I think we need to re-look at how we are going to do church in this future. We are going to look at it. I have six years on here. We are going to look at this baby, and I am sure before I get off of here, and it is going to be a different church. I think that a lot of our frustration and a lot of the feeling that this church has in terms of a lack of momentum, or depressive feeling, or whatever is going on, maybe the Holy Spirit is trying to tell us something. The Holy Spirit does not promise us to be successful, but hopefully it helps us to be effective. And I think it is time for us and I have to turn to the bishop that I have in the Eastern North Dakota Synod by the name of Rick [Richard J.] Foss who is just turning that synod upside down. Power is not something that is just limited, and, if I give you power, I lose power, but, in Rick's mind, power is something that, if I empower you, we both are more powerful. And I think we have to start thinking in this church in a different category. So, we can talk about sexuality. Hopefully, we do not bleed all over all over the place about interpretation of the Bible, but I think we have another agenda: `How are we going to do church?'"

Chair Magnus: "Thank you, David. Mark?"

D. Mark Klever: ". . . I am going to write every one of those people that sent me a letter. I am going to respond to every one of

them and I think that that would surprise them a lot, if they received 33 of them. Lorrie [Bergquist], on your proposal, I think I heard you say that the present committee–task force–would not be in existence anymore. And I guess I have problems with that, in that that implies to me and other people that they screwed up and the document is screwed up. And I do not necessarily want to give that impression. Chuck [Charles S. Miller Jr.] . . . has made this proposal and he has told us today that he is now the lightning rod. And, I guess, I would be in favor of following our new lightning rod leader."

Chair Magnus: "Thanks, Mark. Jim?"

Rev. James G. Cobb: "I wanted to just share some impressions also, in the sense that there have been kind of two waves that have come across. And, I think, it is born out by the letters and the references that Bishop Chilstrom read and then by what others, the rest of us, have experienced in a similar way. The first was the wave of upset and a great deal of anger and all that that has meant. The second wave has been the more studied–the taking a chance to get into the script and the content and do some reflecting. And, in other words, there is a process that is beginning to work after an initial first wave that poured over everyone. And what has started to come is a sense, I think, that people in love have to sometimes learn to fight. And that is one of the ways to do church and do it in a way that can be alright. We have seen some ways in which that fight is not alright. But, one of the ways to do church, one of the ways to get at differences in terms of biblical hermeneutics, will be how to learn to fight with each other in a way in which we still remain the family for each other. So, that is the challenge. What I have not heard is an echo of some sentiments that we have had from pastor groups that have expressed appreciation for about 90 percent of the report. Ten percent is what we are all talking about, if you want to go through the text and lift out some pieces. Ninety percent has to do with a tremendously affirming view of marriage, some excellent statements about abstinence and celibacy as guidelines to some very focused alternatives that the church will make and give. And there is some good stuff within it. So, we are looking at where the real lightning-rod points of this church are.

"Now, one of the things in this second wave of the studied and reflective people that are beginning now to take hold is the sense that the Lutheran church is a church that was born in an academic community that knows how to sink the buckets deep, pay attention, do its homework, reflect on the Scriptures, invite in a wide community, talk to one another, pray, invoke the guidance of the Spirit, and get it right. And Lutherans do not produce junk. And what I hope is that, when we get to the product, it is the best, it is held up in the Church catholic, and that people that look at and read and absorb it and are going to experience a lot of this in their lives are going to say, `That is the best statement of the Gospel with that Jesus Christ and the cross and the sinner–all these issues that we have been, that we can possibly proclaim in an ambiguous world with ambiguous choices, as Frank [Franklin J. Fry] mentioned. So, I do not expect junk to be produced. We have to go forward with the process."

"I realize that it is now going forward into a study. It does have our attention. We are paying attention. Congregations have it. [Regarding] the critiques I have [received], I think I am in agreement with people that say there must be now an expansion of the people that do the review. A great deal of confidence that this will be looked at across our seminaries and by our teaching theologians and that the piece of the conversation is brought to bear on it much more than it seems to be at this point. There are other minor points to mention. I think some of the writing is pejorative. I think, when you get three responses to the gays in the document, they lead you in a certain way. You can adopt response one, but you can adopt the rationale for response two and not leave it set up the way the document wanted it to. To say that, if you are in one, here is the way you look and act and are, because that is just not so. And I think that somehow as a study document that goes out, there has got to be an easier way for people to respond to it. So far, both in the original thick document of a couple of years ago and in this script text of the draft, the questions at the end that are calling for response are much too general. It is difficult for study groups, because when we have done this with pastors, just in the last couple of weeks. It is difficult to know how to get into the document for the kind of response feedback that you want to have forthcoming. I think that is sort of an educational process question that needs to be in there, too. But right now, I think the process has got to go forward, as a study. Let her rip. But, to expand the review panel, I am open on that, and I think that there will have to be some additions to include a wider community for that to happen."

Chair Magnus: "Thank you, Jim. Nelson?"

Rev. Nelson T. Strobert: "I think that we need to be responsible to ourselves and trust ourselves and trust the process, which means that, I would have to agree with option number six. We have had a process and we are experiencing part of that process–the debate, the discussion, which is part of our Reformation tradition. And I do not want to lose that. And it sends a very bad message, if we disband a group that we, as a group, have entrusted, because the same people who send, who are sending, letters, are the same people who in 1995 or 1997 are going to pass or reject this. It is not our document. It is the church's document. And I think we all need to be reminded of that. And we (I think from what we have in the sheets in [council agenda Exhibit P.1.d., etc.] have checks and balances. And we have heard what people have said and I think we have made an attempt, so I would go with option number six."

Chair Magnus: "Thank you, Nelson. Peter? Bishop Peter."

Bishop Peter Rogness: "Several things have already been said, so I do not need to say them. I agree that we need to continue to lead the church into a time of discussing this and not backing off from it. I think that would be the wrong signal. I would also agree we ought not dismiss the task force, even though, at the same time, we acknowledge that the church's confidence in that task force is shaken at this point. But, they have done good work and they are good people, and the document has much to commend itself. So, I would be in favor of staying the course with them as well. I agree with Chuck Miller's analysis. His assumptions on his first page, which I think were very well stated, particularly the second, that the most critical issue we are facing right now, over these three days of the meeting, is the crisis of trust in the church. So, the key issue for us, it seems to me, is what signal does this meeting send that can reinforce or reestablish a sense of trust or confidence throughout the church for what is going on? I like the idea of the consulting panel, but there is not a lot of sophistication out there about who appoints what and who reports to whom here. The crisis of trust is over the fact that a document came out that they do not think reads the church well and did not listen to them well and they do not know a lot about who produced it, but whoever produced that, they do not have much confidence in anymore. My concern about the consulting panel as it is proposed is that it basically comes out of and reports back to the very same entities in the church that now are suffering from lack of confidence. So, I would like to see it appointed, but not appointed by the board for Church in Society, but by the entities that were to work with the board. I also am concerned at the top of page three where it says its authority would be limited to advice and counsel to the new staff team, the task force, and the board, period. I think that could have almost the reverse effect of what we are hoping that it would have. That is, if what we have done, if the only step this meeting takes is to appoint a consulting panel and then limit its authority and role to speaking to those entities that produce the document we now have, I think that would be interpreted throughout the church as a very controlling step. Instead, we ought to appoint a kind of consulting panel or advisory panel or critiquing panel that would have full authority to critique the work, be in dialogue with the task force, critique its work, but have a fully free hand to do and say what it wants. That is, it may affirm paragraphs 1, 3, 5, and 7, and seek to re-write paragraphs 2, 4, and 6, that whether it is the Church Council, or the whole Churchwide Assembly, or whoever, it has several drafts in front of it. That may mess up the process. That is, we do not have

"a" document that comes straight–kind of all packaged and ready to go–but, it will foster the kind of open and free-wheeling conversation throughout this church that I think the church will benefit from. So if we do put together a consulting panel, I would hope we give it a greater degree of independence than what the proposal suggests."

Chair Magnus: "Thank you, Peter. Deb?"

Deborah S. Yandala: "I have two points I would like to comment on. One is, I think one of the things that we should be celebrating is that we are the kind of church that can allow this kind of process to take place. We do not just issue a statement and that is it. And people have to live with it or else. In my own congregation, which has struggled to have an adult education class, there are suddenly 20 people there on Sunday mornings looking at this statement. And I think that kind of teaching moment, as we have said, is so very important that that process needs to go on. The second point I would like to make is a point that I have struggled with a little bit sitting as a representative of this Church Council on the Peace Task Force. On that task force–it is a wonderful group of people–but one–of them is a parish pastor. They are experts in the field of international relations. They live and they breathe the kind of work that that task force is doing. And the gap that I see there, that I think that task force is trying to work through–that I think there is a gap here too–is not having more parish pastors and more lay people in the parish that are not experts on the topic. And I think, if we put together a second consulting panel, those kinds of voices need to be there–people that can say, 'We are educators in the parish. We are people who can help word things so that they will be understood by people in the parish.' I think that includes both pastors and lay people that need to be as well represented as some of the other people on that kind of committee."

Chair Magnus: "Thank you, Deb. Chuck?"

Charles A. Adamson: "Just, very quickly, one of the things that Patsy mentioned, it seems to me that we have to address, and that is–and I am not suggesting that the task force does not have any credibility–but that is the perception, I think, that may be out there. On the other hand, you know, I read the preamble to this and, you know, those folks worked for four years hard on this and it just seems to me to be so unfair to kill the messenger here. But, somehow the credibility of the task force, I think, has to be reinforced for the benefit of our constituents, so to speak. And one thing that Mark [D. Mark Klever] mentioned I think we should all do, is that–you know, I have not counted the letters I have here, but there is a lot of them. . . . I have letters here from terrific people. You know, these are not flaky people. Bishop Spring and I were talking about that during the break. I mean, these people are, not only, obviously, a part of the body of Christ, but they are concerned people, they are people of faith, who are asking us questions and they certainly deserve a response–not just simply to acknowledge that we got their letter, but to answer some of the questions that they put to us. So, I think the sense of the group here is that this has got to go forward, but we cannot do it with a tank that runs over all these fine people that have asked us to stop it. We have got letters from real, responsible people–people that I would love to have on the witness stand as witnesses for anybody–that are saying `Stop this. Just plain stop it.' And I just do not feel that we can thumb our nose at them. Frank [Rev. Franklin D. Fry] is the one that said that, you know, `What do we know?' . . . in houses. So, again, I mean, if the process goes forward, I do not think we should kill the messenger, but, by the same token, we have to respond to the people to restore the credibility that I believe these people deserve, but have somehow, through this process, lost. And that, just to repeat myself, we just cannot thumb our nose at these fine people who are making strong objections.

Chair Magnus: "Thank you, Chuck. David A?"

Rev. David A. Andert: "Some of the people when this first came out asked, `Why are we doing such a thing?' I asked the question, `Do we want a statement?' With all of the voices that are speaking about sexuality, my response was, `You had better believe

I want my church to say something about the issue and to be a light shining in what is often a very dark world.' Whether that should be a social statement or some other kind of teaching document, or just lifting up the issues with some direction given without it being a statement, I am not really sure how I feel about that. It may be that we would be better off with something other than a social statement. We need to ask ourselves the question of the purpose of either a teaching or a social statement: It is not meant simply to reflect the majority view or the most vocal view. I expect the church to give me something that will teach and guide, and it might not be something that I am really happy to get, but it will be something that shows thought and study and faithfulness; and sometimes that makes me angry, but that is how I learn.

"The question of whether the task force should be disbanded–if we propose something like that, what are we asking about the four years of study and all of the presentations that have gone into the work of that task force? If we start with a new group, are we saying the only important contribution is the convictions that these individuals have, rather than research in the study? I do not think we want to say that. I do not want to say that, anyway. I like the idea of adding somebody else into the process. I am not sure who that would be or how that should be done. The proposal that we have makes me ask the practical question–three more staff people and an additional panel of 11 people is going to be a significant cost–will be, at some point, hear that addressed?"

Chair Magnus: "Yes, you will."

Pastor Andert: "I thought so."

Chair Magnus: "Rick?"

Rev. Richard G. Deines: "Kathy [Chair Magnus], when you started, you used two words. You said `respect' and you said `safe place' and that has given me permission, I think, to share it tonight in a way that I normally would not have. Because as the discussion has gone on, a few things have, some folks have said, I began to feel some defensiveness, and I wanted to check myself on that, because I knew that was not going to be helpful. And it reminded me that I have got to become a lot better at beginning everything I do with the confession, with complicity, because I identified with some of the remarks people said about, `We've got good people out there' and so forth. I do believe that, but I think the way you connect is through one making his or her own confession of complicity in everything we are doing here. It is not like some of us are better than others or we are not going to ask somebody else to do something that we are not willing to do ourselves. And it seems to me that that is what trust is based on. I think that trust is based in our faith on mutual confession in the light of the Word. And I think, so, for me, you know, as I struggle with, you know, having a conversation with 75 people and looking, if this is going to be four years, then I agree with whoever said we are going to be at this for a long time. In terms of deciding what being church is about, I am going to have, in order to build a relationship with folks here–if Herb [Bishop Herbert W. Chilstrom] is right when he said that the lightning rod in this is homosexuality–that all parts of Scripture are at equal, all parts of the statement are at equal. People in this room have no idea what I think or do not think about homosexuality, and I do not have any idea what anybody else in here thinks about that. If Herb is right–and I believe he is–that that is the lightning rod, at some point, we will have to talk with each other about homosexuality.

Chair Magnus: "Thank you, Rick. Bill E.?"

William H. Engelbrecht: "Are you still looking for options?"

Chair Magnus: "Yes, I am."

Mr. Engelbrecht: "I would like this to be known as option six and a half. And that would be–and it looks very much like we are going toward six–that we have a consulting panel consisting of three persons appointed by the Church Council, three persons appointed by the Conference of Bishops, three by the seminary presidents, and three parish pastors."

Chair Magnus: "By whom would you–who would appoint those, Bill?"

Mr. Engelbrecht: "The Church Council–the board of directors of this church."

Chair Magnus: "Thank you. Jeanne?"

Jeanne W. Rapp: "I would speak to in favor of going ahead with the draft study that is happening. I think we have congregations excited about it now. They are in the process of studying it. And in some of our congregations, that is probably the most excitement we have seen for a long time. And that is to be affirmed. In looking at the document that we have from Chuck [Rev. Charles S. Miller Jr.], and the consulting panel that is being suggested, I would speak to the representation [issue] as there have already been some speakers before me. There has been a lot of talk tonight about the partnership we have with the congregations–talk about how we are not happy with the we/they conversation that goes on. We have talked about the trust that we have, or lack of trust that we feel from congregations. And the words are used that this would be a vital role that this consulting panel would have in order that we might show the members of this church that a wider circle of persons is engaged in the process. I wonder, you know, at the people that it is suggested would be a part of that. Could we even risk considering naming a Jane or a John from the congregational pew?"

Chair Magnus: "Susan?"

Susan Huber Stapell: Just two quick comments. One, as those of you who were here last time know, I have not been a Lutheran all my life, but one of the reasons I am is because of the fact that everything is not either all right or all wrong, but that we are called to study and to seriously look at the issues and to make some decisions and that we are not handed easy answers. The second thing, and I guess I need to just check myself because I have been doing this for six years now, but, it seems to me that there has not been a meeting where my mailbox has not been hit hard before I have come here with letters from people telling me what to do and how to do it. And this has not been any different in that sense. And I am not sure that I have gotten all that much more mail this time than I have on other occasions when I have come here for meetings. And, I guess, I am not sure why we are overreacting or reacting more than at other meetings over the same amount of mail. You know, I get comments from my mailman about what do I do that I get this kind of mail– seriously! So, I guess, why is this time different from the last times?"

Chair Magnus: "Thank you, Susan. Loren?"

Loren W. Mathre: "A comment on what Bishop Paull [E. Spring] had said about a learning statement and I do think we have a learning opportunity, or teaching opportunity. And I think that, if we have another panel or we have other advice, as stated here, to advise the committee, I think it would be well received–other advice to congregational levels studying that–that they could see there are difference of opinion, and that is okay, that information, like we have received, could go to study groups saying it is okay to say there is difference of opinion."

"The other quick comment, is a question, and it is technical. In here it says, released December 1 will be a video tape. Has that been produced yet?"

Chair Magnus: "Is it possible for us to have that on at noon someplace tomorrow? Eric [Shafer]?"

Rev. Eric C. Shafer: "The video?"

Chair Magnus: "The video."

Eric Shafer: "Yes. They are also for sale downstairs in the store."

Chair Magnus: "As I said, would it be possible for us to have one to view tomorrow. Alright, we will make arrangements and let you know where you could have a viewing. . . . I want to thank you from the bottom of my heart for living up to my expectations this evening. You debated with a good deal of risk in several instances, and with a good deal of honesty, I think, person by person. And I, as your chair, am deeply appreciative of that. It shows maturity on our part as a council. It shows that we as Christian Lutherans can agree to disagree in this place and move forward in leadership. I would beg you this evening to pray, and to talk, to think, and, if you get an option, round about 4:30, get yourself out of bed and write it down.

"... the directions that have been opened up for us this evening are good windows, I think, for us to be able to move through tomorrow. The document will come to you tomorrow afternoon for action. There is going to need to be a good deal of thinking and conversation before we are ready to move it yet in some directions. So, we are going to need some work. ...

"We will recess until tomorrow at 7:00. From 7:00 until 8:30, breakfast is served out here in the hallway. At 7:30, the Executive Committee will meet for breakfast and meeting in the Pentecost Room. At 8:30, your committees meet. ... Let us stand and pray together the Lord's Prayer."

Plenary Session II concluded with the Lord's Prayer. The Church Council recessed at 9:53 P.M.

Executive Session

The Church Council reconvened in Executive Session on December 4, 1993, at 12:34 P.M. for the purpose of electing a unit director for the Department for Synodical Relations and discussing litigation.

The Church Council reconvened in plenary session at 1:08 P.M.

Nominations and Elections

1. Nominating Ballot for Executive Committee of Church Council

Council Action: Chair Magnus reviewed the process for selection of the Executive Committee of the Church Council by nominating ballot. She then directed that nominating ballots be distributed to the members of the Church Council and subsequently declared balloting to be closed. The results of the election are reported elsewhere in these minutes.

2. Vacancies on Churchwide Boards and Committees

Background: Between meetings of the Church-wide Assembly, the Church Council has the responsibility of electing persons to fill unexpired terms on churchwide boards (for example, those that occur because of resignations). The Church Council also is the electing body for steering committees of churchwide commissions and certain advisory committees.

The Church Council's Executive Committee, which serves as the Nominating Committee for the council, met on Friday evening, December 3, and Saturday morning, December 4, 1993, to prepare a slate of nominees for consideration by the council. The committee received suggestions for nominees from the affected divisions, commissions, departments, and other units; other names were submitted to the secretary of this church also were available for possible nomination by the Executive Committee.

Council Action: Chair Magnus reviewed the nomination process and then directed that biographical information for the slate of nominees submitted by the council's Executive Committee be distributed to the members of the Church Council. She then invited

additional nominations from the floor. Secretary Lowell G. Almen explained the rationale for representational and other restrictions requisite to specific vacancies. There being no nominations from the floor, Chair Magnus declared nominations for each vacancy to be closed seriatim. She directed that balloting proceed and subsequently declared balloting to be closed.

The results of the election are reported elsewhere in these minutes.

3. Director of the Department for Synodical Relations

Chair Magnus announced the election of the Rev. Michael L. Cooper-White (Oakland, Calif.) as the director of the Department for Synodical Relations. The election took place during the council's executive session held earlier this afternoon.

Chair Magnus reviewed the agenda for the remainder of this plenary session.

4. Appointments to Boards: Lutheran General HealthSystem

Background: The Evangelical Lutheran Church in America serves as a corporate member of certain affiliated social ministry organizations. The role of the corporate member includes the responsibility to elect or approve a majority of the members of the board of directors and to approve amendments to the governing documents.

The Lutheran General HealthSystem, Park Ridge, Illinois, is an organization for which the Evangelical Lutheran Church in America serves as a corporate member. The Division for Church in Society is the churchwide unit through which the Evangelical Lutheran Church in America relates to this health-care organization. The division requests Church Council action to elect the following board members for this organization.

Council Action: The Church Council adopted the following recommendation by *en bloc* action, as reported elsewhere in these minutes:

EN BLOC   [CC93.12.121]

To elect Richard L. Phillips, M.D., Mary Ann McDermott, R.N., ED.D., Donald S. Peterson, Carl J. Schnakenberg, and Sarah Payne Naylor, with terms expiring in 1996, to the board of Lutheran General HealthSystem, Park Ridge, Illinois.

5. Lutheran Immigration and Refugee Service

Background: The Evangelical Lutheran Church in America also serves as a corporate member of Lutheran Immigration and Refugee Service. The Division for Church in Society is the churchwide unit through which this church relates to LIRS. The division requests that the Church Council take the following action.

Council Action: The Church Council adopted the following recommendation by *en bloc* action, as reported elsewhere in these minutes:

EN BLOC   [CC93.12.122]
    To elect the Rev. Carl Thomas and Barbara Yoshioka Wheeler, with terms expiring in 1996, to the board of Lutheran Immigration and Refugee Service.

Social Teaching Statement on the Church and Human Sexuality (continued)

Background: In the weeks following the release of the initial draft of a social teaching statement on the church and human sexuality, there was substantial communication between churchwide staff and leaders through this church, in particular, synodical bishops. Reflecting on the churchwide reaction to this document and the advice received, the Division for Church in Society, after consultation with the bishop of this church, submitted the document, "Report of the Division for Church in Society on the Development of a Social Statement on Human Sexuality."

Council Action: Chair Magnus drew attention to the recommendation that had been distributed to council members. She indicated that parts of the recommendation originated with the executive committee of the board of the Division for Church in Society and was refined further by the churchwide officers in consideration of the council's deliberations on Friday evening, December 3, 1993. Secretary Lowell G. Almen read the recommendation, noting several emendations.

MOVED;
SECONDED: To acknowledge the strong reaction and widespread concern expressed by numerous members and congregations throughout the Evangelical Lutheran Church in America in response to the content and manner of release of the first draft of a possible "Social Statement on the Church and Human Sexuality–a Lutheran Perspective";

    To recognize, at the same time, those throughout this church who have voiced appreciation for the preparation of this first draft and the hope that the process will proceed for development of a subsequent draft and possible proposal of a social statement on human sexuality for a future Churchwide Assembly;

    To underscore that the current version of the statement is, indeed, a first draft, subject to study and comment by members, congregations, faculties, and institutions throughout the church, with such responses to inform the process for revisions for any subsequent draft;

    To affirm continuation of the process for possible development of a social statement on human sexuality for possible action at a future Churchwide Assembly, emphasizing that such work shall be in keeping with the doctrinal acknowledgement of and confession by this church of the Triune God (ELCA constitutional provision 2.01.), of "Jesus Christ as Lord and Savior and the Gospel as the power of God for the salvation of all who believe" (2.02.), of "Jesus Christ [as] the Word of God incarnate" (2.02.a.), of the "proclamation of God's message to us as both Law and Gospel" (2.02.b.), and "of the Old and New Testaments as the inspired Word of God and the authoritative source and norm of its proclamation, faith, and life" (2.03.);

    To express gratitude to members and congregations who have conveyed their concerns and convictions in this matter and especially to those who have recommended specific changes in the first draft to assist in the process of revision;

    To indicate the conviction that the Church Council would recommend to a future Churchwide Assembly only such a draft of a social statement on human sexuality that would stand on biblical foundations and the confessional tradition of this church and that would merit the study, consideration, thoughtful reflection, and widespread support within this church;

    To acknowledge that the broad interest and intense reactions to the first draft represent a strategic opportunity for study, reflection, and thought on how we as Lutherans read and embrace Scripture and how members of this church understand and respond to issues and concerns related to sexuality in communities and society;

    To indicate the conviction that the process for development of a possible social statement on human sexuality will require significant modifications in order for the process to be widely trusted and accepted throughout this church and in order to assure that responses will be respected and employed in the preparation of a subsequent draft;

    To acknowledge strong signs that trust in the current task force has been impaired and yet to indicate that, in view of the lengthy study, preparation, and dedicated work of the members of the task force to date, it is deemed unwise at this time to direct the board of the Division for Church in Society to disband the current task force;

    To respond to the executive committee of the board of the Division for Church in Society with appreciation for the general direction reflected in the revised proposal for the process of study, revision, and development of a social statement (as shown in council agenda council agenda Exhibit P, Part 1d);

    To affirm the need for greater participation of leadership groups of various perspectives in the development process for enhanced trust and partnership in the development of possible subsequent drafts;

    To determine that the present process will be supplemented by selecting a consulting panel to widen the circle of persons officially engaged in the preparation of a revised draft, with such a consulting panel:
1.   to be mutually accountable to the board of the Division for Church in Society and to the Church Council;
2.   to be expected to provide regular reports directly to the board, the Church Council, and Conference of

Bishops of the panel's work with appropriate staff and the task force; and

3. to be composed of 11 persons appointed by the Church Council, including:

   a. three ELCA seminary faculty members, named by the Church Council upon recommendation of the presidents of ELCA seminaries;

   b. three pastors of ELCA congregations, named by the Church Council;

   c. two lay members of ELCA congregations, named by the Church Council;

   d. two members of the Conference of Bishops, named by the Conference of Bishops; and

   e. one member of the Church Council, named by the Church Council;

   and

To direct that this consultation panel shall have access to all materials received from members, congregations, and others in response to the study document and first draft, shall be charged to give advice and counsel related to the opinions within the church and shall provide advice, counsel, and critique–including the ways in which Scripture is used–in the development of any subsequent drafts;

To affirm the plan of the executive committee of the board of the Division for Church in Society for appointment of a staff team, under the supervision of the executive director of the Division for Church in Society, to carry out responsibilities with the task force and consulting panel for development of any subsequent drafts;

To express appreciation for the development of a plan for recording and providing both statistical and narrative summaries of responses received to the first draft, which shall be reported periodically to the Conference of Bishops and the Church Council; and

To urge renewed commitment to mutual conversation, correction, and consolation among and between sisters and brothers in Christ within the Evangelical Lutheran Church in America, remembering that members of this church are united through Christ and are together by our primary convictions grounded in Scripture, the creeds of the church, the Augsburg Confession, and the other doctrinal writings of the Lutheran Reformation.

Bishop Paull E. Spring stated that the concerns he had expressed had been more than satisfied in the current recommendation. The Rev. Franklin D. Fry suggested that in the fourth, sixth, and eighth paragraphs, the phrase, "and study materials," be added in order to acknowledge the possibility that not all issues related to the development process necessarily be treated in the final text of the proposed social statement. He then moved the following:

MOVED;
SECONDED: To insert the words, *and study materials*, in paragraphs four, six, and eight following the words, "social statement."

The Rev. Donald M. Hallberg requested response from the division. The Rev. Charles S. Miller Jr., executive director of the Division for Church in Society, observed, regarding inclusion of the proposed phrase in the sixth paragraph, that it would not be standard practice to transmit study documents through the Church Council to the Churchwide Assembly. Charles A. Adamson suggested that paragraph seven be amended to reflect Pastor Fry's concern, in lieu of the paragraphs specified in the proposed amendment. Pastor Fry replied, "It is going to be awkward wherever we put it [the emendation] in, because the basic premise of the document is only [development of] a social statement." Secretary Almen observed that the concept of the development of study materials already was implied in paragraph seven. The Rev. John O. Knudson concurred with Pastor Miller that the proposed emendation was not apropos to paragraph six. Chair Magnus directed that by consensus reference to the sixth paragraph be deleted from the proposed amendment. Bishop Herbert W. Chilstrom observed that paragraph four also pertains to transmission of materials to the Churchwide Assembly. Secretary Almen suggested that the emendation of paragraph four read, "preparation of study materials and possible development of a social statement." Deborah S. Yandala objected to the repeated use of the word, "possible." In response, Secretary Almen suggested that paragraph four read, "To affirm continuation of a process for the preparation of study materials and the development of a possible social statement . . .." Bishop Paull E. Spring commented that the Conference of Bishops had recognized that it may not be possible for this church to develop a social statement on the topic of human sexuality. Pastor Fry suggested the wording, ". . . and the development of a social statement on human sexuality, *which may be presented* . . .." Chair Magnus indicated that Pastor Fry's rendering would be accepted by consensus. Edith M. Lohr (and subsequently Bishop Lyle G. Miller) requested confirmation that the amendment proposed for paragraph eight in the original motion was withdrawn. Chair Magnus responded affirmatively.

MOVED
SECONDED;
CARRIED: To amend paragraph four to read: "To affirm continuation of the process for preparation of study materials and the development of a social statement on human sexuality, which may be presented for action at a future Churchwide Assembly . . .."

The Rev. Stephen M. Youngdahl requested that council members receive copies of the final action prior to adjournment.

Lorraine G. Bergquist stated that she remained convinced that the motion she had presented on Friday evening, December 3, 1993, was relevant. She then moved the following:

MOVED;

SECONDED: To substitute the following for the recommendation:

That the Church Council declare the work of the task force responsible for the development of the social statement, "The Church and Human Sexuality: A Lutheran Perspective," to be ended; and

That the social statement, "The Church and Human Sexuality: A Lutheran Perspective," not come before the 1995 Churchwide Assembly; and

That a study committee be established to receive responses from members and congregations of the Evangelical Lutheran Church in America, faculties of the ELCA theological seminaries as well as other theologians within this church, and additional interested parties. This study committee shall consist of two parish pastors of the Evangelical Lutheran Church in America, two seminary professors named by the joint seminary presidents, two bishops named by the Conference of Bishops, two persons named by the Division for Church in Society, and three persons named by the Church Council. Staffing for the Study Committee shall be provided by the Division for Church in Society in consultation with the Office of the Bishop; and

That the study committee be charged to articulate faithfully and clearly the mind of the church as faithful people of God; consider seriously the social statements of the predecessor church bodies, the LCA "Sex, Marriage, and Family" (1970) and the ALC "Human Sexuality and Sexual Behavior" (1980), as well as the paragraph on page 13 of "Vision and Expectations: Ordained Ministers in the Evangelical Lutheran Church in America" regarding sexual conduct, and the work of the task force on the draft of the social statement, "The Church and Human Sexuality: A Lutheran Perspective"; and

That the study committee produce a report that will be provided to congregations and rostered persons, synods, and the churchwide organization of the Evangelical Lutheran Church in America. The report from the study committee will be received by the Church Council at its March 31-April 2, 1995, meeting and will be reported to the 1995 Churchwide Assembly as information.

Ms. Bergquist indicated that the first paragraph of her motion was intended "to address the issue of distrust that has arisen with the task force." She noted that paragraph two "allows time to do further work, and would not impinge upon the election of the churchwide bishop in 1995." The third paragraph addresses the matter of funding for additional development and review procedures. Paragraph four provides for "listening and respecting respondents as caring members . . . and they have a real concern for this church and what is going on; I do not want to take that lightly," she said. She urged that double standards not be set up for the conduct of

clergy and the laity, and that the deliberations of predecessor churches not be lost. The last paragraph recognizes that the outcome need not be a social statement, and would alleviate perceptions of the binding quality of such documents on the conscience. Ms. Bergquist finally raised the question of whether there was further need to clarify the distinction between social "teaching" and social "practice" statements.

Chair Magnus indicated that deliberation would first perfect the main motion, and then proceed to the substitute.

William H. Engelbrecht moved to amend the third paragraph of the main motion as follows:

MOVED;

SECONDED: To amend the third paragraph of the main motion to read, "To underscore that the current version is the FIRST DRAFT OF A STUDY DOCUMENT ONLY (and not policy of the Evangelical Lutheran Church in America), subject to . . .."

Mr. Engelbrecht observed that many people perceive the document to be the policy of this church and not a draft document. "I do not think that we can emphasize enough that this is only a first draft of a study document," he stated. Pastor Miller noted that in actuality the draft was not one of a study document, but of a social statement. Secretary Almen suggested that the emendation read, "To underscore that the current version of the statement is, indeed, a first draft (and not official policy of the Evangelical Lutheran Church in America), and as a first draft is subject to study . . .." Mr. Engelbrecht received the suggestion as a friendly amendment, and requested that the word, "continued," be inserted before the word, "study." He also requested that the parenthetical phrase be printed in an emphatic typeface.

MOVED;

SECONDED;

CARRIED: To amend the third paragraph of the main motion to read, "To underscore that the current version of the statement is, indeed, a first draft (and ***not official policy*** of the Evangelical Lutheran Church in America), and as a first draft is subject to continued study . . .."

The Rev. David A. Andert questioned the potential of the task force to redraft the proposed social statement and "with a clear conscience produce something quite different than that." Pastor Miller responded, "While I do believe that the task force is quite capable of [making] significant alterations to the first draft . . ., it will be aided considerably by the consulting panel and the new staff team that will bring a fresh perspective to what, I think, are some of the chief concerns about the first draft." Edith M. Lohr, a member of the task force, reflected that members of the task force in four years have grown in their understanding, "and are devoted to the church [and] very concerned. I do not believe that it was the intention of the task force to put something forward that would be controversial, but [that] was where after four years they came out. The entire church has not had the benefit of that process. I would clearly feel confident that the task force is very interested in seeing a document come forward that will be helpful to the church–and they can do that job," she said.

Charles A. Adamson observed that in the fourth paragraph from the end of the main motion, the two documents cited were not sufficiently differentiated ("study document" and "first draft"). Chair Magnus directed that the titles of the specific documents be added editorially for identification purposes. Edith M. Lohr verified that at some 3,000 responses had been received by the task force. "Everyone of those comments was summarized for the task force and our experience in reading those comments was much the same experience that Bishop [Herbert W.] Chilstrom shared with us yesterday, in that people were on both sides of the issue." Lorraine G. Bergquist suggested that the dates of the two documents in question be included for additional clarification. Chair Magnus concurred.

D. Mark Klever inquired about the working relationship between the task force and the consulting panel. Pastor Miller indicated that the board of the division, the task force, and the consulting panel would first need to agree on mission and objectives, et al.

Ramona S. Rank expressed concern that too much deference might be being given to people who have raised strenuous objection to various parts of text. "The people who put this together . . . are as faithful Lutheran people as any of us sitting around here or those Lutheran folks that were concerned and in the congregations raising these issues. I want to make sure that we are not sending the message that it is sort of a slap on the wrist, because I want to commend them for their work. It was a tough job," she commented.

Bishop Lyle G. Miller raised the issue of authority and relationships between the groups that would be involved in the statement's development. He commended expectations for a collaborative process, and commented, "I hope it works and that people can and will indeed buy into that commonness of mission and purpose." Pastor Miller responded that the task force will need to recall that it was the creation of the board and "not just accountable to it, but its partner in creating something hopefully of value to the church. And so it would be in that sense that I would be saying to both the task force, the consulting panel, and the new staff team that they have to see themselves as partners, rather than as independent contractors who somehow have to end up discovering how to collaborate; so we will begin with that spirit," he said. Bishop Miller further inquired about the time table and whether it would provide for such a collaborative process. Pastor Miller confirmed that the task indeed can be accomplished by the 1995 Churchwide Assembly.

The Rev. Nelson T. Strobert inquired in reference to item 3.c. of the main motion whether one of the two lay members from congregations be appointed from one of official lay rosters? Chair Magnus responded that such

would not be precluded. J. David Ellwanger observed that the intention was that representation be provided by "the person in the pew." Pastor Strobert stated concern "for that group [associates in ministry, et al.], which very often feels disenfranchised." D. Mark Klever suggested that the issue be addressed by adding lay-rostered members as a separate category. Pastor Miller noted that the added cost would be $550 per individual per meeting. The Rev. Philip L. Natwick suggested that the representative from the Church Council on the consulting panel be a rostered lay person. Pastor Strobert sought to move the following:

MOVED: To amend item 3.c. of the main motion to specify, "one of whom is from the official lay rosters."

The motion, however, died for lack of a second. Patsy Gottschalk expressed concern about the cost of including 28 persons in the development process and its impact on the entire churchwide budget. Pastor Miller reviewed the budget (income and expense) projected for 1994.

The Rev. Stephen M. Youngdahl inquired how the members the consulting panel would be selected. He observed that the matter would become a critical perception problem. Secretary Almen suggested two options– assign the task to the Executive Committee, or delay the initial meeting of consultation until after the spring 1994 meeting of the Church Council. He noted the additional considerations that the Conference of Bishops would not meet until early March 1994, and the desirability of timing the appointment of the consulting panel and initial meetings of both the panel and task force to coincide with the spring 1994 meeting of the board of the Division for Church in Society.

Bishop Peter Rogness commented that, in view of the aforementioned necessities, there may be a need to "revisit" the viability of the time line for transmission of a proposed social statement (and perhaps delay it until 1997). He also raised the question of whether the format of a social teaching statement was the desirable format for appropriate treatment of the subject matter. "I think it would be very helpful for the church for us to say very clearly in this official action that both of those issues are now a part of the process"–namely, that the time line and format would be reexamined. Bishop Rogness commented further that "the signal that comes out of this [is] essentially a signal that will or will not serve the function of restoring the credibility and the confidence of the church in this process." He observed that the proposed composition of the consultation panel had shifted from persons known and trusted throughout this church (namely, members of the Conference of Bishops and seminary faculties) to individuals who would be essentially unknown to this church's constituency. He cautioned that in adopting the main motion, therefore, "we risk endangering the goal of renewing confidence by broadening this consulting group in that way."

Nominations and Elections (continued)

1. Nominating Ballot for Executive Committee of Church Council

Chair Magnus indicated that the results of the nominating ballot had been tabulated and the first ballot for selection of the Executive Committee prepared. She directed that ballots be distributed and cast prior to the afternoon recess.

Social Teaching Statement on the Church and Human Sexuality (continued)

William T. Billings moved to amend the main motion by adding from substitute motion as follows:

MOVED;
SECONDED;
DEFEATED: To insert after paragraph seven the following:

> To consider seriously the social statements of the predecessor church bodies, the LCA "Sex, Marriage, and Family" (1970) and the ALC "Human Sexuality and Sexual Behavior" (1980), as well as the paragraph on page 13 of "Vision and Expectations: Ordained Ministers in the Evangelical Lutheran Church in America" regarding sexual conduct.

During discussion of the foregoing motion, Mr. Billings commended "the task force that worked so hard on it [the draft statement] for two years." He stated that he would support not disbanding the task force altogether, but continuing development of the social statement by instituting another study group, because doing so would give the wrong impression, namely, that it was thought that another body could be more capable or more responsible in producing the desired statement than the present task force. Although he favored the main motion, it omitted "affirmation of the basis for our belief," which, he said, was articulated clearly in the substitute motion offered by Ms. Bergquist. Terry L. Bowes observed that the present draft already in fact quoted the documents in question.

The Rev. James G. Cobb questioned whether the proposed action, which would establish a review panel, would be sufficient to satisfy those who had objected to the draft statement. He observed that the Division for Church in Society and the Church Council both serve as "wrap around" groups that function as review and consultative panels and which already are in place. He stated that he had hoped at this meeting to critique the text of the document more specifically. Pastor Cobb urged that the function of the proposed statement be clearly distinguished with respect to the social teaching of this church versus the social practice within the actual life of the congregation. He cautioned that the practice within this church not become the teaching of this church, and advocated rather that the teach-ing of this church become

its practice. He reiterated the concern that Church Council actually consider the text of the document at this meeting.

Bishop Chilstrom noted that the concept of a review panel had been modeled after the process utilized in the development of the *Lutheran Book of Worship*. He observed that time was not available to permit the council to review the text of the document in sufficient detail and recommended that council members submit in writing their own responses to those assigned responsibility for development of the text. Pastor Cobb stated that, rather than establishing a review panel, he would prefer that the Church Council give instruction directly to the task force.

The Rev. David G. Gabel stated that he shared some of Pastor Cobb's concerns. He proposed that the council delay its action, in order that it might discuss the content of the document–possibly at its April 1994 meeting–and then decide whether to retain or dissolve the task force. "I think that is being very responsible," he commented.

Pastor Miller commented that delaying transmission of the proposed social statement to the Churchwide Assembly in 1997 would extend the service of task force members to eight years, which he considered to be an extraordinary request. Bishop Chilstrom observed that this church's membership expects that "this meeting is going to be very constructive in terms of some sort of recommendation." He stated that in his opinion, the proposed action "would be greeted with very positive response." Edith M. Lohr commented that delaying development of the statement would complicate the study process in congregations with respect to the deadline for response.

Karen M. Dietz spoke in favor of the main motion, and inquired whether a mail ballot might suffice for selection of the consultation panel. Chair Magnus expressed the opinion that a mail ballot was "a doable kind of thing." Ms. Dietz then moved to amend the main motion as follows:

MOVED;
SECONDED: To amend the item labeled "3.b." to read: "Two pastors of ELCA congregations and one associate in ministry."

The Rev. Nelson T. Strobert offered as a friendly amendment substitution of the phrase, "person from the official lay roster of the Evangelical Lutheran Church in America," for the phrase, "associate in ministry," in order to indicate more specifically inclusion of deaconesses and other rostered lay persons.

MOVED;
SECONDED;   YES–16; NO–17
DEFEATED: To amend the item labeled "3.b." to read: "Two pastors of ELCA congregations and one person from the official lay roster of the Evangelical Lutheran Church in America."

Bishop Paull E. Spring stated his continued endorsement of the main motion, noting the it addressed most of the major objections to the draft statement that have been voiced. Bishop Lyle G. Miller concurred, by reason of the direct role that now would be exercised by the Church Council in the development process. Charles A. Adamson also concurred, noting that the recommendation addressed most of the questions raised in correspondence he had received.

Robert S. Schroeder observed that the text of the document was not before the council for action at this time, but rather that an action proposed by the Division for Church in Society was under consideration. Pastor James G. Cobb suggested that one alternative approach was to model the response of the Conference of Bishops, which expressed appreciation, but also noted reservations with the text. He reiterated his concern that the Church Council deal with the text itself and address the task force directly.

Cynthia P. Johnson inquired whether members of the consulting panel would have pertinent training and expertise. Chair Magnus indicated that the Church Council would determine requisite qualifications.

The Rev. David K. Johnson stated, ". . . There is nothing wrong with the task force. I have confidence in these people; the ones I know personally I admire. I think they are fine people. I do not want to say anything derogatory. For four years they went through a process. They worked hard, and they gave it their best shot, . . . and they presented it before the church. I think that we have to admit that the church has reacted to the content, but I think also the truth can be said that we have arrived at a teaching moment. Moses did not make it all the way to the promised land. Maybe a task force cannot make it to the promised land. Maybe the best thing that the task force could do for us and for the church is to say, 'We have done our best. We have nothing to be ashamed of, and with dignity we now turn the matter over and allow the church to deliberate it from here.' That would be a tough thing for them to do, but I think it could help us all a great deal right now."

J. David Ellwanger spoke in favor of the main motion, saying, "I feel we have something to be very proud of, if we should adopt this [motion]." He observed that creation of a review panel would solve the "political problem" of being responsive to the concerns of this church's constituents. Chair Magnus then called for the orders of the day.

Deliberations on this matter resume later in these minutes.

Nominations and Elections (continued)

1. Nominating Ballot for Executive Committee of Church Council

Chair Magnus indicated that the ballot previously cast contained typographical errors. She ordered the ballot to be recast and subsequently declared balloting to be closed.

ELCA Pension and Other Benefits Program

1. Amendments to Medical-Dental Plan– Managed Care

Background: Following a six-month study of the ELCA health plan, recommendations were presented to the trustees of the Board of Pensions in July 1993. The board adopted in principle a resolution to revise the ELCA Medical and Dental Benefits Plan effective January 1, 1995, in order to implement a managed-care arrangement and other cost-containment features under the plan. A memorandum describing the proposed managed-care plan was provided in council agenda Exhibit J, Part 1. [A preliminary discussion on this matter was held at the August 1993 meeting of the Church Council; discussions also have been held with the Conference of Bishops.]

At its October 15-16, 1993, meeting, the Board of Pensions took the following action:

1. RESOLVED, that the Board approve in principle a revision of the ELCA Medical and Dental Benefits Program, to be effective January 1, 1995, and to include the following elements:
    a. A point-of-service arrangement would be phased in over three to five years. Initial areas for implementation of the point-of-service arrangement would include Minneapolis/St. Paul, Minnesota, and Chicago, Illinois.
    b. Those members not covered by the point-of-service arrangement would be covered by the ELCA "managed indemnity" arrangement, which would be our current plan, but which would include additional modifications of an inpatient pre-certification/utilization review program, additional large case management and a simplified reimbursement schedule for chiropractic, out-patient psychotherapy and major dental care.
    c. The supplement to the Medical and Dental Benefits Plan would be eliminated.
    d. The point-of-service and managed indemnity arrangements would be components of the same, national ELCA health plan.
    e. The plan would continue to be bundled with the other ELCA benefit plans.
    f. The in-network benefits of the point-of-service arrangement would be reimbursed at 90 percent of eligible expenses or 100 percent with a small co-payment per physician visit, while the out-of-network benefits would be reimbursed at 70 percent of eligible expenses after a deductible. The out-of-area indemnity arrangement would continue to provide for a reimbursement of 80 percent after a deductible.
    g. Contributions from congregations and other employers would be calculated upon a percent of salary basis, but the subsidy of family rates and the surcharge on member only rates would be phased out over a period of years. However, the low income subsidy would be maintained.
    h. A single rate structure would apply to all congregations and employers.
2. RESOLVED further, that staff be directed to draft and release "Requests for Information" to potential vendors and to engage in preliminary discussions with the vendors.
3. RESOLVED further, that these resolutions be forwarded to the ELCA Church Council to consider approval in principle by its December 1993 meeting.

4.   RESOLVED further, that, if the Church Council approves in principle the revisions to the ELCA Medical and Dental Benefits Plan, staff be directed to draft documenting amendments, to be considered by the Board at its first scheduled meeting in 1994.

At its December 1993 meeting, the Church Council was asked to adopt, in principle, the foregoing changes in the ELCA health plan. The board would then proceed with implementation of the managed-care plan. If the council were to adopt the changes, in principle, documenting plan amendments would be forwarded to the council for consideration at its April 1994 meeting.

Council Action: Chair Magnus called upon John G. Kapanke, president of the Board of Pensions, to introduce the recommendation printed below, subsequently adopted by the Church Council. President Kapanke introduced Kathryn A. Helmke, vice president for medical-dental administration, who was present to respond to questions. He reviewed the elements of the proposed program as presented in council agenda Exhibit J, Part 1. President Kapanke observed that the Board of Pensions is operating in a changing economic and social environment. The board had retained an outside consulting firm that identified and prioritized the key risks and challenges facing the Board of Pensions. Goals for the medical-dental plans were: 1) to reduce the cost of escalation (although a 0.7 percent reduction in premium rates for the medical-dental plan would be realized in 1994, previously, double-digit rate increases were necessary); 2) to maintain high membership in the plan (95 percent of eligible members are plan participants); 3) to continue to improve the financial integrity of the plan (previously, the plan has not had sufficient operating surpluses to satisfy governmental regulations); and 4) to position the plan for the future (especially in light ments do not apply to predecessor plans or to non-medicare eligible persons.

President Kapanke noted that the board values the input of the Church Council, Conference of Bishops, Board of Pensions. In March 1993, the board had surveyed plan members, as well as members of the Church Council and Conference of Bishops, and staff and trustees of the Board of Pensions, in order to assess their experience and preferences with respect to the medical-dental plan. The survey indicated strong support for the existing plan. Respondents indicated that the plan meets their needs and is competitively priced, affirmed the low-income subsidy, and gave high marks to claims processing staff members. Plan members hoped that the plan would reduce their out-of-pocket expenses, address the rising health-care cost issue, and provide freedom of choice; but, they also indicated a willingness to utilize a primary-care physician. The survey resulted in refined recommendations for amending the exiting plan. It was determined that the percent of salary contribution with a low income subsidy should be retained; the member-only surcharge should be eliminated; freedom of choice would be maintained; and the possibility would be considered for a member-only waiver for spouse's group coverage following actuarial evaluation.

President Kapanke reviewed the design of the proposed plan, including the "point of service" component; the managed indemnity plan; and the common benefit component. The savings achieved would be shared by all members, he said. During the first five years of the plan, cost savings of $44 million were anticipated.

Concluding the presentation, President Kapanke addressed the issue of apparent advantages for urban and large-city members. Sixty percent or more of those members would be required to change current health-care providers. Therefore, there are some "trade offs," but nonetheless, "common benefits for all," he said, and implementation of the plan actually would prove to be "cost neutral." The board has not yet received significant feedback on this issue from those who would be served through the indemnity plan; but those whose freedom of choice would be limited by the managed-care approach "overwhelmingly" have raised question. Nevertheless, indemnity plans are becoming extinct, he said.

Loren W. Mathre inquired about the claims process for the point-of-service care. William T. Billings inquired about differences in cost for individual and family coverages, emergency room coverage, and the provision of customer service to plan members. He recommended that, in site visits to HMO providers, Board of Pensions staff members evaluate service by observing waiting rooms. W. Jeanne Rapp inquired about the effect of the proposed federal health-plans on the future of the ELCA plans. Could it be advantageous to delay implementation of the proposed amendments until more is known about the U.S. government plan, she asked. President Kapanke observed that implementation of the federal plan would not occur immediately, and significant savings would result in the meantime. The Rev. John O. Knudson inquired about ceilings on reimbursement for certain types of coverage.

An unidentified council member called the question.

MOVED;
SECONDED;
CARRIED: To move the previous question.

VOTED: **CC93.12.77**
   WHEREAS, the ELCA Board of Pensions administers the ELCA Medical and Dental Benefits Plan ("Plan"), which is funded through the ELCA Medical and Dental Benefits Trust ("Trust"); and
   WHEREAS, the ELCA Board of Pensions has recommended to the ELCA Church Council that it approve, in principle, proposed revisions to the Plan and Trust to be effective January 1, 1995, the main elements of which are set forth in resolutions adopted by the ELCA Board of Pensions on July 17, 1993, and presented to the Church Council; and
   WHEREAS, the Church Council acknowledges that, in order to obtain information about the feasibility of such revisions, the ELCA Board of Pensions has solicited potential vendors and

engaged in preliminary discussions and negotiations with such vendors; and

WHEREAS, the Church Council wishes to adopt the recommendation of the ELCA Board of Pensions; therefore, be it

RESOLVED, that the Church Council hereby adopts the recommendation of the ELCA Board of Pensions and approves, in principle, the proposed revisions to the Plan and Trust, the main elements of which are as follows:

1. A point-of-service managed care arrangement would be phased in over two to three years for the 50 percent of ELCA plan members who reside in a metropolitan area. Approximately 12 sites would be included in the initial implementation of the point-of-service arrangement, including Minneapolis/St. Paul, Minnesota, and Chicago, Illinois.

2. The point-of-service arrangement would retain freedom of provider choice but offer enhanced benefits for use of network providers. The in-network benefits of the point-of-service arrangement would be 90 percent of eligible expenses or 100 percent with a small co-payment per physician visit, while the out-of-network benefits would be reimbursed at 70 percent of eligible expenses after a deductible. The lower benefits for those electing to use out-of-network providers are intended to cover the added cost of unlimited provider choice.

3. Those members not covered by the point-of-service arrangement would be covered by the ELCA "managed indemnity" arrangement, which would be the current ELCA health plan, but modified to include an inpatient pre-certification/utilization review program, expanded large case management and a simplified reimbursement schedule for chiropractic, out-patient psychotherapy and major dental care. The indemnity arrangement would continue to provide for a reimbursement at 80 percent after a deductible. The supplement to the Medical and Dental Benefits Plan would be eliminated.

4. The point-of-service and managed indemnity arrangements would be components of the same, national ELCA health plan. The plan would continue to be bundled with the other ELCA benefit plans.

5. A single rate structure would apply to all congregations and employers. Contributions from congregations and other employers would be calculated upon a percent of salary basis, but the subsidy of family rates and the surcharge on member only rates would be phased out over a period of years. However, the low income subsidy would be maintained.

And be it further

RESOLVED, that the Church Council hereby acknowledges that, if it adopts, in principle, the changes to the ELCA health plan, documenting plan amendments will be considered by the Church Council at its meeting in April 1994.

2. Amendments to the Bylaws of the Board of Pensions of the Evangelical Lutheran Church in America

The proposed amendment to Section 6.9 of Article 6 of the Bylaws was a technical amendment to bring the bylaws into conformity with the actual practices of the corporation: The treasurer does not present the annual report to the trustees either at the fall annual meeting or at other meetings of the board.

The proposed amendment to Section 7.7 of Article 7 of the bylaws would add a Personnel and Compensation Committee to the Board of Trustees.

Council Action:

EN BLOC   [CC93.12.115]

To adopt the amendments to Section 6.9 of Article 6 and Section 7.7 of Article 7 of the bylaws of the Board of Pensions . . . ..

3. Proposed Restatement of The ALC Continuation Trust

a. Restatement

The Board of Pensions has proposed that the trust that serves as a funding vehicle for the ELCA Continuation of The ALC Medical-Dental Plan for Retired Participants be restated:

WHEREAS, this board considers it desirable that the ELCA Continuation of the ALC Major Medical-Dental Trust for Retired Participants ("Trust") be restated effective October 16, 1993, in the form attached hereto (council agenda Exhibit J, Part 3);

RESOLVED, that this board recommends to the ELCA Church Council that the ELCA Church Council take action to authorize any officer of the ELCA to execute the restatement of the Trust; and be it

RESOLVED, that this board hereby authorizes and ratifies the execution of the restatement of the Trust by the trustees, who shall be the members of this board as of October 16, 1993.

According to the board's action, the name of the restated trust would be the "ELCA Continuation of the ALC Major Medical-Dental Trust for Retired Participants."

The following resolution was commended to the Church Council by the Board of Pensions.

Council Action:

EN BLOC   [CC93.12.116]

WHEREAS, the ELCA maintains the "ELCA Continuation of the ALC Medical-Dental Plan for Retired Participants" ("Plan"), which is funded through the "ELCA Continuation of the ALC Major Medical-Dental Trust for Retired Participants" ("Trust"); and

WHEREAS, the ELCA Board of Pensions has recommended to the Church Council that it approve a restatement of the Trust and authorize any officer to execute the Trust on behalf of the Evangelical Lutheran Church in America; and

WHEREAS, the Church Council wishes to adopt the recommendation of the ELCA Board of Pensions; now, therefore, be it

RESOLVED that the document titled, "ELCA Continuation of the ALC Major Medical-Dental Trust for Retired Participants," which has been presented to the Church Council (and ordered filed with a record of this resolution), is hereby approved and the officers of the Evangelical Lutheran Church in America are hereby authorized, and directed, to execute the same on behalf of the Evangelical Lutheran Church in America.

b.   Related Amendment of the "ELCA Continuation of the ALC Major Medical-Dental Trust for Retired Participants."

At its October 1993 meeting, the Board of Pensions took the following action:

WHEREAS, the ELCA Continuation of the ALC Major Medical-Dental Trust for Retired Participants ("Trust") was restated effective October 16, 1993; and

WHEREAS, this board considers it desirable that the Trust now be amended to coordinate the terms of the Trust in certain respects with other trusts maintained by the Evangelical Lutheran Church in America; now, therefore, be it

RESOLVED, that this board recommends to the ELCA Church Council that the amendment to the Trust attached hereto (council agenda Exhibit J, Part 4) be adopted.

These proposed amendments would make the trust consistent with the other ELCA trusts.

Council Action:

EN BLOC   [CC93.12.117]

To adopt the amendments to the ELCA Continuation of the ALC Major Medical-Dental Trust for Retired Participants . . . .

4.   Proposed Miscellaneous Amendments

a.   ELCA Medical and Dental Benefits Plan

The Board of Pensions proposed that several technical amendments be adopted in conjunction with the implementation of the Managed Mental-Health and Chemical- Dependency Program effective January 1, 1994.

Council Action:

EN BLOC   [CC93.12.118.a.]

To adopt the amendments to the ELCA Medical and Dental Benefits . . . .

b.   ELCA Continuation of the LCA Ministerial Health Benefits Plan for Retired Members

The Board of Pensions proposed to eliminate the provision for 100 percent reimbursement of expenses incurred during the final days of a member's lifetime.

Council Action:

EN BLOC   [CC93.12.118.b.]

To adopt the amendments to the ELCA Continuation of the LCA Ministerial Health Benefits Plan for Retired Members . . . .

c.   ELCA Disability Benefits Plan

The Board of Pensions proposed that the ELCA Disability Benefits Plan be restated to (1) revise the definition of disability to apply a more rigorous standard following the first 24 months of disability; and (2) provide for a partial earnings offset during the first 24 months of disability, with a full offset thereafter.

Council Action:

EN BLOC   [CC93.12.118.c.]

To adopt the amendments to the ELCA Disability Benefits Plan . . . .

d.   Chaplaincy Amendments

The Board of Pensions proposed amendments to the various plans of the ELCA Pension and Other Benefits Program that would extend eligibility for clergy in specialized ministries for an additional year.

Council Action:

EN BLOC   [CC93.12.118.d.]

To adopt the amendments to the ELCA Pension and Other Benefits Program . . . .

e.   Government Chaplaincy Plans

The Board of Pensions proposed that the Pension and Welfare Government Chaplaincy Plans that currently exist in three separate sets of documents (ELCA, ALC, and LCA) be consolidated.

Council Action:

EN BLOC   [CC93.12.118.e.]

To adopt the consolidation of the Pension and Welfare Government Chaplaincy Plans . . . .

f.   Master Institutional Savings Plan

The Board of Pensions proposed an expansion of flexibility for employers participating in the Master Institutional Savings Plan.

Council Action:

EN BLOC   [CC93.12.118.f.]

To adopt the amendments to the Master Institutional Savings Plan . . . .

g.   ELCA Medical and Dental Benefits Plan

The Board of Pensions proposed to delete references to the previously-terminated Institutional Benefits Program.

Council Action:

EN BLOC   [CC93.12.118.g.]

To adopt the amendments to the ELCA Medical and Dental Benefits Plan . . . .

h. ELCA Survivor Benefits Plan

The Board of Pensions proposed to delete references to the previously-terminated Institutional Benefits Program.

Council Action:

EN BLOC   [CC93.12.118.h.]

To adopt the amendments to the ELCA Survivor Benefits Plan . . ..

Nominations and Elections (continued)

1. Nominating Ballot for Executive Committee of Church Council

Chair Magnus announced that the following persons had been elected to the Executive Committee of the Church Council: Lorraine G. Bergquist, the Rev. Stephen M. Youngdahl, William E. Diehl, and Carlos Peña. She reported that three vacancies remained. The third ballot for election of the Executive Committee of the Church Council was cast. Chair Magnus subsequently declared the ballot to be closed.

2. Vacancies on Churchwide Boards and Committees

Chair Magnus declared the following persons to be elected to vacancies on churchwide boards and committees:

VOTED: CC93.12.78

To elect the following persons to respective vacancies on churchwide boards and committees to the terms indicated:

Board of the Division for Ministry–
Lay Male (term 1997)
   John R. Graff (8G) - replaces Wayne E. Engel

Steering Committee of the Commission for Multicultural Ministries–
White Committee Members:
   Lay Female (term 1999)
      *L. DeAne Lagerquist (3I) - reelected
   Lay Male (term 1999)
      *LeRoy Zimmerman (4B) - reelected
African-American Committee Members:
   Clergy (term 1999)
      *Rev. Callon Holloway (6F) - reelected
   Lay Female (term 1999)
      Audrey Russell (7F) - replaces Ellen Torrey
Asian Committee Members:
   Clergy (term 1999)
      Rev. Margrethe S. C. Kleiber (2C) - replaces Rev. Linda Hostetter
   Lay Male (term 1999)
      *Alfred Sager (6B) - reelected

Steering Committee of the Commission for Women–
Clergy (term 1995)
   Rev. Loren E. Halvorson (3G) - replaces Rev. David E. Nelson
Clergy (term 1999)
   Rev. Ann M. Tiemeyer (7A) - replaces Rev. Jean Larson Hurd

Lay Female (term 1999)
   1. Patricia Lemmerman (7E) - replaces Robert Brorby
   2. *Venice R. Williams (5J) - reelected
Lay Male (term 1999)
   *Ronald Jacobson (1B) - reelected

Advisory Committee of the Department for Communication–
Clergy - PC/L (term 1999)
   Rev. Barbara Berry-Bailey (7E) - replaces Rev. Clement Lee
Lay Female (term 1999)
   Eva Reque David (7B) - replaces Cathy McMullen
Lay Male (term 1999)
   *Cliff Albert (2C) - reelected

Advisory Committee of the Department for Ecumenical Affairs–
Clergy (term 1999)
   *Rev. Stephen Swenson (6C) - reelected
   Rev. David F. Lindblom (3G) - replaces Rev. J. Christian Quello

Advisory Committee of the Department for Human Resources–
Lay Female (term 1997)
   Doris Pagelkopf (3G) - replaces Mary Alice Bjork
Lay Male (term 1999)
   *Larry Smith (3G) - reelected

Advisory Committee of the Department for Research and Evaluation–
Lay Male (term 1999)
   *F. Paul Carlson (3G) - reelected

Committee of Hearing Officers (term 1999)–
Kathryn E. Baerwald (8G) -
      replaces *Bonnie Block 5K
*Kathleen Kelly (2A) - reelected

Advisory Committee of *The Lutheran*–
Lay Female (term 1999) - Nominated by *The Lutheran*:
      Jean M. LemMon (5D) -
         replaces Regina Sherard
Lay Female (term 1999) - Nominated by the Publishing House:
      Hazel H. Reinhardt (3G) - replaces Paula Kadel
Lay Male (term 1999) - Nominated by the Publishing House:
      Scott Bosley (7A) -
         replaces Myrvin Christopherson
Lay Male (term 1995) - Board of the Publishing House Representative:
      Mark A. Staples (7F) - replaces A. Jean Lesher

Board of Directors of the Mission Investment Fund (term 1995)–
Nominated by the Division for Outreach:
   1. *H. W. Pfennig (4F)
   2. *Rev. William J. Hanson (3G)
   3. *Patricia J. Hardwick (7F)
   4. *Theatrice Williams (3G)
Nominated by the Division for Church in Society:
   5. *Rev. Donald M. Hallberg (5A)

Nominated by the Budget and Finance Committee of the Church Council:

6. *Gail L. Mathews (5A)
7. *Tulia Hamilton (4B)
8. *David E. Johnson (3H)
9. *Raymond S. Caughman (9C)
10. *Rev. John O. Knudson (2C)
11. *Frank R. Jennings (1B)

---

* Incumbent

ELCA Pension and Other Benefits Program (continued)

5. South Africa-Related Matters

Background: The 1987 ELCA Constituting Convention and the 1989 Churchwide Assembly called for divestment of all Board of Pensions' investments in companies doing business with South Africa (CA89.6.26). After consultation with the Board of Pensions and other churchwide units, the Church Council voted in April 1990 to create ELCA South Africa Free Funds (equity, bond and balanced). These funds have no holdings in companies doing business directly in South Africa nor in those strategic companies doing business indirectly in that country. Recognizing the desirability of individuals sharing in investment choices, the Board of Pensions continued to maintain the following additional funds:

ELCA Alternative Funds (what had been the ELCA equity, bond and balanced funds). These funds have been managed under the divestment policy established by the Board of Pensions, with information on these funds being provided to the Church Council. At its April 1990 meeting, the Church Council acknowledged that funds managed under the present policy would likely not become fully South Africa free.

ELCA Social Purpose Funds (equity, bond and balanced) (CC90.4.15). As authorized by the Church Council, the council's Executive Committee received and adopted plan documents to implement these changes in the ELCA Pension and Other Benefits Program, which were prepared by the Board of Pensions.

Since that time, the situation in South Africa has changed radically. Multi-racial elections are scheduled for April 1994. The South African Council of Churches has called for an end to international economic sanctions against South Africa, and pension plans of other denominations, as well as state and local governments, have dropped their South Africa investment screens. Consultation among staff of the Division for Church in Society, Division for Global Missions, and Board of Pensions has continued as conditions have changed in South Africa.

During fall 1993, the boards of the three units that carry out responsibilities related to South Africa took separate actions relating to the changed environment in that country.

At its September 30-October 3, 1993, meeting, the board of the Division for Church in Society took action to recommend that:

1. the bishop of this church convey to the South African Council of Churches the commitment of the ELCA to advocate for the use of the "Code of Conduct for Business Operating in South Africa";
2. the Church Council of the ELCA call for all American-based companies doing business in South Africa to endorse this code of conduct and so communicate this action to those companies

with which the ELCA or its related organizations have investments;
3. the Church Council request the Board of Pensions, the Division for Church in Society, and the Division for Global Mission to collaborate together in a discussion about the changing situation in South Africa, particularly as it relates to corporate social responsibility, and return to the Church Council with a report and recommendations on how this church, through the Division for Church in Society, the Board of Pensions, and other appropriate units:
   a) will respond to the situation in South Africa regarding just economic development; and
   b) will provide opportunities for members of this church to participate in the growth of democracy and economic stability in South Africa;
4. and further, that the board of the Division for Church in Society indicates to the Church Council its interest and willingness to work with the Board of Pensions and Division for Global Mission in the implementation of these recommendations.

The Advisory Committee on the Church's Social Responsibility, which met subsequent to the division's board meeting by conference call, indicated its intent to consider the development of a screen for positive reinvestment in South Africa. Following consideration by the Church Council, this screen would be recommended to the Board of Pensions for possible application to the Social Purpose Fund. The Board of Pensions at its October 16, 1993, meeting authorized its executive committee to act as circumstances developed, after appropriate consultation.

The board of the Division for Global Mission took the following action at its October 28-30, 1993, meeting:

That the board of the Division for Global Mission of the Evangelical Lutheran Church in America, while recognizing the ongoing struggle to resolve conflicts in South Africa:

Celebrates that significant change toward democratic rule has taken place in South Africa with the creation of a Transition Executive Council;

Acknowledges the call to cease economic isolation of South Africa made by the churches and the democratic movement in South Africa;

Stands in continued solidarity with the people of South Africa who are engaged in the process of building a just and democratic society;

Calls for the suspension of sanctions and the cessation of other economic actions to isolate South Africa;

Urges investors to invest in South Africa in a responsible way by observing the South African Council of Churches' "Code of Business Conduct"; and

Works together with the Division for Church in Society and the Board of Pensions of the ELCA and urges the Church Council to take appropriate steps in the implementation of these recommendations.

The actions taken by the executive committee of the Board of Pensions at its November 12, 1993, meeting were described in council agenda Exhibit J, Part 6b. Specifically, the Board of Pensions has:

1. eliminated the South Africa criteria from the Social Purpose funds for the ELCA Regular Pension Plan and the ELCA Master Institutional Regular Pension Plan; and acknowledged that it will continue to receive advice from the Advisory Committee on the Church's Corporate Social Responsibility regarding the development and/or modification of social criteria for the Social Purpose funds.

2. eliminated the April 5, 1991, policy statement of the Board of Pensions (council agenda Exhibit J, Part 6d, p. 8). The board will continue to inform all plan members of their opportunities to transfer accumulations among the South Africa Free, Social Purpose, and Alternative funds; it will manage as directed the investment of various funds belonging to other units of the church; and it will continue to receive advice from the Advisory Committee on the Church's Corporate Social Responsibility on shareholder resolutions relating to South Africa and other social issues.

3. recommended adoption by the ELCA Church Council of proposed amendments to the ELCA Regular Pension Plan which would
   a. allow pensioners to transfer their assets out of the South Africa Free funds; and
   b. eliminate the South Africa Free funds if the aggregate value of those funds falls below $20 million.

Council Action: The Church Council adopted the following recommendation without discussion:

VOTED: CC93.12.79
   To celebrate that significant change toward democratic rule that has taken place in South Africa with the creation of a Transition Executive Council, while recognizing the ongoing struggle to resolve conflicts in South Africa;

   To acknowledge the call to cease economic isolation of South Africa made by the churches and the democratic movement in South Africa;

   To stand in continued solidarity with the people of South Africa and the South African Council of Churches who are engaged in the process of building a just and democratic society;

   To urge investors to invest in South Africa in a responsible way by observing the South African Council of Churches' "Code of Business Conduct."
                           † † †
   To express appreciation for the action taken by the Board of Pensions . . .; and

   To adopt the amendments to the ELCA Regular Pension Plan . . ., which would:
   ● **allow pensioners to transfer their assets out of the South Africa Free funds; and**
   ● **provide for the elimination of the South Africa Free funds if the aggregate value of those funds falls below $20 million.**
                           † † †
   To encourage the Board of Pensions, the Division for Global Mission, and the Division for Church in Society to continue discussion through normal staff channels on:
   1. **issues relating to the continuation of the South Africa Free Funds;**
   2. **the possible development of a screen for the Social Purpose Fund that would provide for investment in companies operating under the**

"Code of Conduct" designed by the South African Council of Churches (in consultation with the Advisory Committee on the Church's Social Responsibility); and
3. **matters relating to shareholder resolutions, within the context of this church's corporate social responsibility;**
and

   To request that a report and any appropriate recommendations be brought to the April 1994 meeting of the Church Council.

Social Teaching Statement on the Church and Human Sexuality (continued)

Deliberations resumed for perfecting the main motion. Discussion related to the substitute motion previously offered by Lorraine G. Bergquist continues below.

The Rev. James G. Cobb sought to move the following:

MOVED: To delete from the main motion the entire section that deals with a consultation panel (paragraphs 12-14).

The motion died for lack of a second.

The Rev. John O. Knudson thanked staff for including in the recommendation his concern in the sixth paragraph regarding assuring this church's membership that the development process would proceed carefully.

There being no further suggestions for perfection of the main motion, consideration of the substitute motion resumed. Loren W. Mathre spoke in favor of the substitute. ". . . I am concerned about our church and about where we are going. I am concerned about the impression we leave as we do things. . . . I think that in any event, no matter what we do, we are going to have people upset with us. . . ." He observed that the draft deviates from traditional Lutheran thought and stated that he would rather receive the document and process as a learning and teaching experience than as a potential social statement.

MOVED;
SECONDED;   *YES–7; No–25*
DEFEATED: To substitute the following for the main motion:

   That the Church Council declare the work of the task force responsible for the development of the social statement, "The Church and Human Sexuality: A Lutheran Perspective," to be ended; and

   That the social statement, "The Church and Human Sexuality: A Lutheran Perspective," not come before the 1995 Churchwide Assembly; and

   That a study committee be established to receive responses from members and congregations of the Evangelical Lutheran Church in America, faculties of the ELCA theological seminaries as well as other theologians within this church, and additional interested parties. This study committee shall consist of two parish pastors of the Evangelical Lutheran Church in America, two seminary professors named by the joint seminary presidents, two bishops named by the Conference of Bishops, two persons named by the Division for Church in Society, and three persons named by the Church Council. Staffing for the Study Committee shall be provided by the Division for Church in Society in consultation with the Office of the Bishop; and

That the study committee be charged to articulate faithfully and clearly the mind of the church as faithful people of God; consider seriously the social statements of the predecessor church bodies, the LCA "Sex, Marriage, and Family" (1970) and the ALC "Human Sexuality and Sexual Behavior" (1980), as well as the paragraph on page 13 of "Vision and Expectations: Ordained Ministers in the Evangelical Lutheran Church in America" regarding sexual conduct, and the work of the task force on the draft of the social statement, "The CHurch and Human Sexuality: A Lutheran Perspective"; and

That the study committee produce a report that will be provided to congregations and rostered persons, synods, and the churchwide organization of the Evangelical Lutheran Church in America. The report from the study committee will be received by the Church Council at its March 31-April 2, 1995, meeting and will be reported to the 1995 Churchwide Assembly as information.

Loren W. Mathre requested that his name be recorded in these minutes as voting in favor of the substitute motion. Ms. Bergquist called for division of the house. The vote tally was *Yes–7; No–25.*

The Rev. William G. Rusch, director of the Department for Ecumenical Affairs, suggested that the word, "confessional," replace the word, "doctrinal," in the final paragraph. Chair Magnus indicated that the suggestion would be received by consensus as an editorial emendation.

VOTED: CC93.12.80A.

A.   To acknowledge the strong reaction and widespread concern expressed by numerous members and congregations throughout the Evangelical Lutheran Church in America in response to the content and manner of release of the first draft of a possible "Social Statement on the Church and Human Sexuality–a Lutheran Perspective";

B.   To recognize, at the same time, those throughout this church who have voiced appreciation for the preparation of this first draft and the hope that the process will proceed for development of a subsequent draft and possible proposal of a social statement on human sexuality for a future Churchwide Assembly;

C.   To underscore that the current version of the statement is, indeed, a first draft (and not official policy of the Evangelical Lutheran Church in America) and as a first draft is subject to continued study and comment by members, congregations, faculties, and institutions throughout the church, with such responses to inform the process for revisions for any subsequent draft;

D.   To affirm continuation of the process for preparation of study materials and the development of a social statement on human sexuality, which may be presented for action at a future Churchwide Assembly, emphasizing that such work shall be in keeping with the doctrinal acknowledgement of and confession by this church of the Triune God (ELCA constitutional provision 2.01.), of "Jesus Christ as Lord and Savior and the Gospel as the power of God for the salvation of all who believe" (2.02.), of "Jesus Christ [as] the Word of God incarnate" (2.02.a.), of the "proclamation of God's message to us as both Law and Gospel" (2.02.b.), and "of the Old and New Testaments as the inspired Word of God and the authoritative source and norm of its proclamation, faith, and life" (2.03.);

E.   To express gratitude to members and congregations of this church who have conveyed their concerns and convictions in this matter and especially to those who have recommended specific changes in the first draft to assist in the process of revision;

F.   To indicate the conviction that the Church Council would recommend to a future Churchwide Assembly only such a draft of a social statement on human sexuality that would stand on biblical foundations and the confessional tradition of this church and that would merit the study, consideration, thoughtful reflection, and widespread support within this church;

G.   To acknowledge that the broad interest and intense reactions to the first draft represent a strategic opportunity for study, reflection, and thought on how we as Lutherans read and embrace Scripture and how members of this church understand and respond to issues and concerns related to sexuality in communities and society;

H.   To indicate the conviction that the process for development of a possible social statement on human sexuality will require significant modifications in order for the process to be widely trusted and accepted throughout this church and in order to assure that responses will be respected and employed in the preparation of a subsequent draft;

I.   To acknowledge strong signs that trust in the current task force has been impaired and yet to indicate that, in view of the lengthy study, preparation, and dedicated work of the members of the task force to date, it is deemed unwise at this time to direct the board of the Division for Church in Society to disband the current task force;

J. To respond to the executive committee of the board of the Division for Church in Society with appreciation for the general direction reflected in the revised proposal for the process of study, revision, and development of a social statement (as shown in council agenda Exhibit P, Part 1d);

K. To affirm the need for greater participation of leadership groups of various perspectives in the development process for enhanced trust and partnership in the development of possible subsequent drafts;

L. To determine that the present process will be supplemented by the selection of a consulting panel to widen the circle of persons officially engaged in the preparation of a revised draft, with such a consulting panel:

1. to be mutually accountable to the board of the Division for Church in Society and to the Church Council;

2. to be expected to provide regular reports directly to the board, the Church Council, and Conference of Bishops of the panel's work with appropriate staff and the task force; and

3. to be composed of 11 persons appointed by the Church Council, including:

   a. three ELCA seminary faculty members, named by the Church Council upon recommendation of the presidents of ELCA seminaries;

   b. three pastors of ELCA congregations, named by the Church Council;

   c. two lay members of ELCA congregations, named by the Church Council;

   d. two members of the Conference of Bishops, named by the Conference of Bishops; and

   e. one member of the Church Council, named by the Church Council; and

M. To direct that this consultating panel shall have access to all materials received from members, congregations, and others in response to the study document, "Human Sexuality and the Christian Faith" (1991), and the first draft, "The Church and Human Sexuality–a Lutheran Perspective" (1993), shall be charged to give advice and counsel related to the opinions within the church, and shall provide advice, counsel, and critique–including the ways in which Scripture is used–in the development of any subsequent drafts;

N. To affirm the plan of the executive committee of the board of the Division for Church in Society for appointment of a staff team, under the supervision of the executive director of the Division for Church in Society, to carry out re-

sponsibilities with the task force and consulting panel for development of any subsequent drafts;

O. To express appreciation for the development of a plan for recording and providing both statistical and narrative summaries of responses received to the first draft, which shall be reported periodically to the Conference of Bishops and the Church Council; and

P. To urge renewed commitment to mutual conversation, correction, and consolation among and between sisters and brothers in Christ within the Evangelical Lutheran Church in America, remembering that members of this church are united through Christ and are bound together by our primary convictions grounded in Scripture, the creeds of the church, the Augsburg Confession, and the other confessional writings of the Lutheran Reformation.

Chair Magnus recognized the Rev. Richard G. Deines who introduced a motion related to homosexuality and the study on human sexuality. He encouraged the Church Council to consider the matter in a posture of mutual confession (WHEREAS paragraph four). He recommended that the council discuss this matter at a future meeting. Pastor Deines asked that the Church Council not act upon, but rather consider the following motion, which the Church Council received as information.

WHEREAS, the release of the draft statement on Human Sexuality has "gotten the attention" of many inside and outside the ELCA; and

WHEREAS, this wake-up call provides the ELCA with a unique opportunity for mutual sharing and consolation and teaching about central dimensions of being human and children of God; and

WHEREAS, human sexuality has been and will continue to be an understandably difficult part of our lives to discuss; and

WHEREAS, confession that we are all in this together is basic to moving ahead; and

WHEREAS, learning from one another's journey regarding how we have been taught and not taught about sexuality s a place where we can being the conversation without judgement; and

WHEREAS, homosexuality appears to be currently the dimension of human sexuality which is most difficult for us to deal with; and

WHEREAS, the purpose of the Statement on Human Sexuality is to engage us in examination and discussion of those realities; and

WHEREAS, the leadership of the ELCA, lay and clergy, all involved in local congregations including ELCA church council members; synod, regional, and national staff; the boards and commissions of the churchwide organization, the Conference of Bishops, the colleges and seminaries and the institutions of this church, can demonstrate leadership in this area; and

WHEREAS, depth discussion of these concerns and sharing from our own experience is more important to the future of the ELCA than meeting a timeline; and

WHEREAS, trust among the various parts of the ELCA community needs great attention and strengthening; and

WHEREAS, homosexuality as a human phenomenon will not disappear, but that persons who are homosexual are members of many if not most congregations and groups in our church, including this Church Council, churchwide staff, and the Conference of Bishops; and

WHEREAS, many if not most members of the ELCA knowingly or not live in home, work, and community settings with persons who are homosexual; and

WHEREAS, basic to all of this discussion from the perspective of the ELCA is the Jesus Christ event and the biblical theology, tradition, and living experience which flows from that happening; now, therefore, be it resolved:

1) That the Church Council communicate to the ELCA that conversations regarding human sexuality need to take place at every level of the ELCA;

2) That these conversations be guided by respect for one another's opinions with the church community, in every expression, becoming safe places for these conversations;

3) That the Church Council identify a process for these conversations to begin with the Church Council itself; (such resources could include the ELCA educational course, "Can We Talk About This?"; suggestion: The Church Council could set aside time at the next meeting to begin this process, perhaps committing ourselves to initiate this in our own congregations with at least one small group.)

4) That every effort be made so that every synod can provide sensitive, quality group leaders to congregations choosing to train their own leaders for these conversations in their local settings (perhaps a few synods are ready to model these conversations beginning with their own discussions at 1994 synod assemblies or other events currently being planned);

5) That the Church Council adopt option #6 as presented by Bishop Chilstrom along with the modifications proposed by the Rev. Charles S. Miller Jr., as a way of continuing to develop a Social Statement alongside the conversation going on across this whole church;

6) That the Church Council emphasize the importance of Bible study and Biblical theology centered in the Jesus Christ event as the basis for our struggle as the church and encourage development of Bible study groups across this church, utilizing quality materials similar to the "Word and Witness" program;

7) That this emphasis on Bible study, however, not obscure nor replace the churchwide conversations on this issues of sexuality in our own lives and those raised by the Statement on Human Sexuality;

8) That recognition of the possible presence of "closet homosexuals" in every church meeting be acknowledged and that persons who are open about their homosexuality be included in these proposed conversations whenever possible;

9) That all groups across the ELCA who are working on the content of the statement be encouraged to submit their findings to the task force and that they also be encouraged to participate in the processes designed to deal with personal and social dimensions of sexuality.

"I offer this as an encouragement for the possibility of creative and effective dialogue in strengthening the witness of our ELCA community," he stated.

Loren W. Mathre commented on the video produced to introduce the draft of the proposed social statement on human sexuality. He raised concern about the interpretation of Scripture evidenced in the video. The Rev. Charles S. Miller Jr., executive director of the Division for Church in Society, responded and indicated that there had been an intentional attempt to express and achieve diversity of opinion and balance in the video. Bishop Chilstrom noted that he had agreed to participate in the video, because it dealt with real individuals and balanced discussion. The Rev. Eric C. Shafer, director of the Department for Communication, subsequently observed that the video had been filmed one year prior to distribution of the initial draft of the social statement, and did not treat directly the text of the statement. The video was made available as an educational resource to facilitate discussion of human sexuality, he said.

Bishop Paul R. Swanson encouraged that the foregoing action of the Church Council be transmitted to synodical offices immediately. Discussion regarding the process for distribution of the council's action throughout this church and to the media ensued. Chair Magnus requested staff of the Department for Communication to report on Sunday, December 5, plans for release of the council's action. Secretary Lowell G. Almen indicated that all synodical offices would be notified by telefax or express mail prior to Tuesday, December 7.

Edith M. Lohr inquired when the council might discuss the text of the draft document. Chair Magnus indicated that a plan would be determined later during this council meeting.

William E. Diehl inquired about the continuing composition of the task force. Pastor Miller indicated that it was his understanding that the task force would continue as constituted. He observed that one or two resignations might be expected. Lorraine G. Bergquist inquired whether those persons would be replaced. Pastor Miller replied that the board of the Division for Church in Society had not yet discussed the matter, but that replacement was not expected.

Nominations and Elections (continued)

1. Nominating Ballot for Executive Committee of Church Council

Chair Magnus announced that the following persons had been elected to serve on the Executive Committee of the Church Council.

VOTED: *CC93.12.81*

To elect the following persons to the Executive Committee of the Church Council for the 1994-1995 biennium:

Lay Female:	Lorraine G. Bergquist
	Deborah S. Yandala
Lay Male:	William E. Diehl
Lay Male (*Person of Color or Language Other than English*):	Carlos Peña
Clergy:	Rev. Stephen M. Youngdahl
	Rev. John O. Knudson
	Rev. Franklin D. Fry

Following several announcements, the Church Council recessed for the day at 6:08 P.M.

Vice President Kathy J. Magnus called Plenary Session III to order at 8:53 A.M., Sunday morning, December 5, 1993. The session was preceded by worship held in the chapel of the Lutheran Center with the Rev. Lowell G. Almen, presiding, the Rev. James G. Cobb, preaching, and Ms. Terry L. Bowes, lector.

Approval of Minutes

Background: The minutes of the March 27-29, 1993, and August 24-25, 1993, meetings of the Church Council had been distributed to the members of the Church Council. The minutes of the October 13, 1993, and November 22, 1993, meetings of the council's Executive Committee have been distributed to council members.

Council Action: Secretary Lowell G. Almen indicated that the following corrections would be made to the protocol copy of the minutes of the council's March 27-29, 1993, meeting: On page 92, the last sentence is to be deleted and replaced with the following: *Chair Magnus declared the motion carried. Subsequently there was as request for a vote by show of hands. On this vote the motion was defeated.*

Chair Magnus inquired whether there were additional emendations. Secretary Almen indicated that the protocol copy of the minutes of the November 22, 1993, meeting of the council's Executive Committee also would be amended to reflect the following correction: On page 16 in the second full paragraph, amend the first phrase of the second line to read: *. . . the current task force be*

dismissed and another group or committee appointed; in addition, four lines from the bottom, replace the word, "process," with the word, "situation."

VOTED: *CC93.12.82*

To approve the minutes of the March 27-29, 1993, and August 24-25, 1993, meetings of the Church Council as corrected; and

To ratify actions of the Executive Committee of the Church Council as indicated in the minutes of the October 13, and November 22, 1993, meetings.

Referrals from 1993 Churchwide Assembly Directed to the Church Council

10. Representational Principles and

11. Voting Membership

Background: REPRESENTATIONAL PRINCIPLES– The following synods adopted memorials related to the ELCA's representational principles at their synod assemblies:

1. Southeastern Texas-Southern Louisiana Synod (4F) [1993 Memorial]

WHEREAS, we believe that discrimination on the basis of race, gender, and ethnic background is always sinful and without justification; and that its price can never be justified by some other cause; and, most importantly, that God has called as to a kingdom in which all persons have standing on the one ground of the grace and call of God in Christ Jesus our Lord, and that God requires us to deal with each other on that basis now; and

WHEREAS, we judge that the Evangelical Lutheran Church in America is very badly served by those constitutional, structural, procedural, and ideological statements, which together establish the so-called "quota system" of racial, gender, and ethnic preference in selection, appointment, and representation of personnel; therefore, be it

RESOLVED, that the Southeastern Texas-Southern Louisiana Synod call upon the Evangelical Lutheran Church in America by memorial at its next assembly:

1. To take all action to end every requirement, process, and record intended or used to give preference in selection, appointment, and representation of persons for any position in the church on the basis of the person's race, gender, or ethnic group or background;

2. To give clear comprehensive expression to the New Testament vision of the kingdom and community of Christ as one in which there is no recognition given to distinctions between people on the basis of their race, gender, or ethnic background; as a community in which preference and prejudgment on the basis of such groupings is condemned as sin; and as one in which there is one head, Jesus Christ the Lord, and all stand before him with one justification, his grace and call alone; and

3. To seek for leaders as widely as possible, among all the diversity of persons whom God calls to the church, for those individuals upon whom the gifts of the Holy Spirit have been lavished, especially where those gifts may have come through life situation and experience unusual among the membership and the leadership at the time; and be it further

RESOLVED, that the Southeastern Texas-Southern Louisiana Synod take all actions necessary:

1. To make the changes in its constitution, rules of procedure, and official statements and practice, which will end the preference, selection, and appointment of persons on the basis of their race,

gender, or ethnic background and origin for any position or task in the synod; and

2. To give clear and deliberate expression of its opposition to any such preference and prejudice on the part of any representative of the synod; and be it further

RESOLVED, that the congregations and rostered leaders of the Southeastern Texas-Southern Louisiana Synod:

1. Be clearly informed that it is the judgment of the synod gathered in assembly that discrimination on the basis of race, gender, or ethnic background in the selection or call of employees and ordained persons, in the election or appointment of parish leaders, and in representatives of the congregation in extra-congregational bodies, is wrong and unacceptable;

2. Be urged by this action and by the synod officers and staff to act to make all changes necessary in constitutions, rules of procedure, and custom to end the practice of racial, gender, or ethnic discrimination wherever it exists in the life of congregations; and

3. Be urged (and assisted, if necessary) by the synod officers and staff to proclaim and teach the sinfulness of race, gender, and ethnic prejudice; and to call and instruct members to the New Testament vision of a single community in Christ wherein there is no longer "Jew or Greek, slave or free, male or female," wherein individuals are to be valued precisely at the point of their uniqueness.

2. Central/Southern Illinois Synod (5C) [1992 Memorial]

WHEREAS, in the 1960s and 1970s the Civil Rights Movement swept across the United States of America; and

WHEREAS, during this time biblical scholars, systematic theologians, and Christian ethicists proclaimed to the Church that to exclude or to give preferential treatment to people on the basis of their race, ethnic background, or primary language was contrary to the will of God; and

WHEREAS, since that time the vast majority of Lutherans have been convinced by the thinking of these Biblical scholars, systematic theologians, and Christian ethicists that to exclude or to give preferential treatment to people on the basis of their race, ethnic background, or primary language is contrary to the will of God; and

WHEREAS, the Evangelical Lutheran Church in America has adopted policies, which seem to be contrary to the above stated position, and which actually give preferential treatment to people on the basis of their race, ethnic background, or primary language; and

WHEREAS, these policies of the Evangelical Lutheran Church in America have not been supported by new evidence from biblical scholars, systematic theologians, or Christian ethicists; and

WHEREAS, these policies are causing confusion among the members of the Evangelical Lutheran Church in America; therefore, be it

RESOLVED, that the Central/Southern Illinois Synod in assembly memorialize the Evangelical Lutheran Church in America to establish a task force of Biblical scholars, systematic theologians, and Christian ethicists to study this policy, which is expressed in the constitution of the Evangelical Lutheran Church in America, articles 5.01.f. and 5.01.g., this task force to be established by January 1, 1994; and be it further

RESOLVED, that this task force report its findings to the Church Council of the Evangelical Lutheran Church in America by January 1, 1995, with the findings to be immediately sent to the congregations of the Evangelical Lutheran Church in America.

3. Metropolitan New York Synod (7C) [1992 Memorial]

RESOLVED, that the Metropolitan New York Synod memorialize the Evangelical Lutheran Church in America to examine the governing documents of this church and that the churchwide agencies, synods and congregations remove all quotas for baptized and confirmed Lutherans so as to affirm what St. Paul said, "So there is no difference between Jews and Greeks, between slaves and free men, between men and women; you are all one in union with Christ Jesus" (Galatians 3:28 [TEV]).

4. Southwestern Pennsylvania Synod (8B) [1993 Memorial]

WHEREAS, we wish to encourage the active participation of all who have gifts and willingness to serve Christ's Church; therefore, be it

RESOLVED, that the Southwestern Pennsylvania Synod memorialize the Evangelical Lutheran Church in America to repeal the present quota system in place.

The Memorials Committee shared the following background information with the Churchwide Assembly:

In formulating the governing documents of the Evangelical Lutheran Church in America, the Commission for a New Lutheran Church recommended that the uniting churches freely undertake the obligation of certain representational principles, beyond those that had been followed previously. Predecessor church bodies allocated percentages of representation for lay persons and for ordained ministers.

The uniting churches approved principles to provide for 60 percent of the voting members of assemblies, councils, boards, and committees of the Evangelical Lutheran Church in America to be lay persons, 50 percent of whom shall be female and 50 percent of whom shall be male. The remaining 40 percent are to be ordained ministers. At least 10 percent of the voting members of such assemblies, councils, boards, and committees are to be persons of color or persons whose primary language is other than English.

The Church is defined as "the assembly of all believers among whom the Gospel is preached in its purity and the holy sacraments are administered according to the Gospel" (Augsburg Confession, Article VII). Further, "it is sufficient for the true unity of the Christian Church that the Gospel be preached in conformity with a pure understanding of it and that the sacraments be administered in accordance with the divine Word" (AC VII).

The Church, however, is not only under the Gospel as the community of believers who are spiritually bound together in the mystical body of Christ. The Church also exists as a human community, seeking to operate in decency and good order as a humanly shaped organization. Within this human community, laws, rules, regulations, policies, and procedures are adopted by this church and followed for the operation of this church as an organization.

As a self-imposed discipline in the practice of inclusive representation, the principles of organization commit this church to ensure in governing bodies that more than half of the voting members (at least 60 percent) shall be lay and shall include both women and men; that the ordained ministers, whenever possible, shall include both men and women; and that 10 percent shall be persons of color or persons whose primary language is other than English.

The memorial of the Central/Southern Illinois Synod calls for appointment of a task force to study this policy. Any such task force would have significant implications for the budget of the churchwide organization.

The memorials from the Southeastern Texas-Southern Louisiana Synod and the Southwestern Pennsylvania Synod requests the removal of all "quotas" for baptized and confirmed Lutherans. This would change the representational principles as required in the ELCA constitutions.

Acting upon the recommendation of the Memorials Committee, which revised its initial recommendation following conversation with voting members, the 1993 Churchwide Assembly voted:

To refer the memorials of the Southeastern Texas-Southern Louisiana Synod, Central/Southern Illinois Synod, Metropolitan New York Synod, and the Southwestern Pennsylvania Synod, to the Church Council;

To instruct the Church Council, in consultation with the Conference of Bishops, to establish a process for reflection by the Church Council, Conference of Bishops, Commission for Women, Commission for Multicultural Ministries, and seminary faculties, and to report any recommendations to the 1995 Churchwide Assembly.

VOTING MEMBERSHIP–The following synods adopted memorials related to the ELCA's representational principles at their synodical assemblies:

1. Southwestern Washington Synod (1C) [1992 Memorial]

WHEREAS, the Southwestern Washington Synod affirms the intent and spirit of section 5.01.g. of the ELCA constitution, which provides that "as nearly as possible" lay membership of the Synod Assembly shall be 50 percent female and 50 percent male; and

WHEREAS, section †S6.04. of the Southwestern Washington Synod Constitution directs the Synod Council to establish a process to ensure that "as nearly as possible" lay membership of the Synod Assembly shall be 50 percent female and 50 percent male; and

WHEREAS, section †S7.21. of the Southwestern Washington Synod Constitution requires each congregation to elect one male and one female voting member to the Synod Assembly; and

WHEREAS, from time to time, it is not possible for congregations to select one female and one male voting member causing said congregations to violate section †S7.21., or be unrepresented, while at the same time, the Southwestern Washington Synod would be in compliance with Section †S6.04., which insures that the Synod Assembly as a whole will have balanced representation; and

WHEREAS, to resolve the conflict between Section †S6.04. and †S7.21., of the Southwestern Washington Synod Constitution, the ELCA bylaws, and the ELCA Model Constitution for Synods will have to be amended; therefore, be it

RESOLVED, that the Southwestern Washington Synod memorialize the Evangelical Lutheran Church in America to amend section 10.41.01.c. of the ELCA bylaws and section †S7.21.c. of the Model Constitution for Synods by:
1. striking the words "of whom" in both places where it appears in the first sentence thereof; and
2. adding the words, "and, whenever possible," after the word "synod" and before the word "one" in the first sentence thereof.

2. East-Central Synod of Wisconsin (5I) [1993 Memorial]

WHEREAS, the constitution of the Evangelical Lutheran Church in America now requires that lay voting members selected to represent their congregations at the Synod Assembly must be equally divided on the basis of gender, one male and one female (S7.21.c.); and

WHEREAS, it is sometimes difficult for congregations to find members who are willing or able to serve as their voting members to the Synod Assembly, and to fulfill this constitutional requirement that their representation must be equally divided on the basis of gender; and

WHEREAS, rather than have a congregation denied the number of voting members it is allowed on the basis of its membership size because of this constitutional requirement; and

WHEREAS, our Lutheran tradition has always been strong in its focus on the freedom we have under the Gospel, and congregations ought to be allowed that same freedom in selecting their Synod Assembly voting members; and

WHEREAS, that freedom under the Gospel could be better exercised by encouraging gender diversity as a guideline rather than an inflexible constitutional requirement; therefore, be it

RESOLVED, that the East-Central Synod of Wisconsin of the Evangelical Lutheran Church in America memorialize the next Churchwide Assembly of the Evangelical Lutheran Church in America to amend the language of the ELCA Constitution for Synods so that gender diversity in congregational representation at

the Synod Assembly is encouraged as a guideline rather than be mandated as a requirement.

3. Northeastern Ohio Synod (6E) [1993 Memorial]

WHEREAS, the constitution of the Evangelical Lutheran Church in America, under "Principles of Organization" (5.01.f.), states "that as nearly as possible, 50 percent of the lay members of their assemblies . . . shall be female and 50 percent shall be male"; and

WHEREAS, some congregations from time to time are legitimately unable to meet this rule and should not be disenfranchised because of such a circumstance; therefore, be it

RESOLVED, that the Northeastern Ohio Synod memorialize the Evangelical Lutheran Church in America to amend bylaw 10.41.01.c., to read: "A minimum of two lay members elected by each congregation related to the synod, one of whom shall be male and one of whom shall be female, shall be voting members and, as nearly as possible, said members shall be one male and one female. The Synod Council shall establish a formula to provide additional lay representation from congregations on the basis of the number of baptized members in the congregation. Additional members from each congregation shall be equally divided between male and female except that the odd numbered member, if any, may be either male or female, as far as possible. Congregations unable to meet this requirement shall submit in writing a request for representative seating to the Credentials Committee of the Synod Assembly."

4. Upstate New York Synod (7D) [1993 Memorial]

WHEREAS, the Church Council of Abiding Savior Lutheran Church affirms resolve of Section 5.01.g. of the ELCA constitution, which provides that "as nearly as possible" 50 percent of the lay members of the synod assemblies (councils, committees, boards or other organizational units) shall be female and 50 percent shall be male; and

WHEREAS, Section S6.04. of the Upstate New York Synod Constitution requires the Synod Council to establish a process to see that, "as nearly as possible, 50 percent of the lay members of the assemblies (councils, committees, boards, or other organizational units) shall be female and 50 percent shall be male"; and

WHEREAS, Section S7.21.c. of the Upstate New York Synod Constitution stipulates that "a minimum of two lay members elected by each congregation related to the synod, one of whom shall be male and one of whom shall be female, shall be voting members" at the Synod Assembly; and

WHEREAS, occasionally it is not possible for small congregations to elect one female and one male delegate, thus denying them full representation; therefore, be it

RESOLVED, that the Upstate New York Synod memorialize the Evangelical Lutheran Church in America to amend Section 10.41.01.c. for the ELCA Bylaws and Section S7.21.c. of the Model Constitution for Synods, by adding the words, "except that congregations of 300 or fewer baptized members may elect two delegates of the same gender if equal female and male representation is not possible" after the words "shall be voting members" in the first sentence thereof.

5. Northeastern Pennsylvania Synod (7E) [1992 Memorial]

RESOLVED, that the Northeastern Pennsylvania Synod memorialize the 1993 Churchwide Assembly of the Evangelical Lutheran Church in America to amend Section †S7.21.c. of the Constitution for Synods by adding the sentence, "except that if equal male and female representation is not possible, a congregation with 150 confirmed members or fewer may elect two delegates of the same gender."

6. Northwestern Pennsylvania Synod (8A) [1993 Memorial]

WHEREAS, the current ELCA practice of requiring one male and one female voting member at synod assemblies results in the underrepresentation of some congregations due to the inability to find appropriate voting members (usually male); and

WHEREAS, some congregations would be willing and able to bring two female voting members but are not permitted under ELCA policy; and

WHEREAS, the denial of seats to additional female voting members is discriminatory and unjust to both congregations seeking to be fully represented in assembly and to women who are willing to serve in these positions but are denied admission as voting members because of their gender; and

WHEREAS, the Scriptures instruct us that as a new creation in Christ there is neither male nor female, but all are one in Christ Jesus (Galatians 3:28) with the clear implication being that the Church should strive to be gender neutral; and

WHEREAS, the problem of being unable to have one voting member of each gender is especially acute among small members congregations who have fewer numbers of volunteers with disposable time from whom to draw; and

WHEREAS, the majority of these congregations tends to be in rural and urban areas where economic marginalization and the realities of work schedules make it more difficult for able men to have the free time necessary to attend the assemblies, the result being that the current ELCA policy discriminates not only on the basis of gender but also on the basis of income and class; and

WHEREAS, the current ELCA policy thus serves to further alienate and discriminate against a significant number of congregations within our church (small churches, average weekly worship attendance under 75), as well as blue-collar workers; and

WHEREAS, the reality is that assembly voting members tend to be disproportionately male since the majority of clergy remains male, which means that the current system, rather than increasing the proportion of women participating in assembly may, in fact, reduce the proportion of women participating in assemblies; and

WHEREAS, many synods have extended the privilege of vote in assembly to retired clergy, meaning that this inequity in the ratio of total male to female voting members has the potential to continue for many years to come; and

WHEREAS, seating additional female lay voting members in assembly would help equalize the ratio of male to female voting members since there are so many male clergy voting members; therefore, be it

RESOLVED, that the Northwestern Pennsylvania Synod memorialize the Evangelical Lutheran Church in America to amend its constitution and whatever other documents are necessary to eliminate any language, which requires congregations to have one male and one female voting member in synod assemblies, substituting instead language, which permits two voting members of either gender, with equal representation of men and women encouraged but not mandated.

7. Upper Susquehanna Synod (8E) [1993 Memorial]

WHEREAS, the constitution of our Evangelical Lutheran Church in America states that "this church accepts the canonical Scriptures of the Old and New Testaments as the inspired Word of God and the authoritative source and norm of its proclamation, faith, and life" (ELCA 2.03.); and

WHEREAS, the Holy Scriptures unequivocally state that "there is neither Jew nor Greek, there is neither slave nor free, there is neither male nor female; for you are all one in Christ Jesus" (Galatians 3:28); and again, "Here there cannot be Greek and Jew, circumcised and uncircumcised, barbarian, Scythian, slave, freeman, but Christ is all and in all" (Colossians 3:11); and in other places also teach us that the Body of Christ is not to be divided into separate and competing groups upon the distinctions of worldly society but is to be united in lowliness, meekness, patience and the unity of the Spirit and bond of peace (Ephesians 4:1-6); and

WHEREAS, the Holy Scriptures further teach us that individual participation in the structures and ministries of the Church should be based upon the gifts of the Spirit (Ephesians 4:11-16; 1 Corinthians 12:4-30) rather than upon participation in ethnic, linguistic, sexual, or any other accidental or sociological consideration; and

WHEREAS, we believe the recapturing of these truths among Lutherans in America is essential to the process of drawing an increasingly diverse leadership from an ever-widening number of races and cultural groups and from both sexes, a process in which our church has established a goal, a process, which can only be hindered by legalistically pitting one group within the church against another; therefore, be it

RESOLVED, that the Upper Susquehanna Synod holds that qualifications for office in the Evangelical Lutheran Church in America should be based upon discerned gifts of the Spirit and not upon arbitrary sociological and sexual considerations; and be it further

RESOLVED, that this synod hereby memorializes the Evangelical Lutheran Church in America to eliminate 5.01.f. and 5.01.g. from the ELCA Constitution, Bylaws, and Continuing Resolutions, and †S6.04. in the Model Constitution for Synods, those sections establishing and mandating gender-based and sociologically-based qualifications for office; and be it further

RESOLVED, that our synodical bishop appoint a person from the Upper Susquehanna Synod delegation to solicit the signatures of 25 voting members to the ELCA Churchwide Assembly from this and other synods (ELCA 22.11.b.) to properly bring this matter to the floor the ELCA Churchwide Assembly.

The Memorials Committee shared with the 1993 Churchwide Assembly the following background information about previous Churchwide Assembly consideration of this matter:

In response to similar memorials to the 1991 Churchwide Assembly, the following rationale was included in the assembly materials for information and background to the voting members:

> The representational principles articulated in Chapter 5 of the ELCA constitution were established by the ELCA Constituting Convention to help this church to implement its commitment to achieving participation by both lay and clergy, male and female, White persons, persons of color and persons whose primary language is other than English. These constitutional categories, and also required considerations relating to geography and synod/congregational membership, help shape the nominating patterns of this church. Taken together, these help this church to reach decisions on its life and work that are shaped by the perspectives of members with different experiences, expertise and perspectives.

> Considerable attention was devoted to this subject by the Commission for a New Lutheran Church. To ensure that the principles of organization of this church would be reflected in the makeup of synod assemblies, the commission proposed and the uniting churches adopted the provision that at least one woman and one man shall serve as lay voting members from each congregation for synod assemblies.

> In addition, similar provision was made for 50 percent women and 50 percent men in lay voting membership for the Churchwide Assembly. The need for inclusive composition for the boards and committees of this church and its synods also was underscored. Any change in these provision may alter, perhaps substantially, the balance in lay representation of women and men in synod assemblies.

> In its review of responsibilities and structures in the Evangelical Lutheran Church in America, undertaken through the "Focusing for Mission" process, the Church Council explicitly affirmed the principles of organization (Chapter 5) as serving the Evangelical Lutheran Church in

America well in its first years. The council declined to recommend any change in these principles–including the representational principle–at this time.

Amendments as proposed in these [1990 and 1991 synod] memorials would alter substantially the statement of this church's commitment to inclusive composition of assemblies, councils, boards, and committees, as specified in the principles of organization.

The 1991 Churchwide Assembly took the following action:

To express support for the guidelines for inclusive representation articulated in the governing documents of the Evangelical Lutheran Church in America; and

To transmit this minute as information to the Lower Susquehanna Synod, Upper Susquehanna Synod, Slovak Zion Synod, Virginia Synod, and Florida Synod (CA91.7.118).

Acting upon the recommendation of the Memorials Committee, which revised its recommendation following conversation with voting members, the 1993 Churchwide Assembly voted

To refer the memorials of the Southwestern Washington Synod, East-Central Synod of Wisconsin, Northeastern Ohio Synod, Upstate New York Synod, Northeastern Pennsylvania Synod, Northwestern Pennsylvania Synod, and Upper Susquehanna Synod, to the Church Council;

To instruct the Church Council, in consultation with the Conference of Bishops, to establish a process for reflection by the Church Council, Conference of Bishops, Commission for Women, Commission for Multicultural Ministries, and seminary faculties, and to report any recommendations to the 1995 Churchwide Assembly.

Council Action: Chair Magnus read the following recommendation, subsequently adopted by the Church Council, which, she noted, would serve as a response to the foregoing synodical memorials. During discussion, the Rev. Franklin D. Fry inquired whether with regard to this church's representational principles and nomination processes, the negative effects of caucusing ought to be addressed also, that is, "the politicizing that then results when we take actions that encourage people to be divided in the church."

VOTED: CC93.12.83

To instruct the Executive Committee of the Church Council, in consultation with the synodical bishops who serve as advisory members of the Church Council, to develop at the committee's January 1994 meeting a time line and process for reflection on the ELCA's representational principles;

To request that the Conference of Bishops, at its March 1994 meeting, provide advice to the Church Council on this proposed process;

To request that the Commission for Multicultural Ministries and the Commission for Women provide advice to the Church Council on this proposed process; and

To instruct the Executive Committee of the Church Council to bring to the April 1994 meeting of the Church Council a report on this effort and a recommendation for council action.

Resolutions from Synods Previously Referred to Churchwide Units

1.   Every-Home Plan for The Lutheran

Saint Paul Area Synod (3H) [1993]

Background: The following resolution of the Saint Paul Area Synod on an Every-Home Plan for *The Lutheran* was transmitted to the Executive Committee at its June 16, 1993, meeting:

WHEREAS, *The Lutheran* is the only direct communication piece between the churchwide expression of the Evangelical Lutheran Church in America and the individual members of the congregations; and

WHEREAS, *The Lutheran* is an excellent news magazine of church news; and

WHEREAS, the every home plan is the most economical communication tool available to the churchwide and synodical expressions of the Evangelical Lutheran Church in America; and

WHEREAS, 270,000 fewer ELCA households received *The Lutheran* in 1993 than in 1988 (1.2 million in 1988; 930,000 in 1993); and

WHEREAS, 40 percent of ELCA households currently do not receive *The Lutheran*; and

WHEREAS, ELCA and Augsburg Fortress Publishers' contributions to *The Lutheran* (approximately $280,000 each in 1993) have declined 50 percent in the last five years and substantial increases in their levels of contributions in the near future are uncertain; therefore, be it

RESOLVED, that the Saint Paul Area Synod of the Evangelical Lutheran Church in America petition the Evangelical Lutheran Church in America to develop a business plan for the Evangelical Lutheran Church in America to provide *The Lutheran* to all ELCA households which would be funded through increased advertising and grant revenues.

The Executive Committee voted:

To refer this resolution of the Saint Paul Area Synod on an Every-Home Plan for *The Lutheran* to *The Lutheran*, the Publishing House of the Evangelical Lutheran Church in America, and the Office of the Treasurer for a report to the December 1993 meeting of the Church Council (ECC93.6.14).

Response from *The Lutheran*:

The intent of the resolution is admirable and positive. It would boost circulation, help accomplish the magazine's purpose of binding the church together and could cut through some of the indifference to the Evangelical Lutheran Church in America which is present in some congregations. Unfortunately, it is not do-able. Sending *The Lutheran* to some 1.5 million households would cost about $8 million annually.

Advertising revenue to *The Lutheran* is increasing, totaling slightly less than $1 million in 1993. Even doubling advertising income is not realistic. Fraternal societies now give about $800,000 to the ELCA churchwide organization; seeking underwriting from them is not feasible.

With the continuing decline of ELCA mission support from congregations through synods, an increased grant from the Evangelical Lutheran Church in America to *The Lutheran* is not forthcoming. Synods might be asked to support their subscriptions, but this likely would defer funds from mission support.

The best response is to pledge to keep costs down, to enlist active support from bishops and pastors, and to move ahead with promotion aimed at preserving existing congregational subscriptions and enlisting congregations, thus increasing subscriptions as much as possible. New personnel, procedures and materials at Augsburg Fortress are helping such an effort move forward.

Council Action: Loren W. Mathre encouraged long-range consideration of the issue. J. David Ellwanger concurred and observed the benefits of communication and connection between congregational members with the churchwide organization. Lorraine G. Bergquist noted that her congregation had opted to eliminate the every-home plan rather than benevolences. Gary J. N. Aamodt, president of the ELCA publishing house, noted that over the past five years, subscriptions to *The Lutheran* have declined and continue to decline each month. He indicated that steps are being taken to address every aspect of the matter.

VOTED: *CC93.12.84*

To request the secretary of the ELCA to convey to the Saint Paul Area Synod the response of *The Lutheran* to the synod's resolution relating to the "Every-Home Plan."

2. Stewardship of Creation

Nebraska Synod (4A) [1992]

Background: The following resolution of the Nebraska Synod on the stewardship of creation was transmitted to the Church Council at its November 1992 meeting:

WHEREAS, human stewardship for God's creation is clearly commended in Scripture (e.g., Genesis 1:26-30, Leviticus 25:1-24); and

WHEREAS, there is an ancient Christian tradition of blessing of fields and prayers for harvest near the end of the Easter season, a tradition that in this country has developed into "Soil and Water Conservation Week" at the end of April and beginning of May; and

WHEREAS, the *Lutheran Book of Worship* provides propers for "Stewardship of Creation'" and

WHEREAS, the first "green" Sunday of Pentecost season seems a natural time to emphasize our stewardship of God's creation; therefore, be it

RESOLVED, that we encourage congregations of our synod to emphasize stewardship of creation on a definite Sunday each year, and to consider the Second Sunday after Pentecost for this purpose, and that we stress concern for environmental issues as part of the ongoing work of the church; and be it further

RESOLVED, that the Nebraska Synod memorialize the Evangelical Lutheran Church in America to establish a churchwide Stewardship of Creation Sunday.

The Church Council voted:

To refer this resolution of the Nebraska Synod on a Stewardship of Creation Sunday to the Division for Congregational Ministries (CC92.11.64).

In the meantime, the 1993 Churchwide Assembly conveyed the following information to the eight synods that had adopted memorials relating to this topic:

The matter of the care of the environment and creation has been addressed in several arenas recently. While many of the concerns in this regard are related to environment and conservation matters, others seem to relate to the agricultural cycle of planting and harvesting along with the need to distribute food resources on an equitable basis.

Traditionally in the Evangelical Lutheran Church in America and the predecessor churches, care of creation has been focused upon through a celebration of Rogation Sunday. Using the *Lutheran Book of Worship*, the Second Sunday after Pentecost has been observed as "Stewardship of Creation" Sunday in congregations. The Division for Congregational Ministries has made available a worship resource entitled "The Stewardship of Creation," which provides assistance to congregations celebrating "Rogationtide," with alternate suggestions for situations where a fixed date would fall outside the planting cycle.

The Division for Church in Society appointed a task force on the environment to prepare a social statement on this subject. This proposed social statement, "Caring for Creation: Vision, Hope, and Justice," will come to the 1993 Churchwide Assembly for discussion and decision. Part V.B.2. in this proposed social statement calls for a continued use of the Second Sunday of Pentecost as "Stewardship of Creation Sunday."

The ELCA Church Council, at its March 1993 meeting, approved a resolution on rural ministry, which originated with the board for the Division for Church in Society. This resolution will come to the 1993 Churchwide Assembly for discussion and action. A part of this resolution relates to the care of creation and directs the Divisions for Congregational Life and Church in Society to "assist rural congregations to become active participants in working with others of goodwill on environmental issues and to be advocates for the care of creation."

The assembly voted:

To transmit this minute as information, and convey the actions of the 1993 Churchwide Assembly on the "Social Statement on Caring for Creation: Vision, Hope, and Justice," and the resolution on rural ministry as the response of the 1993 Churchwide Assembly to the memorials . . . .

Council Action: The Church Council took the following action without discussion:

VOTED: *CC93.12.85*

To request the secretary of this church to convey this information relating to stewardship of creation to the Nebraska Synod in response to the synod's resolution on this subject.

3. Roster Guidelines Regarding Part-Time Pastors

North/West Lower Michigan Synod (6B) [1992]

The following resolution of the North/West Lower Michigan Synod on roster guidelines for part-time pastors was transmitted to the Church Council at its November 1992 meeting:

WHEREAS, there are congregations and ministries that cannot support enough full-time pastors to meet their pastoral needs; and

WHEREAS, the "worker-priest" model is an effective model for some congregations and other ministries; and

WHEREAS, there are clergy who support themselves with non-church jobs and who are willing to serve as part-time pastors ("worker-priest"); and

WHEREAS, some part-time clergy have secular employers who forbid them to be paid by other employers–much less to be paid "commensurate with synod compensation guidelines that apply to persons in full-time positions"; and

WHEREAS, certain congregations and ministries cannot afford to pay part-time pastors "commensurate with synod compensation guidelines that apply to persons in full-time positions"; and

WHEREAS, the current guidelines of the Evangelical Lutheran Church in America requiring a minimum of 20 hours of work per week to be retained on the clergy roster makes the "worker-priest" model impractical to implement in some situations; therefore, be it

RESOLVED, that the North/West Lower Michigan Synod request that the ELCA Church Council revoke the policy concerning shared-time Letters of Call requiring compensation "commensurate with synod compensation guidelines that apply to persons in full-time positions" for those who have primary or significant employment outside this church.

The Church Council voted:

To refer the resolution of the North/West Lower Michigan Synod to the Division for Ministry (CC92.11.75).

The Division for Ministry, through the Task Force on the Study of Ministry, has responded to the questions raised in this resolution. The Churchwide Assembly, in affirming the recommendations of the task force in this area, established non-stipendiary ministries which respond to the specific questions raised in the resolution. The Division for Ministry will, in consultation with the Conference of Bishops and with the approval of the Church Council, develop specific guidelines for implementing those recommendations.

Council Action: The Church Council took the following action without discussion:

VOTED: *CC93.12.86*
      To request the secretary of this church to convey this information relating to Roster Guidelines Regarding Part-Time Pastors to the North/-West Lower Michigan Synod.

Social Teaching Statement on the Church and Human Sexuality (continued)
Public Release of Council Action (continued)

Chair Magnus called upon the Rev. Eric C. Shafer, director of the Department for Communication, to report on plans for a news release on the council's action related to the development of a social statement on the church and human sexuality (see pages 180-181 of these minutes).

He recalled that the release of the draft document resulted in a "teaching moment" for this church. "We had the attention through the news media of the church and the world. With Bishop [Herbert W.] Chilstrom's direction, we have been on a very aggressive outreach program." Additional media coverage was expected, he said. Pastor Shafer distributed an "opinion editorial," which had been prepared by the bishop of this church for distribution to some 70 religion editors of newspapers in key Lutheran areas. He indicated that the Department for Communication had worked with synods in developing media outreach related to this matter. "Many bishops communicated very effectively with local media," he stated. He noted video resources that were in production concerning this matter.

Pastor Shafer indicated that a summary of the council's action was being prepared for distribution to council members prior to adjournment of this meeting. The Office of the Secretary would notify synods on Sunday and Monday, December 6-7, he stated.

Pastor Shafer said that reaction to this matter has varied widely from synod to synod. ". . . Several bishops said, 'We have had no phone calls, no action, no interest,' and some said, 'We have had hundreds [of telephone calls].'" He recommended, therefore, that synodical bishops be assigned responsibility for notifying the clergy of their respective synods of action taken by the council at this meeting.

Edith M. Lohr disagreed with Pastor Shafer's recommendation, since not every synodical bishop would have opportunity to authorize notification within their synods. She favored notification of all pastors from the

churchwide organization, prior to public release of the information. Secretary Lowell G. Almen observed that a notice to clergy might be mailed from the publishing house in Minneapolis on Wednesday, December 8, 1993.

Bishop Lyle G. Miller observed that delivery through synodical offices, rather than by the churchwide organization, would expedite the notification of pastors. Secretary Almen noted that based on past experience "the proximity of synods to pastors within the synod would allow for more prompt receipt" of notification. Mr. Gary J. N. Aamodt, president of the ELCA publishing house, concurred, but stated, "If you should choose that you want us to get it out on Wednesday, we will. You just tell us what you want and we will do it." He noted that the volume of Christmas mail would complicate delivery. Charles A. Adamson reiterated the importance of prompt notification of parish pastors. Bishop Paull E. Spring observed, ". . . This is a churchwide issue. This is a time when the churchwide organization needs to address this matter [rather than synods]. . . . By getting this from the churchwide organization, it would lift up the responsibility of the Church Council, which I think is important." Bishop Peter Rogness concurred and stated, ". . . This is not just a matter of damage control, it is really an opportunity for establishing some very positive relationships. Synod offices are not seen as the source of the document–Chicago is. If this place sent a letter to all pastors with a very positive tone to it, saying we are doing this better, we have heard what we have done, and we are partners with you, it would be an immense opportunity for good."

J. David Ellwanger concurred that notification should be made through the churchwide organization and urged that it should receive priority. He suggested that the release occur as soon as possible, that is, first thing Monday morning, December 6. Pastor Shafer recalled the concern that pastors not receive the news release after the media have received it. Bishop Rogness concurred that notification of pastors take precedence, even if that should result in a "purposeful delay" in releasing information to the news media. Edith M. Lohr moved the following, stating, ". . . We want to prevent what happened the last time; we want to say we have learned from what we did the last time":

MOVED;
SECONDED: To direct that a plan be implemented for distribution by first-class mail as soon as possible to pastors of the ELCA by the churchwide organization of the full text of the action of the Church Council regarding the process for study, response, review, and development of a possible social statement on human sexuality; and

To request that the news release from the Department for Communication related to this action follow the mailing to pastors of the Evangelical Lutheran Church in America.

Lorraine G. Bergquist moved to amend the foregoing motion as follows:

MOVED: To amend the motion to note that the action was not passed unanimously by the Church Council.

She suggested that it is important for the church to recognize that the council struggled with the issue and was not of one mind. Ms. Bergquist subsequently withdrew the motion to amend. Pastor Shafer commented on the relative merits of prompt notification to both pastors and press.

Bishop Robert L. Isaksen suggested that notification be mailed from synods, and the reason for expediting delivery be stated explicitly in the letter. He observed that listing objections to the council's action would be detrimental to the welfare of this church and contribute to division within it. William H. Engelbrecht inquired whether the churchwide mailing would be in addition to notification of synods. He cautioned the "the hurt that is out there" not be under-estimated. Bishop Herbert W. Chilstrom clarified that it was the intention of the members of the Church Council that the full text of the council's action be distributed to pastors with a cover letter. Loren W. Mathre moved the following:

MOVED;
SECONDED: To delete from the motion any reference to delay of the news release.

Ms. Lohr noted that the intent of her motion was that the letter to pastors precede release to the media. The Rev. Edgar R. Trexler, editor of *The Lutheran,* observed that the press may be contacting synodical bishops for information as early as Monday, December 6. Mr. Mathre served notice of his intention to move that there be no delay in releasing information to the press. Bishop Chilstrom noted that immediate release of information to the press "sets us up for another avalanche of letters from pastors who will say, `Once again you blind-sided us; you let the press get this information and our people were reading it before we even knew what was going on.'" Citing two instances, Bishop Rogness noted that he did not consider it to be unusual to delay release of sensitive information to the press. Mr. Gary J. N. Aamodt, president of the ELCA publishing house, requested specific direction from the council with respect to the role of the publishing house in the distribution of notification of the council's action to pastors. He reiterated that delayed delivery of such notice via U.S. mail could not be avoided. He recommended, therefore, that notification be made through synodical offices, rather than by a churchwide mailing.

MOVED;
SECONDED;
DEFEATED: To delete from the motion any reference to delay of the news release.

Bishop Kenneth H. Sauer suggested that cooperation of the synods in notifying pastors would help to make "clear that this is one church . . . and help to solve the credibility problem as well." The Rev. Franklin D.

Fry noted the importance of the contents of the cover letter that would accompany the text of the council's action in conveying "concern for the respect that is being given to parishes and the parish pastors–the attempt to pull us all together." He favored utilization of synod offices in distributing the notice and of delaying the press release. Edith M. Lohr suggested cooperation between the publishing house and synods in carrying out the mailing to pastors. She differed with Pastor Shafer's previous comments, saying, "If my board of directors told me that this was a priority and it had to be done now . . . I would have the staff in to do the job today. If we say that this is an absolute priority, . . . it is the staff's responsibility to get the job done. . . . If your board tells you to do something, it is not helpful to give me six reasons why it is going to be difficult." Secretary Lowell G. Almen indicated that the type of mailing in question was not the responsibility of the Department for Communication, but that of the bishop of this church. Bishop Herbert W. Chilstrom acknowledged, "Let's be clear, folks. We will act as quickly as possible to get the letter out. We will do it in the way that you deem to be the best. . . . I think I hear you saying by defeating Loren's [Mathre] motion that you do in fact want the news release to be delayed somewhat so that there is a good chance that most pastors will have the letter before they read about it in the newspaper." Charles A. Adamson concurred that everything must "be done to get the news to our people in the best possible way . . . ." He disagreed with Ms. Bergquist with respect to issuance of a statement that the council was divided in addressing the issue. Bishop Lyle G. Miller commented on the difficulties related to the notification process and recommended that a summary statement be included in the mailing. In addition, he stated, "I want it clearly understood that this is the action of the Church Council." Therefore, the letter ought to be from both the bishop and the Church Council, he said. He recommended that synodical bishops be apprised that a letter would be sent to all pastors in addition to any early notification they themselves may be able and willing to effect. J. David Ellwanger concurred and reiterated Pastor Fry's concern regarding the contents of the letter that would accompany the notification of the council's action. He recommended that pastors be apprised of "the human dimension of how we arrived at this. . . ."

The Rev. Richard G. Deines called the question.

MOVED;
SECONDED;
CARRIED: To move the previous question.

VOTED: CC93.12.87

To direct that a plan be implemented for distribution by first-class mail as soon as possible to pastors of the Evangelical Lutheran Church in America by the churchwide organization of the full text of the action of the Church Council regarding the process for study, response, review,

and development of a possible social statement on human sexuality; and

To request that the news release from the Department for Communication related to this action follow the mailing to pastors of the Evangelical Lutheran Church in America.

Bishop Herbert W. Chilstrom restated his understanding of the intention of the Church Council regarding the notification procedure. Mr. D. Mark Klever restated the concern that mailing the notification from Minneapolis undoubtedly would delay delivery to pastors. Mr. J. David Ellwanger requested that members of the Church Council receive a copy of the notification. Ms. Ann Hafften, director for news and information in the Department for Communication, requested clarification of expectations regarding release of information to the news media. Chair Magnus observed a distinction between an "embargo" and a "delay" in notifying the media. Mr. Loren W. Mathre spoke against an "embargo" of information. The Rev. Stephen M. Youngdahl stated, "I would disagree with Loren; I think we owe the pastors more than we owe the news media. . . ." Chair Magnus requested that consensus be reached on delay of releasing information to the press until after pastors have been notified. Bishop Peter Rogness concurred with Pastor Youngdahl and recommended that the release to the news media be delayed "at least a day after the mailing has gone out to pastors," rather than specifically on Thursday, December 9. Bishop Kenneth H. Sauer stated that as chair of the Conference of Bishops he would encourage synodical bishops to notify pastors as soon as possible. Bishop Chilstrom restated his understanding of the notification process. The Rev. Robert N. Bacher, executive for administration, inquired of council members, "What do you advise the synod offices say to the press?" Chair Magnus directed that staff prepare a plan prior to the noon recess of the council at which time discussion would conclude. Patsy Gottschalk inquired about the time table for presentation of a proposed social statement on human sexuality to the Churchwide Assembly.

Report of the Executive for Administration

Chair Magnus called upon the Rev. Robert N. Bacher, executive for administration, to present his report on organizational matters and denominational trends in North America. Pastor Bacher began saying, "One of the things I have noticed over the years is that whenever we attempt to [look into the] future . . . it is almost inevitable that the past and the present get in the way." He drew attention to previous observations he had made in his report to the 1993 Churchwide Assembly, and noted that the subject of the future is of interest to many throughout this church, particularly with respect to churchwide structures. He reflected on "three streams of thought" that provide opportunities for learning about

the experience of this church and the future directions it might assume:

(1) Where we are as a church body after six years of experience as a church body–"Are there refinements or changes that need to be made? . . . Maybe it is time to do a little reflection on that experience in a slightly more systematic way . . . and attempt to describe what we have learned, and where we are, where we think we ought to go";

(2) Critical evaluation of the body of commentary on contemporary denominational trends–"While we are doing our thing as a church, others are watching and others are watching other churches like us, and they are writing about it. . . . These are real [apocalyptic] headlines and they create a societal impression among the general public and among religious leaders that things are in decline and that things are not working right"; nevertheless, other observers are beginning to disagree with a pessimistic outlook, as exemplified in the *Christian Century* headline, "A Premature Obituary"; "People react to those dire predictions and those very negative descriptions in what I would have to often say is almost a superficial knee-jerk reaction, and say, therefore, `Okay, I know what needs to be done now'"; Pastor Bacher suggested that commentators be engaged in dialogue with the leadership of this church, in order to elicit recommendations for possible action;

(3) Change, sometimes drastic, is reflected in every institution in contemporary society; there is an increasing call for accountability from nonprofit institutions; the church is the church, but it can learn from the organizational experience of others and those served by it; the church needs "to be very clear about who is being served and how their sets of needs [and mission] are served . . .. It is certainly spelled out in the discussion we have just had about how we deal with the tensions of the needs of pastors and congregations on the one hand and the needs of the press on the other."

"The core elements of what make up the Evangelical Lutheran Church in America seem to be in good shape–the foundational elements. Bishop Chilstrom referred to this the other night with his diagram of what is not negotiable. What is negotiable, what perhaps needs attention, is another set of concerns that are beyond those elements–of our Confession of Faith, of the nature of the Church as we understand it, of the purposes for which we exist, of even the principles of organization that have formed the Evangelical Lutheran Church in America (Chapters 2-5 of the ELCA constitution), [namely,] relationships, common goals and a vision of who we are and what are trying to be–the way in which we deal with each other, the way decisions are made, the way information is shared–those are the places in which perhaps attention is needed. The conclusion would be that if this rings true, there is in the church an opportune moment to tap into what is happening and to do it in a little more systematic way."

Pastor Bacher commented on the fall 1993 synodical-churchwide consultation (as reported in council agenda Exhibit E), noting that it differed in two ways from previous consultations: (1) a single consultation was held in one location; and (2) the theme centered on congregations–how do we serve congregations together? Conclusions reached included an acknowledgement that staffing patterns do not reflect current needs and trends, and need to be revisited. "That event, I think, was significant in doing some reflection together about where we are as a church body and what some of our needs are," he said. He characterized "a sense of movement toward the future" as a key element in effective congregational ministry and concluded, "Perhaps, that is true of the whole church body."

Pastor Bacher then introduced a proposal for further inquiry into the future of this church's organizational structures. "It is not a `restructuring'; please, do not say that . . .. Bacher is not calling for a restructuring of the churchwide organization at this point. It is an inquiry to tap into that conversation to understand what is going on and to do it in several basic ways. We would attempt to ground this theologically, we would attempt to call on people who have a lot of organizational expertise as well as interest in what is happening to the Evangelical Lutheran Church in America and to Protestant bodies in general, we would attempt to put together and to converse with some of those people. The three phases are posited on the understanding of the time we have available to us in the next biennium: (1) We would begin to have that first phase of establishing what the themes and the issues are; (2) secondly, we would go on to doing a little more analysis of those; and (3) thirdly, we would come to some conclusions, but . . . not to say that we are going to restructure this church . . .." Pastor Bacher commented on the role of the Church Council and other entities in such reflection. He concluded, "I think the time is now to do this . . .. I think we could learn from what is going on and offer a gift to the future of the church. I think the need is there, I think the ideas of how to do it are available, I think the energy and the will are operative, I think the resources are available . . .. I think the conclusion would be that now is the time, rather than later, to inquire, to converse, to probe, to dialogue–at best then, to offer some light, as well as heat, as to what is happening in the church bodies and perhaps even a little wisdom about what might be done for the future. The Book of Proverbs talks about listening to advise and instruction that you might have wisdom for the future, and, I guess, that is the way I would characterize this particular proposal."

Council Action: During discussion, William T. Billings raised concern about safeguards for the release of appropriate information to the public media about conclusions and recommendations that may result from the proposed study. Citing the positive group dynamics experienced at the recent synodical-churchwide consultation that had resulted from such a process of reflection,

the Rev. Richard G. Deines affirmed the proposal, the need to proceed at this time, and the significant participation of the Church Council in the reflection process. Terry L. Bowes also concurred and noted that the proposal would address a 1993 Churchwide Assembly referral to the Church Council. Raising the question of interdependence between congregations, synods, and the churchwide organization, William E. Diehl inquired about the correlation of the proposal to synods and their future directions. William H. Engelbrecht observed that "critical self-analysis by any organization is good periodically, but raised concerns about staffing, cost, and funding for accomplishing the task. Pastor Bacher cautioned the members of the Church Council neither to expect too much nor too little from this "modest effort." The Rev. Nadine F. Lehr inquired about the methodology that might be utilized to assure reflection from throughout this church.

VOTED: *CC93.12.88*

To affirm in principle the direction outlined in the proposal "Inquiry: The Future of the Churchwide Organization";

To instruct the Office of the Bishop to develop and implement plans for this initiative, in consultation with the Executive Committee of the Church Council;

To provide for a joint meeting of the Executive Committee and the Program and Structure Committee of the Church Council, immediately prior to the April 1994 Church Council meeting; and

To request that a report on specific plans and activities related to this initiative be provided by the Office of the Bishop to the April 1994 Church Council meeting.

A Proposal
"INQUIRY: THE FUTURE OF THE
CHURCHWIDE ORGANIZATION"
November 1993

The Church Council shall establish an ongoing process to review the function of the structural organization of this church and to develop recommendations for changes (ELCA 5.01.e).

The fashioning of new patterns of [church] organizational life from whatever materials are at hand will require a great deal of imagination, care and even courage (Craig Dykstra and James Hudnut Beumler, 1991).

We are . . . a church so deeply and confidently rooted in the Gospel of God's grace that we are free to give our life joyfully in witness and in service.

Our society and our church are in a period of rapid change. As the year 2000 approaches, and as the pace of change in many areas of life accelerates, our church must confidently address the question: What churchwide, synodical and congregational patterns, activities and structures help us to most effectively "give our live joyfully in witness and service?"

Throughout the spectrum of Christian denominations–and, indeed, throughout the non-profit, governmental and for-profit sectors of society–large national organizations are struggling to redefine how they operate and to sharpen both their self-understanding and the methods they employ to carry out their mission. The growing complexity of social and economic systems, technological advances and the speed of change in all areas of life support the analysis that the process of self-examination and improvement of both structure and processes cannot be a once-in-a-decade effort. Rather, this is a continuous process.

Within this broader context, much attention has been devoted to the "future of national denominations." Commentators on religious life in this country have often focused on national trends from the 1960s, considered the "high point" in American denominationalism. There is a growing body of literature and a widening conversation, both popular and academic, in which the future of mainline denominations is questioned—in particular, the future of national denominational structures. Perhaps in part because of the relatively short historical time frame used by these commentators, a sense that the "sky is falling" sometimes characterizes the analyses of current trends; some commentators even express a conviction of the historic inevitability that national denominations and their churchwide structures will wither away, as localism and radical decentralization become ascendant. While this literature is strong on critique—some better reasoned and grounded than others—there has been little, if any, thoughtful or informed discussion on the range of alternatives or any common agreement on a "preferred future."

At best, the lack of such disciplined discussion is a missed opportunity for shaping the future; at worst, it may allow the future to be shaped by those whose view of the future is doctrinaire, ideological or parochial.

Whether or not the churchwide organization—and its partners in ministry—will change is not an option. The system is changing. Patterns of operation with partners are shifting—at times almost imperceptibly and times with a force that shocks the whole system. Perception of appropriate roles of congregational, synodical and churchwide structures—so linked with broader local, regional and national trends in society—so drives such changes. Finances also drive change, as both synods and the churchwide organization struggle to do more with less money—and as congregations deal with shifting patterns of giving and funding ministries. The breadth, complexity and diversity of the ELCA contribute to the growing acknowledgement that things will not be as they were—nor should they be.

Survival of the churchwide organization cannot and should not be the issue. Service in the common mission is the main issue that must be addressed, as we operate under the assumption that we can and should help to shape our common future—our future as a denomination and the future of the churchwide organization. Being a church steeped in the mind-set of reformation, a sense of confidence and even joy can characterize these discussions.

Church historian and commentator Martin Marty suggests, built into those denominations that stand the best chance of enduring and serving are mechanisms and impulses for reform and renewal. Their significance is less one that can be marked by "decline" and more by something that sounds much simpler but is deliciously more complex: "change."

What is Proposed?

In a word, inquiry: conversation, dialogue, research and study, analysis and evaluation and the development of implications and recommendations for action. The following proposal would provide a means by which this church can in an intentional and thoughtful way reflect on the change that has occurred and will occur—and provide the context for making decisions that will help to shape the change in a way that will best support the mission entrusted to the Evangelical Lutheran Church in America.

The proposed effort is intended to:
- Promote open, honest and careful dialogue and conversation among key partners in the Evangelical Lutheran Church in America based on confidence and hope for the future.
- Establish a common understanding of "where we are," by more establishing more clearly current "realities" and future trends

that implicitly or explicitly affect or influence the whole church's approach to mission.
- Provide a balance in the inquiry between
  - the future of the church in all its expressions with regard to mission and mission priorities; and
  - the role of the churchwide organization and its purpose(s) related to the overall mission of this church.
- Explore new forms for churchwide work in the light of its purpose.

How Will We Approach this Inquiry?

In undertaking this inquiry, we will
- Ground all discussions theologically.
- Employ the best insights from current organizational study and practice.
- Be respectful and affirming of the past, while being open and creative with regard to the future.
- Build on the processes that have shaped churchwide discussion of such matters within the ELCA, specifically:
- The principle embedded in our ELCA constitution of the ongoing review of structure;
- The learnings attained from the organizational streamlining ("Focusing for Mission") which was approved by the 1991 Churchwide Assembly; and
- The internal staff study during the past biennium (some information on which has been shared with the Church Council at past meetings).

How Will the Inquiry be Done?

The process of inquiry will take place in phases directed by a working team established by the Office of the Bishop, in consultation with the Church Council. The working team would coordinate and link each phase of the project, while also maintaining relationships with work on other initiatives. (Such related initiatives include ongoing staffing consultations with synods, other programmatic and financial consultation with synods, and pilot programs relating to quality initiatives undertaken by individual churchwide units, in coordination with the Office of the Bishop.)

Each phase of the project will build upon the previous phase, with the goal of producing several different directional alternatives for the churchwide organization. Once basic directional alternatives are clearly delineated, it will be possible to seek input from a large number of members of the church in a survey phase. It should be noted that these phases may overlap each other—for example, some work in Phase I may continue, even as elements of Phase II begin to move forward.

PHASE I: STARTING THE CONVERSATION AND IDENTIFYING ISSUES AND THEMES
January - June 1994

The initial phase would include structured interviews designed to stake out the territory with regard to "realities," mission, purpose and directional alternatives. The panels for structured interviews would include individuals selected because of their knowledge or perceived strength of opinion in such areas as: theology, congregational ministry, organizational theory and design, Lutheran denominational and religious history, and sociology.

Involvement: Working Groups/Panels/Interview Groups Appointed by the Bishop in Consultation with the Church Council
- Individuals in the categories listed above;
- Church Council;
- Churchwide staff, Planning Team, Cabinet of Executives;
- Members of churchwide boards, steering committees, and advisory committees;
- Synodical bishops;
- Synod Councils and synod staffs;
- Groups of pastors and associates in ministry;
- Theologians;
- Organizational experts;
- Persons associated with church-related institutions.

PHASE II: BROADENING AND DEEPENING THE CONVERSATION
July 1994 - January 1995
        In this phase, the scope of participation in this effort would be widened and the discussion would be particularized –moving toward and assessing directional alternatives for the churchwide organization.

Involvement:
* Continuation of panels of theologians and organizational leaders.
* "Translating" issues and themes into survey questions for broader input; congregations and synods.
* Obtaining additional input from groups listed in Phase I (through such means as telephone, mail, focus groups and teleconferencing).
* Obtaining additional input from selected panels from the churchwide organization, synods, colleges, seminaries and congregational clergy and lay members.

PHASE III: DRAWING IMPLICATIONS AND
MAKING RECOMMENDATIONS
February 1995 - August 1995
        The final phase of the plan would include summarizing implications and developing any recommendations for action, either by the Church Council or the Churchwide Assembly.

Involvement:
        Discussion and dialogue would involve:
* the Church Council;
* the churchwide Planning Team and Cabinet of Executives;
* unit governance bodies;
* Conference of Bishops;
* Panels.
        NOTE: Depending on the nature of the conversations in Phase I and Phase II, Phase III might result in either:
* recommendations developed for action by the Church Council and possibly the 1995 Churchwide Assembly; or
* a foundation upon which the newly elected bishop can plan and act in the 1996-1997 biennium.

How will the Undertaking be Funded?
        Funding application will be made to Aid Association for Lutherans and to Lutheran Brotherhood, both of which have indicated a preliminary interest in assisting in such a process.

        The Rev. Franklin D. Fry expressed caution that central considerations in planning for the future be respected, namely, that such a study be "rooted in the Gospel," lest it "simply rearrange the chairs."

Report of the Program and Structure Committee

        Chair Magnus called upon the Rev. Stephen M. Youngdahl, chair of the Program and Structure Committee, to report on behalf of the committee. Pastor Youngdahl reviewed the recent work of the committee and noted that the Division for Global Mission and the Division for Higher Education and Schools (rather than the ELCA Foundation) would be reviewed during the current biennium. He recommended that a fuller report than previously be transmitted to the 1995 Churchwide Assembly, in order to enhance accountability.

        Pastor Youngdahl noted that the committee had "received with affirmation" a progress report from *The Lutheran* on goals that had been set forth as a result of the committee's 1993 review (council agenda Exhibit G, Part 3). "We appreciate their continuing efforts to work toward this kind of cooperative effort . . .," he said.

1. Commission for Women

        Background: The following action was taken by the Steering Committee of the Commission for Women at its October 1993 meeting:
        WHEREAS, the Commission for Women was established to enable this church to realize the full participation of women; to create equal opportunity for women of all cultures; to foster partnership between men and women; to assist this church to address sexism; and to advocate justice for women in this church and society; and
        WHEREAS, the commission has established processes and priorities to assist this church in developing, understanding, and forming its policies and practices with regard to the full involvement of women in this church; and
        WHEREAS, the commission continues to assist this church to create a safe environment for women in this church and society; and
        WHEREAS, the commission works in cooperation with divisions and other churchwide units to assure that materials and resources are developed to carry out its functions; and
        WHEREAS, in 1988, the ELCA Constituting Convention allocated a $641,868 budget for the Commission for Women to assure that the work of this commission be done; and
        WHEREAS, consistent decreases in spending plans have resulted in a 1994 budget allocation of $375,000; therefore, be it
        RESOLVED, that the Steering Committee of the ELCA Commission for Women request the ELCA Church Council, through the Program and Structure Committee of the Church Council, to call for an immediate moratorium on budget cuts for the Commission for Women and continue through this biennium (CW.93.10.16).

        Council Action: Pastor Youngdahl introduced the following recommendation of the Program and Structure Committee:

        MOVED;
        SECONDED: To request a moratorium on budget reductions for the Commission of Women until April 1994, when the Program and Structure Committee will review the constitutional mandate of the Commission for Women;
        To request that the Steering Committee of the commission for Women prepare options for consideration by the Program and Structure committee at its April 1994 meeting;
        To request that the Budget and Finance Committee review the implication of budget reductions on similarly situated smaller units; and
        To request the Office of the Bishop to provide information relating to the "larger picture," including implications on other units.

        In consideration of the uncertainty of future income levels, the need to maintain flexibility for potential adjustment of the expenditure authorization, and the desirability of developing a "more wholistic approach" to addressing the problem of inadequate funding throughout the churchwide organization, in order to fulfill constitutional mandates, Edith M. Lohr moved to refer the recommendation of the Program and Structure Committee to the Executive Committee of the Church Council:

VOTED: *CC93.12.89*

To refer the following recommendation of the Program and Structure Committee to the Executive Committee of the Church Council:

To request a moratorium on budget reductions for the Commission of Women until April 1994, when the Program and Structure Committee will review the constitutional mandate of the Commission for Women;

To request that the Steering Committee of the Commission for Women prepare options for consideration by the Program and Structure committee at its April 1994 meeting;

To request that the Budget and Finance Committee review the implication of budget reductions on similarly situated smaller units; and

To request the Office of the Bishop to provide information relating to the "larger picture," including implications on other units.

2. Ongoing Review of the Work of Churchwide Units

Background: Each churchwide unit prepared a summary of unit activities, printed in council agenda Exhibit H, Part 1a, and a digest of board and steering committee actions, printed in council agenda Exhibit H, Part 1b.

Council Action: The Church Council received the foregoing as information.

3. Regions

Background: An update on the work of the regions was distributed to council members as council agenda Exhibit H, Part 2.

Council Action: The Church Council received the foregoing as information.

4. Changes Related to Regional Structures

Background: Council agenda Exhibit G, Part 1a, reports changes related to the operation of Region 4; council agenda Exhibit G, Part 1b, reports changes related to Region 5. Both sets of changes have the concurrence of both the related synods and churchwide staff.

During the past few years, budget reductions in several regions have resulted in a reduction from full-time to part-time in the position of regional coordinator. In several regions (2, 4, and 6), the position of a half-time regional coordinator was joined with a half-time position related to the Department for Synodical Relations and the Division for Ministry. Regions 5, 8, and 9 also have moved or are moving to a part-time position. Regions 1, 3, and 7 retain full-time coordinators.

According to ELCA bylaw 18.11.21. and 18.11.31. staffing and governance patterns for regions are to be ratified by the Church Council.

Council Action: The Church Council adopted the following resolution by *en bloc* action:

EN BLOC   [CC93.12.114]

To ratify the changes in regional governance and staffing patterns found in council agenda Exhibit G, Part 1a (Region 4), and 1b (Region 5), as well as the changes in staffing in regions, as described above.

5. Review of the Division for Global Mission and ELCA Foundation

Background: The ELCA governing documents call on the Church Council, through its Program and Structure Committee to:

> establish a process for the review of at least two churchwide units each biennium so as to review all units within a ten-year period. Such review shall include the recommendation for renewal of the mandate for the churchwide unit or recommendation of an alternative structure through which the unit's purposes shall be accomplished (ELCA 14.41.D91.).

As reported above, the Program and Structure Committee discussed the process for review of the two units previously selected for review in this biennium: the Division for Global Mission and the ELCA Foundation. The committee agreed to delay review of the ELCA Foundation in favor of review of the Division for Higher Education and Schools.

Council Action: The Church Council received the foregoing as information.

6. Review of *The Lutheran*

Background: In response to the recommendation of the Program and Structure Committee, which reviewed *The Lutheran* during the past biennium, the Church Council voted at its November 1992 meeting:

> To instruct the staff and the Advisory Committee for *The Lutheran* to give attention to the following ways of deepening and enhancing that partnership [between the magazine and those in leadership positions within the Evangelical Lutheran Church in America]:
> 1) Enhancing Communications
>   a)   To develop improved methods for ongoing communication between *The Lutheran* and churchwide staff, synodical bishops, and Church Council.
>   b)   To encourage the chair of the advisory committee to meet with the executive directors of churchwide units to discuss matters of mutual concern, as raised in the response of the advisory committee to the Program and Structure Committee (CC92.11.91).

The Church Council requested that a progress report on these matters be prepared for its December 1993 meeting. That report was distributed to council members.

Council Action: The Church Council received the foregoing as information.

Resolutions from Synods Directed to the Church Council

At the request of council members, the following resolutions previously had been removed for individual consideration from the en bloc resolution for disposition of certain resolutions from synods.

14. U.S. Embargo Against Cuba

Council Action: William E. Diehl suggested that the division's response to the resolution of the West Virginia-Western Maryland Synod on relations between the United States and Cuba be presented to the Church Council before being transmitted to the synod. He noted the sensitivity of present situation between the United States and Cuba. The Rev. Charles S. Miller Jr., executive director of the Division for Church in Society, indicated that the division would not act precipitously in its response. The following recommendation then was adopted:

VOTED: *CC93.12.90*

To refer the following resolution of the West Virginia-Western Maryland Synod on the U.S. embargo against Cuba to the Division for Church in Society for a report and/or recommendation to the Church Council at its April 1994 meeting for response to the synod:

> WHEREAS, the theme of this assembly is "Many Voices . . . One Song," and, in the words of our "Order for the Opening of an Assembly," "let us pursue justice and peace for mutual understanding"; and
>
> WHEREAS, in light of nutritional, medical, and material goods shortages; therefore, be it
>
> RESOLVED, that this assembly encourage the West Virginia-Western Maryland Synod to support the ministries and work of all Christian congregations in Cuba, and to direct the Synod Council to direct the ELCA Church Council to urge the United States government to end its thirty-two year embargo against Cuba and the Cuban people, and to seek a normalization of relations.

7. Role of the Evangelical Lutheran Church in America And the World Council of Churches

Background: The Southeastern Minnesota Synod Council discussed the resolution printed below, received from the Minnesota River Conference, and voted to forward it to the ELCA Church Council with the following comment:

> We pass this on to the ELCA Church Council with "no great concern" over the issue raised. We feel that our participation in ecumenism through the World Council of Churches far outweighs any minor concerns raised by the *Reader's Digest* article.

Council Action: William E. Diehl suggested that the response of the Department for Ecumenical Affairs be reviewed to the Church Council prior to transmittal to the synod. He subsequently withdrew his objection to the following recommendation:

VOTED: *CC93.12.91*

To refer the following resolution of the Southeastern Minnesota Synod on the World Council of Churches to the Department for Ecumenical Affairs for a report to the synod:

> WHEREAS, the February 1993 issue of *Reader's Digest* published an article containing critical allegations regarding the efforts and expenditures of the World Council of Churches; and

> WHEREAS, in a letter of response to this article, WCC General Secretary Konrad Raiser wrote, "We agree wholeheartedly with the article's concluding suggestion that `ordinary churchgoers' should raise questions about the WCC with their own church leadership"; and
>
> WHEREAS, such questions focus directly on the ELCA participation in the WCC work regarding both programmatic and budgetary support questions; therefore, be it
>
> RESOLVED, that we request that the Evangelical Lutheran Church in America continue to monitor the work and budgetary expenditures of the World Council of Churches, especially in response to public allegations and charges; and be it further
>
> RESOLVED, that if the evaluations of allegations prove true that the Evangelical Lutheran Church in America use all means of protest necessary to get a positive response including the option of cutting levels of financial support to the World Council of Churches; and be it further
>
> RESOLVED, that any money so withheld be placed directly into the World Mission budget of the Evangelical Lutheran Church in America; and be it further
>
> RESOLVED, that the Evangelical Lutheran Church in America make special efforts at publication communication which informs and reassures its membership of the positive results of World Council of Churches' ecumenical efforts, and that the voices of "ordinary churchgoers" are being heard and taken seriously in such concerns; and be it further
>
> RESOLVED, that the Minnesota River Conference in assembly refer this resolution to the Southeastern Minnesota Synod Council for discussion and action; and be it further
>
> RESOLVED, that the Southeastern Minnesota Synod Council forward this resolution to the ELCA Church Council for consideration and possible action.

3. Inclusivity Task Force

Council Action: William E. Diehl suggested that the division's response to the following resolution of the Southern California (West) Synod be presented to the Church Council prior to transmittal to the synod. The Rev. Charles S. Miller Jr., executive director of the Division for Church in Society, outlined the division's proposed response. Mr. Diehl then withdrew his objection.

VOTED: *CC93.12.92*

To refer the following resolution of the Southern California (West) Synod on the establishment of an inclusivity task force to the Division for Church in Society for a response to the synod:

> WHEREAS, the Division for Church in Society of the Evangelical Lutheran Church in America witnesses to the Gospel by seeking justice for all in its commitment to human development and global concerns through service, study, advocacy, moral deliberation, and social analysis in cooperation with congregations, synods, regions, and social ministry organizations; and
>
> WHEREAS, our Southern California (West) Synod has a task force on inclusivity and lesbian and gay orientation; and

WHEREAS, this task force has proved to be beneficial in proving a partnership with and for the advocacy of persons in our congregations of a lesbian or gay orientation; and

WHEREAS, the ELCA Division for Church in Society has not yet established a partnership with and for the advocacy of persons in our congregations of a lesbian or gay orientation, in cooperation with our Synod Task Force on Inclusivity and Lesbian/Gay Orientation; therefore, be it

RESOLVED, that the Southern California (West) Synod request the Evangelical Lutheran Church in America to establish, within the Division for Church in Society, an equivalent to our Synod Task Force on Inclusivity and Lesbian/Gay Orientation.

Report of the Legal and Constitutional Review Committee

1. Terminology Related to Associates in Ministry

Background: In the preparation of the revised document, "Definition and Guidelines for Discipline," the Committee on Appeals noted the legislative history of ELCA bylaw 20.22.01.b., which provides that "Lay persons on official rosters shall be subject to discipline for . . . conduct incompatible with the <u>standards</u> for rostered ministries of this church . . ." [Emphasis supplied]. The Church Council had first recommended the language "conduct incompatible with the character of the ministerial office," *1993 Reports and Records, Volume 1, Part 2,* page 460. The revised recommendation of the Church Council, reported to the Churchwide Assembly in *1993 Reports and Records, Volume 1, Supplement,* page C-12, was adopted as the bylaw above quoted.

In view of this legislative history, the committee concluded that it was advisable that "Definitions and Guidelines for Discipline" use the phrase, "standards for the rostered ministries of this church," with respect to Associates in Ministry, replacing the phrase, "conduct of the ministerial office," used with respect to ordained ministers. However, the Committee on Appeals concluded that the word, "character," was more appropriate than the word, "standards," in 20.22.01.b. and the related language in "Definitions and Guidelines for Discipline."

Because constitutional and bylaw provisions in Chapters 7 and 20 referred to individuals on the official roster of laypersons, the Committee on Appeals concluded that the use of this phrase was required in "Definitions and Guidelines for Discipline." The committee concluded, however, that describing such individuals as "lay ministers," rather than as "laypersons," would be more appropriate in the governing documents and the related language in "Definitions and Guidelines for Discipline."

Council Action: This item was originally scheduled for disposition *en bloc,* but was removed from the *en bloc* resolution for separate consideration. Lorraine G. Bergquist questioned the appropriateness of the terminology employed in the following recommendation with respect to rostered lay persons (*an* official roster, versus *the* official rosters). Secretary Lowell G. Almen indicated

that the referral was proposed to avoid confusion of the function of the ministry of all the laity with the responsibility of a particular group of rostered persons, in accordance with the report of the Task Force on the Study of Ministry. General Counsel David J. Hardy explained the rationale for the recommendation of the Committee on Appeals. Secretary Almen noted that no change of terminology was proposed, because such is determined by the constitution. It was agreed to amend the words, "official roster," to the plural, "official rosters."

VOTED: CC93.12.93
To refer to the Division for Ministry for study and advice the issues of the use of the word "character" rather than "standards" in the context of the phrase "conduct incompatible with the <u>standards</u> of rostered ministries of this church," and the use of the words "lay ministers" rather than "laypersons" as the description of individuals on the official rosters of those who are not ordained.

Speaking in a point of personal privilege, Edith M. Lohr offered apology to the Rev. Eric C. Shafer for previous comments regarding the responsibilities of the Department for Communication in carrying out directives of the Church Council.

2. Confidentiality of Communications with Associates in Ministry

Background: In view of the fact that ELCA constitutional provision 7.45. applies only to ordained ministers, and the absence of a comparable provision applicable to associates in ministry, the Committee on Appeals concluded that it was appropriate that "Definitions and Guidelines for Discipline" as applicable to associates in ministry not have a specific provision related to confidentiality similar to the provision applicable to ordained ministers. The committee concluded, however, that this matter required further study with a view to proposing an appropriate provision concerning confidentiality of communications with Associates in Ministry and related revisions of "Definition and Guidelines for Discipline."

Council Action: The Church Council adopted the following resolution *en bloc,* as reported elsewhere in these minutes:

EN BLOC   [CC93.12.106]
To refer to the Division for Ministry the issue of whether confidentiality of communications with associates in ministry ought to be the subject of a provision in the bylaws and in "Definitions and Guidelines for Discipline."

Policy on Call and Termination of Rostered Lay Ministers

Background: The text printed below is a revision of an earlier policy adopted by the Church Council in October 1990. The new revisions were drafted in response to the following recommendation of the Task Force for the Study of Ministry, as adopted by the 1993 Churchwide Assembly.

> To direct that the process for terminating a congregation's call of a rostered lay person shall be substantially similar to the provisions for termination of a call of an ordained minister found in †S14.13. in the Constitution for Synods of this church.

The new policy would apply to all officially recognized lay ministers. It reflects the language adopted by the Churchwide Assembly in reference to lay rosters.

The change from the earlier document, which appears in paragraph four, gives authority to terminate to a congregation council, rather than a congregational meeting. This recommended change was included at the recommendation of the Conference of Bishops and was approved by the board of the Division for Ministry. It is understood that the required consultation with the synod bishop will protect rostered lay ministers from unjust or unfair termination. This document has been reviewed by the Conference of Bishops and approved by the board of the Division for Ministry.

Council Action: This item was originally scheduled for disposition *en bloc,* but was removed from the *en bloc* resolution for separate consideration. Lorraine G. Bergquist inquired whether the following recommendation addressed concerns raised in a letter to members of the Church Council from an ad hoc advisory group of associates in ministry related to the Division for Ministry. The group had recommended that authority to terminate lay ministers be vested in the congregation meeting, rather than the congregation council. Secretary Lowell G. Almen explained the necessity of and rationale for the proposed policy, which had been developed by the Division for Ministry in consultation with the Conference of Bishops. The Rev. Joseph M. Wagner, executive director of the Division for Ministry, observed that the policy has a primary intention of assuring protection of the ministry of the congregation, as well as the job security of the person serving. The Rev. James G. Cobb noted that the policy was inconsistent with that for termination of ordained ministers serving congregations. He further inquired whether the advisory group of rostered lay persons had been consulted. Pastor Wagner indicated that the group had differed with the opinion of the board of the Division for Ministry on this matter.

William E. Diehl inquired about the language of "a regularly scheduled meeting of the Congregation Council" versus "a specially called meeting." Pastor Wagner indicated that the intent was "a regularly scheduled meeting," and that the division would have no objection to emendation of the policy to reflect that terminology. Bishop Lyle E. Miller noted that the term, "regularly called," refers to a properly called meeting, not a periodic meeting.

William T. Billings requested further clarification on the consistency of the proposed policy with that for ordained ministers.

Lorraine G. Bergquist suggested addition of the option of the Congregation Meeting as the source of call and termination. Secretary Lowell G. Almen noted the

possibility of appeal to the Congregation Meeting in case of dispute. He also observed that a consultation process with the synod was built into the policy in anticipation of the need for mediation.

Loren W. Mathre sought to move the following:

MOVED: To amend the recommendation by deleting the word, "present," in the last line of the proposed policy. The motion died for lack of a second.

General Counsel David J. Hardy suggested substitution of the word, "duly," for the word, "regularly" (see above discussion). The suggestion was received as a friendly emendation.

VOTED: *CC93.12.94*
To adopt the "Policy Statement Regarding the Call and Termination of Associates in Ministry, Deaconesses of the Evangelical Lutheran Church in America, and Diaconal Ministers" as follows:

> Each congregation of this synod shall consult the bishop of this synod before taking any steps leading to the extending of a call to an associate in ministry, a Deaconess of the Evangelical Lutheran Church in America (ELCA), or a diaconal minister listed on this church's official rosters of laypersons or an approved candidate for such rosters.
>
> A congregational call to an associate in ministry, a Deaconess of the ELCA, or a diaconal minister may then be extended following a two-thirds majority vote of members present and voting at a meeting regularly called for that purpose (ELCA 7.52.A93.). When the congregation has voted to issue a call to an associate in ministry, a Deaconess of the ELCA, or a diaconal minister, the letter of call shall be submitted to the bishop of the synod for the bishop's signature.
>
> No associate in ministry, Deaconess of the ELCA, or diaconal minister shall seek or accept a letter of call without first conferring with the bishop of the synod. An associate in ministry, a Deaconess of the ELCA, or a diaconal minister shall respond with an answer of acceptance or declination to a letter of call within 30 days of receipt of such call.
>
> A letter of call from a congregation, when accepted by an associate in ministry, a Deaconess of the ELCA, or a diaconal minister and attested to by the synodical bishop, shall constitute a continuing mutual relationship and commitment which shall be terminated only following consultation with the synodical bishop.
>
> In the case of alleged local difficulties which imperil the effective functioning of the congregation, following appropriate consultation involving all parties, the synodical bishop will recommend a course of action to the pastor, the associate in ministry, Deaconess of the ELCA, or diaconal minister serving under call, and the congregation. If they agree to carry out such recommendations, no further action shall be taken by the synod. If any party fails to assent, the congregation council, after meeting and full consultation with the synodical bishop, may dismiss the associate in ministry, Deaconess of the ELCA, or diaconal minister by a two-thirds majority vote of the voting members present at a duly called meeting.

The Rev. Stephen M. Youngdahl suggested that the executive director of the Division for Ministry apprise the members of the associates in ministry advisory group of the council's deliberations on the foregoing matter.

Vision and Expectations: Commissioned Associates in Ministry

Background: The document printed below replaces an earlier interim document that had been adopted by the board of the Division for Ministry for use in candidacy, pending the completion of the Study of Ministry and decisions related to the forms of lay ministry to be officially recognized by this church. This revised document parallels "Vision and Expectations: Ordained Ministers in the Evangelical Lutheran Church in America," which was adopted by the Church Council in October 1990. The document was being transmitted to the Church Council for adoption prior to distribution to all rostered associates in ministry. It is especially appropriate to distribute Vision and Expectations as a positive teaching document at this time when associates in ministry become subject to new definitions and guidelines for discipline. The document was approved by the board of the Division for Ministry, which recommended adoption by the Church Council.

Council Action: The Church Council adopted the following recommendation in *en bloc* action, as reported elsewhere in these minutes:

EN BLOC [CC93.12.119]

To adopt the following document, "Vision and Expectations: Commissioned Associates in Ministry":

VISIONS AND EXPECTATIONS:
Commissioned Associates in Ministry
Evangelical Lutheran Church in America

This church affirms the universal priesthood of all its baptized members. In its function and its structure this church commits itself to the equipping and supporting of all its members for their ministries in the world and in this church. It is within this context of ministry that this church calls some of its baptized members for specific ministries in this church. Constitution of the Evangelical Lutheran Church in America (7.11.)

Associates in ministry are called to serve in one of the officially recognized lay ministries of this church. Associates in ministry shall be persons whose commitment to Christ, soundness of faith, aptness and ability to serve in programmatic ministries which equip and support the people of God, and whose educational and personal qualifications have been examined and approved in the manner prescribed in the documents of this church; who have been called and commissioned, who accept and adhere to the Confession of Faith of this church; who are diligent and faithful in the exercise of the ministry to which they have been called; and whose lives and conduct are consistent with the Gospel. Associates in ministry shall comply with the constitution of this church.

Associates in ministry, together with the whole people of God, are part of the ministry of the baptized. Partners in ministry with pastors and bishops, diaconal ministers, deaconesses, and laity are called to be faithful to Jesus Christ, knowledgeable of the Word of God and the Confessions of this church, respectful of the people of God, and responsive to the needs of a changing world. Associates

in ministry serve in congregations and other ministries of the Evangelical Lutheran Church in America.

This document designed for associates in ministry and "Vision and Expectations: Ordained Ministers in the Evangelical Lutheran Church in America", seek to state both a vision and expectations for the rostered ministers of this church. This document should not be understood as a juridical standard. Neither is it intended to suggest unrealistic or impossible expectations for those who serve on one of the rosters of this church. Instead, it seeks to express the high value and importance that this church places in those who are called to serve in one of its officially recognized ministries, both lay and ordained. This vision and these expectations are for those who are already on the roster as well as an invitation for reflection and consideration of those who seek to serve as associates in ministry.

The basic standards for service as an associate in ministry are set forth in the constitution and bylaws of the Evangelical Lutheran Church in America. These basic standards are:

- Commitment to Christ;
- Acceptance of and adherence to the Confession of Faith of this church;
- Willingness and ability to serve in response to the needs of this church;
- Academic and practical qualifications for the position;
- Life consistent with the Gospel and personal qualifications including leadership abilities and competence in interpersonal relationships;
- Receipt and acceptance of a letter of call; and
- Membership in a congregation of this church.

During the service of installation and commissioning, the new associate is ministry is asked:

- "Will you assume this ministry in the confidence that it comes from God?"
- "Will you carry out this ministry in accordance with the teachings and practice of the Lutheran Church?"
- "Will you be diligent in your study of the Holy Scriptures and faithful in your use of the means of grace and in prayer?"
- "Will you trust in God's care, seek to grow in love for those you serve, strive for excellence in your skills, and adorn the Gospel of God with a godly life?"

These basic standards and the public statements of commitment contained in the service of installation and commissioning provide a framework for the vision and expectations for those who serve the Evangelical Lutheran Church in America as associates in ministry.

I. SERVING IN FAITHFULNESS

Will you assume this ministry in the confidence that it comes from God?

The Evangelical Lutheran Church in America believes that the Holy Spirit "calls, gathers, enlightens, and sanctifies the whole Christian church on earth and preserves it in union with Jesus Christ in the one true faith" (Small Catechism, Article III). It is the Spirit that provides the church with those persons who are enabled by God to lead the church in carrying out the ministry and mission of the Gospel of Jesus Christ.

The official documents of the ELCA describe the ministries provided by it members in the context of the priesthood of all the baptized. "This church affirms the universal priesthood of all its baptized members. In its function and its structure this church commits itself to the equipping and supporting of all its members for their ministries in the world and in this church. It is within this context of ministry that this church calls some of its baptized for specific ministries in this church" (ELCA Constitution 7.11.).

The Evangelical Lutheran Church in America prepares and approves candidates for commissioning as associates in ministry by setting standards, by providing for theological education through the seminaries and colleges of the church, and by evaluating a person's qualifications for service by a Candidacy Committee. Upon approval for commissioning, a person is eligible to receive a letter of call to serve as a fully recognized and rostered associate in ministry.

The Evangelical Lutheran Church in America, therefore, understands that those who serve this church as associates in ministry are:

- called by the Holy Spirit through this church and are not self-chosen or self-appointed. This ministry is seen as a privilege rather than a right; and
- called to serve this church for a ministry of servanthood in full partnership with the whole people of God, both lay and ordained.

Believing that this ministry comes from God, associates in ministry serve believing that the Holy Spirit will uphold, strengthen, and sustain them as they provide leadership in the church's ministry.

II.   FAITHFULNESS TO THE CHURCH'S CONFESSION

"Will you carry out this ministry in accordance with the teachings and practice of the Lutheran Church?"

All who have been commissioned to serve as associates in ministry in this church are expected to accept and adhere to the Confession of Faith of the Evangelical Lutheran Church in America as stated in Chapter 2 of this church's constitution.

This promise includes confession and teaching the canonical Scriptures of the Old and New Testaments as the inspired Word of God and the authoritative source and norm of its proclamation, faith, and life.

This promise includes acceptance and confession of the ecumenical creeds which are to be taught as true declarations of the faith of this church. The Lutheran Confessions are to be acknowledged as true witnesses and faithful expositions of the Holy Scriptures.

In promising to carry out this ministry in accordance with the teachings and practice of the Lutheran Church, associates in ministry acknowledge that the faith of the church is corporate, catholic and orthodox, and promise to teach nothing "that departs from the Scriptures of the catholic church" (Conclusion to the Augsburg Confession).

III.   FAITHFUL RENEWAL

"Will you be diligent in your study of the Holy Scriptures and faithful in your use of the means of grace and in prayer?"

Associates in ministry, in partnership with ordained clergy, are called upon to enable and equip others in their Christian lives and for their ministry in the world as the baptized people of God. In order to do this, associates in ministry need to develop and nurture a sound knowledge of the Scriptures, both intellectually and devotionally. Associates in ministry will seek regular opportunities for personal participation in the means of grace, including the renewal of baptismal grace in individual confession and absolution, and to receive the sacrament of Holy Communion, thus receiving God's renewing, sustaining, and empowering Spirit both personally and in the practice of ministry.

Associates in ministry engage in daily prayer and encourage others in the practice of regular prayer.

IV.   FAITHFUL LIVING

"Will you trust in God's care, seek to grow in love for those you serve, strive for excellence in your skills, and adorn the Gospel of God with a godly life?"

Associates in ministry must be members of a congregation of the Evangelical Lutheran Church in America. As a member of such a community of faith, the associate in ministry is an integral part of a community in which mutual love and support is given and in which care, forgiveness, and healing occur.

Associates in ministry support not only the work of the congregation, institution or agency in which they are called, but also the synodical and churchwide ministry of the Evangelical Lutheran Church in America. Associates in ministry are expected to work in a collegial relationship with pastors and other associates in ministry, and to share in mutual accountability with those in positions of leadership and oversight in this church. The associate in ministry is willing and able to serve in response to the needs of the church.

Associates in ministry recognize the importance of life-long growth in learning. Such growth is intended to renew, extend, and deepen insight into the Scriptures and the doctrinal teaching of the church, and to enable one to respond to the insights and challenges of the world with greater awareness and a more faithful confession. In an increasingly complex and educated society, the development of an informed intellect and professional skills is crucial to competent ministry. This church expects its ordained and commissioned ministers to participate in regular and disciplined time of personal study, study in the company of others, and in programs of continuing education. Congregations and other entities of this church are expected to provide the time and assistance with the financial resources needed for such study.

Associates in ministry need to be examples of self-care, as well as caring for others. Caring for self includes seeking counseling and/or medical care when needed, as well as adequate time taken for vacation and rest.

Associates in ministry promise to be examples of responsible and faithful living in the exercise of God's gifts of sexuality and family. The qualities of such responsible and faithful living include the following:

- Responsibility to Family. Whether married or single, associates in ministry are expected to uphold an understanding of marriage in their public ministry as well as in private life that is biblically informed and consistent with the teachings of this church. Spouse and children, if any, are to be regarded with love, respect, and commitment. Within the family, forgiveness, reconciliation, healing and mutual care are to be expressed.
- Separation, Divorce and Remarriage. Associates in ministry are expected to keep their marriage inviolate until death, to cultivate love and respect for their spouse, and to seek marital counseling when it is needed. It is recognized that due to human sin and brokenness, in some cases, the marital relationship may have to be dissolved. An associate in ministry seeking to divorce will seek the pastoral care, counsel, and guidance of the synodical bishop. Similarly, an associate in ministry deciding to marry, following a divorce, will seek the counsel and guidance of the synodical bishop.
- Sexual Conduct. The expectations of this church regarding the sexual conduct of its ordained and commissioned ministers are grounded in the understanding that human sexuality is a gift from God and that all baptized Christians are to live in such a way as to honor this gift. All who serve in public ministry are expected to reject sexual promiscuity, the manipulation of others for the purposes of sexual gratification, and all attempts of sexual seduction of others. Single persons are expected to live a chaste life. Married persons are expected to live in fidelity to their spouses, giving expression to sexual intimacy within a marriage relationship that is mutual, chaste, and faithful. Ordained and commissioned ministers who are homosexual in their self-understanding are expected to abstain from homosexual sexual relationships.

Associates in ministry are called to specific ministries which equip and support the ministries of the whole people of God. The charges to witness and minister to the world are given to the church today as it was to the apostles of the early church and to all Christians throughout history. The content of that witness is God's revelation in Jesus Christ: God's creative self-disclosure as the Word made flesh; Jesus Christ victorious over death for the salvation of God's people; and the promise of everlasting life. The testimony of these acts of God's grace and forgiveness are expressed in both word and deed carried out in a lifestyle exemplified by Christ the servant. Called to render a particular service in the church, associates in ministry witness to the world through expressions of compassion, hospitality, patience, and forgiveness; through seeking peace and justice for all people; through care for all of God's creation; and through sharing one's faith in various expressions and functions of ministry.

Our Lord, who came among us as a servant, calls us to faith and a life of loving service to our neighbor. You stand among us as one called to render a particular service, a gift from God go inspire us to love and good works.

Almighty God, our heavenly Father, guide, bless, and keep you, that you may be faithful in the ministry to which you have been called.

(Installation of a Lay Professional Leader, *Lutheran Book of Worship Occasional Services*)

Other Matters Related to Associates in Ministry

Background: The document printed below deals with basic standards, academic and practical requirements, and candidacy procedures leading to commissioning for associates in ministry. This document is a revision of and replaces the 1987 document, "Interim Criteria and Procedures for the Certification of Associates in Ministry in the Evangelical Lutheran Church in America," which was adopted during the transition process that led to the formation of the Evangelical Lutheran Church in America. That document was used in candidacy during 1988-1993, when the Study of Ministry was being carried out. The revisions do not contain substantial changes in the basic requirements from the original document, but do reflect the need for clarity and specificity based on five years of experience with the candidacy process in the ELCA. The revised document also reflects terminology as adopted by the 1993 Churchwide Assembly: call replaces appointment; approval replaces certification; and the entry rite is defined for new associates in ministry as commissioning.

This document applies only to associates in ministry. The academic and practical requirements for diaconal ministers are yet to be developed. This statement was approved by the board of the Division for Ministry, which recommended adoption by the Church Council.

Council Action: The Church Council adopted the following recommendation by *en bloc* action, as reported elsewhere in these minutes:

EN BLOC   [CC93.12.120]
To adopt the document, "Associates in Ministry: Basic Standards, Academic and Practical Requirements, and Candidacy Procedures Leading to Commissioning":

ASSOCIATES IN MINISTRY IN THE
EVANGELICAL LUTHERAN CHURCH IN AMERICA

BASIC STANDARDS
ACADEMIC AND PRACTICAL REQUIREMENTS
PROCEDURES FOR COMMISSIONING

**Division for Ministry
Evangelical Lutheran Church in America**

I. *Introduction*

Associates in ministry are one of three officially recognized and rostered lay ministries in the Evangelical Lutheran Church in America. Diaconal ministers and members of the Deaconess Community of the ELCA also serve as rostered lay ministers. The term "associate in ministry" was adopted by the 1993 Churchwide Assembly to refer to the inherited lay rosters from the three predecessor church bodies that formed the ELCA, and to those persons who are approved and commissioned according to the standards and procedures of this church to serve as ELCA associ-

ates in ministry. Associates in ministry are ELCA members called to specific programmatic ministries which provide leadership and support for the ministries of the whole people of God. Associates in ministry work in partnership with laity, pastors and bishops, diaconal ministers and deaconesses to serve the mission and ministry needs of this church as they carry out responsibilities in congregations, agencies, or institutions of or related to the Evangelical Lutheran Church in America. Through this service associates in ministry provide care and nurture of the people of God in the Christian faith.

Associates in ministry are approved for commissioning through the candidacy process of the ELCA. They have prepared for service through appropriate courses of study which include theological education. They have been guided and approved by the appropriate synodical or multi-synodical Candidacy Committee according to the procedures established by the Division for Ministry. Once approved, associates in ministry are eligible for call and serve under a "Letter of Call" issued by an appropriate expression of this church: congregation, synod council, or ELCA Church Council. Having received the first call, associates in ministry are received onto the roster of the ELCA through a Service of Commissioning authorized by the appropriate synod of this church. An approved and commissioned associate in ministry has met all standards for service as an associate in ministry as established by the ELCA and enters into a relationship of mutual accountability with the calling body and the synodical and churchwide expressions of this church as set forth in the *Constitution, Bylaws and Continuing Resolutions of the Evangelical Lutheran Church in America* (ELCA 7.50. ff).

II. *Basic Standards*

Persons approved, commissioned and rostered as associates in ministry of this church shall satisfactorily meet and maintain the following "Basic Standards" established in the *Constitutions, Bylaws, and Continuing Resolutions of the Evangelical Lutheran Church in America* (ELCA 7.52.11.).
A. Commitment to Christ;
B. Acceptance of and adherence to the Confessions of Faith of this church;
C. Willingness and ability to serve in response to the needs of this church;
D. Academic and practical qualifications for the position;
E. Life consistent with the Gospel and personal qualifications including leadership abilities and competence in interpersonal relationships;
F. Receipt and acceptance of a letter of call; and
G. Membership in a congregation of this church.

III. *Candidacy in the Evangelical Lutheran Church in America*

Candidacy is the churchwide process of discernment, preparation, and approval for the officially recognized and rostered ministries of this church, both lay and ordained. This process of guidance, evaluation, and academic and practical preparation involves the partnership of candidate, congregation, synod, educational institution, and the Division for Ministry.

There are three steps in the candidacy process: Entrance; Endorsement; and Approval.

A. ENTRANCE. The synod office is the first point of contact for all interested persons. Synod staff are prepared to work with potential candidates in a process of early discernment of call to ministry. The synod office will provide interested applicants with a candidate packet which includes an Application for Candidacy. Completion of the application brings a person into contact with the Candidacy Committee of the synod who will arrange the Initial Interview and the Psychological Evaluation and Career Consultation. The candidacy process is the shared responsibility of candidate and committee. The Candidacy Committee will evaluate already completed academic work and make recommendations for future study.

All candidates in the ELCA must be active members of an ELCA congregation for a minimum of one year. The congregation of which the applicant is a member is asked to complete a congregational registration packet that is available from the synod office.

Once the Candidacy Committee has determined the appropriateness for continuing in the candidacy process, the applicant applies for admission to an appropriate college, seminary, or program approved by the Division for Ministry for completion of all academic and theological education requirements.

B. ENDORSEMENT. An applicant becomes a "Candidate" of the ELCA only after being endorsed by a Candidacy Committee. This process normally occurs during the first year of study and includes completion of the endorsement essay and an Endorsement Panel Interview as arranged by the Candidacy Committee.

C. APPROVAL. A candidate must be approved by a Candidacy Committee in order to receive a call to serve on the roster of this church. Following the completion of all academic and practical requirements, the approval process includes an essay and an Approval Interview with the Candidacy Committee. Upon final completion of all academic and field work requirements, approved candidates are presented to the Conference of Bishops for first-call assignment.

In order to be approved, associate in ministry candidates must demonstrate the following:
(1) Knowledge of and ability to articulate and integrate in the ministry setting: biblical study and interpretation, church history, the history and doctrinal teachings of the Lutheran church, and the organization and operating principles of the ELCA;
(2) Ability to articulate one's sense of calling as a baptized Christian and as an associate in ministry;
(3) Commitment to living in accordance with the "Vision and Expectations for Associates in Ministry in the ELCA";
(4) Competence in the area or areas of one's field of specialization; and
(5) At least one year of satisfactory relationship with the appropriate Candidacy Committee.

IV. *Academic and Practical Criteria for Commissioning*

All persons approved and commissioned as ELCA associates in ministry shall meet these basic requirements:

A. A minimum of a bachelor's degree or a graduate degree in a field appropriate to the designated field of specialization (see section V). If the degree is in an unrelated field of study, significant work or competency in the field of specialization must be demonstrated. In some special cases a person not holding a bachelor's degree may be considered for candidacy under the provisions described in section VI: Equivalencies/alternatives in Lieu of Academic Credentials.

B. Basic foundational course-work in theological education shall include a minimum of 20 semester credit hours (or the equivalent quarter hours).

At least one course must be completed in each of the following areas:
● Biblical studies - Old Testament
● Biblical Studies - New Testament
● Lutheran Theology and Confessional Writings
● Introductory Systematic Theology
● North American Lutheran Church History

Additional courses may include Practical Theology appropriate to the specialization. All theological education credits must be earned through courses taken at an accredited college or seminary approved by the Candidacy Committee or through a course of study approved by the Division for Ministry (eg., SELECT). The basic theological education requirement may not be met by equivalency.

C. A satisfactorily completed supervised field experience in the field of specialization as described in the candidacy document, "Guidelines for Supervised Field Experience for Associates in Ministry." The normal duration of the supervised field experience is one year with a minimum of 600 supervised hours.

D. Professional certification when appropriate (eg., day school teachers, counselors, parish nurses, etc.).

V. *Fields of Specialization - Areas of Focus for Ministry*

While an associate in ministry may serve in positions that call for diverse functions and skills, each associate in ministry is expected to have demonstrated training, qualifications, and experience in one or more specialization. Approval in one area does not limit either the associate in ministry or the calling body when determining a position description which overlaps or includes several areas of responsibility. The following four general areas of ministry are recognized for service as an associate in ministry. Examples of positions within each area are included here as illustrative but not exhaustive of each area of ministry.

A. Education

Included in the category are directors of Christian education, youth and family ministers, early childhood educators, Lutheran day school teachers and administrators, librarians, college and seminary faculty.

B. Music and the arts

Included in this category are ministers of music, cantors, teachers of music and drama, liturgical artists and teachers.

C. Administration

Included in the category are church business administrators, parish administrators, volunteer coordinators, administrators in synodical and churchwide expressions and organizations, administrators in social ministry organizations, administrators in ecumenical agencies.

D. Service and General Ministries

Included in this category are campus ministers, outdoor and camping ministers, counselors and lay chaplains, parish workers, parish nurses, and persons in social ministry positions.

VI. *Equivalencies and Alternatives in Lieu of Academic Credentials*

Persons interested in serving as an associates in ministry who have not completed the necessary academic requirement of the bachelor's degree may in some cases be considered for candidacy. This exception is reserved for those persons who, for reason of age and prior experience, may not find it appropriate to complete the bachelor's degree requirement. Such persons may apply for consideration upon evaluation of gifts for ministry, the needs of the church, and the demonstrated abilities of the individual. Age is not the primary criteria for consideration under this provision.

All requests for consideration under this provision will be evaluated by the Division for Ministry. Following evaluation a recommendation will be made to the appropriate Candidacy Committee for an alternative course of study and/or the granting of equivalencies. Evaluations will be based upon experience in non-degree studies and in demonstrated work performance comparable to that expected of a person holding a bachelor's degree.

The following is an outline of the procedure to be followed by those wishing consideration under this provision:
A.   Complete all entrance requirements;
B.   Applicant submits a written request and rationale for consideration under this provision. Based upon this request and all materials submitted, the Candidacy Committee will determine whether the applicant should proceed under this provision.
C.   Upon determination of appropriateness for consideration, the Candidacy Committee shall request a review and recommendation by the Division for Ministry. This request should be forwarded to the Director for Associates in Ministry in the Division for Ministry and include the following material:
(1) A copy of the Application to Candidacy;
(2) A copy of the written request and rationale for consideration;
(3) A detailed listing of the applicant's work experience, including relevant volunteer experience;
(4) A detailed listing of all education completed including related continuing education. All available transcripts should be included;
(5) A current position description if in the employment of a church or church related institution;
(6) Three letters of recommendation from those well acquainted with the candidate's background and work. Letters of

recommendation should include more than character references, and should include knowledge and illustration of the person's demonstrated ability. References should include one's pastor, a congregational leader familiar with the applicant's demonstrated leadership ability and gifts for ministry, and a person with competence and knowledge consistent with the candidate's area of specialization.

Having received the evaluation and recommendation of the Division for Ministry, the final decision regarding equivalency or alternative study rests with the appropriate Candidacy Committee.

Following a decision regarding equivalency or alternative study eligibility, the Candidacy Committee proceeds with endorsement, oversees the designated course of study and appropriate supervised field experience, and makes an approval decision.

Candidates proceeding under this provision must complete the normal requirements for theological education. This provision applies only to the bachelor's degree requirement.

VII. *Service Under Call*

An approved candidate is commissioned upon receipt and acceptance of a valid Letter of Call. All approved candidates participate in the churchwide assignment of candidates for first call through the Conference of Bishops. Those persons currently serving in a position who wish to remain in that position may do so providing that the appropriate call process is followed under the direction of the synodical bishop. The sources of call for associates in ministry are identified in ELCA Continuing Resolution 7.52.A93. of the ELCA *Constitution, Bylaws, and Continuing Resolutions*.

Once called and commissioned, the associate in ministry is placed on the roster of the synod of service and on the ELCA churchwide roster.

Report of the Legal and Constitutional Review Committee (continued)

Chair Magnus called upon William H. Engelbrecht to report on behalf of the Legal and Constitutional Review Committee and thanked him for his service in chairing the committee in the absence of Dale V. Sandstrom.

3. New Process for Indemnification of Certain Persons

Background: ELCA Constitution 21.03., as amended by the recent Churchwide Assembly, provides:

Where a person who, while a Church Council member, officer, employee, division board member, or committee member of this church, is or was serving at the request of this church as (or whose duties in that position involve or involved service in the capacity of) a director, officer, partner, trustee, employee, or agent of another organization, is or was made or threatened to be made a party to a proceeding by reason of such capacity, then such person shall not be entitled to indemnification unless (a) the Church Council has established a process for determining whether a person serving in the capacity described in this section shall be entitled to indemnification in any specific case, and (b) that process has been applied in making a specific determination that such person is entitled to indemnification.

A proposed process prepared by the ELCA's general counsel and reviewed by the Cabinet of Executives, council agenda Exhibit D, Part 6, is printed below.

Council Action: The proposed indemnification process was originally scheduled for adoption *en bloc*. The matter was considered separately due to several emendations made by the council's Legal and Constitutional Review Committee. William H. Engelbrecht noted

several revisions to the proposed process, copies of which had been distributed previously to the Church Council as council agenda Exhibit D, Part 6. General Counsel David J. Hardy commented on the rationale for the proposed process and cited several examples of application of the proposed process.

VOTED: *CC93.12.95*

To approve the following process for indemnification of certain persons serving on behalf of the churchwide organization, as defined in ELCA constitutional provisions 21.03., as amended:

PROCESS FOR DETERMINING PERSONS
ENTITLED TO INDEMNIFICATION UNDER
ELCA CONSTITUTION 21.03.

ELCA Constitution 21.03., as amended at the Third Churchwide Assembly, provides:

Where a person who, while a Church Council member, officer, employee, division board member, or committee member of this church, is or was serving at the request of this church as (or whose duties in that position involve or involved service in the capacity of) a director, officer, partner, trustee, employee, or agent of another organization, is or was made or threatened to be made a party to a proceeding by reason of such capacity, then such person shall not be entitled to indemnification unless (a) the Church Council has established a process for determining whether a person serving in the capacity described in this section shall be entitled to indemnification in any specific case, and (b) that process has been applied in making a specific determination that such person is entitled to indemnification.

The following process is approved by the Church Council of the Evangelical Lutheran Church in America to fulfill the first requisite of 21.03.:

1. One of the principal purposes of separate incorporation is that each organization should be responsible for its own affairs and liabilities and the conduct of its own directors, officers, and other persons whom the organization entrusted with responsibility.
2. However, there are occasions when the interests of ELCA are of sufficient importance that it will agree to indemnify a person who while serving as a Church Council member, officer, employee, division board member, or committee member of ELCA is requested by ELCA to serve in some capacity for another organization.
3. Any person who desires the benefit of indemnification under 21.03. shall make written application setting forth the name of the other organization, whether or not this other organization is incorporated, the position in the other organization that the applicant holds or will hold, and a brief statement as to why the applicants' holding of this position in the other organization is in the interests of ELCA.
4. The application must be signed by the applicant and must be endorsed by either the unit executive or the unit board or committee chair.
5. The applicant may be requested to supply additional information such as the other organization's policy on indemnification, information on the other organization's insurance coverage and financial responsibility, and a description of the responsibilities that the applicant has with relation to the other organization.
6. The application and any requested additional information should be submitted to and will first be reviewed by an administrative committee consisting of the Executive for Administration, the Secretary, the Treasurer, and the General Counsel.
7. The administrative committee shall recommend to the Executive Committee of the Church Council whether the application should be approved. The Executive Committee will decide on behalf of the Church Council. The action of the Executive

Committee will be recorded in its minutes. The applicant will be notified of the Executive Committee's decision.

8. No member of the administrative committee or the Executive Committee shall participate in decisions as to which such member is an applicant.

9. Approval may be granted on a limited basis, examples of which include but are not limited to: the approval may cover the applicant's service as a director but not as an officer of the other organization; the approval may be limited in period of time; the approval may cover civil but not criminal liabilities; the approval may be conditional upon the applicant first seeking indemnification or reimbursement from the other organization or its insurance carrier.

10. If the other organization is not a corporation, indemnification under 21.03. shall be provided only in exceptional cases.

---

4. Reporting of Approvals Made by Officers

Background: At the Church Council meeting of April 22, 1990, several resolutions were approved authorizing a committee consisting of any two of the four elected officers to adopt, on behalf of the Church Council, resolutions concerning routine business transactions or establishing banking accounts. From time to time the Church Council has adopted other resolutions authorizing specified individuals to approve specific transactions.

Council agenda Exhibit D, Part 8, reported approvals given and not previously reported to the Church Council. Copies of these approvals are included with the protocol minutes of this meeting, and the original approvals are maintained in the corporate files in the Office of the Secretary.

Council Action: William H. Engelbrecht introduced briefly the report provided in council agenda Exhibit D, Part 8. The council received the report as information.

5. Amendment of Continuing Resolution 9.52.A87.

Background: As a result of amendments adopted by the 1993 Churchwide Assembly, a continuing resolution (9.52.A87.) related to congregation constitutions needs to be revised to conform the current language of constitutional provision 9.52., which reads: "The governing documents of congregations recognized at the establishment of this church shall continue to govern such congregations. When such a congregation wishes to amend any provision of its governing documents, the governing documents so amended shall conform to 9.25.b. The synod responsible for review of such amendments may permit, for good cause, a congregation to retain particular unamended provisions in the congregation's governing documents that were in force at the establishment of this church." The proposed text for the amended continuing resolution follows (deletions shaded; additions underlined).

Council Action: William H. Engelbrecht introduced the following resolution, which was adopted subsequently by the Church Council without discussion by a greater than two-thirds vote.

2/3 VOTE REQUIRED

VOTED: *CC93.12.96*

To adopt the following continuing resolution as 9.52.A93. to replace previously existing continuing resolution 9.52.A87.:

The Church Council, in cooperation with the synods, shall ~~develop~~ provide an ongoing process for congregations whose governing documents have been accepted into the church under 9.52. to review those documents within four years of the establishment of this church and compare them with the required elements of the Model Constitution for Congregations listed in ~~9.53.01.~~ 9.25.b., applicable to the extent provided in 9.52. to congregations recognized and received by this church as of January 1, 1988. Congregations are encouraged to resolve significant conflicts between their governing documents and the Model Constitution for Congregations.

6. Procedure to Implement †S14.13.c.

Background: During this past year, at the request of one of the synods, the ELCA's general counsel, with suggestions from the ELCA secretary and outside counsel, prepared a proposed Procedure for Dealing with Allegations of Physical or Mental Incapacity of a Pastor under Synodical Constitution †S14.13.b. and c. (and identical provisions of Model Constitution for Congregations C9.05.b. and c.). These synod constitutional provisions read:

b. When allegations of physical or mental incapacity of the pastor . . . have come to the attention of the bishop of the synod, the bishop in his or her sole discretion may, or when such allegations have been brought to the synod's attention by an official recital of allegations by the Congregation Council or by a petition signed by at least one-third of the voting members of the congregation, the bishop shall, investigate such conditions personally in company with a committee of two ordained ministers and one layperson.

c. In case of alleged physical or mental incapacity, competent medical testimony shall be obtained. When such disability is evident, the bishop of the synod with the advice of the committee shall declare the pastorate vacant. Upon the restoration of a disabled pastor to health, the bishop of the synod shall take steps to enable the pastor to resume the ministry, either in the congregation last served or in another field of labor.

The Conference of Bishops, after reviewing the document, recommended to the Church Council that this document be adopted as procedure to be utilized in situations requiring action under †S14.13.c.

Council Action: William H. Engelbrecht introduced the following resolution, subsequently adopted by the Church Council. During discussion, the Rev. Stephen M. Youngdahl commented on the importance of establishing written procedures, and noted that the New England Synod already had adopted a similar set of guidelines.

VOTED: *CC93.12.97*

To adopt the following "Procedure for Dealing with Allegations of Physical or Mental Incapacity of a Pastor Under †S14.13.b. and c. in the Constitu-

tion for Synods of the Evangelical Lutheran Church in America":

PROCEDURES FOR DEALING WITH ALLEGATIONS OF PHYSICAL OR MENTAL INCAPACITY OF A PASTOR UNDER SYNODICAL CONSTITUTION †S14.13.B. AND †S14.13.C.

1. When allegations of physical or mental incapacity of a pastor have come to the attention of the bishop of the synod, the bishop in his or her sole discretion may investigate such conditions personally in company with a committee of two ordained ministers and one lay person.

2. When allegations of physical or mental incapacity of the pastor have been brought to the synod's attention by an official recital of allegations by the congregation council or by a petition signed by at least one-third of the voting members of the congregation, the bishop must investigate such conditions personally in company with a committee of two ordained ministers and one lay person.

3. The committee of three persons who accompany the bishop shall be appointed by the Executive Committee of the Synod Council. These three persons must be members of congregations of the Evangelical Lutheran Church in America, but not necessarily of congregations of the synod in which is rostered the pastor who is the subject of the allegations.

4. The pastor who is the subject of the allegations shall be advised either orally or in writing of the appointment and composition of the committee and the purpose of the committee's inquiry.

5. The cooperation of the pastor shall be solicited by the bishop or other committee member designated by the bishop. To this end, the pastor may be requested to do one or more of the following:

   To execute appropriate releases authorizing his or her own health care providers to provide information to the committee and bishop.

   To execute appropriate releases authorizing hospitals or similar institutions to provide information to the committee and bishop.

   To submit to examination, testing and evaluation by physicians or other professionals designated by the committee and bishop and to execute appropriate releases authorizing such physicians and other professionals to provide the results of such examination, testing, and evaluation to the committee and bishop.

   To provide releases authorizing employers, educational institutions, or others to provide information to the committee and the bishop.

   To provide written information to the committee and the bishop.

   To meet with the committee, the bishop, or both, either separately or at the same time, to respond to questions.

   The cost associated with any of the foregoing, to the extent not reimbursed by the pastor's medical insurance plan, shall be paid by the synod.

6. All information obtained by the committee and the bishop under item 5 (above) shall be shared with the pastor.

7. If the pastor has complied with all of the requests made by the committee and bishop under item 5, the pastor, at his or her own expense, may submit to the committee and bishop the report of physicians or other professionals who, after examining the pastor, are in disagreement with the conclusions of any of the physicians or other professionals whose report was obtained under item 5.

8. If the pastor does not comply with any request made of him or her under item 5, the committee and the bishop may retain one or more competent physicians, psychiatrists, psychologists, or other professionals, who may give testimony to the committee and the bishop based upon available evidence of the pastor's physical or mental condition. Such evidence may include, but is not limited to, written or verbal statements of persons who have observed the pastor. Any testimony given pursuant to this paragraph shall be considered "competent medical testimony" for the purpose of required provision †S.14.13.c of the Constitution for Synods.

9. On the basis of all of the evidence considered, the committee and the bishop shall determine whether physical or mental incapacity of the pastor is evident. The committee and bishop shall find that physical or mental incapacity is evident if, based upon the evidence, the committee and the bishop determine that it is more likely than not that the pastor is physically or mentally incapable of fulfilling adequately his or her duties and responsibilities.

10. If the committee and the bishop decide that the pastor is physically or mentally incapacitated, the bishop shall declare the pastorate vacant, and the status of the pastor shall be on leave from call with the sub-category of medical/temporary disability. The Synod Council shall grant such status.

11. During the period of the pastor's physical or mental incapacity, the bishop or his or her representative shall work with the pastor and the pastor's family to assist the pastor in receiving appropriate care and treatment.

12. Upon restoration of a disabled pastor to health, the bishop shall take steps to enable the pastor to resume ministry, either in the congregation last served if the incapacity has been of short duration or in another field of labor if the incapacity has been of longer duration.

7. Burden of Proof

Background: A resolution introduced at the 1993 Churchwide Assembly by a voting member called for the use of a "clear and convincing" burden of proof standard in cases involving suspension from the clergy roster, and "beyond a reasonable doubt" burden of proof standard in cases involving removal from the clergy roster. This would be in lieu of the "preponderance of the evidence" standard set forth in "Rules Governing Disciplinary Proceedings Against an Ordained Minister or a Congregation of the Evangelical Lutheran Church in America." In accordance with assembly rules, this resolution was submitted to the Committee of Reference and Counsel, which recommended that the resolution be referred to the Church Council for consideration after consultation with the Conference of Bishops and the general counsel. The assembly adopted the committee's recommendation.

The Legal and Constitutional Review Committee discussed this matter at its December 4, 1993, meeting, prior to council consideration.

Council Action: William H. Engelbrecht introduced the following recommendation of the Legal and Constitutional Review Committee, subsequently adopted by the Church Council without discussion:

VOTED: *CC93.12.98*

To request the General Counsel to prepare an analysis of the issues involved in the burden of proof standard in discipline cases for review by the Conference of Bishops through its Committee on Liaison with the Church Council; and

To request the Conference of Bishops to review this analysis and make a report and recommendation to the Church Council at its April 1994 meeting.

8. Establishment of the Endowment Fund Of the Evangelical Lutheran Church in America

Approval of Incorporation

Background: The 1993 Churchwide Assembly authorized the establishment of a separately incorporated Endowment Fund of the Evangelical Lutheran Church in America. This separate corporation can include the operations heretofore conducted by the ELCA Foundation on an expanded basis. It is believed that a separate corporation fulfilling these functions is desirable for various reasons.

Certain of the existing activities of the Foundation are subject to governmental reporting and regulation. Experience with the separately incorporated Mission Investment Fund of the Evangelical Lutheran Church in America clearly demonstrates that compliance with such governmental reporting and regulation would be much easier for the ELCA Foundation, if it were separately incorporated.

Separate incorporation will enable the ELCA Foundation to prepare financial statements that will be less complicated. In contrast, where the Foundation and endowment funds are not separately incorporated, these assets and operations must be presented as part of the financial presentation of the entire churchwide organization, including the liabilities and contingent liabilities of the churchwide organization.

A major opportunity for this church is to provide investment services on the fee basis for the management of the endowment funds of congregations and institutions. Furnishing these services requires compliance with federal and state laws regulating investment service. Compliance with these laws will be easier, if the ELCA Foundation is separately incorporated.

The annual filing with the Internal Revenue Service of the ELCA's Group Exemption was due on November 1, 1993. In order for Endowment Fund of the Evangelical Lutheran Church in America to be included in this filing, it was necessary that Articles of Incorporation first be filed with the Minnesota Secretary of State. Accordingly, this action was taken, using Articles of Incorporation that were closely patterned after the articles of incorporation of other separately incorporated organizations, namely, the Board of Pensions, the Publishing House of the ELCA, and the Mission Investment Fund—all Minnesota nonprofit corporations.

Council Action: William H. Engelbrecht introduced the following recommendation of the Legal and Constitutional Review Committee, subsequently adopted by the Church Council without discussion:

VOTED: CC93.12.99

To approve the filing of Articles of Incorporation of the Endowment Fund of the Evangelical Lutheran Church in America, printed in council agenda Exhibit D, Part 4, in keeping with amendments to the Constitution, Bylaws, and Continuing Resolutions of the Evangelical Lutheran Church in America, as adopted by the 1993 Churchwide Assembly.

Bylaws of the Endowment Fund

William H. Engelbrecht introduced the following recommendation of the Legal and Constitutional Review Committee, subsequently adopted by the Church Council without discussion:

VOTED: CC93.12.100

To approve the bylaws for the separately incorporated Endowment Fund of the Evangelical Lutheran Church in America, printed in council agenda Exhibit D, Part 5.

Transfer of Assets

Background: To effectuate the establishment of the separately incorporated Endowment Fund of the Evangelical Lutheran Church in America, it is appropriate that the Church Council authorize the transfer of certain assets to this new corporation.

Council Action: William H. Engelbrecht introduced the following recommendation of the Legal and Constitutional Review Committee, subsequently adopted by the Church Council without discussion:

VOTED: CC93.12.101

To approve the transfer of appropriate assets to the separately incorporated Endowment Fund of the Evangelical Lutheran Church in America;

To authorize the secretary and treasurer of this church to execute the appropriate documents for this transfer; and

To authorize the secretary and treasurer to take such other actions as may be required to effect this transfer.

9. Revision of Rules Governing Disciplinary Proceedings

Background: Pursuant to ELCA bylaw 20.21.16., the Church Council approved on November 10, 1991, *Rules Governing Disciplinary Proceedings Against an Ordained Minister or a Congregation of the Evangelical Lutheran Church in America* (rules), as that document had been developed by a subcommittee of the Committee on Appeals (subcommittee). At the same time that such approval was given, the Church Council authorized the subcommittee to initiate further revisions in the rules, as experience demonstrated advisable. In addition, the 1993 Churchwide Assembly approved the recommendation from the Study on Ministry that associates in ministry be subject to the same disciplinary process as ordained ministers.

A revision of the rules has been prepared by the subcommittee (Pastors Karen G. Bockelman, Victor L. Brandt, Philip L. Wahlberg). The subcommittee solicited comments from the Conference of Bishops on a draft of revised rules prepared by the subcommittee. The Committee of Hearing Officers also was provided with copies and was invited to share comments. A revision of rules incorporating the recommendations from the Conference of Bishops was distributed to council members as council agenda Exhibit D, Part 1.

Council Action: William H. Engelbrecht introduced the following recommendation of the Legal and Constitutional Review Committee, subsequently adopted by the Church Council. General Counsel David J. Hardy noted that the Legal and Constitutional Review Committee had recommended revision in two of the rules, i.e., D3.e., and H6.

VOTED: CC93.12.102

To adopt the following "Rules Governing Disciplinary Proceedings against an Ordained Minister or a Congregation of the Evangelical Lutheran Church in America" in keeping with action of the 1993 Churchwide Assembly related to recommendations of the Study of Ministry:

RULES GOVERNING DISCIPLINARY PROCEEDINGS
AGAINST AN ORDAINED MINISTER, A ROSTERED LAYPERSON,
OR A CONGREGATIONOF THE
EVANGELICAL LUTHERAN CHURCH IN AMERICA

[As recommended to the Church Council by a Subcommittee of the Committee on Appeals Reflecting suggestions by the Conference of Bishops. Additions underlined; deletions shaded.]

INDEX

A. Preface
B. Introductory Matters
C. Temporary Suspension Without Prejudice of Ordained Ministers or Rostered Laypersons
D. Consultation: The Process Before Charges Are Brought by the Synodical Bishop
E. Dismissal of Charges When Brought by Someone Other than the Synodical Bishop
F. Discipline Hearing Committee–Preliminary Matters
G. The Hearing Officer of a Discipline Hearing Committee
H. Facilitators
I. The Hearing Before the Discipline Hearing Committee
J. Due Process in Discipline Proceedings
K. Discipline Committee - Post Hearing Matters
L. Appeals
   Reference Table

[Proposed Revision]
[Additions underlined; deletions shaded]

Rules Governing Disciplinary Proceedings
Against an Ordained Minister, a Rostered Layperson,
Or a Congregation of the
Evangelical Lutheran Church in America

A.   Preface
     Chapter 20 of the Constitution, Bylaws, and Continuing Resolutions ("governing documents") of the Evangelical Lutheran Church in America ("ELCA") and these rules set forth the ecclesiastical process by which this church determines who will preach and teach in its name. This process reflects the faith of this church and this church's understanding of its nature and mission. The freedom of this church to decide for itself who will minister in its name is a precious one that is safeguarded by the First Amendment to the United States Constitution. Therefore, this church will seek to protect its ecclesiastical disciplinary process from interference by secular authorities.

Chapter 20 of the governing documents of the Evangelical Lutheran Church in America (ELCA) sets forth a juridical process for the discipline of This process may be invoked when ordained ministers, rostered laypersons, and or congregations that fail to maintain ELCA standards. The governing documents (20.21.16.) specifically provide for rules of procedure for the performance of duties of hearing officers and discipline hearing committee. Sections F1 through K15 specifically constitute these rules.

The Church Council of the ELCA has concluded that this process will be facilitated if the material (that has been developed by the same process prescribed in 20.21.16.) found in Sections B1 through E6 and L1 through L23 is available to those who are involved in the discipline process–bishops, bishop's assistants, members of consultation and advisory panels, discipline and appeals committees, hearing officers, facilitators, accuser(s) and accused, their respective representatives, complaining witnesses, and their friends or advocates.

A number of the rules–indicated by an asterisk–are quotations from, or paraphrases of, ELCA constitutional, bylaw or continuing resolution provisions. A reference table at the end of the rules indicates the constitutional, bylaw or continuing resolution provision on which such rules are based.

B.   Introductory Matters
   *B1. Ordained ministers of the ELCA shall be subject to discipline for:
        a.   preaching and teaching in conflict with the faith confessed by this church;
        b.   conduct incompatible with the character of the ministerial office;
        c.   willfully disregarding or violating the functions and standards established by this church for the office of Word and sacrament; or
        d.   willfully disregarding the provisions of the constitution or bylaws of this church.
   *B2. Charges against an ordained minister which could lead to discipline must be specific and in writing, subscribed to by the accuser(s), and be made by one or more of the following:
        a.   at least two-thirds of the members of the Congregation cCouncil of the congregation to of which the ordained minister is under call, submitted to the synodical bishop;
        b.   at least one-third of the voting members of such congregation, submitted to the synodical bishop;
        c.   at least two-thirds of the members of the governing body to which the ordained minister, if not a parish pastor, is accountable, submitted to the synodical bishop;
        d.   at least 10 ordained ministers of the synod on whose roster the accused
             ordained minister is listed, submitted to the synodical bishop; or
        e.   the synodical bishop.
   *B3. Lay persons on official rosters shall be subject to discipline for:
        a.   confessing and teaching in conflict with the faith confessed by this church;
        b.   conduct incompatible with the standards for rostered ministries of this church;
        c.   willfully disregarding or violating the functions and standards established by this church for the lay roster or rosters; or
        d.   willfully disregarding the provisions of the constitution or bylaws of this church.
   B4.   A rostered layperson is one who is on one of the rosters maintained under authority of ELCA Bylaws 7.51.02., 7.51.03., 7.51.04., and 7.51.05.

*B5. Charges against a lay person on an official roster that could lead to discipline must be specific and in writing, subscribed to by the accuser(s), and be made by one or more of the following:

   a.   at least two-thirds of the members of the Congregation Council of the congregation in which the lay person is serving, submitted to the synodical bishop;

   b.   at least one-third of the voting members of the congregation of which the lay person is serving, submitted to the synodical bishop;

   c.   at least two-thirds of the members of the governing body to which the lay person, if not serving a congregation, is accountable, submitted to the synodical bishop;

   d.   at least 10 ordained ministers or lay persons on official rosters of the synod on whose roster the accused lay person is listed, submitted to the synodical bishop; or

   e.   the synodical bishop.

*B3̶6. Congregations of the ELCA shall be subject to discipline for:

   a.   departing from the faith confessed by this church;

   b.   willfully disregarding or violating the criteria for recognition as congregations of this church; or

   c.   willfully disregarding or violating the provisions of the constitution or bylaws of this church.

*B4̶7. Charges against a congregation which could lead to discipline must be specific and in writing, subscribed to by the accuser(s), and be made by one or more of the following:

   a.   at least one-fifth of the voting members of the congregation, submitted to the synodical bishop;

   b.   at least three other congregations of the synod, submitted to the synodical bishop;

   c.   the Synod Council; or

   d.   the synodical bishop.

B5̶8. As used in these rules, "accused" refers to an ordained minister, rostered layperson, or congregation against whom charges have been made under Rules B2, or B4 5, or B7 and "accuser" means a person(s) who signed such charges. An accuser need not necessarily have direct, firsthand knowledge of the alleged acts, conduct or instances that are set forth as specifications in the charges nor is an accuser necessarily required to testify at a subsequent hearing. A̶n̶ person individual who has firsthand knowledge of alleged acts, conduct, or instances and who is identified in the charges is sometimes referred to as a "witness" or a "complaining witness".

B6̶9. Charges shall set forth the offense of which the accused is alleged to be guilty. An offense is an act or conduct set forth either in e̶i̶t̶h̶e̶r̶ ELCA Bylaw 20.21.01. (Rule B1) in the case of ordained ministers, Bylaw 20.23.01. (Rule B3) in the case of rostered laypersons, or 20.31.01. (Rule B3̶6) in the case of congregations or described in the definitions and guidelines approved by the Church Council pursuant to ELCA Bylaw 20.71.11. The specification(s) contained in the charges shall state what the accused is alleged to have done which, if true, constitutes an instance(s) of the offense(s).

B7̶10. T̶h̶e̶ r̶ Resignation from the roster of ordained ministers, or from a roster of laypersons, terminates any disciplinary action that is pending or that might otherwise be brought against an ordained minister or a rostered layperson.

B11. When the resignation occurs after a synodical bishop has brought written charges, or when charges are brought other than by the synodical bishop and have not been withdrawn or dismissed or otherwise disposed of as provided in ELCA Bylaw 20.21.06. (Rule E4), a copy of the charges shall be forwarded to the secretary of the ELCA for retention as provided in ELCA Bylaw 7.41.17. When the resignation occurs earlier than as specified in the preceding sentence, the synodical bishop shall decide to what extent a record of the matter shall be preserved.

B8̶12. Where these rules provide that notice is to be given or delivered to, or service is to be made upon, the accused or the accuser(s), such notice or service may be by personal delivery, by telephone, by facsimile transmission, by courier delivery, by commercial overnight delivery, or by U.S. mail. The use of registered or certified mail with restricted return receipt requested is recommended as the means of establishing the date when mail was actually received by a person.

B13. When a party is represented by an attorney, notice that is given to that attorney shall be deemed to have been given to that party, and documents provided to that attorney shall be deemed to have been provided to that party. However, parties may communicate directly with one another, notwithstanding the fact that one or more of them are represented by attorneys.

B9̶14. The synod of jurisdiction for disciplinary proceedings against an ordained minister or a rostered layperson shall always be the synod on whose c̶l̶e̶r̶g̶y̶ roster such ordained minister's or rostered layperson's name appears at the time t̶h̶e̶ d̶i̶s̶c̶i̶p̶l̶i̶n̶a̶r̶y̶ p̶r̶o̶c̶e̶e̶d̶i̶n̶g̶s̶ a̶r̶e̶ c̶o̶m̶m̶e̶n̶c̶e̶d̶ that written charges are filed, even though specific allegations may involve p̶r̶i̶o̶r̶ events that occurred when the o̶r̶d̶a̶i̶n̶e̶d̶ m̶i̶n̶i̶s̶t̶e̶r̶ individual was on the c̶l̶e̶r̶g̶y̶ roster of another synod.

B1̶0̶15. The synod of jurisdiction for disciplinary proceedings against a congregation shall always be the synod on whose roster of congregations such congregation appears at the time t̶h̶e̶ d̶i̶s̶c̶i̶p̶l̶i̶n̶a̶r̶y̶ p̶r̶o̶c̶e̶e̶d̶i̶n̶g̶s̶ a̶r̶e̶ c̶o̶m̶m̶e̶n̶c̶e̶d̶ that written charges are filed.

B16. Many of the provisions of Rules D1 through E6 are based on provisions of ELCA Bylaw 20.21.04. through 20.21.06. that by their express terms are applicable to ordained ministers. These same bylaw provisions have been made applicable to rostered laypersons by virtue of ELCA Bylaw 20.23.04. and to congregations by virtue of ELCA Bylaw 20.31.04. Accordingly, Rules D1 through E6 are applicable regardless of whether the individual or entity is an ordained minister, a rostered layperson, or a congregation.

B17. Many of the provisions of Rules F1 through K16 are based on provisions of ELCA Bylaw 20.21.07. through 20.21.22. that by their express terms are applicable to ordained ministers. These same bylaw provisions have been made applicable to rostered laypersons by virtue of ELCA Bylaw 20.23.05. and to congregations by virtue of ELCA Bylaw 20.31.05. Accordingly, Rules F1 through K16 are applicable regardless of whether accused is an ordained minister, a rostered layperson, or a congregation.

B18. Any right extended to any party under Chapter 20 of the governing documents or by these rules may be waived by that party. It is preferable that any such waiver be in writing, but not necessary, unless otherwise provided under Chapter 20 of the governing documents or under these rules.

C. Temporary Suspension Without Prejudice of Ordained Ministers or Rostered Laypersons

*C1. If there are indications that a cause for discipline exists or if in the course of the proceedings it should become apparent to the bishop of the synod that the pastoral office cannot be conducted effectively in the congregation(s) being served by the ordained minister due to local conditions or that local conditions may be adversely affected by the continued service by the ordained minister, the bishop of the synod may temporarily suspend the pastor from service in the congregation(s) without prejudice and with compensation including benefits provided through a joint churchwide/synod fund and with housing provided by the congregation(s).

*C2. If there are indications that a cause for discipline exists or if in the course of the proceedings it should become apparent to the bishop of the synod that the role and function of the associate in ministry, Deaconess of the Evangelical Lutheran Church in America, or diaconal minister cannot be conducted effectively in the congregation(s) being served by such rostered layperson due to local conditions or that local conditions may be adversely affected by the continued service by a rostered layperson, the bishop of the synod may temporarily suspend a rostered layperson from service in the congregation(s) without prejudice and with compensation including benefits provided through a joint churchwide-synod-congregation fund.

C2̶3̶. Notwithstanding the preceding rule either Rule C1 or C2, the congregation may continue agree to provide some or all of the compensation including benefits of an ordained minister or rostered layperson who has been temporarily suspended, thereby releasing to such extent the obligation upon churchwide and synod funds.

C4. For the purposes of C1 and C2 the term "benefits" shall include only (a) those payments required to be made to the Board of Pensions of the Evangelical Lutheran Church in America for participation in the pension, medical, and other insurance plans of such Board for the account of an ordained minister or rostered layperson who is a sponsored member in such plans, or (b) the actual payments made for the purpose of providing pension, medical, and other insurance benefits for an ordained minister or rostered layperson who is not a sponsored member, but not in an amount that would exceed the amount described in clause (a) hereof if such person were a sponsored member.

*C3̶5̶. If there are indications that a cause for discipline exists or if in the course of proceedings, it becomes apparent to the bishop of the synod that the circumstances require, the bishop of the synod may temporarily suspend an ordained minister serving under letter of call issued other than by a congregation from the office and functions of ordained ministry without prejudice and without affecting compensation and housing.

*C6. If there are indications that a cause for discipline exists or if in the course of proceedings it becomes apparent to the bishop of the synod that the circumstances require, the bishop of the synod may temporarily suspend a rostered layperson serving under letter of call issued other than by a congregation from the office and functions of a rostered layperson without prejudice and without affecting compensation.

C4̶7̶. If there are indications that a cause for discipline exists or if in the course of proceedings, it becomes apparent to the bishop of the synod that the circumstances require, the bishop of the synod may temporarily suspend an ordained minister who is without call from the office and functions of ordained ministry without prejudice.

C8. If there are indications that a cause for discipline exists or if in the course of proceedings it becomes apparent to the bishop of the synod that the circumstances require, the bishop of the synod may temporarily suspend a rostered layperson who is without call without prejudice.

C5̶9̶. If there are indications that a cause for discipline exists, or if in the course of proceedings it becomes apparent to the bishop of the synod that the circumstances require, the bishop of the synod may temporarily suspend a retired ordained minister from the office and functions of ordained ministry without prejudice.

C10. If there are indications that a cause for discipline exists or if in the course of proceedings it becomes apparent to the bishop of the synod that the circumstances require, the bishop of the synod may temporarily suspend a retired rostered layperson without prejudice.

C11. The term "without prejudice" as used in Rules C1, C2, and C5 through C10 requires that the discipline hearing committee shall not consider the fact that the accused has been temporarily suspended in deciding whether the charges against the accused are true.

D. Consultation: The Process Before Charges Are Brought by the Synodical Bishop

*D1. When there is an indication that a cause for discipline exists, efforts shall be made by the bishop of the synod to resolve the situation by consultation; for assistance in these efforts, the bishop may utilize either a consultation panel or an advisory panel.

D2. The decision to utilize a consultation panel or an advisory panel or neither belongs solely to the synodical bishop.

D2. In addition to, or in lieu of, a consultation panel or an advisory panel, a synodical bishop may utilize the assistance of one of his or her assistants or other staff persons or any other individual appointed by the synodical bishop for this purpose.

D3. A consultation panel or advisory panel does not conduct a formal hearing, nor can such a panel take formal action against any person. Rather, such a panel exists solely to assist the synodical bishop in efforts to resolve the situation by consultation and/or to advise the synodical bishop whether he or she should submit charges and thereby initiate the formal disciplinary process. In other words, a consultation panel or advisory panel merely functions as a group of trusted advisors to the synodical bishop. As a result:

a. The decision to utilize a consultation panel, an advisory panel, or not to utilize either, belongs solely to the synodical bishop.

b. The due process rights provided in the formal disciplinary process–such as the right to specific written notice of the charges, the right to be represented by counsel, and the right to confront witnesses–do not apply to the informal consultation process.

c. The synodical bishop shall decide to what extent he or she should participate in the interviews and/or deliberations of a consultation panel or an advisory panel. The synodical bishop shall not be deemed a member of a consultation panel or advisory panel for purposes of Rule D18 or for any other purpose, even if the synodical bishop participates in any or all of the interviews and deliberations of a panel.

d. Neither a consultation panel nor an advisory panel can take formal action against a person. Such a panel can merely make recommendations to the synodical bishop.

e. The synodical bishop need not follow or even disclose the recommendations made by a consultation panel or advisory panel, even when the synodical bishop participates in any or all of the interviews and deliberations of a panel.

D3̶4. With the exception of the procedures set forth in Rules E1 through E6, the only difference between a consultation panel and an advisory panel is the method of appointment and the eligibility of persons to serve on the panel.

*D4̶5. The Consultation Committee shall consist of 12 persons, of whom five shall be ordained ministers and seven shall be lay persons, who shall each be elected by the Synod Assembly for a term of six years without consecutive reelection.

*D5̶6. When requested by the synodical bishop, a consultation panel consisting of five persons (three ordained ministers and two lay persons) appointed from the members of the Consultation Committee of the synod by the synodical bishop, or, at the request of the synodical bishop, by the Synod Executive Committee or other committee authorized to do so by the Synod Council, shall assist the synodical bishop in efforts to resolve a situation by consultation.

*D6̶7. When requested by the synodical bishop, an advisory panel consisting of five persons (three ordained ministers and two lay persons) appointed by the synodical bishop shall assist the synodical bishop in efforts to resolve a situation by consultation.

D7̶8. One member of the panel may be designated as the chair by the appointer of the panel.

D8̶9. While lay members of an advisory panel must be members of an ELCA congregation, that congregation need not be on the roll of congregations of the synod in which disciplinary proceedings must be brought. While clergy members of an advisory panel must be on the clergy roster of the ELCA, they need not be on the clergy roster of the synod in which disciplinary proceedings must be brought. An advisory panel may include as some of its members, members of the Consultation Committee Members of the Consultation Committee may be appointed to an advisory panel.

D9. No individual can serve as a member of a consultation panel or advisory panel if such individual is related (as defined in ELCA Bylaw 19.61.04.) to the bishop whom the panel is to advise or to the concerned ordained minister or is a member or former member of the concerned congregation.

*D10. When appointed at the request of the synodical bishop, a consultation panel or advisory panel shall advise the synodical bishop as to whether or not the bishop should bring charges or may make other recommendation for resolution of the controversy that would not involve proceedings before a discipline hearing committee.

D11. Since the purpose of a consultation panel or advisory panel is to assist a synodical bishop in efforts to resolve a matter through consultation, the panel's advice to the bishop is never binding upon the bishop,

who must decide whether or not to bring charges or to pursue some other method to resolve the matter.

D1̶2̶11. The consultation or advisory panel may recommend through the bishop that the ordained minister or the rostered layperson resign from the current call or resign from the clergy roster or from the appropriate roster of laypersons.

D1̶3̶12. Whenever possible, a consultation panel or an advisory panel shall endeavor to resolve the controversy through recommendations that are pastoral and therapeutic and that if accepted by the parties and others concerned will eliminate the necessity for proceedings before a discipline hearing committee.

D14. A consultation panel or advisory panel does not conduct a formal hearing. Accordingly, the due process provisions that apply before a discipline hearing committee are not applicable to the work of a consultation or advisory panel.

D1̶5̶13. When the subject of a consultation or advisory panel's inquiry concerns an ordained minister or a rostered layperson, its meetings should be closed sessions, except in unusual circumstances and at the direction of the bishop. When the subject of the panel's inquiry concerns a congregation, its meetings may be open or closed sessions at the discretion direction of the panel bishop.

*D1̶6̶14. The panel may meet with complaining witnesses, as well as with the concerned ordained minister, concerned rostered layperson, or leadership of the concerned congregation, or any other persons who have information that the panel wishes to consider.

D1̶7̶15. A consultation panel or advisory panel may be flexible in dealing with a particular matter. FF23or example, in one case it may be desirable to meet with interview complaining witnesses and the concerned ordained minister or concerned rostered layperson at the same time and place, while in another case it may be preferable that the panel meet interview separately with the complaining witnesses and the concerned ordained minister or concerned rostered layperson.

D1̶8̶16. An individual or congregation may decline to appear before be interviewed by a consultation or advisory panel.

D17. Any individual who does appear before is interviewed by a consultation or advisory panel may be accompanied by a spouse, friend, relative, advocate or representative; however such spouse, friend, relative, advocate or representative shall not participate in discussion with the panel. Members of a congregation chosen to represent it may appear before be interviewed by the panel.

D1̶9̶18. Members of a consultation or advisory panel may not testify in subsequent proceedings before a discipline hearing committee as to statements made by an ordained minister or by representatives of a congregation in discussion with the panel. Evidence, witnesses or testimony identified as a result of statements made by an ordained minister or by representatives of a congregation to members of the panel may be used by the accuser in subsequent proceedings before a discipline hearing committee in which such ordained minister or congregation is the accused regarding any statement they heard or information they learned while serving as members of the committee. However, any witnesses or evidence identified as the result of the statements or information presented to a panel may be presented in subsequent proceedings before a discipline hearing committee.

*D2019. If requested by the synodical bishop, members of the panel may also assist, as representatives of the accuser, in the presentation of accuser's case and examination of witnesses before a discipline hearing committee.

D2120. Members of a consultation panel or advisory panel shall refrain from discussing matters considered by the panel except as required to discharge the duties of the panel.

E. Dismissal of Charges When Brought by Someone Other than the Synodical Bishop

E1. Most frequently, formal disciplinary proceedings are commenced when a synodical bishop brings charges. Rules E1 through E6 provide a special process that a bishop may invoke in the less frequent cases when charges have been brought pursuant to ELCA Bylaw 20.21.03. (Rule B2), ELCA Bylaw 20.23.03. (Rule B4), or ELCA Bylaw 20.31.03. (Rule B46) by someone other than the bishop.

E2. The invocation of the provisions of ELCA Bylaw 20.21.06. (Rule E4) is always discretionary with the synodical bishop. The bishop may, but is not required to, utilize a consultation panel when charges are filed by someone of the other than the bishop, persons or entities authorized to bring charges under ELCA Bylaw 20.21.03. (Rule B2), ELCA 20.23.03. (Rule B4), or ELCA Bylaw 20.31.03. (Rule B46).

E3. The provisions of ELCA Bylaw 20.21.06. (Rule E4), if utilized by the synodical bishop, require the use of a consultation panel, constituted in the manner described in ELCA Bylaw 20.21.04.a. (Rule D56). The provisions of ELCA Bylaw 20.21.06. (Rule E34) cannot be utilized by an advisory panel described in ELCA Bylaw 20.21.04.b. (Rule D67).

*E4. When charges are brought by someone authorized to do so, other than by the synodical bishop, the synodical bishop may refer such charges to a consultation panel as provided in appointed in accordance with 20.21.04.a. (Rule D56):

a. If as a result of meeting with a consultation panel the charges are withdrawn by the accuser(s), no further proceedings shall be required.

b. Upon recommendation of the consultation panel that the charges be dismissed, the synodical bishop may dismiss the charges, in which case no further proceedings shall be required.

c. Upon recommendation of the consultation panel that some of the allegations supporting the charges be stricken, the synodical bishop may strike some or all of such allegations, and further proceedings shall be required on the remaining allegations.

d. In the case of charges that do not anticipate disciplinary action, the consultation panel shall submit a report in writing to the synodical bishop that sets forth the action or actions recommended by the consultation panel, and the synodical bishop shall convey the recommendations to the parties. If either party does not accept the recommendations, that party may appeal to the Synod Council, whose decision shall be final.

e. In the case of charges that anticipate disciplinary action that have not been withdrawn or dismissed as a result of 20.21.06.a. or b. above, the charges shall be referred to a discipline hearing committee for a hearing.

f. The work of a consultation panel under this section should shall be completed within 30 days from the time the panel was constituted.

*E5. While the synodical bishop is not required to follow the recommendations of a consultation panel, the bishop has authority to dismiss the charges or strike certain of the allegations supporting the charges only when so recommended by a consultation panel.

E6. No individual can serve as member of a consultation panel if (i) such individual is related (as defined in ELCA Bylaw 19.61.04.) to the accused if an individual or to any of the accuser(s) if an individual(s),; (ii) such individual is a member or a former member of a congregation that is the accused or accuser, or ; (iii) such member is a member of the Synod Council who is the accuser; or (iv) such individual is an accused or accuser.

F. Discipline Hearing Committee–Preliminary Matters

*F1. A discipline hearing committee shall be convened to conduct a hearing whenever charges are brought by the synodical bishop, or are brought by others and have not been withdrawn or dismissed under the process described in ELCA Bylaw 20.21.06. (Rule E4). The voting members of this committee shall be composed of 12 persons of whom six shall be the members of the Committee on Discipline of the synod and six shall be selected from the churchwide Committee on Discipline under the process described in ELCA Bylaw 20.21.12. (see Rules F11 and F14). A hearing officer selected from the churchwide Committee of Hearing Officers under the process described in ELCA Bylaw 20.21.14. (Rule F15), shall preside as the nonvoting chair of the discipline hearing committee.

*F2. The Committee on Discipline of the synod shall consist of six persons of whom three shall be ordained and three shall be lay persons, who shall each be elected by the Synod Assembly for a term of six years without consecutive reelection.

*F3. The churchwide Committee on Discipline shall consist of 21 28 persons elected by the Churchwide Assembly for a term of six years, each without consecutive reelection, to serve as needed on a discipline hearing committee in any of the synods in this church.

*F4. The churchwide Committee of Hearing Officers shall consist of six persons elected by the Church Council for a term of six years, each without consecutive reelection, to serve as needed on a discipline hearing committee in any of the synods in this church.

*F5. When charges are brought by a synodical bishop, or when charges are brought other than by a synodical bishop and have not been withdrawn or dismissed or otherwise disposed of as provided in ELCA Bylaw 20.21.06. (Rule E4), the synodical bishop shall deliver a copy of the charges to the accused and the secretary of this church.

F6. The secretary of the ELCA shall obtain from the synod of roster of the accused a list of the members of the Committee on Discipline of the synod.

F7. The secretary of the ELCA shall communicate with each of the members of the Committee on Discipline of the synod of roster of the accused to ascertain whether the member is not disqualified from serving, and is available to serve on a discipline hearing committee.

F8. The secretary of the ELCA shall communicate with each of the members of the churchwide Committee on Discipline to ascertain whether the member is not disqualified from serving, and is available to serve on a discipline hearing committee.

F9. The secretary of the ELCA shall communicate with each member of the churchwide Committee of Hearing Officers to ascertain whether the member is not disqualified from serving, and is available to serve on a discipline hearing committee.

F10. No member of the Committee on Discipline of the synod, the churchwide Committee on Discipline, or the churchwide Committee of Hearing Officers shall serve on a discipline hearing committee if (i) such member is related (as defined in ELCA Bylaw 19.61.04.) to the accused if an individual or to the accuser(s) if an individual(s); (ii) such member is a member or a former member of a congregation that is the accused or accuser, or; (iii) such member was a member of a congregation at the time that such congregation employed the accused or accuser; (iv) such member is a member of the Synod Council who is the accuser; (v) such member is an accused or accuser; or (vi) the participation of such member may give rise to the appearance of partiality, even if the member would in fact be impartial. A member of the Committee on Discipline of the synod, the churchwide Committee on Discipline, or the churchwide Committee of Hearing Officers may also voluntarily disqualify himself or herself from serving on the discipline hearing committee.

*F11. The Ssecretary of the ELCA shall notify (as provided in Rule B811) the accused that a discipline hearing committee will hear the case and that the accused has the right to select two (one clergy and one lay) of the 12 committee members who will serve on such committee (and in addition, if the accused so desires, an a first alternate and a second alternate of the same lay or clergy status for each of the two selected members). Such two persons (as well as the alternates) so selected shall be from the 21 28 members of the churchwide Committee on Discipline. The secretary of the ELCA shall also notify the accused that this right must be to exercised this right, the secretary must receive the names of those selected by the accused within 15 20 days from the receipt of date that the secretary's notice is given.

F12. The secretary of the ELCA shall notify the vice president of the ELCA of the need for a meeting of the Executive Committee of the Church Council to select six members from the churchwide Committee on Discipline to serve on a discipline hearing committee.

F13. The secretary of the ELCA shall notify the bishop of the ELCA of the need to appoint a hearing officer to serve as nonvoting chair of a discipline hearing committee.

*F14. If within the time prescribed, the accused has selected two members of the discipline hearing committee, the Executive Committee of the Church Council shall select the four additional members from the churchwide Committee on Discipline so that, together with the two members selected by the accused, the total of six persons selected consists of three ordained ministers and three laypersons. If within the time prescribed the accused shall have failed to exercise the right to select two members, or any of the members or alternates selected by the accused are disqualified from serving or are unable to serve, the Executive Committee of the Church Council shall select an

additional one or two members from the churchwide Committee on Discipline, so that the total of six persons selected consists of three ordained ministers and three laypersons.

*F15. Not later than at the time that the Executive Committee of the Church Council makes its selection as provided in Rule F14, the bishop of the ELCA shall select one member of the churchwide Committee of Hearing Officers to serve as the nonvoting chair of a discipline hearing committee. The bishop shall so advise the secretary of the ELCA.

F16. At the same time as the hearing officer of a discipline hearing committee is selected, tThe bishop of the ELCA shall also select another member of the churchwide Committee of Hearing Officers to serve as the nonvoting chair of a discipline hearing committee in the event of an emergency that precludes the person selected under Rule F15 from discharging his or her duties. The bishop shall so advise the secretary of the ELCA who shall notify the individual so selected and the hearing officer first selected.

*F17. The secretary of the ELCA (or other person authorized by the Executive Committee of the Church Council) shall notify (as provided in Rule B811) the hearing officer of the discipline hearing committee, the accused, and the accuser of the names of the six members of the churchwide Committee on Discipline and the six members of the Committee on Discipline of the synod who will serve on the discipline hearing committee.

*F18. The discipline hearing committee shall be constituted on the date that the secretary of the ELCA gives notice to the hearing officer of the discipline hearing committee, the accused and the accuser(s) of the six members from the churchwide Committee on Discipline and the six members of the Committee on Discipline of the synod who will serve on the discipline hearing committee.

F19. Vacancies in the voting membership of a discipline hearing committee that occur for any reason following the constituting of the committee, as provided in Rule F18, shall reduce the size of the committee and shall not be otherwise filled.

*F20. Any member of the churchwide Committee on Discipline who has been appointed to serve on a discipline hearing committee to hear a particular pending case shall continue to serve to discharge that appointment notwithstanding that his or her successor has been subsequently elected at a Churchwide Assembly.

*F21. Any member of a Committee on Discipline of the synod who has been appointed to serve on a discipline hearing committee to hear a particular pending case shall continue to serve to discharge that appointment notwithstanding that his or her successor has been subsequently elected at a Synod Assembly.

F22. Any member of the churchwide Committee of Hearing Officers who has been appointed to serve on a discipline hearing committee to hear a particular pending case shall continue to serve to discharge that appointment notwithstanding that his or her successor has been subsequently elected by the Church Council.

F2123. The quorum for the discipline hearing committee shall be a majority six of its voting members, and must include at least one member of the churchwide Committee on Discipline and one member of the Committee on Discipline of the synod.

*F2224. Prior to and at the hearing, decisions of the discipline hearing committee shall be made by a majority of its members present. Following the hearing, decisions of the discipline hearing committee shall be made by a majority of its members who were present at the hearing. Any member who was not present for the entire hearing shall not be eligible to participate in any deliberations subsequent to the hearing.

F2325. Either the accused or the accuser may challenge the participation of a hearing officer or any voting member on a discipline hearing committee for cause, and present documentation to support such challenges under Rule F10. A party raising such a challenge shall be permitted to support the challenge with argument and evidence. The other party may, but need not, submit argument and evidence in support of or in opposition to the challenge. The remaining voting members of the committee, even though also challenged, shall determine whether the challenged has merit, in which case the member so challenged shall be removed from the committee hearing officer or member shall be disqualified. The challenged hearing officer or member may participate in the deliberations on whether he or she should be disqualified, but only the remaining members shall vote upon the challenge. This vote shall be by secret ballot if the committee has met in person or by individual poll by the hearing officer or facilitator if the committee has met by telephone conference call.

F2426. Members of a discipline hearing committee shall refrain from discussing matters considered by the committee except as required to discharge the duties of the committee.

F27. Any written statements in the accuser's possession that relate to the subject matter of the charges and have been written, dictated, signed, or subscribed to by a complaining witness who is identified in the charges are for the exclusive use of the accuser and the representatives of the accuser. Such statements shall not be shared with the accused unless consented to by the complaining witness or required in secular judicial proceedings.

G. The Hearing Officer of a Discipline Hearing Committee

G1. After consulting with the secretary of the church concerning the availability of members of the discipline hearing committee, Tthe hearing officer of the discipline hearing committee shall contact the accused, and the accuser(s) (and their representatives, if known) and the members of the discipline hearing committee to determine possible dates and places for a hearing.

G2. The hearing officer of the discipline hearing committee shall set the date and time of the hearing before the discipline hearing committee within the time parameters described in Rule G3 and Rule G4. The hearing officer shall also select the place of the hearing.

*G3. Written notice of the date, time, and place of the hearing and a copy of the charges shall be delivered by the hearing officer to the accused and to the accuser(s) at least 20 days prior to the date of the hearing.

*G4. In each specific case for which a discipline hearing committee has been constituted, the committee shall, within 60 days after the secretary of this church has given notice of the selection by the Executive Committee of the members of the churchwide Committee on Discipline to serve on a discipline hearing committee,

meet with the accused and the accuser(s) to hold a hearing and render its written decision.

G5. The hearing officer of a discipline hearing committee may request that one or more facilitator(s) be appointed by the bishop of the ELCA.

G6. The hearing officer of a discipline hearing committee shall direct the appointed facilitator(s) to make arrangements and to provide assistance as provided in Rules H1 through H6.

G7. The hearing officer shall distribute to ascertain that all members of the discipline hearing committee have available, and shall distribute to the accuser and the accused and or their representatives, the Constitution, Bylaws, and Continuing Resolutions of the ELCA, these Rules Governing Disciplinary Proceedings, Definitions and Guidelines for Discipline adopted pursuant to ELCA Bylaw 20.71.11., and such other documents reflecting policies of the ELCA as may be applicable to the case requested by the parties.

G8. Discovery, as that term is understood in secular judicial proceedings, is not permitted in disciplinary proceedings. Neither the accused nor the accuser shall be compelled to provide any information or documents to the other, except as specifically required by Chapter 20 of the governing documents or by these rules. Members of the discipline hearing committee may take into account the inability of the parties to engage in discovery in deciding what weight or importance to give to particular evidence.

G9. No fewer than two and no more than nine days before the discipline hearing is scheduled to begin:

a. Each party shall provide the other party and the hearing officer with a list of the names of the witnesses that the party intends to call on direct examination (as distinguished from on rebuttal) and shall briefly describe the subject matter of each witness' expected testimony. Each party shall be permitted to call on direct examination only those persons who appeared on that party's witness list, unless the discipline hearing committee finds that there was good cause for the party's failure to identify the witness.

b. Each party shall provide the other party and the hearing officer with copies of all documents that the party intends to introduce on direct examination (as distinguished from on cross or on rebuttal). Each party shall be permitted to introduce on direct examination only those documents that were so disclosed, unless the discipline hearing committee finds that there was good cause for the party's failure to disclose the document. The hearing officer shall not provide copies of any document to the members of the discipline hearing committee until that document is introduced into evidence at the hearing.

G810. The hearing officer of a discipline hearing committee may conduct pre-hearing conferences, either by telephone conference call or by actual meeting, with the accuser(s) and the accused and/or their representatives for the purpose of discussing the need for supplemental rules of procedure (G911), providing for written submissions or briefs on points requested by either the accused or the accuser(s) or by the hearing officer, lists of direct (as distinguished from rebuttal) witnesses, and written offers of proof or testimony (G1012) or similar matters.

G911. The discipline hearing committee, upon request of the accused, the accuser(s) or the hearing officer, or upon its own motion, may adopt additional rules of procedure which are appropriate for consideration of a particular dispute, provided such rules do not conflict with Chapter 20 of the Constitution, Bylaws, and Continuing Resolutions of the ELCA governing documents or with these rules. Copies of such rules shall be furnished to the accused and the accuser(s) promptly after adoption.

G10̶12. The hearing officer of a discipline hearing committee may direct the accuser(s) and the accused or their representatives to prepare written offers of testimony or of other proof that either proposes to offer at the hearing when the hearing officer believes that the testimony or other proof would be only cumulative or of questionable relevancy or of such other nature that the discipline hearing committee may decide to exclude it as evidence at the hearing, or to admit it as evidence only in the form of the written offer. If such testimony or other proof is excluded by the committee, it the written offer of testimony or of other proof shall upon request of a party, made in timely fashion, be included as a part of the record on appeal.

G13. The hearing officer shall avoid imposing unnecessary burdens or costs upon the parties. For example, the hearing officer shall not require the parties to submit written briefs or stipulated facts unless it is clear that the benefits to the committee of such a written submission will outweigh the burdens imposed upon the parties.

G11̶14. The hearing officer of the discipline hearing committee shall be responsible for arrangements for a verbatim record of the hearing to be made by a stenographer or court reporter. If both parties and the hearing officer agree, the hearing may be recorded or by audio/ or video tape recording instead of by a stenographer or court reporter. The stenographer or court reporter shall not produce a transcript of the proceedings unless and until one or both parties appeals the decision of the discipline hearing committee. If the hearing is recorded on audio or video tape, the tapes shall be available to no one other than the hearing officer unless and until one or both parties appeals the decision of the discipline hearing committee. In the event of an appeal, the transcript or tape recordings shall be made available only to the accused, the accuser, and the Committee on Appeals. Use of a court reporter is encouraged. This The transcript or tape shall be the property of this church., but copies shall be made available to the accused and the accuser in the event of an appeal.

G12̶15. The hearing officer of a discipline hearing committee may convene the committee for a telephone conference meeting to decide important matters requiring discussion or decision prior to the scheduled hearing before the committee. The accuser(s) and the accused and their representatives may participate in such telephone conference, if at all, only to the extent determined by the hearing officer.

G13̶16. The hearing officer of a discipline hearing committee may convene the committee for a preliminary meeting on the day preceding or the day on which the hearing is scheduled to begin in order to review important matters requiring discussion or decision prior to the hearing before the committee. The accuser(s) and the accused and their representatives may participate in such preliminary meeting, if at all, only to the extent determined by the committee upon recommendation of the hearing officer.

G14̶17. As a nonvoting member of a discipline hearing committee, the hearing officer shall preside at all meetings of the committee, including the hearing and the deliberation. In presiding during deliberations, the hearing officer shall endeavor to permit reasonable discussion on the part of members of the committee, while keeping the committee focused upon its purposes and the necessity for timely decisions. In presiding at the hearing, the hearing officer shall endeavor to permit reasonable questioning on the part of members of the committee, while allowing both the accuser(s) and the accused to present their cases without unnecessary interruptions.

G15̶18. The hearing officer of a discipline hearing committee shall at all times endeavor to assure that due process, as more fully described in Rules J1 through J4, is observed. In particular, the hearing officer shall observe, and endeavor to have committee members observe, the requirement that both the accuser(s) and the accused are to be allowed to present their cases without unnecessary interruptions. The hearing officer shall also endeavor at all times to maintain decorum during the hearing and for this purpose may order the exclusion at either a public or closed hearing of persons whose conduct is disruptive or distracting. The hearing officer shall avoid written communications to either the accused or the accuser(s) or their respective representatives without copy to the other. The hearing officer shall avoid oral communications with either the accused or the accuser(s) or their respective representatives outside of the presence of the other.

G16̶19. The hearing officer of a discipline hearing committee may exclude offers of testimony or evidence, subject to appeal to the committee upon motion of a committee member, whether following or in the absence of an objection of the accuser(s) or the accused or their representatives.

G17̶20. Subject to the directions and decisions of the discipline hearing committee, the hearing officer of the committee shall be responsible following the hearing for the preparation and appropriate distribution of the committee's written report in conformity with the requirements of ELCA Bylaw 20.21.21. (Rule K89).

G18̶21. The hearing officer of a discipline hearing committee shall be responsible for maintaining material that will constitute the record on appeal (as defined in the rules of the churchwide Committee on Appeals), and for certifying and delivering such material to the churchwide Committee on Appeals in the event that an appeal is timely made by either the accuser(s) or the accused.

G19̶22. In the event of an emergency that requires Tthe hearing officer of a discipline hearing committee to withdraw from a pending matter, the hearing officer shall, if possible, first inform keep the individual selected under Rule F16 sufficiently informed so that if any emergency requires, that individual can promptly assume the duties of, and act as, the hearing officer of the committee.

H. Facilitators
*H1. The bishop of this church may appoint one or more persons as facilitators to make arrangements for, and to provide technical assistance to, a discipline hearing committee.

H2. At all times, the facilitator(s) shall be subject to the directions of the hearing officer of a discipline hearing committee.

H3. Subject to Rule H2, examples of arrangements for which a facilitator may be responsible are travel and hotel arrangements of members of the discipline hearing committee, site arrangements, media relations on behalf of the hearing officer and the committee, and arrangements for a court reporter, and providing secretarial and clerical support for the hearing officer both before and during the hearing.

H4. Subject to Rule H2, examples of technical assistance that a facilitator may provide are identifying and supplying documents setting forth policies of the ELCA and identifying responsible individuals who can testify as to the procedures or policies of the ELCA. Information so furnished by a facilitator to members of a discipline hearing committee shall be shared with the accuser(s) and the accused or their representatives.

H5. Facilitators shall refrain from discussing matters involved in a disciplinary proceeding except as required in the discharge of their duties.

H6. Whenever a facilitator needs to communicate with either the accuser(s) or the accused or their representatives regarding substantive matters (such as evidence relating to the charges), written communication may be made with one only with copy to the other and oral communication may be made with one only in the presence of the other, except in specific instances, with the prior express consent of the other. The facilitator may communicate in writing with either party without sending a copy of the communication to the other party, and the facilitator may communicate orally with either party outside of the presence of the other party, but only regarding non-substantive matters (such as hotel reservations or scheduling of telephone conference calls).

H7. The facilitator may attend sessions of the hearing before the discipline hearing committee if the hearing officer concludes that the facilitator's attendance will expedite the work of the hearing officer or of the committee.

I. The Hearing Before the Discipline Hearing Committee
I1. In the proceedings before the discipline hearing committee there shall be a presumption of innocence in favor of the accused. Among other things this requires that (i) the committee shall reach its decision and make judgment solely on the basis of the evidence presented at the hearing before the committee; (ii) the accuser has the burden of proof as provided in Rule I23; and (iii) the evidence presented at the hearing, as well as the entire process before the committee, shall be in conformity with the requirements of the governing documents and these rules, including specifically the due process requirements set forth in Rules J1 through J5.

I2. The hearing before the discipline hearing committee shall commence at the time and place set forth in the notice issued pursuant to Rule G3, unless in the judgment of the hearing officer, after consultation, if possible, with the accuser and the accused or their representatives, an emergency, such as snowstorm, flood, or airline strike, necessitates a postponement or change of site of the hearing.

*I13. The hearing before the discipline hearing committee shall not be open to the public unless both the accuser(s) and the accused agree to a public hearing.

*I24. In a hearing not open to the public,
a. the accuser and the accused may each be represented by not more than two representatives who may present or assist in the presentation of the evidence, and
b. the discipline hearing committee may permit attendance by a limited number of persons chosen by the accused, provided that persons whose presence may reasonably be expected to intimidate, frighten, or distress a witness, shall not be permitted to attend.
c. a witness may be accompanied by a spouse and by a friend or advocate.

*I35. Irrespective of whether a hearing is or is not open to the public, the discipline hearing committee may decide that witnesses (other than the accused and the accuser) shall be permitted in the hearing only when testifying. A witness may be accompanied by a friend or advocate.

I46. The friend or advocate who accompanies a witness Persons permitted to attend the hearing under Rule I. 4. b. and c. shall not have any role in the proceedings, unless specifically authorized by an additional rule adopted by the discipline hearing committee in a particular case.

I57. The accuser (or if there be more than one, the accusers collectively) and the accused may each have no more than two other persons (the "representatives") present who may act on behalf of either of them. These representatives may, but need not, be attorneys. Subject to the limit of two, representatives of a synod bishop who is an accuser may include persons who served as members of a consultation or advisory panel.

*I68. A verbatim record shall be made by a stenographer or court reporter, or by an audio or video tape recording of the hearing.

I79. The accuser(s) and the accused or their representatives may, but need not, present brief opening statements. Opening statements shall be limited to no more than one hour per side. The accuser, as the party with the burden of proof, shall be permitted to give the first opening statement.

I810. The accuser(s) shall first call witnesses, including the accuser(s) if appropriate, to present evidence in support of the charges.

I911. The accuser(s) may present documentary evidence in support of the charges.

I1012. After the accuser(s) has called witnesses and offered any documentary evidence, the accused may call witnesses and offer documentary evidence.

I13. After the accused has called witnesses and offered any documentary evidence, first the accuser, and then the accused, for purposes of rebuttal, may call witnesses and offer documentary evidence.

I14. The accused may not call as a witness a physician, psychologist, or other expert who has examined the accused for the purpose of preparing to testify on the accused's behalf unless (i) the accused notifies the accuser of the accused's intention to call such an expert witness not later than 30 days after the accused is notified that charges have been filed as provided in Rule F5., and (ii) the accused agrees to be examined by a physician, psychologist, or other expert designated by the accuser. The expert designated by the accuser may testify at the discipline hearing whether or not the expert designated by the accused also testifies.

I15. The accuser may not call as a witness a physician, psychologist, or other expert who has examined a complaining witness for the purpose of preparing to testify on the accuser's behalf unless (i) the accuser notifies the accused of the accuser's intention to call such an expert witness not later than 30 days after the accused is notified that charges have been filed as provided in Rule F5., and (ii) the complaining witness agrees to be examined by a physician, psychologist, or other expert designated by the accused. The expert designated by the accused may testify at the discipline hearing whether or not the expert designated by the accuser also testifies.

I16. Nothing in Rules I14 and I15 shall exclude the testimony of a physician, psychologist, or other expert who is called only as a fact witness, such as a treating psychologist who is called to testify that a statement was made by the accused or a complaining witness during a therapy session.

I17. No party to proceedings before a discipline hearing committee may refer in any manner to a polygraph test. For example, no party may refer to the results of a polygraph test or to the fact that a party or a complaining witness either took or did not take a polygraph test. If any reference is made to a polygraph test in violation of this rule, the committee shall ignore the reference and prevent its decision from being in any way influenced by the reference.

I~~11~~18. The accused has the right to testify or to remain silent.

I19. The accuser may call the accused to testify as part of the accuser's direct case, but only after all other witnesses that the accuser intends to call on direct examination have testified. If the accuser calls the accused to testify at the conclusion of the accuser's direct case, and the accused exercises the accused's right not to testify, the accused shall not be permitted to testify later in the proceedings.

I~~12~~20. Whenever a witness (including the accused or the accuser) testifies, the party who has called the witness shall first question the witness and then the other party may question the witness on any matter relevant to the charges. Then the party calling the witness may again question the witness, followed by the other party questioning the witness, with respect to matters previously testified about by the witness. A representative of a party, in lieu of the party, may question any witness. Committee members may also question the witness for the purpose of clarification.

I21. The accuser(s) and the accused or their representatives may, but need not, present brief closing statements. Closing statements shall be limited to no more than one hour per side. The accuser, as the party with the burden of proof, shall be permitted to give the last closing statement.

I~~13~~22. The rules of evidence and other rules used in secular judicial proceedings shall not apply in the hearing; however, the parties may argue the weight or importance which should be given to any of the testimony or documentary evidence disciplinary proceedings. Testimony or documentary evidence shall not be excluded merely because it would be excluded under such secular rules. For example, evidence shall not be excluded merely because it is hearsay, although individual members of a discipline hearing committee may choose to give hearsay evidence little or no weight or importance. Nothing in this rule shall restrict the authority of a hearing officer of a discipline hearing committee or a discipline hearing committee to exclude offers of testimony or evidence under Rule G12 or Rule G19.

I~~14~~23. The accuser(s) shall have the burden of proving by a preponderance of the evidence the allegations contained in the charges. Preponderance means such evidence as, when weighed with that opposed to it, has more convincing force and the greater probability of truth proof. The discipline hearing committee shall not find that any allegation contained in the charges is true unless the accuser has proven that it is true by a preponderance of the evidence. An allegation has been proven true by a preponderance of the evidence if the committee, after weighing all of the evidence presented at the hearing, believes it more likely than not that the allegation is true.

I~~15~~24. At any time during the hearing the discipline hearing committee at its discretion may meet in executive session for deliberations, either with or without the participation of the accuser(s) and the accused and their respective representatives.

I~~16~~25. If the accused and the accused's representative should fail to appear at the scheduled hearing before the discipline hearing committee, the committee, after making a record that the accused was given notice of the date, time and place of the hearing, and other information relevant to the accused's absence of which the committee has knowledge, may either (i) proceed to hear the testimony and evidence offered by the accuser(s) and render its written decision or (ii) if the committee concludes that the absence is justified, adjourn the hearing to a rescheduled date in which case the period between the originally scheduled date and the rescheduled date shall not be counted for purposes of the 60 day period referred to in ELCA Bylaw 20.21.17. (Rule G4).

J. Due Process in Discipline Proceedings
*J1. The process of discipline governing ordained ministers, persons on other official rosters, and congregations shall assure due process and due protection for the accused, other parties and this church.
*J2. "Due process" means and includes:
   a. the right to be given specific written notice of charges;
   b. in the case of the accused, the right to testify in person or remain silent;
   c. the right to call witnesses;
   d. the right to introduce documentary evidence concerning the pending charges;
   e. the right to confront and cross-examine all witnesses;

f. the right to a hearing by a discipline hearing committee;

g. the right to a hearing closed to the public unless both the accuser and the accused agree to a public hearing;

h. the right to a written decision of the discipline hearing committee; and

i. the right to be treated with fundamental procedural fairness.

*J3. "Fundamental procedural fairness" means and includes:

a. avoidance by committee members of written communications to or from either accused or accuser(s) without copy to the other;

b. avoidance by committee members of oral communications with either the accused or the accuser(s) outside of the presence of the other;

c. maintaining decorum during the hearing;

d. allowing both the accuser(s) and the accused to present their cases without unnecessary interruptions;

e. keeping a verbatim record of the hearing, either made by a stenographer or court reporter or by audio or video tape recording;

f. allowing both the accuser(s) and the accused to be accompanied at the hearing by a representative (who may, but need not, be an attorney) who may also participate in the proceedings;

g. impartiality of the committees which consider the charges; and

h. the right to be treated in conformity with the governing documents of the ELCA.

J4. "Due process" and "fundamental procedural fairness" shall be defined without regard to how these concepts may be defined in secular civil or criminal proceedings. "Due process" and "fundamental procedural fairness" shall mean nothing more and nothing less than what is provided in Rule J2 and Rule J3, respectively.

*J4̶5. Once a charge against a person or entity has been considered by a discipline hearing committee, that person or entity shall not be required to answer that charge again except under the circumstances set forth in ELCA Bylaws 20.14.01. and 20.14.02.

K. Discipline Committee - Post-Hearing Matters

K1. For the purpose of reaching its decision and judgment, the discipline hearing committee, including its hearing officer, shall meet without the presence of the accused, the accuser(s), their representatives or any other person who is not a committee member.

K2. The quorum for the discipline hearing committee shall be a majority of its voting members.

*K3. The decision of the discipline hearing committee shall be made by a majority vote of its voting members who were present at the entire hearing.

K4. The discipline hearing committee shall determine by the preponderance of the evidence (as defined in Rule I1̶4̶23) whether the accused committed the offense(s) charged. In the event that the discipline hearing committee finds that the accused committed the offense(s) charged, it shall determine the appropriate disciplinary action. If the discipline hearing committee finds that the accused did not commit any of the offenses charged, it shall dismiss the charges.

*K5. The disciplinary actions which may be imposed upon an ordained minister are:

a. private censure and admonition by the bishop of the synod;

b. suspension from the office and the functions of the ordained ministry for a designated period or until there is satisfactory evidence of repentance and amendment; or,

c. removal from the ordained ministry of this church.

*K6. The disciplinary actions which may be imposed upon a rostered layperson are:

a. private censure and admonition by the bishop of the synod;

b. suspension from the role and functions as an associate in ministry, a Deaconess of the Evangelical Lutheran Church in America, or a diaconal minister for a designated period or until there is satisfactory evidence of repentance and amendment; or

c. removal from the appropriate official roster for lay persons of this church.

*K6̶7. The disciplinary actions which may be imposed upon a congregation are:

a. censure and admonition by the bishop of the synod;

b. suspension from this church for a designated period, the consequences of such suspension being the loss of voting rights of any member (including ordained ministers) of the congregation at synod or churchwide assemblies, the loss of the right to petition, and the forfeiture of eligibility by any member of the congregation to serve on any council, board, committee or other group of this church, any of its synods or any other subdivision thereof;

c. suspension of the congregation from this church for a designated period (with the same consequences as in b.) during which the congregation shall be under the administration of the synod provided that a congregation may refuse to accept such administration in which case it shall be removed from the roll of congregations of this church; or

d. removal from the roll of congregations of this church.

K7̶8. The Synod Council may terminate synod administration at any time, or may decline to accept synod administration, in which case suspension shall continue for the designated period with the consequences set forth in ELCA Bylaw 20.31.02.b. (Rule K6̶7.b).

*K8̶9. The discipline hearing committee shall render its decision in writing. The written decision shall be in two parts:

a. Findings of Fact. In this part, the committee shall set forth what it has found to be the relevant facts–that is, what it believes to be the truth of the matter.

b. Determination. In this part, the committee shall state whether, based upon the facts that it has found, it believes discipline should be imposed and, if so, what discipline it has chosen to impose.

K9̶10. Subject to the directions and decisions of the discipline hearing committee, following the hearing the hearing officer of the committee shall be responsible for the preparation of the committee's written report in conformity with the requirements of ELCA Bylaw 20.21.21. (Rule K8̶ 9).

*K1̶0̶11. The discipline hearing committee must complete the hearing and render its written decision within 60 days from the time the committee was constituted as defined in Rule F18.

K1112. The hearing officer of the discipline hearing committee shall give notice (as provided in Rule B811) to the accused, the accuser(s), the bishop (if not an accuser) of the synod on whose roster the accused is listed and the secretary of ELCA of the judgment of the discipline hearing committee, and provide to each a copy of the committee's written decision. Such notice must be given, but need not be received, within the 60 day period specified in ELCA Bylaw 20.21.17. (Rules F18, G4 and K1011).

*K1213. Either the accuser(s) or the accused may appeal to the Committee on Appeals of the ELCA within 30 days after receiving the written decision of the discipline hearing committee.

*K1314. The decision of the discipline hearing committee shall be final unless, within 30 days of receipt of the written decision, one of the parties appeals to the Committee on Appeals. The decision of the Committee on Appeals shall be final.

K1415. In event of an appeal, the hearing officer of the discipline hearing committee shall furnish the record on appeal (as defined in the rules of the Committee on Appeals), and certify to the completeness and accuracy of such record.

K1516. In the event there is no appeal, 75 days after giving the notice referred to in Rule K1112. the hearing officer of the discipline hearing committee shall make the following disposition of the material which would have constituted the record on appeal:

a. If the charges were not sustained and disciplinary action was not imposed, documentary and physical evidence presented at the hearing shall be returned to the party who presented the same and all the balance of the material shall be destroyed.

b. If the discipline hearing committee sustained the charges and imposed disciplinary action, (i) documentary and physical evidence shall be returned to the party who presented it;; (ii) the written charges, the written decision of the discipline hearing committee and certification or other proof of notice given under Rule K1112 above shall be delivered to the secretary of the ELCA to be held as provided in ELCA Bylaw 7.41.17.; and (iii) all other material shall be destroyed.

L. Appeals
*L1. The decision of a discipline hearing committee may be appealed to the Committee on Appeals by:
a. the accuser(s) who brought charges upon which a discipline hearing committee has acted;
b. an ordained minister upon whom discipline has been imposed by a discipline hearing committee; or
c. a congregation upon whom discipline has been imposed by a discipline hearing committee.; or
d. a rostered layperson upon whom discipline has been imposed by a discipline hearing committee.

L2. Any error made in the application of Chapter 20 of the governing documents or in the application of these rules may be deemed harmless. A harmless error shall not provide the basis for affording relief to a party or for reversing the decision of a discipline hearing committee. An error shall be deemed harmless if it is clear beyond a reasonable doubt that the outcome of the disciplinary proceeding was not or will not be affected by the error.

L23. Rules governing the scope of and procedure for appeals are set forth in the rules of the Committee on Appeals which appear as ELCA Continuing Resolution 20.61.A92., a copy of which may be obtained from the secretary of the ELCA.

Table Referencing Disciplinary Rules to Governing Documents

Rule	Governing Documents Provision
*B1	20.21.01.
*B2	20.21.03.
*B3	20.22.01.
*B4	20.22.03.
*B35	20.31.01.
*B46	20.31.03.
*C1	20.21.23.
*C2	20.22.06.
*C35	20.21.24.
*C6	20.22.07.
*D1	20.21.04. intro
*D45	†S11.02.
*D56	20.21.04.a.
*D67	20.21.04.b.
*D10	20.21.05.
*D1614	20.21.05.
*D2019	20.21.05.
*E4	20.21.06.
*E5	20.21.06.b. and 20.21.06.c.
*F1	20.21.08.
*F2	†S11.03.
*F3	20.21.11.
*F4	20.21.13.
*F5	20.21.07.
*F11	20.21.12.
*F14	20.21.12.
*F15	20.21.14.
*F17	20.21.17.
*F18	20.21.17.
*F20	19.11.22.A91.
*F22	20.21.22.

10. Revisions of "Definitions and Guidelines for Discipline"

Background: In November 1989, the Church Council approved a document called "Definitions and Guidelines for Discipline" that had been developed by the Committee on Appeals as authorized by ELCA Bylaw 20.71.11. (formerly 19.41.11.). The recent Churchwide Assembly approved the recommendation of the Study on Ministry that associates in ministry be subject to substantially the same guidelines as are applicable in the case of ordained clergy. The Committee on Appeals has prepared a revised document consistent with the Churchwide Assembly action. The document was distributed to council members as council agenda Exhibit D, Part 2.

Council Action: William H. Engelbrecht introduced the following recommendation of the Legal and

Constitutional Review Committee, subsequently adopted by the Church Council without discussion:

VOTED: *CC93.12.103*

To adopt the following revised "Definitions and Guidelines for Discipline" in keeping with action of the 1993 Churchwide Assembly related to recommendations of the Study of Ministry:

DEFINITIONS AND GUIDELINES FOR DISCIPLINE OF ORDAINED MINISTERS[2]

As an expression of its life in the Gospel of Jesus Christ, this church embraces disciplinary processes of counseling, admonition, and correction, with the objective of forgiveness, reconciliation, and healing.

Simultaneously, out of deep concern for effective extension of the Gospel, this church remains alert to the high calling of discipleship in Jesus Christ. The ordained ministers of this church, as persons charged with special responsibility for the proclamation of the Gospel, are to seek to reflect the new life in Christ, avoiding that which would make them stumbling blocks to others. To that end, this church recognizes that there is behavior that is deemed to be incompatible with ordained ministry, and that calls for disciplinary action.

The following definitions and guidelines do not set forth the high expectations this church has of its ordained ministers. (A document of such expectations has been developed by the Division for Ministry for this church.) The normative expectations of this church for its ordained ministers focus upon faithful and effective exercise of ministerial leadership. In all matters of morality and personal ethics, this church expects its ordained ministers to be exemplary in conduct.

These definitions and guidelines describe the grounds for which ordained ministers may be subject to discipline according to the practice of this church. Their purpose is juridical: to assist in the processes of consultation, discipline, and appeals.

Grounds for discipline of ordained ministers are as follows:

a.   Preaching or teaching in conflict with the faith confessed by this church is grounds for discipline of ordained ministers. A summary of the faith confessed by this church is found in Chapters 2 and 3 of this church's constitution.

b.   Conduct incompatible with the character of the ministerial office is grounds for discipline of ordained ministers. These guidelines define and describe kinds of behavior which are incompatible with the character of the ministerial office.

1)   Confidential Communications

Ordained ministers must respect privileged and confidential communication and may not disclose such communication, except with the express permission of the person who has confided it or if the person is perceived to intend great harm to self or others.

2)   Professional Attention to Duties

An ordained minister of this church has made commitments through ordination and through acceptance of a letter of call. Continued neglect of or indifference toward such duties constitutes conduct incompatible with the character of the ministerial office.

3)   Relationship to Family

This church is committed to the sanctity of marriage and the enhancement of family life. Ordained ministers of this church, whether married or single, are expected to uphold Christian ideals of marriage in their public ministry as well as in private

life. Spouse and children, if any, are to be regarded with love, respect, and commitment.

Any departure from this normative behavior may be considered conduct incompatible with the character of the ministerial office. Such departure might include any of the following:

a)   Separation or divorce that occurs without consultation with the synodical bishop's office and appropriate implementation of such consultation. Each such relationship must be considered pastorally.

b)   Desertion or abandonment of spouse or children.

c)   Abuse of spouse or children.

d)   Repeated failure to meet legally determined family support obligations.

4)   Sexual Matters

The biblical understanding which this church affirms is that the normative setting for sexual intercourse is marriage. In keeping with this understanding, chastity before marriage and fidelity within marriage are the norm. Adultery, promiscuity, the sexual abuse of another, or the misuse of counseling relationships for sexual favors constitute conduct that is incompatible with the character of the ministerial office.

Practicing homosexual persons are precluded from the ordained ministry of this church.

5)   Substance Abuse

Misuse of alcohol or mind-altering substances impairs the ability of an ordained minister to perform the duties of the office with full effectiveness. The approach of this church in dealing with such a problem is to recommend and enable effective treatment. However, failure to accept treatment or to follow through on treatment and abide by the terms of such treatment and the consequent impairment of performance is conduct incompatible with the character of the ministerial office.

6)   Fiscal Responsibilities

Ordained ministers of this church are expected to conduct their fiscal affairs in accordance with ethical and legal requirements. Among those fiscal activities which may be considered conduct incompatible with the character of the ministerial office are:

a)   Indifference to or avoidance of legitimate and neglected personal debts.

b)   Embezzlement of money or improper appropriation of the property of others.

c)   Using the ministerial office improperly for personal financial advantage.

7)   Membership in Certain Organizations

This church has specifically declared in ELCA bylaw 7.47.01. that discipline may be administered to any of its ordained ministers who belongs to any organization other than the church which claims to possess in its teaching and ceremonies that which the Lord has given solely to the Church.

8)   Conviction of a Felony

The society in which this church ministers has placed a high premium upon the role of law in regulating the rights and duties of individuals to promote the common good. This includes laws which define certain conduct as felonies. Pleading guilty to, or being convicted of, a felony is grounds for discipline as conduct incompatible with the character of the ministerial office, but may not be grounds for discipline in those instances where the violation of law was to protest or to test a perceived unjust law or as an expression of civil disobedience.

---

[2] Originally approved on November 19, 1989, and subsequently approved in this revised version on December 5, 1993, by the Church Council of the Evangelical Lutheran Church in America, pursuant to ELCA bylaw 20.71.11.

c. Willfully disregarding or violating the functions and standards established by this church for the office of Word and sacrament is grounds for discipline of ordained ministers. Such functions and standards established by this church are found in Section 7.20. through 7.47.01. of this church's constitution, bylaws, and continuing resolutions.

d. Willful disregard of the constitution or bylaws of this church is grounds for discipline of ordained ministers.

DEFINITIONS AND GUIDELINES FOR DISCIPLINE OF ASSOCIATES IN MINISTRY, MEMBERS OF THE DEACONESS COMMUNITY, AND DIACONAL MINISTERS[3]

As an expression of its life in the Gospel of Jesus Christ, this church embraces disciplinary processes of counseling, admonition, and correction, with the objective of forgiveness, reconciliation, and healing.

Simultaneously, out of deep concern for effective extension of the Gospel, this church remains alert to the high calling of discipleship in Jesus Christ. The individuals on the official roster of laypersons of this church, as persons charged with special responsibility for the Gospel in the ministries to which they are called, are to seek to reflect the new life in Christ, avoiding that which would make them stumbling blocks to others. To that end, this church recognizes that there is behavior that is deemed to be incompatible with the standards for the rostered ministries of this church, and that calls for disciplinary action.

The following definitions and guidelines do not set forth the high expectations this church has of individuals on the official roster of laypersons of this church. (A document of such expectations has been developed by the Division for Ministry for this church.) The normative expectations of this church for individuals on the official roster of laypersons of this church focus upon faithful and effective exercise of their leadership. In all matters of morality and personal ethics, this church expects individuals on the official roster of laypersons of this church to be exemplary in conduct.

These definitions and guidelines describe the grounds for which individuals on the official roster of laypersons of this church may be subject to discipline according to the practice of this church. Their purpose is juridical: to assist in the processes of consultation, discipline, and appeals.

Grounds for discipline of individuals on the official roster of laypersons of this church are as follows:

a. Confessing or teaching in conflict with the faith confessed by this church is grounds for discipline of individuals on the official roster of laypersons of this church. A summary of the faith confessed by this church is found in Chapters 2 and 3 of this church's constitution.

b. Conduct incompatible with the standards for the rostered ministries of this church is grounds for discipline of individuals on the official roster of laypersons of this church. These guidelines define and describe kinds of behavior which are incompatible with the standards for these rostered ministries.

   1) Professional Attention to Duties
       An individual on the official roster of laypersons of this church has made commitments through the appropriate liturgical rite and through acceptance of a letter of call. Continued neglect of or indifference toward such duties constitutes conduct incompatible with the standards for the rostered ministries of this church.

   2) Relationship to Family
       This church is committed to the sanctity of marriage and the enhancement of family life. Individuals on the official roster of laypersons of this church,

whether married or single, are expected to uphold Christian ideals of marriage in their public ministry as well as in private life. Spouse and children, if any, are to be regarded with love, respect, and commitment.

Any departure from this normative behavior may be considered conduct incompatible with the standards for the rostered ministries of this church. Such departure might include any of the following:

   a) Separation or divorce that occurs without consultation with the synodical bishop's office and appropriate implementation of such consultation. Each such relationship must be considered pastorally.

   b) Desertion or abandonment of spouse or children.

   c) Abuse of spouse or children.

   d) Repeated failure to meet legally determined family support obligations.

   3) Sexual Matters
       The biblical understanding which this church affirms is that the normative setting for sexual intercourse is marriage. In keeping with this understanding, chastity before marriage and fidelity within marriage are the norm. Adultery, promiscuity, the sexual abuse of another, or the misuse of counseling relationships for sexual favors constitute conduct that is incompatible with the standards for the rostered ministries of this church.

       Practicing homosexual persons are precluded from the rostered ministries of this church.

   4) Substance Abuse
       Misuse of alcohol or mind-altering substances impairs the ability of an individual on the official roster of laypersons of this church to perform the duties of the office with full effectiveness. The approach of this church in dealing with such a problem is to recommend and enable effective treatment. However, failure to accept treatment or to follow through on treatment and abide by the terms of such treatment and the consequent impairment of performance is conduct incompatible with the standards for the rostered ministries of this church.

   5) Fiscal Responsibilities
       Individuals on the official roster of laypersons of this church are expected to conduct their fiscal affairs in accordance with ethical and legal requirements. Among those fiscal activities which may be considered conduct incompatible with the standards for the rostered ministries of this church are:

       a) Indifference to or avoidance of legitimate and neglected personal debts.

       b) Embezzlement of money or improper appropriation of the property of others.

       c) Using one's position improperly for personal financial advantage.

   6) Conviction of a Felony
       The society in which this church ministers has placed a high premium upon the role of law in regulating the rights and duties of individuals to promote the common good. This includes laws which define certain conduct as felonies. Pleading guilty to, or being convicted of, a felony is grounds for discipline as conduct incompatible with the standards for the rostered ministries, but may not be grounds for discipline in those instances where the violation of law was to protest or to test a perceived unjust law or as an expression of civil disobedience.

c. Willfully disregarding or violating the functions and standards established by this church for the rostered ministries

---

[3] Approved on December 5, 1993, by the Church Council of the Evangelical Lutheran Church in America, pursuant to ELCA bylaw 20.71.11.

of this church is grounds for discipline of individuals on the official roster of laypersons of this church. Such functions and standards established by this church are found in Section 7.52. through 7.53. of this church's constitution, bylaws, and continuing resolutions.

d. Willful disregard of the constitution or bylaws of this church is grounds for discipline of individuals on the official roster of laypersons of this church.

DEFINITIONS AND GUIDELINES FOR DISCIPLINE OF CONGREGATIONS[4]

a. Departing from the faith confessed by this church is grounds for discipline of a congregation of this church. A summary of the faith confessed by this church is found in Chapters 2 and 3 of this church's constitution.

b. Willfully disregarding or violating any of the criteria for recognition as congregations of this church is grounds for discipline of a congregation of this church. These criteria are set forth in provisions 9.21. and 9.22. of this church's constitution.

c. Willfully disregarding or violating the provisions of the constitution or bylaws of this church is grounds for discipline of a congregation of this church.

---

11. Southwestern Pennsylvania Synod Memorial

Background: At the March 1993 meeting of the Church Council, a resolution from the Synod Council of the Southwestern Pennsylvania Synod was referred to the Office of the Bishop for exploration of ways of reducing or sharing the cost of disciplinary proceedings incurred by any particular synod. This matter has received consideration in the Office of the Bishop and the Office of the Secretary, particularly from the standpoint of the implications for the legal staffing of discipline cases.

In connection with this meeting of the Church Council, the secretary and the ELCA's general counsel met with the advisory bishops who also serve as the Conference of Bishop's Committee on Liaison with the Church Council. A proposed response to this resolution will be shared with the Conference of Bishops in March 1994, and subsequently reported to the Church Council.

Council Action: The Church Council received the foregoing as information.

12. State of Incorporation of Synods

Background: When Evangelical Lutheran Church in America was formed, the new ELCA synods in any one region were incorporated under the laws of one state in that region, with several exceptions. Several synods have since changed their state of incorporation, with the prior approval of the Church Council. In Region 9 the chosen state of incorporation was North Carolina. The South Carolina Synod and the Florida-Bahamas Synod have requested approval to be incorporated in South Carolina and Florida, respectively. This requires Church Council approval, since a synod is not permitted to amend its

articles of incorporation or to merge with other corporations without the prior approval of the Church Council.

Council Action: The following recommendation of the Legal and Constitutional Review Committee was adopted *en bloc*, as reported elsewhere in these minutes:

EN BLOC   **[CC93.12.107]**

To ratify changes in the restated articles of incorporation of the South Carolina Synod and the Florida-Bahamas Synod to permit the incorporation of the South Carolina Synod in the State of South Carolina, and the Florida-Bahamas Synod in the State of Florida.

13. Change of Name for Synod 4F: Texas-Louisiana Gulf Coast Synod

Background: The 1993 Churchwide Assembly approved amendment of ELCA bylaw 10.01.11. to permit a change in the name of Synod 4F from the Southeastern Texas-Southern Louisiana Synod to the Texas-Louisiana Gulf Coast Synod.

Council Action: The following recommendation of the Legal and Constitutional Review Committee was adopted *en bloc*, as reported elsewhere in these minutes:

EN BLOC   **[CC93.12.108]**

To ratify amendment of the articles of incorporation of Synod 4F to change the synod name from the Southeastern Texas-Southern Louisiana Synod to the Texas-Louisiana Gulf Coast Synod.

14. Indemnification by Certain Synods

Background: The Churchwide Assembly approved a new Chapter 16 dealing with indemnification as required provisions in the Constitution for Synods. In the process of preparing these amendments, it was ascertained by legal counsel that for synods incorporated under the laws of Texas (*Central States Synod; Arkansas-Oklahoma Synod; Northern Texas-Northern Louisiana Synod; Texas-Louisiana Gulf Coast Synod; and Southwestern Texas Synod*), and Washington (*Alaska Synod; Northwest Washington Synod; Southwestern Washington Synod; Eastern Washington-Idaho Synod; Oregon Synod; and Montana Synod*) this constitutional amendment will not be effective unless it is also included in a synod's articles of incorporation. Under a synod's existing articles of incorporation, the synod is required to amend its articles as directed by the Churchwide Assembly or, following consultation, by the Church Council.

Council Action: The following recommendation of the Legal and Constitutional Review Committee was adopted *en bloc*, as reported elsewhere in these minutes:

EN BLOC   **[CC93.12.109]**

To inform the synods incorporated under the laws of Texas (Central States Synod; Arkansas-Oklahoma Synod; Northern Texas-Northern Louisiana Synod; Texas-Louisiana Gulf Coast Synod; and Southwestern Texas Synod), and

---

[4] Originally approved on November 19, 1989, and subsequently approved in this revised version on December 5, 1993, by the Church Council of the Evangelical Lutheran Church in America, pursuant to ELCA bylaw 20.71.11.

Washington (Alaska Synod; Northwest Washington Synod; Southwestern Washington Synod; Eastern Washington-Idaho Synod; Oregon Synod; and Montana Synod) that required constitutional amendments of Chapter 16 in the Constitution for Synods will not be effective unless such amendments also are included in a synod's articles of incorporation; and

To direct that each of these synod amend its respective articles of incorporation in accord with the required constitutional amendments regarding indemnification.

15. Policy Concerning Synods Involved in Litigation

Background: In litigation concerning sexual misconduct of clergy, ELCA's general counsel is involved where a synod is a party, even though the churchwide organization is not a party, under the "Procedure for Joint Representation of Churchwide Organization and Synod in Certain Litigation Matters." This procedure was reported to the Church Council at its November 18-19, 1989, meeting as council agenda Exhibit D, Part 1.

Synods or separately incorporated units occasionally become involved in other types of litigation, either as plaintiff or as defendants. Some of these lawsuits may involve the interpretation of a provision from the governing documents of this church or the application of a policy adopted by the Church Council.

The misinterpretation of such provision or the misapplication of such policy in these cases can have ramifications beyond the particular lawsuit that could adversely affect other synods or the churchwide organization.

Council Action: The following recommendation of the Legal and Constitutional Review Committee was adopted *en bloc*, as reported elsewhere in these minutes:

EN BLOC [CC93.12.110]

To approve the following "Procedure for Joint Representation of Churchwide Organization and Synod in Certain Litigation Matters":

POLICY CONCERNING INVOLVEMENT OF
ELCA GENERAL COUNSEL IN CERTAIN LITIGATION

This policy is directed to litigation (not including litigation arising out of the clergy sexual misconduct[5]) in which a synod, but not the churchwide corporation, is a party, either as plaintiff or defendant.

It is expected that a synod that contemplates filing a lawsuit will notify the ELCA general counsel prior to such filing.

It is expected that a synod that is threatened to be sued or is sued will notify the ELCA general counsel as promptly as possible. This expectation extends to cases being defended by attorneys selected by the insurance carrier for the synod.

Whenever in the judgment of the ELCA general counsel, litigation to which a synod is a party involves the interpretation of

provisions of ELCA governing documents or the application of policies adopted or approved by the Church Council, and upon request made to a synod by the ELCA General Counsel, the synod is expected to designate the ELCA general counsel as (one of) the synod's co-counsel for purposes of the pending litigation. The purpose of so designating ELCA General Counsel is to enable his/her participation with respect to issues involving the interpretation of ELCA governing documents and the application of ELCA policies and procedures.

This designation shall not be understood to entitle the ELCA general counsel to information as to which the synod wishes to assert a privilege so as to prevent disclosure to the churchwide organization. Nor shall this designation preclude the appointment of a synod's own counsel or co-counsel.

No payment is required or expected from any synod with respect to time or expenses of the ELCA general counsel while serving as co-counsel for a synod pursuant to this policy.

16. Ratification of Amendments to Synodical Constitutions

Background: ELCA constitutional provision 10.12. stipulates that amendments to synodical constitutions must be submitted to the Church Council for ratification. Such amendments become effective upon ratification.

Council Action: The following recommendation of the Legal and Constitutional Review Committee was adopted *en bloc*, as elsewhere in these minutes:

EN BLOC [CC93.12.111]

To ratify, in accord with churchwide constitution provision 10.12., amendments to the constitutions of the Southwestern Washington Synod (in keeping with communication with the synod by the secretary of this church); Sierra Pacific Synod (S9.04.); Northeastern Minnesota Synod (S10.06., S12.02., and S14.12.); Southwestern Texas Synod (S9.04.); Texas-Louisiana Gulf Coast Synod (S9.07.); Western Iowa Synod (S3.01. and S7.28.); East-Central Synod of Wisconsin (†S6.03., †S15.11., †S17.02., and Chapter 18 [title]); Greater Milwaukee Synod (in keeping with communication with the synod by the secretary of this church); North/West Lower Michigan Synod (S8.51.); Northwestern Ohio Synod (S9.03.); Northeastern Ohio Synod (S11.04.); Northeastern Pennsylvania Synod (S7.24., S10.03.d., S10.05., and S11.05.); Southeastern Pennsylvania Synod (S9.08.); Slovak Zion Synod (S1.21.); Allegheny Synod (revised provisions in accord with †S18.12.); Delaware-Maryland Synod (†S18.13.a. and other revised provisions in accord with †S18.12.); and Southeastern Synod (in affirmation of communication with the synod by the secretary of this church).

17. Guide for Revision of Congregation Constitutions

Background: Under continuing resolution 9.52.A87., the Church Council is responsible for development of a process to assist congregations in the revision of their constitutions. This process has been adminis-

---

[5] With respect to litigation arising out of clergy sexual misconduct, see "Procedure for Joint Representation of Churchwide Organization and Synod in Certain Litigation Matters," reported to the Church Council at its November 18-19, 1989, meeting, as Agenda Exhibit D, Part 1.

tered by the secretary of this church and has included a guide for distribution by synods to congregations. After each Churchwide Assembly, the guide has been revised to conform to amendments by the assembly to the Model Constitution for Congregations.

A revised edition was prepared, subsequent to the 1993 Churchwide Assembly (council agenda Exhibit A, Part 2b). It was provided to synods with copies of the printed edition of the Model Constitution for Congregations.

Council Action: The following recommendation of the Legal and Constitutional Review Committee was adopted *en bloc*, as reported elsewhere in these minutes:

EN BLOC *[CC93.12.112]*

To approve the 1993 edition of the "Guide for Use of the Model Constitution for Congregations of the Evangelical Lutheran Church in America" for the process required by ELCA continuing resolution 9.52.A87.

Resolutions from Synods Directed to the Church Council (continued)

1. Board of Pensions
Montana Synod (1F)

RESOLVED, that the Montana Synod, assembled June 11-13, 1993, recommend to the ELCA Church Council, in consultation with the ELCA Board of Pensions, to study and make recommendations for a pension plan retirement pay structure which would not penalize retired pastors who serve under a Letter of Call, and accomplish these tasks and report to the 1995 Churchwide Assembly.

Council Action:

EN BLOC *[CC93.12.105.a.]*

To refer the resolution of the Montana Synod on retirement pay structure to the Board of Pensions and request that a report and/or recommendation be brought to the April 1994 meeting of the Church Council.

2. Violence and Misuse of Firearms
Southern California (West) Synod (2B)

WHEREAS, the communities of our Southern California (West) Synod daily experience violence and homicides; and

WHEREAS, the misuse of firearms is a concern of Christians because of the physical pain, mental suffering and anguish, and spiritual grief which result; and

WHEREAS, many of our congregations carry out ministry in neighborhoods of frequent gunfire; and

WHEREAS, violence in schools and homes, including the use of firearms, is increasing; and

WHEREAS, there appears to be a disturbing relation between guns in the home and the use of these weapons in suicide and family disputes, as well as avoidable gun accidents involving children; and

WHEREAS, the medical, psychological and spiritual care of victims of violence imposes a significant economic cost to taxpayers, communities, and society; and

WHEREAS, violent behavior repeatedly depicted in the communication and entertainment industries may be having a profound psychological impact on American children; and

WHEREAS, law enforcement and public health leaders have called for greater restriction of easy availability of firearms; therefore, be it

RESOLVED, that the Southern California (West) Synod urge its members and congregations to participate in community and family violence prevention programs; and be it further

RESOLVED, that the Southern California (West) Synod memorialize the Evangelical Lutheran Church in America to urge its constituency to support legislation which would require:
1) the registration of all firearms;
2) the licensing of all users of firearms; and
3) the development of a list of approved sporting, hunting, personal protection, and antique guns which citizens may lawfully possess;
    and be it further

RESOLVED, that the Southern California (West) Synod memorialize the Evangelical Lutheran Church in America to develop, consistent with the *Mission90* emphasis on children at risk, a social message or social statement that defines Lutheran perspectives on the problem of community and family violence, including the misuse of firearms, and responses to the problem, including, but not limited to, such measures as community awareness, education and organizing, and public policy advocacy.

Council Action:

EN BLOC *[CC93.12.105.b.]*

To refer the resolution of the Southern California (West) Synod on community violence to the Division for Church in Society for a response to the synod which shall include:

(1) action taken by the 1993 Churchwide Assembly on this matter; and

(2) the timeline for the development of the message on community violence.

4. Racism and Social Injustice
Eastern North Dakota Synod (3B)

WHEREAS, we as Christians are called to "bring good news to the poor, proclaim release to the captivesb. . . to let the oppressed go free" (Luke 4:18-19); and

WHEREAS, the ELCA model Constitution for Synods mandates the church to "Serve in response to God's love to meet human needs, . . . advocating for dignity and justice for all people, working for peace and reconciliation among the nations, and standing with the poor and powerless, and committing itself to their needs (S6.02.c.); and

WHEREAS, recent events reveal deeply ingrained racism and systematic injustice at the expense of the oppressed and the powerless; and

WHEREAS, due process of the law is not equally available to all ethnic, racial, and social, economic groups in our land; therefore be it

RESOLVED, that the Eastern North Dakota Synod of the Evangelical Lutheran Church in America take a serious look at how it can change its programs to include persons of many cultures and many races in active roles within the church body; and be it further

RESOLVED, that a strenuous effort be made to support programs within the churchwide organization to reach out to those who are victims of injustice, poverty, and racism wherever they may be; and be it further

RESOLVED, that the church body maintain or increase its level of financial support for programs which uphold these aims; and be it further

RESOLVED, that this resolution be referred to the ELCA Church Council for its consideration and disposal.

Council Action:

EN BLOC [CC93.12.105.c.]
To refer the resolution of the Eastern North Dakota Synod on racism and social injustice to the Office of the Bishop and the Church Council Budget Development Committee as information in the budget-development process.

5. Support for Eastern European Farmers
Northwestern Minnesota Synod (3D)

WHEREAS, the people of Eastern Europe are experiencing political, social, and economic upheaval, resulting in emotional and spiritual turmoil; and

WHEREAS, a component of this upheaval is inefficient techniques of agricultural production and distribution; and

WHEREAS, our Lord has commissioned the church to promote physical and spiritual well-being for all people; and

WHEREAS, many members of the Evangelical Lutheran Church in America have the expertise to assist its Eastern neighbors to practice more sustainable agricultural techniques and to offer spiritual support; therefore, be it

RESOLVED, that the Northwestern Minnesota Synod in assembly memorialize the ELCA Church Council to seek opportunities for members of the Evangelical Lutheran Church in America to teach more sustainable agricultural techniques and to offer spiritual support to the people of Eastern Europe.

Council Action:

EN BLOC [CC93.12.105.d.]
To refer the resolution of the Northwestern Minnesota Synod on sustainable agricultural techniques in eastern Europe to the Division for Global Mission for a response to the synod.

6. Conflicts of Interest
Minneapolis Area Synod (3G)

WHEREAS, the Church Council of the Evangelical Lutheran Church in America in 1988 adopted policies and procedures to address and resolve issues involving "conflicts of interest" at the churchwide level, and recommended adoption of an amendment to the churchwide bylaws to provide that

Except [for churchwide officers and synod bishops, who are ex officio members with voice and no vote], employees of the churchwide organization, including those serving under call, appointment, employment agreement, or contract, shall not be eligible for election and service as voting members of the Churchwide Assembly (ELCA 12.41.15.); and

WHEREAS, the provisions of current ELCA bylaw 12.41.15. quoted above were adopted by the 1989 Churchwide Assembly by a vote of "Yes--819; No–9" (CA89.4.22–13.41.15.); and

WHEREAS, it is also important for the Evangelical Lutheran Church in America to adopt policies and procedures to address and resolve issues involving conflicts of interest at the level of the synods of this church as well; and

WHEREAS, the model Constitution for Synods of the Evangelical Lutheran Church in America contains no provision regarding conflicts of interest; and

WHEREAS, amendments to the mandatory provisions of the ELCA Constitution for Synods are subject to the same procedures for amendment as amendments to the ELCA Constitution (ELCA 10.13.), and may be proposed by the Church Council for adoption by the Churchwide Assembly (ELCA 22.11.a.); therefore, be it

RESOLVED, that the Minneapolis Area Synod request the Church Council (pursuant to ELCA 14.21.11.) to address "conflicts of interest" at the level of synods and to make such recommendations for synod policies and procedures, including any necessary amendments to synod constitutions and bylaw provisions (pursuant to ELCA 22.11.a.) as the Church Council shall deem appropriate.
Council Action:

EN BLOC [CC93.12.105.e.]
To refer the resolution of the Minneapolis Area Synod on conflicts of interest to the Office of the Secretary and the Church Council's Legal and Constitutional Review Committee, for a report and/or recommendation to the April 1994 meeting of the Church Council.

8. First United and St. Francis Lutheran Churches
Metropolitan Chicago Synod (5A)
This memorial addresses the Churchwide Assembly, in its last paragraph, and the Church Council, in the first "Resolved" paragraph.

WHEREAS, two congregations of the Evangelical Lutheran Church in America, St. Francis and First United, both of San Francisco, California, are currently under suspension for having called as pastors individuals who are not on the clergy roster of the Evangelical Lutheran Church in America; and

WHEREAS, the sole purpose of the suspensions as set forth in the open letter from the Discipline Committee, was to allow time, prior to the expulsion of the two congregations, for a ``faithful examination of ELCA policies on the ordination of homosexuals''; and

WHEREAS, the timetable for ELCA Churchwide Assembly consideration of a social statement on sexuality has been extended to 1995, and a study on the question of ordination of gay and lesbian persons has not begun; and

WHEREAS, the whole church will be the poorer if the Evangelical Lutheran Church in America allows the two congregations to be expelled without giving the issues the serious study for which the Discipline Committee pleaded; therefore, be it

RESOLVED, that the Metropolitan Chicago Synod of the Evangelical Lutheran Church in America hereby call upon the ELCA Church Council to postpone the expulsion of St. Francis and First United, now scheduled for December 31, 1995, until the studies called for in the Discipline Committee report have been completed and presented to a Churchwide Assembly; and be it further

RESOLVED, that the Metropolitan Chicago Synod memorialize the ELCA Churchwide Assembly to instruct the Division for Ministry of the Evangelical Lutheran Church in America to begin immediately the studies called for in the open letter from the Discipline Committee; and be it further

RESOLVED, that the Metropolitan Chicago Synod memorialize the Churchwide Assembly to call for postponing the expulsion of St. Francis and First United until such time as those studies are completed and the results and commendations have been reported to a subsequent Churchwide Assembly.

NOTE: the 1993 Churchwide Assembly transmitted the following background information to synods that had called for an extension of the discipline process in the matter relating to St. Francis and First United Lutheran churches in San Francisco.

In its decision dated July 18, 1990, a Committee on Discipline, which met in the Sierra Pacific Synod, ruled that St. Francis and First United Lutheran churches in San Francisco be suspended "from the rights and privileges of a congregation of the Evangelical Lutheran Church in America . . . until December 31, 1995. If, at that time or sooner," the congregations are "in compliance with the criterion for recognition" in regard to the calling of ordained ministers on the roster of this church or properly approved candidates for the roster of ordained ministers, "the suspension shall be lifted . . .. If as of December 31, 1995", those congregations are "not in compliance", they "shall be removed from the roll of congregations of the Evangelical Lutheran Church in America."

The "criteria for recognition" of congregations of this church require (ELCA 9.21.d.) that congregations "agree to call pastoral leadership from the clergy roster of this church in accordance with the call procedures of this church except in special circumstances and with the approval of the synodical bishop." Provision for "special circumstances" relates to the calling of candidates who had been approved, in conformity with the governing documents of this church and who have received and accepted a properly issued letter of call for ordained, pastoral ministry in this church.

The Committee on Discipline in the Sierra Pacific Synod rendered its decision regarding the two congregations. No appeal was filed during the time period provided for such an appeal. Therefore, the decision stands as issued (ELCA Bylaw 19.15.05.d., 1989 edition, subsequently amended as ELCA Bylaw 20.21.22., 1991 edition).

The matter could be resolved if the two congregations were to come into "compliance with the criterion for recognition" in regard to the calling of ordained ministers on the roster of this church or properly approved candidates for the roster of ordained ministers, as the Committee on Discipline ruled.

The Churchwide Assembly does not have the authority to suspend, amend, or otherwise alter a decision of a Committee on Discipline or the Committee on Appeals (ELCA 12.11. and 20.21.22.).

The decision in the Sierra Pacific Synod discipline matter related to the violation by the two cited congregations of "criteria for recognition" of congregations of this church. The memorial of the Southern California (West) Synod also refers to "participating in dialogue with gay and lesbian persons on the issue of ordination of practicing homosexuals." The memorials of the Metropolitan Chicago Synod, Southeast Michigan Synod, and Northeastern Ohio Synod refer to proposed studies.

It should be noted in regard to the matter of proposed studies that, even though the Committee on Discipline in the Sierra Pacific Synod encouraged the Evangelical Lutheran Church in America to study the ordination of practicing homosexual persons, such a study was not a condition for the decision that was rendered by the committee regarding the two congregations in San Francisco.

In response to previous resolutions, the Church Council has determined that a proposed study of the ordination of practicing homosexual persons not take place until the report and possible social statement prepared by the Task Force on the Study of Human Sexuality have been completed and received attention by the Churchwide Assembly. This report and possible social statement are scheduled for the 1995 Churchwide Assembly. In the judgment of the Division for Ministry, the Church Council has wisely delayed any study of the ordination of practicing homosexual persons until the more foundational social statement on human sexuality has been completed. The Division for Ministry is not authorized to begin such a study until directed to do so by the Church Council.

Council Action:

EN BLOC   [CC93.12.105.f.]
To request the ELCA secretary to convey to the Metropolitan Chicago Synod the response transmitted by the 1993 Churchwide Assembly to synods that called for an extension of the discipline process in the matter relating to St. Francis and First United Lutheran churches in San Francisco.

9. Prescription Costs
Northwest Synod of Wisconsin (5H)
WHEREAS, on January 1, 1993, the ELCA Pension and Other Benefits Plan introduced a prescription medications program which encourages members to purchase maintenance medications through a mail order pharmaceutical company; and

WHEREAS, members are encouraged to utilize mail order service by a fee structure which charges plan participants a small service fee for mail order service and a charge of 50% of the cost of the prescription for those who purchase medications at a local pharmacy; and

WHEREAS, a majority of ELCA congregations are located in small communities and rural areas which are already facing a reduction in local provision of necessary services; and

WHEREAS, the ELCA Pension and Other Benefits Plan program for provision of maintenance medication bypasses local pharmacies, further reducing the viability of local providers and thereby reducing the likelihood that pharmaceutical counseling and the other valuable services of local pharmacies would remain available in many communities; and

WHEREAS, cost containment is an important issue for both ELCA congregations and plan participants; therefore, be it
RESOLVED, that the Northwest Synod of Wisconsin, in its 1993 assembly, memorialize the ELCA Church Council to take such action as would urge the Board of Pensions to amend their policy, making it possible for local pharmacies to participate in the program for maintenance medication under the same cost formula as the mail order provider of pharmaceuticals, namely, the cost of ingredients plus a dispensing fee.

Council Action:

EN BLOC   [CC93.12.105.g.]
To refer the resolution of the Northwest Synod of Wisconsin on prescription costs to the Board of Pensions for a response to the synod, and a report and/or recommendation to the April 1994 meeting of the Church Council.

10. First United and St. Francis Churches in San Francisco
North/West Lower Michigan Synod (6B)
WHEREAS, two congregations of the Evangelical Lutheran Church in America, St. Francis and First United, both of San Francisco, California, are currently under suspension for having called as pastors individuals who are not on the clergy roster of the Evangelical Lutheran Church in America; and

WHEREAS, the sole purpose of the suspensions, as set forth in the open letter from the Discipline Committee, was to allow time, prior to the expulsion of the two congregations, for a "faithful examination of ELCA policies on the ordination of homosexuals"; and

WHEREAS, the Evangelical Lutheran Church in America has postponed the study on sexuality and has not even begun to study the other issues set forth in the report of the Discipline Committee; and

WHEREAS, the whole church will be poorer if the Evangelical Lutheran Church in America allows the two congregations to be expelled without giving the issues the serious study for which the Discipline Committee pleaded; therefore, be it
RESOLVED, that the North/West Lower Michigan Synod of the Evangelical Lutheran Church in America hereby calls upon the ELCA Church Council to undertake the studies called for in the Discipline Committee report; and be it further
RESOLVED, that the North/West Lower Michigan Synod calls upon the ELCA Church Council to instruct the Division for Ministry of the Evangelical Lutheran Church in America to

immediately begin the studies called for in the open letter from the Discipline Committee.

NOTE: The background information related to this resolution is found following resolution #8.

Council Action:

EN BLOC   [CC93.12.105.h.]

To request the secretary of this church to convey to the North/West Lower Michigan Synod the response transmitted by the 1993 Churchwide Assembly to synods that called for an extension of the discipline process in the matter relating to St. Francis and First United Lutheran churches in San Francisco.

11. Study of Ministry
New England Synod (7B)

RESOLVED, that the New England Synod Assembly endorse the recommendation amending the Final Report of the Task Force on the Study of Ministry made by the ELCA Church Council to continue use of a Rite of Ordination for only those persons entering in upon a pastoral ministry of Word and Sacrament.

Council Action:

EN BLOC   [CC93.12.105.i.]

To refer the resolution of the New England Synod on the Study of Ministry to the Division for Ministry as information.

12. Board of Pensions Policy on Adoptions
Metropolitan New York Synod (7C)

WHEREAS, the Evangelical Lutheran Church in America at its Churchwide Assembly adopted the "Social Teaching Statement on Abortion" in which it stated that "We encourage and seek to make it possible for people of diverse cultural and racial backgrounds and with limited financial means to adopt children"; and

WHEREAS, the ELCA Board of Pensions currently makes no provision for financial assistance in the costs of adopting a child, while costs for adoption increase steadily each year; and

WHEREAS, the Board of Pensions is more than a simple insurance carrier and pension program; and

WHEREAS, by virtue of a public nature of the office of ministry of Word and Sacrament pastors and their families can be seen as positive role models in this issue; therefore, be it

RESOLVED, that the Synod Council of the Metropolitan New York Synod of the Evangelical Lutheran Church in America request that the ELCA Church Council refer this matter to the Board of Pensions; and be it further

RESOLVED, that the Board of Pensions make a careful study of this situation, based upon the "Social Teaching Statement on Abortion" of the Evangelical Lutheran Church in America and upon the practices of other organizations that assist financially with adoptions, to determine the reasonable and customary costs of adoption; such information would then be used to provide coverage for plan members who adopt a child.

Council Action:

EN BLOC   [CC93.12.105.j.]

To refer the resolution of the Metropolitan New York Synod on the Board of Pensions policy on adoption to the Board of Pensions for a report and/or recommendation to the April 1994 meeting of the Church Council.

13. Homosexual Clergy
Metropolitan Washington, D.C., Synod (8G)

WHEREAS, the 1991 assembly of this synod referred to the synod's Division for Ministry a resolution (SA91.6.37) concerning the synod's readiness and desire "to accept among its clergy homosexual persons who are living in a committed monogamous sexual and affectional relationship"; and

WHEREAS, after study by a task force appointed by the Division for Ministry, this synod's Division for Ministry has concluded that resolution SA91.6.37, though faithfully raising issues of a profound and serious nature, may not in fact represent the actual thought and conviction of many members of the synod; and

WHEREAS, the question of the ordination and public ministry of persons living in these homosexual relationships may be divisive within the congregations of the synod and among the people who strive to be of one mind in the Holy Spirit; therefore, be it

RESOLVED, that this assembly call upon the ELCA Church Council to request the theological seminaries of this church to study the policy of this church on the certification or ordination and public ministry of "homosexual persons living in a committed monogamous sexual and affectional relationship" and make these studies available to the church; and be it further

RESOLVED, that this study by the theological seminaries of this church also include such related issues as a strategy to insure that the same language and expectations of relationship decorum are applied to both heterosexual and homosexual candidates for ordination, and a study of the appropriateness of a rite which affirms and recognizes loving, committed monogamous relationships of gay and lesbian couples; and be it further

RESOLVED, that this assembly request the bishop of this synod to secure from the ELCA Division for Ministry and to disseminate through the synod a description of the history and rationale of the ELCA's present policy on the ordination and public ministry of homosexual persons; and be it further

RESOLVED, that this assembly request the synod's Division for Ministry to provide opportunities for people of the synod to meet and, with prayer for God's guidance, to study and discuss the ordination and public ministry of "homosexual persons living in a committed monogamous sexual and affectional relationship."

Council Action:

EN BLOC   [CC93.12.105.k.]

To refer the resolution of the Metropolitan Washington, D.C., Synod to the secretary of this church and request that the secretary convey to the synod the prior decision made by the Church Council that study of the ordination of "homosexual persons living in a committed monogamous sexual and affectional relationship" will not occur until after the churchwide deliberation on a more foundational study on human sexuality is completed.

15. Churchwide Offering
Indiana-Kentucky Synod (6C)

The Indiana-Kentucky Synod Assembly in 1993 addressed a memorial to the 1993 ELCA Churchwide Assembly as follows:

WHEREAS, the ELCA Church Council is requesting a special churchwide offering to raise additional income for churchwide ministries; and

WHEREAS, this ELCA churchwide solicitation is being addressed by mail directly to all ELCA congregations and gifts are to be received directly by the churchwide office; therefore, be it

RESOLVED, that the Indiana-Kentucky Synod Assembly of the ELCA:
a. affirms that mission of the ELCA and the integrity of the established benevolence process;
b. recognizes the reality of limited resources and the need for special offerings when warranted by unique circumstances such as natural disasters, war, events beyond ELCA control, etc; and
c. upholds partnership as being reciprocal in nature as demonstrated by churchwide ministries, faithful synodical benevolence and appropriate synodical representation churchwide; and be it further

RESOLVED, that the Indiana-Kentucky Synod Assembly memorialize the ELCA Churchwide Assembly that, except for situations warranted by unique circumstances, future requests for special offerings or appeals coming from the churchwide expressions of the ELCA involve prior consultation with the synod councils; and be it further

RESOLVED, that copies of this memorial be forwarded by the secretary of this synod to the synod councils and bishops of the other 64 synods of the ELCA.

A.   Southeastern Minnesota Synod (3I)

Diane McNally Forsyth, vice president, Southeastern Minnesota Synod, forwarded the following resolution to Kathy J. Magnus on June 25, 1993, in a letter which stated:

. . . the Synod Executive Committee voted to support this resolution recently at our meeting. I am writing to communicate the Southeastern Minnesota Synod's support of the enclosed resolution.

B.   Northern Texas-Northern Louisiana Synod (4D)

The following memo, dated July 24, 1993, is addressed to the ELCA Church Council from the Northern Texas-Northern Louisiana Synod Council Executive Committee, Nancy Hicks, Secretary:

The NTNL Synod Executive Committee, in session on July 16, 1993, reviewed and discussed the resolution submitted by the Indiana-Kentucky Synod concerning special offerings and appeals coming from the churchwide expressions of the ELCA.

We have communicated our support of this resolution to the delegates of NTNL.

Our concern is that special offering appeals do not support the understanding of stewardship that we as a church strive to teach our members. If we are giving all that we are able through our weekly offerings, when additional special requests are made and we are able to respond, does that not say that we have not given all that we can. Instead of special offering requests should we not be teaching our members to respond with the fullest gift in the first passing of the plate.

We of NTNL are certainly in support of the ministries that extend beyond our synod throughout the church and urge our members to support these ministries with our prayers, our time and certainly with our financial resources which are all a gift from God. Let us encourage all to give the one full gift each and every week and if churchwide programs discover urgent needs we would ask that all such special requests be first a consultation with all synod councils.

God's blessing and peace be with y'al as you give of your time and energy . . . and resources . . . to the ELCA. Thank you.

C.   Northern Illinois Synod (5B)

Northern Illinois Synod passed the resolution at its 1993 Synod Assembly, substituting "Northern Illinois Synod" for "Indiana-Kentucky" Synod.

NOTE: the 1993 Churchwide Assembly addressed this issue, taking the following action:

1. To receive with appreciation the "Financial Stewardship Strategy";
2. To endorse the general directions described in the report and the related programs and activities that are intended to:
   a. help members of the Evangelical Lutheran Church in America to develop faith-filled lives;
   b. articulate the compelling story of the ELCA's mission;
   c. equip and nurture lay and rostered leaders, so that they will guide the church as it funds its mission activities;
   d. affirm, coordinate, and develop new and current methods of financial support for this church's mission;
   e. coordinate partnerships among all manifestations and expressions of this church; and
   f. support the tithe as a guideline for a joyful response to God's love.
3. To instruct the Church Council of the Evangelical Lutheran Church in America to oversee and guide the further development of the various elements of the Financial Stewardship Strategy, with the support of the Division for Congregational Ministries and other churchwide units;
4. To affirm the Church Council's establishment of a "Vision for Mission Fund" for global and domestic ministries;
5. To establish an annual celebrative churchwide offering, in partnership with our synods, to be held in the spring of each year, as a component of this fund, in order to receive congregational and individual gifts given over and above their primary partnership support for global and domestic ministries;
6. To instruct the Church Council of the Evangelical Lutheran Church in America to cause the Division for Ministry and the Division for Congregational Ministries, in cooperation with the seminaries of the Evangelical Lutheran Church in America, to develop specific, intentional programs to strengthen instruction in the theology of stewardship, recognizing it as a primary faith issue, and in the ecclesiology of the Evangelical Lutheran Church in America to the end that pastors and other teachers and leaders of this church have a fuller personal understanding of stewardship and ecclesiology, and are better equipped to help members of this church develop and grow in their understanding; and
7. To commend the document, "Financial Stewardship Strategy: Report and Recommendations," to synods and congregations of this church for their reflection and action.

Council Action:

EN BLOC   [CC93.12.105.l.]

To refer the resolutions of the Southeastern Minnesota, Northern Texas-Northern Louisiana, and Northern Illinois synods on churchwide offerings to the Division for Congregational Ministries; and

To request that the Division for Congregational Ministries respond directly to these synods, sharing information on the action taken by the 1993 Churchwide Assembly and on current plans for a churchwide offering that address the concerns raised by these resolutions.

16. Possible Reinstatement of Rostered Leaders

Southeastern Pennsylvania Synod (7F)

RESOLVED, that the Synod Council of the Southeastern Pennsylvania Synod petition the ELCA Church Council to request that the Division for Ministry, in consultation with the Conference of Bishops, develop a churchwide policy of support for reinstated leaders that provides for supervision and public accountability for the privilege of serving the church as an ordained or certified leader; and be it further

RESOLVED, that the implementation of the policy of support shall:

a. empower reinstated pastors and associates in ministry to be honest about their history of sexual misconduct and of maintaining proper boundaries, transference and counter-transference issues and of their personal ongoing readiness and ability to provide ministry;

b. assist congregations and agencies of the church who have called reinstated pastors and associates in ministry to set appropriate boundaries as safeguards while working mutually with reinstated leaders in proclaiming the gospel and in calling these leaders to be accountable;

c. assist bishops in being reasonably assured that reinstated leaders were providing faithful and effective exercise of their ministry in all matters of morality and personal ethics. The bishop shall receive regular reports of supervision and evaluation of the pastor/associate in ministry; and

d. give assurance to the general community in which the reinstated pastor/associate in ministry serves that the Evangelical Lutheran Church in America is actively supervising and regularizing the activities of the reinstated leaders so that there is a positive move towards complete restoration.

Council Action:

EN BLOC   [CC93.12.105.m.]
To refer the resolution of the Southeastern Pennsylvania Synod on possible reinstatement of rostered leaders to the Division for Ministry; and

To request that the Division for Ministry, in consultation with the Conference of Bishops, provide a report and recommendation on this matter to the Church Council at its April 1994 meeting.

DECISION OF THE DISCIPLINE COMMITTEE
(IN THE MATTER OF THE DISCIPLINARY PROCEEDINGS AGAINST THE CONGREGATIONS OF ST. FRANCIS LUTHERAN CHURCH AND FIRST UNITED LUTHERAN CHURCH OF SAN FRANCISCO, FILED JULY 18, 1990)

Please refer to Item #8 and Item #10 of these minutes.

This decision resolves charges filed against St. Francis Lutheran Church and First United Lutheran Church of San Francisco by Bishop Lyle G. Miller and the Synod Council of the Sierra Pacific Synod within the Evangelical Lutheran Church in America ("ELCA"). The charges allege that the congregation willfully disregarded criteria for recognition as ELCA congregations by failing to call pastoral leadership in accordance with church call procedures.

The Discipline Committee has received oral and written testimony from over 100 witnesses in a consolidated hearing of these charges. It has also reviewed documentary evidence including many governing documents of the ELCA, items of correspondence, and other exhibits. Because all parties have acted in a spirit of cooperation, mutual respect, and Christian love, it was possible for the committee to study much of this large body of material in advance of formal proceedings and to complete hearings within three days.

Most of the operative facts are beyond dispute. First United called an openly gay man to serve as a pastor; St. Francis called a lesbian couple to serve as pastors. At the time they were called, none of the three were certified for ordination under ELCA procedures. Because of their opposition to ELCA ordination policy, they did not seek to obtain or retain certification. Under that policy, while homosexual orientation does not bar ordination, practicing homosexual persons are precluded from ordained ministry within the church. The accused congregations joined these

three candidates in their opposition to ELCA policy, issued letters of call to them, and accepted them as ordained ministers. They called the three to initiate an outreach ministry in the gay/lesbian community.

The decision of the committee is expressed in three sections of the document. First, there are statements of decision dealing with the charges against each congregation. Second, there is a memorandum summarizing the reasons for the decisions. The foregoing sections represent the views of a majority of the members of the committee as to the matters discussed. Third, the committee has addressed an open letters to all persons affected by or interested in this dispute which offers its thoughts concerning many things needful that go beyond a strict analysis of the charges. The open letter is endorsed by all committee members. Finally, in addition to this document, individual members of the committee who chose top do so have submitted their concurring, dissenting, or other views. These are also included with the decision.

In summary, the committee has sustained the charges against both congregations. Because of certain ambiguities in the development and communication of ELCA policy that may have affected First United, the decision establishes certain conditions which may eventually lead to a dismissal of the charges in its case.

Discipline has been imposed on both congregations. The first element of discipline is a suspension. The consequences of suspension described in a memorandum prepared by the Secretary of the ELCA have been adopted by the committee for purposes of this dispute. During the period of suspension, the congregations as entities will be deprived of certain rights and privileges such as sending voting lay delegates to synod assemblies and petitioning the church. The pastors of the congregations who are now on the clergy roster of the ELCA will continue in that status in all respects, including as voting delegates to synod assemblies. The individual members of the congregation can continue to be participants in the life of the ELCA through service on its councils, boards, and committees and as nonvoting persons at conventions.

The suspension period will expire on December 31, 1995. This five-year period allows time for: (1) study and dialogue within the ELCA with respect to its practices regarding ordination of homosexual persons; and (2) action at one or more Churchwide Assemblies. If by that date or sooner, the practices of these congregations are in accord with the pastoral leadership criterion of recognition, they will be restored to full membership in the church. If such an accord does not occur by the end of the suspension period, the congregations will be removed from the roll of ELCA congregations.

The discipline imposed is severe, as a majority of the committee believes it must be when a basic criterion of ELCA membership has been and continues to be disregarded. At the same time, the committee's decision affords a much needed opportunity for study, dialogue, reconciliation, and progress toward a more unified understanding within the ELCA with respect to the matters in dispute. In the committee's view, that opportunity is essential if the church is to serve as the body of Christ and as a witness to his saving love and continuing presence with us.

En Bloc Disposition of Certain Agenda Items

Background: The following *en bloc* resolution includes agenda items which were considered on the last day of the Church Council meeting. Inclusion of these items in the *en bloc* action reflects a judgment that these items are relatively non-controversial in nature and may not require a plenary discussion and separate vote.

Each of the items is noted as *EN BLOC* in the body of the agenda. On the first day of the council meeting, the chair provided an opportunity for members to express whether they wish to discuss separately any of the items listed in the *en bloc* resolution; any such item was removed from the *en bloc* resolution and discussed at the appropriate point in the agenda.

The chair did not call for a discussion or separate vote on those items that were not removed from the *en bloc* resolution by the end of the first day of plenary sessions.

VOTED: *CC93.12.104*

To take action *en bloc* on the items listed below, the full texts of which are printed in . . . [these minutes]:

CC93.12.105.a.-m.	Synod Resolutions Directed to the Church Council;
CC93.12.106	Confidentiality of Communication with Associates in Ministry;
CC93.12.107	State of Incorporation of Synods;
CC93.12.108	Change in Synod's Name (4F);
CC93.12.109	Indemnification by Certain Synods;
CC93.12.110	Policy Concerning Synods Involved in Litigation;
CC93.12.111	Ratification of Amendments to Synodical Constitutions;
CC93.12.112	Guide for Revision of Congregation Constitutions;
CC93.12.113	Review and Confirmation of Church Council Designated Funds;
CC93.12.114	Changes Related to Regional Structures;
CC93.12.115	Amendments to the Bylaws of the Board of Pensions of the ELCA;
CC93.12.116	Proposed Restatement of The ALC Continuation Trust;
CC93.12.117	Related Amendment of the ELCA Continuation of The ALC Major Medical-Dental Trust for Retired Participants;
CC93.12.118.a.-h.	Proposed Miscellaneous Amendments in the Plans of ELCA Health and Benefits Program;
CC93.12.119	Vision and Expectations: Commissioned Associates in Ministry;
CC93.12.120	Other Matters Related to Associates in Ministry;
CC93.12.121	Appointments to Board of Lutheran General HealthSystem; and
CC93.12.122	Appointments to Board of Lutheran Immigration and Refugee Service.

The Church Council recessed at 12:40 P.M. and reconvened at 1:36 P.M.

Report of the
Budget and Finance Committee

Chair Magnus called upon Edith M. Lohr, chair of the Budget and Finance Committee, to report on behalf of the committee.

1. 1993 Expenditure Authorization

Background: At its August 1993 meeting, the Church Council took the following action lowering the 1993 spending authorization for the churchwide organization:

To revise the 1993 current fund spending authorization from $75,900,000 to $74,900,000, or 98.9 percent of the revised 1993 current fund income estimate; and

To reaffirm the 1993 World Hunger spending of $12,000,000, or 100 percent of the revised World Hunger estimate.

Council agenda Exhibit F, Part 1, detailed the revised 1993 current operating fund income estimate, which totals $76,700,000. The estimated income for mission support (formerly called "proportionate share") has been reduced by $1,000,000. Current receipts from synods in 1993 for mission support, which are displayed in council agenda Exhibit A, Part 3b, have prompted this reduction. It is now estimated that mission support from synods will be approximately $400,000 *less* than what was actually received in 1992.

The World Hunger income estimate remains at the $12,000,000 originally anticipated.

Council agenda Exhibit F, Part 2, detailed the revised current operating fund allocations to units, which total $74,900,000; $1,800,000 will be returned to the Mission Operating Fund (operating reserve).

In making the revised unit allocations, staff of the Office of the Bishop and the Office of the Treasurer requested from units at their quarterly budget reviews information on any possible unit underspending this year due to special circumstances (e.g., staff vacancies, delayed program development). Such planned underspending became the first reductions made for the remainder of the 1993 fiscal year. In calculating future reductions, it was agreed that these reductions were considered *non-recurring*, that is, they would not be considered as unit baseline adjustments when considering unit allocations for 1994 and beyond. Achieved in this manner was $611,075 of the needed $1,000,000 reduction. In allocating the remaining $388,925 in unit reductions, the following were among the factors that were weighed:

- stated budgetary priorities of global mission, planting and supporting congregations, and theological education;
- certain fixed costs; and
- spreading the reductions across units to avoid major, late-in-the-year reductions that could disrupt partners in ministry.

Council Action: The Church Council received the foregoing as information.

2. Synodical-Churchwide Consultations on Mission Support

Background: The responsibility for directing synodical-churchwide consultations on mission support (formerly, "proportionate-share commitments") was assigned to a coordinator for mission support (the Rev. Mark R. Moller-Gunderson, who also serves as executive director of the Division for Congregational Ministries). The Budget and Finance Committee has two important tasks related to mission support:

a. To review and act on 1994 synod mission support commitments, and

b. To review the process and time-line for 1995 synod commitments.

At its March 1993 meeting, the Church Council agreed to the Budget and Finance Committee's recommendation:

1. To refer action on the 1994 synod proportionate-share commitments to the Executive Committee after:
   - additional written responses are received from synods, and;
   - continued conversations between the Office of the Bishop and synods in the face of the lowering of income estimates for 1993.

No action was taken by the Executive Committee of the Church Council on mission support between council meetings. Further revisions and confirmations from synods as to their 1994 commitments, however, have been received. The latest information from synods is shown on the Synodical 1994 Mission Support Commitments Worksheet (council agenda Exhibit F, Part 3a). This exhibit displays each synod by region for the years 1992-1994, with the proposed goals for 1995. Attention should be paid to the variance columns for dollar and percentage changes between 1993 and 1994 revised estimates.

Staff prepared for review of the Budget and Finance Committee and subsequently the Church Council recommendations for action in this area. The options for the Church Council are to approve, disapprove, or approve with conditions (e.g., special consultation visits) the commitments of each synod.

The Synodical-Churchwide Consultation on Mission Support for 1995 took place on October 9, 1993, within the context of a larger meeting that explored the needs of congregations, staffing issues, and funding concerns. Every synod received a workbook of information regarding mission support for 1995. Samples of information from the workbook are shown in council agenda Exhibit F, Part 3b. Included in this exhibit is the Process and Timeline for 1995 Mission Support Consultations, which notes Church Council involvement in items 4, 5, 8 and 9. This process calls for a strengthened role for the Budget and Finance Committee and the Church Council regarding their partnership with synods as levels of mission support are determined.

The Budget and Finance Committee discussed these matters before referring them to the December 1993 Church Council meeting related recommendations for action.

Council Action: Edith M. Lohr introduced the following recommendation of the Budget and Finance Committee, which was subsequently adopted by the Church Council. During discussion, William T. Billings inquired about the manner in which the action of the Church Council would be transmitted to synods. Ms. Lohr indicated that the action related to each respective synod would be forwarded to the synod together with a cover letter of detailed explanation.

VOTED: *CC93.12.123*
To request the Office of the Bishop to notify the synods of the following actions:

(1) *The following synods have increased their dollar commitment and either increased or held constant the percentage shared with the churchwide organization of unrestricted mission support they receive from the congregations in their synods.*
The Church Council expresses thanks and approval for their steady support and strong partnership in the Gospel.
Caribbean, Arkansas-Oklahoma, Metropolitan New York, Montana, Eastern Washington-Idaho, Northeastern Iowa, Northeastern Minnesota, North/West Lower Michigan, Northeastern Ohio, Sierra Pacific, Northern Great Lakes, Northeastern Pennsylvania, Central States, South-Central Synod of Wisconsin, Delaware-Maryland, Southeastern Pennsylvania, South Dakota, Upstate New York, Southern California (West), Eastern North Dakota, Southeastern Minnesota, Western Iowa, New England, Northwestern Minnesota, Texas-Louisiana Gulf Coast, Lower Susquehanna, Southeastern, Pacifica, Northwestern Ohio, Nebraska, Southwestern Pennsylvania, East-Central Synod of Wisconsin, and Southwestern Texas.

(2) *The following synods have increased their dollar commitment and lowered their percentage shared with the churchwide organization of unrestricted mission support they receive from the congregations in their synods. Their mission support percentage is below the 55-percent level.*
The Church Council expresses thanks to the following synods and approval, with concern about reductions that lower their percentage of mission support dollars. Further information and consultation with the Office of the Bishop is requested.
Oregon, Slovak Zion, Rocky Mountain, South Carolina, New Jersey, Saint Paul Area, Southeastern Iowa, Southern Ohio, Grand Canyon, North Carolina, and Indiana-Kentucky.

(3) *The following synods have increased their dollar commitment and lowered their percentage shared with the churchwide organization of unrestricted mission support they receive from the congregations in their synods. Their mission support percentage remains at or above the 55-percent level.*
The Church Council expresses thanks to the following synods and approval for their 1994 synodical commitment to mission support and partnership in the Gospel, with a desire to explore further the implications about reductions in the percentage shared, even though their percentage remains in excess of 55-percent:
LaCrosse Area, Minneapolis Area, and Greater Milwaukee.

(4) *The following synod has decreased its dollar commitment and increased its percentage shared with the churchwide organization of unrestricted mission support received from congregations. Its mission support percentage exceeds the 55-percent level.*
The Church Council expresses thanks to the following synod and approval for its 1994 synodical commitment to mission support and partnership in the Gospel. Additional information and consultation is requested by the Office of the Bishop to understand the reasons for the decrease in anticipated dollars.
Southeast Michigan.

(5) *The following synods have decreased their dollar commitment and held constant their percentage shared with the churchwide organization of unrestricted mission support they receive from the congregations in its synod.*
The Church Council expresses thanks to the following synods and approval, with concern for their

1994 synodical commitment to mission support and partnership in the Gospel. Additional information and discussion with the Office of the Bishop on synodical income estimates is requested.

> **Northwestern Pennsylvania, Southwestern Minnesota, Northern Illinois, Metropolitan Washington, D.C., and Central/Southern Illinois.**

(6) *The following synods have decreased their dollar commitment and decreased their percentage shared with the churchwide organization of unrestricted mission support they receive from the congregations in its synod. Their percentage continues below the 55-percent level.*

> **The Church Council expresses concern about the lowering of the percentage commitments by the following synods.** *Approval is withheld* **until consultations with the Office of the Bishop can be held. Final action is referred to the Executive Committee.**

> **Southwestern Washington, Northwest Washington, and Northern Texas-Northern Louisiana.**

(7) *The following synod has decreased its dollar commitment and decreased its percentage shared with the churchwide organization of unrestricted mission support received from congregations. Its percentage continues above the 55-percent level.*

> **The Church Council expresses thanks and** **approval to the following synod for its 1994 synodical commitment to mission support and partnership in the Gospel, with a desire to explore further the implications about the synod's reduction in percentage. Additional information concerning synodical income estimates is requested.**

> **Northwest Synod of Wisconsin.**

(8) *The following synods have held constant their dollar commitment and increased their percentage shared with the churchwide organization of unrestricted mission support they receive from the congregations in its synod.*

> **The Church Council expresses thanks and** **approval for their steady support and strong partnership in the Gospel.**

> **Western North Dakota and West Virginia-Western Maryland.**

(9) *The following synods have held constant their dollar commitment and held constant the percentage shared with the churchwide organization of unrestricted mission support they receive from congregations. The mission support percentage is below the 55-percent level.*

> **The Church Council expresses thanks to the following synods and** **approval for their 1994 synodical commitment to mission support and partnership in the Gospel. Encouragement is given for these synods to increase their percentage of mission support by one-half of a percent in 1995.**

> **Allegheny and Florida-Bahamas.**

(10) *The following synods have held constant their dollar commitment and decreased the percentage shared with the churchwide organization of unrestricted mission support they receive from congregations. The mission support percentage is below the 55-percent level.*

> **The Church Council expresses thanks to the following synods and** **conditional** **approval with concern for their 1994 synodical commitment to mission support and partnership in the Gospel. Final**

action is referred to the Executive Committee, pending further consultation with the Office of the Bishop.

> **Upper Susquehanna and Virginia.**

(11) *The following synods have indicated new information concerning their 1994 commitment is forthcoming.*

> **The Church Council refers action on the 1994 synod mission support commitment for the following synods to the Executive Committee until additional information is received from the synods.**

> **Alaska and Metropolitan Chicago.**

3. 1994 Expenditure Authorization

Background: The 1993 Churchwide Assembly approved option one of the 1994 budget proposal:

> To approve a 1994 current fund budget proposal of $78,790,000, with an initial Mission Operating Fund allocation of $1,500,000;

> To approve a 1994 World Hunger budget proposal of $12,250,000; and

> To authorize the Church Council to establish the spending authorization after review of 1993 actual income and 1994 revised income estimates.

Action on the budget followed assembly debate and approval of the Financial Stewardship Strategy, which authorized an annual churchwide offering. The budget that was approved by the assembly includes an income estimate of $1,000,000 to be received from this annual churchwide offering. This $1,000,000 is to be applied to the current ongoing mission of the church, as expressed in the churchwide budget.

Income: Since income estimates for mission support (proportionate share) from synods have been revised downward, it was necessary to likewise revise downward the 1994 spending authorization. The original 1994 projections for mission support had included a modest increase of $600,000 from the 1993 estimate. When added to the $1,000,000 reduction in the income estimate for 1993, a reduction of $1,600,000 in income is anticipated for 1994. Thus, the income estimate for 1994 was reduced to $77,190,000. Council agenda Exhibit F, Part 4, displays the revised estimated current operating fund income that the churchwide organization may anticipate for the 1994-1995 biennium.

Anticipated income for the World Hunger budget remains at $12,250,000.

Spending: Council agenda Exhibit F, Part 5, detailed the revised current fund unit allocations after considering the lowered income estimate. The proposed level of spending is $75,690,000. This plan also retains the original 1994 proposal of $1,500,000 being returned to the Mission Operating Fund.

Revised 1994 allocations for the Division for Congregational Ministries, Division for Ministry, Division for Outreach and the Division for Global Mission reflect the budget priorities that were affirmed by the 1993 Churchwide Assembly in its action on the 1994-1995 budget proposal. According to the 1994-1995 Budget Proposal Narrative: The 1994 budget proposal . . . gives relative priority in funding to the following critical areas of the ELCA's life and work:

- global mission;
- theological education; and
- establishing new congregations and ministries, and supporting and equipping existing congregations as they reach out with the Gospel in their communities.

When considered together with the reductions in 1993 and 1994 in other units, the 1994 unit allocations truly reflect a shift in the spending authorization towards these priorities. Reductions in other units ranged from 1-2 percent from the original 1994 allocations.

A total of $216,000 remains to be distributed for the implementation of strategies approved by the Churchwide Assembly. The following nine strategies have been approved by churchwide assemblies since 1989: theological education; study of ministry; women and children living in poverty; sexual abuse; sacramental practices; stewardship; evangelism; confirmation ministry; and the multicultural ministry strategy.

The $216,000 is not sufficient to fund all of those strategies to the extent envisioned by those studies. The Office of the Bishop has been working with the Planning Team to develop a plan for distribution of the available funds to implement those strategies, taking into consideration the availability of outside funding for the strategies. This process was made all the harder by the recent decision of the Lilly Foundation not to fund the final two years of the Study of Theological Education. The Division for Ministry had anticipated receiving $200,000 over the final two years of the study. The results of the process for distribution of the funds earmarked for implementation of strategies was shared with the Church Council at its December 1993 meeting.

Council Action: Edith M. Lohr introduced the following recommendation of the Budget and Finance Committee, subsequently adopted by the Church Council without discussion:

VOTED: *CC93.12.124*
To approve an initial 1994 fiscal year spending authorization of $77,190,000, with an initial Mission Operating Fund allocation of $1,500,000;

To approve an initial 1994 World Hunger spending authorization of $12,250,000; and

To authorize the Church Council Executive Committee to change the 1994 spending authorization, after review and recommendation of the Church Council Budget and Finance Committee, between meetings of the full Church Council.

4. 1994 Capital Budget: Mission Investment Fund

Council Action: Edith M. Lohr introduced the following recommendation of the Budget and Finance Committee, which subsequently was adopted by the Church Council. Treasurer Richard L. McAuliffe reviewed the line items of the budget and commented, "These loans have take-out commitments from the fraternal insurance companies; they are excellent loans; the return is significant to the profitability of the Mission

Investment Fund." The Rev. John O. Knudson commended Treasurer McAuliffe for his management of the fund.

VOTED: *CC93.12.125*
To approve the 1994 capital budget of $50,650,000 for the Mission Investment Fund.

5. Audit Committee

Council Action: Edith M. Lohr introduced the following recommendation of the Budget and Finance Committee, subsequently adopted by the Church Council without discussion:

VOTED: *CC93.12.126*
To approve the report of Audit Committee attached as council agenda Exhibit F, Part 7.

6. ELCA Foundation

Council Action: Edith M. Lohr introduced the semiannual report of the ELCA Foundation, printed in council agenda Exhibit H, Part 1a, which was received by the Church Council as information. William T. Billings inquired about the rationale for the designation of life annuities as gifts? The Rev. Harvey A. Stegemoeller, executive director of the ELCA Foundation, responded.

7. Review and Confirmation of Church Council Designated Funds

Background: The authority to designate funds within the Evangelical Lutheran Church in America rests with the Church Council in its capacity as the board of directors of the churchwide organization. Designations are reviewed annually by the Church Council following recommendation by the Budget and Finance Committee. Exhibit F, Part 8 displays the current designation of such funds.

Council Action: The following recommendation of the Budget and Finance Committee was adopted *en bloc*, as reported elsewhere in these minutes:

EN BLOC   [CC93.12.113]
To ratify the designation of existing Church Council designated funds, as displayed in Exhibit F, Part 8.

8. Keystones Project

Background: At the March 1993 meeting of the Church Council, information was shared about the Keystones Project. The Budget and Finance Committee was authorized by the council to review the business plan for this project and make appropriate recommendations to the bishop. At its December 4, 1993, meeting, the Budget and Finance Committee continued this process of review and subsequently reported any recommendations to the Church Council.

Council Action: The Church Council received the foregoing as information. During discussion, D. Mark Klever requested clarification of the differences in expenditure levels between 1993 and 1994. The Rev. Donald M. Hallberg inquired whether John Giles (Atlanta, Ga.), a consultant for the Keystones Project, was still under contract. Edith M. Lohr indicated that he was not.

Chair Magnus thanked Ms. Lohr and the members of the Budget and Finance Committee for their work.

Report of the Coordination and Services Committee

Chair Magnus called upon William E. Diehl, chair of the Coordination and Services Committee, to report on behalf of the committee. Mr. Diehl indicated that, in order to facilitate communication, the cost of providing telefax machines to council members was being explored. The committee is requesting that a memorandum be transmitted to council members regarding actions taken by the Conference of Bishops.

In reference to the work of the Department for Communication, Mr. Diehl reported that a new logo for this church is under development; William T. Billings inquired about the approval process for the new logo. The response indicated that a work group would propose a design to Bishop Chilstrom for his approval.

Mr. Diehl noted that a Christmas "Story Barn" video may be aired by NBC affiliate stations. He encouraged council members to contact various affiliates that had declined to air the video.

Mr. Diehl indicated that the Coordination and Services Committee would be reviewing changes to the ELCA personnel policies proposed by the Department for Human Resources. "I think you, as the board of directors of this organization, should have a little more knowledge about what some of the personnel issues are . . . and so we intend to bring them to you at future meetings," he stated.

Mr. Diehl reported that the Department for Research and Evaluation has discontinued the "Lutherans Say . . ." survey in favor of the sampling of congregations.

The committee is recommending that the directors of departments be given voice at council meetings regarding the concerns of the units. Chair Magnus expressed appreciation to Women of Evangelical Lutheran Church in America, many members of which had encouraged the airing of the "Story Barn" video in their local areas.

Social Teaching Statement on the Church and Human Sexuality (continued)

The Rev. Eric C. Shafer, director of the Department for Communication, reviewed a proposed account regarding the council's action on the first draft of the proposed social statement on human sexuality:

"The ELCA Church Council took action to continue the process of consideration of "The Church and Human Sexuality—A Lutheran Perspective" with major adjustments. A copy of the council's resolution with a cover letter from Bishop Herbert W. Chilstrom will be mailed first-class to all rostered leaders on Wednesday, December 8, 1993. A news release on the council's action will be distributed following this mailing."

For the sake of clarity, Robert S. Schroeder suggested addition of the phrase, "to the process," at the end of the first sentence.

Pastor Shafer indicated that the information regarding the council's action would be released according to the following schedule:

Monday, December 6	Faxed to 65 bishops;
Wednesday December 8	Mailed to rostered leaders;
Thursday, December 9	News release.

Robert S. Schroeder inquired, "Can I presume that we have learned from our October experience, in that, before the news release is released on Thursday, someone will telephone [the ELCA publishing house] to find out that it really got mailed?" Pastor Shafer answered affirmatively.

Copies of two letters addressed respectively to synodical bishops and to the other rostered persons of this church concerning this matter was distributed to council members. Several suggestions were offered for perfection of the text.

William H. Engelbrecht then moved for the sake of clarity the following:

MOVED;
SECONDED;
CARRIED: To amend the announcement cited above to read: "The ELCA Church Council took action to continue the process of study of the first draft of the document . . .".

The Rev. Donald M. Hallberg thanked the bishop of this church and his staff for quickly responding to the council's directive regarding the notification of synods and rostered persons concerning the council's deliberations on this matter.

1993 Churchwide Assembly Evaluation

Chair Magnus called upon Kenneth W. Inskeep, director of the Department for Research and Evaluation, to highlight findings of an evaluation instrument related to the 1993 Churchwide Assembly. Chair Magnus also reminded council members that a form for evaluation of this meeting had been distributed to council members.

The Rev. Franklin D. Fry noted an issue, which had been discussed on the floor of the 1993 Churchwide Assembly, "namely, concern about the balance between presentations . . . and the assembly as the church's highest legislative assembly." He observed that many assembly members had felt that insufficient emphasis was placed on the deliberative function of the assembly. Bishop Paull E. Spring concurred. He observed that too much of the assembly's time was consumed in procedural matters.

J. David Ellwanger inquired about the degree of participation of lay persons in the planning of assemblies. He observed that most lay members were present by virtue of vacation time off work, and encouraged shortening the duration the assemblies by two days. He concluded that there was too much "down time," and insufficient time devoted to deliberation. The Rev. Stephen M. Youngdahl inquired about consideration of a triennial assembly. He also encouraged the streamlining of parliamentary procedure, particularly with respect to consideration of proposed social statements. Secretary Lowell G. Almen indicated that the duration of assemblies in 1995 and 1997 had been shortened by one day from previous years. Erin Cram observed that voting members who are students also incur conflict with attendance at school.

Social Teaching Statement on the Church and Human Sexuality (continued)

Appointment of Consulting Panel

Chair Magnus invited discussion of criteria for selection of members of the consulting panel. She invited nominations to be submitted by January 15, 1994. Suggestions for criteria included:

- Terry L. Bowes: Inclusive geographical representation; moderate people who have compassion and who are understanding that some mediating needs to be done for the process to continue.
- Charles A. Adamson: Expressed cautioned regarding moderate members, do not "write off" people who have voiced strong opinions.
- Rev. John O. Knudson: Give synodical bishops opportunity to submit names.
- Rev. Paull E. Spring: Church Council should nominate candidates independently of the Conference of Bishops.
- William H. Engelbrecht: Suggested that recommendations the deadline for nominations from seminaries be set prior to that for Church Council nominations. Nominees should agree to serve prior to nomination.
- William E. Diehl: People on the panel should be seen as being trustworthy.
- Rev. Stephen M. Youngdahl: Spread out geographic and synodical representation as much as possible, not duplicating task force membership. "It should not be an upper-Midwest document."
- Lorraine G. Bergquist: Persons with known preconceived viewpoints should not utilized. "Advocates should not be part of the study team."
- Ramona S. Rank: Campus pastors and young adults should be included.

- Rev. Nadine M. Lehr: Concurred with Ramona S. Rank.
- Rev. James G. Cobb: Expressed value for strongly opinionated persons.
- Rev. David A. Andert: Do not let geographical representation exclude input from seminary faculties.

Chair Magnus inquired whether synodical bishops ought to be solicited for nominations. William H. Engelbrecht suggested that council members consult with synodical bishops prior to submitting nominations. William T. Billings observed that such a procedure would not guarantee participation of all synodical bishops. The Rev. Franklin D. Fry cautioned that possible expectations about eventual appointments to the panel be discouraged. Erin Cram concurred, but encouraged cultivation of a wide ownership by this church's constituency of the study process. Bishop Kenneth H. Sauer counseled that bishops would not be disappointed, if they were not officially solicited.

Chair Magnus inquired whether there were objections to the selection process she had outlined. The Rev. David A. Andert proposed a mail ballot, rather than selection by the council's Executive Committee. Loren W. Mathre inquired about the amount of time commitment required. The Rev. Charles S. Miller Jr., executive director of the Division for Church in Society, responded. The Rev. Stephen M. Youngdahl moved:

VOTED: CC93.12.127

To appoint by mail ballot a consulting panel for the continued development of a social teaching statement on the church and human sexuality.

Unfinished Business

Secretary Lowell G. Almen moved the following:

VOTED: CC93.12.128

To refer any remaining items in the agenda and exhibits for this Church Council meeting that may require action to the Office of the Bishop for proper disposition and, as appropriate, for reporting to a future meeting of the Church Council.

Adjournment

The Church Council adjourned at 3:13 P.M. Bishop Herbert W. Chilstrom offered the closing prayer.

April 1994

The twentieth meeting of the Church Council of the Evangelical Lutheran Church in America was held in the Church Council Room of the Lutheran Center at Chicago, Ill., April 16-18, 1994. Vice President Kathy J. Magnus, chair of the Church Council, called the meeting to order at 8:32 A.M. Ms. Magnus then led the opening devotions.

Adoption of Agenda

Chair Magnus reviewed the meeting's agenda, which had been distributed by mail to members of the Church Council prior to their arrival. Additional business and informational materials were distributed during the meeting.

VOTED:

CC94.4.1 **To adopt the agenda and to permit the chair to call for consideration of agenda items in the order she deems most appropriate.**

Report of the Bishop

Chair Magnus called upon the Rev. Herbert W. Chilstrom, bishop of the Evangelical Lutheran Church in America, who presented his report. Bishop Chilstrom commented briefly on the first part of his report, which had previously been distributed to council members. He then read Part 2 of his report.

REPORT OF THE BISHOP OF THE CHURCH
to
The ELCA Church Council (Part 1)

Whither Denominations?

Last month I attended the annual meeting of U.S. Church Leaders. It is the most ecumenical meeting in North America, embracing denominational leaders ranging from Roman Catholic to mainline Protestant, to historic African American churches, to Seventh Day Adventist, to Lutheran Church-Missouri Synod, to evangelical conservative churches. In these off-the-record meetings one soon learns that in spite of our apparent differences, we all have much in common. All are struggling with financial issues, most are looking at falling membership, most are in some stage of reorganization, and all are wrestling with the question: *What is the future of denominations in America?* I want to devote a major part of this report to that question, adding to the reflections and observations already shared with the Church Council by Robert Bacher at its last meeting.

We tend to hear most often about Loren Mead's book, *The Once and Future Church.* It is the case, however, that many books and articles have addressed the same subject and that the spectrum of opinion is very broad.

Douglas John Hall, for example, traces our current problem back to the post-World War II era. Many of us thought those years—1945 to 1965—were the halcyon days of churches in the United States. A record number of new congregations were organized, budgets grew substantially, membership increased, ecumenical organizations flourished. Hall says it was all quite superficial. The world around us changed dramatically during that period while we lived in denial in the churches. What emerged, he argues, was a cultural denominationalism that had little to do with the radical nature of apostolic Christianity.

Though he knows as little as anyone about the future of churches, Hall is convinced that what must emerge is a remnant church whose primary focus is service and prophecy. We will finally have to come to terms with the fact that we do not live in a "Christian" culture, but are, in fact, living in a nation that is alien to Christian values.

How can we prepare ourselves to this future? Hall isn't sure. He offers no plans or strategies for us.

Langdon Gilkey, whom I cited at the December 1993 Church Council meeting, ties the decline of some denominations to a general decline in Western civilization. The church is a part of the broader culture. Whatever we see around us will inevitably have an impact on the churches. As we see the West losing ground politically in the world, so our predominant religion—Christianity—is also losing ground. How shall we meet this challenge? Gilkey isn't sure, except to suggest that it may be through spiritual renewal—especially in worship—that we will find our identity and mission.

Loren Mead, mentioned above, makes a good analysis of what has happened to many denominations—decline in membership, decline in resources for work beyond the local congregation, decline in Sunday worship attendance, and many other signs of malaise. But one looks in vain to Mead for any concrete suggestions on how churches can prepare themselves for an uncertain future.

Martin Marty tends to be more optimistic. While he recognizes that change is the order of the day, he places great emphasis on the gathering of the faithful in local congregations. Those who predicted 30 years ago that congregations would be dead by the turn of the century were wrong. So long as believers come together in these local settings there will always be a need to have denominational structures. What shape will they take? Marty isn't sure. But he is not anxious about the matter. Denominations will change, but will not disappear.

Robert Wuthnow from Princeton University may be the foremost expert in the field of analysis of religious movements in America. He sees a major restructuring of denominations as inevitable. He observes what is obvious to us in the ELCA, that the tensions today are not so much <u>between</u> denominations as they are <u>within</u> denominations. This, in turn, only reflects the deep rift we see in the prevailing culture. On the one side stand those who see the world as so complex and confusing that the only way to cope is to find easy, direct answers. On the other side are those who acknowledge the complexity and insist that we must be open to new and innovative ways of looking at issues and dealing with them.

I save the observations of William McKinney for last because I tend to agree most with his approach. Like Marty, he is confident that denominations will survive in some form. The hope for the future may lie in careful rethinking of who we are. McKinney wonders, for example, if we are spending too much time listening to the fringes and not enough time paying attention to the broad middle in our churches. Taking human sexuality as just one example, McKinney asserts that 80% of the members of our churches are not greatly concerned over the issues that are discussed. In fact, they are confused that there is so much agitation over the question. It is true that there are those who seek the simple answer. "Preach the Gospel and let other matters take their course; look to the Bible for answers to all questions," these folks are saying. And it is also true that there are others who believe we must make a radical break from tradition if we are to address the issues of the day.

McKinney rightly observes, however, that most members of our churches feel quite at home embracing both emphases. They stand in the middle. That is to say, they affirm the need to embrace evangelical values and, at the same time, are fully committed to the church's call to deal with complex social issues. McKinney says it is time for those who love the church to declare an armistice between the extremes and to work for what he calls "a reinvigorated center." This does not mean bringing the two extremes together. That may be impossible. It means, rather, a new consensus on the part of those who are concerned about <u>both</u> evangelism and social action. "It is time," suggests McKinney, "for some old churches to think some new thoughts."

This means that business as usual is out of the question. It means that if this church—the Evangelical Lutheran Church in America—has a future, we must move into it without losing our anchor with the past. What the Canadian economist Dian Cohen says about her country can be applied equally to our situation in the United States:

> Let's lay it out up front: this recession isn't going to end. It isn't going to end because this isn't a recession. What this is is the total restructuring of our economy and our society.

Change: Forced or Planned?

If change is inevitable, my strong hope is that it can be planned rather than forced upon us. In the first three years of our life together in this church we had to live with the estimates of those who planned as best they could. When those estimates proved to be faulty, we were forced to change. We undertook "Focusing for Mission," a deliberate process which resulted in a planned streamlining of our regional and churchwide structure. While questions were raised about changes in synodical patterns, little or no action resulted from it.

Now we need to move again into a planning process. We call it "Inquiry." It is spelled out in some detail in one of the exhibits. What I need to say here is three-fold. First, this process is one of gathering the kind of information my successor and staff will need in order to make needed changes. It would be presumptuous for me—unless forced to do so—to call for changes that would tie the hands of my successor. Under the guidance of the Church Council and with input from the Inquiry Advisory Group, chaired by Dr. H. George Anderson, we will together ascertain the mind of the church as best we can. What challenges face us in the remainder of this decade? What resources can we expect to have? What kind of church do we want to be?

Second, we must be prepared for changes that will reach beyond the churchwide structure. The churchwide organization has been streamlined to the point where we can no longer reduce the budget in certain functions, such as, for example, the Office of the Treasurer. The cost of subsidizing health care benefits for retired clergy continues to escalate. This means that any further reduction in program dollars will have a direct impact on services to synods and congregations. It means, inevitably, that we cannot indefinitely put off the question of reduction of the number of synods. While that action may lie beyond my time in office, I would not be accountable if I did not raise the question now. In the meantime, synods and the churchwide organization must continue to ask questions about how we can share even more effectively our staff and program responsibilities.

The third question is for congregations to consider. The head of another denomination has named the issue "creeping congregationalism." This is not a new phenomenon. Many trace its beginning to the 1960s, the time when two of our predecessor churches came together. In his book "Commitment to Unity," W. Kent Gilbert tells the story of what happened in one of them.

> LCA benevolence receipts fell far short of budget projections in the years 1963 through 1965. As early as the 1964 church convention, the Executive Council pointed to disturbing signs: steadily increasing costs . . .; an actual shortfall in 1963 . . .; the increasing share of benevolence receipts retained by synods. The . . . aim of "an attainable budget" for the 1965-66 biennium soon proved unattainable. The Report of the President to the 1966 convention in Kansas City devoted more than four pages to describing the "grim budgets" proposed for the next two years.
>
> The hoped-for increases in giving to churchwide causes did not materialize . . . in the magnitude needed. People were giving, but a greater proportion was being retained to meet needs at the congregational level ... the total dollars received by the church-at-large actually went down from 1968 to 1969. Obviously, a dramatic shift in the way

the gifts of members were being divided among congregational, synodical, and churchwide causes was occurring.

For decades there has been a gradual but continuing decline, year after year, in the percentage of congregational income that is shared with synod and churchwide mission. During the early 1980s we were deluded into thinking the trend had reversed itself. District, synod, and churchwide budgets grew substantially during those years. The record shows, however, that as a percentage of local income, there was an actual decline.

In the meantime, local income continues to grow. Since the formation of the ELCA, income, when measured by the offering plate, has exceeded the Consumer Price Index. We can give thanks for the generosity of our people. But when more and more dollars stay in the congregation we can only ask what the end result will be for us as a church.

It is little comfort to know it is happening to others as well as to us. We must ask ourselves, in this church, "Is this—the direction we are going—the kind of church we want to be?" If the direction we have been drifting for decades continues, we will soon be a very different church than the interdependent one we envisioned when we were born. We could become little more than a federation of 11,000 congregations with an ecclesiology like that of the Southern Baptists and with the potential to become as fragmented as churches of that kind.

It is for this reason that the question about the future of this church must not be seen only in terms of how we structure the churchwide organization. This must be an analysis that touches the whole church if we are to be one church with one mission.

In the Meantime: Another Grim Story

Treasurer Richard L. McAuliffe will spell out for both the synod bishops and the Church Council the grim report for 1993. The prospects for 1994 and beyond are even more distressing. The one bit of good news in the reports is that we actually finished 1993 with an excess of income over expense. But that is only because of careful stewardship of resources by the churchwide staff, and the use of the funds we had intended to put into our reserve resources. Thus, it really isn't good news at all. The $1,743,000 drop in mission support from 1992 to 1993 means that we must take strong steps to bring 1994 expenditures into line with anticipated income. The fact that other major church bodies are having to take similar measures is only of small comfort to us. When we must release staff persons, reduce grants to our colleges and seminaries, and eliminate important programs, it brings keen disappointment.

As you can see from the report of the treasurer, the pattern for income in 1993 is very uneven from synod to synod. In several cases, the drop has been precipitous. I would caution you, however, to read the report with care. In several cases, synods dipped into reserve funds in order to meet their commitment to the churchwide mission in 1992, hoping for an increase in gifts from congregations in 1993. When that did not happen, and when reserve funds were no longer available, the drop was dramatic.

It also needs to be said that in most cases the synods have been faithful in honoring their promises of division of income from congregations for synodical and churchwide needs. To put it another way, the same strains and stresses we see on the work of the churchwide organization are being felt by the synods.

This leads to the inevitable questions: Can the congregations of the ELCA do more to support synod and churchwide work in order that, among other things, we might serve them more effectively? Is it naive to think that this 30-year trend will bottom out and that we can begin to see movement in the other direction? Has the combination of increase in local expenses, the trend toward giving directly to causes and institutions, the need to be more involved in the local and regional community, the loss of denominational identity, taken a toll that cannot be reversed? If, in spite of our efforts to convey the mission of the whole church, resources continue to diminish, how shall we reshape this church? At this juncture, the immediate financial picture and the long range question of the shape of the church come together. Loren Mead is right when he states that while the future remains uncertain, we cannot go on with business as usual.

The Lutheran: an Exceptional Magazine

Falling income for the churchwide work is matched by falling subscriptions to The Lutheran magazine. In some ways, this is understandable. When local congregations and synods need to take cost-cutting measures it is quite tempting to think, "The magazine is not as essential to our work as other items in the budget."

We need to rethink the value of the magazine in the life of the ELCA. It is, in my judgment, the best vehicle we have to bring the word about the mission of this church to the grassroots. The drop in subscriptions from 1,200,000 to 800,000 is disturbing. Where we could once boast that the magazine went to two-thirds of our ELCA homes, it now goes to only one-half of them.

Two years ago the Conference of Bishops sent a strong message to the editor suggesting that news stories and headlines conveyed an unnecessarily negative image of the ELCA. I believe that message was heard and heeded. The news is balanced and presented in a more positive manner. Along with excellent feature stories, well-written Bible studies, thoughtful editorials, and other strong features, we have a treasure in The Lutheran magazine that is recognized as by far the best church periodical in the country.

For all these reasons, I urge the members of the Church Council and the Conference of Bishops to do everything possible to stop this trend and move it in the direction of recovering lost subscriptions.

Human Sexuality: a Search for the Middle

The first draft of the proposed Statement on Human Sexuality continues to bring mail to my desk and to the Division for Church in Society. Now that congregations and individuals are studying the actual draft rather than depending on news reports, the reactions are more mixed. It is apparent, however, that opinions continue to be very divided among those who respond. I underscore these words because of the remarks noted above from Dr. William McKinney. My suspicion is that his judgment about churches in general applies well to the ELCA. Can we say with certainty that the reaction of those who have written is typical of the broad spectrum of this church? It is difficult to say. I tend to believe we have a "broad middle" in this church which wants us to affirm traditional sexual and family values. But I am equally convinced that this same substantial majority wants to be part of a church which is mature enough, secure enough, and courageous enough to tackle complex issues of the day.

I have already given to the Church Council and the Conference of Bishops my assessment of the draft and my hopes for future revisions. I am grateful for synod bishops who responded to my request, spelling out affirmations and reservations about the draft. I also am thankful for the work of the division, whose staff is helping us to assess the responses to the first draft. Of equal significance is the fact that our colleges and seminary faculties, both corporately and individually, are providing us with insightful resource studies on human sexuality.

I will limit my comments to four areas.

First, I am grateful for the willingness of Dr. Roland Martinson and the consulting panel to enhance the work of the task force as we move through the next stage of development. While there was strong pressure to abandon the process, I believe the action of the Church Council in December 1993 to continue the process—an action encouraged by a strong majority of the synod bishops—was the right decision.

Second, we have learned how difficult it is at times to get word to our pastors before an item hits the headlines. Serious mistakes by churchwide staff were acknowledged and corrected when it happened the first time. After our December 1993 council meeting, we took steps to make sure the pastoral letter was in the hands of parish pastors before it was in the newspapers. Again, however, it was in the news before many pastors received my letter. This time the news passed from a synod office to the press. It leads

me to question whether we have raised expectations too high in regard to keeping things from the press —especially when volatile issues are involved.

Third, a word about the hundreds of letters and statements that have come to my desk. Most are written with legitimate concern and many with deep love for this church. There are some, however, that frighten me.

There are those that want this church to put its stamp of approval on most any kind of sexual behavior.

Then there are those that charge that the first draft does, in fact, endorse sexual immorality. While the document surely needs clarification in some parts, it is patently false to say that the draft encourages irresponsible, immoral behavior.

Some who write have looked carefully at the text of the Bible, but fail completely to deal with the pastoral issues that confront us in our everyday work in the church. Is it enough to ask, "What did Paul say then?" Must we not also ask, in the light of everything he wrote, "What would Paul say today?"

Finally, there are those letters which exude such a vile attitude toward all gay and lesbian persons that I can only describe the attitude of the writers as "demonic." I know the power of hate. It is written everywhere. But it is hard for me to believe that there can be such hatred in the hearts of those who claim to be followers of Jesus Christ.

Fourth, I continue to believe that our Lutheran insistence on the balance of Law and Gospel will be our way to a satisfying resolution of issues surrounding human sexuality. If I may refer to that "broad middle" again, they surely are not urging that we approve irresponsible living. They understand the importance of the Law as a guide for living. They do not want us to deal in "cheap grace." At the same time, I also sense from these members of our church a equally strong desire that we acknowledge the brokenness of our world and learn to speak Gospel words of understanding and hope.

Vision for Mission: a Positive Venture

All of us on the Church Council and among the synod bishops support this church in many ways. Our first and most important gift is the one we place in the offering plate of our local congregation on Sunday morning.

Most of us, however, have the means to do more than that. And we experience the joy of supporting the work of this church is many ways. For that reason, I am delighted to announce that the Vision for Mission Fund, approved by the Church Council, is now in place and is already receiving gifts. As you recall, the primary purpose of this fund is to give members of this church an opportunity to support two of our priority areas—global mission, and evangelism and outreach work in this land. As we move toward the annual offering in May in the congregations of the ELCA all of us in leadership positions will have the opportunity to share special gifts. Corinne and I ask you to consider this request and to join us in making a significant gift to the Vision for Mission Fund.

When One Suffers

Since we last met as a council and conference I have been to the Los Angeles area to survey the damage from the earthquake. You have read reports elsewhere about the visit, the damage to our churches and homes of our members, and the impact on the work of our synod. Thank you for all you have done to encourage support for the Inter-Lutheran Disaster Relief Fund. We are aware of the enormous toll the human and natural disasters have taken in the Los Angeles area in the past two years. We are grateful for the efforts of the synod staff, the social service agencies and of all our pastors and lay leaders in the synod.

May I also say a word about giving to the Inter-Lutheran Disaster Relief Fund rather than sharing direct gifts with a specific congregation. While it is gratifying for congregations and individuals to give in this latter way, we are learning again that this often leads to imbalance in meeting needs. Some congregations get too much, others too little. There is value in giving through the Inter-

Lutheran Disaster Relief Fund so that resources can be distributed more evenly.

Mission90: a Bonding Experience

"*Mission90: Making Christ Known*" events continue to unfold across the church and draw good attendance in most places. I am impressed with the variety of ways in which the synods are planning and carrying out these gatherings. I continue to believe that it is one of the best uses of my time. Meeting with our pastors and key lay leaders is a privilege. Sharing with them a vision of what we can be, leading them in Bible study, and listening to their hopes and dreams is always a source of encouragement for me.

Sacramental Practices

Our Division for Congregational Ministries, in cooperation with the Conference of Bishops, is in the early stages of development of the first draft of a proposed statement on sacramental practices. It will not be reviewed by pastors and congregations until a later stage. We need to be aware, however, that the early materials you have received will have several elements that may stir active discussion among us. Among them are: communion of the baptized; use of the common cup; weekly celebration of the Eucharist. We can aid the process by studying the document carefully, offering suggestions, and being pro-active in urging response to the early draft when it is released to pastors and congregations in the fall of this year.

The Global Scene

Although this report has of necessity focused on internal matters, we have not forgotten the needs of the world and our partnership in mission with churches everywhere. Liberia, the scene of a large investment in mission through the years, continues to suffer from civil war. The work of the Lutheran Church in Liberia has suffered unimaginable pain, and our own partnership with them has ground to a near halt.

In South Africa we wait in hope for the birth of a new nation where there will be greater equality and where our churches can flourish. In the former Yugoslavia we work through the Lutheran World Federation to bring relief to the suffering. In the Middle East we look for the fragile peace efforts to bring understanding between Israeli and Palestinian. We pray for El Salvador, asking that the nation will come together in a peaceful election. Many other places, including companion synods, come to mind. And, as always, we hold up the needs of those who suffer from hunger and poverty throughout the world.

The Central Committee of the World Council of Churches met in South Africa in January. In its ongoing effort to confront racism, staff of the WCC have visited member churches, including the ELCA, to heighten our awareness of this global issue. The WCC voted to have its eighth assembly in 1998 in Zimbabwe.

The Executive Committee of the Council of the Lutheran World Federation met in February for its regular mid-year session. The decision of the LWF to hold its next assembly in Hong Kong in 1997 was affirmed. It was reported that a comprehensive "China Study" has been funded and will be launched soon. The search for a successor to General Secretary Gunnar Staalsett has continued. The election will take place at the meeting of the full Council in Geneva in June.

Before we meet again, the Lutheran World Federation Executive Council will meet in Geneva in June 1994. A major feature of this year's meeting will be a "Church Leaders Convocation" to be held immediately prior to the council. It is expected that more than 100 heads of Lutheran churches around the world will be in attendance.

For those interested in the history of the Lutheran World Federation I recommend reading the newly-published biography of a former general secretary, Dr. Carl Lund-Quist. It is available through Bethany College, Lindsborg, Kansas.

Welcome and Farewell

At this meeting of the Conference of Bishops we heartily welcome our new director of the Department for Synodical Relations, The Rev. Michael Cooper-White. He began his work in mid-January and is already well-integrated into churchwide staff. Our thanks to Dr. Harold Lohr who served so effectively as interim director and who has given Michael helpful orientation to the position.

We also welcome to the Conference of Bishops, Bishop Allan Bjornberg and his wife Vianne. Allan's installation as bishop of our Rocky Mountain Synod was a high point for me in my winter travels. And we thank the four bishops whose terms are ending before the conference meets again: Charles Anderson, Robert Herder, Lyle Miller and Robert Studtmann. "Well done, good and faithful servants." Our thanks as well to your spouses: Shirley, Mildred, Sonia, and Barbara. We will miss you. And we will envy you. We follow you with our prayers for good health and joy in new ventures.

To all of you on the Church Council and in the Conference of Bishops, my thanks for partnership and support in days that often stretch all of us to the limit.

Grace is sufficient!

REPORT OF THE BISHOP
Part 2

Since you received Part 1 of my report, there have been several developments that need comment. Most of Part 2, however, will be devoted to the unfolding discussion of the human sexuality issue.

Well Done, Faithful Servants

On Good Friday morning we received word that John Kaitschuk, bishop of the Central Southern Illinois Synod, had died. After a more than three-year struggle with cancer, the word came as not surprise and with a degree of relief. As I said at his funeral service on the day after Easter Sunday, John was a person who did not take himself too seriously, who could laugh at his own shortcomings, and who was often his own most severe critic. But he had deep confidence in the power of the Gospel. He took his office and the mission of the church with utter seriousness. We commend him to the cloud of witnesses in the church triumphant as we continue to remember his wife Jan and her children in our prayers.

We have also learned in recent days that Henry Schulte, bishop of the Southwestern Texas Synod, has decided to return to the parish ministry. We thank him and his wife Francis for their faithful service.

We also welcome to the circle of bishops the Rev. Robert Mattheis, newly-elected head of the Sierra Pacific Synod. Although the process took the full seven ballots, it was clear by then that Mattheis has the strong majority support of the members of that synod.

Painful Adjustments

In Part 1 of my report and in the report of the treasurer you have factual information about churchwide income in 1993 and the actions taken by my office and the Executive Committee to bring 1994 expenditures into line with anticipated income.

Given reports in our daily newspapers of adjustments in business and industry, it should not surprise us that churches also are faced with the need for downsizing. Nevertheless, when the action is taken it leaves demoralization, confusion and anger in its wake. Now we are not just talking numbers; we are dealing with real persons and real programs. "How can you eliminate the only staff position devoted to peace education?," ask several letter writers. Others question the reduction to one-half time the position of the person who works with specialized ministries. Church camping was reduced by half. The Office of the Bishop staff was reduced by 25 percent, with the work shared with remaining staff. The program and staff adjustments in the Commission for Multicultural Ministries have caused particular unhappiness. For the first time in several decades, this church (including its predecessor churches) has no full-time Native American in an executive staff position lifting up the needs of that community. Reducing the ethnic desks from staff positions to consultant relationships has caused some to ask whether this church has lost its vision to become an inclusive people of God. When combined with the action of the Kansas City assembly to revisit the issue of representational principles, there has been a wave of doubt that has swept through the communities of color in this church.

We have tried our best to put matters into broader perspective. In all these adjustments we have sought to be faithful and realistic: faithful to the priorities set by the Church Council and Churchwide Assembly; realistic about the income available for our common work. Neither is easy. We discover again that in a time of limited resources there are varying convictions about what should be our priorities in this church. We also face the perception of those who seem to see little connection between what congregations and synods share with the churchwide mission and what we are able to do. Congregations share less and less with synod and churchwide ministries. Synods continue to decrease the percentage of what they share with the churchwide organization—often without consultation. Because we must operate within available resources, we have no option other than to make these hard decisions. In the meantime, of course, we bend every effort to increase those resources, such as, for example, the annual churchwide offering. I trust that all of you on the Church Council will join me and the churchwide staff in responding generously to this challenge.

Human Sexuality: Support for the Process

Let me begin our discussion of the issue of human sexuality with several remarks about the decision made by the board of the Division for Church in Society at its March meeting.

I believe the process they have outlined gives us the optimal chance of bringing a document to a churchwide assembly that could receive approval from that body, the highest legislative authority in the ELCA. The process is outlined elsewhere. Let me simply say that the broadened base on which future drafts will be developed is what is needed at this juncture.

As we do so, we will need to exercise care not to lose the positive elements of the first draft. The initial response to the first draft was predominantly negative. In recent weeks, however, my own mail has seen much more balance between positive and negative replies. And we must not forget that in spite of hundreds of letters, we have still heard from only a small percentage of the pastors and lay members of the ELCA.

At the same time, it is apparent from responses from many groups in the church that the approach needs to be modified. As we look forward to a comprehensive statement, we also must understand that not every issue related to human sexuality can be addressed in detail and not every issue can be settled in the near future.

If those working on the process can bring us a second draft in the fall of 1994 and a final proposal in the spring of 1995, I would strongly urge that we try to finish the process at the 1995 assembly. Yet, we must not rush the process. We are aware of the action of the Conference of Bishops, urging that we take the time needed to insure a thorough process, even if it means looking beyond 1995 for action on a recommended draft.

Let me go on to make some general comments. My remarks in Part 1 of my report that was mailed earlier were made before I had an opportunity to study some of the more substantial responses to the first draft that have come from individuals and groups within the community of the teaching theologians of the church, synod bishops, college and seminary faculties, pastors and lay persons.

Impressive Efforts and Areas of Agreement

I am impressed with the effort that so many have invested in their responses. Drawing on deep biblical and theological roots, paper after paper reflects a prayerful and thoughtful concern that makes me proud to be head of a church in which so many take so seriously our call for their insights.

In these responses there are many areas of broad agreement, including the following:

- That marriage and family be affirmed and that this church use its energies to strengthen these bonds.
- That we affirm those who are single, whether involuntarily or by choice.
- That we deal compassionately with families that experience separation and divorce.
- That we urge our youth to refrain from sexual intercourse until they have made a life-long commitment in marriage.
- That we speak out forcefully against sexual abuse of all kinds, prostitution, pornography, spreading sexually-transmitted disease, and the use of sex for commercial purposes.

Strong Differences of Opinion

Having noted these areas of consensus, it is readily apparent that there is also a very deep division of opinion in other areas. Predecessor church body background makes no difference. The rift runs down the middle of most any group one can identify in the ELCA. It seems to have little relationship to one's competence in biblical, confessional, or historical studies. Persons of equally high competence in these and other disciplines come out at radically different points. Graduates of the same seminary show no common attitude. Members of the same congregation are often at odds with one another. Indeed, even within some families and among some friends the division of opinion runs deep.

There is strong disagreement, for example, regarding teen sex. While we agree that we should urge abstinence from sexual intercourse, we are not of one mind regarding what advice to give those who disagree with that stance. Some would counsel, "Just say no," and let the matter rest at that. Others say it is irresponsible not to provide education regarding prevention of sexually transmitted diseases and unwanted pregnancies. Neither are we of one mind regarding pre-marital sex by those who intend to marry.

But, by far, the greatest area of disagreement is in our approach to the issue of homosexuality.

Let me illustrate some of these strong differences of opinion from the responses I have read:

- The heads of two of our predecessor church bodies have joined hundreds who signed a response to the first draft which states, among other things, that "a publicly declared, legally binding marriage between one woman and one man remains the one appropriate place for genital sexual relations." The other predecessor church body head has identified himself with the Network, an alliance of hundreds of other ELCA members who are working for the open acceptance of gay and lesbian persons, including the ordination of otherwise qualified persons who are living in homosexual relationships.
- ELCA college religion professors differ sharply. One says the draft is "excellent in all parts." After more than 30 years of struggle with the issue, this person affirms "the acceptability of a loving, faithfully committed and permanent relationship... between two genetically homosexual people." Another says of the first draft that "the interpretation of the Bible on homosexuality is outrageously tendentious."
- One lay person asserts that the first draft rests on solid Lutheran tradition and reflects "a consistent approach to Scripture." Another, after extensive analysis of the draft, urges his synod bishop "to use whatever influence is yours to see to it that the task force and the statement are summarily disregarded."
- Parish pastors are divided. One castigates the task force for "the manner in which you so easily dismiss and explain away the biblical references to homosexual practice...." Another, having counseled with homosexual persons and their families, affirms the first draft, calling it "a document of hope and comfort."
- Synod bishops span the gamut. One believes that a change of a paragraph or two would make the first draft fully acceptable. Many have stated that they agree with most of it. Others

support the opinion of a bishop who asserts that "the credibility of the churchwide organization will be restored only if the draft is completely redone."

- A teaching theologian at a non-ELCA college sharply criticized the bishop of the church for not stopping the release of the first draft. Another in a similar setting calls it "a remarkably sound, well-substantiated, and forward-looking document."

- Women ELCA seminary professors stand at opposite poles. One uses Luther's Small Catechism to argue that the quality of a relationship is what is of highest importance, "whether that relationship is heterosexual or homosexual." Another, writing as "a teacher of the church, a minister, and a parent of adolescents" calls for the task force to "apologize to the church at large for having released this document in its present form. . . ."

- Two ELCA theologians, both retired from the deanship of prestigious interdenominational seminaries, come to opposite conclusions. One says "the document either distorts or fails to explore the consequences of basic biblical and Lutheran doctrines." The other affirms the accent in the first draft on both fidelity and mutuality in marriage, suggesting that "While the church traditionally has been forceful in teaching fidelity, the church's record on mutuality has been weak indeed." He goes on to state that these same elements—fidelity and mutuality—also apply "to those who have come to know themselves as homosexual (persons). . . ."

- From the same seminary faculty come two diametrically opposed responses. One groups states that "The report's use of Scripture, especially in the section on homosexuality, is disturbing. Various interpretations are introduced in ways that obscure, relativize, and sometimes reverse the plain sense of the text." The other group maintains that "the recognition and acceptance of same gender loving, committed relationships is good for the neighbor and in fact serves the health and well-being of the community. . . ."

We may ask of this representative group of reactors to the first draft, "Who are they? Do they stand at the fringes of this church? Do they share anything in common?"

We would reply, "Yes, they share much in common! No, not one of them stands at the fringe. They are bedrock Lutherans, committed to Jesus Christ, faithful worshipers in our congregations, dedicated in their leadership roles, and bound together by a 'Confession of Faith' that is written into the governing documents of every expression of this church."

The Task of the Church Council

All of this only underscores the seriousness of the task that faces the Church Council. We are not a papal church. Final authority does not reside in the office of the bishop of this church. Many have appealed to me to act decisively—so long as it is in accord with their own opinion! Others have urged me to speak out in a prophetic way, setting out my personal stance on all matters related to the issue of human sexuality.

I have refused for what I hope are obvious reasons. The moment I were to take that step the debate in the church would galvanize around my opinion rather than on drafts and the orderly process we have approved for the development of a social teaching statement. Furthermore, potential candidates for election to this office a year hence would be judged by their agreement or disagreement with my views.

What about this council? We are charged to act on behalf of this church between assemblies. What are our options?

We could, of course, revisit the question of whether to stop this entire process. Given the division of opinion among committed members from all corners of this church, and the possibility that any final draft—unless it be without substance—will likely meet with strong opposition, we could declare a moratorium on all further attempts to develop a statement. We could say, in effect, "This issue is too hot for us to handle. Let's put it aside and focus our energies on other matters."

I hope, however, that you will agree with the recommendation I made at the beginning of this report. I believe it is imperative that we affirm the integrity of the process, that we give our full support to the recommendation of the board of the Division for Church in Society, and that we judge future drafts of a potential statement on the merits of those drafts themselves. The Conference of Bishops, by a strong majority, has urged that the process move forward. Though most synod assemblies are yet to be held, at least two have taken action to recommend that the drafting process continue.

In the meantime, I would urge that we exercise our leadership mandate, calling on the entire church to give itself prayerfully and in unity to the ongoing process. In so doing, let us also call on those congregations and individuals who have chosen to withhold their contributions to the church to reconsider that decision. Those who understand the process will surely not withhold their support for the full mission of this church.

The Perspective of History

Finally, a word about perspective. I began Part 1 of my report with a review of the literature regarding the future of denominations. Let me conclude Part 2 with some brief reflections on the history of conflicts in the churches. Whenever we are in the midst of a given moment of stress in the church we tend to forget that each generation has had its own unique issue. In the mid-1800s Lutherans were deeply divided by the slavery question. Not only was there disagreement between Lutherans in the North and the South; Lutherans in the North also were divided. At least one of our Lutheran colleges was founded by Lutheran who thought slavery to be wrong. Supporters of another college in the area were convinced that the Bible did not forbid slavery.

By the end of the century the debate centered on the atonement and predestination. Local churches, regional churches, national churches—all were engaged in the battle. And at all levels the church was divided into separate entities over this issue.

In the 1920s and 1930s the church reacted to the advances of science by trying to protect the Bible from attack. Some insisted that we must claim "in errancy" for the Bible, meaning that every word was "dictated" by the Spirit and was of equal value with every other word. Others embraced the term, but gave it a different meaning. Still others rejected it. Lutherans were divided.

In the 1950s the issue was Communism. Any church leader who claimed that there were Christian believers behind the Iron Curtain was held in suspicion. There were intense debates over this question.

For some of our predecessor churches the "in errancy" issue continued into the 1960s and was not settled until well into the decade of the 1970s. In fact, some of my mail tells me that the question is still alive in some places in the ELCA.

I mention only these few issues of conflict to illustrate a point. We are seldom without a potentially divisive question in the church. In this decade it happens to be human sexuality. Much as we might like to have it go away, I doubt it will.

United by Confession

For this reason, we as leaders must keep reminding ourselves and this church that the "glue" which holds us together is our "Confession of Faith." Regardless of our opinion on one or another of the elements of the human sexuality question, we are united by our common confession that God is revealed as Father, Son, and Holy Spirit; that Jesus Christ is the living Word of God; that God's Word comes to us as both Law and Gospel; that the Bible is the inspired Word of God and our guide for faith and life; that the ancient Creeds are a faithful declaration of our faith; that the Augsburg Confession is a true witness to the Gospel.

If we can keep ourselves centered in this Confession I am confident we can be a mature and united church, no matter what the issue may be at a given moment.

HERBERT W. CHILSTROM, *Bishop*
Evangelical Lutheran Church in America

During discussion, William E. Diehl inquired whether sexuality issues and the election of a churchwide bishop at the 1995 Churchwide Assembly might be detached. Bishop Chilstrom responded that even if consideration of the study of human sexuality were to be postponed until the 1997 assembly, nominees for the Office of Bishop were certain to be questioned about their stances on the matter. "I do not see any way to avoid that," he said. Bishop Paull E. Spring commented that many pastors of his synod fear the direction this church appears to be heading, and express apprehension about continuing ministry within this church. Bishop Chilstrom acknowledged that "the disagreement is among folks who are at the heart of this church. . . . We have deep disagreement on the part of very well-qualified and deeply committed people." Patsy Gottschalk observed that the proposed document on human sexuality might be presented to the Churchwide Assembly as a study document rather than as a social statement. Several staff and council members commented on deliberations on the issue held at various recent synodical assemblies.

The Rev. Donald M. Hallberg affirmed "*Mission 90*: Making Christ Known" events held in the Metropolitan Chicago Synod at which Bishop Chilstrom had presented a Bible study. Loren W. Mathre commented on sections of the bishop's printed report devoted to "where are we going as a church." He recommended that the functions of church bodies need to be re-examined, so that this church will accurately reflect "exactly what people want to happen." Bishop Chilstrom commented that the issue Mr. Mathre noted was a perception and communication problem that would be addressed by the "Inquiry" process. He observed that the value of a churchwide organization is not always immediately apparent to congregational members.

The Rev. John O. Knudson commented on the "mutual ministry" (spiritual and emotional) needs of pastors and asked whether the Office of the Bishop was addressing the similar needs of synodical bishops. Bishop Chilstrom responded that management of sexual-abuse issues has made service in the office of synodical bishop "extremely debilitating" for some bishops. That office "is never an easy job, but probably harder now than it has ever been," he said.

William T. Billings observed that this church seems to be reacting to the present reality of limited financial resources by seeking to "downsize" synods and the churchwide organization, rather than by making this church's structure reflect more relevantly current congregational giving patterns. Citing several examples of the trend for congregations to contribute to attractive local and other causes directly, Bishop Chilstrom stated, "If this trend continues, we [may need to] become a different kind of church than we have been until now. . . . I raise the question, Bill; I do not have an easy answer to it." D. Mark Klever commented that "localism" is not only the current predisposition of laity, but an outlook sometimes encouraged by clergy.

Report of the Vice President

Vice President Magnus noted a recent ecumenical journey to Geneva, Istanbul, Rome, London, and other European cities in which she and 11 other ELCA members had participated, and reflected on how that trip pertained to the work of the Church Council. She commented on the need for ELCA members to recognize their historical roots among Christians today and throughout the ages. "We are a people of hope, and we are connected in so many ways that we have not even considered, but that we hope we will continue to discover."

Chair Magnus also commented on the process of the council's Executive Committee in determining the membership of the consulting panel for the Study of Human Sexuality. "Our work was significantly intentional and deliberative as we sought to create that group. It was a task that was approached with care and not the nonchalance that has been [reported]. . . . I want to set the record straight with you," she stated.

Chair Magnus noted the usefulness of the ELCA's computer networks in accessing timely news and information about this church, as well as discerning the perceptions and opinions of ELCA members. She invited council members to consider the potential usefulness of electronic communications in facilitating the work of the Church Council.

Report of the Secretary

Chair Magnus called upon the Rev. Lowell G. Almen, secretary of the Evangelical Lutheran Church in America, to present his report. Secretary Almen commented on his written report.

Commenting on the ecumenical journey previously cited in the report of the vice president, Secretary Almen stated, "I think the experience overall was sobering in a number of respects. It was particularly sobering to realize once again the role and responsibility of the Evangelical Lutheran Church in America in the area of ecumenical developments, because this church is looked to for leadership in that area not only because of our size, but also because of the quality of the dialogues that have taken place in North America over the past quarter century." Secretary Almen noted the optimism of the Vatican regarding a proposal, which may be implemented as early as 1997, lifting the mutual condemnations of the sixteenth century related to justification. He observed that other ecumenical developments also would be important for conversation in ELCA congregations and for consideration by this church in 1997, including relationships with Reformed churches, with the Episcopal Church, and with Roman Catholics. Secretary Almen expressed pride in those who had made the ecumenical journey, concerning their preparation, their probing questions, and their insightful observations.

Secretary Almen commented on the death of his mother on January 23, 1994, and how quickly one can be "plunged into that deep valley of the shadow and the sorrow that comes with it. But, I discovered again in the midst of that valley that one is repeatedly surprised by grace—grace reflected in the care of people who take the time to express their concern and support." Secretary Almen acknowledged the many expressions of support received by his family throughout those difficult days.

During discussion of the secretary's report, William T. Billings inquired about "missed savings" that result when travelers fail to make reservations in advance or refuse the lowest possible fare. Secretary Almen indicated the executive directors and director, as well as the secretary, treasurer, and executive for administration, monitor closely matters of travel cost.

Nominations and Elections

Background: Between meetings of the Church-wide Assembly, the Church Council has the responsibility of electing persons to fill unexpired terms on churchwide boards (for example, those which occur because of resignations). The Church Council also is the electing body for steering committees of churchwide commissions and certain advisory committees.

The following is a list of elections that were scheduled to occur at the April 1994 meeting of the Church Council:

1. Board of the Division for Global Mission
    a. Lay Female (term 1997) (resignation of Fern Lee Hagedorn)
2. Advisory Committee for the Department for Communication
    a. Clergy (term 1997) (resignation of the Rev. Stephen J. Cornils)
    b. Lay Female (term 1995) (resignation of Karen Anderson)
3. Standing Committee for the Commission for Multicultural Ministries
    a. Native American lay male (term 1995) (resignation of Charles Tucker Jr.)

Materials related to those elections were distributed to Church Council members as council agenda Exhibit C, Part 1.

Council Action: Chair Magnus called upon Secretary Lowell G. Almen, who reported on behalf of the Executive Committee of the Church Council, which serves as the council's nominating committee. He reviewed the nomination process and noted that the committee took careful account of the geographical distribution of board members, particularly in reference to the boards of the Division for Church in Society and Division for Global Mission. Secretary Almen noted that vacancies on the advisory board of the Department for Communication and the Commission for Multicultural Ministries also the responsibility of the Church Council.

Patsy Gottschalk inquired whether any of the nominees had been listed on the ballot of 1993 Church-wide Assembly. Chair Magnus confirmed that a majority of the present nominees in fact had been nominated by the churchwide Nominating Committee as candidates for churchwide boards and committees for election by the 1993 assembly. The Executive Committee had determined that the present nomination of such persons respected the work of the churchwide Nominating Committee.

Nominations from the floor were invited. There being none, Chair Magnus declared nominations for each vacancy to be closed *seriatim*.

En Bloc Approval of Certain Agenda Items

Chair Magnus requested that council members who desired to remove an item from the *en bloc* resolution for disposition of non-controversial business items for individual consideration notify the secretary prior to the beginning of the afternoon plenary session.

Report of the Treasurer

Chair Magnus called upon ELCA Treasurer Richard L. McAuliffe to present his report. Treasurer McAuliffe reviewed his written report regarding year-end fiscal 1993 (ending January 31, 1994). He indicated that although total revenue in fiscal 1993 was down some $2.4 million from the previous year, actual expenses were less than budgeted. Net revenue and expense, therefore, was favorable by $36,000 over the previous 1992 fiscal year. He explained that the decline in revenue from the previous year was attributable in part to receipts in 1992 from the 1991 Special Offering and Ingathering 1992, as well as a decline in mission support from congregations to the churchwide organization through synods. With respect to restricted revenue, he noted that the decline in receipts from designated gifts had been offset slightly by increased receipts from bequests and trusts. Treasurer McAuliffe then reviewed briefly the charts and balance sheets accompanying his written remarks.

During discussion the Rev. Stephen Youngdahl inquired about the variance in assets in the current fund as of the beginning of fiscal year attributable to cash and cash equivalents in 1994 over 1993. Treasurer McAuliffe cited several variable factors. He also noted that it was not necessary for this church to borrow monies during 1993 in order to pay outstanding operating expenses, and expressed gratitude to executive directors for their prudence in spending $1 million less than budgeted.

William E. Diehl asked why the special offering in 1993 generated less income that the special offering in 1992. Treasurer McAuliffe responded that there was not as much advance time to prepare for the special offering and fewer congregations participated in the effort.

Study of Human Sexuality

Chair Magnus called upon Ms. Fran Burnford, associate executive director of the Division for Church in Society, to introduce the "response library," which had been assembled in the Council Room for the information of council members. She expressed gratitude for the overwhelming number of responses to the initial draft of a possible social statement on human sexuality received to date by the division from various sources—individuals, congregations, and institutions. Ms. Burnford invited the council members to inspect and examine the responses during the course of this meeting.

Report of the Conference of Bishops

Chair Magnus called upon Bishop Kenneth H. Sauer, chair of the Conference of Bishops, to present the report of the conference. Bishop Sauer referred to his written report.

Drawing on the words of Charles Dickens, Bishop Sauer described the work of the Conference of Bishops, since its last report to the Church Council as both the worst of times and the best of times. The worst of times, he said, occurred on Good Friday when word was received that Bishop John P. Kaitschuk (Central/Southern Illinois Synod) had been "called to the Church triumphant." He also expressed regret that four other synodical bishops would retire from the conference in 1994, two of who had decided not to seek re-election due to the newly increased length of terms to six-years. Plans are under way, he indicated, for orientation programs for bishops newly elected by 1994 synodical assemblies.

Bishop Sauer also drew attention to the response of the Conference of Bishops regarding the continued development of the possible social statement on human sexuality. The conference urged that provision be made for adequate study and conversation throughout this church, even if that would not permit completion of the study prior to the Churchwide Assembly in 1995.

The worst of times also is reflected in financial matters for, like the churchwide organization, every synod must address the difficult problem of setting fiscal priorities, he stated. Another matter of growing concern, he noted, was the increased number of graduating seminarians who had placed restrictions on where they would be available for call.

On matters related to the best of times, Bishop Sauer expressed appreciation that 23 synodical bishops were present for Bishop Kaitschuk's funeral, sharing in their support of his family and indicating the cohesiveness of the Conference of Bishops. He also acknowledged the vigor and enthusiasm evident in congregations throughout this church, and the high morale shown by pastors and synodical bishops, in addressing seriously and faithfully the various matters before this church— human sexuality, sacramental practices, ecumenism, the future of this church.

Bishop Sauer then called upon the Rev. Michael L. Cooper-White, newly appointed executive director of the Department of the Synodical Relations, to bring greetings. Pastor Cooper-White expressed his gratitude to the synodical bishops and to members of the churchwide staff for their hospitality.

During discussion, the Rev. Nelson T. Strobert asked whether there were suggestions for addressing the problem of restrictions placed by seminarians on first-call placement, because seminaries face this same difficulty during internship placement. Pastor Cooper-White noted that a working document, distinguishing genuine restrictions from personal preferences, was being developed for distribution to first-year seminarians so that the expectations of the church in meeting leadership needs are stated from the onset of seminary preparation. The Rev. James

G. Cobb recommended that such expectations be shared even earlier by candidacy committees with prospective seminarians.

D. Mark Klever inquired why the conference, in its response to the initial draft of the possible social statement on the issue of the human sexuality statement (council agenda Exhibit A, Part 4A, page 5, item 3) had not provided a more substantive response with respect to the matter of homosexuality. Bishop Sauer explained that, because the conference had not yet been afforded sufficient time to discuss the issue in depth, it would be more appropriate to restrict its comments to matters of process, rather than substance, and to focus on the subject at subsequent meetings of the conference. "We did not want to deal with it in a cavalier way," he said.

Referrals from the 1993 Churchwide Assembly

The following actions taken by the 1993 Churchwide Assembly were referred to the Church Council for consideration.

1. Election of the Bishop of this Church

Background: Two motions regarding the process for election of the ELCA bishop were referred by the 1993 Churchwide Assembly to the Church Council for consideration. At its December 1993 meeting, the council voted:

To refer the resolution of the 1993 Churchwide Assembly on the election of the bishop of the Evangelical Lutheran Church in America to the Executive Committee of the Church Council; and

To request that the Executive Committee develop a response and/or recommendation for action to be reported to the April 1994 meeting of the Church Council (in consultation with the Legal and Constitutional Review Committee, if appropriate) (CC93.12.69).

At its January 25-26, 1994, meeting, the Executive Committee discussed this matter, made recommendations, and referred the matter to the staff of the Office of the Bishop for further work. Following further discussion of the assembly resolutions, the Executive Committee agreed:

To reaffirm the ecclesiastical ballot as the process for election of the bishop of the Evangelical Lutheran Church in America;

To develop a process for reflection at 1995 synod assemblies on the role, functions, and responsibilities of the churchwide bishop to the Churchwide Assembly and Church Council in the life of this church as this church prepares to elect a new bishop at the 1995 Churchwide Assembly; and to request staff of the Department for Research and Evaluation and the Department for Synodical Relations to develop a process and draft a study piece for use as these assemblies;

To review this draft and bring a recommendation for action to the November 1994 Church Council meeting.

Council Action: Chair Magnus reviewed the work of the Executive Committee of the Church Council on this matter and some of the proposals considered regarding the election process, particularly educating voting members about the roles, functions, and responsibilities of the bishop of this church. She noted that the Executive Committee had reaffirmed the ecclesiastical ballot as the means of the electing the bishop and had suggested that a educational process be devised for possible use at

1995 synodical assemblies as groundwork for the Church-wide Assembly, a suggestion endorsed by the Conference of Bishops.

The Rev. David A. Andert expressed appreciation for the Executive Committee's response and asked whether the similar materials might be available in time for use by synodical assemblies in the election process related to synodical bishops. Chair Magnus received Pastor Andert's comment as advice as materials are prepared. Bishop Kenneth H. Sauer noted the Commission for Women already had prepared a helpful resource on this matter. Pastor Andert observed that various special interest groups and related periodicals were engaged in electioneering efforts, and asked whether an official response discouraging such endeavors had been prepared. Bishop Chilstrom advised that no response be made, since such responses rarely are effective. Lorraine G. Bergquist suggested that information be added to the "job description" regarding the relationship of the bishop to the Churchwide Assembly and to the Church Council. Chair Magnus noted the suggestion. Loren W. Mathre asked whether the names (and biographical data) of possible nominees would be included in the proposed educational material. Chair Magnus responded that it would devoted solely to a description of the bishop's functions (demands and expectations placed upon the bishop), in order to preserve the integrity of the ecclesiastical-ballot process. She noted that the ecclesiastical-ballot process would permit sufficient opportunity for biographical information to be distributed of persons nominated. Cynthia P. Johnson inquired whether a list of the qualifications necessary for persons to be elected to the office of ELCA bishop would be included in the educational materials. Chair Magnus responded that constitutionally the only qualification required is that the person be listed on the roster of ordained ministers.

2. Nomination Form for 1995 Churchwide Assembly

Background: The 1993 Churchwide Assembly voted:

WHEREAS, the current ELCA nomination form emphasizes employment, advanced formal education, and positions in church and community service; and

WHEREAS, this leads to overlooking new talent as well as persons with years of experience in non-salaried positions; and

WHEREAS, the nomination form does not identify a nominees' interests, commitment, or expertise; therefore be it

RESOLVED, that the Church Council develop a new nomination form for use with the 1995 Churchwide Assembly, in consultation with the Commission for Women, the Commission for Multicultural Ministries, the board of the Lutheran Youth Organization, the Office of the Secretary, and persons with expertise in recruitment; and be it further

RESOLVED, that the Church Council provide for a consistent way of summarizing the biographical information from the nomination form to the Report of the Nominating Committee (CA93.8.100)

The Church Council referred the matter to the Executive Committee. At its January 25-26, 1994, meeting the Executive Committee voted:

To request the Office of the Secretary to solicit the groups cited in the resolution of the 1993 Churchwide Assembly to provide recommendations to the Executive Committee on revision of the nomination form prior to its April 1994 meeting (EC94.1.4).

Council Action: Chair Magnus called upon Secretary Lowell G. Almen to review proposed changes in nomination form, shown in council agenda Exhibit A., Part 2g. Secretary Almen enumerated the numerous constitutional requirements related to the composition of churchwide boards and committees. A survey of nominating committee members indicated by a substantial margin that the biographical information previously submitted for each nominee was sufficient, that the information received from divisions about the expertise they needed was adequate, and that issues related to representational principles and staff support was adequate. In response to that survey, it was determined that a new item be added to the nomination form; namely, the listing of three factors or experience that the nominee believes may have equipped that person for service on the churchwide board, committee, or council. Secretary Almen noted that the Executive Committee of the Church Council had recommended that the item related to employment be listed further toward the end of the form, while the item related to participation in congregational and synodical activities be listed earlier. Secretary Almen asked that council members keep in mind that the biographical data is maintained and accessed through a complicated computer program, and that the present form had evolved based on comments and requests received during previous churchwide assemblies.

During discussion Terry L. Bowes noted that the concern at 1993 Churchwide Assembly focused on women and persons of color who perhaps did not have the educational or employment history that would obviously qualify them for service, but who did possess life experience that would enable them to contribute appropriately to the work of a board. She recommended that the new item be listed toward the beginning of the form. Secretary Almen observed that the category related to education also provides for the possibility of listing life experience. He noted that strong reaction was voiced during the 1989 assembly that education was not included as an item on the nomination form for that assembly. Youth Adviser Erin Cram observed that life experience was a significant factor for encouraging diversity of age in board composition with respect to young people who may be able to list education as a qualification for service.

J. David Ellwanger stated that while he did not have concerns to raise about the nomination form *per se*, he wished to recommend that abbreviations be avoided in printing the biographical data; he also objected that the amount information listed for each individual was too limited in scope. The Rev. John O. Knudson suggested that the category labeled, "employer," be retitled, "employment."

Implementation of Rural Resolution

Background: In response to a resolution developed by the Division for Outreach, the 1993 Churchwide Assembly voted (CA93.3.5.):

(A) LEADERSHIP

WHEREAS, rural congregations have been faithful in the proclamation of the Gospel and in support of the Evangelical Lutheran Church in America and its predecessor bodies, and are now facing a critical crisis in leadership caused by a shortage of clergy available for town and country ministry; and

WHEREAS, the projected shortage of ordained pastoral leadership and lack of available financial resources for town and country congregations may require lay leaders to assume the responsibilities formerly performed by clergy; and

WHEREAS, this church needs to recruit ordained and lay leaders who will see rural ministry as an opportunity for service and will make long-term commitments to this ministry; and

(B) CONGREGATIONAL DEVELOPMENT

WHEREAS, the presence of the unchurched in rural areas serves as opportunity to develop new congregations to provide a full ministry of nurture, witness, and service; and

WHEREAS, there is a demonstrated need among rural congregations for trained consultants to assist them for networking and in the development of cooperative ministries; and

(C) COMMUNITY ISSUES

WHEREAS, the percentage of rural poverty is higher than in urban areas and opportunities for employment are diminishing; and

WHEREAS, factors including the lack of access to social services, low commodity prices, marketing systems, housing, financial practices, reduced real-estate values, sluggish economy, government farm programs, and declining income have contributed to the ruralization of poverty; and

WHEREAS, rural communities are distressed economically and are being targeted as dumping grounds for toxic, industrial, and municipal wastes, thereby threatening the environment and health of rural people; and

(D) CARE OF CREATION

WHEREAS, urban communities benefit from the natural resources and hard labor of sisters and brothers in Christ who live in rural areas; and

WHEREAS, rural congregations are in unique positions to lift up the need for wise stewardship of creation to those who depend upon the land; and

WHEREAS, love demands that we care for and uphold the viability and integrity of the whole of creation—people and the rest of creation, the living creation and the non-living creation—which sustains life; therefore, be it

RESOLVED, that

(1)   this church affirm its commitment to ministries in the rural setting;

(2)   this church assist congregations to move beyond congregational independence and biases toward better communication and cooperation among ministries in related communities, including ecumenical possibilities; and assist in developing creative responses to changing situations;[1]

(3)   the seminaries of this church use instruction by extension and other instructional methods as ways for developing pastors and lay leaders in rural ministry, and that synods coordinate communication of Lutheran and ecumenical opportunities for continuing education events related to rural ministry, and to inform rostered persons serving in rural ministries of those opportunities;[2]

(4)   synods, in cooperation with churchwide units, develop and train teams of indigenous, lay leaders to serve and provide leadership for worship, evangelism, community service, and Christian care;

(5)   resource materials in evangelism for and with rural congregations be developed;[3]

(6)   this church provide resources to assist multi-point congregations in the development of "articles of agreement" for well-defined operations and relationships;[4]

(7)   the publications of the Evangelical Lutheran Church in America, synods, and other entities of this church recognize and tell the story of multi-point parishes;

(8)   this church give encouragement to rural congregations to become more inclusive and to understand what gospel inclusivity and cultural diversity mean in the rural setting;[5]

(9)   this church has an opportunity to foster a sense of community in the rural setting and should assist congregations in developing skills in the areas of community and economic development;[6]

(10) this church assist rural congregations to become active participants in working with others of goodwill on environmental issues and to be advocates for the care of creation;[7]

(11) this church assist in the formation of partnerships of prayer, presence, understanding, and resource sharing between rural and urban congregations in particular;[8] and

(12) this church advocate for people suffering the effects of economic and social conditions that exist throughout the countryside.[9]

---

[1] Particularly synods, the Division for Outreach, the Division for Congregational Ministries, and the Department for Ecumenical Affairs.

[2] Particularly the Division for Ministry.

[3] Particularly the Division for Congregational Ministries.

[4] Particularly synods and the Division for Outreach.

[5] Particularly synods, the Commission for Multicultural Ministries, and other churchwide units.

[6] Division for Church in Society.

[7] Synods, the Division for Church in Society, and the Division for Outreach.

[8] Synods.

[9] Synods, the Division for Church in Society, and the Division for Outreach.

Council Action: Chair Magnus called upon the Rev. Malcolm L. Minnick Jr., executive director of the Division for Outreach, to introduce plans for the implementation of the foregoing resolution. Pastor Minnick observed that the strategy would require the collaboration of a number of churchwide units and synods. He acknowledged that implementation of the resolution's concerns would be determined by consultation, funded by a Lutheran Brotherhood grant of $20,000, with ELCA members living in rural areas. He noted that the functional definition of "rural" varies from one geographic locale to another.

During discussion, Robert S. Schroeder requested further information on such varying definitions of the concept of "rural." The Rev. James G. Cobb inquired whether additional concerns were missing from the resolution. Pastor Minnick replied that although the resolution was comprehensive in scope, additional concerns may surface during its implementation. The Rev. David G. Gabel commented that he chaired the hearing on the rural resolution held at the 1993 Churchwide Assembly and confirmed that all the concerns raised there had been well addressed in the implementation strategy. Bishop Glenn W. Nycklemoe noted an often voiced concern that pastors called to rural ministries often have urban or suburban backgrounds. He inquired whether a need for increased rural awareness was being addressed by ELCA seminaries and synodical candidacy committees. Pastor Minnick indicated that while such concerns were addressed in the implementation strategy under the category of "Leadership," fewer persons with rural experience are entering ELCA seminaries. He expressed appreciation that some seminaries have established intentional programs that immerse students in rural experiences. Edith M. Lohr commented on the significance of Bishop Kenneth H. Sauer's earlier remarks, regarding restrictions seminarians seek to impose on first-call placement, for the implementation strategy. She noted the value of rural communities as "pastor growing places" where first-call ordinands have opportunity to develop nascent pastoral skills. Bishop Robert L. Isaksen advised discretion in engaging "suburban people" to serve rural (and urban) ministries, and recommended that more rural (and urban) persons be recruited for ministries in like settings. Pastor Minnick concurred with the importance of providing a proper match between the pastor and the setting in which the pastor serves.

Development of Urban Resolution

The Rev. Malcolm L. Minnick Jr., executive director of the Division for Outreach, provided a progress report on the development of a resolution on urban ministry for transmission to the 1995 Churchwide Assembly. Pastor Minnick stated that although urban ministry previously has focused on the core city, the core city has changed. Such ministry now must be understood to encompass the entire metropolitan area, which themselves differ in diverse geographical areas across this church. Bishop Paull E. Spring urged that concern for the inner city must nevertheless continue. William E. Diehl observed that the title of the resolution might better be phrased, "Metropolitan Resolution." Pastor Minnick concurred.

Introductions: ELCIC Vice President

Chair Magnus introduced Ms. Janet Morley, the vice president of the Evangelical Lutheran Church in Canada (ELCIC), noting the major organizational restructuring presently under way in that church body. Ms. Morley brought greetings from the ELCIC Church Council. The renewal process, she said, presently occurring in that church seeks to fulfill four major goals: increased communication, flexibility for mission, a simplified decision-making process, and greater cost effectiveness, in order to better meet the needs of people today. She commended the Evangelical Lutheran Church in America for its interchurch and ecumenical efforts in North America, particularly with respect to human rights in Central America.

The Church Council recessed at 12:22 P.M. and reconvened at 1:33 P.M.

Nominations and Elections (continued)

Chair Magnus directed that ballots be distributed for elections to fill the following vacancies on churchwide boards and committees.

Board of the Division for Church in Society
    (clergy-term 1997):
        Rev. L. Edward Knudson, Portland, Ore. (1E)
        Rev. Carol A. Peters, Scottsdale, Ariz. (2D)

Board of the Division for Global Mission:
    To replace Fern Lee Hagedorn, resignation (lay female-term 1997):
        Mary C. Jones, Portland, Ore.. (1E)
        Diana M. Valdez, Spokane, Wash. (1D)

Advisory Committee for the Department for Communication:
1.   To replace the Rev. Stephen Cornils, resignation (clergy-term 1997):
        Rev. George W. Carlson, San Diego, Calif. (2C)
        Rev. Randall R. Lee, Evanston, Ill. (5A)
2.   To replace Karen Anderson, resignation (lay female-term 1995):
        Janice Haley-Schwoyer, Allentown, Pa. (7E)
        Gloria L. Jensen, Moorhead, Minn. (3D)

Standing Committee for the
Commission for Multicultural Ministries
        To replace Charles Tucker Jr., resignation (Native American lay male-term 1995):
        Erik Phelps, Eau Claire, Wis. (5H)
        Larry Thiele, Tokio, N.Dak. (3B)

Chair Magnus subsequently declared balloting to be closed. The results of the election are reported elsewhere in these minutes.

Referrals from the
1993 Churchwide Assembly (continued)
3.   Representational Principles

Background: In response to a number of memorials requesting the Evangelical Lutheran Church in America to reconsider its representational principles, the 1993 Churchwide Assembly voted (CA93.7.47):

To instruct the Church Council, in consultation with the Conference of Bishops, to establish a process for reflection by the Church Council, Conference of Bishops, Commission for Women, Commission for Multicultural Ministries, and seminary faculties, and to report any recommendations to the 1995 Churchwide Assembly.

At its December 1993 meeting, the Church Council voted:

To instruct the Executive Committee of the Church Council, in consultation with the synodical bishops who serve as advisory members of the Church Council, to develop at the committee's January 1994 meeting a time line and process for reflection on the ELCA's representational principles;

To request that the Conference of Bishops, at its March 1994 meeting, provide advice to the Church Council on this proposed process;

To request that the Commission for Multicultural Ministries and the Commission for Women provide advice to the Church Council on this proposed process; and

To instruct the Executive Committee of the Church Council to bring to the April 1994 meeting of the Church Council a report on this effort and a recommendation for council action (CC93.12.83).

Following consultation with advisory bishops on the Church Council and representatives of commissions, the

Executive Committee engaged in substantial discussion of this issue at its January 25-26, 1994, meeting. It shared its preliminary proposal with the Conference of Bishops and two commissions, prior to their March 1994 meetings. (Note: The Commission for Multicultural Ministries expressed concern that the proposed process does not provide for the opportunity for dialogue and reflection among the commissions, the Conference of Bishops, and ELCA seminaries.)

Council Action: Chair Magnus called upon Secretary Lowell G. Almen to introduce the following recommendation of the Executive Committee of the Church Council subsequently adopted by the council, regarding a time line and process for responding to 1993 Churchwide Assembly actions related to this church's representational principles.

During discussion Bishop Kenneth H. Sauer inquired about the scheduled participation of seminary faculties.

VOTED: CC94.4.2
To approve the following time line and process for responding to the referrals by the 1993 Churchwide Assembly related to representational principles:

March 1994
The Conference of Bishops, Commission for Women, and Commission for Multicultural Ministries review the proposed time line and process.

April - May 1994
The Executive Committee receives input from the Conference of Bishops, Commission for Women, and Commission for Multicultural Ministries and makes any necessary revisions in its recommendation.

The Church Council discusses and affirms proposed time line and process.

The Executive Committee develops basic background information related to the representational principles for distribution to those involved in this process.

May - October 1994
Conference of Bishops, Commission for Women, Commission for Multicultural Ministries, and Division for Ministry, in consultation with seminary faculties, develop and implement processes for reflection on the representational principles within their organizations and/or communities.

October 15, 1994
The results of these processes of reflection and any proposed recommendations for action are submitted to the Executive Committee of the Church Council.

October - November 1994
The Executive Committee of the Church Council reviews the information/recom-mendations received from the above-named groups and develops a initial report and recommendation for Church Council consideration at its November 1994 meeting.

November 1994 - April 1995
Any additional work related to this issue, including further conversation among those listed above, or further refinement of the Church Council's recommendation to the 1995 Churchwide Assembly, will be undertaken.

April 1995
Church Council will convey its recommendation to synods and to the 1995 Churchwide Assembly.

August 1995
The Churchwide Assembly will take action on any recommendations.

ELCA Pension and Other Benefits Program

1.   Managed-Care Program

Background: At its December 1993 meeting, the Church Council approved in principle a recommendation from the Board of Pensions to implement a national managed-care program under the ELCA health plan beginning on January 1, 1995. That action follows:

WHEREAS, the ELCA Board of Pensions administers the ELCA Medical and Dental Benefits Plan ("Plan") which is funded through the ELCA Medical and Dental Benefits Trust ("Trust"); and

WHEREAS, the ELCA Board of Pensions has recommended to the ELCA Church Council that it approve, in principle, proposed revisions to the Plan and Trust to be effective January 1, 1995, the main elements of which are set forth in resolutions adopted by the ELCA Board of Pensions on July 17, 1993, and presented to the Church Council; and

WHEREAS, the Church Council acknowledges that, in order to obtain information about the feasibility of such revisions, the ELCA Board of Pensions has solicited potential vendors and engaged in preliminary discussions and negotiations with such vendors; and

WHEREAS, the Church Council wishes to adopt the recommendation of the ELCA Board of Pensions; therefore, be it

RESOLVED, that the Church Council hereby adopts the recommendation of the ELCA Board of Pensions and approves, in principle, the proposed revisions to the Plan and Trust, the main elements of which are as follows:

(A)   A point-of-service managed care arrangement would be phased in over two to three years for the 50 percent of ELCA plan members who reside in a metropolitan area. Approximately 12 sites would be included in the initial implementation of the point-of-service arrangement, including Minneapolis/St. Paul, Minnesota, and Chicago, Illinois.

(B)   The point-of-service arrangement would retain freedom of provider choice but offer enhanced benefits for use of network providers. The in-network benefits of the point-of-service arrangement would be 90 percent of eligible expenses or 100 percent with a small co-payment per physician visit, while the out-of-network benefits would be reimbursed at 70 percent of eligible expenses after a deductible. The lower benefits for those electing to use out-of-network providers are intended to cover the added cost of unlimited provider choice.

(C)   Those members not covered by the point-of-service arrangement would be covered by the ELCA "managed indemnity" arrangement, which would be the current ELCA health plan, but modified to include an inpatient pre-certification/utilization review program, expanded large case management and a simplified reimbursement schedule for chiropractic, out-patient psychotherapy and major dental care. The indemnity arrangement would continue to provide for a reimbursement at 80 percent after a deductible. The supplement to the Medical and Dental Benefits Plan would be eliminated.

(D)   The point-of-service and managed indemnity arrangements would be components of the same, national ELCA health plan. The plan would continue to be bundled with the other ELCA benefit plans.

(E)   A single rate structure would apply to all congregations and employers. Contributions from congregations and other employers would be calculated upon a percent of salary basis, but the subsidy of family rates and the surcharge on member only rates would be phased out over a period of years. However, the low income subsidy would be maintained.

and be it further

RESOLVED, that the Church Council hereby acknowledges that, if it adopts, in principle, the changes to the ELCA health plan, documenting plan amendments will be considered by the council at its meeting in April 1994 (CC93.12.77).

At its March 1994 meeting, the board of trustees of the Board of Pensions considered a recommendation of a carrier for the national point-of-service program, a vendor for the pre-certification and utilization review program under the Managed Indemnity arrangement and proposed plan amendments to implement the managed-care program.

Council agenda Exhibit J, Part 1a, contained the managed-care report and recommendations that were discussed by the board at its March 12-13, 1994, meeting. The amendments considered by the board were printed in council agenda Exhibit J, Part 1b. Only those plan sections pertaining to enrollment in the point-of-service networks and proposed benefits under the point-of-service, managed-indemnity and common benefits arrangements are being submitted by the board to the Church Council at this time.

The reason for this action is two-fold: (1) Church Council action is required on the benefit design to enable board staff to present that information during the town meetings to be held during April and May 1994; and (2) carrier-specific provisions will be added to the plan document once a carrier has been selected. It is not practical to make significant changes to the plan document at this time when further revisions will be proposed prior to January 1, 1995. The "final" proposed plan document will be presented to the Church Council for consideration at its November 1994 meeting.

The following is a summary of the current proposed changes to the ELCA Medical and Dental Benefits Plan:

(A)   The philosophy of the proposed changes is that, whenever possible, the benefits available to members residing in point-of-service network areas are identical to those for members covered by the managed-indemnity arrangement. The reimbursement percentages of those benefits, however, would vary depending upon whether the member was in the point-of-service network or in the managed-indemnity arrangement.

(B)   Many terms are defined throughout the various sections of the plan document. An amendment to Sec. 1.04 is recommended to clarify that the defined terms appearing in the various sections are capitalized.

(C)   Sections 9.01 through 9.05 establish eligibility for participation in the point-of-service and managed-indemnity arrangements. Section 9.01 permits individuals to "opt into" the point-of-service network if they are not already within the network area by virtue of their home Zip Codes.

(D)   Section 9.06 sets forth the indexing of the deductible, maximum reimbursement amount and maximum out-of-pocket amounts. Currently, dental benefits are indexed according to the dentists-services component of the Consumer Price Index for All Urban Consumers (CPI[U]). The new Section 9.06 provides that dental deductibles and maximum reimbursement amounts would be indexed according to the All-Medical-Care Component of the CPI(U). This recommendation would result in a somewhat faster increase in the dental deductibles and maximum reimbursement amounts than under the current structure, but would also ensure that the dental benefits remain consistent with similar medical benefits (e.g., chiropractic care).

(E)   Section 9.07 sets forth the $1 million maximum reimbursement limit.

(F)   Sections 10.01 to 10.04 set forth the proposed benefits for in-network and out-of-network benefits.

(G)   Section 10.05 contemplates the move of a plan member from managed-indemnity to the point-of-service network. It is recommended that the managed indemnity deductibles transfer to the in-network out-of-pocket amount (not the out-of-network amount). Also, the change would occur on the first day of the next following month. (See Section 9.01.)

(H)   Section 10.06(c) defines "In-Network Eligible Medical Expenses." Each of the four items may be explained as follows: (1) this is the individual who provides the basic care to plan members and serves as a gatekeeper to other types of providers; (2) this means a referral by a primary-care physician to a network specialist or hospital; (3) this means a referral by a network specialist to another network specialist or hospital; and (4) this means a referral out of the network by the primary-care physician, upon approval of the carrier.

(I)   Section 10.06(f) clarifies that the board will not assign a member to a primary-care physician, if the member does not select one.

(J)   Section 10.07 outlines the transitional benefits that would be available for members enrolling in the point-of-service network effective January 1, 1995.

(K)   Sections 11.01 to 11.03 set forth the proposed benefits under the managed-indemnity arrangement.

(L)   Section 11.04 contemplates the transfer of members from the point-of-service network to the managed-indemnity arrangement. It is recommended that all of the in-network and out-of-network out-of-pocket amounts be transferred to the managed-indemnity out-of-pocket amounts in recognition that to do otherwise would penalize the member.

(M)   Section 13.05 sets forth the proposed preventative services to be covered under the point-of-service and managed-indemnity arrangements.

(O)   Sections 13.07(t) and (z) set forth, respectively, (1) the elimination of routine immunizations as excluded services, because routine immunizations are now covered as preventative services under Sec. 13.05, and (2) the $200 non-notification penalty for failure to receive pre-authorization prior to inpatient admission.

(P)   Sections 13.09 and 13.10 set forth the pre-certification and concurrent review (i.e., large case management) programs applicable both the point-of-service and to the managed-indemnity arrangements.

(Q)   Article XIV describes the common benefits available to dental, chiropractic, and mental health/chemical dependency applicable to all members.

(R)   Article XV sets forth the prescription drug benefits. It is recommended that prescription drugs purchased through (1) the point-of-service program, or (2) the ELCA mail service pharmacy (EPS), be subject to a $5 generic or $12 brand-name copayment. All medications purchased at the local pharmacy by plan members in the managed-indemnity arrangement would be reimbursed at 50 percent.

The Board of Pensions also recommended that The ALC and LCA Continuation Plans contain identical benefits to the ELCA Medical and Dental Benefits Plan for prescription drugs. Proposed amendments to The ALC and LCA Continuation Plans to make the prescription drug benefits identical to those proposed for the ELCA plan are printed in council agenda Exhibit J, Part 1d. If adopted by the board and subsequently by the Church Council, these amendments would also become effective January 1, 1995.

1.   *Vendors for point-of-service arrangement.* The board selected Aetna as the national vendor for the point-of-service (POS) arrangement. It was planned to imple-

ment POS networks in 24 areas on January 1, 1995, covering 38 percent of plan members, and in 20 additional areas on January 1, 1996, covering another 12 percent of plan members.

2. *Vendor for pre-certification and utilization review program.* Healthmarc was selected as the pre-certification/utilization vendor for the managed indemnity arrangement, which becomes effective January 1, 1995.

3. *Reciprocity Agreement.* The board of trustees of the Board of Pensions authorized staff to enter into a reciprocity agreement with Evangelical Lutheran Church in Canada to facilitate transfers of pastors and lay employees between the two Lutheran bodies.

Council agenda Exhibit J, Part 4a, contained a rationale for the proposed changes related to covered outpatient mental-health providers. Council agenda Exhibit J, Part 4b, contained the proposed plan amendments. Note that additional information from Towers Perrin was offered to Church Council members upon request.

Council Action: Chair Magnus called upon John G. Kapanke, president of the Board of Pensions, to introduce proposed amendments to the bylaws of the Board of Pensions regarding managed care to become effective January 1, 1995. The next step in the process, Mr. Kapanke commented, would be a series of town meetings to respond to the proposals. The goal is to have a managed-care point-of-service form of health care operative in 24 points across this church.

During discussion, Edith M. Lohr expressed appreciation for the work of the staff and members of the Board of Pensions in planning implementation of the managed-care program. She requested clarification about a situation in which a pastor who had met waiver requirements and in fact had waived participation in the plan. In the event that the plan member died, would the spouse and family be able to re-enter the plan? she asked. Mr. Kapanke responded affirmatively. The Rev. Stephen M. Youngdahl asked whether town meetings were scheduled in places other than point-of-service locations, in order to assure plan members in places where implementation of managed care is not a possibility that the quality of their coverage would continue. Mr. Kapanke said such information would be conveyed particularly at synod assemblies. He noted that there were 40 town meetings already scheduled. Bishop Robert L. Isaksen inquired whether the only grounds for waiver from participation in the plan was spousal health coverage. Mr. Kapanke responded affirmatively, although, he acknowledged, exceptions would be possible. The Rev. John O. Knudson inquired whether there was an additional deductible for chiropractic and similar services. Mr. Kapanke responded affirmatively. The Rev. Donald M. Hallberg expressed his appreciation for the attentiveness of the Board of Pensions to concerns expressed about the plan. He also noted a need for this church to cover some Lutheran social service professionals who presently are excluded because some states do not formally license such professionals.

Mr. Kapanke also clarified that the plan would not go into effect until January 1, 1995. He noted that additional work also needed to be done so that a certain level of consistency is achieved with respect to Lutheran Social Service (LSS) agencies.

VOTED: *CC94.4.3*
To adopt amendments to the ELCA Medical and Dental Benefits Plan and to The ALC and LCA Continuation Plans that implement a managed-care program for the Evangelical Lutheran Church in America, ...

2.   Member Waiver Amendments
Background: At its March 12-13, 1994, meeting, the board of trustees of the Board of Pensions considered proposed amendments to permit members who are covered by other employer-provided group coverage to waive ELCA health-plan coverage but remain in the pension, disability, and survivor plans. For members who waive ELCA plan coverage, congregations would pay a "waived coverage charge." The amount of this charge, and how it will be assessed, is to be announced with the 1995 contribution rates in August 1994. Proposed amendments to the ELCA's Medical and Dental Plan were distributed to council members as council agenda Exhibit J, Part 2b.

Council Action: The Church Council adopted the following recommendation without debate:

VOTED: *CC94.4.4*
To adopt the amendments to the ELCA Medical and Dental Plan printed in council agenda Exhibit J, Part 2b, (Member Waiver Amendments).

3.   ELCA Master Institutional Pension Plan and ELCA Master Institutional Savings Plan
Contributions and Earnings: The proposed amendments clarified the methods of crediting contributions and earnings. They would eliminate inconsistencies between plan language and administrative procedures. Interest units have never been credited to Institutional Pension Plan accounts; annuities are based on an annual assumed interest rate of 4.5 percent, not 3.5 percent; and Savings Plan matching contributions are credited directly to the chosen investment funds.

EN BLOC   *[CC94.4.44]*
To adopt the amendments to the Institutional Pension Plan printed in council agenda Exhibit J, Part 3a.

4.   ELCA Medical and Dental Benefits Plan
Covered Outpatient Mental Health Providers: council agenda Exhibit J, Part 4a, contained a rationale for the proposed changes related to covered outpatient mental-health providers. Council agenda Exhibit J, Part 4b, contained the proposed plan amendments. Note that

additional information from Towers Perrin was offered to Church Council members upon request.

EN BLOC   [CC94.4.45]
To adopt the amendments to the ELCA Medical and Dental Plan printed in council agenda Exhibit J, Part 4b.

Managed Mental Health and Chemical Dependency Program: The amendments printed in council agenda Exhibit J, Part 5, clarified benefits under the managed mental-health/chemical-dependency program. They were recommended in connection with the managed mental-health and chemical-dependency program that became effective January 1, 1994.

EN BLOC   [CC94.4.46]
To adopt the amendments to the ELCA Medical and Dental Benefits Plan printed in council agenda Exhibit J, Part 5.

Subrogation Provisions: Council agenda Exhibit J, Part 6a, was a memo from Robert H. Rydland, counsel to the Board of Pensions, which provides a rationale for the proposed changes related to subrogation. Council agenda Exhibit J, Part 6b, contained the actual amendments to the ELCA Medical and Dental Benefits Plan that would implement the proposed change.

EN BLOC   [CC94.4.47]
To adopt the amendments to the ELCA Medical and Dental benefits Plan printed in council agenda Exhibit J, Part 6b.

5.   ELCA Medical and Dental Benefits Plan and The ALC and LCA Continuation Plans

Coverage of Convalescent Care: The health-benefit plans administered by the Board of Pensions exclude services that are not "medically necessary," but do not specifically define when care is custodial, rather than medically necessary. These amendments would define (1) an eligible convalescent facility, and (2) custodial care. The proposed amendments would also limit confinement in a convalescent facility to 120 days per calendar year. This limit is consistent with Medicare and insurance industry practices. Council agenda Exhibit J, Part 7, contained amendments clarifying coverage of convalescent care.

EN BLOC   [CC94.4.48]
To adopt the amendments to the ELCA Medical and Dental Benefits Plan and The ALC and LCA Continuation Plans printed in council agenda Exhibit J, Part 7.

6.   South Africa

Background: Significant developments have occurred in South Africa during the past year. The prospects of free elections and majority rule in South Africa have altered dramatically the context of the work of the church in that nation. Recognizing these developments, the Church Council, at its December 3-5, 1993, meeting, voted:

To encourage the Board of Pensions, the Division for Global Mission, and the Division for Church in Society to continue discussion through normal staff channels on:
1.   issues related to the continuation of the South Africa Free Funds;
2.   the possible development of a screen for the Social Purpose Fund that would provide for investment in companies operating under the "Code of Conduct" designed by the South African Council of Churches (in consultation with the Advisory Committee on the Church's Social Responsibility); and
3.   matters related to shareholder resolutions, within the context of this church's corporate social responsibility; and

To request that a report and any appropriate recommendations be brought to the April 1994 meeting of the Church Council (CC93.12.79).

Consideration of these matters continues within the respective units in relation to the particular responsibilities of each unit.

Council Action: The Church Council received the foregoing as information.

7.   Synod Resolutions Referred to the Board of Pensions

Council agenda Exhibit J, Part 8, contained the response of the Board of Pensions to synod resolutions referred to the board by the Church Council or Executive Committee at previous meetings.

EN BLOC   [CC94.4.49]
To approve *en bloc* the actions in Exhibit J, Part 8.

8.   Amendment to the Bylaws of the Board of Pensions

Background: Council agenda Exhibit J, Part 9, contained a proposed amendment to Sec. 9.4 of Article 9 of the bylaws of the ELCA Board of Pensions. This change would give the board of trustees the flexibility to authorize individuals to sign checks drawn on the funds of the corporation. At the present time, only benefit payment checks may be signed by one authorized individual. All other checks require signatures from two officers, a procedure that has become overly burdensome, given the size of the organization.

Council Action: The Church Council adopted the following recommendation without discussion:

VOTED: CC94.4.5
To adopt the amendment to Sec. 9.4 of Article 9 of the Bylaws of the Board of Pensions printed in council agenda Exhibit J, Part 9.

Report of the Legal and Constitutional Review Committee

1. Cycle of Churchwide Assemblies

Background: In January 1994, the Executive Committee of the Church Council discussed the relative merits of biennial and triennial churchwide assemblies. Materials related to this matter were printed in council Exhibit D, Part 1. Following that discussion, the Executive Committee voted:

> To recommend to the Church Council amendment of ELCA constitutional provision 12.31. to provide for establishment of triennial churchwide assemblies (EC94.1.3).

Council Action: Chair Magnus called upon Dale V. Sandstrom, chair of the council's Legal and Constitutional Review Committee, to introduce the committee's recommendation on the frequency of churchwide assemblies. He noted that the recommendation did not carry the full support of the committee. Chair Magnus, therefore, asked that the recommended be moved from the council floor.

MOVED;

SECONDED: To recommend to the 1995 Churchwide Assembly the following action:

> To adopt the following amendment to the *Constitutions, Bylaws, and Continuing Resolutions of the Evangelical Lutheran Church in America*:
>
> 12.31. The assembly shall meet ~~biennially~~ triennially in regular session. Special meetings may be called by a two-thirds vote of the Church Council. The purpose for a special meeting shall be stated in the notice. (The assembly shall meet triennially, beginning in 1997); and
>
> To request that additional implementing amendments be prepared for consideration by the Church Council at the November 1994 meeting.

During discussion, the Rev. Stephen M. Youngdahl asked whether, if the proposed constitutional amendment were to be implemented, the first term of the churchwide bishop elected in 1995 would be for five, rather than six years. Mr. Sandstrom noted that related proposals would need to be developed after a decision to transmit proposed change to the Churchwide Assembly had been made by the council. Secretary Lowell G. Almen noted that, if the council wished to propose the change at this time, the council's action would be distributed as soon as possible to synodical assemblies for their consideration, as well as to the Conference of Bishops for discussion at its October 1994 meeting. The Rev. David A. Andert inquired whether the recommendation could be emended at a later date in light of possible new information. Secretary Almen answered affirmatively and noted that the referral could be withdrawn from the assembly's agenda as late as April 1995. William T. Billings noted his opposition to the proposal because he believed the proposal was motivated solely for financial reasons and would distance the church from the people in the pew. Carlos Peña favored the proposal, because, he observed, an assembly gathers only approximately 1,000 congregational members.

Loren W. Mathre inquired about the frequency pattern of synodical assemblies. Secretary Almen responded that almost all synods hold annual meetings, although some support for changing that pattern is being shown. The Rev. Franklin D. Fry asked whether parliamentarily the council could simply refer the matter to the assembly without a specific recommendation. General Counsel David J. Hardy responded that Minnesota not-for-profit statutes, under which this church is incorporated, require a recommendation of some kind. Pastor Fry noted reluctance to support the measure, because it may appear that the council was encroaching upon the assembly's responsibility to itself. Ramona S. Rank expressed disappointment with the proposal, citing the importance of the assembly to those who attend as well as many others. The Rev. David A. Andert concurred, and noted that such a move might encourage those who wish to expand the size of the Church Council to advocate for such a change, thereby undercutting the savings. William E. Diehl said he believed it was important for the council to transmit a recommendation because it would be asking the assembly to make a self-interested decision about itself, while the council should make a recommendation based on what is good for this church.

Patsy Gottschalk supported the measure based on remarks voiced by assembly members in 1993. J. David Ellwanger noted that following the lead of another church body was not a good reason to support the proposal. The Rev. Stephen M. Youngdahl noted the possibility of scheduling a legislative assembly every three years with another kind of gathering in other years that could generate even more positive feelings. Bishop Paull E. Spring cautioned that great pressure would be exerted to increase the size of the Church Council for the sake of increased representation, if a triennial assembly were to be proposed.

The question was called.

VOTED: *CC94.4.6*

To recommend to the 1995 Churchwide Assembly the following action:

> To adopt the following amendment to the *Constitutions, Bylaws, and Continuing Resolutions of the Evangelical Lutheran Church in America*:
>
> 12.31.   **The assembly shall meet ~~biennially~~ triennially in regular session. Special meetings may be called by a two-thirds vote of the Church Council. The purpose for a special meeting shall be stated in the notice. (The assembly shall meet triennially, beginning in 1997); and**
>
> **To request that additional implementing amendments be prepared for consideration by the Church Council at the November 1994 meeting.**

2. Length of Terms of Synodical Officers

Background: Acting upon the recommendation of its Committee of Reference and Counsel, the 1993 Churchwide Assembly voted (CA93.8.113):

> To refer the following motion to the Church Council for consideration with other constitutional provisions: "To amend

ELCA bylaw 10.31.05. and section †S8.51. in the Constitution for Synods [regarding the length of terms for synodical vice presidents, secretaries, and treasurers] by substituting the word, "six," for the word, "four."

At the December 3-5, 1993, meeting of the Church Council, the council voted:

To refer the resolution of the 1993 Churchwide Assembly on the length of terms of synodical officers to the Legal and Constitutional Review Committee of the Church Council; and

To request that the committee recommend a response to the council at its April 1994 meeting (CC93.12.70).

In preparing a response, the secretary of this church surveyed the Conference of Bishops. The survey provided three options for the length of terms of synodical vice presidents, secretaries, and treasurers: six-year terms; four-year terms; or determination of length of term by each synod. In the survey forms that were returned, 24 synods expressed preference for the present pattern of four-year terms for synodical vice presidents, secretaries, and treasurers; 21 indicated a preference for synodical option on the length of these terms; and one recommended shifting to six-year terms.

By a slight margin, support was expressed for maintaining the present pattern of four-year terms for synodical vice presidents, secretaries, and treasurers. In view of the strong preferences expressed either for the present pattern of four-year terms for synodical officers or for synodical option on the length of such terms, flexibility may be appropriate here. Therefore, the Legal and Constitutional Review Committee provided the following recommendation:

To recommend the following amendments to the 1995 Churchwide Assembly for churchwide bylaw 10.31.05. and †S8.51.b. in the *Constitution for Synods* regarding the terms for synodical vice presidents, secretaries, and treasurers:

Bylaw 10.31.05.   (second sentence to read, " . . . Each other officer shall be elected to a term of four years as defined by each synod but not to exceed six years and may be reelected.";

and

†S8.51   in the *Constitution for Synods* to read, "The vice president, secretary, and treasurer of this synod shall be elected to a term of four _____ years and may be reelected.

Council Action: Mr. Sandstrom reviewed the history of the issue and noted that the language in the recommendation was designed to permit synods to set length of terms of office, but not to exceed six years. The Rev. James G. Cobb inquired whether the issue of limitation on the number of terms was addressed. Mr. Sandstrom responded that it was not discussed. Secretary Lowell G. Almen noted that some 20 synods do have limits for bishops as well as some other officers.

VOTED: *CC94.4.7*
To recommend the following amendments to the 1995 Churchwide Assembly for churchwide bylaw 10.31.05. and †S8.51.b. in the *Constitution for Synods* regarding the terms for synodical vice presidents, secretaries, and treasurers:
Bylaw 10.31.05.   (second sentence to read, " . . . Each other officer shall be elected to a term of four years as defined by each synod but not to

exceed six years and may be reelected.";
and

†S8.51   in the *Constitution for Synods* to read, "The vice president, secretary, and treasurer of this synod shall be elected to a term of four _____ years and may be reelected.

3. Conflicts of Interest

Background: The Church Council received the following resolution from the Minneapolis Area Synod regarding conflicts of interest at the level of synods:

WHEREAS, the Church Council of the Evangelical Lutheran Church in America in 1988 adopted policies and procedures to address and resolve issues involving "conflicts of interest" at the churchwide level, and recommended adoption of an amendment to the churchwide bylaws to provide that

Except [for churchwide officers and synod bishops, who are ex officio members with voice and no vote], employees of the churchwide organization, including those serving under call, appointment, employment agreement, or contract, shall not be eligible for election and service as voting members of the Churchwide Assembly (ELCA 12.41.15.); and

WHEREAS, the provisions of current ELCA bylaw 12.41.15. quoted above were adopted by the 1989 Churchwide Assembly by a vote of "Yes—819; No—9" (CA89.4.22—13.41.15.); and

WHEREAS, it is also important for the Evangelical Lutheran Church in America to adopt policies and procedures to address and resolve issues involving conflicts of interest at the level of the synods of this church as well; and

WHEREAS, the model Constitution for Synods of the Evangelical Lutheran Church in America contains no provision regarding conflicts of interest; and

WHEREAS, amendments to the mandatory provisions of the ELCA Constitution for Synods are subject to the same procedures for amendment as amendments to the ELCA Constitution (ELCA 10.13.), and may be proposed by the Church Council for adoption by the Churchwide Assembly (ELCA 22.11.a.); therefore, be it

RESOLVED, that the Minneapolis Area Synod request the Church Council (pursuant to ELCA 14.21.11.) to address "conflicts of interest" at the level of synods and to make such recommendations for synod policies and procedures, including any necessary amendments to synod constitutions and bylaw provisions (pursuant to ELCA 22.11.a.) as the Church Council shall deem appropriate.

At its December 3-5, 1993, meeting the Church Council voted:

To refer the resolution of the Minneapolis Area Synod on conflicts of interest to the Office of the Secretary and the Church Council's Legal and Constitutional Review Committee for a report and/or recommendation to the April 1994 meeting of the Church Council (CC93.12.105.3).

Exploration of this matter to date has revealed substantial complexity, in view of varied circumstances and situations. The resolution will receive further study at the April 1994 meeting of the council's Legal and Constitutional Review Committee.

Council Action: Mr. Sandstrom noted some of the difficulties in making a decision on this issue at this time as background to the specifics of the recommendation of the Legal and Constitutional Review Committee.

VOTED: *CC94.4.8*
To offer at this time no policy statement or proposed constitutional amendments for all synods of this church regarding potential issues of "conflict of interest";

To call to the attention of the Minneapolis Area Synod the provisions of the section dealing with director conflicts of interest found in 317A.255 of the Minnesota Nonprofit Corporation Act, which is the statute of incorporation for the Minneapolis Area Synod and several other synods; and

To request the secretary of this church to inform the Minneapolis Area Synod of this action.

4. Amendment of
Continuing Resolution 15.11.E91.

Name of the Department of Information Management Services;

Change to Department for Information Technology

The development of electronic communication, computer use, data storage and transmission, and other technological possibilities continues at a rapid pace. From the Data Management Staff Team a recommendation has emerged that what has been known as the "Department for Information Management Services" be renamed the "Department for Information Technology." This change would create greater consistency with the department names for that function in both this church's Board of Pensions and the Publishing House of the Evangelical Lutheran Church in America.

2/3 VOTE REQUIRED

VOTED: CC94.4.9

To amend churchwide continuing resolution 15.11.E91., as follows:

15.11.E91.94. *Department for Information Management Services Technology*
The treasurer shall provide for an information management system technology that shall include... [with the remainder of the continuing resolution remaining unchanged].

5. Definition of Ecclesiastical Ballot

Background: Various synods have noted that, although the *Constitution for Synods* provides a model for use of an "ecclesiastical ballot" in the election of a synodical bishop (S9.04.), that provision does not contain a definition of what constitutes an ecclesiastical ballot. For purposes of consistency in constitutional interpretation, such a definition would be helpful.

Council Action: Mr. Sandstrom introduced the following recommendation of the Legal and Constitutional Review Committee, subsequently adopted by the Church Council. He noted that the recommendation consisted of two parts: one addressed to synods that employ an ecclesiastical ballot (but not requiring synods to use an ecclesiastical ballot) and the other addressing the election of the bishop of this church. During discussion the Rev. Franklin D. Fry observed that under most usages of the ecclesiastical ballot, names cannot be withdrawn. Mr. Sandstrom noted that *Robert's Rules of*

Order does not apply here, because it is in force only when are no other procedural rules are in force. General Counsel David J. Hardy stated that ecclesiastical ballots usually are dictated by tradition and the purpose of the proposed amendment was to specify the received tradition.

Edith M. Lohr inquired whether nominees could withdraw their names, which, according to Mr. Sandstrom, could not be done after the second ballot. Ms. Lohr suggested that the wording of item "g" be expanded for the sake of clarity. Secretary Lowell G. Almen commented further on the implications of speeches during election processes. The Rev. James G. Cobb inquired whether it was common practice to have representatives speak for a nominee. Secretary Almen noted that such has rarely happened, but the provision was included to allow flexibility in the face of an unusual circumstance. He also noted that in the case of a short definition such as this it is not possible to nail down every contingency. Bishop Robert L. Isaksen inquired whether the proposed definition would affect those synods that employ a modified ecclesiastical ballot. Mr. Sandstrom noted that the purpose of this amendment was to define only an ecclesiastical ballot, not other instances.

Ramona S. Rank called the question.

MOVED;
SECONDED;   *2/3 VOTE REQUIRED*
CARRIED: To move the previous question.

2/3 VOTE REQUIRED
VOTED: CC94.4.10

To define an "ecclesiastical ballot" for the election of a bishop in synods of the Evangelical Lutheran Church in America as an election process:

1. In which on the first ballot the name of any eligible individual may be submitted for nomination by a voting member of the assembly;
2. Through which the possibility of election to office exists on any ballot by achievement of the required number of votes cast by voting members of the assembly applicable to a particular ballot;
3. That precludes spoken floor nominations in the assembly prior to or following the casting of the first ballot;
4. In which the first ballot is considered a nominating ballot if no election occurs on the first ballot;
5. In which the first ballot defines the total slate of nominees for possible election on a subsequent ballot, with no additional nominations permitted following the casting of the first ballot;
6. That does not preclude, at some point subsequent to the reporting of the first ballot, the

right of persons nominated on such a ballot to withdraw their names prior to the casting of the second ballot;

7. In which the name of any individual that appears on any ballot subsequent to the second ballot may not be withdrawn;

8. That does not preclude an assembly's adoption of rules that may permit, at a defined point in the election process and for a defined period of time, speeches to the assembly by nominees or their representatives and/or a question-and-answer forum in which the nominees or their representatives participate; and

9. In which the number of names that appear on any ballot subsequent to the second ballot shall be determined in accordance with provisions of the governing documents (or, if the governing documents are silent, in accordance with rules adopted by the assembly);

and

To adopt a new churchwide continuing resolution 19.61.A94. to read:

An "ecclesiastical ballot" for the election of officers (other than treasurer) of the churchwide organization of the Evangelical Lutheran Church in America is hereby defined as an election process:

a. *In which on the first ballot the name of any eligible individual may be submitted for nomination by a voting member of the assembly;*

b. *Through which the possibility of election to office exists on any ballot by achievement of the required number of votes cast by voting members of the assembly applicable to a particular ballot;*

c. *That precludes spoken floor nominations in the assembly prior to or following the casting of the first ballot;*

d. *In which the first ballot is considered a nominating ballot if no election occurs on the first ballot;*

e. *In which the first ballot defines the total slate of nominees for possible election on a subsequent ballot, with no additional nominations permitted following the casting of the first ballot;*

f. *That does not preclude, at some point subsequent to the reporting of the first ballot, the right of persons nominated on such a ballot to withdraw their names prior to the casting of the second ballot;*

g. *In which the name of any individual that appears on any ballot subsequent to the second ballot may not be withdrawn;*

h. *That does not preclude an assembly's adoption of rules that may permit, at a defined point in the election process and for a defined period of time, speeches to*

the assembly by nominees or their representatives and/or a question-and-answer forum in which the nominees or their representatives participate; and

i. *In which the number of names that appear on any ballot subsequent to the second ballot shall be determined in accordance with provisions of the governing documents.*

6. Burden of Proof in Disciplinary Proceedings

Background: Council agenda Exhibit D, Part 2a, contained a resolution introduced at the 1993 Churchwide Assembly by a voting member. The resolution called for the use of a "clear and convincing evidence" burden of proof standard in cases involving admonition or suspension from the roster, and "beyond a reasonable doubt" burden of proof standard in cases involving removal from the roster. This would be in lieu of the "preponderance of the evidence" standard set for in *Rules Governing Disciplinary Proceedings Against an Ordained Minister, a Rostered Layperson, or a Congregation of the Evangelical Lutheran Church in America* (Rules). In accordance with assembly rules, this resolution was submitted to the Committee of Reference and Counsel, which recommended that the resolution be referred to the Church Council for consideration in consultation with the Conference of Bishops. By amendment from the floor, the recommended action was to include consultation with the general counsel of this church. The assembly adopted the committee's recommendation as amended.

Upon recommendation of the Legal and Constitutional Review Committee, the Church Council at its December 3-5, 1993, meeting acted:

To request the general counsel to prepare an analysis of the issues involved in the burden of proof standard in discipline cases for review by the Conference of Bishops through its Committee on Liaison with the Church Council; and

To request the Conference of Bishops to review this analysis and make a report and recommendation to the Church Council at its April 1994 meeting (CC93.12.98).

The ELCA general counsel has chosen to have the analysis of the issues done by outside counsel with great experience in both ELCA litigation cases and ELCA discipline cases. A copy of this analysis, prepared by Patrick J. Schiltz of the firm of Faegre & Benson (Minneapolis, Minn.), was presented as council agenda Exhibit D, Part 2b. The general counsel has reviewed this analysis and is in agreement that the existing standard of "preponderance of the evidence" should be retained as the burden of proof requirement in the "Rules."

At its March 1994 meeting, the Conference of Bishops, after reviewing this analysis, recommended that the existing "preponderance of the evidence" standard be retained in disciplinary proceedings.

Council Action: Mr. Sandstrom introduced the following recommendation of the Legal and Constitutional Review Committee not to change the burden of proof standard related to disciplinary matters, subsequently adopted by the Church Council without discussion:

VOTED: *CC94.4.11*

To retain the "preponderance of the evidence" as a burden of proof standard in proceedings before discipline hearing committees.

7. Costs in Disciplinary Proceedings

Background: The Southwestern Pennsylvania Synod Council submitted to the Church Council the following memorial:

To request the Church Council of the Evangelical Lutheran Church in America to consider the best manner for handling the legal expenses that result from discipline proceedings within synods, and to develop a plan for responding to these expenses, e.g., ELCA budget item, assessment to synods, or insurance coverage.

At its March 27-29, 1993, meeting, the Church Council voted:

To refer the resolution of the Southwestern Pennsylvania Synod jointly to the Office of the Bishop and the Conference of Bishops for advice; and

To request that a report and a possible recommendation for action be brought to the December 1993 meeting of the Church Council (CC93.3.41).

This memorial was referred by the Church Council to the Office of the Bishop and the Conference of Bishops. The Office of the Bishop in turn requested the involvement of the general counsel. Matters related to this resolution were discussed with the Conference of Bishop's Committee on Liaison with the Church Council in December 1993 and March 1994.

Council agenda Exhibit D, Part 3, was a report prepared by the general counsel. The report presents information about costs in existing disciplinary proceedings, and discusses alternatives for allocation or sharing of those costs and options for reducing the costs. The Conference of Bishops at its March 1994 meeting reviewed this report and recommended that it was an appropriate response to the memorial.

Council Action: Mr. Sandstrom introduced the following recommendation of the Legal and Constitutional Review Committee regarding participation of synods in the Shared-Risk Fund, subsequently adopted by the Church Council without debate:

VOTED: *CC94.4.12*

To accept the report, attached as council agenda Exhibit D, Part 3, on disciplinary costs and options for the sharing and reducing of such costs as the Church Council's response to the memorial from the Southwestern Pennsylvania Synod Council;

To encourage all synods to participate in the Shared-Risk Fund; and

To ask the Shared-Risk Fund Committee of the Conference of Bishops to consider the advantages and disadvantages of making mandatory participation in the Shared-Risk Fund by all synods.

8. Correction of Inconsistency in Disciplinary Rules

Background: In the "Rules Governing Disciplinary Proceedings against an Ordained Minister, a Rostered Layperson, or a Congregation of the Evangelical Lutheran Church in America," adopted in November 1991, a quorum requirement was stated twice, once in Rule F21 and again in Rule K2, both of which were identical.

The reason for the quorum requirement being twice stated was to make clear that the same requirement continues to apply, even though in deliberations of a discipline hearing committee subsequent to the hearing, only the committee members who participated through the entire hearing were to participate in any post-hearing deliberations.

In the revised "Rules . . . " adopted by the Church Council in December 1993, on recommendation of the subcommittee appointed under ELCA 20.21.16. and the Conference of Bishops, the quorum requirement in Rule F23 (formerly Rule F21 from the 1991 version) was revised to read as follows:

The quorum for the discipline hearing committee shall be six of its voting members, and must include at least one member of the churchwide Committee on Discipline and one member of the Committee on Discipline of the synod.

Through oversight, however, Rule K2 was not revised, resulting in inconsistent quorum requirements between the two rules. The recommended action will again make the quorum requirement in the two rules consistent.

Council Action: Mr. Sandstrom introduced the following recommendation of the Legal and Constitutional Review Committee, subsequently adopted by the Church Council without debate:

VOTED: *CC94.4.13*

To amend Rule K2 in "Rules Governing Disciplinary Proceedings Against an Ordained Minister, a Rostered Layperson, or a Congregation of the Evangelical Lutheran Church in America," adopted by the Church Council on December 5, 1993, to read as follows:

The quorum for the discipline hearing committee shall be six of its voting members, and must include at least one member of the churchwide Committee on Discipline and one member of the Committee on Discipline of the synod.

Mr. Sandstrom reported that the Legal and Constitutional Review Committee concurred with the recommendation of the Budget and Finance Committee concerning the change of synodical fiscal years.

Nominations and Elections (continued)

Chair Magnus called upon Secretary Lowell G. Almen who announced that the following persons had been elected to positions on churchwide boards and committees:

VOTED: *CC94.4.14*

To elect the following persons to fill vacancies on the respective churchwide boards and committees and for the terms indicated:

Board of the Division for Church in Society (clergy-term 1997):

Rev. L. Edward Knudson, Portland, Oreg. (1E)

Board of the Division for Global Mission (lay female-term 1997; resignation of Fern Lee Hagedorn):

Diana M. Valdez, Spokane, Wash. (1D)

Advisory Committee for the Department for Communication (clergy-term 1997;
●**resignation of the Rev. Stephen Cornils):**

Rev. Randall R. Lee, Evanston, Ill. (5A)
●**(lay female-term 1995; resignation of Karen Anderson):**

Gloria L. Jensen, Moorhead, Minn. (3D)

Standing Committee for the Commission for Multicultural Ministries (Native American lay male-term 1995; resignation of Charles Tucker Jr.):

Erik Phelps, Eau Claire, Wis. (5H)

Chair Magnus declared the foregoing persons to have been duly elected to the positions indicated.

Report of the
Executive for Administration

Chair Magnus called upon the Rev. Robert N. Bacher, the executive for administration, to present his report. Pastor Bacher highlighted the first portion of his printed report, which was devoted to a meeting of church body administrators, and which was presented as council agenda Exhibit E, Part 1. Commenting on the second part of his report, Pastor Bacher pointed to the beginning of the "Inquiry" process. Regarding the budget, he stated that he does not want to become accustomed to annual budget reductions and that he was confident that the churchwide organization was characterized by both good stewardship and good development efforts. He noted that our understanding of mission is what drives us beyond the congregation in order to help us to implement that vision.

Pastor Bacher called upon the Rev. Lee S. Thoni, executive assistant to the bishop, to report on regional conversations. Pastor Thoni commented that the synodical-churchwide conversations are intended to move beyond the present relationships between synods and the churchwide organization in order to make ministry leaders and congregations more effective in their work. Clearly a major insight was that everyone must be mission-driven, rather than reactionary. Driving the discussion was the question, "What are we going to do, if current trends continue?" The next steps, he reported, is to complete the process with the two remaining regional meetings, combine the findings, and report to the Confer-

ence of Bishops and be shared in the mission-support consultations in the fall of this year.

During discussion, J. David Ellwanger asked about the composition of the "Inquiry" committee. Pastor Bacher reported that Athornia Steele (Columbus, Ohio) and Kay Conrad (Winston Salem, N.C.) had been added to the committee.

Report of the
Coordination and Services Committee

Chair Magnus called upon William E. Diehl, chair of the committee, who reported on the most recent meeting of the committee. Mr. Diehl noted that the committee met with the Rev. Michael L. Cooper-White, executive director of the Department for Synodical Relations. A major issue to be addressed was the Good Samaritan Fund, which currently is underfunded. Suggestions were made on how this issue could be addressed. The committee also met with staff members of the Department for Human Resources.

Mr. Diehl commented on an amendment, as approved by the committee to personnel policy section 16.0 regarding "Conduct in the Work Place." Secretary Almen suggested revising 11.6. to read: "The unit is to provide time and costs for all rostered members of its staff, ~~including active associates in ministry, members of the Deaconess Community of the Evangelical Lutheran Church in America, and diaconal ministers, under call, on the lay roster or rosters of the synod~~ to attend, once in each four-year period, the assembly in which his or her membership is maintained." He noted that formerly only ordained ministers were accorded the benefit, and that the change to read "all rostered members" without further specification was sufficient. The suggestion was adopted as a friendly amendment.

Members of the Church Council also indicated their interest in receiving reports from the various units submitted to the committee.

Executive Session

The Church Council recessed into executive session at 4:50 P.M., for the purpose of hearing a progress report on current litigation. The Church Council recessed for the day at 5:07 P.M.

Sunday Session

The Church Council reconvened on Sunday, April 17, 1994, at 9:25 A.M. The plenary session was preceded with a Service of Holy Communion held in the chapel of the Lutheran Center. The Rev. Paul R. Nelson, director for worship and the arts in the ELCA Division for Congregational Ministries, served as presiding minister; the Rev. Lowell G. Almen, preacher; Mr. Dale V. Sanderson, lector; Ms. Edith M. Lohr, cantor; and the Rev. William L. Smith, pianist.

Vice President Kathy J. Magnus, chair of the Church Council, thanked Secretary Lowell G. and Mrs.

Sally Clark Almen for hosting dinner on Saturday evening, April 16, 1994, at their residence.

Approval of Minutes

Background: The minutes of the December 3-5, 1993, meeting of the Church Council and the minutes of the January 5, 1994, and March 2, 1994, meetings of the council's Executive Committee were distributed to council members prior to the council's April meeting.

Council Action: Secretary Lowell G. Almen announced a correction to page six of the minutes for the December 3-5, 1993, meeting of the Church Council, noting that the last word on the page, "agencies," was omitted.

VOTED: CC94.4.15

To approve the minutes of the December 3-5, 1993, meeting of the Church Council; and

To ratify actions of the council's Executive Committee as indicated in the minutes of the January 5, 1994, and March 2, 1994, meetings.

Study of Human Sexuality

Background: At its December 1994 meeting, the Church Council took the following action related to the development of a first draft of a social statement on human sexuality:

(A) To acknowledge the strong reaction and widespread concern expressed by numerous members and congregations throughout the Evangelical Lutheran Church in America in response to the content and manner of release of the first draft of a possible "Social Statement on the Church and Human Sexuality—a Lutheran Perspective";

(B) To recognize, at the same time, those throughout this church who have voiced appreciation for the preparation of this first draft and the hope that the process will proceed for development of a subsequent draft and possible proposal of a social statement on human sexuality for a future Churchwide Assembly;

(C) To underscore that the current version of the statement is, indeed, a first draft (*and not official policy* of the Evangelical Lutheran Church in America) and as a first draft is subject to continued study and comment by members, congregations, faculties, and institutions throughout the church, with such responses to inform the process for revisions for any subsequent draft;

(D) To affirm continuation of the process for preparation of study materials and the development of a social statement on human sexuality, which may be presented for action at a future Churchwide Assembly, emphasizing that such work shall be in keeping with the doctrinal acknowledgment of and confession by this church of the Triune God (ELCA constitutional provision 2.01.), of "Jesus Christ as Lord and Savior and the Gospel as the power of God for the salvation of all who believe" (2.02.), of "Jesus Christ [as] the Word of God incarnate" (2.02.a.), of the "proclamation of God's message to us as both Law and Gospel" (2.02.b.), and "of the Old and New Testaments as the inspired Word of God and the authoritative source and norm of its proclamation, faith, and life" (2.03.);

(E) To express gratitude to members and congregations of this church who have conveyed their concerns and convictions in this matter and especially to those who have recommended

specific changes in the first draft to assist in the process of revision;

(F) To indicate the conviction that the Church Council would recommend to a future Churchwide Assembly only such a draft of a social statement on human sexuality that would stand on biblical foundations and the confessional tradition of this church and that would merit the study, consideration, thoughtful reflection, and widespread support within this church;

(G) To acknowledge that the broad interest and intense reactions to the first draft represent a strategic opportunity for study, reflection, and thought on how we as Lutherans read and embrace Scripture and how members of this church understand and respond to issues and concerns related to sexuality in communities and society;

(H) To indicate the conviction that the process for development of a possible social statement on human sexuality will require significant modifications in order for the process to be widely trusted and accepted throughout this church and in order to assure that responses will be respected and employed in the preparation of a subsequent draft;

(I) To acknowledge strong signs that trust in the current task force has been impaired and yet to indicate that, in view of the lengthy study, preparation, and dedicated work of the members of the task force to date, it is deemed unwise at this time to direct the board of the Division for Church in Society to disband the current task force;

(J) To respond to the executive committee of the board of the Division for Church in Society with appreciation for the general direction reflected in the revised proposal for the process of study, revision, and development of a social statement;

(K) To affirm the need for greater participation of leadership groups of various perspectives in the development process for enhanced trust and partnership in the development of possible subsequent drafts;

(L) To determine that the present process will be supplemented by the selection of a consulting panel to widen the circle of persons officially engaged in the preparation of a revised draft, with such a consulting panel:

   (1) to be mutually accountable to the board of the Division for Church in Society and to the Church Council;

   (2) to be expected to provide regular reports directly to the board, the Church Council, and Conference of Bishops of the panel's work with appropriate staff and the task force; and

   (3) to be composed of 11 persons appointed by the Church Council, including:

      (a) three ELCA seminary faculty members, named by the Church Council upon recommendation of the presidents of ELCA seminaries;

      (b) three pastors of ELCA congregations, named by the Church Council;

      (c) two lay members of ELCA congregations, named by the Church Council;

      (d) two members of the Conference of Bishops, named by the Conference of Bishops; and

      (e) one member of the Church Council, named by the Church Council; and

(M) To direct that this consulting panel shall have access to all materials received from members, congregations, and others in response to the study document, "Human Sexuality and the Christian Faith" (1991), and the first draft, "The Church and Human Sexuality—a Lutheran Perspective" (1993), shall be charged to give advice and counsel related to the opinions within the church, and shall provide advice, counsel, and critique—including the ways in which Scripture is used—in the development of any subsequent drafts;

(N) To affirm the plan of the executive committee of the board of the Division for Church in Society for appointment of a staff team, under the supervision of the executive director of the Division for Church in Society, to carry out responsibilities with the task force and consulting panel for development of any subsequent drafts;

(O)	To express appreciation for the development of a plan for recording and providing both statistical and narrative summaries of responses received to the first draft, which shall be reported periodically to the Conference of Bishops and the Church Council; and

(P)	To urge renewed commitment to mutual conversation, correction, and consolation among and between sisters and brothers in Christ within the Evangelical Lutheran Church in America, remembering that members of this church are united through Christ and are bound together by our primary convictions grounded in Scripture, the creeds of the church, the Augsburg Confession, and the other confessional writings of the Lutheran Reformation (CC93.12.80).

Subsequent to the December 1994 meeting, the Church Council was sent several mailings related to this process, including the actions taken by the board of the Division for Church in Society at its March 1994 meeting.

Members of the council were asked to bring these materials with them to the April 1994 meeting, at which time the council would receive an update of recent events and future plans. Materials related to this agenda item were distributed to council members.

The Executive Committee of the Church Council discussed this matter at a meeting on April 14, 1994, and recommended the motion printed below.

Council Action: The Rev. Charles S. Miller Jr., executive director of the Division for Church in Society, introduced the Rev. Roland D. Martinson, professor of pastoral theology at Luther Northwestern Theological Seminary (Saint Paul, Minn.), who serves as consultant to the division's executive director for the study of human sexuality. Pastor Martinson shared some initial observations concerning public responses to the first draft of a possible social statement on human sexuality. He elaborated on a written report, which had been distributed to council members.

Pastor Miller drew attention to a report concerning the current status of the development of the statement. He commented on the profundity with which this church has received the initial draft, as well as the profoundness of the issue itself, and stated that this church is engaged in a "teaching moment" far beyond the hope and expectations of the division. Pastor Miller commented on the appointment of the Rev. Kenneth C. Senft (Gettysburg, Pa.) as project director for the study and on the selection of the writing team.

Pastor Miller reviewed the actions of the board of the Division for Church in Society at its March 1994 meeting. He noted that the March meeting of the board was the first opportunity the board had to convene in full and to discuss the document. Pastor Miller underscored that the function and contribution of the task force had been neither devalued nor diminished. He acknowledged disagreement by some members of the task force with that conclusion, and expressed the expectation that "as the spring and summer unfold, we will be able to take significant strides in rebuilding the relationship [between

the task force, the board of the Division for Church in Society, and staff] and, I believe, capitalizing on the wealth of contributions still to be made by the task force in this process."

Pastor Miller recognized the Rev. Melissa M. Maxwell-Doherty (Grand Forks, N.D.), chair of the consulting panel.

During discussion, the Rev. H. George Anderson inquired about the intended meaning of the word, "strong," in the phrase, "some make *strong* arguments from Scripture and tradition" [emphasis added] in Pastor Martenson's report, that is, strong in the sense of vigorous, or strong in apposition to weak. Bishop Paull E. Spring expressed reservation regarding the ability of this church to follow the proposed time line cited in Pastor Miller's report. The Rev. David G. Gabel inquired about the "intervention" (as cited in Pastor Miller's report) of the board of the Division for Church in Society with respect to the process for the development of the statement and "departure" from the process presented to the Church Council at its December 1994 meeting. Pastor Miller indicated that the continuance of the development process and the rebuilding of trust by this church's membership were more complex than earlier realized.

The Rev. David A. Andert requested distribution of papers produced by the members of the consulting panel regarding pertinent biblical and theological questions. He also observed that the initial draft had been "perceived as an advocacy document." "Will the social statement itself . . . be an advocacy document or a description of the various viewpoints that are held within the Evangelical Lutheran Church in America?" he asked. Pastor Miller indicated that it was too early in the writing process to determine that. "The only piece of advice that seems to be arriving consistently is that whatever else happens the document must be more pastoral and must address more of the realities of pastoral and congregational life than it currently does," he commented.

Lorraine G. Bergquist inquired about when the second draft of the proposed statement would be released to congregations. Pastor Miller reviewed the proposed time line.

D. Mark Klever requested further explanation of the changing responsibilities of the task force. Pastor Miller acknowledged that, although some task force members might disagree with his perspective, "I do not think their role has been significantly altered; only the sequence of tasks. . . . Sequentially, what has changed is that the writing team will do some work first before the task force begins to get engaged. But, in every other respect, I believe that they will be integrally involved in the development of the content."

William E. Diehl raised concern about a possible gap between the opinions and understandings of "Lutheran theologians" and scholars, and the experience of the membership of this church in general. Pastor Miller acknowledged that such opinion must be conveyed in ways that are "not alarming to the church and divisive." "We need to admit that there is a much larger teaching responsibility here than can ever be contained in a social statement. And so, only one aspect of our church's struggle with human sexuality is cared for by the hopeful eventuality of adopting a social statement. There is much more to be done," he observed. Pastor Martinson responded: "If I have read and understood the [synodical] bishops' responses, the teaching theologians' responses—those at universities, seminaries, and so on—I see deeply held, well-developed positions on section three (e.g., on homosexuality and homosexual expression). I would be very surprised, if during the next six months—nine months, 18 months, those people can come to agreement (i.e., middle ground) on such matters. I see very deep differences among people that I have read widely and known for many years and the significant work (careful scholarship) that will be required for these people to engage in conversation. I believe that your observations are very perceptive in that they are reflected widely in the material; for example, I find that clergy are regularly making arguments from Scripture in regard to these matters using a variety of exegetical and hermeneutical insights; I find that lay persons . . . do not make arguments from Scripture in the same way. Generally, there is a tendency to read the Scriptures literally, and take it at that, or to dismiss the Scriptures as having anything to say about this particular contemporary question, because of the nature of the difference in the span of time."

Bishop Herbert W. Chilstrom requested clarification regarding the "ownership" of the draft; that is, was the authorship of the current document attributable to the task force or to the Division for Church in Society board? Pastor Miller responded that it was to be considered a document of the board.

The Rev. James G. Cobb observed that the next essential task of this church would be the question of contemporary biblical interpretation and hermeneutics. He also inquired about the reception the study had received at recent synodical assemblies. Bishop Peter Rogness inquired about the "benchmarks" that would determine the feasibility of transmitting a final document to the 1995 Churchwide Assembly. Pastor Miller indicated that the March 1995 meeting of the board of the Division for Church in Society would be critical for that determination. The Rev. Franklin D. Fry commented on the circumscribed ability of congregations to engage in scholarly biblical study. He urged that the nomenclature, "academic theologian," be employed, in preference to "teaching theologian." He observed further a lack of appropriate printed materials for congregational use with regard to biblical hermeneutics and theology. Bishop Chilstrom commented on the difficulty of developing appropriate study materials, noting that the "Word and Witness" Bible-study series had been criticized as being too difficult for the lay reader. Referring to several historical instances in American Lutheranism in which dogmatic disputes had been settled by unusual means, Bishop Chilstrom alluded to a possible analogous outcome for present circumstances as "an agreement to disagree."

Chair Magnus introduced the following recommendation of the council's Executive Committee:

MOVED;

SECONDED: To affirm the action of the board of the Division for Church in Society, in which that board, at its March 10-13, 1994, meeting defined the roles, tasks and accountabilities of the board, task force on human sexuality, consulting panel and staff, including the understandings that:

1. The role of the board of the Division for Church in Society is to establish direction and set policy; its task is to oversee staff management of the entire list of projects; its accountability is to the Church Council;

2. The role of the task force on human sexuality is to recommend content for the social statement; its task is to study and respond to the church's deliberation about the topics to be addressed in the social statement; its accountability is to the board of the Division for Church in Society; its work is directly with division staff assigned by the executive director;

3. The consulting panel's role is to advise the board of the Division for Church in Society and staff on key issues, themes, and content pertaining to the social statement; its task is to critique the first draft and future statement renditions and to make recommendations to the staff and board of the Division for Church in Society in this regard; its accountability is to the Church Council and the division's board; its work is directly with division staff assigned by the executive director; and

4. The role of the executive director (and staff, current or seconded, assigned by the executive director) is to provide leadership for all aspects of this endeavor; the task is to guide and support persons engaged in these processes, and to identify writers; the executive's accountability is to the board of the Division for Church in Society and the bishop of this church;

To recall that the 1989 Churchwide Assembly of the Evangelical Lutheran Church in America established a process for the development of social statements (CA89.3.14), including directing that:

1. "The board . . . oversee the study process leading to a social statement, assuring that an appropriate group be named to study the issue and that ways be found to encourage broad participation by the congregations and members of our church";

2. "The board . . . review, if need be revise, and approve proposed social teaching statements, and recommend through the Church Council . . . that they be adopted by the Churchwide Assembly . . ."; and

3. "The Church Council shall review and act upon the recommendations of the board . . .; [and that] the Church Council may offer a report expressing its observations and recommendations on social teaching statements for the consideration of the Churchwide Assembly . . .";

To acknowledge the action of the Conference of Bishops of the Evangelical Lutheran Church in America on March 7, 1994, which (CB94.3.3):

1. Noted "with great encouragement the many examples of healthy deliberation taking place in congregations and synods of this church (in spite of attempts by some inside and outside this church to polarize this discussion in unhelpful and unuseful ways), and [noted] with particular joy the new contributions being made to the discussion by teachers of the Church (seminary and college faculty, pastors, and bishops)";

2. Affirmed the "effort to return the work toward a statement on human sexuality to its proper place in the life of this church, recognizing the significance this statement can have for our life together, but also affirming the primary work of this church, which is to be engaged in God's mission through the proclamation of the Gospel in witness and service";

3. Declared "great reluctance to rush to a conclusion in this matter, and...[urged that] this church to take the time necessary to engage fully its membership in this process, even if this means the work will not be completed before the Churchwide Assembly in 1995"; and

4. Expressed "the expectation that, in the midst of strong and sometimes conflicting views on these matters, members of this church will let zeal for their viewpoints be informed by compassion, humility, and grace";

To express as the Church Council of the Evangelical Lutheran Church in America gratitude for the constructive attention that members of congregations, pastors, seminary and college and university teachers, and others have devoted to the review and responses to the first draft of a possible social statement on the church and human sexuality; and

To solicit and affirm the continuing cooperation and contributions of the board of the Division for Church in Society, members of the task force on human sexuality, members of the consultation panel, the project director, the writing team, and others for the preparation of a second draft of a social statement on the church and human sexuality.

During discussion, Terry L. Bowes observed that the Church Council did not adequately express appreciation to the task force for its work. She moved the following:

MOVED;
SECONDED;
CARRIED: To amend the penultimate paragraph of the motion to read:

To express . . . gratitude to the task force on human sexuality for the time, effort, and expertise that task force members have devoted to developing the first draft of a human sexuality statement and . . .

During discussion of the foregoing amendment, Ramona S. Rank, who also serves on the consulting panel, concurred, noting the difficult and trying deliberations held by the council at its fall 1994 meeting. Edith M. Lohr, who also serves on the task force, also concurred, noting that the task force desired to function at the forefront of the development process.

The Rev. Nadine F. Lehr requested additional clarification about the functions of the various committees in developing the text of the document. The Rev. David G. Gabel observed that the writing team was not cited in the proposed resolution. Pastor Miller explained that the writing team functioned as staff under the direction of the executive director of the division. Pastor Gabel urged that the functions and responsibilities of the various parties involved be defined clearly. William E. Diehl requested additional clarification regarding the responsibilities of the writing team and other parties involved in the development of the text of the statement. Lorraine G. Bergquist inquired about the authorship of the first draft. Pastor Miller indicated that the Rev. Karen L. Bloomquist was the principal writer of the document at the direction of the task force. Edith M. Lohr underscored that the task force considered itself to be the author of the document. Bishop Peter Rogness inquired about the role of the executive director of the division in the writing of the document. Bishop Chilstrom observed that, despite authorship, the second draft ultimately would become the responsibility of the board of the Division for Church in Society. Pastor Miller noted that the board intended to exercise through the division's executive director greater oversight of the further development of the second draft. Cynthia P. Johnson inquired about the methodology in developing the eventual document as an evolving design process. Loren W. Mathre asked about the divisional staffing related to the study.

Pastor Gabel inquired about the implications of the development time line with respect to the function of the Church Council in authorizing release of the second draft. Chair Magnus indicated that the Executive Committee of the Church Council had considered the matter and would introduce a recommendation for council action later during this meeting.

Secretary Lowell G. Almen reviewed the proposed time line for such authorization. J. David Ellwanger expressed concern that the members of the Church Council would not have sufficient opportunity to respond to the text of the document. Chair Magnus explained that the Church Council would transmit its recommendations together with the document *per se* to the Churchwide Assembly. The Rev. David K. Johnson expressed reluctance to assign the responsibility of approving release of the document to the council's Executive Committee. Bishop Glenn W. Nycklemoe commented on the time line and recommended that completion of the task be expedited. Mr. Mathre observed that the time line may not be sufficient to result in adequate response and council approval through its Executive Committee. Ms. Bergquist requested further clarification of the critical "benchmarks" enabling eventual completion of the task and transmission to the Churchwide Assembly in 1995. The Rev. Stephen M. Youngdahl, speaking as a member of the Executive Committee, expressed reticence to approve distribution of the document without a clear perception of the preponderance of the council's opinion on the matter. William E. Diehl noted with caution the possibility that the text of the second draft could be released to the public by the board of the Division for Church in Society without Church Council's approval. The Rev. H. George Anderson gave notice of his desire to comment on the question of the length of the document. Patsy Gottschalk inquired about the use of congregational critique to the second draft in perfecting the final text, in view of the time line given for such response.

VOTED: *CC94.4.16*

To affirm the action of the board of the Division for Church in Society, in which that board, at its March 10-13, 1994, meeting defined the roles, tasks and accountabilities of the board, task force on human sexuality, consulting panel and staff, including the understandings that:

1. The role of the board of the Division for Church in Society is to establish direction and set policy; its task is to oversee staff management of the entire list of projects; its accountability is to the Church Council;
2. The role of the task force on human sexuality is to recommend content for the social statement; its task is to study and respond to the church's deliberation about the topics to be addressed in the social statement; its accountability is to the board of the Division for Church in Society; its work is directly with division staff assigned by the executive director;
3. The consulting panel's role is to advise the board of the Division for Church in Society and staff on key issues, themes, and content pertaining to the social statement; its task is to critique the first draft and future statement renditions and to make recommendations to the staff and board of the Division for Church in Society in this regard; its accountability is to the Church Council and the division's board; its work is directly with division staff assigned by the executive director; and
4. The role of the executive director (and staff, current or seconded, assigned by the executive director) is to provide leadership for all aspects of this endeavor; the task is to guide and support persons engaged in these processes, and to identify writers; the executive's accountability is to the board of the Division for Church in Society and the bishop of this church;

To recall that the 1989 Churchwide Assembly of the Evangelical Lutheran Church in America established a process for the development of social statements (CA89.3.14), including directing that:

1. "The board . . . oversee the study process leading to a social statement, assuring that an appropriate group be named to study the issue and that ways be found to encourage broad participation by the congregations and members of our church";
2. "The board . . . review, if need be revise, and approve proposed social teaching statements, and recommend through the Church Council . . . that they be adopted by the Churchwide Assembly . . ."; and
3. "The Church Council shall review and act upon the recommendations of the board . . .; [and that] the Church Council may offer a report expressing its observations and recommendations on social teaching statements for the consideration of the Churchwide Assembly . . .";

To acknowledge the action of the Conference of Bishops of the Evangelical Lutheran Church in America on March 7, 1994, which (CB94.3.3):

1. Noted "with great encouragement the many examples of healthy deliberation taking place in congregations and synods of this church (in spite of attempts by some inside and outside this church to polarize this discussion in unhelpful and unuseful ways), and [noted] with particular joy the new contributions being made to the discussion by teachers of the Church (seminary and college faculty, pastors, and bishops)";
2. Affirmed the "effort to return the work toward a statement on human sexuality to its proper place in the life of this church, recognizing the significance this statement can have for our life together, but also affirming the primary work of this church, which is to be engaged in God's mission through the proclamation of the Gospel in witness and service";
3. Declared "great reluctance to rush to a conclusion in this matter, and...[urged that] this church to take the time necessary to engage fully its membership in this process, even if this means the work will not be completed before the Churchwide Assembly in 1995"; and
4. Expressed "the expectation that, in the midst of strong and sometimes conflicting views on these matters, members of this church will let zeal for their viewpoints be informed by compassion, humility, and grace";

To express as the Church Council of the Evangelical Lutheran Church in America gratitude to the task force on human sexuality for the time, effort, and expertise that task force members have devoted to developing the first draft of a human sexuality statement and for the constructive attention that members of congregations, pastors, seminary and college and university teachers, and others have devoted to the review and responses to the first draft of a possible social statement on the church and human sexuality; and

To solicit and affirm the continuing cooperation and contributions of the board of the Division for Church in Society, members of the task force on human sexuality, members of the consultation panel, the project director, the writing team, and others for the preparation of a second draft of a social statement on the church and human sexuality.

The Rev. H. George Anderson inquired about how the limitation of the length of the document was determined. He recommended that there be flexibility in restricting the length of the text.

Secretary Almen moved the following recommendation of the Executive Committee:

MOVED;
SECONDED: To authorize the Executive Committee of the Church Council, contingent upon favorable action by the board of the Division for Church in Society on a second draft of a social statement on the church and human sexuality, to affirm distribution of such a second draft to the congregations of the Evangelical Lutheran Church in America.

During the discussion of the foregoing motion, Pastor Youngdahl inquired whether the response of the Conference of Bishops would be available to council members prior to the decision of the Executive Committee. Mr. Ellwanger inquired further about the function of the Executive Committee in this matter. He moved the following:

MOVED;
SECONDED;
CARRIED: To postpone consideration until after lunch.

Recognition of Relationship of Independent Lutheran Organizations

Background: The *Constitution, Bylaws, and Continuing Resolutions of the Evangelical Lutheran Church in America* assigns to the Division for Global Mission the following task: "be responsible for this church's relationship to mission societies, organizations, and movements in North America that focus on mission in other countries: (ELCA continuing resolution 16.11.F91.b.).

The *Constitution, Bylaws, and Continuing Resolutions of the Evangelical Lutheran Church in America* assigns the responsibility for establishing criteria and policies for relationships with independent Lutheran organizations to the Department for Ecumenical Affairs,

the Church Council, and the Churchwide Assembly: "This church, through its Department for Ecumenical Affairs and by action of the Churchwide Assembly, shall establish the general policies to govern official relationships with independent Lutheran organizations that seek to relate with this church while maintaining their independence and autonomy" (ELCA bylaw 8.51.01.).

Further, a bylaw provides: "The Church Council shall establish the criteria and policies for the relationships between this church and independent, cooperative, and related Lutheran organizations. The policies adopted by the Church Council shall be administered by the appropriate unit of the churchwide organization. The fiscal determination of which organization shall relate to a specific unit of the churchwide organization shall be made by the Church Council" (ELCA bylaw 14.21.05.).

In the absence of any relevant policies provided by the ELCA Church Council, the Department for Ecumenical Affairs, or the Churchwide Assembly, it became necessary for the Division for Global Mission to establish a policy, criteria, and process for recognition of relationship with independent Lutheran organizations that wish to formalize their relationship with ELCA Division for Global Mission. It is assumed that these are organizations that relate to mission purposes and geographic areas assigned to the Division for Global Mission by the Evangelical Lutheran Church in America. The terminology, "recognition of relationship," is used, rather than terms such as "endorsement" or "approval."

The board of the Division for Global Mission voted to approve the "Process for Recognition of Relationship of Independent Lutheran Organizations with the Division for Global Mission, Evangelical Lutheran Church in America," as amended, and the "Criteria for Reviewing an Organization for Recognition of Relationship with Division for Global Mission, the Evangelical Lutheran Church in America," as the policy by which independent Lutheran organizations will receive recognition of relationship with the Division for Global Mission, the Evangelical Lutheran Church in America. The process and criteria for recognition of relationship were printed in council agenda Exhibit Q, Part 1.

Council Action: Chair Magnus called upon the Rev. Mark W. Thomsen, executive director of the Division for Global Mission, to introduce the following resolution:

VOTED: CC94.4.17
To accept as interim operational guidelines the "Process for Recognition of Relationship of Independent Lutheran Organizations with the Division for Global Missions, Evangelical Lutheran Church in America," and the "Criteria for Reviewing an Organization for Recognition of Relationships with the Division for Global Mission, the Evangelical Lutheran Church in America"; and

To refer this matter to the Office of the Secretary for further consideration as part of the review of the overall policy governing the relationships between the Evangelical Lutheran Church in America and independent Lutheran organizations.

PROCESS FOR RECOGNITION OF RELATIONSHIP OF INDEPENDENT LUTHERAN ORGANIZATIONS WITH THE DIVISION FOR GLOBAL MISSION, THE EVANGELICAL LUTHERAN CHURCH IN AMERICA

Step 1. The organization inquires for information from the division.

Step 2. The division shares relevant information including the process toward *recognition of relationship*, questions to be answered, material to be supplied by the organization.

Step 3. The organization submits requested information to the division.

Step 4. A division staff screening committee reviews the request and makes recommendation to the executive staff.

Step 5. The executive staff recommends to the board for action.

Step 6. The division informs the organization of the board's decision and takes appropriate steps for implementation, including the development of a *Memorandum of Agreement*.

Questions
(to be answered in writing to the Division for Global Mission)

1. Why does your organization seek *recognition of relationship* with the Division for Global Mission?

2. In fulfilling its mission commitments, how would your organization assist the Division for Global Mission?

3. How does your organization carry out global mission commitments and activities that the Division for Global Mission is unable to fulfill?

4. How would your organization use the *recognition of relationship* with ELCA/DGM in its interpretation and fund-raising publicity?

5. Describe your organization's relationship to other church's ecumenical agencies. Have you requested recognition from any other church agency?

Materials to be Submitted to the Division by the Requesting Organization

1. Copies of relevant descriptive documents such as constitution, purpose statement, policies, guidelines, budget.

2. Samples of publicity and fund-raising materials.

3. List of staff, leaders, board members or other persons involved in the organization.

CRITERIA FOR REVIEWING AN ORGANIZATION FOR RECOGNITION OF RELATIONSHIP WITH THE DIVISION FOR GLOBAL MISSION, THE EVANGELICAL LUTHERAN CHURCH IN AMERICA

(This criteria is to be used by the staff and board in considering the requests for recognition of relationship.)

1. **Compatibility with ELCA**. The organization's purpose and activities are compatible with the following sections of the ELCA constitution: Confession of Faith, Nature of the Church, Statement of Purpose and Principles of Organization.

2. **Focus for Mission.** The organization's purpose and activities are compatible with the commitments to mission as envisioned and stated in the board's policy documents.

3. **Global Focus.** The organization's activities are global in their scope.

4. **Extends DGM's ministry.** The organization fulfills ministries that expand or extend ELCA/DGM's outreach; they fulfill a function ELCA/DGM is unable to provide.

5. **Documents.** The organization has a constitution or a purpose statement.

6. **Overseas' program and partners.** The organization's purpose and activities are compatible with DGM's overseas program; the organization is acceptable to ELCA/DGM's partner(s) in the country(s) where the activities are being conducted.

7. **Constituency.** The organization's membership is church-wide in its scope. If it is primarily local or regional, DGM will suggest it seek *recognition of relationship* with the ELCA synod and/or region where it resides.

8. **Leadership.** The organization is intentional in securing leadership on its board and staff that is diverse in gender, culture and ethnicity.

9. **Funding.** The organization's financial operation is transparent; the method and scope of its fund-raising is compatible with ELCA funding processes.

10. **Accountability.** The organization will agree to appropriate methods of accountability to ELCA/DGM in return for *recognition of relationship*. Such agreements might include DGM representation on its board and periodic programmatic and financial reports.

11. **Reciprocity.** The organization commits itself to the principle of reciprocity in its relationship to the ELCA/DGM; that is, support of the ELCA/DGM in its goals for mission and refraining from publicity or fund-raising techniques that diminish the ELCA/DGM's public image or effectiveness in mission.

12. **Publicity.** The organization and ELCA/DGM agree to the specific phraseology that describes the relationship to the ELCA/DGM in the organization's publicity.

13. **Review of Relationship.** The organization agrees to review the relationship every three years.

During discussion of the foregoing resolution, the Rev. Franklin D. Fry inquired about the vulnerability of this church to legal liability as a result of its adoption. General Counsel David J. Hardy explained that the document defining the relationship between this church and such organizations. Secretary Lowell G. Almen commended the division for its responsible management of this matter.

Stewardship Survey

Chair Magnus distributed a questionnaire to council members. The Church Council recessed at 12:17 P.M. The Church Council reconvened 1:35 P.M. The Rev. Mark R. Moller-Gunderson commented on the stewardship survey that council members had been requested to complete.

Study of Human Sexuality

During the previous session, Secretary Lowell G. Almen had moved the following motion on behalf of the Executive Committee of the Church Council:

MOVED;
SECONDED: To authorize the Executive Committee of the Church Council, contingent upon favorable action by the board of the Division for Church in Society on a second draft of a Social Statement on the Church and Human Sexuality, to affirm distribution of such a second draft to the congregations of the Evangelical Lutheran Church in America.

Chair Magnus reviewed the following schedule recommended by the Executive Committee of the Church Council:

Schedule for Church Council Approval
Of Distribution of Second Draft of
Proposed Document on Human Sexuality

Late September	Embargoed draft sent to board of Division for Church in Society, Church Council, and Conference of Bishops.
Sept. 29-Oct. 1	Division for Church in Society board meets.
October 3-4	Conference of Bishops discusses document and adopts possible response.
October 4	Church Council is faxed actions of the board and Conference of Bishops.
October 5-6	Church Council members telephone assigned Executive Committee members.
October 6	(10:00 P.M. Eastern Time) Executive Committee telephone conference call; Executive Committee authorizes distribution of second draft in accordance with the opinion of two-thirds of council members responding in agreement with such distribution.

Dale V. Sandstrom inquired who would determine the content of the final document delivered to the board of the Division for Church in Society. The Rev. Charles S. Miller Jr., executive director of the Division for Church in Society, responded that the executive director and the writing team would be responsible for that content. The Rev. Richard G. Deines questioned the realism of the time line for completion of the task. Chair Magnus indicated that the Executive Committee had considered that issue and favored expedition of completion. The Rev. H. George Anderson observed that the Church Council was acting in order to afford congregations as much opportunity as possible to study and respond to the second draft; the Church Council would have opportunity to act again on the matter at its April 1995 meeting. The Rev. James G. Cobb observed that the Church Council's final recommendation might be determined as late as its August 1995 meeting should additional time to perfect the document is required.

VOTED: **CC94.4.18**

To authorize the Executive Committee of the Church Council, contingent upon favorable action by the board of the Division for Church in Society on a second draft of a social statement on the church and human sexuality, to affirm distribution of such a second draft to the congregations of the Evangelical Lutheran Church in America.

Report of the
Budget and Finance Committee

Chair Magnus called upon Edith M. Lohr, chair of the Budget and Finance Committee, to report on behalf of the committee.

1.   Keystones Project

Background: At its March 1993 meeting, the Church Council took the following action:

To authorize, contingent upon approval of a business plan by the Budget and Finance Committee and the bishop, the development

of a pilot project coordinated by the Division for Ministry as recommended by the Stewardship Strategy Development Committee, "Keystones: A Partnership Program of Interpretation, Learning, and Support for Theological Education in the Evangelical Lutheran Church in America" (Exhibit F, Part 4) [CC93.3.20].

Council Action: Ms. Lohr noted that no further action on the Keystones Project was anticipated. She stated that the Budget and Finance Committee had determined that any further reconsideration of the project would begin with examination of a business plan.

2.   1994 Expenditure Authorization

Background: At its December 1993 meeting, the Church Council took the following action in regard to the 1994 spending authorization:

To approve an initial 1994 fiscal year spending authorization of $77,190,000, with an initial Mission Operating Fund allocation of $1,500,000;

To approve an initial 1994 World Hunger spending authorization of $12,250,000; and

To authorize the Church Council Executive Committee to change the 1994 spending authorization, after review and recommendation of the Church Council Budget and Finance Committee, between meetings of the full Church Council (CC93.12.124).

The final receipts from synods in the form of mission support totaled $63,052,852, or approximately $1.7 million less than was received in fiscal 1992 and $1.35 million less than the revised 1993 income estimate. After review of this and other sources of income, the 1994 income estimate was reduced by $1,800,000. This included a reduction in the 1994 estimate for mission support to approximately the amount received in fiscal 1993, or $63,000,000. Along with other reductions, the total income estimate was reduced $2,000,000, offset by an increase in the estimate income from the newly established annual churchwide offering. The net reduction is $1,800,000.

Acting upon the recommendation of the Budget and Finance Committee, the Executive Committee took the following action:

To approve a revised 1994 fiscal year spending authorization of $75,390,000, with a Mission Operating Fund allocation of $1,500,000; and

To authorize the Office of the Bishop and the Office of the Treasurer to change the 1994 World Hunger spending authorization after review of final 1993 operating results.

World Hunger income estimates need to be lowered as well. After reviewing the final income amounts for 1993 and discussion with the inter-unit staff team for world hunger, the spending authorization was reduced to 93 percent ($11,392,500) of the original $12,250,000 income estimate.

Following the March 2, 1994, telephone conference call of the Executive Committee, unit allocations—council agenda Exhibit F, Part 1a—were implemented. Specific unit reductions enumerated in council agenda Exhibit F, Part 1b were reviewed by unit boards and steering committees at their spring meetings.

At its March 2, 1994, meeting the Executive Committee recommended that the Church Council engage in a discussion of budgetary priorities. In this round of budget cuts, the following areas received priority, in consonance with the prior action of the Church Council:

- starting new congregations, supporting urban and rural ministries, and providing support for congregations in evangelism and worship;
- missionary compensation; and
- grants to seminaries.

These functions were reduced by approximately one percent. Since these priorities total $20,902,395 of the $75,690,000 current budget for churchwide units, a one percent level of reduction has meant that other churchwide functions received far heavier reductions—approximately 4.5 percent on balance—as the $1.8 million spending reduction was implemented. The Executive Committee suggested that the Church Council discuss the degree to which the aforementioned priorities should be maintained, given the impact on other important churchwide functions. The impact on small units is also an issue to be considered, in response to the request of the Program and Structure Committee, made at the council's December 1993 meeting.

Council Action: The Church Council received the foregoing as information.

3. Budget Reduction for the Commission for Women

Background: At its October 1993 meeting, the Steering Committee of the Commission for Women voted the following:

RESOLVED, that the Steering Committee of the ELCA Commission for Women request the ELCA Church Council, through the Program and Structure Committee of the Church Council, to call for an immediate moratorium on budget cuts for the Commission for Women and continue through the biennium.

The Program and Structure Committee reviewed this request and recommended that the Church Council take the action noted below. The Church Council voted:

To refer the following recommendation of the Program and Structure Committee to the Executive Committee of the Church Council:

To request a moratorium on budget reductions for the Commission for Women until April 1994, when the Program and Structure Committee will review the constitutional mandate of the Commission for Women;

To request that the Steering Committee of the Commission for Women prepare options for consideration by the Program and Structure Committee at its April 1994 meeting;

To request that the Budget and Finance Committee review the implication of budget reductions on similarly situated smaller units; and

To request the Office of the Bishop to provide information related to the "larger picture," including implications on other units.

At its March 2, 1994, meeting, the Executive Committee discussed this recommendation when it reviewed the revised unit allocations for 1994, which were recommended by the Office of the Bishop. However, the committee did not authorize a moratorium on budget reductions for the commission. The issue of the impact of further reductions on smaller units was discussed at the pre-council meeting of the Budget and Finance Committee, in preparation for the council's discussion of budgetary priorities and their impact on other churchwide functions.

Council Action: The Church Council received the foregoing as information. Further discussion of this matter is recorded below.

4. Synodical Fiscal Year

Background: The following information was received from the Upper Susquehanna Synod:

The Synod Council of the Upper Susquehanna Synod requests that the ELCA Church Council take appropriate action to begin the constitutional process of changing the financial year of the synods of the Evangelical Lutheran Church in America from a fiscal year beginning February 1 and ending January 31, to the calendar year.

There are two primary reasons for this request. First, changing the synods to a calendar year would remove a great deal of confusion that arises as one tries to explain the different congregational income figures that appear in synod treasurers' reports (congregations' calendar year giving figures and the synod's fiscal year figures). This presents difficulty not only for Synod Council members as we plan for future budgets, but also for voting members and pastors at the assembly. This makes a process, which is already difficult, even harder to understand. There can also be a sense that the "church is playing games" with budgets.

Second, changing the synods to a calendar year would simplify matters for the synod staff person who is responsible for the bookkeeping, specifically, in reporting to congregations and in all matters related to payroll, i.e., FICA payments to clergy persons [and] calculating salaries for entry into the computer, in order to obtain the correct gross salary at the end of the year.

When this matter was discussed in the March 1993 meeting, the Church Council noted that final action on any possible amendment of ELCA 10.73., which sets the beginning of the fiscal year, could not be accomplished prior to the 1995 Churchwide Assembly, according to ELCA 22.11. The council voted:

To refer the resolution of the Upper Susquehanna Synod on the synodical fiscal year to the Office of the Bishop;

To request that the Office of the Bishop, in consultation with the Office of the Treasurer and Conference of Bishops, bring a report and possible recommendation through the Budget and Finance Committee and subsequently through the Legal and Constitutional Review Committee to the April 1994 meeting of the Church Council; and

To request the ELCA secretary to convey this action to the Upper Susquehanna Synod (CC93.3.42).

This matter was considered at the March 1994 meeting of the Conference of Bishops. By a "straw vote," the bishops overwhelmingly indicated their desire that the timing of the beginning and ending of the fiscal year remain unchanged.

Council Action: The Church Council adopted the following recommendation of the Budget and Finance Committee without discussion:

VOTED: *CC94.4.19*

To decline to change the financial year for synods, as requested by the Upper Susquehanna Synod; and

To request the secretary of this church to convey this information to the Upper Susquehanna Synod.

5. Executive Committee Authorization

Council Action: The Church Council adopted the following recommendation of the Budget and Finance Committee without discussion:

VOTED: *CC94.4.20*
To authorize the Church Council Executive Committee, upon recommendation from the Church Council Budget and Finance Committee, to establish spending authorizations between Church Council meetings.

6. 1994 and 1995 Synodical Mission-Support Commitments

Background: The Budget and Finance Committee discussed the following matters at its April 15, 1994, meeting:

- Follow-up on the Church Council's responses to 1994 commitments, made at its December 1993 meeting;
- Revisions in 1994 synod commitments made since the December 1994 Church Council meeting; and
- Response to 1995 synod commitments.

The latest information from synods on these matters was distributed to council members in the "Synodical Mission Support Commitments Worksheet" (council agenda Exhibit A, Part 3i). That exhibit displayed each synod by region for the years 1992-1995.

During its February 1993 conference call, the Budget and Finance Committee requested the preparation of a report comparing ELCA financial trends of support through congregations with similar denominations. The committee also requested an analysis of the 1993 results. This report (council agenda Exhibit F, Part 3) provided information related to the proposed action on commitments from synods for 1995 mission support and revisions in the 1994 commitments.

Synods commonly have revised their estimated income and, therefore, the amount they anticipate forwarding to the churchwide organization of unrestricted income received from congregations. Synods have not been uniform in their practice of informing the churchwide organization of these changes. Notification usually has been received only when synods were specifically asked for revisions or by happenstance in general conversations. With increasing regularity, synods also change the percentage of congregational mission support shared with the churchwide organization. Since the December 1993 Church Council meeting, six synods have decreased their percentage amounts and one has increased it.

1994 Requested Responses to Church Council Action

At its December 1993 meeting, the Church Council developed eleven different categories of response to the "1994 synodical mission-support commitments." In four of those categories, additional information or discussion was requested; in three, action was referred to the council's Executive Committee pending additional discussion and information. Information has been received and discussions were held with synods since the December 1993 Church Council meeting. Synods have suggested that the time period between synod council action on the 1994 commitments and Church Council action does not allow synods time to alter their 1994 plans already under way. Discussions will continue with all synods in order to find a pattern for holding discussions in a way that allows for all parties to act in a practical time frame. Given the circumstances, changes in percentages for those synods are highly improbable.

Council Action: During discussion of the following recommendation of the Budget and Finance Committee, Loren W. Mathre inquired whether the original commitments had been approved previously on the basis of percentage. Ms. Lohr responded affirmatively.

VOTED: *CC94.4.21*
To approve the 1994 mission support for the following synods, recognizing the circumstances surrounding the decisions made on 1994 mission support; continued consultation is requested before mission-support levels for 1995 can be approved:

Alaska, Southwestern Washington, Northwest Washington, and Northern Texas-Northern Louisiana.

To remove the word "conditional" in its earlier approval of the 1994 synodical commitment for the following synods, granting approval for the 1994 commitment:

Upper Susquehanna and Virginia.

To express thanks to the following synod and *approval* for its 1994 synodical commitment to mission support and partnership in the Gospel:

Metropolitan Chicago.

1994 Synod Revisions Since Church Council Response

Background: The Church Council was required to respond to changes and revisions in 1994 synodical mission support made by synods since the council's last meeting. Further revisions and confirmations of their 1994 commitments were received from thirty-two synods. As noted above, six synods lowered the percentage of unrestricted congregational income they anticipate sharing with the churchwide organization; only one increased the percentage. All revisions resulted in lowered dollar estimates for mission support. While changes in estimated income by synods are understandable, changing the *percentage* to be shared with the churchwide organization after Church Council approval has been given, is problematic at worst, troublesome at least.

Council Action: During discussion of the following recommendation of the Budget and Finance Committee, Loren W. Mathre inquired about the nature of the adjustments being made by the synods to their commitments. Treasurer Richard L. McAuliffe noted that the revised commitments represent an almost $3 million decrease.

Discussion turned to the reasons for requests from synods for adjusting their mission support commitments. Carlos Peña requested examples of the stated reasons for such reductions. Treasurer McAuliffe drew attention to council agenda Exhibit F, Part 3, which listed contributing factors. The Rev. Mark R. Moller-Gunderson, executive director of the Division for Congregational Ministries, who authored the exhibit, elaborated. D. Mark Klever inquired about the impact of the possible social statement on human sexuality on such reductions. W. Jeanne Rapp inquired about the affect of the lowered commitments on the current expenditure authorization.

VOTED: **CC94.4.22**

To acknowledge the revised income estimates for the following synods, which remain consistent with the agreement approved by the Church Council in December 1993:

> Northwest Washington, Sierra Pacific, Pacifica, Rocky Mountain, South Dakota, Minneapolis Area, Nebraska, Arkansas-Oklahoma, Texas-Louisiana Gulf Coast, Metropolitan Chicago, Northwest Synod of Wisconsin, Indiana-Kentucky, Northwestern Ohio, Southern Ohio, New Jersey, New England, Metropolitan New York, Slovak Zion, Southwestern Pennsylvania, Upper Susquehanna, Delaware-Maryland, North Carolina, Southeastern, and Florida-Bahamas.

VOTED: **CC94.4.23**

To request consultation with the Office of the Bishop, for changes made in the percentage of mission support from the following synods, since approval was given at the December 1993 Church Council meeting:

> Northwestern Minnesota, Saint Paul Area, Eastern North Dakota, Northeastern Ohio, Southeastern Minnesota, and Southeast Michigan.

VOTED: **CC94.4.24**

WHEREAS, the North/West Lower Michigan Synod has decreased the dollar estimate for mission support and *increased* the percentage the mission support represents of unrestricted congregational income; therefore, be it

RESOLVED, that the Church Council acknowledges the revised estimate of mission support of the North/West Lower Michigan Synod and expresses its gratefulness for synodical commitment to mission support and partnership in the Gospel.

1995 Synodical Mission-Support Commitments

Background: At its December 1993 meeting, the Budget and Finance Committee reviewed and acted on 1994 synod mission-support commitments and reviewed the process and time line for 1995 synod commitments. According to that time line, the Church Council is to act on "1995 synodical mission-support commitments" at the April 1994 meeting.

Changes in the percentage of mission support for 1995 have occurred in some synods. For others, however, action must be delayed until final resolution of the 1994 agreements.

Council Action: The following recommendations of the Budget and Finance Committee was adopted without further discussion:

> NOTE: *Approval for 1995 mission support for the following synods needed to be delayed (1) because of the resolution of their 1994 mission support levels; and (2) because they have reduced the mission-support percentage to levels requiring further consultation:*

VOTED: **CC94.4.24**

To withhold approval until consultations can be held, with final approval anticipated during the November 1994 Church Council meeting for the following synods:

> Northwestern Minnesota, Saint Paul Area, Eastern North Dakota, Northeastern Ohio, Southeastern Minnesota, Southeast Michigan, Alaska, Southwestern Washington, Northwest Washington, Northern Texas-Northern Louisiana, Northwestern Pennsylvania, Montana, Texas-Louisiana Gulf Coast, and Florida-Bahamas.

VOTED: **CC94.4.25**

> NOTE: *The following synods slightly decreased the mission support percentage shared with the churchwide organization.*

To express thanks and *approval* to the following synods for their 1995 synodical commitments to mission support and to encourage these synods to increase their percentage of mission support in 1996:

> Upper Susquehanna, North Carolina, South Carolina, Southwestern Pennsylvania, Sierra-Pacific, Western Iowa, Virginia, New Jersey, and Central States.

> NOTE: *The following synods held the percentage of mission support shared with the churchwide organization at levels consistent with the past.*

To express thanks and approval to the following synods for their 1995 synodical commitment to mission support:

Upstate New York, Southern Ohio, Southeastern, East-Central Synod of Wisconsin, Minneapolis Area, Metropolitan Washington, D.C., Lower Susquehanna, Oregon, Southwestern Minnesota, Northern Great Lakes, Northeastern Minnesota, Northern Illinois, Central/Southern Illinois, Pacifica, North/West Lower Michigan, Northeastern Pennsylvania, Allegheny, South Dakota, Delaware-Maryland, Nebraska, Southeastern Iowa, Northwestern Ohio, Eastern Washington/Idaho, New England, Indiana-Kentucky, Northwest Synod of Wisconsin, Metropolitan New York, West Virginia-Western Maryland, and LaCrosse Area.

NOTE: The following synods have increased the percentage of mission support shared with the churchwide organization.

To express thanks and approval for their steady support to the following synods for their 1995 synodical commitment to mission support:

Southwestern Texas, South-Central Synod of Wisconsin, Greater Milwaukee, Grand Canyon, Metropolitan Chicago, Rocky Mountain, Southeastern Pennsylvania, Southern California (West), Northeastern Iowa, Arkansas-Oklahoma, and Western North Dakota.

The following synod has not yet responded concerning its 1995 synod commitment for mission support:

VOTED: *CC94.4.26*
To refer action on the 1995 synod mission-support commitment for the following synod to the Church Council's Executive Committee until additional information is received from the synod: Caribbean.

The following synod submitted a proposal for 1995 synodical mission support based on a plan to operate in a fiscally sound manner while returning mission support to previous levels in the near future.

VOTED: *CC94.4.27*
To approve the 1995 synod mission-support commitment of the following synod: Slovak-Zion.

7. Mission Support Policy

Council Action: Ms. Lohr introduced the following recommendation of the Budget and Finance Committee, subsequently adopted by the Church Council:

VOTED: *CC94.4.28*
To request representation from the Conference of Bishops to work with churchwide staff on the process and formula for mission support, to be reported to the 1995 Churchwide Assembly.

During discussion of the foregoing action, William T. Billings requested additional information about the composition of the work group assigned to this matter. Ms. Lohr explained that the resolution was intended to encourage the members of the Conference of Bishops to continue in conversation about this matter.

Discussion of Budget Priorities

The Rev. Robert N. Bacher, executive for administration, introduced discussion of express areas of budgetary priority. He highlighted a discussion paper on how decisions regarding budgetary priorities are determined and applied.

During discussion, William E. Diehl stated that at the time the council adopted the three areas of budgetary priority (global mission; theological education; and establishing and supporting outreach ministries), he did not fully realize the degree of impact the decision would have on the work of other churchwide ministries. He questioned whether the present level of priority for the three areas should be maintained or adjusted at this time. Edith M. Lohr stated that the Budget and Finance Committee had determined to request unit directors to prioritize the work of their units in preparation of the 1996-1997 budget proposal. Carlos Peña inquired about what specific strategies were in place to address the matter with respect to the income side of the budget and synodical mission-support commitments. The Rev. Franklin D. Fry inquired about the patterns of congregational giving and benevolence in other church bodies.

Secretary Lowell G. Almen observed that synodical assemblies have expressed affirmation of the council's action in setting the three areas of budgetary priority.

William E. Diehl moved the following, in order "to test the degree of priority" that should be placed upon the three stated budgetary areas:

MOVED;
SECONDED: To stipulate that, should future operating reductions need to be made, the average percentage of reduction in non-protected areas not exceed two-times the average percentage of reduction in priority areas.

Edith M. Lohr inquired whether the intent was to limit the motion to the current biennium. Mr. Diehl stated that it was. Treasurer Richard L. McAuliffe questioned whether the motion was achievable. Loren W. Mathre spoke against the motion in deference to the desires of congregations. The Rev. Donald M. Hallberg also spoke against the motion, requesting factual data.

The Rev. Franklin D. Fry moved the following:

MOVED;
SECONDED: To refer the motion to appropriate staff for study and recommendation at a future meeting of the Church Council.

J. David Ellwanger spoke against the motion to refer, in order to conserve staff time and because he believed the original motion would fail. Edith M. Lohr spoke against referral, stating that the Budget and Finance Committee would be required to act on this issue prior to the next meeting of the Church Council. William T. Billings supported the motion to refer.

Deborah S. Yandala recommended that the motion be amended to refer the matter to the Budget and Finance Committee and the Executive Committee of the Church Council, rather than full Church Council. The suggestion was received as a friendly amendment. Edith M. Lohr observed that the referral was redundant, because staff already were addressing the matter.

MOVED;
SECONDED;
DEFEATED: To refer the motion to appropriate staff for study and recommendation to the Budget and Finance Committee and Executive Committee of the Church Council.

Karen M. Dietz commented that the council must place its trust in the persons making decisions about specific budgetary adjustments and protecting those areas the council has determined to have priority. William T. Billings inquired about the achievability the proposed resolution with respect to the specification, "average." Pastor Bacher responded affirmatively. J. David Ellwanger stated that, in his opinion, the priority areas should not be reduced at all. The Rev. Stephen M. Youngdahl noted that future budgetary adjustments to the priority areas could in theory exceed the one percent of the most recent reductions.

MOVED;
SECONDED;
DEFEATED: To stipulate that, should future operating reductions need to be made, the average percentage of reduction in non-protected areas not exceed two-times the average percentage of reduction in priority areas.

Chair Magnus recognized Robert S. Schroeder who stated a concern that theological education was a broader concept than seminary education *per se* and that theological education in the broadest sense was not being treated as a protected budgetary priority. He moved:

MOVED;
SECONDED: To make restoration of grants to non-seminary theological education areas, including continuing education centers and scholarships for theological study, a priority for distribution of 1994 annual church-wide offering [Vision for Mission] receipts.

Edith M. Lohr indicated that the motion would have no effect until those receipts exceeded $1.2 million dollars, which already were committed to the general budget. The Rev. Joseph M. Wagner stated that the issue facing the Church Council was to set priorities. He was not prepared to comment on the priority of continuing education in deference to other budgetary needs. The Rev. Donald M. Hallberg cautioned against micro-management of the budget. Mr. Schroeder stated that the intent of his motion was to redefine theological education in a broader sense.

MOVED;
SECONDED;
DEFEATED: To make restoration of grants to non-seminary theological education areas, including continuing education centers and scholarships for theological study, a priority for distribution of 1994 annual church-wide offering ["Vision for Mission"] receipts.

A division of the house was called, which indicated that the motion had failed [7—Yes; 22—No].

The Rev. David G. Gabel observed that ELCA stewardship materials "were not up to par," and requested that the Church Council consider the matter of marketing. D. Mark Klever concurred that the issue should be addressed. Chair Magnus recommended that discussion of the question be deferred until staff members of the Division for Congregational Ministries were scheduled to report on matters related to that unit.

The Rev. Franklin D. Fry requested information on additional expenses related to the release of the initial draft of a possible social statement on human sexuality. The Rev. Charles S. Miller Jr. stated that cost related in the past biennium totaled approximately $27,000. He stated that the costs in 1994 were expected to be greater, but that such costs would be absorbed by the unit's personnel budget. Robert S. Schroeder observed that the cost of the study to this church was beyond monetary costs. The Rev. Philip L. Natwick commented on the need to keep the matter of the election of a new bishop of this church before the church's consciousness.

Report of the Program and Structure Committee

1. **Review of the Division for Global Mission and Division for Higher Education and Schools**
   Background: The ELCA governing documents call on the Church Council, through its Program and Structure Committee to "establish a process for the review of at least two churchwide units each biennium so as to review all units within a ten-year period. Such review shall include the recommendation for renewal of the mandate for the churchwide unit or recommendation of an alternative structure through which the unit's purposes shall be accomplished" (ELCA continuing resolution 14.41.D91.).

   The Program and Structure Committee has begun a review of the Division for Global Mission. The committee's plan includes a review of the Division for Higher Education and Schools during the 1993-1995 biennium.

Council Action: Chair Magnus called upon the Rev. Stephen M. Youngdahl, chair of the Program and Structure Committee, to report on behalf of the committee. He indicated that the committee's review of the Division for Global Mission would be transmitted to the Church Council in April 1995. He reported that the review of the Division for Higher Education and Schools was being delayed in light of the "Inquiry" study.

The Church Council received the foregoing as information.

2. Matters Related to Commissions

Council Action: Pastor Youngdahl indicated that the committee had considered the ramifications for the ministry of this church with respect to the recent restructuring of the Commission for Multicultural Ministries due to budgetary restrictions.

The Church Council received the foregoing as information.

3. Ongoing Review of the Work of Churchwide Units

Background: Each churchwide unit has prepared a summary of unit activities (council agenda Exhibit H, Part 1a), and a digest of board and steering committee actions (council agenda Exhibit H, Part 1b).

The Church Council received the foregoing as information.

4. Regions

Background: An update on the work of the regions was presented as council agenda Exhibit H, Part 2.

The Church Council received the foregoing as information.

5. Changes Related to Regional Structures

The Steering Committee of Region 4 took the following action at its meeting January 24, 1994:

To recommend to the Church Council that the Steering Committee of Region 4 be comprised of the six synodical bishops and a churchwide representative, effective August 1, 1994.

To recommend that this action be ratified by the six synod councils of Region 4.

According to ELCA 18.11.21. and 18.11.31., staffing and governance patterns for regions are to be ratified by the Church Council.

Council Action: The Church Council approved the following recommendation in *en bloc* action take at the conclusion of this meeting.

EN BLOC   [CC94.4.43]

To approve the change in the composition of the Steering Committee of Region 4 to be comprised of the six synodical bishops and a churchwide representative, effective August 1, 1994, pending ratification by the six synod councils of Region 4 prior to August 1, 1994.

Inquiry: The Future of the Churchwide Organization

Background: A proposal, "Inquiry: The Future of the Churchwide Organization," was discussed at the December 1993 meeting of the Church Council. That document was printed in council agenda Exhibit B, Part 1a. *[Note: This document was distributed earlier to council members as council agenda Exhibit E, Part 1e, of the December 1993 agenda.]*

After discussion of this proposal, the council voted:

To affirm in principle the direction outlined in the proposal "Inquiry: The Future of the Churchwide Organization";

To instruct the Office of the Bishop to develop and implement plans for this initiative, in consultation with the Executive Committee of the Church Council;

To provide for a joint meeting of the Executive Committee and the Program and Structure Committee of the Church Council immediately prior to the April 1994 Church Council meeting; and

To request that a report on specific plans and activities related to this initiative be provided by the Office of the Bishop to the April 1994 Church Council meeting (CC93.12.88).

Since the council's December 1993 meeting, the Executive Committee discussed this matter with the Office of the Bishop and reviewed preliminary tools that could be used in the inquiry process. Following the committee's conversation at its January 24-25, 1994, meeting, Bishop Herbert W. Chilstrom appointed the following persons to serve on an advisory committee for the inquiry process:

- Rev. H. George Anderson (*Chair*), President, Luther College, Decorah, Iowa;
- Rev. Paul J. Blom, Bishop, Texas-Louisiana Gulf Coast Synod, ELCA, Houston, Tex.;
- Kay Conrad, Winston Salem, N.C.;
- Charles Y. Glock, former Professor of Sociology of Religion, University of California, Berkeley, retired, Sand Point, Idaho;
- Rev. Laura L. Klick, Pastor, Grace Lutheran Church, Allentown, Pa.;
- Kathy J. Magnus, ELCA Vice President, Denver, Colo.;
- Rev. Gerald W. Nelson, Pastor, Our Saviour's Lutheran Church, Naperville, Ill.;
- Athornia Steele, Columbus, Ohio; and
- David L. Tiede, President, Luther Northwestern Theological Seminary, St. Paul, Minn.

The following persons will staff this process:
- Robert N. Bacher, Executive for Administration, Office of the Bishop;
- Kenneth W. Inskeep, Director, Department for Research and Evaluation; and
- Lita Brusick Johnson, Assistant to the Bishop, Office of the Bishop.

On Thursday, April 14, 1994, the Church Council's Executive Committee and the Program and Structure Committee met jointly to discuss the inquiry process, and used the instrument for gathering information that was printed in council agenda Exhibit B, Part 1b. The committees discussed the process and time line for the inquiry printed in council agenda Exhibit B, Part 1c.

Council Action: Chair Magnus called upon the Rev. Robert N. Bacher, executive for administration, to initiate discussion on the "inquiry" process. He reviewed several themes that had emerged as a result of initial reflection on the issues by members of the Church Council through the use of evaluation instrument developed by the Department for Research and Evaluation. Such themes included leadership roles and functions, valuation of wide participation, and a preference in society for support of local causes. The question of funding and the distribution of limited resources soon will come to the forefront of the discussion, he said.

J. David Ellwanger commented that the redesign of the churchwide organization is "too important to be left to theologians." He urged that the composition of the task force be expanded to include laypersons with particular management expertise.

The Rev. John O. Knudson commented on personal experience versus Scripture as the basis of authority. The Rev. David G. Gabel expressed appreciation for the opportunity to use the evaluation instrument. William E. Diehl questioned whether the workbook might be to complicated for general application. Deborah S. Yandala commented on the benefits of the workbook experience for church leadership.

Declining Circulation of The Lutheran

Background: Information related to a decline in the circulation of *The Lutheran* was printed in council agenda Exhibit R, Part 1. This matter was discussed by the advisory committee for *The Lutheran*.

Council Action: Chair Magnus called upon the Rev. Edgar R. Trexler, editor of *The Lutheran*, and Gary J. N. Aamodt, president of the Publishing House of the Evangelical Lutheran Church in America, to report on declining circulation of *The Lutheran*. Pastor Trexler noted that the declining circulation of church periodicals is a trend in most all church bodies. He invited members of the Church Council to consider the matter in relationship to *The Lutheran*'s circulation and service to this church. Mr. Aamodt reviewed circulation statistics and indicated that the level at which the decline in circulation might cease cannot be predicted. He acknowledged the significance of the every-home plan in underwriting the cost of the magazine, and the importance of the support of clergy in promoting that plan.

Bishop Paull E. Spring expressed strong support for the present configuration of *The Lutheran*. He acknowledged that the magazine has been responsive to previous criticism. Youth advisor Erin Cram commented on the value of the synod supplements despite their high cost. She noted that the journals most read are those containing cross-word puzzles. William T. Billings, in reference to promotion of the every-home plan, suggested that creative marketing approaches be utilized, such as reduced initial subscription rates. He observed that *The Lutheran* is not an Augsburg Fortress sale item. He also recommended that *The Lutheran* be made available to visitors to the Lutheran Center chapel. The Rev. David

G. Gabel commended the excellence of *The Lutheran*. The Rev. Stephen M. Youngdahl commended the magazine, but cautioned against changing to a "Lutheran living" format. D. Mark Klever acknowledged enjoyment of the magazine, and encouraged reception of new copy concepts. Loren W. Mathre offered several ideas for increasing the magazine's circulation. The Rev. James G. Cobb suggested relaxing restrictions to the every-home plan. Pastor Gabel inquired whether local or other Lutheran magazines or tabloids affect *The Lutheran*'s circulation. The Rev. Franklin D. Fry observed that viewing the magazine as an outreach tool enabled his congregation to maintain the every-home plan. The Rev. Nadine F. Lehr drew attention to the resolution of the advisory committee for *The Lutheran* printed on page three of council agenda Exhibit R. Bishop Herbert W. Chilstrom raised the issue of how in an information age, people wish to have immediate access to news.

Matters Related to the Division for Church in Society

1. Working Principles for Welfare Reform

Background: Council agenda Exhibit P, Part 2, contained a set of principles adopted by the board of the Division for Church in Society that will guide this church's advocacy efforts in the upcoming congressional debate on welfare reform.

Council Action: The Rev. Charles S. Miller Jr., executive director of the Division for Church in Society, highlighted a document adopted by the board of the division on working principles for addressing welfare reform.

The Church Council received the foregoing as information.

2. Social Statement on Peace: First Draft

Background: At its March 1994 meeting, the board of the Division for Church in Society authorized the printing and distribution of the first draft of the proposed "Social Statement on Peace: God's Gift, Our Calling." That draft statement was shared with the Conference of Bishops when the conference met in March 1994; no objections to the draft were made at that meeting. The finalized version, which includes several "friendly amendments" approved by the board of the division, also was shared with synodical bishops.

The March 1994 issue of "Seeds for the Parish" described the plan for distribution of this draft statement. In early April 1994, the draft was made available from the ELCA Distribution Service. Congregations will receive a copy of this draft in the May-June Action Packet.

The Church Council received the foregoing as information.

3. Economic Justice Social Statement: Advisory Committee Members

Background: Council agenda Exhibit P, Part 5, listed persons appointed by the board of the Division for Church in Society to serve on the task force that will be developing a statement on economic justice. The statement is scheduled to be transmitted to the 1997 Churchwide Assembly for possible action. Also included in that exhibit is additional information related to the development of the economic justice statement.

The chair of the Church Council appointed the Rev. Donald M. Hallberg to serve on the task force as liaison from the council.

Council Action: Pastor Miller announced further appointments of members to the task force. The board of the division requested that an additional member be appointed, specifically, a women of color, who lives or has had experience living in poverty. Deborah S. Yandala observed that there is a need to include on the membership of task forces persons, such as pastors, who are able to interpret statements produced to "the person in the pew." Youth adviser Erin Cram advocated for the inclusion of youth on such task forces. Bishop Kenneth E. Sauer recommended that nominees to task forces be reviewed by synodical staff prior to appointment. Bishop Glenn W. Nycklemoe recommended that the formation and initial work of task forces be given full interpretation to this church's membership.

4. Resolution on Cuba

Background: The Minneapolis Area Synod forwarded the following memorial to the 1993 Churchwide Assembly:

WHEREAS, our faith calls us to love our neighbor and to work for justice, peace and reconciliation; and

WHEREAS, for the past 32 years there has been alienation between the United States and Cuba; and

WHEREAS, the economic embargo against Cuba, imposed by the United States, is causing great suffering, especially for children and the elderly; and

WHEREAS, the ELCA "Churchwide Blueprint for Action on Central America and Caribbean Concerns" seeks:

1. to oppose politicization of humanitarian assistance in the region (1.4);
2. to advocate normalization of relations between the United States and other nations in the region (1.6.); and
3. to promote and develop mutually supportive relationships between Lutheran churches in the region and those in the United States (2.4.);

and

WHEREAS, lifting the blockade against Cuba, the provision of humanitarian help, and the promotion of dialogue between churches in Cuba and the United States are measures called for by the National Council of Churches of Christ in the U.S.A., [NCC], the Caribbean Council of Churches, the Latin American Council of Churches, the ELCA Metropolitan New York Synod, and others; and

WHEREAS, the Evangelical Lutheran Confession in Cuba, while experiencing growth and excitement in ministry, also is calling for the lifting of the U.S. embargo; therefore, be it

RESOLVED, that the Minneapolis Area Synod memorialize the 1993 Churchwide Assembly:

1. to support Lutheran congregations in Cuba through prayer, information sharing and material support, in cooperation with the ELCA Division for Global Mission and the Lutheran Coalition on Latin America;
2. to participate in sending humanitarian aid to Cuba through organizations such as Lutheran World Relief, Church World Service, and Pastors for Peace; and
3. to petition the U.S. government to end its embargo against Cuba, and seek further reconciliation and normalization of relations between the United States and Cuba.

The 1993 Churchwide Assembly voted (CA93.7.53):

To refer the memorial of the Minneapolis Area Synod on relations between the United States and Cuba to the Division for Church in Society to study the issues raised by this memorial, especially the ramifications in #3 of the Resolved paragraph, and to report its recommendations to the Church Council in November 1994.

The 1993 West Virginia-Western Maryland Synod transmitted the following resolution to the Church Council, which also addresses the Cuban situation:

WHEREAS, the theme of this assembly is "Many Voices ... One Song," and, in the words of our "Order for the Opening of an Assembly," let us pursue justice and peace for mutual understanding"; and

WHEREAS, in light of nutritional, medical and material goods shortages; therefore be it

RESOLVED, that this assembly encourage the West Virginia-Western Maryland Synod to support the ministries and work of all Christian congregations in Cuba, and to direct the Synod Council to direct the ELCA Church Council to urge the United States government to end its thirty-two year embargo against Cuba and the Cuban people, and to seek a normalization of relations.

At its December 1993 meeting the ELCA Church Council voted (CC93.12.90):

To refer the resolution of the West Virginia-Western Maryland Synod on the U.S. embargo against Cuba to the Division for Church in Society for a report and/or recommendation to the Church Council at its April 1994 meeting for response to the synod.

The board of the Division for Church in Society discussed this matter at its March 1994 board meeting, having received the following information about the issue from staff:

1. Church-to-Church Relationships

The Evangelical Lutheran Church in America has both bilateral relations with the Lutheran Church in Cuba, known as the Evangelical Church of the Lutheran Confession in Cuba (ECLCC), as well as multilateral relationships with that church and other churches in Cuba through the Ecumenical Council of Cuba, the Lutheran World Federation (LWF), the National Council of the Churches of Christ in the U.S.A. (NCC), and the World Council of Churches (WCC). The Ecumenical Council and the ECLCC have had increasing contact with the Evangelical Lutheran Church in America in recent years as well as with the Lutheran World Federation.

It should be noted that the ELCA "Churchwide Blueprint for Action on Central America and Caribbean Concerns" was adopted by ELCA Church Council in November 1989. The relevant provisions are cited in the Minneapolis Area Synod resolution.

During a fraternal visit to U.S. churches in February 1993, members of the Executive Committee of the Latin American Council of Churches urged the U.S. churches to: "end the embargo that the United States has maintained arbitrarily against the government and population of Cuba" and "provide humanitarian aid so that the people of this nation [Cuba] can continue to take the steps—without counter-productive outside intervention— considered necessary and opportune to improve its own situation, to improve relations with the U.S., and to benefit the Cuban population resident in the U.S., while preserving the social progress achieved through the revolution."

In a pastoral letter dated 17 May 1993, the bishop of the Salvadoran Lutheran Synod, Medardo Gómez, described his visit to

Cuba on the invitation of the Ecumenical Council of Cuba. He saw "a consistent church, rich in spirituality: a church of the poor and with the poor, which, inspired in Christ, in the word of God, nourishes the people in their faith and hope, against the uneasiness produced by the material limitations of a poverty imposed by the [U.S.] boycott." In conclusion, Gómez wrote: " . . . therefore, in the name of the poor, suffering and humble people of Cuba, and in virtue of the call I feel from God, ask our Christian brothers and sisters who belong to the ecumenical councils, to speak to the world, asking the government of the United States, over which Mr. Bill Clinton presides, to lift the embargo and blockade against Cuba."

On November 10, 1993, the General Board of the National Council of Churches adopted a resolution on Cuba, which, among other provisions, asked its member churches to: (1) continue humanitarian aid to the Cuban people through the Cuban churches; and (2) increase their pastoral accompaniment of the churches in Cuba to strengthen dialogue, increase information flow, theological formation, and ecumenical unity. It also called for prayer for the Cuban people and the governments of Cuba and the U.S. The member churches were asked to support proposals in Congress to build a new U.S.-Cuba relationship. The National Council of Churches also was asked to support the Cuban churches in their dialogue with their government "in the search for necessary changes in Cuba and the preservation of social gains which have been made to date." The U.S. government was asked to lift the embargo against Cuba and other restrictions; halt interference in the trade of other nations with Cuba; and provide humanitarian aid to the Cuban people.

The life of the Lutheran congregations in Cuba was recently described in an article, "Lutherans in Cuba Try to Reconcile," in the January 1994 issue of *The Lutheran* (page 54).

The Lutheran World Federation Department for World Service issued an appeal on January 21, 1994, to churches and their related agencies to provide medicines to those in need in Cuba through the Ecumenical Council of Cuba.

2. Church-to-Government Relationships

Until the action by the 1993 Churchwide Assembly, the relationship of the Evangelical Lutheran Church in America to the U.S. government with respect to Cuba was understood to be governed by the provisions in the 1989 Blueprint adopted by the Church Council, i.e., that the Evangelical Lutheran Church in America supported the normalization of relations between the U.S. government and that of Cuba. This position reflected the view that normal governmental relations would facilitate contact between members of the Evangelical Lutheran Church in America and Christians in Cuba in furtherance of the other goal of promoting and developing "mutually supportive relationships between Lutheran churches in the region and those in the United States."

When the policy was proposed in 1989 by an inter-unit staff team and endorsed by the Advisory Committee on Central America and the Caribbean, both groups were mindful of the long-standing U.S. embargo against Cuba. Even so, it was believed that despite the situation in Cuban concerning human rights and other social conditions, it was in the interest of the churches and the Cuban people to build better relations between peoples by calling for the normalization of relations.

3. Government-to-Government Relationships

Bilateral contacts between the governments of the United States and Cuba, for more than thirty years, have not been normal. The most recent version of the prohibitions against Cuba are covered in the "Cuba Democracy Act of 1992" (Title XVII of Public Law 102-484). These include: 1) U.S. sanctions that may be imposed against countries assisting Cuba; 2) prohibitions on contracts with Cuba; 3) prohibitions on use of ships that have recently entered Cuban ports; 4) and restrictions on the travel of Cubans to the United States.

The embargo exempts food donations to non-governmental organizations and individuals in Cuba; most medicines and medical supplies; telecommunications services and facilities; and mail delivery. It also excludes financial penalties, which might otherwise be imposed under the Trading with the Enemy Act, for educational and religious activities or those of human rights organizations "that are reasonably limited in frequency, duration, and number of participants."

The sanctions could be waived by the U.S. President, if he determines and reports to Congress that Cuba: (1) has held free and fair elections; (2) has permitted opposition parties to campaign for such elections; (3) is respecting civil liberties and human rights of its citizens; (4) is moving to a free market economy; and (5) has committed itself to constitutional change to ensure free and fair elections.

The U.S. embargo against Cuba has been discussed in recent years at the United Nations. The result has been increased isolation of the U.S. in votes in the General Assembly. For example in 1992 the vote on the resolution calling for an end to the embargo was 59-3 with 71 abstentions and in 1993 the vote was 88-4 with 57 abstentions.

These resolutions have been adopted while the UN has also criticized the human rights situation in Cuba, including Cuba's non-cooperation with the UN Special Rapporteur on human rights in Cuba. The vote in 1992 criticizing Cuba's record was 69-18 with 4 abstentions. In 1993, the vote was 74-20 with 61 abstentions. The UN Special Rapporteur, Ambassador Carl-Johan Groth of Sweden, in a late October 1993 interim report, reiterated his previous recommendations that Cuba: (1) ratify the International Covenants on Civil and Political Rights as well as Economic, Social and Cultural Rights; (2) cease persecuting and punishing its citizens for reasons related to freedom of peaceful expression and association; (3) permit independent groups (e.g. human rights and labor) to operate; (4) respect guarantees of due process; (5) better treat its prisoners and allow inspection of prisons by the Red Cross and independent national groups; (6) review sentences imposed for offenses related to political affiliation and attempts to leave the country illegally; and (7) expedite procedures to allow people to leave and enter the country and avoid retaliation against applicants who apply for such permission. He cited also a September 1993 pastoral letter from Cuban bishops raising similar concerns. Even so, he offered the view that, "the most constructive measures, in the international context, for improving the human rights situation in Cuba should start by eliminating, as soon as possible, the vestiges of the cold war as they relate to Cuba while endeavoring, instead, to promote the country's return to the regional and world system of cooperation and settlement of conflicts." He also said, "The international community must encourage a reform program designed to improve productivity and efficiency in the economy."

Conclusions

The lack of normal relations between the U.S. and Cuba has not assisted the church in promoting reconciliation between the U.S. and Cuban peoples. Indeed it has inhibited, though not prohibited, communication and exchanges. Better communication and exchanges could provide more information and encourage respect for human rights in Cuba, which would help build a more democratic society and one that will challenge restrictive policies.

The Evangelical Lutheran Church in America should continue to support human rights and criticize their violation wherever they may occur. In the present context this means that the Evangelical Lutheran Church in America may raise questions about Cuba's commitment to civil and political rights, but also needs to remind the U.S. government that it must work to promote and protect the economic and social rights of the Cuban people—i.e., not harm their right to an adequate standard of living, including adequate food, clothing and housing, their right to freedom from hunger, as well as their right to the highest attainable standard of physical and mental health, etc. (which are effectively inhibited, if not violated, by the present U.S. policy).

Many would argue that the present U.S. embargo policy with its sanctions against other nations that assist Cuba is a clear violation of customary international law. While some nations have ignored the threat of sanctions, smaller nations are less able to do so, which raises the matters of both fairness and the use of coercion by more powerful nations against weaker ones. The policy, which places a greater burden on a weaker country to remedy its human rights situation while other countries (which are more powerful or deemed to be strategically significant to perceived U.S. interests) continue to violate the rights of their citizens, raises questions about equity and selectivity on the part of the U.S. vis-á-vis other countries.

The Evangelical Lutheran Church in America should join the conclusion of the members of the Executive Committee of the Latin American Council of Churches that change in Cuba will be achieved most effectively by Cubans themselves without external interference, such as the embargo and related restrictions.

The board of the Division for Church in Society, at its March 1994 meeting, recommended that the Church Council take the following action.

To act affirmatively on the 1993 memorial of the Minneapolis Area Synod and the 1993 resolution of the West Virginia-Western Maryland Synod;

To request that relevant entities of the Evangelical Lutheran Church in America:

(1) Support Lutheran congregations in Cuba through prayer, information sharing, and material support, in cooperation with the ELCA Division for Global Mission and the Lutheran Coalition on Latin America;

(2) Participate in sending humanitarian aid to Cuba through such organizations as Lutheran World Relief, Church World Service, and Pastors for Peace; and

(3) Petition the U.S. government to end its embargo against Cuba, and to seek further reconciliation and normalization of relations between the United States and Cuba.

To request the secretary of this church to communicate this action to the Minneapolis Area Synod and the West Virginia-Western Maryland Synod.

Council Action: Pastor Miller introduced the foregoing recommendation of the board of the Division for Church in Society.

During discussion, Dale V. Sandstrom spoke passionately against the proposal, observing that the action of the Churchwide Assembly did not call for support of economic aid to Cuba and the Castro regime. He stated, "I have no problem at all with the support of Lutheran congregations in Cuba, but the effect of the remainder of this proposal is to prop up the Castro regime in Cuba. For nearly one-third of a century the Castro regime has been maintained with massive economic aid from the [former] Soviet Union. Now that the communist order in Eastern Europe has collapsed and the Soviet Union is no more, Castro's continuation is in jeopardy. The thrust of this, although it labels it as humanitarian aid, is economic aid for Cuba and Castro regime. Normalization of relations is additional support for the Castro regime in Cuba. I believe that the people of Cuba would be better served by the end of the Castro regime and hopefully the establishment of democracy. I do not think we serve the cause of human freedom by propping up a communist regime in Cuba. . . . This body, and this church before it, talked about the importance of economic sanctions to help bring about just governments around the world. I do not believe that propping up the Castro regime is an action that serves causes that this church should be promoting. I am deeply concerned that if we adopt this resolution as it is before us, it will only serve to reinforce the perception throughout this country of a national church that is radical and out of touch with our people. I would urge the defeat of this resolution or simply adopting the first item for continued support of Lutheran congregations in Cuba . . .."

The Rev. Nadine F. Lehr disagreed, stating that seeking normalization of relations between the U.S. and Cuba did not necessarily imply economic aid. Bishop Paull E. Spring observed that "normalization" usually is applied to diplomatic relations. Bishop Isaksen drew attention to a distinction between sending aid to the Cuban government, and humanitarian aid to the people. He suggested that the resolution specify the provision of aid through the Ecumenical Council of Cuba, that is vis-a-vis church-to-church sources. The Rev. Franklin D. Fry inquired about the opinion of Central American churches on this matter.

Edith M. Lohr moved the following:

MOVED;
SECONDED;
CARRIED: To postpone further discussion until Monday, April 18, 1994.

In the meantime, Chair Magnus appointed a committee of three—Dale V. Sandstrom, Bishop Robert L. Isaksen, and the Rev. Charles S. Miller Jr.—to consider the matter further.

5. Women and Children Living in Poverty

Background: A report on the implementation of the resolution related to women and children living in poverty, adopted by the 1993 Churchwide Assembly, was printed in council agenda Exhibit P, Part 6.

Council Action: Pastor Miller introduced the aforementioned update on "Women and Children Living in Poverty." The Church Council received the foregoing as information.

The Church Council recessed at 5:45 P.M. Bishop Herbert W. Chilstrom offered the closing prayer.

Monday Session

The Church Council reconvened on Monday, April 18, 1994, at 8:35 A.M. Opening devotions were offered by Vice President Kathy J. Magnus, chair of the Church Council. Chair Magnus then reviewed the agenda for the day and made several announcements.

Matters Related to the Division for Higher Education and Schools
ELCA Colleges and Universities and the Mission of the Church

Background: A document describing the distinctive mission of ELCA colleges and universities and their contributions to our church's ministry was reviewed by the board of the Division for Higher Education and Schools.

Council Action: Chair Magnus called upon the Rev. W. Robert Sorensen, executive director of the

Division for Higher Education and Schools, to introduce a report concerning the relationship between the educational institutions of this church to the various expressions of this church. He announced the planning process for the "Sittler symposium" devoted to the distinctive mission of ELCA colleges, universities, and seminaries as they relate to the strategic mission of this church. The conference would be held in Columbus, Ohio, August 5-7, 1994. Pastor Sorensen asserted that although the level of the relationship between this church and its colleges varies from institution to institution, in each of the 29 colleges of this system, the desire to enhance the relationship is lively, vital, and strong. He then reviewed the seven functions of the colleges listed in the report.

During discussion, William T. Billings inquired about "wholistic education," specifically asking whether the colleges foster a Christian life for the students with regard to morality and ethics. Pastor Sorensen cited campus ministries and the departments of religion as the major factors in fostering Christianity on campus. The Rev. Nadine F. Lehr observed the rich worship life of the campus communities. Bishop Herbert W. Chilstrom commented on the importance of the ELCA college and university presidents in fostering the connection between the institutions and this church, and expressed appreciation for their commitment.

Matters Related to the Division for Congregational Ministries

1. Sacramental Practices

Background: At the 1989 Churchwide Assembly, "A Statement on Communion Practices," originally prepared and adopted by predecessor church bodies in 1978, was approved for continued use as the policy of the Evangelical Lutheran Church in America (CA89.4.23). The 1989 Churchwide Assembly also approved a response to memorials of six synods regarding a study on sacramental practices. The response indicated that the Conference of Bishops had "recommended that a statement on sacramental practices be prepared as a guide to the Evangelical Lutheran Church in America" and that "such a study would be carried out by a committee including persons representing the Conference of Bishops, the teaching theologians of this church, the Division for Ministry, the Division for Congregational Life [Ministries], and the Office [Department] for Ecumenical Affairs." At its April 1989 meeting, the Church Council requested that the Conference of Bishops prepare a time line and process for this study for consideration by the council at its November 1989 meeting. In its specific response, the 1989 Churchwide Assembly referred the memorials from synods "to the Conference of Bishops for use in the development of a study on sacramental practices" (CA89.8.119).

Because of budget reductions, implementation of the study process was delayed. In response to the delay, the 1991 Churchwide Assembly took the following action related to a study of sacramental practices:

To direct the Conference of Bishops, Division for Congregational Ministries, and the Budget Development Committee of the Church Council to develop and report to the 1993 Churchwide Assembly a strategy for funding and conducting a communion practices study and statement (CA91.7.47).

Upon recommendation of the board of the Division for Congregational Ministries, the Department for Synodical Relations (Conference of Bishops) and the Office of the Bishop, the Church Council took the following action at its November 1992 meeting:

To designate the Division for Congregational Ministries as the lead unit in preparing the report and possible recommendation on a sacramental practices study and statement, in consultation with the Conference of Bishops and the Budget and Finance Committee of the Church Council, for presentation to the 1993 Churchwide Assembly (CC92.11.108).

Council agenda Exhibit L, Part 1b, contained preliminary materials prepared by the task force on sacramental practices. This material was shared with the Conference of Bishops and board of the Division for Congregational Ministries, as described in the time line. The task force will meet in June 1994 to develop a first draft for possible distribution to congregations in fall 1994. Members of the Church Council were invited to share their responses with the task force by May 15, 1994.

Council Action: Chair Magnus called upon the Rev. Mary Ann Moller-Gunderson, executive director of the Division for Congregational Ministries, to report on the initial work of the drafting committee of a possible statement on sacramental practices. She reviewed the work of the task force to date and stressed the preliminary nature of the materials. Pastor Moller-Gunderson also reviewed the group of persons invited to serve as reviewers of the document, and the time line. She noted that the major purpose of the document was dialogue and study, and she invited written responses from the members of the Church Council by May 15.

Pastor Moller-Gunderson called upon the Rev. Paul R. Nelson, director for worship in the Division for Congregational Ministries, to review the major points of the document. He noted that the spirit of this proposal is particularly important to watch. He pointed to several significant features, particularly a deeply-rooted confessional background, which encourages the Word and the sacraments as the norms for the worship life of this church. Three kinds of material are evident: brief descriptive statements on worship practice; statements yet to be prepared (commentary); and a need for supporting papers on why a change in policy is being requested by this task force.

During discussion, Dale V. Sandstrom asked what the effect of this statement would be. Pastor Nelson stated that such remained something of an open question for the task force. Secretary Lowell G. Almen suggested one possibility was developing a document that would present basic expectations, but also would allow room for individual congregational expression. The Rev. John O. Knudson expressed concern about the brief time allotted to congregations for study of the matter and an expectation that congregations will move into new practice without time for significant conversation. Pastor Moller-Gunderson agreed, and explained that the schedule was dictated primarily by economics. She noted that teaching tools would be prepared to allow congregations to study the issues both before and after presentation to the Churchwide Assembly. Patsy Gottschalk expressed concern about the time line for present recommendations to the 1995 Churchwide Assembly, because the study of human sexuality also might be before that assembly. Bishop Kenneth H. Sauer urged continued conversation with the Evangelical Lutheran Church in Canada (ELCIC) on how its congregations responded to that church's recent statement on sacramental practices.

The Rev. Philip L. Natwick asked about distribution of the materials developed to date, to which Pastor Moller-Gunderson responded that they were too preliminary to be considered even as a first draft. Robert S. Schroeder inquired about the audience for which the document would be directed, and urged the use of appropriate language. Pastor Nelson responded that materials would be read by various audiences, but expressed a desire that they would be utilized in the teaching life of congregations, as well as by church leaders who are responsible for the worship life of this church.

Bishop Glenn W. Nycklemoe urged the task force to make the document deeply pastoral and cited, as an example, the policy on communing children. The Rev. James G. Cobb expressed appreciation for the layout of the initial materials with their short, crisp sentences. Bishop Paull E. Spring said that he did not believe this study would be as controversial as the study of human sexuality, because of the consultative process being utilized here. Bishop Herbert W. Chilstrom inquired about what issues would be most conflicted. Bishop Sauer commented that the communion of the baptized would be controversial, but even more important would be the practice of congregations that differ from one another. Bishop Robert L. Isaksen observed that change often comes slowly, but noted the dramatic changes that have been made during the last 20 years. He also urged that the Eucharist be viewed as proclamation as is the Word, and that the frequency of public confession and absolution be addressed.

2. Annual Churchwide Offering

Chair Magnus called upon the Rev. Mark R. Moller-Gunderson to introduce discussion of the "Vision for Mission Fund" and the annual churchwide offering. He reviewed the process for soliciting gifts in 1994 and reported that three weeks into the offering, the ELCA had received $159,000 from 35 congregations and more than 1,000 individuals. The average gift per individual was $100. Pastor Moller-Gunderson expressed gratitude to the members of the Church Council for their leadership in giving and for making an opportunity for giving directly to the work of the churchwide organization possible.

Pastor Moller-Gunderson also reported initial results of the stewardship survey of council members conducted on Sunday, April 17. In a response to a question raised previously, Pastor Moller-Gunderson said the stewardship campaign included education, interpretation, and response categories. He cited several examples to illustrate the inter-relationship of those three aspects of the program. He noted that a fundamental piece of the strategy would be to convince congregations that the churchwide organization was providing the resources that they need in conducting comprehensive stewardship programs.

The Rev. David G. Gabel expressed appreciation for the presentation, but objected that the "Vision for Mission Fund" materials were not helpful in providing a way to encourage congregations to "go the extra mile" to support the "Vision for Mission" program. Pastor Moller-Gunderson responded that, if more congregations provided the leadership Pastor Gabel was providing, the program would not be necessary; nonetheless, it was being made available in order to give ELCA members another opportunity to give. Pastor Gabel recommended that other reporting mechanisms be utilized to demonstrate that people are giving to a variety of causes.

Bishop Herbert W. Chilstrom observed that several letters were received stating that this was a new program, which it was not. The Rev. James G. Cobb commented that Lutheran Laity Movement for Stewardship (LLM) in the past often had distributed materials, and that those efforts were more effective in making materials available to congregational members. Pastor Moller-Gunderson responded that, while many pieces of material were produced in the first five years of this church's life, there was no evidence that such materials were effective. He also commented that other denominations utilize a cost-recovery basis for producing stewardship materials.

3. Constitution of the Lutheran Laity Movement for Stewardship

Background: According to ELCA 16.11.A91.f.4., the Division for Congregational Ministries is to:

relate to the Lutheran Laity Movement for Stewardship, which shall be recognized as being an association within this church, which shall be self-supporting financially, and which shall provide specialized stewardship services to this church in consultation with and through cooperation with this division. This association shall administer its affairs in conformity with the applicable policies of this church and shall coordinate its operations with the Division for Congregational Ministries. The specific function of this association shall be enumerated in its constitution and bylaws. The constitution and bylaws of the Lutheran Laity Movement for Stewardship, and amendments thereto, after review by this division, may be amended by a two-thirds vote of the Church Council.

The proposed amendments to the constitution of the Lutheran Laity Movement for Stewardship, were reviewed by the board of the Division for Congregational Ministries, which recommended approval by the Church Council.

Council Action: Pastor Mark R. Moller-Gunderson reviewed the changes in board membership being proposed in the LLM constitution, requiring Church Council approval.

VOTED:

2/3 VOTE REQUIRED
CC94.4.29

To adopt the amendments to the constitution of the Lutheran Laity Movement for Stewardship printed in council agenda Exhibit L, Part 3.

4. Matters Related to Worship

Background: In the coming months, the worship staff of the Division for Congregational Ministries will devote attention to:

- Development of occasional services for the commissioning of associates in ministry and the consecration or commissioning of diaconal ministers;
- Revision of the lectionary used in the Evangelical Lutheran Church in America.

Under the guidelines approved by the Church Council for review of worship materials, the Church Council has a role in these matters. Both activities are at the early stages of discussion. Preliminary plans of the Division for Congregational Ministries will be shared with the Church Council at its April 1994 meeting.

Council Action: Chair Magnus called upon the Rev. Paul R. Nelson, director for worship in the Division for Congregational Ministries, to introduce two proposals concerning the relationship between churchwide staff and the staff of the ELCA publishing house. The first concerned the development of trial resources to supplement the continued use of *Lutheran Book of Worship.* The second new direction was related to the possible revision of the lectionary, intended to parallel the revised lectionary prepared by the ecumenical Consultation on Common Texts. The rationale for such a revision arose, because of problems with the present lectionary, and particularly, because the Lutheran lectionary is "out of sync" with the ecumenical consensus, especially in the Sundays after Pentecost.

During discussion, the Rev. David A. Andert inquired about the kinds of resources to be published for congregations. Pastor Nelson said such issues had not been resolved. The Rev. Nelson T. Strobert asked what other denominations have accepted the common lectionary. Pastor Nelson indicated that the United Church of Christ, the Presbyterian Church (U.S.A.), and the United Methodist Church already had adopted the lectionary; the Episcopal Church would decide the issue during summer 1994.

The Rev. James G. Cobb observed that one critique from pericope study groups was the need for a fuller use of Scripture in the lectionary. The Rev. Franklin D. Fry suggested that as new resources are published, determination should be made, not simply on the basis of what sells in a competitive market, but on what this church desires to provide for the benefit of its own congregations.

Matters Related to the Division for Ministry

1. Guidelines Related to Non-Stipendiary Ministry

Background: The 1993 Churchwide Assembly of the Evangelical Lutheran Church in America acted "to determine that this church may have stipendiary and non-stipendiary ministers among its rostered ministries." This action was part of the proposals of the Task Force on the Study of Ministry related to flexibility for mission. The Division for Ministry was directed by the assembly to develop churchwide standards for non-stipendiary ministers. The assembly further adopted bylaw 7.41.14., which states:

> When it is deemed necessary for the mission needs of this church, a letter of call may be issued by the Synod Council—according to criteria, policies, and procedures recommended by the Division for Ministry, reviewed by the Conference of Bishops, and adopted by the Church Council—to a pastor as a ordained minister for non-stipendiary service after the Synod Council has sought and received approval by the Conference of Bishops. Care is to be exercised so that positions that can be filled adequately and appropriately by the laity in this church and in the world not be filled by pastors as ordained ministers for their convenience, status, or personal preference. A call to non-stipendiary service is to be reviewed at least annually by the Synod Council and continued only as warranted for the ministry needs of this church. Such a call may be terminated by the Synod Council when it is deemed to be fulfilling no longer the mission needs of this church.

The Division for Ministry has developed criteria, policy, and procedures for partial and non-stipendiary service for ordained ministers in this church. The Division for Ministry believes that the same criteria, policy, and procedures could apply in a parallel manner to associates in ministry, deaconesses, and diaconal ministers. Should such a parallel policy for rostered lay ministers be sought by this church, appropriate bylaw language would need to be prepared.

Guidelines related to non-stipendiary ministry in the Evangelical Lutheran Church in America, "Non-Stipendiary Ministry—The Evangelical Lutheran Church in America," were printed in council agenda Exhibit M, Part 1. They were reviewed by the Conference of Bishops and the board of the Division for Ministry, which recommended Church Council approval.

Council Action: Chair Magnus called upon the Rev. Joseph M. Wagner, executive director of the Division for Ministry, to present various matters related to the Study for Ministry approved by the 1993 Churchwide Assembly. Major changes in the "topography" of ministry are evident in these days of the church's life and in this society, he said. The goal of the division is to be responsive to these changes and develop new approaches.

Pastor Wagner introduced the proposed guidelines related to non-stipendiary ministry. He expressed a conviction that the primary issue here was that such ministries be used for the sake of the mission and ministry of the whole church, rather than simply the desires of the individuals involved.

During discussion, Bishop Peter Rogness observed that the purpose of the calls issued by synod councils is to validate that such ministry is conducted as the legitimate ministry of the congregation. It is a safeguard to make sure that such ministry is not based simply on a cozy relationship between a congregation and a pastor who is now involved in another form of service, he said. Bishop Robert L. Isaksen commented that, while this church is seeking new forms of ministry for the sake of flexibility, a variety of restrictions are being imposed. Pastor Wagner noted that the proposed material is in accord with the bylaws already approved by the Churchwide Assembly.

VOTED: *CC94.4.30*
To adopt the document, "Non-Stipendiary Ministry—The Evangelical Lutheran Church in America," [as] printed in council agenda Exhibit M, Part 1.

NON-STIPENDIARY MINISTRY
EVANGELICAL LUTHERAN CHURCH IN AMERICA

I.   Definition and Criteria for Non-Stipendiary Ministry
Non-stipendiary ministry in the Evangelical Lutheran Church in America is understood to be service as a rostered minister without regard to compensation for such service. It may be either service for no stipend (or for reimbursed expenses only) or for a token stipend that is not commensurate with the normal salary guidelines for rostered ministry. Non-stipendiary calls are not eligible for participation in the ELCA Pension and Health Benefits Plan, therefore it is also understood that such non-stipended service is possible only when there is clear evidence that the ordained minister has adequate alternative income and health insurance.

A letter of call to non-stipendiary ministry in the Evangelical Lutheran Church in America may be issued only by a Synod Council following approval by the Conference of Bishops. The ordained minister serving in a non-stipendiary call shall be accountable to the synod bishop and Synod Council in the carrying out of this ministry. A call to non-stipendiary service shall be a one-year term call that may be renewed by the Synod Council only on the basis of the satisfactory fulfillment of the established criteria. A call to non-stipendiary ministry neither qualifies as an initial call to congregational service required for ordination nor does it imply any employment relationship or contractual obligation to the Synod Council (7.43. and 7.43.01.). The criteria under which a Synod Council may issue a letter of call to an ordained minister for non-stipendiary service include the following:

A.   There shall be a clearly defined statement of the need for this pastor to provide for Word and sacrament ministry in the synod and a rationale for this call to be for non-stipendiary service, including an annual ministry plan;

B.   The minimum commitment by the ordained minister shall be a monthly average of 10 hours per week to the ministry to which called;

C.   The ordained minister shall meet the criteria and standards of this church for its ordained ministers;

D.   The Synod Council must determine that a call to non-stipendiary service is extended in order to carry out a specific ministry on behalf of the synod.

II.   Action by the Synod Bishop and Synod Council
When the synod bishop and Synod Council believe that the criteria for a non-stipendiary letter of call are met by a specific ministry, the Synod Council may propose by a majority vote a letter of call. Final action to extend such a letter of call is contingent upon the approval of the Conference of Bishops. The Synod Council forwards its proposal, together with the rationale for issuing the call to non-stipendiary ministry, to the Conference of Bishops.

Should the Conference of Bishops approve the request and the ministry begin the Synod Council will conduct an annual review of the non-stipendiary call. Annual Synod Council action is required in order to continue the call to non-stipendiary ministry.

III.   Action by the Conference of Bishops
The Roster Committee of the Conference of Bishops receives all requests from Synod Councils for calls to non-stipendiary ministry. The Roster Committee reviews these requests and reports its recommendations to the Conference of Bishops. The Conference of Bishops, in a regular meeting of the conference, by a majority vote acts upon requests for calls to non-stipendiary ministry. It reports its decision to the Synod Council seeking such approval. When approval is given by the Conference of Bishops the Synod Council may proceed with the issuance of a letter of call to non-stipendiary ministry and may annually renew such a call without subsequent action by the Conference of Bishops.

2.   Guidelines Related to On-Leave-from-Call Status

Background: The 1993 Churchwide Assembly of the Evangelical Lutheran Church in America acted (CA93.6.17, Section VI.C.):

> to provide for the possibility that ordained persons rostered by this church but no longer holding a letter of call from a source officially recognized by this church may continue on the roster subject to careful annual synodical review for the church's mission, under specific policy to be developed by the Division for Ministry, reviewed by the Conference of Bishops, and approved by the Church Council. Retention on the roster beyond three years must be approved by the Conference of Bishops.

In regard to pastors, the ELCA constitution states:
On Leave from Call. A pastor as an ordained minister of this church, serving under a regularly issued letter of call, who leaves the work of that ministry without accepting another regularly issued letter of call, may be retained on the roster of ordained ministers of this church, upon endorsement by the synodical bishop, by action of the Synod Council in the synod of which the pastor as an ordained minister is a member under policy developed by the Division for Ministry, reviewed by the Conference of Bishops, and adopted by the Church Council. Thereafter, by annual action of the Synod Council in the synod of which a member, upon endorsement by the synodical bishop, a pastor as an ordained minister who is without a current letter of call may be retained on the roster of ordained ministers of this church for a maximum of three years beginning at the completion of an active call. Exception to this limit for the purpose of serving the needs of this church may be granted by the Synod Council in the synod of current roster after having received approval by the Conference of Bishops.

By annual recommendation by the Division for Ministry and action of the Synod Council in the synod of which a member, with the approval of the synodical bishop, a pastor as an ordained minister engaged in graduate study, in a field of study that will enhance service in the ordained ministry, may be retained on the roster of ordained ministers of this church for a maximum of six years. Exception to this limit for the purpose of serving the needs of this church may be granted by the Synod Council in the synod of current roster after having received approval by the Conference of Bishops (ELCA 7.31.16.).

In regard to associates in ministry, the ELCA constitution states:
On Leave from Call. An associate in ministry [understood here to include all officially rostered lay ministers including associates in ministry, deaconesses, and diaconal ministers], serving under a regularly issued letter of call, who leaves the work of that call without accepting another regularly issued letter of call, may be retained on the roster of associates in ministry of this church, upon endorsement by the synodical bishop, by action of the Synod Council in the synod of which a member. Thereafter, by annual action of the Synod Council in the synod of which a member, upon endorsement by the synodical bishop, an associate in ministry who is

without a current letter of call may be retained on the roster of associates in ministry of this church for a maximum of three years beginning at the completion of an active call. Exception to this limit for the purpose of serving the needs of this church may be granted by the Synod Council of current roster after having received approval by the Conference of Bishops.

By annual recommendation by the Division for Ministry and action by the Synod Council in the synod of which a member, with the approval of the synodical bishop, an associate in ministry engaged in graduate study appropriate for service in this church may be retained on the roster of associates in ministry for a maximum of six years. Exception to this limit for purpose of serving the needs of this church may be granted by the Synod Council in the synod of current roster after having received approval by the Conference of Bishops (ELCA 7.52.22.).

Council agenda Exhibit M, Part 2, "On Leave from Call—Rostered Ministers," spelled out in some detail those criteria and related processes. The document was reviewed by the Conference of Bishops and the board of the Division for Ministry at their March 1994 meetings.

Council Action: Chair Magnus invited the Rev. Joseph M. Wagner, executive director of the Division for Ministry, to continue his report. Pastor Wagner introduced the Rev. A. Craig Settlage, director for candidacy in the Division of Ministry, to introduce the proposed policy related to persons on leave from call. The new policy provides for the possibility that this status can be extended beyond the present practice of three years (or six years in the case of those involved in graduate study). Pastor Settlage stated that the primary, though not exclusive, reason for this policy is to respond to those involved in parenting children.

During discussion, Bishop Paull E. Spring commented that the bylaw providing for transfer from one synod to another while rostered persons are on leave from call needs to be addressed.

VOTED: CC94.4.31

To adopt the document, "On Leave from Call—Rostered Ministers," [as] printed in council agenda Exhibit M, Part 2.

ON LEAVE FROM CALL:
ROSTERED MINISTERS IN THE
EVANGELICAL LUTHERAN CHURCH
IN AMERICA

I. Definition and Criteria for on Leave from Call

Ordained ministers, associates in ministry, deaconesses, and diaconal ministers on leave from call are retained on the roster of the synod where they held their last call. On leave from call status, if granted by the Synod Council upon approval by the synod bishop, begins the day the rostered minister is no longer serving under a regularly issued letter of call. A rostered minister on leave from call cannot be transferred to another synod while on leave from call.

A rostered minister must provide a written request to the Synod Council to apply for on leave from call status. An annual decision of the Synod Council in the synod of which the rostered minister is a member, together with the approval of the synod bishop, is necessary for a rostered minister to remain on leave from call.

A rostered minister on leave from call must be an active member of a congregation of this church and be available to contribute to the mission and ministry needs of this church. A rostered minister on leave from call remains accountable to the synod bishop and must be willing to meet the criteria and standards of this church for its rostered ministers.

A rostered minister on leave from call for more than three years (six years in the case of approved graduate study) may be retained on the roster of this church, upon approval by the synod bishop, by action of the Synod Council, and by action of the Conference of Bishops. Continued on leave from call status must contribute to the ministry and mission of this church, and the special circumstances of the ministry provided must warrant an exception to the normal three year limitation.

Graduate Study: A rostered minister engaged in graduate study, in a field of study that will enhance service in the rostered ministry of this church, may be retained on the roster of this church for a maximum of six years by annual recommendation by the Division for Ministry, annual action of the Synod Council and approval of the synod bishop in the synod of which the rostered minister is a member.

II. Criteria for Continuation of On Leave from Call

A rostered minister who seeks to remain on leave from call beyond three years must provide a written request to the synod bishop and Synod Council for the continuation of that status. This request must be received no later than six months prior to the end of the third year of on leave from call status. This request must state clearly the reason(s) for such a request and how these reasons relate to the church's ministry and mission. The request must include the following information:

A. The rationale for the rostered minister's remaining on leave from call, including a statement of the rostered minister's commitment to be available for a letter of call, and an articulation of how the rostered minister's gifts and circumstances can contribute to the ministry and mission of this church;

B. The anticipated date when the rostered minister will be available for a letter of call;

C. A statement describing the ability and willingness of the rostered minister to provide ministry services at the direction of the synod bishop, consistent with the ministry and mission needs of the synod;

D. The rostered minister's plan for continuing education while on leave from call;

E. A statement describing the rostered minister's current participation in the life of a congregation of this church.

Graduate Study: A rostered minister engaged in graduate study who seeks to remain in the "on leave from call" status beyond six years must first seek the approval of the Division for Ministry for such continuation. The written request must indicate clearly the educational goals of the rostered minister, the time line of when the completion of study is anticipated, and a statement of commitment that the rostered minister intends to be available for a letter of call within this church upon completion of the graduate study. Should the Division for Ministry indicate its approval concerning continued graduate study the request for continuation of the on leave from call status is made by the rostered minister to the Synod Council in the synod of which the rostered minister is a member. This request, together with the recommendation of the Division for Ministry, is then considered by the synod bishop and Synod Council.

III. Action by the Synod Bishop and Synod Council

The synod bishop reviews the request for continuation of the on leave from call status beyond three years and forwards that request to the Synod Council together with the bishop's evaluation of the request. The Synod Council considers the request of the rostered minister. Should the decision of the Synod Council be to recommend approval, the Synod Council shall make such a request to the Conference of Bishops. The Synod Council forwards its decision, together with the statement of the rostered minister and the rationale of the Synod Council in recommending approval, to the Conference of Bishops.

At the request of the synod bishop, the Synod Council may initiate consideration of continued on leave status with a rostered minister for the sake of the mission and ministry in the synod.

A rostered minister on leave from call must provide an annual written request to the Synod Council for continuation of that status. The Synod Council must act annually on a request to remain on leave from call beyond the three year norm (six years for graduate study).

IV.   Action by Conference of Bishops

The Roster Committee of the Conference of Bishops receives requests from Synod Councils for the continuation of on leave from call status beyond the three year norm. The Roster Committee reviews such requests and reports its recommendations to the Conference of Bishops. The Conference of Bishops, in a regular meeting of the conference, by a majority vote acts upon requests for continuation of on leave from call status. It shall report its decision to the Synod Council seeking such a continuation. Conference of Bishops action in approving the request by a Synod Council is valid for two years. A Synod Council may act to continue the on leave from call status for a second year before requesting the Conference of Bishops for subsequent action.

3.   Leadership Development Strategy

Background: The Division for Ministry, as mandated in a churchwide continuing resolution, shall:

coordinate, in consultation with other churchwide units, synods, and institutions, this church's efforts in leadership development and in the formation of persons preparing for and serving in rostered ministries (ELCA16.11.B91.a.3).

At its January 1991 meeting, the Church Council voted:

To request the Division for Ministry, in consultation with other appropriate churchwide units, to develop an initial plan for developing a comprehensive leadership recruitment and development strategy for the Evangelical Lutheran Church in America to be reported to the Church Council at its April 1994 meeting" (CC91.1.8).

"A Proposal for Leadership Development within the Evangelical Lutheran Church in America" was presented to the Church Council at its November 1991 meeting by the Division for Ministry.

At its March 1993 meeting, the Church Council voted:

To reaffirm the need for an intensified churchwide effort to develop a leadership strategy (that would include recruitment, development and support), as mandated by the Church Council in January 1991; and to request that the interunit staff team on leadership development, which is carrying out this assignment and is convened by the Division for Ministry, report its progress to the council at its December 1993 meeting (CC93.3.11).

The Division for Ministry recommended Church Council adoption of the following resolution.

Council Action: Pastor Settlage reported on behalf of an inter-unit staff team convened to address this issue. He characterized the project as one of the most interesting and challenging assignments he has had, because of the broad range of understanding of leadership development within the churchwide organization. He said that the most significant development, therefore, was the determination of a definition of leadership development that is focused on the mission of the church and the intentional recruitment and training of persons for service.

During discussion, the Rev. John O. Knudson inquired whether the most recent consultations on this issue also could be applied to recruitment in rural areas. Pastor Settlage responded affirmatively. Patsy Gottschalk commented that the development of this policy seemed to be an unusually labor-intensive effort. The

Rev. Richard G. Deines inquired whether the recruitment of persons of color, particularly in urban areas, was addressed. Pastor Settlage responded that that matter was being considered with a focus on the development of lay leadership.

VOTED: *CC94.4.32*

To receive the "Report on the ELCA Leadership Recruitment and Development Strategy" as fulfillment of the requests of the Church Council in its January 1991 and March 1993 meetings concerning the development of "a leadership strategy that would include recruitment, development, and support," specifically affirming:

1.   the need for a continued commitment to the recruitment and development of faithful leaders in the Evangelical Lutheran Church in America;

2.   the "Definition of Leadership Recruitment and Development" printed in the report; and

3.   the need for continued inter-unit consultation and coordination of activities related to leadership recruitment and development in the Evangelical Lutheran Church in America as described in the "next steps" of the report.

4.   Study of Theological Education
Financial Support of Theological Education; Clustering of Seminaries

Council Action: Pastor Wagner introduced the Rev. Phyllis B. Anderson, director for theological education in the Division for Ministry, who presented a progress report on the Study of Theological Education, particularly with an emphasis on the financial support of theological education in this church and the clustering of seminaries. Pastor Anderson reviewed the developments that have occurred since the February 1994 report was issued, particularly the response of seminaries. Luther Northwestern Theological Seminary (St. Paul, Minn.) and Pacific Lutheran Theological Seminary (Berkeley, Calif.) have agreed, by board action in September 1993, to form a cluster. Lutheran School of Theology at Chicago and Wartburg Theological Seminary are expected to take a similar action in the next few weeks. Lutheran Theological Seminary at Philadelphia, Lutheran Theological Seminary at Gettysburg, and Lutheran Theological Southern Seminary (Columbia S.C.) have considered formation of an east-coast cluster. If that occurs, Trinity Lutheran Seminary (Columbus, Ohio) is expected to act to be considered a cluster of one, making it responsible for developing a full range of programs to train those in its geographical area. Assignment of synods to these clusters will need to be considered no matter what the eventuality of the alignments. Preparation for clustering includes the development of a business plan on costs and possibilities for raising funds.

Turning to the issue of seminary funding, Pastor Anderson reported that some 25 synods have had meetings to look at this issue, along with four of the seminary boards. Nonetheless, no easy way to raise money has been found, and the financial situation has become even more acute since the report on seminary funding was written. The report supports present patterns of funding and depends on financial savings through clustering. Pastor Anderson reviewed a variety of responses to this proposal that surfaced through the consultations already held.

During discussion, the Rev. James G. Cobb asked about recent meetings of seminary boards. Pastor Anderson responded that the boards of the seminaries at Philadelphia, Gettysburg, and Columbia had voted to continue in conversation. Pastor Cobb also inquired about the proposal that Trinity Lutheran Seminary be a cluster of one. Pastor Anderson commented that such a plan was anticipated as a possibility from the beginning, "in order to allow flexibility for the seminaries really to make choices that would work for them." Pastor Cobb asked whether the task force, board of the Division for Ministry, or Church Council would have an opportunity to be more directive in expressing a preference to align the seminary with other institutions. Pastor Anderson responded that such was an appropriate idea. She noted that while the seminaries would have the right to choose their alignments, the division's board would take action to approve such decisions. She observed that any action the Church Council may take to encourage the institutions to engage seriously in the clustering process, as approved by the Churchwide Assembly, would be welcome. Bishop Paull E. Spring expressed concern about the east-coast configuration, noting that it would not help to integrate the various ecclesial traditions this church had inherited. Carlos Peña noted a concern of his Synod Council that synods may divert churchwide mission support funds in order to support seminaries. Bishop Kenneth H. Sauer confirmed that Trinity Seminary would prefer to be involved with another seminary in a new configuration and would be grateful for suggestions on how that might be possible.

The Rev. Franklin D. Fry questioned churchwide support for seminaries, stating that he believed such funding would be lodged more appropriately in synods, because it is easier to raise money for the local institution than for theological education in general. The Rev. H. George Anderson asked about the proportion of revenue raised through tuition and fees. Pastor Anderson responded that, although the cost to students would increase, it would be offset by expanded availability of financial aid.

Robert S. Schroeder asked when the task force would address funding for theological education in areas other than seminaries. Pastor Anderson responded that seminaries will be engaging in theological education in broader ways than previously. Through the clustering program, seminaries will design new relationships with the colleges of this church so that both are part of the delivery system.

Dale V. Sandstrom inquired whether, if a system of theological education were to be built from scratch now, would it look like the present system. Pastor Anderson

replied that a new system would be quite different, with perhaps four large seminaries located across the church. But, she cautioned, such a change would obliterate the well developed loyalties that are presently in place. Loren W. Mathre expressed concern that 50 percent of seminary funding would come from a seminary's constituency, and that, if traditional loyalties are broken, it would endanger the ability of this church to fund theological education. Bishop Robert L. Isaksen noted that Trinity Seminary was open to being part of the east-coast cluster but that that had not happened. Pastor Anderson indicated that Trinity's participation was presently being discussed.

The Rev. James G. Cobb offered the following motion:

VOTED: CC94.4.33
To encourage the inclusion of Trinity Theological Seminary, Columbus, Ohio, in a cluster (either east or west).

Bishop Kenneth H. Sauer recommended that the foregoing resolution be directed to all the seminaries of this church. The Rev. John O. Knudson noted that seminaries do not have the financial resources to provide the kinds of scholarships that colleges are able to offer. Pastor Anderson responded that a large percentage of financial aid funds come from seminary endowments restricted to scholarship purposes and such endowments need to be increased.

5. Special Needs Retirement Fund

Background: The 1993 Churchwide Assembly voted (CA93.8.100):

To establish in consultation with the ELCA Board of Pensions a special fund to provide both additional pension contributions for pastors in situations of low compensation, and for pensions who are receiving at or near the minimum pension. This will be a churchwide program to encourage support throughout the Evangelical Lutheran Church in America.

To recommend that the Division for Ministry—in consultation with the Division for Congregational Ministries, the Division for Outreach, and representatives from synods and rostered leaders—propose additional strategies for improving the ability of congregations to understand and respond to the interconnected issues of congregational mission and ministry, particularly as they relate to rostered leadership; and to request that a report be prepared for transmission to the 1994 Churchwide Assembly; and

To recommend that the Division for Ministry—in consultation with the Conference of Bishops—discuss constructive strategies that might be helpful in the present circumstances to address effects of low compensation on pastors, associates in ministry, and congregations.

Staff of the Division for Ministry, Division for Congregational Ministries, and Board of Pensions have developed a plan to implement the fund authorized by the Churchwide Assembly. This plan was reviewed by the Board of Pensions and the board of the Division for Ministry, and was shared as information with the Church Council.

Council Action: Pastor Wagner presented a progress report on the development of a "Special Needs

Retirement Fund." The Church Council received the foregoing as information.

6. Reinstatement of Rostered Leaders

Background: The Southeastern Pennsylvania Synod submitted the following resolution to the Church Council:

RESOLVED, that the Synod Council of the Southeastern Pennsylvania Synod petition the ELCA Church Council to request that the Division for Ministry, in consultation with the Conference of Bishops, develop a churchwide policy of support for reinstated leaders that provides for supervision and public accountability for the privilege of serving the church as an ordained or certified leader; and be it further

RESOLVED, that the implementation of the policy of support shall:

a. empower reinstated pastors and associates in ministry to be honest about their history of sexual misconduct and of maintaining proper boundaries, transference and counter-transference issues and of their personal ongoing readiness and ability to provide ministry;

b. assist congregations and agencies of the church who have called reinstated pastors and associates in ministry to set appropriate boundaries as safeguards while working mutually with reinstated leaders in proclaiming the gospel and in calling these leaders to be accountable;

c. assist bishops in being reasonably assured that reinstated leaders were providing faithful and effective exercise of their ministry in all matters of morality and personal ethics. The bishop shall receive regular reports of supervision and evaluation of the pastor/associate in ministry; and

d. give assurance to the general community in which the reinstated pastor/associate in ministry serves that the Evangelical Lutheran Church in America is actively supervising and regularizing the activities of the reinstated leaders so that there is a positive move towards complete restoration.

At its December 1993 meeting the Church Council voted:

To refer the resolution of the Southeastern Pennsylvania Synod on possible reinstatement of rostered leaders to the Division for Ministry; and

To request that the Division for Ministry, in consultation with the Conference of Bishops, provide a report and recommendation on this matter to the Church Council at its April 1994 meeting (CC93.12.105.m.).

Staff of the Division for Ministry and the Conference of Bishops, together with the ELCA general counsel, have reviewed the resolution submitted to the Church Council by the Southeastern Pennsylvania Synod regarding the development of a churchwide policy for reinstated leaders, which would provide for supervision and public accountability of those persons. The reinstatement of ordained ministers to the roster of the Evangelical Lutheran Church in America is presently guided by a process developed by the Division for Ministry, reviewed by the Conference of Bishops, and adopted by the Church Council in November 1992. That policy already requires that a very thorough evaluation of candidates for reinstatement be made by the candidacy committee of the synod, including such actions as a review of all records and information concerning the applicant and verification of synodical records concerning the reason for removal from the roster. The candidacy committee is instructed to interview the applicant and to explore all concerns related to reinstatement, including:

1. The circumstances surrounding the removal of the applicant from the roster of ordained ministers, including the applicant's reasons for leaving the roster.

2. The applicant's reasons for requesting reinstatement to the roster of ordained ministers, with special emphasis upon what has changed in the person's life, faith, attitudes and circumstances since the time of removal.

3. Discussion of the applicant's understanding of ordained ministry in the Evangelical Lutheran Church in America, and the applicant's willingness to serve in response to the needs of this church.

4. Discussion of "Vision and Expectations—Ordained Ministers in the Evangelical Lutheran Church in America," and the applicant's commitment to live according to the expectations of this church.

The policy states, "If an applicant who was removed from the roster as the result of the official disciplinary process of this church (or who resigned from the roster in order to avoid the official disciplinary process) is approved for reinstatement, the candidacy committee must report its decision to the Executive Committee of the Synod Council. Authorization of the approval requires a two-thirds majority vote of the total membership of the Executive Committee. If such an applicant is denied reinstatement by the candidacy committee, its decision is final."

The policy states, "In the case of an applicant whose removal from the roster was the result of the official disciplinary process of this church (or a resignation from the roster to avoid the disciplinary process), a minimum of five years must elapse after the removal from the roster before an application for reinstatement may be considered. The elapse of five years does not guarantee reconsideration, however."

The intent of the Southeastern Pennsylvania Synod resolution appears to be focused upon assuring congregations, the bishop, and the general community that pastors and associates in ministry who may have been guilty of sexual misconduct in the past will not repeat such conduct in the future. Although this is an understandable desire, the churchwide staff who have reviewed the recommendations do not believe that the strategies proposed can accomplish that end. Further, there is the inference that persons reinstated, because of the conditions under which they were removed from the roster, should be reinstated with some conditions attached to that reinstatement. Again, while such conditions may be appropriate, they are best established on a case-by-case basis by the synod bishop who bears supervisory responsibility for the rostered leaders of the synod, reinstated or not. The synod bishop is already empowered to develop whatever guidelines or individual understandings he or she may deem appropriate in regard to such cases. Procedures and common understandings among bishops and synod staffs also make it highly unlikely that a person's ministerial history will be unknown by those presently responsible for oversight.

It is the judgment of staff of the Division for Ministry and the Conference of Bishops that sufficient protections exist in the policies of the Evangelical Lutheran Church in America in regard to the reinstatement of formerly-rostered persons, and that synod bishops are already empowered to develop whatever additional guidelines or supervisory relationships they may deem appropriate to individual persons on the rosters of the Evangelical Lutheran Church in America. It is, therefore, recommended that the resolution from the Southeastern Pennsylvania Synod be received as useful advice by the Division for Ministry and the Conference of Bishops, but that no new policies be developed in response to this resolution.

Council Action: Pastor Wagner introduced the following recommendation, subsequently adopted by the Church Council without discussion.

VOTED: *CC94.4.34*
To request the secretary of the Evangelical Lutheran Church in America to convey this information on reinstatement of rostered leaders to the Southeastern Pennsylvania Synod.

7.   Guidelines Related to Diaconal Ministers
Background: The 1993 Churchwide Assembly of the Evangelical Lutheran Church in America adopted the following (CA93.6.17, Section III.):

To establish a diaconal ministry as part of the officially recognized, rostered ministries of the Evangelical Lutheran Church in America.

To designate, as recommended by the board of the Division for Ministry, such a diaconal ministry as part of the lay rostered ministries of this church for which individuals would be approved for the roster of diaconal ministers, according to the criteria, standards, policies, and procedures of this church.

To declare that diaconal ministers be called by this church to a public ministry that exemplifies the servant life, equips and motivates others to live it, and shares the Word of God in Law and Gospel through word and deed wherever possible and in a great variety of ways, in order to serve officially in interdependence with other laity, pastors, and bishops of this church, sharing with them responsibility for the Word of God in service to the Church and the world, to empower, equip, and support all the baptized in the ministry and mission of Jesus Christ—with an initial and illustrative, but not an exhaustive, list of categories of diaconal ministry to include education, mission and evangelism, care, administration, and music and the arts.

To assign the care and guidance of candidates for diaconal ministry to this church's candidacy system, with the Division for Ministry to provide appropriate assistance and training for synodical candidacy committees to deal with diaconal candidates.

To affirm that the specific requirements for approval be developed by the Division for Ministry, reviewed by the Conference of Bishops, and adopted by the Church Council.

To direct the Division for Ministry, in consultation with the Conference of Bishops and with the approval of the Church Council—and in consultation with the appropriate officials of the Evangelical Lutheran Church in Canada—make the necessary revisions in related documents for their application to diaconal ministers.

To direct the Division for Ministry to hold a consultation(s) with persons engaged in diaconal ministry of various kinds in this church and with those engaged in training persons for diaconal service in this and other churches as part of the design and preparation of programs for training ELCA diaconal ministers.

The 1993 Churchwide Assembly adopted bylaw 7.51.05., regarding diaconal ministers:

This church shall establish and maintain a lay roster of diaconal ministers who shall be called by this church to positions that exemplify the servant life and that seek to equip and motivate others to live it. Such diaconal ministers shall seek in a great variety of ways to empower, equip, and support all the baptized people of God in the ministry of Jesus Christ and the mission of God in the world.

(a)   Upon certification and approval as a candidate for the lay roster of diaconal ministers, and upon receipt and acceptance of a valid, regularly issued letter of call, the candidate shall be designated, according to the service orders of this church, as a lay diaconal minister.

(b)   All constitutional provisions, bylaws, and continuing resolutions regarding associates in ministry of the Evangelical Lutheran Church in America shall apply to those on the lay roster of diaconal ministers of the Evangelical Lutheran Church in America.

In response to the actions of the 1993 Churchwide Assembly, the Division for Ministry held a consultation on the preparation and training of diaconal ministers. This consultation was held at the churchwide offices in Chicago, January 27-29, 1994. Participants included Division for Ministry staff and board representation; a representative from the Conference of Bishops liaison committee; representatives from the eight ELCA seminaries; representatives from the Roman Catholic Church, Episcopal Church, United Methodist Church, and the Evangelical Lutheran Church in Canada; and representatives from current Lutheran expressions of diaconal Ministry—Diakonia, ELCA Deaconess Community, and Lutheran Deaconess Association.

Two distinctive models for diaconal ministry were identified during this consultation. The Roman Catholic and Episcopal models are an ordained, non-stipended model of servant ministry combined with liturgical functioning for which diocesan specific programs of training and preparation are developed. This is the model used to fashion the Diakonia lay program that serves in the Metropolitan New York Synod of the Evangelical Lutheran Church in America. The second model of a consecrated, stipended, leadership model for diaconal ministry was represented by the United Methodist Church and the two Lutheran deaconess communities. These expressions require academic training and preparation for ministry. A third model found in American Protestantism but not represented at this consultation is that of a congregational deacon (Baptist and others).

Following the consultation, staff of the Division for Ministry has developed "Diaconal Ministers in the Evangelical Lutheran Church in America: Standards, Preparation, Approval, and Call." These standards include a description of diaconal ministry in the Evangelical Lutheran Church in America and the requirements for preparation and approval for service as a diaconal minister.

The Conference of Bishops discussed those standards at its March 1994 meeting and referred the document back to committee. Acknowledging this action, the board of the Division for Ministry, at its meeting later in the month, recommended that the Church Council adopt council agenda Exhibit M, Part 6, as a working document. Following additional conversations, a final document will be reviewed by the Conference of Bishops at its October 1994 meeting, prior to consideration by the board of the Division for Ministry. The Church Council will then take action on the finalized version of this document at its November 1994 meeting.

Council Action: Pastor Wagner introduced Madelyn H. Busse, director for associates in ministry in the Division for Ministry, who introduced the following recommendation, subsequently adopted by the Church Council:

VOTED: CC94.4.35
To adopt "Diaconal Ministers in the Evangelical Lutheran Church in America: Standards, Preparation, Approval, and Call," printed in council agenda Exhibit M, Part 6, as a working document subject to final review by the Conference of Bishops, final recommendation by the board of the Division for Ministry, and final adoption by the Church Council.

During discussion, Chair Magnus inquired about the inclusion of the word, "diaconal," in the Item B.3. of the Exhibit ("Be committed and prepared to equip the baptized for diaconal ministry in the world and in the church."). Ms. Busse explained, "Diaconal ministry is something to which the whole church is called. . . . Just as we have the priesthood of all believers, we are all called to share in diaconal ministry. . . ." William T. Billings inquired about usage of the terminology, "consecration," and how it relates to ordination. Ms. Busse noted that "consecration" refers to induction into an ecclesiastical office through a ceremony (Webster). Edith M. Lohr inquired about life-long consecration in relationship to roster status and call to specific ministry. Patsy Gottschalk asked about the educational requirements for diaconal service. The Rev. Franklin D. Fry inquired about the appropriate function of diaconal ministers in working both within and without this church proper. He recommended that the matter be addressed in the document as it is developed.

Following several announcements, the Church Council recessed 12:25 P.M.

The Church Council reconvened on Monday, April 18, 1994, at 1:30 P.M.

Letters of Call for Associates in Ministry

Robert S. Schroeder sought to move the following:

MOVED: To extend letters of call to all associates in ministry to whom letters of appointment previously had been extended by the Church Council.

The motion died for lack of a second.

Matters Related to the Department for Ecumenical Affairs

1.   Study on Lutheran-Jewish Declaration

Background: At the 1993 Churchwide Assembly, the following memorials were received from the Northwestern Minnesota Synod and from the New England Synod:

WHEREAS, because of their common heritage and Scripture, Christians and Christianity have a unique relationship with Jews and Judaism; and

WHEREAS, the attitude of Christians toward Jews has often been hostile, lacking in love and respect; and

WHEREAS, the fundamental witness of Christians is reconciliation and peace; and

WHEREAS, the Evangelical Lutheran Church in America has not adopted a statement on Lutheran-Jewish relations; therefore, be it

RESOLVED, that the Northwestern Minnesota Synod memorialize the 1993 Churchwide Assembly of the Evangelical Lutheran Church in America to form a task force through its Department for Ecumenical Affairs to develop a statement on Lutheran-Jewish relations; and

RESOLVED, that the New England Synod Assembly memorialize the Evangelical Lutheran Church in America in its 1993 Churchwide Assembly to direct the Department for Ecumenical Affairs:

1. To prepare a statement of instruction and guidance on Jewish-Lutheran relations for the Evangelical Lutheran Church in America for consideration by the Evangelical Lutheran Church in America at its next churchwide assembly in 1995; and
2. To prepare a separate declaration directed to our friends in the Jewish community:
   a. deploring and repudiating the anti-Judaic recommendations and coarse rhetoric employed by Martin Luther in theological controversies in the sixteenth century and the baleful effect that these had on subsequent generations and their use in Germany under the National Socialists; and
   b. affirming our desire as Lutheran Christians to live out our faith in Jesus Christ as Lord and Savior in love and respect for the Jewish people by pledging ourselves to increased efforts at the eradication of anti-Semitism in the United States and throughout the world, and continuing efforts at improving understanding and relations with our Jewish friends in this country individually and as congregations and church judicatories.

In response to these memorials, the 1993 Churchwide Assembly voted (CA93.7.46):

To request the Department for Ecumenical Affairs to prepare a declaration addressed to the Jewish community (1) repudiating the anti-Judaic rhetoric and violent recommendations of Martin Luther and grieving the tragic affects of such words on subsequent generations; and (2) affirming our desire to live out our faith in Jesus Christ in love and respect for the Jewish people by pledging to oppose the deadly working of anti-Semitism in church and society; such a declaration is to be reported to the Church Council for action;

To receive and affirm as a member church of the Lutheran World Federation the section of the statement of the 1984 assembly of Lutheran World Federation regarding Martin Luther's anti-Judaic writings, that statement having been commended by the assembly to its member churches;

To refer the statement of the 1984 Lutheran World Federation Assembly of the Department for Ecumenical Affairs to be used as one of the bases of the department's work on the subject of Lutheran-Jewish relations in the 1994-1995 biennium within the context of the worldwide communion of Lutheranism;

To refer the memorials of the Northwestern Minnesota and New England Synod to the Department for Ecumenical Affairs as the department continues its work on the subject of Lutheran-Jewish relations in the 1994-1995 biennium; and

To transmit this minute as information as the response of the 1993 Churchwide Assembly to the memorials of the Northwestern Minnesota Synod and the New England Synod.

Subsequent to the 1993 Churchwide Assembly, staff of the Department for Ecumenical Affairs developed a procedure to handle the memorial from the Churchwide Assembly. On November 9, 1993, the Consultative Panel on Lutheran-Jewish relations met and discussed the ecumenical-affairs staff proposal, concurred with the proposed time line and offered some suggestions regarding the text of the declaration.

The advisory committee of the Department for Ecumenical Affairs reviewed this material at its subsequent meeting, refined the text of a suggested statement and took the following action:

That

1. "The Declaration" *[see below]* be conveyed to the Church Council for review and action at its April 1994 meeting.
2. A study group to develop a study guide on "The Declaration" be formed by the Department for Ecumenical Affairs and that this guide be reviewed by the advisory committee in 1995.
3. The Department for Ecumenical Affairs continue its work in the area of Lutheran-Jewish relations with the expectation that as soon as funds are available the department would fulfill the commitment made in "Ecumenism: The Vision of the ELCA" and prepare a document on Lutheran-Jewish relations including as resources the 1974 American Lutheran Church statement, the 1984 Lutheran World Federation statement and the 1971 statement of the Lutheran Council USA, "Some Observations and Guidelines for Conversations between Lutherans and Jews," as well as recent efforts of various expressions of this church.

"The Declaration of the Evangelical Lutheran Church in America to the Jewish Community," as approved by the advisory committee of the Department for Ecumenical Affairs, was as follows:

In the long history of Christianity there exists no more tragic development than the treatment accorded the Jewish people on the part of Christian believers. Very few Christian communities of faith were able to escape the contagion of anti-Judaism and its modern successor, anti-Semitism. Lutherans belonging to the Lutheran World Federation and the Evangelical Lutheran Church in America feel a special burden in this regard because of certain elements in the legacy of the reformer Martin Luther and the catastrophe suffered by Jews in places where the Lutheran churches were strongly represented.

The Lutheran communion of faith is linked by name and heritage to the memory of Martin Luther, teacher and reformer. Honoring his name in our own, we recall his bold stand for truth, his earthy and sublime words of wisdom, and above all his witness to God's saving Word. Luther proclaimed a gospel for people as we really are, bidding us to trust a grace sufficient to reach our deepest shames and address the most tragic truths.

In the spirit of that truth-telling, we who bear his name and heritage must with pain acknowledge also Luther's anti-Judaic diatribes and violent recommendations of his later writings against the Jews. As did already many of Luther's own companions, we reject this violent invective, and yet more do we express our deep and abiding sorrow over its tragic effects on subsequent generations. In concert with the Lutheran World Federation, we particularly deplore the appropriation of Luther's words by modern anti-Semites for the teaching of hatred toward Judaism or toward the Jewish people in our day.

Grieving the complicity of our own tradition within this history of hatred, moreover, we express our urgent desire to live out our faith in Jesus Christ with love and respect for the Jewish people. We recognize in anti-Semitism a contradiction and an affront to the Gospel, a violation of our hope and calling, and we pledge this church to oppose the deadly working of such bigotry, both within our own circles and in the society around us. Finally, we pray for the continued blessing of the Blessed One upon the increasing cooperation and understanding between Lutheran Christians and the Jewish community.

Council Action: Chair Magnus called upon the Rev. William G. Rusch, executive director of the Department for Ecumenical Affairs, to introduce discussion of the proposed declaration. The Rev. Daniel F. Martensen, associate director of the Department for Ecumenical Affairs, also was present for the discussion.

Bishop Robert L. Isaksen termed the action a "great response" to the action of 1993 Churchwide Assembly. He proposed two friendly amendments, which were then moved by the Rev. Stephen M. Youngdahl:

MOVED;

SECONDED: To amend the text of the proposed declaration as follows:

• Paragraph one, line 7, add "of the holocaust"; and
• Paragraph three, line 3, strike "already" and add "in the sixteenth century" after the word, "companions."

The Rev. H. George Anderson asked whether the word, catastrophe, referred only to the Holocaust. The Rev. Nadine F. Lehr stated discomfort with confining catastrophe only to the Holocaust. She stated, "Any kind of anti-Semitism that comes out of a Christian context is not appropriate," and moved the following amendment:

MOVED;

SECONDED: To amend the motion to read:

To amend the text of the proposed declaration as follows:

• Paragraph one, line 7, ". . . and the catastrophe suffered by the Jews in the places where the Lutheran churches were strongly represented, including the Holocaust of the twentieth century; and
• Paragraph three, line 3, strike "already" and add "in the sixteenth century" after the word, "companions."

The Rev. James G. Cobb commended the amendment, because it addresses both the specificity of the Holocaust and the general difficulty of Jewish-Christian relations. Secretary Lowell G. Almen recommended that the motion be emended by placing the final clause after the word, "catastrophe." Pastor Rusch recommended changing the word, catastrophe, to the plural, catastrophes. The proposed emendations were received as friendly amendments.

MOVED;

SECONDED;

CARRIED: To amend the motion to read:

To amend the text of the proposed declaration as follows:

- Paragraph one, line 7, ". . . and the catastrophes, including the Holocaust of the twentieth century, suffered by the Jews in the places where the Lutheran churches were strongly represented; and
- Paragraph three, line 3, strike "already" and add "in the sixteenth century" after the word, "companions."

MOVED;
SECONDED;
CARRIED: To amend the text of the proposed declaration as follows:

- Paragraph one, line 7, ". . . and the catastrophes, including the Holocaust of the twentieth century, suffered by the Jews in the places where the Lutheran churches were strongly represented; and
- Paragraph three, line 3, strike "already" and add "in the sixteenth century" after the word, "companions."

VOTED: CC94.4.36
To affirm the continuing work in this area by the Department for Ecumenical Affairs; and

To adopt "The Declaration" as a statement on Lutheran-Jewish Relations, as follows:

THE DECLARATION OF THE
EVANGELICAL LUTHERAN CHURCH IN AMERICA
TO THE JEWISH COMMUNITY

In the long history of Christianity there exists no more tragic development than the treatment accorded the Jewish people on the part of Christian believers. Very few Christian communities of faith were able to escape the contagion of anti-Judaism and its modern successor, anti-Semitism. Lutherans belonging to the Lutheran World Federation and the Evangelical Lutheran Church in America feel a special burden in this regard because of certain elements in the legacy of the reformer Martin Luther and the catastrophes, including the Holocaust of the twentieth century, suffered by Jews in places where the Lutheran churches were strongly represented.

The Lutheran communion of faith is linked by name and heritage to the memory of Martin Luther, teacher and reformer. Honoring his name in our own, we recall his bold stand for truth, his earthy and sublime words of wisdom, and above all his witness to God's saving Word. Luther proclaimed a gospel for people as we really are, bidding us to trust a grace sufficient to reach our deepest shames and address the most tragic truths.

In the spirit of that truth-telling, we who bear his name and heritage must with pain acknowledge also Luther's anti-Judaic diatribes and violent recommendations of his later writings against the Jews. As did many of Luther's own companions in the sixteenth century, we reject this violent invective, and yet more do we express our deep and abiding sorrow over its tragic effects on subsequent generations. In concert with the Lutheran World Federation, we particularly deplore the appropriation of Luther's words by modern anti-Semites for the teaching of hatred toward Judaism or toward the Jewish people in our day.

Grieving the complicity of our own tradition within this history of hatred, moreover, we express our urgent desire to live out our faith in Jesus Christ with love and respect for the Jewish people. We recognize in anti-Semitism a contradiction and an affront to the Gospel, a viola-tion of our hope and calling, and we pledge this church to oppose the deadly working of such bigotry, both within our own circles and in the society around us. Finally, we pray for the continued blessing of the Blessed One upon the increasing cooperation and understanding between Lutheran Christians and the Jewish community.

The Rev. Franklin D. Fry stated that, while this church has placed itself on record in a salutary way on this issue, this church will be hosting a global mission event at Howard University, which recently had provided a controversial meeting place for followers of Louis Farrakhan and the Nation of Islam. Pastor Fry cautioned that this church not identify itself with the position of the university. The Rev. Mark W. Thomsen, executive director of the Division for Global Mission, responded that negotiations have been ongoing for three years for holding a global mission event on the campus of an African American university. Consultation with people living in the area indicated that moving the event did not seem to be necessary, because the official position of the university was, in fact, not represented by Minister Farrakhan. Pastor Fry stated he was not trying to move the global mission event, but to underscore the need to bear witness intentionally to the newly adopted ELCA declaration during the event.

The Rev. James G. Cobb asked about the distribution of declaration.

2.   Lutheran-Orthodox Dialogue
Pastor Rusch also reported that the Rev. Robert L. Wilken (Charlottesville, Va.) recently had resigned from the Lutheran-Orthodox dialogue committee. He announced that Bishop Herbert W. Chilstrom had appointed the Rev. Carl A. Voltz of Luther Northwestern Theological Seminary (St. Paul, Minn.) to fill the vacancy.

Matters Related to the Division for Church and Society (continued)
4.   Resolution on Cuba
Chair Magnus called upon the Rev. Charles S. Miller Jr., executive director of the Division for Church and Society, to continue discussion of the proposed resolution on U.S. relations with Cuba. He drew attention to council agenda Exhibit P, Part 7, pages 1 and 2, regarding the involvement of Lutheran World Relief (LWR) in humanitarian relief in Cuba, and the issue of petitioning the U.S. government to end its embargo against Cuba. He referred specifically to LWR activities in Cuba and to the ELCA "Churchwide Blueprint for Action on Central America and the Caribbean," a document approved by the Church Council in 1989. Pastor Miller also noted that the United States has had normalized relations with other nations that were communist or considered oppressive.

Pastor Miller suggested a division of the question. Loren W. Mathre then moved to divide the question by paragraph:

MOVED;
SECONDED;
CARRIED: To consider the second "resolve" in the motion on Cuba item by item.

During discussion, J. David Ellwanger noted that an embargo against Cuba has been opposed by every democracy in Central and South America, based in part on the belief that Fidel Castro's days as dictator are numbered. He also asserted that regardless of that situation, humanitarian aid ought to be offered to suffering people.

MOVED;
SECONDED;
CARRIED: To approve item (1) as follows:

To request that relevant entities of the Evangelical Lutheran Church in America:
(1)   Support Lutheran congregations in Cuba through prayer, information sharing, and material support, in cooperation with the ELCA Division for Global Mission and the Lutheran Coalition on Latin America.

Bishop Robert L. Isaksen suggested the following amendment to item (2), which subsequently was moved by a voting member of the council:

MOVED;
SECONDED;
CARRIED: To amend item (2) to read:

(2)   Participate in sending humanitarian aid to people aided by the churches of Cuba through such organizations as Lutheran World Relief, Church World Service, and Pastors for Peace; and

During discussion of the foregoing item, Loren W. Mathre inquired about the organization, Pastors for Peace.

During discussion of item (3), Dale V. Sandstrom urged disapproval of the motion. The Rev. Stephen M. Youngdahl moved the following amendment to item (3):

MOVED;
SECONDED;
CARRIED: To delete the phrase, "end its embargo against Cuba, and" from item (3).

Mr. Sandstrom reiterated his concern that the Castro regime be ended as soon as possible. The Rev. Richard G. Deines spoke against the amendment, observing that, as in the case of Nicaragua, the embargo affects people living in poverty rather than the governing regime.

MOVED;
SECONDED;
CARRIED: To approve item (3) as amended:

(3)   Petition the U.S. government to seek further reconciliation and normalization of relations between the United States and Cuba;

VOTED: *CC94.4.37*
To act affirmatively on the 1993 memorial of the Minneapolis Area Synod and the 1993 resolution of the West Virginia-Western Maryland Synod.
To request that relevant entities of the Evangelical Lutheran Church in America:
(1)   Support Lutheran congregations in Cuba through prayer, information sharing, and material support, in cooperation with the ELCA Division for Global Mission and the Lutheran Coalition on Latin America.
(2)   Participate in sending humanitarian aid to people aided by the churches of Cuba through such organizations as Lutheran World Relief, Church World Service, and Pastors for Peace; and
(3)   Petition the U.S. government to seek further reconciliation and normalization of relations between the United States and Cuba; and
To request the secretary of this church to communicate this action to the Minneapolis Area Synod and the West Virginia-Western Maryland Synod.

5.   50th Anniversary of the United Nations

Background: At its March 1994 meeting, the board of the Division for Church in Society adopted the following resolution calling for study, reflection, renewal, new visioning, and recommitment to the United Nations throughout the Evangelical Lutheran Church in America on the occasion of the UN's 50th anniversary in 1995. This resolution also reaffirmed the division's activities to further these activities and urged the Church Council to participate in this effort.

WHEREAS, in 1995 the 50th anniversary of the founding of the United Nations will be commemorated; and

WHEREAS, 1995 will mark also 50 years [after] the end of World War II, the initiation of the atomic era, the beginning of the manifestations of the Cold War, such as the division of Korea, the launching of the process of decolonization, and the start of discussions which led to the adoption of the International Bill of Human Rights; and

WHEREAS, the churches, corporately through the Federal Council of Churches' Commission on a Just and Durable Peace, subsequently, the National Council of the Churches of Christ in the U.S.A., the World Council of Churches, and denominational efforts supported the founding of the United Nations and have continued to support the United Nations' ongoing work; and

WHEREAS, the principles enunciated in the Six Pillars of Peace, adopted by the Federal Council of Churches' Commission on a Just and Durable Peace in 1942, continue to be vital for today, i.e.,

(1)   The peace must provide the political framework for continuing collaboration of the United Nations and, in due course, of neutral and enemy nations.

(2) The peace must make provision for bringing within the scope of international agreement those economic and financial acts of national governments which have widespread international repercussions.

(3) The peace must make provision for an organization to adapt the treaty structure of the world to changing underlying conditions.

(4) The peace must proclaim the goal of autonomy for subject peoples and it must establish an international organization to assure and to supervise the realization of that end.

(5) The peace must establish procedures for controlling military establishment everywhere.

(6) The peace must establish in principle, and seek to achieve in practice, the right of individuals everywhere to religious and intellectual liberty.

WHEREAS, in the year 1995, the scope of the mission of the United Nations will be manifest in the World Summit for Social Development, the Fourth World Conference of Women, the Review Conference on the Non-Proliferation Treaty, and the United Nations Year of Tolerance; and

WHEREAS, the General Board of the National Council of the Churches of Christ in the U.S.A. has adopted a resolution calling the attention of the churches to the UN's 50th anniversary,

THEREFORE, the board of the Division for Church in Society of the Evangelical Lutheran Church in America;

(1) Anticipates 1995 as a year of study, reflection, renewal, new visioning, and recommitment;

(2) Commits itself to full participation in those processes already commenced by the National Council of Churches, noting in particular the themes adopted by Friendship Press for 1995 on Europe and the United Nations;

(3) Urges the Church Council to call upon congregations of the Evangelical Lutheran Church in America to join actively in these related activities, summoning renewed vigor in commitment to justice, peace, and the integrity of creation;

(4) Pledges to work, in coordination with the Department of Ecumenical Affairs, with the World Council of Churches to take the lead internationally to rally the Christian community to this cause;

(5) Requests the Division for Church in Society to advocate with the U.S. government a renewal of the U.S.'s full commitment to the United Nations as a primary channel for conflict resolution and for responding to global problems;

(6) Reaffirms the 1993-1994 Lutheran Office for Governmental Affairs Advocacy Plan, which seeks U.S. ratification of human rights instruments not yet approved by the U.S. Senate:
   (a) the International Convention on the Elimination of All Forms of Racial Discrimination;
   (b) the International Convention on the Elimination of All Forms of Discrimination Against Women;
   (c) the International Convention on the Rights of the Child;
   (d) the International Covenant on Economic, Social and Cultural Rights; and
   (e) the American Convention on Human Rights;
   and encourages ELCA congregations to communicate support for these instruments to their Senators and the Administration;

(7) Calls upon the U.S. and all other UN member states to recommit themselves to the principles outlined in the preamble to the Charter and the purposes stated in Article I;

(8) Commits the Evangelical Lutheran Church in America to work with the National Council of the Churches of Christ in the U.S.A., other faith communities, and like-minded organizations to support the principles and goals of the United Nations; and

(9) Calls upon members of the Evangelical Lutheran Church in America to join with members of other communions to pray for and support the United Nations in its preventive diplo-

macy, peacekeeping, peace-making, peace-building agenda, and its work for social justice and development.

Council Action: Pastor Miller introduced the following recommendation of the board of the Division for Church in Society, commemorating the 50th anniversary of the United Nations, subsequently adopted by the Church Council:

VOTED: **CC94.4.38**

To affirm the plans of the Division for Church in Society to join with ecumenical and interfaith organizations, and with others of good will, to commemorate the 50th anniversary of the founding of the United Nations;

To call upon congregations of the Evangelical Lutheran Church in America to participate in activities related to this anniversary, summoning renewed vigor in commitment to justice, peace, and the integrity of creation; and

To call upon members of the ELCA to join with members of other communions to pray for and support the United Nations in its preventive diplomacy, peacekeeping, peace-making, peace-building agenda and its work for social justice and development.

During discussion of the foregoing resolution, Loren W. Mathre inquired about related budgetary implications.

6.   Message on Community Violence

Background: The 1993 Churchwide Assembly voted to refer several memorials that deal with community violence and gun control to the Division for Church in Society, "instructing it about the urgency of developing a 'Message' on the subject of guns, community violence, and alternatives to violence, for adoption by the ELCA Church Council at its spring 1994 meeting." The assembly requested that this message "be used as the basis for a process of deliberation throughout the Evangelical Lutheran Church in America on the subject of guns, community violence, and alternatives to violence, and proposed legislation, in preparation for possible action on this matter by the 1995 Churchwide Assembly."

Council agenda Exhibit P, Part 3, contained the text of "A Message on Community Violence," which was reviewed by the board of the Division for Church in Society at its March 1994 meeting and commended by the board to the Church Council for adoption.

Council Action: Pastor Miller provided background on the technical understanding of "message" in this church, namely, an action of the Church Council, not the Churchwide Assembly, which will authorize and encourage further deliberation in this church on a particular issue. He further noted that the assembly had taken action on gun control, but directed the division and the Church Council to prepare a message. He then introduced the Rev. Karen L. Bloomquist, director for studies in the Division for Church in Society, who commented on the text of the message. Pastor Bloomquist reviewed the process for the development of this text. She noted that more than 30 reviewers had contributed substantive commentary on the initial draft, which was incorporated in the present text. The focus of the message was to help congregations to understand how conversations can be enhanced. She noted that the message would not establish new advocacy, but seeks to draw connections between previous social teaching statements and those presently being prepared for discussion in this church.

During discussion, Patsy Gottschalk suggested that children be included in those listed as the targets of educational efforts. She then moved the following:

MOVED;
SECONDED;
CARRIED: To amend, under the section, "As a community of education and service," the third bulleted item to read: ". . . educating ~~people~~ <u>children and adults</u> in how to deal with . . . ."

The Rev. Richard G. Deines expressed enthusiastic appreciation for the message, for the practical impact it will have on a variety of local issues, and for the favorable reception it will receive in the ecumenical community, which admires the timely nature of what this church is doing. He also thanked the authors for rooting the message and this church's deliberation on social issues in the cross and resurrection, that is, in this church's worship life of Word and Sacrament.

VOTED:
CC94.4.39 **To adopt as amended "A Message on Community Violence":**

A MESSAGE ON COMMUNITY VIOLENCE

The Church Council of the Evangelical Lutheran Church in America calls on members of this church to consider how they might become more involved in countering the reality and fear of violence in their communities.

The reality and fear of violence today

Violence between humans is an age-old mark of sin. Cain slew Abel; Shechem raped Dinah; David plotted the death of Uriah. Massacres, raids, and widespread abuse of peoples have been a part of our history. Those in power have often extended their racial, sexual, economic, and/or political domination through violent means. Violence is woven in and through the distinctive stories that have shaped us as Americans.

If there is something timeless about violence, there are also disturbingly new aspects. Today the word *violence* evokes images of random shootings and muggings on city streets and country lanes; savage abuse of women, men, and children; senseless brutality depicted in movies, TV shows, and video games. The breakdown of families and communities is a widespread fact of life, and violence one of its wages. For some women and children, home is less safe than the street.[1] Hate crimes continue.[2] Neighborhood,

schoolyard, workplace, or family disputes spark into violence and become lethal. They become headlines news, reinforcing the atmosphere of violence and inspiring profitable entertainment media.

People who are poor and vulnerable have long experienced life as "nasty, brutish, and short;" now those who thought they were privileged and protected are also haunted by violence. Many of the young, who previously were sheltered from exposure to violence, are now not only "entertained" by violence, but increasingly are both its victims and perpetrators. People who are poor, who are of color, or who live in inner cities are typically the most pervasively and deeply affected by violence. However, disintegrating social structures and values have occasioned turbulence that affects people of *every* class, color, and locality.

Even when experienced as stark and brutal, the causes of violence are complex. Different forms of violence have distinctive dynamics and remedies. Social as well as individual factors are involved. The collapse of families, economic injustices, breakdown of community institutions, unemployment, inadequate moral formation and guidance, personal irresponsibility, racism and sexism, inability to deal with anger and conflict, homophobia, low self-esteem, psychological problems, biochemical imbalances, and substance abuse—these and other factors lie behind the incidence of violent crime today. Fear, anxiety, and alienation are expressed through readily-available weapons of destruction.

Violence breeds more violence. Incidents of violence stir up anger and a craving for vengeance. Fear festers an attitude of "we're not going to take it anymore." Increasingly, our national mood has been described as one of "getting mad and getting even." Possessing a gun is viewed by many ordinary citizens as their last line of defense against the chaos in society, or at least a means by which to get some respect. Harsher, more vindictive sentences (including the death penalty) have much popular appeal, despite their expense and failure to deter further crime.[3]

"Tough on crime" policy stances are often proposed in response to the fear of violent crimes. Such stances have their place, but also their limits. Although police and prisons help to protect society, they have no real effect on the *causes* of violence. More prison cells and larger police forces do not necessarily lead to greater security. The United States has the highest imprisonment rate in the world, but that has not significantly affected its high rate of violent crime. Instead of addressing the root causes of violence, "tough on crime" measures can blind us to the injustices that breed violence in the first place. People of color or those who do not speak English have long been suspicious of the protection and justice that police and criminal justice systems claim to provide. Prisons can often become "schools" that harden criminals, making them even more disillusioned and enraged.

Violence and rumors of violence continue to spread—feared yet also expected in daily life. In the face of this, what are we as a church called to be and do? What resources of our faith can we bring to bear on this apparently intractable predicament? How shall we respond to both victims and perpetrators of violence? What shall we do in cooperation with others as together we seek to counter violence in our communities?

Responding out of the faith we confess

In the face of violence, God's resolve for peace in human communities is unshakable. Deliberate acts to harm or kill innocent people violate God's intention for human community. God's commandment is "You shall not murder" (Exodus 20:13). In proclaiming God's law, we declare that all people are accountable before God and the community to honor and respect the life God has given.

Before God, we all are in captivity to sin, and in need of God's mercy. Some have committed acts of violence. Others have been sinned against through acts of violence. Still others are overwhelmed by fears of violence. In proclaiming the gospel of Jesus Christ's forgiveness, healing, and new life, the church addresses the

---

[1] "Ministry to Abusive Families," (1990, Division for Congregational Ministries), a resource on domestic violence is available from the ELCA Distribution Service (code: 34-10030-2100).

[2] See "No Hate Allowed," A Resource for Congregations for Action Against Racial Hate Crimes (1993, ELCA Commission for Multicultural Ministries), available from the ELCA Distribution Service (code: 69-7007).

[3] See the ELCA social statement, "The Death Penalty," (1991).

ultimate root of violence. Through his death, Christ broke down the dividing walls of hostility, fear, and violence between people, reconciling us to God and one another (Ephesians 2:13-17). God's reign of peace has come in Jesus Christ, and will be complete in a "new heaven and new earth" where death and pain "will be no more" (Revelation 21:1,4).

The Holy Spirit works among us to wrench us from violence, hate, greed, and fear, and transforms us into people who are called to trust God and live in community with one another. In doing so, we need to confront the violent tendencies within ourselves and our society, and find ways to cultivate the practice of nonviolence. Christians, as salt of the earth (Matthew 5:13) and light of the world (Matthew 5:14), are called to respond to violent crime in the restorative ways taught by Jesus (Matthew 5:38-39) and shown by his actions (John 8:3-11).[4] Rather than reacting out of fear, or out of a vengeful desire to "get even" with those we consider our "enemies," (Luke 6:27ff) we realize they are our neighbors. We are empowered to take up the challenge to prevent violence and to attack the complex causes that make violence so pervasive.

According to Lutheran theology, society is to be ruled by the civil use of the Law. Government is responsible under God for the protection of its citizens and the maintenance of justice and public order.[5] Just laws and their proper enforcement by police and courts are necessary to restrain violence. But laws and their enforcement are often corrupted by sin. As citizens in a democracy, we have the responsibility to join with others to hold government accountable for protecting society and ensuring justice for all, and to seek changes in policies and practices toward these ends.

Pursuing our commitment to counter community violence
As a community of worship
The cross and resurrection have broken the cycle of violence, freeing us for God's future and for one another. We confess how we have sinned and been sinned against through violence. Through prayer and absolution, the power of what God has promised is able to disarm our captivity to violence. Gathered around word and sacrament, we remember and celebrate this gift of peace given the world in Jesus Christ. We are nourished and strengthened to make peace and to embrace:

- those who are victims of violence and often feel silenced. They need to speak of their pain and lingering fears, and to hear the word of new life in ways that are effective in healing the pain and overcoming the fears;
- those who have done violence to others, and their families, who often feel frozen out of the community of faith. They need to hear God's law and gospel in their lives, so that they might turn and walk in the newness of life;
- those who protect and defend society, enforce laws, settle disputes, and maintain domestic tranquillity. They need to be supported as they live out their vocation for the sake of the common good.

As a community of education and service
Communities of faith, on their own, through social ministry organizations, and in partnership with others, are called to minister to those in captivity to violence through such efforts as:

- providing a "safe place," counseling, and other services that enable people to face and deal with the realities and fears of violence in their lives;
- mediating to achieve just and peaceful solutions to social conflicts in their communities;
- educating children and adults in how to deal with anger, disagreement, discrimination, and disappointment in nonviolent ways;
- assisting those affected by poverty, racism, family instability, domestic violence, and unemployment as they seek to deal with these challenges;

---

[4] "The Death Penalty," p. 2.

[5] For example, see Article 16 of the Augsburg Confession.

- organizing activities and programs that are effective in moving youth, especially those attracted to gangs and hate groups, from disillusionment to hope;
- supporting organizing efforts that empower communities to effect change;
- ministering with persons who have committed violent crimes so that they might be restored as productive participants in their communities;
- building relationships of trust between neighborhood residents and law enforcement officers;
- enabling people to reclaim their violence-plagued communities, especially through community economic development.

As a community of advocacy
The Evangelical Lutheran Church in America is committed to:

work with and on behalf of the poor, the powerless, and those who suffer, using its power and influence with political and economic decision-making bodies to develop and advocate policies that seek to advance justice, peace, and the care of creation.[6]

In service of its commitment to counter violence, the ELCA publicly advocates in opposition to the death penalty because the death penalty perpetuates violence, its actual use is not fair, and it fails to make society better or safer.[7] The ELCA also advocates in favor of gun control.[8] These stances alone, however, cannot presume to stop the tide of violence, much less address the causes.

Violent crime and those who perpetuate it must be stopped. The challenge is to restrain violence in ways that effectively limit it, and that do not simply repay violence with more violence. Some violence is a reminder of the failure to ensure justice for all members of a society. Many people—due to race, language, economic class, gender, or sexual orientation—have not received the protection and justice necessary for human well-being. Others suffer from individual pathologies. Attention must be given to those especially vulnerable because of the breakdown of families and other communities of moral formation. Short-term measures to counter violence are needed, as well as long-term measures to counter social and economic inequalities and the brokenness that contribute to violence.

As we move toward a more comprehensive address of community violence, we join with other religious communities in anti-violence initiatives that:

- offer vital spiritual and moral resources for replacing fear and violence with hope and reconciliation in our homes, communities, and nation;
- stem the proliferation of guns in our streets, schools, and homes;
- counter the "culture of violence" that pervades our national culture and media;
- build strong anti-violence coalitions in our neighborhoods and communities;
- develop peer mediation skills in the schools;
- protect our youth from the epidemic of violence through equitable law enforcement, and the promotion of education,

---

[6] ELCA Social Statement, "The Church in Society: A Lutheran Perspective" (1991), p. 7.

[7] On the basis of the ELCA Social Statement on "The Death Penalty" (1991).

[8] On the basis of a resolution on community violence adopted by the 1993 Churchwide Assembly, which called for "passage and strict enforcement of local, state, and national legislation that rigidly controls manufacture, importation, exportation, sale, purchase, transfer, receipt, possession and transportation of handguns, assault weapons and assault-like weapons and their parts, excluding rifles and shotguns used for hunting and sporting purposes, for use other than law enforcement and military purposes."

social programs, anti-drug programs, and real job opportunities.[9]

We also join with others in working through government and with the advertising and media industries to find ways to respect free expression while abhorring and seeking appropriate ways to limit expressions of violence in electronic media and film.[10]

As a community of ongoing deliberation

As a church committed to "contribute toward the up-building of the common good and the revitalizing of public life through open and inclusive processes of deliberation,"[11] we call for public discussions of violence that:

- continue to examine the appropriateness and effectiveness of measures such as the death penalty and gun control;
- question a one-sided approach to violence, which would make persecution and punishment the primary remedies;
- object to the manipulation of fear of violence by some who hold or seek public office;
- deplore how "toughness on crime" can play into the racism infecting and affecting all in this society;[12]
- explore specific ways violence has shaped and influenced our history;
- challenge the logic of winning by destroying one's opponents, which Scripture has sometimes been used to justify;
- explore how depictions of violence in the media (typically apart from the pain and anguish) affect actual violence in society;
- consider not only short-term measures, but also long-term address of the recalcitrant discrimination and injustices that lie behind many expressions of violence.

We call on members and congregations of the ELCA to consider the international dimensions of violence and militarism by studying and discussing drafts of the social statement, "Peace: God's Gift, Our Calling."[13] Communities of faith are also encouraged to explore some of the wider economic issues related to community violence by participating in processes leading to the development of an economic social statement.[14]

Guiding us is a vision of the age-to-come in which people are free from violence, justice is done, and the common good is realized. "They shall not hurt or destroy on all my holy mountain, says the Lord" (Isaiah 65:25). May that promise stir us to challenge and heal violence in our day!

8. Economic Justice Social Statement: Advisory Committee Members

Patsy Gottschalk expressed concern about the full agenda before the Division for Church and Society. She moved the following:

---

[9] These items are from a religious leaders' letter on violence to President Clinton, December 10, 1993 (National Council of Churches of Christ, USA).

[10] See "Violence in Electronic Media and Film," A Policy Statement adopted by the General Board of the National Council of Churches of Christ in the USA, November 11, 1993.

[11] "The Church in Society: A Lutheran Perspective," p. 8.

[12] ELCA Social Statement, "Freed in Christ: Race, Ethnicity, and Culture" (1993).

[13] Responses to the first draft of this statement (code:69-7345) are requested during 1994. The proposed statement is to be considered at the 1995 Churchwide Assembly. The related study booklet, "Peace: God's Gift, Our Task," (1993) is available from the ELCA Distribution Service (code: 69-7349).

[14] Work on this statement begins in 1994. For information as to how you can be involved contact the Department for Studies, Division for Church in Society, ELCA.

MOVED;

SECONDED: To recommend to the board of the Division for Church and Society that further development of a possible social statement on economic justice be delayed for one year.

Pastor Miller expressed surprise that the motion was being offered. He commended the work of the division's staff and expressed a conviction that staff members could ably carry out the present assignment. He noted that the project "does not add an extraordinary burden to our budget for 1994 . . . and we would not achieve significant savings by delaying." He also noted that the process would need to begin now, if a document were to be readied for presentation to the 1997 Churchwide Assembly. He advised that the motion not be adopted.

Deborah S. Yandala expressed a related concern that congregations were being overly burdened with expectations for their serious participation in numerous studies (sacramental practices, human sexuality, peace, et al.) Loren W. Mathre expressed a similar concern, particularly because such involvement may detract from other priority tasks, particularly evangelism. The Rev. James G. Cobb supported from the parish point of view the concerns expressed. Edith M. Lohr observed that delay now may postpone Churchwide Assembly consideration until the year 2000. Pastor Miller pointed out that this proposed statement would not reach parishes until March 1996, well after congregational consideration of the sacramental practices and human sexuality documents would have concluded. The Rev. Robert N. Bacher, executive for administration, indicated that the concerns being raised regarding the participation of congregations in churchwide programs already were being addressed by churchwide staff. He noted that such expectations also affect the work of synods. The Rev. Donald M. Hallberg observed that postponement now would delay too long this church's commentary on a crucial issue.

MOVED;

SECONDED;

DEFEATED: To recommend to the board of the Division for Church and Society that further development of a possible social statement on economic justice be delayed for one year.

En Bloc Approval of Certain Agenda Items

Background: The following *en bloc* resolution includes agenda items, which were considered on the last day of the Church Council meeting. Inclusion of these items in the *en bloc* action reflects a judgment that these items were relatively non-controversial in nature and would not require a plenary discussion and separate vote.

Each of the items is noted as *EN BLOC* in the body of the agenda. On the first day of the council meeting, the chair provided an opportunity for members to express whether they wish to discuss separately any of the items listed in the *en bloc* resolution; such items were removed from the *en bloc* resolution and discussed at the appropriate point in the agenda.

The chair did not call for a discussion or separate vote on those items that were not removed from the *en bloc* resolution by the end of the first day of plenary sessions. The items remaining in the *en bloc* resolution was considered as the last item of council business.

VOTED: *CC94.4.40*
To take action *en bloc* on the items listed below, the full texts of which are found in the body of the agenda or in an Exhibit . . .:

CC94.4.41 **Synod Resolutions Directed to the Church Council: Draft on Human Sexuality;**
CC94.4.42 **Synod Resolutions Directed to the Church Council: Call and Appointment Process;**
CC94.4.43 **Changes Related to Regional Structures;**
CC94.4.44 **ELCA Master Institutional Pension Plan and ELCA Master Institutional Savings Plan: Contributions and Earnings;**
CC94.4.45 **ELCA Medical and Dental Benefits Plan: Covered Outpatient Mental Health Providers;**
CC94.4.46 **ELCA Medical and Dental Benefits Plan: Managed Mental Health/Chemical Dependency Program;**
CC94.4.47 **ELCA Medical and Dental Benefits Plan: Subrogation Provisions;**
CC94.4.48 **ELCA Medical and Dental Benefits Plan and The ALC and LCA Continuation Plans: Coverage of Convalescent Care; and**
CC94.4.49 **Synod Resolutions Referred to the Board of Pensions.**

Synodical Resolutions Directed to the Church Council

1. Draft on Human Sexuality

Background: At its December 2, 1993, meeting, the Synod Council of the Southeastern Pennsylvania Synod passed the following resolution, asking that it be forwarded to the Church Council:

RESOLVED, that the Southeastern Pennsylvania Synod Council indicates its support of a process of churchwide education and deliberation of the draft statement on human sexuality as it moves toward consideration of a final draft at the 1995 Churchwide Assembly.

Council Action: The Church Council adopted the following response by *en bloc* action:

EN BLOC   *[CC94.4.41]*
To refer the resolution of the Southeastern Pennsylvania Synod to the Division for Church in Society, as it facilitates discussion throughout this church related to the development of a social statement on human sexuality.

2. Call and Appointment Process

Background: At its November 1992 meeting, the Church Council received the following resolution on the call and appointment process from the 1992 Synod Assembly of the Northern Illinois Synod:

WHEREAS, the intent of the call process within the Evangelical Lutheran Church in America includes the concern for making all clergy available to all congregations of the whole church; and

WHEREAS, the present call process often has negative effects on the morale of congregations:
1. feeling unsupported by the Evangelical Lutheran Church in America and the synods involved; and
2. experiencing frequently the deterioration of congregational life and ministry during a prolonged vacancy; and

WHEREAS, the present call process often has negative effects on the morale of candidates for ordination and ordained clergy, with special concern for those who do not have a present call and for whom a long wait means:
1. feeling unsupported by the Evangelical Lutheran Church in America and the synods involved; and
2. experiencing personal and family stress and difficulty in meeting financial obligations; and

WHEREAS, at present many candidates for ordination and ordained clergy are experiencing long waits for calls or for changes of calls; and

WHEREAS, the church is suffering because the gifts and talents of candidates awaiting calls are not being fully utilized to serve God's people; and

WHEREAS, there is no working limit on the time a congregation has exclusive rights to a candidate; and

WHEREAS, there is inconsistency among the synods:
1. some allow congregations to interview multiple candidates and some do not; and
2. some place candidates for ordination in competition with experienced clergy and some do not; and

WHEREAS, some candidates for ordination have experienced long waits for calls because they are allowed to be considered by only one synod and one congregation at a time; therefore, be it

RESOLVED, that the Northern Illinois Synod request the Church Council to direct the Conference of Bishops and the Division for Ministry of the Evangelical Lutheran Church in America to examine, evaluate, and standardize the call/appointment process for synods and congregations, in order to enhance the mobility of ordained ministers/associates in ministry.

The Church Council referred this resolution to the Division for Ministry and the Conference of Bishops, and requested that a report on this matter be brought to the Church Council.

Following is a response prepared by the Department for Synodical Relations. Attempts being carried out by the Division for Ministry and Department for Synodical Relations/Conference of Bishops to enhance mobility include:

(1) Encouragement of synodical bishops and staffs to share clergy and AIM mobility forms with the deployed DSR/DM staff persons. These staff persons consult with each other and with the director of the department via monthly conference telephone calls; sharing of information regarding clergy and AIMS open for call occurs through this monthly forum.

(2) In several regions, mobility consultations involving bishops are held on a regular basis by the deployed staff of the department. In some cases, mobility forms are discussed by the bishops and DSR/DM deployed staff persons. In other regions, clergy and AIMS open for call are invited for in-person interviews to make known their gifts and availability to bishops throughout a region. The Division for Ministry provides a monthly listing to all synods of AIMS available for call.

(3) In an effort to facilitate "computer-literate" clergy and AIMS in completing mobility forms, staff of the Department for Synodical Relations are working to provide diskettes with the

form outlines. These will soon be available (following review by the Office of the Secretary).

(4) In order to provide greater flexibility for candidates and synods in the first call process, the Conference of Bishops has adopted revised guidelines for reassignment of candidates if no call is received in the synod of original assignment within 90 days of assignment. These guidelines also allow for brief "contingency" assignments, whereby a candidate assigned to one synod can be considered in another by agreement of both synodical bishops.

(5) Constitutional authority for "consulting in the calling process for ordained ministers and associates in ministry" resides with synods (S6.03.a.4.). There is no constitutional authority for the Division for Ministry or Department for Synodical Relations "to standardize" the call process.

(6) Staff will recommend to the Conference of Bishops agenda committee discussion of the call process and additional means to enhance mobility at a future meeting of the conference.

Council Action: The Church Council adopted the following response by *en bloc* action:

EN BLOC [CC94.4.42]

To request the secretary of this church to convey this information to the Northern Illinois Synod, in response to its resolution related to mobility of clergy.

Matters Related to the Division for Congregational Ministries

5. **Transmission from Lutheran Youth Organization**

Council Action: Chair Magnus recognized the Rev. Mary Ann Moller-Gunderson, executive director of the Division for Congregational Ministries (DCM), who introduced the Rev. Walter J. (Mark) Knutson, director for youth ministries and the Lutheran Youth Organization (LYO). Pastor Knutson introduced a resolution adopted by the board of the Lutheran Youth Organization at its March 1994 meeting, which had been affirmed and transmitted to the Church Council by the board of the Division for Congregational Ministries:

RESOLVED, that the LYO board, recognizing the Church Council's commitment to young leaders in having included the name of a youth on the ballot for the Consulting Panel on Human Sexuality, encourage the Church Council to affirm the long-term goal [of the Lutheran Youth Organization] of having youth on every board, committee, and council of the church by appointing a young person to the Consulting Panel on Human Sexuality at the spring 1994 Church Council meeting.

Secretary Lowell G. Almen noted that awareness of the LYO representational goal has been reflected by synods, which increasingly are including youth as voting members at synodical and churchwide assemblies, and by the Nominating Committee for the Churchwide Assembly, which has included youth on the slates of nominees for churchwide boards and committees. He observed that the LYO resolution combines two issues, the most immediate one being the request to reconsider the composition of the consulting panel. Secretary Almen suggested two possible responses to the LYO request: (1) the Church Council might agree to reconsider the compo-

sition of the consulting panel by directing that an additional person be added in the category of youth; or (2) the council could decline to reconsider the composition of the panel at this time.

The Rev. James G. Cobb noted several difficulties related to responding to the LYO request at that point in time, particularly that the work of the panel already was in progress. The Rev. Stephen M. Youngdahl noted that the Executive Committee had nominated a youth to sit on the panel, but that person was not elected by the Church Council. He noted that the Executive Committee had determined that it would not be possible to make the composition of the panel representative of all constituencies within this church. Deborah S. Yandala concurred and observed that despite its composition, the consulting panel (and other entities involved) would be expected to consider all viewpoints in the review process, including those of youth.

William T. Billings commented that while he agreed with the intent of the LYO request, changing the composition of the consulting panel would be problematic at this time. He urged that the participation of youth be considered routinely in all actions taken by the Church Council. Terry L. Bowes expressed gratitude for the participation of the council's youth advisory members in the deliberations of the council, and to the Lutheran Youth Organization for bringing this issue to the council's attention.

Deborah S. Yandala moved the following:

VOTED: CC94.4.50

To affirm the intent of the action of the Lutheran Youth Organization related to the participation of youth in the membership of the consulting panel to the Study of Human Sexuality;

To decline to change the composition of the consulting panel at this time; and

To request that the consulting panel include a process for listening intentionally to the young people of this church.

ELCA Pension and Other Benefits Plan (continued)

9. **Physical Examinations as Reimbursable Item**

Background: The Northern Illinois Synod (5B) submitted the following resolution regarding physical examinations to the 1993 Churchwide Assembly:

WHEREAS, sound Trinitarian Lutheran theology teaches that God prizes creation and our created body; and

WHEREAS, preventive health practices have been proven to minimize illness and therefore expenses; therefore, be it

RESOLVED, that the Great Northwest Conference memorialize the Northern Illinois Synod to memorialize the Evangelical Lutheran Church in America to request the Board of Pensions to develop a program to cover physical examinations for all persons covered in the Board of Pensions health-care program.

The Board of Pensions submitted the following information to the Churchwide Assembly:

The purpose of the ELCA Medical and Dental Benefits Plan is to provide financial protection from major expenses arising from medically necessary treatment of existing or suspected illness or injury. In addition, certain services designed for early detection of illness have been identified by the Board of Pensions as covered expenses because it has determined those services will result in cost savings to the plan. Those preventive services covered currently are: (1) annual pap smear for women of any age; (2) annual routine mammograms for individuals age 35 and over; (3) annual routine proctosigmoidoscopies for individuals age 40 and over; (4) routine well child care through age five (including immunizations); and (5) preventive dental care.

Prior to 1990, the ELCA Medical and Dental Benefits Plan also provided for coverage of a portion of the cost of periodic routine physical examinations (where no illness is present) for certain individuals age 44 and over. That portion was the first $75 in 1988 and the first $80 in 1989. Effective January 1, 1990, the routine physical examination benefit was eliminated because: (1) no statistical evidence has been collected in the medical-insurance industry to date to confirm that routine physical examinations result in early detection of illness and, consequently, reduce benefit plan costs; and (2) removal of the benefit was expected to save approximately 1.7 percent in costs for the plan.

The United States Preventive Services Task Force recommends that individuals in the following age categories receive periodic routine preventive physician care as follows:

- Infants, adolescents and children: preventive visits at ages 2, 4, 6, 15, and 18 months, 2 years and 4 years, and once or twice between ages 9 and 18;
- Adults aged 19 through 39: preventive visits every 1 to 2 years;
- Adults aged 40 to 64: women should have a preventive visit every year, men should have a visit every 1 to 3 years; and
- Adults age 65 and over: annual preventive visits.

The consulting actuary to the Board of Pensions was requested to estimate the cost impact to the Medical and Dental Benefits Plan, if routine physical examinations were covered by the plan. Assuming: (1) coverage would be limited to periodic visits in certain age groups; (2) eligible expenses would include the cost of examinations and any related tests (i.e., laboratory, EKG); and (3) the expenses would be subject to the deductible and copayment provisions of the plan, monthly plan cost would increase by $4.50 to $6.25 (or about three percent) for each member, spouse, and child covered under the plan.

The Board of Pensions regularly reviews the benefits of and costs for the ELCA Medical and Dental Benefits Plan. As consideration is given to future arrangements for health-care benefits for plan members and their families, the feasibility of including coverage for physical exams could be included in these reviews.

The 1993 Churchwide Assembly voted (CA93.7.81):

To refer the memorial of the Northern Illinois Synod on physical examinations to the Board of Pension as information in their review of the ELCA Medical and Dental Benefits Plan; and

To request that the Board of Pensions report its recommendation to the Church Council at its April 1994 meeting.

The Board of Pensions considered coverage of routine physical examinations, adult immunizations, and preventive tests as it developed the recommended benefit design of the revised ELCA Medical and Dental Benefits Plan to be effective January 1, 1995. A recommendation to cover physical examinations, immunizations, and preventive tests was approved by the Board of Pensions at its March 12-13, 1994, meeting. The enabling plan amendments were approved by the Church Council at its April 16-18, 1994, meeting.

VOTED: *CC94.4.51*
To request the secretary of the Evangelical Lutheran Church in America to convey information provided by the Board of Pensions related to physical examinations to the Northern Illinois Synod, as a response to its memorial to the 1993 Churchwide Assembly.

Adjournment

Secretary Lowell G. Almen noted as information that the Office of the Secretary and Division for Ministry would explore the question of reissuing letters of call (formerly, appointment) to associates in ministry.

VOTED: *CC94.4.52*
To adjourn.

The Church Council adjourned with the singing of the common doxology at 3:02 P.M.

November 1994

The twenty-first meeting of the Church Council of the Evangelical Lutheran Church in America was held in the Church Council room of the Lutheran Center at Chicago, Illinois, on November 12-14, 1994. The meeting opened with the Service of the Word led by Susan Huber Stapell and the Rev. David G. Gabel in the chapel of the Lutheran Center at 8:30 A.M.

Vice President Kathy J. Magnus, chair of the Church Council, called the meeting to order at 9:47 A.M. She thanked staff members for their involvement in dinner meetings hosted by churchwide units for council members and unit staff members held on the preceding evening.

Adoption of the Agenda

Chair Magnus reviewed the agenda for this meeting, which had been distributed by mail to members of the Church Council prior to their arrival. Additional business and informational materials were distributed during the meeting.

VOTED: *CC94.11.53*
To adopt the agenda and to permit that chair to call for consideration of agenda items in the order she deems most appropriate.

En Bloc Approval of Certain Agenda Items

Chair Magnus requested that council members who desired to remove items from the *en bloc* resolution for disposition of non-controversial business times for individual consideration notify the secretary prior to the beginning of the afternoon plenary session.

Report of the Bishop

Chair Magnus called upon the Rev. Herbert W. Chilstrom, bishop of the Evangelical Lutheran Church in America, who presented his report. Bishop Chilstrom commented briefly on the first part of his report, which had previously been distributed to council members.

Bishop Chilstrom then reflected on the differences between events in the life of this church a year ago and events now. He noted with appreciation a number of spiritually uplifting gatherings that were held across this church and that had contributed positively to this church's ministry. He commented specifically on the recent meeting of synodical vice presidents, the "Making the Connections" conference sponsored by the Division for Congregational Ministries, the meeting of synodical communicators sponsored by the Department for Communication, and the Multicultural Mission Institute held in the Twin Cities. In addition he mentioned several *Mission90* gatherings in which he had personally participated.

Commenting on the recent meeting of the Committee on Lutheran Cooperation, Bishop Chilstrom noted that the meeting focused on reports submitted by the faculties of the seminaries of The Lutheran Church—Missouri Synod regarding this church's conversations with the Episcopal Church and the Reformed churches in this country. At the heart of these reports, he said, were theological questions suggesting that the Evangelical Lutheran Church in America could no longer be considered a member of the Lutheran family in this country, if it were to enter into fellowship agreements with any of those church bodies. Refuting such a deduction, Bishop Chilstrom pointed to the historic forms of cooperation between Lutherans and members of other Christian traditions in Europe. On a more positive note, Bishop Chilstrom expressed appreciation for the high levels of cooperation that continue to exist among American Lutherans in such ministries as Lutheran World Relief and Lutheran Immigration and Refugee Service.

Bishop Chilstrom commented on the recent installation of eight synodical bishops. During the spring of 1995, he observed, almost 40 synods would hold elections for bishop, and in 12 of those synods the present bishop would not stand for re-election. In addition, the election of the bishop of this church will be a major component of the 1995 Churchwide Assembly. He asked the members of the Church Council to pray for the guidance of the Holy Spirit as the various elections are conducted.

Bishop Chilstrom reported that he had left the meeting of the governing board of the National Council of the Churches of Christ in the U.S.A. in order to attend this meeting of the Church Council. He said that the major item of conversation centered on the upcoming vote to approve reorganization of that council, a move driven primarily by finances. Bishop Chilstrom paid tribute to NCCC General Secretary Joan Brown Campbell and the NCCC executive staff, which, he said, had put together a very workable structure for the future. He reported that appreciation was expressed during that meeting for the counsel of the Rev. Robert N. Bacher, executive for administration, in formulating those plans.

Bishop Chilstrom also reported on his work as chair of a special NCCC committee that has been engaged in conversation with Roman Catholics and various evangelical and Pentecostal groups regarding the future of the ecumenical movement.

He also commented on his involvement in the Religious Alliance Against Pornography, an ecumenical committee charged with addressing the increasingly problematic issue of pornography in the media. The group is sponsoring an international consultation in January 1995, to be held in Manila, to discuss the response of the religious community to this problem.

Finally, Bishop Chilstrom expressed concern for the suffering of other churches around the world, especially in Liberia, where complete anarchy has resulted from the fighting between ethnic communities. He also deplored the famine that had struck again in Ethiopia and northern Tanzania, where the Lutheran World Federation already was assisting in the on-going Rwandan situation. The Lutheran community on the Israeli West Bank and in Jordan of approximately 4,000 members in seven congregations also was in need of continued prayer, he said.

Nominations and Elections

Background: Between meetings of the Churchwide Assembly, the Church Council has the responsibility of electing persons to fill unexpired terms on churchwide boards (for example, those which occur because of resignations). The Church Council is also the electing body for steering committees of churchwide commissions and certain advisory committees.

The Executive Committee of the Church Council serves as the council's Nominating Committee. At its November 11-14, 1994, meeting, the Executive Committee developed the following slates of nominees for vacancies on churchwide boards and committees to be filled by the Church Council.

1.   **Board of the Division for Outreach**
     Clergy [term 1995] [to replace the Rev. Donald M. Haven]:
     The Rev. Robert L. Hock
          (Winter Park, Fla.) 9E; and
     The Rev. Ronald K. Johnson
          (Minneapolis, Minn.) 3G.

2.   **Steering Committee for the Commission for Multicultural Ministries:**
     Background: ELCA continuing resolution 16.22.A91.g. specifies:
     Members of the steering committee [of the Commission for Multicultural Ministries] shall be nominated and elected for their experience and expertise in relation to the commission's responsibilities. Each community shall nominate two of its members to serve on the commission's steering committee. In addition, the board of each division shall nominate one African American, or one Asian, or one Hispanic, or one Native American member for the steering committee. The Church Council shall elect the members of the steering committee.

     The Executive Committee received the following nominations to the steering committee of the Commission for Multicultural Ministries from the ELCA Association of Hispanic Ministries:
     a.   Clergy [term 1997], Hispanic Committee member [to replace the Rev. Maria Valenzuela]:
               The Rev. Ivis LaRiviere-Mestre
                    (Allentown, Pa.) 7E;
     b.   Lay male [term 1997], Hispanic Committee member [to replace Pablo Jose Quiñones]:
               Mr. Ezekiel Martin
                    (Santa Ana, Calif.) 2C.
     Council Action: Chair Magnus called upon Secretary Lowell G. Almen, who reported on behalf of the Executive Committee of the Church Council, which serves as the council's nominating committee. He reviewed the nomination process and also noted that

council's responsibility to ratify the election of members of the steering committee for the Commission for Multicultural Ministries, who are selected by the various ethnic communities

Nominations from the floor for the position on the board of the Division for Outreach were invited. There being none, Chair Magnus declared nominations closed.

Report of the Secretary

Chair Magnus called upon the Rev. Lowell G. Almen, secretary of the Evangelical Lutheran Church in America, to present his report. Secretary Almen commented on his written report.

Drawing attention to the parochial statistics for 1993, Secretary Almen said worship participation in the 11,023 congregations of this church decreased by 31,000 people per Sunday, or about three people per congregation. Approximately 30 percent of congregational members attend worship each Sunday, he said, but a decrease of 22,000 in communing-contributing membership, or two persons per congregation, also was noteworthy. Nearly 170,000 members disappeared "out the back door," he said.

Other factors of concern include the context for congregational life, especially the disturbing statistic that there are now fewer than two million farms in the USA, the lowest number since the Civil War. The majority of the ELCA's baptized membership is concentrated in traditionally rural areas, he said, especially in Regions 3, 6, and 8. We need to ask, he suggested, where our members are on Sunday mornings and whether the church has contributed to misunderstandings that keep people from attending worship. The answers are complex, he said, and no one churchwide program or strategy will make a significant different. Clearly, however, people who are not in worship are soon off the church's rolls, and people who do not worship also do not contribute to support this church's ministry. Worship poorly done along with empty preaching will not draw them back. Yet, he takes hope, he said, in the biblical promise that God's Word will not return empty.

Turning to informational items, Secretary Almen reported that

•   the 1995 ELCA yearbook would be available on approximately November 15, 1994;

•   a mailing would soon be sent to all church leaders and voting members of the 1995 Churchwide Assembly inviting nominations for the Church Council and boards and committees; and

•   new computer software is being tested to improve record keeping on this church's roster and candidates for ministry.

Secretary Almen also noted that the impending arrival of the church's newly appointed associate general counsel, Philip H. Harris, had necessitated rearrangement of the floor space in the Office of the Secretary. He reported that plans were being formulated to make all the written materials pertaining to the

Secretary. He reported that plans were being formulated to make all the written materials pertaining to the Churchwide Assembly more accessible, even as the pace of planning for the assembly was increasing.

During discussion, William E. Diehl observed that the average age of ELCA congregants is 51 years, which is well above the average age of the population. That situation necessitates outreach to the "baby boomers" that must be both creative and of excellent quality, he said. Mr. Diehl then inquired whether nominations to fill vacancies on the Church Council by the 1995 Churchwide Assembly should reflect the present representational and demographic distribution of those whose terms are expiring and, if so, whether such would "freeze" the geographic composition of the council. Secretary Almen explained that only gender and clergy or lay considerations are specified by the ELCA's governing documents, together with the provisions that (1) not more than one person from any one synod may serve concurrently; (2) not more than two-thirds of the synods in any one region may have council members serving concurrently; and (3) at least one council member must serve from each region. The Rev. John O. Knudson inquired whether the demographics of this church's membership are to be reflected in the composition of the Church Council. Noting the aforementioned restrictions, Secretary Almen commented that previously the Nominating Committee has been sensitive to issues of demographics.

The Rev. Mary Ann Moller-Gunderson, executive director of the Division for Congregational Ministries, commented on the need for this church to reach out to "baby boomers" and others, noting that the issue is more complicated than the relationship between worship and evangelism. For example, issues of education and evangelism also must be addressed. She said that a first step was being made by publishing a new worship supplement that attempts to "add to rather than take from" the tradition represented by the *Lutheran Book of Worship*. The Rev. Franklin D. Fry expressed appreciation for the emphasis on adult education and urged that new materials designed for people who have little or no background in the faith be developed. William E. Diehl noted that the "hook" for his congregation was religious education for children and that the provision of professional child care appealed to parents. J. David Ellwanger reported that the Chief Justice of the Supreme Court, who had been unchurched, became an active member of a Lutheran congregation because his daughter was invited to attend Sunday School and she then invited her parents to accompany her.

Chair Magnus invited the Rev. W. Robert Sorensen, executive director of the Division for Higher Education and Schools, to comment on this church's ministry to the young. He noted that 42,000 young adults are enrolled in ELCA colleges and universities, while campus ministry reaches out to another 250,000 young people. He also commented that congregations with elementary schools reportedly grow by some 10 adults per year.

Report of the Vice President

Vice President Kathy J. Magnus called attention to her written report.

Report of the Treasurer

Chair Magnus called upon ELCA Treasurer Richard L. McAuliffe to present his report. Treasurer McAuliffe reviewed his written report regarding the eight-month period ending September 30, 1994. He indicated that increased revenues and decreased expenses resulted in improvement in the seasonal operating deficit. Because of this church's seasonal income pattern, heavily weighted to the end of the fiscal year, deficits are to be expected until late in the church's fiscal year. Receipts for the eight month period totaled $46,065,000 compared with $45,416,000 in 1993, an increase of $649,000. Expenses related to those funds amounted to $47,134,000, a decrease of $1,616,000. The resulting deficit for the period of $1,069,000 compares with the $3,334,000 deficit experienced for the similar period last year. Income from congregations through synods in the form of mission support decreased $238,000. Other funds, both restricted and unrestricted, rose $887,000, primarily because of increased bequests and the annual Vision for Mission offering.

During discussion, the Rev. John O. Knudson noted that to date only 1,700 congregation had participated in the 1994 Vision for Mission offering. William H. Engelbrecht inquired about the mortgage on the Lutheran Center and whether principal was being paid. Treasurer McAuliffe responded that, in the initial years, only interest payments were required. That pattern changes in fiscal 1996, when principal payments also will be made. The Rev. Stephen M. Youngdahl noted that the treasurer's report seemed to indicate moderately good news. Treasurer McAuliffe concurred, because revenue was ahead of last year; nonetheless, he cautioned that the sources of revenue cannot necessarily be counted upon. He also noted that ELCA mission support has not plummeted to the same degree that it has in other church bodies, and continues to account for some 70 percent of the churchwide budget.

Edith M. Lohr commended the Cabinet of Executives for controlling spending and expressed appreciation to the staff members of the ELCA Foundation for their efforts. Loren W. Mathre inquired about the nature of income from bequests. The Rev. Harvey A. Stegemoeller, executive director of the ELCA Foundation, responded that a bequest in the amount of $926,000 had been received this year. Other bequests are of more modest amounts, he said. D. Mark Klever asked how such gifts are allocated. Pastor Stegemoeller explained that most bequests are designated for the Division for Global Mission or Division for Outreach, as well as the endowment fund. The Rev. Franklin D. Fry inquired about the disposition of undesignated bequests. Pastor Stegemoeller reported that those funds presently are placed in the church's current operating fund, with the hope that in the future all such receipts will be able to placed in the endowment fund. The Rev. Donald M. Hallberg supported that goal.

Report of the Conference of Bishops

Chair Magnus called upon Bishop Charles H. Maahs, vice-chair of the Conference of Bishops, to present the report of the conference. Bishop Maahs drew attention to the written report of Bishop Kenneth H. Sauer, chair of the Conference of Bishops.

Bishop Maahs commented on the fall 1994 meeting of the conference in Door County, Wisconsin. He noted that discussion of the second draft of a possible statement on human sexuality and of this church's representational principles constituted a major portion of the agenda. Bishop Maahs reported that the conference had approved a proposal permitting representational exceptions in the selection of congregational representatives to synod assemblies, but rejected a proposal for increasing the ordained membership of the Churchwide Assembly. He observed that worship and Bible study are always important elements of the conference's agenda. The Rev. Donald H. Juel of Luther Seminary (St. Paul, Minn.) served as study leader. Finally, Bishop Maahs commented that the mood of the conference was "upbeat" and that morale and energy were high in the synods, despite continuing perplexity about financial support.

Referral from the 1993 Churchwide Assembly: Deaf Ministry

Background: Acting upon the recommendation of the Reference and Counsel Committee, the 1993 Churchwide Assembly took the following action related to a resolution, which was submitted by a voting member of the assembly:

To refer the following resolution to the Church Council for appropriate action after conferring with the person who submitted the resolution, the Division for Church and Society, and the Commission for Multicultural Ministries; and

To request that a response regarding ministry with the deaf community be transmitted to the 1995 Churchwide Assembly.

WHEREAS, the language and culture of the deaf population is unlike any in this nation; and

WHEREAS, the language of the deaf, American Signed Language (ASL), is truly a language other than English, being strongly based in a French signing system, and is the primary language of members of the deaf culture; and

WHEREAS, 94 percent of the deaf population in the United States is unchurched; and

WHEREAS, specialized ministry, skills, and sensitivity are necessary to reach this population; and

WHEREAS, four years ago the deaf community asked the Churchwide Assembly to view them not as "persons with handicapping conditions" but rather as a unique and diverse community and as such to be "inclusive" in the work of the church through the efforts of the Commission for Multicultural Ministries; and

WHEREAS, this was subsequently addressed by the Church Council at its April 1991 meeting affirming the uniqueness of the deaf community and then resolved to take a "multi-unit" approach leaving the Division for Social Ministry Organizations or its successor carrying the responsibility; and

WHEREAS, this approach has continued to confuse the issue of the deaf as either a community or as individuals with handicapping conditions; and

WHEREAS, further attempts were made by the deaf community at the 1991 Churchwide Assembly to ensure that a desk position be created for deaf ministry to serve the deaf community by advocating the "Multicultural" approach to this ministry; and

WHEREAS, the Division for Social Ministry Organizations or its successor unit has chosen not to create a desk position because of financial constraints; and

WHEREAS, Women of the Evangelical Lutheran Church in America at its recent assembly enthusiastically recognized deaf culture as a culture of its own and American Signed Language (ASL) as the primary language of this culture; and

WHEREAS, the Metropolitan Chicago Synod has successfully included the deaf community in its Commission for Multicultural Ministries for several years; therefore, be it

RESOLVED, that the 1993 Churchwide Assembly, after hearing several years of prayerful requests from the deaf community, open its arms to this unique community, to affirm this ministry by giving it the visibility and "voice" of being one of the five emphasis groups in the Commission for Multicultural Ministries.

At its November 1993 meeting the Church Council voted:

To refer the matter of the inclusion of the deaf community as an additional community served by the Commission for Multicultural Ministries jointly to the commission and the Division for Church in Society;

To request that a report and recommendation on this matter be developed following consultation with the ELCA deaf community and with the Division for Outreach and the Office of the Bishop; and

To request that this report and recommendation be brought through the Program and Structure Committee to the November 1994 meeting of the Church Council (CC93.12.71).

The following report was prepared by the Division for Church in Society:

The 1989 Churchwide Assembly debated a memorial adopted by the Metropolitan Chicago Synod, which called for shifting of the responsibility for addressing the concerns of the deaf from the Division for Social Ministry Organizations to the Commission for Multicultural Ministries. The assembly referred the memorial to the Division for Social Ministry Organizations for discussions with persons who are deaf and with the Commission for Multicultural Ministries. The assembly also called for a report and recommendations to the Church Council.

A dialogue including deaf persons and staff of the Division for Social Ministry Organizations and the Commission for Multicultural Ministries resulted in the following recommendation from the Division for Church in Society, which was adopted by the Church Council at its April 1991 meeting:

To affirm the following statement, which articulates the relationship between the churchwide organization and the deaf community:

Deafness has led to the creation of a unique language and culture, worthy of respect and affirmation within the Evangelical Lutheran Church in America.

Responsibility for promoting the inclusion of deaf people in all aspects of ministry within the Evangelical Lutheran Church in America rests with the Divisions for Congregational Life, Education, Ministry, Outreach, and Social Ministry Organizations and with the Commission for Multicultural Ministries. The Division for Social Ministry Organizations or its successor unit will carry lead responsibility for this multi-unit approach. Assistance will be provided to the deaf community in the Evangelical Lutheran Church in America to organize and to make known the unique ministry needs and opportunities resulting from their distinct language and culture (CC91.4.52).

In response to this action, the Division for Church in Society, through the work of the director for disability ministries, has provided leadership and funding for the following activities:

- The formation of the Evangelical Lutheran Deaf Association (ELDA);
- Annual gatherings of deaf ELCA members and the clergy ministering in deaf ministry settings;
- Consultation to ELCA deaf ministry sites by the Rev. Mark J. Hendrickson, Bread of Life Lutheran Church (Deaf) in Minneapolis;
- Efforts to identify potential deaf seminarians, including facilitation of interpreter services at Lutheran Theological Seminary at Philadelphia for a deaf student during 1992-1993;
- Representation by deaf ELCA members at annual NCCC Deaf Ministry task-force meetings and leadership-training events (three ELCA deaf members have assumed leadership roles on the steering committee for this NCCC task force);
- Financial Support to Ephphatha Heartland, a deaf ministry under the direction of Lutheran Social Services of South Dakota; and
- Support for an intern at Ephphatha Heartland (1994-1995).

An interunit effort is preceding as well:

- The Division for Outreach is regularly represented at ELDA meetings, has held a consultation of deaf leaders and pastors in deaf ministry, provides financial and consultative support to deaf congregations, and is preparing a "Strategy for Deaf Ministry."
- The Division for Ministry has been active in developing alternate routes to ordination for deaf persons and is regularly represented at ELDA meetings.
- The Division for Congregational Ministries is regularly represented at ELDA meetings and is especially interested in worship forms appropriate to deaf culture.
- The Commission for Multicultural Ministries is providing assistance in the organizational development of ELDA as an ELCA organization, is assisting with planning for cross-cultural training for hearing pastors in deaf ministry, and is represented by the executive director at ELDA meetings.

The location of responsibility for deaf ministry in the churchwide offices has been a topic discussed at the past four Evangelical Lutheran Deaf Association meetings. Each time this discussion takes place, deaf members are divided on this issue—although a large majority favors retention of the present structure. Those who favor placement of deaf ministry in the Commission for Multicultural Ministry argue that such placement is the only response possible by the Evangelical Lutheran Church in America to acknowledge fully deaf culture. By not adding the deaf as a fifth culture within the Commission for Multicultural Ministries, the deaf would be seen as similar to persons of Norwegian, Swedish, or German descent. A much larger number of deaf representatives, however, favors the current arrangement. Their position is based upon the feeling that much progress is taking place and that the transfer of responsibility to the Commission for Multicultural Ministries might result in the loss of momentum of progress. In 1991, the group made clear that any resolution to the 1991 Churchwide Assembly calling for a shift of responsibility to the Commission for Multicultural Ministries would not represent the majority of those present. At its 1994 meeting, representatives at the ELDA meeting stated that they were tired of this discussion and asked that this issue not be made part of any future ELDA business meetings. The resolution brought to the floor of the 1993 Churchwide Assembly represented the position of one deaf individual and did not represent a formal position of the Evangelical Lutheran Deaf Association.

At its September 30-October 1, 1994, meeting, the board of the Division for Church in Society voted:

To recommend to the Church Council that it reaffirm its April 1991 statement regarding deaf culture in the Evangelical Lutheran Church in America, as a response to the resolution from the 1993 Churchwide Assembly.

At its October 7-8, 1994, meeting the Standing Committee of the Commission for Multicultural Ministries took similar action:

That the Commission for Multicultural Ministries Steering Committee recommends to the Church Council that it reaffirm its April 1991 statement regarding deaf culture and ministry in the in Evangelical Lutheran Church in America, as a response to the resolution from the 1993 Churchwide Assembly.

Council Action: Chair Magnus called upon the Rev. Stephen M. Youngdahl, chair of the council's Program and Structure Committee, to present the following recommendation, subsequently adopted by the Church Council:

VOTED: CC94.11.54

To reaffirm the following statement, which articulates the relationship between the church-wide organization and the deaf community (and which was originally adopted by the Church Council at its April 1991 meeting):

Deafness has led to the creation of a unique language and culture, worthy of respect and affirmation within the Evangelical Lutheran Church in America.

Responsibility for promoting the inclusion of deaf people in all aspects of ministry within the Evangelical Lutheran Church in America rests with the Divisions for Congregational Ministries, Church in Society, Higher Education and Schools, Ministry, and Outreach, and with the Commission for Multicultural Ministries. The Division for Church in Society will carry lead responsibility for this multi-unit approach. Assistance will be provided to the deaf community in the Evangelical Lutheran Church in America to organize and to make known the unique ministry needs and opportunities resulting from their distinct language and culture.

and

To report this response to the 1995 Churchwide Assembly.

Referral from the 1993 Churchwide Assembly: Calls to Interim Ministry

Background: Acting upon the recommendation of the Committee of Reference and Council, the 1993 Churchwide Assembly took the following action:

To refer the following motion to the Church Council for consideration, in consultation with the Conference of Bishops, Board of Pensions, and Division for Ministry, and to report back to 1995 Churchwide Assembly.

To adopt a new bylaw, ELCA 7.41.13., and renumber existing bylaws accordingly, to provide for uniform standards of call status for pastors serving in interim positions at the request of their synods, as follows:

7.41.13.   **Calls to Interim Ministry.** Pastors as ordained ministers serving as interim pastors, at the request of the synod, shall serve under letter of call, if the pastor so requests. This shall be a term call extended by the Synod Council. The period of call shall be defined by the Synod Council upon recommendation of the office of the synodical bishop. An ordained minister serving under call as interim pastor will be reviewed annually by the synodical bishop.

At its November 1993 meeting the Church Council voted:

To refer the proposed amendment of ELCA 7.41.13. to the Conference of Bishops (Department for Synodical Relations) and Division for Ministry;

To request that a report and/or recommendation be developed by the Conference of Bishops, the Division for Ministry, and the Board of Pensions, for Church Council consideration (following review by the Church Council's Legal and Constitutional Review Committee); and

To request that this recommendation be brought to the Church Council for consideration at its November 1994 meeting (CC93.12.72).

The following report conveys the response of staff of the Conference of Bishops, Division for Ministry, and Board of Pensions related to this topic:

Constitutional provisions regarding interim pastors include:

* The *Model Constitution for Congregations* states, "At a time of pastoral vacancy, an interim pastor shall be appointed by the bishop of the synod with the consent of the congregation or the Congregation Council" (*C9.06.);

* The Synod Constitution states, "During service to a congregation, an interim pastor shall have the rights and duties in the congregation of a regularly called pastor. . . " (S14.17.); and

* In 7.44.A.93.b.1.5 the ELCA constitution lists the source of call for interim pastors as the synod council.

At the present time, some synods issue calls to ordained ministers serving as interim pastors and others do not issue such calls. Synods that issue calls to interim pastors do not have common guidelines and criteria by which to evaluate requests for such calls. This disparity among synods appears to create feelings of inequity and unfairness among pastors who serve in interim ministry.

With the synod council as the source of call, interim pastors serve "under contract" or interim agreement with the congregation served.

The Board of Pensions takes no exception to the proposed bylaw.

Staff of the Division for Ministry and Conference of Bishops feel there is merit in implementing a bylaw that would serve to encourage synods to consider issuing calls to interim ministry and require churchwide guidelines under which such calls would be issued. It is believed that synods should have final determination whether or not to issue calls to interim ministry. The initially proposed wording of the bylaw would appear to make such calls mandatory, "if the pastor so requests." Accordingly, a suggested revision of the proposed bylaw has been transmitted to the Office of the Secretary.

The proposed amendment to the ELCA's governing documents (bylaw 7.41.11.b.) was reviewed by the council's Legal and Constitutional Review Committee at its pre-council meeting. The committee's recommendation and subsequent council action in approving the bylaw amendment is reported elsewhere in these minutes.

Council Action: During discussion, Bishop Robert L. Isaksen commented that the use of the terminology, "interim ministry" or "interim pastor" in the ELCA constitution was unclear, because the terms can refer both to a pastor of a neighboring congregation who may assume pastoral responsibilities during a vacancy in a nearby congregation and to a person who is trained to serve congregations on a part-time basis during a vacancy. The Rev. Joseph M. Wagner, executive director of the Division for Ministry, noted that this terminology usually refers to ordained ministers who are specially trained to serve parishes during a pastoral vacancy. Secretary Lowell G. Almen noted that the terminology has been used in an omnibus way in ELCA governing documents. Bishop Isaksen suggested that the terminology referring to those functions be distinguished in future constitutional revisions. Lorraine G. Bergquist asked how the issue related to persons on leave from call. Secretary Almen responded that, if a person were to be called by a synod to serve as an interim pastor, the three-year limitation of leave status would be affected. Most synods, however, provide for interim ministries on a contract for services basis, which would not interrupt the pastor's rostered leave status, he said. Secretary Almen observed that practices regarding interim ministry vary from synod to synod. The Rev. Michael L. Cooper-White, director of the Department for Synodical Relations, recommended that common guidelines be developed for use in all synods following the adoption of related bylaw amendment.

VOTED: *CC94.11.55*

To receive the report requested by the Church Council (CC93.12.72) from the Conference of Bishops, Division for Ministry, and Board of Pensions on interim ministry as information.

Referral from the 1993 Churchwide Assembly: Financial Support of Church Workers on Leave from Call

Background: The Minneapolis Area Synod, at its 1993 assembly, adopted the following memorial:

WHEREAS, pastors of the Evangelical Lutheran Church in America are not eligible for unemployment compensation; and

WHEREAS, a pastor's profession is unique, in that opportunities to seek calls may be limited; and

WHEREAS, circumstances sometimes arise in which a call is erminated, leaving a pastor with no sustainable income; therefore, be it

RESOLVED, that the Minneapolis Area Synod memorialize the 1993 Churchwide Assembly to request the Board of Pensions to develop a plan to provide basic financial support to pastors and other self-employed church professionals who are on unrequested or involuntary leave from call or appointment and are without other sources of sustainable income.

The following background information was provided by the Memorials Committee to the 1993 Churchwide Assembly:

The Board of Pensions of the Evangelical Lutheran Church in America could develop and administer an Unemployment Compensation Plan. A plan administered by the Board of Pensions would ordinarily be a "contractual" arrangement under which each covered member of the plan would be entitled to benefits, regardless of need. Before such a plan can be devised, however, many issues would need to be resolved and clarified. Some of the more important issues include:

1. It should be determined whether there is consensus among the synod bishops for the establishment of an unemployment compensation plan. The concept should be introduced to the Conference of Bishops for consideration prior to the development of a proposed plan.

2. It needs to be determined whether a proposed unemployment compensation plan should be optional or mandatory for ELCA pastors, associates in ministry, and lay employees and/or for congregations, synods, seminaries, ELCA churchwide units, and other ELCA affiliated organizations. The matter of coverage for ELCA ordained ministers serving non-ELCA organizations also would need to be considered.

3. It needs to be determined how the proposed plan would be financed. While the Board of Pensions would be able to administer a plan, the board could only administer a plan that was adequately financed. A determination would need to be made as to whether the cost for the plan would be paid from ELCA benevolence, from synod budgets, or from assessments of congregations. Considerations for the financing mechanism are very closely related to the considerations for the makeup of the group of eligible persons and the participation requirements for the congregations and other employing organizations.

   If it is believed that congregations should pay the premiums for the coverage, it needs to be determined whether those premiums would be assessed on a per member basis, a flat fee per covered individual, etc. It also would need to be determined whether coverage would be lost or what other consequence would occur if a congregation did not remit the required payments on a timely basis.

   It should be determined whether the unemployment compensation benefits would be based on a percentage of salary, a flat dollar amount, or some other formula.

   The ELCA Pension and Other Benefits Program is mandatory only for synods, seminaries, and churchwide units (other than the publishing house). This fact would add to the challenge of establishing a viable plan applicable to all persons in need.

4. Would the ELCA be the sponsor of the plan? The plan sponsor is the entity that would be committed to covering any financial shortfall.

5. The resolution refers to support for persons who are without other sources of sustainable income. The ELCA Department for Synodical Relations administers a Good Samaritan Program to assist ELCA pastors, associates in ministry, and lay employees with emergency financial needs. If the Unemployment Compensation Plan would have a needs test, consideration should be given to financing the plan through the existing Good Samaritan Program. In cooperation with the synod bishops, the program already provides assistance to persons based on their need.

   Before such a plan could be designed, determination would be needed on whether there would be support for such a plan throughout the Evangelical Lutheran Church in America and on whether it be deemed to be economically feasible.

Upon recommendation of the Memorials Committee, the 1993 Churchwide Assembly took the following action:

To refer the memorial of the Minneapolis Area Synod on financial support of pastors and other professional staff to the Church Council and the Board of Pensions to determine the financial feasibility and wisdom for such a plan and to provide a report to the 1995 Churchwide Assembly.

At its November 1993 meeting the Church Council voted:

To request that the Board of Pensions, following consultation with the Conference of Bishops and the Office of the Bishop, bring to the November 1994 meeting of the Church Council a report and possible recommendation for action on this resolution relating to financial support of church workers on leave from call (CC93.12.73).

In responding to this action, the Board of Pensions consulted with the Office of the Bishop and the Department for Synodical Relations. The following is the report provided by the Board of Pensions:

A key issue raised by this memorial is whether providing a plan of financial support to pastors and other self-employed church professionals who are on unrequested or involuntary leave from call or appointment is an insurable event.

In the secular world, unemployment insurance is primarily provided by state unemployment insurance programs operated under federal guidelines to alleviate certain types of unemployment. The federal government provides grants to states to administer the unemployment insurance programs. A federal tax is levied on employers' payrolls, which is generally offset by the tax employers pay the states under the existing state law. Employers with favorable benefit cost experience pay less than employers with unfavorable cost experience.

Generally, people are eligible for temporary benefits if their job is eliminated or if they are fired for reasons other than cause. Benefits under state programs to unemployed workers are based on the requirement that not only are such persons unemployed but they are actively seeking and willing to work, and that they have not refused suitable work in other areas. As a result, such programs usually benefit low-skilled workers who often find it difficult to find other work. Such programs are generally not intended to benefit professionals who, for a variety of non-economic reasons, may find it difficult to succeed at their chosen professions. A professional faced with the loss of employment in his/her chosen profession may need to consider alternative types of employment.

The purpose of insurance is to bring together large numbers of persons who are exposed to a particular financial loss that is unpredictable for each individual but is predictable for the group in aggregate. Each member of the group incurs a small predictable loss (the premium) in exchange for protection from a large unpredictable loss (e.g., loss of income due to involuntary unemployment). Here, the risk of unemployment is not similar for all members of the group. The risk is more closely related to one's suitability for the ministry than it is to unpredictable economic factors. As a result, even with a large group, losses for the group are not readily predictable. Mandatory participation by all congregations would help, but is not consistent with the ELCA's approach to the Pension and Other Benefits Program.

Temporary financial support for pastors whose employment is interrupted is best provided through a needs-based welfare or charity fund. The Evangelical Lutheran Church in America already has established a Good Samaritan Fund, which is utilized for clergy and other church workers for short-term emergency financial needs. Although the Good Samaritan Fund currently is not funded with benevolence dollars, it would seem that, if a need exists for persons who are temporarily without financial support as a result of unrequested or involuntary leave from call or appointment, the Good Samaritan Fund could be the vehicle for this need. Benevolence funding for such a program would be required if the Good Samaritan Fund were to be used for this purpose.

Based on these initial observations, the Board of Pensions recommends against conducting a feasibility study as requested by the Memorials Committee. The Board of Pensions believes that this type of program falls outside of its mandate and to expend assets of the Board of Pensions to conduct a feasibility study would be inappropriate.

Council Action: Chair Magnus called upon John G. Kapanke, president of the Board of Pensions, to introduce the recommendation of the board that the Church Council decline to act upon the request of the Minneapolis Area Synod. During discussion, William E. Diehl suggested that some persons in reading the report from the Board of Pensions may assume that the Good Samaritan is large enough to meet the financial-support needs of unemployed pastors. He cautioned that the fund does not have sufficient funds to address the matter in the manner sought by the memorial of the Minneapolis Area Synod.

VOTED: *CC94.11.56*
     To decline to act upon the recommendation of the Minneapolis Area Synod on the financial support of church workers on leave from call;
     To convey this action to the 1995 Churchwide Assembly; and
     To request the secretary of the Evangelical Lutheran Church in America to communicate this action and the rationale provided by the Board of Pension to the Minneapolis Area Synod.

Referral from the 1993 Churchwide Assembly: Roster Leaders Mobility Needs and Data Bank

     Background: Acting on a memorial from the Indiana-Kentucky Synod, the 1993 Churchwide Assembly voted:
     To continue to pursue the establishment of a roster leaders mobility needs and data bank, pending available budget and staff resources, and to report its progress to the Church Council in the fall of 1994.
     The Department for Synodical Relations submitted the following response:
     Present departmental efforts to facilitate mobility of rostered persons include the following: (a) monthly staff conference calls in which the needs of synods for candidate and mobility forms of persons open for call are shared; (b) regional mobility conferences in which bishops and synod staff persons have opportunity for personal interviews with rostered persons open for call; and (c) distribution of mobility forms at the request of synods.
     Working together with the Department for Information Technology, the Department for Synodical Relations has developed a computer disk version of the standard mobility forms. This new resource is presently being "field tested" with first-call candidates; it will likely be available for general distribution early in 1995. This is the first step toward development of an electronic mobility system.
     Council Action: During discussion, the Rev. Michael L. Cooper-White, director of the Department for Synodical Relations, indicated that three issues have dominated the discussion: (1) the readiness of all involved to use such a system; (2) the availability of technology; and (3) provision for staffing. He reported that a survey of the Conference of Bishops indicated support for more standardization in the call process and for establishment of such a data base. At the moment, he said, the computer software was being field tested, while exploration of implications for staffing such a system and the use of the wide-area communications network continues.

VOTED: *CC94.11.57*
     To request that the Department for Synodical Relations converse with the Indiana-Kentucky

Synod regarding the establishment of a rostered leaders mobility-needs and data bank to determine whether plans underway address concerns expressed by the synod.

Referral from the 1993 Churchwide Assembly: ELCA Representational Principles

     Background: In response to a number of synodical memorials requesting the Evangelical Lutheran Church in America to reconsider representational principles, the 1993 Churchwide Assembly voted:
     To instruct the Church Council, in consultation with the Conference of Bishops, to establish a process for reflection by the Church Council, Conference of Bishops, Commission for Women, Commission for Multicultural Ministries, and seminary faculties, and to report any recommendations to the 1995 Churchwide Assembly.
     At its December 1993 meeting, the Church Council voted:
     To instruct the Executive Committee of the Church Council, in consultation with the synodical bishops who serve as advisory members of the Church Council, to develop at the committee's January 1994 meeting a time line and process for reflection on the ELCA's representational principles;
     To request that the Conference of Bishops, at its March 1994 meeting, provide advice to the Church Council on this proposed process;
     To request that the Commission for Multicultural Ministries and the Commission for Women provide advice to the Church Council on this proposed process; and
     To instruct the Executive Committee of the Church Council to bring to the April 1994 meeting of the Church Council a report on this effort and a recommendation for council action (CC93.12.83).
     Following consultation with advisory bishops to the Church Council and representatives of the churchwide commissions, the Executive Committee of the Church Council engaged in substantial discussion of this issue at its January 25-26, 1994, meeting. It shared its preliminary proposal with the Conference of Bishops and the two commissions, prior to their March 1994 meetings.
     At its April 1994 meeting the Church Council adopted the following resolution, upon recommendation of its Executive Committee:
     To approve the following time line and process for responding to the referrals by the 1993 Churchwide Assembly relating to the representational principles:
March 1994
     The Conference of Bishops, Commission for Women, and Commission for Multicultural Ministries review the proposed time line and process.

April-May 1994
     The Executive Committee receives input from the Conference of Bishops, Commission for Women, and Commission for Multicultural Ministries and makes any necessary revisions in its recommendation.
     The Church Council discusses and affirms proposed time line and process.
     The Executive Committee develops basic background information relating to the representational principles for distribution to those involved in this process.

May-October 1994

Conference of Bishops, Commission for Women, Commission for Multicultural Ministries, and Division for Ministry, in consultation with seminary presidents, develop and implement processes for reflecting on the representational principles within their organizations/communities.

October 15, 1994

The results of these processes of reflection and any proposed recommendations for action are submitted to the Executive Committee.

October-November 1994

The Executive Committee of the Church Council reviews the information/recommendations received from the above-named groups and develops an initial report and recommendation for Church Council consideration at its November 1994 meeting.

November 1994-April 1995

Any additional work relating to this issue, including further conversation among those listed above, or further refinement of the Church Council recommendation to the 1995 Churchwide Assembly, will be undertaken.

April 1995

Church Council will convey its recommendation to synods and to the 1995 Churchwide Assembly.

August 1995

The Churchwide Assembly will take action on any recommendations.

The Conference of Bishops and the steering committees of the Commission for Women and the Commission for Multicultural Ministries engaged in discussion of the ELCA representational principles at their fall 1994 meetings. The action taken at the Conference of Bishops was as follows:

The Conference of Bishops encourages this church to maintain its present representational principles, with a revision to allow synods limited exception from the present formula for male and female representation in synodical assemblies. For example, synod documents should be amended whereby an assembly committee could grant occasional waivers when congregations present a compelling rationale why the normal requirements cannot be met (CB94.10.11).

A report from the Division for Ministry on behalf of the seminary communities, described the process of deliberation that will be carried forward in that setting. A report and/or recommendations from the seminary communities will be shared with the Conference of Bishops and commissions prior to the April 1995 meeting of the Church Council; it will subsequently be included in the agenda of the council's April 1995 meeting.

At the Church Council's November 1994 meeting, preliminary discussion on representational principles was scheduled.

In providing advice to the council, the Conference of Bishops, the Commission for Multicultural Ministries, and the Commission for Women did not recommend major changes in this church's system of representation. The bishop of this church and the Conference of Bishops did suggest, however, that the Church Council consider a constitutional amendment to provide synods with additional flexibility in dealing with one part of the constitutional requirement for representation at synodical assemblies: the current requirement that each congregation elect one lay male and one lay female voting member to synodical assemblies. The proposed constitutional change was placed on the agenda of the November 1994 council meeting, in order to allow the council the opportunity to meet the six-month requirement for notification to synods of constitutional changes; delaying consideration of that proposal until April 1995 would mean that final action on such an amendment would not be possible until the 1997 Churchwide Assembly.

Council Action: Chair Magnus indicated the Council would initiate discussion of this issue in small groups, an exercise also employed by the Conference of Bishops. She called upon Secretary Lowell G. Almen to introduce the discussion.

Secretary Almen urged wise and cautious discussion of an issue that does not concern the core of the faith or the Confession of Faith of this church. There are theological implications to these issues, he said, but principally these are practical matters related to how we have chosen to organize ourselves within the human structure of this church. After reviewing the present constitutional provisions, Secretary Almen said that, in the small-group discussions, there should be concern about how we are heard, as well as about what we are saying. For example, he noted the importance that everyone understand how this discussion is heard by women, who have indicated that under the present principles there is some assurance of more adequate participation by women than has occurred in the past. The same sensitivity applies to persons of color or whose primary language is other than English. He also noted that the very discussion of this issue may raise unrealistic expectations of change. He reminded the council members that there are certain perceptions of primarily white middle-aged pastors who harbor feelings of being shunted aside. Some difficulty has been expressed by congregations who must elect male and female voting members for synod assemblies.

Secondly, Secretary Almen cautioned council members to bear in mind that these discussions do not deal with the ELCA's central organizational principle. He observed that the principle of inclusive representation is shaped and informed by the more basic principles of the unity of this church under Christ, confessional integrity, and interdependence.

Care, he said, must be demonstrated in how this question is defined. This is an organizational issue whose theological dimensions are framed by the Lutheran notion that there is no absolute, divinely given model for church order. While this freedom is one of the marvelous gifts of the Reformation, once a decision on how the church is to be organized has been made, Lutherans have historically appreciated having church structures well organized. He went on to note that Lutherans in North America have always had some kind of representational principles, a practice that began with the Ministerium of Pennsylvania and included the ELCA's three predecessor church bodies. He noted that a number of synod memorials have been offered to eliminate constitutional provisions 5.01.f. and 5.01.g., but without specifying what aspect of these representational principles should be changed. Simple elimination of these constitutional sections would make it impossible to decide such basic issues as how to elect the Church Council or even voting members of assemblies.

Finally, Secretary Almen reviewed the contents of the exhibit, pointing to responses from the Commission for Multicultural Ministries, Commission for Women, and Conference of Bishops. He also noted that the seminary faculties had been invited to comment on this issue, with responses due to be received prior to the April 1995 meeting of the Church Council.

Chair Magnus made several announcements. The Church Council recessed at 12:26 P.M.

Referrals from the 1993 Churchwide Assembly: Representational Principles

The Church Council reconvened at 1:30 p.m. in small groups in order to discuss this church's representational principles. The council reconvened into plenary session at 2:33 p.m.

Referrals from the 1993 Churchwide Assembly: Election of the Bishop of this Church

Background: Acting upon the recommendation of the Committee of Reference and Counsel, the 1993 Churchwide Assembly took the following action related to two resolutions submitted by a voting member of the assembly:

To refer the following resolutions to the Church Council for such consideration as it deems advisable.

Resolution 1:

WHEREAS, Bishop Herbert W. Chilstrom has declared his resolve to conclude his service as bishop of the church in 1995; and

WHEREAS, the choice of a new bishop for the Evangelical Lutheran Church in America will be one of the most important decisions of the Churchwide Assembly in 1995; and

WHEREAS, some voting members in synod assemblies who have participated in electing a synod bishop have expressed the desire to be better prepared to make this decision and have asked for some planned means for giving careful consideration to it in advance of voting; and

WHEREAS, some synods have experience with processes which help to surface names of persons who might be considered and give opportunity for church members to talk together in various settings about the needs of the church for leadership at this time and to pray together in preparation for making a decision; therefore, be it

RESOLVED, that this assembly direct the Church Council to develop a process in the period prior to the next Churchwide Assembly that will facilitate an open and prayerful consideration of persons who might serve as the next bishop of this church, with the understanding that the provisions of the constitution and bylaws governing election of the bishop (specifically 19.31.01.a.) will not be changed in any way.

Resolution 2

WHEREAS, Bishop Herbert W. Chilstrom has served this church faithfully and with distinction since its founding; and

WHEREAS, Bishop Herbert W. Chilstrom has declared that he will not seek reelection in 1995; and

WHEREAS, the times continue to call for an open and informed discussion throughout this church of our mission, our vision, and the role of leadership; therefore, be it

RESOLVED, that the Church Council appoint a select committee to receive names of persons who might faithfully and competently serve as a successor to Bishop Herbert W. Chilstrom, selecting from among them four to eight persons to engage in a thoughtful, public dialogue on the mission of the Evangelical Lutheran Church in America, a vision for our future, and the leadership role of the bishop of this church; and be it further

RESOLVED, that the work of the select committee will begin no sooner than November 1, 1994, and will conclude no later than June 1, 1995.

At its December 1993 meeting the council voted:

To refer the resolution of the 1993 Churchwide Assembly on the election of the bishop of the Evangelical Lutheran Church in America to the Executive Committee of the Church Council; and

To request that the Executive Committee develop a response and/or recommendation for action to be reported to the April 1994 meeting of the Church Council (in consultation with the Legal and Constitutional Review Committee, if appropriate) (CC93.12.69).

Following conversation with the Office of the Bishop, the Church Council's Executive Committee agreed:

• To reaffirm the ecclesiastical ballot as the process for election of the bishop of the Evangelical Lutheran Church in America.

• To develop a process for reflection at 1995 synod assemblies on the role, functions, and responsibilities of the churchwide bishop in the life in this church as this church prepares to elect a new bishop at the 1995 Churchwide Assembly; and to request staff of the Department for Research and Evaluation and the Department for Synodical Relations to develop a process and draft a study piece for use at these assemblies;

• To review this draft and bring a recommendation for action to the November 1994 Church Council meeting.

That action was reported to the Church Council at its April 1994 meeting.

A possible process for reflection at 1995 synodical assemblies was developed by staff of the Department for Research and Evaluation and the Department for Synodical Relations. The process was reviewed by the Church Council's Executive Committee at its pre-council meeting.

In addition, a report on the process and timing of ballots in the election of the bishop at the 1995 Churchwide Assembly was provided to the Church Council members.

Council Action: Chair Magnus called upon the Rev. Michael L. Cooper-White, director of the Department for Synodical Relations, to report on behalf of the staff team on synodical services and resources, which has been asked to design a process for reflection throughout this church on the roles, functions, and responsibilities of the churchwide bishop and synodical bishops, in preparation for elections forthcoming in 1995 during synodical assemblies and the Churchwide Assembly. Pastor Cooper-White introduced the text of a document, "Choosing a Bishop," and accompanying memorandum that had been prepared for possible distribution to synods. He reviewed emendations to the draft that previously had been distributed to council members. The revised text was the result of suggestions offered by the Executive Committee of the Church Council at its pre-council meeting of November 11, 1994.

"We saw our work . . . as a task of spiritual direction to assist this church in moving into a space where the Spirit may speak—where we may listen, where we may deliberate prayerfully, and invoke the Spirit's guidance upon the important decisions that lie before the Churchwide Assembly, as well as synodical assemblies electing bishops this coming spring," he said.

Pastor Cooper-White noted that the document, "Choosing a Bishop," begins with a litany invoking the Holy Spirit. He then drew attention to several emendations that had been recommended by the Executive Committee of the Church Council during its pre-council meeting. These included changing terminology from "What is the office of bishop" to "What is the ministry of bishop," in order to clarify that this church recognizes but one office of ministry. Pastor Cooper-White said that we need to look closely at the mission and direction for this church, as well as at the faith and vision of the nominees proposed for the office of bishop. In order to avoid politicizing the elections, the staff team deliberately used language reflecting a call to Spirit-led service. Practical matters related to the qualifications for office and the process of conducting the elections also are included in the document.

During discussion, Bishop Robert L. Isaksen suggested that relevant portions related to the installation of a bishop in the *Occasional Services Book* and in the *Commentary to the Occasional Services Book* be included in the document for the convenience of the reader. The Rev. Franklin D. Fry offered an editorial emendation. Cynthia P. Johnson questioned whether voting members could be assured that persons nominated indeed would have the qualifications cited in the document. "Are you assuming that they would have those skills?" she asked. Chair Magnus drew attention to a document, "Election Process—ELCA Officers," which provided rationale for various proposed election processes. Referring to the ELCA constitution, William T. Billings requested clarification of the distinction between the role of ordained minister and bishop. Pastor Cooper-White responded that there is a fine line of distinction. "We need to avoid separating the role of pastor and bishop," he said. Secretary Almen explained further that the word, "office," carries different connotations when used in an ecclesiastical sense, than when used in a secular organization. Edith M. Lohr commented that ELCA members need to exhibit a high level of trust in the constitution of this church and in the persons submitting names for the ballot.

Chair Magnus asked council members whether, in their opinion, the proposed document, "Choosing a Bishop," was a document that would well serve this church? Bishop Glenn W. Nycklemoe expressed some disappointment with the document, noting that his synod

had developed its own guidelines. The Rev. James G. Cobb asked at what point during the assembly the biographies of nominees would be distributed to voting members? Secretary Almen responded that vitae would be distributed before the third or fourth ballot, depending on rules adopted by the assembly.

Bishop Paull E. Spring observed that the agenda of his synod's assembly would not permit deliberate study of the election process related to synodical and the churchwide bishops. Chair Magnus suggested several arenas in which issues related to the election process might be raised. Pastor Cooper-White suggested that small groups and forums be convened for this purpose, even if there is no time for the entire synod assembly to participate in the study.

Terry L. Bowes wished to know whether the names of possible nominees would be lifted up prior to the ecclesiastical ballot (see the referral from the 1993 Churchwide Assembly, Resolution #2, reprinted above). Chair Magnus responded that the council's Executive Committee and the staff team on synodical services and resources were, in effect, recommending that no individual names be surfaced prior to the assembly. Ms. Bowes recommended that such needs to be stated clearly. "We have looked at this request from the Churchwide Assembly and have said, 'No, we will not submit names,'" she said.

Lorraine G. Bergquist offered a suggestion that two documents be developed—one for use in conjunction with synodical elections and another for elections during the Churchwide Assembly. Pastor Cooper-White responded that the staff team had considered that, but had concluded that two documents would create more confusion. Patsy Gottschalk observed that several synods have developed their own process and would not welcome another document. Deborah S. Yandala affirmed the document as an informative resource, even if only read privately by voting members. Pastor Cooper-White stated that the staff team wanted to be sensitive to the political climate. "We do not want to appear to have a hidden agenda or candidate," he cautioned.

During further discussion, the Rev. Stephen M. Youngdahl inquired about plans for distribution of the document. Secretary Almen indicated that it would be mailed to voting members with other pre-assembly print materials. Several council members recommended that it be distributed separately for emphasis.

VOTED: *CC94.11.58*
To affirm the process for reflection and deliberation related to the election of a new bishop, "Choosing a Bishop"; and

To commend to the synods this process for their use.

ELCA Pension and Other Benefits Program

1. Restatement of ELCA Medical and Dental Benefits Plan

Background: Council agenda Exhibit J, Part 1, documented the recommended restatement of the ELCA Medical and Dental Benefits Plan to incorporate the previously approved Point-of-Service, Standard and Common Benefits, and to reflect the elimination of the medical supplement plan.

A summary of the proposed provisions is set forth below. Where appropriate, the proposed plan sections are contrasted with the provisions adopted by the Church Council at its meeting in April 1994:

a. The philosophy of the proposed changes is that, whenever possible, the Point-of-Service Benefits are identical to the Standard Benefits. The reimbursement percentages of the benefits, however, would vary depending upon whether the member was covered by Point-of-Service Benefits or by Standard Benefits.

b. Many terms are defined throughout the various sections of the plan document, in addition to the definitions stated in Article XVIII. An amendment to Sec. 1.04 was previously adopted by the Church Council to clarify that the defined terms appearing in the various sections are capitalized.

c. All references to the plan's Supplemental Coverage have been deleted from the draft as the Supplement will terminate on December 31, 1994.

d. A new term, "Coverage Continuation Member," has been added to describe plan members who are eligible for benefits but who are no longer sponsored by an employer. The term appears throughout the enclosed draft. It is needed to establish "head of household" status for purposes of assigning ZIP Codes for Point-of-Service Benefits.

e. Throughout the document it is indicated that, in addition to the Board of Pensions, the POS administrator is responsible for determining the eligibility of claims.

f. Sec. 3.02 provides that ELCA clergy serving in specialized ministry may continue to be sponsored in the plan during 1995.

g. The current provisions of the plan do not clearly establish enrollment in the plan, and subsequent waiver of that coverage, by plan members, spouses, and children. The proposed language in Sec. 3.03 and Article IV addresses enrollment in the plan by plan members, spouses, and children and then permits them to waive coverage.

h. Sec. 4.06(b) clarifies that a child who purchases coverage because s/he no longer meets the eligibility requirements is deemed to be an eligible child. This permits the deductible and out-of-pocket amount for the child to be applied toward the family's deductible and out-of-pocket amount.

i. Article IX establishes eligibility for Point-of-Service and Standard Benefits. Sec. 9.01 provides that spouses or children who reside out of the members' Point-of-Service network areas are covered for Standard Benefits unless they opt into the network where they reside. The other provisions in Article IX have been modified only slightly from that which was previously adopted, principally to include reference to Coverage Continuation Members.

The plan provisions pertaining to (1) the $1 million maximum reimbursement limit, (2) indexing of deductibles and out-of-pocket amounts, (3) coordination of benefits, (4) Medicare coverage, and (5) subrogation also appear in Article IX.

j. Article X sets forth Point-of-Service Benefits:
   i. Section 10.02(c) clarifies that the copayment for urgent care is $15 (the provision previously adopted provided for a $50 urgent care copayment).
   ii. Sec. 10.02(e) provides for a reduced copayment for injections received in the physician's office.
   iii. Sec. 10.06 clarifies coverage for individuals outside of the United States.
   iv. Sec. 10.07 contemplates the move of a plan member from Standard to Point-of-Service Benefits. This provision is identical to the one previously adopted by the Church Council.
   v. Secs. 10.08(c) and (i) include language pertaining to urgent and emergency care.
   vi. Sec. 10.09 sets forth the transitional benefits that would be available to plan members covered for Point-of-Service Benefits on January 1, 1995. The list has been revised and expanded from the list previously adopted by the Church Council, following input from Aetna's utilization management and medical director staff. Transition benefits will be available for up to one year, depending upon the duration of medically necessary care approved by Aetna.
   vii. Sec. 10.10 sets forth Aetna's Institutes of Excellence program, which is available only to members with Point-of-Service Benefits.

k. Article XI sets forth Standard Benefits. Sec. 11.04 contemplates the move of a member from Point-of-Service to Standard Benefits. This provision is identical to the one previously adopted by the Church Council.

l. Article XII sets forth Common Benefits. The provisions are identical to those previously adopted by the Church Council.

m. With the exception of the preventive services set forth in Sec. 13.07, the provisions of Article XIII have not previously been considered by the Church Council:
   i. Secs. 13.01 - 13.06 are provisions contained within the current plan document.
   ii. Sec. 13.07 was previously adopted by the Church Council, but has been clarified to

limit eligible expenses for non-preferred and Standard Benefits OB/GYN exams to $100.

   iii. Sec. 13.08 contains provisions from the current plan document, but also clarifies coverage for occupational and physical therapy (13.08(e)); durable medical equipment (13.08(f)); hospice care (13.08(l)); home health care (13.08(m)); and speech therapy (13.08(p)).

   iv. Sec. 13.09 contains provisions from the current plan document. In addition, the provision pertaining to services or supplies that are experimental or investigational, 13.09(b), has been expanded to incorporate Aetna's standard.

n. Secs. 13.10 and 13.11 set forth the seven-day notice requirement to pre-certify inpatient admissions and certain outpatient procedures. This language was approved by Aetna and Healthmarc.

o. Article XIV sets forth eligible Common Benefits expenses. These provisions are contained within the current plan document.

p. With the exception of the following sections, the provisions of Article XV have already been adopted by the Church Council:

   i. Sec. 15.01 clarifies that prescription drugs purchased at a network pharmacy are limited to a 30-day supply, and that medications purchased for an emergency are not reimbursed at an enhanced benefit level (previously adopted).

   ii. Secs. 15.03(a) and (b) describe the copayments applicable for drugs purchased under Point-of-Service Benefits.

q. Sec. 16.02 clarifies the appeals procedure with regard to (1) the Board of Pensions, (2) Aetna, (3) Healthmarc, and (4) Value Behavioral Health. While plan members ultimately will appeal to the board, they should first exhaust the appeal procedures of the specific vendors.

r. Article XVII is contained within the current plan document.

s. Most of the definitions in Article XVIII are contained within the current plan document. However, the definitions of "Coverage Continuation Member" and "Reasonable and Customary" are new and the definition of "Medically Necessary" has been expanded to incorporate Aetna's standard.

t. Appendices A, B, C, and D are from the current plan document.

Council Action: Chair Magnus called upon John G. Kapanke, president of the Board of Pensions, to introduce the proposed restatement of the ELCA Medical and Dental Benefits that would enable the implementation of point-of-service, standard, and common benefits, as previously approved by the Church Council, as well as the elimination of the medical supplement plan. He noted that nothing new was being recommended, but rather the recommendation represented the start of the managed-care system,

effective January 1, 1995. Enrollment cards would be mailed to plan members during the last week of November 1994, he said.

During discussion, D. Mark Klever inquired about special provisions that may be necessary for travellers who need medical attention when away from their point-of-service location. Mr. Kapanke explained procedures for meeting such emergencies. The Rev. John O. Knudson inquired about provisions for quality control. "Is it to assist participants, or to save money?" he asked. Mr. Kapanke responded that the performance of the plan, as administered by the carrier, Aetna Health Plans, would be monitored.

VOTED: *CC94.11.59*
To adopt the plan document, ELCA Medical and Dental Benefits Plan . . ..

2. Elimination of South Africa Free Funds

Background: Council agenda Exhibit J, Part 2, represents proposed amendments to the ELCA Regular Pension Plan, ELCA Regular Pension Trust, ELCA Master Institutional Regular Pension Plan, and ELCA Master Institutional Regular Pension Trust to eliminate the South Africa Free Funds. With these changes, as of April 1, 1995, the plan and trusts will have the same funds that existed prior to the implementation of the South Africa Free Funds. The default for members who do not make a choice, however will be the Balanced Fund instead of the Bond Fund.

Council Action: Mr. Kapanke introduced the following recommendation of the Board of Pensions, subsequently adopted by the Church Council. During discussion William E. Diehl asked how the South Africa Free Funds had performed relative to other funds, and whether there would be a penalty for transferring them? Mr. Kapanke responded that social purpose funds in general have performed in a manner comparable to other funds, sometimes having performed better. "It is not the screens, but the way the funds are managed, that determines performance," he said. "We use controlled risk environments."

VOTED: *CC95.11.60*
To eliminate South Africa Free Funds by adopting the amendment to the ELCA Regular Pension Plan, ELCA Regular Pension Trust, ELCA Master Institutional Regular Pension Plan, and ELCA Master Institutional Regular Plan Trust.

Items 3.a.-c. and 4.a.-e. were adopted by *en bloc* at the conclusion of this meeting of the Church Council, as reported on page 136 of these minutes.

3. Miscellaneous Proposed Amendments (May 1994)

a. **ELCA Continuation of the ALC Medical-Dental Plan for Retired Participants and ELCA Continuation of the LCA**

Ministerial Health Benefits Plan for Retired Members

The proposed amendments better facilitate the Board of Pensions' ability to recover expenses from parties legally responsible for injuries to our members.

EN BLOC   *[CC94.11.104]*
To adopt the amendments to the ELCA Continuation of the ALC Medical-Dental Plan for Retired Participants and ELCA Continuation of the LCA Ministerial Health Benefits Plan for Retired Members . . ..

b.   ELCA Medical and Dental Benefits Plan

The proposed amendments make a technical correction to a cross reference regarding pre-existing conditions.

EN BLOC   *[CC94.11.105]*
To adopt the amendments to the ELCA Medical and Dental Benefits Plan . . ..

c.   ELCA Master Institutional Regular Pension Plan

The proposed amendments enable more frequent investment of employer pension contributions.

EN BLOC   *[CC94.11.106]*
To adopt the amendments to the ELCA Master Institutional Regular Pension Plan . . ..

4.   Miscellaneous Proposed Amendments (August 1994)
   a.   ELCA Regular Pension Plan, ELCA Survivor Benefits Plan and ELCA Disability Benefits Plan

The proposed amendments extend the eligibility for clergy in specialized ministries.

EN BLOC   *[CC94.11.107]*
To adopt the amendments to the ELCA Regular Pension Plan, ELCA Survivor Benefits Plan and ELCA Disability Benefits Plan . . ..

b.   ELCA Regular Pension Plan

The proposed amendments reduce the lag in computing equity fund unit values.

EN BLOC   *[CC94.11.108]*
To adopt the amendments to the ELCA Regular Pension Plan . . ..

c.   ELCA Disability Benefits Plan

The proposed amendments delay the offset for Social Security retirement benefits.

EN BLOC   *[CC94.11.109]*
To adopt the amendments to the ELCA Disability Benefits Plan . . ..

d.   ELCA Medical and Dental Benefits Plan

The proposed amendments revise (1) the definition of a covered outpatient mental health therapist, and (2) the penalty for failure to contact the Managed Health Administrator. This language also appears in the restated medical plan to be effective January 1, 1995.

EN BLOC   *[CC94.11.110]*
To adopt the amendments to the ELCA Medical and Dental Benefits Plan . . ..

e.   ELCA Regular Pension Plan, ELCA Survivor Benefits Plan, ELCA Disability Benefits Plan and ELCA Medical and Dental Benefits Plan

The proposed amendments revise the definition of "defined compensation."

EN BLOC   *[CC94.11.111]*
To adopt the amendments to the ELCA Regular Pension Plan, ELCA Survivor Benefits Plan, ELCA Disability Benefits Plan and ELCA Medical and Dental Benefits Plan . . ..

5.   Other Items
   a.   Contribution Rates for 1995
Background: Council agenda Exhibit J, Part 5a, detailed 1995 rate recommendations for the ELCA Medical and Dental Benefits Plan for both non-retired members and retired members, the ALC and LCA Continuation Plans, and Survivor and Disability Benefits Plans.
Council Action: The Church Council received the foregoing as information.

   b.   Contribution Rates for Early Retirees
Council Action: Mr. Kapanke commented on proposed contribution rates for early retirees. He reported that there are 2,000 plan members who are retired, but under age 65. Medicare is not available to them. The Board of Pensions has priced their participation in ELCA Medical-Dental Benefits Plans as a stand alone plan, resulting in high premiums. Such costs can keep people, who may wish to retire, from retiring. Instead, they may activate leave-from-call status, which places them into a different premium category. Mr. Kapanke reviewed several alternative ways for shifting the cost of coverage for this group, as explained in council agenda Exhibit J, Part 5b. Although the Board of Pensions is empowered to act on the matter, it is asking synodical bishops and Church Council members to evaluate the various alternatives.
During discussion, several council members inquired about the that may cause plan participants to

seek early retirement. He explained that such reasons range from emotional fatigue to favorable financial outlooks. The Rev. Stephen M. Youngdahl expressed the opinion that, if a person chooses to retire early, he or she should bear some of the financial responsibility for insurance premiums. Mr. Kapanke responded that the board would not recommend free coverage. Whatever the formula, they would be paying their way, he stated. The Rev. H. George Anderson encouraged the Board of Pensions not to set up walls that discourage people from retiring. Several council members expressed agreement with the conclusion of the Conference of Bishops that options one and three in council agenda Exhibit J, Part 5b, are preferable and encouraged the Board of Pensions to develop the formula.

Nominations and Elections

Chair Magnus called for ballots to be distributed for elections to fill vacancies on churchwide boards and committees. Subsequently, she declared balloting to be closed. The results of the elections are reported elsewhere in these minutes.

Report of the Coordination and Services Committee

Chair Magnus called upon William E. Diehl, to report on behalf of the Coordination and Services Committee. Commenting on the activities of churchwide departments, Mr. Diehl announced that a new approach to the performance appraisal system was being developed by the Department for Human Resources. A universal, computerized, position-posting service also was being considered. Kenneth W. Inskeep, director of the Department for Research and Evaluation, and the Rev. A. C. ("Chris") Stein, director of the Department for Human Resources, reflected on the results of a questionnaire related to the attitudes of churchwide staff. Mr. Diehl then introduced the concept of the Wide Area Network System for linking computers. A demonstration of the network was presented to the Church Council subsequently, on Sunday, November 13, 1995.

Report of the Legal and Constitutional Review Committee

Chair Magnus called upon Dale V. Sandstrom, chair of the Legal and Constitutional Review Committee of the Church Council, to present the committee's report.

1. Cycle of Churchwide Assemblies: Options on Council and Board Terms

Background: The Church Council, at the April 1994 meeting, recommended to the 1995 Churchwide Assembly amendment of churchwide constitutional provision 12.31. to provide for triennial, rather than biennial, regular meetings of the Churchwide Assembly. At the same time, the council requested that the ELCA secretary prepare implementing amendments for consideration by the November 1994 meeting of the council.

The primary impact of a triennial assembly would relate to terms of churchwide officers as well as council and board members.

Under amendments proposed for consideration by the 1995 Churchwide Assembly is the recommendation that the terms of the vice president, secretary, and treasurer be made consistent with that of the bishop—six years. A pattern of six-year terms fits both a biennial and a triennial meeting schedule for the Churchwide Assembly.

Council and board terms currently are for six years without reelection. If the Churchwide Assembly were to meet on a triennial schedule with six-year terms for council and board members, half the membership of the council and half the membership of churchwide board would change after each assembly. At the present time, some boards have indicated that a changeover of one-third of board membership each biennial offers some problems for continuity. A changeover of one-half the membership of a board every three years would further complicate continuity.

Council Action: Mr. Sandstrom reviewed the following three options considered by the Legal and Constitutional Review Committee: (1) nine-year terms for council and board members, with one-third the membership changing each triennium; (2) continuing the current pattern of six-year terms, but with the possibility of election to one additional six-year term for a maximum of 12 continuous years on the council or any given board; or (3) continuing the current pattern of six-year terms without possibility of reelection.

Option 1: To recommend to the 1995 Churchwide Assembly, contingent upon approval by the Churchwide Assembly of regular meetings of the assembly on a triennial basis, amendment of the following constitutional provisions and bylaws:

14.32. Church Council members shall be elected to one ~~six~~ nine-year term and shall not be eligible for consecutive election.

16.11.13. Each division board shall be composed of 21 persons elected to one ~~six~~ nine-year term, with no consecutive reelection, and with one-third of the board members being elected every ~~biennium~~ triennium, as provided in Chapter 19. . . .

17.51.01. This publishing house shall have a board of trustees of 21 members, elected for one ~~six~~ nine-year term with no consecutive reelection and with one-third elected every ~~two~~ three years as provided in Chapter 19. . . .

17.61.03. This board shall have a board of trustees composed of 21 persons elected to one ~~six~~ nine-year term with no consecutive reelection and with one-third elected each ~~biennium~~ triennium as provided in Chapter 19. . . .

19.04. Other than elections of officers and executive directors of units, elections shall be for one ~~six~~ nine-year term, without consecutive reelection, and with one-third of the members of the Church Council and of each board elected each ~~biennium~~ triennium.

Option 2: To recommend to the 1995 Churchwide Assembly, contingent upon approval by the Churchwide Assembly of regular meetings of the assembly on a triennial basis, amendment of the following constitutional provisions and bylaws:

14.32. Church Council members shall be elected to ~~one~~ a six-year term and shall ~~not~~ be eligible for ~~consecutive~~ reelection once.

16.11.13. Each division board shall be composed of 21 persons, each elected to ~~one~~ a six-year term, with ~~no consecutive~~ reelection permitted for one consecutive term, and with approximately one-third of the board members being elected every ~~biennium~~ triennium, as provided in Chapter 19. . . .

17.51.01. This publishing house shall have a board of trustees of 21 members, elected for ~~one~~ a six-year term with ~~no consecutive~~ reelection permitted for one consecutive term, and with one-third elected every ~~two~~ three years as provided in Chapter 19. . . .

17.61.03. This board shall have a board of trustees composed of 21 persons elected to ~~one~~ a six-year term with ~~no consecutive~~ reelection permitted for one consecutive term, and with one-third elected each ~~biennium~~ triennium as provided in Chapter 19. . . .

19.04. Other than elections of officers and executive directors of units, elections shall be for ~~one~~ a six-year term, without ~~consecutive~~ reelection permitted for one consecutive term, and with approximately one-third of the members of the Church Council and of each board elected each ~~biennium~~ triennium.

Option 3: To recommend to the 1995 Churchwide Assembly, contingent upon approval by the Churchwide Assembly of regular meetings of the assembly on a triennial basis, amendment of the following constitutional provisions and bylaws:

14.32. Church Council members shall be elected to one six-year term and shall not be eligible for consecutive reelection.

19.04. . . . and with ~~one-third~~ one-half of the members of the Church Council and of each board elected each ~~biennium~~ triennium.

16.11.13. Each division board shall be composed of 21 persons elected to one six-year term, with no consecutive reelection, and with ~~one-third~~ one-half of the board members being elected every ~~biennium~~ triennium, as provided in Chapter 19. . . .

17.51.01. This publishing house shall have a board of trustees of 21 members, elected for one six-year term with no consecutive reelection and with ~~one-third~~ one-half elected every ~~two~~ three years as provided in Chapter 19. . . .

17.61.03. This board shall have a board of trustees composed of 21 persons elected to one six-year term with no consecutive reelection with ~~one-third~~ one-half elected each ~~biennium~~ triennium as provided in Chapter 19. . . .

Mr. Sandstrom reported that the committee recommended the third option.

VOTED: *CC94.11.61*

To recommend to the 1995 Churchwide Assembly, contingent upon approval by the Churchwide Assembly of regular meetings of the assembly on a triennial basis, amendment of the following constitutional provisions and bylaws:

14.32. Church Council members shall be elected to one six-year term and shall not be eligible for consecutive reelection.

19.04. . . . and with ~~one-third~~ one-half of the members of the Church Council and of

each board elected each ~~biennium~~ triennium.

16.11.13. Each division board shall be composed of 21 persons elected to one six-year term, with no consecutive reelection, and with ~~one-third~~ one-half of the board members being elected every ~~biennium~~ triennium, as provided in Chapter 19. . . .

17.51.01. This publishing house shall have a board of trustees of 21 members, elected for one six-year term with no consecutive reelection and with ~~one-third~~ one-half elected every ~~two~~ three years as provided in Chapter 19. . . .

17.61.03. This board shall have a board of trustees composed of 21 persons elected to one six-year term with no consecutive reelection with ~~one-third~~ one-half elected each ~~biennium~~ triennium as provided in Chapter 19. . . .

2. Cycle of Churchwide Assemblies: Method of Implementation of Staggered Terms

Background: In the event of adoption of a triennial pattern for the Churchwide Assembly and in view of the possibility of maintaining six-year terms for council and board members, an implementing constitutional amendment would be required.

Council Action: Mr. Sandstrom introduced the following recommendation of the Legal and Constitutional Review Committee, subsequently adopted by the Church Council. He noted that the implementation of the provision with respect to staggered terms would not be effected fully until the year A.D. 2003.

VOTED: *CC94.11.62*

To recommend to the 1995 Churchwide Assembly, contingent upon approval by the Churchwide Assembly of regular meetings of the assembly on a triennial basis and contingent on possible decisions to maintain six-year terms for Church Council and board members, amendment of the following new constitutional provision:

19.06. One-half of those persons elected as members of the Church Council and boards by the 1997 Churchwide Assembly shall be elected to three-year terms with the possibility of reelection to one six-year term, and one-half of those persons elected as members of the Church Council and boards by the 1997 Churchwide Assembly shall be elected to six-year terms, notwithstanding with provisions to the contrary in the governing documents.

3. Cycle of Churchwide Assemblies: Term of the Editor of *The Lutheran*

Background: The four-year term of the editor of *The Lutheran* magazine also would be affected by a change in the frequency of Churchwide Assemblies.

Council Action: Mr. Sandstrom introduced the following three options considered by the Legal and Constitutional Review Committee: (1) a three-year term; (2) a six-year term; or (3) election by the Church Council to a four-year term.

Option 1: To recommend to the 1995 Churchwide Assembly, contingent upon approval by the Churchwide Assembly of regular meetings of the assembly on a triennial basis, amendment of the following bylaws:

17.21.02.   . . . shall be elected to a ~~four~~ <u>six</u>-year term. <u>(Notwithstanding this or other constitutional provisions or bylaws to the contrary, an election of an editor to a six-year term shall occur at the first triennial Churchwide Assembly in A.D. 2000. This parenthetical stipulation shall expire at the completion of that election.)</u>

19.51.04.   The editor of the church periodical shall be elected to a ~~four~~ <u>six</u>-year term by the Churchwide Assembly. . .

Option 2: To recommend to the 1995 Churchwide Assembly, contingent upon approval by the Churchwide Assembly of regular meetings of the assembly on a triennial basis, amendment of the following bylaws:

17.21.02.   . . . shall be elected to a ~~four~~ <u>three</u>-year term. <u>(Notwithstanding this or other constitutional provisions or bylaws to the contrary, an election of an editor to a three-year term shall occur at the first triennial Churchwide Assembly in A.D. 2000. This parenthetical stipulation shall expire at the completion of that election.)</u>

19.51.04.   The editor of the church periodical shall be elected to a ~~four~~ <u>three</u>-year term by the Churchwide Assembly. . . .

Option 3: To recommend to the 1995 Churchwide Assembly, contingent upon approval by the Churchwide Assembly of regular meetings of the assembly on a triennial basis, amendment of the following bylaws:

17.21.02.   The ~~Churchwide Assembly~~ <u>Church Council</u> shall elect the editor of the church periodical. . . . shall be elected to a four-year term.

19.51.04.   The editor of the church periodical shall be elected to a four-year term by the ~~Churchwide Assembly~~ <u>Church Council</u>. . . .

Mr. Sandstrom reported that the committee recommended the first option, subsequently adopted by the Church Council without discussion.

VOTED: *CC94.11.63*

To recommend to the 1995 Churchwide Assembly, contingent upon approval by the Churchwide Assembly of regular meetings of the assembly on a triennial basis, amendment of the following bylaws:

17.21.02.   . . . shall be elected to a ~~four~~ <u>six</u>-year term. <u>(Notwithstanding this or other constitutional provisions or bylaws to</u>

<u>the contrary, an election of an editor to a six-year term shall occur at the first triennial Churchwide Assembly in A.D. 2000. This parenthetical stipulation shall expire at the completion of that election.)</u>

19.51.04.   **The editor of the church periodical shall be elected to a ~~four~~ <u>six</u>-year term by the Churchwide Assembly. . . .**

4. Cycle of Churchwide Assemblies: Terms of Churchwide Officers

Background: The bishop of this church is to be elected in 1995, under constitutional provision 13.22. as amended by the 1993 Churchwide Assembly, to a six-year term. The vice president and secretary are to be elected in 1995 to a four-year term or, if amendments are adopted to change the term, to a six-year term.

If the 1995 Churchwide Assembly were to approve proposals to move to a triennial pattern for regular meetings of the Churchwide Assembly, officers elected in 1995 would either need to have their respective terms extended or implementing amendments would need to be approved to provide for elections at the A.D. 2000 Churchwide Assembly.

Council Action: Mr. Sandstrom introduced the following recommendation of the Legal and Constitutional Review Committee, subsequently adopted by the Church Council without discussion:

VOTED: *CC94.11.64*

To recommend to the 1995 Churchwide Assembly, contingent upon approval by the Churchwide Assembly of regular meetings of the assembly on a triennial basis, amendment of the following constitutional provisions:

13.22.b.   <u>In the event that the term of the bishop expires in a year in which a regular meeting of the Churchwide Assembly is not held, that term shall end, as provided in the bylaws, at the regular meeting of the Churchwide Assembly prior to the expiration of the term. (This provision shall expire on September 1, 2000.)</u>

19.07.   <u>In the event that the terms of the vice president, secretary, or editor of the church periodical expire in a year in which a regular meeting of the Churchwide Assembly is not held, the respective terms shall end, as provided in the bylaws, at the regular meeting of the Churchwide Assembly prior to the expiration of the term. (This provision shall expire on September 1, 2000.)</u>

5. Discipline Process in Congregations

Background: The following memorial was adopted by the Lower Susquehanna Synod at its 1992 assembly:

WHEREAS, we are of the opinion that the Congregation Council must be formally involved in efforts to resolve disputes within the congregation before the dispute is brought to the synodical bishop, and we do not believe that informing the congregation president that the bishop is being contacted in the event of disagreements would serve the containment and resolution of difficulties as well as the procedure outlined below; and

WHEREAS, Chapter 15 of the *Model Constitution for Congregations* has been changed from "Discipline of Members" to "Discipline of Members and Adjudication," it would appear consistent that, in addition to the subtitle, "Adjudication," that now appears at C15.10., there be a subtitle, "Discipline of Members," perhaps C15.00.; and

WHEREAS, paragraphs pertaining to discipline of members have been well defined over time, it would be good if the sections devoted to adjudication could be just as carefully worked out; therefore be it

RESOLVED, that to clarify procedural matters, the following paragraphs be proposed to replace C15.11.:

C15.11.   When there is disagreement among factions within this congregation on a substantive issue that cannot be resolved by the parties, members of this congregation shall refer the disagreement to the Congregation Council.

C15.12.   Should the disagreement not be resolved by the Congregation Council in a manner that is satisfactory to the parties involved and the Congregation Council, members of this congregation shall have access to the synodical bishop for consultation.

C15.13.   Should the disagreement not be resolved with the help of the bishop in a manner that is satisfactory to the parties involved and the Congregation Council, the disagreement shall be referred to the synodical Consultation Committee.

C15.14.   Should the disagreement not be resolved by the Consultation Committee in a manner that is satisfactory to the parties involved and the Congregation Council, the disagreement shall be referred to the Synod Council. The decision of the Synod Council shall be final and binding upon the parties involved and the Congregation Council.

The following background information was supplied to the 1993 Churchwide Assembly by the Memorials Committee:

Provision C15.11. in the *Model Constitution for Congregations* regarding "Adjudication" is identical to required provision †S17.11. in the *Constitution for Synods*. Both relate to stipulations in constitutional provision 20.84. in the churchwide constitution.

Although the *Model Constitution for Congregations* may be amended by the Churchwide Assembly in the manner provided for the bylaws of this church (ELCA 9.53.02.), mandatory provisions in the *Constitution for Synods* that incorporate constitutional provisions of this church may be amended only in the manner prescribed for amendments to the constitution of this church (ELCA 10.13.).

In view of the fact that final action on such proposed amendments could not be completed by the 1993 Churchwide Assembly and in recognition of the need for study of the implications of such amendments, the 1993 Churchwide Assembly acted upon the Memorials Committee recommendation and adopted the following resolution:

To refer the memorial of the Lower Susquehanna Synod on adjudication related to members of congregations to the Legal and Constitutional Review Committee of the Church Council for study in connection with preparation of any possible amendments to be proposed by the Church Council to the 1995 Churchwide Assembly.

Subsequently, the Church Council, at the December 1993 meeting, voted:

To refer this resolution to the Office of the Secretary; and

To request that a report and/or recommendation be prepared for review by the Church Council, through the Legal and Constitutional Review Committee of the Church Council, at the November 1994 Church Council meeting.

Experience throughout this church does not appear to point to a pressing need for such a detailed amendments to the *Model Constitution for Congregations*. Further, the Lower Susquehanna Synod, in a memorial adopted by the 1994 Synod Assembly, has urged that the number of amendments to the *Model Constitution for Congregations* be reduced and restricted. The detailed steps outlined in the 1992 memorial may be addressed later in proposing possible rules of procedure to synods regarding such adjudication.

Council Action: Mr. Sandstrom introduced the following recommendation of the Legal and Constitutional Review Committee, subsequently adopted by the Church Council following several inquires for additional clarification:

VOTED: *CC94.11.65*

To decline, in keeping with the request of the 1994 memorial of the Lower Susquehanna Synod Assembly, to propose amendments to the *Model Constitution for Congregations* for the additional provisions requested in the 1992 memorial of the Lower Susquehanna Synod Assembly; and

To request the secretary of this church, in consultation with the general counsel, to explore the possibility of developing model rules of procedures that may be submitted to synods for consideration and possible use in adjudication processes.

6. Ratification of Synodical Constitutions

Background: Churchwide constitutional provision 10.12. indicates, "Each synod shall have a constitution, which shall become effective upon ratification by the Church Council. Amendments thereto shall be subject to like ratification...."

Council Action: Mr. Sandstrom introduced the following recommendation of the Legal and Constitutional Review Committee, subsequently adopted by the Church Council without discussion:

VOTED: *CC94.11.66*

To ratify, in accord with †S18.13. in the Constitution for Synods, amendments to the constitutions of the following synods: Oregon (1E); Sierra Pacific (2A); Southern California (2B); Eastern North Dakota (3B); Texas-Louisiana Gulf Coast (4F); Indiana-Kentucky (6C); Lower Susquehanna (8D); and Delaware-Maryland (8F); and

To ratify S9.04. as an amendment to the Minneapolis Area Synod Constitution, except for the words, "by ecclesiastical ballot," permitting

implementation of the amended S9.04.a. through d., including related bylaws; and to convey again to the Minneapolis Area Synod the previous action of the Church Council in defining the meaning of an ecclesiastical ballot (CC94.4.10).

7. Amendment on Lay Voting Membership in Synodical Assemblies

Mr. Sandstrom commented briefly on the issues relevant to the recommendation of the Legal and Constitutional Review Committee regarding lay representation at synodical assemblies. The council's consideration of this matter continues elsewhere in these minutes.

8. Amendments to the Constitutions, Bylaws, and Continuing Resolutions

Background: Under this church's governing documents, the Church Council may propose amendments to the constitutions, bylaws, and continuing resolutions for consideration by the Churchwide Assembly. Constitutional amendments that are sent as "an official notice to...the synods at least six months prior to the next regular meeting of the Churchwide Assembly" may be adopted by the assembly without presentation to a previous meeting of the assembly (see churchwide constitutional provision 22.11.a.) The process for amendment of churchwide bylaws is provided in churchwide constitutional provision 22.21., for the Constitution for Synods, 10.13., and for the *Model Constitution for Congregations*, 9.53.02.

The Legal and Constitutional Review Committee has the responsibility for examining proposed amendments and submitting them for consideration by the Church Council.

Council Action: Mr. Sandstrom introduced the following recommendation of the Legal and Constitutional Review Committee, subsequently adopted by the Church Council. During discussion, the Rev. John O. Knudson inquired about the conclusion of terms of office for members of the board of the Mission Investment Fund. William E. Diehl inquired about the terminology, "commissioned/consecrated," in ELCA 7.52. and following. He raised a question regarding the application of ELCA 19.61.05. to persons under contract. General Counsel David J. Hardy suggested that the question be explored prior to the 1995 spring meeting of the Church Council. Lorraine G. Bergquist raised several technical question regarding the text of certain provisions. Consequently, it was noted that the text of the proposed amendment to ELCA 20.13. would be perfected prior to the 1995 spring meeting of the Church Council with respect to the question of how a congregation makes a decision on the matter of agreeing to a closed hearing.

Pastor Knudson inquired about the application of proposed bylaw 9.23., which reads:

Proposed 9.23.   In accord with constitutional provision 9.21.d. and bylaw 9.21.01. and without invoking the provisions of Chapter 20, a congregation that maintains as its pastor an ordained minister who has been removed from this church's roster of ordained minister by disciplinary action or that calls as its pastor one who has not been approved for the roster of ordained ministers shall be removed from the roster of congregations of this church by the Synod Council.

Subsequently, proposed bylaw 9.23. was removed from the recommendation of the Legal and Constitutional Review Committee for further consideration.

VOTED: *CC94.11.67*

To propose for possible adoption by the 1995 Churchwide Assembly the following amendments to the *Constitutions, Bylaws, and Continuing Resolutions of the Evangelical Lutheran Church in America*:

[Note: The text of the proposed amendments will be printed in Volume 2 of the 1995 Pre-Assembly eport.]

EXECUTIVE SESSION

The church council recessed into executive session at 5:17 P.M. for the purpose of hearing a presentation on legal matters by General Counsel David J. Hardy. The Church Council recessed for the day at 5:52 P.M.

The Church Council reconvened on Sunday, November 13, 1994, at 9:47 A.M. The plenary session was preceded with a service of Holy Communion held in the chapel of the Lutheran Center. The Rev. H. George Anderson served as presiding minister and the Rev. John O. Knudson was the preacher. Vice President Kathy J. Magnus opened the meeting by thanking those who had participated in the worship service just concluded.

Report of the Executive for Administration

Chair Magnus called upon the Rev. Robert N. Bacher, executive for administration of the Evangelical Lutheran Church in America, for his report. Pastor Bacher selected, for the attention of the council, several items related to two conferences he had attended.

1.   The Leadership Network sponsored a conference called "Summit: the Futures of Denominations." Peter Drucker, professor of social sciences at Claremont Graduate School at Claremont, Calif., and Lyle Schaller, church consultant, were presenters at this conference. Most of the conference participants were pastors of large, independent congregations. According to Pastor Bacher, the mood of this conference was expressed in the assumption that denominations are not worth reforming. The participants did not feel that denominations are useful now and thought they would become even less useful in the future. Professor Drucker questioned this assumption, however, stating that small and mid-sized congregations will still need to rely on denominations for support.

2. Eli Lilly, Inc. again sponsored a conference for executives for administration from eleven denominations. At the conclusion of this conference, James Lewis, of Eli Lilly Endowment, thanked the participants for their openness and observed, favorably, that he perceived no denial on their part regarding the serious situation in which denominations find themselves. Mr. Lewis complimented the participants saying, "There seems to be a healthy attitude, celebrating and affirming what is working and not bemoaning what is not." Continuing this observation, Pastor Bacher quoted Bishop Peter Rogness who had written in his synodical newsletter of how congregations and the denomination are affirming the past while looking for new ways to proceed. At this conference the emphasis was on providing resources and supporting congregations for mission. People talked about the practical implications of the increased diversity within congregations. Pastor Bacher said that alternative ways have been identified to do almost everything that denominations now do, with the exception, perhaps, of endorsing candidates for ministry.

Pastor Bacher noted that the language used when describing restructuring is important. Changes should not be made to effect stability, but to provide greater flexibility. The pendulum view of history is not a good model. We can remember and give thanks for the past, but it is not the goal for our future. We must avoid being imprinted with a denominational model circa 1965, he said, which is often looked upon as the peak year for most denominations. Unfortunately, the literature focusing on the crisis in denominations can become a self-fulfilling prophecy. "Why support them if they are already useless?" can become a refrain that makes denominations easy targets for thoughtless criticism. Loren Mead, former head of the Alban Institute, offered a kind of apology for his book, *Once and Future Church*, observing that it could be used to deny support to denominations.

Pastor Bacher commented on some of the random suggestions that had been offered at the conference: Perhaps, like the early church, we should call decision-making assemblies only as often as needed. Leadership styles may change as we transcend ethnic traditions and engage more women in leadership roles. The expectations placed upon our middle entities (synods) also may change. Communication technology is changing so many facets of our lives. Will the virtual congregation be a reality in the future, and if not, what, for example, would be the implications for Christian education in the home?

The choices, according to Pastor Bacher, are two: to shut down or to understand the alternatives with which we are faced, and then take faithful and courageous action.

Pastor Bacher called the council's attention to the various activities in which we are now engaged that have implications for how we address the future. He highlighted three teams: the Social Statement Develop-

ment Team, chaired by Secretary Lowell G. Almen; the New Technology Team, chaired by Lita B. Johnson; and the Synodical Services Team, chaired by the Rev. Michael L. Cooper-White, that are at work on cross-functional concerns. Some individual units also are doing long-range planning for the work in their areas. He noted that the Department for Communication recently sponsored a training workshop for staff who are editors of newsletters and magazines. The workshop emphasized how to produce a quality product that attracts people's attention.

Chair Magnus invited questions from the council members. William E. Diehl inquired whether other church bodies also are struggling with the matter of defining their own distinctiveness among the denominations? Pastor Bacher responded that individuals attending the conference were able to define how their faith traditions affect them personally, but they thought that their church bodies have not been able to articulate such distinctions clearly. Lyle Schaller stressed the importance of each denomination displaying its specific identity very clearly. Mr. Diehl followed with observations from a Mennonite conference, which he had attended, at which participants kept repeating, "This is what we used to do, or used to be, but we don't now know who we are anymore." Pastor Bacher responded that the Church of the Brethren has been engaged in a conscious effort to articulate who they are, and the process has been very positive for their own commitment. For example, they have consciously decided not to change their name.

Bishop Paul R. Swanson asked about the status of proposed organizational changes in the Evangelical Lutheran Church in Canada (ELCIC). Secretary Almen responded that structural proposals would presented to the ELCIC forthcoming assembly in July 1995. Such proposed changes relate very directly to the Canadian context and size of the ELCIC. Implications of those plans in relation to the ELCA are limited.

Inquiry Process

Pastor Bacher called upon the Rev. H. George Anderson, chairman of the Inquiry Committee, to report on the work of that committee.

Pastor Anderson began his presentation by defining the term, "inquiry," noting that one may find it open in one sense and threatening in another. Originally, the committee had addressed itself to the purpose of finding a better structure to fit the needs and resources of this church. It intended, and still plans, to present the church's newly elected bishop with recommendations based on its findings. The committee members thought that structural change must be proposed in an open process or lack of trust would be generated. The committee also concluded also that the churchwide officers, who would have to implement such changes, must have opportunity to provide input for the entire process. Noting that the inquiry is intended to be a spiritual process, the committee is proposing that the bishop of this church call it to prayer about the future. "God has a purpose for this church," Pastor Anderson said, "and we can trust the leading of the Holy Spirit."

Pastor Anderson offered some historical and personal reflections. It is not wise to focus on the 1950s as the height of the church's life, he said, for even then, many said that contemporary piety was hollow and would not last. Rather, we must remember that we are always at a crossroad. The first generation of immigrants lost the support of an established church and were forced to learn about volunteerism. The second generation had to deal with the issue of language. The third generation became vulnerable to the modernism and fundamentalism of U.S. culture. Succeeding generations were confronted with wars and the civil rights movement. We are always at the crossroads. Pastor Anderson cited Loren Mead, who has said that the church today is not simply faced with a problem, but with a "mess." It exists not in a spiritual desert, but in a "spiritual jungle" full of religions. Pastor Anderson counseled that whenever the church has begun to feel comfortable, God has nudged her. God's Church will persevere and survive. The question is, "Will we be the Church?"

Chair Magnus, also a member of the Inquiry Committee, added, "I don't think we have even figured out the questions. I hope that we will always be in inquiry." She also noted that the committee is seeking input from across this church. Organizational change is no longer the driving force, she added. The inquiry is a journey not destined for one specific outcome. She concluded her remarks with a call for prayer and reflection.

Responding to Pastor Anderson's presentation, Bishop Herbert W. Chilstrom told council members that he was not a member of this Inquiry Committee because he does not want to establish a mandate for his successor. He said, however, that he was pleased with what is happening. We are always looking at reorganization, he said, specifically for ways "to do it better."

During discussion, Edith M. Lohr pointed out that the matter of "who we are" can be defined, but "what we do" will change from day to day in our current environment. Loren W. Mathre said that he liked the broad approach described by Pastor Anderson. "I grew up knowing more about who I wasn't than who I was." We need to establish a consensus around clearly defined goals, he said. Terry L. Bowes, observing that the future is "scary," called on the Church Council for a time of prayer. She also asked that the members of the council listen to what people around them are saying. The Rev. Nelson T. Strobert reminded council members that an emphasis on our confessional roots would help us to be open to the future. The Rev. Franklin D. Fry cautioned that it is not the task of our congregations to emulate other faith communions. If we just copy others, we impoverish the whole church, he said. We each have to find out what we need to be and do within our own communities.

Report of the Bishop

Chair Magnus called upon the Rev. Herbert W. Chilstrom, bishop of the Evangelical Lutheran Church in America, to continue his report. Bishop Chilstrom distributed the second part of his report pertaining to the issue of financing the mission of the churchwide organization.

REPORT OF THE BISHOP OF THE CHURCH TO THE ELCA CHURCH COUNCIL (PART 1B)

In this second part of my report to you I want to share three reflections on how we finance the mission of the churchwide organization.

1. I begin with the question, "Is the pattern of giving in 1994 a harbinger of what is to come?" You see that pattern in the report of the treasurer. Income from mission support from congregations through the 65 synods continues to show a gradual decline. In spite of the efforts of our synods, our stewardship staff and others to increase the flow of gifts from this source, it has remained level, at best, since 1988 and has declined in several of those years. I see nothing in what has happened in this or other churches which gives me reason to expect a change in the foreseeable future.

At the same time, we have seen an increase in giving for designated causes and in what we have received from larger gifts, wills, and bequests.

Not as evident in the report, but increasingly significant for all Lutheran church bodies are the grants we receive from the fraternal organizations—Aid Association for Lutherans and Lutheran Brotherhood.

Judging from the observations of Dr. Loren Mead in his latest book, *Transforming Congregations for the Future*, we would be unwise to expect the flow of funds from congregations to increase in the future. Mead observes that most denominations have done well in "pledged annual giving." "Mainline church members now talk about proportional giving and even tithing. An increasing number practice one or the other. Some . . . denominations . . . have experienced remarkable growth of pledged giving with strong leadership from the top down and the bottom up."

We could say the same of the ELCA. The increase in giving of more than $94 million since 1988 is evidence of deep commitment on the part of pastors and people.

What has happened in all churches, however, is that most of the increase has stayed in the local congregation or the local community—a pattern consistent with our experience. We have spent more than enough energy analyzing why this is so—increased costs, especially for medical coverage for church workers; remodeling for aging buildings; suspicion of any large or distant organizations; preference for designated giving; sensitivity to needs in the immediate community; and more. The point is that no one sees any change on the horizon.

What it means for us is that our decision to expand our ELCA Foundation staff and to put greater emphasis on planned giving is a wise one. According to Mead, dependence on a single source of giving—so-called "pledged annual giving"—is crippling most of our churches at every expression: local, regional, and national.

Mead reminds us of what you may have heard in other places. In the next 15 to 20 years $6 *trillion* will be passed from one generation to the next. He puts it bluntly: "If the churches ever had an opportunity to develop resources for the future, the time is now. The time is not likely to return. The clock is ticking."

2. Does this mean we should pay less attention to "planned annual giving?" No, surely not. In spite of a substantial increase in this kind of giving in the past several years, members of the ELCA still lag far behind members of other churches in what they give for the mission of this church. Stewardship education needs to be kept as strong as ever in the Evangelical Lutheran Church in America.

What troubles me as much, however, is how the gifts from members of our congregations are passed from congregation to synod to churchwide organization. Those of us who served on the Commission for a New Lutheran Church remember well the discussion. Which pattern shall we follow? That of the American Lutheran Church, where congregations sent some of those dollars directly to the district and some to the national church? Or that of the Lutheran Church in America, where all monies went to the synods and the synods, by agreed-upon formula, sent part of them to the national church? The latter prevailed. Those of us out of the former LCA felt good about that decision because that method had worked well in that church. Thus, it was agreed at the time of our formation that synods would share 55 percent of mission support income with the churchwide expression and retain 45 percent for the synodical mission. We also agreed, however, to negotiate exceptions when a particular situation in a synod called for a different division of those funds.

In my judgment, it has not worked as well as we had hoped. Our decision was based on the assumption that mission support would increase year by year. As that resource has shrunk, synods have been under pressure to change the formula. While most have respected the original agreement and have negotiated changes in an appropriate way, others have acted unilaterally. There seems to be an attitude in some places that the mission support dollars from congregations are the sole "property" of the synod and that the synod is free to decide on its own when the formula for division is changed. All of this is in sharp contrast to what is embedded in the governing documents of this church, namely, that those mission-support dollars are for the mission of the whole church, both synodical and churchwide ministries. Furthermore, the biblical principle that when one member suffers, the whole body suffers, is not without application. If our congregations cannot or will not give the support we expect, then we must share the burden of that shortage of funding.

All of this underscores the importance of our recent council decision to look carefully at this matter. Our commitment to interdependence calls us to talk about this issue openly, forthrightly and honestly. We must ask how we can arrive at a process that is based on mutual respect, mutual understanding, and mutual accountability.

3. The Vision for Mission Fund and the annual offering to support it are now firmly in place. With a minimum of cost in promotion the fund has received nearly $2.5 million through the annual offering and other gifts and bequests in the first three quarters of 1994. In his report to the Budget and Finance Committee, our treasurer reports that "some [synods] made highly visible efforts, while others did virtually nothing to promote the fund." He observes that when members received special offering envelopes many responded with generous gifts.

Treasurer Richard L. McAuliffe's key comment is that when given an opportunity, members respond. In the unfolding pattern of support for our ELCA mission, I am convinced that the annual offering for the Vision for Mission Fund will play an increasingly important role. Again, I call for the council—and the synods—to give it full support.

During discussion of the bishop's report, William T. Billings asked whether members were free to share this document with their synod assemblies. They were encouraged to disseminate the information widely. The Rev. James G. Cobb asked Bishop Chilstrom how one goes about inviting for bequests. Bishop Chilstrom responded that Mr. Jerry Olstad has joined the staff of the ELCA Foundation to work full time in securing bequests. Foundation staff members also are working to make people more aware of the "Vision for Mission Fund," Bishop Chilstrom said, noting that the needs of global missions and the birthing of new congregations always has appeal to ELCA members.

Treasurer Richard L. McAuliffe reminded the members of the council that donors need a focus when they are approached for gifts.

Synodical-Churchwide Consultations

Background: Materials related to synodical-churchwide consultations, including a schedule, proposed guidelines for partnership, and a preliminary report on the early consultations, were presented. All 65 synods will participate in these consultations, which will be held in 11 different regional settings, from October 12, 1994, through January 18, 1995. These consultations will include up to five representatives from each synod and up to three representatives from the churchwide organization. The consultation agenda includes mission-support discussions (for 1996), the Inquiry process, and agreement on expectations during the current time of transition. The Church Council will receive a report of synodical 1996 mission-support commitments at its April 1995 meeting.

Council Action: Chair Magnus called upon the Rev. Mark R. Moller-Gunderson, executive director of the Division for Congregational Ministries, to report on the 1994 synodical-churchwide consultations. Pastor Moller-Gunderson said that the regional meetings include up to five leaders from each synod and two or three churchwide staff members. The deadline for each synod to return its statement of intent is March 15, 1995, he said. Synodical leaders also have been asked to gather and discuss the distribution of unrestricted funds. The principle question, he said, is how do our principles match the reality of our distributions? All these conversations have been respectful, candid, and substantive, he said. He also noted that there is a wide range of practice and performance in this church regarding mission support. Many synods are at the "high end" and hold there, he said, and generally speaking, stability with these synod partners can be anticipated for the future. There are, however, some negative pockets where a drop in mission support has been experienced. A few of these have been accompanied by additions to synod staff and other local expansion, he said, while other synods are simply stretched to the point of breaking.

Pastor Moller-Gunderson also reported that several synods questioned the authority of the Church Council to inquire about their reductions in mission support. He also observed that while some synods abide by the fifty-five percent formula and treated it as a fixed expectation, others do not. The amount of independent giving to church agencies also has an impact on this. He reminded the council members that there are major and long-term shifts in the way people support religious and other institutions. Having grieved this change, we must now accept, adapt, and adjust, he said. Several synods also are seeking new sources of funds, with some synods even establishing development offices. While the Evangelical Lutheran Church in America is a mission-driven church, how this mission is funded will determine how this church is perceived. Pastor Moller-Gunderson concluded, "We are walking together. I sense some call to adventure in the time of change, not just doom and gloom."

During discussion, the Rev. Franklin D. Fry suggested that others in addition to churchwide staff be included in the consultation process with synods. This would help alleviate the negative impression that churchwide staff members were involved in the process principally to enforce the funding directives as defined in this church's constitution and bylaws, he said.

Ms. Lorraine G. Bergquist inquired whether it would be possible to ask synods to consult with the churchwide office when they plan to expand their staff, especially if such expansion affects their financial commitment to churchwide ministries. Pastor Moller-Gunderson responded that they can be asked to do so, but also noted that synods are not obliged to discuss their staffing decisions with the churchwide office. He also observed that synod staffing arrangements affect the way we allocate responsibilities in this church in non-financial ways as well. The Rev. Donald M. Hallberg asked what policies are in place for the receipt and disposition of money received by this church through estates and trusts, and reminded council members that demographics show that the potential for this source of funds will be great in the next decade and beyond.

ECUMENICAL MATTERS

1. "Lifting" of Mutual Condemnations: Request to the Lutheran World Federation

Background: The following information was provided by the Department for Ecumenical Affairs:

Concerning the Evangelical Lutheran Church in America's request to the Lutheran World Federation that staff share with our coordinating committee the declaration now being prepared in cooperation with the Pontifical Council for the Promotion of Christian Unity in Rome:

The Lutheran-Roman Catholic Coordinating Committee felt that what we do here in the U.S.A. related to the "lifting" of the mutual condemnations recorded in the 16th century Lutheran Confessions and the Decrees of the Council of Trent must be done in close cooperation with the world-level efforts.

The U.S.A. Bishop's Conference (Roman Catholic) will be making the same request of the Vatican.

The Lutheran members of the Lutheran-Roman Catholic Coordinating Committee at its meeting of October 21-23, 1994, recommended that the Church Council adopt the resolution printed below, subsequently adopted by the Church Council.

Council Action: Chair Magnus called upon the Rev. William G. Rusch, director of the Department for Ecumenical Affairs, and Darlis J. Swan, associate director, to brief the council on the issue of "full communion." Using video images to underscore their message, Ms. Swan referred to John 10:30, in which Jesus states, "the Father and I are one," and concludes Jesus' discussion of one flock and one shepherd. She observed that Christians are called to live out their unity for the sake of the world. The concept of full communion recognizes that we share a common witness based in a relationship between churches—not organic merger. "A relationship brings gifts to all of the partners," she said. This relationship is energized, she noted, by a mutual lifting of condemnations and a mutual recognition of each other's clergy committed to evangelism and service. She asked, "How would entering full communion with another church affect you?" and proceeded to explain that many of the decisions made or ratified by the council have ecumenical implications. She cited particularly issues such as sacramental practice, lectionary development, ordination of women, determination of qualifications for admission to the roster of ordained ministers, representational principles, and matters related to human sexuality. Such decisions are made not only as and for Lutherans, but also as Christians living in communion with other Christians, she said.

Chair Magnus reminded council members that important ecumenical decisions await the Churchwide Assembly in 1997. During discussion, Bishop Paull E. Spring asked about the status of the doctrinal consensus related to Lutheran-Reformed conversations. Bishop Chilstrom referred to a recent meeting of the National Council of the Churches of Christ in the U.S.A. and cautioned, "There is far too much judgment based on anecdotal information. That is why we have to look at the documents to see what each church believes."

The Rev. Franklin D. Fry inquired about the implications of "mutual recognition and availability of clergy," and asked if that implies interchangability of clergy? He asked, "Are there no gates to the office of Word and Sacrament any more? Can we set aside the distinctiveness of our ordination vows to conform to others?" Bishop Robert L. Isaksen observed that other denominations have difficulty reaching consensus on many of these issues within their own church bodies. He asked whether there was a confessional basis in the Episcopal Church similar to the one in the Lutheran Church. Pastor Rusch indicated that the difficulties to be overcome in our relationship with the Episcopal Church were more organizational than theological. William T. Billings asked what "full communion" means to the person in the pew. Ms. Swan referred to the video, which is available through the ELCA Distribution Service, depicting mutual sharing of the sacraments, and all aspects of faith, life, and witness. Bishop Chilstrom added that we would no longer duplicate new mission starts. Robert S. Schroeder inquired about the meaning of apostolic succession. Pastor Rusch responded that all Christian churches are in *apostolic* succession; the office of Word and Sacrament in this church is an apostolic office. We do not have bishops in *episcopal* succession. We anticipate exchanging only where there are parallels.

VOTED: *CC94.11.68*

To request that the Lutheran World Federation make every effort to coordinate its work related to the inapplicability of the mutual 16th century condemnations on justification with the work of the coordinating committee;

To request that the present and successive drafts of the Joint Declaration on the Doctrine of Justification of the Lutheran World Federation and the Roman Catholic Church be shared with the Bishops' Committee for Ecumenical and Interreligious Affairs-Evangelical Lutheran Church in America Coordinating Committee; and

To make these requests with the assurance that confidentiality (within the coordinating committee) will be maintained.

Nominations and Elections

Chair Magnus announced the result of the ballot to fill vacancies on churchwide boards and committees. She declared the following persons elected to the respective positions indicated:

VOTED: *CC94.11.69*
To elect the following persons to fill respective vacancies on the churchwide boards and committees as indicated:
1. **Board of the Division for Outreach**
    Clergy [term 1995] [to replace the Rev. Donald M. Haven]:
        The Rev. Ronald K. Johnson (Minneapolis, Minn.) 3G.
2. **Steering Committee for the Commission for Multicultural Ministries:**
    a. **Clergy [term 1997], Hispanic Committee member [to replace the Rev. Maria Valenzuela]:**
            The Rev. Ivis LaRiviere-Mestre (Allentown, Pa.) 7E;
    b. **Lay male [term 1997], Hispanic Committee member [to replace Pablo Jose Quiñones]:**
            Mr. Ezekiel Martin (Santa Ana, Calif.) 2C.

The Church Council recessed at 12:32 P.M. and reconvened at 1:34 P.M.

Report of the
Budget and Finance Committee

Chair Magnus called upon Ms. Edith M. Lohr, chair of council's Budget and Finance Committee, to report on behalf of the committee. She provided a historical overview of the budget development and financial support of this church since this church's 1987 constituting convention. She observed that an initial 14-month budget of $112 million had been reduced by 1994 to $85.8 million for the 12-month year. She noted the difficult decisions made in facing such reductions responsibly in light of the mission of this church, "so that it can witness into the future." "But we are still a vital and absolutely marvelous church," she said, "full of people committed to doing the very best we can."

1.   1994 Expenditure Authorization

Background: At its April 1994 meeting, the Church Council took the following action related to changes in spending authorization for the churchwide organization:

To authorize the Church Council Executive Committee, upon recommendation from the Church Council Budget and Finance Committee, to establish spending authorizations between Church Council meetings.

In late August 1994 the Office of the Treasurer reviewed the estimate of revenue that could be reasonably assumed to be received during this fiscal year. The forecasted changes were:

Mission Support	($1,000,000)
Vision for Mission	(400,000)
Missionary Sponsorship	(200,000)
Unrestricted Gifts	(50,000)
Miscellaneous unrestricted	(25,000)
Bequests (Restricted & Unrestricted)	500,000
Investment Income	175,000
Total	($1,000,000)

The Office of the Bishop and the Office of the Treasurer, together with members of the Planning Team, are using *planned underspending* by units as a way to bring spending in line with the lowered estimate of 1994 revenue. At the quarterly budget reviews in early September 1994 held by the Office of the Treasurer, each unit identified the savings that could be anticipated this fiscal year. A total of $808,000 was identified through this process. In dealing with the 1994 situation, it is the bishop's expectation that the identified savings in units will be realized; the bishop also asked units to try to underspend *more* than they had identified. (Several units expressed a willingness to take a second look at their expenditure levels.) If absolutely necessary, however, $192,000 less might be returned to working capital in 1994 than was originally anticipated. This "voluntary" approach to the 1994 situation will be reviewed should income estimates change.

No changes were made to the current estimate of World Hunger income at this time. Close monitoring of the revenue received and dollars expended on a continuous basis will allow the World Hunger program to operate at levels appropriate to the income received.

Council Action: The Church Council received the foregoing as information.

2.   Mission-Support Commitments

Background: The ELCA Church Council has the responsibility of reviewing and approving or withholding approval for synods regarding mission-support commitments.

At its April 1994 meeting, upon recommendation of the Budget and Finance Committee, the Church Council withheld approval for and requested further consultation with 16 synods. Following the Church Council meeting, a letter was sent to those synods, informing them of the Church Council action and subsequent follow-up. Since that time, conversations have been held with each synod by phone, mail, or in person. The majority of the consultations requested will take place in face-to-face settings during the fall round of synodical-churchwide consultations, at which the 1996 mission-support commitments also will be discussed. A full report of the status of all 16 synods was distributed at the Church Council meeting. At its April 1995 meeting, the Church Council will receive a report of 1996 synodical mission support commitments.

Council Action: During discussion, the Rev. David G. Gabel asked for a synod-by-synod listing of the percentages of mission-support commitments. Ramona S. Rank inquired about the definition of a "significant percentage" of reduction in mission support. The Rev. Mark R. Moller-Gunderson, executive director of the Division for Congregational Ministries, replied that in most cases the reduction amounts to a drop of one percentage point, but in some cases a "significant" change of four to six percentage points has been experienced. Loren W. Mathre inquired about the authority of the Church Council to enforce fulfillment of synodical commitments. Secretary Lowell G. Almen read the related constitutional provision that indicates the percentage of mission support to be remitted to the churchwide organization is determined by the Churchwide Assembly, with individual exceptions being allowed by the Church Council upon request by a specific synod. The Rev. Stephen M. Youngdahl suggested that consultations be held with full synod councils, rather than small groups synodical representatives. The Rev. Robert N. Bacher, executive for administration, noted that, if consultations were to be cyclical (e.g., biennial or triennial), it would be possible to meet with full synodical councils. William T. Billings suggested that synods be reminded of the relevant constitutional provisions when addressing this matter with synods; assuming a knowledge of these provisions should not be assumed, he cautioned. Ms. Lohr noted the importance of maintaining a trust relationship between synods and the churchwide organization. Mr. Billings advocated the need for synods to respect their commitments in accordance with pre-established policy and procedures. Bishop Glenn W. Nycklemoe noted that most synods consult with the Office of the Treasurer continuously. Treasurer Richard L. McAuliffe suggested a need to proceed cautiously in consulting with synods and of achieving a positive tenor and outcome. Carlos Peña observed that synod council members do not always recognize the impact of commitment reductions for the overall work of this church, and noted the importance of informing them accordingly.

VOTED: *CC94.11.70*

To take the following action related to synodical mission support commitments for 1994 and 1995:

1. **Alaska Synod**
   Acknowledge with concern reductions in 1994 and 1995. Encourage restoration to previous level. Request continuing conversations regarding long-term ramifications.

2. **Northwest Washington Synod**
   Acknowledge the reduction in 1994. Affirm proposed increase in 1995. Encourage restoration to previous level.

3. **Southwestern Washington Synod**
   Acknowledge with concern the reduction in 1994. Affirm proposed dollar increase in 1995. Encourage restoration to previous level. Request continuing conversation regarding long-term ramifications.

4. **Montana Synod**
   Acknowledge with concern the reduction in 1995. Encourage restoration to previous level.

5. **Eastern North Dakota Synod**
   Acknowledge the reduction in 1994. Thank the synod for its commitment to restore to previous level in 1995 and following years.

6. **Northwestern Minnesota Synod**
   Acknowledge with concern reductions for 1994 and 1995, with review following face-to-face consultation on November 15, 1994.

7. **Saint Paul Area Synod**
   Acknowledge reductions in 1994 and 1995, with review following consultation on November 15, 1994.

8. **Southeastern Minnesota Synod.**
   Acknowledge reductions in 1994 and 1995, with review following consultation on November 15, 1994.

9. **Northern Texas-Northern Louisiana Synod**
   Acknowledge with concern the reduction in 1994. Encourage restoration to previous level.

10. **Texas-Louisiana Gulf Coast Synod**
    Acknowledge with concern the percentage drop in 1995. Encourage restoration to 55 percent and increase in dollar amount in 1995.

11. **Southeast Michigan Synod**
    Acknowledge with the concern the percentage reduction for 1994. Affirm the plans to increase actual dollar amount in 1995. Encourage restoration to 55 percent.

12. **Northwestern Ohio Synod**
    Acknowledge with concern the reduction for 1995. Encourage restoration to previous level. Request continuing conversation with synodical leadership.

13. **Northeastern Ohio Synod**
    Acknowledge with concern the reduction in percentage for 1994 and 1995. Affirm the proposed increase in actual dollars remitted for 1995.

14. **Southern Ohio Synod**

Acknowledge with concern the reduction in percentage. Affirm the proposed increase in actual dollar amount for 1995. Encourage restoration to 55 percent.

15. **Northwestern Pennsylvania Synod**

Acknowledge with concern the reduction in percentage in 1995. Affirm the proposed increase in actual dollars remitted. Encourage restoration to 50 percent level.

16. **Florida-Bahamas Synod**

Acknowledge reduction in percentage for 1995. Affirm proposed increase in actual dollars remitted in 1995. Encourage restoration to 52 percent.

3. Vision for Mission Fund

Background: Since the April 1994 Church Council meeting, Jerry Olstad has been appointed as full-time director for the Vision for Mission Fund to give direction to this effort, under the supervision of the Division for Congregational Ministries. Synodical relationships and work with individual donors will be a major part of this effort.

Early evaluation of the Vision for Mission initiative suggests the following:

(1) Synods were not uniform throughout this church in their emphasis on or encouragement of this initiative. Some synods made highly visible efforts, while others did not actively promote the fund.

(2) When members received envelopes, by and large the response was fairly good.

(3) The "leader mailing" received about a 10 percent response, with an average gift of $93.

(4) Over 90 percent of the respondents checked off, "Use As Needed" or "Now", which showed evidence of trust for the churchwide organization to make decisions, even when individuals were given multiple options.

(5) The option for synods to piggyback mission efforts in their territory did not receive an overwhelming response.

(6) Many of the largest gifts came from churchwide staff in Chicago.

While the Vision for Mission Fund is an ongoing effort throughout the year, an offering emphasis in May 1995 is being planned. Attempts will be made to simplify the fund so that it is more "user-friendly," to work more closely with synods, and to find ways to give all families in the ELCA the opportunity to participate in this effort.

The Vision for Mission Fund is a long-term effort, not a short-term fix. While the Annual Offering provides substantial income, the other main benefit of this effort is the acquisition of names to build a donor base for major gifts. That effort is well under way, but it will take years for the results of careful cultivation and invitation to become apparent.

Staff is working closely with a consulting firm to focus energies more sharply on overall financial development strategies at the churchwide level. This

may include, but is not limited to, direct mail efforts, major gifts, database management, donor relations, case developments, and other components of solid development strategies.

Council Action: The Church Council received the foregoing as information.

4. 1995 Spending Authorization

Background: The projected level of income for the churchwide organization in 1995 has been reduced by $1,465,000 from the 1994 budgeted levels. (This is *not* in addition to the $1,000,000 reduction for 1994 described above.)

• Mission support is anticipated to be level with the *revised* 1994 estimate, therefore, $1,000,000 lower than the original 1994 budgeted levels.

• Vision for Mission income is projected at $1,000,000, a reduction of $200,000 from the original 1994 estimate and $200,000 higher than the *revised* 1994 estimate.

• Missionary Sponsorship is estimated to be $200,000 less than the original 1994 estimate, which is level with the *revised* 1994 estimate.

On the expense side, two items will result in significant *savings* for the churchwide organization. The first and largest is a reduction of $900,000 in the amount that must be transferred to the Board of Pensions for retirees' medical claims. Corresponding reductions between 8 percent for full family coverage and 17 percent for single coverage in premiums paid for current employees will be realized in unit expenditures. It is anticipated that this will result in savings in the range of $400,000-$450,000 in the budget.

The second major reduction in expenses results from the elimination of fidelity-bond coverage for congregations. This coverage and expense is being eliminated as of March 1995. The ELCA's insurance brokers have worked to provide congregations with the opportunity to continue coverage at affordable rates. This action will save the churchwide organization an estimated $175,000 in 1995.

Additional *cost pressures* on our resources have been identified at a level of $868,000. The largest impact on expenses is an allowance for three percent compensation increases ($670,000 in 1995). Other increases in budgeted expenditures are due to long-term debt obligations: principal and interest payments on the Archives building and, beginning in September 1995, the minimal principal payments on the Lutheran Center. Together, these total $198,000.

Additional budget pressure could result from commitments to help fund assemblies of the Lutheran World Federation and World Council of Churches, costs associated with the separate incorporation of the ELCA Foundation, and options the churchwide organization faces related to the application of emerging technologies.

These changes in income and expenses will require a reduction in 1995 of $1,258,000 from the original spending authorization for 1994. Since the $1,000,000 in reduced 1994 spending is to be achieved through planned underspending, some of which is related to "one-time" circumstances, those savings were *not* included in the base when defining 1995 adjustments.

The success of the cooperative efforts of churchwide units in achieving significant reductions in 1994 encouraged the Office of the Bishop and the Office of the Treasurer to build on that process for 1995. The 1995 expenditure authorization proposal was reviewed by the Budget and Finance Committee at its pre-council meeting.

Council Action: Ms. Lohr introduced the recommendation of the Budget and Finance Committee printed below, subsequently adopted by the Church Council.

During discussion, Robert S. Schroeder inquired about the drop of fidelity bonding for congregations. Treasurer McAuliffe explained that the insurance carrier no longer wished to carry the program and subsequently it was determined that congregations would be better served by carrying their own fidelity insurance. He noted that only one out of 11,000 ELCA congregations had expressed concern to date. Pastor Schroeder raised the possibility that the added expense to congregations would result in the designation of less mission support to synods and the churchwide organization. D. Mark Klever, speaking as an insurance professional, concurred that the cost to congregations would not be substantial.

VOTED: CC94.11.71

To approve an initial 1995 fiscal year spending authorization of $73,925,000, with an initial Mission Operating Fund allocation of $1,500,000; and

To approve an initial 1995 World Hunger spending authorization of $11,400,000.

5. Requests for Restoration of 1994 Reductions in 1995

Background: Council agenda Exhibit B, Part 1a, detailed requests from the Chicago Metropolitan Synod and the Washington, D.C., Synod for the restoration of funding to the Commission for Multicultural Ministries so that the four ethnic "desks" might be restored. In that same exhibit, the request of the Northeastern Iowa Synod for the restoration of funding for the Peace Education Department in the Division for Church and Society is found. Finally, the Southeastern Synod requested the restoration of the staff reduction in the area of specialized pastoral care in the Division for Ministry.

Council agenda Exhibit F, Part 5a, contained reports from the Commission for Multicultural Ministry, the Division for Church in Society, and the Division for Ministry describing the context in which those reductions were made.

The Budget and Finance Committee considered the matter of budgetary priorities, as it reviewed action related to the 1994 and 1995 expenditure authorizations and began its discussion of the 1996-1997 budget

proposal. An exhibit shared at the council's April 1994 meeting, which was a "discussion paper" on budget choices and budget priorities, was provided to council members. The categories described in that exhibit continue to shape our discussion of churchwide budget priorities.

At its pre-council meeting, the Budget and Finance Committee will develop a response to the actions taken by the synods listed above.

Council Action: Ms. Lohr introduced the following recommendation of the Budget and Finance Committee, subsequently adopted without discussion.

VOTED: CC94.11.72

To receive the requests of the Southwestern Washington Synod, Sierra Pacific Synod, Central States Synod, Metropolitan Chicago Synod, Southeastern Pennsylvania Synod, and Metropolitan Washington, D.C., Synod (related to budget cuts in the Commission for Multicultural Ministries); from the Northeastern Iowa Synod and Greater Milwaukee Synod (related to budget cuts in the Division for Church in Society); and from the Northwestern Ohio Synod, Northeastern Pennsylvania Synod, and Southeastern Synod (related to budget cuts in the Division for Ministry);

To recognize the validity of the concern of these synods about the impact of the reduction in funds available for churchwide ministries, specifically the elimination of churchwide staff positions serving:

●the ethnic desks in the Commission for Multicultural Ministries,

●the peace education program in the Division for Church in Society, and

●specialized pastoral care in the Division for Ministry;

To request the Office of the Bishop to share with these synods the three areas that were earmarked for priority treatment within the budget of the churchwide organization: global mission, planting and supporting congregations, and theological education. These functions are distributed across unit lines. Most of this work, however is housed in four divisions: the Division for Global Mission, Division for Outreach, Division for Congregational Ministries, and Division for Ministry. These priorities were established by action of the Church Council and the Churchwide Assembly as budgetary priorities. The consequent actions, we believe, were in concert with these priorities and these choices were made with great difficulty.

To decline to restore funding for specific churchwide programs, noting that such restorations would by necessity be at the expense of other churchwide programs or grants to synods and other partners in ministry;

To request the Commission for Multicultural Ministries to share with the Southwestern Washington Synod, Sierra Pacific Synod, Central States Synod, Metropolitan Chicago Synod, Southeastern Pennsylvania Synod, and Metropolitan Washington, D.C., Synod information that indicates the measures that were taken to continue the work related to these responsibilities;

To request the Division for Church in Society to share with the Northeastern Iowa Synod and Greater Milwaukee Synod information that indicates the measures that were taken to continue the work related to these responsibilities;

To request the Division for Ministry to share with the Northwestern Ohio Synod, Northeastern Pennsylvania Synod, and Southeastern Synod information that indicates the measures that were taken to continue the work related to these responsibilities; and

To thank these and all synods for their ongoing support for churchwide ministries and encourage them to continue to discuss with their members and congregations the connection between declining levels of income shared with the wider church and the elimination or reduction of churchwide programs that support ministry in synods and congregations.

6. 1996-1997 Budget Proposal Guidelines

Background: The lack of clear and consistent financial patterns in the early life of the Evangelical Lutheran Church in America makes planning two and three years in advance difficult at best. On the basis of past experience, the Office of the Bishop has proposed a somewhat different approach to the development of the 1996-1997 budget proposal, which will be substituted to the 1995 Churchwide Assembly for adoption. Should the Church Council affirm this approach, the assembly would be presented with a "two-tiered" expense budget for the coming biennium, rather than the unitary budget proposal that has been the pattern at the last three churchwide assemblies.

For 1996, a $2 million increase in income is projected over 1995 revised levels ($1 million in increased mission support and $1 million in the Vision for Mission Fund). While past history does not make budget planners sanguine about either increase, this projection represents only a modest increase that would barely keep abreast of inflation. In the current financial context, however, this would represent a "challenge" budget for use in conversations with synods and in their conversations with congregations.

The first "tier" of the "two-tiered" expense budget would reflect income anticipated at the revised 1995 budget level for all units. A second "tier" would be the $2 million in estimated increased income. Allocations from the increased income would *not* be made until there is certainty that the income will be available. The newly-elected bishop would recommend to the Church Council

in the fall of 1995 how funds in this second tier would be distributed.

This approach has the following advantages:

- It continues the relative priorities established by past churchwide assemblies during a potential "transition period" (1996-1997). During this period, the results of the "Inquiry" process will be analyzed and necessary changes in churchwide processes and structure may be developed.

- It provides a process that could provide *additions* to unit spending rather than *reductions*, which would provide stability both for churchwide programs and for those receiving grants through the churchwide organization.

- It would provide to the new bishop and to the new Church Council the opportunity to help shape budgetary priorities in the early months of their tenure.

Council Action: The Church Council received the foregoing as information.

7. Mission Support: Alternative Formula Progress Report

Background: The 1993 Churchwide Assembly instructed the churchwide organization to come to the 1995 assembly with a recommendation for the formula and process for mission support. A working group, chaired by the Rev. Mark R. Moller-Gunderson as ELCA coordinator for mission support has been assembled to fulfill that assignment. The following persons are members of this working group:

Ms. Edith M. Lohr (Budget and Finance Committee, Church Council);

The Rev. James S. Aull (Bishop, South Carolina Synod);

The Rev. Robert W. Kelley (Bishop, Northeastern Ohio Synod);

The Rev. Robert N. Bacher (Office of the Bishop);

The Rev. Michael L. Cooper-White (Department for Synodical Relations); and

Messrs. Richard L. McAuliffe and Gary K. Brugh (Office of the Treasurer).

The working group met on September 16, 1994. After reviewing current research and exploring ten different models, the working group recommends a set of principles upon which formula decision making should be based. The working group also recommends that specific guidelines be suggested for congregations, synods, the churchwide organization, and agencies and institutions. Additional research is being done to assist the working group in its task. This progress report was reviewed by the Budget and Finance Committee at its pre-council meeting. Final recommendations, which will be directed to the 1995 Churchwide Assembly, will be presented at the April 1995 meeting of Church Council.

Council Action: The Church Council received the foregoing as information.

8. Mission Investment Fund: 1995 Capital Budget Recommendation

Background: A joint staff committee comprised of staff from the Division for Outreach and the Office of the Treasurer prepares annually for the Mission Investment Fund a capital budget based on projected availability of capital funds and projected requirements for loans and real property acquisition for ministry development, church building programs, or other approved capital needs. The capital budget of $54,740,000 for 1995 was presented to the October 20, 1994, meeting of the board of the Division for Outreach, and the November 10, 1994, meeting of the board of the Mission Investment Fund of the Evangelical Lutheran Church in America.

Council Action: The Church Council adopted the following resolution through *en bloc* action taken at the conclusion of this meeting:

EN BLOC   *[CC94.11.100]*
To approve the 1995 capital budget of $54,740,000 for the Mission Investment Fund . . ..

9. Audit Committee

Council Action: The Church Council adopted the following resolution through *en bloc* action taken at the conclusion of this meeting:

EN BLOC   *[CC94.11.101]*
To approve the Report of the Audit Committee . . ..

10. ELCA Foundation

Background: The ELCA Foundation is to report semi-annually to the Church Council through the Budget and Finance Committee. Reports of the ELCA Foundation was provided to council members.

Council Action: The Church Council received the foregoing as information.

11. Review and Confirmation of Church Council Designated Funds

Background: The authority to designate funds within the ELCA churchwide organization rests with the Church Council in its capacity as the board of directors of the ELCA churchwide organization. Such designations are reviewed annually by the Church Council following recommendation by the Budget and Finance Committee. Council agenda Exhibit F, Part 9, displayed the current designation of such funds, which required Church Council ratification.

Council Action: The Church Council adopted the following resolution through *en bloc* action taken at the conclusion of this meeting:

EN BLOC   *[CC94.11.102]*
To approve the designation of existing Church Council designated funds described in [council agenda] Exhibit F, Part 9.

12. Election of Assistant Treasurer

Background: Gift annuities and various other documents require the signature of a treasurer or assistant treasurer. Since an assistant treasurer has not been elected, he/she cannot sign in the absence of the treasurer. Because obtaining the required signature may delay such transactions for several days, Church Council appointment of an assistant treasurer is recommended.

Council Action: The Church Council adopted the following resolution through *en bloc* action taken at the conclusion of this meeting:

EN BLOC   *[CC94.11.103]*
To elect Kenneth L. Murken as assistant treasurer of the Evangelical Lutheran Church in America.

13. Process to Determine Who Is Entitled to Certain Bequests

Background: Occasionally, a bequest is received from an estate of a decedent whose will was executed prior to January 1, 1988, and was not subsequently revised. Less occasionally, the decedent's will was executed prior to January 1, 1988, and names a predecessor church body as a beneficiary. Likewise, a will, whether executed prior to or after January 1, 1988, may name a judicatory of a predecessor church body. In all of these cases, the question is who is now entitled to the bequest. A decision-making process is needed when the answer to that question is not free from doubt.

Council Action: Ms. Lohr introduced the following resolution, subsequently adopted by the Church Council without discussion:

VOTED: *CC94.11.73*
To approve the following process for determining who is entitled to certain bequests:

PROCESS FOR DETERMINING WHO IS ENTITLED TO CERTAIN BEQUESTS

Occasionally, a bequest is received from an estate of a decedent whose will was executed prior to January 1, 1988, and was not subsequently revised. Less occasionally, the decedent's will was executed prior to January 1, 1988, and names a predecessor church body as a beneficiary. Likewise, a will, whether executed prior to or after January 1, 1988, may name a judicatory of a predecessor church body. In all of these cases, the question is who is now entitled to the bequest. A decision-making process is needed when the answer to that question is not free from doubt.

In all cases, the fundamental issues for resolution are, first, what did the decedent intend and, second, how would the decedent have reflected this intent, given the nomenclature, structure, and boundaries that became effective on January 1, 1988.

When all parties who are potential beneficiaries can agree upon the answers to these questions, the agreement of the potential beneficiaries should prevail. If one or more of the potential beneficiaries cannot agree, however, then who makes the decision should depend upon who are the potential beneficiaries, as follows:

1. When the potential beneficiaries are units of the churchwide expression or include the churchwide expression itself, but do not include any synods as potential beneficiaries, the decision should be made by the Church Council, consistent with the existing ELCA 20.82. and 20.83.

2. When the potential beneficiaries are two or more synods, but do not include the churchwide expression or units thereof, the decision should be made by the Church Council, consistent with ELCA 20.82. as proposed to be amended (see Church Council Agenda, November 12-14, 1994, page 39; revised November 11, 1994).

3. When the potential beneficiaries include one or more synods *and* the churchwide expression or units thereof, the decision should be made by the Committee on Appeals, with right to appeal to the Churchwide Assembly, consistent with the newly-proposed ELCA 20.84. (see Church Council Agenda, November 12-14, 1994, page 39; revised November 11, 1994).

14. Other Matters

William H. Engelbrecht inquired about the number of global mission personnel now serving overseas. Loren W. Mathre commented on the need to keep before congregations their individual participation in the outreach ministries of this church. The Rev. James G. Cobb expressed appreciation for Ms. Lohr's introductory remarks. He also raised concern that congregations may bypass synods in contributing designated giving to missionary outreach.

Pastor Cobb expressed further concern regarding the lodging of stewardship functions in the Division for Congregational Ministries. He observed that the bulk of responsibility seems to be shifting to a matter of synodical relationships. It was noted that the responsibility for synodical-churchwide consultations is shared among several churchwide units. Bishop Glenn W. Nycklemoe said that synods are doing their best to avoid reductions in mission-support commitments and to cooperate with the churchwide organization. Bishop Chilstrom concurred with this observation.

The Rev. H. George Anderson inquired about the trend toward establishment of endowment funds. Bishop Robert L. Isaksen cautioned against competition among such funds, which is detrimental to all. Bishop Peter Rogness commented on the establishment of the "Vision for Mission Fund" and the climate of support (or lack thereof) for the annual churchwide offering. Pastor Anderson suggested that the intent of his question was to ask how the Church Council might help to alleviate tensions and increase the partnerships between synods and the churchwide organization.

Report of the
Program and Structure Committee

Chair Magnus called upon the Rev. Stephen M. Youngdahl, chair of the council's Program and Structure Committee, to report on behalf of the committee.

1. Specialized Pastoral Care Ministry

Background: The following resolutions on staffing levels related to specialized pastoral care in the Division for Ministry were received from synods and directed to the council's Executive Committee for disposition:

1. Northwestern Ohio Synod (6D)

WHEREAS, the ELCA Division for Ministry Board, effective May 1, 1994, reduced the only staff support position for ELCA specialized pastoral care from full-time to half time; and

WHEREAS, this severely diminishes the support, education and outreach efforts of a significant domestic mission composed of some 800-plus chaplains, counselors, pastoral care educators and other ministers serving in hospitals, rehabilitation centers, nursing home/retirement centers, dependency treatment programs, prisons and other caring agencies; and

WHEREAS, this decision was made by the Division for Ministry Board without contact or consultation with the Specialized Pastoral Care Advisory Committee which the board itself appointed to advise the division on specialized pastoral care issues; therefore be it

RESOLVED, that the Northwestern Ohio Synod gathered in Assembly request that the ELCA Division for Ministry Board suspend its decision to reduce the specialized pastoral care staff position to half-time, and re-evaluate, in consultation with its advisory committee, the options for full-time staffing of the position; and be it further

RESOLVED, that the ELCA, in its "inquiry" process related to church organizational structure, be strongly encouraged to re-evaluate whether support for specialized pastoral care might better be placed in another division of organizational unit of the ELCA.

The Executive Committee voted:

To transmit this resolution of the Northwestern Ohio Synod on specialized pastoral care ministry to the Division for Ministry and Office of the Bishop; and

To request that the Program and Structure Committee review the suggestion that support for specialized pastoral care be placed in another churchwide unit, and provide a report to the November 1994 meeting of the Church Council; and

To request that the Office of the Bishop bring a report on this matter to the November 1994 meeting of the Church Council, as part of the broader discussion related to budgetary priorities (EC94.8.21i).

2. Northeastern Pennsylvania Synod (7E)

WHEREAS, the Evangelical Lutheran Church in America Division for Ministry has reduced from full-time to half-time the position of director for specialized pastoral care and clinical education, effective May 1, 1994; and

WHEREAS, the reduction of that position makes it virtually impossible for the ELCA to ensure that uniform standards be maintained for the training, calling and endorsing of Lutheran chaplains and pastoral counselors; and

WHEREAS, a very severe cut of staffing already occurred at the forming of the ELCA when the responsibility for direction of Lutheran chaplains and pastoral counselors was reduced to one position; and

WHEREAS, bishops, synod councils, board and executives of social ministry organizations and other health care and counseling centers, as well as the people receiving direct pastoral care, benefit from the gifts of pastoral service which come from professional training and certification of chaplains and pastoral counselors; and

WHEREAS, executives and boards of health care and counseling institutions and agencies not affiliated with the church often look to the denominational judicatories for signs of denominational support, or lack thereof, in making decisions to support or not to support chaplaincy and pastoral counselling positions; therefore be it

RESOLVED, that the Northeastern Pennsylvania Synod in Assembly request that the ELCA Division for ministry restore funding for a full time director for specialized pastoral care and clinical education with a budget and support staff sufficient to fulfill this vital mission of the church.

The Executive Committee voted:

To transmit the resolution of the Northeastern Pennsylvania Synod on the specialized pastoral care position to the Division for Ministry for a response to the synod (EC94.7.16m)

Council Action: Pastor Youngdahl introduced the foregoing information, which the Church Council received as information.

2. Review of Churchwide Units

Pastor Youngdahl reported the positive support of the committee for the work of the Commission for Multicultural Ministries, and specifically for its work in reevaluating its structure. He also commented on the extensive conversations with the Rev. W. Robert Sorensen, executive director of the Division for Higher Education and Schools. A progress report will be brought to the April 1995 meeting of the Church Council.

3. Resolution on Violence Toward Women

Background: With the coordination of the Commission for Women, several churchwide units have developed resolutions related to violence against women that have been approved by their boards and steering committees. These resolutions were presented in their entirety in council agenda Exhibit G, Part 2b.

A response to these resolutions was reviewed by the Program and Structure Committee.

Council Action: Chair Magnus called upon Joanne Chadwick, executive director of the Commission for Women, highlighted several resolutions adopted by the governing boards of various churchwide units. The Church Council then adopted the following resolution without discussion:

VOTED: CC94.11.74

To approve the following motion and to commend it to the 1995 Churchwide Assembly for adoption:

WHEREAS, violence against women is a tragic reality that pervades societies worldwide, expressing itself in not only extreme forms (such as beating, sexual abuse, rape, torture, and killing,) but also cultural practices (such as discrimination, female infanticide, genital mutilation, dowry, and widow deaths); and

WHEREAS, Jesus Christ calls each Christian and the whole Church into a mission of love and compassion toward all peoples, and the Holy Scriptures repeatedly call the people of God to do justice, love kindness, and walk humbly with God; and

WHEREAS, the Evangelical Lutheran Church in America, participating in God's mission, commits itself in its constitution to "lift its voice in concord and work with forces for good, to serve humanity, cooperating with church and other groups participating in activities that promote justice, relieve misery,

and reconcile the estranged" (churchwide constitution provision ELCA 4.03.g.); and

WHEREAS, the Lutheran World Federation Council at its meeting in Kristiansand, Norway, in June 1993, asked the member churches to provide educational programs on the different forms of violence against women, to offer social support and practical aid for women, and to advocate for social policies and laws that protect women; and

WHEREAS, by action of the Church Council in April 1988, the Evangelical Lutheran Church in America joined with other Christian churches in the "Ecumenical Decade: Churches in Solidarity with Women," the focus of which is on:
- "the full participation of women in both church and society,"
- "the commitment to justice and peace for all," and
- "theology and spirituality which flow out of women's faith and life experience" (Church Council minutes, CC88.4.53); and

WHEREAS, widespread discrimination against women continues to permit the rationalization of violence against women and may result in a violation of their human rights; and

WHEREAS, the report from the United Nations World Conference on Human Rights, held in June 1993 in Vienna, Austria, calls for action by governments and non-governmental organizations to prevent violence against women, e.g., domestic violence, abuse, rape, and killing of women during civil wars and at refugee camps, and considers these abhorrent acts as violations of the human rights of women; and

WHEREAS, 130 nations have ratified the International Convention Against the Discrimination of Women, but the United States is among the minority that have not; and

WHEREAS, the United Nations has drafted a Declaration Against Violence Against Women and the U.N. Commission on Human Rights has appointed a Special Rapporteur on Violence Against Women; and

WHEREAS, the international relief and development agencies with whom the ELCA cooperates have identified the suffering of women as a major concern and have called upon churches and global institutions to respond; therefore be it

RESOLVED, that the 1995 Churchwide Assembly of the Evangelical Lutheran Church of America:

- denounce and combat the beating, sexual abuse, raping, and killing that threaten the life and safety of women everywhere;
- encourage greater awareness among members of the ELCA about all forms of violence that threaten the life and safety of all women;
- encourage all members of the Evangelical Lutheran Church in America to make their homes, schools, and places of employment safe places where all may be free from physical abuse and those elements of the mass media that extol violence and the exploitation of women;
- support the efforts of all members and congregations of this church, synods, churchwide units, and church-related agencies and institutions that seek to provide both justice and security for women in church and society through law, policy, care, service, and support within the Body of Christ;
- encourage the development of culture-specific resources and programs that advise and educate women who may experience violence in their lives;
- express appreciation to the United States Senate for the ratification of the International Convention on the Elimination of All Forms of Racial Discrimination on June 24, 1994;
- encourage the U.S. government to ratify the Convention on the Elimination of Discrimination Against Women (CEDAW) and encourage church leaders and members, congregations, synods, the churchwide organization, and church-related agencies and institutions to advocate for the ratification of this important agreement;
- affirm the call made by the Lutheran World Federation to combat violence against women.

4. Review of Division for Global Mission

Pastor Youngdahl expressed appreciation on behalf of the committee for the evaluation and self-study process employed by the staff of the Division for Global Mission. He further noted that specific recommendations will be brought to the April 1995 meeting of the Church Council.

Matters Related to the Division for Church and Society

1. Proposed Merger of Lutheran General HealthSystem and Evangelical Health System

Background: The Evangelical Lutheran Church in America, acting through its Church Council, serves as a corporate member of the Lutheran General Health-System (LGHS). The Division for Church in Society is the churchwide unit through which the Evangelical Lutheran Church in America relates to LGHS. The role of corporate member includes the responsibility to act on the recommendation from LGHS that approval be granted for it to enter into a merger with EHS Health Care, Oak Brook, Illinois. Under the proposed merger, as of January 1, 1995, the Evangelical Lutheran Church in America and the Illinois congregations of the United Church of Christ would each appoint representatives to a Member Council that would constitute the corporate members of the faith-based, values-driven integrated health system serving Chicagoland.

At its September 29-October 1, 1994, meeting, the board of the ELCA Division for Church in Society voted:

To recommend to the Church Council of the ELCA the merger of Evangelical Health System and Lutheran General HealthSystem, subject to the review of documents and actions in connection with the merger requiring ELCA approval by the executive committee of the board of the Division for Church in Society and recommendation of such documents and actions by the executive committee of the board of the Division for Church in Society to the ELCA Church Council.

During October 1994, conversations between Lutheran General HealthSystem, the Evangelical Health System, and the executive committee of the board of the Division for Church in Society continued. Final review of documents was completed by the executive committee of the board for the Division for Church in Society, and also by ELCA general counsel.

Council Action: Chair Magnus called upon the Rev. Charles S. Miller Jr., executive director of the Division for Church in Society, who introduced the following guests: Ms. Mary Ann McDermott, chair of the board of Lutheran General HealthSystem; Mr. Stephen Ummel, president and chief executive officer; the Rev. James Wylie, senior vice president for mission; and Ms. Elizabeth O'Kelley, legal counsel, who shared background information and rationale for the proposed merger. Ms. McDermott indicated that the board had to consider many options, especially whether the hospital could maintain its independence and viability in the future or whether sale of the system would be in the best interest of the hospital and of this church. Partnerships, joint ventures, and a variety of different configurations of joining with other institutions came to the board as invitations from outside and as overtures from within the board. A strong management recommendation that a total asset merger with a leading like-minded health system was the option considered in depth over the past eighteen months. She complemented the management staff in maintaining the present system and concurrently pursuing this and an alternate contingency plan. She requested the Church Council to entertain the proposal for merger with an open heart.

Mr. Ummel discussed the "fundamental economic transformation" of health care in the United States. He noted that economics, rather than quality or access, was fundamentally driving health-care reform today. He also said that the decline in high-tech intervention and of hospital occupancy, decreasing reimbursements to health-care providers, and decline in the need for specialized care, coupled with the high-profit margin of insurance providers were significant factors affecting the industry today. He indicated that managed-care is hastening economic restructuring. Employers are exerting more pressure for health-care providers to bring about economic relief on their behalf. Initiatives and incentives from within and without the health-care industry promote restructuring of health-care providers.

Mr. Ummel explained the affect of the above trends on LGHS in particular. He described the planning endeavor resulting in the merger proposal. He commented on the advantages of the merger, including the lowest costs to patients of network providers in the Chicago area, the largest geographical area, the state's largest primary care physician production, and the largest pool of available primary-care physicians (1200).

Pastor Wiley stated that LGHS sees itself as a mission-driven institution whose ministry is characterized by the phrase, "faith-based, values-driven." Ms. O'Kelley outlined the next steps in completing the proposed merger (a combination agreement was signed on October 21, 1994, which served as a road map for the rest of the transaction): (1) Creation of a parent organization (January 1, 1995); and (2) Merger in two to three years following IRS approval. Ms. O'Kelley noted that several procedural agreements would need to be finalized prior to closure of the merger. She described the governance structure for the new organization and then introduced the recommendation before the council.

During discussion, William T. Billings inquired whether the term, "liquidation," implied that LGHS would be sold. Ms. McDermott explained that such wording was meant only to provide for possible future contingencies. Mr. Billings inquired whether further mergers were planned. Ms. McDermott responded that at this time various relationships with other potential partners were being identified and cited examples of such partnerships. At the request of William H. Engelbrecht, ELCA General Counsel David J. Hardy observed that the interests of the Evangelical Lutheran Church in America had been "guarded at every step." Mr. Engelbrecht then asked Mr. Hardy to explain the proposed corporate structure. Mr. Engelbrecht inquired further about the extent of the assets of each parent corporation. He observed that corporate mergers have both up-and-down sides, and asked, "What is the down-side of this?" Mr. Ummel responded, "We do not think there are many formidable, major downsides or we would not have proceeded with [the merger]." He noted that LGHS would have a minority of board members, but all other

governance committees would be equal, and the two chief executive officers of the parent companies would be retained. Mr. Hardy stated that in his opinion the merger provisions were well considered with adequate safe-guards for ELCA-related assets.

Bishop Herbert W. Chilstrom concurred that the merger had been carefully planned. He inquired how the Lutheran General Medical Group was valued as an asset and how vulnerable would its existence be post-merger. Mr. Ummel and Ms. McDermott responded, confirming the value of such multi-specialty medical groups as "precious assets" both now and in the future. Mr. Ummel predicted that, as a result of the proposed merger, LGHS medical group would double in size during the next several years.

Edith M. Lohr inquired how the name of new corporation would reflect faith values and a Lutheran identity. Mr. Ummel explained that an outside firm had been engaged to "find a [new system] name that satisfies those rigorous criteria"; nonetheless, the various merging institutions were expected to retain their current names. Bishop Robert L. Isaksen requested further general information about EHS Health Care. Mr. Ummel responded. The Rev. Donald M. Hallberg offered "congratulations to the governance body and to Mr. Ummel and all his colleagues for bringing us to this place." He voiced strong concern that the eventuality of Lutheran General Medical Group be resolved before the final merger agreement is effected.

VOTED: *CC94.11.75*
To adopt the following recommendation:
WHEREAS, on June 13, 1994, Lutheran General HealthSystem ("LGHS") and EHS Health Care ("EHS") entered into a Letter of Intent to merge LGHS and EHS; and

WHEREAS, a Combination Agreement, dated as of October 1, 1994, (the "Combination Agreement") has been entered into among EHS, LGHS, Lutheran General Hospital ("LGH"), and Evangelical Hospitals Corporation ("EHC") setting forth the agreements of the parties; and

WHEREAS, the Evangelical Lutheran Church in America ("ELCA") is the Sole Corporate Member of LGHS and has certain reserve powers over LGHS; and

WHEREAS, pursuant to the Combination Agreement, LGHS and EHS will form an Illinois not-for-profit corporation to be initially named "EHS/LGHS Co." (as such entity may be named from time to time, referred to herein as "EHS/LGHS Co."); and

WHEREAS, the Board of Directors of EHS/LGHS Co. will consist of eighteen (18) members: nine (9) appointed by the United Church of Christ ("UCC"), at least five (5) of whom must be UCC members (the "UCC Members"); seven (7) appointed by ELCA, at least four (4) of whom must be ELCA members (the "ELCA Directors"); and the two (2) Co-Chief Executive Officers, who shall serve as ex officio members of the Board of Directors; and

WHEREAS, it is contemplated that as of closing of the Combination Agreement, anticipated to be January 1, 1995, or shortly thereafter (the "Closing"), EHS/LGHS Co. will become the Corporate Member of LGHS and EHS; and

WHEREAS, the Combination Agreement includes certain conditions which must be satisfied or waived in order for Closing to occur; and

WHEREAS, the Combination Agreement also provides for the Members of EHS/LGHS Co., to consist of twenty-four (24) people, twelve (12) of whom will be appointed by ELCA (the "ELCA Members"), and twelve (12) of whom will be appointed by UCC; and

WHEREAS, on October 7 and October 18, 1994, the Board of Directors of LGHS nominated the following individuals to ELCA for appointment as the ELCA Directors of EHS/LGHS Co. to serve effective as of Closing for the terms indicated:

	Term
William J. Arnold, M.D.	1988,
Rev. Sherman G. Hicks	1998,
Donald R. Hollis	1999,
Mary Ann McDermott, R.N., Ed.D.	2000,
Richard L. Phillips, M.D.	1998,
Carl J. Schnakenberg	2000, and
Sarah M. Stegemoeller	1999;

and

WHEREAS, it will be necessary to amend the current Bylaws and Articles of Incorporation of LGHS effective as of the Closing to reflect the Corporate Member of LGHS as EHS/LGHS Co. and to grant certain reserved powers to EHS/LGHS Co.; and

WHEREAS, it will be necessary to establish EHS/LGHS Co. which will grant the following reserved powers to the Members:

1. Approval of formal statements of philosophy, values, and mission of EHS/-LGHS Co.
2. Approval of certain amendments to the Articles of Incorporation by Bylaws of EHS/LGHS Co. as proposed by the Board of Directors of EHS/LGHS Co. related to the Members and certain changes to Board configuration. Changes to Board configuration which would require Member approval are: (i) change in the ratio of UCC Director positions to ELCA Director positions; and (ii) change to the requirement that a majority of the Board of Directors must be UCC Directors and ELCA Directors.
3. Approval of any merger, consolidation, liquidation, or dissolution of EHS/LGHS Co. or sale of all or substantially all of its assets.
4. Appointment by the associated Member delegate group of the Directors of EHS/-LGHS Co. from among those nominated by the Board of Directors of EHS/LGHS Co. and removal of such Directors at any time, with or without cause, also by the associated Member delegate group.

and

WHEREAS, the ELCA appointed Members shall also have the right to appoint one (1) clergy and one (1) lay representative to a "Governing Council" or similar body established with respect to LGH at such time such Governing Council or similar body is established; and

WHEREAS, an additional Illinois not-for-profit corporation will be formed to be initially named "EHS/LGHS Hospital Co." (as such entity may be named from time to time, referred to herein as "Hospital Co.") into which LGHS and EHS, as well as LGH and EHC, will be merged upon the satisfaction or waiver of conditions set forth in the Combination Agreement (the "Merger Conditions"); and

WHEREAS, EHS/LGHS Co. and Hospital Co. will be Illinois not-for-profit corporations that will apply for tax-exempt status under the Internal Revenue Code; and

WHEREAS, upon receipt of the Internal Revenue Service ("IRS") determinations that EHS/LGHS Co. and Hospital Co. qualify for tax-exempt status and redeterminations of tax-exempt status for those entities affected by the reorganization and confirmation that the other Merger Conditions are waived or satisfied, LGHS, EHS, LGH, and EHC will merge into Hospital Co.; and

WHEREAS, pursuant to the Bylaws of LGHS, ELCA shall approve all amendments to the Articles of Incorporation of LGHS as proposed by the Board of Directors of LGHS, and any amendments to Sections 2.1 and 10.1 of the Bylaws of LGHS before the amendments may become effective; and

WHEREAS, pursuant to the Bylaws of LGHS, ELCA shall approve, before it may become effective, any merger of LGHS; and

WHEREAS, the Board of Directors of LGHS met on October 18, 1994, and submitted the amendments to the Articles of Incorporation, Bylaws of LGHS and the Plan of Merger, which are set forth in Agenda Exhibit P, Parts 4c, 4e, and 4d, respectively, to ELCA for approval in its capacity as Sole Corporate Member of LGHS; therefore be it

RESOLVED, that the Church Council of ELCA hereby approves the amendments to the Bylaws and Articles of Incorporation of LGHS as set forth in Agenda Exhibit P, Parts 4e and 4c; such amendments to become effective as of the Closing; and be it further

RESOLVED, that the Church Council of ELCA hereby approves the appointment of the following individuals, effective as of the Closing, to serve as the ELCA Directors of EHS/LGHS Co. with the terms indicated:

	Term
William J. Arnold, M.D.	1988,
Rev. Sherman G. Hicks	1998,
Donald R. Hollis	1999,
Mary Ann McDermott, R.N., Ed.D.	2000,
Richard L. Phillips, M.D.	1998,
Carl J. Schnakenberg	2000, and
Sarah M. Stegemoeller	1999;

and be it further

RESOLVED, that the Church Council of ELCA hereby approves the appointment of the following individuals to serve as the ELCA Members of EHS/LGHS Co., effective as of Closing, and for the terms indicated:

	Term
Sally Clark Almen	1997,
Ruth H. Bengsten	1996,
Josselyn Bennett	1998,
Bishop Herbert W. Chilstrom	1996,
Ingrid Christiansen	1996,
Rev. Donald M. Hallberg	1996,
Loretta Horton	1997,
Richard L. McAuliffe	1997,
Rev. Charles S. Miller Jr.	1998,
Donald Peterson	1997,
Julie Schlueter	1998,
Dr. Jerry Seidel	1998;

and be it further

RESOLVED, that the Church Council of ELCA hereby approves the merger of LGHS and EHS into Hospital Co., upon the satisfaction or waiver of the Merger Conditions, pursuant to a Plan of Merger substantially similar in form to the Plan of Merger set forth in Agenda Exhibit P, Part 4d; and be it further

RESOLVED, that the Church Council of ELCA hereby delegates to the Executive Committee of the Church Council authority to consider and approve, on behalf of the Church Council, any amendments proposed by LGHS to the documents approved herein subsequent to the date of these Resolutions; and be it further

RESOLVED, that the Church Council of ELCA hereby approves that the proper officers of ELCA be authorized to take all such further actions and execute and deliver all such further documents as shall be necessary or desirable to carry out the foregoing resolutions and the transactions contemplated thereby, such necessity or desirability shall be conclusively evidenced by the execution and delivery of these documents by the proper officers of ELCA.

Treasurer Richard L. McAuliffe abstained and asked that his abstention be noted in these minutes.

Report of the Program and Structure Committee (continued)

4. Review of the Division for Global Mission

On behalf of the Program and Structure Committee, Chair Magnus called upon the Rev. Mark W. Thomsen, executive director of the Division for Global Mission, to comment on the process for the review of the unit. Pastor Thomsen drew attention to Council agenda Exhibit Q, Part 2. He commented on several trends documented therein within the work of the unit since this church's inception, including outreach to other faith communities, particularly the Moslem community and Asian peoples; increased personnel in Eastern Europe; a decrease in the funding of traditional evangelism personnel, but a correlative increase in the funding of leadership development and scholarships with partner churches; increased partnership with "South-South" churches as they reach out to other churches; relief and development programs through ELCA Hunger Program; and a drastic reduction of missionaries due to funding reductions, compensated by expanding volunteer program.

Representational Principles

Chair Magnus noted that the Church Council would not make a final recommendation to the 1995 Churchwide Assembly until April 1995, when the report from ELCA seminaries would be available. She invited the recorders from the small groups that had met earlier during this meeting to report on their findings:

Group 1 (Deborah S. Yandala reporting)
- The representational principles were valued highly, having forced a recognition of diversity within this church.
- The principles are rooted both theologically and in the organization of this church.
- Significant discussion in the question related to male and female representation.
- The real issue is not representational principles, but a feeling of distance of some persons and populations

from the churchwide expression; the Church Council ought to address of that matter further.

Group 2 (Carlos Peña)

- The group agreed fully with the representational principles and their value to this church; voices have been heard not otherwise heard before; the goals encourage greater attention to the issue.
- Representational goals encourage greater inclusivity.
- With respect to male and female representation at synodical assemblies; two-thirds of the group responded in favor; the concern seems to be economically driven.
- Lay and clergy representation: Same matter needs to be addressed with respect to all rostered persons.

Group 3 (Lorraine G. Bergquist)

- Although representational principles encourage wider participation, geographic issues are important.
- Forcing the issue at times, in the impression of color first, and then talents.
- Recognition that the matter has recreated a morale problem among white male clergy.
- Concern expressed that known persons of color are being overly utilized.
- Concern that some people have been overlooked by virtue of the "quota system."
- With respect to male and female representation, a suggestion was voiced that the word, normally, be included in the constitutional and bylaw references to synodical assemblies.

Group 4 (The Rev. Franklin D. Fry)

- Strongly affirmed concept of representational principles.
- Affirmed male and female representation with provision for flexibility.
- The dilemma of expertise and credentials was voiced; we need to do a better job of identifying qualified persons.
- Pastor Fry expressed a wish that the conversation could be "turned away from the pitting of rights of one group against the rights of another group . . . and could rather see this in the sense that it is a fearsome thing to think that we would stand before the living God and tell God that God may not serve his Church and his people through various persons simply because of accident of their identification; that the issue is . . . pitting ourselves against the lavish goodness of God as he seeks to bestow it upon us through all persons."

Group 5 (William E. Diehl)

- Diversity among us at assemblies is wonderful.
- The issue is basically basically one of color.
- The issue basically an organizational, theological, and political issue.
- The issue is a social necessity, if church growth is to be achieved.
- With respect to male and female representation, suggestions included exemption for small congregations, and for special exemptions for greater flexibility.

During discussion, the Rev. John O. Knudson posited a need for the Church Council to advocate for and speak positively of the tremendous gift that this has brought to us. Terry L. Bowes reported the passionate response of participants at a multicultural town meeting held in the Rocky Mountain Synod. Concerns voiced at that meeting included the critical nature of the issue, representation as a theological issue, this church's self-identity, and the relationship of its members with one another (as well as with God).

Report of the Legal and Constitutional Review Committee (continued)

7. Amendment on Lay Voting Membership in Synodical Assemblies

Background: Council Agenda Exhibit B, Part 1, contained the texts of various synodical memorials to Churchwide Assemblies that have sought amendment of †S7.21.c. regarding the election of lay voting members for synodical assemblies.

Given the apparently widespread desire for greater flexibility in this matter, consideration was given to proposing constitutional and bylaw amendments that would assign responsibility for implementation of the lay representational principles at synodical assemblies to the respective synods.

After discussion of this church's representational principles during the October 1-6, 1994, meeting of the Conference of Bishops, members voted to adopt the following resolution:

The Conference of Bishops encourages this church to maintain its present representational principles, with a revision to allow synods limited exception from the present formula for male and female representation in synodical assemblies. For example, synod documents should be amended whereby an assembly committee could grant occasional waivers when congregations present a compelling rationale why the normal requirements cannot be met (CB94.10.11).

In view of the variety reflected on this matter in memorials and resolutions at previous churchwide assemblies and the content of some memorials already received for the 1995 Churchwide Assembly, it may be wise to offer the voting members of the 1995 Churchwide Assembly two options on this matter, one of which could be chosen, if the assembly so determines, for the amendment of the governing documents.

Council Action: Chair Magnus called upon Secretary Lowell G. Almen to review the two options that might be presented to the Churchwide Assembly for its consideration. Option One would add the word, "normally," to the present bylaw, while Option Two also would provide for the election of a minimum of one rather than two voting members by congregations with fewer than 175 baptized members:

Option 1:

†S7.21.c.   A minimum of two lay members elected by each congregation related to this synod, normally one of whom shall be

male and one of whom shall be female, shall be voting members. The Synod Council shall establish a formula to provide additional lay representation from congregations on the basis of the number of baptized members in the congregation. The Synod Council shall seek to ensure that, as nearly as possible, 50 percent of the lay members of the assembly shall be female and 50 percent shall be male. Additional members from each congregation normally shall be equally divided between male and female except that the odd-numbered member, if any, may be either male or female.

10.41.01.c. A minimum of two lay members elected by each congregation related to the synod, normally one of whom shall be male and one of whom shall be female, shall be voting members. The Synod Council shall establish a formula to provide additional lay representation from congregations on the basis of the number of baptized members in the congregation. The Synod Council shall seek to ensure that, as nearly as possible, 50 percent of the lay members of the assembly shall be female and 50 percent shall be male. Additional members from each congregation normally shall be equally divided between male and female except that the odd-numbered member, if any, may be either male or female.

Option 2:

†S7.21.c.   A minimum of one lay member elected by each congregation with fewer than 175 baptized members and a minimum of two lay members elected by each congregation with more than 175 baptized members related to this synod,. . . [with the remainder as above], and

10.41.01.c. A minimum of one lay member elected by each congregation with fewer than 175 baptized members and a minimum of two lay members elected by each congregation with more than 175 baptized members related to the synod,. . . [with the remainder as above].

Dale V. Sandstrom, chair of the council's Constitutional Review Committee, commented that the above options represented two issues that should be addressed separately by the assembly in order to avoid confusion. William T. Billings noted a need for additional textual clarity. Secretary Almen indicated that the wording of the resolution would need to be perfected in order to separate clearly the two issues.

On behalf of the committee, Mr. Sandstrom moved Option 1 for discussion purposes of the addition of the word, "normally.":

MOVED;

SECONDED: To recommend to the 1995 Churchwide Assembly the following constitutional and bylaw amendments:

†S7.21.c.   A minimum of two lay members elected by each congregation related to this synod, normally one of whom shall be male and one of whom shall be female, shall be voting members. The Synod Council shall establish a formula to provide additional lay representation from congregations on the basis of the number of baptized members in the congregation. The Synod Council shall seek to ensure that, as nearly as possible, 50 percent of the lay members of the assembly shall be female and 50 percent shall be male. Additional members from each congregation normally shall be equally divided between male and female except that the odd-numbered member, if any, may be either male or female.

10.41.01.c. A minimum of two lay members elected by each congregation related to the synod, normally one of whom shall be male and one of whom shall be female, shall be voting members. The Synod Council shall establish a formula to provide additional lay representation from congregations on the basis of the number of baptized members in the congregation. The Synod Council shall seek to ensure that, as nearly as possible, 50 percent of the lay members of the assembly shall be female and 50 percent shall be male. Additional members from each congregation normally shall be equally divided between male and female except that the odd-numbered member, if any, may be either male or female.

Robert S. Schroeder recommended that the issue be revisited after several years to determine the affect of the term, "normally." Mr. Sandstrom commented on the rationale for the proposed addition. The Rev. Stephen M. Youngdahl observed that by not acting at this meeting *per se*, the council would in effect be affirming the present representational principles. Chair Magnus explained that a delay by the council in a recommendation would mean that any change in constitutional provisions could not take effect until 1997. Adopting the recommendation of the Legal and Constitutional Review Committee would permit implementation in 1996.

The Church Council adopted the following resolution as Option One:

VOTED: *CC94.11.76*

To recommend to the 1995 Churchwide Assembly the following constitutional and bylaw amendments:

†S7.21.c.   A minimum of two lay members elected by each congregation related to this synod, <u>normally</u> one of whom shall be male and one of whom shall be female, shall be voting members. The Synod Council shall establish a formula to provide additional lay representation from congregations on the basis of the number of baptized members in the congregation. <u>The Synod Council shall seek to ensure that, as nearly as possible, 50 percent of the lay members of the assembly shall be female and 50 percent shall be male.</u> Additional members from each congregation <u>normally</u> shall be equally divided between male and female except that the odd-numbered member, if any, may be either male or female.

10.41.01.c.   A minimum of two lay members elected by each congregation related to the synod, <u>normally</u> one of whom shall be male and one of whom shall be female, shall be voting members. The Synod Council shall establish a formula to provide additional lay representation from congregations on the basis of the number of baptized members in the congregation. <u>The Synod Council shall seek to ensure that, as nearly as possible, 50 percent of the lay members of the assembly shall be female and 50 percent shall be male.</u> Additional members from each congregation <u>normally</u> shall be equally divided between male and female except that the odd-numbered member, if any, may be either male or female.

Mr. Sandstrom moved on behalf of the committee Option Two:

VOTED: *CC94.11.77*
To recommend to the 1995 Churchwide Assembly the following constitutional and bylaw amendments:

†S7.21.c.   A minimum of <u>one lay member elected by each congregation with fewer than 175 baptized members and a minimum of</u> two lay members elected by each congregation <u>with</u> <u>more than 175 baptized members</u> related to this synod, . . . [*with the remainder as above*].

10.41.01.c.   A minimum of <u>one lay member elected by each congregation with fewer than 175 baptized members and a minimum of</u> two lay members elected by each congregation <u>with more than 175 baptized members</u> related to the synod, . . . [*with the remainder as above*].

Matters Related to the Division for Outreach
Criteria for Synodically Authorized Worshiping Communities

Background: In response to synodical memorials, the 1993 Churchwide Assembly adopted a churchwide bylaw (10.02.03.) and a provision in the *Constitution for Synods* (S7.26.) to permit synodical recognition of authorized worshiping communities:

Within the territory of each geographic synod, the synod, in keeping with criteria and procedures proposed by the Division for Outreach and approved by the Church Council, may acknowledge certain authorized worshiping communities—such as developing ministries, preaching points, or chapels—as related to the synod and part of the synod's life and mission. Such authorized worshiping communities of the synod shall accept and adhere to the Confession of Faith and Statement of Purpose of this church, shall be served by leadership under the criteria of this church, and shall be subject of the discipline of this church (ELCA 10.02.03.).

The secretary of this church has worked with the executive director and staff of the Division for Outreach in the development of the criteria and procedures required by the cited bylaw. The board of the Division for Outreach, following review and approval by the Conference of Bishops, recommends adoption of the policy document.

Council Action: Chair Magnus called upon the Rev. Malcolm L. Minnick Jr., executive director of the Division for Outreach, to introduce the recommendation printed below, subsequently adopted by the Church Council. During discussion, the Rev. Nadine F. Lehr inquired about the annual renewal of letter of call by the synod. Ramona S. Rank inquired about implications of the proposed policy for ecumenical settings. Bishop Paull E. Spring objected to the terminology, "Synodically Authorized Worshiping Communities." Pastor Minnick explained that such communities are known colloquially as "chapels."

VOTED: *CC94.11.78*
To adopt the following "Policy on Criteria for Synodically Authorized Worshiping Communities":

POLICY ON CRITERIA FOR SYNODICALLY AUTHORIZED WORSHIPING COMMUNITIES

1.   Basis
The possibility of synodically authorized worshiping communities being acknowledged by synods exists on the basis of churchwide bylaws and an optional provision in the Constitution for Synods.

Churchwide bylaw 10.02.03. says: "Within the territory of each geographic synod, the synod, in keeping with criteria and procedures proposed by the Division for Outreach and approved by the Church Council, may acknowledge certain authorized worshiping communities—such as developing ministries, preaching points, or chapels—as related to the synod and part of the synod's life and mission. Such authorized worshiping communities of the synod shall accept and adhere to the Confession of Faith and Statement of Purpose of this church, shall be served by leadership under the criteria of this church, and shall be subject to the discipline of this church."

Further, churchwide bylaw 10.41.04. indicates: "Synods may establish processes that permit representatives of authorized worshiping communities of the synod, under bylaw 10.02.03., to serve as voting members of the Synod Assembly, consistent with bylaw 10.41.01."

In the Constitution for Synods, S7.26., if adopted by the synod, provides: "This synod may establish processes through the Synod Council that permit representatives of authorized worshiping communities of the synod, under ELCA bylaw 10.02.03., to serve as voting members of the Synod Assembly, consistent with †S7.21. Such authorized worshiping communities, acknowledged under criteria and procedures of the ELCA Division for Outreach and the Church Council of the Evangelical Lutheran Church in America, shall accept and adhere to the Confession of Faith and Statement of Purpose of this church, shall be served by leadership under the criteria of this church, and shall be subject to the discipline of this church."

2. **Criteria**
   a. The primary criteria for acknowledgment of such synodically authorized worshiping communities, under the governing documents of this church, include agreement to:
   (1) Accept and adhere to the Confession of Faith of this church (Chapter 2 of the churchwide constitution);
   (2) Accept and adhere to the Statement of Purpose of this church (Chapter 4 of the churchwide constitution);
   (3) Be served by leadership appointed or called on an annual basis by the synod under the criteria of this church;
   (4) Be subject to the discipline of this church; and
   (5) Be evaluated annually by the synod to determine next year's status.
   b. Other criteria for such synodically authorized worshiping communities (hereafter known as "chapels," unless otherwise designated) include:
   (1) Participatory worship for the chapel, consistent with Lutheran expectations, provided under the leadership of a pastor of this church or a licensed lay person;
      (2) Ability to be a financially self-supporting ministry, unless other arrangements are made in accord with Division for Outreach policies on developing ministries;
   (3) Participation in benevolent ("mission support") giving to the synod and churchwide organization, with the expectation that 15 percent of the offerings of such chapels will be provided to the respective synod as a sign of commitment to the overall ministry of this church;
   (4) Commitment to evangelical outreach to unchurched persons within the area of the chapel;
   (5) Authorization by the synod for a specified duration, generally for one year, subject to possible renewal following evaluation jointly by the synod and Division for Outreach;

   (6) Maintenance by the leadership appointed or called to serve the chapel of a listing of regular participants to be filed annually with the synod[1];
   (7) Proper recording of such pastoral acts as baptism (see item 4.b.1.); and
   (8) If an authorized worship community is discontinuing, refer remaining participants to a regularly recognized congregation of this church for possible membership.

3. **Examples of Chapels and Other Authorized Worshiping Communities**
   Generic designation—*Chapels*: Such gatherings of small groups sometimes are known as preaching points and places where the population base is insufficient to establish or maintain a congregation, as defined in the *Constitution, Bylaws, and Continuing Resolutions of the Evangelical Lutheran Church in America* (9.11., 9.21., 9.23., 9.25, and 9.31.).
   a. *Former congregation*: A small group that has dissolved as a congregation and who can no longer call a pastor, but who may continue worshiping as a chapel.
   (1) An authorized worshiping community may be a way in which the synod may continue to serve a group of people in an area where a congregation has dissolved or where several congregations have dissolved.
   (2) Before being identified as an authorized worshiping community, an existing congregation that may no longer be viable would have to complete the necessary steps for dissolution as a congregation.
   b. *Small groups*: A small group of Lutherans may request Lutheran worship in an area where the potential for growth is limited and could not be expected to achieve a self-reliant congregation nor to call a full-time pastor. This group, however, could generate enough income to pay for worship costs and the service of a part-time pastor or other synodically authorized leader.
   c. *Test a Field*: An opportunity may be sought to test the potential of a new development prior to the commitment of churchwide resources for development of a congregation. This may be a vehicle for experimentation to reach a specialized community of people whose population base is not sufficient to guarantee viable development of a congregation.
   d. *Seasonal and Recreational Ministries*: In situations where recreational and vacation communities exist, seasonal worship needs might be met, even though a year-round worship schedule would not be possible.
   e. *A Former Ministry Development*: A former ministry under development may not have developed sufficiently for formal organization as a recognized congregation. Yet a long-term commitment was found within a group of loyal "members." They may be organized into a chapel as participants in such an authorized worshiping community.

4. **Listing of Chapels and Other Authorized Worshiping Communities**
   a. Upon acknowledgment by the Synod Council in the synod to which the chapel is related, the synod shall report such acknowledgment to the Office of the Secretary of the Evangelical Lutheran Church in America for recording on the list of acknowledged

---

[1] A temporary roster of participants is to be filed annually with the synod. The synod will use this listing in determining status as to voting rights at the Synod Assembly. Records also are to be maintained of any official pastoral acts [see item 4.b.(1) below].

chapels and other authorized worshiping communities.

(1) A number will be assigned to the authorized worshiping community by the Office of the Secretary.

(2) The community will be listed in the ELCA churchwide organization's annual report to the Internal Revenue Service, to be covered by the ELCA Group Exemption Number for nonprofit status.

(3) Each synodically authorized worshiping community is to obtain an Employer Identification Number to be used for payment of the salary and benefits of the pastor or other leader serving the authorized worshiping community.

b. Records shall be maintained on an annual basis of the regular participants of each acknowledged chapel and of all pastoral acts conducted within each chapel, the latter retained on a permanent basis.

(1) For retention on a permanent basis, the synod shall designate an existing congregation as a congregation of record for the recording of all pastoral acts conducted within a synod's authorized worshiping communities.

(2) Those participants in an authorized worshiping community who are received by affirmation of faith or adult baptism shall be recorded as members in the congregation of record (cited immediately above) for the duration of participation in the authorized worshiping community.

(3) Those participants in an authorized worshiping community who already are members of an existing congregation shall continue to be listed as members of such an existing congregation during the period of their participation in the authorized worshiping community.

5. *Provisions for Property, Finances, and Insurance*

a. If any real property is involved, care must be taken to assure appropriate maintenance, insurance, management, liability protection, and other matters.

b. Title to any real property is to be held in the name of the synod, which may develop arrangements with the Division for Outreach to provide insurance coverage.

c. Each authorized worshiping community is to make provision for bond coverage for the handling of finances in the authorized worshiping community.

6. *Procedures*

The authorized worshiping community:

a. may select a steering committee from the list of participants to work with the synodically designated leader.

b. should develop and approve an annual spending plan, including the commitment to 15 percent of all offerings to benevolence ("mission support").

c. should prepare and adopt a governing document that includes: fully and without alteration or amendment the Confession of Faith and Statement of Purpose of the Evangelical Lutheran Church in America; a statement of the community's relationship to the synod; agreement to be served by leadership appointed or called by the synod; agreement to be subject to the discipline of this church; agreement to be reviewed by the synod and the Division for Outreach annually to determine the next year's status; and any definition of internal organization and decision-making.

d. may elect representation to the Synod Assembly, if such provision is made in the synod's constitution.

7. *Changing Status*

Status may be shifted from a synodically authorized worshiping community to a congregation under development or a recognized congregation:

a. When the population of the community has sufficient potential to warrant full-time mission development, this ministry may be declared a congregation under development by the synod and the Division for Outreach.

b. When the participants of this ministry are of a sufficient number and leadership ability and when they have fulfilled the organizing steps leading to recognition and reception as a congregation, then the synod and the Division for Outreach may complete the process for the reception and reception of a congregation of this church, in accord with churchwide constitutional provision 9.25.

8. *In Event of Discontinuance of Authorization*

a. A plan, effective upon discontinuance of authorization, should be established for the transfer of any remaining participants to regular membership in congregations of this church.

b. Arrangements, in consultation with the synod, should be made for the orderly disposition of any supplies and other material.

c. Records and historical materials of the chapel should be gathered and transferred to the synod for archival filing.

Chair Magnus then reviewed the agenda for the remainder of the meeting.

1995 CHURCHWIDE ASSEMBLY

Chair Magnus called upon the Rev. Lee S. Thoni, executive assistant to the bishop, to introduce plans for the 1995 Churchwide Assembly. He reviewed four significant components: (1) the election of churchwide officers; (2) the 25th anniversary of the ordination of Lutheran women in the U.S.; (3) business before the assembly; and (4) the Festival Gathering.

The Rev. Franklin D. Fry recommended that during the assembly introductory presentations of the various business items be minimized and that legislative discussion be maximized.

Publishing House of the Evangelical Lutheran Church in America

Gary J. N. Aamodt, president of the Publishing House of the Evangelical Lutheran Church in America commented on recent actions of the board of the publishing house to terminate the in-house printing operations and to consolidate order and distribution facilities.

During discussion, Edith M. Lohr asked about the economic advantage this church in general will have as a result of the changes. William E. Diehl inquired whether centralized printing services would continue to be provided for churchwide units through the publishing house. William T. Billings inquired about the sale of printing equipment.

Lutheran World Federation

The Rev. Franklin D. Fry recommended that a letter be sent to the retiring general secretary and newly elected general secretary of the Lutheran World Federation. The suggestion was approved by consensus.

VOTED: *CC94.11.79*
To request the secretary of this church to send greetings on behalf of this church to the retiring general secretary and newly elected general secretary of the Lutheran World Federation.

Following announcements, the Church Council recessed for the day at 5:36 P.M. with the singing of the Doxology.

The Church Council reconvened on Monday, November 14, 1994, at 8:34 A.M. Opening devotions were offered by the Rev. David K. Johnson, a member of the Church Council. Vice President Kathy J. Magnus, chair of the Church Council, then reviewed the agenda for the day and made several announcements.

Corporate Responsibility

Chair Magnus called upon the Rev. James G. Cobb, who offered the following motion:

MOVED;
SECONDED: To refer to the Church Council's Legal and Constitutional Review Committee a request to list for the Church Council the names of corporate entities for which the Church Council has direct responsibilities and to make commentary on what would be required to dissolve such direct responsibilities.

During discussion, Pastor Cobb called attention to the direct responsibility of the Church Council for decisions relating to this church's oversight of various corporate entities, such as Lutheran General HealthSystem. Clarity on the full dimensions of those relationships would be helpful as background when the council is asked to make significant decisions regarding them. William H. Engelbrecht noted that, if colleges and universities were to be included in this resolution, the task would be herculean. Pastor Cobb responded that such was an example of the serious need for that kind of discovery. J. David Ellwanger agreed that such a review would be beneficial. The Rev. H. George Anderson said the present resolution would not address the church colleges, because the four college corporation meetings that are convened concurrently but independently during the course of the Churchwide Assembly (with the assembly serving as sole voting member) would not be covered by the resolution. The Rev. Franklin D. Fry noted that, if only organizations are included for which the churchwide expression has responsibility, the task

would be manageable. William H. Engelbrecht suggested it would be presumptuous for the committee to propose changes to those entities. Chair Magnus appointed William J. Engelbrecht, the Rev. David A. Andert, David J. Hardy, and the Rev. James G. Cobb as a committee to discuss these issues and present an alternative motion after midday recess.

Matters Related to the Division for Church in Society
2. Draft Statement on Human Sexuality

Background: Between meetings of the Church Council, members have received numerous mailings relating to the development of a working draft of a possible social statement on human sexuality.

Council Action: Chair Magnus called upon the Rev. Charles S. Miller Jr., executive director of the Division for Church in Society, to introduce an update on the draft statement on human sexuality. She also expressed thanks to the Church Council's Executive Committee for input on the second draft of the statement and celebrated the process that led to the release of the document. She also expressed appreciation to the staff of the division whom she said have endured much in the past year, and to the Department for Communication that handled the pubic media well.

Pastor Miller noted that more than 30,000 copies of the draft statement were distributed on October 25, 1994, and a press conference was held on November 4, 1994. He expressed appreciation for Bishop Chilstrom's comments during the press conference and said the text of Bishop Chilstrom's remarks also was placed on the LutherLink computer network. Commenting on the newly established process for responding to the document, he noted the period of response has been extended to June 30, 1995, with a "progress report" to be presented at the 1995 Churchwide Assembly. To date, responses have been very modest, he said, and have been diverse, with no specific pattern of response emerging. But he did say interest in the document is high with some 8,100 copies having been ordered, along with the social statements of the predecessor church bodies. He expressed appreciation to the inter-unit staff team on social statement development and the Department for Communication for leading the process for releasing the document. He also expressed thanks to the writing team, project director, consultant, and editor of the document who together contributed 119 person days to its development.

In the immediate future, Pastor Miller said, statistical reports will be received from the Department for Research and Evaluation and, in the meantime, commentary will be organized by category as it is received in individual correspondence. Responses to the working draft will not be acknowledged because of cost, he said. He also noted that there is no intention to publish a monthly update, but an interim report consisting of statistical data categorizing responses will be provided to the Conference of Bishops, the Church Council, and the board of the Division for Church in Society in the spring of 1995. Materials for synods desiring a workshop at synod assemblies also will be prepared. He further noted that the Spanish language version of the document is due in January 1995. The Church Council will receive a report in August 1995 concerning plans for the development of a "final draft" of the social statement.

Pastor Miller commented that the net cost of preparing a possible social statement on human sexuality in 1992 was $12,000, $14,000 in 1993, and $80,000 in 1994. The higher level of expenditure in 1994 was accrued as temporary staff members were hired to acknowledge and catalogue responses to the first draft, and to cover costs of meetings of the consulting panel, the writers and editor, and others. He noted that the budget for this project was just over $36,000 and said the gap has been filled by drawing on an unfilled position in the studies department, which also will be used to cover 1995 expenditures. He also said that the process has led to the development of a special committee on the process and form of such statements. The committee is due to report in 1996.

Difficulties associated with the development of this possible draft, especially related to the inhumane timeline imposed, has taken a toll on the entire staff, Pastor Miller said. The present task is to repair relationships within the division, he said, as well as with the members of the consulting panel.

Chair Magnus called upon Edith M. Lohr to reflect on the relationship between the members of the original task force and the division staff and the writing team of the second draft. Ms. Lohr expressed her concern not to misrepresent the feelings of members of the task force. She noted that the task force perceives it has completed its work and noted that while they had the opportunity to meet with the writing team, the members thought they the did not have a significant amount of influence on what the final result would be. In the last six months the relationship has been neutral, she said, but the task force has indeed struggled in relating to the division. For example, she said it was especially difficult for the task force to accept that it would not be allowed to review the second draft before it was distributed. In the future, Ms. Lohr said, it would be helpful to define specifically the nature of a task force's work and its relationship to others involved in a project.

Chair Magnus noted that council agenda Exhibit P, Part 1, a memo from the secretary of this church concerning the actions that led to the release of the second draft, was distributed to the Church Council at the request of the chair. This is a valuable document in helping to define what the role of a consulting panel would be. Ramona S. Rank expressed appreciation for the opportunity to serve as a member of the consulting panel. She noted this was generally a difficult time for all concerned. She said the consulting panel consisted of good people, serious about their task, but that the parameters of the assignment itself was rather nebulous from their perspective. Thus, they needed to decide how they would relate to the task force and the division and

then how to proceed and to say a good word to this church. She also noted that there was no one driving force on the panel. She said the model of appointing a consulting panel is a helpful one, but the Church Council must be very specific about its responsibilities in the charge to such a group.

During discussion, Pastor Miller reported that technically the work of the consulting panel is not completed. The resolution forming the panel states that it has responsibility for all subsequent drafts of a possible social statement. The contractual agreements with the members of the writing team and the project director expired at the end of September 1994, he said, though he intends to speak with them about a new contract for the next chapter of this work, suggesting that Division for Church in Society staff, the writing team, and the consulting panel will continue to be involved in this work. Finally, Pastor Miller commented that the division's board has not officially determined that the work of the task force is completed.

William E. Diehl asked for clarity on the timeline imposed on the writing team and the consulting panel. Pastor Miller responded that the consulting panel received the final draft that also was sent to the division board. The panel then met by telephone conference call to determine if the final version of the working draft would force them to change their previous recommendation and voted that the document should not be released. Dale V. Sandstrom noted that the costs of preparing these documents do not account for staff time. Edith M. Lohr suggested that the process following the release of the first draft was unfortunate because the members of the task force became the scapegoat. Nonetheless, the task force members made themselves available for a variety of forums to present or respond to the first draft. Because of that, she thought there was a definite level of unfairness in not allowing the task force to have a hand in the next phase of the work. Consequently, they should have been dismissed much sooner. The Rev. David G. Gabel expressed the opinion that the Church Council needs to take some responsibility for these feelings of frustration between the consulting panel and the task force because it had created the consulting panel.

J. David Ellwanger commented that this process has allowed this church to address quite successfully the perceived "mutiny in the pew" but not nearly as well with the issue of sexuality. Deborah S. Yandala urged that a larger spectrum of people be involved in analyzing the responses to broaden perspectives. Lorraine G. Bergquist commented on the difficulty of even preparing a possible social statement. Pastor Miller said the issue is simply living with the ambiguity that comes from dealing with social issues, on the one hand, and the problem this church has of speaking authoritatively on a long list of social concerns, on the other hand. Work must go on, he said, while discussion continues on whether this is the best form for this church to do this work. The Rev. John O. Knudson asked if experience with previous social statements in general could in fact be applied to this statement. Pastor Miller responded yes, and noted that a review of the process already had been planned.

William E. Diehl recalled that when the consulting panel was created it was in response not only to the content of the first draft but to the issue of the composition of the task force, an issue that would not have gone away. The Rev. Nadine F. Lehr said she assumed, however, that the consulting panel was created with the idea that the task force would still be intimately involved in the process. Charles A. Adamson expressed his dismay about this as well. Chair Magnus explained that the consulting panel was created by the Church Council and reports to the council, while the task force was created by the Division for Church in Society board, implying a different relationship. Pastor Miller said again that no official action has been taken concerning the task force. He said members of the task force had indicated their willingness to live with the ambiguity of the present situation, which in reality meant the end of their responsibility. But the division board has not acted one way or the other. Pastor Miller also noted that the present situation does not represent an ordinary process and as an extraordinary one is being "patched together" as we go along. He also said that no plan on how to proceed from this point has been developed. The Rev. Nadine F. Lehr said the issue is not really the various levels of responsibility between the task force and the consulting panel but the issue of trust. Ramona S. Rank agreed and maintained this is the primary reason to be specific concerning such relationships in the charge to a newly appointed group. The intended collegiality between the consulting panel and the task force did not happen, but the resolution establishing the panel does not specify such a relationship. Charles S. Adamson asked about the future of the panel. Chair Magnus responded that the Church Council would need to discuss the issue. She pointed to the assumption of the division board's that the consulting panel would continue to function, but the relationship of the panel to the Church Council needs to be clarified. Furthermore, she said, unless the Church Council takes action the panel will not continue, and then the Executive Committee will need to deal with issues of reporting.

D. Mark Klever asked about the length and accessibility of the document. Pastor Miller responded that after the response period has ended, the next key event is the report to the 1995 Churchwide Assembly. Then the writing team and consulting panel will go back to work to produce any possible subsequent drafts of a document that could lead to consideration by the Church Council no later than spring of 1997. Whether other drafts will be produced is open to question, he said. The goal is to have the final document be half the length of the current document. The social statement itself in the present document is in the neighborhood of 9,000 words; a final draft needs to be about half that. Pastor Miller also suggested that, in subsequent drafts, the background and foundational materials may not need to be included. Deborah S. Yandala observed that the problem was that a task force must be involved, in order to honor the

process of preparing social statements, but at the present time such a task force would not by functioning. She asked, "Who will pick up that role?" Pastor Miller responded that formally this church's documents assume only that the division will bring together a group to study an issue. Everything that has been done in this process is simply a way to live out that one sentence, he said, and corresponds to the practice implemented in other instances. Because this is such an extraordinary issue, however, he suggested that relying on ordinary practice is perhaps not helpful.

Bishop Paull E. Spring said the Church Council must address the issue of process in April 1995. Terry L. Bowes said she is uncomfortable with leaving this meeting without ensuring that the consulting panel will continue its work, and without asking the division board to clarify the role of the task force. Edith M. Lohr recalled that previous practice has dictated that the members of the task force be listed in social statements. She noted that this document does not include such a listing because Pastor Miller agreed this would not be appropriate in this case. William E. Diehl agreed that clarity must be given to the ongoing role of the consulting panel and moved, therefore, the following:

VOTED: *CC94.11.80*
To request the Executive Committee of the Church Council to meet during the midday recess, in order to prepare a resolution giving guidance to the consulting panel.

William T. Billings requested a report from the Executive Committee on the responses of Church Council members to the second draft of the human sexuality document.

3.   Process for the
     Development of Social Statements
Background: Council agenda Exhibit B, Part 2, contained the response of the Division for Church in Society to a 1994 resolution of the Nebraska Synod related to the process by which social statements are developed in the Evangelical Lutheran Church in America. At its September 29-October 1, 1994, meeting, the board of the Division for Church in Society took the following action:

WHEREAS, it has been five years since the understandings and procedures for developing social statements were adopted ("Social Statements in the ELCA"); and

WHEREAS these understandings and procedures have served as the basis for successful completion and adoption of five ELCA social statements; and

WHEREAS, discussions continue regarding the basis, purpose, procedures, and authority of social statements; therefore be it

RESOLVED, that

a.   the board authorize the Division for Church in Society to assemble a committee to review the bases, purposes, procedures, and authority of social statements in the Evangelical Lutheran Church in America:

b.   this Social Statement Review Committee be composed of two members from the board of the Division for Church in Society, two members from the Church Council, two members from the Conference of Bishops, two theologians/ethicists appointed by the Division for Church in Society in consultation with seminar presidents, two staff persons from the Division for Church in Society, and one person from the Office of the Bishop. Included in (or in addition to) the above should be persons with in-depth knowledge and experience in current and predecessor church traditions and practices regarding social policy development, and those who have led congregations in their consideration of social statements.

c. this committee give attention to the following:

1. The Evangelical Lutheran Church in America has committed itself to develop social statements as one of the ways through which the ELCA carries out its mission in society. Considering what has been done already, should this commitment be reconsidered? On what basis?

2. Are the current assumptions, understandings, and multiple purposes of social statements still tenable? (For example, they have theological, teaching, ethical reflection, deliberative and policy-establishing purposes.)

3. What have been the strengths and weaknesses of the current procedures, processes, and uses of social statements? (For example, the respective roles of task forces, board of the Division for Church in Society, Church Council, Conference of Bishops, theological faculties, congregational deliberation and response.)

4. What recommendations should be proposed for changes in the policy and practices regarding social statements (i.e., for changes in the procedural document, "Social Statements in the Evangelical Lutheran Church in America")?

d. this committee be charged to bring a report to the board of the Division for Church and Society and the Church Council no later than the fall of 1996.

Council Action: During discussion, William E. Diehl asked about the appointment of two theologians, questioning whether this church would perceive that theological content might be tipped in one way or another. He suggested it would be more helpful for a more neutral body to appoint the theologians. Lorraine G. Bergquist agreed and suggested the same perception surrounds the appointment of the consulting panel working with the development of the possible social statement on human sexuality. The Rev. Stephen M. Youngdahl concurred, but pointed out that the resolution on the floor did not originate with the Church Council. He suggested that the board of the Division for Church in Society broaden the areas of responsibility. Edith M. Lohr suggested the Church Council was engaging in micro-management rather than trusting the work of boards and divisions. The Rev. Donald M. Hallberg agreed and said it would send dangerous signals to second guess the work of boards.

VOTED: *CC94.11.81*

To affirm the action taken by the board of the Division for Church in Society to review the policies and procedures related to the development of social statements; and

To authorize the chair of the Church Council, in consultation with the Executive Committee, to appoint two persons to serve on this committee.

4. Update on World Hunger

The Rev. Charles S. Miller Jr. introduced this information by emphasizing that the division does more than studies. This report underscored the Lutheran contribution to relief work in Rwanda. Since the report was written, ELCA support has risen to $600,000, he said, half of which has been channeled through Lutheran World Federation World Service. Since September 15, 1994, some 150 flights have occurred to provide food. Lutheran World Relief has sent 60,000 pounds of soap, thousands of quilts, and other resources. Pastor Miller then introduced a brief video presentation on the Rwandan relief effort.

5. Affiliated Lutheran Social Ministry Organizations

Background: Council agenda Exhibit P, Part 3, contained information related to the scope of activity of the Lutheran Social Service system.

Council Action: The Rev. Charles S. Miller Jr. introduced this information item, observing that this does not include hospitals because that is such a large category in itself. He said that the Lutheran corporate social ministry presence is the largest not-for-profit human service system in the United States. More than 1.8 million persons were served by 80,000 employees and over 80,000 volunteers providing five million volunteer hours. Income generated throughout the system is $2.3 billion while expenses total $2.2 billion. Of the total program service expenses, approximately 65 percent constitutes service to older adults. The assets of these agencies is $3.2 billion with investments of $565 million. Finally, he said, this system faces great challenges in the future. A blue-ribbon committee to articulate a churchwide vision for this ministry and to outline subsequent strategies has been established. This group has completed half its work, and has set a goal of presenting a final report to the Church Council in November 1995, with the hope of calling this church to an even stronger vision of this work.

6. Appointments to Boards of Social Ministry Organizations

Background: The Evangelical Lutheran Church in America serves as the corporate member of certain affiliated social ministry organizations. The role of the corporate member includes the responsibility to elect or approve a majority of the members of the board of directors and to approve amendments to the governing documents.

Lutheran General HealthSystem, Park Ridge, Ill., and Martin Luther Home, headquartered in Lincoln, Nebr., are organizations for which the Evangelical Lutheran Church in America serves as corporate member. The Division for Church in Society is the churchwide unit through which the Evangelical Lutheran Church in America relates to these social ministry health-care organizations. The division requests Church Council action to elect the following board members for these organizations.

Council Action: The Church Council took the following action *en bloc* at the conclusion of this meeting.

a. Martin Luther Home Society, Inc.

EN BLOC   *[CC94.11.112]*

To elect the Rev. Robert Nelson to the board of directors of Martin Luther Home Society, Inc., for a term ending in 1997.

b. Lutheran General HealthSystem

EN BLOC   *[CC94.11.113]*

To reelect Jerry Bauer, M.D., Christine K. Cassel, M.D., and Donald R. Hollis, to the board of directors of the Lutheran General HealthSystem, for terms ending in 1997; and

To elect Mary E. Aquina and John C. Gienapp, Ph.D., to the board of directors of the Lutheran General HealthSystem, for terms ending in 1997.

Matters Related to the Division for Ministry

1. Study of Theological Education

Background: A copy of the September 1994 draft of the report of the Study of Theological Education was provided as council agenda Exhibit M, Part 1. After further study and revision, this report will be presented to the 1995 Churchwide Assembly,

At its October 1994 meeting, the Conference of Bishops discussed this draft of the report and adopted the following resolution:

The Conference of Bishops expresses its appreciation for the consultation, planning, and recommendations represented in *Theological Education for a Church in Mission*, the report being proposed by the Division for Ministry for the 1995 Churchwide Assembly;

The Conference of Bishops especially affirms the report's focus upon "enhancing essential revenue streams to support the preparation of mission leaders;"

The Conference of Bishops advises the Church Council of its encouragement and support for enhancing revenue streams; and

The Conference of Bishops encourages each bishop to begin now to take leadership in proposing the best ways possible for the synod to accept responsibility for the increased funding needed to support seminary clusters.

Council Action: Chair Magnus called upon the Rev. Joseph M. Wagner, executive director of the Division for Ministry, who described new directions of this church in areas of ministry and theological education. He introduced a new resource entitled, "What Shall I Say?," a tool to help people discern their call to ministry. Pastor Wagner then called upon the Rev. Phyllis B. Anderson, director for theological education, who presented the latest draft of a report on Study on Theological Education. Pastor Anderson pointed to the theme of mission in the report and highlighted several points. First, seminary clusters have been developed, one in the east (The Lutheran Theological Seminary at Philadelphia

[Pa.], Lutheran Theological Southern Seminary [Columbia, S.C.], and Lutheran Theological Seminary at Gettysburg [Pa.]), one titled the Western Mission cluster (Luther Seminary [St. Paul, Minn.] and Pacific Lutheran Theological Seminary [Berkeley, Calif.]), and a "Heartland" cluster (Lutheran School of Theology at Chicago [Ill.] and Wartburg Theological Seminary, [Dubuque, Iowa; including a covenant relationship with Trinity Lutheran Seminary [Columbus, Ohio]]). She also reported that the board of the Division for Ministry extended the deadline for developing these clusters to enable the "heartland" cluster to finalize its plans. The report notes that theological education is being refocused, Pastor Anderson said, to address more adequately the changed ministry scene, to include lay theological education, and to encourage the development of extension centers and other forms of education to reach under-served regions. Enhancing revenue streams to the seminaries is also a major part of the report, she commented. Seminaries recently proposed to the task force that the resolution of funding issues be delayed in order to develop a comprehensive business plan, with work to begin in the spring of 1995.

During discussion, the Rev. Donald M. Hallberg asked for clarity on the relationship of Trinity Seminary to the other seminaries in the cluster. Pastor Anderson described the new relationship and how the seminaries are attempting to fit the criteria for clustering. Patsy Gottschalk asked why Trinity Seminary (Columbus, Ohio) was not willing to engage more quickly in this relationship. Pastor Anderson responded that the seriousness of this concept, including consolidated organizational structures and pooled funding required thorough study and commitment. Robert S. Schroeder asked for further explanation for the emphasis on continuing education. Pastor Wagner responded that decreased funding from this church to these centers has prompted them to seek alternative funding, suggesting that while some attrition is expected, the strategy of networking resources should provide the necessary tools. Treasurer McAuliffe expressed apprecation for the work on funding theological education, and urged the task force to be aware of synodical and churchwide funding priorities.

2. Seminary Clusters

Background: Council agenda Exhibit M, Part 2a, contains "Criteria for the Formation of Seminary Clusters," which were approved by the board of the Division for Ministry at its October 14-16, 1994, meeting.

Additional information related to the process of ratification of the formation of seminary clusters was provided to council members.

The board of the Division for Ministry commended the action printed below, subsequently adopted by the Church Council.

Council Action: During discussion Loren W. Mathre observed that historic relationships out of Florida with Trinity Seminary (Columbus, Ohio) will be changed. Pastor Wagner noted that at a meeting of the synods in regions 6 and 9 it was agreed that present funding campaigns will continue, as will solicitation from alumni around the country, but that this does represent a new pattern. Pastor Anderson suggested that Trinity Seminary will actually benefit from this new arrangement.

VOTED: CC94.11.82

To affirm that, pending final action on the formation of an Eastern Cluster by the boards of the seminaries and the Division for Ministry, the synods of Region 6 be assigned to Trinity Lutheran Seminary (Columbus, Ohio) and the synods of Region 9 be assigned to Lutheran Theological Southern Seminary (Columbia, S.C.) for the purposes of funding and governance as of January 31, 1996.

3.   25th Anniversary of the Lutheran Ordination of Women

Background: The 1993 Churchwide Assembly voted:

WHEREAS, 1995 marks the 75th anniversary of the first decision by Lutherans worldwide (Evangelical Lutheran Church of the Kingdom of the Netherlands) to ordain women; and

WHEREAS, this anniversary will be observed by Lutherans around the world; and

WHEREAS, 1995 marks the 25th anniversary of the ordination of Lutheran women in North America; and

WHEREAS, plans are under way for a churchwide celebration of this anniversary; and

WHEREAS, as of December 1992, women represented 8.7 percent (1,522) of the ordained ministers of the Evangelical Lutheran Church in America; and

WHEREAS, this church rejoices in its decision to ordain women and is blessed through the leadership and ministries of those whom it has called to serve as pastors; and

WHEREAS, this church yet recognizes the need to continue to grow to full acceptance and appreciation of the gifts of women in ordained ministry; therefore be it

RESOLVED, that the 1993 Churchwide Assembly of the Evangelical Lutheran Church in America:

1.   urge synods and seminaries to plan activities, events, and emphases to involved ELCA members in observing these anniversaries;

2.   encourage congregations, especially those which have not had women as pastors, to plan activities to meet and to get to know ordained women;

3.   request, in the 1993-1995 biennium, that the Division for Ministry, the Commission for Women, the Conference of Bishops, Women of the Evangelical Lutheran Church in America, synods, and seminaries collaborate on strategies and materials that build familiarity and receptivity to the ministry of ordained women in congregations that have not yet had that experience;

4.   request that ELCA events held in 1995, the calendar of emphases, and the 1995 Churchwide Assembly include opportunities for men and women to reflect on and to celebrate these anniversaries;

5.   encourage congregations and synods to find ways to assist persons to attend the 1995 churchwide celebration of the 25th anniversary of the ordination of Lutheran women in North America; and

6.   offer prayers of thanksgiving to God for the ministries of lay and ordained women, past and present.

Council agenda Exhibit M, Part 3, contained information about a special churchwide event, scheduled August 14-16, 1995, to celebrate the 25th anniversary of the ordination of women.

Council Action: Pastor Wagner briefly commented on the foregoing information concerning a celebratory event, which is scheduled to precede the 1995 Churchwide Assembly.

4.   Guidelines for Diaconal Ministry

Background: The 1993 Churchwide Assembly of the Evangelical Lutheran Church in America adopted the following:

• To establish a diaconal ministry as part of the officially recognized, rostered ministries of the Evangelical Lutheran Church in America.

• To designate, as recommended by the board of the Division for Ministry, such a diaconal ministry as part of the lay rostered ministries of this church for which individuals would be approved for the roster of diaconal ministers, according to the criteria, standards, policies, and procedures of this church.

• To declare that diaconal ministers be called by this church to a public ministry that exemplifies the servant life, equips and motivates others to live it, and shares the Word of God in Law and Gospel through word and deed wherever possible and in a great variety of ways, in order to serve officially in interdependence with other laity, pastors, and bishops of this church, sharing with them responsibility for the Word of God in service to the Church and the world, to empower, equip, and support all the baptized in the ministry and mission of Jesus Christ—with an initial and illustrative, but not an exhaustive, list of categories of diaconal ministry to include education, mission and evangelism, care, administration, and music and the arts.

• To assign the care and guidance of candidates for diaconal ministry to this church's candidacy system, with the Division for Ministry to provide appropriate assistance and training for synodical candidacy committees to deal with diaconal candidates.

• To affirm that the specific requirements for approval be developed by the Division for Ministry, reviewed by the Conference of Bishops, and adopted by the Church Council.

• To direct the Division for Ministry, in consultation with the Conference of Bishops and with the approval of the Church Council—and in consultation with the appropriate officials of the Evangelical Lutheran Church in Canada—make the necessary revisions in related documents for their application to diaconal ministers.

• To direct the Division for Ministry to hold a consultation(s) with persons engaged in diaconal ministry of various kinds in this church and with those engaged in training persons for diaconal service in this and other churches as part of the design and preparation of programs for training ELCA diaconal ministers.

The 1993 Churchwide Assembly adopted churchwide bylaw 7.51.05., regarding diaconal ministers:

This church shall establish and maintain a lay roster of diaconal ministers who shall be called by this church to positions that exemplify the servant life and that seek to equip and motivate others to live it. Such diaconal ministers shall seek in a great variety of ways to empower, equip, and support all the baptized people of God in the ministry of Jesus Christ and the mission of God in the world.

(a)   Upon certification and approval as a candidate for the lay roster of diaconal ministers, and upon receipt and acceptance of a valid, regularly issued letter of call, the candidate shall be designated, according to the service orders of this church, as a lay diaconal minister.

(b)   All constitutional provisions, bylaws, and continuing resolutions regarding associates in ministry of the

Evangelical Lutheran Church in America shall apply to those on the lay roster of diaconal ministers of the Evangelical Lutheran Church in America.

Following extensive discussion and consultation, the Division for Ministry developed the document, "Diaconal Ministers in the Evangelical Lutheran Church in America: Standards, Preparation, Approval and Call." These standards include a description of diaconal ministry in the Evangelical Lutheran Church in America and the requirements for preparation and approval for service as a diaconal minister. The Conference of Bishops subsequently discussed these standards at its March 1994 meeting and referred the document to a committee for further refinement.

Acknowledging this action and acting upon the recommendation of the board of the Division for Ministry, the Church Council voted in April 1994:

To adopt "Diaconal Ministers in the Evangelical Lutheran Church in America: Standards, Preparation, Approval, and Call" as a working document subject to final review by the Conference of Bishops.

Conversation about this material continued between meetings of the Church Council. The Conference of Bishops reviewed this document at its October 1994 meeting and voted to adopt the following resolution:

The Conference of Bishops indicates its positive review of the document, "Diaconal Ministers in the Evangelical Lutheran Church in America: Standards, Preparation, Approval and Call," with the recommendation that all references to *consecrating* and *consecration* be changed to *commissioning* and *commission*.

At its October 1994 meeting, the board of the Division for Ministry removed references to consecration or commissioning from its document, which was provided as council agenda Exhibit M, Part 4. The board determined that further intensive conversations with the Conference of Bishop were needed before a recommendation on *commissioning/consecration* would be brought to the Church Council.

The board recommended, however, that the Church Council approve the rest of the document (Exhibit M, Part 4), since that material now has been approved by the board and affirmed by the Conference of Bishops. A final recommendation on the matter of consecration or commissioning of diaconal ministers will be brought to the Church Council at its April 1995 meeting.

Council Action: Pastor Wagner called upon Madelyne H. Busse, director for rostered lay ministries in the Division for Ministry, to introduce the recommendation of the board of the Division for Ministry on this matter. The working document has been under development since April 1994, Ms. Busse said, with an emphasis on the candidacy process for diaconal ministers. She reported that Lutheran Theological Seminary at Gettysburg has been selected as the major site for training diaconal ministers and is responsible for preparing the curriculum for this work. She also noted that developing the entrance rite for diaconal ministers has been separated from the issue of guidelines and preparations. She also promised that a progress report will be offered in April 1995 on the relationship between diaconal ministers and deaconesses and associates in ministry.

During discussion, the Rev. Nadine F. Lehr asked about basic issues related to these ministries. Ms. Busse said that candidacy committees in the synods are responsible for the entrance, endorsement, and approval processes of diaconal ministers as well as pastors. She outlined a number of possibilities for the arenas of ministry in which these people might serve and said the documents have avoided naming these possibilities in order not to limit the scope for developing ministries in which diaconal ministers might serve. She also noted that suggestions about internships and other issues are presently being developed. William T. Billings asked for a definition of the term "diaconal bias." Ms. Busse said diaconal ministry is the natural outgrowth of the ministry of Word and Sacrament, providing leadership for the Word and service. She also observed that the boundaries between the two, as well as with associates in ministry, are not clear. To speak of "diaconal bias," she said, flows from concepts such as a bias for the poor, which helps to define the ministry of deacons. Experimentation will be a part of the process of developing the understanding of this ministry for this church.

Patsy Gottschalk expressed concern regarding the requirement that training for this lay ministry must be done in a theological center. Ms. Busse said the recommendation of the Task Force for the Study for Ministry asserted that deeply rooting someone in the Word of God happens best in one of the seminaries of this church or in another accredited seminary. Associates in ministry may do this on the undergraduate level or through correspondence. The Rev. David A. Andert observed that the standards being proposed are very similar to those required for the pastoral office (clinical pastoral education, internship, etc.). Ms. Busse said the underlying concern was for providing adequate theological education for this form of service and has nothing to do with whether this will be a lay or ordained office. She said that practical preparation makes sense for a form of service that is essentially practical in nature, and that action and reflection models for education also are being discussed. Pastor Wagner noted that this is different from models for more informal diaconal patterns that will be distinguished by a licensing process for indigenous leaders who do not have an academic background. The Rev. Franklin D. Fry noted the importance of the ministry of the laity in the world, which he termed, "sacred secularity," to be rooted theologically and to possess ecclesiastical responsibility. He also suggested that internships for such positions could be in society rather than in the church.

VOTED: *CC94.11.83*
To adopt the following "Diaconal Ministers in the Evangelical Lutheran Church in America: Standards, Preparation, Approval, and Call":

DIACONAL MINISTERS IN THE EVANGELICAL LUTHERAN CHURCH IN AMERICA: STANDARDS, PREPARATION, APPROVAL AND CALL STANDARDS FOR DIACONAL MINISTERS

I. Introduction

"This church shall establish and maintain a lay roster of diaconal ministers who shall be called by this church to positions that exemplify the servant life and that seek to equip and motivate others to live it. Such diaconal ministers shall seek in a great variety of ways to empower, equip, and support all the baptized people of God in the ministry of Jesus Christ and the mission of God in the world" (ELCA Constitution, Bylaws, and Continuing Resolutions 7.51.05.).

Significant features of the proposal to establish diaconal ministry included the following:

- Diaconal ministers will be ministers of the Word of God. They will be publicly charged to transmit, defend, and teach it and to be spokespersons for the faith of the Church. The message and its expression in service are not to be separated. In diaconal ministry, the work of God in specialized service and witness is primary.
- Diaconal ministers will be charged to equip the baptized for service in all aspects of their life.
- Diaconal ministry will strengthen the ELCA in the fulfillment of its declared mission. Among the components of that mission are:
- "Proclaim God's saving Gospel of justification by grace for Christ's sake through faith alone, according to the apostolic witness in the Holy Scripture, preserving and transmitting the Gospel faithfully to future generations" (ELCA churchwide constitutional provision 4.02.a.).
- "Carry out Christ's Great Commission by reaching out to all people to bring them to faith in Christ and by doing all ministry with a global awareness consistent with the understanding of God as Creator, Redeemer, and Sanctifier of all" (ELCA churchwide constitutional provision 4.02.b.).
- "Serve in response to God's love to meet human needs, caring for the sick, and the aged, advocating dignity and justice for all people, working for peace and reconciliation among the nations, and standing with the poor and powerless and committing itself to their needs" (ELCA churchwide constitutional provision 4.02.c.).
- "Lift its voice in concord and work in concert with forces for good, to serve humanity, cooperating with church and other groups participating in activities that promote justice, relieve misery, and reconcile the estranged" (ELCA churchwide constitutional provision 4.03.g.).
- "Study social issues and trends, work to discover the causes of oppression and injustice, and develop programs of ministry and advocacy to further human dignity, freedom, justice, and peace in the world" (ELCA churchwide constitutional provision 4.03.l.)

Recognizing that all the ministries of this church are committed to this mission, these purposes still confront the Church with many unfulfilled challenges. Diaconal ministers are call to provide leadership which signals a commitment to new ways of augmenting our present ministries. Diaconal ministers will serve as a sign of Christ's ministry which calls the whole Church to ministries of service and witness exemplifying service in Christ's name in the world.

II. Basic Standards

Persons admitted to and continued as diaconal ministers of this church shall satisfactorily meet and maintain the following:

a) commitment to Christ;
b) acceptance of and adherence to the Confession of Faith of this church;
c) willingness and ability to serve in response to the needs of this church;
d) academic and practical qualifications for ministry;
e) life consistent with the Gospel and personal qualifications including leadership abilities and competence in interpersonal relationships;
f) receipt and acceptance of a letter of call; and
g) membership in a congregation of this church.

III. Definition

Diaconal ministers shall:

1. Be rooted in the Word of God: Diaconal ministers are ministers of the Word of God, committed to Christ, and called to be spokespersons for the Gospel, the apostolic faith, and the theological emphasis of this church to God's world.

2. Be trained to carry out a particular service: Diaconal ministers carry out a public ministry of service and witness. With demonstrated competence and expertise in a particular discipline, diaconal ministers may serve both within and outside of congregational settings, in each case bearing responsibility for making the linkages between church and world. Programmatic ministries within congregational settings should be marked by extension of the witness and service of the church into the wider community.

3. Be committed and prepared to equip the baptized for ministry in the world and in the church: Diaconal ministers along with pastors are called to lead and equip the baptized for ministry. Diaconal ministers support the ministry of the baptized through appropriate programmatic ministries and by working with the laity in discerning and encouraging their gifts for ministry.

4. Give particular attention to ministries at the boundaries between church and world: Diaconal ministers carry public responsibility to speak for the needs of God's world to the church as well as taking God's saving Gospel to the needs of the world through the actions of God's people both individually and collectively.

5. Exemplify the life of Christ-like service addressing all forms of human need: The call to diaconal ministry is a lifelong commitment which supports and complements the ministry of Word and sacrament, focusing on ministry to the whole person. This "diaconal bias" provides the lens and vision for developing the diaconal mission of the church carried out among and through its members.

6. Be grounded in community: Diaconal ministers need the support and shared vision of a community of leaders committed to a common calling. This grounding in a diaconal community serves as the reminder to seek to build community in all ministry settings.

IV. Preparation and Training

The definition of diaconal ministry requires the following components to be included in any preparation and educational program designed to equip persons for this leadership role:

1. Knowledge and understanding of the Word of God.
2. A Lutheran understanding of the Gospel.
3. Knowledge and understanding of the Lutheran Confessions.
4. Theological reflection on issues of faith and life.
5. Personal spiritual formation and ministry identity.
6. Communication and planning skills necessary for effective witness, both verbally and in action.
7. Specific training and skill in an identified area of service.

These components will be addressed through a comprehensive program of preparation that includes:

1. Theological education;
2. Formation for ministry; and
3. Skill training.

V. Preparation, Approval, and Call

Except as otherwise provided, a candidate for diaconal ministers shall have:

1. Membership in a congregation of this church, and registration, by its pastor and congregation council, of the candidate with the candidacy committee;

2. Been granted entrance to candidacy by and under the guidance and supervision of the appropriate committee for at least a year before being approved for entry into diaconal ministry.

3. Demonstrated competence in at least one area of specialization or expertise according to guidelines established by the Division for Ministry.

4. Satisfactorily completed a first theological degree from an accredited theological school in North America.

5. Satisfactorily completed approved work in Lutheran studies as defined by the Division for Ministry.

6. Satisfactorily completed the formational component of the preparation program for Lutheran diaconal ministry as defined by the Division for Ministry.

7. Satisfactorily completed an approved internship or practical preparation as defined by the Division for Ministry.

8. Been examined and approved by the appropriate committee according to criteria, policies, and procedures established by the Division for Ministry (candidacy process).

9. Been recommended for call by the bishop of the synod to which the candidate has been assigned for first call in accordance with procedures recommended by the Division for Ministry, reviewed by the Conference of Bishops, and adopted by the Church Council.

10. Received and accepted a properly issued and attested letter of call.

5. Matters Related to the Deaconess Community

a. Relationship to Evangelical Lutheran Church in Canada (ELCIC)

Background: At its October 1994 meeting, the board of the Division for Ministry received the document, "ELCA Deaconess Community—Relationships and Statements of Agreement in the Evangelical Lutheran Church in Canada." At its October 1994 meeting the board of the Division for Ministry voted:

> To approve "ELCA Deaconess Community—Relationships and Statements of Agreement with the Evangelical Lutheran Church in Canada" for adoption by the Church Council.

Council Action: Pastor Wagner noted the relationships between the Deaconess Community of the Evangelical Lutheran Church in America and the deaconesses serving in the Evangelical Lutheran Church in Canada. These historic relationships are now being clarified in light of the policies and practices now introduced in the ELCA. He pointed particularly to a change in paragraph one which now reads, "set apart according to the entry rite of that church."

VOTED: *CC94.11.84*

To approve the following statement, "ELCA Deaconess Community - Relationships and Statements of Agreement with the Evangelical Lutheran Church in Canada:"

ELCA DEACONESS COMMUNITY
RELATIONSHIPS AND STATEMENTS OF AGREEMENT
WITH THE EVANGELICAL LUTHERAN CHURCH IN CANADA

(1) Members of the Evangelical Lutheran Church in Canada (ELCIC) will be approved, set apart according to the entry rite of that church, and rostered by the ELCIC.

(2) The Deaconess Community of the Evangelical Lutheran Church in America (ELCA) will serve both churches for the purpose of formation and community support and will relate to the candidacy process of both churches according to the guidelines established by each church.

(3) The Deaconess Community of the ELCA will include members of both the Evangelical Lutheran Church in America and the Evangelical Lutheran Church in Canada.

(4) Deaconesses serving in the Evangelical Lutheran Church in Canada shall be in a relationship of accountability for discipline, call and mobility with the Evangelical Lutheran Church in Canada according to the practices of that church.

(5) There shall be mutual transferability for deaconesses who are members of the Deaconess Community of the ELCA between both churches as presently exists for ordained ministers.

(6) The question of rostering needs to be determined by each church. While only members of the ELCA can be listed on the roster of the ELCA, it will be requested that the Yearbook listing of members of the Deaconess Community of the ELCA include members of the Evangelical Lutheran Church in Canada with appropriate designation of which church roster they are a member. The Evangelical Lutheran Church in Canada will determine how to list its deaconesses—which may be as "diaconal ministers."

b. Consecration of Deaconesses

Background: Following recommendation by the Deaconess Community related to June 29, 1994, consultations, the board of the Division for Ministry, at its October 1994 meeting, recommended:

> That the board of the Division for Ministry recommend to the Church Council that approved candidates for the roster deaconesses of the Evangelical Lutheran Church in America enter that ministry by "consecration," consistent with historical practice, thus replacing the current service of "Setting Apart of a Deaconess" with a service of "consecration."

Council Action: Pastor Wagner noted that approval of entry rites for deaconesses, called the "setting apart of a deaconess," needs to be reviewed in light of the question of the entry rite being conducted in other areas, in consultation with the Conference of Bishops.

VOTED: *CC94.11.85*

To refer the matter of terminology related to entrance rites for deaconesses ("setting apart" versus "consecration") to the Division for Ministry for further consultation with the Conference of Bishops; and

To request that a report on this issue be brought to the Church Council at its April 1995 meeting.

6. Service Rites for Ordination, Commissioning, and Consecration

Background: Acting upon the recommendation of the Deaconess Community of the Evangelical Lutheran Church in America, the board of the Division for Ministry, at its October 1994 meeting, voted:

> To recommend to the Church Council referral to the department for worship in the Division for Congregational Ministries and to the Office of the Secretary a study and review with possible revision of the service rites for ordination, commissioning, and consecration. Such study should include the following: (1) clarification of terminology related to "office," so that it is clear that persons are ordained, consecrated, or commissioned to a particular ministry and called to carry out the functions inherent in a designated office or position; and (2) consideration of "laying on of hands" as appropriate for consecration and commissioning as well as ordination.

Council Action: The Church Council took the following action *en bloc* at the conclusion of this meeting.

EN BLOC   [CC94.11.114]

To refer the request of the Division for Ministry concerning the development of rites for ordination, commissioning, and consecration jointly to the Division for Congregational Ministries and the Office of the Secretary;

To encourage continuing conversation between the Division for Congregational Ministries, the Office of the Secretary, the Division for Ministry, and the Conference of Bishops on this matter;

To request that reports and recommendations be brought to the Church Council as appropriate.

7.   **Admission to the Roster of Ordained Ministers Of Persons Ordained in Another Lutheran Church or Another Christian Tradition**

Background: At its October 1994 meeting, the board of the Division for Ministry voted:

To approve the revised policy, "Admission to the Roster of Ordained Ministers of Persons Ordained in Another Lutheran Church or Another Christian Tradition," consistent with the ELCA statement on ecumenism.

Council Action: During discussion, the Rev. David G. Gabel asked for clarification on the interim policy. Secretary Almen responded that the last paragraph related to ecumenical matters dealing with the "time between the times" because we do not have mutual exchangeablility of ministers is not possible because we do not have full communion with these other churches. If we were to enter into a full communion relationship with a church body in which we needed to ordain a person, he said, these proposals would apply. The Rev. A. Craig Settlege, director for candidacy, responded that at present the rite of entry is determined by the synod bishop in consultation with the bishop of this church. The Rev. Nadine F. Lehr expressed the desire to delete the phrase. The Rev. Franklin D. Fry suggested striking only "and exchangeability."

Secretary Almen noted the necessity of removing this item from *en bloc.* As a matter of information, he also commented that the text before the Church Council has been used since 1989.

MOVED;

SECONDED: To delete the following penultimate paragraph from the proposed policy statement [text printed below].

The Rev. Franklin D. Fry served notice that, if the recommendation was defeated, he would move to remove the words "and exchangeability."

MOVED;

SECONDED;

CARRIED: To delete the following penultimate paragraph of the proposed policy statement:

This policy is to be considered an interim one until such time as the Evangelical Lutheran Church in America is in full communion with another Christian church and, as such, shares in a mutual recognition and exchangeability of ordained ministers.

VOTED: *CC94.11.86*

To adopt, as amended, the following policy, "Admission to the Roster of Ordained Ministers of Persons Ordained in Another Lutheran Church or Another Christian Tradition," consistent with Statement on Ecumenism of the Evangelical Lutheran Church in America:

ADMISSION TO THE ROSTER OF ORDAINED MINISTERS OF PERSONS ORDAINED IN ANOTHER LUTHERAN CHURCH OR ANOTHER CHRISTIAN TRADITION

This policy is the process by which the Evangelical Lutheran Church in America approves for the roster of ordained ministers those person previously ordained by another Lutheran church body or another Christian tradition. In the case of ordained ministers of the Evangelical Lutheran Church in Canada, they shall be received by transfer upon acceptance of a valid call from a congregation, Synod Council, churchwide board, or the Church Council of this church following the certification of their good standing on the roster of the Evangelical Lutheran Church in Canada and with the approval of the bishop of the synod in which they are to serve.

This policy shall apply to those who are citizens of the United States as well as those who seek to immigrate to the United States.

Basic Standards for Ordained Ministers

Persons admitted to and continued in the ordained ministry of this church shall satisfactorily meet and maintain the following:
a.   commitment to Christ;
b.   acceptance of and adherence to the Confession of Faith of this church;
c.   willingness and ability to serve in response to the needs of this church;
d.   academic and practical qualifications for ministry;
e.   life consistent with the Gospel and personal qualifications including leadership abilities and competence in interpersonal relationships;
f.   receipt and acceptance of a letter of call; and
g.   membership in a congregation of this church.

Any person seeking admission to the ordained ministry of this church must be able to meet and maintain the above standards. In the case of a person previously ordained by another Lutheran church body or another Christian tradition it is implicit that the applicant is familiar with the Confession of Faith of this church and is committed to it.

Initial Application

The applicant registers with the synod of residence. In the case of an applicant who does not reside in the United States registration may be made to a synod where there is a familial or mentor relationship, or request may be made to the Conference of Bishops for a synod assignment.

The applicant is to provide the synod with the following information:
1.   "Application to the Roster of Ordained Ministers of the Evangelical Lutheran Church in America."
2.   Academic transcripts for all post-secondary education (degree or non-degree).
3.   Certificates of study (if any).
4.   Documentation of supervised field experience, i.e. internship, clinical education, etc.

5. Statement or certificate of ordained status in another Lutheran church body or Christian tradition.
6. Letter of reference from applicant's current or former ecclesiastical supervisor.
7. Documentation of the Immigration and Naturalization Service (for those seeking to immigrate to the United States).
8. Copy of at least one recent sermon.
9. A personal statement, including the theological rationale, on why the applicant seeks to serve on the ordained roster of the Evangelical Lutheran Church in America.
10. A recent photograph.

Upon receipt of this information the synod bishop, in consultation with the candidacy committee of the synod, arranges an interview with the applicant. The purpose of this interview is to determine the applicant's readiness to enter the candidacy process of this church. Entrance into the candidacy process is based upon the adequacy of the information provided by the applicant and the applicant's statement of intention to serve in the ordained ministry of the Evangelical Lutheran Church in America. If the applicant comes from a church overseas with which this church is related, the Division for Global Mission will be consulted by the synod. The purpose of this consultation is to receive any additional information regarding the applicant that is available from the applicant's church body. After the completion of the interview and the receipt of the required information, the applicant is considered for endorsement by the candidacy committee.

Endorsement for Candidacy

The candidacy committee has the responsibility to act on the endorsement of the applicant. The applicant ordinarily shall be requested to participate in a psychological evaluation, according to the procedures of the Division for Ministry. The candidacy committee may request the applicant to prepare the Endorsement Essay. The committee may interview the applicant. When the applicant has completed the necessary steps the committee takes action on the endorsement of the applicant. Upon a positive decision the applicant is to be considered a candidate for the ordained ministry of the Evangelical Lutheran Church in America.

Review Panel

Following the endorsement of the candidate, the chairperson of the candidacy committee forwards the candidate's file to the Division for Ministry. Division for Ministry staff will review the candidate's file and on the basis of that file convene a Review Panel. This panel will include faculty members of a seminary of this church trained for the review process and, as needed, persons appropriate to the cultural or language background of the candidate, chosen in consultation with the Commission for Multicultural Ministries and/or the Division for Global Mission. This panel, together with representation from the Division for Ministry staff, will interview the candidate. An interpreter will be present when necessary.

The panel will review with the candidate the academic and practical work that must be completed in order to fulfill the standards for ordained ministry. The panel may require study at an Evangelical Lutheran Church in America seminary, language proficiency study, a supervised in-service assignment, or other appropriate preparation.

The decision options of the panel include the following:
1. Immediate recommendation for approval of the candidate upon receipt and acceptance of a letter of call.
2. Recommendation for approval of the candidate upon the satisfactory completion of the recommended work and the receipt and acceptance of a letter of call.
3. A decision to reconsider the candidate upon the satisfactory completion of the recommended work.
4. A decision to recommend that the candidate not be approved.

The panel informs the candidate of its decision at the earliest possible time. In the case of a decision to require further study or preparation, the candidacy committee will continue an on-going relationship with the candidate. When financial assistance is needed the candidacy committee will work with the candidate in securing this assistance. The Division for Ministry, together with

other churchwide units and the seminaries of this church, is a resource to the candidate and candidacy committee during the time of preparation.

Approval

Upon the successful completion of the required work and the recommendation of the panel, the candidate is considered for approval by the candidacy committee. A positive recommendation by the panel normally shall be necessary if the candidacy committee is to approve the candidate. In the case of a candidate who has been denied a positive recommendation by the panel, the candidacy committee must consult directly with the Division for Ministry. The Division for Ministry will arrange for a member of the panel to be present at the Approval Interview and to participate in the committee's deliberations. The approval decision is reported in writing to the Conference of Bishops. The candidate is assigned to a region and synod for consideration for a letter of call.

Ordination or Reception of the Candidate

After receipt and acceptance of a letter of call by the candidate, the synod bishop is to consul with the Office of the Bishop of the Evangelical Lutheran Church in America concerning the reception of the candidate. The Evangelical Lutheran Church in America will receive ordained ministers from churches which believe, teach, and confess the Apostles', the Nicene, and the Athanasian Creeds. Those from other traditions will be ordained according to the Service of Ordination of this church. The determination of how this policy applies in the case of each candidate is made by the Office of the Bishop of the Evangelical Lutheran Church in America.

The basis for this policy is the recognition that while ordination is into the Church catholic it is always particularized in a specific tradition of the Church and never in the abstract. As the Evangelical Lutheran Church in America determines its ecumenical vision and policy, it is necessary to avoid the impression that this church is taking unilateral action that implies the recognition or exchangeability of ordained ministers of another Christian tradition. At the same time it is important to give a clear witness to this church's willingness to affirm the ordination of those churches which believe, teach, and confess the ecumenical creeds.

Pastoral Care and Support

The beginning of service for those who come to the Evangelical Lutheran Church in American from other churches is an important time. It is a time to establish significant relationships of support and growth. During the early years of service, it is recommended that the synod bishop offer the newly rostered pastor a mentor who would assist the bishop in providing this support and nurture.

8. Reinstatement to the Rosters of the Evangelical Lutheran Church in America

Background: The board of the Division for Ministry took the following action at its October 1994 meeting:

[To] approve the revised policy, "Reinstatement to the Rosters of the Evangelical Lutheran Church in America," for adoption by the Church Council.

Council Action: The Church Council adopted the following resolution through *en bloc* action at the conclusion of this meeting:

EN BLOC   [CC94.11.115]

To approve the revised policy, "Reinstatement to the Rosters of the Evangelical Lutheran Church in America,"

REINSTATEMENT TO THE ROSTERS OF THE EVANGELICAL LUTHERAN CHURCH IN AMERICA

I. Reinstatement Process

A. Reinstatement to the rosters of the Evangelical Lutheran Church in America is the responsibility of the Candidacy Committee of the synod where the applicant was last under call as an ordained minister, associate in ministry, deaconess or diaconal minister of the Evangelical Lutheran Church in America.

B. In the case of an applicant whose rostered ministry was last in one of the ELCA predecessor churches, the successor ELCA synod has the responsibility.

C. The reinstatement process may be transferred from one synod to another, with the written concurrence of both candidacy committees and both synod bishops. In every case, the process begins in the synod from which the applicant left the roster.

II. Application

A. The applicant provides the completed "Application for Reinstatement" to the appropriate roster of the Evangelical Lutheran Church in America" to the synod, and a copy is sent to the Division for Ministry for information.

B. Upon receipt of the application, the synod bishop arranges an interview with the applicant. The purpose of this interview is to determine the acceptability of the applicant's request for reinstatement.

C. The applicant is considered for reinstatement by the Candidacy Committee when the application is forwarded to the committee by the bishop.

D. The bishop will notify the Office of the Secretary of the Evangelical Lutheran Church in America and request any pertinent information concerning the applicant.

E. In the case of an applicant whose removal from the roster was the result of the official disciplinary process of this church (or resignation from the roster to avoid the disciplinary process), a minimum of five years must elapse after the removal from the roster before an application for reinstatement may be considered. The elapse of five years does not guarantee reconsideration, however.

F. In the case of an applicant whose inappropriate conduct or misjudgment led to resignation from the roster, the synod bishop is to determine that suitable corrective action has been taken by the applicant before proceeding with the reinstatement process.

G. Any person removed from a lay roster that existed on December 31, 1987, who seeks to return to active lay roster status must apply for acceptance to a roster of this church under the standards, criteria, policies, and procedures that apply to the roster of associates in ministry, as identified in ELCA churchwide bylaw 7.51.13.a. This same requirement shall apply to those certified during the period of January 1, 1988, through September 1, 1993, as associates in ministry of this church.

III. Candidacy Committee

A. The Synod Candidacy Committee shall receive and review the registration by the pastor and congregation council of the congregation of which the applicant is a member in good standing. The registration attests that the applicant is an active member of an ELCA congregation.

B. The committee shall determine that all records and information concerning the applicant have been received, including verification of synodical records concerning the reason for removal from the roster. If synodical records are incomplete, this verification may include conferring with the former bishop or staff concerning knowledge of the circumstances for removal.

C. The applicant prepares the Approval Essay and submits it to the Candidacy Committee for use in the approval process.

D. In the case of an applicant who has been off the roster for more than five years, the Candidacy Committee shall require the applicant to participate in the Psychological Evaluation and Career Consultation according to the policies of the Division for Ministry. The expense of this evaluation is the responsibility of the applicant.

E. The Candidacy Committee interviews the applicant to explore all concerns related to reinstatement, including:

(1) the circumstances surrounding the removal of the applicant from the roster including the applicant's reason(s) for leaving the roster,

(2) the applicant's reason(s) for requesting reinstatement to the roster with special focus upon what has changed in the person's life, faith, attitudes and circumstances since the time of removal;

(3) discussion of the applicant's understanding of ordained, commissioned or consecrated ministry in the Evangelical Lutheran Church in America, and the applicant's willingness to serve in response to the needs of this church;

(4) discussion of "Vision and Expectations" and the applicant's commitment to live according to the expectations of this church.

F. The Candidacy Committee may request the Division of Ministry to convene a Review Panel to determine the applicant's theological readiness for ordained ministry. The Review Panel will make a recommendation to the committee following the procedures developed by the Division for Ministry.

IV. Decision

A. The Candidacy Committee shall make a decision concerning the applicant's suitability to serve as a rostered minister of this church. This decision is one of the following:

(1) approval of the candidate upon receipt and acceptance of a letter of call;

(2) postponement of approval with specific recommendations for remedial or developmental work prior to further consideration for reinstatement;

(3) denial of approval for reinstatement.

B. If an applicant who was removed from the roster as the result of the official disciplinary process of this church (or who resigned from the roster in order to avoid the official disciplinary process) is approved for reinstatement, the Candidacy Committee must report its decision to the Executive Committee of the Synod Council. Authorization of the approval requires a two-thirds majority vote by the total membership of the Executive Committee. If such an applicant is denied reinstatement by the Candidacy Committee, its decision is final.

V. Approval

A. If approved, the candidate will complete the normal candidacy documents and will participate in the churchwide assignment process through the Department for Synodical Relations.

B. An approved candidate is eligible for a call for a period of one year after approval.

C. The process for renewal of approval, as defined by the Division for Ministry(Candidacy Manual), is the same as that for other candidates for ordained ministry.

D. Upon receipt and acceptance of a properly issued and duly-attested letter of call, the candidate is reinstated to the appropriate roster of this church.

Plans for an ELCA Wide-Area Network

Background: The Evangelical Lutheran Church in America is called to be an interdependent church, with all expressions working together to "bear witness to God's creative, redeeming and sanctifying activity in the world." The sheer number of ELCA congregations, synods and staff, separated by space and time differences, however, presents a major communication challenge.

Large organizations, including the Evangelical Lutheran Church in America, are prone to problems of physical and psychological distance that can make difficult the development of the types of *relationships* that can enhance mutual understanding and support. For the sake of the mission entrusted to this church, new communication technologies and resources need to be assessed in the light of their potential contributions to the development of such critical relationships.

At its November 1994 meeting, the Church Council had the opportunity to discuss plans for an expanded ELCA wide-area network (WAN), which offers the ability for broad-based, ongoing, *interactive group communication*—communication that is virtually impossible through any other medium. The computer-based communication system being proposed has the potential to draw ELCA members and leaders together in a dynamic electronic community, allowing them to focus on common goals of witness and service.

The 1992 parochial report of the congregations of this church showed that 7,248 congregations had access to personal computers. Prices for high-speed modems to carry out computer-based communication have dropped low enough to be within reach of most congregations.

The ELCA churchwide organization plans to implement a Unix-based wide area network host at the Lutheran Center, using Internet-standard communication tools to provide electronic mail and conferencing to ELCA members and staff. The host also will interconnect with a broader, ecumenical, wide-area network. Ecunet, a cooperative of faith-group networks, is proposing a plan for co-hosts that can exchange information on a worldwide basis. This effort builds on the experience with the current Wide-Area Network "prototype" (LutherLink), in which almost 600 persons now participate.

Over the past year, the Office of the Bishop and the Department for Human Resources convened an inter-unit team to plan for churchwide applications of emerging technology. This team developed prototype "screens" describing possible applications in an expanded ELCA wide-area network. (Both current capabilities and anticipated new applications were demonstrated at the November 1994 Church Council meeting.) While many units have participated and have expressed a keen interest in this effort, key roles in the development of this project have been played by the Department for Information Technology, Department for Communication, and Division for Congregational Ministries. In addition, advice from a network advisory group representing a variety of ELCA

Council Action: Chair Magnus called upon Lita Brusick Johnson, executive assistant to the bishop, to present plans for a wide-area network, which is designed to harness technologies for the ministry for this church. Ms. Johnson described the proposal as "ministry at the edge of cyberspace." The purpose of the proposal is to link ministers and institutions in order to allow them to

resource one another, to receive information from the wider church, and from the worldwide Lutheran family. She introduced Paul D. Edison-Swift, director for resource information and networks in the Department for Communication; the Rev. Michael R. Rothaar, director for planning and congregational studies for the Division for Congregational Ministries; Ken F. Aicher, director for information management services for the Department for Information Technology; and the Rev. A. C. ("Chris") Stein, director of the Department for Human Resources.

Mr. Edison-Swift introduced a demonstration on computer networking. Pastor Rothaar continued the demonstration with an emphasis on congregational resources available. Pastor Stein described the use of technology for ministry, and to strengthen the ties within this church.

VOTED: *CC94.11.87*
To affirm continuing development of plans, in conversation with synods and other partners in ministry, for the expansion of a Lutheran wide-area network; and

To encourage continued exploration of emerging technologies that can assist this church in carrying out the mission entrusted to it.

During discussion of the foregoing resolution, William H. Engelbrecht asked about budget commitments. It was reported that the budget approved earlier during this meeting of the Church Council included $45,000 for this work, and a grant proposal was being prepared in the range of $300,000, with the goal to make it self-supporting within two years.

The Church Council recessed at 12:46 P.M. with prayer offered by Secretary Almen. The Church Council reconvened at 1:34 P.M. on Monday afternoon, November 14, 1994.

Approval of Minutes

The minutes of the April 16-18, 1994, meeting of the Church Council and the minutes of the May 13, 1994, July 19, 1994, August 19, 1994, October 6, 1994, and October 18, 1994, meetings of the council's Executive Committee were distributed to council members prior to the council's November 1994 meeting.

VOTED: *CC94.11.88*
To approve the minutes of the April 16-18, 1994, meeting of the Church Council.

During discussion of the foregoing resolution, two typographical errors in the text of the minutes were noted: On the bottom of page four, in the last paragraph under the "Report of the Bishop" the word, "not," was inadvertently omitted (i.e., ". . . I do *not* have an easy answer to it."); and on page 15 under the section "3. Representational Principles," in the second full paragraph, the year was incorrectly cited as "1994," rather than 1993 (i.e., "At its December 1993 meeting the Church Council voted: . . ..").

VOTED: *CC94.11.89*

To ratify actions of the council's Executive Committee as indicated in the minutes of the May 13, 1994, July 19, 1994, August 19, 1994, October 6, 1994, and October 18, 1994, meetings.

Appointments

Chair Magnus announced the appointment of Church Council members to the Memorials Committee and the Committee of Reference and Council for the 1995 Churchwide Assembly.

VOTED: *CC94.11.90*

To confirm the appointment of the following persons respectively to the Memorials Committee and the Committee on Reference and Counsel for the 1995 Churchwide Assembly:

Memorials Committee

Rev. Joseph L. Carucci (Paradise Valley, Ariz.)
Rev. Susan L. Gamelin (Clearwater, Fla.)
Rev. Donald M. Hallberg (Des Plaines, Ill.), *co-chair*
Mr. D. Mark Klever (Dayton, Iowa)
Rev. Nadine F. Lehr (Gettysburg, Pa.), *co-chair*
Mr. Harold Light (St. Louis, Mo.)
Ms. Diane Melbye (Dickinson, N.Dak.)
Bishop Mark R. Ramseth (Great Falls, Mont.)
Ms. W. Jeanne Rapp (Pontiac, Ill.)
Mr. Douglas Reeves (Cheyenne, Wyo.)
Ms. Mary Ann Shealy (Newberry, S.C.)
Bishop Harold S. Weiss (Wescosville, Pa.)
Ms. Deborah S. Yandala (Akron, Ohio)

Committee of Reference and Counsel

Rev. James W. Addy (Clinton, S.C.)
Rev. David A. Andert (Duluth, Minn.)
Ms. Lorraine G. Bergquist (Seattle, Wash.), *co-chair*
Ms. Terry L. Bowes (Longmont, Co.)
Mr. J. David Ellwanger (Plano, Tex.)
Ms. LeRoy R. Hamlett Jr. (Charlottesville, Va.)
Bishop Gerhard I. Knutson (Rice Lake, Wis.)
Bishop A. Donald Main (Lewisburg, Pa.)
Ms. Joanne Negstad (Minneapolis, Minn.)
Mr. Carlos Peña (Galveston, Tex.), co-chair
Rev. Elizabeth A. Platz (College Park, Md.)
Ms. Ramona S. Rank (Portland, Oreg.)
Mr. Nel Vos (Maxatawny, Pa.)

Matters Related to the Division for Church in Society (continued)

2. Draft Statement on Human Sexuality

Earlier during this meeting the council's Executive Committee had been requested to confer regarding the role of the "consulting panel" in the further development of a possible social statement on human sexuality. Reporting on behalf of the Executive Committee, Chair Magnus offered the following motion, subsequently adopted by the Church Council:

VOTED: *CC94.11.91*

To express thanks to the consulting panel, which was established by the Church Council at the December 1993 meeting, for its role in the process for developing a possible social statement on the church and human sexuality; and

To request that the consulting panel continue in its role until further notice, with the expectation that more specific instructions regarding its role will be developed and transmitted following the Church Council's April 1995 meeting.

Chair Magnus then reported on the Executive Committee's work in surveying the members of the Church Council on the dissemination of the second draft of a possible social statement on human sexuality. She noted that while the survey was conducted by the committee members in different ways, a strong consensus emerged for the action taken. She expressed appreciation to the Rev. Charles S. Miller Jr., executive director of the Division for Church in Society, for leading this process effectively.

Matters Related to the Division for Congregational Ministries

1. Sacramental Practices

Background: At the 1989 Churchwide Assembly, "A Statement on Communion Practices," originally prepared and adopted by predecessor church bodies in 1978, was approved for continued use as the policy of the Evangelical Lutheran Church in America (CA89.4.23). The 1989 Churchwide Assembly also approved a response to memorials of six synods regarding a study on sacramental practices. The response indicated that the Conference of Bishops had "recommended that a statement on sacramental practices be prepared as a guide to the Evangelical Lutheran Church in America" and that "such a study would be carried out by a committee including persons representing the Conference of Bishops, the teaching theologians of this church, the Division for Ministry, the Division for Congregational Life [Ministries], and the Office [Department] for Ecumenical Affairs." At its April 1989 meeting, the Church Council requested that the Conference of Bishops prepare a time line and process for this study for consideration by the council at its November 1989 meeting.

In its specific response, the 1989 Churchwide Assembly referred the memorials from synods "to the Conference of Bishops for use in the development of a study on sacramental practices" (CA89.8.119). Because of budget reductions, implementation of the study process was delayed. In response to the delay, the 1991 Churchwide Assembly took the following action related to a study of sacramental practices:

To direct the Conference of Bishops, Division for Congregational Ministries, and the Budget Development Committee of the Church Council to develop and report to the 1993 Churchwide

Assembly a strategy for funding and conducting a communion practices study and statement (CA91.7.47).

Upon recommendation of the board of the Division for Congregational Ministries, the Department for Synodical Relations (Conference of Bishops), and the Office of the Bishop, the Church Council took the following action at its November 1992 meeting:

To designate the Division for Congregational Ministries as the lead unit in preparing the report and possible recommendation on a sacramental practices study and statement, in consultation with the Conference of Bishops and the Budget and Finance Committee of the Church Council, for presentation to the 1993 Churchwide Assembly (CC.92.11.108).

Information on the proposed scope and time line for the development of a sacramental practices statement was shared with the 1993 Churchwide Assembly. At its April 1994 meeting, the Church Council reviewed preliminary materials prepared by the task force on sacramental practices. This material also was shared with the Conference of Bishops and Division for Congregational Ministries Board.

In June 1994, after consultation with the bishop of this church, the executive committee of the board of the Division for Congregational Ministries expanded the anticipated time for congregational response to proposed drafts of a sacramental practices statement. The new time line anticipates the completion of this statement at the 1997 Churchwide Assembly. Given the other items that were on the agenda for congregational discussion during 1994-1995, the division suggested that working toward final action at the 1995 Churchwide Assembly would not have permitted the type of thorough conversation throughout the congregations of this church that this important topic warrants. Information on this change, together with a revised time line, was shared with the Church Council, synodical bishops, and Cabinet of Executives in June 1994. At its October 1994 board meeting, the full board of the Division for Congregational Ministries affirmed this action.

Council Action: Chair Magnus called upon the Rev. Mary Ann Moller-Gunderson, executive director of the Division for Congregational Ministries. She reported that the division board was excited about the possibility of developing this statement because it allows congregations a substantial amount of time to respond to drafts of this document. She noted the importance of allowing congregations the opportunity to engage in a study of Word and Sacrament and their place at the center of our life together. She also said that the second draft of the proposed statement will be available in time to be studied at synod assemblies before the 1997 Churchwide Assembly. Pastor Moller-Gunderson reported that the editorial committee will be meeting next week, and a first draft of the statement is expected to result from the meeting of the task force in January 1995. She also expressed the hope that this process would achieve a greater consensus in our understanding of the means of grace in this church.

Bishop Robert L. Isaksen inquired about the status of the first draft of the statement. Pastor Moller-Gunderson reported that it has been significantly re-

shaped and continues to be re-written. The structure, however, in three sections related respectively to Word, Baptism, and Holy Communion, remains.

2. Amendments to the Governing Documents of the Lutheran Youth Organization

Background: ELCA 16.11.A91.f.2. provides that:
The constitution of the Lutheran Youth Organization shall be approved by the Church Council.

Council agenda Exhibit L, Part 2, detailed changes to the Lutheran Youth Organization's governing documents that were recommended by the organization and the board of the Division for Congregational Ministries, which oversees and supports the work of the Lutheran Youth Organization.

Council Action: The Church Council took the following action *en bloc* at the conclusion of this meeting:

EN BLOC   [CC94.11.116]
To adopt the amendments to the governing documents of the Lutheran Youth Organization . . . .

3. Revised Common Lectionary

Background: Council agenda Exhibit L, Part 3, contained a report and recommendations to the Church Council on proposed changes related to the *Revised Common Lectionary.* An accompanying statement from staff of Augsburg Fortress was printed on page 10 of that exhibit.

Under the guidelines approved by the Church Council for review of worship materials, the Church Council has a role in dealing with these matters. These guidelines were originally adopted by the Church Council in April 1991.

The board of the Division for Congregational Ministries, which met October 14-16, 1994, commended the following action to the Church Council for adoption.

Council Action: Pastor Moller-Gunderson introduced the Rev. Karen M. Ward, associate director for worship in the Division for Congregational Ministries and a member of the Consultation on Common Texts, to respond to questions regarding the revised common lectionary. During discussion, Bishop Paull L. Spring asked whether a full series of lessons could be developed for Reformation Day. Pastor Ward said that such a recommendation could be presented to the Consultation on Common Texts. Bishop Robert L. Isaksen expressed a similar concern that the appointed texts for dedication and anniversary of a congregation in the *Lutheran Book of Worship* could be expanded. The Rev. John O. Knudson inquired whether we are losing our Lutheran identity in adopting the new common lectionary. Pastor Ward commented that the Roman Lectionary for Mass has already served as the basis for the *Lutheran Book of Worship* lectionary, and the current revision of the common lectionary had been presented to the Vatican for possible use.

VOTED: *CC94.11.92*

To affirm the recommendation of the board of the Division for Congregational Ministries:

That the Revised Common Lectionary (1992) of the Consultation on Common Texts be authorized for use by the congregations of this church beginning with the First Sunday of Advent 1995;

That the typological (not the continuous) first lesson be the preferred option for use in the Evangelical Lutheran Church in America; and

That where the existing calendar of the church (*Lutheran Book of Worship*, 1978) provides for festivals or commemorations not included in the Revised Common Lectionary, readings for those observances be provided from *Lutheran Book of Worship*.

Corporate Responsibility (continued)

Earlier during this meeting, the Rev. James G. Cobb had offered the following motion:

MOVED;

SECONDED: To refer to the Church Council's Legal and Constitutional Review Committee a request to list for the Church Council the names of corporate entities for which the Church Council has direct responsibilities and to make commentary on what would be required to dissolve such direct responsibilities.

Chair Magnus then appointed an *ad hoc* committee to study the matter. Chair Magnus now recognized Pastor Cobb, who moved the following recommendation of the *ad hoc* committee:

VOTED: *CC94.11.93*

To request the Church Council's Legal and Constitutional Review Committee to prepare a listing, for distribution to the members of the Church Council, of the names of corporate entities for which the churchwide organization, Church Council, or Churchwide Assembly have control or corporate membership responsibilities; and

To request that a brief commentary be prepared on the source and history or background of such agencies and institutions.

Report of the Legal and Constitutional Review Committee

Chair Magnus called upon Dale V. Sandstrom, chair of the council's Legal and Constitutional Review Committee, to continue the committee's report.

8. Amendments to the Constitutions, Bylaws, and Continuing Resolutions

Background: Earlier during this meeting various amendments to the governing documents of this church were proposed for adoption by the Church Council in an *en bloc* resolution. During discussion, proposed bylaw 9.23. was removed from the recommendation of the Legal and Constitutional Review Committee for further consideration.

Proposed 9.23. In accord with constitutional provision 9.21.d. and bylaw 9.21.01. and without invoking the provisions of Chapter 20, a congregation that maintains as its pastor an ordained minister who has been removed from this church's roster of ordained minister by disciplinary action or that calls as its pastor one who has not been approved for the roster of ordained ministers shall be removed from the roster of congregations of this church by the Synod Council.

Council Action: Mr. Sandstrom introduced the following recommendation of the Legal and Constitutional Review Committee, which sought to provide for flexibility for the synodical bishop in responding to particular circumstances.

VOTED: *CC94.11.94*

To propose for possible adoption by the 1995 Churchwide Assembly the following amendment to the *Constitutions, Bylaws, and Continuing Resolutions of the Evangelical Lutheran Church in America:*

To add a new constitutional provision, numbered 9.23. regarding congregations that fail to acknowledge and practice in regard to pastoral leadership this church's criteria for recognition and to renumber existing constitutional provision 9.23. as 9.24.:

9.23. In accord with constitutional provision 9.21.d. and bylaw 9.21.01. and without invoking the provisions of Chapter 20, a congregation that maintains as its pastor an ordained minister who has been removed from this church's roster of ordained ministers by disciplinary action or that calls as its pastor one who has not been approved for the roster of ordained ministers may be removed from the roster of congregations of this church by the Synod Council upon recommendation of the synodical bishop.

9. Discipline of Congregations

Background: The following memorial was adopted by the Lower Susquehanna Synod at its 1992 assembly:

WHEREAS, we are of the opinion that the Congregation Council must be formally involved in efforts to resolve disputes within the congregation before the dispute is brought to the synodical bishop, and we do not believe that informing the congregation president that the bishop is being contacted in the event of disagreements would serve the containment and resolution of difficulties as well as the procedure outlined below; and

WHEREAS, Chapter 15 of the *Model Constitution for Congregations* has been changed from "Discipline of Members" to "Discipline of Members and Adjudication," it would appear consistent that, in addition to the subtitle, "Adjudication," that now appears at C15.10., there be a subtitle, "Discipline of Members," perhaps C15.00.; and

WHEREAS, paragraphs pertaining to discipline of members have been well defined over time, it would be good if the sections devoted to adjudication could be just as carefully worked out; therefore be it

RESOLVED, that to clarify procedural matters, the following paragraphs be proposed to replace C15.11.:

C15.11. When there is disagreement among factions within this congregation on a substantive issue that cannot be resolved by the parties, members of this congregation shall refer the disagreement to the Congregation Council.

C15.12. Should the disagreement not be resolved by the Congregation Council in a manner that is satisfactory to the parties involved and the Congregation Council, members of this congregation shall have access to the synodical bishop for consultation.

C15.13. Should the disagreement not be resolved with the help of the bishop in a manner that is satisfactory to the parties involved and the Congregation Council, the disagreement shall be referred to the synodical Consultation Committee.

C15.14. Should the disagreement not be resolved by the Consultation Committee in a manner that is satisfactory to the parties involved and the Congregation Council, the disagreement shall be referred to the Synod Council. The decision of the Synod Council shall be final and binding upon the parties involved and the Congregation Council.

The following background information was supplied to the 1993 Churchwide Assembly by the Memorials Committee:

Provision C15.11. in the *Model Constitution for Congregations* regarding "Adjudication" is identical to required provision †S17.11. in the *Constitution for Synods*. Both relate to stipulations in constitutional provision 20.84. in the churchwide constitution.

Although the *Model Constitution for Congregations* may be amended by the Churchwide Assembly in the manner provided for the bylaws of this church (ELCA 9.53.02.), mandatory provisions in the *Constitution for Synods* that incorporate constitutional provisions of this church may be amended only in the manner prescribed for amendments to the constitution of this church (ELCA 10.13.).

In view of the fact that final action on such proposed amendments could not be completed by the 1993 Churchwide Assembly and in recognition of the need for study of the implications of such amendments, the 1993 Churchwide Assembly acted upon the Memorials Committee recommendation and adopted the following resolution:

To refer the memorial of the Lower Susquehanna Synod on adjudication related to members of congregations to the Legal and Constitutional Review Committee of the Church Council for study in connection with preparation of any possible amendments to be proposed by the Church Council to the 1995 Churchwide Assembly.

Subsequently, the Church Council, at the December 1993 meeting, voted:

To refer this resolution to the Office of the Secretary; and

To request that a report and/or recommendation be prepared for review by the Church Council, through the Legal and Constitutional Review Committee of the Church Council, at the November 1994 Church Council meeting.

Experience throughout this church does not appear to point to a pressing need for such detailed amendments to the *Model Constitution for Congregations*. Further, the Lower Susquehanna Synod, in a memorial adopted by its 1994 Synod Assembly, has urged that the number of amendments to the *Model Constitution for Congregations* be reduced and restricted. The detailed steps outlined in the 1992 memorial may be addressed later in proposing possible rules of procedure to synods regarding such adjudication.

Council Action: During discussion Bishop Paul R. Swanson noted that a similar case covered by this provision has currently cost the synod $25,000 and another $10,000-15,000 will be spent on hearings and related needs.

VOTED: CC94.11.95

To decline, in keeping with the request of the 1994 memorial of the Lower Susquehanna Synod Assembly, to propose amendments to the *Model Constitution for Congregations* for the additional provisions requested in the 1992 memorial of the Lower Susquehanna Synod Assembly; and

To request the secretary of this church, in consultation with the general counsel, to explore the possibility of developing model rules of procedures that may be submitted to synods for consideration and possible use in adjudication processes.

6.   Policy and Procedural Manual for Rosters

Background: In 1987 and 1989, a booklet of "Guidelines for the Management of Rosters of the Evangelical Lutheran Church in America" was compiled and distributed to synods by the ELCA secretary. The content of the guidelines had been received as the policy document for such matters by the Conference of Bishops in December 1987.

During the past years, more detailed policies have been developed—as required by the bylaws—by the Division for Ministry. These have been reviewed by the Conference of Bishops and subsequently adopted by the Church Council.

The secretary and general counsel have been working with staff of the Division for Ministry to compile a current edition of such policies. These are to be issued as a "Manual of Policies and Procedures for the Management of the Rosters of the Evangelical Lutheran Church in America." The content of the manual will be the policies adopted by the council, plus additional texts of procedures, where applicable.

Council Action: Mr. Sandstrom introduced the following recommendation, subsequently adopted by the Church Council without discussion:

VOTED: *CC94.11.96*

To approve the "Manual of Policies and Procedures for the Management of the Rosters of the Evangelical Lutheran Church in America" and authorize its distribution for use by synodical bishops, synodical staff members, and others who hold responsibilities for such matters in this church; and

To authorize the secretary to provide periodic updates reflecting new or revised policies subsequently adopted by the Church Council.

7. Lay Voting Membership in Synodical Assemblies (continued)

Council Action: During the council's previous discussion of proposed amendments to †S7.21.c., *et al.*, regarding the election of lay voting members for synodical assemblies, a question was raised about whether the revised provisions would be effective in 1996. Mr. Sandstrom reported that implementation of the amended provision would depend on current bylaws of each synod. He noted that the Legal and Constitutional Review Committee had prepared revised wording that would provide for immediate implementation in all synods, should Church Council members choose to reconsider the council's previous action. No further action on this matter was taken.

Installation of the Bishop of this Church

Background: According to the current schedule, the Church Council is to meet December 1-4, 1995. In order to avoid the cost of additional travel, consideration was given at the Conference of Bishops' meeting to changing the dates of the fall 1995 meeting of the Conference of Bishops to November 28-December 3, thereby providing the common date of December 2 at which both the members of the Church Council and the members of the Conference of Bishops would be in Chicago for the installation of the new bishop of this church.

During discussion, however, it was noted that during the first weekend of December, many ELCA colleges and universities present Christmas concerts. Members of the Conference of Bishops suggested that scheduling the installation of the bishop of the church on that weekend would preclude attendance by many college presidents and other representatives from this church's colleges and universities.

Alternative dates were suggested: Tuesday, November 14, through Sunday, November 19, 1995, for the Conference of Bishops; and Friday, November 17, through Monday, November 20, 1995, for the Church Council. Following such a schedule would mean that the installation of the bishop could occur on Saturday afternoon, November 18, likely followed by a banquet in the evening. Such a date also would permit people from throughout the area to attend the service.

Council Action: Chair Magnus called upon Secretary Lowell G. Almen to introduce the following recommendation, subsequently adopted by the Church Council without discussion:

VOTED: *CC94.11.97*

To establish November 17-20, 1995, as the dates for the regular fall meeting of the Church Council;

To designate November 14-19, 1995, as the dates for the regular fall meeting of the Conference of Bishops;

To set November 18, 1995, as the date for the installation of the bishop of the Evangelical Lutheran Church in America; and

To request the Office of the Bishop to extend appropriate advance invitations to officials of the Lutheran World Federation and ecumenical entities, to the bishop of the Evangelical Lutheran Church in Canada, and to the leaders of other church bodies for this event.

Follow-Up on Letters of Call

Background: During the spring 1994 meeting of the Church Council, council member Robert S. Schroeder inquired about the possibility of issuing Letters of Call to persons on the official lay rosters of this church who previously had received Letters of Appointment for their service in the churchwide organization. Secretary Lowell G. Almen then indicated that the matter would be explored with the Division for Ministry. Following conversation, it has been determined that such Letters of Call will be prepared by the Office of the Secretary, upon request, for those who wish to replace their previous Letter of Appointment.

Council Action: Chair Magnus called upon Secretary Lowell G. Almen to introduce the foregoing report, which the Church Council received as information.

Synod Resolutions Directed to the Church Council

Background: Council agenda Exhibit B, Part 1a, contained synod resolutions that were directed to the Church Council from Synod Councils. Council agenda Exhibit B, Part 1b, contained responses to synod resolutions previously referred to units. Recommendations for appropriate referrals also are printed in these exhibits.

Council Action: The Church Council took the following action *en bloc* at the conclusion of this meeting.

EN BLOC   *[CC94.11.98]*

To approve *en bloc* the following disposition of synod resolutions directed to the Church Council:

Section I: Budget Cuts

A. Staffing in the Commission for Multicultural Ministries

Southwestern Washington Synod (1C)

WHEREAS, a ten year commitment was made by the constituting assembly of the ELCA to the people of color and/or language; and

WHEREAS, that commitment was for a minimum of ten (10) percent inclusion in the membership of the ELCA; and

WHEREAS, that commitment created the Commission for Multicultural Ministries with four director positions of ethnic ministries, Asian, African, Hispanic, and Native America, to work with other churchwide organizations to achieve that goal; and

WHEREAS, after six years, the growth factor is 1.5 to 2 percent; and

WHEREAS, as of April 1994 the four director positions of ethnic ministries ceased to exist; therefore be it

RESOLVED, that the Southwestern Washington Synod Assembly direct the Synod Council to forward this resolution to the Church Council to reinstate the four director positions of ethnic ministries of the Commission for Multicultural Ministries and to reinstate the budget for Commission for Multicultural Ministries at 1993 levels.

B. Office of Peace Education

Northeastern Iowa Synod (5F)

WHEREAS, "we of the Evangelical Lutheran Church in America share with people around the globe the longing for a more peaceful and just world"; and

WHEREAS, "the biblical narrative shapes our vision of peace. Baptism gives us our identity as peacemakers and Word and Sacrament nurture and sustain our calling"; and

WHEREAS, "in our time, we face the uncertain futures of nations undergoing vast economic and political changes. The scope, rate and character of these changes significantly redefine how we human beings live, setting conditions for the prospect of peace in a new century"; and

WHEREAS, "it belongs to the church's identity to be a community of peace. God's resolve for peace, we confess, stands behind and before our responsibility for peace." (Peace: God's Gift, Our Calling, First Draft of a Proposed Social Statement of the Evangelical Lutheran Church in America); and

WHEREAS, the ELCA in the Division for Church in Society has eliminated the Office for Peace Education; and

WHEREAS, the Mission90 theme for 1996 is to be peace and justice; therefore be it

RESOLVED, that

1. the ELCA Northeastern Iowa Synod, now assembled, encourage the church to fulfill the mandates coming from is own identity to help create an environment conducive to peace through faithfulness in its life and activities as a community for peace; and

2. congregations clarify and strengthen their understanding of our call to be peacemakers by educating and equipping the faithful to act for peace in all their communities; and

3. members and congregations be encouraged to study, discuss and comment on the first draft of the proposed social statement, "Peace: God's Gift, our Calling"; and

4. the ELCA re-establish the Office of Peace Education to assist, support, and expand all ELCA peacemaking ministries, fulfilling its mission as witness to Jesus Christ who frees us to do justice and give our lives in service; and

5. this resolution be forwarded to the ELCA Church Council and the Division for Church in Society.

C. Staffing for the Commission for Multicultural Ministries

Metropolitan Washington, D.C., Synod (8G)

WHEREAS, the ELCA, in its constituting assembly, committed itself to the creation of an inclusive church; and

WHEREAS, the Commission for Multicultural Ministry was established and staffed with four full-time positions to advocate for and establish partnership with the African American, Asian American, Native American, and Hispanic American communities; and

WHEREAS, the dream of an increase to 10 percent representation of these groups in the membership of the ELCA is far from being realized; and

WHEREAS, in spite of our failure to achieve this stated vision, the positions of directors of African American, Asian American, Native American and Hispanic American ministries have been eliminated in the current churchwide budget; therefore be it

RESOLVED, that the Metropolitan Washington, D.C., Synod Assembly memorialize the ELCA Church Council to restore and fund the positions of directors of African American, Asian American, Native American and Hispanic American ministries within the Commission for Multicultural Ministry in the churchwide body.

D. Specialized Pastoral Care Position

Southeastern Synod (9D)

WHEREAS, the Evangelical Lutheran Church in America has traditionally committed itself to overseeing the service of those persons who professionally demonstrate the church's mission to people whose spiritual needs must be met outside of the parish in specialized ministry settings; and

WHEREAS, the Evangelical Lutheran Church in America and its predecessor church bodies have historically been leaders in providing rostered persons in a diversified number of areas of specialized pastoral ministry settings; and

WHEREAS, the Evangelical Lutheran Church in America has had only one staff person, (Director for Specialized Pastoral Care and Clinical Education,) who directly serves as a liaison, coordinator and administrative link between the Evangelical Lutheran Church in America and the 850 rostered persons of the church engaged in specialized ministry; and

WHEREAS, the Division for Ministry has recently reduced that position to a half-time position without consultation with the Advisory Committee for Specialized Pastoral Care and Clinical Education or any of the 850 rostered persons engaged in ministry in specialized settings in order to seek alternatives to this position reduction; and

WHEREAS, the decentralization and proliferation of any duties of the Director for Specialized Pastoral Care and Clinical Education will greatly defuse and further fragment communication, the connection and relationship of 850 rostered persons in specialized pastoral ministry with the Evangelical Lutheran Church in America; therefore be it

RESOLVED, that the Church Council request the Division for Ministry to restore the position of Director for Specialized Pastoral Care and Clinical Education to a full-time position; and be it further

RESOLVED, that the Church Council request that the Division for Ministry consider a re-evaluation of the Office for Specialized Pastoral Care and Clinical Education which may include the possibility of the formation of grassroots networks of rostered specialized pastoral care persons and bishops within and between synods; the networks would relate to the Evangelical Lutheran Church in America Division for Ministry and the Office for Pastoral Care and Clinical Education through synodical bishops; and be it further

RESOLVED, that the Southeastern Synod Assembly direct the Southeastern Synod Council to forward this resolution to the Church Council for consideration and possible action.

Council Action:

EN BLOC   *[CC94.11.99a]*
To request the Office of the Bishop to share with the Southwestern Washington Synod, Northeastern Iowa Synod, Metropolitan Washington, D.C. Synod, and Southeastern Synod the action of the Church Council relating to budgetary priorities in the development of the 1995 spending plan and the 1996-97 budget proposal, together with other appropriate information relating to these resolutions.

Section II: Social Statements—Part 1: Process for the Development of Social Statements

A.   Adoption of Social Statements
Southern California (West) Synod (2B)

WHEREAS, the release of two press releases, dated October 11, 1993, and October 15, 1993, to the Associated Press, and the release of a copy of the document, "The Church and Human Sexuality: A Lutheran Perspective," to the Associated Press even before the rostered staff and congregations of the ELCA received a copy, created confusion and gave the impression to members of our congregations and our communities that this document was established ELCA policy, rather than a first-draft copy for study and discussion; therefore be it

RESOLVED, that the Southern California (West) Synod Assembly direct the bishop to write a letter to the ELCA Church Council strongly encouraging that the review of the process for handling social statements that is currently being undertaken by the churchwide office be made a high priority, and that, as part of the review, consideration be given to the question of whether and/or when copies of first drafts of social statements should be released to the press or other media.

B.   **Release of Social Statements**
Southwestern Pennsylvania Synod (8B)

WHEREAS, the process by which the study document, "The Church and Human Sexuality: A Lutheran Perspective," was released reflected an alarming lack of accountability, including the disregard for the counsel of the ELCA's Conference of Bishops; and

WHEREAS, the media fiasco surrounding the release of this statement resulted in a woeful distortion and sensationalization; and

WHEREAS, this hindered the church's deliberative process by diverting its attention from the substance of the issue; therefore be it

RESOLVED, that the Southwestern Pennsylvania Synod memorialize the ELCA Churchwide Assembly that in the future any social statement produced by the ELCA be subject to approval for release by the ELCA's Conference of Bishops prior to its release for further study; and be it further

RESOLVED, that the Southwestern Pennsylvania Synod Council be directed to memorialize this resolution to the ELCA Church Council.

C.   **Revisions in Governing Procedures for Social Statements**
Metropolitan Washington, D.C., Synod (8G)

WHEREAS, we underscore that members of the ELCA, before God, are free to exercise their citizenship responsibly without the church speaking for them, just as before God we affirm our freedom to live in the church and practice our faith without the state imposing its will upon our religious life; and

WHEREAS, the ELCA has experienced a time of turmoil and distress because of statements made or proposed by agencies of the ELCA; and

WHEREAS, we come to the church with love, respect and the deepest regard for what Christian community means in our personal and congregational lives; and

WHEREAS, documents have been made available with time lines believed by some to be too short for congregational study and response, or released to the general public and congregations without the study and concurrence of the synodical bishops; and

WHEREAS, the church that is to continue is "the congregation of saints, in which the Gospel is rightly taught and the Sacraments are rightly administered" (*Augsburg Confession, Article VII: Of the Church*); and

WHEREAS, the church which is known as a communion of saints in which "all brothers and sisters" are "so closely united that a closer relationship cannot be conceived," (Martin Luther, *Weimar, I, 756*) is also a community of moral deliberation ("The Church in Society: A Lutheran Perspective); and

WHEREAS, central to the church are its "preaching, teaching, the sacraments, Scripture, and 'mutual conversation and consolation'" among the members of its congregations (*The Church in Society and Smalcald Articles, Part III, Art. IV*); and

WHEREAS, the Gospel partnership between congregations, synodical bishops and the national church must be constant and preserved for the church to exist as a viable institution; and

WHEREAS, the ELCA continues to affirm the separation of church and state in a manner that leads us to "work with civil authorities in areas of mutual endeavor, maintaining institutional separation of church and state in a relation of functional interaction" (ELCA 4.03.); therefore be it

RESOLVED, that the Metropolitan Washington, D.C., Synod memorialize the Church Council to review the ELCA's organizational structure, methods of operation and policies and procedures contained in "Social Statements in the Evangelical Lutheran Church in America" and that the following guidelines be affirmed or established for conversation, study and deliberation in the ELCA:

1.   Approved social statements and other position papers that inform the conscience or shape the life of the ELCA shall be developed by an orderly study process that deliberately incorporates participation by congregations and synodical bishops.

2.   Public advocacy, when done within the limits of positions held in the various documents and statements of the ELCA, shall be done with the acknowledgement that significant disagreement within the church, which may be valid before God, may be present on any public issue.

3.   The statements, studies, and proposed actions of any unit, task force, or study group of the church affecting the life and ministry of congregations shall be reviewed formally by the Conference of Bishops and serious consideration shall be given to remedial action for any concerns which they might express. If a majority of the Conference of Bishops does not concur

with the proposed statement, study or action, the responsible unit, task force, or study group shall diligently make every reasonable effort to overcome these objections before proceeding.

4. The variety of the roles played by congregations, synods, and the ELCA, (including its assemblies, councils, offices, divisions, departments, commissions, and other agencies) shall be examined so that the partnership of all expressions of the church has an identifiable and specific role and function in moral deliberations, and so that the unity of a large a complex religious community can be acknowledged and strengthened.

Council Action:

EN BLOC   *[CC94.11.99b]*
To refer these resolutions on the process for development of social statements from Southern California (West) Synod, Southwestern Pennsylvania Synod, and Metropolitan Washington, D.C., Synod to the Division for Church in Society; and

To request that the division provide directly to the synods information relating to the process for release of subsequent drafts of a statement on human sexuality and plans for a review of the overall process of social statement development, as affirmed by the Church Council.

Section II: Social Statements—Part 2: Draft Statement on the Church and Human Sexuality
A.   The Draft Statement on the Church and Human Sexuality
Western North Dakota Synod (3A)
WHEREAS, the constitution of the Evangelical Lutheran Church in America accepts ". . . the canonical Scriptures of the Old and New Testaments as the inspired word of God and the authoritative source and norm for its proclamation, faith and life" (ELCA 2:03.); and

WHEREAS, the historical teaching of the Christian Church and the ELCA through its inherited statements from the American Lutheran Church and the Lutheran Church in America on the issue of sexuality, based on Genesis 2, Matthew 19, 1 Corinthians 6 and 7, and other passages, supports sexual expression within heterosexual marriage and abstinence outside of marriage; and

WHEREAS, the draft document entitled "The Church and Human Sexuality: A Lutheran Perspective" produced by the Division for Church in Society obscures, relativizes, and occasionally reverses the plain meaning of the Scripture, and departs from the historic teaching of the Christian Church in matters of human sexuality as stated above; and

WHEREAS, the Conference of Bishops recognizes that there is no basis in Scripture or tradition for the blessing of a homosexual marriage; therefore be it

RESOLVED, that the Western North Dakota Synod in Assembly instruct its Synod Council to request the ELCA Church Council Executive Committee to require the Division for Church in Society to be accountable to Scripture, tradition, and confessional documents in the second draft of the document, "The Church and Human Sexuality: A Lutheran Perspective"; and be it further

RESOLVED, that the second draft of the document be distributed by the Division for Church in Society to congregations six months prior to the 1995 Churchwide Assembly, and be it further

RESOLVED, that the Western North Dakota Synod in Assembly adopt the following statement as it summary of teaching on human sexuality:

God created people male and female and provided for them to become one within the context of marriage. Heterosexual marriage one woman, one man — faithfulness within marriage; abstinence outside of marriage — these constitute the Christian standard. When we fall short we are invited to repent, receive the forgiveness of God, and amend our lives. As members of the body of Christ we are called to daily repentance for all have sinned and fall short of the glory of God.
and be it further

RESOLVED, that this assembly instruct the synod council to request the ELCA Church Council to refuse to submit to the 1995 Churchwide Assembly any statement on human sexuality which does not reflect the aforesaid summary of teaching; and be it further

RESOLVED, that this assembly request the 1995 Churchwide Assembly to reject any statement on human sexuality which does not reflect the aforesaid summary of teaching.

B.   Process for the Development of the Human Sexuality Statement
Northern Illinois Synod (5B)
WHEREAS, the first draft of "The Church and Human Sexuality: A Lutheran Perspective" generated negative publicity because of an ill-timed news release; and

WHEREAS, 64 percent of lay responses and 42 percent of clergy responses to the first draft are negative, (according to an article in the June 1994 issue of *The Lutheran*); and

WHEREAS, a great benefit of the process of developing a social statement is to encourage congregational members to explore the issues in dialogue with one another; and

WHEREAS, the current process approved by the Church Council calls for a second draft to be released on November 1, 1994, and responses are due by January 31, 1995; therefore be it

RESOLVED, that the Northern Illinois Synod express appreciation to the Division for Church in Society for undertaking the process of developing a social statement on human sexuality and for the opportunity to dialogue that has resulted; and be it further

RESOLVED, that the Northern Illinois Synod request the ELCA Church Council to revise the process for development of a social statement on human sexuality so that congregations and individuals have more time to engage in dialogue, reflect and respond to the second draft and develop greater consensus; and be it further

RESOLVED, that the churchwide office develops and recommends study materials for discussion regarding the second draft of the human sexuality statement; and be it further

RESOLVED, that the final proposal of a social statement on the church and human sexuality come no sooner than the 1997 Churchwide Assembly.

C.   The Draft Statement on the Church and Human Sexuality
Northwest Synod of Wisconsin (5H)
WHEREAS, the Conference of Bishops' Committee on Theological and Ethical Concerns has carefully studied the first draft of the ELCA proposed statement on human sexuality and has agreed upon a response which states:

The "gift of sexual expression finds its highest intended fulfillment in heterosexual, monogamous marriage;" and

The study's three characterizations of the ELCA responses to homosexuality are "neither accurate nor helpful;" and

"As a church we have neither a definitive word on the biological and/or behavioral origins or nature of homosexuality, nor are we able to say with unanimity what the church's faithful response should be to persons who understand their homosexual orientation to be a given;" and

WHEREAS, the statement of this committee is both positive and reflective of the response of many lay and clergy members of the church; therefore be it

RESOLVED, that the Northwest Synod of Wisconsin endorses this response and memorializes the ELCA Church Council to delay any action on a human sexuality statement until the rewritten draft has once again been submitted to the congregations for their further study and response.

D. The Draft Statement on the Church and Human Sexuality
Northeastern Ohio Synod (6E)

WHEREAS, the first draft of the social statement, "The Church and Human Sexuality: A Lutheran Perspective," deals with delicate issues and has evoked such strong response; and

WHEREAS, the Evangelical Lutheran Church in America has been forthright and intentional about soliciting a grass roots response from the people of the ELCA; and

WHEREAS, there has been a ground swell of emotion and response to the issues confronted in the first draft document; and

WHEREAS, the ELCA task force which composed this document, together with the leadership of ELCA, has stated clearly their intent to incorporate the response(s) in the evaluation of the first draft and utilize this feedback in the subsequent draft; and

WHEREAS, the ELCA has established a rather narrow time frame, namely, November 1994 until December 15, 1994, for the purpose of evaluating responses and incorporating this feedback into the second draft; and

WHEREAS, the timing of the evaluation and composition period comes during the holiday seasons of Thanksgiving, Advent, and Christmas; and

WHEREAS, this vital issue merits our full consideration and attention; therefore be it

RESOLVED, that the Northeastern Ohio Synod meeting in tri-synodical assembly, June 23-25, 1994, in Columbus, Ohio, encourage the ELCA Church Council to extend this time frame to January 30, 1995, to allow congregations a more adequate opportunity for evaluation and response.

E. The Draft Statement on the Church and Human Sexuality
North Carolina Synod (9B)

WHEREAS, the use of media promotion in the release of the first draft of the statement, "The Church and Human Sexuality," has given a widespread public image of the ELCA as a sexually permissive church; and

WHEREAS, both the Conference of Bishops and the ELCA Church Council have recognized the task force's questionable use of Scripture as a factor in an acknowledged impairment of trust among the ELCA constituency; and

WHEREAS, the written response to the ELCA draft statement on "The Church and Human Sexuality" by members of the faculty of the Luther Northwestern Seminary has received wide support from ELCA college and seminary faculty members, synod bishops, and many lay people and pastors, including former LCA and ALC bishops; therefore be it

RESOLVED that the paragraph in the Luther Northwestern response which states and affirms the basic biblical teachings on marriage and sexual relations, namely that:

> God created people male and female, and provided for the marriage relationship in which two may become one. A publicly declared, legally binding marriage between one woman and one man remains the one appropriate place for genital sexual relations. Heterosexual marriage, faithfulness within marriage, abstinence outside of marriage— these constitute the Christian standard. When we fall short, we are invited to repent, receive the forgiveness of God, and amend our lives.

be affirmed by the North Carolina Synod and commended to the ELCA Division for Church in Society as the basic orientation in

the production of a position statement on human sexuality; and be it further

RESOLVED that the North Carolina Synod Assembly direct the Synod Council to forward this resolution to the Church Council for consideration and possible action to use the same statement as the standard for advocacy and judgment in matters related to human sexuality until such time as a more complete statement can be formulated and adopted by the Churchwide Assembly of the ELCA.

F. The Draft Statement on the Church and Human Sexuality
Florida-Bahamas Synod (9E)

WHEREAS, the first draft of the social statement, "The Church and Human Sexuality: A Lutheran Perspective," has engendered debate in and outside the church; and

WHEREAS, debate is healthy as the significant issue of human sexuality and its relation to the Christian faith and ethics is explored; and

WHEREAS, discussion gives the church the opportunity to restate and reaffirm issues of faith and ethics; and

WHEREAS, the Florida-Bahamas Synod of the ELCA affirms the canonical Scripture of the Old and New Testaments as the inspired Word of God and the authoritative source and norm of its proclamation, faith, and life, as stated in the ELCA constitution; therefore be it

RESOLVED, that we affirm that the Gospel of forgiveness and salvation by God's grace through faith in Jesus Christ is inclusive and is for all people regardless of gender, race, class, or sexual orientation; and be it further

RESOLVED, that we affirm marriage as a covenant relationship of fidelity and commitment between male and female; and be it further

RESOLVED, that we affirm the standard of sexual ethics to be fidelity in marriage and chastity outside marriage; and be it further

RESOLVED, that the Florida-Bahamas Synod in Assembly direct the Synod Council to forward this resolution to the Church Council for proper referral and disposition under the bylaws and continuing resolutions of this church.

Council Action:

EN BLOC   **[CC94.11.99c]**

To refer these resolutions on the draft statement on the church and human sexuality from the Western North Dakota Synod, Northern Illinois Synod, Northwest Synod of Wisconsin, Northeastern Ohio Synod, North Carolina Synod, and Florida-Bahamas Synod to the Division for Church in Society; and

To request the Division for Church in Society to convey to the Western North Dakota Synod, Northern Illinois Synod, Northwest Synod of Wisconsin, Northeastern Ohio Synod, North Carolina Synod, and Florida-Bahamas Synod the action taken on this matter by the board of the Division for Church in Society, the Conference of Bishops and the Church Council.

Section III: Accountability for Policies and Public Statements
A. Accountability for Policies and Public Statements
Metropolitan Washington, D.C., Synod (8G)

WHEREAS, the Church, including the ELCA, has the "treasure of the Gospel "in earthen vessels" (2 Corinthians 4:7) and we, therefore, acknowledge the institutional church as fallible; and

WHEREAS, we are cautioned by our Lord to "be wise as serpents and innocent as doves" (Matthew 10:16) in making our way as Christ's witnesses in the world; and

WHEREAS, we have agreed to arrive at positions to guide "this portion of Christ's Church through participatory processes of moral deliberation," (The Church in Society: A Lutheran Perspective); and

WHEREAS, significant distress, confusion and disruption has been caused within congregations and among the members of our church by the manner in which statements have been released to our congregations and to the world on behalf of the ELCA; and

WHEREAS, we are committed to the judgment that the Gospel provides its counsel to us through "mutual conversation and consolation" (Smalcald Article, Part III, Art IV.). We are led to offer the following resolution to assist the ELCA, its synods, congregations and various agencies, departments, divisions and commissions to promulgate social statements and other policies in a way that ensures thoughtful consideration, provides accountability, and promotes responsibility; therefore be it

RESOLVED, that the Metropolitan Washington, D.C., Synod in Assembly memorialize the Church Council to establish the following policy:

Whenever a unit of this church desires to release to the public statements in which are contained generalizations that characterize the Evangelical Lutheran Church in America as holding one or another opinion or position, such general characterizations be released only after verification by the bishop. This same process and level of accountability for the process shall apply to the bishops regarding statements released by synodical committees and other agencies.

Council Action:

EN BLOC   **[CC94.11.99d]**

To refer this resolution of the Metropolitan Washington, D.C., Synod on release of and accountability for policies and public statements jointly to the Division for Church in Society and the Office of the Bishop; and

To request that the Division for Church in Society and the Office of the Bishop bring a report and/or recommendation to the April 1995 meeting of the Church Council.

Section IV: Election Procedures for Churchwide Offices
A.   Election Procedures for Churchwide Officers
Rocky Mountain Synod (2E)

WHEREAS, the ELCA constitution states, "The Church Council shall establish an ongoing process to review the function and the structural organization of this church and to develop recommendations for changes" (ELCA 5.01.e.); and

WHEREAS, the ELCA constitution states, "This church shall function as people of God through congregations, synods, and the churchwide organization, all of which shall be interdependent. Each part, while fully the church, recognizes that it is not the whole church and therefore lives in a partnership relationship with others" (ELCA 8.11.); and

WHEREAS, the size of the ELCA in both membership and geography makes it imperative that constant attention be given to strengthening relationships between the various parts of the church and between the churchwide organization and the membership; and

WHEREAS, throughout its brief history the ELCA has experienced a significant shortfall in financial support as compared to initial projections, and has suffered from an oft-expressed perception of its membership that it is distant from the congregations and the concerns of the membership; and

WHEREAS, the interdependent character of this church might be strengthened, and the sense of relationship enhanced, through wider participation in the selection of persons to serve in elected positions, such as members of boards and committees; and

WHEREAS, all who serve in such capacities, regardless of the means by which they have come to such service, are to regard themselves as servants of Christ and representatives of the whole people of God; and

WHEREAS, the perception of a "top-down" church is increased by the holding of an excessive number of elections at churchwide assemblies, a task which many voting members find difficult and frustrating; therefore be it

RESOLVED, that the Rocky Mountain Synod Assembly direct the Rocky Mountain Synod Council to forward this resolution to the ELCA Church Council to review the election procedures of the Evangelical Lutheran Church in America and consider amendments to the documents of this church with a goal of minimizing the number of persons elected at churchwide assemblies and expanding the number of persons elected at the synod level, and bring its recommendations to the 1997 Churchwide Assembly.

Council Action:

EN BLOC   **[CC94.11.99e]**

To refer this resolution of the Rocky Mountain Synod on election procedures for churchwide officers to the Executive Committee of the Church Council; and

To request that a report and/or recommendation be brought to the Church Council at its April 1995 meeting.

Section V: Representational Principles
A.   Representational Principles
Western North Dakota (3A)

WHEREAS, the 1990 census shows the population of the United States to be 80.3 percent white and 19.7 percent non-white (0.8 percent Native American, 12.1 percent Black, and 6.8 percent other); and

WHEREAS, the 1990 census shows the population of North Dakota (638,800) to be 94.57 percent white (604,142), and 5.4 percent non-white (4.06 percent Native American [25,917], 0.55 percent Black [3,524], and 0.82 percent other [5,217]); and

WHEREAS, this same 1990 census shows that the Western North Dakota Synod is 93.8 percent white and further that more than half of the counties in the synod are 99 percent (or higher) white, and further that only 4 counties have a white population of less than 90 percent; and

WHEREAS, according to the 1990 census figures, the people of North Dakota are already 75.9 percent adherents of a church; therefore be it

RESOLVED, that the Western North Dakota in Assembly instruct its Western North Dakota Synod Council to request the Church Council of the Evangelical Lutheran Church in America to look again at its goals for 10 percent minority membership by 1997 in its synod assemblies, councils, committees, boards and/or other organizational units considering the demographics of some synods, and the Church Council report back to the synods by December 31, 1994, and allow such synods as have similar demographics to drop sections *S6.04. and S6.04.A87. of their synod constitutions and to amend the ELCA constitution to reflect such circumstances.

B.   Representational Principles
Northeastern Minnesota Synod (3E)

WHEREAS, the constitution of the Evangelical Lutheran Church in America in 10.41.01.c. requires that lay voting members selected to represent their congregations at the Synod Assembly must be equally divided on the basis of gender, one male and one female; and

WHEREAS, section †S7.21.c. of the Northeastern Minnesota synod constitution requires each congregation to elect one male and one female voting member to the Synod Assembly; and

WHEREAS, it is sometimes not possible for congregations to find one person of each gender to represent them, thus causing them to be in violation of †S7.21., or be unrepresented; therefore be it

RESOLVED, that the Synod Council of the Northeastern Minnesota Synod request the Church Council of the Evangelical Lutheran Church in America to amend section 10.41.01.c. of the ELCA bylaws and section †S7.21.c. of the Model Constitution for Synods by adding "normally" after the words "one of whom" so as to read, "the synod, one of whom normally shall be male and one of whom normally shall be female," and forward it to the 1995 ELCA Churchwide Assembly for adoption.

C. Representational Principles
Northern Great Lakes Synod (5G)

WHEREAS, the 1995 ELCA Churchwide Assembly will revisit the matter of multicultural representation policies currently in practice; and

WHEREAS, the Northern Great Lakes Synod and its predecessors have long and often expressed support for multicultural inclusion in decision making at all levels of our church; and

WHEREAS, in S.6.04. of the Northern Great Lakes Synod Constitution, the Synod Council is required to insure that at least 60 percent of the members of the synod assemblies, councils, committees, boards, and other organizational units shall be lay persons; that, as nearly as possible, 50 percent of the lay members of the assemblies, councils, committees, boards, or other organizational units shall be female and 50 percent shall be male, and that where possible, the representation of ordained ministers shall be both male and female; and also to reach a minimum goal that 10 percent of the members of its assemblies, councils, committees, boards, or other organizational units, be persons of color and/or persons whose primary language is other than English; and

WHEREAS, one of the Northern Great Lakes Synod's partnership organizations, the Lutheran Human Relations Association, has encouraged widespread communication with churchwide leaders and the 1995 Churchwide Assembly urging continuation of broad and inclusive multicultural representation at all levels of our church; therefore be it

RESOLVED, that the Northern Great Lakes Synod Assembly encourage the ELCA Church Council to recommend to the 1995 ELCA Churchwide Assembly to continue its broad representation policies.

D. Repeal of Gender Representative Requirements for Synod Assemblies
Allegheny Synod (8C)

WHEREAS, St. Paul has written in Galatians 3:28, "There is neither Jew nor Greek, there is neither slave nor free, there is neither male nor female; for you are all one in Christ Jesus; and

WHEREAS, this statement by St. Paul declares our unity in Christ Jesus, and that while ethnic, social, and gender differences do not vanish, being in Christ makes these differences before God irrelevant; and

WHEREAS, current requirements in ELCA governing documents (ELCA 10.41.01.c. and S7.21.c.) may restrict congregations from electing voting members best able to serve the congregation; therefore be it

RESOLVED, that the Allegheny Synod memorialize the 1995 ELCA Churchwide Assembly to amend sections 10.41.01.c. and S7.21.c. to delete all references to "males" and "females"; and be it further

RESOLVED, that the Allegheny Synod send a recommendation to the ELCA Church Council to amend sections 10.41.01.c. and S7.21.c. to delete all references to "males" and "females."

E. Repeal of Representational Principles
Allegheny Synod (8C)

WHEREAS, the constitution of the Evangelical Lutheran Church in America states that "this church accepts the canonical Scriptures of the Old and New Testaments as the inspired Word of God and the authoritative source and norm of its proclamation, faith and life" (ELCA 2.03.); and

WHEREAS, the Holy Scriptures unequivocally state that "There is neither Jew nor Greek, there is neither slave nor free, there is neither male nor female; for you are all one in Christ Jesus" (Galatians 3:28); and again, "Here there cannot be Greek and Jew, circumcised and uncircumcised, barbarian, Scythian, slave, freeman, but Christ is all and in all" (Colossians 3:11); and in other places also teach us that the body of Christ is not to be divided into separate and competing groups based upon the distinctions of worldly society, but is to be united in lowliness, meekness, patience, and the unity of the spirit and the bond of peace (Ephesians 4:1-6); and

WHEREAS, the Holy Scriptures further teach us that the individual participation in the structures and ministries of the church should be based upon the gifts of the Spirit (Ephesians 4:11-16, 1 Corinthians 12:4-30); and

WHEREAS, in the church we are called to represent not ourselves, but Christ who is Lord of the Church (Philippians 1:3-11); therefore be it

RESOLVED, that the Allegheny Synod memorialize the 1995 ELCA Churchwide Assembly to strike from its constitution sections 5.01.f. and 5.01.g. (which mandate the "quota system" throughout the church,) while continuing to strive for the inclusion of all peoples at all levels of service in the church; and be it further

RESOLVED, that the Allegheny Synod send a recommendation to the ELCA Church Council to strike from the ELCA constitution sections 5.01.f. and 5.01.g. (which mandate the "quota system" throughout the church,) while continuing to strive for the inclusion of all peoples at all levels of service in the church.

F. Representation of Lay Voting Members from Congregations
South Dakota Synod (3C)

Since there are some congregations in the South Dakota synod who each year are legitimately unable to meet the gender provision [found in ELCA bylaw 10.41.01.c.], the South Dakota Synod Council requests the ELCA Church Council to recommend the revision of constitutional documents to the Churchwide Assembly so that synod documents could be amended allowing for the granting of occasional waivers when congregations have compelling reasons for not meeting the requirement.

Council Action:

EN BLOC   [CC94.11.99f]

To request the secretary of the Evangelical Lutheran Church in America to inform the Western North Dakota Synod, South Dakota Synod, Northeastern Minnesota Synod, Northern Great Lakes Synod, and Allegheny Synod of the process currently being carried out by the Church Council to review the ELCA's representational principles as mandated by the 1993 Churchwide Assembly; and

To refer these resolutions of the Western North Dakota Synod, South Dakota Synod, Northeastern Minnesota Synod, Northern Great Lakes Synod, and Allegheny Synod on representational principles to the Executive

Committee of the Church Council, as it develops a report/recommendation for the 1995 Churchwide Assembly

Section VI: Immigration
A. Immigration
Metropolitan Washington, D.C., (8G)

WHEREAS, our Hebrew ancestors were encouraged to practice hospitality by the Scriptures which counseled, "For the Lord your God . . . renders justice for the orphans and the widows, and befriends the aliens, feeding and clothing them, so you, must befriend the aliens, for you were once aliens yourselves" (Dt.10:17-19); and

WHEREAS, for generations, our churches have faithfully welcomed and assisted newcomers, including refugees, asylum-seekers and immigrants to the United States, and, by doing so, have assisted and identified with them on their difficult journeys, while recalling our own origins; and

WHEREAS, respect for people and their human dignity, family relationships, the strength arising from diverse cultures, and the commitment to the common good for our society are placed in jeopardy when we too easily reject the sojourners, strangers, and aliens in our midst; and

WHEREAS, we recognize the need for and support the development of appropriate and fair immigration control measures; and

WHEREAS, we believe that documented refugees and immigrants in the United States should have access to essential services without which they would experience physical, economic and social jeopardy; therefore be it

RESOLVED, that the Metropolitan Washington, D.C., Synod urge its congregations to strive to make their communities models of social justice by serving as advocates of hospitality; and be it further

RESOLVED, that the Metropolitan Washington, D.C., Synod urge its congregations actively to oppose measures which would curtail health care, education, welfare and other human services to refugees and immigrants, as follows:

Health Care Reform: Support full coverage for all immigrants and refugees as an essential feature of a national health care program which provides genuine access and supports existing limited emergency services to undocumented persons.

Welfare Reform: Strongly oppose efforts to eliminate benefits for all residents and refugees in any financing plan for welfare reform and urge that services to refugees be developed within the traditional public assistance (AFDC) system, giving special attention to the transitional needs of refugees.

Educational Benefits: Advocate upholding current mandated policy that primary and secondary educational benefits be provided to all children.

and be it further

RESOLVED, that the Metropolitan Washington, D.C., Synod advocate the protection of asylum-seekers who come to United States shores seeking protection from human rights abuses and violence in their homelands and for any asylum system that allows prompt and fair consideration of asylum claims; and be it further

RESOLVED, that the Metropolitan Washington, D.C., Synod memorialize the Church Council of the Evangelical Lutheran Church in America to advocate, through the Lutheran Office for Governmental Affairs and Lutheran Social Services of the National Capitol Area, for the development of a citizenship program that invites newcomers to complete the process of becoming full participants in United States' society, and that supports birthright citizenship as a continuing part of our United States' constitution.

Council Action:

EN BLOC   *[CC94.11.99g]*

To refer this resolution of the Metropolitan Washington, D.C., Synod on immigration to the Division for Church in Society, and through it to Lutheran Immigration and Refugee Service, as they continue their ongoing advocacy in this area.

To request that the Division for Church in Society respond directly to the synod with information relating to the synod's request.

Section VII: International Concerns
A. Conflict in Former Yugoslavia
Southeastern Minnesota Synod (3I)

WHEREAS, compelling evidence exists to indicate that non-combatants caught in the conflict in the former Yugoslavia are being targeted, both accidentally and deliberately, by uniformed military personnel; therefore be it

RESOLVED, that the Southeastern Minnesota synod encourage Bishop Glenn Nycklemoe to communicate with the leaders of all major Christian faith communities of the former Yugoslavia that in the name of Jesus Christ this faith community, ELCA Southeastern Minnesota Synod, encourages such leaders to instruct all military personnel under their guidance to work to assure the safety of, and to refrain from targeting, any and all non-combatants caught in the conflict; and be it further

RESOLVED, that the Southeastern Minnesota Synod memorialize the Church Council of the ELCA to encourage the bishop of the ELCA to communicate a similar message to the leaders of the major Christian faith communities of the former Yugoslavia.

Council Action:

EN BLOC   *[CC94.11.99h]*

To refer this resolution of the Southeastern Minnesota Synod on the conflict in the former Yugoslavia to the Division for Global Mission in consultation with the Office of the Bishop; and

To request that the Division for Global Mission respond directly to the Southeastern Minnesota Synod on this matter.

B. Relationship with Cuba
Metropolitan Washington, D.C., Synod (8G)

WHEREAS, our faith calls us to love our neighbor and to work for justice, peace and reconciliation among all peoples; and

WHEREAS, the economic embargo imposed by the United States is causing great suffering in Cuba, especially for children and the elderly; and

WHEREAS, the ELCA's "A churchwide Blueprint for Action on Central America and Caribbean Concerns" states as goals in section 3:

1. oppose the politicization of humanitarian assistance in the region and advocate its unrestricted delivery (1.4,); and
2. advocate the normalization of diplomatic relations between the U.S. and other nations in the region where this is not the case (1.6.); and
3. listen and respond to the voices from the churches in the region (2.1.); and
4. promote and develop mutually supportive relationships between the Lutheran churches in the region and those in the U.S., and promote, between churches in the region and other partners in the region, self-sufficient, interdependent efforts and relationships among the churches and peoples (2.3.); and

WHEREAS, the representatives of the Lutheran World Federation, the Council of Churches of Canada, the National Council of Churches of Christ in the U.S.A., the Caribbean Council of Churches, the Latin American Council of Churches and the Ecumenical Council of Cuba, in their meeting in Havana in December 1991 called for the lifting of the U.S. embargo against Cuba, the provisions of humanitarian help (especially food and medicines), and promotion of dialogue and exchanges of people and information between the churches in Cuba and in our country; and

WHEREAS, Evangelical Church of the Lutheran Confession in Cuba, while experiencing growth and excitement in ministry, is also calling for a lifting of the U.S.> embargo which is cause for s much pain among the people; therefore be it

RESOLVED, that congregations of the Metropolitan Washington, D.C., Synod recognize and be encouraged to support the Lutheran congregations in Cuba through prayer, information-sharing and material support through the ELCA Division for Global Mission; and be it further

RESOLVED, that congregations be urged to participate in the current humanitarian appeal of Lutheran world Relief/Church World Service to send shipments of medical and food supplies to Cuba through Lutheran World Relief; and be it further

RESOLVED, that the Metropolitan Washington, D.C., Synod urge congregations to become familiar with the ELCA's "A Churchwide Blueprint for Action on Central America and Caribbean Concerns" and the goals stated therein; and be it further

RESOLVED, that the Metropolitan Washington, D.C., Synod memorialize the Church Council of the ELCA to forward to the appropriate churchwide unit(s) the appeal of this synod that the Cuban government conduct its affairs informed by full respect for the human rights of all Cuban citizens and engage in meaningful dialogue with human rights organizations on the island; and be it further

RESOLVED, that the Metropolitan Washington, D.C., Synod:
1. Memorialize the Church Council of the ELCA, through the appropriate divisions and programs of the church, to work toward ending the United States embargo against Cuba, and to seek further reconciliation and the establishment of normal relations between the United States and Cuba; and
2. Urge all members of the synod, through letters to congressional and delegate offices, to encourage the lifting of this embargo for humanitarian purposes and to encourage steps, to whatever degree possible, toward normalization of the relationships of the United States and Cuba.

Council Action:

EN BLOC   [CC94.11.99i]

To refer the resolution of the Metropolitan Washington, D.C., Synod on relationships with Cuba to the Division for Church in Society for a response directly to the synod.

Section VIII: Children and Families
A.   The Church's Ministry with Children and Families
Northwestern Ohio Synod (6D)

WHEREAS, America's children are this nation's most valuable resource; and

WHEREAS, the very core of support and nurture for children is the family unit, whatever its structure; and

WHEREAS, the effects of much of modern American culture and society (i.e., violent crime, racism, teen pregnancy, substance abuse, materialistic message of media,) upon the family unit seems to be destruction, rather than support and encouragement; and

WHEREAS, the message of the Gospel compels us to view ourselves as a community which works for unity, health, and mutual growth in Jesus Christ in all relationships including families: "Bear with one another charitably, in complete selflessness, gentleness, and patience. Do all you can to preserve the unity of the Spirit by the peace that binds you together ... If we live by the truth and in love, we shall grow in all ways into Christ, who is the head by whom the whole body is fitted and joined together, every member adding its own strength, for each separate part to work according to its function. And so the body grows until it has built itself up in love" (Ephesians 4:2-3, 16-16); and

WHEREAS, many parents and caregivers who strive to live their Christian faith and impart Christian values to their children are seeking support from their churches in the forms of (but not limited to) reading material, family Bible studies and devotions, edifying television programs, parenting support groups, development of mentors for parents and youth, etc.,; therefore be it

RESOLVED, that the Northwestern Ohio Synod of the Evangelical Lutheran Church in America gathered in assembly request that the Church Council of the Evangelical Lutheran Church in America commit the ELCA to a churchwide emphasis on the family, the purpose of which would be to continually and consistently communicate with and stimulate all members of this church and the greater United States society to work for the values and priorities that support and nurture children and families; and be it further

RESOLVED, that the Northwestern Ohio Synod in assembly request that the Church Council direct all divisions and boards which develop and offer information and support materials for Christian parenting and family life to promote them in a unified publication for dissemination through a variety of methods to the membership of this church; and be it further

RESOLVED, that the Northwestern Ohio Synod in assembly publicly affirm the work of the Women of the Evangelical Lutheran Church in America in its triennial emphasis on "Women and Children in Poverty."

Council Action:

EN BLOC   [CC94.11.99j]

To refer this resolution of the Northwestern Ohio Synod on the church's ministry with children and families to the Division for Church in Society; and

To request that the Division for Church in Society, with other churchwide units, provide a report and/or recommendation on this matter to the Church Council at its April 1994 meeting.

Section X: Pension Plan
A.   Cost of Medical Insurance for Persons Who Retire Before Age 65
Southwestern Texas Synod

WHEREAS, the cost of medical insurance for an ELCA Pension Plan member on roster status and spouse, who retire before age 65, is $661.00 per month; and

WHEREAS, the maximum cost of any active member and spouse, regardless of salary, is $597.00 per month in 1994; and

WHEREAS, John Kapanke of the Board of Pensions states that the Benefits Committee discussed this issue and decided not to do anything about it; and

WHEREAS, he stated that the only way to proceed with any attempt to change this would be through the Church Council or the Conference of Bishops or by resolution to the ELCA; therefore be it

RESOLVED, that the Southwestern Texas Synod, in assembly, urge the Board of Pensions of the ELCA to change this inequity; and be it further

RESOLVED, that the Southwestern Texas Synod Assembly direct the Synod Council to forward this resolution to the Church Council for consideration and action.

Council Action:

EN BLOC   [CC94.11.99k]

To refer this resolution of the Southwestern Texas Synod on the cost of medical insurance for persons who retire before age 65 to the Board of Pensions; and

To request the Board of Pensions to provide a report and/or recommendation to the Church Council at its April 1995 meeting.

Resolutions from Synods
Previously Referred to Churchwide Units

A. ELCA Medical and Dental Benefits Plan
Alaska Synod (1A)

Background: The following resolution of the Alaska Synod on the ELCA Medical and Dental Benefits Plan was transmitted to the Church Council's Executive Committee at its November 22, 1993, meeting:

WHEREAS, each ELCA congregation provides health insurance for pastors throughout the Evangelical Lutheran Church in America; and

WHEREAS, since the merger, the cost to congregations has risen substantially every year; and

WHEREAS, benefits have decreased and deductibles increased; and

WHEREAS, the Board of Pensions refuses to see the rural Alaskan situation as being different from other areas like Minneapolis; and

WHEREAS, the Board of Pensions no longer allows coverage for travel from rural (remote) locations to Anchorage, Fairbanks, or Seattle for emergency or for necessary medical care by specialists; and

WHEREAS, it seems the Board of Pensions operates independently and without any real accountability to the rest of the Evangelical Lutheran Church in America; and

WHEREAS, this trend in cost increases is becoming a burden to small struggling congregations; and

WHEREAS, in many cases pastors in small struggling congregations who are likely to already be below synod-recommended salary guidelines are having to forego salary increases so that the congregation can meet the medical premium increases; therefore, be it

RESOLVED, that the Alaska Synod request that the Alaska Synod Council transmit this resolution to the ELCA Church Council Executive Committee for referral in order to set in motion a means to completely review the current policies of the ELCA Board of Pensions; and to do a careful reevaluation and reconsideration of its policies pertaining to Alaska and other rural (remote) areas of the church with respect to higher medical costs and transportation for medical care; and be it further

RESOLVED, that the Alaska Synod request the Alaska Synod Council to request that the ELCA Executive Committee of the ELCA Church Council put in motion a means to reconsider the concept that the Board of Pensions be independent from any control of the church body of the Evangelical Lutheran Church in America.

The Executive Committee voted:

To refer this resolution of the Alaska Synod on health insurance for pastors to the Board of Pensions for a response to the April 1994 meeting of the Church Council (EC93.11.27.1.)

The following response from the Board of Pensions follows conversation between the Board and representatives of the Alaska Synod on matters relating to the ELCA Medical and Dental Benefits Plan.

Through its consultant, Towers Perrin, the Board of Pensions has researched the services provided by other insurance carriers in the state of Alaska. Based on those inquiries, it has been confirmed that: 1) there is a significant diversity in the charge patterns of physicians throughout the state, and 2) there is a notable lack of reliable physician data in the outlying areas. As a result of the fact that other insurance carriers do differentiate

in the administration of benefits in Alaska versus the "lower 48" states, the Board of Pensions is reviewing the application of the Reasonable and Customary data applied to Alaska.

Reimbursement of travel expenses incurred by plan members who receive services either in urban areas of Alaska or in Seattle also has been a major issue for plan members in Alaska. Currently, the ELCA plan provides for coverage of air ambulance to the nearest facility that can treat the patient's condition in the event of an emergency situation. Since the Board of Pensions will utilize Healthmarc as its pre-certification vendor effective January 1, 1995, non-emergency travel expenses will be managed through this pre-certification process. Therefore it is possible that some non-emergency travel expenses could be reimbursed if care that must be provided is not available in the local community. Approval will be accomplished on a case-by-case basis as part of the pre-certification process.

Conversations with the bishop of the Alaska Synod are scheduled to take place during the week of October 3, 1994, at the Conference of Bishops meetings in Door County, Wisconsin.

Council Action:

EN BLOC   *[CC94.11.99l]*

To request that the Board of Pensions provide an update of its response to the concerns raised by the Alaska Synod to the April 1995 meeting of the Church Council.

B. Pension Plan Retirement Pay Structure
Montana Synod (1F)

The following resolution of the Montana Synod on retirement pay structure was transmitted to the Church Council at its December 12, 3-5, 1993, meeting:

RESOLVED, that the Montana Synod, assembled June 11-13, 1993, recommend to the ELCA Church Council, in consultation with the ELCA Board of Pensions, to study and make recommendations for a pension plan retirement pay structure which would not penalize retired pastors who serve under a Letter of Call, and accomplish these tasks and report to the 1995 Churchwide Assembly.

The Church Council voted:

To refer the resolution of the Montana Synod on retirement pay structure to the Board of Pensions and request that a report and/or recommendation be brought to the April 1994 meeting of the Church Council (CC93.102.105.a).

Representatives of the Board of Pensions, Division for Ministry and Department for Synodical Relations have reviewed and discussed the Montana Synod resolution. The Board of Pensions' position with respect to this memorial is that the roster status should determine eligibility for retirement pension. Currently a person under age 70½ is not eligible to receive a pension unless he/she is in a retired status. Plan members are not eligible to receive a pension while serving under a call if under age 70½. To conform to Internal Revenue Service regulations, a monthly pension must begin following age 70½ for active plan members.

A revision to the Board of Pension's eligibility requirements for a retirement pension would involve significant issues which must be reviewed within the church since change could have undetermined effects on retirement patterns in the ELCA. Before any such change is initiated, it is recommended that this issue be explored further with the Conference of Bishops for input and advice.

Council Action:

EN BLOC   *[CC94.11.99m]*

To request that the Board of Pensions consult with the Conference of Bishops on the issues raised by the resolution of the Montana Synod and provide a report and/or recommendation to the Church Council at its April 1995 meeting.

C. Development of Social Statements
Nebraska Synod (4A)

The Nebraska Synod submitted a resolution on the draft statement on the church and human sexuality which included the following resolution:

RESOLVED, that the Nebraska Synod request the ELCA Church Council to reconsider the process for the development, review and release of social statements in light of the experience gained through the release of the draft statement on human sexuality.

At its July 19, 1994, meeting the Executive Committee of the Church Council voted:

To transmit this resolution of the Nebraska Synod on the draft statement on human sexuality to the Division for Church in Society, as the second draft of the statement, "The Church and Human Sexuality: A Lutheran Perspective," is developed; and

To request that the Division for Church in Society make a report to the Church Council at its November 1994 meeting.

The Division for Church in Society provided the following response from its Department for Studies:

**A CURRENT ASSESSMENT OF
HOW ELCA SOCIAL STATEMENTS
ARE DEVELOPED**

The principles and procedures for the development of ELCA social statements ("Social Statements in the ELCA," adopted by the 1989 Churchwide Assembly) were developed in 1988-89, based on a careful assessment of the legacy of social statement development in the ALC and LCA (e.g., the paper "Building on Our Legacy," available from the Department for Studies), of input from and discussion with a number of theologians and church leaders with experience in this area, of a special consultation with representatives from each synod (December, 1988), and informed by a number of other discussions in ELCA settings.

Since that time, the Department for Studies has been involved in periodic discussions with many people and assessments as to how various aspects of the prescribed procedures have functioned in practice. In these discussions and assessments:

- What is not negotiable is the clear, ongoing need to develop documents like social statements to carry out the confessional and constitutionally-mandated purposes of the ELCA. Our faith and purpose as a church call us to address the changing circumstances and issues of our world in light of God's living word. Guidance is needed for members as they live out their vocation as well as to direct the institutional expressions of the ELCA. The ethical challenges facing us continue to change, and the meaning of our faith in relation to these challenges needs to be explored in ever-new contexts.
- The theological bases and ecclesial commitments for why and how the church speaks and acts on social issues have been set forth and developed in the first or foundational social

statement, "The Church in Society: A Lutheran Perspectives," adopted by the 1991 Churchwide Assembly.

- The overall record of the development and approval of social statements has been quite positive, with the first five statements, (including controversial topics such as abortion and the death penalty,) having each been adopted by approximately a 90 percent-plus vote at a churchwide assembly.
- A task force appointed by and accountable to the board of the Division for Church in Society (and drawing from nominations received from throughout the ELCA) has worked with staff on the development of each statement. Each task force has been composed of ELCA members with the kinds of diverse perspectives and necessary topic-specific expertise referred to in the foundational social statement. Because a social statement is viewed, first of all, as a theological document, a significant proportion of each task force has been composed of persons with professional/graduate degrees in theological areas (e.g., 10 out of 17 members of the task force on human sexuality, in addition to staff). A task force typically is appointed and begins its work approximately three years prior to the anticipated adoption of a social statement, and usually meets twice a year in as economical a site and time span as possible.
- The basic process has involved the development of a study document for the purposes of study, deliberation, and response from ELCA members and congregations and the subsequent development of (usually) a first and second draft of a social statement. Critiques have been heard that the time for responding to a study document has been too brief, and that many respond to a first draft apart from having participated in any deliberation of the study document. Consequently, in the process of developing the next social statement (on economic life), plans are for the study document and first draft to be distributed at the same time rather than sequentially. This will occur approximately a year before the proposed social statement is ready.
- Although the initiation of work on each social statement has been based on an assessment on why it is important to give priority to addressing certain issues, in the case of the statement on economic life, this is being sought in a more intentional and systematic way through a series of listening posts in various geographical areas of the ELCA, in cooperation with synods. The intent is to discern more clearly how ELCA members experience, perceive, and interpret the economic realities that affect them and their communities, so that the work on the statement can be framed and approached in ways that will be most helpful.
- The expertise on social issues among ELCA members, especially through their ministries in daily life, is considerable. This needs to be more effectively tapped early on in the process of developing a statement. Because only a limited amount of that expertise is likely to be present on a task force, intentional efforts are being made to consult with and receive input and critique from those with particular areas of expertise regarding economic life during the first stages as well as the subsequent development and implementation of this statement. The current plan is that a large group of such consultants, theologians, and other church leaders would be invited to respond to an early embargoed version of the study/first draft-in-process sometime before it is revised, completed, authorized, and released for widespread distribution in the ELCA (this occurred with a pre-first draft of the sexuality statement in May/June of 1993).
- From the beginning, ELCA seminary and college faculties as well as the Conference of Bishops have been encouraged to study, discuss, and respond to drafts. The sexuality statement is where this has occurred to the fullest degree, with these responses having been published in "A Collection of Responses..." Discussions are occurring with seminary faculties as to how their perspectives and expertise might contribute to the early shaping of the theological approach and content of statement

drafts (e.g., Trinity/Capital are planning series of symposia correlated with and making a contribution toward the developing economic life statement in 1995).

• Structures and procedures are now in place (e.g., through the inter-unit staff team on social statements) to assure that drafts of studies/statements are printed and in the hands of pastors and other church leaders prior to their release to the press. Pastors and congregations are kept informed ahead of time (e.g., through *Seeds for the Parish*) as to when such documents will be available so that timely study and response to such might be planned in congregations and other settings.

• There has been an increasing awareness of and participation in social statement deliberations by ELCA members and congregations, with a growing sense of what it means and the challenges involved in being "a community of moral deliberation." The first draft of the sexuality statement had an all-time rate of participation for any ELCA process, with hundreds of reports from congregations as to how important the process had been for them. Many pastors and congregational leaders have not felt sufficiently prepared (e.g., in linking their faith with public issues, and in how Lutherans do ethics), and are seeking education and resources that can help with their leadership in this area. One of DCS' major program directions for the remainder of this decade seeks to address this need, along with other units and institutions of the church.

• The lack of consensus among ELCA members as to how biblical authority is understood and functions, what sources Lutherans draw upon and how in addressing ethical issues, and the polarizing climate for dealing with social issues our society today (particularly those that are sexual) have complicated the challenge of moral deliberation. Plans call for DCS (through Studies) to continue to give attention to these underlying factors, in collaboration with other units and institutions of the church.

• What frequently has been discussed, but has not yet been officially changed, is whether there should be two types of social statements (social teaching and social practice) or only one. The subtle distinction between the two has been misunderstood by many (e.g., as if they had different kinds of authority), and has not proven to be that helpful an operational distinction. Only one statement adopted thus far, on "The Death Penalty." has been officially classified as a social *practice* statement (its focus is on a particular public policy position) with all the others being social *teaching* statements.) During the past three years, these distinctions have in actual practice and reference been downplayed, and all the current processes are being referred to as "social statements," developed according to the basic procedures set forth for social "teaching" statements, but also as establishing the bases for the church's "practice." If the original conception of a social practice statement were to be dropped (namely, that it defines and develops priorities and directives for this church's advocacy and corporate social responsibility practices), the question is what vehicle would be used in its stead. One possibility is the kind of "working principles" document developed in relation to the NAFTA and welfare reform issues.

Continuing the Review of Policies and Procedures Related to Social Statements

Recognizing the ongoing need to review the policies and procedures related to how social statements are developed, the Department for Studies of the Division for Church in Society brought to the DCS board the following resolution, which was adopted on October 1, 1994:

WHEREAS, it has been five years since the understandings and procedures for developing social statements were adopted ("Social Statements in the ELCA"); and

WHEREAS, these understandings and procedures have served as the basis for successful completion and adoption of five ELCA social statements; and

WHEREAS, discussions continue regarding the basis, purpose, procedures, and authority of social statements; therefore be it RESOLVED, that

a. the board authorize the Division for Church in Society to assemble a committee to review the bases, purposes, procedures, and authority of social statements in the ELCA;

b. this Social Statement Review Committee be composed of two members from the DCS board, two members from the Church Council, two members from the Conference of Bishops, two theologians/ethicists appointed by the Division for Church in Society in consultation with seminar presidents, two DCS staff persons, and one person from the Office of the Bishop. Included in (or in addition to) the above should be persons with in-depth knowledge and experience in current and predecessor church traditions and practices regarding social policy development, and those who have led congregations in their consideration of social statements;

c. this committee give attention to the following:

1. The ELCA has committed itself to develop social statements as one of the ways through which the ELCA carries out its mission in society. Considering what has been done already, should this commitment be reconsidered? On what basis?

2. Are the current assumptions, understandings, and multiple purposes of social statements still tenable? (For example, they have theological, teaching, ethical reflection, deliberative *and* policy-establishing purposes.)

3. What have been the strengths and weaknesses of the current procedures, processes, and uses of social statements? (For example, the respective roles of task forces, DCS board, Church Council, Conference of Bishops, theological faculties, congregational deliberation and response.)

4. What recommendations should be proposed for changes in the policy and practices regarding social statements? (i.e., for changes in the procedural document, "Social Statements in the ELCA.")

d. this committee be charged to bring a report to the board of the Division for Church and Society and the Church Council no later than the fall of 1996.

Council Action:

EN BLOC [CC94.11.99n]

To request the secretary of this church to convey to the Nebraska Synod the report of the Division for Church in Society relating to the development of social statements, together with the related action of the Church Council, as a response to that synod's resolution on this matter.

D. Lutheran-Reformed Dialogue

Background: At its August 19, 1994, meeting, the Church Council's Executive Committee received two resolutions regarding the Lutheran-Reformed dialogue:

(1) *Lower Susquehanna Synod*

WHEREAS, a task force is currently working on the reception and implementation of "A Common Calling: The Witness of Our Reformation Churches in North America Today," the results of the Lutheran-Reformed dialogue in the United States; and

WHEREAS, that dialogue calls for "full communion" between the ELCA and the three Reformed Churches, (Presbyterian Church USA, United Church of Christ, Reformed Church in America,) engaged in that dialogue; and

WHEREAS, the chief treasure of this full communion would be mutual sharing in the Sacrament of the Eucharist and the mutual recognition of ministers of the Sacrament of the Eucharist; and

WHEREAS, the Sacrament of Holy Communion is the Lord's Table to which he calls all sinners to the banquet of grace and forgiveness, and to be united in the common fellowship (koinonia, communion) of the Holy Spirit of our Lord Jesus Christ in the bread of his body and the wine of his blood, such that the common celebration and communion at the Lord's Table is precisely the Lord's gracious gift of the healing of our divisions; therefore be it

RESOLVED, that the Lower Susquehanna Synod request the ELCA Church Council to encourage and exhort the task force on the reception and implementation of the Lutheran-Reformed dialogue to follow the pattern of ecumenical communion established by the Lutheran-Episcopal dialogue for the last decade, namely, not to move hastily to full communion but to establish a period of "interim sharing of the Eucharist" between our various churches; and be it further

RESOLVED, that this period of "interim sharing of the Eucharist" be intentionally observed, studied, and evaluated as a time of controlled and regulated joint services of Holy Communion so as to see how far the Holy Spirit might take us in communion and how long the Holy Spirit will take in bringing us to full communion; and be it further

RESOLVED, that no move to full communion be made until, in the judgment of the churches with clear theological and sacramental evaluation, it is seen that the Holy Spirit is guiding these churches into the relationship of full communion.

The Executive Committee voted:

To transmit this resolution of the Lower Susquehanna Synod on the reception and implementation of the Lutheran-Reformed dialogue to the Department for Ecumenical Affairs; and

To request that the Department for Ecumenical Affairs bring to the November 1994 meeting of the Church Council a report and/or recommendation on this matter.

and

(2) *Delaware-Maryland Synod*

WHEREAS, the ELCA and its predecessor bodies have been exploring "full communion" with churches of the Reformed tradition (i.e., the Presbyterian Church USA, the Reformed Church in America, and the United Church of Christ,) and have actively engaged in theological dialogue with the churches of the Reformed tradition; and

WHEREAS, "full communion" has been defined to mean full recognition of each other as churches in which the Gospel is rightly taught and the sacraments rightly administered according to the Word of God, including open sharing of the sacraments among its members and orderly exchange of ordained ministers among its congregations; and

WHEREAS, the United Church of Christ in its constitution manual on ministry and service of ordination requires no confessional subscription or accountability for its ordained pastors; and

WHEREAS, the ELCA affirms the unaltered Augsburg Confession to be a true witness to the Gospel and an authoritative norm for the life of the church; and

WHEREAS, the unaltered Augsburg Confession declares "For the true unity of the church it is enough to agree concerning the teaching of the Gospel and the administration of the sacraments"; and

WHEREAS, full communion between the ELCA and any body, such as the churches of the Reformed tradition, depends on establishing true unity of the churches in the sense defined by the unaltered Augsburg Confession; and

WHEREAS, the churches of the Reformed tradition teach that Christ is present in a spiritual mode, reserving the corporeal mode to existing in heaven; and

WHEREAS, the churches of the Reformed tradition teach that Christ is received in the Sacrament of Holy Communion in the Spirit alone, thus being received only by believers; and

WHEREAS, these teachings of the churches of the Reformed tradition reveal that the ELCA and the Reformed churches still have fundamental differences over the person of Christ and His presence in the church and in the sacrament; and

WHEREAS, these fundamental differences exhibit a failure to agree concerning the teaching of the Gospel and the administration of the sacraments, thus demonstrating a lack of true unity; therefore be it

RESOLVED, that the Delaware-Maryland Synod Assembly request the ELCA to refrain from establishing full communion with churches of the Reformed tradition until such time as substantial agreement has been reached on issues of the person of Christ and His presence in the Church and the sacrament, on the expectations of ordained ministers, and "true unity" between the churches has been obtained; and be it further

RESOLVED, that the Delaware-Maryland Synod Assembly request the ELCA to continue to dialogue with the Reformed churches regarding issues of sacramental theology and ordained ministry, while at the same time celebrating the faith in Jesus Christ that the two traditions already hold in common; and be it further

RESOLVED, that the Delaware-Maryland Synod Assembly direct the Synod Council to forward this resolution to the ELCA Church Council for consideration and action.

The Executive Committee voted:

To transmit this resolution of the Delaware-Maryland Synod on consideration of full communion with reformed churches to the Department for Ecumenical Affairs; and

To request that the Department for Ecumenical Affairs bring to the November 1994 meeting of the Church Council a report and/or recommendation on this matter.

The Department for Ecumenical Affairs has provided the following response to the synod memorials:

The Department for Ecumenical Affairs has shared with the Lutheran-Reformed Coordinating Committee the resolutions from the Lower Susquehanna Synod and the Delaware-Maryland Synod, and the actions of the Executive Committee of the Church Council. The coordinating committee greatly appreciates the opportunity to make a Lutheran-Reformed response to the request from the Church Council.

The committee reviewed these resolutions in light of the discussion and action at the 1993 ELCA Churchwide Assembly, which voted:

To affirm that the recommendations for full communion between the Evangelical Lutheran Church in America, the Presbyterian Church (U.S.A.), the Reformed Church in America, and the United Church of Christ, made by the Lutheran-Reformed Committee for Theological Conversations in *A Common Calling: The Witness of Our Reformation Churches in North America Today*, be voted on by the respective communions (church bodies) in the same year, not earlier than 1995 and not later than 1997; and

To request that the ecumenical staffs of the Evangelical Lutheran Church in America, the Presbyterian Church (U.S.A.), the Reformed Church in America, and the United Church of Christ convene a meeting of the heads of communion of these churches prior to the next meeting of the Lutheran-Reformed Coordinating Committee to seek their guidance in this matter of determining timing of such a vote (CA93.6.6.).

Subsequently the heads of communion affirmed 1997 as a time for decision.

The Lutheran-Reformed Coordinating Committee has concluded that no new arguments are being raised by the resolutions from the Lower Susquehanna Synod and Delaware-Maryland Synod. Therefore the committee recommends that the response to the synods be the 1993 action of the Churchwide Assembly, especially in view of the present and future work being undertaken by the coordinating committee.

The coordinating committee would recommend that the two synods be in consultation with the Department for Ecumenical Affairs as the ELCA takes part in the reception process and churchwide study of "A Common Calling" utilizing its companion study document, "A Common Discovery." It is envisioned that this process also will include a "Formula of Agreement" which addresses concerns raised in these resolutions.

Council Action:

EN BLOC   *[CC94.11.99o]*

To request the secretary of this church to convey to the Lower Susquehanna and Delaware-Maryland Synods the response of the Department for Ecumenical Affairs to the resolutions on the Lutheran-Reformed Dialogue.

EN BLOC ITEMS

The following *en bloc* resolution includes agenda items that were considered on the last day of the Church Council meeting. Inclusion of these items in the *en bloc* action reflects a judgment that these items were relatively non-controversial in nature and may not have required a plenary discussion and separate vote.

Each of the items is noted as *EN BLOC* in the body of the agenda. On the first day of the council meeting, the chair provided an opportunity for members to express whether they wished to discuss separately any of the items listed in the *en bloc* resolution; any such item will be removed from the *en bloc* resolution and discussed at the appropriate point in the agenda.

The chair did not call for a discussion or separate vote on those items that were not removed from the *en bloc* resolution by the end of the first day of plenary sessions.

VOTED: *CC94.11.98*

To take action *en bloc* on the items listed below, the full texts of which are printed in the body of these minutes or in an exhibit as noted:

CC94.11.99	Synod Resolutions Directed to the Church Council;
CC94.11.100	Mission Investment Fund: 1995 Capital Budget Recommendation;
CC94.11.101	Audit Committee;
CC94.11.102	Review and Confirmation of Church Council Designated Funds;
CC94.11.103	Election of Assistant Treasurer;
CC94.11.104	ELCA Continuation of the ALC Medical-Dental Plan for Retired Participants and ELCA Continuation of the LCA Ministerial Health benefits Plan for Retired Members;
CC94.11.105	ELCA Medical and Dental Benefits Plan;
CC94.11.106	ELCA Master Institutional Regular Pension Plan;
CC94.11.107	ELCA Regular Pension Plan, ELCA Survivor Benefits Plan and ELCA Disability Benefits Plan;
CC94.11.108	ELCA Regular Pension Plan;
CC94.11.109	ELCA Disability Benefits Plan;
CC94.11.110	ELCA Medical and Dental Benefits Plan;
CC94.11.111	ELCA Regular Pension Plan, ELCA Survivor Benefits Plan, ELCA Disability Benefits Plan and ELCA Medical and Dental Benefits Plan;
CC94.11.112	Martin Luther Home Society Inc., Election of board members;
CC94.11.113	Lutheran General HealthSystem, Election of board members;
CC94.11.114	Service Rites for Ordination, Commissioning, and Consecration;
CC94.11.115	"Reinstatement to the Rosters of the ELCA"; and
CC94.11.115	Amendment of Lutheran Youth Organization Governing Documents

Compensation of Women

Background: The following action was taken by the board of the Women of the Evangelical Lutheran Church in America at its October 1994 meeting:

WHEREAS, women clergy, women lay professionals, and support staff are often offered lower compensation and benefits than males in comparable positions; and

WHEREAS, recognition for women's previous work experience, whether in professional fields, volunteer work, or homemaking, is often not taken into account; and

WHEREAS, the contribution of women is integral to the whole economic structure of family and society; therefore, be it

RESOLVED, that the Evangelical Lutheran Church in America through congregational units, institutions, affiliated ministries, agencies, synods and the churchwide organization examine current salary levels and benefits of women employed and called to serve throughout the Evangelical Lutheran Church in America in order to achieve equity in compensation, making salary adjustments as needed and offering benefits to those not presently covered; and be it further

RESOLVED, that the Women of the ELCA executive board transmit this resolution to the ELCA Church Council for action.

Council Action: The following recommendation was offered:

MOVED;
SECONDED: To refer the resolution on the compensation of women jointly to the Commission for Women and the Women of the Evangelical Lutheran Church in America; and

To request that those units, in consultation with the Division for Church in Society and the Department for Human Resources, bring a recommendation for action to the Church Council at its April 1995 meeting.

During discussion, Edith M. Lohr recommended that greater responsibility for the matter be given the Department for Human Resources.

MOVED;
SECONDED: To amend the motion to read:

To refer the resolution on the compensation of women jointly to the Commission for Women, the Women of the Evangelical Lutheran Church in America, and the Department for Human Resources; and

To request that those units, in consultation with the Division for Church in Society, bring a recommendation for action to the Church Council at its April 1995 meeting.

VOTED: *CC94.11.117*

To refer the resolution on the compensation of women jointly to the Commission for Women,

the Women of the Evangelical Lutheran Church in America, and the Department for Human Resources; and

To request that those units, in consultation with the Division for Church in Society, bring a recommendation for action to the Church Council at its April 1995 meeting.

Election Procedures for Churchwide Officers

Background: The following resolution was transmitted to the Church Council by the Rocky Mountain Synod Assembly:

WHEREAS, the ELCA constitution states, "The Church Council shall establish an ongoing process to review the function and the structural organization of this church and to develop recommendations for changes" (ELCA 5.01.e.); and

WHEREAS, the ELCA constitution states, "This church shall function as people of God through congregations, synods, and the churchwide organization, all of which shall be interdependent. Each part, while fully the church, recognizes that it is not the whole church and therefore lives in a partnership relationship with others" (ELCA 8.11.); and

WHEREAS, the size of the ELCA in both membership and geography makes it imperative that constant attention be given to strengthening relationships between the various parts of the church and between the churchwide organization and the membership; and

WHEREAS, throughout its brief history the ELCA has experienced a significant shortfall in financial support as compared to initial projections, and has suffered from an oft-expressed perception of its membership that it is distant from the congregations and the concerns of the membership; and

WHEREAS, the interdependent character of this church might be strengthened, and the sense of relationship enhanced, through wider participation in the selection of persons to serve in elected positions, such as members of boards and committees; and

WHEREAS, all who serve in such capacities, regardless of the means by which they have come to such service, are to regard themselves as servants of Christ and representatives of the whole people of God; and

WHEREAS, the perception of a "top-down" church is increased by the holding of an excessive number of elections at churchwide assemblies, a task which many voting members find difficult and frustrating; therefore be it

RESOLVED, that the Rocky Mountain Synod Assembly direct the Rocky Mountain Synod Council to forward this resolution to the ELCA Church Council to review the election procedures of the Evangelical Lutheran Church in America and consider amendments to the documents of this church with a goal of minimizing the number of persons elected at churchwide assemblies and expanding the number of persons elected at the synod level, and bring its recommendations to the 1997 Churchwide Assembly.

Council Actions: During discussion of the following recommendation, Lorraine G. Bergquist inquired whether it might be more appropriate for the Church Council to consider the matter, rather than referring the resolution to the council's Executive Committee.

VOTED: *CC94.11.118*
To refer the resolution of the Rocky Mountain Synod on election procedures for churchwide offices to the Executive Committee of the Church Council; and

To request that a report and/or recommendation be brought to the Church Council at its April 1995 meeting.

Adjournment

VOTED: *CC94.11.119*
To adjourn.

The Church Council adjourned at 2:19 P.M. Bishop Herbert W. Chilstrom offered the closing prayer and expressed thanks to the council for the leadership and guidance provided by council members.

April 1995

The twenty-second meeting of the Church Council of the Evangelical Lutheran Church in America was held in the Church Council Room of the Lutheran Center at Chicago, Illinois, on April 1-3, 1995. The meeting opened with the Service of the Word in the Lutheran Center chapel at 8:30 A.M. The service was led by Ms. Cynthia P. Johnson and Bishop Charles H. Maahs, with Mr. Loren W. Mathre serving as lector.

Vice President Kathy J. Magnus, chair of the Church Council, called the meeting to order at 9:31 A.M.

Opening Remarks

At the beginning of the meeting, Vice President Magnus invited written evaluations and suggestions from council members of the function on the council's committees and the council during the past biennium.

Adoption of the Agenda

Agenda items had been distributed by mail and additional items were distributed at the meeting to the members of the Church Council and invited resource persons.

VOTED: CC95.4.1
To adopt the agenda and to permit the chair to call for consideration of agenda items in the order she deems most appropriate.

En Bloc Approval of Certain Items

Chair Magnus requested that council members who desired to remove items from the *en bloc* resolution for disposition of non-controversial business items for individual consideration notify the secretary by noon of Saturday, April 1, 1995.

Report of the Bishop

Vice President Magnus called upon Bishop Herbert W. Chilstrom to present his report. Bishop Chilstrom reminded the members of the council that he would leave office seven months from this date. He, then, read the text of his report.

Bishop Chilstrom quoted Tony Campolo, a Baptist minister and evangelist who teaches at Eastern College in St. Davids, Pennsylvania. Campolo recently said in an interview in the *Christian Century*: ". . . mainline churches are about to experience a revitalization, a renewal, a dynamic explosion. . . . They are recovering balance. Without abandoning their social agenda they are becoming increasingly concerned about bringing people into that personal, transforming relationship with Christ. [They] are still talking about the important issues of our time, but they are also remembering that the church has a pastoral role as well as a prophetic one."

Asked Bishop Chilstrom: "Can this be said of us, the Evangelical Lutheran Church in America?" His response was, "Yes," as he cited several reasons, including that way in which "we have sought to live out a Christ-centered vision of our church—'a church, so deeply and confidently rooted in the Gospel of God's grace, that we are free to give our life joyfully in witness and service.'"

He continued, "We have kept our focus at a time when all churches have been tested by many and varied demands. At the very beginning of our life together, we committed ourselves to churchwide reflection on what it means for us to be Christians; to individual prayer and daily reflection on the Scriptures; to tithing as a joyful response to God's grace; to congregational Bible study and evangelical witness by our members; to justice for women and children in poverty; to strengthening linkages with churches throughout the world through the companion-synod program."

Reviewing the past eight years, he said, "We have made enormous adjustments in these early years. Every aspect of our work has been streamlined. Though the demands on those serving in churchwide ministries have increased, they have been faithful."

Bishop Chilstrom cited several important developments including achievement of "stability in our church-wide ministries."

Complex issues, he observed, have tested our unity, including the death penalty, ecumenical relationships, the environment, racism, abortion. He continued, "As you are aware, we are now in the midst of formulating our position on what is surely the most controversial issue of all—human sexuality. A second draft of a possible social statement is in the hands of our members. I trust that pastors and lay leaders are even now sharing the draft with their congregations and that they will be as faithful in responding to the second draft as with the first. We continue to remind our members that responses should be submitted by June 30, 1995, and we look toward the possibility of further work toward a social statement in this important area."

Said Bishop Chilstrom: "My time in office is winding down. But my hope and expectation for the future of the Evangelical Lutheran Church in America grow stronger as I reflect on the possibilities that lie ahead for this church," including synodical and church-wide elections, possible approval of a social statement on peace, study of a sacramental practices draft, critical decisions about the future of theological education in our church, important ecumenical decisions facing our church, and funding churchwide and global ministries for the future.

Acknowledging that this was his last regular meeting with the Church Council while in office as bishop of this church, he said: "I can assure you that I will follow your work and the mission of this church with keen interest and with my fervent prayers. You can always count on me to speak a positive, supportive word on behalf of this church and its leadership."

Report of Vice President

The report of Vice President Kathy J. Magnus was presented in the form of a time outline in the anticipated sequence of items on the agenda.

Nominations to Fill Unexpired Terms on Division Boards

Background: Between meetings of the Churchwide Assembly, the Church Council has the responsibility of electing persons to fill unexpired terms on churchwide boards (for example, those which occur because of resignations). The Church Council is also the electing body for steering committees of churchwide commissions and certain advisory committees. Materials related to the election to boards were printed in council agenda Exhibit C, Part 1. The following lists elections that were required at this meeting of the Church Council:

1. Board of the Division for Congregational Ministries—clergy [term 1999]—to replace the Rev. Judith A. Spindt;
2. Board of the Division for Outreach—lay female [term 1997]—to replace Ms. Barbara S. Rudisill; and
3. Board of the Division for Outreach—clergy [term 1997]—to replace the Rev. Dale C. Trautman.

The Executive Committee of the Church Council serves as the council's nominating committee. The following slates were submitted. Motions were approved to close nominations.

1. Division for Congregational Ministries (unexpired term to 1999); it was noted that continuing service of board members by regions includes: 1-2; 2-1; 3-3; 4-1; 5-2; 6-2; 7-3; 8-0; 9-6.
   Clergy
   - a. Rev. David R. Hauck, Washingtonville, Pa. (8E)
   - b. Rev. Robert L. Miller, State College, Pa. (8C)
2. Division for Outreach (unexpired terms to 1997); continuing service by regions includes: 1-2; 2-1; 3-2; 4-2; 5-1; 6-2; 7-5; 8-3; 9-1.
   Lay female
   - a. Marlene M. Case, Rochester, Minn. (3I)
   - b. Caroline Wolff, Erie, Pa. (8A)
   Clergy
   - a. Rev. Dennis N. Nelson, Gillett, Wis. (5I)
   - b. Rev. Richard W. Owens, Bismarck, N.Dak. (3A)

Churchwide Nominating Committee

Secretary Lowell G. Almen presented action of the Executive Committee of the Church Council. It was noted that incumbents with continuing terms on the churchwide Nominating Committee are as follows: Region 1—one person; Region 2—zero; Region 3—two persons; Region 4—two persons; Region 5—one person; Region 6—two persons; Region 7—one person; Region 8—two persons; and Region 9—one person.

A motion was approved to close the nominations. Subsequently, the Church Council voted to approve the slate.

VOTED: CC95.4.2

To transmit the following slate for the churchwide Nominating Committee for possible election by the 1995 Churchwide Assembly:

Lay Female
1. a. Carolyn Thomas, Broomfield, Colo. (2E)
   b. Barbara J. Eaves, Phoenix, Ariz. (2D)
Lay Female
2. a. Deborah R. Joncas, Newark, N.J. (7A)
   b. Roberta C. Schott, Princeton Junction, N.J. (7A)
Lay Male
3. a. Keith P. Brown, Roanoke, Va. (9A)
   b. Clifton W. Anderson, Charlottesville, Va. (9A)
Lay Male (PC/L)
4. a. Fred B. Renwick, New York, N.Y. (7C)
   b. Willis H. Hines, Matawan, N.J. (7A)
Clergy
5. a. Rev. James Braaten, Yakima, Wash. (1D)
   b. Rev. Darrel O. Lundby, Beaverton, Oreg. (1E)
Clergy (Region 5)
6. a. Rev. Jerald L. Wendt, Whitewater, Wis. (5K)
   b. Rev. Robert L. Vogel, Waverly, Iowa (5F)

The Church Council recessed at 10:29 A.M. and reconvened at 10:51 A.M.

Balloting for Board Positions

Chair Magnus invited council members to cast ballots to fill unexpired terms on two of the division boards. Subsequently, she declared the ballot closed.

Inquiry Process

Background: A proposal, "Inquiry: The Future of the Churchwide Organization," was discussed at the December 1993 meeting of the Church Council. At that meeting, the council voted:

> To affirm in principle the direction outlined in the proposal "Inquiry: The Future of the Churchwide Organization";
>
> To instruct the Office of the Bishop to develop and implement plans for this initiative, in consultation with the Executive Committee of the Church Council; . . . (CC93.12.88).

During its April 1994 meeting, the Church Council's Executive Committee and the Program and Structure Committee met jointly to discuss the inquiry process; the full council engaged in discussion of this effort as well.

Since that time, discussions relating to the Inquiry have occurred at the fall 1994 meeting of the Conference of Bishops and at the synodical-churchwide consultations held during fall 1994 and winter 1995.

The Inquiry Advisory Committee, chaired by the Rev. H. George Anderson, has met several times, most recently March 9-10, 1995. The chair of the Church Council, Kathy J. Magnus, also serves on this committee. A report of current plans for the Inquiry was presented in council agenda Exhibit B, Part 3a. Bishop Chilstrom's call to prayer and reflection on the future was provided as council agenda Exhibit B, Part 3b.

Council Action: Chair Magnus called upon the Rev. H. George Anderson to present a progress report on the "Inquiry" process. He stated that the first phase, dealing with discovery of issues and questions, hopes and conflicts to be addressed, had been completed. He drew attention to the section on "Themes . . . and Questions" (page three of the exhibit), which provided a summary of some of the findings thus far. "The situation in the United States is so different today that we really need to formulate a new, a different, concept of mission, because everyone talks about mission, but there are very few people who agree exactly on what that might be. And so, not only do we need to reformulate, to find new images and new possibilities, but we also have to form one mind about the mission and the adjustments that will be necessary to carry it out. In fact, we need to increase the levels of trust and connectedness within this church, in order to move forward, so that we can do so together with some feeling of positive progress.

"We discovered that resources and energy at many levels of the church are at the breaking point, and that most members of this church—people in the pew, so to speak—seem to be blissfully unaware that these stresses and strains even exist. Now, our church certainly does not lack for calls to action, calls to faithfulness, shouts of warning, or cries for attention. What it does lack is conversation—serious, deep, respectful, prayerful conversation among all the partners, conversation about what it means to be faithful to God's mission in terms of programs and priorities for this generation and the next, conversation on how to develop the type of leadership, lay and clergy, that this mission requires, conversation that will develop and maintain trusting relationships, that is, relations that will hold through the stresses and strains that change require.

"So, we have begun by asking Bishop [Herbert W.] Chilstrom to call the whole Evangelical Lutheran Church in America to participate in a period of prayer and reflection as we consider our future and select leaders . . .. We thank Bishop Chilstrom for a very helpful and theological call to prayer and reflection. Then, in August 1995, the Churchwide Assembly will provide forums for voting members to engage in conversation regarding the future of this church. Next fall, every congregation will have the opportunity to share its hopes and suggestions with the wider church. In addition, such conversations, of course, can be fairly shallow, so in order to help us go deeper into some of the tougher questions, we have proposed two series of conferences. One will be called, 'Dialogue Conferences.' These are to involve clergy and laity in local areas of this church in conversation. The other series, called 'Future Search Conferences,' is longer in duration and seeks to bring together partners from the whole system—from congregations, from auxiliaries, from institutions of this church, from synods, and from the churchwide expression—all to talk together about the future and about what kinds of explorations are needed toward common ground for the future. I want to emphasize that one of the things the advisory committee has found most important is to ground and embed all of this process in a context of worship and prayer, in order to be open to the Spirit of God to whom the future really belongs. We have become quite excited about the possibilities for worship and prayer as an integral part of the cycle of these conferences.

"Now, it is hoped that all of these activities will result in a report to the new bishop by late 1995 and that report, of course, will be shared with synods and congregations. It will be a report, probably, on the state of the church, on the hopes of the church, and on some possibilities for the future. What happens from then on, however, will not be decided by the 'Inquiry' process, but by the new bishop and the Church Council. It is our hope that the 'Inquiry' process will create a foundation and a climate for those changes that most certainly do lie ahead."

During discussion, Cynthia P. Johnson inquired how the conference sites were selected, who (e.g., synodical representatives) would facilitate discussion within congregations, and what might be the format of those conversations. Kenneth W. Inskeep, director of the Department for Research and Evaluation, responded. William E. Diehl questioned the use of random selection in identifying conference participants, and recommended that participation be opened to all interested parties.

D. Mark Klever asked why synodical assemblies would not be directly involved in the conversations. Mr. Inskeep noted that financial restrictions had a significant impact on the overall design of the process. "In some ways, we are still searching for what the issues are and how those issues need to be addressed. We wanted to have a longer, more focused dialogue, so that we could get a better sense of how these discussions might take place and around what kinds of issues. It is not going to be helpful for us to collect large amounts of data that we do not understand, nor know how to use. It is our belief that these will be ongoing conversations. . .," he said. Chair Magnus noted that synodical assemblies already had been requested to add to their agendas significant time for reflection on elections to be held at those assemblies, as well as at the Churchwide Assembly.

Mr. Klever inquired further about a shift in focus and time table from the 'Inquiry' process as originally conceived. Pastor Anderson indicated that as the committee examined the task, it became apparent that the bishop elected by the Churchwide Assembly in August 1995 should be involved in the process, and that the time line should be relaxed in order to amplify the participatory nature of the process. He noted that the random process was intended as a means to "reach out and pull in" persons who otherwise might not choose to participate. W. Jeanne Rapp requested further details about the random process and criteria for selecting conference participants. Terry L. Bowes recommended the participation of Church Council members in the conferences. William T. Billings commended the committee's call for prayer and reflection, "because we often forget that we have one unique source of inspiration and guidance. . . ." He admonished that such a focus not become "lost" in the deliberative process.

Report of the Treasurer

Treasurer Richard L. McAuliffe called attention to his written report, presented as council agenda Exhibit A, Part 4. Receipts totaled $76.2 million for fiscal year 1994. At the same time, contributions to the ELCA World Hunger Appeals were $11.5 million, and the ELCA Disaster Response income, $2.4 million.

For fiscal 1994, the year ended with a favorable net variance of $3.3 million. Mission-support income declined some $310,000 from the previous year. Restricted bequests, however, increased substantially.

The report of the Mission Investment Fund of the Evangelical Lutheran Church in America also was provided as council agenda Exhibit A, Part 4g.

Referral on Representational Principles

Background: In response to a number of synod memorials requesting the ELCA to reconsider representational principles, the 1993 Churchwide Assembly voted:

> To instruct the Church Council, in consultation with the Conference of Bishops, to establish a process for reflection by the Church Council, Conference of Bishops, Commission for Women, Commission for Multicultural Ministries, and seminary faculties, and to report any recommendations to the 1995 Churchwide Assembly (CA93.7.47).

A description of the process that has been followed and documentation on responses that have emerged from this reflection are found as follows:

> Exhibit B, Part 2a: Report of the Church Council to the 1995 Churchwide Assembly;
> Exhibit B, Part 2b: Context of Representational Principles;
> Exhibit B, Part 2c: Response of the Seminary Faculties;
> Exhibit B, Part 2d: Response of the Commission for Multicultural Ministries;
> Exhibit B, Part 2e: Response of the Commission for Women; and
> Exhibit B, Part 2f: Response of the Conference of Bishops.

The Executive Committee of the Church Council reviewed this material in its meeting on March 10, 1995, and prepared the following recommendation:

> To recommend to the 1995 Churchwide Assembly adoption of the following resolution:
>> To receive with appreciation the theological study, analyses, historical review, and descriptions of experiences provided by the Church Council, Conference of Bishops, seminary faculties, Commission for Multicultural Ministries, Commission for Women, and others in regard to the representational principles applied to councils, boards, and committees throughout the synods and churchwide organization of the Evangelical Lutheran Church in America;
>> To consider the discussion and materials an appropriate response to the resolution of the 1993 Churchwide Assembly that directed the Church

Council "to establish a process for reflection" on the representational principles and recommendations to the 1995 Churchwide Assembly (CA93.7.47);

To affirm the judgment that the current representational principles do not compromise the Gospel but rather reflect an appropriate pattern for good order within the practice of this church's ecclesiology and polity;

To recognize that the current representational principles are not an end in themselves but are a means appropriate to this time in this church's history that have been chosen to allow for more complete and more inclusive participation by members of the ELCA in this church's decision-making processes;

To acknowledge the perceived need in various synods for greater flexibility in relation to the composition of voting membership from congregations in Synod Assemblies, with such appropriate flexibility being anticipated through constitutional and bylaw amendments;

To urge continued attention to community outreach and ministry by all congregations of this church so that each congregation may grow in awareness of being a mission center within its community as well as increase in commitment to the wider mission of this church throughout the respective synods and the churchwide ministries; and

To express gratitude for the salutary results that have emerged thus far through the practice of this church's representational principles.

Council Action: Bishop Paull E. Spring asked about how the seminary responses were developed. The Rev. Joseph M. Wagner explained that a committee from three seminaries (Trinity in Columbus, Ohio; Lutheran School of Theology at Chicago [Ill.]; and Wartburg in Dubuque, Iowa) was asked to do a draft, which was reviewed by all the seminaries. Bishop Spring responded that he was "surprised that seminary response did not have more depth."

The Rev. James Cobb suggested that a presentation by Bishop Herbert W. Chilstrom on the subject of this church's representational principles, "The Call to be Inclusive," also be included in the report to the 1995 Churchwide Assembly. The address was presented at Augsburg College in Minneapolis, Minn., on October 15, 1988. It was agreed that members of the Executive Committee would review the text for possible inclusion in the report. Subsequently, Vice President Magnus announced that the committee recommended that the address be attached to related material for the Churchwide Assembly. The following, therefore, will constitute the council's response to the referral from the 1993 Churchwide Assembly on representational principles:

> Exhibit B, Part 2a: Report of the Church Council to the 1995 Churchwide Assembly;
> Exhibit B, Part 2b: Context of Representational Principles;
> Exhibit B, Part 2c: Response of the Seminary Faculties;
> Exhibit B, Part 2d: Response of the Commission for Multicultural Ministries;
> Exhibit B, Part 2e: Response of the Commission for Women;
> Exhibit B, Part 2f: Response of the Conference of Bishops;
> Exhibit B, Part 2g: "The Call to be Inclusive" by Bishop Chilstrom.

Dale V. Sandstrom proposed the following as a friendly amendment, which was subsequently received by the council:

To acknowledge statements by ~~the perceived need in~~ various synods regarding the need for greater flexibility in relation to the composition of voting membership from congregations in synodical assemblies, with such appropriate flexibility being anticipated through constitutional and bylaw amendments;

VOTED: CC95.4.3

To recommend to the 1995 Churchwide Assembly adoption of the following resolution:

To receive with appreciation the theological study, analyses, historical review, and descriptions of experiences provided by the Church Council, Conference of Bishops, seminary faculties, Commission for Multicultural Ministries, Commission for Women, and others in regard to the representational principles applied to councils, boards, and committees throughout the synods and churchwide organization of the Evangelical Lutheran Church in America;

To consider the discussion and materials an appropriate response to the resolution of the 1993 Churchwide Assembly that directed the Church Council "to establish a process for reflection" on the representational principles and recommendations to the 1995 Churchwide Assembly (CA93.7.47);

To affirm the judgment that the current representational principles do not compromise the Gospel, but rather reflect an appropriate pattern for good order within the practice of this church's ecclesiology and polity;

To recognize that the current representational principles are not an end in themselves, but are a means appropriate to this time in this church's history that has been chosen to allow for more complete and more inclusive participation by members of the Evangelical Lutheran Church in America in this church's decision-making processes;

To acknowledge statements by various synods regarding the need for greater flexibility in relation to the composition of voting membership from congregations in synodical assemblies, with such appropriate flexibility being anticipated through constitutional and bylaw amendments;

To urge continued attention to community outreach and ministry by all congregations of this church so that each congregation may grow in awareness of being a mission center within its community as well as increase in commitment to the wider mission

of this church throughout the respective synods and the churchwide ministries; and

To express gratitude for the salutary results that have emerged thus far through the practice of this church's representational principles.

Matters Related to the Division For Church in Society

1. Proposed Social Statement on Peace

Background: At its March 1995 meeting, the board of the Division for Church in Society reviewed the proposed social statement, "For Peace in God's World." The board recommended that the statement, and the related recommendations for action, be placed on the agenda of the 1995 Churchwide Assembly.

Council Action: Chair Magnus called upon the Rev. Charles S. Miller Jr., executive director of the Division for Church in Society, to introduce the proposed social statement on peace, which, he observed, was transmitted "unanimously and enthusiastically" to the Church Council by the division's board. Pastor Miller then introduced the Rev. John R. Stumme, associate director for studies in the Division for Church in Society, and Ms. Katherine M. Kidd, co-chair of the task force on peace with the late Rev. Carl H. Mau Jr. Ms. Kidd reviewed the composition of the 16-member task force and the process for development of the statement. She acknowledged grants provided by the Stanley Foundation (Muscatine, Iowa), which underwrote the cost of research, consultants, and nine hearings held across this church.

Ms. Kidd characterized the group as "uncommonly civil" in the development of the statement. She said that the task force had voted unanimously to submit the statement to the board of the Division for Church in Society. That board, in turn, approved the statement with only "a few minor changes" before transmitting the text to the Church Council.

Highlighting portions of the document, she indicated that controversial elements may include the discussion of the "violent God" as portrayed in parts of the Old Testament; the way the concept of "shalom" is employed (although the word, "shalom," itself is not employed throughout the statement; and in section 4.A., support of traditional Lutheran leanings toward the just-unjust theory of war, even though the "richness and importance of the pacifist tradition" in the life of the Church is acknowledged. "We firmly believe, as a task force that we are a church in the just-unjust war tradition and that that tradition still has much to offer us, especially if we study and use it," she commented. Other controversial points include section 5.B., which insists that peace and economic justice belong together; also in that section there is a controversial phrase supporting "sustainable growth and fair distribution." Section 5.C. explores conflict between non-intervention principles and issues of human rights, an issue that is "a very serious problem for the international community and . . . for the church as we try to balance the need to stand up when individuals' rights are being violated, and the need to respect the sovereignty of governments within the borders of their own states. I do not think it is possible for us, given that overarching conflict in international law to resolve this issue within our social statement," Ms. Kidd stated. The issue the effectiveness of collective security has engendered considerable comment; the present draft is careful, she said, in expressing optimism relative to the role of collective security (e.g., the peace-keeping activities of the United Nations) in international affairs. Finally, in the last section, "the idea that we can call upon God to fulfill God's divine purpose and to give God no rest until peace comes" has received significant critique, both pro and con.

Commenting on the document, Ms. Kidd observed that the proposed statement clearly indicates that this church is one with a global perspective and a history of global involvement. It also makes a positive statement about what is required to be peacemakers and builders of peace. Special focus is given to peacemaking tasks prior to the outbreak of violence. Ms. Kidd characterized the Evangelical Lutheran Church in America as a "peace church," in that "an understanding of peace is central to our church." A long-term perspective is reflected in the statement; an effort was made to avoid examples that might "date" the document. The statement seeks to balance the need to be hopeful and the need to be realistic with respect to the achievement of peace in our time. Finally, Ms. Kidd noted that the task force attempted to address specifically the role of the United States in peace and international affairs, even though the document will have wider application within the global Lutheran community.

Chair Magnus invited questions. Several comments followed with respect to the document's liturgical and educational bearings.

VOTED: CC95.4.4

To recommend adoption by the 1995 Churchwide Assembly of the following resolution:

1. To adopt "For Peace in God's World" as a social statement of this church to be used in accordance with the understanding outlined in "Social Statements in the Evangelical Lutheran Church in America: Principles and Procedures" (adopted at the 1989 Churchwide Assembly; CA89.3.14).

2. To call on members of this church to renew our prayer for peace, our identity as a community for peace, and our study of the scriptural witness to the God of Peace, using this statement to help them form their judgments and carry out their commitment to live a faith active for peace.

3. To call on our congregations and professional leaders to give renewed attention to how our liturgy, preaching, hymnody, and prayers embody God's will for peace and our calling for peace.

4. To commend the education, service, and advocacy ministries of this church in their work for peace on our behalf; to direct churchwide units to review their programs and major program directions in light of this social statement with the intention of strengthening this church's witness to global peace; and to call upon members to support these ministries.

5. To direct the Division for Church in Society, in cooperation with other units, particularly the Division for Congregational Ministries, to provide leadership, consultation, and educational and worship resources for congregations on the basis of this statement.

6. To call upon members to give generously to the Evangelical Lutheran Church in America and its World Hunger Appeal, so that the Lutheran World Federation, Lutheran World Relief, Lutheran Immigration and Refugee Service, and our partner ecumenical agencies might do more in helping to alleviate the causes and consequences of war, to resolve conflicts, and to build peace; and to call upon members to participate actively in these ministries.

7. To call upon the educational institutions of this church—day schools, colleges, seminaries, centers of continuing education, and camps—to review their programs in light of this statement, so as to further the study of peace and global affairs.

8. To call upon the members and leaders of this church to support our youth in their struggle to define their identity and vocation as present and future peacemakers, and to call upon pastors and educators to encourage our youth to consider various forms of volunteer service that contribute to peace.

9. To share this social statement with other churches of the Lutheran World Federation, the World Council of Churches, and our other ecumenical partners as a sign of our commitment to work together for peace with justice.

10. To send this social statement to the President of the United States, to our elected representatives in the United States Senate and House of Representatives, to the United States Secretary of State, and to the Secretary General of the United Nations as a sign of our commitment to work with them for a more peaceful world.

William E. Diehl inquired about responses to hate groups. The Rev. Frederick E. N. Rajan, executive director of the Commission for Multicultural Ministries, announced the availability of a printed resource. Charlotte E. Fiechter, executive director of Women of the Evangelical Lutheran Church in America, noted the theme of the organization's next Triennial Convention, "Proclaim God's Peace."

Elections to Unexpired Terms

Vice President Magnus declared elected ("*") those who received a greater-than-majority number of votes in the balloting:

1. Division for Congregational Ministries (clergy term to 1999):
   a. The Rev. David R. Hauck, Washingtonville, Pa. (8E) -- 14
   b. *The Rev. Robert L. Miller, State College, Pa. (8C) -- 23
2. Division for Outreach (clergy term to 1997):
   a. The Rev. Dennis N. Nelson, Gillett, Wis. (5I) -- 16
   b. *The Rev. Richard W. Owens, Bismarck, N.Dak. (3A) -- 20
3. Division for Outreach (lay female term to 1997):
   a. *Ms. Marlene M. Case, Rochester, Minn. (3I) -- 23
   b. Ms. Caroline Wolff, Erie, Pa. (8A) -- 14

Announcements and Recess

Chair Magnus announced that the memorial service for the Rev. Carl H. Mau Jr., former general secretary of the Lutheran World Federation, would be held on Friday, April 7, at Grace Lutheran Church, Des Moines, Washington, at 4:00 P.M.

Following several announcements, the council recessed for lunch at 12:34 P.M., with instructions to return at 1:30 P.M. to meet in executive session.

Resumption of Executive Session

The Church Council entered into an executive session at 1:32 P.M. for purposes of a briefing on legal matters and personnel factors. Because no action was taken in executive session, no separate minutes exist for the session. The executive session ended at 2:29 P.M.

Matters Related to the Division For Church in Society

1. Possible Social Statement on Human Sexuality

Following a progress report on the development of a possible social statement on human sexuality by the Rev. Charles S. Miller Jr., executive director of the Division for Church in Society, the council explored "next steps" in anticipation of the 1995 Churchwide Assembly and subsequent to that assembly.

A written report, which was council agenda Exhibit P, Part 2, provided information related to action taken by the Church Council in November 1994 and by the board of the Division for Church in Society at the board's March 1995 meeting. In November 1994, the council had voted:

> To express thanks to the consulting panel, which was established by the Church Council at the December 1993 meeting, for its role in the process for developing a possible social statement on the church and human sexuality; and
>
> To request that the consulting panel continue in its role until further notice, with the expectation that more specific instructions regarding its role will be developed and transmitted following the Church Council's April 1995 meeting (CC94.11.91).

Discussion ensued. Pastor Miller suggested that, if development of a social statement on human sexuality were not pursued at this time, other steps could be considered. They could include development of an educational plan with seminaries and colleges and universities, resources on biblical interpretation prepared, and a study and listening process undertaken by the Division for Church in Society, and on the basis of current social statements, on some advocacy issues related to hospitality and justice issues.

William H. Engelbrecht moved adoption of the following recommendation:

MOVED;
SECONDED: To receive as information the action of the board of the Division for Church in Society to:

(a) "acknowledge the desirability for this church to consider and adopt a social statement on human sexuality";

(b) "acknowledge the constraints of scheduling the date for the adoption of such a statement to a Church-wide Assembly at this time" [in view of the allocation of staff time and funds];

(c) "ask the executive director to construct a time table and list activities that would lend to the adoption of a social statement, taking into consideration the total responsibilities" of the Division for Church in Society; and

(d) "ask the executive director [of the Division for Church in Society] to present a list of activities related to the subject of human sexuality to the September 1995 meeting [of the board of the Division for Church in Society] that the division will pursue to facilitate this church in its moral deliberation, its practice of hospitality and advocacy for justice in society in this interim until a statement is presented, such a list to be based on observations that can be made from the responses received to the first draft and the working draft of the social statement, and the board's discussion during its session held March 11, 1995";

To express the gratitude of the Church Council of the Evangelical Lutheran Church in America to those congregations that have undertaken or still plan to undertake a study of and prepare a response, by June 30, 1995, to the current working draft of a possible social statement on human sexuality;

To request the executive director of the Division for Church in Society to convene by telephone the members of the consulting panel to provide advice to the division and the Church Council on possible subsequent steps for the development of a social statement on human sexuality for consideration by the 1997 Churchwide Assembly or a later assembly; and

To direct the Executive Committee of the Church Council to review in late July or early August the report prepared by the Division for Church in Society for submission to the 1995 Churchwide Assembly on responses to the working draft and to make recommendations regarding the report to the Church Council at the council's August 15, 1995, meeting in connection with transmittal of the report to the 1995 Churchwide Assembly.

The Rev. Stephen M. Youngdahl suggested that the chair of the division's board be included in the conference call with the consulting panel. He also noted the need to define who would write the report. The suggestion was accepted as a friendly amendment. Pastor Miller said that the executive director would write the report with a draft distributed to the division's board prior to meeting with board's executive committee for transmittal of the report to the Church Council.

Questions of sexuality "are not a duckable issue," the Rev. Franklin D. Fry said. There is a need to admit, however, when we do not know the answers to certain questions. Both drafts make too many absolute statements. Nothing escapes Genesis 3, he argued. "We have got to come clean on what we believe and teach and stake our lives on."

Ramona S. Rank moved the following:

MOVED;
SECONDED;
CARRIED: To postpone further consideration until Sunday, April 2, 1995.

Matters Related to the Division for Ministry

1. Study of Theological Education

Background: The final report of the Study of Theological Education is "Faithful Leaders for a Changing World–Theological Education for Mission in the ELCA." At its March 16-18, 1995, meeting, the board of the Division for Ministry reviewed that report and the related recommendations. The board recommended that the Church Council affirm the report and recommendations and transmit them to the 1995 Churchwide Assembly for adoption.

Council Action: The Rev. Joseph M. Wagner, executive director of the Division for Ministry, characterized the document as being a "strong and broad report." Pastor Wagner introduced Dorothy J. Marple, chair of the study task force, and the Rev. Phyllis B. Anderson, director for theological education in the Division for Ministry.

Ms. Marple observed that she was presenting the "final" report of the task force. She noted that there is "something special about the word, final,…, but in reality" no education is final. "It is an ongoing story." The report is an account of what has been accomplished since the 1993 Churchwide Assembly and anticipates what may come before the 1997 Churchwide Assembly, she indi-

cated. Already 59 of 65 synods are engaging in structured programs of first-call theological education.

Ms. Marple then recognized Pastor Anderson who offered several observations and responded to questions. The strategy will provide a clearer picture on funding potentials, she said. It also may reveal where there may be "strategic abandonments," as well as additional allocation of specific resources. It will portray various potential "revenue streams" for the support of theological education in this church moving into the new century.

Questions and comments by council members followed. Treasurer Richard L. McAuliffe noted that the Budget and Finance Committee of the Church Council needs to become involved, at some point, in the discussion of future funding patterns for theological education.

VOTED: CC95.4.5
To recommend that the 1995 Churchwide Assembly adopt the following resolution:

To receive with appreciation and to affirm the directions outlined in the final report of the Study of Theological Education, "Faithful Leaders for a Changing World–Theological Education for Mission in the ELCA";

To direct the Division for Ministry to report to the 1997 Churchwide Assembly continuing progress of the ELCA seminaries toward fulfilling the 11 imperatives approved by the 1993 Churchwide Assembly;

To require, by the fall of 1997, that all newly rostered pastors and lay leaders participate, throughout their first three years of ministry under call, in structured programs of theological education, designed and supervised by their synods, according to churchwide standards;

To request and encourage the Division for Ministry, together with the Department for Communication, the seminary clusters, and other interested partners, to develop a distance-learning consulting service to be a technological, administrative, and faculty development resource for an ELCA theological education distance-learning network;

To direct the Division for Ministry to report to the 1997 Churchwide Assembly continuing progress by the seminary clusters in meeting the time line approved by the 1993 Churchwide Assembly;

To affirm the decision of the Division for Ministry and the seminaries regarding the expansion of the Study of Theological Education to include programmatic and financial planning for an ELCA system of theological education; and to request that the Division for Ministry prepare by 1997 a case and strategies for this church's increased financial support of a system of theological education;

To urge congregations, synods, and the churchwide organization of the Evangelical Lutheran Church in America to support the efforts of the seminary clusters to increase financial support by granting access to seminary representatives and commending the cause of theological education to potential donors;

To encourage seminary clusters to invest significant time and resources for cultivating participation in deferred giving programs that will build endowments for the future; and

To encourage the seminary clusters, with the support of the Division for Ministry and in coordination with other churchwide units, to initiate regular consultations with their supporting synods regarding program and funding.

2. Ministry of the Baptized (Ministry in Daily Life)

Background: The following action was taken by the 1993 Churchwide Assembly concerning the ministry of the baptized (CA93.6.17):

2a. To reaffirm the universal priesthood of all believers, namely that all baptized Christians are called to minister in the name of Christ and, empowered by the Holy Spirit, to proclaim the promise of God in the world and in their various callings and to bear God's creative and redeeming word to all the world, to meet human needs, work for dignity and justice for all people, and peace and reconciliation among the nations, while praying for one another, hearing confession and forgiving one another, and in emergencies and where authorized, to administer the sacraments of baptism and holy communion.

2b. To direct the Division for Ministry and the Division for Congregational Ministries to lift up and develop further this church's commitment to encourage all baptized members to understand, be equipped for, and live out their ministries in the world and in the church. This church's commitment shall be demonstrated by integrating the emphasis on the ministry of the baptized into the life of this church in and through its various expressions, units, institutions, laity movements, but especially through congregations. The Divisions for Ministry and Congregational Ministries shall make a progress report and appropriate recommendations to the 1995 Churchwide Assembly.

2c. To direct the Division for Ministry to arrange for a two-year period (1993-1995) of theological study and action-reflection on the ministry of the baptized in the world and on the ways in which faithful people are expected to account for their ministries to both God and the community of believers.

In responding to this recommendation during the past biennium, the Division for Ministry engaged in a process of listening to persons throughout this church on matters relating to the ministry of the baptized. Council agenda Exhibit M, Part 2, contained a brief progress report on those conversations. This response to action of the 1993 Churchwide Assembly has complemented the ongoing work in this area being done by the Division for Ministry and the Division for Congregational Ministries,

which shares responsibility for work supporting ministry in daily life.

At its March 1995 meeting, the board of the Division for Ministry determined that these discussions on the ministry of the baptized had not yet reached the point where a specific set of recommendations could be provided to the 1995 Churchwide Assembly. The board expressed its intent to continue and to deepen churchwide conversation on this issue in the coming biennium, so that recommendations may be provided to the 1997 Churchwide Assembly that will move this church forward in its commitment to the ministry of the baptized.

Council Action: Chair Magnus called upon Pastor Wagner to introduce the recommendation that follows, subsequently adopted by the Church Council. He called attention to the broad process that has been under way "to integrate the emphasis on ministry in daily life into the life of this church."

During discussion, William E. Diehl expressed disappointment that the Division for Ministry was not able to develop recommendations in response to action of the 1993 Churchwide Assembly regarding ministry in daily life. He recalled that the "Connections" and the "Word and Witness" programs were not passed into the life of this church. He also observed that the only assignment given to the division by the 1993 assembly that was not completed was that related to ministry in daily life. It might be helpful for some congregations with effective programs of ministry in daily life to dialogue with executive directors and directors of churchwide units, in order to help churchwide staff better understand the needs of 99 percent of the ELCA members, he suggested.

VOTED: CC95.4.6

To transmit to the 1995 Churchwide Assembly the progress report on implementation of the actions of the 1993 Churchwide Assembly that relate to the ministry of the baptized (from the Study of Ministry); and

To recommend that the 1995 Churchwide Assembly adopt the following resolution:

To receive the progress report of the Division for Ministry on matters relating to the ministry of the baptized;

To affirm the plans of the Division for Ministry, in consultation with the Division for Congregational Ministries, to continue and deepen the churchwide conversation on matters relating to the ministry of the baptized in the 1996-1997 biennium; and

To request that the Division for Ministry bring a report and recommendations on this matter to the 1997 Churchwide Assembly.

3. Entry Rite for Diaconal Ministers

Background: The 1993 Churchwide Assembly of the Evangelical Lutheran Church in America established diaconal ministry as part of the officially recognized, rostered ministries of this Church.

This church shall establish and maintain a roster of diaconal ministers who shall be called by this church to positions that exemplify the servant life and that seek to equip and motivate others to live it. Such diaconal ministers shall seek in a great variety of ways to empower, equip, and support all the baptized people of God in the ministry of Jesus Christ and the mission of God in the world.... (ELCA 7.51.05.).

In November 1994, the Church Council adopted the document, "Diaconal Ministers in the Evangelical Lutheran Church in America: Standards, Preparation, Approval, and Call." This document was prepared by the Division for Ministry and affirmed by the Conference of Bishops.

The one outstanding issue upon which the Division for Ministry and the Conference of Bishops had not agreed related to the entry rite for diaconal ministers. At its October 1994 meeting, the Conference of Bishops recommended that diaconal ministers be commissioned. The board of the Division for Ministry, at its October 1994 meeting, received the recommendation for commissioning from the Conference of Bishops. Because of the need for further study before making a final decision, the Division for Ministry board made no recommendation regarding the entry rite for diaconal ministers to the November 1994 Church Council meeting. At its March 1995 meeting, the board of the Division for Ministry recommended that the Church Council affirm the following position:

That diaconal ministers enter service in the Evangelical Lutheran Church in America through a rite of consecration.

The Division for Ministry provided to the Church Council a report describing why it determined that diaconal ministers should be "consecrated"; the Conference of Bishops provided a similar rationale for the use of the word, "commissioning." These were distributed to Church Council members respectively as council agenda Exhibit M, Parts 3a and 3b.

Since the board of the Division for Ministry bears responsibility for recommending policy to the Church Council on this matter, the recommendation that follows, subsequently adopted by the Church Council, was provided for the council's consideration.

Council Action: The Rev. Joseph M. Wagner, executive director of the Division for Ministry, introduced the agenda item. He highlighted the rationale for the recommendation of the board of the Division for Ministry. Bishop Peter Rogness spoke concerning the recommendation of the Conference of Bishops on the matter (council agenda 3b). Two arguments seemed reflected in the action of the bishops: (1) the action of the 1993 Churchwide Assembly in defining these categories as part the lay roster, and the concern that the rite of consecration may cloud that intent; but (2) the dominant reason was carrying forward the apparent intent of the assembly concerning the lay roster.

Discussion followed. The Rev. John O. Knudson moved to amend the recommendation, replacing the word, "consecration," with "commissioning." The motion

was seconded and discussed. The vote on the amendment was: 15—yes; 17—no. The amendment was defeated.

MOVED;
SECONDED;
DEFEATED: To amend the recommendation by replacing the word, "consecration," with "commissioning."

The unamended main motion was approved on a voice vote with audible dissent.

VOTED: CC95.4.7
To affirm that diaconal ministers will enter service in the Evangelical Lutheran Church in America through a rite of consecration.

The council recessed for the day at 5:06 P.M.

Sunday Session
Vice President Kathy J. Magnus called the meeting to order at 9:38 A.M. The session followed the Service of Holy Communion in the Lutheran Center chapel at 8:30 A.M. The service was led by Bishop Paull E. Spring as presiding minister, Ms. Ramona S. Rank as assisting minister, the Rev. David A. Andert as preacher, and Mr. J. David Ellwanger as lector.

Matters Related to the Division for Church in Society
2.   Possible Social Statement on Human Sexuality
Discussion resumed on the motion postponed the previous day regarding a possible social statement on human sexuality:

To receive as information the action of the board of the Division for Church in Society to:
(a)   "acknowledge the desirability for this church to consider and adopt a social statement on human sexuality";
(b)   "acknowledge the constraints of scheduling the date for the adoption of such a statement to a Churchwide Assembly at this time" [in view of the allocation of staff time and funds];
(c)   "ask the executive director to construct a time table and list activities that would lend to the adoption of a social statement, taking into consideration the total responsibilities" of the Division for Church in Society; and
(d)   "ask the executive director [of the Division for Church in Society] to present a list of activities related to the subject of human sexuality to the September 1995 meeting [of the board of the Division for Church in Society] that the division will pursue to facilitate this church in its moral deliberation, its practice of hospitality and advocacy for justice in society in this interim until a statement is presented, such a list to be based on observations that can be

made from the responses received to the first draft and the working draft of the social statement, and the board's discussion during its session held March 11, 1995";

To express the gratitude of the Church Council of the Evangelical Lutheran Church in America to those congregations that have undertaken or still plan to undertake a study of and prepare a response, by June 30, 1995, to the current working draft of a possible social statement on human sexuality;

To request the executive director of the Division for Church in Society to convene by telephone the members of the consulting panel to provide advice to the division and the Church Council on possible subsequent steps for the development of a social statement on human sexuality for consideration by the 1997 Churchwide Assembly or a later assembly; and

To direct the Executive Committee of the Church Council to review in late July or early August the report prepared by the Division for Church in Society for submission to the 1995 Churchwide Assembly on responses to the working draft and to make recommendations regarding the report to the Church Council at the council's August 15, 1995, meeting in connection with transmittal of the report to the 1995 Churchwide Assembly.

The Rev. Franklin D. Fry recommended an amendment for the third part of the resolution to read, ". . . on possible subsequent steps that would be necessary for the development of a possible social statement on human sexuality . . .." The proposed changed was accepted as a friendly amendment.

Mr. William H. Engelbrecht moved to close debate. The motion was seconded and approved.

VOTED: CC95.4.8

To receive as information the action of the board of the Division for Church in Society to:

(a) "acknowledge the desirability for this church to consider and adopt a social statement on human sexuality";

(b) "acknowledge the constraints of scheduling the date for the adoption of such a statement to a Churchwide Assembly at this time" [in view of the allocation of staff time and funds];

(c) "ask the executive director to construct a time table and list activities that would lend to the adoption of a social statement, taking into consideration the total responsibilities" of the Division for Church in Society; and

(d) "ask the executive director [of the Division for Church in Society] to present a list of activities related to the subject of human sexuality to the September 1995 meeting [of the board of the Division for

Church in Society] that the division will pursue to facilitate this church in its moral deliberation, its practice of hospitality and advocacy for justice in society in this interim until a statement is presented, such a list to be based on observations that can be made from the responses received to the first draft and the working draft of the social statement, and the board's discussion during its session held March 11, 1995";

To express the gratitude of the Church Council of the Evangelical Lutheran Church in America to those congregations that have undertaken or still plan to undertake a study of and prepare a response, by June 30, 1995, to the current working draft of a possible social statement on human sexuality;

To request the board chair and the executive director of the Division for Church in Society to convene by telephone the members of the consulting panel to provide advice to the division and the Church Council on subsequent steps that would be necessary for the possible development of a social statement on human sexuality for consideration by the 1997 Churchwide Assembly or a later assembly; and

To direct the Executive Committee of the Church Council to review in late July or early August the report prepared by the Division for Church in Society for submission to the 1995 Churchwide Assembly on responses to the working draft and to make recommendations regarding the report to the Church Council at the council's August 15, 1995, meeting in connection with transmittal of the report to the 1995 Churchwide Assembly.

Matters Related to the Division for Ministry (continued)

4. Entry Rite for Deaconesses

Background: Associates in ministry, deaconesses, and diaconal ministers constitute the rostered lay ministries of this church. Since the entry rites for rostered lay ministries have been reviewed by the Task Force on the Study of Ministry, and since the Division for Ministry, with advice from the Conference of Bishops, also has considered whether diaconal ministers should be commissioned or consecrated, the Division for Ministry took up the question of the entry rites for deaconesses as well.

The current practice of the Evangelical Lutheran Church in America is that deaconesses enter service by being "set apart" (Occasional Services of the *Lutheran Book of Worship*). During fall 1994, the board of the ELCA Deaconess Community requested that consecration be the entry rite for deaconesses to enter upon their official ministries in the Evangelical Lutheran Church in America. The board of the Division for Ministry agreed to recommend this to the Church Council. The rationale for the request of the Deaconess Community, articulated in a January 1995 memo to all bishops, is that consecration has been the historic rite of entry for deaconesses in the Lutheran church. The language of being *set apart*, found in the Occasional Services of the *Lutheran Book of Worship,* is publicly interpreted by the ELCA Deaconess Community as *consecration*, in keeping with practice prior to 1962.

The Division for Ministry sought further advice from the Division for Ministry Liaison Committee of the Conference of Bishops in January 1995. The recommendation of the committee, which was affirmed by the full conference at its March 1995 meeting, is that the entry rite for deaconesses remain the rite of *setting apart*, not consecration or commissioning. The following reasons were provided for this recommendation:

1. While the historic practice is consecration, the official entry rite in the ELCA and its predecessors since 1962 has been setting apart, not consecration. The Occasional Services of the *Service Book and Hymnal,* and of the *Lutheran Book of Worship* make no mention of consecration as the entry rite for deaconesses. The precedent in the ELCA is for setting apart.
2. In addition to this argument of current practice, the retention of setting apart for deaconesses avoids the potential relational problem of having deaconesses consecrated, should associates in ministry and diaconal ministers be commissioned. Those responsible for developing diaconal ministry guidelines have preferred consecration but have agreed to commissioning. To have consecrated deaconesses and commissioned diaconal ministers would be inconsistent and potentially divisive. It is anticipated that these two groups of diaconal workers will be linked very closely in coming years, and they should be able to cooperate without friction regarding their entry rites.
3. When the Study of Ministry brought roster recommendations and the 1993 Churchwide Assembly adopted those recommendations, a principle was observed to maintain the status and patterns of the previously-existing rosters. This principle argues for retaining deaconesses as women set apart for their ministries.

At its March 1995 meeting, the board of the Division for Ministry did not agree with the advice of the Conference of Bishops and took the following action, in support of the request of the ELCA Deaconess Community:

> That consecration be the rite of entry for persons serving in the Deaconess Community of the Evangelical Lutheran Church in America.

The rationale for the board's position is the same rationale for the use of the term, *consecration* in the entry rite for diaconal ministers.

Council Action: The Rev. Joseph M. Wagner, executive director of the Division for Ministry, presented some background information on the proposal.

VOTED: CC95.4.9
To affirm that the rite of entry for persons serving in the Deaconess Community of the Evangelical Lutheran Church in America be "consecration."

5.   Report on Rostered Leaders' Compensation

Council agenda Exhibit M, Part 7, contained the report to the 1995 Churchwide Assembly on clergy compensation, which had been prepared by the Division for Ministry in response to action taken at the 1991 and 1993 churchwide assemblies. The recommendation was moved and seconded, and subsequently carried.

VOTED: CC95.4.10
To transmit to the 1995 Churchwide Assembly the report of the Division for Ministry on Clergy Compensation:

CLERGY COMPENSATION REPORT TO THE
EVANGELICAL LUTHERAN CHURCH IN AMERICA
CHURCHWIDE ASSEMBLY

[*NOTE: The text of the report will appear in Volume 2 of the Pre-Assembly Report.*]

6.   Associates in Ministry and Diaconal Ministers

The 1993 Churchwide Assembly voted:

> "To direct the Division for Ministry to study the relationship between associates in ministry and diaconal ministers, with the results and any recommendations emerging from such a study to be presented to the 1995 Churchwide Assembly" (CA93.6.17).

The board of the Division for Ministry reviewed the report printed in council agenda Exhibit M, Part 9, and recommended that the Church Council transmit this report to the 1995 Churchwide Assembly. Pastor Wagner provided additional background information on the report.

VOTED: CC95.4.11
To transmit the report, "Relationship Between Associates in Ministry and Diaconal Ministers" to the 1995 Churchwide Assembly:

RELATIONSHIP BETWEEN ASSOCIATES IN MINISTRY AND
DIACONAL MINISTERS"

[*NOTE: The text of the report will appear in Volume 2 of the Pre-Assembly Report.*]

ELCA Pension and Other Benefits Program

1.   Medical Rates for Retirees Under Age 65

Chair Magnus called upon Mr. John G. Kapanke, president of the Board of Pensions, to discuss possible options on the setting of rates for retirees under the age of 65. The subject will be considered, he said, by the board of trustees of the Board of Pensions in May 1995.

The Church Council received the report as information.

2.   Pharmacy-Network Evaluation Project

Mr. Kapanke also presented a progress report on a benefit study that may result in recommendations regarding the pharmacy-network programs for covered persons in the Standard Benefit Program of the Board of Pensions. He indicated that the mail-order maintenance drug program had become popular. In the point-of-service program of Aetna, short-term prescription costs are $5, generic, and $12, brand specific. Outside the network, however, only one-half of the cost of short-term prescriptions is reimbursed. The matter is under examination. The Church Council received the report as information.

Report of the Executive for Administration

The Rev. Robert N. Bacher, executive for administration, reflected on five topics, detailed in his written report. The report was received as information.

The mid-morning recess began at 10:56 A.M. The session resumed at 11:13 A.M.

Report of the Budget and Finance Committee

Vice President Magnus recognized Edith M. Lohr, chair of the Church Council's Budget and Finance Committee, for the report. She introduced items in the report.

1. 1995 Expenditure Authorization

At its November 1994 meeting, the Church Council voted:

> To approved an initial 1995 fiscal year spending authorization of $73,925,000, with an initial Mission Operating Fund allocation of $1,500,000; and
>
> To approve an initial 1995 World Hunger spending authorization of $11,400,000 (CC94.11.71).

This action was taken after a review of the revised income estimates and identified cost increases at that time. Preliminary review of the final fiscal 1994 results suggested that no additional adjustments need to be made at this time. Should the income projections change during the course of the 1995 fiscal year, previous action of the Church Council authorizes the Church Council Executive Committee, upon recommendation from the Church Council Budget and Finance Committee, to establish a revised spending authorization between Church Council meetings.

2. 1996-1997 Budget Proposal

Background: A draft of the narrative report describing the 1996-97 budget proposal that will be presented to the 1995 Churchwide Assembly was reviewed. Setting out overview, criteria, influencing factors, desired outcome, and future issues, this narrative was intended to place the budget proposal into context for voting members as they prepare to vote on the recommendation of the Church Council.

Only the 1996 unit expense proposal has been prepared for review by the 1995 Churchwide Assembly, as has been the practice in past budget cycles. Given the erratic patterns of income in recent years, establishing unit allocations for two years in the future (1997) does not allow for the flexibility needed to deal with changing circumstances. In the fall of 1996 the Church Council will review the unit expense allocations for 1997.

The 1996 Summary of Programs and Services by Churchwide Units, council agenda Exhibit F, Part 7, will also be presented to the 1995 Churchwide Assembly. This exhibit defines the major program areas of each churchwide unit, describing the mission goals of each program and the total budgeted dollars allocated to them.

Council Action: Dale V. Sandstrom asked about the basis for any anticipated increased in projected income. Ms. Lohr's response related to the Vision for Mission Fund. The Rev. Mark R. Moller-Gunderson also responded. Mission-support goals are set to be fair, realistic, and yet challenging. The Rev. Nadine F. Lehr inquired about the specifics of budget allocation. William E. Diehl inquired about the Special Needs Retirement Fund.

VOTED: **CC95.4.12**

To recommend to the 1995 Churchwide Assembly adoption of the following resolution:

(a) <u>1996 Budget Proposal</u>

To approve a 1996 current fund budget proposal of $75,325,000, with an initial Mission Operating Fund allocation of $1,500,000, and an Expanded Ministry Fund allocation of $515,000;

To approve a 1996 World Hunger budget proposal of $12,000,000; and

To authorize the Church Council to establish a spending authorization after review of 1995 actual income and 1996 revised income estimates.

and

(b) <u>1997 Budget Proposal</u>

To approve a 1997 current fund budget proposal of $76,325,000, with an initial Mission Operating Fund allocation of $1,500,000;

To approve a 1997 World Hunger budget proposal of $12,200,000; and

To authorize the Church Council to establish a spending authorization after review of 1996 actual income and 1997 revised income estimates.

The Rev. Donald M. Hallberg raised a question about the coordination of fund-raising and stewardship education. Pastor Moller-Gunderson responded from the perspective of the Financial Stewardship Strategy adopted by the 1993 Churchwide Assembly. He noted there are 400 development offices in entities and institutions throughout this church. Coordination may grow slowly.

3. Synodical-Churchwide Consultations on Mission-Support Commitments

Background: The ELCA Church Council has the responsibility of reviewing and approving or withholding approval for synodical mission-support commitments.

1995 Commitments

Revisions to 1995 synod mission-support commitments have been received from 32 synods.

VOTED: CC95.4.13

To adopt the following resolution:

1. The Church Council acknowledges with thanks the revisions to the 1995 synod mission-support commitments that have been made by the following synods:

   Northwest Washington, Southern California (West), Pacifica, Southwestern Minnesota, Southeastern Minnesota, Nebraska, Central States, Metropolitan Chicago, Western Iowa, Northern Great Lakes, Northwest Synod of Wisconsin, East-Central Synod of Wisconsin, Greater Milwaukee, South-Central Synod of Wisconsin, La Crosse Area, Slovak Zion, Upper Susquehanna, Allegheny, West Virginia-Western Maryland, Virginia, North Carolina, and South Carolina; and

2. The Church Council acknowledges with thanks and appreciation the increases in the 1995 synod mission-support commitments (expressed in dollars and/or percentages,) which have been made by the following synods:

   Northwestern Minnesota, Arkansas-Oklahoma, and Southwestern Pennsylvania; and

3. The Church Council requests further consultations with the following synods due to significant change in either dollar or percentage commitments for 1995 mission support:

   Eastern Washington-Idaho, Western North Dakota, Southern Ohio, Northeastern Pennsylvania, Northwestern Pennsylvania, Delaware-Maryland, and Metropolitan Washington, D.C.

1996 Commitments

Synod commitments for mission support in 1996 have been received from 64 synods to date.

VOTED: CC95.4.14

To adopt the following resolution:

1. The Church Council acknowledges with thanks and appreciation the mission support commitment for 1996 of the following synods:

   Northwest Washington, Southwestern Washington, Oregon, Montana, Sierra Pacific, Southern California (West), Pacifica, Grand Canyon, Rocky Mountain, South Dakota, Northwestern Minnesota, Southwestern Minnesota, Minneapolis Area, Saint Paul Area, Southeastern Minnesota, Nebraska, Arkansas-Oklahoma, Southwestern Texas, Texas-Louisiana Gulf Coast, Metropolitan Chicago, Northern Illinois, Central/ Southern Illinois, Southeastern Iowa, Western Iowa, Northeastern Iowa, Northern Great Lakes, Northwest Synod of Wisconsin, East-Central Synod of Wisconsin, Greater Milwaukee, South-Central Synod of Wisconsin, La Crosse Area, Southeast Michigan, North/West Lower Michigan, Indiana-Kentucky, Northwestern Ohio, Northeastern Ohio, New Jersey, New England, Metropolitan New York, Southeastern Pennsylvania, Slovak Zion, Northwestern Pennsylvania, Southwestern Pennsylvania, Allegheny, Lower Susquehanna, Upper Susquehanna, West Virginia-Western Maryland, Virginia, North Carolina, South Carolina, Southeastern, Florida-Bahamas; and Caribbean;

2. The Church Council acknowledges with concern a reduction in either the dollar or percentage mission-support commitments for 1996 made by the following synods:

   Eastern North Dakota, and Central States;

3. The Church Council requests additional consultation concerning the 1996 mission-support commitment with the following synods:

   Alaska, Eastern Washington-Idaho, Western North Dakota, Northeastern Minnesota, Northern Texas-Northern Louisiana, and Delaware-Maryland;

4. The Church Council postpones a decision, pending further clarification of mission-support data, for the following synods:

   Southern Ohio, Northeastern Pennsylvania, and Metropolitan Washington, D.C.; and

5. The Church Council postpones a decision on the 1996 mission-support commit-

ments for the following synod until such commitment is received:

Upstate New York;

To authorize the Church Council Executive Committee to respond to those synods for which further consultation or data is to be anticipated; and

To request the Coordinator for Mission Support to notify each synod of the response of the Church Council.

4. Vision for Mission Fund: Financial Development and Progress Report

Background: Council agenda Exhibit F, Part 9, reflected the status of the Vision for Mission Fund at the preliminary close of the 1994 fiscal year. This exhibit showed funds received from all sources identified as Vision for Mission. The Church Council received the report as information. The Rev. Mark R. Moller-Gunderson, executive director of the Division for Congregational Ministries, reported that about 25 synod "piggy-back" appeals.

Council Action: The Church Council received the report as information.

5. Mission Support–Alternative Formula and Process Report

Background: Council agenda Exhibit F, Part 10, was the report, "Mission Support–Alternative Formula and Process." It was reviewed by the Conference of Bishops at its March 1995 meeting.

Council Action: The Rev. Mark R. Moller-Gunderson, executive director of the Division for Congregational Ministries, reviewed the historical development of the report and its key features.

VOTED: **CC95.4.15**

To approve the revised report, "Mission Support–Alternative Formula and Process," for submission to and possible approval at the 1995 Churchwide Assembly.

VOTED: **CC95.4.16**

To recommend that the 1995 Churchwide Assembly adopt the following resolution:

To receive the report, "Mission Support—Alternative Formula and Process"; and

To approve the procedures, outlined in the report, "Mission Support—Alternative Formula and Processes," as the means for fulfillment of the required determination— under ELCA churchwide constitutional provision 10.71. and †S15.12. in the Constitution for Synods—of the sharing between synods and the churchwide organization of mission-support funds submitted by congregations for support of synodical and churchwide ministries.

6. ELCA Foundation

The ELCA Foundation reports to the Church Council through the Budget and Finance Committee semi-annually. The ELCA Foundation report was provided as council agenda Exhibit H, Part 1a, page 30 ff.

The session recessed at 12:27 P.M. for lunch. The meeting resumed at 1:35 P.M.

Nomination of the Editor of *The Lutheran*

In regard to *The Lutheran* magazine, churchwide bylaw 17.21.01. provides, "The advisory committee, in consultation with the bishop of this church and the Church Council, shall nominate the editor for the church periodical." The subsequent bylaw (17.21.02.) specifies, "The Churchwide Assembly shall elect the editor of the church periodical." Election is to a four-year term (17.21.02. and 19.51.04.), beginning "on the first day of the third month after election" (19.51.04.). Further, according to bylaw 19.11.01., "For the position of editor of *The Lutheran*, a majority of the legal votes cast shall be necessary for election."

Meeting on October 28, 1994, the advisory committee for *The Lutheran* voted "that the Rev. Edgar R. Trexler be nominated as editor of *The Lutheran*, for a four-year term."

The Church Council has the responsibility for transmitting this nomination by the advisory committee to the Churchwide Assembly.

VOTED: **CC95.4.17**

To transmit to the 1995 Churchwide Assembly the nomination by the advisory committee for *The Lutheran* of the Rev. Edgar R. Trexler for election to a four-year term as editor of *The Lutheran* magazine.

Terms of Executive Directors and Department Directors

The election of a new bishop of the Evangelical Lutheran Church in America in 1995 affects the timing of the process by which executive directors, department directors, and the treasurer are asked to continue when their terms expire, or new persons are selected to fill those positions. The new bishop assumes responsibility on November 1, 1995. The process of evaluation of the executive directors of commissions and department directors, together with the possible selection of new staff, may require more time than would be available to the new bishop between November 1 and the November 17-20, 1995, Church Council meeting. In addition, board meetings, at which the elections of executive directors of divisions occur, are generally scheduled before November 1.

Council agenda Exhibit C, Part 3, contained a listing of all incumbent executive directors, department directors, and their terms. The following schedule for election of key staff would provide for an orderly election process for these staff.

1. Treasurer

The following provision of the ELCA governing documents describes the process providing for the election of the treasurer of this church:

> The treasurer shall be elected by the Church Council to a four-year term and shall be a voting member of a congregation of this church (ELCA 13.52.).

The term of the incumbent treasurer expires February 1, 1996, with election for the new term scheduled for the November 1995 meeting of the Church Council.

This was received as information.

2. Executive Directors of Divisions

The following provision of the ELCA's governing documents relates to the election of the executive directors of divisions:

> Each board shall elect its executive director to a four-year term in consultation with and with the approval of the bishop of this church. Nomination of a candidate for election by the board shall be made jointly by the bishop of this church and the search committee of the board. . . . Executive directors shall be eligible for reelection (ELCA 16.11.21.).

a. Division for Global Mission and Division for Outreach

Background: The Rev. Mark W. Thomsen, executive director of the Division for Global Mission, has announced his retirement. A selection process is under way, which would provide for conversation between the board and the bishop-elect during September 1995. A joint nomination will be made to the board of the division, which meets in October 1995.

The term of the incumbent executive director of the Division for Outreach, the Rev. Malcolm L. Minnick Jr., expires on July 15, 1997.

Council Action: The foregoing was received as information. Chair Magnus suggested, based on discussion of the Church Council's Executive Committee, that the Church Council's Coordination and Services Committee might examine whether policy should be developed that would preclude a board restriction consideration to an ordained minister.

The Rev. Nadine F. Lehr moved:

MOVED;
SECONDED: To request that the Church Council's Coordination and Services Committee meet with the board of the Division for Global Mission to revisit the question of an ordination requirement as a criterion for the executive director's position of that unit.

The Rev. Stephen M. Youngdahl moved to substitute the following:

MOVED;
SECONDED: To direct the Church Council's Coordination and Services Committee, at the November 1995

meeting, to review the relationship and responsibilities of the unit board, the Office of the Bishop, and the Church Council in establishing the criteria for, and selection of, unit directors."

Chair Magnus called for the vote on the substitution. The motion to substitute was adopted and became the main motion. The council then voted on the main motion.

VOTED: CC95.4.18

To direct the Church Council's Coordination and Services Committee, at the November 1995 meeting, to review the relationship and responsibilities of the unit board, the Office of the Bishop, and the Church Council in establishing the criteria for, and selection of, unit directors.

J. David Ellwanger suggested the revisiting of titles, namely, only one executive director for the churchwide organization with division directors.

Questions were asked on the plan for staffing the executive director position with two part-time persons in the Division for Congregational Ministries. Pastor Youngdahl asked that that be part of the review requested in the above resolution. Edith M. Lohr suggested that the topic was a management issue and not a matter for consideration by the board of directors. Lorraine G. Bergquist indicated that she believed some discussion by the Church Council was needed on the subject.

b. Division for Higher Education and Schools, Division for Ministry, Division for Church in Society, and Division for Congregational Ministries

The terms of incumbent executive directors expire on the following dates:

Division for Higher Education and Schools	September 1, 1995;
Division for Ministry	October 1, 1995;
Division for Church in Society and	October 31, 1995;
Division for Congregational Ministries	December 31, 1995.

In order to allow for an ordered process of review and consultation with the new bishop, the Office of the Bishop recommends that the boards of these divisions vote on new terms at their winter-spring 1996 meetings.

VOTED: CC95.4.19

To extend the term of the incumbent executive directors of the Division for Congregational Ministries, Division for Ministry, Division for Higher Education and Schools, and Division for Church in Society until the winter-spring 1996 meetings of their respective boards; and

To schedule the election of the executive directors of these units at their winter-spring 1996 meetings, following consultation with the bishop of the Evangelical Lutheran Church in America

3. Commission for Women and Commission for Multicultural Ministries

The following provision of the ELCA's governing documents relates to the election of the executive directors of commissions:

Each commission shall have an executive director who shall be elected by the Church Council to a four-year term in consultation with and with the approval of the bishop of this church. Nomination of a candidate for election by the council shall be made jointly by the bishop of this church and the steering committee (ELCA 16.22.14.).

The term of the current executive directors expire on the following dates:

Commission for Multicultural Ministries   January 16, 1996;
Commission for Women   January 15, 1996.

VOTED: **CC95.4.20**
To extend the term of the incumbent executive directors of the Commission for Multicultural Ministries and the Commission for Women until the April 1996 meeting of the Church Council; and

To schedule the election of the executive directors of these units at the April 1996 Church Council meeting.

4. Directors of Departments

The following provision of the ELCA's governing documents relates to the election of the directors of departments:

The director for this department shall be nominated by the bishop and elected by the Church Council to a four-year term. The director shall be eligible for reelection (ELCA 15.31.B91.b.—*example from the Department for Communication*).

The terms of the current department directors expire as follows:

Department of Human Resources and
    Management Services   November 1995;
Department for Communication   April 1997;
Department for Ecumenical Affairs   November 1995;
Department for Research and Evaluation   November 1995;
Department for Synodical Relations   January 1998.

In order to provide for a smooth transition with a newly elected bishop, the Office of the Bishop recommends the following.

VOTED: **CC95.4.21**
To schedule the election of the directors of the Department for Ecumenical Affairs, Department for Human Resources and Management Services, and Department for Research and Evaluation at the November 1995 meeting of the Church Council.

5. President of the Board of Pensions

The bylaws governing the process for the election of the executive director of the Board of Pensions, a separately incorporated unit, provide that:

The president shall be elected by the board of trustees of the Board of Pensions to a four-year term in consultation with and with the approval of the bishop of this church. Nomination of a candidate for president shall be made jointly by the bishop of this church and the search committee of the board (ELCA 17.61.06.).

The term of the president of the Board of Pensions expires October 1, 1995, with election for the new term scheduled for the August 3-4, 1995, meeting of the Board of Pensions.

This was received as information.

6. Providing for Flexibility in the Election Schedule

The following resolution would provide the bishop-elect the means to suggest changes in this time line for election of executive and department directors between the August and November 1995 meetings of the Church Council.

VOTED: **CC95.4.22**
To authorize the Executive Committee of the Church Council to make adjustments in this schedule of election of executive and department directors, upon the request of the bishop-elect.

Matters Related to the Division for Congregational Ministries

1. Statement on Sacramental Practices

Chair Magnus introduced three resource persons: the Rev. Mary Ann Moller-Gunderson, executive director of the Division for Congregational Ministries; the Rev. Michael R. Rothaar, interim director for worship in that division; and the Rev. Charles H. Maahs, bishop of the Central States Synod and a member of the Task Force on Sacramental Practices. Ms. Magnus noted that this is Pastor Moller-Gunderson's last regular meeting with the Church Council in her role as executive director of the Division for Congregational Ministries.

A copy of the first draft of a proposed statement on sacramental practices was mailed to members of the Church Council in early February 1995. After that mailing, the statement was reviewed by the Conference of Bishops, which provided advice to the Division for Congregational Ministries. The board of the Division for Congregational Ministries reviewed the draft at its March 10-12, 1995, meeting and made some changes.

A copy of the revised statement, "The Use of the Means of Grace–A Statement on the Practice of Word and Sacrament" (with Commentary), as approved by the board of the Division for Congregation Ministries, was provided to council members.

Pastor Moller-Gunderson expressed the hope that the statement would foster common practice and caution against careless practice in regard to the sacramental life of this church. The statement provides a firm stand on the Communion of the baptized. It urges hospitality between and among congregations with differing practices.

Bishop Maahs summarized responses to the document provided by the Conference of Bishops. "Flash points" identified by the bishops were (1) weekly communion as the norm; (2) communion of the baptized; (3) its attitude toward use of grape juice; and (4) how the document will be perceived and used in this church. The members of the conference expressed appreciation for the teaching tone of the document. Forty-seven changes were suggested, most of which were included in the document.

Pastor Moller-Gunderson indicated that the board of the Division for Congregational Ministries made some editorial changes and requested the Church Council to authorize distribution. She outlined the publication and distribution dates:

- Distribution to congregations by mail no later than April 24, 1995
- Release to Lutherlink and the media three days after mailing to congregations
- Availability of June 1, 1995, supplemental resource packet from Division for Congregational Ministries
- Deadline for response to document June 1, 1996

Discussion followed. The recommendation of the board of the Division for Congregational Ministries was moved and seconded. Further discussion followed. Dale V. Sandstrom expressed concern about reaction of this church to the document. He expressed "great reservations" about distributing it.

Chair Magnus declared the meeting to be in recess at 3:40 P.M. The session resumed at 3:55 P.M.

Edith M. Lohr moved:

MOVED;
SCONDED: That all individual comments be limited to two minutes per person for the rest of the agenda for this meeting.

The motion was seconded, and subsequently lost.

Bishop Charles H. Maahs responded to the concern expressed before the break by Mr. Sandstrom. He indicated that the members of the Conference of Bishops did discuss that concern, but generally felt that the tone of the document might assist congregations in dealing with this in a positive way.

Mr. Sandstrom proposed that section C.3.6.a. be changed. A question was raised as to whether the document was open to amendment. Mr. Sandstrom proposed to delete the words, "Since the baptized are welcomed . . ." through the words, ". . . gift of Christ in the supper"; and to change next sentence to read, "The age for this beginning communion may vary . . .." J. David Ellwanger urged that the original wording be retained.

The question was called by Edith M. Lohr, and debate subsequently was closed. The Church Council then voted on the motion.

VOTED: CC95.4.23
To affirm the recommendation of the board of the Division for Congregational Ministries to distribute the first draft of the statement, "The Use of the Means of Grace–A Statement on the Practice of Word and Sacrament" (with Commentary); and

To encourage congregations to engage in careful study of this document and to share with the Division for Congregational Ministries their

response to this draft, in preparation for the second draft of this statement in 1996.

Report of the Conference of Bishops

Bishop Kenneth H. Sauer, chair of the Conference of Bishops, was introduced for the report of the Conference of Bishops. He elaborated on parts of the written report. He addressed specifically the responsibility of bishops for fidelity to the confessions of this church.

1995 Churchwide Assembly

Chair Magnus introduced the Rev. Lee S. Thoni, executive assistant to the bishop, to present information on plans for the 1995 Churchwide Assembly, to be held in Minneapolis August 16-22.

1. Rules of Organization and Procedure

The proposed rules of organization and procedure for the 1995 Churchwide Assembly then were presented.

VOTED: CC95.4.24
To commend the "Rules of Organization and Procedure" to the 1995 Churchwide Assembly for adoption:

RULES OF ORGANIZATION AND PROCEDURE
FOR THE 1995 CHURCHWIDE ASSEMBLY
[NOTE: The text of the rules will appear in
Volume 2 of the Pre-Assembly Report.]

and

To authorize the bishop and the secretary of this church to make appropriate changes in the day, date, and hour provisions, and other necessary adjustments as the agenda and program of the assembly are finalized.

2. Recognition of Upsala College

A request from the board of the Division for Higher Education and Schools for recognition of Upsala College was introduced.

VOTED: CC95.4.25
To request that the Division for Higher Education and Schools work with the Office of the Bishop to arrange an appropriate observance during the 1995 Churchwide Assembly in recognition and gratitude for the 102 years of history and service of Upsala College, East Orange, N.J.

Report of the
Program and Structure Committee
1. Report on Multicultural Mission Strategy

Chair Magnus called upon the Rev. Stephen M. Youngdahl, chair of the Program and Structure Committee, to report on behalf of the committee.

VOTED: CC95.4.26

To transmit to the 1995 Churchwide Assembly the report on the Multicultural Mission Strategy. . ..

[*NOTE: The text of the rules will appear in Volume 2 of the Pre-Assembly Report.*]

Report of the Legal and Constitutional Review Committee

Dale V. Sandstrom, chair of the Legal and Constitutional Review Committee, began the report of the committee.

1. Mission Investment Fund Amendments

The Division for Outreach and the Office of the Treasurer have engaged in extended conversations to refine the administrative operation of the Mission Investment Fund. In view of agreed-upon changes and adjustments, the time has come for amendment of the relevant continuing resolutions that guide the operation of the Mission Investment Fund.

Churchwide constitutional provision 22.31. stipulates that: "Provisions relating to the administrative functions of this church shall be set forth in the continuing resolutions." Such continuing resolutions "may be adopted or amended . . . by a two-thirds vote of the Church Council."

Proposed revisions of continuing resolutions related to the Mission Investment Fund were approved by a greater than two-thirds vote.

2/3 VOTE REQUIRED

VOTED: CC95.4.27

To amend continuing resolution 15.21.A91. as follows and renumber as 15.21.A95.:

15.21.A9**15**.   Operation of Mission Investment Fund of the ELCA

a. The Mission Investment Fund of the Evangelical Lutheran Church in America shall have primary responsibility for promotion of Mission Investments.

b. The provisions of 15.11.D91. shall apply to the Mission Investment Fund of the ELCA.

c. The board of directors **trustees** of the Mission Investment Fund of the ELCA shall be eleven in number, who shall be elected by the Church Council for two **six**-year terms and shall be eligible for re-election, with six members nominated by the Church Council's Budget and Finance Committee, four members nominated by the board of the Division for Outreach, and

one member nominated by the board of the Division for Church in Society.

d. Staff services for the Mission Investment Fund of the ELCA shall be provided by staff of the Office of the Treasurer.

e **d.** Relationship to Division for Outreach: This **The** Mission Investment Fund of the ELCA shall relate to the Division for Outreach. The Division for Outreach shall have staff responsible **request** for real estate acquisition and disposition for new and/or existing ministries within the limits of the capital funds available and within criteria established jointly by the Division for Outreach and the Mission Investment Fund of the ELCA. The Mission Investment Fund of the ELCA, through the Office of the Treasurer, shall provide expertise for management of real property and execute all necessary documents for the acquisition and disposition of such property.

f **e.** Capital Budget Development: An annual capital budget for ministry development shall be established. The budget shall be prepared by a joint staff committee comprised of staff from the Division for Outreach and the Office of the Treasurer **Mission Investment Fund**. This budget is to be based on projected availability of capital funds and projected requirements for loans and real property acquisition for ministry development, church building programs, or other approved capital needs. This capital budget, upon recommendation of the joint staff committee, will be submitted to the board of the Division for Outreach and the board of the Mission Investment Fund of the ELCA for approval and recommendation to the Church Council. Following approval, the capital budget shall be monitored by the joint staff committee.

g̶ f. Within guidelines established jointly by the Division for Outreach and the Mission Investment Fund of the ELCA, the Division for Outreach <u>Mission Investment Fund</u> shall have the responsibility for determining which congregations shall receive loans, the amount of each loan, and the repayment schedule. The Division for Outreach shall supervise the collection of said loan. Upon order of the Division for Outreach, the Mission Investment Fund of the ELCA shall execute the loan, ensure safekeeping for the legal documents, and provide accounting services for the repayment<u>, supervise collection, and confer with the Division for Outreach on any exceptions to established loan policies</u>.

g. <u>The Mission Investment Fund shall offer building and architectural consultative services to new congregations entering first-unit construction, to congregations relocating with synodical approval, to other congregations, and to campus ministry programs of the Division for Higher Education and Schools.</u>

and

To amend continuing resolution 16.11.C91. as follows:

16.11.C91.　Division for Outreach
This division shall provide leadership and support for this church as it reaches out in witness to the Gospel in the areas served by the synods of this church by developing new ministries and congregations; supporting existing ministries and congregations in transition or with special needs; <u>and working with synods in developing area strategies for outreach; and administering capital funds for loans, real-estate acquisition, and building programs in support of new ministries and congregations.</u>
To fulfill these responsibilities, this division shall:

a. develop and recommend policy for, and then assist in the development of new ministries and congregations, the support of existing ministries and congregations in transition or with special needs, and of urban and rural coalitions. To do so, this division will:
1) function in cooperation with synods and congregations.
2) have primary responsibility in working with synods to determine where and when new congregations of this church shall be developed and to recommend ministries for recognition and reception as congregations of this church.
3) be responsible for the churchwide Mission Partners program and Mission Builders program, in coordination with synods and appropriate churchwide units.
4) <u>relate to the Mission Investment Fund in accord with the applicable continuing resolutions and policies that govern the operation of the Mission Investment Fund.</u>

b. develop and carry out programs of evangelism in the development of new ministries, working in coordination with the Division for Congregational Ministries as the Division for Congregational Ministries develops programs and resources to nurture evangelism efforts of existing congregations.

c. establish, support, and plan, in consultation with the Commission for Multicultural Ministries and the Division for Congregational Ministries, for the outreach of this church among persons of color and those whose primary language is other than English.

d. provide staff services and financial grants to assist synods or groups of synods in the development of area strategies for outreach, in coordination with the Division for Church in Society and the Division for Congregational Ministries.

e. provide for appropriate training and support, in cooperation with synods, for persons in outreach ministries of development and re-development, and those in urban, rural, and area ministries.

f. develop, in consultation with the Office of the Treasurer Mission Investment Fund, an annual capital budget and administer the use of these capital funds for loans, real-property acquisition, and building programs in support of the development of new ministries and congregations. It also shall support investment in the Mission Investment Fund of the ELCA. Criteria for real-estate acquisition and disposition for new or existing ministries within the limits of capital funds available shall be established jointly by the Division for Outreach and the Office of the Treasurer Mission Investment Fund. Within jointly established guidelines, this division the Mission Investment Fund shall determine which congregations shall receive loans, the amount of each loan, and the repayment schedule. This division also shall supervise collection of such loans. To do so, this division will:

1) have staff responsible for real-property work in the acquisition and disposition of property for new and/or existing ministries within the limits of the capital funds available and within criteria established jointly by the Division for Outreach and the Mission Investment Fund of the ELCA through the Office of the Treasurer. The real-property staff of this division shall provide expertise to the Division for Higher Education and Schools in support of campus-ministry facility development.

2) offer building and architectural consultative services to new congregations entering first- unit construction, to congregations relocating with synodical approval, and to other congregations.

g. be responsible for representing this church in churchwide cooperative planning for outreach together with other church bodies and ecumenical organizations serving in the geographic territory of this church's synods.

h. cooperate, under the coordination of the Division for Global Mission, with Lutheran church bodies based in other nations that desire to carry out ministry in the U.S.A., and consult with synods of this church in planning and implementing such ministry.

i. cooperate with the Division for Global Mission, the Division for Congregational Ministries, the Division for Higher Education and Schools, and the synods of this church in providing programs of education for mission and for witness to persons of other faiths.

j. relate to congregationally based community organizations that are associated with outreach ministries supported by this division and assist in the development of such organizations, under the coordination of the Division for Church in Society and synods.

2. Recommendation of Amendments to the 1995 Churchwide Assembly

As a follow-up to the Study of Ministry and actions regarding it at the 1993 Churchwide Assembly, some additional bylaw amendments are to be considered by the forthcoming assembly. In addition, review of the governing documents has suggested some other amendments for clarification.

VOTED: CC95.4.28
To recommend to the 1995 Churchwide Assembly the following resolution:

To adopt the following proposed amendments to the *Constitutions, Bylaws, and Continuing Resolutions of the Evangelical Lutheran Church in America*:

To amend the final section of existing bylaws 7.31.16. and 7.52.22. regarding "on leave" status for study:

7.31.16.   By annual recommendation of the Division for Ministry and action of the Synod Council in the synod of which a member, with the approval of the synodical bishop and in consultation with the Division for Ministry, a pastor as an ordained minister engaged in graduate study, in a field of study that will enhance service in the ordained ministry, may be retained on the roster... *[with the remainder of the bylaw unchanged]*.

7.52.22.   By annual ~~recommendation of the Division for Ministry and~~ action of the Synod Council in the synod of which a member, with the approval of the synodical bishop and in consultation with the Division for Ministry, an associate in ministry, deaconess, or diaconal minister engaged in graduate study appropriate for service in this church may be retained on the roster of associates in ministry, deaconesses, and diaconal ministers... *[with the remainder of the bylaw unchanged].*

To adopt a new bylaw regarding non-stipendiary service for lay rostered ministries:

7.52.26.   When necessary for the mission needs of this church, a letter of call may be issued by the Synod Council—according to criteria, policies, and procedures recommended by the Division for Ministry, reviewed by the Conference of Bishops, and adopted by the Church Council—to an associate in ministry, deaconess, or diaconal minister for non-stipendiary service after the Synod Council has sought and received approval by the Conference of Bishops. A call to non-stipendiary service is to be reviewed at least annually by the Synod Council and continued only as warranted for the ministry needs of this church. Such a call may be terminated by the Synod Council when it is deemed to be fulfilling no longer the mission needs of this church.

To adopt a new bylaw concerning various synodically authorized deacon programs:

7.61.02.   When needed to provide for diaconal ministry as part of a congregation or ministry of this church where it is not possible for such ministry to be provided by appropriately rostered lay ministry, the synodical bishop—acting with the consent of the congregation or ministry, in consultation with the Synod Council, and in accord with standards and qualifications developed by the Division for Ministry, reviewed by the Conference of Bishops, and approved by the Church Council—may authorize a non-rostered person who is a member of a congregation of the Evangelical Lutheran Church in America to offer such non-sacramental ministry. Such an individual shall be supervised by an ordained minister appointed by the synodical bishop and shall be trained and authorized to fulfill a particular ministry for a specific period of time in a given location only. Authorization, remuneration, direct supervision, and accountability are to be determined by the appropriate synodical leadership according to churchwide standards and qualifications for this type of ministry. Authorization for such service shall be renewed annually and renewed only when a demonstrated need remains for its continuation.

To amend churchwide bylaw 8.51.01. to reflect more accurately the actual pattern for handling such matters:

8.51.01.   This church, through its Department for Ecumenical Affairs and by the secretary of this church and ~~action of the Churchwide Assembly~~ Church Council, shall establish the general policies to govern official relationships with independent Lutheran organizations that seek to relate with this church while maintaining their independence and autonomy.

To add a new bylaw, 14.21.09., to reflect the requirements of other constitutional provisions and bylaws in the governing documents:

14.21.09.   The Church Council may adopt policies in accord with this church's consti-

tutions, bylaws, and continuing resolutions.

and,

To amend S7.32. to clarify its intent and to make the provision consistent with churchwide bylaw 12.31.09.:

S7.32. **Robert's Rules of Order, latest edition, shall govern parliamentary procedures of the Synod Assembly, unless otherwise ordered by the assembly.**

3. Amendments Related to Discipline Process

Extensive review has been undertaken regarding possible refinements in the consultation and discipline process defined by Chapter 20 in the Constitution, Bylaws, and Continuing Resolutions of the Evangelical Lutheran Church in America. General Counsel David J. Hardy particularly has consulted at length with the Conference of Bishops in this process. As a result of that review and consultation, the following amendments are proposed.

VOTED: CC95.4.29
To recommend to the 1995 Churchwide Assembly the following resolution:

To adopt the following proposed amendments to the *Constitutions, Bylaws, and Continuing Resolutions of the Evangelical Lutheran Church in America*:

[The full text of the proposed amendments will appear in Volume 2 of the Pre-Assembly Report.]

The session recessed at 5:02 P.M.

Monday Session

Vice President Kathy J. Magnus, chair of the Church Council, called the plenary session to order at 8:33 A.M. She invited Bishop Kenneth H. Sauer, chair of the Conference of Bishops, to offer the morning prayer.

Chair Magnus outlined the anticipated schedule for items to be considered throughout the morning's deliberations. She then called on Dale V. Sandstrom, chair of the Legal and Constitutional Review Committee, to complete the committee's report.

Report of the Legal and Constitutional Review Committee (Continued)

4. Adjudication Policy

Synodical constitutions include the following mandatory sections in the adjudication provision of Chapter 17:

†S17.01. The synodical bishop and the Executive Committee of the Synod Council shall be available to give counsel when disputes arise within this synod.

†S17.02. The synodical bishop and the Executive Committee of the Synod Council shall receive expressions of concern from ordained ministers, associates in ministry or other persons on the official lay roster of this church, congregations, and organizations within this synod; provide a forum in which the parties concerned can seek to work out matters causing distress or conflict; and make appropriate recommendations for their resolution. When the matter at issue cannot be resolved in this manner, the prescribed procedures for investigation, decision, appeal, and adjudication shall be followed. Allegations or charges that could lead to the discipline of an ordained minister or a person on the official lay roster of this church shall not be addressed by the Executive Committee but shall be resolved through the disciplinary process set forth in the Constitution, Bylaws, and Continuing Resolutions of the Evangelical Lutheran Church in America.

At the request of the Conference of Bishops, legal counsel, in consultation with the secretary of this church and the director of the Department for Synodical Relations, prepared a draft policy related to †S17.02., which was reviewed by the Conference of Bishops at its March 1995 meeting. The conference recommends Church Council approval of this policy, which was distributed to council members as council agenda Exhibit D, Part 2.

VOTED: CC95.4.30
To adopt the following policy related to †S17.02.:

A POLICY STATEMENT
EXPLAINING THE PROCESSES CONTEMPLATED BY †S17.02.
AS IT RELATES TO SYNODICAL BISHOPS,
EXECUTIVE COMMITTEES OF SYNOD COUNCILS, AND
SYNOD COUNCILS

1. **Background**

The governing documents of the Evangelical Lutheran Church in America (ELCA) provide for a variety of processes for decision making or dispute resolution. Examples of such processes include (parenthetical reference to ELCA Constitution and Bylaws):
Discipline of ordained ministers and rostered laypersons (20.20.);
Discipline of congregations (20.30.);
Discipline of members of congregations (20.40.);
Dispute resolution between factions within a congregation (20.84.; †S17.04.; *C15.11.);
Dispute resolution for entities within a synod (†S17.03. and †S17.04.);
Dispute resolution for units within the churchwide organization (20.82. and 20.83.);
Termination of a pastor's or AIM's call from a congregation (†S14.13.b.); and
Termination of a pastor's call for reasons of physical or mental incapacity (†S14.13.c.).

Common to all of these processes is the concept that a final decision is to be made by the entity within this church so identified and with rights of appeal only as specifically authorized.

Another of these processes for decision making/dispute resolution is †S17.02., a mandatory provision contained in the constitutions of all of the synods[1]. This provision reads:

The synodical bishop and the Executive Committee of the Synod Council shall receive expressions of concern from ordained ministers, associates in ministry, or other persons on the official lay roster of this church, congregations, and organizations within this synod; provide a forum in which the parties concerned can seek to work out matters causing distress or conflict; and make appropriate recommendations for their resolution. When the matter at issue cannot be resolved in this manner, the prescribed procedures for investigation, decision, appeal, and adjudication shall be followed. Allegations or charges that could lead to the discipline of an ordained minister or a person on the official lay roster of this church shall not be addressed by the Executive Committee but shall be resolved through the disciplinary process set forth in the Constitution, Bylaws, and Continuing Resolutions of the Evangelical Lutheran Church in America.

In one sense the process set forth in †S17.02. is the "catchall" provision that can cover any situation not governed by one or more of the particular processes, such as some of those earlier identified. Clearly, †S17.02. cannot be used either to override, or to preempt, the regular process that should be utilized to resolve the matter. But, for the good of the church, the process set forth in †S17.02. can be utilized to promote understanding, to attempt reconciliation, and to provide a forum for the airing of differences of opinion.

†S17.02., as the "catchall" provision, can no doubt cover a variety of expressions of concerns, including those expressions that center upon the actions (including decisions not to act) of the synodical bishop.

The purpose of this document is to offer guidance to synodical bishops, Synod Councils, and Executive Committees of Synod Councils on the application and utilization of †S17.02. While this document will center upon dealing with expressions of concern relating to a synodical bishop's actions or inactions, the concepts set forth herein would be equally applicable to dealing with expressions of concern on other matters where there is not a process directly applicable.

2. **Bishop's Election for a Specified Term and Recall Provisions**

In the Evangelical Lutheran Church in America, synodical bishops are elected at Synod Assemblies for a term of six years. Subject to term limitations that each synod is free to adopt, a synodical bishop may stand for reelection at the conclusion of the six year term.

There is a process–set forth in a Continuing Resolution (CR)–by which a synodical bishop may be removed from office before the end of his or her term. This process is essentially a termination for cause, and the determination that proper cause exists is made by the churchwide Committee on Appeals as set forth in CR 20.53.A92.

3. **The Discretionary Nature of the Bishop's Actions**

It is important to understand that the governing documents of the Evangelical Lutheran Church in America and of its synods require much of its synodical bishops. And, in many instances, the governing documents grant to a synodical bishop the discretion to take or not take certain action. Examples of matters left to a bishop's discretion

include (comparable examples relating to associates in ministry omitted):

a. Recommending or not recommending an ordained minister to a congregation in its call process.

b. Recommending or not recommending an ordained minister to a bishop of another synod for consideration for call.

c. Recommending or not recommending an approved candidate for ordination to a congregation for call as provided in 7.31.13.g.

d. In the absence of an official recital by the Congregation Council or by a petition signed by at least one-third of the voting members of the congregation as provided in †S14.13.b., investigating or not investigating allegations of physical or mental incapacity of an ordained minister as contemplated by †S14.13.b. and c.

e. In the absence of an official recital by the Congregation Council or by a petition signed by at least one-third of the voting members of the congregation as provided in †S14.13.b., investigating or not investigating allegations of ineffective conduct of the pastoral office and making recommendations as contemplated by †S14.13.b. and d.

f. Exercising or not exercising the power to suspend temporarily and without prejudice an ordained minister from service in a congregation under ELCA Bylaw †S14.13.f.

g. Making or not making written charges, thereby invoking the formal discipline process under ELCA Bylaws 20.21.03.e., 20.22.03.e., or 20.31.03.d.

h. Appointing or not appointing an advisory or consultation panel as permitted under ELCA Bylaw 20.21.04. and 20.21.05.

i. Exercising or not exercising the power to suspend temporarily and without prejudice an ordained minister from service in a congregation under ELCA Bylaw 20.21.23.

j. Exercising or not exercising the power to suspend temporarily and without prejudice an ordained minister from service in a setting other than a congregation under ELCA Bylaw 20.21.24.

k. Filing or not filing a petition for removal of another officer of the synod, as permitted under Continuing Resolution 20.53.A92.c.

l. Referring or not referring to a consultation panel as permitted in 20.21.06., disciplinary written charges made by other than the synodical bishop.

m. When recommended by a consultation panel as permitted in 20.21.06., dismissing or modifying or not dismissing or not modifying, disciplinary written charges as permitted in 20.21.06.b. and c.

n. Endorsing or not endorsing an ordained minister's retention on the roster in the status of on leave from call as provided under 7.31.16.

o. Authorizing or not authorizing licensure status to a layperson as permitted under 7.61.01.

The Executive Committee has no authority to reverse or set aside a decision made by a synodical bishop within the exercise of his or her discretion. Simply because a person disagrees with how a synodical bishop has decided to exercise his or her discretion in taking or not taking a particular action (such as any of those listed above) is not basis for an Executive Committee making any recommendation to the bishop. In some cases, however, the Executive Committee may provide a forum through which the persons expressing concern may be better informed of the process or of the basis by which the bishop decided to take or not take a particular action.

---

[1] From 1987 until September 1991 this provision appeared as 19.62. in the ELCA Constitution; the Churchwide Assembly at Orlando (1991) transferred this provision to the Synod Constitution.

4. Timelines for Resolution of the Concern

The Executive Committee should take care not to interfere with the synodical bishop's ministry as defined by the synod constitution. Expressions of concern are prematurely made when the bishop has not concluded his or her decision making in a particular process. For the Executive Committee to consider these concerns prematurely may actually interfere with the process that should be followed. Executive Committees are cautioned that sometimes persons expressing concern do so for the purpose of attempting to influence or to "pressure" the bishop. An Executive Committee should not entertain such premature expressions of concern.

The final sentence of †S17.02. makes explicit that the process therein outlined is never to be used when the disciplinary processes under Chapter 20, particularly 20.10. through 20.31.05., are available. While not explicit, the same principle applies when there are other and more specific processes that should be utilized for decision making. Never should †S17.02. be utilized as a substitute for a more particular or appropriate process established by this church.

5. The Role of the Executive Committee

a. *Overview of Executive Committee's function.* Under †S17.02., the Executive Committee has three functions:

   1) to receive expressions of concern;
   2) to provide a forum in which the parties concerned can seek to work out matters causing distress or conflict;
   3) to make appropriate recommendations for the resolution of matters causing distress or concern.

b. *Receiving Expressions of Concern.* Unless the Executive Committee has designated some other member, the expression of concern should be made directly to the vice president of the synod who serves as the chair of the Synod Council. The vice president, or other designated member, may require that the expression of concern be in writing. The vice president, or other designated member, discharges his or her function by acknowledging receipt of the expression and by distributing the expression to other Executive Committee members, including the bishop.

c. *The Forum to be Provided.* It is exclusively within the province of the Executive Committee to decide, with respect to each case, how, and what kind of, a forum shall be provided to persons making expressions of concern. The Executive Committee may decide to consider the expressions of concern only in writing without any opportunity for personal appearance. Or the Executive Committee may decide to provide an opportunity for a personal appearance by one or more persons expressing concern on the same subject. Where personal appearance is afforded, this forum may be before the entire Executive Committee or it may be before one or more persons designated by the Executive Committee to hear the concerns.

d. *The Role of the Synodical Bishop.* Affording the synodical bishop an opportunity to address the issue is critical, since those persons bringing expressions of concerns, may not know—indeed frequently have no right to know—confidential information important to the decision making of the bishop. The Executive Committee shall decide whether persons expressing concern shall be present when the bishop informs the Executive Committee, or shall be informed of some or all of the content of the bishop's information, or neither. The Executive Committee shall also decide whether it is appropriate that the bishop be present when the Executive Committee considers the expressions of concern presented to it.

e. *Recommendations of the Executive Committee.* The third responsibility of an Executive Committee is to make recommendations to any of the parties when in the judgment of the Executive Committee resolution of the concerns may be enhanced by doing so. There may be some situations when an Executive Committee concludes that no useful purpose would be served by making any recommendations; in such cases no recommendations need to be made. The Executive Committee shall also decide whether and to what extent the synodical bishop may participate in the formation of these recommendations.

f. *Dissemination of Recommendations.* The Executive Committee alone shall decide which of its recommendations shall be communicated and to whom. It may decide that some or all of its recommendations be communicated to the Synod Council, or to the congregations and roster leadership of the entire synod. It may decide that all of its recommendations shall be communicated to only some or all of the parties who have made, or are most affected by, the expressions of concern. It may decide that one or more of its recommendations shall be communicated to only some of the parties. It may decide to communicate one or more of its recommendations to only one of the parties.

6. Further "Prescribed Procedures"

In the Constitution for Synods, †S17.02. recognizes that the process, as described above, may not resolve every matter. In such cases, "the prescribed procedures for investigation, decision, appeal, and adjudication shall be followed." No attempt in this document is made to identify the "prescribed procedures" in all cases that may appropriately be presented under †S17.02., other than where the issue centers upon the conduct of the bishop. In cases where the issue is so centered upon the conduct of the bishop, the "prescribed procedures" refer to the process for Recall or Dismissal of a Synod Officer as set forth in continuing resolution 20.53.A92.

It is within the discretion of the Executive Committee to recommend to the entire Synod Council that a written petition be filed seeking removal of the synodical bishop under continuing resolution 20.53.A92. Authorization for filing of such petition requires an affirmative vote of at least two-thirds of the elected council members present and voting [continuing resolution [20.53.A92.b.1.] The petition must set forth the grounds for recall or dismissal and must contain specific allegations. A hearing before the churchwide Committee on Appeals is then required, at which the petitioner must prove the allegations set forth in the petition. A two-thirds vote of the members, present and voting, of the churchwide Committee on Appeals is required to grant the petition and thereby remove the synodical bishop.

7. Nonavailability of Judicial Review by the Civil Courts

The religion clauses of the First Amendment to the U.S. Constitution, as interpreted in a series of decision by the U.S. Supreme Court and other federal courts, preclude civil courts–federal or state–from reviewing decisions made by ecclesiastical bodies pursuant to ecclesiastical procedures. This church jealously protects the constitutional rights afforded to it and to its decisions under the First Amendment. Any attempt to resort to civil courts by persons who are dissatisfied with decisions of synodical bishops or with the Executive Committee's handling of their expressions of concern, will be vigorously resisted. The General Counsel of ELCA should be informed of any threatened or actual litigation.

5. Ratification of Synodical Constitutions

Churchwide constitutional provision 10.12. indicates, "Each synod shall have a constitution, which shall become effective upon ratification by the Church Council. Amendments thereto shall be subject to like ratification . . . ."

The following action was adopted *en bloc* at the conclusion of this meeting .

To ratify amendment †1.21. in the constitution of the Slovak Zion Synod; and

To ratify amendments to the constitution of the Northwest Washington Synod and the Montana Synod, contingent upon fulfillment of required changes and corrections, as indicated in the review by the secretary of this church and reported by the secretary to the Northwest Washington Synod and the Montana Synod (CC95.4.47l).

6. Independent Lutheran Organizations

At the Church Council meeting in November 1989, a "Report Concerning Certain Lutheran Organizations Which Relate to the ELCA" was received. The report sought to address the various types of independent organizations in regard to the provision in churchwide governing documents for relationships with such entities (ELCA 8.51. and ELCA 8.51.01.).

The council at that meeting voted (CC89.11.172): ". . . To identify other organizations presently related to the Evangelical Lutheran Church in America through a particular unit so that the elements of the relationship can be reported to the Church Council by the appropriate unit; and to request that the secretary of this church maintain a roster of such organizations related to the Evangelical Lutheran Church in America, with the unit through which the relationship is maintained." By that action, the council assigned the Institute for Mission, Columbus, Ohio, to the Division for Outreach, and the Evangelical Lutheran Educational Association to the Division for Higher Education and Schools.

Subsequently, at its April 1994 meeting, the Church Council voted to accept as interim operational guidelines the "Process for Recognition of Relationship of Independent Lutheran Organizations with the Division for Global Mission" and "Criteria for Reviewing an Organization for Recognition...," which had been prepared by that division. The council also voted: "To refer this matter to the Office of the Secretary for further consideration as part of the review of the overall policy governing the relationships between the Evangelical Lutheran Church in America and independent Lutheran organizations."

The matter is specifically related to independent Lutheran organizations. Cooperative Lutheran organizations, such as Lutheran World Relief and Lutheran Immigration and Refugee Service, are owned jointly by the Evangelical Lutheran Church in America and The Lutheran Church—Missouri Synod and are governed by documents previously approved by the Church Council (October 1987).

In addition, directly related entities—as defined in the *Constitution, Bylaws, and Continuing Resolutions of the Evangelical Lutheran Church in America*—include the seminaries of this church, colleges and universities of this church, certain schools, social-ministry organizations, and the Lutheran Student Movement.

The matter of a consistent policy on relations with independent Lutheran organizations has been studied. The following document is proposed as a general policy to guide units in any "official relationships" with independent Lutheran organizations that seek to relate with this church.

VOTED: **CC95.4.31**

To adopt the following operational policy regarding the process and criteria for recognition of relationships with independent Lutheran organizations:

PROCESS AND CRITERIA FOR RECOGNITION OF RELATIONSHIP OF INDEPENDENT LUTHERAN ORGANIZATIONS

SECTION I—Process: The process for recognition of a relationship of an independent Lutheran organization to a unit of the churchwide organization of the Evangelical Lutheran Church in America includes:

A. The following preliminary steps normally will occur in the process for any "official relationship with independent Lutheran organizations that seek to relate with this church while maintaining their independence and autonomy" (ELCA churchwide bylaw 8.51.01.):

    1. The organization seeks information from an appropriate unit regarding possible recognition.

    2. The unit provides relevant information, including the criteria for recognition of a relationship, questions to be answered by the organization, and a list of material to be supplied by the organization.

        a. Questions to be answered include:

           (1) Why does the organization seek recognition of a relationship with a churchwide unit?

           (2) How does the organization, in fulfilling its commitments, work compatibly and assist the respective churchwide unit in the unit's work?

           (3) Does the organization fulfill particular activities that the respective unit is unable to accomplish?

           (4) How would the organization use the recognition of a relationship in its interpretation and fund-raising activities?

           (5) What is the organization's relationship to other church-related ecumenical entities?

        b. Materials to be submitted include:

           (1) A copy of relevant descriptive documents, such as a constitution, corporate bylaws, purpose statement, policies, guidelines, and budget.

           (2) Samples of publicity and fund-raising materials.

           (3) A list of staff, leaders, and board members as well as a description of the method of election for board members.

           (4) Documentation of the organization's independent status and insurance coverage for any existing or potential liabilities of such an organization.

B. The organization submits the requested information and material to the unit.

C. The unit reviews the request and formulates a recommendation for possible action by the respective unit's board or steering committee.

D. The action of the board or steering committee is reported to the Church Council for ratification.

SECTION II—Criteria: The criteria for reviewing an organization for possible recognition of a relationship with a unit of the churchwide organization of the Evangelical Lutheran Church in America include:

A. Determination of compatibility with the ELCA: The organization's statement of faith, purpose, and activities are compatible with the ELCA's governing documents, specifically the sections on Confession of Faith, Nature of the Church, Statement of Purpose, and Principles of Organization.

B. *Focus:* The organization's purpose and activities are compatible with the program and policy of the churchwide unit proposing such a recognition of relationship.

C. *Extension of ministry:* The organization undergirds or extends the work of the churchwide unit that proposes such a recognition of relationship.

D. *Documents:* The organization has a constitution or bylaws and an purpose statement, and is an officially recognized nonprofit entity.

E. *Constituency:* The organization's membership is churchwide in its scope. If the constituency is primarily local or regional, any relationship more appropriately would be to a synod or group of synods.

F. *Leadership:* As appropriate, the organization seeks leadership on its board and staff that is diverse in gender, culture, and ethnicity.

G. *Funding:* The organization's financial operation is open for inspection and appropriately audited; the method and scope of its fund-raising is compatible with ELCA funding processes.

H. *Accountability:* The organization will agree to appropriate methods of accountability to the unit proposing recognition. Such agreement might include periodic programmatic and financial reports. Further, the organization agrees to protect the ELCA churchwide organization and any related entities from liability or financial demands.

I. *Commitment:* The organization agrees to support the purposes and goals of the churchwide organization and to refrain from publicity or fund-raising techniques that diminish the public image of the churchwide organization, its financial resources, and its effectiveness in mission.

J. *Publicity:* The organization agrees to use of specific phraseology in any publicity that describes the recognized relationship with the appropriate churchwide unit.

K. *Review of Relationship:* The unit and organization agree to review the relationship every three years.

7. Approval of Ecumenical Proposals by the 1997 Churchwide Assembly

The Department for Ecumenical Affairs anticipates that the following proposals will come before the 1997 Churchwide Assembly:

• full communion with the Episcopal Church;
• full communion with three Reformed churches: the Presbyterian Church (USA), the Reformed Church in America, and the United Church of Christ; and
• the declaration that the sixteenth century mutual condemnations between Lutherans and Roman Catholics on justification no longer apply to the present ecumenical partner.

All three actions would be groundbreaking and without parallel for the Evangelical Lutheran Church in America and its predecessor bodies. Neither the constitution nor the bylaws of this church anticipated such actions; they provide no specific guidance in this regard.

Staff of the Department for Ecumenical Affairs has been in consultation with the Office of the Secretary about this matter. This matter also has been discussed by the various coordination committees. The closest analogy to these proposals may be the provisions for amendment to the constitution and by-laws of this church. These changes require an affirmative vote by two-thirds vote of the voting members present.

The bishop and the Department for Ecumenical Affairs discussed with the department's advisory committee their recommendation that the 1995 Churchwide Assembly should by formal action indicate that the votes taken on these matters by the 1997 Churchwide Assembly will require a two-thirds vote. The advisory committee concurred with this recommendation.

The Legal and Constitutional Review Committee considered the matter at its pre-council meeting and recommended the following:

> To recommend to the 1995 Churchwide Assembly adoption of a new section and bylaw:

Official Church-to-Church Relationships

8.71.01. This church may establish official church-to-church relationships and agreements. Establishment of such official relationships and agreements shall require a two-thirds vote of the voting members of the Churchwide Assembly.

Discussion followed. The Rev. William G. Rusch, director of the Department for Ecumenical Affairs, raised questions of interpretation. A possible addition was submitted that would add, following "relationships and agreements," the words, "that result in full communion or removal of obstacles to full communion."

Terry L. Bowes moved that the foregoing language be added after "relationships and agreements." Charles A. Adamson seconded the motion. The Rev. Stephen M. Youngdahl questioned whether we would gain anything from language. A motion was made to refer the matter to the Legal and Constitutional Review Committee for further consideration. The Rev. Franklin D. Fry noted the importance of this assembly taking action on the matter. Karen M. Dietz moved to table the matter. The motion was seconded and carried.

8. Board Membership at Certain Church Colleges

Churchwide bylaw 8.32.06. defines the required minimum number of board members who must be Lutheran at certain colleges of the Evangelical Lutheran Church in America. The board of the Division for Higher Education and Schools has requested an amendment of that bylaw.

The Rev. Franklin D. Fry expressed concern about the council being the appropriate place for action on this matter. Some matters are obviously synodical or regional issues, he said. He characterized the issue as an anachronism of the past totally inappropriate in the context of this church.

The Rev. W. Robert Sorensen, executive director of the Division for Higher Education and Schools, provided additional background information.

VOTED: **CC95.4.32**

To recommend to the 1995 Churchwide Assembly adoption of the following bylaw amendment:

8.32.06.   **Subject to approval by the appropriate synods, a college or university may be owned by a not-for-profit corporation that has voting members at least 90 percent of whom shall consist of members of the biennial Churchwide Assembly. Meetings of such corporations shall be held in conjunction with the Churchwide Assembly for the purpose of electing or ratifying members of the governing board and approving amendments in the governing documents. At least ~~75~~ 60 percent of the members of the governing boards of such corporations shall be Lutheran and at least a majority shall be members of this church.**

The Rev. Franklin D. Fry requested that his abstention be recorded in these minutes.

9.   Required Provisions in the Model Constitution for Congregations

The Northeastern Ohio Synod Council submitted the following resolution regarding required provisions in the model constitution for congregations:

WHEREAS, the decisions of the 1993 ELCA [Churchwide] Assembly mandate that all required provisions in the *Model Constitution for Congregations* must be inserted *verbatim*, without alteration or amendment of the text, into the constitution of every congregation revising its governing documents; and

WHEREAS, such requirements make it impossible for a congregation to insert language into a required provision that might reflect that congregation's history and practice, even though neither that language nor the spirit of the congregation's provision is in conflict with the intent or spirit of the governing documents of the ELCA or the synod (i.e., the content of the provision satisfies the "principle of comparability" with ELCA governing documents); and

WHEREAS, it is necessary for all congregations to agree on the matters of faith, doctrine and practice which affect our interrelatedness, yet some matters appear within the required provisions that are either matters of the congregation's internal governance or *adiaphora*, "things indifferent" (Art. X, "Epitome, Formula of Concord"), and do not impinge upon the congregation's interrelationship with others in the church; and

WHEREAS, the only constitutional response available to the Synod Council in the case of a congregation's unwillingness to revise its proposed governing documents in matters of internal governance or *adiaphora* is to discipline the congregation; and

WHEREAS, seeking absolute textual conformity in matters considered *adiaphora* or of internal governance elicits the perception that the ELCA is acting in a legalistic manner; and

WHEREAS, paragraph two of ELCA Bylaw 9.53.03. indicates that "The synod shall recognize that congregations may organize themselves in a manner which they deem most appropriate and that there are a variety of ways in which the required elements may be stated"; and

WHEREAS, ELCA 9.22. indicates that "The judgment on whether a congregation meets the criteria listed in 9.21. shall be made by this church through the synod of this church in whose territory the congregation is located"; therefore, be it

RESOLVED, that the 1995 Northeastern Ohio Synod Assembly memorialize the 1995 Churchwide Assembly to (1) restrict the required provisions of the *Model Constitution for Congregations* to those that most immediately affect our interrelatedness, and (2) in required provisions containing matters "indifferent" or of internal governance, allow congregations to use variant language in the practical aspects of them; and be it further

RESOLVED, that each respective Synod Council be allowed to respond to variant language in congregation constitutions with a greater degree of its own discretion, exercising its good judgment, determining whether or not the congregations meet the criteria for recognition and reception as congregations of the ELCA (9.20.), and determining whether or not a congregation's governing documents satisfy the "principle of comparability" with ELCA and synod governing documents.

The resolution had been transmitted by the Northeastern Ohio Synod Council for a response from the Church Council.

VOTED: **CC95.4.33**

To respond to the resolution submitted by the Northeastern Ohio Synod Council regarding required provisions in the Model Constitution for Congregations by noting:

1.   **That several assertions in the "WHEREAS" clauses of the resolution contain misleading or incorrect information and require clarification or correction;**

2.   **That all congregations are NOT required to amend their constitutions to include the required language, because, as provided by ELCA churchwide constitutional provision 9.52., "The governing documents of congregations recognized at the establishment of this church shall continue to govern such congregations. When such a congregation wishes to amend a particular provision of its governing documents, the provision so amended shall be consistent with the governing documents of this church.";**

3.   **That the 1993 Churchwide Assembly approved the designation of certain provisions in the Model Constitution for Congregations as required at the point of amendment for a congregation in conformity with the governing documents of this church and in response to expressed needs throughout this church;**

4.   **That the action of the 1993 Churchwide Assembly occurred after a study by the Church Council of the need for required provisions and that such a study was undertaken at the request of the 1991 Churchwide Assembly that emerged from numerous requests of congregations and synods in the**

initial years of the ELCA for clarification of which provisions are required to conform to the governing documents of this church, as stipulated by ELCA churchwide constitutional provision 9.52.;

5. That the required provisions do not involve sections related to the internal governance and operation of a congregation but rather are those that concern matters of faith, unity, doctrine, and practice that affect the interrelatedness of the three primary expressions of this church, namely, congregations, synods, and the churchwide organization;

6. That only congregations that desire to amend any provision of their constitutions are now required to amend all of those provisions that relate to the subject matter of the required provisions but not their whole constitution;

7. That a congregation may continue to choose to retain in unamended form its constitution that was in effect on December 31, 1987, or its constitution as amended prior to September 1, 1993;

8. That congregations may freely adopt bylaws, in addition to the required constitutional provisions, and that such bylaws may reflect the congregation's practice and history so long as those bylaws are not in conflict with any of the required constitutional provisions, if such provisions have been adopted by the congregation;

9. That each congregation is free to determine its pattern of internal governance and organizational structures;
and

To decline at this time to propose any further amendments of Chapter 9, "Congregations," in the Constitution, Bylaws, and Continuing Resolutions of the Evangelical Lutheran Church in America or of the Model Constitution for Congregations.

Mission Investment Fund

Chair Magnus introduced the Rev. Arnold O. Pierson, vice president for marketing of the Mission Investment Fund, to report on progress in development of the fund. In 1988, the fund totaled $63 million. Last week, that amount had climbed to $128 million. Loans have been let in 47 states, plus Puerto Rico and the Virgin Islands. The fund is used for the establishment of new congregations. Twenty-three percent of ELCA congregations have invested in the fund. Pastor Pierson invited Church Council members to become involved in the fund.

ELCA Pension and Other Benefits Program (Continued)

3. Abortion Medical Coverage (continued)

John G. Kapanke, president of the Board of Pensions, was introduced to provide background information on current developments with respect to medical coverage of abortion procedures. He indicated that under the current code developed by the American Medical Association (AMA), abortion is considered to be a reimbursable procedure. Abortion procedures are classified under 13 separate codes. Although the ELCA benefit program is based on a medically necessary model, the Board of Pensions has not routinely questioned medical diagnosis cited on bills submitted for reimbursement. "If you were to ask me, does the Board of Pensions cover [elective] abortions, we could not tell by going back and looking at individual statements. The only way we can really tell [whether a procedure was elective] is to ask the plan member straight out or possibly through the doctor . . . Up until now, the board has simply not asked the question," he said. Mr. Kapanke noted that the issue had been raised during contractual negotiations with AETNA for point-of-service coverage, and that the Board of Pensions has entered into conversation with the Division for Church in Society relative to compliance with the ELCA social statement on abortion.

During discussion, William E. Diehl asked whether it was standard practice that the board does not pursue interpretations under the AMA code. Mr. Kapanke said that sometimes clarification is requested. Usually, claims are processed on the basis of the code. Edith M. Lohr noted that such questions generally arise when unusual claims are submitted for reimbursement. Bishop Paull E. Spring inquired about the frequency of therapeutic abortions. William T. Billings requested additional clarification about the 13 different AMA-coded procedures under the broad category of abortion.

Deborah S. Yandala asked how widespread was this concern. She said she would be hesitant to inquire into confidential matters between patient and physician. Mr. Kapanke indicated that to date the Board of Pensions had received several letters supporting both sides of the issue, in addition to numerous telephone inquiries. Charles A. Adamson inquired about waiver of doctor-patient confidentiality. The Rev. Charles S. Miller Jr., executive director of the Division for Church in Society, stated that the division has received about a half-dozen letters. In addition, 57 telephone calls were received, primarily from pastors asking for information.

Edith M. Lohr commented on the briefing on this matter of representatives of the Board of Pensions who attend 1995 synodical assemblies. Robert S. Schroeder offered a closing comment on the implementation of the social statement on abortion in the practices of this church.

Matters Related to the Department for Ecumenical Affairs

1. Ecumenical Proposals before the 1995 Churchwide Assembly

Chair Magnus noted the following action of the Executive Committee adopted at its March 31, 1995, meeting (EC95.3.9):

> To direct the Department for Ecumenical Affairs to prepare:
>
> (1) a one-page document of questions and direct, simple answers on the key theological and practical ("flash point") issues in the Lutheran-Episcopal proposals for a declaration of full communion, including reference citations to sections of the relevant documents, and
>
> (2) a one-page document of questions and direct, simple answers on the key theological and practical ("flash point") issues in the Lutheran-Reformed proposals for a declaration of full communion, including reference citations to sections of the relevant documents, for review by the Executive Committee of the Church Council by mid-April 1995 and possible distribution to the 1995 synodical assemblies.

2. 1997 Ecumenical Proposals, Documentation, and Resources

The following was information provided by the Department for Ecumenical Affairs:

> As 1997 approaches, additional resources and documentation are being produced. In the area of Lutheran-Episcopal relations, two volumes have been published that provide background and explanation for the Concordat: *A Commentary on "Concordat of Agreement,"* council agenda Exhibit K, Part 1; and *Concordat of Agreement: Supporting Essays,* council agenda Exhibit K, Part 2.
>
> Concerning Lutheran-Reformed relations, the Joint Coordinating Committee has prepared *A Formula of Agreement,* council agenda Exhibit K, Part 3, which along with *A Common Calling,* council agenda Exhibit K, Part 4, could come before the 1997 Churchwide Assembly for action. Any reactions or suggestions for emendation by members of the Church Council would be most helpful at this state of the process.
>
> Finally, the International Lutheran-Roman Catholic Task Force has produced the first draft of a declaration whose acceptance would result in the inapplicability of 16th century condemnations on justification: *Joint Declaration on the Doctrine of Justification Between the Lutheran World Federation and the Roman Catholic Task Force,* council agenda Exhibit K, Part 5. Here, too, reactions and comments from members of the Church Council at this early stage in the process would be helpful. Also being shared with the Church Council are two items recently produced by the Department for Ecumenical Affairs: *The Condemnations of the 16th Century on Justification—Do They Still Apply Today,* council agenda Exhibit K, Part 6, and *Mutual Condemnations: What Are They?,* council agenda Exhibit K, Part 7.

Chair Magnus introduced the Rev. William G. Rusch, director of the Department for Ecumenical Affairs, to present background information. He underscored that ". . . what we have is a two-year time frame to reflect about these very important proposals—three actually—that will be before the Evangelical Lutheran Church in America. I think we have an advantage in that we do not have to make any quick decisions, but in fact we can carefully reflect about the nature of these three proposals—what they are and what they are not. So I welcome very much the questions that have been formulated by a subcommittee of your Executive Committee. We will share these questions with the appropriate coordinating committees in the next few weeks, and you will receive from those coordinating committees, which have the responsibility of overseeing the reception process, their response to your questions. But, what I would like to do very briefly now is just . . . to point out a couple of things. First of all, you have just received a document that we are preparing for synodical bishops . . . and others who will have responsibility in studying these proposals. You will notice, I hope, several things about this document. It reminds folks about the three decisions in 1977, it encapsulates the description of `full communion' for the Statement on Ecumenism of our church, it says how each of the three proposals would affect reports of the dialogues, then additional study sources, and it finally reminds people that the department is available at any time to assist them in this process. Then, you will notice that there is a chart of three pages, which lists and summarizes according to categories all the materials that are available before this church that we have produced; there are other materials in addition to these, but these are the materials that we have produced to encourage people to study the nature of the proposals."

Members of the Executive Committee had prepared a list of questions for consideration and response, including:

1. How will acceptance of these proposals enhance the mission of this church in congregational, synodical, and churchwide settings?
2. What are some examples of how acceptance of these proposals will affect the life of congregations, synods, and the churchwide organization?
3. How does full communion differ from merger?
4. How will pastors and the call process be affected by full communion?
   - Do parishes automatically get the names of pastors from other rosters?
   - To what extent will names of clergy be made available to other denominations?
   - Will the candidacy process change?
   - Are there barriers to those who go through our candidacy requirements, but do not meet the requirements of other denominations?
5. Do pastors remain in their own pension and medical plan no matter where they serve?
6. How will the understanding of the role of bishops change?
7. Could an ELCA candidate be ordained without an Episcopal bishop present?
8. Will the liturgical process and doctrinal heritage of a congregation be honored by a pastor from a different tradition? Include comments on:
   - How congregational life may or may not be affected (worship, education, confirmation, etc.);
   - Would Episcopal priests called by Lutheran congregations still be called "Father"?
9. How will theological and pastoral "quality control" be provided by bishops and synods for Episcopal and Reformed clergy when they are called to serve a Lutheran congregation?
10. How might theological education change in response to acceptance of these proposals for all of the churches involved?
11. What are the similarities and differences in the understanding of communion among the churches involved in these proposals? Would the liturgical practice of the respective church be honored in the parishes served?
12. Can members retain primary membership in one denomination while they are active in a church of another denomination?

13. Can a pastor from Episcopalian or Reformed traditions be elected to serve as a Lutheran bishop?
14. Is there a relationship between the Episcopal Church and Reformed churches?
15. Can we share a common witness in the church today short of full communion?
16. Will our "Visions and Expectations" document apply to clergy from other traditions serving in our congregations?
17. Will rostered lay persons from other denominations be required to meet the same educational stipulations as that which exist for ELCA-rostered lay persons?
18. Describe the resources that will assist congregations to engage in conversation regarding the proposals for full communion.
19. What additional interpretive materials will be available?
20. What is the process for dealing with responses from congregations?
21. How will responses from Conference of Bishops, seminary faculties, and others be addressed?

Pastor Rusch continued, "What I would like to do very quickly, is look at the questions from the Executive Committee and, I will not go into the sub-questions, but just very quickly say a word to two about many of them, so that people see where we are coming from and then maybe that will promote some discussion. The first item is actually not a question, but a comment—a brief history. I would remind all of our folks that these proposals rest on 30 years or more of ecumenical work by this church and its predecessor church bodies, and that, in fact, if we are able to vote positively on these three proposals, we will be moving in harmony with the Lutheran world community. No, that is not the reason alone why we should vote yes; but, I think it is a cautionary note that we need to reflect upon very carefully why we want to vote no. To move positively on these three will put us in harmony with either where the world Lutheran communion is, or where we perceive it is moving. In terms of questions one and two, which in some ways are very much alike, there are numerous examples that we could give in the department, that synodical bishops could give, about how the mission of the church could be enhanced, if churches can enter into a relationship of full communion. . . . In terms of question three, full communion is a goal; it is not a model. It is a goal that we hold out in our ecumenical relationships. It is not anywhere near close to organizational merger. All of these churches would keep their own identity and their own lives, but they would reflect far more fully to those around them that Christ's Church is one. The call process within the Evangelical Lutheran Church in America would not change in any way. The standards—the methods—would all remain in place. In terms of any ELCA pastor wishing to serve in one of the other churches in full communion, I would imagine that that person would have to indicate to his or her synodical bishops that he or she was willing to be considered for such a call. The candidacy process for us would not change. Similarly, in terms of [question] five, I would think that pastors would, in fact, remain on their own pension and medical plans no matter where they serve. But, remember, in these proposals for full communion, there is provision for a continuation committee to oversee this new kind of relationship that we would all be entering into. Now in terms of [question] six, how would the understanding of the role of bishops change?— in no significant way, I think. The process of election, election for a term, would continue. The only difference would be, it seems to me, we would more faithfully reflect Article XIV of the `Apology to the Augsburg Confession,' and practically, that would be spelled out in the sense that bishops who are no longer serving actively in office could attend and participate in the Conference of Bishops. [Question] seven, could an ELCA candidate be ordained with an Episcopal bishop being present?—Certainly, there is no provision that an Episcopal bishop has to be present at the ordination of an ELCA candidate who is being ordained as a pastor. And [question] eight, certainly the liturgical and doctrinal heritage of the congregation would be honored. Would an Episcopal priest, called by an ELCA congregation, still be called, Father?—I imagine she would not wish so to be called. [Question] nine, the theological and pastoral quality controls would remain in place. In terms of [question] 10, theological education would change in relationships of full communion; for example, we would commit ourselves that our ordinands would study the *Book of Common Prayer*, and the Episcopal Church would pledge itself that its candidates for ordination would study the Lutheran confessions, particularly, the `Augsburg Confession' and the `Small Catechism.' And that church has indicated already that it would make a mandatory question on its general ordination exam dealing with the Lutheran confessions. [Question 11], indeed, there are both similarities and differences in the understanding of communion, the Lord's Supper, among these churches, but the thrust of the work of 30 years of dialogue is that these differences are no longer a rationale to keep the churches divided. Certainly, the liturgical practices of the respective churches are honored in full communion. In terms of [question] 12, it seems to me that, while provision is made of the exchangeability, the transfer of members, members would find their place in one of the churches. That is where the membership would be, but that does not mean that they could not worship obviously in other churches—as continues today. [Question] 13, I think the answer is, no. An Episcopal priest or a Reformed minister could not automatically be elected a bishop in the ELCA. [Question] 14, the Episcopal Church and the Reformed churches are both members of the Consultation on Church Union (COCU) in the United States. They do not have a particularly impressive record of bilateral dialogue between them. I imagine, in full communion, one of the results would be that those two traditions would have to be much more related, because they would both be in full communion to us—not to each other, obviously, but to us. [Question] 15, indeed, we do share a common witness, short of full communion; there are many examples of that, but that would be enhanced and lifted up in full communion. Yes, any clergy coming to serve in the Evangelical Lutheran Church in America would be subject to our discipline and regulations, if that is what is behind [question] 16. [Question] 17 would not apply; the ecumenical proposals concern only ordained ministers of the tradition; rostered lay people would not be included in these provisions. In terms of [question] 18, I need quickly to say several things—I am puzzled by the material in bold print because, in fact, there are several study guides and they are, in fact, all finished; they are completed. There is a study guide on *Implications of the Gospel*, there is a study guide to the churchwide study on Lutheran-Episcopal relations, there is a study guide on *A Common Calling*, called, *A Common Discovery*. They are written at a level of approximately tenth grade and these materials have been developed in consultation with [the Department for] Research and Evaluation and the folks in [the Department for] Communication. Almost everything in that column on the page that deals with interpretive resources has either been field tested or discussed with our colleagues in those other units. I think [question] 19 is provided for in terms of the three pages of charts that you have; you see the interpretive materials that will be available. [Question 20], the process for dealing with responses from congregations really falls to our friends in [the Department for] Research and Evaluation; they will be handling that for us. And then we intend, in terms of [question] 21, certainly to keep you, the Conference of Bishops, and others, addressed as we perceive where the constituency of the Evangelical Lutheran Church in America is about these proposals. So, I hope that at least begins to answer some of those concerns. There are many other questions; in fact, we have prepared a sheet of what we perceive as they key theological questions on these proposals and that is also available."

During discussion, Secretary Lowell G. Almen questioned whether the department intended to fulfill the directive of the Executive Committee. Bishop Paull E. Spring cautioned against the tendency to anecdotalize these processes. "We have got to move beyond that into the documentary level, that is, what do we say, what is in the documentation, what do we affirm, what do we confess—not only we but they . . .?" he said. The Rev. Robert N. Bacher, executive for administration, observed that the committee's concern was whether people would understand the issues from the documents produced by the various ecumenical dialogues.

The Rev. David G. Gabel asked, "How do we know when we are there [that is, when full communion has been reached]? Pastor Rusch responded, "I think that at its best full communion is a developing relationship that is hard to plot out on a grid. I suspect that in many places in this church with several churches we are well along the road to full communion. But, part of the unfolding of that process, it seems to me, is certain judicial actions that have to be taken to affirm that process." Pastor Gabel question the necessity of such judicial actions and said, "Maybe we just need to let that happen . . ." rather than legislating it.

Patsy Gottschalk commented, "I just do not see how the person in the pew is going to relate to this issue and why it is so important, and to what advantage." She also questioned the comprehensibility of the various official documents. The Rev. Nadine F. Lehr inquired about the

implications of election of synodical bishops to life occupancy in the office of bishop. She also raised questions about the status of the "Augsburg Confession" in the *Concordat of Agreement*. William E. Diehl asked how such practical questions as contributions to pension plans and continuing theological education would be determined. Pastor Rusch indicated that the coordinating committees would explore such considerations as relationships develop. Mr. Diehl cautioned that such questions would be important to people attending synodical assemblies where the full communion proposals may be discussed. The Rev. Franklin D. Fry concurred with the directive of the Executive Committee to the Department for Ecumenical Affairs and noted that assisting readers with accessible language to identify issues would be of prime importance. Bishop Peter Rogness commented on the need for a one-page summation ("primer") to be prepared for distribution at synodical assemblies. Observing that 60 percent of the voting membership of the Churchwide Assembly is laity, he stated, "We have got to figure out some way to trigger some curiosity about it [the full-communion proposals] on the part of lay people. . . ." He urged that this church's membership be assisted in focusing on the key issues.

J. David Ellwanger inquired about the differences between the present relationship of "interim full communion" with the Episcopal Church and the proposals now under consideration. Discussion continued and included a request for a brief summary of "flash point" issues in the proposals.

Lorraine G. Bergquist noted that the Executive Committee of the Church Council was concerned that there be resources for clarification and greater understanding in congregations of what is actually being proposed and what the implications may be of such actions. Bishop Herbert W. Chilstrom noted that what is being presented emerges out of more than a quarter century of dialogues and conversations. The primary is not primary enough, he said.

Pastor Rusch confirmed, "We will bring together all the resources to give you what you have asked for."

The council recessed at 10:31 A.M. and reconvened at 10:50 A.M.

Report of the Program and Structure Committee (Continued)

Chair Magnus introduced the Rev. Stephen M. Youngdahl, chair of the Program and Structure Committee, to present the committee's report.

2. Review of the Division for Global Mission

The ELCA governing documents call on the Church Council, through its Program and Structure Committee to:

establish a process for the review of at least two churchwide units each biennium so as to review all units within a ten-year period. Such review shall include the recommendation for renewal of the mandate for the churchwide unit or recommendation of an alternative structure through which the unit's purposes shall be accomplished (ELCA 14.41.D91.).

Council agenda Exhibit G, Part 1, contained material related to the review of the Division for Global Mission, which was the focus of the work of the Program and Structure Committee this year. At its pre-council meeting, the Program and Structure Committee reviewed this material. and adopted the following recommendation to the Church Council for consideration.

Council Action: Pastor Youngdahl introduced the Rev. Mark W. Thomsen, executive director of the Division for Global Mission, and the Rev. Bonnie L. Jensen, director for planning and evaluation and program director for Papua New Guinea and the South Pacific, who highlighted the division's work by means of a seven-minute slide presentation on the division's constitutional mandate. Ms. Tanya Anderson, a staff member of the division, also was present for the presentation.

VOTED: CC95.4.34

To affirm the renewal of the mandate of the Division for Global Mission; and

To express deep appreciation to the staff and board of the Division for Global Mission for their ongoing service in this ministry of the Evangelical Lutheran Church in America.

VOTED: CC95.4.35
1.   To affirm the continuation of global mission as a budgetary priority of the churchwide organization.
2.   To express appreciation and support for the following five priorities of the Division for Global Mission (DGM), which were adopted previously by the division's board:
   a.   *Evangelism.* The primary involvement of the Division for Global Mission will be evangelism, specifically a holistic witness among people who have not heard or who have not fully heard the Gospel of Jesus Christ. Building on its strategic presence within the Muslim world and in Asia, the Division for Global Mission will give priority to engagement with Muslims and to witness within the world of Buddhism, Hinduism, and secularism in Asia.
   b.   *Cooperation . . . Leadership.* All the churches in which the Division for Gobal Mission relates identify more and better leadership as one of their most critical needs. This priority allocates Division for Global Mission resources to the discovery, formation, and undergirding of persons who are or can be leaders, especially women.
   c.   *South-South Relationships.* The Division for Global Mission gives priority to the developing, facilitating, and nurturing of exchanges, relationships, coopera-

tion, and mutual involvement in mission among churches of the southern hemisphere—Africa, the Middle East, Asia, and Latin America.
   d.   *Poverty, Ill Health, and Oppression.* Within the scope of God's mission to this world, people who suffer from poverty, preventable diseases, and oppression have a special claim upon the concern, commitment, and resources of the Evangelical Lutheran Church in America.
   e.   *Mission to the ELCA.* The Division for Global Mission education program will work to increase the concern and the involvement of every member and every congregation in Christ's mission to the world: expanding awareness, renewing prayer life, and increasing support for the ELCA global mission program. The primary methodology will be strategies that enable ELCA members to receive and experience the gifts and witness of members of churches with whom the ELCA cooperates.
3.   To affirm the work of the Division for Global Mission in mission education, to encourage the division, in cooperation with other churchwide units, to explore new ways to share information about the global mission work being undertaken by the ELCA, and to enable members of the ELCA to participate in the life and mission of the body of Christ.
4.   To express appreciation and support for the Companion Synod Program and to encourage continuing conversations between the Division for Global Mission and synods to further this effort.
5.   To affirm the ongoing work of the Division for Global Mission in addressing the concerns and needs of women and in lifting up the role of women in many cultures.
6.   To affirm the division's commitment to building relationships with African Americans, Asians, Hispanics, and Native Americans.
7.   To express strong affirmation of the ELCA World Hunger Program and continuing commitment to strengthening this important churchwide effort; to affirm the continuation of the current practice of special appeals to respond to domestic and international disasters; and to express continuing support for the 70-75 percent allocation for the international hunger program, which was determined by the 1987 ELCA Constituting Convention; and to transmit to the Office of the Bishop without recommendation the following action taken by the board of the Division for Global Mission:

That the board request the ELCA Church Council and the Office of the Bishop to communicate to the Interunit Hunger Staff Team that it would be the board's desire that the 72.4 percent allocated to the international program be maintained or increased.

8. **To request that the Office of the Bishop engage in conversation with the Division for Global Mission and other appropriate church-wide units about designated giving initiatives and bring a report and possible recommendations for action to the November 1995 meeting of the Church Council; to request that this report address the issue of coordination among churchwide units and other partners in ministry as they approach congregations for designated gifts; and to refer to the Office of the Bishop the following action by the board of the Division for Global Mission:**

That the board of the Division for Global Mission of the Evangelical Lutheran Church in America seek the cooperation and approval of the Church Council, the Office of the Bishop, and the Conference of Bishops to explore with the Division for Congregational Ministries and other churchwide units of the ELCA new avenues and sources of funding for global mission and to develop further opportunities for designated giving to global ministries over and above the division's annual budget.

9. **To receive with appreciation the board's identification of ongoing issues and to request that results of the survey of missionaries be shared with the Program and Structure Committee.**

Bishop Glenn W. Nycklemoe thanked the division for awakening new interest in mission outside this church through its companion-synod program.

Pastor Thomsen expressed appreciation to J. David Ellwanger, who had represented the Division for Global Mission and the Office of the Treasurer on the board of the Ecumenical Development and Cooperative Society, which originated with the World Council of Churches. Mr. Ellwanger reported on the investment and development work of the society in third-world countries. He noted that this church related to the society by reason of an outstanding $1.2 million loan that The American Lutheran Church [predecessor church body] had made to the society. Mr. Ellwanger also expressed appreciation for the opportunity to serve on the Church Council.

Report of the Legal and Constitutional Review Committee (continued)

7. **Approval of Ecumenical Proposals by the 1997 Churchwide Assembly**

A matter previously tabled, a proposal for adoption by the 1995 Churchwide Assembly of a new bylaw regarding official church-to-church relationships, was returned for consideration. Mr. Dale V. Sandstrom, chair of the Legal and Constitutional Review Committee, reported that consultation on revisions had been undertaken. The conclusion of such conversations was to recommend the original text of the proposed bylaw, as submitted by the committee.

Chair Magnus requested that there be unanimous consent that the amendment that was proposed be withdrawn. There being no objection, the original proposal was presented.

VOTED: **CC95.4.36**
    To recommend to the 1995 Churchwide Assembly adoption of a new section and bylaw:

8.70.01.   Official Church-to-Church Relationships
8.71.01.   This church may establish official church-to-church relationships and agreements. Establishment of such official relationships and agreements shall require a two-thirds vote of the voting members of the Churchwide Assembly.

Report of the Coordination and Services Committee

Chair Magnus called upon William E. Diehl, chair of the Coordination and Services Committee, to present the committee's report.

1. **Matters Related to Departments**

Mr. Diehl reported that the Department for Synodical Relations was providing transition assistance to synods with newly elected bishops. The Department for Communication had provided for committee members a demonstration of this church's participation on Internet, linking Lutherans around the world. The Evangelical Lutheran Church in America received numerous awards from the Religious Public Relations Council, he said, including awards for *Seeds for the Parish*, *Mosaic* video magazine, and the campus ministry poster for the ELCA Youth Gathering. In addition Women of the Evangelical Lutheran Church in America received an award for *Lutheran Woman Today*; the Board of Pensions received an award for its "Board Talk" newsletter; Luther Seminary (St. Paul, Minn.) received four awards for its publications; Lutheran World Relief received an award for its "Rwanda Exodus" video; the South-Central Synod of Wisconsin received an award for missionary prayer cards; and St. John's Lutheran Church (Northfield,

Minn.) received an award for its 125th anniversary booklet. The Department for Research and Evaluation reported that trend analysis for individual congregations is now available on the Lutheran Center's computer network. The Department for Human Resources is working to revise the employee evaluation process.

Mr. Diehl reported that the committee also had approved minor changes to the personnel policies of the churchwide organization

2. Matters Related to the
Department for Synodical Relations
Special Needs Retirement Fund

Council agenda Exhibit I, Part 2, contained a report from an inter-unit churchwide working group on the Special Needs Retirement Fund. Representatives from the Department for Synodical Relations, Office of the Treasurer, Division for Ministry, Board of Pensions, and ELCA Foundation participated in this working group.

The Coordination and Services Committee, at its pre-council meeting, had discussion in regard to the fund. The discussion centered around two foci. First, there was concern about whether the current plans will ever gather sufficient funds to guarantee additional income to low-income retirees. It was reported that $375,000 was needed to institute the plans. After one quarter, only $50,000 has been collected. Secondly, the committee questioned whether additional pension contributions will ever be added to the accounts of persons in low compensation situations to alleviate the problems in the future.

Mr. Diehl introduced the committee's recommendation. Discussion followed. Edith M. Lohr noted the issue of permitting pension participants to determine investment patterns, and factors related to those who opt out of Social Security.

VOTED: **CC95.4.37**
To request the Board of Pensions to explore, in dialogue with the Special Needs Retirement Fund Management Committee, additional avenues to address the immediate and long-term needs of low-income retirees in the ELCA Pension Program.

Loren W. Mathre moved the following motion, subsequently adopted by the Church Council. During discussion, a suggestion was made that the session include goal setting.

VOTED: **CC95.4.38**
To devote up to one day of the November 1995 meeting of the Church Council to a planning session with the bishop of this church so that the members of the Church Council may be incorporated into the "Inquiry" process.

3. Cross-Denominational Study on Giving

The results of a recent study on denominational giving patterns was distributed to council members as council agenda Exhibit I, Part 3. The Church Council received the foregoing as information.

Matters Related to the
Division for Congregational Ministries (continued)
2. Lutheran Laity Movement for Stewardship

According to the ELCA's governing documents, the constitution and bylaws of the Lutheran Laity Movement for Stewardship, and amendments thereto, after review by [the Division for Congregational Ministries], may be amended by a two-thirds vote of the Church Council (ELCA 16.11.A91.f.4.).

The amendments to the governing documents of Lutheran Laity Movement for Stewardship (LLM), council agenda Exhibit L, Part 2, proposed by the LLM board, were reviewed by the board of the Division for Congregational Ministries.

The Rev. Mark R. Moller-Gunderson, executive director of the Division for Congregational Ministries, introduced the following recommendation of the division's board, subsequently adopted by the Church Council.

2/3 VOTE REQUIRED
VOTED: **CC95.4.39**
To approve the amendments to the constitution and bylaws of the Lutheran Laity Movement for Stewardship . . ..

3. Youth Gathering

The board of the Division for Congregational Ministries evaluated the 1994 Youth Gathering. On the basis of that positive evaluation, the board recommended that another Youth Gathering be held in 1997.

During discussion, the Rev. Nadine F. Lehr inquired about the possibility of scheduling several gatherings in light of the large number of people attending previous events (34,000 in 1994). Pastor Moller-Gunderson reported that the division had contemplated multiple gatherings, but had determined that a single event would be preferable. "We will work for a ceiling that provides a level of safety for participants," he said, noting that multiple events would continue to be considered in the future. The Rev. James G. Cobb commented on the difficulties of holding both the Churchwide Assembly and a youth gathering during the same summer, and encouraged that the schedule for those events be staggered.

VOTED: **CC95.4.40**
To express appreciation to all those whose time and efforts made the 1994 Youth Gathering a great success and a gift to the whole church; and
To authorize the Division for Congregational Ministries to hold a Youth Gathering in 1997.

4. Resolutions from the Convention of the
Lutheran Youth Organization

Karris Golden, vice president of the Lutheran Youth Organization (LYO), presented the following resolutions, adopted by the 1994 convention of the

Lutheran Youth Organization. The resolutions were reviewed by the board of the Division for Congregational Ministries and were transmitted to the Church Council and the 1995 Churchwide Assembly for possible action.

A. Americans with Disabilities Act

WHEREAS, the Americans with Disabilities Act was passed by Congress in 1990 laying out requirements for provision of access for persons with disabilities, and

WHEREAS, business, schools, and transportation companies are required to provide access to persons with disabilities as specified in the ADA but churches are exempt under the Act, and

WHEREAS, persons with disabilities are an integral part of the ministry of the LYO and the ELCA, and have valuable talents to offer the church; and

WHEREAS, people with disabilities are often blocked from full participation in the church by lack of access; and

WHEREAS, provision for access for disabled people is not an act of charity; but rather an act of justice; therefore, be it,

RESOLVED, that the LYO strongly encourage all congregations and organizations in the church to make buildings and events accessible to persons with disabilities, according to the provisions indicated in the ADA, and be it further

RESOLVED, that the LYO strongly encourage all congregations and organizations to make themselves also attitudinally accessible to persons with disabilities, and be it further

RESOLVED, that the LYO request the board of the Division for Congregational Ministries to transmit to the Churchwide Assembly the request that the assembly take similar action.

VOTED: **CC95.4.41**

To recommend that the 1995 Churchwide Assembly adopt the following resolution:

To affirm the action taken by the Lutheran Youth Organization regarding Americans with disabilities; and

To reaffirm the commitment of the Evangelical Lutheran Church in America to make all aspects of its life and work accessible to persons with disabilities.

B. Post-High School Youth

WHEREAS, the youth of the church are more than the future of the Church and are an integral part of the full communion of Christ; and

WHEREAS, the Church has made strides in ministering with the youth of the church through organizations such as the Evangelical Lutheran Church in America's Lutheran Youth Organization and other ELCA youth ministry organizations, Lutheran Campus Ministries, and the Lutheran Student Movement; and

WHEREAS, the Church is the body of believers (Romans 12:5) and all members of the body are important for the continued mission of Christ's Church on earth; and

WHEREAS, the Evangelical Lutheran Church in America hgh school age groups; and

WHEREAS, the post-high school age youth of the Church have consistently shown great drive, ideals, and energy fostered from previous involvement in the ELCA LYO on all levels; and

WHEREAS, these young adults have things to say, ideas to implement, and energy to change and move forward; and

WHEREAS, the Evangelical Lutheran Church in America to provide any intentional ministry for those youth who have recently graduated from high school and are not pursuing a college career; and

WHEREAS, this age (post-high school) is the time when these people are making life decisions, becoming integral parts of society, and longing for a place not only to be accepted, but to be empowered; and

WHEREAS, a majority of the nominees appearing in *The Delegate Handbook* for the twelve positions on the churchwide LYO Board have graduated from high school before completing the first year of their term if elected; and

WHEREAS, several of the members of the current churchwide LYO Board are post-high school age; therefore, be it

RESOLVED, that the Lutheran Youth Organization of the Evangelical Lutheran Church in America memorialize the 1995 Churchwide Assembly of the ELCA with the intention of forming programs for and ministering to youth that have recently graduated from high school, regardless of their educational or occupational plans for the future; and be it further

RESOLVED, that the LYO ensures that efforts be made to welcome, reach out to, and encourage post-high school age youth of the congregational, synodical, and churchwide expression of the Evangelical Lutheran Church in America.

VOTED: **CC95.4.42**

To recommend that the 1995 Churchwide Assembly adopt the following resolution:

To affirm the action taken by the Lutheran Youth Organization regarding post-high school youth;

To encourage all congregations to create programs for and minister to youth who have recently graduated from high school, regardless of their educational or occupational plans for the future; and

To encourage congregations, synods, and the churchwide organization to welcome, reach out to, and encourage post-high school age youth.

C. Nomination Process

The board of the Division for Congregational Ministries, at its March 1995 meeting, transmitted to the Church Council the following resolution from the board of the Lutheran Youth Organization:

That the Churchwide Assembly adopt a policy of replacing "other" with a multi-ethnic option and provide space to list cultures on forms that request ethnic identification.

VOTED: **CC95.4.43**

To refer the resolution of the Lutheran Youth Organization on the nomination process to the secretary of this church; and

To request that a report on this matter be brought to the November 1995 meeting of the Church Council.

D. Representational Principles

The board of the Division for Congregational Ministries, at its March 1995 meeting, transmitted the following resolution from the board of the Lutheran Youth Organization to the Church Council:

That the LYO (Lutheran Youth Organization) strongly encourage the Churchwide Assembly to continue to maintain or exceed the current representational principles in the Evangelical Lutheran Church in America.

VOTED: **CC95.4.44**

To request the secretary of the ELCA to report this action of the board of the Lutheran

Youth Organization to the 1995 Churchwide Assembly as part of the Church Council's report on representational principles.

The Rev. Franklin D. Fry expressed concern about fund raising activities.

Matters Related to the Division for Outreach
Urban Initiative

Background: Earlier in the 1994-1995 biennium, the board and staff of the Division for Outreach indicated their intent to present an Urban Resolution to the 1995 Churchwide Assembly. The process for developing such a resolution included work with urban pastors, coalitions, and groups such as City Lutherans in Action and the Urban Guild. As this discussion process went forward, participants questioned the need for an urban resolution. In addition, various groups and sections of the country expressed a variety of understandings as to what should be emphasized in a resolution, should such a resolution be developed.

In addition to the input coming from those involved in urban ministry, the division itself has reordered its way of providing services to synods and ministries in the urban setting. The creation of an Urban Ministry Staff Team and the plan to develop networks of ministry advisers is only one part of this change in direction.

At its March 17-19, 1995, meeting, the board of the Division for Outreach decided to withdraw its plans for an urban resolution to be presented to the Churchwide Assembly in 1995. In its place, the board affirmed the "Urban Initiative" found in council agenda Exhibit N, Part 1. The board requests this Urban Initiative be reported to the 1995 Churchwide Assembly as an information item.

Council Action: The Rev. Malcolm L. Minnick Jr., executive director of the Division for Outreach, provided background. "It had been our hope and intent to move to the 1995 [Churchwide] Assembly with an urban resolution similar to what we did in 1993 with the rural resolution. As we began to work in the diversity of what is urban and rural America and with groups that represent those settings, we began to find that a great deal more was needed in the way of work and a different approach than what we were using. Because of that find, we developed what we call and urban initiative, which lays out a process that will be used by the division in reaching not only those who minister in the inner city, but also those that are ministering in urban settings and in metropolitan settings. We not only have the oppression of those who are poor and those who are oppressed in our inner cities, but we also have a great strength in our Lutheran witness in the cities of America. All of this needs to be brought together as a total resource to develop a direction for this church that can be helpful. In order to do that, we have developed an urban team that is composed of three of our staff persons. Those people will be doing a marketing analysis over the next year

with the people who are in urban ministry. Out of that we hope to develop not only an awareness of the true needs and opportunities for ministry there, but also to identify those ministry practitioners, whom we would call ministry advisers, who can lead to the development of the kind of networking where people in urban ministry can be aiding other people who need assistance in urban ministry. It is to carry the concept of coalition, such as we have in Milwaukee, to a much broader stance by seeing that it is something that can work throughout the entire country and in different regions of the country.

"Another facet of the urban initiative is that we are already seeking funds from one of the fraternals to bring together for the first time our leaders in urban ministry, not only inner city but also congregations that have strength in the urban setting as well. We hope to do just that before the 1997 Churchwide Assembly in Philadelphia, and we feel it is very fitting that the wind-up and report of this urban initiative would then come to the 1997 assembly in Philadelphia. It was in one of the predecessor church bodies that the real work in urban ministry began in the 1960s and would seem to be a very appropriate place for us to look to the future as it pertains to the work of the church in the urban setting. . . ."

VOTED: CC95.4.45
To transmit to the 1995 Churchwide Assembly the "Urban Initiative" . . .; and
To recommend that the 1995 Churchwide Assembly adopt the following action:

To receive the "Urban Initiative" prepared by the Division for Outreach; and

To request that the Division for Outreach bring to the 1997 Churchwide Assembly a report on the implementation of this initiative during the 1996-1997 biennium.

Department for Research and Evaluation

Chair Magnus introduced Kenneth W. Inskeep, director of the Department for Research and Evaluation, who made a presentation on "Findings on Twenty-two Hypotheses on Religious Giving." Mr. Inskeep noted that the department participated in a study conducted by Dean R. Hoge at Catholic University (Washington, D.C.) funded by the Lilly Foundation to the extent of $500,000. The study, the data of which are not yet fully analyzed, examined giving patterns in five denominations [Assemblies of God, Evangelical Lutheran Church in America, selected Roman Catholic archdioceses, Presbyterian Church (U.S.A.), and Southern Baptist Convention]. The hypotheses upon which Mr. Inskeep commented follow:

FINDINGS ON
TWENTY-TWO HYPOTHESES ON RELIGIOUS GIVING
Adapted from *Religious Giving in Five Denominations*
(Dean R. Hoge, Charles Zech, Patrick McNamara, and Michael Donohue, 1993)
Prepared by the Department for Research and Evaluation
Evangelical Lutheran Church in America

Hypothesis 1: Persons of higher income, higher education, older age, and fewer dependent children give more.

- As income increases, the level of giving goes up.
- Assemblies and Baptists increase their giving sooner.
- Increases in income impact giving least for Roman Catholics.
- Higher education means higher giving except for Roman Catholics.
- Highest giving levels occur between ages 45 and 65. After 65, giving decreases.
- The number of dependent children does not directly impact giving levels.

Hypothesis 2: Married members give more than single or widowed members, and married members whose spouses attend the same church give more.

- Members who give the most are married with their spouses attending the same congregation.

Hypothesis 3: Members whose children attend five-day-a-week religious schools give less to the congregation or parish.

- Applies primarily to Roman Catholics and Assemblies of God. Giving levels with children attending religious schools are about the same as persons of the same ages without children attending religious schools.

Hypothesis 4: Members who perceive more democratic decision-making regarding the use of church funds give more.

- Dissatisfaction with the decision-making process is mildly associated with lower giving.

Hypothesis 5: Members who perceive adequate accountability by congregational and denominational leaders regarding use of funds give more.

- This is true primarily at the congregational level. At the denominational level, results were mixed.

Hypothesis 6: Members who have doubts about honesty and openness in the handling of church funds give less.

- Levels of trust are so high in almost all the churches that the factor is unimportant.

Hypothesis 7: Members who are actively involved in congregational life give more.

- People who attend church more and participate actively in the church clearly give more money.

Hypothesis 8: Members who feel they have adequate communication with congregational and denominational leaders and are more enthusiastic about them give more.

- The hypothesis is true at both the congregational and denominational level but the impact is very modest. It is a secondary factor in giving, not a main one.

Hypothesis 9: Members who believe the congregational or denomination has serious needs give more. Members of congregations in debt or in the midst of capital campaigns give more and members of congregations with endowments give less.

- The belief that congregations have serious needs does not consistently impact giving.
- The belief that denominations have serious needs does encourage higher giving.
- Congregations with debts experience higher levels of giving among Baptists, Lutherans, and Presbyterians.
- Only among Lutheran churches do capital campaigns increase giving.
- Endowments are not associated with levels of giving.

Hypothesis 10: Members with stronger and more traditional doctrinal beliefs give more, and members believing that tithing is important for righteousness or salvation give more.

- The relationship between strong and more traditional doctrinal beliefs is strongly related to giving except among Roman Catholics.

Hypothesis 11: Members feeling alienated from denominational leadership and teachings give less.

- The hypothesis was supported only for Baptists who oppose the ordination of women and homosexuals.

Hypothesis 12: Members who plan their giving by the year or by the month give more than those who decide week to week.

- People who decide about giving for an entire year give much more than those who decide week by week. Those who are most likely to decide for a year tend to be the regular attenders.

Hypothesis 13: Younger and more educated members tend to prefer designated giving to specific missions over unified giving to denominational missions, and persons preferring designated giving give more.

- Younger and more educated members do prefer designated giving, but those who prefer that the denomination choose give more among Lutherans and Baptists. Presbyterians and Assemblies of God that prefer designated giving give more. Among Roman Catholics it makes no difference.

Hypothesis 14: Smaller congregations have higher per-member giving.

- The results of the test were inconsistent.

Hypothesis 15: Members of congregations with a wide array of programs give more.

- The impact of having more programs is moderate and grows weaker with controls for congregational size.

Hypothesis 16: Congregations using annual pledge drives and pledge cards have a higher level of giving.

- Members that pledge give more money even after controls for regular church attendance, higher income, and size of congregation.

Hypothesis 17: Congregations which provide explicit reports on expenditures of funds and which send out monthly or quarterly reports to members on the amount received from them have a higher level of giving.

- The hypothesis was not supported.

Hypothesis 18: Congregations in which laypersons handle the finances have a higher level of giving than those in which clergy handle the finances.

- Members who prefer lay handling of finances actually give more than others, and denominations currently having lay control over finances have higher levels of giving.

Hypothesis 19: Congregations using stewardship programs and stressing stewardship as an aspect of Christian living, rather than fund-raising to support programs, have a higher level of giving.

- Stewardship programs have a modest effect on giving.

Hypothesis 20: Congregations or denominations which stress giving as an obligatory aspect of Christian living have a higher level of giving.

- There are very few congregational effects but the differences between denominations are important. Denominations that stress giving as an obligatory aspect of Christian living have higher levels of giving.

Hypothesis 21: Denominations or congregations which maintain distinctive life-styles have a higher level of giving.
- There are very few congregational effects but the differences between denominations are important. Denominations that maintain the necessity of distinctive life-styles have higher levels of giving.

Hypothesis 22: Congregations or parishes with five-day-a-week religious schools have a lower level of giving to the congregation or parish.
- Congregations or parishes with five-day-a-week religious schools have giving levels that are similar to those without the schools.

Report of the Secretary

Secretary Lowell G. Almen presented his formal report and commented on elements of it.

The council recessed for lunch at 12:41 P.M. The meeting reconvened at 1:25 P.M.

Matters Related to the Division for Church in Society (continued)

3. Study Guide on Political Life

The Division for Church in Society will be developing a teaching and discussion resource for congregational use on the subject of political life. No message of concern will be brought to the Church Council on this matter. The division considers such study materials the best medium to meet the needs of congregations in 1995-1996.

The Church Council received the foregoing as information.

4. Women and Children in Poverty

The 1993 Churchwide Assembly took action on a wide range of recommendations related to women and children living in poverty. It requested that the Division for Church in Society bring annual reports to the Church Council and biennial reports to the Churchwide Assembly on this issue.

VOTED: **CC95.4.46**

To transmit the report on women and children living in poverty . . . to the 1995 Churchwide Assembly.

[The text of the report will appear in Volume 2 of thge Pre-Assembly Report.]

5. "Blue Ribbon Committee" Vision and Strategies for the Corporate Social Ministry of the ELCA

Background: The environment in which not-for-profit human service organizations operate is changing dramatically. New and complex challenges abound for this church's social ministry organizations.

In 1993, the board of the Division for Church in Society appointed a Blue Ribbon Committee to address

these challenges. Council agenda Exhibit P, Part 4, was an interim report of the committee to the board of the division and the Church Council. A final report accompanied by recommendations and a strategic plan will be presented to the division's board in September 1995 and the Church Council in November 1995.

Council Action: Issues outlined by the Rev. Charles S. Miller Jr., executive director of the Division for Church in Society, included (1) church identity; (2) need to bring organizations into a system (collaborative organization); and (3) servant-leadership development for the future.

He reported that the Association of Lutheran Social Ministry Organizations was being created to serve as a forum for the leadership of ELCA-affiliated social ministry organizations.

Discussion followed.

6. Corporate Social Responsibility

An update on recent activities related to the ELCA's activities in the arena of corporate social responsibility was distributed to council members as council agenda Exhibit P, Part 5 and was received as information.

7. Advocacy Plan

The advocacy plan of the Division for Church in Society for 1995-1996 was distributed to council members as council agenda Exhibit P, Part 6.

Pastor Miller stated that the work in the advocacy plan is driven by actions of the Churchwide Assembly and the Church Council and by the social statements of this church and its predecessor bodies, as noted in the document itself.

The Church Council received the foregoing as information.

Women of the ELCA: Resolution on Compensation for Women

Background: The following action was taken by the board of the Women of the Evangelical Lutheran Church in America at its October 1994 meeting:

WHEREAS, women clergy, women lay professiona,ls and support staff are often offered lower compensation and benefits than males in comparable positions; and

WHEREAS, recognition for women's previous work experience, whether in professional fields, volunteer work, or homemaking, is often not taken into account; and

WHEREAS, the contribution of women is integral to the whole economic structure of family and society; therefore be it

RESOLVED, that the ELCA through congregational units, institutions, affiliated ministries, agencies, synods and the churchwide organization examine current salary levels and benefits of women employed and called to serve throughout the ELCA in order to achieve equity in compensation, making salary adjustments as needed and offering benefits to those not presently covered; and be it further

RESOLVED, that the Women of the ELCA Executive Board transmit this resolution to the ELCA Church Council for action.

At its November 1994 meeting the Church Council voted:

To refer the resolution on the compensation of women jointly to the Commission for Women, the Women of the Evangelical

Lutheran Church in America, and the Department for Human Resources; and

To request that those units, in consultation with the Division for Church in Society, bring a recommendation for action to the Church Council at its April 1995 meeting (CC94.11.114).

Council Action: Chair Magnus called upon Charlotte E. Fiechter, executive director of Women of the Evangelical Lutheran Church in America, to report on the resolution.

Lutheran Brotherhood Lutheran Community Foundation

Chair Magnus and the Rev. Mark R. Moller-Gunderson, executive director of the Division for Congregational Ministries, reported on the Lutheran Community Foundation being formed by Lutheran Brotherhood.

The Rev. Donald M. Hallberg expressed disappointment on the Lutheran Brotherhood action.

Report of the Program and Structure Committee (continued)

3. Regional Reports

An update on the work of the regions was distributed to council members as council agenda Exhibit H, Part 2a. The Church Council received the foregoing as information.

Update on Upsala College

The Rev. W. Robert Sorensen, executive director of the Division for Higher Education and Schools, reported on the closing of Upsala College, which was established in 1893 at East Orange, N.J. Are there "more Upsalas" in our future, he asked. The future is unpredictable, he answered. It is a difficult decade for higher education in this country. Pastor Sorensen cautioned against taking church colleges and universities for granted.

En Bloc Approval of Certain Agenda Items

VOTED: **CC95.4.47**

To take action *en bloc* on the items listed below, the full texts of which are found in the body of the agenda or in an exhibit as noted:

CC95.4.47a-k	Synod Resolutions Directed to the Church Council
CC95.4.47l	Ratification of Synodical Constitutions
CC95.4.47m	Changes in the Structure of Region 3
CC95.4.47n	ELCA Medical and Dental Benefits Plan Regarding Pre-Certification of Outpatient Procedures
CC95.4.47o	ELCA Medical and Dental Benefits Plan Regarding Services Excluded from Mental Health and Chemical Dependency Coverage
CC95.4.47p	ELCA Medical and Dental Benefits Plan Regarding the Order of Benefit Determination in the Case of Divorced Parents
CC95.4.47q	ELCA Medical and Dental Benefits Plan and ELCA Continuation of the ALC Medical-Dental Plan
CC95.4.47r	ELCA Continuation of the LCA Ministerial Health Benefits Plan and ELCA Continuation of the ALC Medical and Dental Benefits Plan

CC95.4.47s	Technical Amendments
CC95.4.47t	Synodically Authorized Ministries
CC95.4.47u	Nonstipendiary Ministries for Lay Rosters
CC95.4.47v	Policy for Rostered Persons: On Leave From Call for Study
CC95.4.47w	Election of Corporate Members
CC95.4.47x	Recognition of Relationship of Independent Lutheran Organizations to the Division for Global Mission

Synodical Resolutions

1. Clergy Mobility

Southwestern Texas Synod (4E)

WHEREAS, the Evangelical Lutheran Church in America is divided into 65 synods, each synod having its own policies on receiving candidates for potential placement; and

WHEREAS, clergy seeking call in more than one synod face the potential of great expense in visiting with placement committees within the synod offices of each individual synod; and

WHEREAS, a unified placement form has been developed and is widely used by the synods of the Evangelical Lutheran Church in America; and

WHEREAS, clergy mobility in a national church is desirable; now, therefore, be it

RESOLVED, that the Southwestern Texas Synod direct the Synod Council to communicate to the ELCA Church Council this synod's recommendation that a biennial conference of the synod bishops be convened in Chicago for the purpose of interviewing pastoral candidates for synodical calls in the central location; and be it further

RESOLVED, that this process be given a trial in 1996, and follow with biennial centrally located interviews after that year should this conference prove to be effective in enabling bishops to interview potential candidates and for candidates to interview with multiple synods at one time.

The following action was adopted *en bloc* at the conclusion of this meeting:

EN BLOC   **[CC95.4.47a]**

To refer the resolution of the Southwestern Texas Synod on clergy mobility to the Department for Synodical Relations for discussion with the Conference of Bishops.

2. Peace Education Office

Northeastern Ohio Synod (6E)

WHEREAS, the most fervent prayer of religious people everywhere is for peace in the world; and

WHEREAS, as the followers of the Prince of Peace, we pray weekly in our worship services for the peace of the whole world; and

WHEREAS, according to the words of Christ himself we are called to be peacemakers, working for peace in addition to praying for it; and

WHEREAS, our ELCA social statement clearly and urgently calls the church and its people to be active peacemakers; therefore be it

RESOLVED, that the Northeastern Ohio Synod of the Evangelical Lutheran Church in America (ELCA) memorialize the Evangelical Lutheran Church in America to re-establish a peace education office within the [ELCA churchwide] Division for Church in Society; and be it further

RESOLVED, that this [peace education] office provide additional materials to aid in the understanding and application of the principles espoused by the social statement as new peace-threatening events occur in the world; and be it further

RESOLVED, that the peace education office develop materials for use in congregations and agencies of our church and that materials be developed that are appropriate for use among children, by high school youth groups, by men's organizations, by women's organizations, and in adult forums, etc.; and be it further

RESOLVED, that the materials reflect a peace ethic that connects peace within the family, peace within society, and peace between nations; and be it further

RESOLVED, that the peace education office cooperate with other divisions, commissions, and offices of the ELCA [churchwide organization] and other peace organizations in the pursuit of these policies.

The following action was adopted *en bloc* at the conclusion of the meeting:

EN BLOC   [CC95.4.47b]
To request the Office of the Bishop to share with the Northeastern Ohio Synod the action of the Church Council related to budgetary priorities in the development of the 1995 spending plan and the 1996-1997 budget proposal, together with other appropriate information related to these resolutions; and

To request the Division for Church in Society to respond directly to the synod on concerns raised about the production of resources for peace education.

3. Re-Imagining Conference
Slovak Zion Synod (7G)

WHEREAS, we, the Slovak Zion Synod, affirm the authority of Scripture and the Lutheran Confessions; and

WHEREAS, we recognize that the Evangelical Lutheran Church in America also upholds Scripture and the Lutheran Confessions in its Statement of Faith as found in our constitution; and

WHEREAS, we are concerned that certain biblical concepts have been misused at the Re-Imagining Conference in the support of heretical, non-confessional theology; now therefore be it

RESOLVED, that Slovak Zion Synod, in assembly, register with the Evangelical Lutheran Church in America its strong objections to the way it has used funds to further causes inconsistent with the integrity of the Lutheran Confessions and the authority of Scripture.

The following action was adopted *en bloc* at the conclusion of this meeting:

EN BLOC   [CC95.4.47c]
To refer the resolution of the Slovak Zion Synod on the Re-Imagining Conference to the Office of the Bishop for response directly to the Slovak Zion Synod.

4. Biennial Churchwide Assemblies
Upper Susquehanna Synod (8E)

WHEREAS, biennial churchwide assemblies of the Evangelical Lutheran Church in America continue to allow opportunities for lay persons and pastors to experience a gathering of the churchwide expression; and

WHEREAS, there is a need for members of the Evangelical Lutheran Church in America to assemble physically as the body of the church to "touch" the churchwide expression and learn how the Evangelical Lutheran Church in America functions as a part of us throughout the world; to build relationships with ELCA staff and brothers and sisters of the Evangelical Lutheran Church in America; to receive spiritual and personal renewal and edification with and among our brothers and sisters in the other 11,000-plus

congregations of the ELCA; to experience variety in worship and ministry as it exists among our multicultural church; etc. All of these activities enhance the partnership and interdependency of the various expressions of the Evangelical Lutheran Church in America; therefore, be it

RESOLVED, that the Synod Council of the Upper Susquehanna Synod of the Evangelical Lutheran Church in America encourage the Church Council of the Evangelical Lutheran Church in America to retain its current schedule of biennial churchwide assemblies.

The following action was adopted en bloc at the conclusion of this meeting:

EN BLOC   [CC95.4.47d]
To receive the resolution of the Upper Susquehanna Synod on biennial churchwide assemblies;

To request the secretary of this church to convey to the Upper Susquehanna Synod the rationale for the Church Council's recommendation on this matter; and

To encourage full discussion of this recommendation at the 1995 Churchwide Assembly.

Resolutions from Synods Previously Referred to Churchwide Units

1. ELCA Medical and Dental Benefits Plan
Alaska Synod (1A)

The following resolution of the Alaska Synod on the ELCA Medical and Dental Benefits Plan was transmitted to the Church Council's Executive Committee at its November 22, 1993, meeting:

WHEREAS, each ELCA congregation provides health insurance for pastors throughout the Evangelical Lutheran Church in America; and

WHEREAS, since the merger, the cost to congregations has risen substantially every year; and

WHEREAS, benefits have decreased and deductibles increased; and

WHEREAS, the Board of Pensions refuses to see the rural Alaskan situation as being different from other areas like Minneapolis; and

WHEREAS, the Board of Pensions no longer allows coverage for travel from rural (remote) locations to Anchorage, Fairbanks, or Seattle for emergency or for necessary medical care by specialists; and

WHEREAS, it seems the Board of Pensions operates independently and without any real accountability to the rest of the Evangelical Lutheran Church in America; and

WHEREAS, this trend in cost increases is becoming a burden to small struggling congregations; and

WHEREAS, in many cases pastors in small struggling congregations who are likely already to be below synod-recommended salary guidelines are having to forego salary increases so that the congregation can meet the medical premium increases; therefore, be it

RESOLVED, that the Alaska Synod request that the Alaska Synod Council transmit this resolution to the ELCA Church Council Executive Committee for referral in order to set in motion a means to review completely the current policies of the ELCA Board of Pensions; and to do a careful reevaluation and reconsideration of its policies pertaining to Alaska and other rural (remote) areas of the church with respect to higher medical costs and transportation for medical care; and be it further

RESOLVED, that the Alaska Synod request the Alaska Synod Council to request that the ELCA Executive Committee of the ELCA Church Council put in motion a means to reconsider the concept that the Board of Pensions be independent from any control of the church body of the Evangelical Lutheran Church in America.

The Executive Committee voted:

To refer this resolution of the Alaska Synod on health insurance for pastors to the Board of Pensions for a response to the April 1994 meeting of the Church Council (EC93.11.27.1).

The following response from the Board of Pensions was presented to the Church Council at its November 1994 meeting:

Through its consultant, Towers Perrin, the Board of Pensions has researched the services provided by other insurance carriers in the state of Alaska. Based on those inquiries, it has been confirmed that: (1) there is a significant diversity in the charge patterns of physicians throughout the state, and (2) there is a notable lack of reliable physician data in the outlying areas. As a result of the fact that other insurance carriers do differentiate in the administration of benefits in Alaska versus the "lower 48" states, the Board of Pensions is reviewing the application of the "reasonable and customary" data applied to Alaska.

Reimbursement of travel expenses incurred by plan members who receive services either in urban areas of Alaska or in Seattle also has been a major issue for plan members in Alaska. Currently, the ELCA plan provides for coverage of air ambulance to the nearest facility that can treat the patient's condition in the event of an emergency situation. Since the Board of Pensions will utilize Healthmarc as its pre-certification vendor effective January 1, 1995, non-emergency travel expenses will be managed through this pre-certification process. Therefore it is possible that some non-emergency travel expenses could be reimbursed if care that must be provided is not available in the local community. Approval will be accomplished on a case-by-case basis as part of the pre-certification process.

Conversations with the bishop of the Alaska Synod took place in October 1994 and at its November 1994 meeting, the Church Council voted:

To request that the Board of Pensions provide an update of its response to the concerns raised by the Alaska Synod to the April 1995 meeting of the Church Council.

Following is the updated response from the Board of Pensions regarding the concerns raised by the Alaska Synod.

- **Reasonable and Customary Expenses**

Effective January 1, 1992, the Board of Pensions implemented "reasonable and customary" guidelines for all physician, x-ray and laboratory fees. Under the guidelines, the portion of the expense that exceeds the amount usually charged by 80 percent of the providers performing the same service in the same geographic area is denied.

In response to the 1993 Alaska Synod resolution, the Board of Pensions requested its consultant, Towers Perrin, to revisit the application of the guidelines in Alaska in the context of typical insurance practices in Alaska, without regard to the benefit programs of national employers. Based upon this analysis, Towers Perrin indicated that the "reasonable and customary" guidelines should be eliminated for plan members in Alaska because health-care delivery is very different in Alaska than in the lower 48 states.

This information was presented to the board of trustees of the Board of Pensions at its November 1994 meeting. The board

of trustees of the Board of Pensions voted to authorize staff to suppress the "reasonable and customary" fee guidelines for claims incurred in Alaska. This means that all medical claims for professional fees are processed for benefit reimbursement based upon the fees charged by physicians and other health care providers. Plan members in Alaska were notified of the change on November 23, 1994.

- **Travel Expenses:** Plan members in Alaska also raised questions concerning how travel expenses are reimbursed under the ELCA Medical and Dental Benefits Plan.

In the case of emergencies, the ELCA plan has always provided for coverage of air ambulance service from remote areas to the nearest facility that can treat the patient's condition. When no emergency has been involved, coverage of air transportation has generally not been covered because the transportation has not been "medically necessary." Towers Perrin has advised us that employer plans generally cover non-emergency air transportation only when it has been pre-approved as medically appropriate during the pre-certification of care process.

Effective January 1, 1995, plan members in Alaska are covered under the ELCA Medical and Dental Benefits Plan for Standard Benefits. The Standard Benefits program contains a health-care pre-certification/utilization review component administered by Healthmarc.

During the pre-certification process for members in Alaska, Healthmarc evaluates each specific case and recommends the most appropriate "medically necessary" treatment available. If air transportation is appropriate in a particular case, Healthmarc will pre-certify the care and recommend that the transportation expense be covered under the ELCA plan. Healthmarc will not authorize air transportation for out-patient services.

- **Cost of Coverage:** Contribution rates in 1995 for the ELCA Medical and Dental Benefits Plan decreased an average of 16 percent from 1994 when there was a two percent decrease. It is estimated that the contribution-rate decreases will result in a total dollar savings to congregations and other employing organizations of approximately $9 million. The savings are attributed to overall favorable trend rates, along with the Board of Pensions' efforts to control medical costs through managed-care programs, such as the prescription drug program, the managed mental-health program, and the ELCA managed-care program that was implemented January 1, 1995. The savings were shared with all congregations, regardless of where they are located. Therefore, congregations in Alaska shared in the savings.

- **Summary:** The Alaska Synod has raised numerous and legitimate concerns that the Board of Pensions has researched during the past year. The Board of Pensions has implemented measures that have addressed these concerns, as noted in its response to the Alaska Synod resolution.

The following action was adopted *en bloc* at the conclusion of this meeting:

EN BLOC   **[CC95.4.47e]**

To request the secretary of this church to transmit the foregoing minute to the Alaska Synod as a response to its resolution regarding the ELCA Medical and Dental Benefits Plan.

2. Pension Plan Retirement Pay Structure
Montana Synod (1F)

The following resolution of the Montana Synod on retirement pay structure was transmitted to the Church Council at its December 1993 meeting:

Resolved, that the Montana Synod, assembled June 11-13, 1993, recommend to the ELCA Church Council, in consultation with the ELCA Board of Pensions, to study and make recommendations for a pension plan retirement pay structure which would not penalize retired pastors who serve under a Letter of Call, and accomplish these tasks and report to the 1995 Churchwide Assembly.

At its December 1993 meeting the Church Council voted:

To refer the resolution of the Montana Synod on retirement pay structure to the Board of Pensions and request that a report and/or recommendation be brought to the April 1994 meeting of the Church Council (CC93.12.105.a).

The following information was presented to the November 1994 meeting of the Church Council:

Representatives of the Board of Pensions, Division for Ministry, and Department for Synodical Relations have reviewed and discussed the Montana Synod resolution. The Board of Pensions' position with respect to this memorial is that the roster status should determine eligibility for retirement pension. Currently a person under age 70½ is not eligible to receive a pension unless he or she is in a retired status. Plan members are not eligible to receive a pension while serving under a call if under age 70½. To conform to Internal Revenue Service regulations, a monthly pension must begin following age 70½ for active plan members.

A revision to the Board of Pension's eligibility requirements for a retirement pension would involve significant issues that must be reviewed within this church since change could have undetermined effects on retirement patterns in the ELCA. Before any such change is initiated, it is recommended that this issue be explored further with the Conference of Bishops for input and advice.

At its November 1994 meeting the Church Council voted:

To request that the Board of Pensions consult with the Conference of Bishops on the issues raised by the resolution of the Montana Synod and provide a report and/or recommendation to the Church Council at its April 1995 meeting.

The following response is provided by the Board of Pensions:

As a follow-up to action of the Church Council at the November 12-14, 1994, meeting, representatives of the Department for Synodical Relations and the Board of Pensions have consulted on the issues raised in the resolution. Because of the time constraints on the agenda of the Conference of Bishops for the March 1995 meeting, it was determined that the issues raised in the Montana Synod resolution would be on the agenda for the November 1995 Conference of Bishops meeting. The issues that need to be addressed in the resolution could have a significant impact on the call process and retirement patterns in general. Therefore, adequate time is necessary to review thoroughly the ramifications of any proposed changes with the Conference of Bishops and perhaps other churchwide units.

Currently, the Board of Pensions is involved in a strategic planning project related to the development of the Pension-Investment Strategy. Issues related to the commencement of a pension are under review and it is anticipated that the board of trustees of the Board of Pensions will review recommendations at the board's May 1995 meeting. The issues raised in the Montana Synod resolution are being explored as part of the Pension-Investment Strategy Project. Consultations with the Conference of Bishops are scheduled for the November 1995 meeting of the Conference of Bishops.

The following action was adopted *en bloc* at the conclusion of this meeting:

EN BLOC   [CC95.4.47f]

To request that the Board of Pensions, in consultation with the Department for Synodical Relations, following the November 1995 meeting of the Conference of Bishops, prepare a report to be presented to the Church Council at its November 1995 meeting; and

To request the secretary of this church to transmit the foregoing minute to the Montana Synod in response to its resolution on the pension plan retirement pay structure.

3. Election Procedures for Churchwide Offices
Rocky Mountain Synod (2E)

The following resolution of the Rocky Mountain Synod on election procedures for churchwide offices was transmitted to the Church Council at its November 1994 meeting:

WHEREAS, the ELCA constitution states, "The Church Council shall establish an ongoing process to review the function and the structural organization of this church and to develop recommendations for changes" (ELCA 5.01.e.); and

WHEREAS, the ELCA constitution states, "This church shall function as people of God through congregations, synods, and the churchwide organization, all of which shall be interdependent. Each part, while fully the church, recognizes that it is not the whole church and therefore lives in a partnership relationship with others" (ELCA 8.11.); and

WHEREAS, the size of the ELCA in both membership and geography makes it imperative that constant attention be given to strengthening relationships between the various parts of the church and between the churchwide organization and the membership; and

WHEREAS, throughout its brief history, the ELCA has experienced a significant shortfall in financial support as compared to initial projections, and has suffered from an oft-expressed perception of its membership that it is distant from the congregations and the concerns of the membership; and

WHEREAS, the interdependent character of this church might be strengthened, and the sense of relationship enhanced, through wider participation in the selection of persons to serve in elected positions, such as members of boards and committees; and

WHEREAS, all who serve in such capacities, regardless of the means by which they have come to such service, are to regard themselves as servants of Christ and representatives of the whole people of God; and

WHEREAS, the perception of a "top-down" church is increased by the holding of an excessive number of elections at churchwide assemblies, a task that many voting members find difficult and frustrating; therefore, be it

RESOLVED, that the Rocky Mountain Synod Assembly direct the Rocky Mountain Synod Council to forward this resolution to the ELCA Church Council to review the election procedures of the Evangelical Lutheran Church in America and consider amendments to the documents of this church with a goal of minimizing the number of persons elected at churchwide assemblies and expanding the number of persons elected at the synod level, and bring its recommendations to the 1997 Churchwide Assembly.

At its November 1994 meeting the Church Council voted:

To refer this resolution of the Rocky Mountain Synod on election procedures for churchwide offices to the Executive Committee of the Church Council; and

To request that a report and/or recommendation be brought to the Church Council at its April 1995 meeting (CC94.11.118).

The resolution of the Rocky Mountain Synod Assembly poses issues of ecclesiology, polity, and procedure. Taken literally, the resolution could be seen as suggesting a change in the polity of this church into what could be seen as a confederation of synods. Further, the churchly role of the voting members of the Churchwide Assembly in making decisions on behalf of this whole church is embraced in the existing governing documents of the Evangelical Lutheran Church in America.

As to procedural problems, several may be cited, including how determination would be made on the allocation of seats on various boards and committees to synods, in order to (1) ensure fulfillment of the representational principles, (2) achieve geographic distribution on boards and committees, (3) provide for necessary experience and expertise from the perspective of the specific needs of a division or other unit, (4) achieve some rotation on board memberships for persons from synods, (5) fill unexpired terms, and (6) recognize the responsibility of the Churchwide Assembly, and the Church Council in the interim, for overseeing the programs, policies, and directions of divisions and other units.

Experience in one predecessor church is instructive. That church body had divisional board membership for each national division sufficient to provide one board member from each "district," a geographical entity now known in the Evangelical Lutheran Church in America as "synod." Seldom was there general awareness in the congregations of a district as to who served on what national board. Such a pattern of district election did fit that church body not only in terms of number of board positions available, but also from the perspective that, technically, the ecclesiastical reality of the national church was viewed only as limited and delegated by member congregations.

The process of election for churchwide boards and committees of the churchwide organization of the Evangelical Lutheran Church in America reflects this church's polity as one church, respects the responsibilities of voting members of the Churchwide Assembly, fulfills the needs of boards and committees regarding representational principles and necessary experience and expertise, and allows for gradual rotation and geographic distribution of council, board, and committee memberships throughout the 65 synods of this church.

The following action was taken *en bloc* at the conclusion of this meeting:

EN BLOC   [CC95.4.47g]
To affirm the concern of the Rocky Mountain Synod resolution for embracing and acknowledg-

ing the principle of interdependence in the polity of the Evangelical Lutheran Church in America;

To urge that each synod make greater effort to raise the visibility within the synod of those who serve on the churchwide council and churchwide boards, committees, work groups, task forces, and other groups, by introducing such individuals in synodical assemblies and inviting such individuals, as appropriate, to bring information to meetings of the Synod Council;

To encourage each synod to foster more extensive reporting by voting members of the Churchwide Assembly to congregations and conferences or clusters following each Churchwide Assembly;

To underscore the importance of synodical participation in the process of seeking potential nominees for consideration by the churchwide Nominating Committee in preparation for each Churchwide Assembly; and

To decline to propose changes in the ecclesiology, polity, and processes of nomination and election for the churchwide organization of the Evangelical Lutheran Church in America.

4. Cost of Medical Insurance for Persons Who Retire Before Age 65
Southwestern Texas Synod (4E)

The following resolution on the cost of medical insurance for persons who retire before age 65 was transmitted to the Church Council at its November 1994 meeting:

WHEREAS, the cost of medical insurance for an ELCA Pension Plan member on roster status and spouse, who retire before age 65, is $661.00 per month; and

WHEREAS, the maximum cost of any active member and spouse, regardless of salary, is $597.00 per month in 1994; and

WHEREAS, John Kapanke of the Board of Pensions states that the Benefits Committee discussed this issue and decided not to do anything about it; and

WHEREAS, he stated that the only way to proceed with any attempt to change this would be through the Church Council or the Conference of Bishops or by resolution to the ELCA; therefore, be it

RESOLVED, that the Southwestern Texas Synod, in assembly, urge the Board of Pensions of the Evangelical Lutheran Church in America to change this inequity; and be it further

RESOLVED, that the Southwestern Texas Synod Assembly direct the Synod Council to forward this resolution to the Church Council for consideration and action.

At its November 1994 meeting the Church Council voted:

To refer this resolution of the Southwestern Texas Synod on the cost of medical insurance for persons who retire before age 65 to the Board of Pensions; and

To request the Board of Pensions to provide a report and/or recommendation to the Church Council at its April 1995 meeting.

The response of the Board of Pensions follows:

Medical-dental contribution rates for retirees under age 65 continue to be a source of concern for plan members. While most ELCA medical rates were reduced for 1995, rates for retirees under age 65 remain the same as in 1994. The Conference of Bishops and the Church Council are both concerned with this issue and have asked for further advice and recommendations from the Board of Pensions.

At its meeting in May 1994, the benefits committee of the board of trustees of the Board of Pensions, discussed the current rating policy for retirees under age 65. Under this policy, congregations pay for sponsored members while retirees pay for their own coverage (with ELCA subsidies for post-65 coverage). Rates are determined for three separate rating classes -- sponsored (and coverage continuation) members, retired members under age 65 (and not eligible for Medicare), and retired members over 65 (and eligible for Medicare). Because of the high average age and the absence of Medicare, the rates for retirees under age 65 are substantially higher than rates for retirees over 65, and also substantially higher than rates for sponsored members.

While concerned about this issue, the benefits committee recognized that any change that produces lower rates for retirees under age 65 will, inevitably, raise rates for other plan members. Without some direction from the Church Council and the Conference of Bishops, the committee determined that it was inappropriate for the Board of Pensions to change rating practices.

In October 1994, John G. Kapanke, president of the Board of Pensions, discussed this issue with the Conference of Bishops. By a strong consensus, the bishops urged the Board to review alternatives for reducing the early retiree rates.

In November 1994, President Kapanke also discussed this issue with the Church Council. The Church Council indicated a strong interest in pursuing alternatives that would bring some rate relief to retirees under age 65. While affirming the current medical plan rating policy, it encouraged the Board of Pensions to exercise some flexibility in implementing that policy. In particular, the Church Council is comfortable with having congregations absorb the cost of providing some degree of rate relief for retirees under age 65. The Church Council was not eager to increase the ELCA's obligation to finance post-retirement benefits.

The Church Council has asked the Board of Pensions to address this issue further and to develop recommendations that can be implemented in 1996. At its February 1995 meeting, the benefits committee discussed several alternative approaches along with suggested evaluation criteria. The staff of the Board of Pensions is now developing illustrative 1995 active and retired rates for two or three alternative approaches considered worthy of further analysis. Staff will present its recommendations to the board of trustees in May 1995. If approved by the board of trustees of the Board of Pensions and the Church Council, these recommendations will be implemented as part of the 1996 rate structure.

The following action was adopted en bloc at the conclusion of this meeting:

EN BLOC   [CC95.4.47h]
To request the Board of Pensions to provide a report and/or recommendation to the Church Council at its November 1995 meeting; and

To request that the secretary of this church transmit this minute to the Southwestern Texas Synod.

5. The Church's Ministry with Children and Families
Northwestern Ohio Synod (6D)
The following resolution of the Northwestern Ohio Synod on the church's ministry with children and fami-

lies was transmitted to the Church Council's November 1994 meeting:

WHEREAS, America's children are this nation's most valuable resource; and

WHEREAS, the very core of support and nurture for children is the family unit, whatever its structure; and

WHEREAS, the effects of much of modern American culture and society (i.e., violent crime, racism, teen pregnancy, substance abuse, materialistic message of media,) upon the family unit seems to be destruction, rather than support and encouragement; and

WHEREAS, the message of the Gospel compels us to view ourselves as a community which works for unity, health, and mutual growth in Jesus Christ in all relationships including families: "Bear with one another charitably, in complete selflessness, gentleness, and patience. Do all you can to preserve the unity of the Spirit by the peace that binds you together.. . . If we live by the truth and in love, we shall grow in all ways into Christ, who is the head by whom the whole body is fitted and joined together, every member adding its own strength, for each separate part to work according to its function. And so the body grows until it has built itself up in love" (Ephesians 4:2-3, 5-16); and

WHEREAS, many parents and care givers who strive to live their Christian faith and impart Christian values to their children are seeking support from their churches in the forms of (but not limited to) reading material, family Bible studies and devotions, edifying television programs, parenting support groups, development of mentors for parents and youth, etc.; therefore be it

RESOLVED, that the Northwestern Ohio Synod of the Evangelical Lutheran Church in America gathered in assembly request that the Church Council of the Evangelical Lutheran Church in America commit the ELCA to a churchwide emphasis on the family, the purpose of which would be to communicate continually and consistently with and stimulate all members of this church and the greater United States society to work for the values and priorities that support and nurture children and families; and be it further

RESOLVED, that the Northwestern Ohio Synod in assembly request that the Church Council direct all divisions and boards that develop and offer information and support materials for Christian parenting and family life to promote them in a unified publication for dissemination through a variety of methods to the membership of this church; and be it further

RESOLVED, that the Northwestern Ohio Synod in assembly publicly affirm the work of the Women of the Evangelical Lutheran Church in America in its triennial emphasis on "Women and Children Living in Poverty."

At its November 1994 meeting the Church Council voted:

To refer this resolution of the Northwestern Ohio Synod on the church's ministry with children and families to the Division for Church in Society; and

To request that the Division for Church in Society, with other churchwide units, provide a report and/or recommendation on this matter to the Church Council at its April 1994 meeting (CC94.11.99j.).

The Division for Church in Society has provided the following response:

The churchwide office of the Evangelical Lutheran Church in America, through several units, has had a commitment to ministry with children and families. In partnership with Augsburg Fortress, Publishers, multiple resources (print and video) have been produced to support and nurture children and families. In 1991, for the Family Week Celebration, a resource guide for the family was produced. This guide needs to be updated with all the family resources currently available. Each year, a family week packet is produced and sent out in the "Action Packet" to all congregations and others in leadership. The themes over the past years were as follows:

1987 Celebrating Families
1988 Christian Families and Electronic Media
1989 Families Celebrating and Creating the Future
1990 Families Renewed by the Word
1991 Families 2000: Exploring Challenges for the Church
1992 Created in God's Image Male-Female
1993 Economic Justice for Families
1994 International Year of the Family: "Family: Resources and Responsibilities in a Changing World"
1995 Strengthening Families for Change.

A few 1995 packets are still available. Each year, new resources were added to the Family Resources Series. Currently about 23 titles are still available through the Division for Congregational Ministries, which has arranged for distribution from the DESCAR National Clearing House, Concordia University (address below).

The learning-ministries program of the Division for Congregational Ministries also has directed a cooperative project with The Lutheran Church–Missouri Synod, called "DESCAR" (Dedicated Early Support for Children At Risk). Newsletters, resource listings under various topics, and more information are available at the DESCAR National Clearinghouse, Concordia University, P.O. Box 22B, River Forest, IL 60305-1499 (708.488.4104). A congregational handbook, called "Rising Above At-Risk: The Congregation's Ministry With Young Children," will be available from the ELCA Distribution Service in May 1995 (order number 69-2610).

Another effort is under way between several ELCA churchwide units to respond to concerns, such as those expressed in the Northwestern Ohio Synod assembly resolution. A group of staff and church leaders who relate to issues of children and families, especially those at-risk, are exploring the feasibility of a vision statement or message to the church about congregations as "sanctuaries for childhood." This would likely be a project of the "Women and Children Living in Poverty" strategy, directed by the Division for Church in Society.

A project under development focuses on helping congregations equip and empower parents and guardians to nurture the spiritual life of their children. Initial exploration and research has been undertaken by the Learning Ministries program in the Division for Congregational Ministries, Augsburg Fortress staff, Augsburg Youth and Family Institute, and Luther Seminary in St. Paul, Minnesota. This cooperative venture will expand to include other ELCA churchwide units and various agencies as it develops resources and leadership support for congregations.

The Committee on Family Violence has received funding to pilot the project, "Stop the Violence: Healing Hurting Families." The project will provide training and resources for congregations to begin two kinds of support ministries: (1) for women struggling with abusive relationships; and (2) for men seeking help to deal with their own anger and violence.

As a part of the new resources produced by Augsburg Fortress, Publishers, "The Good News Explorer Enrichment Starters Kit" contains "Family Newsletters" on computer disk and "Inter-Generational Sessions." Augsburg Fortress also has provided a listing of resources available on marriage and family life in the "Basic Church and Sunday School Library List 1994-1995."

The Women of the Evangelical Lutheran Church in America have had an emphasis on "Women and Children Living in Poverty," since their Triennial Assembly in 1990. The 1993 ELCA Churchwide Assembly approved a strategy on "Women and Children Living in Poverty," and a project director was hired. The project director and project team have been at work on the implementation of the strategy. A report on the progress of the strategy will be presented to the 1995 Churchwide Assembly. The Women of the ELCA have continued to work in harmony with the strategy of this church.

While much has been done and resources produced over the life of this church, we are still very concerned about children and families and support the need to continue lifting up children and families and providing resources. We will work toward the development of a unified publication on materials for Christian parenting and family life.

The following action was adopted en bloc at the conclusion of this meeting:

EN BLOC   **[CC95.4.47i]**
To request the secretary of this church to transmit to the Northwestern Ohio Synod this information from the Division for Church in Society concerning this church's ministry with children and families.

6. Support for Treatment of Addiction and Co-Dependency
Southeastern Pennsylvania Synod (7F)

The following resolution was transmitted to the Church Council's Executive Committee at its October 18, 1994, meeting:

WHEREAS, the ELCA Board of Pensions has elected to use an HMO for attending to the medical and emotional issues of clergy, associates in ministry, other religious professionals and their dependents; and

WHEREAS, the benefits of this program seriously limit treatment for chemical dependency; and

WHEREAS, the program excludes treatment of other legitimate addiction issues such as sex and love addiction and co-dependency programs; and

WHEREAS, the program excludes treatment for families, thereby denying that addiction is a family problem; and

WHEREAS, without adequate family treatment the family members continue to manifest the addictive behaviors in their lives and carry these behaviors and potential for generational transfer of addiction; therefore, be it

RESOLVED, that the Southeastern Pennsylvania Synod in assembly direct the Synod Council to request that the Church Council of the Evangelical Lutheran Church in America express our concerns to the Board of Pensions of the ELCA regarding the gross inequities in the matter of treatment for addiction and co-dependency and provide support and payment for healing, rather than turning our backs on these brothers and sisters who have been victimized by the addiction process; and be it further

RESOLVED, that Nationally Certified Addictions counselors be approved as treatment providers, both in the initial outpatient or inpatient treatment and for a two-year period of continuing care following their discharge from initial treatment, in addition to medical and/or mental health professionals who have often had no training in addictions treatment.

At its October 18, 1994, meeting the Executive Committee voted:

To refer this resolution of the Southeastern Pennsylvania Synod on support for treatment of addiction and co-dependency to the Board of Pensions; and

To request that the Board of Pensions bring a report and/or recommendation on this matter to the spring 1995 meeting of the Church Council (EC94.10.29b).

The following is the response from the Board of Pensions:

Effective January 1, 1994, the Board of Pensions implemented a managed mental-health program for plan members of the ELCA Medical and Dental Benefits Plan. Value Behavioral Health (VBH) is the administrator of the program and advises the Board of Pensions regarding the medical necessity of mental health and chemical dependency care. This program is not a health maintenance organization (HMO), but does require pre-certification and case management for all inpatient psychiatric hospitalizations and subsequent outpatient treatment, and for chemical dependency treatment at all levels of care. After a psychiatric or chemical dependency diagnosis is established by a qualified therapist, VBH evaluates the proposed treatment and, if appropriate, refers the patient to a provider in VBH's national preferred provider network.

The terms of the ELCA health plan also limit coverage under the plan to "medically necessary" treatment of an existing or suspected illness or injury. In the area of mental health, coverage is limited to treatment of diagnosable mental-health disorders, as defined in the Diagnostic and Statistical Manual of Mental Disorders (DSM-IV) published by the American Psychiatric Association. The DSM-IV is the nationally recognized reference for defining and describing psychiatric disorders.

Sex and love addiction, as well as co-dependency, are not included in the DSM-IV. This means they are not accepted psychiatric disorders. In contrast, chemical dependency, known as substance-related disorders, is included in the DSM-IV. Treatment for chemical dependency, including involvement by family members, is covered under the plan. Treatment for sexual addiction or co-dependency is not covered under the plan.

Effective July 1, 1994, the ELCA health plan was amended to expand the list of therapists eligible to provide mental-health treatment. Nationally Certified Addictions counselors are covered providers under the plan only if they also possess one of the eligible postgraduate clinical degrees. As noted above, however, therapy is covered only for treatment of a mental-health disorder with a DSM-IV diagnosis.

The following action was adopted en bloc at the conclusion of this meeting:

EN BLOC   [CC95.4.47j]
To request the secretary of this church to transmit to the Southeastern Pennsylvania Synod this information from the Board of Pensions concerning treatment for addiction and co-dependency.

7. Accountability for Policies and Public Statements
Metropolitan Washington, D.C., Synod (8G)

The following resolution regarding accountability for policies and public statements was submitted to the Church Council at its November 1994 meeting:

WHEREAS, the Church, including the Evangelical Lutheran Church in America, has the "treasure" of the Gospel "in earthen vessels" (2 Corinthians 4:7) and we, therefore, acknowledge the institutional church as fallible; and

WHEREAS, we are cautioned by our Lord to "be wise as serpents and innocent as doves" (Matthew 10:16) in making our way as Christ's witnesses in the world; and

WHEREAS, we have agreed to arrive at positions to guide "this portion of Christ's Church through participatory processes of moral deliberation," ("Statement on the Church in Society–A Lutheran Perspective"); and

WHEREAS, significant distress, confusion, and disruption has been caused within congregations and among the members of our church by the manner in which statements have been released to our congregations and to the world on behalf of the Evangelical Lutheran Church in America; and

WHEREAS, we are committed to the judgment that the Gospel provides its counsel to us through "mutual conversation and consolation" (*Smalcald Article, Part III, Article IV*). We are led to offer the following resolution to assist the Evangelical Lutheran Church in America, its synods, congregations and various agencies, and its [churchwide] departments, divisions, and commissions to promulgate social statements and other policies in a way that ensures thoughtful consideration, provides accountability, and promotes responsibility; therefore be it

RESOLVED, that the Metropolitan Washington, D.C., Synod in assembly memorialize the Church Council to establish the following policy:

Whenever a unit of this church desires to release to the public statements in which are contained generalizations that characterize the Evangelical Lutheran Church in America as holding one or another opinion or position, such general characterizations be released only after verification by the bishop. This same process and level of accountability for the process shall apply to the bishops regarding statements released by synodical committees and other agencies.

At its November 1994 meeting, the Church Council voted:

To refer this resolution of the Metropolitan Washington, D.C., Synod on release of and accountability for policies and public statements jointly to the Division for Church in Society and the Office of the Bishop; and

To request that the Division for Church in Society and the Office of the Bishop bring a report and/or recommendation to the April 1995 meeting of the Church Council (CC94.11.99d.).

The Division for Church in Society and the Office of the Bishop have provided the following response:

The resolution of the Metropolitan Washington, D.C., Synod addresses the process by which public statements are made in the Evangelical Lutheran Church in America. The synod's resolution would require a process of "verification" by the churchwide bishop for any "public statements in which are contained generalizations that characterize the Evangelical Lutheran Church in America as holding one or another opinion or position." A parallel process of "verification" by synodical bishops would be imposed on all synods for "statements released by synodical committees and other agencies."

The Office of the Bishop and the Division for Church in Society recommend that the ELCA Church Council not approve the process outlined in the synod's resolution for the following reasons:

(1) ***There is no clear need for this process to be implemented.***

   Churchwide Perspective: The current process of oversight of the work of churchwide units is adequate to address specific issues that may arise.

   Unit directors are responsible both to their boards and to the Office of the Bishop for ensuring that the policies of the Evangelical Lutheran Church in America are represented appropriately. The Office of the Bishop holds quarterly reviews with each executive director; ongoing conversation and consultation occurs as need arises, sometimes on a daily basis. There already are strong channels of communication between units and the bishop about emerging issues and about controversial issues.

   In addition, synods that object to a specific position taken may, through their bishop or through a synodical resolution, engage in conversation directly with the unit involved and with the Office of the Bishop. The synod may then bring concerns about a specific situation it feels has not been addressed adequately to the Church Council or the Churchwide Assembly. Such synodical actions are taken seriously and contribute to the ongoing oversight process. The questions and concerns raised by individual ELCA members also provide helpful feedback.

   Synodical Perspective: No request has been received from any other synod to institute a process for requiring that the synodical bishop "verify" all positions taken by synodical committees and boards. Such an action could be viewed as an imposition on all synods of one process that may or may not take into account the histories or needs of individual synods.

(2) ***This process would lay an unnecessary administrative burden on the bishop of this church and synodical bishops.***

   The churchwide bishop and the synodical bishops have numerous important responsibilities in addition to oversight of the work of churchwide units or synodical committees. To "verify" positions reached by units, committees, or agencies would require the churchwide bishop and each synodical bishop to have a deep knowledge of all subject areas *and* of all of the actions of previous churchwide assemblies or synodical assemblies. The bishop of this church and the synodical bishops currently implement their oversight responsibilities in a variety of ways, some of which place less of an administrative burden on the bishop.

(3) ***The current governance patterns embedded in the ELCA's governing documents provide for adequate accountability. The new proposal could involve the churchwide bishop in "micro-management" of the clearly defined work of churchwide units. This proposal also could involve synodical bishops in a type of oversight over the work of synodically related entities that is not spelled out in the synod's or the agencies' governing documents.***

   Churchwide Perspective: The ELCA's governing documents set forth clearly the responsibilities of units and their boards, within the context of the oversight of the Office of the Bishop and the ELCA Church Council. Units are "assigned responsibility for a major, identified portion of the program of this church" (ELCA churchwide constitutional provision 16.11.).

   Division for Church in Society: "This division shall assist this church to. . . a) develop and coordinate this church's theological and ethical study and analysis of social issues as part of its social witness. . . b) develop this church's social statements for action by the Church Council and the Churchwide Assembly; and prepare, in consultation with the Office of the Bishop and appropriate churchwide units, messages and resolutions on social issues for action by the Church Council" (ELCA continuing resolution 16.11.E91.).

   The procedures by which the development of social statements occur is governed by "Social Statements in the Evangelical Lutheran Church in America," adopted as policy by the 1989 Churchwide Assembly. The Office of the Bishop is kept informed regularly regarding the development of study documents and early drafts. The bishop normally sees and is invited to comment on early drafts even prior to the consideration of such by the board of the Division for Church in Society.

   Synodical bishops are sent copies of early drafts prior to consideration by the board of the Division for Church in Society. A synodical bishop has served on every task force that has worked on a social statement. Requests regularly have been made for discussion of early documents at meetings of the Conference of Bishops. In other words, the basic practice is to encourage early comment and counsel from the synodical bishops so that the position eventually proposed for adoption will be enhanced by such input.

   The Division for Church in Society is also to "direct and implement this church's public-policy advocacy to national and international governmental bodies, in consultation with other churchwide units, and coordinate its public-policy advocacy to state governmental bodies" (ELCA continuing resolution 16.11.E91.i.).

   The board of the division recommends policy and develops strategies in its particular area of responsibility (ELCA churchwide bylaw 16.11.31.)–in this instance, through its advocacy plan, which is reviewed by the board and reported to the Church Council. This, together with other policy, procedures and programs of churchwide units are reviewed by the Church council "in order to assure conformity with the governing documents of this church and with Churchwide Assembly actions" (ELCA churchwide bylaw 16.11.11.).

   It is difficult to ascertain what "verification by the bishop" would add to these procedures, or what would be entailed. The current participatory processes already provide an effective means for achieving the intent of the synod's resolution: the development of positions in a way that "ensures thoughtful consideration, provides accountability, and promotes responsibility." The current process does not hinge on the "verification" of one person– although the judgment of the bishop of this church is an important element in this process.

   Early drafts, as well as officially-adopted statements, and the subsequent messages, resolutions, and advocacy positions that are based on them do not claim to reflect an opinion poll of ELCA members, but recognize their freedom to dissent from or disagree with the positions adopted.

   Synodical Perspective: It is unclear whether the synodical bishop could require agencies in the synod to submit all of their public statements that interpret ELCA actions to a process of "verification" by the bishop, given existing governing documents.

The Office of the Bishop and the Division for Church in Society encourage the Metropolitan Washington, D.C., Synod to engage in further conversations with churchwide units or with the Office of the Bishop concerning specific issues that are of concern to it.

The following action was adopted *en bloc* at the conclusion of this meeting:

EN BLOC [CC95.4.47k]

To decline to adopt the policy on "Accountability for Policies and Public Statements" that is recommended by the Metropolitan Washington, D.C., Synod; and

To request the secretary of this church to transmit to the Metropolitan Washington, D.C., Synod this action, as well as the information provided by the Office of the Bishop and the Division for Church in Society on this matter.

Ratification of Synodical Constitutions

Amendments to the constitutions of synods, adopted under †S18.13., are subject to ratification by the Church Council prior to becoming effective. This is in accord with ELCA churchwide constitutional provision 10.12. The following action was adopted *en bloc* at the conclusion of this meeting:

EN BLOC [CC95.4.47l]

To ratify amendment †S1.21. in the constitution of the Slovak Zion Synod; and

To ratify amendments to the constitutions of the Northwest Washington Synod and the Montana Synod, contingent upon fulfillment of required changes and corrections, as indicated in the review by the secretary of this church and reports by the secretary to the Northwest Washington Synod and the Montana Synod.

Changes in the Structure of Region 3

According to the ELCA's governing documents, the Church Council is to ratify changes in the governance structure of regions. Council agenda Exhibit H, Part 2b, contained the changes recommended by the synods of Region 3, in partnership with the churchwide organization. The following action was adopted *en bloc* at the conclusion of this meeting:

EN BLOC [CC95.4.47m]

To ratify the changes in the governance and structure of Region 3 . . . .

ELCA PENSION AND OTHER BENEFITS PROGRAMS

1. ELCA Medical and Dental Benefits Plan: Pre-Certification of Outpatient Procedures

Council agenda Exhibit J, Part 1, contained a proposed amendment to revise the outpatient procedures subject to pre-certification review by Aetna and Healthmarc. The following action was adopted *en bloc* at the conclusion of this meeting:

EN BLOC [CC95.4.47n]

To adopt the amendment to the ELCA Medical and Dental Benefits Plan . . . regarding outpa-

tient procedures subject to pre-certification review by Aetna and Healthmarc.

2. ELCA Medical and Dental Benefits Plan: Services Excluded from Mental Health and Chemical Dependency Coverage

Council agenda Exhibit J, Part 2, contained a proposed amendment to revise the services excluded from mental health and chemical dependency coverage. T h e following action was adopted *en bloc* at the conclusion of this meeting:

EN BLOC [CC95.4.47o]

To adopt the amendment to the ELCA Medical and Dental Benefits Plan . . . regarding the services excluded from the mental health and chemical dependency coverage.

3. ELCA Medical and Dental Benefits Plan: Order of Benefit Determination in the Case of Divorced Parents

Council agenda Exhibit J, Part 3, contained a proposed amendment to revise the order of benefit determination in the case of divorced parents. The following action was adopted *en bloc* at the conclusion of this meeting:

EN BLOC [CC95.4.47p]

To adopt the amendment to the ELCA Medical and Dental Benefits Plan . . . regarding the order of benefit determination in the case of divorced parents.

4. ELCA Medical and Dental Benefits Plan and ELCA Continuation of the ALC Medical-Dental Plan

Council agenda Exhibit J, Part 4, contained a proposed amendment to revise the definition of an eligible dental care provider. The following action was adopted *en bloc* at the conclusion of this meeting:

EN BLOC [CC95.4.47q]

To adopt the amendment to the ELCA Medical and Dental Benefits Plan and ELCA Continuation of the ALC Medical-Dental Plan . . . to revise the definition of an eligible dental care provider.

5. ELCA Continuation of the LCA Ministerial Health Benefits Plan and ELCA Continuation of the ALC Medical and Dental Benefits Plan

Council agenda Exhibit J, Part 5, contained a proposed amendment to make the prescription drug benefits consistent with the ELCA Medical and Dental Benefits Plan. The following action was adopted *en bloc* at the conclusion of this meeting:

EN BLOC [CC95.4.47r]

To adopt the amendment to the ELCA Continuation of the LCA Ministerial Health Benefits Plan and ELCA Continuation of the ALC Medical and Dental Benefits Plan . . . to make the prescription

drug benefits consistent with the ELCA Medical and Dental Benefits Plan.

6. Technical Amendments

Council agenda Exhibit J, Part 6, contained technical amendments to correct omissions or inconsistencies in the various plan documents.

The following action was adopted *en bloc* at the conclusion of this meeting:

EN BLOC   **[CC95.4.47s]**

To adopt the technical amendments found in [council agenda] Exhibit J, Part 6.

Matters Related to the Division for Ministry (Continued)
7. Synodically Authorized Ministries

Council agenda Exhibit M, Part 5, contained proposed "Guidelines Related to Synodically Authorized or Licensed Ministries." The proposed guidelines were reviewed by the Conference of Bishops and the board of the Division for Ministry. The following action was adopted *en bloc* at the conclusion of this meeting:

EN BLOC   **[CC95.4.47t]**

To adopt as policy the "Guidelines Related to Synodically Authorized or Licensed Ministries":

GUIDELINES RELATED TO SYNODICALLY AUTHORIZED OR LICENSED MINISTRIES

These guidelines relate to bylaws 7.61.01. and proposed 7.61.02. dealing with synodically authorized ministries. These ministries include licensed ministry of Word and Sacrament, as well as diaconal ministry authorized by the synod. These ministries exist to provide pastoral or diaconal leadership for a congregation or other ministry of this church when needs exist within a synod which exceed those which can be met by rostered persons. Those who provide such ministry within a synod are not rostered by the Evangelical Lutheran Church in America (unless already serving on a roster of this church) but are authorized by the synod to provide a specific ministry within a particular setting for a specific period of time.

1. Identification of Need

Mission and ministry needs within the synod that are unable to be met by rostered persons are identified by the synod.

2. Invitation to Service

An individual who demonstrates the potential for service is identified and invited to consider entering a program of preparation for service within the synod. This invitation is normally made by the person's pastor or congregation council; it may also come from the synodical bishop or synod staff person. Such persons are not self-selected.

3. Qualifications

Normally, a person invited to prepare for a synodically authorized ministry has been an active member of an ELCA congregation for at least one year. Prior to entering the synod's program of preparation an individual must have:
   A. Been recommended by the individual's pastor and congregation council;
   B. Consulted with synodical staff and the synodical committee responsible for the synod's program of preparation; and

   C. The ability and willingness to participate in a program of preparation leading to possible service in a synodically authorized ministry.

4. Synodical Committee for Authorized Ministry

An appropriate synodical board or committee shall be appointed by the Synod Council to provide the synodical bishop with recommendations concerning the authorization and accountability for authorized ministries within the synod. This committee may be a sub-committee of the synodical candidacy committee; its functions, however, are distinct from that of the candidacy committee.

The synodical committee determines the program of preparation within the synod for persons considered for service in an authorized ministry, determines the eligibility for individuals to enter a program of preparation, and advises the bishop on the suitability of an individual for service in a synodically authorized ministry.

5. Program of Preparation

The synod defines the program of preparation leading to either a licensed ministry of Word and Sacrament or another synodically authorized ministry. Such programs of preparation normally include study in the following areas:
   A. Bible;
   B. Lutheran theology, polity, and the Confessions;
   C. Worship;
   D. Spiritual discernment and faith development;
   E. Leadership expectations and identity;
   F. Contextual understanding; and
   G. Skill development, e.g., preaching, catechetics, worship leadership, visitation, pastoral care, missions.

The program of preparation can be accomplished in a variety of ways including educational programs that utilize current rostered leaders within the synod, ELCA seminaries and continuing education centers, the ELCA *Select* curriculum, and other identified resources.

Upon satisfactory completion of the synodical program of preparation, an individual may be certified as available for service within the synod. There is no guarantee of service within the synod and completion of a program of preparation does not mean that authorization for service will follow.

Persons may participate in a synodical program of preparation to be enriched and equipped to serve within their congregations and in the world in the ministry of the baptized with no intention of becoming licensed or authorized.

6. Authorization for Service

Upon satisfactory completion of the synod's program of preparation, and where a specific need exists, an individual may be authorized for service within the synod. The synod bishop, at the request and recommendation of the appropriate synodical committee established to oversee synodically authorized ministries, may then authorize an individual to serve in a congregation or other ministry within the synod. Such service shall fulfill assigned responsibilities and shall be for a specific period of time not to exceed one year, unless terminated earlier. Authorized or licensed ministries that may be considered include:
   A. Lay Minister of the Word
   B. Lay Minister of Word and Sacrament
   C. Worship Leader
   D. Catechist
   E. Evangelist
   F. Synodical Missionary
   G. Synodical Deacon

Persons who are considered for a synodically authorized ministry must meet the criteria for public ministry within a congregation or other ministry of this church, namely:

A. evidence of mature Christian faith and commitment to Christ;

B. satisfactory completion of the synodical program of preparation, including demonstration of appropriate ministry skills;

C. knowledge and acceptance of the Confession of Faith of this church; and

D. willingness to meet this church's expectations concerning the personal conduct and behavior of persons serving in public ministry ("Visions and Expectations").

A person authorized by the synodical bishop is then installed in such service.

7. Supervision and Accountability

Accountability and supervision for synodically authorized ministry in a congregational setting is the direct responsibility of the congregation council. Accountability and supervision for a synodically authorized ministry in a non-congregational setting with a synod is the direct responsibility of the governing body of the entity that conducts that ministry, or if there is no such entity, the Synod Council. In all cases, a synodically authorized ministry is to be under the direct supervision of an ordained minister appointed by the appropriate governing body with the concurrence of the synodical bishop. The supervising ordained minister shall report to the governing body and may seek the advice and counsel of the synodical bishop or appropriate synodical staff person.

8. Renewal and Revocation

Renewal of authorization after one year is given only when a demonstrated need remains for its continuation. This need is determined by the synodical bishop at the request and with the consent of the congregation or other ministry within the synod being served, after consultation with the appropriate committee and a review of both the ministry setting and the service of the authorized minister.

Authorization to provide ministry within the synod may be revoked at any time by the synodical bishop, who need not specify the reason.

9. Letter of Authorization

The authorization of license may be evidenced by an appropriate letter describing the terms and conditions of the authorization or license. The description also may limit or prohibit activities to be conducted.

10. Relation to Other Policy

Nothing in these guidelines shall limit the authorization of a synodical bishop to license lay persons as permitted under this church's policy on sacramental practices.

11. Other Matters

Persons may serve in a synodically authorized or licensed ministry only within the synod that has authorized that ministry. A synod may consider for authorization an individual trained and authorized by another synod, based on the individual's qualifications and ability to meet the new synod's criteria for authorized ministry. Persons authorized for such ministries will not wear clerical garb (e.g., clerical collars) or clerical stoles. The title "Pastor" is reserved for ordained ministers of Word and Sacrament, "Associate in Ministry" is reserved for commissioned associates in ministry, "Diaconal Minister" for rostered diaconal ministers, and "Deaconess" for rostered ELCA deaconesses, and are titles not to be used by synodically authorized ministers. Synodically authorized or licensed ministers are not to offer counseling as a part of their ministries.

Existing Bylaw 7.71.01.

When need exists to render Word and Sacrament ministry of a congregation or ministry of this church where it is not possible to provide appropriate ordained pastoral leadership, the synodical bishop—acting with the consent of the congregation or ministry, in consultation with the Synod Council, and in accord with standards and qualifications developed by the Division for Ministry, reviewed by the Conference of Bishops, and approved by the Church Council—may authorize a person rostered in other rostered ministry, or a non-rostered person who is a member of a congregation of the Evangelical Lutheran Church in America to offer ministry. Such an individual shall be supervised by a pastor appointed by the synodical bishop, such service shall be rendered during its duration under the sacramental authority of the bishop as the synod's pastor. Such an individual will be trained and licensed to fulfill this ministry for a specified period of time and in a given location only. Authorization, remuneration, direct supervision, and accountability are to be determined by the appropriate synodical leadership according to churchwide standards and qualifications for this type of ministry. Authorization for such service shall be reviewed annually and renewed only when a demonstrated need remains for its continuation.

Proposed Bylaw 7.61.02.

When need exists to make provision for diaconal leadership as part of a congregation or ministry of this church where it is not possible for such ministry to be provided by appropriate rostered lay ministry, the synodical bishop—acting with the consent of the congregation or ministry, in consultation with the Synod Council, and in accord with standards and qualification developed by the Division for Ministry, reviewed by the Conference of Bishop, and approved by the Church Council—may authorize a non-rostered person who is a member of a congregation of the Evangelical Lutheran Church in America to offer such non-sacramental ministry. Such an individual shall be supervised by an ordained minister appointed by the synodical bishop and shall be trained and authorized to fulfill a particular ministry for a specific period of time in a given location only. Authorization, remuneration, direct supervision, and accountability are to be determined by the appropriate synodical leadership according to churchwide standards and qualifications for this type of ministry. Authorization for such service shall be reviewed annually and renewed only when a demonstrated need remains for its continuation.

8. Nonstipendiary Ministries for Lay Rosters

Council agenda Exhibit M, Part 6, contained guidelines related to non-stipendiary lay ministry, which were reviewed by the board of the Division for Ministry at its March 16-18, 1995, meeting. The board commended these guidelines to the Church Council for adoption. The following action was adopted *en bloc* at the conclusion of this meeting:

EN BLOC   **[CC95.4.47u]**

To adopt as policy the following "Guidelines Related to Non-Stipendiary Rostered Lay Ministry":

GUIDELINES RELATED TO NON-STIPENDIARY ROSTERED LAY MINISTRY

I. Definition

Non-stipendiary ministry in the Evangelical Lutheran Church in America is understood to be service as a rostered minister without regard to compensation for such service. It may be either service for no stipend (or for reimbursed expenses only) or for a token stipend that is not commensurate with the normal salary guidelines for rostered ministry. Non-stipendiary calls are not eligible for participation in the ELCA Pension and Health Benefits Plan; therefore, it also is understood that such non-stipended service is possible only when there is clear evidence that the associate in ministry, deaconess, or diaconal minister has adequate alternative income and health insurance.

A letter of call to non-stipendiary ministry in the Evangelical Lutheran Church in America may be issued only by a Synod Council following approval by the Conference of Bishops. The rostered lay minister serving in a non-stipendiary call shall be accountable to the synod bishop and Synod Council in the carrying out of this ministry. A call to non-stipendiary service shall be a one-year term call that may be renewed by the Synod Council only on the basis of the satisfactory fulfillment of the established criteria. A call to non-stipendiary ministry neither qualifies as an initial call to congregational service nor does it imply any employment relationship or contractual obligation to the Synod Council (7.43. and 7.43.01.). The criteria under which a Synod Council may issue a letter of call to an associate in ministry, deaconess, or diaconal minister for non-stipendiary service include the following:

A. There shall be a clearly defined statement of the need for this rostered lay minister to provide for ministry in the synod and a rationale for this call to be for non-stipendiary service, including an annual ministry plan;

B. The minimum commitment by the rostered lay minister shall be a monthly average of 10 hours per week to the ministry to which called; and

C. The rostered lay minister shall meet the criteria and standards of this church for its rostered lay ministers;

D. The Synod Council must determine that a call to non-stipendiary service is extended in order to carry out a specific ministry on behalf of the synod.

II. Action by the Synod Bishop and Synod Council

When the synod bishop and Synod Council believe that the criteria for a non-stipendiary letter of call are met by a specific ministry, the Synod Council may propose by a majority vote a letter of call. Final action to extend such a letter of call is contingent upon the approval of the Conference of Bishops. The Synod Council forwards its proposal, together with the rationale for issuing the call to non-stipendiary ministry, to the Conference of Bishops.

Should the Conference of Bishops approve the request and the ministry begin, the Synod Council will conduct an annual review of the non-stipendiary call. Annual Synod Council action is required in order to continue the call to non-stipendiary ministry.

III. Action by the Conference of Bishops

The Roster Committee of the Conference of Bishops receives all requests from Synod Councils for calls to non-stipendiary ministry. The Roster Committee reviews these requests and reports its recommendations to the Conference of Bishops. The Conference of Bishops, in a regular meeting of the conference, by a majority vote acts upon requests for call to non-stipendiary ministry. It reports its decision to the Synod Council seeking such approval. When approval is given by the Conference of Bishops, the Synod Council may proceed with the issuance of a letter of call to non-stipendiary ministry and may annually review such a call without subsequent action by the Conference of Bishops.

---

9. Policy for Rostered Persons: On Leave From Call for Study

Council agenda Exhibit M, Part 8, contained a description from the Division for Ministry of the current process of approval for rostered persons who wish to go on leave from call in order to engage in further study. Following consultation with the Conference of Bishops, the board of the Division for Ministry recommends that the relevant ELCA bylaw and the appropriate guidelines be altered to make explicit the role of the division in this process. The following action was adopted *en bloc* at the conclusion of this meeting:

EN BLOC   [CC95.4.47v]
To amend the current "Guidelines Related to On-Leave-From-Call Status" as follows:

> **A rostered minister engaged in graduate study, in a field of study that will enhance service in the rostered ministry of this church, may be retained on the roster of this church for a maximum of six years by annual action of the Synod Council, *in consultation with the Division for Ministry*.**

Matters Related to the Division for Church in Society (continued)
8. Election of Corporate Members

The Evangelical Lutheran Church in America serves as a corporate member of certain affiliated social ministry organizations. The role of the corporate member includes the responsibility to elect or approve a majority of the members of the board of directors and to approve amendments to the governing documents.

Lutheran Medical Center, Brooklyn, New York, is an organization for which the Evangelical Lutheran Church in America serves as a corporate member. The Division for Church in Society is the churchwide unit through which the Evangelical Lutheran Church in America relates to this social ministry health care organization. The division requests Church Council action to elect the following board members for these organizations. The following action was adopted *en bloc* at the conclusion of this meeting:

EN BLOC   [CC95.4.47w]
To elect the following to the Board of Directors of Lutheran Medical Center, Brooklyn, New York:
a. **for terms ending in 1999—John J. Bennett Jr., Harold T. Fries Jr., Frank O. McNally, Daniel J. Schaefer, and Florence M. Sullivan; and**
b. **for terms ending in 2000—Walter Jensen, Joseph G. Kearns, the Rev. Elizabeth J. S. Nebrasky, the Rev. Nitza Rosario, and Andrew Varela.**

Matters Related to the Division for Global Mission
Recognition of Relationship of Independent Lutheran Organizations to the Division for Global Mission

After following the review process proposed by the board of the Division for Global Mission and affirmed by the Church Council at their spring 1994 meetings, the board of the division recommends that the relationship with the following independent Lutheran organizations be formally recognized: Operation Bootstrap and Christians Linked in Mission. Council agenda Exhibit Q, Part 1a, contained the full text of the actions taken by the board of the Division for Global Mission. The following action was adopted *en bloc* at the conclusion of this meeting:

EN BLOC   [CC95.4.47x]

To ratify the action taken by the board of the Division for Global Mission to recognize the relationship with the following independent Lutheran organizations: Operation Bootstrap; and Christians Linked in Mission.

Adoption of Minutes

The minutes of the November 12-14, 1994, meeting of the Church Council had been distributed to council members as well as the minutes of the December 15, 1994, January 19, February 15, and March 10, 1995, meetings of the council's Executive Committee.

VOTED: CC95.4.48

To approve the minutes of the November 12-14, 1994, meeting of the Church Council; and

To ratify actions of the council's Executive Committee as indicated in the minutes of the December 15, 1994, January 19, February 15, and March 10, 1995, meetings.

Personal Privilege: Bishop Herbert W Chilstrom

Speaking in a point of personal privilege, Bishop Herbert W. Chilstrom stated, "Thank you for the wonderful evening last night." A banquet had been held at the Rosewood Restaurant in Rosemont, Ill., Sunday evening, April 2, in honor of the bishop, who retires October 31, 1995, at the conclusion of his second term of office.

Evaluation

Chair Magnus invited reflections upon the work of the council during the current biennium.

Adjournment

The meeting of the Church Council adjourned at 2:22 P.M. on Monday, April 3, 1995.

ELCA GOVERNING DOCUMENTS

Constitutions, Bylaws, and Continuing Resolutions

The text of the *Constitutions, Bylaws, and Continuing Resolutions of the Evangelical Lutheran Church in America* as amended by the 1993 Churwide Assembly follows. When referring to continuing resolutions, note the emendations cited below.

Emendation of Continuing Resolutions

During the 1993-1995 biennium, the Church Council of the Evangelical Lutheran Church in America acted to adopt, amend, or delete continuing resolutions from the *Constitutions, Bylaws, and Continuing Resolutions* of this church as follows:

Action Number	Council Action
CC93.12.96	Amendment of continuing resolution 9.52.A87., renumbered as 9.52.A93.
CC94.4.9	Amendment of continuing resolution 15.11.E91., renumbered as 15.11.E94.
CC94.4.10	Adoption of new churchwide continuing resolution 19.61.A94.
CC95.4.27	Amendment of continuing resolution 15.21.A91., renumbered as 15.21.A95.; and amendment of continuing resolution 16.11.C91.

The texts of those provisions, as adopted or amended, follows:

9.52.A93. *The Church Council, in cooperation with the synods, shall provide an ongoing process for congregations whose governing documents have been accepted into the church under 9.52. to review those documents and compare them with the required elements of the Model Constitution for Congregations listed in 9.25.b., applicable to the extent provided in 9.52. to congregations recognized and received by this church as of January 1, 1988. Congregations are encouraged to resolve significant conflicts between their governing documents and the Model Constitution for Congregations.*

15.11.E94. *Department for Information Technology*
The treasurer shall provide for information technology that shall include . . . [with the remainder of the continuing resolution remaining unchanged].

15.21.A95. *Operation of Mission Investment Fund of the ELCA*
a. *The Mission Investment Fund of the Evangelical Lutheran Church in America shall have primary responsibility for promotion of Mission Investments.*
b. *The provisions of 15.11.D91. shall apply to the Mission Investment Fund of the ELCA.*
c. *The board of trustees of the Mission Investment Fund of the ELCA shall be eleven in number, who shall be elected by the Church Council for six-year terms and shall be eligible for reelection, with six members nominated by the Church Council's Budget and Finance Committee, four members nominated by the board of the Division for Outreach, and one member nominated by the board of the Division for Church in Society.*
d. *Relationship to Division for Outreach: The Mission Investment Fund of the ELCA shall relate to the Division for Outreach. The Division for Outreach shall request real estate acquisition for new and existing ministries within the limits of the capital funds available and within criteria established jointly by the Division for Outreach and the Mission Investment Fund of the ELCA. The Mission Investment Fund of the ELCA shall provide expertise for management of real property and execute all necessary documents for the acquisition and disposition of such property.*
e. *Capital Budget Development: An annual capital budget for ministry development shall be established. The budget shall be prepared by a joint staff com-*

mittee composed of staff from the Division for Outreach and the Mission Investment Fund. This budget is to be based on projected availability of capital funds and projected requirements for loans and real property acquisition for ministry development, church building programs, or other approved capital needs. This capital budget, upon recommendation of the joint staff committee, will be submitted to the board of the Division for Outreach and the board of the Mission Investment Fund of the ELCA for approval and recommendation to the Church Council. Following approval, the capital budget shall be monitored by the joint staff committee.

f. Within guidelines established jointly by the Division for Outreach and the Mission Investment Fund of the ELCA, the Mission Investment Fund shall have the responsibility for determining which congregations shall receive loans, the amount of each loan, and the repayment schedule. The Mission Investment Fund of the ELCA shall execute the loan, ensure safekeeping for the legal documents, provide accounting services for the repayment, supervise collection, and confer with the Division for Outreach on any exceptions to established loan policies.

g. The Mission Investment Fund **shall offer building and architectural consultative services to new congregations entering first-unit construction, to congregations relocating with synodical approval, to other congregations, and to campus ministry programs of the Division for Higher Education and Schools.**

16.11.C91. *Division for Outreach*
This division shall provide leadership and support for this church as it reaches out in witness to the Gospel in the areas served by the synods of this church by developing new ministries and congregations; supporting existing ministries and congregations in transition or with special needs; _and_ working with synods in developing area strategies for outreach. To fulfill these responsibilities, this division shall:
a. develop and recommend policy for, and then assist in the development of new ministries and congregations, the support of existing ministries and congre-

gations in transition or with special needs, and of urban and rural coalitions. To do so, this division will:
1) function in cooperation with synods and congregations.
2) have primary responsibility in working with synods to determine where and when new congregations of this church shall be developed and to recommend ministries for recognition and reception as congregations of this church.
3) be responsible for the churchwide Mission Partners program and Mission Builders program, in coordination with synods and appropriate churchwide units.
4) relate to the Mission Investment Fund in accord with the applicable continuing resolutions and policies that govern the operation of the Mission Investment Fund.

b. develop and carry out programs of evangelism in the development of new ministries, working in coordination with the Division for Congregational Ministries as the Division for Congregational Ministries develops programs and resources to nurture evangelism efforts of existing congregations.

c. establish, support, and plan, in consultation with the Commission for Multicultural Ministries and the Division for Congregational Ministries, for the outreach of this church among persons of color and those whose primary language is other than English.

d. provide staff services and financial grants to assist synods or groups of synods in the development of area strategies for outreach, in coordination with the Division for Church in Society and the Division for Congregational Ministries.

e. provide for appropriate training and support, in cooperation with synods, for persons in outreach ministries of development and re-development, and those in urban, rural, and area ministries.

f. develop, in consultation with the Mission Investment Fund, an annual capital budget for loans, real-property acquisition, and building programs in support of the development of new ministries and congregations. It also shall support investment in the Mission Investment Fund of the ELCA. Criteria for real- estate acquisition for new or existing ministries within the limits of capital funds available shall be established jointly by the Division for Outreach and the Mission Investment Fund. Within jointly established guidelines, the Mission Investment Fund shall determine which congregations shall receive loans, the amount of each loan, and the repayment schedule.

g. be responsible for representing this church in churchwide cooperative planning for outreach together with other church bodies and ecumenical organizations serving in the geographic territory of this church's synods.

h. cooperate, under the coordination of the Division for Global Mission, with Lutheran church bodies based in other nations that desire to carry out ministry in the U.S.A., and consult with synods of this church in planning and implementing such ministry.

i. cooperate with the Division for Global Mission, the Division for Congregational Ministries, the Division for Higher Education and Schools, and the synods of this church in providing programs of education for mission and for witness to persons of other faiths.

j. relate to congregationally based community organizations that are associated with outreach ministries supported by this division and assist in the development of such organizations, under the coordination of the Division for Church in Society and synods.

19.61.A94. ***Ecclesiastical Ballot***

An "ecclesiastical ballot" for the election of officers (other than treasurer) of the churchwide organization of the Evangelical Lutheran Church in America is hereby defined as an election process:

a. In which on the first ballot the name of any eligible individual may be submitted for nomination by a voting member of the assembly;

b. Through which the possibility of election to office exists on any ballot by achievement of the required number of votes cast by voting members of the assembly applicable to a particular ballot;

c. That precludes spoken floor nominations in the assembly prior to or following the casting of the first ballot;

d. In which the first ballot is considered a nominating ballot if no election occurs on the first ballot;

e. In which the first ballot defines the total slate of nominees for possible election on a subsequent ballot, with no additional nominations permitted following the casting of the first ballot;

f. That does not preclude, at some point subsequent to the reporting of the first ballot, the right of persons nominated on such a ballot to withdraw their names prior to the casting of the second ballot;

g. In which the name of any individual that appears on any ballot subsequent to the second ballot may not be withdrawn;

h. That does not preclude an assembly's adoption of rules that may permit, at a defined point in the election process and for a defined period of time, speeches to the assembly by nominees or their representatives and/or a question-and-answer forum in which the nominees or their representatives participate; and

i. In which the number of names that appear on any ballot subsequent to the second ballot shall be determined in accordance with provisions of the governing documents.

Evangelical Lutheran Church in America

CONSTITUTIONS, BYLAWS, AND CONTINUING RESOLUTIONS

as adopted by the Constituting Convention
of the Evangelical Lutheran Church in America
(April 30, 1987)

and

as amended by the
First (1989), Second (1991), and Third (1993)
Churchwide Assemblies
of the Evangelical Lutheran Church in America

Edition current as of September 1993

CONTENTS

Revised as of September 1, 1993 / This edition printed November 1993

INTRODUCTION

The basic commitments of the Evangelical Lutheran Church in America (ELCA) as well as its organizational outline, structural patterns, and rubrics of governance are reflected by this church's constitutions, bylaws, and continuing resolutions. These documents govern our life together as congregations, synods, and churchwide organization.

We find ourselves consulting these documents again and again to guide, direct, and assist us. They express for us, as a church body, our understanding of the nature of the church. They contain our statement of purpose and our principles of organization. They define our membership, our relationships, and our operating patterns.

While we recognize that the Evangelical Lutheran Church in America officially began operation as a church body on January 1, 1988, through the uniting of three predecessor bodies, we realize that our roots reach deep into the soil of the Lutheran Confessions and we draw constant nourishment from our biblical foundations. So we really are an old church with a different name and structure from those of our three predecessor church bodies. We are a particular gathering of people known as the Evangelical Lutheran Church in America. As part of the whole Church of Christ, we announce and declare the teachings of the prophets and apostles and seek to confess in our time the faith once delivered to the saints.

THE REV. LOWELL G. ALMEN
Secretary

Day of commemoration
for Henry Melchior Muhlenberg
October 7, 1993

RESTATED
ARTICLES OF INCORPORATION
OF
EVANGELICAL LUTHERAN CHURCH
IN AMERICA

ARTICLE I

The name of this corporation shall be:

EVANGELICAL LUTHERAN CHURCH IN AMERICA

ARTICLE II

This corporation (sometimes referred to herein as the "Church") is organized and shall be operated exclusively for religious purposes and, specifically, this corporation shall constitute a Lutheran church the purpose and functions of which shall be as specified from time to time in the Constitution of this corporation.

Within the framework and limitations of these purposes, the Church is organized and shall be operated exclusively for religious purposes and shall have such powers as are consistent with the foregoing purposes, including the power to acquire and receive funds and property of every kind and nature whatsoever, whether by purchase, conveyance, lease, gift, grant, bequest, legacy, devise, or otherwise, and to own, hold, expend, make gifts, grants, and contributions of, and to convey, transfer, and dispose of any funds and property and the income therefrom for the furtherance of the purposes of the Church hereinabove set forth, or any of them, and to lease, mortgage, encumber, and use the same, and such other powers which are consistent with the foregoing purposes and which are afforded to the Church by the Minnesota Nonprofit Corporation Act, and by any future laws amendatory thereof and supplementary thereto.

(9-93) ARTICLES OF INCORPORATION / 11

ARTICLE III

This corporation shall not afford pecuniary gain, incidentally or otherwise, to its members, and no part of the net income or net earnings of this corporation shall inure to the benefit of any member, private shareholder, or individual, and no substantial part of its activities shall consist of carrying on propaganda, or otherwise attempting to influence legislation. This corporation shall not participate in, or intervene in (including the publishing or distributing of statements), any political campaign on behalf of any candidate for public office.

This corporation shall not lend any of its assets to any officer, director or member of this corporation or guarantee to any other person the payment of a loan made to an officer, director or member of this corporation.

All references in these Articles of Incorporation to sections of the Internal Revenue Code of 1954 include any provisions thereof adopted by future amendments thereto and any cognate provisions in future Internal Revenue codes to the extent such provisions are applicable to this corporation.

ARTICLE IV

The period of duration of corporate existence of this corporation shall be perpetual.

ARTICLE V

The registered office of this corporation shall be located at 405 Second Avenue South, Minneapolis, Minnesota 55401.

ARTICLE VI

The management and direction of the business of the Church shall be vested in a board of directors which shall be known and designated as the Church Council. The terms of office, method of election, powers, authorities and duties of the members of the Church Council, the time and place of their meetings, and such other regulations with respect to them as are not inconsistent with the express provisions of these Articles of Incorporation shall be as specified from time to time in the bylaws of the Church, which shall be known to the Church as its Constitution.

ARTICLE VII

The Church Council shall consist of thirty-seven (37) persons. The names and addresses of the members of the Church Council and the expiration date of their respective terms of office, are as follows:

Name	Post Office Address	Expiration Date of Term— Close of the Church's Convention in the Year:

Names of the members of the Church Council elected at the Constituting Convention of the Evangelical Lutheran Church in America and, in the case of the treasurer, at the first meeting of the Church Council were filed in the Restated Articles of Incorporation and appear in the minutes of the convention and council meeting.

ARTICLE VIII

Except as otherwise provided in the Church's Constitution, the Church shall have no members with voting rights.

Whenever, and to the extent that, the Church's Constitution provides that voting rights shall be exercised by individuals elected, appointed or otherwise designated to serve as voting members of an assembly of the Church, then the voting members of this Church for purposes of the laws of the State of Minnesota shall be the persons who were most recently seated as the voting members of an assembly of the Church.

Members of congregations of the Church shall not, as such, have any voting rights with respect to this corporation.

ARTICLE IX

For purposes of the laws of the State of Minnesota, only the Church's Constitution shall be treated as the bylaws of this corporation, and none of this corporation's governing documents other than these Articles of Incorporation and the Church's Constitution need be subject to the procedures specified by law or otherwise for the amendment of articles of incorporation or bylaws.

ARTICLE X

Members of this corporation shall not be personally liable for the payment of any debts or obligations of this corporation of any nature whatsoever, nor shall any of the property of the members be subject to the payments of the debts or obligations of this corporation to any extent whatsoever.

ARTICLE XI

This corporation shall have no capital stock.

ARTICLE XII

These Articles of Incorporation may be amended from time to time in the manner prescribed by law.

ARTICLE XIII

In the event of the dissolution of this corporation any surplus property remaining after the payment of its debts shall be disposed of by transfer to one or more corporations, associations, institutions, trusts, community chests or foundations organized and operated exclusively for one or more of the purposes of this corporation, and described in section 501(c)(3) of the Internal Revenue Code of 1954, in such proportions as the Church Council of this corporation shall determine. Notwithstanding any provision herein to the contrary, nothing herein shall be construed to affect the disposition of property and assets held by this corporation upon trust or other condition, or subject to any executory or special limitation, and such property, upon dissolution of this corporation, shall be transferred in accordance with the trust, condition or limitation imposed with respect to it.

CONSTITUTION, BYLAWS, AND CONTINUING RESOLUTIONS
of the
EVANGELICAL LUTHERAN CHURCH IN AMERICA

CONSTITUTION, BYLAWS, AND CONTINUING RESOLUTIONS

of the

EVANGELICAL LUTHERAN CHURCH IN AMERICA

CODIFICATION EXPLANATION

The provisions of the Constitution, the Bylaws, and the Continuing Resolutions that pertain to the same matter have been placed together. This arrangement requires that the three types of material be identified by means other than physical separation.

The three types of provisions are identified by the following devices:

a. All constitutional provisions are in **bold face type.**

b. All bylaw provisions are printed in light face type.

c. All continuing resolutions are printed in *italic* type.

d. A numerical codification indicates general subject, constitutional provisions, bylaw provisions, and continuing resolutions.

Major sections are designated as chapters. The chapters are numbered 1 through 22. The chapter designation becomes the first number in the codification sequence and is followed by a period. Thus provisions in "Chapter 14. Church Council" are preceded by "14.".

General subjects normally are titled and designated by a number ending in zero. Thus, a subdivision of Chapter 16 that contains provisions regarding the divisions and commissions is codified and titled "16.10. Divisions." When subjects that are bylaw provisions only are titled, the same principles would apply within the third number sequence, e.g., 16.11.10. Division Boards.

Constitutional provisions are codified with two sets of numbers. The chapter number and a two-digit number preceding the second period in the codification. Thus, one constitutional provision related to the bishop of this church is 13.21.

Bylaw provisions are codified with three sets of numbers, the chapter number, the related constitutional provision number, and a two-digit number. Thus, one bylaw provision related to the secretary of this church is codified as 13.41.01.

Continuing resolutions also are codified with three sets of numbers except that the third set is preceded by a capital letter. Thus, a continuing resolution might be numbered 16. to designate the chapter; 16.11. to designate the subject matter within the chapter; and the third set might be numbered A91. in the codification 16.11.A91. to indicate by the "A" that it is the first continuing resolution regarding that subject and by the "91" that it was adopted in 1991.

When many related provisions are parts of a unit that are considered inseparable, they are normally lettered "a," "b," "c," etc. When related provisions are part of a unit but considered separable, such as a list of duties, they are normally numbered in sequence. If the related provisions cannot be clearly judged to be separable or inseparable, preference will be given to a number sequence.

If chapter numbers are considered the major sequence number, constitution numbers as a fraction of the chapter number, and bylaw numbers as a fraction of the constitution number, then the codification can be said to provide a progressive sequence. Thus, 8.31. will precede 8.33.01., and 9.21.01. will precede 9.22.

Provisions in the Constitution for Synods are prefaced with "S," and those in the Model Constitution for Congregations with "C."

In these governing documents, with the exception of the "Restated Articles of Incorporation," "Church" with a capital letter is used in references to the one, holy, catholic, and apostolic Church. In references to the Evangelical Lutheran Church in America, the words "church" and "this church" in lower case letters are employed.

PREAMBLE

Convinced that the Holy Spirit is leading us toward unity in the household of God, we of The American Lutheran Church, The Association of Evangelical Lutheran Churches, and the Lutheran Church in America give thanks to God for the faith we share together in Christ and, by adopting this constitution, form a new church, in the name of the Father, the Son, and the Holy Spirit.

Chapter 1.
NAME, INCORPORATION, SEAL, AND LOCATION

1.01. **The name of this church shall be Evangelical Lutheran Church in America.**

1.01.01. The name, Evangelical Lutheran Church in America, as used herein, refers, in general references, to this whole church, including its three primary expressions—congregations, synods, and the churchwide organization. The name, Evangelical Lutheran Church in America, is also the name of the corporation of the churchwide organization to which specific references are made herein.

1.02. **For the purposes of this constitution and the accompanying bylaws, the Evangelical Lutheran Church in America is hereafter designated as "this church."**

1.11. **This church shall be incorporated.**

1.21.01. The seal of this church is a cross with three united flames emanating from the base of the cross and three entwined circles beside the cross. The year of the constituting convention of this church is included at the base of the cross. The name of this church forms the circular outer edge of the seal.

1.31.01. The principal office of this church shall be located in Chicago, Illinois.

1.31.02. This church may maintain offices in such other locations as the Church-wide Assembly or the Church Council shall determine.

Chapter 2.
CONFESSION OF FAITH

2.01. **This church confesses the Triune God, Father, Son, and Holy Spirit.**

2.02. **This church confesses Jesus Christ as Lord and Savior and the Gospel as the power of God for the salvation of all who believe.**

a. **Jesus Christ is the Word of God incarnate, through whom everything was made and through whose life, death, and resurrection God fashions a new creation.**

b. **The proclamation of God's message to us as both Law and Gospel is the Word of God, revealing judgment and mercy through word and deed, beginning with the Word in creation, continuing in the history of Israel, and centering in all its fullness in the person and work of Jesus Christ.**

c. **The canonical Scriptures of the Old and New Testaments are the written Word of God. Inspired by God's Spirit speaking through their authors, they record and announce God's revelation centering in Jesus Christ. Through them God's Spirit speaks to us to create and sustain Christian faith and fellowship for service in the world.**

2.03. **This church accepts the canonical Scriptures of the Old and New Testaments as the inspired Word of God and the authoritative source and norm of its proclamation, faith, and life.**

2.04. **This church accepts the Apostles', Nicene, and Athanasian Creeds as true declarations of the faith of this church.**

2.05. **This church accepts the Unaltered Augsburg Confession as a true witness to the Gospel, acknowledging as one with it in faith and doctrine all churches that likewise accept the teachings of the Unaltered Augsburg Confession.**

2.06. **This church accepts the other confessional writings in the Book of Concord, namely, the Apology of the Augsburg Confession, the Smalcald Articles and the Treatise, the Small Catechism, the Large Catechism, and the Formula of Concord, as further valid interpretations of the faith of the Church.**

2.07. **This church confesses the Gospel, recorded in the Holy Scriptures and confessed in the ecumenical creeds and Lutheran confessional writings, as the power of God to create and sustain the Church for God's mission in the world.**

Chapter 3.
NATURE OF THE CHURCH

3.01. All power in the Church belongs to our Lord Jesus Christ, its head. All actions of this church are to be carried out under his rule and authority.

3.02. The Church exists both as an inclusive fellowship and as local congregations gathered for worship and Christian service. Congregations find their fulfillment in the universal community of the Church, and the universal Church exists in and through congregations. This church, therefore, derives its character and powers both from the sanction and representation of its congregations and from its inherent nature as an expression of the broader fellowship of the faithful. In length, it acknowledges itself to be in the historic continuity of the communion of saints; in breadth, it expresses the fellowship of believers and congregations in our day.

Chapter 4.
STATEMENT OF PURPOSE

4.01. The Church is a people created by God in Christ, empowered by the Holy Spirit, called and sent to bear witness to God's creative, redeeming, and sanctifying activity in the world.

4.02. To participate in God's mission, this church shall:

a. Proclaim God's saving Gospel of justification by grace for Christ's sake through faith alone, according to the apostolic witness in the Holy Scripture, preserving and transmitting the Gospel faithfully to future generations.

b. Carry out Christ's Great Commission by reaching out to all people to bring them to faith in Christ and by doing all ministry with a global awareness consistent with the understanding of God as Creator, Redeemer, and Sanctifier of all.

c. Serve in response to God's love to meet human needs, caring for the sick and the aged, advocating dignity and justice for all people, working for peace and reconciliation among the nations, and standing with the poor and powerless and committing itself to their needs.

d. Worship God in proclamation of the Word and administration of the sacraments and through lives of prayer, praise, thanksgiving, witness, and service.

e. Nurture its members in the Word of God so as to grow in faith and hope and love, to see daily life as the primary setting for the exercise of their Christian calling, and to use the gifts of the Spirit for their life together and for their calling in the world.

f. Manifest the unity given to the people of God by living together in the love of Christ and by joining with other Christians in prayer and action to express and preserve the unity which the Spirit gives.

4.03. To fulfill these purposes, this church shall:

a. Receive, establish, and support those congregations, ministries, organizations, institutions, and agencies necessary to carry out God's mission through this church.

b. Encourage and equip all members to worship, learn, serve, and witness; to fulfill their calling to serve God in the world; and to be stewards of the earth, their lives, and the Gospel.

c. Call forth, equip, certify, set apart, supervise, and support an ordained ministry of Word and sacrament and such other forms of ministry that will enable this church to fulfill its mission.

d. Seek unity in faith and life with all Lutherans within its boundaries and be ready to enter union negotiations whenever such unity is manifest.

e. Foster Christian unity by participating in ecumenical activities, contributing its witness and work and cooperating with other churches which confess God the Father, Son, and Holy Spirit.

f. Develop relationships with communities of other faiths for dialogue and common action.

g. Lift its voice in concord and work in concert with forces for good, to serve humanity, cooperating with church and other groups participating in activities that promote justice, relieve misery, and reconcile the estranged.

h. Produce and publish worship materials for corporate, family, and personal use and resources for education, witness, service, and stewardship.

i. Establish and maintain theological seminaries, schools, colleges, universities, and other educational institutions to equip people for leadership and service in church and society.

j. Assure faithfulness to this church's confessional position and purpose and provide for resolution of disputes.

k. Publish a periodical and make use of the arts and public communication media to proclaim the Gospel and to inform, interpret, and edify.

l. Study social issues and trends, work to discover the causes of oppression and injustice, and develop programs of ministry and advocacy to further human dignity, freedom, justice, and peace in the world.

m. Establish, support, and recognize institutions and agencies that minister to people in spiritual and temporal needs.

n. Work with civil authorities in areas of mutual endeavor, maintaining institutional separation of church and state in a relation of functional interaction.

o. Provide structures and decision-making processes for this church that foster mutuality and interdependence and that involve people in making decisions that affect them.

p. Support the mission of this church by arranging for and encouraging financial contributions for its work, management of its resources, and processes of planning and evaluation.

q. Provide fair personnel practices and adequate compensation, benefits, and pensions for those employed by this church.

Chapter 5.
PRINCIPLES OF ORGANIZATION

5.01. The Evangelical Lutheran Church in America shall be one church. This church recognizes that all power and authority in the Church belongs to the Lord Jesus Christ, its head. Therefore, all actions of this church by congregations, synods, and the churchwide organization shall be carried out under his rule and authority in accordance with the following principles:

a. The congregations, synods, and churchwide organization shall act in accordance with the Confession of Faith set forth in Chapter 2 of this constitution and with the Statement of Purpose set forth in Chapter 4.

b. This church, in faithfulness to the Gospel, is committed to be an inclusive church in the midst of division in society. Therefore, in their organization and outreach, the congregations, synods, and churchwide units of this church shall seek to exhibit the inclusive unity that is God's will for the Church.

c. The congregations, synods, and churchwide organization of this church are interdependent partners sharing responsibly in God's mission. In an interdependent relationship primary responsibility for particular functions will vary between the partners. Whenever possible, the entity most directly affected by a decision shall be the principal party responsible for decision and implementation, with the other entities facilitating and assisting. Each congregation, synod, and separately incorporated unit of the churchwide organization, as well as the churchwide organization itself, is a separate legal entity and is responsible for exercising its powers and authorities.

d. Each congregation and synod in its governing documents shall include the Confession of Faith and Statement of Purpose and such structural components as are required in this constitution. Beyond these common elements, congregations and synods shall be free to organize in such manner as each deems appropriate for its jurisdiction.

e. The Church Council shall establish an ongoing process to review the function of the structural organization of this church and to develop recommendations for changes.

f. Except as otherwise provided in this constitution and bylaws, the churchwide organization, through the Church Council, shall establish processes that will ensure that at least 60 percent of the members of its assemblies, councils, committees, boards, and other organizational units shall be laypersons; that as nearly as possible, 50 percent of the lay members of these assemblies, councils, committees, boards, or other organizational units shall be female and 50 percent shall be male, and that, where possible, the representation of ordained ministers shall be both female and male. At least 10 percent of the members of these assemblies, councils, committees, boards, or other organizational units shall be persons of color and/or persons whose primary language is other than English. Processes shall be developed that will assure that in selecting staff there will be a balance of women and men, persons of color and persons whose primary language is other than English, laypersons, and persons on the roster of ordained ministers. This balance is to be evident in terms of both executive staff and support staff consistent with the inclusive policy of this church.

g. Except as otherwise provided in this constitution and bylaws, synods, through synodical councils, shall establish processes that will ensure that at least 60 percent of the members of their assemblies, councils, committees, boards, and other organizational units shall be laypersons; that, as nearly as possible, 50 percent of the lay members of their assemblies, councils, committees, boards, or other organizational units shall be female and 50 percent shall be male, and that, where possible, the representation of ordained ministers shall be both female and male. Each synod shall establish processes that will enable it to reach a minimum goal that 10 percent of the membership of its assemblies, councils, committees, boards, or other organizational units be persons of color and/or persons whose primary language is other than English.

h. Leaders in this church should demonstrate that they are servants by their words, life-style, and manner of leadership. Leaders in this church will recognize their accountability to the Triune God, to the whole Church, to each other, and to the organization of this church in which they have been asked to serve.

i. As a steward of the resources that God has provided, this church shall organize itself to make the most effective use of its resources to accomplish its mission.

j. Each assembly, council, committee, board, commission, task force, or other body of the churchwide organization or any churchwide units shall be conclusively presumed to have been properly constituted, and neither the method of selection nor the composition of any such assembly, council, committee, board, commission, task force, or other body may be challenged in a court of law by any person or be used as the basis of a challenge in a court of law to the validity or effect of any action taken or authorized by any such assembly, council, committee, board, commission, task force, or other body.

5.01.A87. *It shall be a goal of this church that within 10 years of its establishment its membership shall include at least 10 percent people of color and/or primary language other than English.*

5.01.B87. *With regard to the minimum goal that 10 percent of the membership of synod assemblies, councils, committees, boards, and/or other organizational units be persons of color and/or persons whose primary language is other than English, it is understood that initially there may be exceptions to the attainment of this goal based on the makeup of the membership within a particular synod. By the time of its second assembly, each synod shall establish a plan to attain this goal within 10 years.*

5.01.C89. *The term, "persons of color and/or persons whose primary language is other than English," shall be understood to mean Asian, African American, Black, Hispanic, and Native American, including Native Alaskan, people. This definition, however, shall not be understood as limiting this church's commitment to inclusive participation in its life and work.*

Chapter 6.
MEMBERSHIP

6.01. The members of this church shall be the baptized members of its congregations.

6.02. The voting members of this church shall be those persons elected to serve as members of the Churchwide Assembly. Membership in a congregation does not, in itself, confer voting rights in this corporation.

Chapter 7.
MINISTRY

Ministry of the Baptized People of God

7.10. This church affirms the universal priesthood of all its baptized members. In its function and its structure this church commits itself to the equipping and supporting of all its members for their ministries in the world and in this church. It is within this context of ministry that this church calls or appoints some of its baptized members for specific ministries in this church.

7.11. The roster of pastors as ordained ministers of the Evangelical Lutheran Church in America shall be composed of:

7.11.01.

1) those persons on the Clergy Roster of The American Lutheran Church, the Clergy Roster of The Association of Evangelical Lutheran Churches, and the Roll of Ordained Ministers of the Lutheran Church in America as of December 31, 1987; and

2) those persons who are added to the roster of ordained ministers following that date pursuant to section 7.20. *et seq.* of the Constitution of the Evangelical Lutheran Church in America.

Ordained Ministry

7.20. Within the people of God and for the sake of the Gospel ministry entrusted to all believers, God has instituted the office of ministry of Word and sacrament. To carry out this ministry, this church calls and ordains qualified persons.

7.21.

7.22. A pastor as an ordained minister of this church shall be a person whose commitment to Christ, soundness in the faith, aptness to preach, teach, and witness, and educational qualifications have been examined and approved in the manner prescribed in the documents of this church; who has been properly called and ordained; who accepts and adheres to the Confession of Faith of this church; who is diligent and faithful in the exercise of the ministry; and whose life and conduct are above reproach. A minister shall comply with the constitution of this church.

7.23. The standards for acceptance and continuance of pastors in the ordained ministry of this church shall be set forth in the bylaws.

7.24. The secretary of this church shall maintain a roster containing the names of pastors as ordained ministers who qualify on the basis of constitutional provisions 7.22., 7.23., 7.30., and 7.31., and related bylaws.

Standards for Pastors as Ordained Ministers

7.30.

7.31. In accordance with the description of an ordained minister stated in 7.22., pastors as ordained ministers shall be governed by the following standards, policies, and procedures.

7.31.10.

7.31.11. Basic Standards

Persons admitted to and continued as pastors in the ordained ministry of this church shall satisfactorily meet and maintain the following, as defined by this church in its governing documents and in policies developed by the Division for Ministry, reviewed by the Conference of Bishops, and adopted by the Church Council:

a. commitment to Christ;

b. acceptance of and adherence to the Confession of Faith of this church;

c. willingness and ability to serve in response to the needs of this church;

d. academic and practical qualifications for ministry;

e. life consistent with the Gospel and personal qualifications including leadership abilities and competence in interpersonal relationships;

f. receipt and acceptance of a letter of call; and

g. membership in a congregation of this church.

7.31.12. Consistent with the faith and practice of the Evangelical Lutheran Church in America,

a. Every pastor as an ordained minister shall:

1) preach the Word;

2) administer the sacraments;

3) conduct public worship;

4) provide pastoral care;

5) seek out and encourage qualified persons to prepare for the ministry of the Gospel;

6) witness to the Kingdom of God in the community, in the nation, and abroad; and

7) speak publicly to the world in solidarity with the poor and oppressed, calling for justice and proclaiming God's love for the world.

b. Each pastor as an ordained minister with a congregational call shall, within the congregation:

1) offer instruction, confirm, marry, visit the sick and distressed, and bury the dead;

2) supervise all schools and organizations of the congregation;

3) impart knowledge of this church and its wider ministry through distribution of its periodicals and other publications;

4) endeavor to increase the support given by the congregation to the work of the churchwide organization and synod of the Evangelical Lutheran Church in America;

5) install regularly elected members of the Congregation Council; and

6) with the council, administer discipline.

7.31.13. Preparation and Approval. Except as provided below, a candidate for ordination as a pastor shall have:

a. membership in a congregation of this church and registration, by its pastor and council, of the candidate with the candidacy committee;

b. been endorsed by and under the guidance and supervision of the appropriate committee for at least a year before being approved for ordination;

c. satisfactorily completed the requirements for the Master of Divinity degree from an accredited theological school in North America, including practical preparation as defined by the Division for Ministry such as internship and supervised clinical work;

d. completed at least one year of residency in a seminary of this church, except when waived by the appropriate committee in consultation with the faculty of a seminary of this church;

e. been recommended for approval by the faculty of a seminary of this church;

f. been examined and approved by the appropriate committee according to criteria, policies, and procedures established by the Division for Ministry after consultation with the Conference of Bishops and adoption by the Church Council;

g. been recommended to a congregation or other entity by the bishop of the synod to which the candidate has been assigned for first call in accordance with the procedures recommended by the Division for Ministry, reviewed by the Conference of Bishops, and adopted by the Church Council; and

h. received and accepted a properly issued and attested letter of call.

7.31.14. Admission under Other Circumstances. Candidates for ordination as pastors or for reception who by reason of (a) age and prior experience, (b) ordination in another Lutheran church body, or (c) ordination in another Christian church body, whether in North America or abroad, shall be approved by the appropriate committee for ordination or reception according to criteria, policies, and procedures recommended by the Division for Ministry, reviewed by the Conference of Bishops, and adopted by the Church Council. In preparing such criteria, policies, and procedures, the Division for Ministry shall consult with the seminaries of this church and, as appropriate, with the Division for Outreach, the Division for Global Mission, and the Commission for Multicultural Ministries.

7.31.15. Reinstatement. Persons seeking reinstatement to the ordained ministry as pastors, whether having served previously in this church or in one of its predecessor bodies, shall be registered with the candidacy committee by the pastor and council of the congregation of which a member and interviewed, examined, and approved by the appropriate committee under criteria, policies, and procedures recommended by the Division for Ministry, reviewed by the Conference of Bishops, and adopted by the Church Council. In this process, the committee shall review the circumstances related to the termination of earlier service together with subsequent developments. The person is reinstated after receiving and accepting a letter of call to serve as a pastor in this church.

7.31.16. **On Leave from Call.** A pastor as an ordained minister of this church, serving under a regularly issued letter of call, who leaves the work of that ministry without accepting another regularly issued letter of call, may be retained on the roster of ordained ministers of this church, upon endorsement by the synodical bishop, by action of the Synod Council in the synod of which the pastor as an ordained minister is a member, under policy developed by the Division for Ministry, reviewed by the Conference of Bishops, and adopted by the Church Council. Thereafter, by annual action of the Synod Council in the synod of which a member, upon endorsement by the synodical bishop, a pastor as an ordained minister who is without a current letter of call may be retained on the roster of ordained ministers of this church for a maximum of three years beginning at the completion of an active call. Exception to this limit for the purpose of serving the needs of this church may be granted by the Synod Council in the synod of current roster after having received approval by the Conference of Bishops.

By annual recommendation by the Division for Ministry and action of the Synod Council in the synod of which a member, with the approval of the synodical bishop, a pastor as an ordained minister engaged in graduate study, in a field of study that will enhance service in the ordained ministry, may be retained on the roster of ordained ministers of this church for a maximum of six years. Exception to this limit for the purpose of serving the needs of this church may be granted by the Synod Council in the synod of current roster after having received approval by the Conference of Bishops.

7.40. **Calls for Pastors as Ordained Ministers**

7.41. **Letters of Call.** Letters of call to pastors as ordained ministers of this church or properly approved candidates for this church's roster of ordained ministers shall be issued in keeping with this church's constitutions, bylaws, and continuing resolutions as well as policies regarding such calls developed by the Division for Ministry, reviewed by the Conference of Bishops, and approved by the Church Council.

7.41.10. **General Categories**

7.41.11. **Service under Call.** A pastor as an ordained minister of this church shall serve under letter of call properly extended by a congregation, a synodical council or assembly, the Church Council, or the Churchwide Assembly. Calls may be extended for stated periods of time and for shared-time ministry by the appropriate calling body under criteria recommended by the Division for Ministry, reviewed by the Conference of Bishops, and adopted by the Church Council.

7.41.12. **Initial Call to Congregational Service.** Because the responsibilities of the office of the ordained ministry are most clearly focused in the congregational pastorate, experience in which is deemed by this church to be invaluable for all other ordained service, initial service of at least three years shall be in the parish ministry. Exceptions may be granted under criteria and procedures recommended by the Division for Ministry, reviewed by the Conference of Bishops, and adopted by the Church Council.

7.41.13. **Calls to Non-Congregational Service.** Calls to serve in institutions, agencies, and other entities inside and outside this church may be extended where there is an identifiable relationship of the work to the purpose of the ordained ministry. Such calls involve, for example, the care of the Word, the administration of the sacraments, pastoral care, and activities closely associated with those tasks including oversight in the church and in inter-Lutheran and inter-church agencies and institutions. Care is to be exercised so that positions which can be filled adequately and appropriately by the laity in the church and in the world not be filled by ordained ministers for their convenience or status. Synodical councils and the Church Council may seek the advice of the Conference of Bishops in specific situations.

7.41.14. **Non-Stipendiary Service Under Call.** When it is deemed necessary for the mission needs of this church, a letter of call may be issued by the Synod Council—according to criteria, policies, and procedures recommended by the Division for Ministry, reviewed by the Conference of Bishops, and adopted by the Church Council—to a pastor as an ordained minister for non-stipendiary service after the Synod Council has sought and received approval by the Conference of Bishops. Care is to be exercised so that positions that can be filled adequately and appropriately by the laity in the church and in the world not be filled by pastors as ordained ministers for their convenience, status, or personal preference. A call to non-stipendiary service is to be reviewed at least annually by the Synod Council and continued only as warranted for the ministry needs of this church. Such a call may be terminated by the Synod Council when it is deemed to be fulfilling no longer the mission needs of this church.

7.41.15. **Calls to Serve in Unusual Circumstances.** When it is deemed to be in the interests of this church in the care of the Gospel, pastors as ordained ministers may be called for a stated period of time, not to exceed three years, to minister on behalf of this church while employed in an occupation outside the traditional range of the ordained ministry. Such calls may be extended by a Synod Council or the Church Council upon recommendation by the Conference of Bishops according to criteria and procedures recommended by the Division for Ministry, reviewed by the Conference of Bishops, and adopted by the Church Council. Such calls shall be reviewed annually.

7.41.16. Calls in Predecessor Church Bodies. Accountability for specific calls to service extended in predecessor church bodies shall be exercised according to the policies and procedures of this church.

7.41.17. Retirement. Pastors as ordained ministers may retire upon attainment of age 60, or after 30 years on the roster of ordained ministers of this church or one of its predecessor bodies, or upon disability, and continue to be listed on the roster of ordained ministers of this church.

7.41.18. Retention of Personnel Records. When a pastor as an ordained minister is removed from that roster of this church, the personnel record shall be retained by the secretary of this church and the synodical bishop shall invite the person at the time of removal to provide, annually, appropriate current information for the personnel record.

7.42. Each pastor on the roster of ordained ministers of this church shall be related to that synod:

a. of which the congregation issuing the call to the ordained minister is related;

b. which issues a letter of call to the ordained minister;

c. on whose roster the ordained minister was listed at the time of the issuance of a letter of call from the Church Council;

d. on whose roster the ordained minister, if a seminary teacher or administrator, was assigned by the seminary board and Synod Council of each affected synod, to approval by the synodical bishop and Synod Council of each affected synod, to assure proportionate representation of faculty and administration in each synod of its region;

e. on whose roster the ordained minister was listed at the time of the issuance of a call to federal chaplaincy or on the roster of the synod of current address, if approved by the synod bishop and received by the Synod Council;

f. in which the ordained minister, upon receiving a call from this church, serves as a deployed staff person or on the roster of one of the synods to which the ordained minister is deployed;

g. on whose roster the ordained minister was listed when placed on leave from call; or

h. on whose roster the ordained minister was listed when last called or the synod of current address, if retired or disabled.

7.42.01. If the service of a pastor as an ordained minister who receives and accepts a letter of call from this church, under 7.42.c., would be enhanced through transfer of roster status from the previous synod of roster to the synod of current address, such as an ordained minister who is president of a college or university of this church or a chaplain in an educational or social service institution, such a transfer may be authorized upon mutual agreement of the synodical bishops involved after consultation with and approval by the secretary of this church.

7.43. A letter of call issued by a Synod Council or the Church Council to a pastor as an ordained minister of this church shall be either co-terminus with, or not longer than, the duration of the service or employment for which the call was issued. With the exception of persons designated as employees of a synod or the churchwide organization, such a call does not imply any employment relationship or contractual obligation in regard to employment on the part of the Synod Council or Church Council issuing the call. The recipient of such a call remains subject to this church's standards and discipline for ordained ministry, as contained in this church's constitution, bylaws, and continuing resolutions and in the policy and procedure documents of this church.

7.43.01. When the Synod Council or the Church Council, as the calling source, determines that the service or employment no longer fulfills the criteria under which a call was issued, the Synod Council or the Church Council shall vacate the call and direct that the individual be placed on leave from call or, if such leave status is not granted, the individual shall be removed from the roster of pastors as ordained ministers.

7.44. Each synod shall maintain a roster containing the names of those pastors as ordained ministers who are related to it on the basis of 7.42. of this constitution.

7.44.A93. *Sources of Calls for Ordained Ministers*

a. Principles for Sources of Calls

The following principles shall govern calls in this church:

1) A "call" is an action by an organizational unit of this church through which it asks a person to serve in a specified ministry and which is attested in a "letter of call."

2) Interdependence within the body of this church suggests that any action of one of its entities affects other entities. Therefore, interdependence is expressed in all calls extended by any organizational unit within this church.

3) A call expresses a relationship between this church and the person called involving mutual service, support, accountability, supervision, and discipline. The calling entity, in cooperation with the synod and other appropriate entities, bears a primary responsibility for this relationship on behalf of this church.

4) A letter of call is issued by that organizational unit of this church authorized to do so which is most directly involved in accountability for the specified ministry.

5) Decisions on calls for ministries in unusual circumstances not otherwise provided for but deemed to be in the interests of this church's care of the Gospel are referred to the Conference of Bishops for recommendation to the appropriate calling body.

(9-93)   ELCA CONSTITUTION—CHAPTER 7 / 33

ELCA CONSTITUTION—CHAPTER 7   (9-93)

b. Table of Sources of Calls for Ordained Ministers

Setting	Calling Body
1.0 Congregational ministry	
1.1 Single congregation	Congregation meeting
1.11 Pastor	
1.12 Senior pastor	
1.13 Associate/assistant pastor	
1.14 Co-pastor	
1.15 Shared-time pastor	
1.2 Multiple-congregation parish	Congregation meetings, acting on a common proposal
1.21 Pastor	
1.22 Other pastoral arrangements	
1.3 Coalition and cluster ministry	Synod Council
1.4 Congregations beyond ELCA	
1.41 Independent Lutheran congregation	Synod Council
1.42 Overseas independent Lutheran congregation	Church Council upon request of board of Division for Global Mission
1.43 Other	Synod Council or Church Council
1.5 Interim pastor	Synod Council
1.6 Pastor in a congregation under development	Synod Council
2.0 Synodical ministry	
2.1 Bishop	Synod Assembly
2.2 Assistant to bishop	Synod Council
2.3 Shared staff by two or more synods	One of the participating synods
2.4 Synod staff partially supported by grants from churchwide units	Synod Council
3.0 Regional ministry	
3.1 Staff	Church Council
3.2 Shared synodical-churchwide staff	Church Council
4.0 Churchwide ministry	
4.1 Bishop and secretary	Churchwide Assembly
4.2 Editor of the church periodical	Churchwide Assembly
4.3 Treasurer	Church Council
4.4 Bishop's staff	Church Council
4.5 Office staff	Church Council
4.6 Division and commission staff	Church Council upon request of appropriate board or committee
4.7 Other churchwide unit staff	Church Council
5.0 Chaplaincy and institutional ministry	
5.1 Institution/agency related or unrelated to a synod	Synod Council
5.2 Institution/agency related to more than one synod	Synod Council of one of the synods
5.3 ELCA-related institution/agency	Church Council upon request of board of Division for Church in Society
5.4 Federal agency/institution	Church Council
5.5 Military	Church Council
6.0 Campus ministry	
6.1 Staff	Synod Council
7.0 Church camp ministry	
7.1 Staff	Synod Council
8.0 Ecumenical ministry	
8.1 Related to a synod	Synod Council
8.2 Related to more than one synod	Synod Council of one of the synods
8.3 National/international organization	Church Council
9.0 Inter-Lutheran ministry	
9.1 Related to a synod	Synod Council
9.2 Related to more than one synod	Synod Council of one of the synods
9.3 National/International	Church Council
10.0 Educational ministry	
10.1 ELCA-related seminary chaplain/faculty/administrator	Church Council upon request of board of Division for Ministry
10.2 Chaplain/faculty/administrator of a seminary unrelated to ELCA	Church Council upon request of board of Division for Ministry
10.3 ELCA-related college chaplain/faculty/administrator	Synod Council of the synod in which college is located

7.47. **Pastors as ordained ministers shall be subject to discipline as set forth in Chapter 20 of this constitution and bylaws.**

7.47.01. After the organization of this church, no person who belongs to any organization other than the church which claims to possess in its teachings and ceremonies that which the Lord has given solely to the Church shall be ordained or otherwise received into the ministry of this church, nor shall any person so ordained or otherwise received by this church be retained in its ministry who subsequently joins such an organization. Violation of this rule shall make such minister subject to discipline.

Official Rosters of Laypersons

7.50. **This church may establish rosters of laypersons on which the names may be listed of those who qualify for such according to the bylaws and continuing resolutions of the Evangelical Lutheran Church in America.**

7.51. The standards of acceptance and continuance on the lay rosters of this church as defined herein shall be included in the bylaws.

7.51.01. Under constitutional provision 7.51., those persons previously rostered as commissioned church staff (The American Lutheran Church), deaconesses (The Association of Evangelical Lutheran Churches), deaconesses (The American Lutheran Church), deaconesses (the Lutheran Church in America), deacons (The Association of Evangelical Lutheran Churches), lay professional leaders (the Lutheran Church in America), and commissioned teachers (The Association of Evangelical Lutheran Churches) shall be retained as associates in ministry of this church (except for removals in accord with the governing documents, criteria, policies, and procedures of this church) in the recognized category of ministry of their previous church body for as long as they are in good standing according to the standards, criteria, policies, and procedures of this church. Accountability for specific calls shall be exercised according to the policies and procedures of this church. Such persons may resign from the roster or may elect to be rostered in another ELCA category by meeting the appropriate criteria established by the Evangelical Lutheran Church in America and by relinquishing their previous roster category.

7.51.02. The lay roster of associates in ministry, in addition to those listed in bylaw 7.51.02., shall be composed of:

a. those certified during the period of January 1, 1988, through September 1, 1993, as associates in ministry of the Evangelical Lutheran Church in America; and

b. those who are certified, subsequent to September 1, 1993, as associates in ministry in this church according to the standards, criteria, and requirements of this church, as defined herein and in policies and procedures developed by the Division for Ministry, reviewed by the Conference of Bishops, and adopted by the Church Council.

(9-93) ELCA CONSTITUTION—CHAPTER 7 / 37

10.4 Chaplain/faculty/administrator of a college unrelated to ELCA	Synod Council of the synod in which college is located
10.5 ELCA-related school chaplain/faculty/administrator	Congregation of which the school is a part or, if related to several congregations, Synod Council of the synod in which the school is located
10.6 Chaplain/faculty of a school unrelated to ELCA	Synod Council of the synod in which the school is located
10.7 Director/staff of a continuing education center related to Division for Ministry	Synod Council in which the main office of center is located upon the request of the board of Division for Ministry
11.0 Missionary ministry	
11.1 Outside United States	Church Council upon request of board of Division for Global Mission
11.2 Within United States	Church Council upon request of board of Division for Outreach
12.0 Other	
12.1 Non-stipendiary service under call	Synod Council upon approval by the Conference of Bishops
12.2 Unusual ministries (as in conjunction with occupations and in approved situations not otherwise specified)	Synod Council or Church Council upon recommendation by Conference of Bishops

7.45. **In keeping with the historic discipline and practice of the Lutheran church and to be true to a sacred trust inherent in the nature of the pastoral office, no ordained minister of this church shall divulge any confidential disclosure received in the course of the care of souls or otherwise in a professional capacity, nor testify concerning conduct observed by the ordained minister while working in a pastoral capacity, except with the express permission of the person who has given confidential information to the ordained minister or who was observed by the ordained minister, or if the person intends great harm to self or others.**

7.46. **The provisions for termination of the mutual relationship between a pastor as an ordained minister and a congregation shall be included in †S14.13. of the Constitution for Synods.**

1) commitment to Christ;

2) acceptance of and adherence to the Confession of Faith of this church;

3) willingness and ability to serve in response to the needs of this church;

4) academic and practical qualifications for the position;

5) life consistent with the Gospel and personal qualifications including leadership abilities and competence in interpersonal relationships;

6) receipt and acceptance of a letter of call; and

7) membership in a congregation of this church.

b. **Preparation and Approval.** Except as provided below, a candidate for certification shall have:

1) membership in a congregation of this church and registration by its pastor and council;

2) been endorsed by and under the guidance and supervision of the appropriate committee for at least a year before being approved by the committee for certification;

3) completed the academic and practical preparation for the work for which certified according to criteria and procedures established by the Division for Ministry; and

4) been examined and approved by the appropriate committee according to procedures established by the Division for Ministry after consultation with the seminaries and colleges of this church which offer programs designed to prepare persons for certification as associates in ministry.

7.52.12. **Certification under Other Circumstances.** A candidate may, for reasons of age or prior experience, be granted certification under criteria and procedures which permit certain equivalencies as defined by the Division for Ministry.

7.52.13. **Reinstatement.** Persons seeking reinstatement as associates in ministry, whether having previously served in this church or in one of its predecessor bodies, shall be endorsed by the pastor and council of the congregation of this church of which a member and interviewed, examined, and approved for reinstatement by the appropriate committee under criteria and procedures recommended by the Division for Ministry, reviewed by the Conference of Bishops, and adopted by the Church Council. In this process, the committee shall review the circumstances related to the termination of earlier service together with subsequent developments. The person is reinstated after receiving and accepting a letter of call in this church.

a. Any person removed from a lay roster that existed on December 31, 1987, as cited herein, who seeks to return to active lay roster status must apply for acceptance to a roster of this church under the standards, criteria, policies, and procedures that apply to the roster of

Upon receipt and acceptance of a valid, regularly issued letter of call, a newly certified candidate shall be commissioned, according to proper service orders of this church, as an associate in ministry.

Accountability for specific calls shall be exercised according to the policies and procedures of this church. Such persons may resign from the roster or may elect to be rostered in another ELCA category by meeting the appropriate criteria established by the Evangelical Lutheran Church in America and by relinquishing their previous roster category.

7.51.04. This church shall maintain a lay roster of the members of the Deaconess Community of the Evangelical Lutheran Church in America of those set apart—according to the standards, criteria, policies, and procedures of this church—for such service within the life of this church.

a. A newly approved candidate for this roster shall be set apart, according to the service orders of this church, as a member of the Deaconess Community of the Evangelical Lutheran Church in America.

b. All constitutional provisions, bylaws, and continuing resolutions regarding associates in ministry of the Evangelical Lutheran Church in America, except for the service order of setting apart for the Deaconess Community, shall apply to those on the lay roster of this church as members of the Deaconess Community of the Evangelical Lutheran Church in America.

7.51.05. This church shall establish and maintain a lay roster of diaconal ministers who shall be called by this church to positions that exemplify the servant life and that seek to equip and motivate others to live it. Such diaconal ministers shall seek in a great variety of ways to empower, equip, and support all the baptized people of God in the ministry of Jesus Christ and the mission of God in the world.

a. Upon certification and approval as a candidate for the lay roster of diaconal ministers, and upon receipt and acceptance of a valid, regularly issued letter of call, the candidate shall be designated, according to the service orders of this church, as a lay diaconal minister.

b. All constitutional provisions, bylaws, and continuing resolutions regarding associates in ministry of the Evangelical Lutheran Church in America shall apply to those on the lay roster of diaconal ministers of the Evangelical Lutheran Church in America.

7.52. **The standards of acceptance and continuance as associates in ministry of this church shall be included in the bylaws.**

7.52.10. **Standards for Associates in Ministry.**

7.52.11. Associates in ministry shall be governed by the following:

a. **Basic Standards.** Persons certified and continued as associates in ministry of this church shall satisfactorily meet and maintain the following:

associates in ministry, as identified in 7.51.03.b. This same requirement shall apply to those certified during the period of January 1, 1988, through September 1, 1993, as associates in ministry of this church.

b. A person on the roster of a previous church body or a person on the roster of associates in ministry of this church, who was so certified during the period between January 1, 1988, and September 1, 1993, shall relinquish such a roster category upon being received and accepted on another roster of this church.

7.52.14. **Maintenance of Lay Rosters.** Each synod shall maintain a lay roster or rosters containing the names of those related to the synod as members of its congregations who have been approved as associates in ministry, members of the Deaconess Community of the Evangelical Lutheran Church in America, and diaconal ministers—according to the bylaws and continuing resolutions of this church—for inclusion on such a roster or rosters.

7.52.15. The secretary of this church shall maintain a lay roster or rosters of associates in ministry, members of the Deaconess Community of the Evangelical Lutheran Church in America, and diaconal ministers on which shall be listed the names of those who qualify according to the constitution, bylaws, and continuing resolutions of this church.

7.52.20. **Service as Associates in Ministry**

7.52.21. **Service under Call.** An associate in ministry shall serve under a letter of call properly extended by a congregation, synod, or the churchwide organization. Calls may be extended either for indefinite or stated periods of time by the appropriate calling body for service in a congregation, synod or churchwide unit, in an institution or agency of this church, or in another setting in a category of work. Regular, valid calls in this church shall be in accord with criteria, policies, and procedures recommended by the Division for Ministry, reviewed by the Conference of Bishops, and adopted by the Church Council. An associate in ministry serving under call to a congregation shall be a member of that congregation. In a parish of multiple congregations, an associate in ministry shall be a member of one of the congregations being served.

7.52.22. **On Leave from Call.** An associate in ministry, serving under a regularly issued letter of call, who leaves the work of that call without accepting another regularly issued letter of call, may be retained on the roster of associates in ministry of this church, upon endorsement by the synodical bishop, by action of the Synod Council in the synod of which a member. Thereafter, by annual action of the Synod Council in the synod of which a member, upon endorsement by the synodical bishop, an associate in ministry who is without a current letter of call may be retained on the roster of associates in ministry of this church for a maximum of three years beginning at the completion of an active call. Exception to this limit for the purpose of serving the needs of this church may be granted by the Synod Council of current roster after having received approval by the Conference of Bishops.

By annual recommendation by the Division for Ministry and action by the Synod Council in the synod of which a member, with the approval of the synodical bishop, an associate in ministry engaged in graduate study appropriate for service in this church may be retained on the roster of associates in ministry of this church for a maximum of six years. Exception to this limit for the purpose of serving the needs of this church may be granted by the Synod Council in the synod of current roster after having received approval by the Conference of Bishops.

7.52.23. **Issuance and Termination of the Call of an Associate in Ministry.**

a. A letter of call to an associate in ministry of this church shall be issued in keeping with this church's constitutions, bylaws, and continuing resolutions as well as policies regarding such calls developed by the Division for Ministry, reviewed by the Conference of Bishops, and approved by the Church Council. In the case of alleged local difficulties that imperil the effective functioning of the congregation, the synodical bishop, following appropriate consultation, will recommend a course of action to the pastor, associate in ministry, and the congregation. If they agree to carry out such recommendations, no further action shall be taken by the synod. If any party fails to assent, the congregation may dismiss the associate in ministry under criteria, policies, and procedures recommended by the Division for Ministry, reviewed by the Conference of Bishops, and adopted by the Church Council.

b. A letter of call issued by a Synod Council or the Church Council to an associate in ministry of this church shall be either co-terminus with, or not longer than the duration of, the service or employment for which the call was issued. With the exception of persons designated as employees of a synod or the churchwide organization, such a call does not imply any employment relationship or contractual obligation in regard to employment on the part of the Synod Council or Church Council issuing the call. The recipient of such a call remains subject to this church's standards and discipline for associates in ministry, as contained in this church's constitution, bylaws, and continuing resolutions and in the policy and procedure documents of this church.

c. When the Synod Council or the Church Council, as the calling source, determines that the service or employment no longer fulfills the criteria under which a call was issued, the Synod Council or the Church Council shall vacate the call and direct that the individual be placed on leave from call or, if such leave status is not granted, the individual shall be removed from the roster of associates in ministry.

7.52.24.   **Retirement.** Associates in ministry may retire upon attainment of age 60, or after 30 years on a roster of this church or one of its predecessor bodies, or upon disability, and continue to be listed on the roster of associates in ministry of this church.

7.52.25.   **Retention of Personnel Records.** When an associate in ministry is removed from the roster of this church, the personnel record shall be retained by the secretary of this church and the synodical bishop shall invite the person at the time of removal to provide, annually, appropriate current information for the personnel record.

7.52.A93.   *Sources of Calls for Associates in Ministry*

a. *The principles governing sources of calls for ordained ministers shall, as appropriate, also govern sources of letters of call for associates in ministry.*

b. *Table of Sources of Call for Associates in Ministry*

Setting	Calling Body
1.0 *Congregational ministry*	
1.1 *Single congregation*	*Congregation meeting*
1.2 *Multiple-congregation parish*	*Congregation meetings, acting on a common proposal*
1.3 *Coalition and clusters*	*Synod Council*
1.4 *Other congregations*	
1.41 *Independent Lutheran*	*Synod Council*
1.42 *Other*	*Synod Council*
2.0 *Synodical ministry*	*Synod Council*
3.0 *Regional ministry*	*Church Council*
4.0 *Churchwide ministry*	
4.1 *Bishop's/office's staff*	*Church Council*
4.2 *Division's and commission's staff*	*Church Council upon request of appropriate division board or commission committee of the churchwide organization*
4.3 *Other churchwide organization's staff*	*Church Council*
5.0 *Social ministry institutions*	
5.1 *Institution/agency related or unrelated to a synod*	*Synod Council*
5.2 *Institution/agency related to more than one synod*	*Synod Council of one of the synods*
5.3 *ELCA-related institution/ agency*	*Church Council upon request of board of Division for Church in Society*
5.4 *Other*	*Church Council*
6.0 *Campus ministry*	
6.1 *Staff*	*Synod Council*
7.0 *Church camp ministry*	
7.1 *Staff*	*Synod Council*
8.0 *Ecumenical ministry*	
8.1 *Related to a synod*	*Synod Council*
8.2 *Related to more than one synod*	*Synod Council of one of the synods*
8.3 *National/international organization*	*Church Council*
9.0 *Inter-Lutheran ministry*	
9.1 *Related to a synod*	*Synod Council*
9.2 *Related to more than one synod*	*Synod Council of one of the synods*
9.3 *National/international organization*	*Church Council*
10.0 *Educational ministry*	
10.1 *ELCA-related seminary*	*Church Council upon request of board of Division for Ministry*
10.2 *Seminary unrelated to ELCA*	*Church Council upon request of board of Division for Ministry*
10.3 *ELCA-related college*	*Synod Council of the synod in which the college is located*
10.4 *College unrelated to ELCA*	*Synod Council of the synod in which the college is located*
10.5 *ELCA-related school*	*Synod Council of which the school is a part or, if related to several congregations, Synod Council of the synod in which the school is located*
10.6 *School unrelated to ELCA*	*Synod Council of the synod in which the school is located*
10.7 *Director/staff of a continuing education center related to Division for Ministry*	*Synod Council of the synod in which the main office of center is located upon the request of the board of Division for Ministry*
11.0 *Missionary ministry*	
11.1 *Outside United States*	*Church Council upon request of board of Division for Global Mission*
11.2 *Within United States*	*Church Council upon request of board of Division for Outreach*
12.0 *Unusual ministries*	*Synod Council or Church Council upon recommendation by Conference of Bishops*

7.53.   **Persons on the lay rosters of this church as defined herein shall be subject to discipline as set forth in the Constitution, Bylaws, and Continuing Resolutions of the Evangelical Lutheran Church in America.**

Licensure

7.60.01.

7.61.01.   When need exists to render Word and Sacrament ministry for a congregation or ministry of this church where it is not possible to provide appropriate ordained pastoral leadership, the synodical bishop—acting with the consent of the congregation or ministry, in consultation with the Synod Council, and in accord with standards and qualifications developed by the Division for Ministry, reviewed by the Conference of Bishops, and approved by the Church Council—may authorize a person rostered in other rostered ministry, or a non-rostered person who is a member of a congregation of the Evangelical Lutheran Church in America to offer this ministry. Such an individual shall be supervised by a pastor appointed by the synodical bishop; such service shall be rendered during its duration under the sacramental authority of the bishop as the synod's pastor. Such an individual will be trained and licensed to fulfill this ministry for a specified period of time and in a given location only. Authorization, remuneration, direct supervision, and accountability are to be determined by the appropriate synodical leadership according to churchwide standards and qualifications for this type of ministry. Authorization for such service shall be reviewed annually and renewed only when a demonstrated need remains for its continuation.

Chapter 8.
RELATIONSHIPS

8.10. Relationship between Congregations, Synods, and the Churchwide Organization

8.11. This church shall seek to function as people of God through congregations, synods, and the churchwide organization, all of which shall be interdependent. Each part, while fully the church, recognizes that it is not the whole church and therefore lives in a partnership relationship with the others.

8.11.01. References herein to the nature of the relationship between the three primary expressions of this church—congregations, synods, and the churchwide organization—as being interdependent or as being in a partnership relationship describe the mutual responsibility of these expressions in God's mission, and the fulfillment of the purposes of this church as described in Chapter 4, and do not imply or describe the creation of partnerships, co-ventures, agencies, or other legal relationships recognized in civil law.

8.12. The congregation shall include in its mission a life of worship and nurture for its members, and outreach in witness and service to its community.

8.13. The synod shall provide for pastoral care of the congregations, ordained ministers, and associates in ministry within its boundaries. It shall develop resources for the life and mission of its people and shall enlarge the ministries and extend the outreach into society on behalf of and in connection with the congregations and the churchwide organization.

8.14. The churchwide organization shall implement the extended mission of the Church, developing churchwide policies in consultation with the synods and congregations, entering into relationship with governmental, ecumenical, and societal agencies in accordance with accepted resolutions and/or in response to specific agreed-upon areas of responsibility.

8.15. Since congregations, synods, and the churchwide organization are partners that share in God's mission, all share in the responsibility to develop, implement, and strengthen the financial support program of this church.

8.16. In faithful participation in the mission of God in and through this church, congregations, synods, and the churchwide organization—as interdependent expressions of this church—shall be guided by the biblical and confessional commitments of this church. Each shall recognize that mission efforts must be shaped by both local needs and global awareness, by both individual witness and corporate endeavor, and by both distinctly Lutheran emphases and growing ecumenical cooperation.

(9-93) ELCA CONSTITUTION—CHAPTER 8 / 45

44 / ELCA CONSTITUTION—CHAPTER 7 (9-93)

Relationship through Other Organizational Units

8.20.

8.21. The regions shall serve to foster interdependent relationships among the churchwide organization, the synods, and the congregations and to assist them in exercising their mutual responsibilities.

8.22. Conferences, clusters, coalitions, or other area subdivisions shall serve to assist the congregations and synods in exercising their mutual responsibilities.

Relationship with Institutions and Agencies

8.30.

8.31. Seminaries. This church shall own, govern, and support seminaries for the preparation of persons for the ordained and other ministries and for continuing study on the part of ordained ministers and laypersons.

8.31.01. Each seminary shall be a seminary of this church, shall be incorporated, and shall be governed by its board of directors consistent with policies established by the Division for Ministry.

8.31.02. The board of directors of each seminary shall be nominated and elected in cooperation with the seminary involved, and consist of approximately 20-24 members, elected as follows:

a. One-fifth (rounded off to the nearest whole number) by the Division for Ministry.

b. Two members by the bishops of the supporting synods from among their number.

c. The remaining members by the supporting synods. The number to be elected by each synod and the length of the term shall be set forth in the governing documents of the seminary.

Elections shall be so arranged that the terms of all directors of any given seminary elected in any year shall commence simultaneously.

8.31.03. In accordance with the governing documents of each seminary, the board of directors shall elect the president of the seminary in consultation with the bishop of this church and the board of the Division for Ministry, elect and retain faculty and administrative officers, and approve educational policies and programs for persons preparing for public ministry.

The board shall exercise all other normal governance functions, including the granting of degrees, holding title to and managing all seminary property and assets, receiving gifts and bequests, establishing salaries for faculty and administrative officers, providing for the financial resources and fiscal contracts required to operate the seminary, and shall have authority to recruit students throughout this church.

8.31.04. The seminaries shall receive churchwide and synodical financial support. The amount of such support shall be determined annually through a consultation process involving seminaries, synods, and the Division for Ministry.

8.31.05. To implement financial support by this church, synods shall be assigned to specific seminaries in such manner as to attain equitable distribution of synods. Normally, all synods in a given region will be assigned to one seminary. Churchwide funds shall be distributed by the Division for Ministry, in order to ensure equitable financial support.

8.31.06. Seminaries shall provide their remaining financial requirements through tuition, fees, endowment income, and fund-raising programs. Fund-raising in the congregations of supporting synods, however, shall be conducted only upon approval of the synods. Funds for special churchwide tasks assigned to a seminary by the Division for Ministry shall be raised through the cooperative effort of the seminary and the Division for Ministry.

8.31.07. Aid to students preparing for the ministries of this church shall be administered by the seminaries under guidelines established by the Division for Ministry.

8.31.A87. *This church adopts the following goal: that it shall provide at least 50 percent of the support of each seminary's educational and general operating budget through a combination of churchwide and synodical appropriations.*

8.32. **Colleges and Universities. This church shall express its responsibility for higher education through its colleges and universities, its Division for Higher Education and Schools, and its synods. While variation is possible in college relationships across this church, this church recognizes the desirability of some degree of uniformity of relationship for colleges within the same region. Therefore, synods shall determine initial policies and thereafter review periodically such policies consistent with recommendations from the board of the Division for Higher Education and Schools and in consultation with that board and the colleges and universities within the region with respect to and consistent with the bylaws, as set forth herein.**

8.32.01. A variety of relationship patterns is possible including relationship with the Churchwide Assembly, the Division for Higher Education and Schools, a synod assembly, or a corporation whose voting members are, or have been elected by, synodical assemblies, other organizational units (conferences, clusters, etc.), or congregations.

8.32.02. Primary responsibility for recruiting members for its board belongs to each college. This responsibility is best exercised when appropriate structures of this church are substantially involved.

8.32.03. The college and the appropriate synods shall determine how many of the college board members are to be elected or ratified by the approved form of relationship as provided in 8.32.01.

8.32.04. The responsibility for initiating changes in constitutional documents rests with each college. Each college will reach agreement with the appropriate structures of this church as identified in 8.32.01. regarding changes in constitutional documents. This church's participation may range from prior consultation to final approval.

(9-93)   ELCA CONSTITUTION—CHAPTER 8 / 47

ELCA CONSTITUTION—CHAPTER 8   (9-93)

8.32.05. Representation of members of this church on college boards, limitation of terms for board members, whether or not college presidents shall be members of this church, and representation of bishops of synods on college boards shall be determined by each college and the appropriate synods.

8.32.06. Subject to approval by the appropriate synods, a college or university may be owned by a not-for-profit corporation that has voting members at least 90 percent of whom shall consist of members of the biennial Churchwide Assembly. Meetings of such corporations shall be held in conjunction with the Churchwide Assembly for the purpose of electing or ratifying members of the governing board and approving amendments in the governing documents. At least 75 percent of the members of the governing boards of such corporations shall be Lutheran and at least a majority shall be members of this church.

8.32.A91. *The relationship of this church to its colleges and universities shall be guided by policies fostering educational institutions dedicated to the Lutheran tradition wherein such institutions are an essential expression of God's mission in the world: faithful to the will of God as institutions providing quality instruction in religion and a lively ministry of worship, outreach, and service; diligent in their preparation of leaders committed to truth, excellence, and ethical values; and pledged to the well-being of students in the development of mind, body, and spirit.*

8.33. **Institutions and Agencies. This church shall seek to meet human needs through encouragement of its people to individual and corporate action, and through establishing, developing, recognizing, and supporting institutions and agencies that minister to people in their spiritual and temporal needs.**

8.33.01. Through its Division for Church in Society, this church shall, with church-affiliated agencies and institutions, develop criteria for their ministries, establish affiliations both within this church and within society, and carry out a comprehensive social ministry outreach.

8.40. **Relationship with Interchurch Agencies, Institutions, and Councils**

8.41. **The congregations, synods, social ministry institutions and agencies, and churchwide organization may establish or affiliate with interchurch agencies and councils in relationships that will reflect this church's objectives of sharing with other faith communities in study, dialogue, and common action, in accordance with adopted policies governing such associations.**

8.41.01. Policies governing ecumenical, inter-Lutheran, and interfaith activities shall be recommended by the bishop of this church to the Churchwide Assembly for its adoption.

8.41.02. Formal membership in interchurch agencies and/or councils shall be by action of the Churchwide Assembly in all relationships involving

national or international involvement, by the Synod Assembly in its geographic area, and by congregations in community settings, with each affiliation by any congregation, synod, or churchwide organization to be in accordance with the policies of this church.

Relationship with Independent Lutheran Organizations

8.50.

8.51. **This church may relate to independent Lutheran organizations.**

8.51.01. This church, through its Department for Ecumenical Affairs and by action of the Churchwide Assembly, shall establish the general policies to govern official relationships with independent Lutheran organizations that seek to relate with this church while maintaining their independence and autonomy.

Special Interest Conferences

8.60.

8.61. **This church cherishes the diversity of cultural and linguistic groups as they are brought together in the geographic synods, recognizing, however, that certain groups, for historical reasons, may be able to meet needs and share resources through special interest conferences, which for the present cannot occur in the regular life within the geographic synods.**

8.61.01. Because of both official and informal international contacts with other churches, the Danish Special Interest Conference, Finnish (Suomi) Special Interest Conference, German Lutheran Conference in North America, and Hungarian Special Interest Conference shall relate to this church through the Department for Ecumenical Affairs under the authority of the bishop of this church. Official contacts and relationships of the special interest conferences with leaders and representatives of other churches shall be coordinated through the Department for Ecumenical Affairs.

Chapter 9.
CONGREGATIONS

9.10. **Definition**

9.11. A congregation is a community of baptized persons whose existence depends on the proclamation of the Gospel and the administration of the sacraments and whose purpose is to worship God, to nurture its members, and to reach out in witness and service to the world. To this end it assembles regularly for worship and nurture, organizes and carries out ministry to its people and neighborhood, and co-operates with and supports the wider church to strive for the fulfillment of God's mission in the world.

9.20. **Criteria for Recognition and Reception**

9.21. This church shall recognize, receive, and maintain on the roster those congregations which by their practice as well as their governing documents:

 a. preach the Word, administer the sacraments, and carry out God's mission;

 b. accept this church's Confession of Faith;

 c. agree to the Statement of Purpose of this church;

 d. agree to call pastoral leadership from the clergy roster of this church in accordance with the call procedures of this church except in special circumstances and with the approval of the synodical bishop;

 e. agree to be responsible for their life as a Christian community; and

 f. agree to support the life and work of this church.

9.21.01. Approval of the synodical bishop, as required in 9.21.d., involves the bishop's attesting that a candidate for the roster of ordained ministers of this church has been approved, in conformity with the governing documents and policies of this church, through the synodical candidacy process for first call as a seminary graduate or for call in this church through approval for reception into this church from another Lutheran church body or another Christian church body. Consultation with the synodical bishop in accordance with the call procedures and governing documents of this church and the synod is required for the calling of pastoral leadership from among persons on the roster of ordained ministers of this church or persons who are approved as eligible candidates for the roster of ordained ministers of this church.

9.21.A87. *Congregations which are members of The American Lutheran Church, The Association of Evangelical Lutheran Churches, and the Lutheran Church in America on December 31, 1987, and so certified by said church bodies shall be recognized as congregations of this church.*

9.22. All congregations of this church shall abide by the provisions of 9.21., 9.62., and 7.46. The judgment on whether a congregation meets the criteria listed in 9.21. shall be made by this church through the synod of this church in whose territory the congregation is located.

9.23. A recognized and received congregation that is part of this church shall, when legally possible, be incorporated and may:

 a. own property and be responsible for its care; and

 b. call or employ staff.

9.25. A congregation newly formed by this church and any congregation seeking recognition and reception by this church shall:

 a. Accept the criteria for recognition and reception as a congregation of this church, fulfill the functions of the congregation, and accept the governance provisions as provided in Chapter 9 of the ELCA constitution and bylaws.

 b. Adopt governing documents that include fully and without alterations the Preamble, Chapter 1, where applicable, and all provisions of Chapters 2, 3, 4, 5, 6, 7, 8, 9, 15, 16, 17, and 18 in the Model Constitution for Congregations consistent with requirements of this constitution and the constitution for synods of this church. Bylaws and continuing resolutions, appropriate for inclusion in these chapters and not in conflict with the required provisions in the Model Constitution for Congregations, the constitution of the synod, or the Constitution, Bylaws, and Continuing Resolutions of the Evangelical Lutheran Church in America, may be adopted as described in Chapters 16 and 18 of the Model Constitution for Congregations.

 c. Accept the commitments expected of all congregations of the ELCA as stated in C6.01., C6.02., and C6.03. of the Model Constitution for Congregations.

If a congregation is a member of another church body, the leaders of the congregation first should consult with the appropriate authorities of that church body before taking action to leave its current church body. After such consultation, leaders of the congregation should make contact with the ELCA synod bishop or staff where the congregation is located.

Recognition and reception into this church of transferring or independent congregations by the Evangelical Lutheran Church in America is based on the judgment of the synod and action by the synod through the Synod Council and Synod Assembly. The synod bishop shall provide for prompt reporting of such additions to the secretary of this church for addition to the register of congregations.

9.30. **Reservation of Authority**

9.31. Congregations of this church shall have authority in all matters that are not assigned by the constitution and bylaws of this church to synods and the churchwide organization.

9.40. **Functions**

9.41. The congregation shall:

a. Provide services of worship at which the Word of God is preached and the sacraments are administered.

b. Provide pastoral care and assist all members to participate in this ministry.

c. Challenge, equip, and support all members in carrying out their calling in their daily life and in their congregation.

d. Teach the Word of God.

e. Witness to the reconciling Word of God in Christ, reaching out to all people.

f. Respond to human need, work for justice and peace, care for the sick and the suffering, and participate responsibly in society.

g. Motivate its members to provide financial support for the congregation's ministry and the ministry of the synod and the churchwide organization.

h. Foster and participate in interdependent relationships with other congregations, the synod, and the churchwide organization.

i. Foster and participate in ecumenical relationships consistent with churchwide policy.

9.50. **Governance**

9.51. Each congregation shall structure itself in such a way as to involve its members in fulfilling the definition, purpose, and functions of a congregation.

9.52. The governing documents of congregations recognized at the establishment of this church shall continue to govern such congregations. When such a congregation wishes to amend any provision of its governing documents, the governing documents of that congregation shall be so amended as to conform to 9.25.b. The synod responsible for the review of such amendments may permit, for good cause, a congregation to retain particular unamended provisions in the congregation's governing documents that were in force at the establishment of this church.

9.52.A87. *The Church Council, in cooperation with the synods, shall develop a process for congregations whose governing documents have been accepted into the church under 9.52. to review those documents within four years of the establishment of this church and compare them with* the elements of the *Model Constitution for Congregations* listed in 9.53.01. *Congregations are encouraged to resolve significant conflicts between their governing documents and the Model Constitution for Congregations.*

9.53. **Each congregation shall have governing documents, no terms of which shall conflict with provision 9.21. Subject to the provisions of 9.52., these documents shall contain the elements listed in the bylaws.**

9.53.01. The governing documents of congregations shall include:

a. the Confession of Faith;

b. the Statement of Purpose;

c. provisions describing the congregation's relationship to this church;

d. a process for calling a pastor;

e. a listing of the duties of a pastor;

f. provisions describing the role of the pastor in the governance of the congregation;

g. a process for removal of a pastor;

h. provisions regulating the disposition of property;

i. a legislative process;

j. an enumeration of officers with definition of authority and functions of each;

k. a definition of each structural component (e.g., committees, boards); and

l. a process for the discipline of members.

9.53.02. A Model Constitution for Congregations shall be provided by this church. Amendments to the Model Constitution for Congregations shall be made in the same manner as prescribed in Chapter 22 for amendments of the bylaws of this church.

9.53.03. Each congregation shall provide a copy of its governing documents to the synod. All proposed changes in the constitution or incorporation documents of a congregation shall be referred to the synod with which the congregation is affiliated. The synod shall approve or disapprove the proposed changes within 120 days of receipt thereof, and shall notify the congregation of its decision; in the absence of a decision, the changes shall go into effect.

The synod shall recognize that congregations may organize themselves in a manner which they deem most appropriate and that there are a variety of ways in which the required elements may be stated.

9.53.04. Each congregation shall take the necessary steps to protect its members and this church from liability.

9.53.05. Congregations shall normally maintain a fiscal year of January 1 through December 31.

9.53.06. A congregation considering a relocation shall confer with the bishop of the synod in which it is territorially located before any steps are taken leading to such action. The approval of the Synod Council shall be received before any such action is effected.

9.53.07. Congregations shall have the right to petition this church. Petitions shall be addressed to the synod to which the congregation relates for response by the synod, or, at the discretion of the synod, for forwarding to the Churchwide Assembly.

Termination of Relationship

9.60.

9.61. The relationship between a congregation and this church may be terminated in one of the following ways:

a. The congregation takes action to dissolve.

b. The congregation ceases to exist.

c. The congregation is no longer recognized by this church under the disciplinary provisions of Chapter 20.

d. The congregation terminates its relationship according to the procedure outlined in 9.62.

e. The membership of the congregation becomes so scattered or diminished in numbers as to make it impracticable for such congregation to fulfill the purposes for which it was organized. In such case, the synod, in order to protect the property from waste and deterioration, through the Synod Council or trustees appointed by it, may take charge and control of the property of the congregation to hold, manage, and convey the same on behalf of the synod. The congregation shall have the right to appeal the decision to the Synod Assembly.

9.62. A congregation may terminate its relationship with this church by the following procedure:

a. A resolution indicating desire to terminate its relationship must be adopted at a legally called and conducted special meeting of the congregation by a two-thirds majority of the voting members present.

b. The secretary of the congregation shall submit a copy of the resolution to the synodical bishop and shall mail a copy of the resolution to voting members of the congregation. This notice shall be submitted within 10 days after the resolution has been adopted.

c. The bishop of the synod shall consult with the congregation during a period of at least 90 days.

d. If the congregation, after consultation, still desires to terminate its relationship, such action may be taken at a legally called and conducted special meeting by a two-thirds majority of the voting members present, at which meeting the synodical bishop or an authorized representative shall be present. Notice of the meeting shall be mailed to all voting members at least 10 days in advance of the meeting.

e. A certified copy of the resolution to terminate its relationship shall be sent to the synodical bishop, at which time the relationship between the congregation and this church shall be terminated.

f. Notice of termination shall be forwarded by the synodical bishop to the secretary of this church and published in the periodical of this church.

g. Congregations which had been members of the Lutheran Church in America shall be required, in addition to the foregoing provisions in 9.62., to receive synodical approval before terminating their membership in this church.

h. Congregations that are established by the Evangelical Lutheran Church in America shall be required, in addition to the foregoing provisions in 9.62., to receive synodical approval before terminating their membership in this church.

Ownership of Property

9.70.

9.71. Subject to the provisions of 9.52., the following shall govern the ownership of property by congregations of this church:

a. Title to property shall reside in the congregation. The congregation may dispose of its property as it determines, subject to any self-accepted indebtedness or other self-accepted restrictions.

b. Title to the undisposed property of a congregation that ceases to exist shall pass to the synod of this church to which the congregation is related.

c. Title to the property of a congregation that is no longer recognized by this church as a result of discipline shall continue to reside in the congregation.

d. Title to the property of a congregation that has acted to terminate its relationship with this church by the provisions of 9.62. to relate to another Lutheran church body shall continue to reside in the congregation.

e. Title to the property of a congregation that has acted to terminate its relationship with this church by the provisions of 9.62. to become independent or to relate to a non-Lutheran church body shall continue to reside in the congregation only with the consent of the Synod Council. The Synod Council, after consultation with the congregation by an established synodical process, may give approval to the request to become independent or to relate to a non-Lutheran church body, in which case title shall remain with the majority of the congregation. If the Synod Council fails to give such approval, title shall remain with those members who desire to continue as a congregation of this church.

9.80. Discipline of Congregations

See Chapter 20.

Chapter 10.
SYNODS

10.01. This church shall be divided into synods, the names and boundaries of which shall be determined by the Churchwide Assembly and included in the bylaws.

10.01.10. Names and Boundaries

10.01.11. The names and boundaries of the synods shall be:

Synod 1.A—Alaska. The state of ALASKA.

Synod 1.B—Northwest Washington. The counties of Island, King (north), San Juan, Skagit, Snohomish, Whatcom in the state of WASHINGTON.

Synod 1.C—Southwestern Washington. The counties of Clallam, Clark, Cowlitz, Grays Harbor, Jefferson, King (south), Kitsap, Lewis, Mason, Pacific, Pierce, Skamania, Thurston, Wahkiakum in the state of WASHINGTON.

Synod 1.D—Eastern Washington-Idaho. The state of IDAHO; the counties of Adams, Asotin, Benton, Chelan, Columbia, Douglas, Ferry, Franklin, Garfield, Grant, Kittitas, Klickitat, Lincoln, Okanogan, Pend Oreille, Spokane, Stevens, Walla Walla, Whitman, Yakima in the state of WASHINGTON.

Synod 1.E—Oregon. The state of OREGON.

Synod 1.F—Montana. The state of MONTANA; and the counties of Park and Washakie in the state of WYOMING.

Synod 2.A—Sierra Pacific. The counties of Alameda, Alpine, Amador, Butte, Calaveras, Colusa, Contra Costa, Del Norte, El Dorado, Fresno, Glenn, Humboldt, Inyo, Kings, Lake, Lassen, Madera, Marin, Mariposa, Mendocino, Merced, Modoc, Mono, Monterey, Napa, Nevada, Placer, Plumas, Sacramento, San Benito, San Francisco, San Joaquin, San Mateo, Santa Clara, Santa Cruz, Shasta, Sierra, Siskiyou, Solano, Sonoma, Stanislaus, Sutter, Tehama, Trinity, Tulare, Tuolumne, Yolo, Yuba in the state of CALIFORNIA; the counties of Churchill, Douglas, Elko, Eureka, Humboldt, Lander, Lyon, Mineral, Pershing, Storey, Washoe, White Pine and the consolidated municipality of Carson City in the state of NEVADA.

Synod 2.B—Southern California (West). The counties of Kern, Los Angeles, San Luis Obispo, Santa Barbara, Ventura in the state of CALIFORNIA.

Synod 2.C—Pacifica. The counties of Imperial, Orange, Riverside, San Bernardino, San Diego in the state of CALIFORNIA; the state of HAWAII.

Synod 2.D—Grand Canyon. The state of ARIZONA; the counties of Clark, Esmeralda, Lincoln, Nye in the state of NEVADA.

Synod 2.E—Rocky Mountain. The states of COLORADO; NEW

MEXICO; UTAH; and WYOMING, excluding the counties of Park and Washakie; the counties of Brewster, Culberson, El Paso, Hudspeth, Jeff Davis, Loving, Presidio, Reeves, Ward, Winkler in the state of TEXAS.

Synod 3.A—Western North Dakota. The counties of Adams, Benson (the town/parishes of Esmond), Billings, Bottineau, Bowman, Burke, Burleigh, Divide, Dunn, Emmons, Golden Valley, Grant, Hettinger, Kidder (excluding the Woodworth Parish of Pettibone), Logan (excluding the towns/parishes of Fredonia and Gackle), McHenry, McIntosh, McKenzie, McLean, Mercer, Morton, Mountrail, Oliver, Pierce (excluding the Wolford Parish in the northeastern part), Renville, Rolette, Sheridan, Sioux, Slope, Stark, Towner, Ward, Wells, Williams in the state of NORTH DAKOTA; and the parishes of Lemmon, Lodgepole, Ralph, and Shadehill in the state of SOUTH DAKOTA.

Synod 3.B—Eastern North Dakota. The counties of Barnes, Benson (east of and including the towns/parishes of Maddock and Leeds), Cass, Cavalier, Dickey, Eddy, Foster, Grand Forks, Griggs, Kidder (the Woodworth Parish of Pettibone), LaMoure, Logan (the towns/parishes of Fredonia and Gackle), Nelson, Pembina, Pierce (the northeastern part including the Wolford Parish), Ramsey, Ransom, Richland, Sargent, Steele, Stutsman, Traill, Walsh in the state of NORTH DAKOTA.

Synod 3.C—South Dakota. The state of SOUTH DAKOTA with the exception of the township of Sioux Valley in Union County.

Synod 3.D—Northwestern Minnesota. The counties of Becker, Beltrami, Clay, Clearwater, Douglas, Grant, Hubbard, Kittson, Lake of the Woods, Mahnomen, Marshall, Norman, Otter Tail, Pennington, Polk, Red Lake, Roseau, Todd, Traverse, Wadena, Wilkin in the state of MINNESOTA.

Synod 3.E—Northeastern Minnesota. The counties of Aitkin, Carlton, Cass, Cook, Crow Wing, Itasca, Kanabec, Koochiching, Lake, Mille Lacs, Morrison, Pine, St. Louis in the state of MINNESOTA.

Synod 3.F—Southwestern Minnesota. The counties of Benton, Big Stone, Brown, Chippewa, Cottonwood, Jackson, Kandiyohi, Lac qui Parle, Lincoln, Lyon, McLeod, Martin, Meeker, Murray, Nicollet, Nobles, Pipestone, Pope, Redwood, Renville, Rock, Sherburne (part), Sibley, Stearns, Stevens, Swift, Watonwan, Wright (part), Yellow Medicine in the state of MINNESOTA.

Synod 3.G—Minneapolis Area. The counties of Anoka, Carver, Hennepin, Isanti, Scott, Sherburne (part), Wright (part) in the state of MINNESOTA.

Synod 3.H—Saint Paul Area. The counties of Chisago, Dakota, Ramsey, Washington in the state of MINNESOTA.

Synod 3.I—Southeastern Minnesota. The counties of Blue Earth, Dodge, Faribault, Fillmore, Freeborn, Goodhue, Houston, Le Sueur, Mower, Olmsted, Rice, Steele, Wabasha, Waseca, Winona in the state of MINNESOTA.

Synod 4.A.—Nebraska. The state of NEBRASKA.

Synod 4.B—Central States. The states of MISSOURI and KANSAS.

Synod 4.C—Arkansas-Oklahoma. The states of ARKANSAS and OKLAHOMA.

Synod 4.D—Northern Texas-Northern Louisiana. The counties of Andrews, Archer, Armstrong, Bailey, Baylor, Bell, Borden, Bosque, Bowie, Briscoe, Brown, Callahan, Camp, Carson, Cass, Castro, Childress, Clay, Cochran, Coke, Coleman, Collin, Collingsworth, Comanche, Concho, Cooke, Coryell, Cottle, Crosby, Dallam, Dallas, Dawson, Deaf Smith, Delta, Denton, Dickens, Donley, Eastland, Ector, Ellis, Erath, Falls, Fannin, Fisher, Floyd, Foard, Franklin, Gaines, Garza, Glasscock, Gray, Grayson, Gregg, Hale, Hall, Hamilton, Hansford, Hardeman, Harrison, Hartley, Haskell, Hemphill, Henderson, Hill, Hockley, Hood, Hopkins, Howard, Hunt, Hutchinson, Irion, Jack, Johnson, Jones, Kaufman, Kent, King, Knox, Lamar, Lamb, Lampasas, Limestone, Lipscomb, Lubbock, Lynn, McCulloch, McLennan, Marion, Martin, Midland, Mills, Mitchell, Montague, Moore, Morris, Motley, Navarro, Nolan, Ochiltree, Oldham, Palo Pinto, Panola, Parker, Parmer, Potter, Rains, Randall, Reagan, Red River, Roberts, Rockwall, Runnels, Rusk, San Saba, Scurry, Shackelford, Sherman, Smith, Somervell, Stephens, Sterling, Stonewall, Swisher, Tarrant, Taylor, Terry, Throckmorton, Titus, Tom Green, Upshur, Van Zandt, Wheeler, Wichita, Wilbarger, Wise, Wood, Yoakum, Young in the state of TEXAS; the parishes of Bienville, Bossier, Caddo, Caldwell, Catahoula, Claiborne, Concordia, DeSoto, East Carroll, Franklin, Grant, Jackson, LaSalle, Lincoln, Madison, Morehouse, Natchitoches, Ouachita, Red River, Richland, Sabine, Tensas, Union, Webster, West Carroll, Winn in the state of LOUISIANA.

Synod 4.E—Southwestern Texas. The counties of Aransas, Atascosa, Bandera, Bastrop, Bee, Bexar, Blanco, Brooks, Burnet, Caldwell, Calhoun, Cameron, Comal, Crane, Crockett, De Witt, Dimmit, Duval, Edwards, Frio, Gillespie, Goliad, Gonzales, Guadalupe, Hays, Hidalgo, Jackson, Jim Hogg, Jim Wells, Karnes, Kendall, Kenedy, Kerr, Kimble, Kinney, Kleberg, La Salle, Lavaca, Lee, Live Oak, Llano, McMullen, Mason, Maverick, Medina, Menard, Milam, Nueces, Pecos, Real, Refugio, San Patricio, Schleicher, Starr, Sutton, Terrell, Travis, Upton, Uvalde, Val Verde, Victoria, Webb, Willacy, Williamson, Wilson, Zapata, Zavala in the state of TEXAS.

Synod 4.F—Texas-Louisiana Gulf Coast. The counties of Anderson, Angelina, Austin, Brazoria, Brazos, Burleson, Chambers, Cherokee, Colorado, Fayette, Fort Bend, Freestone, Galveston, Grimes, Hardin, Harris, Houston, Jasper, Jefferson, Leon, Liberty, Madison, Matagorda, Montgomery, Nacogdoches, Newton, Orange, Polk, Robertson, Sabine, San Augustine, San Jacinto, Shelby, Trinity, Tyler, Walker, Waller, Washington, Wharton in the state of TEXAS; the parishes of Acadia, Allen, Ascension, Assumption, Avoyelles, Beauregard, Calcasieu,

Cameron, East Baton Rouge, East Feliciana, Evangeline, Iberia, Iberville, Jefferson, Jefferson Davis, Lafayette, LaFourche, Livingston, Orleans, Plaquemines, Pointe Coupee, Rapides, St. Bernard, St. Charles, St. Helena, St. James, St. John the Baptist, St. Landry, St. Martin, St. Mary, St. Tammany, Tangipahoa, Terrebonne, Vermilion, Vernon, Washington, West Baton Rouge, West Feliciana in the state of LOUISIANA.

Synod 5.A—Metropolitan Chicago. The counties of Cook, DuPage, Kane, Lake in the state of ILLINOIS.

Synod 5.B—Northern Illinois. The counties of Boone, Bureau, Carroll, De Kalb, Grundy, Henderson, Henry, Jo Daviess, Kendall, Knox, La Salle, Lee, McHenry, Mercer, Ogle, Putnam, Rock Island, Stephenson, Warren, Whiteside, Will, Winnebago in the state of ILLINOIS.

Synod 5.C—Central/Southern Illinois. The counties of Adams, Alexander, Bond, Brown, Calhoun, Cass, Champaign, Christian, Clark, Clay, Clinton, Coles, Crawford, Cumberland, De Witt, Douglas, Edgar, Edwards, Effingham, Fayette, Ford, Franklin, Fulton, Gallatin, Greene, Hamilton, Hancock, Hardin, Iroquois, Jackson, Jasper, Jefferson, Jersey, Johnson, Kankakee, Lawrence, Livingston, Logan, McDonough, McLean, Macon, Macoupin, Madison, Marion, Marshall, Mason, Massac, Menard, Monroe, Montgomery, Morgan, Moultrie, Peoria, Perry, Piatt, Pike, Pope, Pulaski, Randolph, Richland, St. Clair, Saline, Sangamon, Schuyler, Scott, Shelby, Stark, Tazewell, Union, Vermilion, Wabash, Washington, Wayne, White, Williamson, Woodford in the state of ILLINOIS.

Synod 5.D—Southeastern Iowa. The counties of Appanoose, Benton, Boone, Cedar, Clarke, Clinton, Dallas (east), Davis, Decatur, Des Moines, Henry, Iowa, Jackson (south), Jasper, Jefferson, Johnson, Jones, Keokuk, Lee, Linn, Louisa, Lucas, Madison, Mahaska, Marion, Marshall, Monroe, Muscatine, Polk, Poweshiek, Scott, Story (south), Tama (south), Van Buren, Wapello, Warren, Washington, Wayne in the state of IOWA.

Synod 5.E—Western Iowa. The counties of Adair, Adams, Audubon, Buena Vista, Calhoun, Carroll, Cass, Cherokee, Clay, Crawford, Dallas (west), Dickinson, Emmet, Fremont, Greene, Guthrie, Hamilton (west), Hancock, Harrison, Humboldt, Ida, Kossuth, Lyon, Mills, Monona, Montgomery, O'Brien, Osceola, Page, Palo Alto, Plymouth, Pocahontas, Pottawattamie, Ringgold, Sac, Shelby, Sioux, Taylor, Union, Webster, Winnebago, Woodbury, Wright (west) in the state of IOWA, and the township of Sioux Valley, Union County, in the state of SOUTH DAKOTA.

Synod 5.F—Northeastern Iowa. The counties of Allamakee, Black Hawk, Bremer, Buchanan, Butler, Cerro Gordo, Chickasaw, Clayton, Delaware, Dubuque, Fayette, Floyd, Franklin, Grundy, Hamilton (east), Hardin, Howard, Jackson (north), Mitchell, Story (north), Tama (north), Winneshiek, Worth, Wright (east) in the state of IOWA.

Synod 5.G—Northern Great Lakes. The counties of Florence, Forest, Iron, Marinette, Oneida, Vilas in the state of WISCONSIN; the counties in the Upper Peninsula in the state of MICHIGAN.

Synod 5.H—Northwest Synod of Wisconsin. The counties of Ashland, Barron, Bayfield, Buffalo (north), Burnett, Chippewa, Clark, Douglas, Dunn, Eau Claire, Jackson (north), Marathon (west), Pepin, Pierce, Polk, Price, Rusk, St. Croix, Sawyer, Taylor, Trempealeau (north), Washburn, Wood (northwest corner) in the state of WISCONSIN.

Synod 5.I—East-Central Synod of Wisconsin. The counties of Brown, Calumet, Door, Fond Du Lac, Green Lake, Kewaunee, Langlade, Lincoln, Manitowoc, Marathon (east), Marquette, Menominee, Oconto, Outagamie, Portage, Shawano, Waupaca, Waushara, Winnebago, Wood (southeast) in the state of WISCONSIN.

Synod 5.J—Greater Milwaukee. The counties of Kenosha, Milwaukee, Ozaukee, Racine, Sheboygan, Washington, Waukesha in the state of WISCONSIN.

Synod 5.K—South-Central Synod of Wisconsin. The counties of Columbia, Dane, Dodge, Grant, Green, Iowa, Jefferson, Lafayette, Rock, Sauk, Walworth in the state of WISCONSIN.

Synod 5.L—LaCrosse Area. The counties of Adams, Buffalo (south), Crawford, Jackson (south), Juneau, La Crosse, Monroe, Richland, Trempealeau (south), Vernon in the state of WISCONSIN.

Synod 6.A—Southeast Michigan. The counties of Genesee, Lapeer, Lenawee, Livingston, Macomb, Monroe, Oakland, Saint Clair, Shiawassee, Washtenaw, Wayne in the state of MICHIGAN.

Synod 6.B—North/West Lower Michigan. The counties of Alcona, Allegan, Alpena, Antrim, Arenac, Barry, Bay, Benzie, Berrien, Branch, Calhoun, Cass, Charlevoix, Cheboygan, Clare, Clinton, Crawford, Eaton, Emmet, Gladwin, Grand Traverse, Gratiot, Hillsdale, Huron, Ingham, Ionia, Iosco, Isabella, Jackson, Kalamazoo, Kalkaska, Kent, Lake, Leelanau, Manistee, Mason, Mecosta, Midland, Missaukee, Montcalm, Montmorency, Muskegon, Newaygo, Oceana, Ogemaw, Osceola, Oscoda, Otsego, Ottawa, Presque Isle, Roscommon, St. Joseph, Saginaw, Sanilac, Tuscola, Van Buren, Wexford in the state of MICHIGAN.

Synod 6.C—Indiana-Kentucky. The states of INDIANA and KENTUCKY.

Synod 6.D—Northwestern Ohio. The counties of Allen, Auglaize, Crawford, Defiance, Erie, Fulton, Hancock, Hardin, Henry, Huron, Lucas, Marion, Mercer, Morrow, Ottawa, Paulding, Putnam, Sandusky, Seneca, Van Wert, Williams, Wood, Wyandot in the state of OHIO.

Synod 6.E—Northeastern Ohio. The counties of Ashland, Ashtabula, Carroll, Columbiana, Cuyahoga, Geauga, Harrison, Holmes, Jefferson, Lake, Lorain, Mahoning, Medina, Portage, Richland, Stark, Summit, Trumbull, Tuscarawas, Wayne in the state of OHIO.

Synod 6.F—Southern Ohio. The counties of Adams, Athens, Belmont, Brown, Butler, Champaign, Clark, Clermont, Clinton, Coshocton, Darke, Delaware, Fairfield, Fayette, Franklin, Gallia, Greene, Guernsey, Hamilton, Highland, Hocking, Jackson, Knox, Lawrence, Licking, Logan, Madison, Meigs, Miami, Monroe, Montgomery, Morgan, Muskingum, Noble, Perry, Pickaway, Pike, Preble, Ross, Scioto, Shelby, Union, Vinton, Warren, Washington in the state of OHIO.

Synod 7.A—New Jersey. The state of NEW JERSEY.

Synod 7.B—New England. The states of CONNECTICUT; MAINE; MASSACHUSETTS; NEW HAMPSHIRE; RHODE ISLAND; and VERMONT; and the counties of Clinton, Essex, and Franklin in the state of NEW YORK.

Synod 7.C—Metropolitan New York. The counties of Bronx, Dutchess, Kings, Nassau, New York, Orange, Putnam, Queens, Richmond, Rockland, Suffolk, Sullivan, Ulster, Westchester in the state of NEW YORK.

Synod 7.D—Upstate New York. The counties of Albany, Allegany, Broome, Cattaraugus, Cayuga, Chautauqua, Chemung, Chenango, Columbia, Cortland, Delaware, Erie, Fulton, Genesee, Greene, Hamilton, Herkimer, Jefferson, Lewis, Livingston, Madison, Monroe, Montgomery, Niagara, Oneida, Onondaga, Ontario, Orleans, Oswego, Otsego, Rensselaer, St. Lawrence, Saratoga, Schenectady, Schoharie, Schuyler, Seneca, Steuben, Tioga, Tompkins, Warren, Washington, Wayne, Wyoming, Yates in the state of NEW YORK.

Synod 7.E—Northeastern Pennsylvania. The counties of Berks, Bradford, Carbon, Lackawanna, Lehigh, Luzerne, Monroe, Northampton, Pike, Schuylkill, Sullivan, Susquehanna, Wayne, Wyoming in the state of PENNSYLVANIA.

Synod 7.F—Southeastern Pennsylvania. The counties of Bucks, Chester, Delaware, Montgomery, Philadelphia in the state of PENNSYLVANIA.

Synod 7.G—Slovak Zion. A non-geographic synod consisting of congregations distinctively Slovak in language or antecedents.

Synod 8.A—Northwestern Pennsylvania. The counties of Armstrong (part), Cameron, Clarion, Crawford, Elk, Erie, Forest, Indiana, Jefferson, McKean, Mercer, Potter, Venango, Warren in the state of PENNSYLVANIA.

Synod 8.B—Southwestern Pennsylvania. The counties of Allegheny, Armstrong (part), Beaver, Butler, Fayette, Greene, Lawrence, Washington, Westmoreland in the state of PENNSYLVANIA.

Synod 8.C—Allegheny. The counties of Bedford, Blair, Cambria, Centre, Clearfield, Huntingdon, Somerset in the state of PENNSYLVANIA.

Synod 8.D—Lower Susquehanna. The counties of Adams, Cumberland, Dauphin, Franklin, Fulton, Lancaster, Lebanon, Perry, York in the state of PENNSYLVANIA.

Synod 8.E—Upper Susquehanna. The counties of Clinton, Columbia, Juniata, Lycoming, Mifflin, Montour, Northumberland, Snyder, Tioga, Union in the state of PENNSYLVANIA.

Synod 8.F—Delaware-Maryland. The state of DELAWARE; the city of Baltimore and the counties of Allegany, Anne Arundel, Baltimore, Caroline, Carroll, Cecil, Dorchester, Frederick, Harford, Howard, Kent, Queen Anne's, Somerset, Talbot, Washington, Wicomico, Worcester in the state of MARYLAND; the counties of Accomack, Northampton in the state of VIRGINIA.

Synod 8.G—Metropolitan Washington, D.C. The District of Columbia; the counties of Calvert, Charles, Montgomery, Prince Georges, St. Mary's in the state of MARYLAND; the counties of Arlington, Fairfax, Loudoun, Prince William and the independent cities within the territory of these counties in the state of VIRGINIA; BERMUDA.

Synod 8.H—West Virginia-Western Maryland. The county of Garrett in the state of MARYLAND; the state of WEST VIRGINIA.

Synod 9.A—Virginia. The counties of Albemarle, Alleghany, Amelia, Amherst, Appomattox, Augusta, Bath, Bedford, Bland, Botetourt, Brunswick, Buchanan, Buckingham, Campbell, Caroline, Carroll, Charles City, Charlotte, Chesterfield, Clarke, Craig, Culpeper, Cumberland, Dickenson, Dinwiddie, Essex, Fauquier, Floyd, Fluvanna, Franklin, Frederick, Giles, Gloucester, Goochland, Grayson, Greene, Greensville, Halifax, Hanover, Henrico, Henry, Highland, Isle of Wight, James City, King and Queen, King George, King William, Lancaster, Lee, Louisa, Lunenburg, Madison, Mathews, Mecklenburg, Middlesex, Montgomery, Nelson, New Kent, Northumberland, Nottoway, Orange, Page, Patrick, Pittsylvania, Powhatan, Prince Edward, Prince George, Pulaski, Rappahannock, Richmond, Roanoke, Rockbridge, Rockingham, Russell, Scott, Shenandoah, Smyth, Southampton, Spotsylvania, Stafford, Surry, Sussex, Tazewell, Warren, Washington, Westmoreland, Wise, Wythe, York and the independent cities within the territory of these counties in the state of VIRGINIA.

Synod 9.B—North Carolina. The state of NORTH CAROLINA.

Synod 9.C—South Carolina. The state of SOUTH CAROLINA.

Synod 9.D—Southeastern. The states of ALABAMA; GEORGIA; MISSISSIPPI; and TENNESSEE.

Synod 9.E—Florida-Bahamas. The state of FLORIDA; the BAHAMAS.

Synod 9.F—Caribbean. The commonwealth of PUERTO RICO; the territory of the VIRGIN ISLANDS.

10.02. **Each congregation, except those which are in partnership with the Slovak Zion Synod, shall establish a relationship with the synod in whose territory it is located.**

10.02.01. The Slovak Zion Synod shall continue as a nongeographic synod of this church. In all other respects it shall be bound by the provisions of the constitution and bylaws of this church. In addition, it shall enter into relationships with geographic synods in order to provide opportunities for congregations, ordained ministers, and other leaders to share in the programmatic services of such synods, workshops, and conferences. It shall also periodically review and evaluate its ministries to ascertain their continuing effectiveness.

10.02.02. Any congregation in a border area desiring to change its synod relationship may do so upon approval of the synod assemblies of the synods concerned, which shall report any such change to the Churchwide Assembly.

10.02.03. Within the territory of each geographic synod, the synod, in keeping with criteria and procedures proposed by the Division for Outreach and approved by the Church Council, may acknowledge certain authorized worshiping communities—such as developing ministries, preaching points, or chapels—as related to the synod and part of the synod's life and mission. Such authorized worshiping communities of the synod shall accept and adhere to the Confession of Faith and Statement of Purpose of this church, shall be served by leadership under the criteria of this church, and shall be subject to the discipline of this church.

10.10. **Incorporation and Constitution**

10.11. Each synod shall be incorporated. The articles of incorporation of each synod in existence on January 1, 1988, shall continue to govern such synods. The articles of incorporation of each synod organized after December 31, 1987, shall be submitted to the Church Council for ratification before filing. Amendments to the articles of incorporation of all synods shall be submitted to the Church Council for ratification before filing.

10.12. Each synod shall have a constitution, which shall become effective upon ratification by the Church Council. Amendments thereto shall be subject to like ratification, provided, however, that an amendment which is identical to a provision of the Constitution for Synods shall be deemed to have been ratified upon its adoption and the Church Council shall be given prompt notification of its adoption.

10.13. The Constitution for Synods contains mandatory provisions that incorporate and record therein provisions of the constitution and bylaws of this church. Amendments to mandatory provisions incorporating constitutional provisions of this church shall be made in the same manner as prescribed in Chapter 22 for amendments to the constitution of this church. Amendments to mandatory provisions incorporating bylaw provisions of this church and amendments to non-mandatory provisions shall be made in the same manner as prescribed in Chapter 22 for amendments to the bylaws of this church.

10.20.

10.21. **Purpose**

Each synod, in partnership with the churchwide organization, shall bear primary responsibility for the oversight of the life and mission of this church in its territory. In fulfillment of this role, the synod shall:

a. Provide for the pastoral care of congregations, ordained ministers, and associates in ministry in the synod, including:

  1) approving candidates for the ordained ministry in cooperation with the appropriate seminaries of this church, which may be done through multi-synodical committees;

  2) authorizing ordinations and ordaining on behalf of this church;

  3) certifying associates in ministry, which may be done through multi-synodical committees;

  4) consulting in the calling process for ordained ministers and in the selection of associates in ministry.

b. Provide for leadership recruitment, preparation, and support in accordance with churchwide standards and policies, including:

  1) nurturing and supporting congregations and lay leaders;

  2) seeking and recruiting qualified candidates for the rostered ministries of this church;

  3) making provision for pastoral care, call or appointment review, and guidance;

  4) encouraging and supporting persons on the rosters of this church in stewardship of their abilities, care of self, and pursuit of continuing education to undergird their effectiveness of service; and

  5) supporting recruitment of leaders for this church's colleges, universities, seminaries, and social ministry organizations.

c. Provide for discipline of congregations, ordained ministers, and persons on the official lay rosters; as well as for termination of call, appointment, adjudication, and appeals consistent with the procedures established by this church in Chapter 20 of the ELCA constitution and bylaws.

d. Foster organizations for youth, women, and men, and organizations for language or ethnic communities.

e. Plan for the mission of this church in the synod, initiating and developing policy, and implementing programs, consistent with churchwide policy, including:

  1) ecumenical guidance and encouragement;

  2) development of new ministries, redevelopment of existing ministries, and support and assistance in the conclusion, if necessary, of a particular ministry;

3) leadership and encouragement of congregations in their evangelism efforts;

4) development of relationships to and participation in planning for the mission of social ministry organizations and ministries;

5) encouragement of financial support for the work of this church by individuals and congregations;

6) provision for resources for congregational life;

7) assistance to the members of its congregations in carrying out their ministries in the world; and

8) interpretation of social statements in a manner consistent with the interpretation given by the churchwide unit which assisted in the development of the statement, and suggestion of social study issues through (a) Synod Assembly memorials to the Churchwide Assembly or (b) resolutions for referral from the Synod Assembly through the Synod Council to the Church Council and (c) Synod Council resolutions addressed to the Church Council or for referral to a unit of the churchwide organization through the Church Council's Executive Committee.

f. Promote interdependent relationships among congregations, synods, and the churchwide organization, and enter into partnership with other synods in the region.

g. Participate in churchwide programs and develop support for the ministry of the churchwide organization.

h. Foster the grouping of congregations in conferences, clusters, coalitions, or other area subdivisions for mission purposes.

i. Support relationships with and provide partnership funding on behalf of colleges, universities, and campus ministries.

j. Foster relationships with and provide partnership funding on behalf of social ministry organizations.

k. Maintain relationships with and provide partnership funding on behalf of seminaries and continuing education centers.

l. Foster supporting relationships with camps and other outdoor ministries.

m. Foster supporting relationships with preschools, elementary schools, and secondary schools operated by congregations of the synod.

n. Interpret the work of this church to congregations and to the public.

o. Respond to human need, work for justice and peace, care for the sick and the suffering, and participate responsibly in society.

p. Provide for archives in conjunction with other synods.

q. Cooperate with other synods and the churchwide organization in creating, using, and supporting regions to carry out those functions of the synod which can best be done cooperatively with other synods and the churchwide organization.

10.22. In the event that this church or any synod of this church is charged with liability for any contingent debt, liability, or obligation arising or resulting from acts or omissions of any synod of the Lutheran Church in America, or The American Lutheran Church, or district of The American Lutheran Church, occurring prior to January 1, 1988, the Church Council is authorized and empowered to determine whether and to what extent this church or such synod of this church shall be indemnified or reimbursed for any such debt, liability, or obligation by one or more synods of this church. In making its determination with respect to indemnification or reimbursement, the Church Council shall consider the nature of the activity which gave rise to the debt, liability, or obligation, the situs of that activity, and such other factors as the Church Council deems appropriate under the circumstances in order that such debt, liability, or obligation may be discharged in a manner that is fair and equitable to this church's congregations, synods, and churchwide organization. For purposes of this provision, a "contingent" debt, liability, or obligation means a debt, liability, or obligation (a) the amount of which had not been ascertained by the Evangelical Lutheran Church in America on December 31, 1987, or (b) the existence of which was unknown to the Evangelical Lutheran Church in America on December 31, 1987.

Officers

10.30. The officers of each synod shall be a bishop, a vice president, a secretary, and a treasurer.

10.31. a. As the synod's pastor, the bishop shall:

1) Oversee and administer the work of the synod.

2) Preach, teach, and administer the sacraments in accord with the faith of this church.

3) Provide pastoral care and leadership for the synod, its congregations, its ordained ministers, and its associates in ministry.

4) Advise and counsel its related institutions and organizations.

5) Be its chief ecumenical officer.

6) Exercise supervision over the work of the other officers.

7) Preside at all meetings of the Synod Assembly and be the chief executive officer of the synod; provide for the preparation of the agenda of the Synod Assembly, Synod Council, and the Executive Committee; see to it that the

constitution and bylaws of the synod are duly observed, and that the actions of the synod in conformity therewith are carried into effect; coordinate the work of all synodical staff members; and appoint all committees for which provision is not otherwise made.

8) Coordinate the use of the resources available to the synod as it seeks to promote the health of this church's life and witness in the areas served by the synod.

9) Exercise solely this church's power to ordain (or provide for the ordination of) approved candidates who have received and accepted a properly issued, duly attested letter of call for the office of ordained ministry; and shall install (or provide for the installation of):

a) the pastors of all congregations of the synod;

b) ordained ministers called to extraparish service within this church; and

c) associates in ministry rostered in the synod.

10) Be ex officio a member of the Churchwide Assembly and a member of all committees and any other organizational units of the synod.

11) Submit a report to each regular meeting of the Synod Assembly concerning the synod's life and work.

12) Interpret and advocate the mission and theology of the whole church.

b. The vice president shall chair the Synod Council. In the event of the death, resignation, or disability of the bishop, the vice president shall convene the Synod Council to arrange for the conduct of the duties of the bishop until a new bishop shall be elected, or, in the case of temporary disability, until the bishop resumes full performance of the duties of the office.

10.31.01. The bishop shall be elected by the Synod Assembly. The bishop shall be a pastor who is an ordained minister of this church. The bishop may have as many assistants as the synod shall authorize. Each synod shall establish a mutual ministry committee to provide support and counsel to the bishop.

10.31.02. The vice president shall be elected by the Synod Assembly. The vice president shall be a layperson. The vice president shall not receive a salary for the performance of the duties of the office.

10.31.03. The secretary shall be elected by the Synod Assembly. The secretary may be either a layperson or an ordained minister.

10.31.04. The treasurer shall be elected by the Synod Assembly. The treasurer may be either a layperson or an ordained minister.

10.31.05. The bishop of the synod shall be elected to a term of six years and may be reelected. Each other officer shall be elected to a term of four years and may be reelected.

10.31.06. Each officer shall be a voting member of a congregation of the synod, except that the bishop need not be a member of a congregation of the synod at the time of election.

Synod Assembly

10.40.

10.41. Each synod shall have a Synod Assembly, which shall be its highest legislative authority, and which shall meet at least biennially. Special meetings may be called as needed. With the exception of ordained ministers on the roster of synods other than their synod of residence, each member of the Synod Assembly, the Synod Council, a board, committee, or other organizational unit of the synod shall be a voting member of a congregation of the synod.

10.41.01. Membership of the Synod Assembly, of which at least 60 percent of the voting membership shall be composed of lay persons, shall be constituted as follows:

a. All ordained ministers under call on the roster of the synod in attendance at the Synod Assembly shall be voting members.

b. All active associates in ministry, members of the Deaconess Community of the Evangelical Lutheran Church in America, and diaconal ministers, under call, on the lay roster or rosters of the synod shall have both voice and vote as lay voting members in the Synod Assembly.

c. A minimum of two lay members elected by each congregation related to the synod, one of whom shall be male and one of whom shall be female, shall be voting members. The Synod Council shall establish a formula to provide additional lay representation from congregations on the basis of the number of baptized members in the congregation. Additional members from each congregation shall be equally divided between male and female except that the odd-numbered member, if any, may be either male or female.

d. Voting membership shall include the officers of the synod.

10.41.02. Synods may establish processes that permit retired ordained ministers on the roster of the synod to serve as voting members of the Synod Assembly, consistent with bylaw 10.41.01.c. above.

10.41.03. Synods may establish processes that permit ordained ministers on the roster of the synod who are on leave from call to serve as voting members of the Synod Assembly, consistent with bylaw 10.41.01.c. above.

10.41.04. Synods may establish processes that permit representatives of authorized worshiping communities of the synod, under bylaw 10.02.03., to serve as voting members of the Synod Assembly, consistent with bylaw 10.41.01.

10.72. Each synod shall arrange to have an annual audit of its financial records conducted by a certified public accountant firm selected by the Synod Council. The audited annual financial report shall be submitted by the synod to the churchwide Office of the Treasurer and to the congregations of the synod. Synodical financial reports shall be in a format approved by the churchwide Office of the Treasurer in order to attain uniformity in reporting.

10.73. Each synod shall have the fiscal year of February 1 through January 31.

Installation

10.80.

10.81.01. The bishop of this church, or a member of the Conference of Bishops appointed by the bishop of this church, shall install into office each newly elected synod bishop.

10.41.05. Synods may establish processes that permit Synod Council voting members who are not otherwise serving as voting members of the Synod Assembly the privilege of both voice and vote as members of the Synod Assembly.

Synod Council

10.50.

10.51. Each synod shall have a Synod Council, which shall be its board of directors, and which shall serve as the interim legislative authority between meetings of the Synod Assembly, except that it may not take any action which is reserved exclusively for the Synod Assembly or which is in conflict with action taken by the Synod Assembly.

10.52. The Synod Council shall consist of the four officers of the synod, 10 to 24 other members, and at least one youth, all elected by the Synod Assembly. Each person elected to the Synod Council shall be a voting member of a congregation of the synod, with the exception of ordained ministers on the roster of the synod who reside outside the territory of the synod. The process for election and the term of office when not otherwise specified herein shall be determined by each synod. A member of the Church Council of the Evangelical Lutheran Church in America from the synod, unless otherwise elected as a voting member of the Synod Council, may serve as an advisory member of the Synod Council with voice but not vote.

Conferences, Clusters, Coalitions, or Other Area Subdivisions, and Committees

10.60.

10.61. Opportunities for groupings of congregations and institutions in specified geographic areas of the synod shall be provided by the synod to foster interdependent relationships among congregations, institutions, the synod, and churchwide units for mission purposes. These groupings may be formed as conferences, clusters, coalitions, or other area subdivisions.

10.62. Each synod may establish such boards, committees, task forces, and other organizational forms as it deems necessary to carry out effectively the functions assigned to the synod.

10.63. Each synod shall have an executive committee, a consultation committee, and a committee on discipline.

10.64. Each synod shall elect or appoint representatives to the steering committee of the region.

Fiscal Policy

10.70.

10.71. Each synod shall remit to the churchwide organization a percentage of all donor unrestricted receipts contributed to it by the congregations of the synod, such percentage to be determined by the Churchwide Assembly. Individual exceptions may be made by the Church Council upon request of a synod.

Chapter 11.
CHURCHWIDE ORGANIZATION—DEFINITION AND PURPOSES

11.10. Definition of the Churchwide Organization

11.11. The Evangelical Lutheran Church in America shall have a churchwide organization that shall function interdependently with the congregations and synods of this church. The churchwide organization shall serve on behalf of and in support of this church's members, congregations, and synods in proclaiming the Gospel, reaching out in witness and service both globally and throughout the territory of this church, nurturing the members of this church in the daily life of faith, and manifesting the unity of this church with the whole Church of Jesus Christ.

11.12. The churchwide organization shall be an instrument for accomplishing the purposes of this church, as defined by Chapter 4 in this constitution, that are shared with and supported by the members, congregations, and synods of this church. In keeping with this church's purposes, it shall develop churchwide policy, set standards for leadership, establish criteria for this church's endeavors, and coordinate the work of this church. It shall be a means for the sharing of resources throughout this church, and shall provide programs and services as determined by this church.

11.20. Purposes of the Churchwide Organization

11.21. In fulfillment of the purposes of this church, the churchwide organization shall:

a. Undergird the worship life of this church as the Word of God is preached and the sacraments are administered.

b. Provide resources to equip members to worship, learn, serve, and witness in their ministry in daily life.

c. Support and establish policy for this church's mission and coordinate planning and evaluation for that mission throughout the world, including participation with other churches.

d. Witness to the Word of God in Christ by united efforts in proclaiming the Gospel, responding to human need, caring for the sick and suffering, working for justice and peace, and providing guidance to members on social matters.

e. Foster interdependent relationships among congregations, synods, and the churchwide organization to implement the mission of this whole church.

f. Provide for the ordained ministry and other rostered ministries of this church.

g. Oversee and establish policy for this church's relationship to seminaries, colleges, universities, schools, and other education endeavors, and provide support as appropriate.

h. Establish and reflect this church's ecumenical stance and its relationship to other churches, and direct this church's policy for relationship with persons of other faiths.

i. Develop and administer policies for this church's relationship to social ministry organizations and cooperate with public and private agencies that enhance human dignity and justice.

j. Determine and implement policy for this church's relationship to governments.

k. Provide for a comprehensive financial support system for this church's mission and for the administration of financial resources necessary for fulfillment of the particular responsibilities of the churchwide organization.

l. Provide planned giving opportunities for the financial support of this church, its congregations, synods, agencies, and institutions through the establishment of a foundation.

m. Provide pension and other benefits plans for this church.

n. Provide a church publishing house.

o. Provide archives for the retention of its valuable records, and coordinate archival activity in the synods, regions, institutions, and agencies of this church.

p. Provide and monitor a system of discipline, appeals, and adjudication.

q. Establish and operate other programs and activities, as determined by this church, on behalf of and in support of the congregations and synods of this church.

Description of the Churchwide Organization

11.30. The legislative function of the churchwide organization shall be fulfilled by the Churchwide Assembly as described in Chapter 12 of this church's constitution, bylaws, and continuing resolutions.

11.31. The Church Council shall exercise interim legislative authority and shall serve as the board of directors of the corporation.

11.32. Leadership of this church shall be vested in the officers, the Churchwide Assembly, the Church Council, boards, and executive directors of churchwide administrative units. The full-time officers shall be the bishop of this church, secretary of this church, and treasurer of this church. The vice president shall be non-salaried and shall serve as chair of the Church Council.

11.33.

11.34. The churchwide organization shall carry out its duties through units known as offices, divisions, commissions, and other churchwide units. Departments shall be sub-units within offices, divisions, and other units that shall accomplish particular responsibilities as part of the respective unit's overall functions on behalf of this church.

12.10. Description and Authority of the Churchwide Assembly

12.11. The Churchwide Assembly shall be the highest legislative authority of the churchwide organization and shall deal with all matters which are necessary in pursuit of the purposes and functions of this church.
The powers of the Churchwide Assembly are limited only by the provisions of the Articles of Incorporation, this constitution and bylaws, and the assembly's own resolutions.

12.20. Duties of the Churchwide Assembly

12.21. The Churchwide Assembly shall:

a. Review the work of the churchwide officers, and for this purpose require and receive reports from them and act on business proposed by them.

b. Review the work of the churchwide units, and for this purpose require and receive reports from them and act on business proposed by them.

c. Receive and consider proposals from synod assemblies.

d. Establish churchwide policy.

e. Adopt a budget for the churchwide organization.

f. Elect officers, board members, and other persons as provided in the constitution or bylaws.

g. Establish churchwide units to carry out the functions of the churchwide organization.

h. Have the sole authority to amend the constitution and bylaws.

i. Fulfill other functions as required in the constitution and by-laws.

j. Conduct such other business as necessary to further the purposes and functions of the churchwide organization.

12.30. Meetings of the Churchwide Assembly

12.31. The assembly shall meet biennially in regular session. Special meetings may be called by a two-thirds vote of the Church Council. The purpose for a special meeting shall be stated in the notice.

12.31.01. The time and place of the Churchwide Assembly shall be determined by the Church Council. The time and place for the next regular assembly normally shall be announced at the preceding assembly.

12.31.02. The secretary shall give notice of the time and place of each regular assembly by publication thereof at least 60 days in advance in this church's periodical. The secretary shall give written notice of a special assembly to the bishop of each synod upon the issuance of a call thereof

---

11.35. Each unit shall be governed by a board, an advisory committee, a steering committee, or a committee of the Church Council. Units shall be responsible to the Churchwide Assembly and the Church Council in the interim between regular meetings of the assembly.

11.36. The churchwide organization shall provide a disciplinary process and an appeal process.

11.40. General Fiscal Policies

11.41. Within the limits established by the Churchwide Assembly in the constitution and bylaws, the Church Council, as the board of directors of the churchwide organization, shall establish the fiscal policies of this church.

11.41.01. A single treasury shall be maintained for the receipt and disbursement of funds for the churchwide organization and its units receiving budgetary support, except as otherwise provided in the constitution and bylaws or as approved by the Church Council.

11.41.02. Within the policies established by the Churchwide Assembly and the Church Council, the management and investment of the funds of the churchwide organization and its units receiving budgetary support shall be the responsibility of the Office of the Treasurer.

11.41.03. On the basis of estimated income, and upon advice of the Office of the Bishop and the Office of the Treasurer, in consultation with the units receiving support from the churchwide budget, the Church Council shall authorize expenditures within the budget for the fiscal year and the units may incur financial obligations up to the specified amounts. Expenditure authorizations shall be subject to revision, in light of changing conditions, by the Church Council, upon the advice of the Office of the Bishop and the Office of the Treasurer.

11.41.04. The Church Council shall establish a working capital fund to be administered by the Office of the Treasurer within the policies established by the Church Council.

11.41.05. The fiscal year for the churchwide organization shall be February 1 through January 31.

11.41.06. No churchwide appeal to congregations or individuals of this church for the raising of funds shall be conducted by this church or churchwide units without the consent of the Churchwide Assembly, following consultation with the Conference of Bishops. No appeal to selected congregations and individuals of this church for the raising of funds shall be conducted by this church or churchwide units without the consent of the Church Council, following consultation with either the Conference of Bishops or specific synods as appropriate. Proposals for such special appeals shall be presented to the Church Council through the appropriate council committee with recommendations by the Office of the Bishop.

12.41.12. The secretary of each synod shall submit to the secretary of this church at least four months before the assembly a certified list of the regular and alternate voting members elected by the synod.

12.41.13. Each voting member of the Churchwide Assembly shall be a voting member of a congregation of this church and shall cease to be a member of the assembly if no longer a voting member of a congregation of this church. The criterion for voting membership in the congregation from which the voting member is elected shall be in effect regarding minimum age for that voting member.

12.41.14. Voting members elected through the process of 12.41.11. through 12.41.13. shall begin serving with the opening of a regular Churchwide Assembly and shall continue serving until voting members are seated at the next regular Churchwide Assembly.

12.41.15. Except as defined in 12.41.21., employees of the churchwide organization, including those serving under call, appointment, employment agreement, or contract, shall not be eligible for election and service as voting members of the Churchwide Assembly.

Ex Officio Members

12.41.20.

12.41.21. The officers of this church and the bishops of the synods shall serve as ex officio members of the Churchwide Assembly. They shall have voice and vote.

Advisory Members

12.41.30.

12.41.31. Members of the Church Council and board chairpersons or their designees, unless elected as voting members, shall serve as advisory members of the Churchwide Assembly. Executive directors of churchwide units, the executive for administration, and executive assistants to the bishop shall serve as advisory members of the Churchwide Assembly.

12.41.32. Advisory members shall have voice but no vote.

Other Non-Voting Members

12.41.40.

12.41.41. Other categories of non-voting members may be established by the Churchwide Assembly.

12.41.A89. *Presidents of the colleges, universities, and seminaries of this church, unless elected as voting members of the assembly, shall have voice but not vote.*

Committees of the Churchwide Assembly

12.50.

12.51. **The Churchwide Assembly shall have a Reference and Counsel Committee, a Memorials Committee, and a Nominating Committee. The description of these committees shall be in the bylaws. The Churchwide Assembly may authorize such other committees as it deems necessary.**

and shall publish the same in this church's periodical at least 30 days in advance of the special assembly. Written notice shall be mailed to all voting members not more than 30 days nor less than 10 days in advance of any meeting.

12.31.03. At least 20 days prior to an assembly the secretary shall prepare and distribute to each congregation and to the voting members-elect a pre-assembly report.

12.31.04. The arrangements for agenda, program, and worship shall be under the supervision of the bishop.

12.31.05. Physical arrangements for churchwide assemblies shall be made by the secretary or by an assembly manager working under the secretary's supervision. Such committees as may be necessary to facilitate the planning for and operation of the assembly may be established by the secretary in consultation with the bishop.

12.31.06. The churchwide organization shall be responsible for the costs of the Churchwide Assembly, including reasonable costs for travel, housing, and board for voting and advisory members.

12.31.07. At least one-half of all persons elected as voting members must be present at a meeting to constitute a quorum for the legal conduct of business. If such a quorum is not present, those voting members present may adjourn the meeting to another time and place, provided that only those persons eligible to vote at the original meeting may vote at the adjourned meeting.

12.31.08. Proxy and absentee voting shall not be permitted at a Churchwide Assembly.

12.31.09. The Churchwide Assembly shall use parliamentary procedures in accordance with Robert's Rules of Order, latest edition, unless otherwise ordered by the assembly.

Members of the Churchwide Assembly

12.40.

12.41. **The voting members of the Churchwide Assembly shall be the voting members of this church. The requirements for voting members of the assembly and other members shall be specified in the bylaws.**

Voting Members

12.41.10.

12.41.11. Each synod shall elect one voting member of the Churchwide Assembly for every 6,500 baptized members in the synod. In addition, each synod shall elect one voting member for every 50 congregations in the synod. The synod bishop, who is ex officio a member of the Churchwide Assembly, shall be included in the number of voting members so determined. There shall be at least two voting members from each synod. The secretary shall notify each synod of the number of assembly members it is to elect.

Reference and Counsel Committee

12.51.10.

12.51.11. A Reference and Counsel Committee, appointed by the Church Council, shall review all proposed changes or additions to the constitution and bylaws and other items submitted that are not germane to items contained in the stated agenda of the assembly.

Memorials Committee

12.51.20.

12.51.21. A Memorials Committee, appointed by the Church Council, shall review memorials from synodical assemblies and make appropriate recommendations for assembly action.

Nominating Committee

12.51.30.

12.51.31. A Nominating Committee, elected by the Churchwide Assembly, shall nominate two persons for each position for which an election will be held by the Churchwide Assembly and for which a nominating procedure has not otherwise been designated in the constitution and bylaws of this church.

Chapter 13.
OFFICERS OF THIS CHURCH

Officers

13.10.

13.11. This church shall have as its officers the bishop, vice president, secretary, and treasurer.

Bishop

13.20.

13.21. This church shall have a bishop who, as its pastor, shall be a teacher of the faith of this church and shall provide leadership for the life and witness of this church. The bishop shall be an ordained minister of this church. The bishop may be male or female, as may all other officers of this church. The bishop shall:

a. Be the president and chief executive officer of the corporation, overseeing the work of the churchwide organization.

b. Be the chief ecumenical officer of this church and its primary representative in the national and international interchurch agencies in which this church holds membership.

c. Provide for the preparation of the agenda for the Churchwide Assembly, Church Council, Executive Committee, Conference of Bishops, and Cabinet of Executives, and preside at the Churchwide Assembly.

d. Provide leadership and care for the bishops of the synods.

e. Supervise the work of the other officers.

f. Provide for the preparation of the budget for the churchwide organization.

g. Nominate and direct the work of the executive for administration.

h. Convene a Cabinet of Executives for common counsel and co-ordination. The cabinet shall meet at least quarterly at the call of the bishop. The cabinet shall be composed of the officers, the executive for administration, the assistants to the bishop, the executive directors of the churchwide units, directors of the departments related to the bishop, and the editor of the church periodical.

i. Appoint members of all churchwide committees for which election procedures are not provided.

j. Be responsible for the chaplaincies of this church in federal agencies, institutions, and armed forces and provide for the pastoral care of those called to these ministries.

k. Recommend legal counsel to the Church Council.

l. Serve as an advisory member, with voice but not vote, on all committees of this church and all boards or committees of divisions, commissions, and other units, or designate a person to serve as the bishop's representative.

13.22. a. **The bishop shall be elected by the Churchwide Assembly to a six-year term.**

b. **The designation of the term of six years for the bishop of this church shall begin upon the next election of the bishop of this church. This item of 13.22. shall expire at the completion of that election.**

13.22.01. The bishop shall be elected as provided in Chapter 19 and shall take office on the first day of the third month after election.

13.22.02. The bishop shall be a full-time, salaried position.

13.30. **Vice President**

13.31. **The vice president of this church shall be a layperson who shall serve as chair of the Church Council and, in the event the bishop is unable to do so, as chair of the Churchwide Assembly. The vice president shall serve under the bishop of this church, providing leadership as specified in provision 11.33. of this church's constitution, bylaws, and continuing resolutions.**

13.32. **The vice president shall be elected by the Churchwide Assembly to a four-year term and shall be a voting member of a congregation of this church.**

13.32.01. The vice president shall be elected as provided in Chapter 19 and shall take office on the first day of the third month after election.

13.32.02. The vice president shall serve without salary.

13.40. **Secretary**

13.41. **The secretary of this church shall serve under the bishop of this church, providing leadership, as specified in Chapter 11 of this church's constitution, bylaws, and continuing resolutions, and shall fulfill the normal functions of the secretary of a corporation.**

13.41.01. The secretary, as the recording officer of this church, shall keep the minutes, have responsibility for rosters, records, and reporting of parochial statistics, oversee the archives, attest to all documents that require such signature, be the custodian of the seal, and perform other duties as prescribed by the Constitutions, Bylaws, and Continuing Resolutions of the Evangelical Lutheran Church in America.

13.41.02. The secretary shall:

a. Be responsible for the minutes and records of the Churchwide Assembly, Church Council, Executive Committee, Conference of Bishops, and Cabinet of Executives, and shall receive complete minutes for permanent record of all boards and advisory and steering committees of the churchwide organization.

b. Maintain the rosters of ordained ministers, all other rostered persons, congregations, and synods.

c. Provide for the publication of official documents and policies of this church, pre-assembly reports, assembly minutes, a directory of congregations, rostered persons, and entities of this church, and other informational and statistical material.

d. Receive the annual report of the congregations in a form devised by the secretary, summarize the information, and make the summary available to this church.

e. Coordinate the use of legal services by the churchwide organization.

f. Be responsible for the archives of this church, including provision for an Archives Advisory Committee.

g. Implement and operate a records management system for the church-wide organization.

h. Arrange for and manage meetings of the Churchwide Assembly and Church Council.

i. Have custody of the seal, maintain a necrology, and attest documents.

13.41.03. The secretary, in consultation with the bishop, shall be responsible for preparation and research of amendments to the Constitution, Bylaws, and Continuing Resolutions of the Evangelical Lutheran Church in America, as well as the Constitution for Synods and the Model Constitution for Congregations, to be proposed by the Church Council for action by the Churchwide Assembly in accordance with provisions of Chapter 22.

13.41.04. The secretary shall prepare interpretations, as necessary, of the Constitutions, Bylaws, and Continuing Resolutions of the Evangelical Lutheran Church in America. If a board, steering committee, advisory committee, or synod disagrees with the interpretations, as rendered, the objecting entity may appeal the secretary's interpretation to the Church Council.

13.41.05. The secretary shall provide staff services to the Nominating Committee of the Churchwide Assembly and the nomination process of the Church Council; shall be responsible for declaring an interim vacancy resulting from the resignation, death, or disability of a member of a board, committee, or council; and shall arrange for an election by the Church Council to fill the vacancy consistent with Chapter 19.

13.42. **The secretary shall be elected by the Churchwide Assembly to a four-year term and shall be a voting member of a congregation of this church.**

13.42.01. The secretary shall be elected as provided in Chapter 19 and shall take office on the first day of the third month after election.

13.42.02. The secretary shall be a full-time, salaried position.

13.42.A91. *Archives Advisory Committee*

a. *The committee shall consist of at least five persons appointed by the secretary in consultation with the archivist.*

b. *The committee shall meet at least annually.*

c. *The committee shall assist the secretary and archivist in maintaining professional standards and procedures for the preservation of records.*

d. *The committee shall assist the secretary and archivist in recommending policy for the archives of this church.*

e. *The committee shall assist the secretary and archivist in encouraging archival activities within the synods, or cooperatively through regions.*

13.50. **Treasurer**

13.51. **The treasurer of this church shall serve under the bishop of this church, providing leadership as specified in Chapter 11 of this church's constitution, bylaws, and continuing resolutions, and shall fulfill the normal functions of the treasurer of a corporation.**

13.51.01. The treasurer shall propose policy for review and action by the Church Council and provide for the implementation, within such policies, of the financial, accounting, insurance, property management, investment and money management systems, and related services for the units of the churchwide organization.

13.52. **The treasurer shall be elected by the Church Council to a four-year term and shall be a voting member of a congregation of this church.**

13.52.01. The treasurer shall be elected as provided in Chapter 19 and shall take office on the first day of the third month after election.

13.52.02. The treasurer shall be a full-time, salaried position.

13.52.03. The Church Council, by a two-thirds vote, may dismiss the treasurer for cause.

13.60. **Death, Resignation, or Disability of an Officer**

13.61. **Should the bishop die, resign, or be unable to serve, the vice president shall convene the Church Council to arrange for the appropriate care of the responsibilities of the bishop until an election of a new bishop can be held or until the bishop is able to serve again. The term of the successor bishop, elected by the next Churchwide Assembly, or a special meeting of the Churchwide Assembly called for the purpose of election, shall be six years, with the subsequent election to take place at the assembly closest to the expiration of such a term.**

13.62. **Should the vice president, secretary, or treasurer die, resign, or be unable to serve, the bishop, with the approval of the Executive Committee of the Church Council, shall arrange for the appropriate care of the responsibilities of the officer until an election of a new officer can be held or until the officer is able to serve again. The term of the successor vice president or secretary, elected by the next Churchwide Assembly, shall be four years. The Church Council shall elect the successor treasurer for a term of four years.**

13.63. **The Executive Committee of the Church Council shall determine whether an officer is unable to serve; the officer may appeal the decision of the Executive Committee by requesting a hearing before the Church Council. A meeting to determine the ability of an officer to serve shall be called upon the request of at least three members of the Executive Committee and prior notice of the meeting shall be given to the officer in question.**

Chapter 14.
CHURCH COUNCIL

Purpose and Meetings

14.10.

14.11. **This church shall have a Church Council which shall be the board of directors of this church and shall serve as the interim legislative authority between meetings of the Churchwide Assembly.**

14.12. **The Church Council shall meet at least two times each year.**

14.13. **"Interim legislative authority" is defined to mean that between meetings of the Churchwide Assemblies, the Church Council may exercise the authority of the Churchwide Assembly so long as:**

a. **the actions of the Church Council do not conflict with the actions of and policies established by the Churchwide Assembly; and**

b. **the Church Council is not precluded by constitutional or bylaw provisions from taking action on the matter.**

14.14. **The Church Council shall elect the treasurer of this church.**

14.15. **The Church Council shall elect advisory committee and steering committee members and, in the event that a vacancy on the council or on a board or committee is declared by the secretary of this church, the Church Council shall elect a member to serve the balance of the term.**

Responsibilities of the Church Council

14.20. **The specific duties of the Church Council shall be listed in the bylaws.**

14.21.

14.21.01. The Church Council shall act on the policies proposed by churchwide unit boards subject to review by the Churchwide Assembly.

14.21.02. The Church Council shall review the procedures and programs of the churchwide units to assure that churchwide purposes, policies, and objectives are being fulfilled.

14.21.03. The Church Council shall review all recommendations from churchwide units for consideration by the Churchwide Assembly.

14.21.04. The Church Council, upon recommendation of the bishop, shall submit budget proposals for approval by the Churchwide Assembly and authorize expenditures within the parameters of approved budgets.

14.21.05. The Church Council shall establish the criteria and policies for the relationship between this church and independent, cooperative, and related Lutheran organizations. The policies adopted by the Church Council shall be administered by the appropriate unit of the churchwide organization. The fiscal determination of which organization shall relate to a specific unit of the churchwide organization shall be made by the Church Council.

14.21.06. The Church Council shall establish ranges for the salaries for the church-wide bishop, secretary, and treasurer.

14.21.07. The Church Council shall adopt personnel policies for this church.

14.21.08. The Church Council shall arrange the process for all elections to boards of churchwide units to assure conformity with established criteria.

14.21.11. The Church Council shall act on resolutions from synod councils.

14.21.12. The Church Council shall provide for the installation of the churchwide officers. At the installation of a newly elected bishop of this church, the presiding minister shall be the retiring bishop of this church or, where that is not possible, a synodical bishop designated by the Church Council.

14.21.13. The Church Council, acting through the Division for Church in Society, shall have responsibility for the corporate social responsibility of this church and shall have the authority to file shareholder resolutions and cast proxy ballots thereon on stocks held by the churchwide units that are not separately incorporated. In addition, the Church Council may make recommendations to the churchwide units that are separately incorporated concerning the filing of shareholder resolutions and the casting of ballots on stocks held by those units.

14.21.14. The Church Council shall report its actions to the Churchwide Assembly.

14.21.15. Proxy and absentee voting shall not be permitted at meetings of the Church Council.

Composition of the Church Council

14.30. **The voting members of the Church Council shall consist of the four churchwide officers and 33 other persons, elected by the Churchwide Assembly.**

14.31. **Church Council members shall be elected to one six-year term and shall not be eligible for consecutive reelection.**

14.32. The Church Council shall have as advisory members nine synodical bishops, each elected by the Conference of Bishops to one four-year term. One bishop shall be elected from each region.

14.32.01. The Church Council shall have two youth advisory members, each elected by the board of the youth organization of this church to a two-year term beginning at the first meeting of the Church Council following each regular meeting of the Churchwide Assembly.

14.32.02. Advisory members of the Church Council shall have voice but not vote.

14.32.03.

Church Council Committees

14.40. **The Church Council shall establish committees and nominate or elect such persons as necessary to carry out the functions assigned to it. The description of such committees shall be set forth in the bylaws and continuing resolutions.**

14.41.

84 / ELCA CONSTITUTION—CHAPTER 14 (9-93)

(9-93) ELCA CONSTITUTION—CHAPTER 14 / 85

14.41.10.

Executive Committee

The Church Council shall have an Executive Committee composed of the churchwide officers and seven members of the Church Council elected by the council. The vice president of this church shall chair this committee. The Executive Committee shall counsel with the churchwide officers and shall perform those functions of the Church Council assigned to it by the Church Council. This committee, with the exception of the officers of this church, shall review the work of the officers and set salaries of the churchwide bishop, secretary, and treasurer within the ranges established by the Church Council. This committee shall demonstrate concern for the spiritual, emotional, and physical well-being of the full-time salaried officers of this church. This committee shall transmit resolutions from synods to the appropriate unit or units of the churchwide organization and shall carry out the responsibilities of the council related to nominations, with staff services provided for the nomination and election processes of the Church Council by the Office of the Secretary.

14.41.11.

14.41.12.

Except as provided in bylaw 14.41.11. regarding the Executive Committee, the officers of this church shall have voice but not vote in all Church Council committees.

14.41.A91.

Budget and Finance Committee

A Budget and Finance Committee shall be composed of members of the Church Council elected by the council and the treasurer of this church as an ex officio member with voice but not vote in the committee. This committee shall have staff services provided by the Office of the Bishop and the Office of the Treasurer. The committee shall prepare and present a comprehensive budget to the Church Council for its consideration and presentation to the Churchwide Assembly. In addition, the committee shall relate to the work of the Office of the Treasurer and the Mission Investment Fund of the ELCA. The executive director of the ELCA Foundation shall relate to the council through this committee. The committee also shall carry out the functions of the Financial Information Committee regarding pension and benefits plans, as specified by bylaw 17.61.02.e.

14.41.B91.

Coordination and Services Committee

A Coordination and Services Committee shall be composed of members of the Church Council elected by the council and shall have staff services provided by the Office of the Bishop. This committee shall evaluate processes for coordination and implementation of churchwide standards related to the work of the departments that have implications for churchwide units, and review provisions for technical and professional services to divisions and other units. This committee also shall review the work of the Department for Communication, Department for Human Resources, Department for Research and Evaluation, and Department for Synodical Relations and shall bring reports and recommend policies to the Church Council related to these areas.

14.41.C91.

Legal and Constitutional Review Committee

A Legal and Constitutional Review Committee shall be composed of members of the Church Council elected by the council, shall include the secretary of this church as an ex officio member with voice but not vote in the committee, and shall have staff services provided by the Office of the Secretary. This committee shall provide ongoing review of legal and constitutional matters. It shall review all proposed amendments to the constitutions, bylaws, and continuing resolutions.

14.41.D91.

Program and Structure Committee

A Program and Structure Committee shall be composed of members of the Church Council elected by the council and shall have staff services provided by the Office of the Bishop. This committee shall be responsible for the ongoing review and evaluation of the programs and the structure of the churchwide organization, making recommendations to the Churchwide Assembly through the Church Council. This committee shall establish a process for the review of at least two churchwide units each biennium so as to review all units within a ten-year period. Such review shall include the recommendation for renewal of the mandate for the churchwide unit or recommendation of an alternative structure through which the unit's purposes shall be accomplished. The women's organization, the Publishing House of the ELCA, the Board of Pensions, the Conference of Bishops, the church periodical, and the ELCA Foundation also shall be reviewed. Commissions established by this church shall relate to the Church Council through this committee.

Chapter 15.
CHURCHWIDE OFFICES AND ADMINISTRATION

15.10. **Offices**

15.11. **An office is a unit of the churchwide organization directly related to and under the authority of a full-time officer of this church. Each office is related to the Church Council through the officer who reports to the Church Council in the interim between regular meetings of the Churchwide Assembly. Each office may have departments to assist the officer in the performance of specified functions that are the responsibility of that officer.**

15.11.01. There shall be the following offices:

   a. Office of the Bishop;

   b. Office of the Secretary; and

   c. Office of the Treasurer.

15.11.A91 *Administrative Team*

The bishop, secretary, treasurer, and executive for administration shall function as an administrative team, directed by the bishop. This administrative team shall assist the bishop in the fulfillment of the bishop's responsibilities for oversight, management, supervision, and coordination in the operation of the churchwide organization.

15.11.B91 *Duties of the Executive for Administration*

The executive for administration, who shall be an assistant to the bishop, shall be accountable to the bishop and shall serve as chief administrator of the churchwide organization. The executive for administration shall be elected by the Church Council upon nomination of the bishop and shall have an appointment coterminous with the term of the bishop. At the direction of the bishop, the executive for administration shall:

   a. Supervise the day-to-day functioning of the churchwide organization and coordinate the work of churchwide units;

   b. Coordinate the day-to-day staff activities within the Office of the Bishop and the functioning of the administrative team;

   c. Oversee the work of the Department for Communication, Department for Human Resources, and Department for Research and Evaluation;

   d. Develop the budget for the churchwide organization and report to the Church Council and the Churchwide Assembly through the Budget and Finance Committee of the Church Council with regard to the preparation of the budget; and

   e. Report to the Church Council through the council's Coordination and Services Committee on matters relating to the departments under the supervision of the executive for administration.

15.11.C91 *Responsibility for Planning and Evaluation*

The Office of the Bishop shall provide coordinated, strategic planning for, and review and evaluation of, the work of the churchwide organization and shall coordinate this planning process with the budget-development process.

15.11.D91 *Responsibilities of the Office of the Treasurer*

   a. This office shall be related to the treasurer, who shall be its full-time executive officer. Matters related to the role, election, and term of the treasurer are contained in provisions 13.51. and following.

   b. This office shall provide for the management of the capital (church property) funds and, when requested and authorized by other churchwide units, shall purchase sites and facilities for new congregations, manage properties for future use, make loans, and secure loans for capital funds.

   c. This office shall provide for a common system of financial reporting from synods and regions.

   d. This office shall provide, upon request, a financial management system for synods.

   e. This office shall provide, upon request, assistance in financial matters to the Publishing House of the ELCA, the Board of Pensions, the women's organization, congregations, synods, regions, and institutions.

   f. This office shall provide for internal audit procedures of the churchwide organization.

   g. This office, through the Budget and Finance Committee of the Church Council, shall recommend to the Church Council a certified public accounting firm to audit the financial records of the churchwide organization. Synodical financial reports shall be submitted to this office for compilation.

   h. This office shall provide legal documents pertaining to the financial and property management matters of the churchwide organization. These legal documents shall be signed by the officers authorized by the Church Council.

   i. This office shall provide and manage insurance (exclusive of life and health) programs for the churchwide organization and shall make available insurance programs to congregations, synods, regions, and related institutions, agencies, and organizations.

   j. This office shall be authorized, within policies established by this church, to purchase or otherwise acquire title to real property; to mortgage, lease, sell, or otherwise dispose of the same; and to act on behalf of the units of the churchwide organization after receiving their direction regarding the purchase or disposition of real property.

k. This office shall manage such other capital loan funds as are established by the Church Council. The management shall be within policies established jointly by the Office of the Treasurer and other affected churchwide units.

l. This office shall have the authority to borrow; issue bonds, notes, certificates, or other evidence of obligation; or increase contingent liabilities within the overall limits determined by the Churchwide Assembly and the more restrictive limits established by the Church Council. No churchwide board shall make a commitment that binds the churchwide organization to an outside lending or other similar institution or which creates a liability of this church to such an institution without prior approval of the Office of the Treasurer.

m. This office shall have the authority and responsibility to establish and maintain banking relationships.

n. Receipt of Gifts: This office, within the policies established by the Church Council, shall assure the implementation of a donor gift acknowledgement process in consultation with the board of the ELCA Foundation.

o. Major Gifts and Deferred Giving: This office, in consultation with the ELCA Foundation's board, shall recommend and implement:

1) approved policy for the valuation process for noncash gifts;
2) the management of assets of life-income agreements;
3) the establishment and management of memorial funds received by the foundation; and
4) the distribution of earned-income payments to remainder beneficiaries as regulated by the life-income, trust, and other fiduciary donor agreements.

15.11.E91. **Department for Information Management Services**
The treasurer shall provide for an information management system that shall include the following:

a. Information services, including data processing for the churchwide units, except as otherwise determined.

b. Data processing links among congregations, synods, and the churchwide organization for communication of information and data base.

c. Guidelines and policies for computer standards, security, application development, data storage, and data retrieval for all congregations, synods, and the churchwide organization of this church.

15.20. **Mission Investment Fund**
of the Evangelical Lutheran Church in America

15.21. **This church shall have a fund, known as the Mission Investment Fund of the Evangelical Lutheran Church in America, to provide**

loans to congregations and units of this church and to organizations and institutions that are affiliated with this church. The Mission Investment Fund of the Evangelical Lutheran Church in America shall be incorporated. The treasurer shall serve as its executive director and shall be president of the corporation.

15.21.A91. *Operation of Mission Investment Fund of the ELCA*

a. The Mission Investment Fund of the Evangelical Lutheran Church in America shall have primary responsibility for promotion of Mission Investments.

b. The provisions of 15.11.D91. shall apply to the Mission Investment Fund of the ELCA.

c. The board of directors of the Mission Investment Fund of the ELCA shall be eleven in number, who shall be elected by the Church Council for two-year terms and shall be eligible for reelection, with six members nominated by the Church Council's Budget and Finance Committee, four members nominated by the board of the Division for Outreach, and one member nominated by the board of the Division for Church in Society.

d. Staff services for the Mission Investment Fund of the ELCA shall be provided by staff of the Office of the Treasurer.

e. Relationship to Division for Outreach: This Mission Investment Fund of the ELCA shall relate to the Division for Outreach. The Division for Outreach shall have staff responsible for real estate acquisition and disposition for new and/or existing ministries within the limits of the capital funds available and within criteria established jointly by the Division for Outreach and the Mission Investment Fund of the ELCA. The Mission Investment Fund of the ELCA, through the Office of the Treasurer, shall provide expertise for management of real property and execute all necessary documents for the acquisition and disposition of such property.

f. Capital Budget Development: An annual capital budget for ministry development shall be established. The budget shall be prepared by a joint staff committee comprised of staff from the Division for Outreach and the Office of the Treasurer. This budget is to be based on projected availability of capital funds and projected requirements for loans and real property acquisition for ministry development, church building programs, or other approved capital needs. This capital budget, upon recommendation of the joint staff committee, will be submitted to the board of the Division for Outreach and the board of the Mission Investment Fund of the ELCA for approval and recommendation to the Church Council. Following approval, the capital budget shall be monitored by the joint staff committee.

g. Within guidelines established jointly by the Division for Outreach and the Mission Investment Fund of the ELCA, the Division for Outreach shall have the responsibility for determining which congregations shall receive loans, the amount of each loan, and the repayment schedule. The Division for Outreach shall supervise the collection of said loan. Upon order of the Division for Outreach, the Mission Investment Fund of the ELCA shall execute the loan, ensure safekeeping for the legal documents, and provide accounting services for the repayment.

Departments

15.30.10.

15.31.11. Departments related to the officers of this church shall develop and implement churchwide standards and provide for coordination of services requiring technical and specific expertise, in support of divisions and other units.

15.31.12. Advisory committees for departments may be established by the Church Council. Advisory committees established under this provision and their responsibility for reporting to the Church Council, consistent with 14.41.B91., shall be described in continuing resolutions. Members of such committees shall be selected for particular experience and expertise related to the responsibilities of the department. Upon two successive absences that have not been excused by the committee, a committee member's position shall be declared vacant by the secretary of this church who shall arrange for election by the Church Council to fill the unexpired term, according to the provisions of Chapter 19.

15.31.13. Names and descriptions of responsibilities of the departments related to officers shall be provided in continuing resolutions.

15.31.A91. Such departments shall function under the administrative team, as defined in continuing resolution 15.11.A91., and as assigned by the bishop of this church with the concurrence of the Church Council.

15.31.B91. *Department for Communication*

a. *This department shall interpret the work of this church, provide for this church's presence in public media, and coordinate the communication activities of this church's divisions, commissions, and, as appropriate, other units. To fulfill these responsibilities, this department shall:*

1) *develop an overall communication strategy for this church and recommend communication policies, procedures, and standards to the Church Council. Upon approval by the Church Council, this department shall be responsible for implementation of such policies, procedures, and standards.*

2) *maintain a news and information service to gather and disseminate news about this church and its members, and respond to inquiries about this church, its policies, and its programs.*

3) *interpret, in cooperation with the divisions, commissions, and other churchwide units, the work of the churchwide organization to the members of this church and the public. This shall include the assignment of interpretation persons to churchwide*

units to provide counsel and to communicate the work of each unit.

4) *develop and carry out in coordination with other churchwide units a communication system for sharing information and resources among congregations, synods, regions, and the churchwide organization.*

5) *coordinate multimedia production for the churchwide organization.*

6) *develop, promote, and distribute public media-ministry programs of this church.*

7) *make appropriate provisions for translation, as determined by policy established by the Church Council, of church communication into languages other than English and into non-visual and non-verbal versions.*

8) *gather, under the coordination of the Department for Research and Evaluation, information to guide and direct the communication policies and strategies of this church, its programs, and its officers.*

9) *provide public relations counsel and support to the officers and units of this church.*

10) *facilitate programs for communication training and media education.*

11) *maintain relationships with communication offices of other church bodies and ecumenical agencies and engage in cooperative efforts as appropriate.*

12) *monitor national and international communication policies and issues, recommending under the coordination of the Division for Church in Society action to this church where appropriate.*

b. *The director for this department shall be nominated by the bishop and elected by the Church Council to a four-year term. The director shall be eligible for reelection. Service of the director may be terminated by the bishop, consistent with the personnel policies of the churchwide organization and in consultation with the Executive Committee of the Church Council.*

c. *This department shall be related to the bishop of this church through the executive for administration.*

d. *The advisory committee of the Department for Communication shall be composed of up to 10 persons elected to six-year terms by the Church Council for particular experience and expertise.*

15.31.C91. *Department for Ecumenical Affairs*

a. *This department shall be related to the bishop of this church, shall coordinate the ecumenical, inter-Lutheran, and interfaith activities of this church, and shall recommend, through the bishop, policies relating thereto to the Churchwide Assembly and Church Council. To fulfill these responsibilities, this department shall:*

1) assist the bishop of this church in carrying out the bishop's role as the chief ecumenical officer of this church.

2) administer the ecumenical, inter-Lutheran, and interfaith discussions (including bilateral dialogues) in which this church is involved.

3) administer (including personnel and financial support) the membership of this church in ecumenical organizations, such as World Council of Churches, National Council of the Churches of Christ in the U.S.A., and Lutheran World Federation.

4) study and advise this church in matters of fellowship and unity with other Lutheran churches.

5) guide the process of reception of theological agreements.

6) encourage the study of theological topics of common concern.

7) assist the synods, congregations, and churchwide units of this church in carrying out their ecumenical, inter-Lutheran, and interfaith responsibilities by giving guidance and by preparing guidelines for action.

8) provide for this church's relationship with independent Lutheran organizations. This church shall not, in any manner, be responsible for nor liable for the actions of any independent Lutheran organization.

b. The director for this department, who shall report to the bishop of this church and shall be an assistant to the bishop, shall be nominated by the bishop and elected by the Church Council to a four-year term. Service of the director may be terminated by the bishop, consistent with the personnel policies of the churchwide organization and in consultation with the Executive Committee of the Church Council.

c. The advisory committee of the Department for Ecumenical Affairs, which shall report to the Church Council through the bishop of this church, shall be composed of 11 members, including the bishop of this church, three members of the Church Council elected by the council, and seven persons elected to six-year terms by the Church Council from outside its membership for particular experience and expertise. A synodical bishop chosen by the Conference of Bishops shall serve as an advisory member of the committee with voice but not vote.

d. The advisory committee for this department shall serve as the U.S.A. National Committee of the Lutheran World Federation. In serving in such capacity, the committee of this department shall be augmented by the members of this church who serve as voting members of the LWF council. One staff member of the Division for Global Mission and one staff member of the Division for Church in Society shall serve as consultants to the U.S.A. National Committee of the Lutheran World Federation.

15.31.D91. *Department for Human Resources*

a. This department shall recommend to the Church Council personnel policies for the churchwide organization except as otherwise determined, including equal-employment opportunity and affirmative action, recruitment, interview, and selection, compensation and benefits, fair-employment practices, staff position description, performance evaluation, and training. To fulfill these responsibilities, this department shall:

1) recommend personnel policies, procedures and standards, and, upon approval by the Church Council, be responsible for the implementation, administration, and evaluation of personnel policies, procedures, and standards for divisions, commissions, offices, and other units, as applicable, of the churchwide organization.

2) guide the recruitment, personnel interviews, and process of selection of staff.

3) authorize necessary research to update compensation packages and make recommendations to the Church Council for upgrading pension and other benefits plans.

4) make employee assistance programs, such as family-crisis counseling and retirement-planning services, available to the employees of this church.

5) recommend policy and procedures to the Church Council for ongoing performance evaluation.

6) provide for just and equitable employee-relations practices, including grievance procedures, and provide employee services appropriate to the churchwide office, such as child-care services.

7) maintain personnel records for all employees, including employee-performance evaluations.

b. This department shall provide management of the facilities for the churchwide organization and coordinate central services for Chicago-based churchwide units.

c. This department shall offer such policies to the synods and congregations as guidelines and be available to counsel and advise the synods as requested.

d. The director for this department shall be nominated by the bishop and elected by the Church Council to a four-year term. The director shall be eligible for reelection. Service of the director may be terminated by the bishop, consistent with the personnel policies of the churchwide organization and in consultation with the Executive Committee of the Church Council.

e. This department shall be related to the bishop of this church through the executive for administration.

f. The advisory committee of the Department for Human Resources shall be composed of five persons elected to six-year terms by the Church Council for particular experience and expertise.

15.31.E91. Department for Research and Evaluation

a. This department shall assist the bishop, other leaders, and staff of the churchwide organization to accomplish their responsibilities by providing reliable and valid research, relevant information, and appropriate evaluation related to the purposes of this church. To fulfill these responsibilities, this department shall:

1) recommend research and evaluation policies, processes, procedures, and standards to the Church Council and implement them upon approval by the Church Council.

2) serve as the center for this church in the area of research and evaluation by:

   a) conducting systematic, ongoing research on issues, attitudes, and contextual developments;

   b) conducting individual research projects on behalf of the churchwide organization and its units;

   c) overseeing the development and execution of research plans for each unit; and

   d) providing consultation to all churchwide units on matters related to research and evaluation.

3) provide interpretation of the results of research conducted or reviewed in support of the work of churchwide units.

4) provide the churchwide organization, its units, and other expressions of the church with demographic data and analysis.

5) offer upon request counsel and advice about research and evaluation to congregations, synods, regions, agencies, and institutions of this church.

b. This department shall provide at the direction of the secretary for the collection and tabulation of the parochial statistics for this church.

c. This department shall provide at the direction of the bishop for coordinated comprehensive research and evaluation of the work of the churchwide organization.

d. The director for this department shall be nominated by the bishop and elected by the Church Council to a four-year term. The director shall be eligible for reelection. Service of the director may be terminated by the bishop, consistent with the personnel policies of the churchwide organization and in consultation with the Executive Committee of the Church Council.

e. This office shall be related to the bishop of this church through the executive for administration.

f. The advisory committee of the Department for Research and Evaluation shall be composed of five persons elected to six-year terms by the Church Council for particular experience and expertise.

15.31.F91. Department for Synodical Relations

a. This department shall coordinate the relationships between the churchwide organization and synods, including regions, develop and implement synodical-churchwide consultations and services, render support for synodical bishops and synodical staff, and provide staff services for the Conference of Bishops. To fulfill these responsibilities, this department shall:

1) relate to the Conference of Bishops in fulfillment of the conference's assigned responsibilities and provide staff services for development of programs and other needs.

2) have a staff member selected by the bishop who shall be an assistant to the bishop of this church for federal chaplaincies in the Veterans Affairs Administration and the armed forces.

3) plan and coordinate synodical-churchwide consultations and provide for services, including assistance to synods for organizational concerns, long-range planning, and ongoing evaluation.

4) coordinate the interaction of churchwide units with synodical responsibilities and programs.

5) implement and monitor churchwide participation in regional steering committees.

b. The director for this department, who shall report to the bishop of this church and shall be an assistant to the bishop, shall be nominated jointly by the bishop of this church and the executive committee of the Conference of Bishops, ratified by the Conference of Bishops, and elected by the Church Council to a four-year term. The director shall be eligible for reelection. Service of the director may be terminated by the bishop, consistent with the personnel policies of the churchwide organization and in consultation with the Executive Committee of the Church Council.

Conference of Bishops

15.40.

15.41. **The Conference of Bishops shall be composed of the bishops of the synods, the bishop of this church, and the secretary of this church.**

15.41.01. This conference shall report to the Church Council, and may make recommendations to the bishop of this church and to the Church Council.

15.41.02. Staff services for the functions and responsibilities of the conference shall be provided by the Department for Synodical Relations.

15.41.03. This conference shall elect its own officers and committees and shall meet at least two times each year. Budget for the work of the conference shall be provided through the Department for Synodical Relations.

15.41.04. The responsibilities of the Conference of Bishops shall be enumerated in a continuing resolution. The resolution may be amended by majority vote of the Churchwide Assembly or by a two-thirds vote of the Church Council. Should the conference disagree with the action of the Church Council, it may appeal the decision to the Churchwide Assembly.

15.41.A91. *Responsibilities of the Conference of Bishops*

a. *This conference shall provide opportunities for worship, spiritual renewal, and theological enrichment for those elected to the office of bishop of a synod, the bishop of this church, and the secretary of this church.*

b. *This conference shall be a forum in which goals, objectives, and strategies may be developed and shared concerning pastoral leadership, care, and counsel for the synods.*

c. *This conference shall review recommendations from the Division for Ministry pertaining to standards for the admission to the rosters of ordained ministers and associates in ministry and for their retention on those rosters.*

d. *This conference shall establish and maintain the processes for first call for candidates for the ordained ministry of this church, first call for persons certified as associates in ministry, mobility of rostered persons, and pastoral care.*

e. *This conference shall review recommendations from the Division for Ministry pertaining to policies related to ordained ministers, associates in ministry, and their families for pastoral care in such areas as call or appointment review, guidance, mobility, intervention, discipline, rehabilitation, and spiritual growth.*

f. *This conference shall develop programs, in consultation with the Division for Ministry, related to ordained ministers, associates in ministry, and their families for pastoral care, including call or appointment review, guidance, mobility, intervention, discipline, rehabilitation, and spiritual growth.*

g. *This conference shall offer programs for orientation and continuing education for bishops, officers, and their spouses.*

h. *This conference shall assist the bishops in their role as teachers by being a forum for serious reflections on the theological and ethical implications of issues that affect the life of this church.*

i. *This conference shall participate with the Department for Ecumenical Affairs in the development and study of ecumenical documents. This conference shall consult with the Department for Ecumenical Affairs to assist the bishops to promote the unity of this church through leadership and ecumenical worship, fellowship, and interaction.*

Staff

15.50.

15.51. **The churchwide units shall employ staff according to churchwide policy.**

15.51.01. The Department for Human Resources shall recommend to the Church Council the personnel policies of this church. Such policies shall be binding on all churchwide units unless exceptions are granted by the Church Council or specified in the constitution and bylaws of this church.

15.51.A91. *Staffing Assumptions*

a. *Wherever practical, staff should be shared between churchwide units and synods, either as deployed staff or shared-time staff. When staff are "deployed" or are "shared synodical-churchwide" staff, this shall occur only after all affected organizations of this church in use of such staff have agreed to the purposes and details of such an arrangement.*

1) *Deployed staff shall be understood to mean fully funded by the deploying churchwide unit(s).*

2) *Shared synodical-churchwide staff shall be understood to mean shared funding by the deploying churchwide unit(s) and the synod(s).*

b. *Where purchase of service is warranted, rather than full-time employment, such options should be encouraged.*

c. *Before new executive staff positions can be added to any unit of the churchwide organization, such unit must present its proposal to the Church Council through the council's Program and Structure Committee.*

d. *Categories of staff allocations are as follows:*

1) *Executive director: the director of the unit.*

2) *Executive staff: all other executives of a unit.*

3) *Full-time equivalents under churchwide personnel policies: contract staff whose services are purchased out of budget allocations within the unit or shared staff the cost of whom are shared with synods or other units.*

4) *Support staff: staff with the responsibility of assisting the executive director, executive staff, and full-time equivalents.*

Chapter 16.
DIVISIONS AND COMMISSIONS OF THE CHURCHWIDE ORGANIZATION

16.10. **Divisions**

16.11. A division is a unit of the churchwide organization to which is assigned responsibility for a major, identified portion of the program of this church.

16.11.10. **Division Boards**

16.11.11. Each board shall be responsible to the Churchwide Assembly and will report to the Church Council in the interim. The policies, procedures, and program of each division shall be reviewed by the Church Council in order to assure conformity with the governing documents of this church and with Churchwide Assembly actions.

16.11.12. Each board, which shall meet at least two times each year, shall function as specified in this church's constitution, bylaws, and continuing resolutions regarding its responsibilities in relation to a particular unit of the churchwide organization.

16.11.13. Each division board shall be composed of 21 persons elected to one six-year term, with no consecutive reelection, and with one-third of the board members being elected every biennium, as provided in Chapter 19. The bishop of this church, or the bishop's designee, shall serve as an advisory member of each board. The Conference of Bishops shall select one bishop to serve as an advisory member of each board.

16.11.14. Proxy and absentee voting shall not be permitted at meetings of any board or any committee of the board.

16.11.20. **Staff of Divisions**

16.11.21. Each board shall elect its executive director to a four-year term in consultation with and with the approval of the bishop of this church. Nomination of a candidate for election by the board shall be made jointly by the bishop of this church and the search committee of the board. Each board, together with the bishop of this church, shall arrange within the policy of this church for an annual review of the executive director. Executive directors shall be eligible for reelection. The employment of the executive director may be terminated jointly by the bishop of this church and the executive committee of the board.

16.11.22. Each board, within churchwide policy, shall authorize staff positions upon recommendation by the executive director and ratify candidates for executive staff upon recommendation by the executive director.

16.11.23. The salary structures of all divisions shall be within the personnel policies of this church, unless exceptions are granted by the Church Council.

16.11.24. Consistent with applicable personnel policies, each board shall establish the salary of the executive director with the concurrence of the bishop of this church and ratify executive staff salaries upon recommendation of the executive director.

16.11.25. Consistent with applicable personnel policies, all divisions will have staff persons, some of whom shall be executive staff and others of whom shall be support staff. In conformity with this church's commitment to inclusive practice, each board will assure that staff include a balance of women and men, persons of color and persons whose primary language is other than English, laypersons, and persons on the roster of ordained ministers. This balance is to be evident in terms of both executive staff and support staff consistent with the inclusive policy of this church.

16.11.30. **Responsibilities Common to Boards**

16.11.31. Each board shall request budget support for programs of the division through the budget-development process. In its review of the division's work, the board shall seek to ensure that the division operates within the expenditure authorization established by the Church Council.

16.11.32. Each board shall recommend policy and develop strategies in its particular areas of responsibility after consultation with other units of the churchwide organization and affected synods, congregations, agencies, and institutions.

a. Policies related to the day-to-day functioning of the unit or to the specific responsibilities of the unit that have no implications for other units, congregations, synods, agencies, or institutions may be adopted by the board, subject to ratification by the Church Council.

b. All other policies shall be submitted to the Church Council for approval.

16.11.33. Each board shall approve and review major program directions for its areas of responsibility in cooperation with the Church Council's Program and Structure Committee, for presentation to the Church Council.

16.11.40. **Establishment of Divisions**

16.11.41. The responsibilities of the divisions shall be enumerated in continuing resolutions. Such continuing resolutions may be amended by a majority vote of the Churchwide Assembly or by a two-thirds vote of the Church Council. Should the board disagree with the action of the Church Council, it may appeal the decision to the Churchwide Assembly.

16.11.42. This church shall have the following divisions:

a. Division for Congregational Ministries
b. Division for Ministry
c. Division for Outreach
d. Division for Higher Education and Schools
e. Division for Church in Society
f. Division for Global Mission

16.11.A91. Division for Congregational Ministries

This division, working in partnership with congregations, synods, regions, and other units of the churchwide organization, shall provide support for congregations as they carry out their ministry; it also shall provide a financial-support program for this church. To fulfill these responsibilities, this division shall:

a. develop integrated programs and provide services, in cooperation with other churchwide units, in support of congregations in such major areas as worship, education, evangelism, stewardship, congregational social ministry, congregational planning, service and justice, and lay leadership.

b. develop and deliver programs to enable members and congregations to respond financially in support of this church's ministry in congregations, synods, agencies, institutions, and the churchwide organization. To do so, this division will:

   1) direct the financial-support program to undergird this church's whole ministry.

   2) direct the churchwide program of designated giving developed in cooperation with other appropriate units of the churchwide organization.

   3) direct, in cooperation with the Division for Church in Society, the ingathering of funds for the hunger appeal.

   4) plan for and implement approved churchwide special appeals in accordance with policies of this church and decisions of the Churchwide Assembly and the Church Council.

   5) provide, upon request, counsel and assistance to congregations, synods, agencies, and institutions of this church to develop and strengthen financial stewardship through contractual or special services.

c. develop resources for congregational use in partnership with the Publishing House of the ELCA and other appropriate churchwide units. To do so, this division will:

   1) participate in resource planning groups with other churchwide units to plan and develop materials to assist members and congregations.

   2) work in coordination with the Women of the ELCA, the Commission for Women, and the Publishing House of the ELCA in development of resources for women.

   3) develop multilingual and culture-specific resources, in cooperation with the Commission for Multicultural Ministries and the Publishing House of the ELCA.

d. develop programs and resources, under the coordination of the Division for Ministry and in cooperation with the Publishing House

of the ELCA, to assist congregations to equip people individually and collectively for ministry in daily life.

e. develop programs to meet specific needs for congregational ministries among families, singles, older adults, children, youth, men, and women.

f. relate to organizations that provide support for congregational ministry. To do so, this division will:

   1) oversee and support the Lutheran Youth Organization, which shall operate with youth leadership elected by its members and with a constitution established by its members. The constitution of the Lutheran Youth Organization shall be approved by the Church Council. Policies and actions of the youth organization shall be subject to review by the board of the Division for Congregational Ministries, and all budget requests shall be submitted through the Division for Congregational Ministries.

   2) oversee and support Lutheran Men in Mission, which shall operate with leadership elected by its members and with a constitution established by its members, which shall become effective upon approval by the Church Council. Policies and actions of Lutheran Men in Mission shall be subject to review by the board of the Division for Congregational Ministries and all budget requests shall be submitted through the Division for Congregational Ministries.

   3) relate to ELCA outdoor ministries and provide support through programs and services.

   4) relate to the Lutheran Laity Movement for Stewardship, which shall be recognized as being an association within this church, which shall be self-supporting financially, and which shall provide specialized stewardship services to this church in consultation with and through cooperation with this division. This association shall administer its affairs in conformity with the applicable policies of this church and shall coordinate its operations with the Division for Congregational Ministries. The specific function of this association shall be enumerated in its constitution and bylaws. The constitution and bylaws of the Lutheran Laity Movement for Stewardship, and amendments thereto, after review by this division, may be amended by a two-thirds vote of the Church Council.

g. assist congregations, in cooperation with the Commission for Multicultural Ministries, in ministry with African Americans, Asians, Hispanics, and Native Americans.

h. cooperate and consult with synods with regard to congregational concerns and engage in research, under the guidance and coordination of the Department for Research and Evaluation and in accord with standards established by the Church Council, to identify and assess the needs of congregations and evaluate churchwide support for such ministry.

i. cooperate with other churchwide units and with the synods to develop strategies for service to congregations, synods, and other ministries. To do so, this division will:

1) provide for delivery systems for congregational programs and resources, working with other appropriate units.

2) seek to inform congregations, working with the Department for Communication, about the availability of programs and resources.

3) inform synodical leadership and work through synodical structures under the coordination of the Department for Synodical Relations.

4) assist the Publishing House of the ELCA in the promotion, introduction, and distribution of published resources.

j. provide for development of congregational social ministry in cooperation with synods, social ministry organizations, the Division for Church in Society, and the Division for Outreach.

16.11.B91. *Division for Ministry*

This division shall be responsible for the policies, programs, organizations, and seminaries of this church that affirm, develop, and support the ministries of the whole people of God, including recognition and support of the ministry of laypersons, ordained persons, and associates in ministry. To fulfill these responsibilities, this division shall:

a. provide leadership to this church in undergirding and supporting the ministry of all the baptized in the church and in the world. To do so, this division will:

1) provide appropriate programs, counsel, and support to congregations, synods, and other entities and institutions in support of the ministry of the laity in daily life, including the development of forums for reflection and study of theology, other disciplines, and society.

2) relate to and provide support for movements and organizations of ministry in daily life and work closely with other churchwide units, especially the Division for Congregational Ministries, in fostering programs and activities in congregations and other settings concerning ministry in daily life.

3) coordinate, in consultation with other churchwide units, synods, and institutions, this church's efforts in leadership development and in the nurture of persons preparing for and serving in rostered ministries.

b. oversee the system of theological education of this church. To do so, this division will:

1) recommend churchwide policies and educational standards for the seminaries of this church to the Church Council and/or Churchwide Assembly, or where appropriate, establish such policies related to the system of theological education in this church.

2) approve amendments to the governing documents of the seminaries.

3) convene annual meetings of seminary presidents, deans, and faculty representatives to promote interseminary communication and cooperation; and consult regularly with the presidents of the seminaries to coordinate this church's program and planning for theological education.

4) advocate on behalf of the seminaries to this church and advocate for this church to the seminaries.

5) encourage the seminaries of this church to use the services of a common auditor.

c. provide leadership to this church in the development of standards, procedures, and policies related to the rostered ministries of this church and foster concern for the care of rostered persons. To do so, this division will:

1) develop, in consultation with the Conference of Bishops, ecclesiastical standards for the admission of persons to and the continuation of persons on the rosters of ordained ministers and associates in ministry.

2) develop and manage programs, in cooperation with the synods and seminaries, for the recruitment, preparation, evaluation, and support of candidates for service as ordained ministers and as associates in ministry, including the development and recommendation of standards for educational programs that prepare ordained ministers and associates in ministry, and coordinate, in consultation with the Division for Higher Education and Schools, the development of programs for the recruitment of candidates for rostered ministries of this church.

3) develop policy governing the relationship with the Deaconess Community of the Evangelical Lutheran Church in America and others on the official lay roster of this church.

4) recommend and provide for programs of continuing theological education and other education and support for ministry for ordained ministers, associates in ministry, and laypersons, in consultation with and with the cooperation of the Conference of Bishops, the Division for Higher Education and Schools, synods, seminaries, continuing education centers, and the colleges and universities of this church.

5) consult with the Conference of Bishops as the conference develops and implements programs for first call, mobility, and pastoral care of rostered persons.

6) develop and manage, in cooperation with the Conference of Bishops, other churchwide units and synods, policies and programs in specialized pastoral care, counseling and clinical education ministries, including development of standards and maintenance of relationships with professional certification entities and other organizations related to ministries of specialized pastoral care and development of programs in such areas as educational preparation, support, advocacy, resources, ministry development, and supervised clinical ministry.

d. initiate, encourage, and promote theological reflection in cooperation with theologians, the Conference of Bishops, the Department for Ecumenical Affairs, the Division for Higher Education and Schools, the Publishing House of the ELCA, lay movements, and others. To do so, this division will:

1) develop and disseminate to this church information concerning significant developments in theological research and trends.

2) develop and edit Lutheran Partners magazine for publication by the Publishing House of the ELCA.

3) provide for a regular and representative convocation of theologians involved in the teaching ministry of this church, through a committee comprised of representatives of this division, seminary faculties including Lutheran faculties teaching at non-Lutheran seminaries and schools of theology, members of this church who teach on college and university religion faculties, and synodical bishops.

e. distribute financial resources provided by this church to seminaries, continuing education centers, associated agencies, and other diverse ministries, providing funds for such items as scholarships and faculty development (especially among women, persons of color, and persons with a primary language other than English), internship support, theological conferences, and educational programs for specialized ministries.

16.11.C91. *Division for Outreach*

This division shall provide leadership and support for this church as it reaches out in witness to the Gospel in the areas served by the synods of this church by developing new ministries and congregations; supporting existing ministries and congregations in transition or with special needs; working with synods in developing area strategies for outreach; and administering capital funds for loans, real-estate acquisition, and building programs in support of new ministries and congregations. To fulfill these responsibilities, this division shall:

a. develop and recommend policy for, and then assist in the development of new ministries and congregations, the support of existing

ministries and congregations in transition or with special needs, and of urban and rural coalitions. To do so, this division will:

1) function in cooperation with synods and congregations.

2) have primary responsibility in working with synods to determine where and when new congregations of this church shall be developed and to recommend ministries for recognition and reception as congregations of this church.

3) be responsible for the churchwide Mission Partners program and Mission Builders program, in coordination with synods and appropriate churchwide units.

b. develop and carry out programs of evangelism in the development of new ministries, working in coordination with the Division for Congregational Ministries as the Division for Congregational Ministries develops programs and resources to nurture evangelism efforts of existing congregations.

c. establish, support, and plan, in consultation with the Commission for Multicultural Ministries and the Division for Congregational Ministries, for the outreach of this church among persons of color and those whose primary language is other than English.

d. provide staff services and financial grants to assist synods or groups of synods in the development of area strategies for outreach, in coordination with the Division for Church in Society and the Division for Congregational Ministries.

e. provide for appropriate training and support, in cooperation with synods, for persons in outreach ministries of development and redevelopment, and those in urban, rural, and area ministries.

f. develop, in consultation with the Office of the Treasurer, an annual capital budget and administer the use of these capital funds for loans, real-property acquisition, and building programs in support of the development of new ministries and congregations. It also shall support investment in the Mission Investment Fund of the ELCA. Criteria for real-estate acquisition and disposition for new or existing ministries within the limits of capital funds available shall be established jointly by the Division for Outreach and the Office of the Treasurer. Within jointly established guidelines, this division shall determine which congregations shall receive loans, the amount of each loan, and the repayment schedule. This division also shall supervise collection of such loans. To do so, this division will:

1) have staff responsible for real-property work in the acquisition and disposition of property for new and/or existing ministries within the limits of the capital funds available and within criteria established jointly by the Division for Outreach and the Mission Investment Fund of the ELCA through the Office of the Treasurer. The real-property staff of this division shall provide expertise

to the Division for Higher Education and Schools in support of campus-ministry facility development.

2) offer building and architectural consultative services to new congregations entering first-unit construction, to congregations relocating with synodical approval, and to other congregations.

g. be responsible for representing this church in churchwide cooperative planning for outreach together with other church bodies and ecumenical organizations serving in the geographic territory of this church's synods.

h. cooperate, under the coordination of the Division for Global Mission, with Lutheran church bodies based in other nations that desire to carry out ministry in the U.S.A., and consult with synods of this church in planning and implementing such ministry.

i. cooperate with the Division for Global Mission, the Division for Congregational Ministries, Division for Higher Education and Schools, and the synods of this church in providing programs of education for mission and for witness to persons of other faiths.

j. relate to congregationally based community organizations that are associated with outreach ministries supported by this division and assist in the development of such organizations, under the coordination of the Division for Church in Society and synods.

16.11.D91. **Division for Higher Education and Schools**

This division shall be responsible for the educational activities of this church through its colleges and universities, its campus ministries, its early childhood education centers, and elementary and secondary schools. It shall advocate to this church for these educational enterprises and for this church to these educational efforts. This division also shall develop programs and recommend policies in response to this church's commitment to mission in education and, thereby, shall help to prepare leaders for church and society. To fulfill these responsibilities, this division shall:

a. encourage, assist, and sustain the colleges and universities of this church, both individually and as a community of institutions. To do so, this division will:

1) render services in policy, planning, and oversight for this church's colleges and universities; distribute churchwide funding in consultation with synodical partners; encourage and provide funding for colleges and universities to use the services of a common auditor; assist colleges and universities in providing health-insurance programs through voluntary employees' beneficiary associations; and provide risk management services for the colleges and universities and, in cooperation with the Division for Ministry, for the seminaries of this church.

2) cooperate with congregations, synods, and the colleges and universities in student recruitment; and work in partnership with

congregations, the ELCA Foundation, other funding sources, and colleges and universities to encourage and develop scholarship opportunities.

3) assist the colleges and universities in the recruitment and development of faculty and administrators.

4) promote relationships between groups of colleges and universities and synods; provide for the creation and support of a council of college presidents; be represented on each college board by an advisory member; and participate in the search for and election of college presidents.

5) make recommendations to the Church Council on long-term educational policy, including the establishment and location of colleges and universities.

6) assist colleges and universities to develop international education opportunities in consultation with the Division for Global Mission.

b. oversee the campus ministry program at state and independent colleges and universities by recommending policy for campus ministry agencies and personnel. To do so, this division will:

1) initiate planning for fulfilling this ministry and coordinate and distribute churchwide funding in consultation with synodical and congregational partners.

2) provide for the purchase and maintenance of campus ministry facilities.

3) provide for the recruitment and development of campus ministry professional staff; conduct regular evaluations of staff performance and ministry; give pastoral support and counsel to professional staff and campus ministry agencies; and develop materials and other resources to support and strengthen the work of campus ministry.

4) coordinate a system of contact pastors and congregations to perform ministry at colleges and universities where professional campus ministry staff are not employed.

5) foster relationships with Lutheran student movements, ecumenical student movements, and other denominational campus ministries.

6) develop strategies for assisting this church to educate and evangelize publicly in higher education settings.

c. undergird Lutheran early childhood education centers, elementary schools, and secondary schools, and recommend policies for their relationship to this church. To do so, this division will:

1) assist the schools of this church to develop appropriate educational and administrative policies and practices.

2) provide for the recruitment, development, and affirmation of teachers and other leaders in schools of this church in consultation with the Division for Ministry.

3) work with the Division for Congregational Ministries and synods to support congregations that operate early childhood education centers and schools, with a special focus on the role of schools in faith formation, community service, and outreach.

4) encourage, in consultation with the Division for Congregational Ministries, the congregations and synods of this church to support and be involved with public and non-public schools of this nation.

d. recruit—in consultation and cooperation with the Division for Ministry, the Commission for Multicultural Ministries and the Commission for Women, the colleges and universities of this church, and this church's campus ministry programs—candidates for ordained and lay ministries of this church and other leaders for congregations, and seek to develop methods for helping students and academic personnel to discover and strengthen their Christian vocation in the church and in the world.

e. represent the colleges, universities, and schools of this church in public policy matters under the coordination of the Division for Church in Society; and encourage, support, and promote relationships with associations and entities related to higher education and to schools.

16.11.E91. *Division for Church in Society*

This division shall assist this church to discern, understand, and respond to the needs of human beings, communities, society, and the whole creation through direct human services and through addressing systems, structures, and policies of society, seeking to promote justice, peace, and the care of the earth. To fulfill these responsibilities, this division shall:

a. develop and coordinate this church's theological and ethical study and analysis of social issues as part of its social witness.

b. develop this church's social statements for action by the Church Council and Churchwide Assembly; and prepare, in consultation with the Office of the Bishop and appropriate churchwide units, messages and resolutions on social issues for action by the Church Council.

c. work in cooperation with the Division for Congregational Ministries and the Division for Ministry to relate this church's social witness to the life of congregations and to the ministry of members in daily life; assist, when appropriate, the Division for Congregational Ministries and the Publishing House of the ELCA in the development of educational resources and strategies.

d. support, encourage, and facilitate communication among formal and informal networks of people throughout this church committed to study, service, and advocacy concerning social issues.

e. provide, in cooperation with other units, leadership, consultation, educational resources, and programmatic activities in the areas of peace and the environment.

f. develop, in cooperation with synods, congregations, and community and social ministry organizations, a comprehensive delivery system for human services to carry out this church's ministry in response to the needs of persons in poverty and other persons with limited options, including persons who are aged, sick, imprisoned, living with disabilities, homeless, infants and children, refugees, and those experiencing disasters. To do so, this division will:

1) establish criteria to grant and maintain affiliation with social ministry organizations through homes, institutions, agencies, hospitals, and other parts of the social ministry system; and recommend overall policy for the social ministry activity of this church.

2) provide for technical and programmatic support and monitoring for new and established social ministry organizations; fund developing social ministry organizations and community organizations; fund pilot and research projects for program development in existing social ministry organizations; and provide emergency funds for social ministry organizations in temporary financial difficulty.

3) maintain a network to enable the sharing of financial assets and personnel among the social ministry organizations; monitor financial matters of the social ministry organizations; and provide recommendations regarding capital expansion.

4) provide for leadership development and standards for executives, staff, and boards of social ministry organizations; and, in cooperation with the Division for Ministry, maintain standards for chaplains serving in affiliated social ministry organizations.

g. coordinate this church's relationship with community organizations and community-economic development activities in cooperation with synods, congregations, the Division for Outreach, the Commission for Multicultural Ministries, and the Commission for Women.

h. assist this church in inclusive ministry with and among persons with disabilities.

i. direct and implement this church's public-policy advocacy to national and international governmental bodies in consultation with other churchwide units, and coordinate its public-policy advocacy to state governmental bodies. To do so, this division will:

1) maintain an office in Washington, D.C., on behalf of this church for advocacy to the U.S. and foreign governments.

2) maintain an office in New York, on behalf of this church, for advocacy to the United Nations and other international and national governmental bodies; and shall represent, at the request of the Lutheran World Federation and in consultation with the U.S.A. National Committee of the Lutheran World Federation, the concerns of the Lutheran World Federation in the United Nations.

3) establish and maintain, in partnership with synods and social ministry organizations, state public-policy offices for advocacy to state governments on behalf of this church.

j. give expression to this church's concern for corporate social responsibility, both in its internal affairs and its interaction in the broader society. To do so, this division will:

1) exercise, at the direction of the Church Council, the rights of this church as a corporate shareholder on issues of social concern on stocks held by the churchwide units that are not separately incorporated. In addition, the Church Council may make recommendations to the churchwide units that are separately incorporated concerning the filing of shareholder resolutions and the casting of proxy ballots on stocks held by those units.

2) facilitate the formation of an Advisory Committee on the Church's Corporate Social Responsibility that will include representatives from the Board of Pensions, the Church Council, and other units of this church and that will give counsel and advice to all appropriate units of this church on corporate social responsibility.

3) work with national ecumenical groups on issues of corporate responsibility.

k. be responsible for this church's program to combat world hunger; administer, in cooperation with the Division for Outreach and other appropriate units, a hunger grants program to combat hunger and poverty in the United States through relief and development; administer hunger education and hunger advocacy grants; and direct this church's hunger education in cooperation with appropriate churchwide units.

l. relate on behalf of this church to Lutheran Immigration and Refugee Service and the Inter-Lutheran Domestic Disaster Response.

m. coordinate this church's domestic disaster response.

16.11.F91. Division for Global Mission

This division shall be responsible for this church's mission in other countries and shall be the channel through which churches in other countries engage in mission to this church and society. To fulfill these responsibilities, this division shall:

a. engage the members and resources of this church in mission outside the territory of this church through involvement in evangelism, witness, education, promotion of justice, service, relief, and development. To do so, the division will:

1) establish relationships and cooperate in mission with Lutheran and other Christian churches, agencies, institutions, mission societies, and movements in other countries.

2) develop and recommend policies and programs for this church's mission in other countries.

3) facilitate contacts and the exchange of human and material resources among churches, institutions, and agencies outside the U.S.A. with which this division cooperates.

4) recruit, call, prepare, and send missionary personnel, including volunteers.

5) develop and administer personnel policies for long-term missionaries and, in consultation with the Department for Human Resources, recommend these policies to the Church Council.

6) participate in development and relief with Lutheran World Relief, the Lutheran World Federation, and other ecumenical organizations and agencies.

7) administer the allocation of funds to combat hunger outside the U.S.A. in cooperation with the Division for Church in Society.

8) cooperate with the global community in promoting justice and the equitable sharing of resources.

b. be responsible for this church's relationship to mission societies, organizations, and movements in North America that focus on mission in other countries.

c. develop and administer international scholarship programs on behalf of this church, the Lutheran World Federation, and churches in other countries.

d. encourage and enable churches in other countries in mission to this church and society and, in cooperation with the Division for Outreach and the Division for Church in Society, be their contact as those churches carry out mission in this country.

e. cooperate with the Division for Outreach and other units of this church in programs of education about and witness to persons of other faiths within the territory of this church.

f. share with this church insights and expertise gained from Christian relationships around the globe and intercultural experiences.

g. provide programs of global mission education for this church in cooperation with the synods of this church, the Division for Outreach, the Division for Congregational Ministries, the Commission for Multicultural Ministries, and other units of this church.

16.20. **Commissions**

16.21. **This church may establish commissions to accomplish specific tasks. Action of the Churchwide Assembly is required to establish a commission or to determine that a commission's mandate has been fulfilled. At the expiration of a commission's mandate, continuing responsibilities related to the particular commission shall be undertaken by the appropriate division of the churchwide organization.**

16.22. **A commission is a unit to which is assigned the responsibility to assist this church in addressing specific tasks of particular urgency by providing advice, counsel, and services in the area of the commission's specific function to the divisions, other churchwide units, Church Council, congregations, and synods of this church.**

Commission Steering Committees

16.22.10.

16.22.11. Each commission shall be governed by a steering committee, whose members shall be selected for their experience and expertise related to the commission's responsibilities. The size of the steering committee and the procedure for election by the Church Council shall be described in the continuing resolutions of each commission. The bishop of this church, or the bishop's designee, shall serve as an advisory member of each steering committee. The Conference of Bishops shall select one bishop to serve as an advisory member of each steering committee.

Steering committee members shall be elected to one six-year term, with no consecutive reelection and with one-third to be elected every biennium.

16.22.12. To assist the commission in carrying out its service to the divisions, one member of the commission executive staff may attend meetings of the board of each division in an advisory capacity with voice but not vote.

16.22.13. Each division of this church may be represented at meetings of the steering committee of each commission by one member of the division executive staff in an advisory capacity with voice but not vote.

16.22.14. Each commission shall have an executive director who shall be elected by the Church Council to a four-year term in consultation with and with the approval of the bishop of this church. Nomination of a candidate for election by the council shall be made jointly by the bishop of this church and the steering committee. The bishop of this church, or the bishop's designee, shall arrange within the policy of this church for an annual review of the executive director in consultation with the chair of the steering committee. Executive directors of commissions shall be eligible for reelection. The employment of the executive director may be terminated jointly by the bishop of this church and the Executive Committee of the Church Council in consultation with the chair of the steering committee, consistent with the personnel policies. In keeping with personnel policies, the salary of the executive director shall be established by the bishop of this church and the salaries of staff members proposed by the executive director shall be ratified by the bishop's representative.

16.22.15. The provisions of 14.21.01. through 14.21.04., 14.21.07., 16.11.23., 16.11.25., 16.11.31., 16.11.32. and 16.11.33. shall apply to each commission.

16.22.16. Each commission steering committee shall meet at least two times each year. Upon two successive absences that have not been excused by the committee, a committee member's position shall be declared vacant by the secretary of this church who shall arrange for election by the Church Council to fill the unexpired term.

16.22.17. The responsibilities of the commissions shall be enumerated in continuing resolutions. Such continuing resolutions may be amended by a majority vote of the Churchwide Assembly or by a two-thirds vote of the Church Council. Should the steering committee in question disagree with the action of the Church Council, it may appeal the decision to the Churchwide Assembly.

16.22.18. This church shall have the following commissions:
a. Commission for Multicultural Ministries; and
b. Commission for Women.

16.22.A91. *Commission for Multicultural Ministries*

a. *This commission shall assist this church in working toward the goal of full partnership and participation of African Americans, Asians, Hispanics, and Native Americans in the life of this church and society. To fulfill these responsibilities, this commission shall:*

1) *assist this church in developing its policies and practices related to this commission's responsibilities. To do so, this commission will:*

  a) *review and monitor program directions and plans of this church.*

  b) *develop and recommend to the Church Council churchwide strategies, plans, policies, and procedures to facilitate realization of goals related to this commission's responsibilities.*

  c) *assist in developing and implementing such strategies.*

  d) *assist in the development and support of African American, Asian, Hispanic, and Native American leadership.*

2) *assist the churchwide organization and other expressions of this church to deal with racism and to minister in a multicultural context.*

3) assist this church in developing and implementing a public-policy advocacy program on racial justice issues under the coordination of the Division for Church in Society.

4) assist this church in assessing and responding to African American, Asian, Hispanic, and Native American needs and opportunities for specific ministry. To do so, this commission will:

a) assist this church in the proclamation of the Gospel among and in the development of partnerships with African Americans, Asians, Hispanics, and Native Americans in cooperation with the Division for Outreach.

b) provide advice, counsel, and recommendations to other churchwide units concerning the development of multicultural and community-specific programs and resources.

c) work cooperatively with the Commission for Women in developing and implementing programs for the full participation and partnership of African American, Asian, Hispanic, and Native American women in the life of this church and society.

5) facilitate dialogue among and between African American, Asian, Hispanic, Native American, and White communities.

6) assist this church in developing and implementing cooperative efforts with the African American, Asian, Hispanic, and Native American communities in society, in other Christian communions, and in other religious traditions.

b. This commission shall develop and convene African American, Asian, Hispanic, and Native American advisory groups to gather advice and information, and to identify subjects and issues for study in these communities. This commission shall interpret such information for use by this church and shall engage in research with these communities under the guidance and coordination of the Department for Research and Evaluation and in accord with standards established by the Church Council.

c. This commission shall assist and support the African American Lutheran Association in the ELCA, the Association of Asians in the ELCA, the Association of Hispanic Ministries in the ELCA, and the Native American Lutheran Association in the ELCA.

d. This commission shall report to the Church Council through the council's Program and Structure Committee.

e. The executive director of this commission shall serve as an advisory member of the steering committee of the Commission for Women with voice but not vote.

f. The steering committee of the Commission for Multicultural Ministries shall have 20 members elected in accord with the representation principles stipulated in 5.01.f., except that four shall be African American, four shall be Asian, four shall be Hispanic, four

shall be Native American, and four shall be White. In addition to advisory members provided in 16.22.11., the executive director of the Commission for Women shall serve as an advisory member of this steering committee with voice but not vote.

g. Members of the steering committee shall be nominated and elected for their experience and expertise in relation to the commission's responsibilities. Each community shall nominate two of its members to serve on the commission's steering committee. In addition, the board of each division shall nominate one African American, or one Asian, or one Hispanic, or one Native American member for the steering committee. The Church Council shall nominate the remaining members. The Church Council shall elect the members of the steering committee.

16.22.B91. Commission for Women

a. This commission shall enable this church to realize the full participation of women; to create equal opportunity for women of all cultures; to foster partnership between men and women; to assist this church to address sexism; and to advocate justice for women in this church and society. To fulfill these responsibilities, this commission shall:

1) assist this church in developing, understanding, and forming its policies and practices with regard to the full involvement of women in this church. To do so, this commission will:

a) promote and facilitate study and dialogue.

b) develop and maintain relationships with other units of this church and with similar units of other church organizations.

c) develop and recommend to the Church Council strategies, plans, policies, procedures, and goals related to the commission's responsibility.

d) assist this church in coordinating the programs related to women.

2) assist this church to create a safe environment for women in this church and society.

3) propose to the Church Council a plan to review, monitor, and report on implementation and progress toward meeting this church's goals in this area.

4) identify subjects and issues for study and action, assist this church to listen to the concerns of women, gather information, and cooperate in research under the guidance and coordination of the Department for Research and Evaluation and in accord with standards established by the Church Council.

5) provide, in cooperation with divisions and other churchwide units, for materials and other resources to carry out the functions of this commission.

17.10. **Other Churchwide Units**

17.11. **This church may establish other churchwide units and organizations to carry out the purpose and functions of this church.**

17.12. **Other churchwide units include:**

a. **the church periodical;**

b. **the ELCA Foundation, operating under the Endowment Fund;**

c. **the Women of the ELCA;**

d. **the Publishing House of the ELCA; and**

e. **the Board of Pensions.**

The Endowment Fund of the Evangelical Lutheran Church in America, the Board of Pensions of the ELCA, the Publishing House of the ELCA, and the Women of the ELCA may be separately incorporated units of this church.

17.20. **Church Periodical**

17.21. **The church periodical, *The Lutheran*, shall be published by this church through the Publishing House of the ELCA and shall be identified as a magazine of this church.**

17.21.01. An advisory committee for *The Lutheran* shall have the responsibility for the church periodical. The advisory committee, in consultation with the bishop of this church and the Church Council, shall nominate the editor for the church periodical.

17.21.02. The Churchwide Assembly shall elect the editor of the church periodical. If the first nominee nominated by the advisory committee is not elected, the advisory committee shall nominate another person. The editor shall be elected to a four-year term.

17.21.03. Should the editor be unable to serve to the completion of the editor's term, the Church Council shall elect an acting editor, upon nomination of the periodical advisory committee, to serve until the next Churchwide Assembly. Dismissal of an editor shall follow the procedure for an officer.

17.21.04. The editor shall be responsible to the Churchwide Assembly through the Church Council and shall report to the Church Council in the interim, in keeping with 14.21.04. through 14.21.04., 14.21.07., 16.11.23., and 16.11.25. The editor shall select the editorial staff of the church periodical. The salary of the editor shall be established by the bishop of this church and salaries of staff members proposed by the editor shall be ratified by the bishop or the bishop's designee.

17.21.05. The publishing house, in consultation with the editor, shall produce and distribute the church periodical, provide staff for circulation, promotion,

6) cooperate with the appropriate agencies and institutions to address issues common to sexism and racism and other attitudes and practices that divide, discriminate, and oppress.

b. The executive director of this commission shall serve as an advisory member to the board of this church's women's organization and of the steering committee of the Commission for Multicultural Ministries with voice but not vote.

c. This commission shall report to the Church Council through the council's Program and Structure Committee.

d. The steering committee of the Commission for Women shall be composed of 12 members, eight of whom shall be lay people and four of whom shall be ordained ministers, elected by the Church Council for their experience and expertise in relation to the commission's responsibilities. Membership of the committee shall include African American, Asian, Hispanic, and Native American persons. In addition to advisory members provided in 16.22.11., the executive director of the Women of the ELCA and the executive director of the Commission for Multicultural Ministries shall serve as advisory members of this steering committee with voice but not vote.

subscription fulfillment, advertising solicitation, billing and collection of accounts, and other services.

17.21.06. The budget for the church periodical shall be prepared by the editor and the executive director of the publishing house for inclusion of the subsidy request in the budget-development process of the Church Council. One-half of the subsidy shall be from the churchwide organization's budget and one-half shall be provided by the publishing house.

17.21.07. Official notices of this church shall be published in the periodical.

17.21.20. **Advisory Committee for the Church Periodical**

17.21.21. The specific responsibilities of the advisory committee shall be specified in a continuing resolution. The continuing resolution may be amended by a majority of the members of the Churchwide Assembly or by a two-thirds vote of the Church Council. Should the committee disagree with the action of the Church Council, it may appeal the decision to the Churchwide Assembly.

17.21.A87. *The advisory committee of the church periodical shall:*

a. *develop editorial and advertising guidelines;*

b. *receive periodic reports from the editor;*

c. *consult with the editor from the perspective of the expertise of committee members;*

d. *receive the periodical's annual budget for transmission of the subsidy request to the Church Council in this church's budget process; and*

e. *be responsible, together with the bishop of this church, for the annual performance review of the editor.*

17.30. **ELCA Foundation**

17.31. **This church shall have a foundation to provide major gift and planned giving programs for individual donors, and educational and support services in major gift and deferred giving programs to congregations, synods, agencies, and institutions of this church. This foundation shall operate under the Endowment Fund of the Evangelical Lutheran Church in America. The Endowment Fund shall be incorporated. Its executive director shall be president of the corporation and shall serve as its chief executive officer, unless the Church Council determines that the treasurer of this church shall be the president of this corporation.**

17.31.01. The Endowment Fund of the Evangelical Lutheran Church in America, operating as the ELCA Foundation, shall have a board of trustees of nine members, elected by the Church Council from a slate of nominees submitted by the council's nomination process. To ensure geographical distribution, there shall be one member of the committee from each region. Board members shall be elected for one six-year term with no consecutive reelection and with one-third elected every two years. The

bishop of this church or the bishop's designated representative, a representative with stewardship responsibilities in the Division for Congregational Ministries, the treasurer of this church, and a synodical bishop elected by the Conference of Bishops shall serve as advisory members of the board with voice but not vote.

17.31.02. The president shall be elected by the board of trustees of the Endowment Fund of the Evangelical Lutheran Church in America to a four-year term in consultation with and with the approval of the bishop of this church. Nomination of a candidate for president shall be made jointly by the bishop of this church and the search committee of the board. The board, together with the bishop of this church, shall arrange for an annual review of the president. The president shall be eligible for re-election. The employment of the president may be terminated jointly by the board of trustees of the Endowment Fund of the Evangelical Lutheran Church in America and the bishop of this church, following recommendation by the executive committee of the board of trustees.

17.31.03. This foundation's executive director shall serve as an advisory member of the board of the Division for Congregational Ministries.

17.31.04. The following constitutional provisions shall apply to the operation of the board: 14.21.01. through 14.21.04., 16.11.12., 16.11.24., and 16.11.25.

17.31.05. The board of trustees shall consult with the Office of the Treasurer with regard to the assessment of management fees or provision of other assets available for the budget of the foundation.

17.31.06. The specific responsibilities of the foundation shall be enumerated in a continuing resolution. The continuing resolution may be amended by a majority vote of the Churchwide Assembly or a two-thirds vote of the Church Council. Should the board disagree with the action of the Church Council, it may appeal the decision to the Churchwide Assembly.

17.31.A91. *Responsibilities of the ELCA Foundation*

a. *This foundation shall conduct—on behalf of this church, its congregations, synods, churchwide units, and institutions—a program of major gifts and planned giving.*

b. *This foundation shall provide consultation, support, and guidance to members of this church in the area of planned giving.*

c. *This foundation shall provide coordination and support in major gifts and planned giving to this church, including congregations, synods, churchwide organization, and agencies and institutions.*

d. *This foundation shall provide educational materials, seminars, and workshops in the area of planned giving.*

e. *This foundation shall coordinate its programs and ministries with the objectives and programs of other stewardship and financial-resource development activities of this church.*

f. *This foundation shall consult with the Office of the Treasurer in the recommendation and establishment within that office of policies and procedures for processes governing valuation of noncash gifts, the management of assets of life-income agreements and endowment funds, and the distribution of earned-income payments to donors and to remainder beneficiaries as regulated by life-income, trust, and other fiduciary donor agreements.*

g. *This foundation, in cooperation with congregations, synods, and agencies and institutions of this church, shall:*
1) *identify and cultivate prospective major and deferred-gift donors;*
2) *seek gifts, bequests, and investments for the Mission Investment Fund of the Evangelical Lutheran Church in America; and*
3) *coordinate the programs of this foundation with the ministry objectives of the synods of this church.*

Women's Organization

17.40.

17.41. **This church shall have a women's organization to assist its women to commit themselves to full discipleship, affirm their gifts, and support each other in their particular callings.**

17.41.01. Membership of this organization shall be women of this church who wish to participate through local and other groupings that affirm the purposes of this organization. This organization shall function in local, synodical, and churchwide settings.

17.41.02. This organization shall be incorporated, self-supporting financially, and shall manage its own assets within the policies of this church.

17.41.03. The provisions of bylaws 16.11.11., 16.11.11., 16.11.12., 16.11.22. through 16.11.24., 16.11.32., and 16.11.33. shall apply to this organization. Bylaw 16.11.25. shall apply to the women's organization with the exception of the balance provisions for women and men and for laypersons and persons on the roster of ordained ministers.

17.41.04. This organization shall have a board of 21 members elected by the assembly of this organization for one three-year term with eligibility for one consecutive reelection. At least 10 percent of the members of this board shall be persons of color or primary language other than English. No more than one elected board member shall be from any one synod. Board members are to serve with the perspective of the interdependence of all units of this church. The Conference of Bishops shall select one bishop to serve as an advisory member of the board of this organization with voice but not vote.

17.41.05. The board of this organization shall meet at least two times per year and shall be responsible to the assembly that elected it. The assembly of this organization shall be representative of local and other groupings of women who are members of the women's organization. Upon two successive absences that have not been excused by the board, a board

member's position shall be declared vacant and the board shall arrange for election to fill the vacancy under Article I, Section 4, Item 9, of the constitution and bylaws of the women's organization.

17.41.06. This organization's board shall elect its executive director to a four-year term in consultation with and with the approval of the bishop of this church. This board, together with the bishop, shall arrange for an annual review of the executive director. The executive director shall be eligible for reelection. The board may terminate the employment of the executive director in consultation with and with the approval of the bishop of this church.

17.41.07. This organization's executive director shall serve as an advisory member to the steering committee of the Commission for Women, with voice but not vote.

17.41.08. The specific responsibilities of the women's organization shall be enumerated in a continuing resolution. The continuing resolution may be amended by a majority of the Churchwide Assembly or two-thirds of the Church Council. Should the board disagree with the action of the Church Council, it may appeal the decision to the Churchwide Assembly.

Responsibilities of the Women's Organization

17.41.A91. a. *This organization shall enable its members to grow through biblical study, theological reflection, and prayer.*

b. *This organization shall cooperate with other units of this church in advocating for the oppressed and voiceless, urging change in systems and structures that exclude and alienate, and working for peace and justice as messengers of hope.*

c. *This organization shall provide for development and distribution of resources for and to its members, including a magazine.*

d. *This organization shall facilitate local initiative in creating programs and identifying alternative structural models that encourage and support flexibility.*

e. *This organization shall design and implement a leadership development program for its members, assisting its members to identify, develop, and express their gifts for ministry.*

f. *This organization, in cooperation with the Commission for Women, shall develop networks for communication among women locally, ecumenically, and globally.*

g. *This organization shall relate to other women's organizations ecumenically and globally.*

h. *This organization shall work interdependently with all units of this church. It shall cooperate and coordinate with the Commission for Women and the Division for Congregational Ministries in program development, research, and planning in order to enhance the ministries and participation of women in church and in society.*

i. *This organization shall develop working arrangements in areas of mutual responsibility with the Publishing House of the Evangelical Lutheran Church in America.*

Publishing House of the ELCA

17.50.

17.51. **This church shall have a publishing house. The Publishing House of the Evangelical Lutheran Church in America shall be incorporated. Its executive director shall be president of the corporation and shall serve as its chief executive officer.**

17.51.01. This publishing house shall have a board of trustees of 21 members, elected for one six-year term with no consecutive reelection and with one-third elected every two years as provided in Chapter 19. The Conference of Bishops shall elect one bishop to serve as an advisory member of the board of the publishing house with voice but not vote.

17.51.02. The provisions of 16.11.11., 16.11.12., 16.11.24., 16.11.25., 16.11.32., and 16.11.33. shall apply to this publishing house.

17.51.03. The president shall be elected by the board of trustees of the Publishing House of the ELCA to a four-year term in consultation with and with the approval of the bishop of this church. Nomination of a candidate for president shall be made jointly by the bishop of this church and the search committee of the board. The board, together with the bishop of this church, shall arrange for an annual review of the president. The president shall be eligible for reelection. The president may be terminated at any time jointly by the board of trustees of the Publishing House of the ELCA and the bishop of this church, following recommendation by the executive committee of the board of trustees.

17.51.04. The specific responsibilities of this publishing house shall be enumerated in a continuing resolution. The continuing resolution may be amended by a majority vote of the Churchwide Assembly or a two-thirds vote of the Church Council. Should the board disagree with the action of the Church Council, it may appeal the decision to the Churchwide Assembly.

17.51.A91. *Responsibilities of the Publishing House of the ELCA*

a. *This publishing house shall be responsible for the publishing, production, and distribution of publications to be sold to accomplish the mission of this church.*

b. *This publishing house shall work in close cooperation with congregations, synods, and the churchwide organization to provide a diversity of published resources.*

c. *This publishing house shall relate to other churchwide units through resource planning groups. Materials published to assist congregations in fulfilling their life in mission shall be developed in coordination with other appropriate churchwide units. Development costs will be paid by the unit developing the publication.*

d. *This publishing house shall develop, produce, and distribute materials required to carry out its functions.*

e. *This publishing house shall be financed from the distribution of materials, not from the budget of this church.*

(9.93)

f. *This publishing house shall create, develop, and publish a diversity of resources in various media; make available other publications, materials, and church supplies; produce the official documents and publications of this church; and produce materials in a manner that assures their ready availability.*

g. *This publishing house shall establish a distribution center for each region, as well as utilize other means for the wide distribution of resources within and beyond this church.*

h. *This publishing house shall manage its finances and other resources in a manner that assures the continuity and extension of its activities. This publishing house shall maintain its own accounting, data processing, personnel, pension, and other functions essential to a cohesive, efficient, and effective operation.*

i. *This publishing house shall identify and nurture talented authors, composers, artists, and others involved in creating various media.*

j. *This publishing house shall produce and distribute the church periodical in accord with provisions of this church's constitution, bylaws, and continuing resolutions.*

k. *This publishing house shall determine its necessary financial reserves, appropriations, and publishing subsidies, and it also shall provide one-half of such subsidy as is necessary for the budget of the church periodical after agreement on the amount of subsidy by both the Church Council and the board of this publishing house.*

l. *This publishing house, in cooperation with the Commission for Multicultural Ministries and the Division for Congregational Ministries, shall make available resources to meet unique language and cultural needs.*

m. *This publishing house shall provide for production and distribution services for materials that originate in churchwide units, including the option of providing for competitive printing costs and delivery from independent printers, with costs for these services paid by the originating unit.*

Board of Pensions

17.60.

17.61. **This church shall have a church pension and other benefits plans unit. This Board of Pensions shall be incorporated. Its executive director shall be president of the corporation and shall serve as its chief executive officer.**

17.61.01. The Churchwide Assembly shall:

a. authorize the creation of the governance structure for this program;

b. approve the documents establishing and governing the program;

c. refer any amendments to the program initiated by the Churchwide Assembly to the Board of Pensions for recommendation before final action by the Church Council, assuring that no amendment shall abridge the rights of members with respect to their pension accumulations; and

   d. direct the establishment of an appeal process within the Board of Pensions to enable participants in the plans to appeal decisions.

17.61.02. The Church Council shall:

   a. review policy established by the board and take action on any policy that would change the documents establishing and governing this program;

   b. approve any changes in the approved program when there is to be:

      1) a significant increase in cost to the employer; or

      2) a significant decrease in benefits to the participant;

   c. refer any amendments to the program initiated by the Church Council to the board for recommendation before final action by the Church Council, assuring that no amendment shall abridge the rights of members with respect to their pension accumulations;

   d. refer, as it deems appropriate, proposed amendments to the Churchwide Assembly for final action; and

   e. appoint a Financial Information Committee, composed of persons not responsible for pension and benefits plans, to evaluate proposed benefit and contribution changes in terms of their economic impact on:

      1) individual congregations;

      2) synods and the churchwide organization; and

      3) long-term cost to contributors.

17.61.03. This board shall have a board of trustees composed of 21 persons elected for one six-year term with no consecutive reelection and with one-third elected each biennium as provided in Chapter 19. In addition, the trustees of this board shall include persons with expertise in investments, insurance, and pensions, and six persons who are participants in the plans, at least one of whom shall be a lay plan participant or lay recipient of plan benefits and at least one of whom shall be an ordained minister who is a plan participant. The Conference of Bishops shall elect one bishop to serve as an advisory member of the Board of Pensions with voice but not vote.

17.61.04. The board shall organize itself as it deems necessary except that it shall have the following committees:

   a. Benefits Committee, including a subcommittee on appeals; and

   b. Investment Committee.

17.61.05. The provisions of 16.11.11., 16.11.12., 16.11.24., 16.11.25., 16.11.32., and 16.11.33. shall apply to this board.

17.61.06. The president shall be elected by the board of trustees of the Board of Pensions in consultation with and with the approval of the bishop of this church. Nomination of a candidate for president

shall be made jointly by the bishop of this church and the search committee of the board. The board, together with the bishop of this church, shall arrange for an annual review of the president. The president shall be eligible for reelection. The president may be terminated at any time jointly by the board of trustees of the Board of Pensions and the bishop of this church, following recommendation by the executive committee of the board of trustees.

17.61.07. The specific responsibilities of the Board of Pensions shall be enumerated in continuing resolutions. Such continuing resolutions may be amended by a majority vote of the Churchwide Assembly or by a two-thirds vote of the Church Council. Should the board disagree with the action of the Church Council, it may appeal the decision to the Churchwide Assembly.

17.61.A91. *Responsibilities of the Board of Pensions*

   a. *This board shall manage and operate the pension and other benefits plans for this church with the design and policy adopted by the Churchwide Assembly and shall invest the assets according to its best judgment.*

   b. *The Investment Committee of the Board of Pensions shall receive advice and counsel from the Advisory Committee on the Church's Corporate Social Responsibility formed by the Division for Church in Society and within the context of fiduciary responsibility make appropriate recommendations to the board.*

   c. *This board shall manage and operate those portions of The American Lutheran Church, The Association of Evangelical Lutheran Churches, and Lutheran Church in America plans requiring continuation in this church.*

   d. *This board shall provide pension, health, and other benefits exclusively for the benefit of eligible members working within the structure of this church and those benefits shall be on the same basis for all the participants.*

   e. *This board shall provide an outline of all benefits to be provided as a part of the fund document.*

   f. *This board shall prepare a statement assessing the financial impact of proposed benefit program changes on individuals, congregations, synods, and the churchwide organization.*

   g. *This board shall report to the Churchwide Assembly through the Church Council, with the Church Council making comments on all board actions needing approval of the Churchwide Assembly.*

   h. *This board shall establish appropriate linkages with other units of this church.*

   i. *This board shall be self-supporting, except for minimum pensions and post-retirement health benefits of certain retirees, with all costs being paid from the administrative and management charges to the employers utilizing the plans and from investment income.*

j. *This board shall manage its finances in a manner that assures an efficient and effective administration of the plans for pension and other benefits. The board shall maintain its own accounting, data processing, personnel, and other administrative functions essential to the ongoing work of this organization.*

k. *This board shall not be responsible, nor assume any liability for, health-insurance programs provided by colleges and universities of this church through voluntary employees' beneficiary associations or similar arrangements.*

Chapter 18.
REGIONS

18.01. **This church shall have regions as a partnership between groups of synods and the churchwide organization for the purpose of exercising mutual responsibilities.**

18.10.10.

Functions

18.11.11. The regions shall be a means for coordinated responses by synods and the churchwide organization to mission and program opportunities within the region.

18.11.A91. *In fulfilling the region's function and the purposes of this church, each region may assist in:*

a. *planning for this church's participation in God's mission in the region, with special attention to the opportunities for outreach with the Gospel;*

b. *providing for ongoing dialogue between the synods of the region and churchwide units for the purpose of identifying functions that may be done together;*

c. *forming resource planning groups to recommend resources and services needed for congregations;*

d. *facilitating, when requested, relationships with colleges, universities, and campus ministries and partnership funding responsibilities of the synods and churchwide organization on behalf of colleges, universities, and campus ministries;*

e. *facilitating gatherings of synodical bishops, synodical staff, and regional staff; and*

f. *coordinating the work of the churchwide staff within the territory of the region.*

18.11.12. The region shall be a forum where the synods and the churchwide organization may study, plan, and share together in developing common programs unique to the region. Responsibilities carried out together will vary from region to region depending on the decision of the synods and churchwide units.

18.11.13. In partnership, the synods and the churchwide organization shall explore the feasibility of carrying out additional functions between and among synods and churchwide units within the region.

18.11.B91. *Additional functions may include:*

a. *relating to seminaries;*

b. *relating to camps and other outdoor ministries;*

c. *developing communication plans and projects;*

d. *planning for and coordinating continuing education programs;*

e. *providing for various services to congregations;*

f. facilitating global mission education and interpretation;

g. providing for stewardship and evangelism events;

h. providing for events for the growth and equipping of God's people for their ministries in the world;

i. compiling lists of personnel that may be used by synods for interim ministries;

j. providing a financial service bureau for the cooperating synods for banking, payroll, accounts payable, and accounts receivable;

k. providing for regional archives, associated with institutions of this church wherever possible;

l. coordinating resources for youth ministry;

m. assisting synods in facilitating the mobility of ordained ministers and associates in ministry and providing such resources as crisis-intervention services and psychodiagnostic-treatment programs;

n. facilitating, when requested, relationships with social ministry organizations and assisting in advocacy work; and

o. addressing other functions, as deemed appropriate by synods and the churchwide organization.

18.11.14. Additional programs or services may be developed in each region upon the request of two or more synods, or upon the request of the churchwide organization and one or more synods, providing that each requesting synod and the churchwide organization supply the necessary financial support for the services requested.

18.11.15. A process for reviewing the ongoing programs of the region every four years shall be established by each regional steering committee.

Governance

18.11.20. Each region shall have a steering committee. The membership of the committee shall be determined jointly by synodical-churchwide consultation, subject to ratification by the Church Council.

18.11.21.

18.11.22. The churchwide organization shall have such representation on the regional steering committee as will provide adequate opportunity for a partnership relationship in shaping and sharing in the programs where responsibility is shared.

Staff

18.11.30. Staffing patterns developed by regions to carry out the basic functions of regional coordination shall be ratified by the Church Council. A full-time salaried coordinator may be appointed by the regional steering committee who will:

a. facilitate processes to accomplish the functions of the region; and

b. receive and carry out tasks assigned by the regional steering committee.

18.11.31.

18.11.32. The region may have such additional staff as the regional steering committee may determine.

Funding

18.11.40.

18.11.41. The funding of the region shall be shared by the participating synods and the churchwide organization according to a cost allocation as decided by the synods and the churchwide organization.

Geography

18.11.50.

18.11.51. The synods and the churchwide organization may evaluate, from time to time, the regional geography and the appropriateness of synodical assignments to the region.

Chapter 19.
NOMINATIONS AND ELECTION PROCESS

19.01.   The Churchwide Assembly shall elect the bishop, vice president, and secretary of this church and such other persons as the constitution and bylaws may require, according to procedures set forth in the constitution and bylaws of this church.

19.02.   The members of the Church Council shall be elected by the Churchwide Assembly. Each biennium the Church Council shall determine how this church's commitment to inclusive representation will affect the next election to the Church Council. The Nominating Committee shall invite each eligible synod to submit suggested nominees and shall then nominate persons who fulfill the categories assigned by the Church Council. Excluding the churchwide officers, there shall not be more than one member of the Church Council from a synod nor shall more than two-thirds of the synods in a region have members on the Church Council at the same time. The Church Council shall have at least one member from each region. The terms of office of persons elected to regular terms on the Church Council by the Churchwide Assembly shall begin at the conclusion of the Churchwide Assembly at which such persons were elected.

19.03.   In the event an interim vacancy on a board, committee, or council is declared by the secretary of this church, the Church Council shall elect a member to serve the balance of the term.

19.04.   Other than elections of officers and executive directors of units, elections shall be for one six-year term, without consecutive reelection, and with one-third of the members of the Church Council and of each board elected each biennium.

19.05.   Each nominee for an elected or appointed position in this church shall be a voting member of a congregation of this church.

19.10.   Nomination and Election Considerations

19.11.01.   In the nomination and election process the following general considerations shall be observed:

a.   It shall be the responsibility of the Church Council to assure that this church maintain its commitment to inclusive representation.

b.   In all elections by the Churchwide Assembly, other than for the bishop, vice president, and secretary, a majority of the votes cast on the first ballot shall be necessary for election. If an election does not occur on the first ballot, the names of the two persons receiving the highest number of votes cast shall be placed on the second ballot. On the second ballot, a majority of the legal votes cast shall be necessary for election. For the position of editor of *The Lutheran*, a majority of the legal votes cast shall be necessary for election.

c.   Members of the Church Council, committees, and the boards of churchwide units who have served less than one-half of a term shall be eligible for election to one full term to be served consecutively upon the conclusion of the partial term.

d.   Before electing a member to a vacancy on a board, the Church Council shall consult with the board.

e.   On the final ballot for the election of the bishop, vice president, and secretary of this church, when only two names appear on the ballot, a majority of the legal votes cast shall be necessary for election.

f.   The Conference of Bishops shall select one bishop from each region to serve a four-year term as an advisory member of the Church Council. Each biennium the Conference of Bishops shall select a bishop to serve as an advisory member of each board, steering committee, and advisory committee of the churchwide organization. No synodical bishop shall serve as a voting member of the Church Council or of a board or committee of any churchwide unit.

g.   The youth organization of this church shall elect for terms of two years two persons to serve as advisory members of the Church Council.

h.   An advisory member of a board, committee, or of the Church Council shall have voice but not vote.

Nominating Committee

19.20.

19.21.01.   There shall be a Nominating Committee consisting of 18 members elected by the Churchwide Assembly. Each member shall be elected to one six-year term and shall not be eligible for consecutive reelection. Six members of the committee shall be elected each biennium. The Church Council shall place in nomination the names of two persons for each position. The committee shall consist of at least one member but no more than three members from any region. Nominations from the floor shall also be permitted, but each floor nomination shall be presented as an alternative to a specific category named by the Church Council and shall therefore meet the same criteria as the persons against whom the nominee is nominated. In the materials provided in advance to each member of the assembly, the Church Council shall set forth the criteria applicable to each category that must be met by persons nominated from the floor.

19.21.02.   The Nominating Committee shall nominate two persons for each council, board, or committee position for which an election will be held by the Churchwide Assembly. Nominations from the floor also shall be permitted, but each floor nomination shall be presented as an alternative to a specific category named by the Nominating Committee and shall therefore meet the same criteria as the persons against whom the nominee is nominated. In the materials provided in advance to each member of the assembly, the Nominating Committee shall set forth the criteria applicable to each category that must be met by persons nominated from the floor.

19.21.03. In each case in which there are floor nominations, there shall be a preliminary ballot that shall include the names of the nominees presented by the Nominating Committee or the Church Council, and the person or persons nominated from the floor. The names of the two persons receiving the highest number of votes cast shall be placed on the final ballot.

19.21.04. It shall be the responsibility of the Church Council to make certain that every synod has at least one person serving on the churchwide boards. Among those persons elected by the assembly, no more than two persons from any one synod shall serve on any one board.

19.21.05. The Nominating Committee shall strive to ensure that all persons nominated for any position possess the necessary competence and experience for the position. All persons elected to any position, whether nominated by the Nominating Committee or not, shall strive to represent this church and not just a particular geographic area.

Election of Officers

19.30.

19.31.01. The churchwide officers shall be elected as follows:

a. The bishop shall be elected by the Churchwide Assembly by ecclesiastical ballot. Three-fourths of the votes cast shall be necessary for election on the first ballot. If no one is elected, the first ballot shall be considered the nominating ballot. Three-fourths of the votes cast on the second ballot shall be necessary for election. The third ballot shall be limited to the seven persons (plus ties) who received the greatest number of votes on the second ballot, and two-thirds of the votes cast shall be necessary for election. The fourth ballot shall be limited to the three persons (plus ties) who receive the greatest number of votes on the third ballot, and 60 percent of the votes cast shall be necessary for election. On subsequent ballots, a majority of the votes cast shall be necessary for election. These ballots shall be limited to the two persons (plus ties) who receive the greatest number of votes on the previous ballot.

b. The vice president shall be elected by the Churchwide Assembly. The election shall proceed without oral nominations. If the first ballot for vice president does not result in an election, it shall be considered a nominating ballot. On the first ballot, three-fourths of the votes cast shall be required for election. Thereafter only such votes as are cast for persons who received votes on the first or nominating ballot shall be valid. On the second ballot, three-fourths of the votes cast shall be necessary for election. On the third ballot, the voting shall be limited to the seven persons (plus ties) receiving the greatest number of votes on the second ballot and two-thirds of the votes cast shall be necessary for election. On the fourth ballot, voting shall be limited to the three persons (plus ties) receiving the greatest number of votes on the previous ballot and 60 percent of the votes cast shall elect. On subsequent ballots, voting

shall be limited to two persons (plus ties) receiving the greatest number of votes on the previous ballot and a majority of votes cast shall elect.

c. The secretary shall be elected by the Churchwide Assembly. The election shall proceed without oral nominations. If the first ballot for secretary does not result in an election, it shall be considered a nominating ballot. On the first ballot, three-fourths of the votes cast shall be required for election. Thereafter only such votes as are cast for persons who received votes on the first or nominating ballot shall be valid. On the second ballot, three-fourths of the votes cast shall be required for election. On the third ballot, the voting shall be limited to the seven persons (plus ties) receiving the greatest number of votes on the second ballot and two-thirds of the votes cast shall be necessary for election. On the fourth ballot, voting shall be limited to the three persons (plus ties) receiving the greatest number of votes on the previous ballot and 60 percent of the votes cast shall elect. On subsequent ballots, voting shall be limited to the two persons (plus ties) receiving the greatest number of votes on the previous ballot and a majority of the votes cast shall elect.

d. The treasurer shall be elected by the Church Council.

Terms of Office

19.40.

19.41.01. The terms of office of persons elected to regular terms on a division board by the Churchwide Assembly shall begin at the conclusion of the assembly at which such persons were elected. The commencement of terms of office of persons elected to regular terms by the Churchwide Assembly on the board of trustees of the Publishing House of the ELCA and the board of trustees of the Board of Pensions shall be specified in the bylaws of these separately incorporated entities.

19.41.02. The terms of office of persons elected to regular terms on the Nominating Committee of the Churchwide Assembly, the Committee on Discipline, and the Committee on Appeals shall begin at the conclusion of the Churchwide Assembly at which such persons were elected, except as may be specified in continuing resolutions with respect to particular pending discipline matters.

19.41.A91. *With respect to committees that consider disciplinary cases or appeals:*

a. Any member of the churchwide Committee on Discipline who has been appointed to serve on a discipline hearing committee for a particular pending case shall continue to serve to discharge that appointment notwithstanding that his or her successor has been subsequently elected at a Churchwide Assembly.

b. Any member of the synodical Committee on Discipline who is serving at the time that the Executive Committee of the Church Council appoints members from the churchwide Committee on Discipline to a discipline hearing committee shall continue as a member of that discipline hearing committee for the particular pending case,

(9-93)   ELCA CONSTITUTION—CHAPTER 19 / 135

notwithstanding that his or her successor has been subsequently elected at a Synod Assembly.

c. *Any member of the Committee on Appeals who is serving at the time that an appeal is made shall continue to serve to decide that appeal, notwithstanding that his or her successor has been subsequently elected at a Churchwide Assembly.*

19.50. Experience and Expertise

19.51.01. The Churchwide Assembly shall elect all members of each division board, the board of the Publishing House of the ELCA, and the board of trustees of the Board of Pensions. The Nominating Committee shall seek to ensure that these boards have within their membership persons with the expertise and experience essential to the fulfillment of the work of the board.

19.51.02. The members of the steering committees for each commission shall be elected by the Church Council and shall have particular experience and expertise that will assist the committee in its work. The terms of office of persons elected by the Church Council to regular terms on a steering committee shall begin at the conclusion of the first regular meeting of the Church Council after each regular meeting of the Churchwide Assembly.

19.51.03. The advisory committee of the church periodical shall be composed of ten members elected by the Church Council.

a. Five members of the advisory committee of the church periodical shall be nominated by the Church Council's nomination process and the remaining five members shall be nominated by the board of the Publishing House of the ELCA. Not more than one person shall be a member of the Church Council and not more than one person shall be a member of the board of the publishing house. The members of the advisory committee shall include persons chosen for their understanding of periodical publishing.

b. The terms of office of persons so elected to regular terms on the advisory committee of the church periodical shall begin on the first day of the month following the first regular meeting of the Church Council after each regular meeting of the Churchwide Assembly.

c. With the exception of a member of the Church Council selected to serve on the advisory committee and with the exception of a member of the board of this church's publishing house selected to serve on the advisory committee, each member of the advisory committee for *The Lutheran* shall be elected for one six-year term, with no consecutive reelection and with one-third of the members elected every two years. A member of the Church Council and a member of the board of the publishing house shall serve two-year terms on the advisory committee, with the possibility of biennial reelection to a maximum of six years.

d. The advisory committee shall elect the chair of the committee from those members who are not members of the Church Council or the board of the publishing house.

e. The Conference of Bishops shall elect one bishop to serve as an advisory member of this committee.

19.51.04. The editor of the church periodical shall be elected to a four-year term by the Churchwide Assembly upon nomination as provided in Chapter 17 and shall take office on the first day of the third month after election.

19.51.05. The Church Council shall elect the members of the board members of the ELCA Foundation as provided in Chapter 17.

19.60. Other Matters Related to Nominations and Elections

19.61.01. The Church Council shall from time to time, by continuing resolution, establish committees and procedures for the conduct of elections at the Churchwide Assembly.

19.61.02. No member of the Church Council, a committee of the Church Council, a board, a steering committee, an advisory committee, or other committee shall receive emolument for such service, nor shall any member be simultaneously an officer of this church, an elected member of the Church Council, or a member of a committee or board of the churchwide organization.

Nothing in this section shall be construed to prohibit the payment by this church of the costs of insurance on behalf of a person who is or was a member of the Church Council, a committee of the Church Council, a board, a steering committee, the board of the ELCA Foundation, or the advisory committee of the church periodical against any liability asserted against and incurred by such person in or arising from that capacity, whether or not this church would have been required to indemnify such person against the liability under provisions of law or otherwise.

19.61.03. No employee of the churchwide organization of this church, of its regions, or individual under contract to any unit of the churchwide organization or a region shall be eligible for nomination to or membership on the Church Council, a steering committee, a board, committees related to the Commission for Multicultural Ministries, church periodical, or archives, the Committee on Appeals, the Committee on Discipline, or the churchwide Nominating Committee during the period of employment or service under contract. (The phrase "under contract" shall not mean short-term contracts for specific, limited purposes, usually not to exceed six months.)

19.61.04. No spouse, parent, son, daughter, sibling, uncle, aunt, niece, nephew, grandparent, grandchild, or in-law (parent, son, or daughter of a spouse, or spouse of a sibling) of an executive director or of an executive staff member of the churchwide organization shall be eligible for nomination

19.61.05. to or membership on the Church Council, board, or committee that oversees the unit in which the person's relative is employed.

No voting member of a board, or persons employed by an entity, agency, or institution supervised by that board, shall be simultaneously an officer of this church, a voting member of the Church Council, or a voting member of another board, steering committee, or advisory committee of this church, except the advisory committee of the church periodical that has representation from the Church Council and the board of the Publishing House of the ELCA. Upon two successive absences that have not been excused by the board, steering committee, or advisory committee, a member's position shall be declared vacant by the secretary of this church who shall arrange for election by the Church Council to fill the unexpired term.

Chapter 20.
CONSULTATION, DISCIPLINE, APPEALS, AND ADJUDICATION

20.10. **Consultation and Discipline**

20.11. There shall be set forth in the bylaws a process of discipline governing ordained ministers, officers, the editor of the church periodical, associates in ministry, persons on other official rosters, congregations, and members of congregations. Such process shall assure due process and due protection for the accused, other parties, and this church. Since synods have responsibility for admittance of persons into the ordained ministry of this church or onto other rosters of this church and have oversight of pastoral/congregational relationships, the disciplinary process shall be a responsibility of the synod on behalf of this church and jointly with it.

20.12. As used in this constitution and bylaws, due process means the right to be given specific written notice of the charges against any person or entity of this church, the right to testify in person or remain silent (at the election of the accused), the right to call witnesses and introduce documentary evidence concerning the pending charges, the right to confront and cross-examine all witnesses in support of such charges, the right to a hearing before a discipline hearing committee as provided in 20.13., the right to a written decision of the discipline hearing committee as provided in the bylaws, and the right to be treated with fundamental procedural fairness. Any violation of these rights shall be grounds for reversal of an unfavorable finding and the right to a new hearing.

20.12.01. "Fundamental procedural fairness" means and includes: avoidance by committee members of written communications to or from either the accused or accuser(s) without copy to the other; avoidance by committee members of oral communications with either the accused or accuser(s) outside the presence of the other; maintaining decorum during the hearing; allowing both the accuser(s) and the accused to present their cases without unnecessary interruptions; keeping a verbatim record of the hearing, either made by a stenographer or court reporter or by tape recording; allowing both the accuser(s) and the accused to be accompanied at the hearing by a representative (who may, but need not, be an attorney) who also may participate in the proceedings; impartiality of the committees that consider the charges; and the right to be treated in conformity with the governing documents of the Evangelical Lutheran Church in America.

20.13. The accused shall be entitled to a hearing before a discipline hearing committee as described in the bylaws. The hearing shall not be open to the public unless both the accuser and the accused agree to a public hearing. At a hearing not open to the public, a limited number of concerned persons may attend as provided in the bylaws.

20.13.01. In a hearing not open to the public,

a. the accuser and the accused may each be represented by not more than two representatives who may present or assist in the presentation of the evidence, and

b. the discipline hearing committee may permit attendance by a limited number of persons chosen by the accused.

20.13.02. Irrespective of whether a hearing is or is not open to the public, the discipline hearing committee may decide that witnesses (other than the accused and the accuser) shall be permitted in the hearing only when testifying. A witness may be accompanied by a friend or advocate.

20.14. Once a charge against a person or entity has been considered by a discipline hearing committee, that person or entity shall not be required to answer that charge again except under the circumstances set forth in the bylaws.

20.14.01. The circumstances in which a person or entity shall be required to answer again charges before a discipline hearing committee shall be limited to the following:

a. The Committee on Appeals has ordered a rehearing as its disposition of a timely appeal to it.

b. The Committee on Appeals has ordered a further hearing after either an accuser or an accused has petitioned for a further hearing on the basis of newly discovered evidence or testimony that was not available at the time of the original hearing.

20.14.02. After a charge against a person or entity has been considered by a discipline hearing committee, evidence related to that charge may be introduced at a subsequent hearing before another discipline hearing committee on a different but related charge. Charges are "related" if they involve similar alleged conduct on the part of the accused.

20.15. The procedures for consultation and discipline set forth in the bylaws shall be the exclusive means of resolving all matters pertaining to the discipline of congregations of this church. Neither this church nor a synod of this church shall institute legal proceedings in which conduct described in provision 20.31.01. is the basis of a request for relief consisting of suspension of that congregation from this church or removal of that congregation from the roll of congregations of this church. A congregation of this church shall not institute legal proceedings against this church or a synod of this church seeking injunctive or other relief against the imposition or enforcement of any disciplinary action against that congregation.

20.16. It is the intent of this church that all matters of discipline should be resolved internally to the greatest extent possible. It is the policy of this church not to resort to the civil courts of this land until all internal procedures and appeals have been exhausted, except for emergency situations involving a significant imminent risk of physical injury or severe loss or damage to property.

20.17. None of the provisions of this chapter is intended nor shall be construed to limit the authority of a Synod Council to remove, under the bylaws of this church, from the rosters of this church an ordained minister or other person who is without regular call and not retired, for any reason, even though such reason might also be the basis for disciplinary proceedings under this chapter.

20.20. Ordained Ministers and Official Lay Rosters

20.21.01. Ordained ministers shall be subject to discipline for:

a. preaching and teaching in conflict with the faith confessed by this church;

b. conduct incompatible with the character of the ministerial office;

c. willfully disregarding or violating the functions and standards established by this church for the office of Word and sacrament; or

d. willfully disregarding the provisions of the constitution or bylaws of this church.

20.21.02. The disciplinary actions which may be imposed are:

a. private censure and admonition by the bishop of the synod;

b. suspension from the office and functions of the ordained ministry in this church for a designated period or until there is satisfactory evidence of repentance and amendment; or

c. removal from the ordained ministry of this church.

20.21.03. Charges against an ordained minister which could lead to discipline must be specific and in writing, subscribed to by the accuser(s), and be made by one or more of the following:

a. at least two-thirds of the members of the congregation's council, submitted to the synodical bishop;

b. at least one-third of the voting members of the congregation, submitted to the synodical bishop;

c. at least two-thirds of the members of the governing body to which the ordained minister, if not a parish pastor, is accountable, submitted to the synodical bishop;

d. at least 10 ordained ministers of the synod on whose roster the accused ordained minister is listed, submitted to the synodical bishop; or

e. the synodical bishop.

20.21.04. When there are indications that a cause for discipline may exist and before charges are made, efforts shall be made by the bishop of the synod to resolve the situation by consultation; for assistance in these efforts, the bishop may utilize either a consultation panel or an advisory panel as herein provided:

a. When requested by the synodical bishop, a consultation panel consisting of five persons (three ordained ministers and two lay persons) appointed from the members of the Consultation Committee of the synod by the synodical bishop, or, at the request of the synodical bishop, by the Synod Council's Executive Committee or other committee authorized to do so by the Synod Council, shall assist the synodical bishop in efforts to resolve a situation by consultation.

b. When requested by the synodical bishop, an advisory panel consisting of five persons (three ordained ministers and two lay persons) appointed by the synodical bishop shall assist the synodical bishop in efforts to resolve a situation by consultation.

20.21.05. If appointed, a consultation panel or advisory panel shall advise the synodical bishop as to whether or not the bishop should bring charges or may make other recommendation for resolution of the controversy that would not involve proceedings before a discipline hearing committee. To these ends, the panel may meet with complaining witnesses as well as with the concerned ordained minister. If requested by the synodical bishop, members of the panel also may assist, as representatives of the accuser, in the presentation of evidence and examination of witnesses before a discipline hearing committee.

20.21.06. When charges are brought other than by the synodical bishop, the synodical bishop may refer such charges to a consultation panel as provided in 20.21.04.a.

a. If as a result of meeting with a consultation panel the charges are withdrawn by the accuser(s), no further proceedings shall be required.

b. Upon recommendation of the consultation panel that the charges be dismissed, the synodical bishop may dismiss the charges, in which case no further proceedings shall be required.

c. Upon recommendation of the consultation panel that some of the allegations supporting the charges be stricken, the synodical bishop may strike some or all of such allegations, and further proceedings shall be required on the remaining allegations.

d. In the case of charges that do not anticipate disciplinary action, the consultation panel shall submit a report in writing to the synodical bishop that sets forth the action or actions recommended by the consultation panel, and the synodical bishop shall convey the recommendations to the parties. If either party does not accept the recommendations, that party may appeal to the Synod Council, whose decision shall be final.

e. In the case of charges that anticipate disciplinary action that have not been withdrawn or dismissed as a result of 20.21.06.a. or b. above, the charges shall be referred to a discipline hearing committee for a hearing.

f. The work of a consultation panel under this section shall be completed within 30 days from the time the panel was constituted.

20.21.07. When charges are brought by a synodical bishop, or when charges are brought other than by a synodical bishop and have not been withdrawn or dismissed or otherwise disposed of as provided in 20.21.06., the synodical bishop shall deliver a copy of the charges to the accused and the secretary of this church.

20.21.08. A discipline hearing committee shall be convened to conduct a hearing. The voting members of this committee shall be composed of 12 persons of whom six shall be the members of the Committee on Discipline of the synod and six shall be selected from the churchwide Committee on Discipline under the process described in 20.21.12. A hearing officer selected from the churchwide Committee of Hearing Officers under the process described in 20.21.14. shall preside as the nonvoting chair of the discipline hearing committee.

20.21.11. The churchwide Committee on Discipline shall consist of 28 persons, 15 of whom shall be laypersons and 13 of whom shall be ordained ministers, elected by the Churchwide Assembly for a term of six years, each without consecutive reelection, to serve as needed on a discipline hearing committee in any of the synods in this church.

20.21.12. The accused shall have the privilege of selecting two persons (one clergy and one lay) of the six persons from the churchwide Committee on Discipline to serve on a discipline hearing committee. The remaining four persons (two clergy and two lay), or six, if the accused does not exercise the privilege, shall be selected by the Executive Committee of the Church Council.

20.21.13. The churchwide Committee of Hearing Officers shall consist of six persons elected by the Church Council for a term of six years, each without consecutive reelection, to serve as needed on a discipline hearing committee in any of the synods of this church.

20.21.14. The bishop of this church shall select one member of the churchwide Committee of Hearing Officers to serve as the nonvoting chair of a discipline hearing committee.

20.21.15. The bishop of this church may appoint one or more persons as facilitators to make arrangements for, and to provide technical assistance to, a discipline hearing committee.

20.21.16. The Church Council shall appoint three members from the Committee on Appeals who shall recommend rules of procedure for the performance of the duties of hearing officers and discipline hearing committees. The rules shall become effective when ratified by the Church Council.

20.21.17. In each specific case for which a discipline hearing committee has been constituted, the committee shall, within 60 days after the secretary of this church has given notice of the selection by the Executive Committee of the Church Council of the members of the churchwide Committee on Discipline to serve on a discipline hearing committee, meet with the accused and the accuser(s) to hold a hearing and render its written decision. The 60-day period may be extended one or more times to a

20.21.18. specified date by a written stipulation signed by the accuser(s), the accused, and the hearing officer prior to the expiration of the original 60-day period or prior to the extended specified date.

20.21.19. Written notice of the date, time, and place of the hearing and a copy of the charges shall be delivered to the accused and to the accuser(s) at least 20 days prior to the date of the hearing.

20.21.20. At the hearing, the accuser(s) may present evidence in support of the charges and thereafter the accused shall be entitled to present evidence. The accused and the accuser(s), or other person acting on behalf of either of them, shall be entitled to question the other party or any of the witnesses appearing on behalf of the other party. A verbatim record shall be made by a stenographer or by tape recording of the hearing.

20.21.21. The discipline hearing committee shall render its decision in writing. The written decision shall be in two parts:

a. Findings of Fact. In this part, the committee shall set forth what it has found to be the relevant facts—that is, what it believes to be the truth of the matter.

b. Determination. In this part, the committee shall state whether, based upon the facts that it has found, it believes discipline should be imposed and, if so, what discipline it has chosen to impose.

20.21.22. The decision of the discipline hearing committee shall be made by a majority vote of its members who were present at the hearing. The decision of the discipline hearing committee shall be final unless, within 30 days, one of the parties appeals to the Committee on Appeals. The decision of the Committee on Appeals shall be final.

20.21.23. If there are indications that a cause for discipline exists or if in the course of the proceedings it should become apparent to the bishop of the synod that the pastoral office cannot be conducted effectively in the congregation(s) being served by the ordained minister due to local conditions or that local conditions may be adversely affected by the continued service by the ordained minister, the bishop of the synod may temporarily suspend the pastor from service in the congregation(s) without prejudice and with pay provided through a joint synodical and churchwide fund and with housing provided by the congregation(s).

20.21.24. If there are indications that a cause for discipline exists or if in the course of proceedings, it becomes apparent to the bishop of the synod that the circumstances require, the bishop of the synod may temporarily suspend an ordained minister serving under letter of call issued other than by a congregation from the office and functions of ordained ministry without prejudice and without affecting compensation and housing.

20.22.01. Lay persons on official rosters shall be subject to discipline for:

a. confessing and teaching in conflict with the faith confessed by this church;

b. conduct incompatible with the standards for the rostered ministries of this church;

c. willfully disregarding or violating the functions and standards established by this church for the lay roster or rosters; or

d. willfully disregarding the provisions of the constitution or bylaws of this church.

20.22.02. The disciplinary actions that may be imposed are:

a. private censure and admonition by the bishop of the synod;

b. suspension from the role and functions of an associate in ministry, a Deaconess of the Evangelical Lutheran Church in America, or a diaconal minister for a designated period or until there is satisfactory evidence of repentance and amendment; or

c. removal from the official roster for lay persons of this church.

20.22.03. Charges against a layperson on an official roster of this church that could lead to discipline must be specific and in writing, subscribed to by the accuser(s), and be made by one or more of the following:

a. at least two-thirds of the members of the Congregation Council of the congregation in which the layperson is serving, submitted to the synodical bishop;

b. at least one-third of the voting members of the congregation of which the layperson is serving, submitted to the synodical bishop;

c. at least two-thirds of the members of the governing body to which the layperson is accountable, submitted to the synodical bishop;

d. at least 10 ordained ministers or laypersons on official rosters of the synod on whose roster the accused layperson is listed, submitted to the synodical bishop; or

e. the synodical bishop.

20.22.04. When there are indications that a cause for discipline exists, efforts shall be made by the bishop of the synod to resolve the situation by consultation in the same manner as set forth above for ordained ministers in 20.21.04. through 20.21.06.

20.22.05. If those efforts fail, the procedures for discipline shall be the same as that set forth above for ordained ministers in 20.21.07. through 20.21.22.

20.22.06. If there are indications that a cause for discipline exists or if in the course of the proceedings it should become apparent to the bishop of the synod that the role and function of the associate in ministry, Deaconess of the Evangelical Lutheran Church in America, or diaconal minister cannot be conducted effectively in the congregation(s) being served by a rostered layperson due to local conditions or that local conditions may be adversely affected by the continued service by a rostered layperson, the bishop of the synod may temporarily suspend a rostered layperson from service in the congregation(s) without prejudice and with pay provided through a joint churchwide-synodical-congregation fund.

20.22.07. If there are indications that a cause for discipline exists or if in the course of proceedings, it becomes apparent to the bishop of the synod that the circumstances require, the bishop of the synod may temporarily suspend a rostered layperson serving under letter of call issued other than by a congregation from the office and functions of a rostered layperson without prejudice and without affecting compensation.

20.30. Congregations

20.31.01. Congregations shall be subject to discipline for:

a. departing from the faith confessed by this church;

b. willfully disregarding or violating the criteria for recognition as congregations of this church; or

c. willfully disregarding or violating the provisions of the constitution or bylaws of this church.

20.31.02. The disciplinary actions which may be imposed are:

a. censure and admonition by the bishop of the synod;

b. suspension from this church for a designated period, the consequences of such suspension being the loss of voting rights of any member (including ordained ministers) of the congregation at synod or churchwide assemblies, the loss of the right to petition, and the forfeiture of eligibility by any member of the congregation to serve on any council, board, committee, or other group of this church, any of its synods, or any other subdivision thereof;

c. suspension of the congregation of this church for a designated period (with the same consequences as in b.) during which the congregation shall be under the administration of the synod, provided that a congregation may refuse to accept such administration in which case it shall be removed from the roster of congregations of this church; or

d. removal from the roster of congregations of this church.

20.31.03. Charges against a congregation which could lead to discipline must be specific and in writing, subscribed to by the accuser(s), and be made by one or more of the following:

a. at least one-fifth of the voting members of the congregation, submitted to the synodical bishop;

b. at least three other congregations of the synod, submitted to the synodical bishop;

c. the Synod Council; or

d. the synodical bishop.

20.31.04. When there are indications that a cause for discipline exists, efforts shall be made by the bishop of the synod to resolve the situation by consultation in the same manner as set forth above for ordained ministers in 20.21.04. through 20.21.06.

20.31.05. If those efforts fail, the procedures for discipline shall be the same as that set forth above for ordained ministers in 20.21.07. through 20.21.22.

20.40. Members of Congregations

20.41.01. The offenses for which a member of a congregation shall be subject to discipline are:

a. denial of the Christian faith;

b. conduct grossly unbecoming a member of the Church of Christ; or

c. persistent trouble-making within the congregation.

20.41.02. Discipline shall be administered by the Congregation Council on behalf of the congregation. The procedure which Christ instructed his disciples to follow (Matthew 18:15-17) shall be adhered to in every case, proceeding through these successive steps:

a. private admonition by the pastor;

b. admonition by the pastor in the presence of two or three witnesses; and

c. written citation to appear before the Congregation Council, serving as a discipline hearing committee, having been received by the member at least 10 days prior to the meeting.

If proposed discipline against a member proceeds beyond counseling and private admonition by the pastor, the charges against a member must be specific and in writing, and shall accompany the written citation.

20.41.03. Members of the Congregation Council who participate in the preparation of the written charges or who present evidence or testimony in the hearing before the Congregation Council are disqualified from voting upon the question of the guilt of the accused member. Should the accused be found guilty by the vote of at least two-thirds of the members of the Congregation Council, who are not disqualified but who are present and voting, and renewed admonition prove ineffectual, the council shall impose one of the following disciplinary actions:

a. censure before the council or the congregation;

b. suspension from stated privileges of membership for a definite designated period of time; or

c. termination of membership.

A resolution of the council suspending or terminating the membership of a member of this congregation shall be delivered to the person in writing.

20.41.04. Appeal from any disciplinary action imposed by the Congregation Council may be made to the Synod Council, whose decision shall be final.

20.41.05. Disciplinary actions may be reconsidered and revoked by the Congregation Council upon receipt of:
a. evidence that injustice has been done; or
b. evidence of repentance and amendment.

20.50. Recall or Dismissal

20.51. The recall or dismissal of the bishop, vice president, or secretary of this church or of the editor of the church periodical and the vacating of office may be effected:
a. for willful disregard or violation of the constitution and bylaws of this church;
b. for such physical or mental disability as renders the officer incapable of performing the duties of office; or
c. for such conduct as would subject the officer to disciplinary action as an ordained minister or as a member of a congregation of this church.

20.52. Proceedings for the recall or dismissal of such an officer shall be instituted by petition by:
a. the Church Council on a vote of at least two-thirds of its elected members; or
b. the Churchwide Assembly on a vote of at least two-thirds of its members.
The petition shall be filed with the chair of the Committee on Appeals and shall set forth the specific charge or charges.

20.52.A92. *Recall or Dismissal of a Churchwide Officer or Editor*
a. *The petition for recall or dismissal described in 20.52. shall be filed with the chair of the Committee on Appeals (in care of the secretary of the Evangelical Lutheran Church in America, 8765 West Higgins Road, Chicago, Illinois 60631, except if the subject of the petition is the secretary, the petition shall be in care of the bishop of this church at the same address).*
b. *In the case of alleged physical or mental incapacity of the officer or the editor,*
1) *with respect to the officer or editor the procedures outlined in 13.63. shall first be followed, and if such officer or editor does not accept the decision of the Church Council, the Church Council may proceed to petition for proceedings for recall or dismissal.*
2) *in the event of such petition, four members of the Committee on Appeals, designated by the committee chair and consisting of two ordained ministers and two lay persons, shall*
   a) *investigate such conditions in person;*
   b) *seek competent medical testimony;*
   c) *seek the counsel and advice of the other officers of this church;*
   d) *submit a written report of their findings to the other members of the Committee on Appeals.*

3) *the members of the Committee on Appeals, other than those who investigated the conditions and other than those who are disqualified, shall review the findings of the investigation committee and by an affirmative vote of at least two-thirds of those present and voting may adopt the findings and grant the petition.*

c. *If the officer or editor is an ordained minister, grounds for recall or dismissal include those set forth in 20.71.11. and 20.71.12. for discipline of ordained ministers. If the officer or editor is a layperson, grounds for recall or dismissal include those set forth in 20.41.01.*

d. *In the case of alleged willful disregard or violation of the constitution and bylaws of this church or of alleged conduct as would subject the officer or editor to disciplinary action, the following procedures shall apply:*
1) *The petition shall be referred to the Committee on Appeals which shall function as the discipline hearing committee that shall conduct a hearing in accordance with the rules provided for in 20.21.16., except to the extent that those rules are in conflict with 20.51., 20.52., 20.53., or with the provisions of this continuing resolution; and*
2) *the members of the Committee on Appeals, other than those who are disqualified, may grant the petition by an affirmative vote of at least two-thirds of those present and voting.*

e. *Upon the filing of a written petition, the Executive Committee of the Church Council may temporarily suspend the officer or editor from service without prejudice, but with continuation of compensation, including benefits, if the officer or editor is a salaried employee. Appeals from such temporary suspension shall be provided in 13.63.*

20.53. **Notice of a decision by the Committee on Appeals that the charges have been sustained shall be given to the accused person, the Church Council shall be notified of the entry of such judgment, and the office shall be vacated.**

20.53.11. The Church Council shall appoint three members from the Committee on Appeals who shall recommend a similar process for the recall or dismissal of an officer of a synod, which process shall become operative when ratified by the Church Council.

20.53.A92. *Recall or Dismissal of a Synod Officer*
a. *The recall or dismissal of the bishop, vice president, secretary, or treasurer of a synod of this church and the vacating of office may be effected:*
1) *for willful disregard or violation of the constitution and bylaws of this church or the constitution and bylaws of the synod:*

2) for such physical or mental disability as renders the officer incapable of performing the duties of office; or

3) for such conduct as would subject the officer to disciplinary action as an ordained minister or as a member of a congregation of this church.

b. Proceedings for the recall or dismissal of a synodical bishop shall be instituted by written petition by:

1) the Synod Council on an affirmative vote of at least two-thirds of its elected members present and voting;

2) the Synod Assembly on an affirmative vote of at least two-thirds of its members present and voting;

3) at least 10 synodical bishops; or

4) the bishop of this church.

The petition shall be filed with the chair of the Committee on Appeals (in care of the secretary of the Evangelical Lutheran Church in America, 8765 West Higgins Road, Chicago, Illinois 60631) and shall set forth the specific charge or charges.

c. Proceedings for the recall or dismissal of an officer of a synod, other than the synodical bishop, shall be instituted by written petition by:

1) the Synod Council on an affirmative vote of at least two-thirds of its elected members present and voting;

2) the Synod Assembly on an affirmative vote of at least two-thirds of it members present and voting; or

3) the synodical bishop.

The petition shall be filed with the chair of the Committee on Appeals (in care of the secretary of the Evangelical Lutheran Church in America, 8765 West Higgins Road, Chicago, Illinois 60631) and shall set forth the specific charge or charges.

d. In the case of alleged physical or mental incapacity of an officer of a synod,

1) the procedures outlined in †8.56 shall first be followed, and if such officer does not accept the decision of the Synod Council, the Synod Council may proceed to petition for proceedings for recall or dismissal.

2) four members of the Committee on Appeals, designated by the committee chair and consisting of two ordained ministers and two lay persons, shall

a) investigate such conditions in person;

b) seek competent medical testimony;

c) seek the counsel and advice of the bishop of this church if such officer is the synodical bishop;

d) seek the counsel and advice of the synodical bishop if such officer is the vice president, secretary, or treasurer of the synod; and

e) submit a written report of their findings to the other members of the Committee on Appeals.

3) the members of the Committee on Appeals, other than those who investigated the conditions and other than those who are disqualified, shall review the findings of the investigation committee and by an affirmative vote of at least two-thirds of those present and voting shall adopt the findings and grant the petition.

e. If the synod officer is an ordained minister, grounds for recall or dismissal include those set forth in 20.21.01. and as defined under the process described in 20.71.11. and 20.71.12. for discipline of ordained ministers.

f. If the synod officer is a layperson, grounds for recall or dismissal include those set forth in 20.41.01.

g. If the case of alleged willful disregard or violation of the constitution and bylaws of this church or the constitution and bylaws of the synod or of alleged conduct as would subject the officer to disciplinary action, the following procedures shall apply:

1) If the proceedings were instituted by the bishop of this church, the synodical bishop, or at least 10 other synodical bishops, the petitioner shall first meet with the Executive Committee of the Synod Council in which the officer serves. The Executive Committee shall function as a consultation panel to give advice to the petitioner;

2) If as a result of the consultation the petition is not filed, no further proceedings shall be required;

3) If as a result of the consultation the petition is filed or if the proceedings were instituted by the Synod Assembly or the Synod Council, the petition shall be referred to the Committee on Appeals which shall function as the discipline hearing committee that shall conduct a hearing in accordance with the rules provided for in 20.21.16. except to the extent that those rules are in conflict with the provisions of this continuing resolution; and

4) the members of the Committee on Appeals, other than those who are disqualified, may grant the petition by an affirmative vote of at least two-thirds of those present and voting.

h. Upon the filing of a written petition, the Executive Committee of the Synod Council may temporarily suspend the officer from service in the synod without prejudice, but with continuation of compensation, including benefits, if the officer is a salaried employee of the synod. Appeals from such temporary suspension shall be provided in †58.56.

i. Written notice of a decision by the Committee on Appeals that the charges have been sustained shall be given to the affected officer. The Synod Council shall be notified of such decision and the office shall be vacated if the charges have been sustained.

Committee on Appeals

20.60.

20.61. There shall be a Committee on Appeals to which may be referred appeals from disciplinary proceedings and petitions for the recall of an officer or the editor of the church periodical. The Church Council shall appoint three members from the Committee on Appeals who shall recommend rules of procedure for the performance of its duties. The rules shall become effective when ratified by the Church Council.

20.61.A92. *Rules of the Committee on Appeals*

a. Any appeal to the Committee on Appeals shall be made in writing within 30 days after the decision of the discipline hearing committee has been delivered to the accused and the accuser(s). Appeals may be made only by the accused or the accuser(s) or the respective designated representative of the accused. Notice of the appeal shall be given by certified or registered letter addressed to the Committee on Appeals (in care of the secretary of this church, 8765 West Higgins Road, Chicago, Illinois 60631), with a copy to the other party.

b. The Committee on Appeals shall normally render its written decision within 60 days from the due date for the last written statement to be submitted under item h. below.

c. The material that shall be reviewed by the Committee on Appeals (herein referred to as the record on appeal) shall consist of the following:

1) a copy of the specific charges referred to the discipline hearing committee;

2) copy of any rules governing the hearing before the discipline hearing committee;

3) information concerning the composition of the discipline hearing committee that heard the case;

4) the verbatim record or the tape recording of the hearing before the discipline hearing committee;

5) all documents or physical evidence presented at the hearing before the discipline hearing committee;

6) the written decision of the discipline hearing committee;

7) proof that the written decision was delivered to the accused and the accuser(s).

d. It shall be the responsibility of the chair of the discipline hearing committee to furnish the record on appeal to the Committee on

e. If the Committee on Appeals has reason to believe that a required action was taken by a discipline hearing committee, but such action is not revealed in the record on appeal, the Committee on Appeals may, by written request to the chair of the discipline hearing committee, with copies to the accused and the accuser(s), solicit written confirmation of such action. Copies of such confirmation shall be supplied to the accused and the accuser(s).

f. The persons or entities who may appeal to the Committee on Appeals are set forth in 20.63.

g. The circumstances for which the Committee on Appeals may reverse or set aside the decision of a discipline hearing committee are set forth in 20.62.01., and consequences of such circumstances are set forth in 20.62.02.

h. The party taking an appeal may present a written statement of reasons why the decision of a discipline hearing committee should be reversed or set aside. The other party shall have an opportunity to make a written response to the Committee on Appeals. The party taking an appeal then may present a written rebuttal. Appropriate limitations and due dates for these statements may be established by the committee chair. In the event of cross appeals, the committee chair may permit the filing of additional statements so that both parties have adequate opportunity to present their respective appeals and respond to the statement of each other. Parties shall promptly give to each other copies of any written statement filed with the Committee on Appeals.

i. Final decisions of the Committee on Appeals require an affirmative vote by at least two-thirds of those present and voting.

j. Notice of decisions of the Committee on Appeals shall be given in writing to the accused, the accuser(s), the chair of the discipline hearing committee, the synodical bishop, and the secretary of this church.

k. The Committee on Appeals also shall prepare a brief summary of each appeal, which shall be presented to the Churchwide Assembly. Such summary shall not disclose the names of the accused, the accuser(s), or any witness. If the decision of the discipline hearing committee was reversed or remanded, the summary shall indicate the reasons for such reversal or remand.

l. The Committee on Appeals shall elect the following officers: chair, vice-chair, secretary, and assistant secretary. In addition to the duties discipline hearing committee. The Committee on Appeals must give due regard to the opportunity of the discipline hearing committee to judge the credibility of the witnesses.

3) Although the Findings of Fact are not clearly erroneous, the discipline hearing committee's Determination is nevertheless one with which no reasonable person, acting objectively, could agree. The committee's Determination may not be reversed simply because the Committee on Appeals, had it been the discipline hearing committee, would have reached a different conclusion. The discipline hearing committee's Determination must be sustained if reasonable people can disagree as to its propriety.

b. Due process has not been followed.

c. New evidence has been submitted by one of the parties, which evidence, in the judgment of the Committee on Appeals, should be considered.

d. The record of the proceedings before the discipline hearing committee is insufficient to permit the Committee on Appeals to determine whether the committee abused its discretion or followed due process.

20.62.02. When the Committee on Appeals has decided to reverse or set aside the decision of the discipline hearing committee, the Committee on Appeals shall proceed as follows:

a. If the Committee on Appeals has determined that one of the conditions listed in 20.62.01.a.1) or 20.62.01.a.2) exists, the Committee on Appeals may return the matter to the discipline hearing committee for further proceedings or render its own decision, which shall be final and unappealable.

b. If the Committee on Appeals has determined that the condition listed in 20.62.01.a.3) exists, it shall render its own decision, which shall be final and unappealable.

c. If the Committee on Appeals has determined that one of the conditions listed in 20.62.01.b., 20.62.01.c., or 20.62.01.d., exists, it shall return the matter to the discipline hearing committee for further proceedings.

20.63. **The decision of a discipline hearing committee may be appealed to the Committee on Appeals by:**

a. **the accuser(s) who brought charges upon which a discipline hearing committee has acted;**

b. **an ordained minister upon whom discipline has been imposed by a discipline hearing committee;**

c. **a congregation upon whom discipline has been imposed by a discipline hearing committee; or**

d. **other persons on the official rosters of this church upon whom discipline has been imposed by a discipline hearing committee.**

---

prescribed in Chapter 20, the chair shall schedule and preside at committee meetings. In the absence of the chair, the vice-chair shall act as chair. The secretary, or assistant secretary, shall keep such record of proceedings of the committee as is necessary.

m. Meetings of the Committee on Appeals may be held in person or by conference telephone call.

n. A majority of the members of the Committee on Appeals who are not disqualified shall constitute a quorum for the conduct of its business at a scheduled meeting, and three-fourths of the members of the Committee on Appeals who are not disqualified shall constitute a quorum for the conduct of its business by conference telephone call.

o. Members of the Committee on Appeals shall refrain from discussing appeals made to the committee, except as required to discharge the duties of the committee membership.

p. No member of the Committee on Appeals shall serve on any case if such a member is related (as defined in 19.61.04.) to the accused, the accuser(s), any witness who testified before the discipline hearing committee, or a member of the consultation or discipline hearing committee that considered the case, or where such member is a member or former member of a congregation that was an accuser or an accused. A member of the Committee on Appeals also may voluntarily disqualify himself or herself.

q. See 20.52.A92. and 20.53.A92. for additional rules of procedure applicable in proceedings for recall or dismissal.

20.62. **The circumstances for which the Committee on Appeals may reverse or set aside the decision of a discipline hearing committee and the consequences of such action shall be set forth in the bylaws.**

20.62.01. The judgment of a discipline hearing committee must be sustained unless the Committee on Appeals finds that one of the following conditions exists:

a. The discipline hearing committee abused its discretion. The discipline hearing committee may not be found to have abused its discretion unless at least one of the following is true:

1) The discipline hearing committee's Determination was not supported by any evidence in the record.

2) One or more of the discipline hearing committee's Findings of Fact is clearly erroneous. A Finding of Fact is clearly erroneous when, although there is evidence to support it, the Committee on Appeals on the entire evidence is left with the definite and firm conviction that a mistake has been committed. The Committee on Appeals may not reverse a finding of the discipline hearing committee simply because the Committee on Appeals concludes that it would have found differently had it been the

Chapter 21.
INDEMNIFICATION

21.01. Except as otherwise provided in this constitution, indemnification of any person who is or was made or threatened to be made a party to any proceeding is prohibited. For purposes of this chapter, the term, "proceeding," means a threatened, pending or completed civil, criminal, administrative, arbitration or investigative proceeding, including a proceeding in the right of this church, any other churchwide unit, or any other organization, but excluding (a) a proceeding by this church and (b) a disciplinary hearing or other proceeding described in Chapter 20. For purposes of this chapter, the term, "indemnification," includes advances of expenses.

21.02. To the full extent permitted from time to time by law, each person who is or was made or threatened to be made a party to any proceeding by reason of the present or former capacity of that person as a Church Council member, officer, employee, division board member, or committee member of this church shall be indemnified against judgments, penalties, fines, settlements, excise taxes, and reasonable attorneys fees and disbursements incurred by that person in connection with the proceeding. While indemnification of any person by reason of that person's capacity as a director, officer, employee or committee member of a separately incorporated churchwide unit, including the Mission Investment Fund of the Evangelical Lutheran Church in America, may be made by such separately incorporated unit, indemnification of such person by this church is prohibited. Indemnification of any person by reason of that person's capacity as a director, officer, employee, or committee member of any other organization is subject to the provisions of section 21.03.

21.03. Where a person who, while a Church Council member, officer, employee, division board member, or committee member of this church, is or was serving at the request of this church as (or whose duties in that position involve or involved service in the capacity of) a director, officer, partner, trustee, employee, or agent of another organization, is or was made or threatened to be made a party to a proceeding by reason of such capacity, then such person shall not be entitled to indemnification unless (a) the Church Council has established a process for determining whether a person serving in the capacity described in this section shall be entitled to indemnification in any specific case, and (b) that process has been applied in making a specific determination that such person is entitled to indemnification.

21.04. This church may purchase and maintain insurance on behalf of itself or any person entitled to indemnification pursuant to this chapter against any liability asserted against and incurred by this church or by such other person in or arising from a capacity described in section 21.02. or section 21.03.

20.64. The Committee on Appeals shall be comprised of six ordained ministers and six laypersons, elected by the Churchwide Assembly for a term of six years, without consecutive reelection.

20.65. The Committee on Appeals shall elect its own officers.

20.66. Decisions of the Committee on Appeals shall be final; an affirmative vote by at least two-thirds of those present and voting shall be necessary to render a decision or opinion. Each decision or opinion shall be reported as soon as practical in writing to the parties concerned and a summary of action taken shall be reported to the Churchwide Assembly.

Definitions and Guidelines

20.70. The Committee on Appeals shall establish definitions and guidelines, subject to approval by the Church Council, to enable clear and uniform application of the grounds for discipline in each of the above categories.

20.71.11.

20.71.12. The Committee on Appeals shall present to the Church Council for consideration and recommendation a process and definitions, as required in bylaw 20.71.11.

Adjudication

20.80.

20.81. The bishop and the Executive Committee of the Church Council shall be available to give counsel when disputes arise within this church.

20.82. When there is disagreement on a substantive issue among churchwide units which cannot be resolved by the parties, the aggrieved party or parties may appeal to the bishop and the Executive Committee of the Church Council for consultation. If this consultation fails to resolve the issue, a petition may be addressed by the parties to the Church Council requesting it to mediate the matter.

20.83. When a component or beneficiary of a churchwide unit has a disagreement on a substantive issue which it cannot resolve with the board of its unit, it may address an appeal to the bishop and the Executive Committee of the Church Council. In this case, the decision of the Executive Committee shall prevail, except that upon the motion of a member of the Church Council, the decision shall be referred to the Church Council for final action.

20.84. When there is disagreement among factions within a congregation on a substantive issue which cannot be resolved by the parties, members of a congregation shall have access to the synodical bishop for consultation after informing the chair of the Congregation Council of their intent. If the consultation fails to resolve the issue(s), the Consultation Committee of the synod shall consider the matter. If the Consultation Committee of the synod shall fail to resolve the issue(s), the matter shall be referred to the Synod Council, whose decision shall be final.

Chapter 22.
AMENDMENTS, BYLAWS, AND CONTINUING RESOLUTIONS

22.10. **Amendments to Constitution**

22.11. The constitution of this church may be amended only through either of the following procedures:

a. The Church Council may propose an amendment, with an official notice to be sent to the synods at least six months prior to the next regular meeting of the Churchwide Assembly. The adoption of such an amendment shall require a two-thirds vote of the members of the next regular meeting of the Churchwide Assembly present and voting.

b. An amendment may be proposed by 25 or more members of the Churchwide Assembly. The proposed amendment shall be referred to the Committee of Reference and Counsel for its recommendation, following which it shall come before the assembly. Adoption of such an amendment shall require passage at two successive regular meetings of the Churchwide Assembly by a two-thirds vote of the members present and voting.

22.20. **Bylaws**

22.21. Bylaws not in conflict with this constitution may be adopted or amended at any regular meeting of the Churchwide Assembly when presented in writing by the Church Council or by at least 15 members of the assembly. An amendment proposed by members of the assembly shall immediately be submitted to the Committee of Reference and Counsel for its recommendation. In no event shall an amendment be placed before the assembly for action sooner than the day following its presentation to the assembly. A two-thirds vote of the members present and voting shall be necessary for adoption.

22.30. **Continuing Resolutions**

22.31. Provisions relating to the administrative functions of this church shall be set forth in the continuing resolutions. Continuing resolutions may be adopted or amended by a majority vote of the Churchwide Assembly or by a two-thirds vote of the Church Council.

CONSTITUTION for SYNODS

CONSTITUTION FOR SYNODS

Chapter 1.
NAME AND INCORPORATION

†**S1.01.** The name of this synod shall be *(name of synod)* of the Evangelical Lutheran Church in America.

†**S1.02.** For the purposes of this constitution and the accompanying bylaws, the *(name of synod)* of the Evangelical Lutheran Church in America is hereafter designated as "this synod" or "the synod."

†**S1.11.** This synod shall be incorporated. Amendments to the articles of incorporation of this synod shall be submitted to the Church Council for ratification before filing.

†**S1.21.** The seal of this synod is *(describe)*.

Chapter 2.
STATUS

†**S2.01.** This synod possesses the powers conferred upon it, and accepts the duties and responsibilities assigned to it, in the Constitution, Bylaws, and Continuing Resolutions of the Evangelical Lutheran Church in America (ELCA or "this church"), which are recognized as having governing force in the life of this synod.

Chapter 3.
TERRITORY

†**S3.01.** The territory of this synod, as determined by the Churchwide Assembly, shall be: _____ .

"Determined by the Churchwide Assembly" is understood to include the reported changes in synod relationship made by any congregation in a border area agreed under ELCA bylaws 10.01.11. and 10.02.02.

---

† Required provisions

(9-93) SYNOD CONSTITUTION / 161

Chapter 4.
CONFESSION OF FAITH

†**S4.01.** This synod confesses the Triune God, Father, Son, and Holy Spirit.

†**S4.02.** This synod confesses Jesus Christ as Lord and Savior and the Gospel as the power of God for the salvation of all who believe.

a. Jesus Christ is the Word of God incarnate, through whom everything was made and through whose life, death, and resurrection God fashions a new creation.

b. The proclamation of God's message to us as both Law and Gospel is the Word of God, revealing judgment and mercy through word and deed, beginning with the Word in creation, continuing in the history of Israel, and centering in all its fullness in the person and work of Jesus Christ.

c. The canonical Scriptures of the Old and New Testaments are the written Word of God. Inspired by God's Spirit speaking through their authors, they record and announce God's revelation centering in Jesus Christ. Through them God's Spirit speaks to us to create and sustain Christian faith and fellowship for service in the world.

†**S4.03.** This synod accepts the canonical Scriptures of the Old and New Testaments as the inspired Word of God and the authoritative source and norm of its proclamation, faith, and life.

†**S4.04.** This synod accepts the Apostles', Nicene, and Athanasian Creeds as true declarations of the faith of this synod.

†**S4.05.** This synod accepts the Unaltered Augsburg Confession as a true witness to the Gospel, acknowledging as one with it in faith and doctrine all churches that likewise accept the teachings of the Unaltered Augsburg Confession.

†**S4.06.** This synod accepts the other confessional writings in the Book of Concord, namely, the Apology of the Augsburg Confession, the Smalcald Articles and the Treatise, the Small Catechism, the Large Catechism, and the Formula of Concord, as further valid interpretations of the faith of the Church.

†**S4.07.** This synod confesses the Gospel, recorded in the Holy Scriptures and confessed in the ecumenical creeds and Lutheran confessional writings, as the power of God to create and sustain the Church for God's mission in the world.

Chapter 5.
NATURE OF THE CHURCH

†**S5.01.** All power in the Church belongs to our Lord Jesus Christ, its head. All actions of this synod are to be carried out under his rule and authority.

†**S5.02.** The Church exists both as an inclusive fellowship and as local congregations gathered for worship and Christian service. Congregations find

their fulfillment in the universal community of the Church, and the universal Church exists in and through congregations. This church, therefore, derives its character and powers both from the sanction and representation of its congregations and from its inherent nature as an expression of the broader fellowship of the faithful. In length, it acknowledges itself to be in the historic continuity of the communion of saints; in breadth, it expresses the fellowship of believers and congregations in our day.

Chapter 6.
STATEMENT OF PURPOSE

†**S6.01.** The Church is a people created by God in Christ, empowered by the Holy Spirit, called and sent to bear witness to God's creative, redeeming, and sanctifying activity in the world.

†**S6.02.** To participate in God's mission, this synod as a part of the Church shall:

a. Proclaim God's saving Gospel of justification by grace for Christ's sake through faith alone, according to the apostolic witness in the Holy Scripture, preserving and transmitting the Gospel faithfully to future generations.

b. Carry out Christ's Great Commission by reaching out to all people to bring them to faith in Christ and by doing all ministry with a global awareness consistent with the understanding of God as Creator, Redeemer, and Sanctifier of all.

c. Serve in response to God's love to meet human needs, caring for the sick and the aged, advocating dignity and justice for all people, working for peace and reconciliation among the nations, and standing with the poor and powerless, and committing itself to their needs.

d. Worship God in proclamation of the Word and administration of the sacraments and through lives of prayer, praise, thanksgiving, witness, and service.

e. Nurture its members in the Word of God so as to grow in faith and hope and love, to see daily life as the primary setting for the exercise of their Christian calling, and to use the gifts of the Spirit for their life together and for their calling in the world.

f. Manifest the unity given to the people of God by living together in the love of Christ and by joining with other Christians in prayer and action to express and preserve the unity which the Spirit gives.

†**S6.03.** To fulfill these purposes, this synod, in partnership with the churchwide organization, shall bear primary responsibility for the oversight of the life and mission of this church in the territory of this synod. In fulfillment of this role, this synod shall:

a. Provide for the pastoral care of congregations, ordained ministers, and associates in ministry in this synod, including:

1) approving candidates for the ordained ministry in cooperation with the appropriate seminaries of this church, which may be done through multi-synodical committees;

2) authorizing ordinations and ordaining on behalf of this church;

3) certifying associates in ministry, which may be done through multi-synodical committees;

4) consulting in the calling process for ordained ministers and in the selection of associates in ministry.

b. Provide for leadership recruitment, preparation, and support in accordance with churchwide standards and policies, including:

1) nurturing and supporting congregations and lay leaders;

2) seeking and recruiting qualified candidates for the rostered ministries of this church;

3) making provision for pastoral care, call or appointment review, and guidance;

4) encouraging and supporting persons on the rosters of this church in stewardship of their abilities, care of self, and pursuit of continuing education to undergird their effectiveness of service; and

5) supporting recruitment of leaders for this church's colleges, universities, seminaries, and social ministry organizations.

c. Provide for discipline of congregations, ordained ministers, and persons on the official lay roster; as well as for termination of call, appointment, adjudication, and appeals consistent with the procedures established by this church in Chapter 20 of the ELCA constitution and bylaws.

d. Foster organizations for youth, women, and men, and organizations for language or ethnic communities.

e. Plan for the mission of this church in this synod, initiating and developing policy and implementing programs, consistent with churchwide policy, including:

1) ecumenical guidance and encouragement;

2) development of new ministries, redevelopment of existing ministries, and support and assistance in the conclusion, if necessary, of a particular ministry;

3) leadership and encouragement of congregations in their evangelism efforts;

4) development of relationships to and participation in planning for the mission of social ministry organizations and ministries;

5) encouragement of financial support for the work of this church by individuals and congregations;

6) provision for resources for congregational life;

7) assistance to the members of its congregations in carrying out their ministries in the world; and

8) interpretation of social statements in a manner consistent with the interpretation given by the churchwide unit which assisted in the development of the statement, and suggestion of social study issues through (a) Synod Assembly memorials to the Churchwide Assembly or (b) resolutions for referral from the Synod Assembly through the Synod Council to the Church Council and (c) Synod Council resolutions addressed to the Church Council or for referral to a unit of the churchwide organization through the Church Council's Executive Committee.

f. Promote interdependent relationships among congregations, synods, and the churchwide organization, and enter into partnership with other synods in the region.

g. Participate in churchwide programs and develop support for the ministry of the churchwide organization.

h. Foster the grouping of congregations in conferences, clusters, coalitions, or other area subdivisions for mission purposes.

i. Support relationships with and provide partnership funding on behalf of colleges, universities, and campus ministries.

j. Foster relationships with and provide partnership funding on behalf of social ministry organizations.

k. Maintain relationships with and provide partnership funding on behalf of seminaries and continuing education centers.

l. Foster supporting relationships with camps and other outdoor ministries.

m. Foster supporting relationships with preschools, elementary schools, and secondary schools operated by congregations of this synod.

n. Interpret the work of this church to congregations and to the public.

o. Respond to human need, work for justice and peace, care for the sick and the suffering, and participate responsibly in society.

p. Provide for archives in conjunction with other synods.

q. Cooperate with other synods and the churchwide organization in creating, using, and supporting regions to carry out those functions of this synod which can best be done cooperatively with other synods and the churchwide organization.

r. Elect members of the Churchwide Assembly in accordance with bylaw 12.41.11. of the constitution and bylaws of the Evangelical Lutheran Church in America and according to procedures specified in the bylaws of this constitution.

S7.14. One-half of the members of the Synod Assembly shall constitute a quorum.

†S7.21. The membership of the Synod Assembly, of which at least 60 percent of the voting membership shall be composed of laypersons, shall be constituted as follows:

a. All ordained ministers under call on the roster of this synod in attendance at this Synod Assembly shall be voting members.

b. Other persons on the rosters of this synod as defined by ELCA bylaw 10.41.01.b. shall be voting members.

c. A minimum of two lay members elected by each congregation related to this synod, one of whom shall be male and one of whom shall be female, shall be voting members. The Synod Council shall establish a formula to provide additional lay representation from congregations on the basis of the number of baptized members in the congregation. Additional members from each congregation shall be equally divided between male and female except that the odd-numbered member, if any, may be either male or female.

d. Voting membership shall include the officers of this synod.

S7.22. The synod may establish processes that permit retired ordained ministers on the roster of this synod to serve as voting members of the Synod Assembly, consistent with †S7.21.c. above.

S7.23. All retired ordained ministers, all ordained ministers on leave from call, and all associates in ministry on leave from call or retired, all of whose names appear on the rosters of this synod, shall have the privilege of voice but not vote at all meetings of the Synod Assembly. The bishop of the Evangelical Lutheran Church in America and such other official representatives of this church as may be designated from time to time by the Church Council shall also have voice but not vote in the meetings of the Synod Assembly. Like privileges shall be accorded to those members of the Synod Council who are not voting members of the Synod Assembly and to those additional persons whom the Synod Assembly or the Synod Council shall from time to time designate.

S7.24. Ordained ministers under call on the roster of this synod shall remain as members of the Synod Assembly so long as they remain under call and so long as their names appear on the roster of ordained ministers of this synod. Associates in ministry under call on the roster of this synod shall remain as members of the Synod Assembly so long as they remain under call and so long as their names appear on the official lay roster of this synod. Lay members of the Synod Assembly representing congregations shall continue as such until replaced by the election of new members or until they have been disqualified by termination of membership. Normally, congregations will hold elections prior to each regular meeting of the Synod Assembly.

(9.93)

---

†S6.04. Except as otherwise provided in this constitution and bylaws, the Synod Council shall establish processes that will ensure that at least 60 percent of the members of the synod assemblies, councils, committees, boards, and other organizational units shall be laypersons; and that, as nearly as possible, 50 percent of the lay members of assemblies, councils, committees, boards, or other organizational units shall be female and 50 percent shall be male; and that, where possible, the representation of ordained ministers shall be both male and female. This synod shall establish processes that will enable it to reach a minimum goal that 10 percent of its assemblies, councils, committees, boards, or other organizational units be persons of color and/or persons whose primary language is other than English.

†S6.04.A87. *It is the goal of this synod that 10 percent of the membership of synod assemblies, councils, committees, boards and/or other organizational units be persons of color and/or persons whose primary language is other than English. By the time of this synod's second assembly, a plan shall be established to attain this goal within 10 years.*

†S6.05. Each assembly, council, committee, board, commission, task force, or other body of this synod or any synodical units shall be conclusively presumed to have been properly constituted, and neither the method of selection nor the composition of any such assembly, council, committee, board, commission, task force, or other body may be challenged in a court of law by any person or be used as the basis of a challenge in a court of law to the validity or effect of any action taken or authorized by any such assembly, council, committee, board, commission, task force, or other body.

Chapter 7.
SYNOD ASSEMBLY

†S7.01. This synod shall have a Synod Assembly, which shall be its highest legislative authority.

†S7.11. A regular meeting of the Synod Assembly shall be held at least biennially.

S7.12. Special meetings of the Synod Assembly may be called by the bishop with the consent of the Synod Council, and shall be called by the bishop at the request of one-fifth of the voting members of the Synod Assembly. The notice of each special meeting shall define the purpose for which it is to be held. The scope of actions to be taken at such a special meeting shall be limited to the subject matter(s) described in the notice.

S7.13. If the special meeting of the Synod Assembly is required for the purpose of electing a successor bishop because of death, resignation, or inability to serve, the special meeting shall be called by the bishop of the ELCA in cooperation with the Synod Council.

Notice of the time and place of all meetings of the Synod Assembly shall be given by the secretary of this synod.

†S7.25. With the exception of ordained ministers on the roster of this synod who reside outside the territory of this synod, each member of the Synod Assembly shall be a voting member of a congregation of this synod.

S7.26. This synod may establish processes through the Synod Council that permit representatives of authorized worshiping communities of the synod, under ELCA bylaw 10.02.03., to serve as voting members of the Synod Assembly, consistent with †S7.21. Such authorized worshiping communities, acknowledged under criteria and procedures of the ELCA Division for Outreach and the Church Council of the Evangelical Lutheran Church in America, shall accept and adhere to the Confession of Faith and Statement of Purpose of this church, shall be served by leadership under the criteria of this church, and shall be subject to the discipline of this church.

S7.27. Duly elected voting members of the Synod Council who are not otherwise voting members of the Synod Assembly under †S7.21. shall be granted the privilege of both voice and vote as members of the Synod Assembly.

†S7.31. Proxy and absentee voting shall not be permitted in the transaction of any business of this synod.

S7.32. Robert's Rules of Order, latest edition, shall govern parliamentary procedure of the Synod Assembly.

S7.33. "Ex-officio" as used herein means membership with full rights of voice and vote unless otherwise expressly limited.

Chapter 8.
OFFICERS

†S8.01. The officers of this synod shall be a bishop, a vice president, a secretary, and a treasurer.

S8.10. Bishop

†S8.11. The bishop shall be elected by the Synod Assembly. The bishop shall be a pastor who is an ordained minister of the Evangelical Lutheran Church in America. This synod shall establish a Mutual Ministry Committee to provide support and counsel to the bishop.

†S8.12. As this synod's pastor, the bishop shall:

a. Oversee and administer the work of this synod.

b. Preach, teach, and administer the sacraments in accord with the faith of this church.

c. Provide pastoral care and leadership for this synod, its congregations, its ordained ministers, and its associates in ministry.

d. Advise and counsel its related institutions and organizations.

e. Be its chief ecumenical officer.

f. Exercise supervision over the work of the other officers.

g. Preside at all meetings of the Synod Assembly and be the chief executive officer of this synod; provide for the preparation of the

agenda for the Synod Assembly, Synod Council, and Executive Committee; ensure that the constitution and bylaws of this synod are duly observed, and that the actions of this synod in conformity therewith are carried into effect; coordinate the work of all synod staff members; and appoint all committees not otherwise provided for.

h. Coordinate the use of the resources available to this synod as it seeks to promote the health of this church's life and witness in the areas served by this synod.

i. Exercise solely this church's power to ordain (or provide for the ordination of) approved candidates who have received and accepted a properly issued, duly attested letter of call for the office of ordained ministry; and shall install (or provide for the installation of):

1) the pastors of all congregations of this synod;

2) ordained ministers called to extraparish service within this church; and

3) associates in ministry rostered in this synod.

j. Attest letters of call for persons called to serve congregations in this synod and letters of call for persons called by the Synod Council.

k. Be ex-officio a member of the Churchwide Assembly and a member of all committees and any other organizational units of this synod.

l. Submit a report to each regular meeting of the Synod Assembly concerning this synod's life and work.

m. Interpret and advocate the mission and theology of the whole church.

n. 1) Provide for preparation and maintenance of synod rosters containing:

a) the names and addresses of all ordained ministers of this synod and a record of the calls under which they are serving or the date on which they become retired or disabled; and

b) the names and addresses of all associates in ministry, members of the Deaconess Community of the Evangelical Lutheran Church in America, and diaconal ministers of this synod and a record of the positions to which they have been called or appointed or the date on which they become retired or disabled;

2) Annually bring to the attention of the Synod Council the names of all ordained ministers on leave from call or engaged in approved graduate study and the names of all associates in ministry, commissioned teachers, and consecrated deacons and deaconesses on leave from appointment or engaged in approved graduate study in conformity with the constitution and bylaws of this church as stated in ELCA 7.31.16. and ELCA 7.52.22. and pursuant to prior action of this synod.

3) Provide for preparation and maintenance of a register of the congregations of this synod and the names of the laypersons who have been elected to represent them.

o. Provide for prompt reporting to the secretary of this church:
1) additions to and subtractions from the rosters of ordained ministers, associates in ministry, commissioned teachers, consecrated deacons and deaconesses, certified and commissioned lay professionals, and the register of congregations;
2) issuance of a certificate of transfer for a pastor as an ordained minister in good standing who has received and accepted a properly issued, duly attested, regular letter of call under the jurisdiction of another synod; and
3) entrance of the names of such persons for whom proper certificates of transfer have been received on the roster of ordained ministers and the rosters of associates in ministry, commissioned teachers, consecrated deacons and deaconesses, and certified and commissioned lay professionals of this synod.

p. Appoint a statistician of this synod, secure the parochial reports of the congregations, collate the same for annual report to this synod, and make the reports available to the secretary of this church.

S8.13. The bishop shall be the president of the synod corporation and be authorized and empowered, in the name of this synod, to sign deeds or other instruments and to affix the seal of this synod.

S8.14. The bishop may have such assistants as this synod shall from time to time authorize.

†S8.15. The bishop of this church, or the appointee of the bishop, shall install into office each newly elected synod bishop.

Vice President

S8.20.

†S8.21. The vice president shall be elected by the Synod Assembly. The vice president shall be a layperson. The vice president shall be a voting member of a congregation of this synod. The vice president shall not receive a salary for the performance of the duties of the office.

S8.22. The vice president shall chair the Synod Council.

S8.23. In the event of the death, resignation, or disability of the bishop, the vice president shall convene the Synod Council to arrange for the conduct of the duties of the bishop until a new bishop shall be elected or, in the case of temporary disability, until the bishop resumes full performance of the duties of the office.

Secretary

S8.30.

†S8.31. The secretary shall be elected by the Synod Assembly. The secretary shall be a voting member of a congregation of this synod. The secretary may be either a layperson or an ordained minister.

†S8.32. The secretary shall:
a. Keep the minutes of all meetings of the Synod Assembly, be responsible for the printing and distribution of such minutes, and perform such other duties as this synod may from time to time direct.
b. Be authorized and empowered, in the name of this synod, to attest all instruments which require the same, and which are signed and sealed by the bishop.
c. In consultation with the bishop, classify and arrange all important papers and documents and deposit them in the archives of this synod.
d. Submit to the secretary of this church at least four months before the Churchwide Assembly a certified list of the regular and alternate voting members elected by the Synod Assembly.

Treasurer

S8.40.

†S8.41. The treasurer shall be elected by the Synod Assembly. The treasurer shall be a voting member of a congregation of this synod. The treasurer may be either a layperson or an ordained minister.

S8.42. The treasurer shall provide and be accountable for:
a. Management of the monies and accounts of this synod, its deeds, mortgages, contracts, evidences of claims and revenues, and trust funds, holding the same at all times subject to the order of this synod.
b. Investment of funds upon the authorization of the Synod Council.
c. Receipt and acknowledgement of offerings, contributions, and bequests made to this synod, collecting interest and income from its invested funds, and paying regular appropriations and orders on the several accounts as approved and directed by the Synod Council. The treasurer shall transmit each month to the treasurer of the Evangelical Lutheran Church in America the funds received by this synod for the general work of this church.
d. Maintenance of a regular account with each congregation of this synod and informing the congregation, at least quarterly, of the status of this account.
e. Rendering at each regular meeting of the Synod Assembly a full, detailed, and duly audited report of receipts and disbursements in the several accounts of this synod for the preceding fiscal year, together with the tabulation, for record and publication in the minutes, of the contributions from the congregations.
f. Giving of corporate surety in the amount determined by the Synod Council, which shall be in the custody of the secretary, and the premium therefore shall be paid by this synod. Fidelity coverage provided by the Evangelical Lutheran Church in America shall be deemed a fulfillment of this requirement.

General Provisions

S8.50.

†S8.51.
  a. The bishop of this synod shall be elected to a term of six years and may be reelected.

  b. The vice president, secretary, and treasurer of this synod shall be elected to a term of four years and may be reelected.

  c. The designation of the term of six years for the bishop shall begin upon the next election of a bishop of this synod. This item c. of †S8.51. shall expire at the completion of that election.

S8.52. The terms of the officers shall begin on the first day of the ——— month following election.

†S8.53. Each officer shall be a voting member in a congregation of this synod, except that the bishop need not be a member of a congregation of this synod at the time of election.

†S8.54. Should the bishop die, resign, or be unable to serve, the vice president shall convene the Synod Council to arrange for the appropriate care of the responsibilities of the bishop until an election of a new bishop can be held or, in the case of temporary disability, until the bishop is able to serve again. Such arrangements may include the appointment by the Synod Council of an interim bishop, who during the vacancy or period of disability shall possess all of the powers and authority of a regularly elected bishop. The term of the successor bishop, elected by the next Synod Assembly or a special meeting of the Synod Assembly called for the purpose of election, shall be six years with the subsequent election to take place at the Synod Assembly closest to the expiration of such a term and with the starting date of a successor term to be governed by constitutional provision S8.52.

S8.55. Should the vice president, secretary, or treasurer die, resign, or be unable to serve, the bishop, with the approval of the Executive Committee of the Synod Council, shall arrange for the appropriate care of the responsibilities of the officer until an election of a new officer can be held or, in the case of temporary disability, until the officer is able to serve again. The term of the successor officer, elected by the next Synod Assembly, shall be four years.

†S8.56. The Executive Committee of the Synod Council shall determine whether an officer is unable to serve; the officer may appeal the decision of the Executive Committee by requesting a hearing before the Synod Council. A meeting to determine the ability of an officer to serve shall be called upon the request of at least three members of the Executive Committee and prior written notice of the meeting shall be given to the officer in question at least ten calendar days prior to the meeting.

†S8.57. The recall or dismissal of an officer may be effected in accordance with the procedure established by the Committee on Appeals of the Evangelical Lutheran Church in America.

Chapter 9.
NOMINATIONS AND ELECTIONS

†S9.01. The Synod Assembly shall elect such officers of this synod and such other persons as the constitution and bylaws may require, according to procedures set forth in the bylaws.

†S9.02. In all elections by the Synod Assembly, other than for the bishop, a majority of the votes cast shall be necessary for election.

S9.03. There shall be a Nominating Committee consisting of ——— members who shall be appointed by the Synod Council to serve for each regular meeting of the Synod Assembly. Additional nominations may be made from the floor for all elections for which nominations are made by the Nominating Committee.

S9.04. The bishop shall be elected by the Synod Assembly by ecclesiastical ballot. Three-fourths of the votes cast shall be necessary for election on the first ballot. If no one is elected, the first ballot shall be considered the nominating ballot. Three-fourths of the votes cast on the second ballot shall be necessary for election. The third ballot shall be limited to the seven persons (plus ties) who received the greatest number of votes on the second ballot, and two-thirds of the votes cast shall be necessary for election. The fourth ballot shall be limited to the three persons (plus ties) who receive the greatest number of votes on the third ballot, and 60 percent of the votes cast shall be necessary for election. On subsequent ballots a majority of the votes cast shall be necessary for election. These ballots shall be limited to the two persons (plus ties) who receive the greatest number of votes on the previous ballot.

S9.05. The Nominating Committee shall nominate at least two persons for vice president; additional nominations may be made from the floor.

S9.06. The Synod Council shall nominate two persons for secretary; additional nominations may be made from the floor.

S9.07. The Synod Council shall nominate two persons for treasurer; additional nominations may be made from the floor.

S9.08. In all elections, except for the bishop, the names of the persons receiving the highest number of votes, but not elected by a majority of the votes cast on a preceding ballot, shall be entered on the next ballot to the number of two for each vacancy unfilled.

S9.09. The result of each ballot in every election shall be announced in detail to the assembly.

S9.11. The Synod Council shall elect or appoint representatives to the steering committee of its region.

Chapter 10.
SYNOD COUNCIL

†S10.01.
a. The Synod Council consisting of the four officers of the synod, 10 to 24 other members, and at least one youth shall be elected by the Synod Assembly. Each person elected to the Synod Council shall be a voting member of a congregation of this synod, with the exception of ordained ministers on the roster of this synod who reside outside the territory of this synod. The process for election and the term of office when not otherwise provided shall be specified in the bylaws. A member of the Church Council of the Evangelical Lutheran Church in America from this synod, unless otherwise elected as a voting member of the Synod Council, may serve as an advisory member of the Synod Council with voice but not vote.

b. The term of office of members of the Synod Council, with the exception of the officers and the youth member, shall be ⸺ years.

†S10.02. The Synod Council shall be the board of directors of this synod and shall serve as its interim legislative authority between meetings of the Synod Assembly. It may make decisions which are not in conflict with actions taken by the Synod Assembly or which are not precluded by provisions of this constitution or the constitution and bylaws of the Evangelical Lutheran Church in America.

S10.03. The functions of the Synod Council shall be to:

a. Exercise trusteeship responsibilities on behalf of this synod.

b. Recommend program goals and budgets to the regular meetings of the Synod Assembly.

c. Carry out the resolutions of the Synod Assembly.

d. Provide for an annual review of the roster of ordained ministers and of other official rosters, receive and act upon appropriate recommendations regarding those persons whose status is subject to reconsideration and action under the constitution and bylaws of the ELCA, and make a report to the Synod Assembly of the Synod Council's actions in this regard.

e. Issue letters of call to ordained ministers and letters of call to associates in ministry, members of the Deaconess Community of the Evangelical Lutheran Church in America, and diaconal ministers as authorized by Chapter 7 of the constitution and bylaws of the ELCA.

f. Fill vacancies until the next regular meeting of the Synod Assembly except as may otherwise be provided in the constitution or bylaws of this synod, and determine the fact of the incapacity of an officer of this synod.

g. Report its actions to the regular meeting of the Synod Assembly.

h. Perform such other functions as are set forth in the bylaws of this synod, or as may be delegated to it by the Synod Assembly.

S10.04. Any proposal to appropriate funds, whether by amendment to the budget or otherwise, which is presented to a meeting of the Synod Assembly without the approval of the Synod Council, shall require a two-thirds vote for adoption.

S10.05. No elected member of the Synod Council shall receive compensation for such service.

S10.06. If a member of the Synod Council ceases to be a member in good standing on a roster of this synod, if an ordained minister, or to be a voting member of a congregation of this synod, if a layperson, the office filled by such member shall at once become vacant.

S10.07. The composition of the Synod Council, the number of its members, and the manner of their selection, as well as the organization of the Synod Council, its additional duties and responsibilities, and the number of meetings to be held each year shall be as set forth in the bylaws.

Chapter 11.
COMMITTEES
(names of other organizational units)

†S11.01. There shall be an Executive Committee, a Consultation Committee, a Committee on Discipline, and such other committees as this synod may from time to time determine. The duties and functions of such committees, or any other organizational units created by this synod, and the composition and organizational structure of such units, shall be as set forth in this constitution or in the bylaws and shall be subject to any applicable provisions or requirements of the constitution and bylaws of the Evangelical Lutheran Church in America.

†S11.02. The Consultation Committee of this synod shall consist of 12 persons, of whom five shall be ordained ministers and seven shall be laypersons, who shall each be elected by the Synod Assembly for a term of six years without consecutive reelection. The functions of the Consultation Committee are set forth in Chapter 20 of the Constitution, Bylaws, and Continuing Resolutions of the Evangelical Lutheran Church in America and in Chapter 17 of this constitution.

†S11.03. The Committee on Discipline of this synod shall consist of six persons of whom three shall be ordained ministers and three shall be laypersons, who shall each be elected by the Synod Assembly for a term of six years without consecutive reelection. The functions of the Committee on Discipline of this synod are set forth in Chapter 20 of the Constitution, Bylaws, and Continuing Resolutions of the Evangelical Lutheran Church in America.

S11.04. This synod shall in its bylaws or by continuing resolution establish a process to ensure that the members of its committees and other organizational units will be persons possessing the necessary knowledge and competence to be effective members of such units, and to meet the requirements of †S6.04. With the exception of ordained ministers on the roster of this synod who reside outside the territory of this synod, each member of a committee of this synod, or any other organizational unit created by this synod, shall be a voting member of a congregation of this synod.

Chapter 12.
CONFERENCES, CLUSTERS, COALITIONS, OR OTHER AREA SUBDIVISIONS

†S12.01. This synod shall establish conferences, clusters, coalitions, or other area subdivisions within its territory as specified in the bylaws. The purpose of such groupings shall be to foster interdependent relationships among congregations, institutions, and synodical and churchwide units for mission purposes.

Chapter 13.
CONGREGATIONS

†S13.01. Each congregation, except those certified as congregations of the Evangelical Lutheran Church in America by the uniting churches, prior to being listed in the register of congregations of this synod, shall adopt the Model Constitution for Congregations or one acceptable to this synod, which is not in contradiction to the constitution and bylaws of the ELCA.

A congregation newly formed by this church and any congregation seeking recognition and reception by this church shall:

a. Accept the criteria for recognition and reception as a congregation of this church, fulfill the functions of the congregation, and accept the governance provisions as provided in Chapter 9 of the ELCA constitution and bylaws.

b. Adopt governing documents that include fully and without alterations the Preamble, Chapter 1, where applicable, and all provisions of Chapters 2, 3, 4, 5, 6, 7, 8, 9, 15, 16, 17, and 18 in the Model Constitution for Congregations consistent with requirements of this constitution and the constitution of this church. Bylaws and continuing resolutions, appropriate for inclusion in these chapters and not in conflict with these required provisions in the Model Constitution for Congregations, the constitution of this synod, or the Constitution, Bylaws, and Continuing Resolutions of the Evangelical Lutheran Church in America, may be adopted as described in Chapters 16 and 18 of the Model Constitution for Congregations.

c. Accept the commitments expected of all congregations of the ELCA as stated in C6.01., C6.02., and C6.03. of the Model Constitution for Congregations.

If a congregation is a member of another church body, the leaders of the congregation first should consult with the appropriate authorities of that church body before taking action to leave its current church body.

After such consultation, leaders of the congregation should make contact with the ELCA synod bishop or staff where the congregation is located.

Recognition and reception into this church of transferring or independent congregations by the Evangelical Lutheran Church in America is based on the judgment of the synod and action by the Synod through the Synod Council and Synod Assembly. The synod bishop shall provide for prompt reporting of such additions to the secretary of this church for addition to the register of congregations.

†S13.02. It shall be the responsibility of each congregation of this synod annually to choose from among its voting members laypersons to serve as members of the Synod Assembly as well as persons to represent it at meetings of any conference, cluster, coalition, or other area subdivision of which it is a member. The number of persons to be elected by each congregation and other qualifications shall be as prescribed in guidelines established by this synod.

S13.11. When a pastor or an associate in ministry resigns, the Congregation Council shall receive the letter of resignation, report it to the congregation, and at once notify the bishop of this synod.

S13.12. A congregation under financial obligation to its former pastor or associate in ministry shall make satisfactory settlement of the obligation before calling a successor.

S13.21. The alignment of congregations in pastoral charges, and all alterations in any alignment, shall be subject to approval by the Synod Assembly or by the Synod Council.

†S13.22. Each congregation of the Evangelical Lutheran Church in America within the territory of this synod, except those which are in partnership with the Slovak Zion Synod, shall establish and maintain a relationship with this synod.

†S13.23. Provision 9.71. of the ELCA constitution shall govern the relationship of this synod and a congregation of this synod regarding the property of the congregation.

S13.24. If any congregation of this synod has disbanded, or if the members of a congregation agree that it is no longer possible for it to function as such, or if it is the opinion of the Synod Council that the membership of a congregation has become so scattered or so diminished in numbers as to make it impractical for such a congregation to fulfill the purposes for which it was organized or that it is necessary for this synod to protect the congregation's property from waste and deterioration, the Synod Council, itself or through trustees appointed by it, may take charge and control of the property of the congregation to hold, manage, and convey the same on behalf of this synod. The congregation shall have the right to appeal the decision to the Synod Assembly.

S13.25. This synod may temporarily assume administration of a congregation upon its request or with its concurrence.

S13.31. Congregations and members of congregations are subject to discipline in accordance with the provisions of Chapter 20 of the ELCA constitution and bylaws.

Chapter 14.
ORDAINED MINISTERS AND ASSOCIATES IN MINISTRY

†S14.01. The time and place of the ordination of those persons properly called to congregations or extraparish service of this synod shall be authorized by the bishop of this synod.

†S14.02. Consistent with the faith and practice of the Evangelical Lutheran Church in America,

a. Every ordained minister shall:
1) preach the Word;
2) administer the sacraments;
3) conduct public worship;
4) provide pastoral care; and
5) speak publicly to the world in solidarity with the poor and oppressed, calling for justice and proclaiming God's love for the world.

b. Each ordained minister with a congregational call shall, within the congregation:
1) offer instruction, confirm, marry, visit the sick and distressed, and bury the dead;
2) supervise all schools and organizations of the congregation;
3) install regularly elected members of the Congregation Council; and
4) with the council, administer discipline.

c. Every pastor shall:
1) strive to extend the Kingdom of God in the community, in the nation, and abroad;
2) seek out and encourage qualified persons to prepare for the ministry of the Gospel;
3) impart knowledge of this church and its wider ministry through distribution of its periodicals and other publications; and
4) endeavor to increase the support given by the congregation to the work of the ELCA churchwide organization and of this ELCA synod.

S14.03. The pastor shall keep accurate parochial records of all baptisms, confirmations, marriages, burials, communicants, members received, members dismissed, or members excluded from the congregation, and shall submit a summary of such statistics annually to this synod.
The pastor shall be a member of the congregation that has extended the letter of call. In a parish of multiple congregations, the pastor shall hold membership in one of the congregations.

S14.04. Whenever members of a congregation move to such a distance that regular attendance at its services becomes impractical, it shall be the duty of the pastor to commend them, upon their consent, to the pastoral care of a Lutheran congregation nearer to their place of residence.

S14.05. Each ordained minister on the roster of this synod shall submit a report of his or her ministry to the bishop of the synod at least 90 days prior to each regular meeting of the synod assembly.

†S14.11. When a congregation of this church desires to call a pastor or a candidate for the pastoral office in the ordained ministry of this church:

a. Each congregation of this synod shall consult the bishop of this synod before taking any steps leading to the extending of a call to a prospective pastor.

b. For issuance of a letter of call to a pastor or pastoral candidate by a congregation of this synod in accord with ELCA constitutional provision 7.41., a two-thirds majority ballot vote shall be required of members of the congregation present and voting at a meeting regularly called for the purpose of issuing such a call.

c. When the congregation has voted to issue a call to a prospective pastor, the letter of call shall be submitted to the bishop of this synod for the bishop's signature.

S14.12. No ordained minister shall accept a call without first conferring with the bishop of this synod. An ordained minister shall respond with an answer of acceptance or declination to a letter of call within 30 days of receipt of such call. In exceptional circumstances with the approval of the bishop of this synod and the chair of the Congregation Council of the congregation issuing the call, an additional 15 days may be granted to respond to a letter of call.

†S14.13.
a. The call of a congregation, when accepted by a pastor, shall constitute a continuing mutual relationship and commitment which, except in the case of the death of the pastor, shall be terminated only following consultation with the synodical bishop and for the following reasons:

1) mutual agreement to terminate the call or the completion of a call for a specific term;
2) resignation of the pastor, which shall become effective, unless otherwise agreed, 30 days after the date on which it was submitted;
3) inability to conduct the pastoral office effectively in that congregation in view of local conditions, without reflection on the competence or the moral and spiritual character of the pastor;
4) the physical or mental incapacity of the pastor;
5) disqualification of the pastor through discipline on grounds of doctrine, morality, or continued neglect of duty;
6) the dissolution of the congregation; or
7) suspension of the congregation as a result of discipline proceedings.

S14.15. The parochial records of each congregation shall be kept in a separate book which shall remain its property. The secretary of the congregation shall attest to the bishop of this synod that such records have been placed in his or her hands in good order by a departing pastor before:

a. installation in another field of labor, or

b. the issuance of a certificate of dismissal or transfer.

S14.16. The pastor shall make satisfactory settlement of all financial obligations to a former congregation before:

a. installation in another field of labor, or

b. the issuance of a certificate of dismissal or transfer.

S14.17. During service to a congregation, an interim pastor shall have the rights and duties in the congregation of a regularly called pastor. The interim pastor may delegate the same in part to an interim supply pastor with the consent of the bishop of this synod. The interim pastor and any ordained ministers who may assist shall refrain from exerting influence in the selection of a pastor. Upon completion of service, the interim pastor shall certify to the bishop of this synod that the parochial records, for the period for which the interim pastor was responsible, are in order.

S14.18. With the approval of the synodical bishop expressed in writing, which sets forth a clear statement of the purpose to be served by such a departure from the normal rule of permanency of the call as expressed in †S14.13., a congregation may call a pastor for a specific term. Details of such calls shall be in writing setting forth the purpose and conditions involved. Prior to the completion of a term, the bishop of this synod or a representative of the bishop shall meet with the pastor and representatives of the congregation for a review of the call. Such call may also be terminated before its expiration in accordance with the provisions of †S14.13.

S14.21. All ordained ministers under a call shall attend meetings of the Synod Assembly, and the pastors of congregations shall also attend the meetings of the conference, cluster, coalition, or other area subdivision to which the congregation belongs.

S14.22. The provisions in the churchwide documents and such provisions as may be developed by the Division for Ministry governing associates in ministry shall apply in this synod.

b. When allegations of physical or mental incapacity of the pastor or ineffective conduct of the pastoral office have come to the attention of the bishop of this synod, the bishop in his or her sole discretion may, or when such allegations have been brought to this synod's attention by an official recital of allegations by the Congregation Council or by a petition signed by at least one-third of the voting members of the congregation, the bishop shall, investigate such conditions personally in company with a committee of two ordained ministers and one layperson.

c. In case of alleged physical or mental incapacity competent medical testimony shall be obtained. When such disability is evident, the bishop of this synod with the advice of the committee shall declare the pastorate vacant. Upon the restoration of a disabled pastor to health, the bishop of this synod shall take steps to enable the pastor to resume the ministry, either in the congregation last served or in another field of labor.

d. In the case of alleged local difficulties that imperil the effective functioning of the congregation, all concerned persons shall be heard, after which the bishop of this synod together with the committee described in †S14.13.b. shall decide on the course of action to be recommended to the pastor and the congregation. If they agree to carry out such recommendations, no further action shall be taken by this synod. If either party fails to assent, the congregation may dismiss the pastor by a two-thirds majority vote of the voting members present at a regularly called meeting after consultation with the bishop.

e. If, in the course of proceedings described in †S14.13.d., the committee concludes that there may be grounds for disciplinary action, the committee shall make recommendations concerning disciplinary action to the synodical bishop who may bring charges, in accordance with the provisions of the constitution and bylaws of the Evangelical Lutheran Church in America and the constitution of this synod.

f. If, following the appointment of the committee described in †S14.13.b. or d., it should become apparent that the pastoral office cannot be conducted effectively in the congregation(s) being served by the ordained minister due to local conditions, the bishop of this synod may temporarily suspend the pastor from service in the congregation(s) without prejudice and with pay provided through a joint synodical and churchwide fund and with housing provided by the congregation(s).

S14.14. Ordained ministers shall respect the integrity of the ministry of congregations which they do not serve and shall not exercise ministerial functions therein unless invited to do so by the pastor, or if there is no duly called pastor, then by the interim pastor in consultation with the Congregation Council.

Chapter 15.
FINANCIAL MATTERS

†S15.01. The fiscal year of this synod shall be February 1 through January 31.

†S15.11. Since the congregations, synods, and churchwide organization are interdependent units that share responsibly in God's mission, all share in the responsibility to develop, implement, and strengthen the financial support program of the whole church. The gifts and offerings of the members of ELCA are given to support all parts of this church and thus partnership in this church should be evidenced in determining each part's share of the gifts and offerings. Therefore:

a. The mission of this church beyond the congregation is to be supported by such a proportionate share of each congregation's annual budget as each congregation determines. This synod shall develop guidelines for determining "proportionate share," and shall consult with congregational leaders to assist each congregation in making its determination.

b. This synod shall receive the proportionate share of the mission support from its congregations, and shall transmit that percentage of each congregation's mission support as determined by the Churchwide Assembly to the treasurer of the Evangelical Lutheran Church in America.

†S15.12. The annual budget of this synod shall reflect the entire range of its own activities and its commitment to partnership funding with other synods and the churchwide organization. Unless an exception is granted upon the request of this synod by the Church Council, each budget shall include the percentage of congregational mission support assigned to it by the Churchwide Assembly.

S15.13. On the basis of estimated income, the Synod Council shall authorize expenditures within the budget for the fiscal year. Expenditure authorizations shall be subject to revision, in light of changing conditions, by the Synod Council.

S15.14. Except when such procedure would jeopardize current operations, a reserve amounting to no more than 16 percent of the sum of the amounts scheduled in the next year's budget for regular distribution to synodical causes shall be carried forward annually for disbursement in the following year in the interest of making possible a more even flow of income to such causes. The exact number of dollars to be held in reserve shall be determined by the Synod Council.

S15.21. No appeal to congregations of this or any other synod of the Evangelical Lutheran Church in America for the raising of funds shall be conducted by congregations or organizations related to or affiliated with this synod without the consent of the Synod Assembly or the Synod Council.

S15.31. This synod shall arrange to have an annual audit of its financial records conducted by a certified public accountant firm selected by the Synod

Council. The audited annual financial report shall be submitted by this synod to the churchwide Office of the Treasurer and to the congregations of this synod. The financial reports shall be in the format approved from time to time by the churchwide Office of the Treasurer.

Chapter 16.
INDEMNIFICATION

†S16.01. Except as otherwise provided in this constitution, indemnification of any person who is or was made or threatened to be made a party to any proceeding is prohibited. For purposes of this chapter, the term, "proceeding," means a threatened, pending, or completed civil, criminal, administrative, arbitration, or investigative proceeding, including a proceeding in the right of this synod or any other organization. Except as otherwise required by law, the term, "proceeding," does not include (a) a proceeding by this synod and (b) a disciplinary hearing or other proceeding described in Chapter 20 of the Constitution, Bylaws, and Continuing Resolutions of the Evangelical Lutheran Church in America. For purposes of this chapter, the term, "indemnification," includes advances of expenses.

†S16.02. To the full extent permitted from time to time by law, each person who is or was made or threatened to be made a party to any proceeding by reason of the present or former capacity of that person as a Synod Council member, officer, employee, or committee member of this synod shall be indemnified against judgments, penalties, fines, settlements, excise taxes, and reasonable attorney's fees and disbursements incurred by that person in connection with the proceeding. Indemnification of any person by reason of that person's capacity as a director, officer, employee, or committee member of any other organization, regardless of its form or relationship to this synod, is subject to the provisions of section †S16.03.

†S16.03. Whenever a person who, while a Synod Council member, officer, committee member, or employee of this synod (or whose duties in that position involve or involved service in the capacity of) a director, officer, partner, trustee, employee, or agent of another organization, is or was made or threatened to be made a party to a proceeding by reason of such capacity, then such person shall not be entitled to indemnification unless (a) the Synod Council has established a process for determining whether a person serving in the capacity described in this section shall be entitled to indemnification in any specific case, and (b) that process has been applied in making a specific determination that such person is entitled to indemnification.

†S16.04. This synod may purchase and maintain insurance on behalf of itself or any person entitled to indemnification pursuant to this chapter against any liability asserted against and incurred by this synod or by such other person in or arising from a capacity described in section †S16.02. or section †S16.03.

Chapter 17.
ADJUDICATION

†S17.01. The synodical bishop and the Executive Committee of the Synod Council shall be available to give counsel when disputes arise within this synod.

†S17.02. The synodical bishop and the Executive Committee of the Synod Council shall receive expressions of concern from ordained ministers, associates in ministry or other persons on the official lay roster of this church, congregations, and organizations within this synod; provide a forum in which the parties concerned can seek to work out matters causing distress or conflict; and make appropriate recommendations for their resolution. When the matter at issue cannot be resolved in this manner, the prescribed procedures for investigation, decision, appeal, and adjudication shall be followed. Allegations or charges that could lead to the discipline of an ordained minister or a person on the official lay roster of this church shall not be addressed by the Executive Committee but shall be resolved through the disciplinary process set forth in the Constitution, Bylaws, and Continuing Resolutions of the Evangelical Lutheran Church in America.

†S17.03. When there is disagreement among units of this synod on a substantive issue that cannot be resolved by the parties, the aggrieved party or parties may appeal to the synodical bishop and the Executive Committee of the Synod Council for a consultation. If this consultation fails to resolve the issue, a petition may be addressed by the parties to the Synod Council requesting it to arbitrate the issue. The decision of the Synod Council shall be final.

†S17.04. When a component or beneficiary of a synod has a disagreement on a substantive issue that it cannot resolve, it may address an appeal to the synodical bishop and the Executive Committee of the Synod Council. In this case the decision of the Executive Committee shall prevail, except that upon the motion of a member of the Synod Council, the decision shall be referred to the Synod Council for final action.

Adjudication in a Congregation

†S17.10.

†S17.11. When there is disagreement among factions within a congregation on a substantive issue that cannot be resolved by the parties, members of a congregation shall have access to the synodical bishop for consultation after informing the chair of the Congregation Council of their intent. If the consultation fails to resolve the issue(s), the Consultation Committee of this synod shall consider the matter. If the Consultation Committee of this synod shall fail to resolve the issue(s), the matter shall be referred to the Synod Council, whose decision shall be final.

Chapter 18.
AMENDMENTS, BYLAWS, AND CONTINUING RESOLUTIONS

Amendments to Constitution

†S18.10.

†S18.11. Certain sections of this constitution incorporate and record therein provisions of the constitution and bylaws of this church. If such provisions are amended by this church, corresponding amendments shall be introduced at once into this constitution by the secretary of this synod upon receipt of formal certification thereof from the secretary of the Evangelical Lutheran Church in America.

†S18.12. Whenever the secretary of the Evangelical Lutheran Church in America officially informs this synod that the Churchwide Assembly has amended the Constitution for Synods, this constitution may be amended to reflect any such amendment by a simple majority vote at any subsequent meeting of the Synod Assembly without presentation at a prior Synod Assembly. An amendment that is identical to a provision of the Constitution for Synods shall be deemed to have been ratified upon its adoption by this synod. The Church Council, through the secretary of this church, shall be given prompt notification of its adoption.

†S18.13. Other amendments to this constitution may be adopted by this synod through either of the following procedures:

a. An amendment may be adopted by a two-thirds vote at a regular meeting of the Synod Assembly after having been presented in writing at the previous regular meeting of the Synod Assembly over the signatures of at least _____ members and been approved by a two-thirds vote of the voting members present and voting at such a regular meeting of the Synod Assembly.

b. The Synod Council may propose an amendment, with notice to be sent to the congregations of this synod at least six months prior to the next regular meeting of the Synod Assembly. Such an amendment shall require for adoption a two-thirds vote of the voting members present and voting at such a regular meeting of the Synod Assembly.

All such amendments shall become effective upon ratification by the Churchwide Assembly or by the Church Council.

Amendments to Bylaws

†S18.20.

†S18.21. This synod may adopt bylaws not in conflict with this constitution nor with the constitution and bylaws of this church. This synod may amend its bylaws at any meeting of the Synod Assembly by a two-thirds vote of voting members of the assembly present and voting. Newly adopted bylaws and amendments to existing bylaws shall be reported to the secretary of this church.

MODEL CONSTITUTION FOR CONGREGATIONS OF THE EVANGELICAL LUTHERAN CHURCH IN AMERICA

1993

Amendments to Continuing Resolutions

†S18.30. This synod may adopt continuing resolutions not in conflict with this constitution or its bylaws. Such continuing resolutions may be adopted or amended by a majority vote of the Synod Assembly or by a two-thirds vote of Synod Council. Newly adopted continuing resolutions

†S18.31. and amendments to existing continuing resolutions shall be reported to the secretary of this church.

INTRODUCTION

This current edition of the *Model Constitution for Congregations of the Evangelical Lutheran Church in America* contains amendments adopted by the 1989, 1991, and 1993 Churchwide Assemblies.

The model is consistent with the requirements of the constitutional governing documents of the ELCA's churchwide organization and synods.

The *Model Constitution for Congregations of the Evangelical Lutheran Church in America* originally was adopted by the Constituting Convention of this church in Columbus, Ohio, on April 30, 1987. This was done as required by the *Constitutions, Bylaws, and Continuing Resolutions of the Evangelical Lutheran Church in America.*

▶ *Required provisions*: Sections of this constitution marked by an asterisk [*] are required when a congregation amends its governing documents. These sections must be used without alteration or amendment of the text in any manner (neither additions nor deletions). This is in keeping with provision 9.52. in the *Constitution, Bylaws, and Continuing Resolutions of the Evangelical Lutheran Church in America.* This provision stipulates that when a congregation of this church "wishes to amend any provision of its governing documents, the governing documents of that congregation shall be so amended to conform to 9.25.b." in the churchwide constitution. The provisions herein marked by an asterisk are those that are indicated as required in ELCA constitutional provision 9.25.b.

▶ *Review by synod*: In keeping with provisions that apply to all congregations of this church, each congregation is to provide a copy of its governing documents to the synod. As specified by ELCA bylaw 9.53.03. (numbering as listed in the 1991 and subsequent editions):

All proposed changes in the constitution or incorporation documents of a congregation shall be referred to the synod with which the congregation is affiliated. The synod shall approve or disapprove the proposed changes within 120 days of receipt thereof, and shall notify the congregation of its decision; in the absence of a decision, the changes shall go into effect.

▶ *Codification explanation*: A numerical codification indicates (a) general subject, (b) constitutional provisions, (c) bylaws, and (d) continuing resolutions.

a. Major sections are designated as chapters. The chapter designation becomes the first number in the codification sequence and is followed by a period. Thus, provisions in "Chapter 8. Membership" are preceded by "8."

b. Constitutional provisions are codified with two sets of numbers: the chapter number and a two-digit number preceding the second period in the codification. Thus, one constitutional provision related to "Membership" is codified *C8.02.

c. Bylaw provisions are codified with three sets of numbers: the chapter number, the related constitutional provision number, and a two-digit number. Thus, one bylaw provision related to "Membership" would be codified C8.02.01. Because bylaws and continuing resolutions normally are so specifically related to details of each congregation's organization, operation, and life, no model set of bylaws or continuing resolutions is provided. Each congregation may develop its own bylaws and continuing resolutions, but no such bylaws or continuing resolutions may conflict with this constitution, the constitution and bylaws of the Evangelical Lutheran Church in America, and the constitution of the synod, as indicated in *C6.03.e.

d. Continuing resolutions also are codified with three sets of numbers except that the third set is preceded by a capital letter. Thus, a continuing resolution might be numbered C13. to designate the chapter; C13.07. to designate the subject matter within the chapter; and the third set might be numbered A93. in the codification C13.07.A93. to indicate by the "A" that it is the first continuing resolution regarding that subject and to indicate by the "93" that it was adopted in 1993.

When many related provisions are parts of a unit that are considered inseparable, they normally are lettered "a," "b," "c," etc. When related provisions are part of a unit but considered separable, such as a list of duties, they are normally numbered in sequence. If the related provisions cannot be judged clearly to be separable or inseparable, preference will be given to a number sequence.

▶ *Ease of use*: The provisions of your congregation's constitution, the bylaws, and the continuing resolutions that pertain to the same matter should be placed together for clarity and ease in use.

If chapter numbers are considered the major sequence number, constitution numbers as a fraction of the chapter number, and bylaw numbers as a fraction of the constitution number, then the codification can be said to provide a progressive sequence. Thus, *C5.01. will precede C5.03.10., and C9.11.16. will precede *C9.13.

All provisions in the Model Constitution for Congregations are prefaced with "C" to distinguish these provisions from comparable ones in the synodical and churchwide constitutions.

▶ *Missing numbers*: As you work with the Model Constitution for Congregations, you may notice that certain numbers seem to be missing from the numbering sequence in some chapters. That is intentional. In the style followed here, the number ".10." and multiples thereof have been reserved for possible use as section headings in

MODEL CONSTITUTION for CONGREGATIONS of the EVANGELICAL LUTHERAN CHURCH IN AMERICA

Copyright 1993
by the Evangelical Lutheran Church in America

future editions. Therefore, in the sequence, for example, of Chapters 1, 9, and 12, these ".10." numbers do not appear.

▶ *Selection of options*: Alternatives are provided in certain places within the model. Those are noted by square brackets. For example, *C9.01. offers the alternative of election of a call committee by the congregation or by the Congregation Council. One alternative should be chosen in each instance where square brackets appear in the text.

Optional texts are provided in separate paragraphs in Chapters 11 and 12 regarding the Congregation Council and its membership. Each congregation will need to select one of those options for council membership or a variation thereof, subject to approval through the synod's constitutional review process.

▶ *References to church*: In the governing documents, "Church" with a capital letter is used in references to the one, holy, catholic, and apostolic Church. In references to the Evangelical Lutheran Church in America, the words "church" and "this church" in lower case letters are employed, although, for clarity in this constitution, the full name or "ELCA" normally is used.

The specific congregation may be identified, as provided in C1.02., as "this congregation."

▶ *Guidelines*: A list of guidelines for a congregation engaging in review and amendment of its constitution is available through each synod office.

The task of amending a constitution is not easy. It is, however, an important endeavor that merits thoughtful work. In your constitutional responsibilities, God grant you wisdom, mutual love, clear understanding of good order, and commitment to the unity of this church in faithful witness to our Lord and Savior, Jesus Christ.

THE REV. LOWELL G. ALMEN
Secretary
Evangelical Lutheran Church in America

September 1, 1993

*PREAMBLE

We, baptized members of the Church of Christ, responding in faith to the call of the Holy Spirit through the Gospel, desiring to unite together to preach the Word, administer the sacraments, and carry out God's mission, do hereby adopt this constitution and solemnly pledge ourselves to be governed by its provisions. In the name of the Father and of the Son and of the Holy Spirit.

Chapter 1.
NAME AND INCORPORATION

C1.01.   The name of this congregation shall be _____ .

C1.02.   For the purpose of this constitution and the accompanying bylaws, the congregation of _____ is hereinafter designated
(Insert full legal name)
as "this congregation."

C1.11.   This congregation shall be incorporated under the laws of the State of _____ .

Chapter 2.
CONFESSION OF FAITH

*C2.01.   This congregation confesses the Triune God, Father, Son, and Holy Spirit.

*C2.02.   This congregation confesses Jesus Christ as Lord and Savior and the Gospel as the power of God for the salvation of all who believe.

a. Jesus Christ is the Word of God incarnate, through whom everything was made and through whose life, death, and resurrection God fashions a new creation.

―――――――――
*Required provisions

b. The proclamation of God's message to us as both Law and Gospel is the Word of God, revealing judgment and mercy through word and deed, beginning with the Word in creation, continuing in the history of Israel, and centering in all its fullness in the person and work of Jesus Christ.

c. The canonical Scriptures of the Old and New Testaments are the written Word of God. Inspired by God's Spirit speaking through their authors, they record and announce God's revelation centering in Jesus Christ. Through them God's Spirit speaks to us to create and sustain Christian faith and fellowship for service in the world.

*C2.03. This congregation accepts the canonical Scriptures of the Old and New Testaments as the inspired Word of God and the authoritative source and norm of its proclamation, faith, and life.

*C2.04. This congregation accepts the Apostles', Nicene, and Athanasian Creeds as true declarations of the faith of this congregation.

*C2.05. This congregation accepts the Unaltered Augsburg Confession as a true witness to the Gospel, acknowledging as one with it in faith and doctrine all churches that likewise accept the teachings of the Unaltered Augsburg Confession.

*C2.06. This congregation accepts the other confessional writings in the Book of Concord, namely, the Apology of the Augsburg Confession, the Smalcald Articles and the Treatise, the Small Catechism, the Large Catechism, and the Formula of Concord, as further valid interpretations of the faith of the Church.

*C2.07. This congregation confesses the Gospel, recorded in the Holy Scriptures and confessed in the ecumenical creeds and Lutheran confessional writings, as the power of God to create and sustain the Church for God's mission in the world.

Chapter 3.
NATURE OF THE CHURCH

*C3.01. All power in the Church belongs to our Lord Jesus Christ, its head. All actions of this congregation are to be carried out under his rule and authority.

*C3.02. The Church exists both as an inclusive fellowship and as local congregations gathered for worship and Christian service. Congregations find their fulfillment in the universal community of the Church, and the universal Church exists in and through congregations. The Evangelical Lutheran Church in America, therefore, derives its character and powers both from the sanction and representation of its congregations and from its inherent nature as an expression of the broader fellowship of the faithful. In length, it acknowledges itself to be in the historic continuity of the communion of saints; in breadth, it expresses the fellowship of believers and congregations in our day.

Chapter 4.
STATEMENT OF PURPOSE

*C4.01. The Church is a people created by God in Christ, empowered by the Holy Spirit, called and sent to bear witness to God's creative, redeeming, and sanctifying activity in the world.

*C4.02. To participate in God's mission, this congregation as a part of the Church shall:

a. Worship God in proclamation of the Word and administration of the sacraments and through lives of prayer, praise, thanksgiving, witness, and service.

b. Proclaim God's saving Gospel of justification by grace for Christ's sake through faith alone, according to the apostolic witness in the Holy Scripture, preserving and transmitting the Gospel faithfully to future generations.

c. Carry out Christ's Great Commission by reaching out to all people to bring them to faith in Christ and by doing all ministry with a global awareness consistent with the understanding of God as Creator, Redeemer, and Sanctifier of all.

d. Serve in response to God's love to meet human needs, caring for the sick and the aged, advocating dignity and justice for all people, working for peace and reconciliation among the nations, and standing with the poor and powerless, and committing itself to their needs.

e. Nurture its members in the Word of God so as to grow in faith and hope and love, to see daily life as the primary setting for the exercise of their Christian calling, and to use the gifts of the Spirit for their life together and for their calling in the world.

f. Manifest the unity given to the people of God by living together in the love of Christ and by joining with other Christians in prayer and action to express and preserve the unity which the Spirit gives.

*C4.03. To fulfill these purposes, this congregation shall:

a. Provide services of worship at which the Word of God is preached and the sacraments are administered.

b. Provide pastoral care and assist all members to participate in this ministry.

c. Challenge, equip, and support all members in carrying out their calling in their daily lives and in their congregation.

d. Teach the Word of God.

e. Witness to the reconciling Word of God in Christ, reaching out to all people.

f. Respond to human need, work for justice and peace, care for the sick and the suffering, and participate responsibly in society.

*C5.04. This congregation annually shall choose from among its voting members to serve as voting members of the Synod Assembly as well as persons to represent it at meetings of any conference, cluster, coalition, or other area subdivision of which it is a member. The number of persons to be elected by the congregation and other qualifications shall be as prescribed in guidelines established by this synod.

Chapter 6.
CHURCH AFFILIATION

*C6.01. This congregation shall be an interdependent part of the Evangelical Lutheran Church in America or its successor, and of the _____ Synod of the Evangelical Lutheran Church in America. This congregation is subject to the discipline of the Evangelical Lutheran Church in America.

*C6.02. This congregation accepts the Confession of Faith and agrees to the Purposes of the Evangelical Lutheran Church in America and shall act in accordance with them.

*C6.03. This congregation acknowledges its relationship with the Evangelical Lutheran Church in America in which:

a. This congregation agrees to be responsible for its life as a Christian community.

b. This congregation pledges its financial support and participation in the life and mission of the Evangelical Lutheran Church in America.

c. This congregation agrees to call pastoral leadership from the clergy roster of the Evangelical Lutheran Church in America in accordance with its call procedures except in special circumstances and with the approval of the bishop of the synod.

d. This congregation agrees to consider associates in ministry for call to other staff positions in the congregation according to the procedures of the Evangelical Lutheran Church in America.

e. This congregation agrees to file this constitution and any subsequent changes to this constitution with the synod for review to ascertain that all of its provisions are in agreement with the constitution and bylaws of the Evangelical Lutheran Church in America and with the constitution of the synod.

*C6.04. Affiliation with the Evangelical Lutheran Church in America may be terminated as follows:

a. This congregation takes action to dissolve.

b. This congregation ceases to exist.

c. This congregation is removed from membership in the Evangelical Lutheran Church in America according to the procedures for discipline of the Evangelical Lutheran Church in America.

d. This congregation follows the procedures outlined in *C6.05.

g. Motivate its members to provide financial support for the congregation's ministry and the ministry of other parts of the Evangelical Lutheran Church in America.

h. Foster and participate in interdependent relationships with other congregations, the synod, and the churchwide organization of the Evangelical Lutheran Church in America.

i. Foster and participate in ecumenical relationships consistent with churchwide policy.

*C4.04. This congregation shall develop an organizational structure to be described in the bylaws. The Congregation Council shall prepare descriptions of the responsibilities of each committee, task force, or other organizational groups and shall review their actions. (Such descriptions shall be contained in continuing resolutions in the section on the Congregation Council.)

*C4.05. This congregation shall, from time to time, adopt a mission statement which will provide specific direction for its programs.

Chapter 5.
POWERS OF THE CONGREGATION

*C5.01. The powers of this congregation are those necessary to fulfill its purpose.

*C5.02. The powers of this congregation are vested in the Congregation Meeting called and conducted as provided in this constitution and bylaws.

*C5.03. Only such authority as is delegated to the Congregation Council or other organizational units in this congregation's governing documents is recognized. All remaining authority is retained by the congregation. The congregation is authorized to:

a. call a pastor as provided in Chapter 9;

b. terminate the call of a pastor as provided in Chapter 9;

c. call or terminate the call of associates in ministry in conformity with the applicable policy of the Evangelical Lutheran Church in America;

d. approve the annual budget;

e. acquire real and personal property by gift, devise, purchase, or other lawful means;

f. hold title to and use its property for any and all activities consistent with its purpose;

g. sell, mortgage, lease, transfer, or otherwise dispose of its property by any lawful means;

h. elect its [officers,] Congregation Council, boards, and committees, and require them to carry out their duties in accordance with the constitution[,] [and] bylaws[,] [and continuing resolutions]; and

i. terminate its relationship with the Evangelical Lutheran Church in America as provided in Chapter 6.

*C6.05. This congregation may terminate its relationship with the Evangelical Lutheran Church in America by the following procedure:

a. A resolution indicating the desire of this congregation to terminate its relationship must be adopted at a legally called and conducted special meeting of this congregation by a two-thirds majority of the voting members present.

b. The secretary of this congregation shall submit a copy of the resolution to the synodical bishop and shall mail a copy of the resolution to voting members of this congregation. This notice shall be submitted within 10 days after the resolution has been adopted.

c. The bishop of the synod shall consult with this congregation during a period of at least 90 days.

d. If this congregation, after consultation, still desires to terminate its relationship, such action may be taken at a legally called and conducted special meeting by a two-thirds majority of the voting members present, at which meeting the bishop of the synod or an authorized representative shall be present. Notice of the meeting shall be mailed to all voting members at least 10 days in advance of the meeting.

e. A certified copy of the resolution to terminate its relationship shall be sent to the synodical bishop, at which time the relationship between this congregation and the Evangelical Lutheran Church in America shall be terminated.

f. Notice of termination shall be forwarded by the synodical bishop to the secretary of this church and published in the periodical of this church.

g. If this congregation was a member of the Lutheran Church in America, it shall be required, in addition to the foregoing provisions in *C6.05., to receive synodical approval before terminating its membership in the Evangelical Lutheran Church in America.

h. If this congregation was established by the Evangelical Lutheran Church in America, it shall be required, in addition to the foregoing provisions in *C6.05., to receive synodical approval before terminating its membership in the Evangelical Lutheran Church in America.

*C6.06. If this congregation is considering relocation, it shall confer with the bishop of the synod in which it is territorially located before any steps are taken leading to such action. The approval of the Synod Council shall be received before any such action is effected.

Chapter 7.
PROPERTY OWNERSHIP

*C7.01. If this congregation ceases to exist, title to undisposed property shall pass to the _____ Synod of the Evangelical Lutheran Church in America.

196 / MODEL CONSTITUTION FOR CONGREGATIONS (9-93)

*C7.02. If this congregation is removed from membership in the Evangelical Lutheran Church in America according to its procedure for discipline, title to property shall continue to reside in this congregation.

*C7.03. If a two-thirds majority of the voting members of this congregation present at a regularly called and conducted special meeting of this congregation vote to transfer to another Lutheran church body, title to property shall continue to reside in this congregation. Before this congregation takes action to transfer to another Lutheran church body, it shall consult with representatives of the _____ Synod.

*C7.04. If a two-thirds majority of the voting members of this congregation present at a regularly called and conducted special meeting of this congregation vote to become independent or relate to a non-Lutheran church body, title to property of this congregation shall continue to reside in this congregation only with the consent of the Synod Council. The Synod Council, after consultation with this congregation by the established synodical process, may give approval to the request to become independent or to relate to a non-Lutheran church body, in which case title shall remain with the majority of this congregation. If the Synod Council fails to give such approval, title shall remain with those members who desire to continue as a congregation of the Evangelical Lutheran Church in America.

Chapter 8.
MEMBERSHIP

*C8.01. Members of this congregation shall be those baptized persons on the roll of this congregation at the time that this constitution is adopted and those who are admitted thereafter and who have declared and maintain their membership in accordance with the provisions of this constitution and its bylaws.

*C8.02. Members shall be classified as follows:

a. *Baptized* members are those persons who have been received by the Sacrament of Holy Baptism in this congregation, or, having been previously baptized in the name of the Triune God, have been received by certificate of transfer from other Lutheran congregations or by affirmation of faith.

b. *Confirmed* members are baptized persons who have been confirmed in this congregation, those who have been received by adult baptism or by transfer as confirmed members from other Lutheran congregations, or baptized persons received by affirmation of faith.

c. *Voting* members are confirmed members. Such confirmed members shall have communed and made a contribution of record during the current or preceding year.

d. *Associate* members are persons holding membership in other Lutheran [Christian] congregations who wish to retain such

(9-93) MODEL CONSTITUTION FOR CONGREGATIONS / 197

membership but desire to participate in the life and mission of this congregation. They have all the privileges and duties of membership except voting rights and eligibility for elected offices or membership on the Congregation Council of this congregation.

*C8.03. All applications for confirmed membership shall be submitted to and shall require the approval of the Congregation Council.

*C8.04. It shall be the privilege and duty of members of this congregation to:

a. make regular use of the means of grace, both Word and sacraments;

b. live a Christian life in accordance with the Word of God and the teachings of the Lutheran church; and

c. support the work of this congregation, synod, and the churchwide organization of the Evangelical Lutheran Church in America through contributions of their time, abilities, and financial support as biblical stewards.

*C8.05. Membership in this congregation shall be terminated by any of the following:

a. death;

b. resignation;

c. transfer or release;

d. disciplinary action by the Congregation Council; or

e. removal from the roll due to inactivity as defined in the bylaws.

Such persons who have been removed from the roll of members shall remain persons for whom the church has a continuing pastoral concern.

Chapter 9.
THE PASTOR

*C9.01. Authority to call a pastor shall be in this congregation by at least a two-thirds majority ballot vote of members present and voting at a meeting regularly called for that purpose. Before a call is issued, the officers, or a committee elected by [this congregation] [the Congregation Council] to recommend the call, shall seek the advice and help of the bishop of the synod.

*C9.02. Only a member of the clergy roster of the Evangelical Lutheran Church in America or a candidate for the roster of ordained ministers who has been recommended for the congregation by the synodical bishop may be called as a pastor of this congregation.

*C9.03. Consistent with the faith and practice of the Evangelical Lutheran Church in America,

a. Every ordained minister shall:
1) preach the Word;
2) administer the sacraments;
3) conduct public worship;

4) provide pastoral care; and
5) speak publicly to the world in solidarity with the poor and oppressed, calling for justice and proclaiming God's love for the world.

b. Each ordained minister with a congregational call shall, within the congregation:
1) offer instruction, confirm, marry, visit the sick and distressed, and bury the dead;
2) supervise all schools and organizations of this congregation;
3) install regularly elected members of the Congregation Council; and
4) with the council, administer discipline.

c. Every pastor shall:
1) strive to extend the Kingdom of God in the community, in the nation, and abroad;
2) seek out and encourage qualified persons to prepare for the ministry of the Gospel;
3) impart knowledge of this church and its wider ministry through distribution of its periodicals and other publications; and
4) endeavor to increase the support given by the congregation to the work of the churchwide organization of the Evangelical Lutheran Church in America (ELCA) and of the _____ Synod of the ELCA.

*C9.04. The specific duties of the pastor, compensation, and other matters pertaining to the service of the pastor shall be included in a letter of call, which shall be attested by the bishop of the synod.

*C9.05. a. The call of a congregation, when accepted by a pastor, shall constitute a continuing mutual relationship and commitment, which, except in the case of the death of the pastor, shall be terminated only following consultation with the synodical bishop and for the following reasons:
1) mutual agreement to terminate the call or the completion of a call for a specific term;
2) resignation of the pastor, which shall become effective, unless otherwise agreed, 30 days after the date on which it was submitted;
3) inability to conduct the pastoral office effectively in the congregation in view of local conditions, without reflection on the competence or the moral and spiritual character of the pastor;
4) the physical or mental incapacity of the pastor;
5) disqualification of the pastor through discipline on grounds of doctrine, morality, or continued neglect of duty;
6) the dissolution of the congregation; or
7) suspension of the congregation as a result of discipline proceedings.

b. When allegations of physical or mental incapacity of the pastor or ineffective conduct of the pastoral office have come to the attention of the bishop of the synod, the bishop in his or her sole discretion may, or when such allegations have been brought to the synod's attention by an official recital of allegations by the Congregation Council or by a petition signed by at least one-third of the voting members of the congregation, the bishop shall, investigate such conditions personally in company with a committee of two ordained ministers and one layperson.

c. In case of alleged physical or mental incapacity, competent medical testimony shall be obtained. When such disability is evident, the bishop of the synod with the advice of the committee shall declare the pastorate vacant. Upon the restoration of a disabled pastor to health, the bishop of the synod shall take steps to enable the pastor to resume the ministry, either in the congregation last served or in another field of labor.

d. In the case of alleged local difficulties that imperil the effective functioning of the congregation, all concerned persons shall be heard, after which the bishop of the synod together with the committee described in *C9.05.b. shall decide on the course of action to be recommended to the pastor and the congregation. If they agree to carry out such recommendations, no further action shall be taken by the synod. If either party fails to assent, the congregation may dismiss the pastor by a two-thirds majority vote of the voting members present at a regularly called meeting after consultation with the bishop.

e. If, in the course of proceedings described in *C9.05.d., the committee concludes that there may be grounds for disciplinary action, the committee shall make recommendations concerning disciplinary action to the synodical bishop who may bring charges, in accordance with the provisions of the constitution and bylaws of the Evangelical Lutheran Church in America and the constitution of this synod.

f. If, following the appointment of the committee described in *C9.05.b. or d., it should become apparent that the pastoral office cannot be conducted effectively in the congregation(s) being served by the ordained minister due to local conditions, the bishop of the synod may temporarily suspend the pastor from service in the congregation(s) without prejudice and with pay provided through a joint synodical and churchwide fund and with housing provided by the congregation(s).

*C9.06. At a time of pastoral vacancy, an interim pastor shall be appointed by the bishop of the synod with the consent of this congregation or the Congregation Council.

*C9.07. During the period of service, an interim pastor shall have the rights and duties in the congregation of a regularly called pastor and may delegate the same in part to a supply pastor with the consent of the bishop of

the synod and this congregation or Congregation Council. The interim pastor and any ordained pastor providing assistance shall refrain from exerting influence in the selection of a pastor.

*C9.08. This congregation shall make satisfactory settlement of all financial obligations to a former pastor before calling a successor. A pastor shall make satisfactory settlement of all financial obligations to this congregation.

*C9.09. When a pastor is called to serve in company with another pastor or pastors, the privileges and responsibilities of each pastor shall be specified in documents to accompany the call and to be drafted in consultation involving the pastors, the Congregation Council, and the bishop of the synod. As occasion requires, the documents may be revised through a similar consultation.

*C9.11. With the approval of the bishop of the synod, the congregation may depart from *C9.05.a. and call a pastor for a specific term. Details of such calls shall be in writing setting forth the purpose and conditions involved. Prior to the completion of a term, the bishop or a designated representative of the bishop shall meet with the pastor and representatives of the congregation for a review of the call. Such a call may also be terminated before its expiration in accordance with the provisions of *C9.05.a.

*C9.12. The pastor shall keep accurate parochial records of all baptisms, confirmations, marriages, burials, communicants, members received, members dismissed, or members excluded from the congregation, and shall submit a summary of such statistics annually to the synod.

The pastor shall be a member of the congregation that has extended the letter of call. In a parish of multiple congregations, the pastor shall hold membership in one of the congregations.

*C9.13. The pastor(s) shall submit a report of his or her ministry to the bishop of the synod at least 90 days prior to each regular meeting of the Synod Assembly.

Chapter 10.
CONGREGATION MEETING

C10.01. The [annual] [semi-annual] [quarterly] meeting of this congregation shall be held at a time specified in the bylaws.

C10.02. A special Congregation Meeting may be called by the pastor, the Congregation Council, or the president of this congregation, and shall be called by the president of the congregation upon the written request of _____ [number] [percent] of the voting members. The call for each special meeting shall specify the purpose for which it is to be held and no other business shall be transacted.

C10.03. Notice of all meetings of this congregation shall be given at the services of worship on the preceding two consecutive Sundays and by mail to all [voting] members at least 10 days in advance of the date of the meeting. The posting of such notice in the regular mail, with the regular postage affixed or paid, sent to the last known address of such members shall be sufficient.

C10.04. _____ voting members shall constitute a quorum.

C10.05. Voting by proxy or by absentee ballot shall not be permitted.

C10.06. All actions by the congregation shall be by majority vote except as otherwise provided in this constitution.

C10.07. Robert's Rules of Order, latest edition, shall govern parliamentary procedure of all meetings of this congregation.

Chapter 11.
OFFICERS

C11.01. The officers of this congregation shall be a president, vice president, secretary, and treasurer.

a. Duties of the officers shall be specified in the bylaws.

b. The officers shall be voting members of the congregation.

c. Officers of this congregation shall serve similar offices of the Congregation Council and shall be voting members of the Congregation Council.

d. If the Congregation Council elects its officers, the president, vice president, and secretary shall be selected from the elected membership of the Congregation Council.

C11.02. The [congregation] [Congregation Council] shall elect its officers and they shall be the officers of the congregation. The officers shall be elected by written ballot and shall serve for one year or until their successors are elected. Their terms shall begin at the close of the annual meeting at which they are elected.

or

The pastor shall be ex officio president of the congregation and the Congregation Council. The [congregation] [Congregation Council] shall elect by written ballot the other officers of the congregation who shall serve for one year or until their successors are elected. Their terms shall begin at the close of the annual meeting at which they are elected.

or

The pastor shall be ex officio president of the congregation and the Congregation Council. The [congregation] [Congregation Council] shall elect by written ballot the other officers of the congregation who shall serve for one year or until their successors are elected. Their terms shall begin on _____ (month and day) and end on _____ (month and day).

or

The officers shall be elected by the [congregation] [Congregation Council] by written ballot and shall serve for one year. The term shall begin on _____ (month and day) and end on _____ (month and day).

C11.03. No officer shall hold more than one office at a time. No elected officer shall be eligible to serve more than two consecutive terms in the same office.

Chapter 12.
CONGREGATION COUNCIL

C12.01. The voting membership of the Congregation Council shall consist of the pastor(s), the officers of the congregation, and not more than _____ members of the congregation. Any voting member of the congregation may be elected, subject only to the limitation on the length of continuous service permitted in that office. A member's place on the Congregation Council shall be declared vacant if the member a) ceases to be a voting member of this congregation or b) is absent from four successive regular meetings of the Congregation Council without cause.

C12.02. The members of the Congregation Council except the pastor(s) shall be elected by written ballot to serve for _____ years or until their successors are elected. Such members shall be eligible to serve no more than two full terms consecutively. Their terms shall begin at the close of the annual meeting at which they are elected.

or

The members of the Congregation Council except the pastor(s) shall be elected at a legally called meeting of the congregation during the month of _____. Their term of office shall be for _____ years, with the term of office beginning on _____ (month and day) and ending on _____ (month and day). Newly elected Congregation Council members shall be installed at worship on the Sunday prior to the date they assume office.

C12.03. Should a member's place on the Congregation Council be declared vacant, the Congregation Council shall elect, by majority vote, a successor until the next annual meeting.

C12.04. The Congregation Council shall have general oversight of the life and activities of this congregation, and in particular its worship life, to the end that everything be done in accordance with the Word of God and the faith and practice of the Evangelical Lutheran Church in America. The duties of the Congregation Council shall include the following:

a. To lead this congregation in stating its mission, to do long-range planning, to set goals and priorities, and to evaluate its activities in light of its mission and goals.

b. To seek to involve all members of this congregation in worship, learning, witness, service, and support.

c. To oversee and provide for the administration of this congregation to enable it to fulfill its functions and perform its mission.

d. To maintain supportive relationships with the pastor(s) and staff and help them annually to evaluate the fulfillment of their calling or employment.

e. To be examples individually and corporately of the style of life and ministry expected of all baptized persons.

f. To promote a congregational climate of peace and goodwill, and, as differences and conflicts arise, to endeavor to foster mutual understanding.

g. To arrange for pastoral service during the sickness or absence of the pastor.

h. To emphasize partnership with the synod and churchwide units of the Evangelical Lutheran Church in America as well as cooperation with other congregations, both Lutheran and non-Lutheran, subject to established policies of the synod and the Evangelical Lutheran Church in America.

i. To recommend and encourage the use of program resources produced or approved by the Evangelical Lutheran Church in America.

j. To seek out and encourage qualified persons to prepare for the ministry of the Gospel.

C12.05. The Congregation Council shall be responsible for the financial and property matters of this congregation.

a. The Congregation Council shall be the board of [trustees] [directors] of this congregation, and as such shall be responsible for maintaining and protecting its property and the management of its business and fiscal affairs. It shall have the powers and be subject to the obligations that pertain to such boards under the laws of the State of _____, except as otherwise provided herein.

b. The Congregation Council shall not have the authority to buy, sell, or encumber real property unless specifically authorized to do so by a meeting of the congregation.

c. The Congregation Council may enter into contracts of up to $_____ for items not included in the budget.

d. The Congregation Council shall prepare an annual budget for adoption by this congregation, shall supervise the expenditure of funds in accordance therewith following its adoption, and may incur obligations of more than $_____ in excess of the anticipated receipts only after approval by a Congregation Meeting. The budget shall include this congregation's full indicated share in support of the wider ministry being carried on in partnership with the synod and churchwide organization.

e. The Congregation Council shall ascertain that the financial affairs of this congregation are being conducted efficiently, giving particular attention to the prompt payment of all obligations and to the regular forwarding of benevolence monies to the synodical treasurer.

f. The Congregation Council shall be responsible for this congregation's investments and its total insurance program.

C12.06. The Congregation Council shall see that the provisions of this constitution[,] [and] its bylaws[,] [and the continuing resolutions] are carried out.

C12.07. The Congregation Council shall provide for an annual review of the membership roster.

C12.08. The Congregation Council shall be responsible for the employment and supervision of the salaried lay workers of this congregation.

C12.09. The Congregation Council shall submit a comprehensive report to this congregation at the annual meeting.

C12.11. The Congregation Council shall normally meet once a month. Special meetings may be called by the pastor or the president, and shall be called by the president at the request of at least one-half of its members. Notice of each special meeting shall be given to all who are entitled to be present.

C12.12. A quorum for the transaction of business shall consist of a majority of the members of the Congregation Council, including the pastor or interim pastor, except when the pastor or interim pastor requests or consents to be absent and has given prior approval to the agenda for a particular regular or special meeting, which shall be the only business considered at that meeting. Chronic or repeated absence of the pastor or interim pastor who has refused approval of the agenda of a subsequent regular or special meeting shall not preclude action by the Congregation Council, following consultation with the synodical bishop.

Chapter 13.
CONGREGATION COMMITTEES

C13.01. The officers of this congregation and the pastor shall constitute the *Executive Committee.*

C13.02. A *Nominating Committee* of six voting members of this congregation, two of whom, if possible, shall be outgoing members of the Congregation Council, shall be elected at the annual meeting for a term of one year. Members of the Nominating Committee are not eligible for consecutive reelection.

C13.03. An *Audit Committee* of three voting members shall be elected by the Congregation Council. Audit Committee members shall not be members of the Congregation Council. Term of office shall be three years, with one member elected each year. Members shall be eligible for reelection.

C13.04. A *Staff Support Committee* (in the absence of a staff support committee, their duties shall be fulfilled by the executive committee) shall be appointed jointly by the president [vice president¹] and the pastor. Term of office shall be two years, with three members to be appointed each successive year. Committee members will hold no other office in the congregation during their term.

C13.05. When a pastoral vacancy occurs, a *Call Committee* of six voting members shall be elected by [this congregation] [the Congregation Council]. Term of office will terminate upon installation of the newly called pastor.

C13.06. Other committees of this congregation may be formed, as the need arises, by decision of the Congregation Council.

C13.07. Duties of committees of this congregation shall be specified in the [bylaws] [continuing resolutions].

Chapter 14.
ORGANIZATIONS WITHIN THE CONGREGATION

C14.01. All organizations within this congregation shall exist to aid it in ministering to the members of this congregation and to all persons who can be reached with the Gospel of Christ. As outgrowths and expressions of this congregation's life, the organizations are subject to its oversight and direction. This congregation at its meeting shall determine their policies, guide their activities, and receive reports concerning their membership, work, and finances.

C14.02. Special interest groups, other than those of the official organizations of the Evangelical Lutheran Church in America, may be organized only after authorization has been given by the Congregation Council [and specified in a continuing resolution].

Chapter 15.
DISCIPLINE OF MEMBERS AND ADJUDICATION

*C15.01. Denial of the Christian faith as described in this constitution, conduct grossly unbecoming a member of the Church of Christ, or persistent trouble-making in this congregation are sufficient cause for discipline of a member. Prior to disciplinary action, reconciliation will be attempted following Matthew 18:15-17, proceeding through these successive steps: a) private admonition by the pastor, b) admonition by the pastor in the presence of two or three witnesses, and c) citation to appear before the Congregation Council.

*C15.02. The process for discipline of a member of the congregation shall be governed as prescribed by the chapter on discipline in the Constitution, Bylaws, and Continuing Resolutions of the Evangelical Lutheran Church in America. A member charged with the offense shall appear before the Congregation Council after having received a written notice,

¹For use if the pastor is president of the congregation under two of the options in C11.02.

specifying the exact charges that have been made against the member, at least 10 days prior to the meeting.

*C15.03. Members of the Congregation Council who participate in the preparation of the written charges or who present evidence or testimony in the hearing before the Congregation Council are disqualified from voting upon the question of the guilt of the accused member. Should the allegations be sustained by a two-thirds majority vote of the members of the Congregation Council, who are not disqualified but who are present and voting, and renewed admonition prove ineffectual, the council shall impose one of the following disciplinary actions:

a. censure before the council or congregation;

b. suspension from membership for a definite period of time; or

c. exclusion from membership in this congregation.

Disciplinary actions b. and c. shall be delivered to the member in writing.

*C15.04. The member against whom disciplinary action has been taken by the Congregation Council shall have the right to appeal the decision to the Synod Council. Such right may not be abridged and the decision of the Synod Council shall be final.

*C15.05. Disciplinary actions may be reconsidered and revoked by the Congregation Council upon receipt of a) evidence that injustice has been done or b) evidence of repentance and amendment.

Adjudication

*C15.10.

*C15.11. When there is disagreement among factions within this congregation on a substantive issue that cannot be resolved by the parties, members of this congregation shall have access to the synodical bishop for consultation after informing the chair of the Congregation Council of their intent. If the consultation fails to resolve the issue(s), the Consultation Committee of the synod shall consider the matter. If the Consultation Committee of the synod shall fail to resolve the issue(s), the matter shall be referred to the Synod Council, whose decision shall be final.

Chapter 16.
BYLAWS

*C16.01. This congregation may adopt bylaws. No bylaw may conflict with this constitution.

*C16.02. Bylaws may be adopted or amended at any legally called meeting of this congregation with a quorum present by a majority vote of those voting members present and voting.

*C16.03. Changes to the bylaws may be proposed by any voting member provided, however, that such additions or amendments be submitted in writing to the Congregation Council at least 60 days before a regular or special Congregation Meeting called for that purpose and that the Congregation Council notify the members of the proposal with its recommendations at least 30 days in advance of the Congregation Meeting.

*C16.04. Approved changes to the bylaws shall be sent by the secretary of this congregation to the synod.

Chapter 17.
AMENDMENTS

*C17.01. Amendments to this constitution may be proposed by at least _____ voting members or by the Congregation Council. Proposals must be filed in writing with the Congregation Council 60 days before formal consideration by this congregation at its regular or special meeting called for that purpose. The Congregation Council shall notify the members of the proposal with the council's recommendations at least 30 days in advance of the meeting.

*C17.02. A proposed amendment to this constitution shall:

    a. be approved at a properly called meeting according to this constitution by a majority vote of those present and voting;

    b. be ratified without change at the next annual meeting by a two-thirds majority vote of those present and voting; and

    c. have the effective date included in the resolution and noted in the constitution.

*C17.03. Any amendments to this constitution shall be sent by the secretary of this congregation to the synod. The amendment shall become effective within 120 days from the date of the receipt of the notice by the synod unless the synod informs this congregation that the amendment is in conflict with the constitution and bylaws of the Evangelical Lutheran Church in America or the constitution of the _____ Synod of the ELCA.

*C17.04. Whenever the Model Constitution for Congregations is amended by the Churchwide Assembly, this constitution may be amended to reflect any such amendment by a simple majority vote at any subsequent meeting of the congregation without presentation at a prior meeting of the congregation, provided that the Congregation Council has submitted by mail notice to the congregation of such an amendment or amendments at least 30 days prior to the meeting. Following the adoption of an amendment, the secretary of the congregation shall submit a copy thereof to the synod, consistent with *C17.03.

Chapter 18.
CONTINUING RESOLUTIONS

*C18.01. The Congregation Council may enact continuing resolutions which describe the function of the various committees or organizations of this congregation.

*C18.02. Continuing resolutions shall be enacted or amended by a two-thirds vote of all voting members of the Congregation Council.

208 / MODEL CONSTITUTION FOR CONGREGATIONS   (9-93)